ONE EUROPE, MANY NATIONS

A Historical Dictionary of European National Groups

James B. Minahan

Greenwood Press
Westport, Connecticut • London

Library of Congress Cataloging-in-Publication Data

Minahan, James.
   One Europe, many nations : a historical dictionary of European national groups / by
James B. Minahan.
      p.   cm.
   Includes bibliographical references and index.
   ISBN 0–313–30984–1 (alk. paper)
   1. Europe—History—Dictionaries.   2. Ethnology—Europe—Dictionaries.   I. Title.
D21.3.M55   2000
940'.0321—dc21   99–046040

British Library Cataloguing in Publication Data is available.

Library of Congress Catalog Card Number: 99–046040
ISBN: 0–313–30984–1

First published in 2000

Greenwood Press, 88 Post Road West, Westport, CT 06881
An imprint of Greenwood Publishing Group, Inc.
www.greenwood.com

Printed in the United States of America

The paper used in this book complies with the
Permanent Paper Standard issued by the National
Information Standards Organization (Z39.48–1984).

10 9 8 7 6 5 4 3 2 1

Contents

Preface

The turn of the twenty-first century, like the beginning of the twentieth century, is overshadowed by the specter of radical nationalism in Europe. As it was a century ago, the European continent remains divided by national identities and therefore remains the focus of efforts to bring peace to the world in the new century. Historical national loyalties and alliances retain the ability to involve states and national groups far beyond Europe's boundaries. This volume addresses the national situation in Europe, with an emphasis on the many possible nationalist conflicts that dot the European landscape. *One Europe, Many Nations: A Historical Dictionary of European National Groups* is the first book to address the Europeans as distinct national groups, not as nation-states and national minorities. The book follows the development of Europe's many national groups from the earliest periods of their national histories to the dawn of the twenty-first century. This book is an essential guide to the national groups that populate the so-called Old World, national groups that continue to dominate world headlines and that present the world community with some of its most intractable conflicts.

The Cold War, which dominated world politics from the end of World War II until the collapse of communism in the last decade of the twentieth century, gave the world a fragile peace, but part of the price for that peace was the suppression of many of the national groups that inhabited the Cold War's most dangerous theater, Europe. In the name of political stability historic identities were buried, and collective rights as European national groups were ignored during the process of maintaining a delicate peace in the ideologically divided continent. Intergroup and interethnic conflicts, which often result from the expression of the historic and human rights of national groups, were also suppressed in the name of state unity and national integrity. Until now few reference books have addressed the post–Cold War nationalist resurgence in Europe, and fewer still have addressed the resurgence by focusing on the most basic element of any nationalism, the nation. The tribal histories of the Europeans are intricate, fluid, and largely unresearched.

This dictionary was prepared to address that deficiency. The book contains nearly 150 surveys of Europe's national groups, short articles highlighting the political, social, economic, and historical evolution of the peoples who are now claiming a distinct identity within an increasingly integrated continent. The worth of the dictionary, in part, derives from its up-to-date information and historical background on the European national groups that are currently making news and those that will produce future headlines and conflicts.

Most recent reference books about Europe approach the subject of nations and nationalism from the perspective of the European Union and the nation-state, relegating the numerous nonstate national groups to the position of national minorities, deserving only an occasional paragraph or footnote. However, selecting the national groups to be included in the dictionary presented numerous problems, not the least of which was the difficulty of applying a uniform criterion to the many distinct groups that inhabit the European continent. Europe's national groups represent a perplexing diversity of peoples who range from the powerful and diverse national groups that dominate the continent's historic nation-states, to the small, virtually unknown groups that have emerged since the collapse of Europe's Cold War stability. The national groups included in this book share just one characteristic: they identify themselves as distinct European nations.

The arduous task of researching Europe's historical diversity was complicated by the lack of a consensus on what constitutes a nation or a nation-state. There is no universally accepted definition of nation, country, or state, particularly in Europe. The controversy continues to generate endless debate and numerous regional and international conflicts. *Webster's Unabridged Dictionary* defines the word "nation" as "a body of people, associated with a particular territory, that is sufficiently conscious of its unity to seek or possess a government particularly its own." Building on this definition the criterion used for selecting the national groups for inclusion in this volume was based on three important factors, modified by the immense diversity of Europe's national groups. The three factors are a national claim to a specific geographic area; the display of the outward trappings of national consciousness; and the formation of specifically nationalist or political organizations that reflect the group's claim to identity as a distinct European national group.

In any compilation of this type, the selection process for choosing which peoples to include is a complex evolution of subtraction and addition. Estimates of the number of distinct national groups in Europe run into the hundreds, making the selection process a difficult process of elimination. The national groups included in this volume therefore represent only the most developed portion of the self-proclaimed nations of Europe, including many that are counted both as part of a larger national group and as distinct European nations.

National sentiment is often difficult to define and is nearly impossible to measure. An attempt to apply the criteria used to distinguish between Europe's nations or national groups and its less numerous nation-states floundered on the numerous anomalies encountered. Size is definitely not a criterion. Over forty world states recognize a building in Rome, covering just 108.7 acres, as an independent European state, but the fewer than 1,000 inhabitants of Vatican City do not constitute a European national group. Nor is membership in the United Nations (UN) the measure of independence: Ukrainians and Belarussians were founding members of the UN in 1945, yet their homelands became independent nation-states only in 1991. One exception to the criterion for inclusion is the Roms or Gypsies. They have evolved a strong national sentiment but, uniquely, without a defined geographic base. The decision to include the Roms is based on the Roms' claim to national status, the well-developed and widely supported Rom national movement, and the fact that the Roms constitute one of Europe's most numerous national groups.

Historically, nationalism in Europe has been defined by the nation-states, and many of the national groups included in this volume played little or no role in European politics before the end of the Cold War. However, since the early 1990s they have increasingly demanded a separate role in the planned continental economic and political system that has developed since the 1950s. Some of the national groups will be familiar, either historically or more recently as news items, and many will be known to millions of the inhabitants of other continents whose immigrant families trace their roots to these historic European nations.

The entry for each national group is divided into several parts or headings: the name and alternative names of the group; simple line drawings of the flag and a map of the national group's homeland; population statistics and continental distribution; geographic location, including the group's state or regional political affiliation; descriptions of the national and other pertinent flags that are not pictured; a brief sketch of the national characteristics of the group; and the nation, including the history and national development of each national group from its historical beginnings to the present.

The flags and maps are presented as visual aids to the text. The flags are not displayed in their proper dimensions, but are accurate as to design. The maps are roughly to scale and present the national homelands in their geographic context with the non-sovereign states and regions shown in italics.

Many of the national groups included in this volume will be familiar as the core nations of powerful nation-states, historically as European nations, or more recently as news items, but the majority are so unfamiliar that many do not have standardized names or spellings in English. Familiar names are often the colonial or imposed names that represented a particularly harsh form of cultural suppression. That situation is now reversing in Europe, with cartographers and geographers attempting to settle on the definitive forms of the names of national groups, territories, and languages. Until that process is completed, many of the names used in this volume not only will be unfamiliar to most readers but may not appear in even the most comprehensive reference sources. Unfamiliar group and place-names used in this volume are most often followed by the more familiar or historic names in parentheses.

The population figures are the author's estimates for the year 2000. The figures are designated by the abbreviation (2000 e) before the appropriate statistics. The figures were gleaned from a vast number of sources, both official and unofficial, representing the latest censuses, official estimates, and, where no other sources were available, nationalist population claims. Where conflicting figures are included, both official and unofficial statistics are presented. Official rates of population growth, unofficial estimates, and other variables were applied to the figures to arrive at the statistics included in the dictionary. Detailed population figures and geographic locations can be found in Appendix A. A list of the principal statistical sources is provided at the end of this section.

The geographic information on the homeland of each national group incorporates, if available, the size of the territory, in both square miles (sq.mi.) and square kilometers (sq.km.). Additional geographic information includes location of the territory in relation to neighboring states and information on the principal geographic features of each homeland.

Information on the national flag or other pertinent flags, if available, is detailed. Flags form an important and very emotional role in the development of a national consciousness, and their use has been widespread in Europe for centuries.

Information on the people, the members of the national group, is an overview of the national characteristics of the national groups. The descriptions highlight the linguistic, religious, cultural, and national influences and affiliations that have shaped each national group.

Each of the newly independent nations has its own particular history, the events and conflicts that have shaped its national characteristics. The largest part of each national survey is therefore devoted to the historical development of the nation. The historical survey follows the evolution and consolidation of the nation from its earliest history to the present, including information on the numerous conflicts and controversies that continue to plague Europeans' attempts at closer continental cooperation and integration.

The two appendixes included in this volume allow the reader to develop a better understanding of the size, historic affiliations, and distribution of Europe's national groups. Appendix A sets the group name, population size, and geographic distribution within the context of Europe. Appendix B provides an overview of the historic affiliations based on language and dialects.

Few of Europe's national groups developed in isolation but were shaped by their relations with various governments and neighboring peoples. To facilitate the reader's identification of nations mentioned in the text that are included as a separate national survey in the dictionary, the name of the nation appears with an asterisk (*). An extensive subject index at the end of the volume provides a convenient way to access desired information. Each entry also includes a short bibliographic list as a guide to sources that pertain to the national group in question.

This dictionary was compiled to provide a guide to Europe's numerous national groups, both the historic peoples associated with long-established nation-states and the many nonstate national groups that are increasingly demanding a distinct identity within the emerging continental political system. This dictionary is presented as a unique reference source to the nationalist phenomenon that is spearheading one of the most powerful and enduring political movements that emerged from the twentieth century, a movement that is set to dominate Europe well into the twenty-first century, the pursuit of democracy's basic tenet, self-determination.

PRINCIPAL STATISTICAL SOURCES

1. National Censuses 1997–2000.
2. World Population Chart 1998 (United Nations).
3. Populations and Vital Statistics 1998 (United Nations).
4. World Tables 1999 (World Bank).
5. World Demographic Estimates and Projections, 1950–2025, 1988 (United Nations).
6. UNESCO [United Nations Educational, Scientific, and Cultural Organization] Statistical Annual 1999.
7. World Bank Atlas 1998.
8. The Economist Intelligence Unit (Country Report series 1998).
9. OMRI [Open Media Research Institute] 1997.
10. Europa Yearbook 1999.
11. U.S. Department of State publications.
12. The CIA [Central Intelligence Agency] World Factbook 1998.
13. United Nations Statistical Yearbook 1998.
14. United Nations Demographic Yearbook 1999.
15. The Statesman's Yearbook 1999.
16. Encyclopedia Britannica.
17. Encyclopedia Americana.
18. Webster's New Geographical Dictionary.
19. National Geographic Society.
20. Royal Geographical Society.
21. World Almanac and Book of Facts 1999.

22. Political Handbook of the World.

23. The Urban Foundation.

24. The Blue Plan.

25. Eurostat, the European Union Statistical Office.

30. International Monetary Fund (IMF) publications.

Introduction

More than any other continent, Europe has been obsessed by its own self-definition. However, Europe, conventionally one of the seven continents of the world, is not a separate continent at all but is actually just a huge peninsula, the western fifth of the Eurasian landmass, which is made up primarily of Asia. Modern geographers generally describe the Ural Mountains, the Ural River, part of the Caspian Sea, and the Caucasus Mountains as forming the main boundary between Europe and Asia. Europe is united by its shared history and culture, but it remains a continent of extraordinary diversity. This diversity, which has withstood centuries of suppression, most characterizes Europe at the threshold of the twenty-first century. The persistent diversity of Europe's ancient national groups must necessarily be a barrier to closer integration unless the continent's diversity is recognized, studied, and accepted.

The twentieth century brought more and faster changes to the map of Europe than all the centuries before. The changes, the result of the growth of nationalist sentiment across the continent during the nineteenth century, continue to threaten the stability of Europe and therefore of the entire world. Perhaps no other subject has inspired the passions that surround nationalism and national sentiment, ideas that evolved from the European experience. In 1900 the European continent and the world were dominated by the empires of Great Britain, France, Germany, Russia, Turkey, Italy, Belgium, the Netherlands, Spain, Austria-Hungary, and Portugal. A century later the empires have disappeared, and the number of European states has grown from fewer than twenty to nearly fifty, many the result of nationalist conflicts. The nineteenth-century growth of nation-states ignored the continent's historic and ethnic diversity, while European nationalism, in its most virulent forms, provoked wars, massacres, terrorism, and genocide. Conflicts between European national groups remain of particular concern to a world community still unsure of post–Cold War alignments. In spite of recent efforts to unite in an economic and political union, Europe remains one of the world's most volatile regions, and a majority of the frictions that threaten the peace of the continent are conflicts between the many national groups.

Europe, in spite of knowing little real peace in its history, has long been a center of great cultural and economic achievement. The ancient Greeks and Romans produced major civilizations, famous for their contributions to philosophy, literature, fine art, and government. The Renaissance, which began in the fourteenth century, was a period of great accomplishment for European artists and architects, and the age of exploration, beginning in the fifteenth century, included voyages to the far corners of the world by European navigators. European states, particularly Spain, Portugal, France, and Great Britain, built large colonial empires, first by dominating neighboring national groups and eventually with vast holdings in Africa, the Americas, and Asia. The descendants of Europe's colonizers now make up a substantial portion of the population of the world while retaining ties to their ancestral homelands in Europe.

The majority of Europe's state and stateless nations have embraced nationalism, but at the threshold of the twenty-first century, most seek greater autonomy or independence within the overarching security of the continental economic and political organization, the European Union. Although the nationalist resurgence that accompanied the collapse of communism and the end of the Cold War in Europe has spawned numerous conflicts, reinforcing the erroneous belief that nationalism is synonymous with extremism and separatism, nationalism is not automatically a divisive force, as it provides citizens with an identity and a sense of responsibility and involvement in an increasingly integrated continental political system.

An offshoot of the eighteenth-century European doctrine of popular sovereignty, nationalism became a driving force in the nineteenth century, shaped and invigorated by the principles of the American and French Revolutions. The first wave of modern nationalism culminated in the breakup of Europe's multinational empires after World War I. The second wave began during World War II and continued as the very politicized decolonization process that engulfed the remaining colonial empires as a theater of the Cold War after 1945. The removal of Cold War factionalism has now released a third wave of nationalism in Europe, which is experiencing both integration on a continental scale and disintegration of the historic nation-states.

Nationalism has become an ascendant ideology that is increasingly challenging the nineteenth-century definition of the unitary European nation-state. The worldwide nationalist revival is an amplified global echo of the nationalism that swept Europe's stateless nations in the late nineteenth and early twentieth centuries. However, the belief that political and economic security could be guaranteed only by the existing European political order faded as quickly as the ideological and political divisions set in place on the continent after World War II. Traditional insistence that national structures conform to the existing international borders for the sake of peace was one of the first casualties of the revolution brought on by the end of the Cold War and Europe's new enthusiasm for democracy and self-determination.

The growth of national sentiment can be based on language, history, culture, territorial claims, geographical location, religion, economics, ethnicity, racial background, opposition to another group, or opposition to bad or oppressive government. The mobilization of national sentiment is most often a complicated mixture of some or all of these components. No one of these factors is essential; however, some must be present for group cohesion to be strong enough to evolve a self-identifying nationalism.

Democracy, although widely accepted as the only system that is able to provide the basis of humane political and economic activity, can be a subversive force. Multiparty democracy often generates chaos and instability as centrifugal forces, an inherent part of a free political system, are set loose. The post–Cold War restoration of political pluralism and democratic process in Europe has given rise to a rebirth of ethnicity and politicized national identity, while the collapse of communism shattered the political equilibrium that had prevailed for over four decades. The Cold War blocs had mostly succeeded in suppressing or controlling the regional nationalisms in their respective spheres, nationalisms that now have begun to reignite old national desires and ethnic rivalries. Across the European continent numerous stateless nations, their identities and aspirations long buried under decades of Cold War tensions, are emerging to claim for themselves the basic principle of democracy, self-determination.

History has a tendency to simplify national reality and to identify it with state structures, but this century's last and most powerful resurgence of nationalism is a movement against the existing state structures, aided and abetted by the construction of continental trading and political blocs. The nationalism of the European nations is most often rooted in the historical mismatch of state frontiers relative to the peoples claiming national status. Very few of the so-called European nation-states are homogeneous, made up of just one nation, but are, in fact multiethnic, multinational, and multireligious political entities increasingly threatened by the aspiration of their constituent nations. Powerful centrifugal forces, held in check by the Cold War, have emerged to challenge the accepted definition of what constitutes a nation and its rights. The doctrine of statism is slowly being superseded by a post–Cold War internationalism that is reshaping the world's view of the unitary nation-state and, what is more important, the world's view of who or what constitutes a nation.

The historical emphasis on the rights of states, rather than the rights of the individuals and nations within them, has dictated international attitudes to nationalism, buttressed by ignorance and failure to understand the nation versus the nation-state. The use of condemnatory labels—separatist, secessionist, rebel, splittist, and so on—has been a powerful state weapon against those who seek a different state structure on behalf of their nations. Two main trends are vying to shape post–Cold War Europe. One is the movement to form a continental economic-political grouping that would allow for smaller political units as members. The other is the emergence of smaller and smaller national units as older states are broken up. The two trends are not mutually exclusive. The traditional European nation-state and its absolute sovereignty are fading and giving way to historical trends, the nation rather than the nation-state, in one direction, and supranational bodies, such as the European Union (EU), on the other.

The rapidly changing political and economic realities have swept aside the old arguments that population size, geographic location, and economic viability are deterrents to national sentiment and eventual self-determination. The revival of nationalism is converging with the emergence of a continental political and economic unit already able to accommodate smaller national units within an overarching political, economic, and security framework. The nationalist resurgence in Europe is inexorably moving continental politics away from the present state system to a new political order more closely resembling Europe's ethnic and historical geography.

The rapid spread of national sentiment, affecting even nations long considered assimilated or quiescent, is attracting considerable attention, but the focus of this attention is invariably on its impact on established governments and its effect on international relations. As the Cold War withered away, it was replaced by a bewildering number and variety of nationalisms that, in turn, spawned a continental movement toward the breakdown of the existing system of nation-states. The impact of the nationalist upsurge has only begun to be felt or studied. The biggest impulse to the recent explosion of nationalism was the end of the Cold War. The fall of communist dictatorships released nationalisms across Europe and the former Soviet Union. That nationalism is now feeding on itself as the freedom won by many historically stateless nations has emboldened others to demand greater self-determination.

The third wave of twentieth-century nationalism in Europe, with its emphasis on democratic self-determination, is set to top the continental agenda well into the twenty-first century. The nationalist revival has strengthened submerged national, ethnic, and regional identities and has shattered the conviction that assimilation would eventually homogenize the existing European nation-states.

The Europeans' grand social, economic, and political experiment, the European Union (EU), gives the continent one of the most sophisticated political systems on earth, but at the same time, parts of Europe are still torn by the entrenched state nationalism and ethnic hatreds that brought war to the continent throughout most of the twentieth century. Europe is united by its shared history and culture, but it remains a continent of extraordinary diversity. This diversity, which has withstood centuries of suppression, most characterizes Europe at the threshold of the twenty-first century.

The political and cultural renaissance spreading through Europe's stateless nations is inexorably moving continental politics away from the present system of sovereign states, each jealously defending its authority, to a new order more closely resembling the continent's true national and historical geography. A

European economic and political community dominated by democracy must inevitably recognize the rights of the stateless nations, including the right to choose their own future. The diffusion and force of contemporary national movements make it imperative that the nationalist phenomenon is studied and understood.

ABAZA

Abazian; Abazin; Abazintsy; Apsua; Ashuwa

POPULATION: Approximately (2000 e) 38,000 Abaza in Europe, mostly in the Russian Federation, plus about 10,000 in Turkey and 150 in Germany.

THE ABAZA HOMELAND: The Abaza homeland lies in the northwestern area of the North Caucasus region of southern European Russia. The Abaza region, called Abazashta, forms a district of the Karachayevo-Cherkess Autonomous Region of the Russian Federation. Abazashta lies in the foothills of the main range of the Great Caucasian Mountains on the upper reaches of the Big and Little Zelenchuk, Kuban, and Kuma Rivers.

Most of the Abaza live in thirteen towns and villages in Abazashta, but some live as far away as Kabarda and Adygea, and in two towns near Kislovodsk farther north in Stavropol Krai. In recent years the Abaza have rallied to the call for a separate autonomous republic of Abazashta as an independent member state of the Russian Federation.

FLAG: The Abaza national flag, a variation of the flag of the Confederation of Caucasian Highland Peoples, has seven green and white horizontal stripes with a red canton on the upper hoist bearing two white stars.

PEOPLE: The Abaza are a West Caucasian people, part of the large group of Caucasian nations that inhabit the Caucasus region that divides Europe and Asia between the Black and Caspian Seas. Abaza or Apsua, which is also used by the closely related Abkhaz, are the names they use for their small nation, while Abazin is the name of their language and the name used by the Russians. The Abaza are very attached to their distinct language and culture. The small Abaza nation is traditionally divided into two distinct kinship groups, the Tapanta and Shkaraua (Ashkharaua).

The Abaza language belongs to the Northwest Caucasian language group spoken by the related Caucasian peoples of the North Caucasus. The language, an Abkhaz-Abazin language of the Abkhazo-Adyghian group of Caucasian languages, is close to Abkhaz but also shows elements characteristic of the Circassian language of the Kabards.* Phonetically and morphologically, the Abaza language is practically the same as that of neighboring Abkhaz. The language is spoken in three major dialects, Tapanta, Ashkaraua, and Bezshagh, and five subdialects, Psyzh-Krasnovostok, Apsua, Kubin-Elburgan, Kuvin, and Abazakt. Tapanta is the main dialect and is the source of the Abaza literary language. Extremely rich in consonants, at least sixty-five, of all the languages spoken in Russia, Abaza phonetics are considered the most difficult. The language is the mother tongue of about 95% of the Abaza, a very high percentage among Russian nationalities. Abazin has literary status in Russia and is written in a modified Cyrillic script; however, in Turkey the Abaza minority use Turkish as their literary language.

The majority of the Abaza are Sunni Muslims, with a small, about 3%, Christian minority. The Muslim religion was embraced in the seventeenth and nineteenth centuries under Turkish influence; however, the Abaza's earlier Christian and pagan beliefs and customs can still be observed in their distinct Muslim traditions. A significant number of Abaza, particularly the Shkaraua, remained nominally Christian until the mid-nineteenth century. In the tradition of most European Muslims, the Abaza's lifestyle is basically European, and Abaza women are liberated and unveiled.

NATION: The Abaza are descended from the proto-Abkhazian tribes, a broad conglomerate of Caucasian tribes that populated the eastern shores of the Black Sea in ancient times. Archaeological evidence of their presence goes back to between 4000 and 3000 B.C. Their homeland, which stretched from present-day Tuapse to Sukhumi, was known to the ancient Greeks* and other peoples of the eastern Mediterranean in the first millennium B.C. The early tribal peoples adopted many cultural and linguistic traits from the Greeks and Romans who controlled the coastal regions. In the sixth century A.D. the tribes mostly accepted Christianity under the influence of Byzantium's emperor Justinian I, who decreed that all pagans in the empire should convert.

Four different tribes, the Apsil, Abazg, Svanig, and Misimian, slowly merged to form the Abkhaz nation in the eighth century, and by the late eighth century or early ninth century, an offshoot had formed, the smaller Abaza nation. The center of the Abaza nation lay in the traditional territory of the Abazgi tribe in the northwestern part of Abkhazia, from the Bsyb River to the present city of Tuapse.

In the thirteenth century there was a mass migration to the highlands of the northern Caucasus region. Some individual clans had been moving into the highlands since the eighth century, but the resettlement of the whole Tapanta tribe began in the thirteenth century, followed by the Shkaraua tribe. In the fifteenth and sixteenth centuries the Abaza were known as a strong and militant nation, their mountain strongholds nearly impossible to take by force, although intertribal quarrels and constant wars with neighboring peoples reduced the small nation to vassalage to Kabard princes in the seventeenth century.

Turkish expansion into the Caucasus brought a new religion to the region, Islam. Under Turkish influence the Abaza converted to Sunni Islam between the sixteenth and eighteenth centuries. The Abaza nobility first embraced the Islamic religion spreading to their homeland from Abkhazia. For about a century after the Abaza majority's conversion to Islam, the rural people retained their pagan and Christian traditions, only slightly changed to accommodate the prevailing religion.

The expanding borders of the Russian Empire reached the Abaza homeland in the late eighteenth century, making Abazashta of strategic concern to both the Russians and the Turks of the Ottoman Empire. To overcome Abaza resistance to outside authority, both powers used arms, but the most effective way became deportation. Whole villages were forcibly resettled in territory controlled by Russia or Ottoman Turkey.

The economic life of the region was shaped by the environment. The Abaza, mostly Shkaraua, living in the mountains rich in pastures mainly raised livestock, with flocks of sheep and goats and herds of famous-pedigree horses. The Tapanta living on the flatter lands were mostly farmers, cultivating millet until corn became the primary crop in the nineteenth century. Abundant free land meant that Abaza farmers could plant a field for two or three years, then abandon it for a new plot.

The Abaza joined the other Caucasian peoples in fiercely resisting the imposition of Russian rule in the region. As a result the Russian forces were forced to take the region valley by valley, stronghold by stronghold. Throughout the decades of war, thousands of Abaza fled to Turkish territory to escape the rule of Christian Russia. The emigration was accelerated by a Russian government decree of 1862 demanding that the Abaza people living between the Labo and Belyi Rivers either move to the Kuban to the north or leave Russian territory. The mass emigration of the Abaza destroyed their former tribal structure and brought the clans and subtribes into closer cooperation in order to survive. The territories emptied by the emigrants were colonized by immigrants from other parts of Russia, mostly ethnic Slavs. An estimated 2 million acres of historically Abaza land were confiscated for Slav settlement. As a result of the exodus only about 9,000 of the 50,000 Abaza remained in Russia by 1880.

The Russian Empire, devastated by nearly three years of war, was swept by revolution in February 1917, leaving Abazashta effectively independent as local government collapsed. A movement to unite with the separatist republic set up in neighboring Abhkazia was put down by local Slav militias. On 7 February 1918 Soviet power was proclaimed in Batalpashinsk, the region that included Abazashta. There were Abaza soldiers fighting in both the Red and White Guard units. Two White mounted regiments, Tapanta and Baskhyag, had achieved considerable fame as fierce fighters before the final White defeat.

Collectivization and the cultural revolution radically changed the Abaza way of life. The imposition of Soviet rule aggravated the antagonism between the different social classes. The Soviet solution was found in the deportation and execution of the class enemies unacceptable to the new authorities. The atmosphere of terror in Abazashta hastened the collectivization and subjugation of the Abaza homeland.

Prior to the advent of Soviet power the only education available to the Abaza was the village school or the mosque. The new Soviet authorities in Abazashta, in 1918, set the goal of universal secondary education in the Abaza language. This goal, however, became possible only after 1923, when Talustan Tabulov created a Latin-alphabet Abaza script. Education in the Abaza language was made available for the first six years of schooling; thereafter, Russian was to be used. In 1938 the Soviet authorities ordered that the Abaza literary language adopt the Cyrillic alphabet and that Russian be made the official language of education. The Abaza language and literature were retained as curriculum subjects. A vernacular prose developed, and an Abaza-language theater was established. In 1938 a newspaper began to publish in the Abaza language.

The Abazashta region was included in the Mountain Republic until 1922, when that Caucasus area was divided into small administrative units. The Abaza region was added to the newly formed Karachayevo-Cherkess Oblast. In 1926 the Abaza region was divided between two new administrative units, the Karachay Autonomous Region and the Cherkess National Area. Abazashta was reunited in 1936 but was again divided during World War II.

Joseph Stalin, an ethnic Georgian and particularly suspicious of the small Muslim nations of the Caucasus, in 1943 prepared a plan to deport the Abkhaz and Abaza to Central Asia, but the plan was later postponed. In 1944 the Karachayevo-Cherkess Autonomous Oblast was abolished following the deportation of the entire Karachai nation. Preparations for the mass deportation of the Abkhaz-Abaza began again in 1953, but due to Stalin's death in that year the two small nations were spared the horrors experienced by other Caucasian peoples deported from their homelands on Stalin's orders.

Abazashta remained administratively divided between the Stavropol Krai of the Russian Federation and the Georgian Soviet Socialist Republic from 1944 until 1957, when the Karachay-Cherkess Autonomous Region was reconstituted. The reunited Abaza region received many new inhabitants, mostly ethnic Slavs resettled from areas devastated during World War II.

Communist policy and propaganda left a marked impact on both the daily lives and the mentality of the Abaza people. The way of life in Abazashta is now basically European, with the Abaza's clothing and household goods reflecting the advance of European culture. During the Soviet era homes could be built in only one of three standardized designs approved by the state, and urban settlements were restructured from the traditional haphazard placement to the Russian-style grid pattern.

The liberalization of Soviet life in the late 1980s initiated a period of reculturation. A religious revival began to slowly reverse the inroads made by the official atheism of the Soviet period. Of the traditional rites and customs formerly observed by the Muslim Abaza, those connected with funerals had been the most resistant to change.

Many Abaza crossed the new international border to fight alongside their Abkhaz kin in neighboring Georgia in 1992. A militant nationalist organization, the Confederation of Caucasian Peoples, supported by most of the small nations of the North Caucasus, organized fighting units to support the Abkhaz bid for independence. For the more militant Abaza minority the goal of the fighting was the unification of Abkhazia and Abazashta in a separate, sovereign republic.

The Abaza have begun to take a greater interest in their own history and culture as the decades of imposed Soviet culture fade. Ties to the ethnically and historically related neighboring peoples have increased since the collapse of the Soviet Union, which has strengthened the small nation's determination to survive. However, two trends that may adversely affect the future of the Abaza nation have accelerated since the disintegration of the Soviet Union in 1991, the growing number of mixed marriages and urbanization.

SELECTED BIBLIOGRAPHY

Abtorkhanov, Abdurahman, and Marie Bennigsen Broxup. *The North Caucasus Barrier: The Russian Advance towards the Muslim World.* 1992.

Baddeley, John F. *Russian Conquest of the Caucasus.* 1997.

Chervonnaeiia, Svetlana Aleksandrovna. *Conflict in the Caucasus: Georgia, Abkhazia, and the Russian Shadow.* 1994.

Coppieters, Bruno, ed. *Contested Borders in the Caucasus.* 1996.

Olson, James S. *An Ethnohistorical Dictionary of the Russian and Soviet Empires.* 1994.

ABKHAZ

Abkhazi; Abkhazians; Apsua

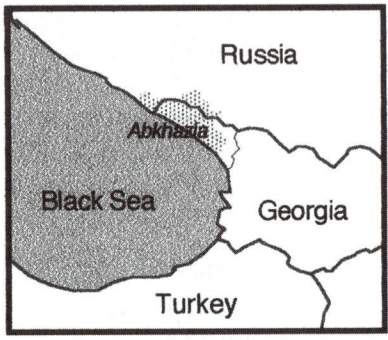

POPULATION: Approximately (2000 e) 122,000 Abkhaz in Europe, mostly in the Causasian breakaway Republic of Abkhazia, and an estimated 35,000 in Turkey. Other large populations live in Syria and Jordan. Smaller numbers live in the United States, Israel, Yugoslavia, Canada, Egypt, the Netherlands, and Germany.

THE ABKHAZ HOMELAND: The Abkhaz homeland occupies a narrow coastal plain on the southeastern coast of the Black Sea, backed by a spur of the western Caucasus Mountains, in northwestern Georgia. The steep mountain slopes give way to a central area of foothills and river valleys that meet a narrow coastal lowland along the shores of the eastern Black Sea. This narrow strip of land is characterized by an extreme variety of natural conditions, including sub-tropical lowlands, mountain lakes, mineral springs, and abundant forests. The natural borders of the Abkhaz homeland are the Psou River in the west, the Ingur in the east, the Black Sea in the south, and the main range of the Caucasus Mountains in the north.

Abkhazia borders the Russian Federation on the north, the Black Sea on the southwest, and the Georgian region of Mingrelia on the southeast. Prior to the outbreak of fighting in the region in 1992, Abkhazia was divided into five regions, only two of which had Abkhaz majorities. The Abkhaz republic, while virtually independent, legally remains an autonomous republic within the Republic of Georgia. *Republic of Abkhazia (Apsny Respublika)*: 3,320 sq.mi.–8,599 sq.km. (2000 e) 307,000. The population breakdown is based on 1992 population estimates made prior to the outbreak of fighting in the region. (92e) Georgians* 44%, Abkhaz 20%, Russians* 16%, Armenians* 6%, Ukrainians* 2%, Pontian Greeks* 2%. The Abkhaz capital and major cultural center, Sukhumi, the official capital of the breakaway republic, had an estimated population of 104,000 in 1999.

FLAG: The Abkhaz national flag, the official flag of the breakaway republic, has seven green and white stripes with a red canton on the upper hoist bearing a white hand below an arch of seven white, five-pointed stripes.

PEOPLE: The Abkhaz are a Northern Caucasian nation encompassing four major geographical and cultural groups, the Muslim Gudauta, Abzhui, and Abaza and the Orthodox Samurzakan. The Abkhaz call themselves Apsua, and their ancient territory they call Ashvy, the Land of the Abkhaz. The Abkhaz population grew very slowly until after World War II. From 1926 to 1939 the population grew by only 2,000, which graphically reflects the impact of collectivization and the excesses of the Soviet repression.

The Abkhaz language belongs to the Abkhazo-Adyghian group of Caucasian languages. Rich in consonants, at least sixty-eight, the Abkhaz language is considered the world's fastest phonetically, with complete information, such as word root and tense, often conveyed by a single consonant. The language is considered one of the most difficult of the languages of the region to learn. The three major dialects of the language are Abzhui, Samurzakan, and Bzyb.

The majority of the Abkhaz are Sunni Muslims; however, the rites and rituals often mix ancient Christian and pagan traditions. Christianity was brought to the region by missionaries in the first century A.D., and the Abkhaz greatly helped the spread of the new religion throughout the Caucasus region. In the sixteenth century the Turks* introduced Islam, which rapidly supplanted the earlier Christianity among a majority of the population.

NATION: The first written mention of the Abkhaz people is believed to be the note on the Abesla tribes living in Asia Minor found in the records of the Assyrian ruler Tiglath-pileser. The early Abkhaz tribes, the Apsil, Misiman, Abazg, and Svanig, were known to the ancient Greek and Roman historians like Hekateus of Miletus, Strabo, and Flavius Arrianus. Greeks colonized the coastal regions as early as the sixth century B.C. Latinized following the Roman conquest of the Greek cities in 65 B.C., the tribes adopted much of the Romans' Latin culture and language, and Christian missionaries later became active in the region.

In the first century A.D. the tribes organized in petty states, which united in the Lazika principality in the fourth century. The tribes soon came under Byzantine cultural and political influence, particularly those tribes living in the coastal regions. During this period the first evidence of a local Christian congregation was recorded when Stratophilus, the archbishop of Pitsunda, took part in the first Council of Nicaea held in A.D. 325.

The consolidation of the Abkhaz nation in the seventh and eighth centuries began with the separation of Abkhazia from Lazika in 740. Prince Leon II united all of present western Georgia into a unitary state with his capital at Kutaisi. Weakened by wars and internal strife, the state declined, and in 978 the Abkhaz throne passed to the dynasty that ruled Georgia.

In the early sixteenth century the Turks began to raid the coast, about the same time that the Abkhaz regained their independence under Prince Shervash-idze. During the rule of the Shervashidze dynasty Turkish influence became paramount, and in 1578 Abkhazia became a protectorate of the Turkish sultanate. Over the next decades a majority of the Abkhaz abandoned Christianity for the Islamic religion of the Turks. As Turkish protection meant mainly an obligation to pay a yearly tribute, in the eighteenth century the Ottoman Turks began the political subordination of Abkhazia. The Shervashidzes turned to Russia for help, and in 1810 Czar Alexander I issued an order declaring Abkhazia a Russian protectorate. For Abkhaz society annexation to Russia meant the final establishment of feudal relations and the consolidation of serfdom. Land rights were consolidated in the hands of *ataua*, dukes and princes; *aamsta*, the nobility; and the clergy.

The Crimean and Caucasian Wars, fought mostly in the Black Sea and Caucasus regions, allowed the Abkhaz to demand greater rights. However, following the final Russian victory over the Caucasian peoples to the east in 1864, Abkhaz autonomy became unnecessary to the Russian government. The last Prince Shervashidze was sent into exile, and czarist power and Russian bureaucracy were established.

Russian attempts to promote assimilation, particularly official efforts to convert the Muslim Abkhaz to Orthodox Christianity, incited a popular uprising in 1866. The Russian military quickly defeated the poorly armed Abkhaz army of 20,000 and subjected the majority of the defeated Abkhaz to virtual serfdom on the Russian and Georgian estates established on confiscated Abkhaz lands. As a result of the brutal suppression following the Abkhaz uprising, many Abkhaz emigrated to Turkish territory, the so-called Manadzhir Movement. Over 70,000 Abkhaz are believed to have left Abkhazia between 1866 and 1878. The tsarist government reacted by banning the name Abkhazia and instituting a program of leasing empty lands to peasants immigrating from other parts of the empire.

The Russian state reforms of 1870 accelerated the development of cash crops in the region. Tobacco, tea, and subtropical fruits became the major crops, and industries began to develop. Health resorts along the coast became fashionable with the tsarist nobility. The overall economic prosperity spurred the growth of a local intelligentsia and eventually the rise of Abkhaz national consciousness.

By the early 1900s a strong nationalist and separatist sentiment had developed among the educated Abkhaz. Following the February Revolution in 1917, Abkhazia became effectively independent as the tsarist bureaucracy collapsed. Abkhaz leaders formed the Abkhaz National Council and asserted their nation's right to autonomy. Occupied by Georgian troops following the Bolshevik coup in October 1917, the Abkhaz organized resistance and in February 1918 rose to expel the invaders. The rebels proclaimed Abkhazia independent on 8 March 1918. Their independent state lasted just forty-two days before Bolshevik troops invaded. In desperation the Abkhaz leaders appealed to the neighboring Georgians for military aid. Once having driven the Bolsheviks out of Abkhazia, the Georgians stayed to incorporate the unwilling Abkhaz nation into their newly independent republic.

The Abkhaz revolted against Georgian rule in early 1921. The resulting chaos within Georgia provided a pretext for the Red Army's subsequent invasion and conquest of both Abkhazia and Georgia. In February 1921 the Abkhaz Soviet Socialist Republic was established and in December of that year was incorporated into the Georgian Soviet Socialist Republic. After Joseph Stalin became leader of the USSR in the late 1920s, Georgian authorities began restricting Abkhazian cultural expression and pressed assimilation.

The Soviet period saw the collectivization of the Abkhaz homeland. From 1929 to 1935 the number of collective farms rose from 14 to 472, and by 1940 collectivization had been applied to over 90% of the region's agricultural lands. The collectivization of the Abkhaz lands was accompanied by the elimination or deportation of the Abkhaz opposition. Many Abkhaz leaders were banished to the notorious coal mines at Tkvarceli. In spite of the hardships and oppression, agricultural production increased rapidly, which, in turn, spurred the growth of the cities and the urbanization of the Abkhaz nation. Only 5% of the Abkhaz lived in urban areas in 1926, but by 1939 over 15% were considered city dwellers.

A Latin-based alphabet, devised in 1862, spurred the growth of Abkhaz education. The first books were published in the Abkhaz alphabet in 1865, and by 1912 a vernacular prose had developed. Soviet policy decreed a change of alphabet to Roman letters in 1928, then the introduction of the Georgian alphabet in 1938, and the Cyrillic alphabet in 1954. Periodicals in Cyrillic script started to appear only in the mid-1950s.

The Soviet leader Joseph Stalin, himself an ethnic Georgian and particularly suspicious of the small Muslim nations of the Caucasus, in 1943, during World War II, prepared a plan to deport the Abkhaz to Central Asia, but the plan was later postponed. Preparations for the mass deportation of the Abkhaz began again in 1953, but due to Stalin's death in that year the Abkhaz were spared the horrors experienced by other Caucasian peoples deported from their homelands on Stalin's orders. However, massive Georgian immigration to Abkhazia, undertaken under Stalin's long dictatorial rule, reduced the Abkhaz to minority status in their homeland by the end of World War II.

Resentment of the Georgians' dominant status fanned tense ethnic relations in the region and stimulated an Abkhaz national revival in the 1970s and 1980s. Led by the educated, urban population, numbering over one-third of the Abkhaz population in 1970, Abkhaz nationalist sentiment developed as a popular anti-Georgian movement. Beginning in 1978, the Soviet government, in an effort to head off growing Abkhaz demands for separation from Georgia, set aside as many as 67% of government and party positions in Abkhazia for native Abkhaz, even though the ethnic Georgian population of the region was some two and a half times larger.

The liberalization of Soviet life in the late 1980s accelerated the growth of Abkhaz nationalism. In 1988 a nationalist popular front organization, Aiglara (Unity), formed, and for the first time since 1921 the Abkhaz National Council was convened. On 18 March 1989 the council called for Abkhaz secession from Georgia, which provoked a strong Georgian nationalist reaction and violent confrontations, particularly severe in June and July 1989.

The Republic of Georgia regained its independence at the disintegration of the Soviet Union in 1991, claiming Abkhazia as part of its national territory. An ethnocentric Georgian national government exacerbated tensions between Georgians and Abkhazians, whose sense of national identity is as strong as that of the Georgians. On 23 July 1992 the Abkhaz legislature, with widespread support, reinstated the republic's 1925 constitution, effectively declaring Abkhazia an independent republic. In response, the Georgian military occupied the region, setting off a bitter war of secession.

The separatist forces slowly drove the Georgian military from the region and in September 1993 took the capital, Sukhumi. Some 200,000 Georgians fled from Abkhazia into western Georgia. In June 1994 the Georgian government reluctantly accepted 3,000 Russian troops on the Abkhaz border, effectively making Abkhazia independent under the de facto protection of the Russians.

On 26 November 1994 the Abkhaz parliament formally proclaimed the sovereign Republic of Abkhazia. The parliament then elected as the republic's first president parliament chairman Vladislav Ardzinba. In 1996 CIS leaders agreed to impose economic sanctions against Abkhazia until it willingly reincorporates itself into the Georgian republic. The republic remains effectively independent, although its sovereignty has not been recognized by any world body or national government.

SELECTED BIBLIOGRAPHY

Benet, Sula. *Abkhasians: The Long Living People of the Caucasus.* 1974.

Chervonnaeiia, Svetlana Aleksandrovna. *Conflict in the Caucasus: Georgia, Abkhazia, and the Russian Shadow.* 1994.

Colton, Timothy, and Robert Levgold, eds. *After the Soviet Union.* 1992.

Coppieters, Bruno, ed. *Contested Borders in the Caucasus.* 1996.

Dins, Sham. *Perestroika and the Nationalities Quest in the USSR.* 1991.

ADYGE

Adygeny; Adyghe; Adyghei;
Adygei

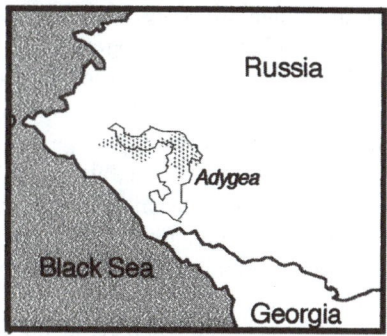

POPULATION: Approximately (2000 e) 128,000 Adyge in Europe, mainly in the Adyge Republic of the Russian Federation. A large Adyge population, estimated to number over 130,000, live in Turkey, with smaller numbers in Syria, Jordan, Iraq, Israel, the United States, and Germany. Adyge nationalists estimate the total number of Adyge at between 275,000 and 300,000.

THE ADYGE HOMELAND: The Adyge homeland lies in the North Caucasus Region of southwestern European Russia, between the Kuban River and the foothills of the Caucasus Mountains. Most of the traditional Adyge homeland is now included in the autonomous republic, the Adyge Republic or Adygea, which was proclaimed a member state of the Russian Federation in 1991. Adygea is surrounded by territory belonging to Krasnodar Krai (Kuban) and is separated from the territories of the other Circassian peoples, the Cherkess* and Kabards,* by the Slav-populated Laba region just east of Adygea.

Its terrain consists of rolling plains in the Kuban River valley and mountains and foothills in the south. The highest peak is Mt. Chugush, which rises to 10,623 ft. (3,238 m.). The republic has abundant forests and fertile black soil in the Kuban lowlands. The region, rich in agricultural output, also produces oil and natural gas. Major products include livestock, wheat, and corn. Other economic assets include lumbering, furniture making, food processing, and machinery manufacture.

Adygea, formerly the Adygei Autonomous Oblast, became a member state of the Russian Federation in 1991. *Republic of Adygea (Respublika Adygea)*: 8,757 sq.mi.–22,686 sq.km. (2000 e) 440,000—Russians* and Kuban Cossacks* 68%, Adyge 24%, Cherkess and Kabards 6%, Nogais* 2%. The Adyge capital and major cultural center, Maykop (Maikop), has a population of (2000 e)165,000 and lies sixty-five miles southeast of Krasnodar.

FLAG: The Adyge national flag, the official flag of the autonomous republic, is a green field bearing three crossed yellow arrows surmounted by three yellow stars under an arc of nine yellow stars.

PEOPLE: The Circassian peoples, who call themselves Adyge, are the oldest indigenous people in the North Caucasus region. The Adyge are a Circassian people, also known as the Lower Circassians or Kiakhs, the most westerly of the three main divisions of the Circassian peoples. The Adyge nation is divided into ten cultural and geographical subgroups. The Adyge first emerged as a distinctive group in the thirteenth century. At that time they had populated the vast region between the Don River, the Black Sea, the Caucasus Mountains, and the Stavropol Plateau.

Their language, Adyge, also called West Circassian or Kiakh, belongs to the Northwestern Caucasian languages and is a Lower Circassian language of the Abkhazo-Adyghian group of Caucasian languages. Its unusual phonological system—an overabundance of consonants and a scarcity of vowels—has stimulated much interest among linguists. The language, although dialectical differences remain, can be understood by the other Circassian peoples, the Cherkess or Middle Circassians, and the Kabards. The language is the mother tongue of an estimated 96% of the Adyge population. The language is spoken in four major, mutually intelligible dialects: Sapsug, Bezhedukh (Bzedug), Abadzeg (Abadzekh), and Temirgoi (Temirgoj). Adyge was made an official literary language, along with Russian, in Adygea in 1994 and is used for instruction in Adyge schools. The Adyge language became a literary language only after the Russian Revolution.

Overwhelmingly and fervently Sunni Muslim, the Adyge adhere to the Shafi or Hanafi rites, a moderate form of Islam that eschews fundamentalist extremes. Their Islamic religion, which shows strong pagan and Christian influences, remains an important part of the Adyge's everyday life.

The Adyge have good relations with the numerous Kuban Cossacks who inhabit the region, but relations with the ethnic Russian population is often strained. The Adyge have lived beside the Cossack population for over two centuries, and many Adyge traditions have become part of the neighboring Kuban Cossack culture.

Known for their exquisite tapestries and other handicrafts, the Adyge have developed a culture influenced by both the Christian and Muslim peoples living in the North Caucasus region. The Adyge are known throughout the region for their skills in breeding horses, cattle, and sheep and are renowned horsemen noted for their marksmanship. Their sheepskins and leathers are prized far beyond their homeland.

NATION: Known to the ancient Greeks as Zyukhoy, the Circassian peoples probably settled the region of the North Caucasus before the sixth century B.C. Possibly the earliest representative of the Caucasian peoples, the Circassian peo-

ples populated a wide area north of the Caucasus Mountains that figured prominently in the legends of ancient Greece. The handsome Adyge, valued in harems
and as slaves, developed a warrior society as protection against the region's
frequent invaders and raids by slavers.

The Adyge homeland, whose rivers drain into the Black Sea, not the Caspian,
has a long history of contact with the Mediterranean world. Greek and Roman
writers described them as fine horsemen. The Adyge tribes traded with Byzantium in horses, honey, agricultural products, and fine jewelry.

Christianity, introduced to the Adyge tribes by Greek monks, began to take
hold in the sixth century A.D. A common religion facilitated the tribes' trade
and diplomatic ties to the Byzantines to the south and the early Slav state,
Kievan Rus, to the north. By the ninth century the tribes carried on an extensive
trade and maintained diplomatic ties with the expanding Slav Empire.

The fierce Circassian tribes, often warring among themselves, were feared by
neighboring peoples. The intertribal wars scattered the tribes across a wide area,
from the Black Sea to the Kuban River and the Greater Caucasus Mountains.

Contact with Byzantium ended with the thirteenth-century Mongol invasion.
Weakened by the Mongol conquest of 1241–42, the tribes came under the rule
of Christian Georgia by the end of the thirteenth century. The majority of the
tribes fought Georgian rule, with rebellions frequent. The tribes' mountain
strongholds frustrated Georgian efforts to completely subdue the Adyge and the
other tribes. The tribes, seeking allies, sought aid from the expanding Ottoman
Empire of the Turks. Turkish influence became predominant in much of the
region.

Russian expansion into the North Caucasus in the sixteenth century was contested by the dominant power in the region, the Ottoman Empire. The Adyge,
along with the other Circassian tribes, generally sided with the Turks in the
series of wars with Russia. By the seventeenth century the majority of the tribes
had adopted the Turks' Islamic religion.

In 1774 the Russians finally established their authority in the region, which
prompted fierce Adyge resistance over the next decades. In 1783 the Adyge
homeland was formally annexed to the Russian Empire. Zaporozhye Cossacks
from the Ukraine were settled in the newly conquered lands in 1792. These
Cossacks, the ancestors of the Kuban Cossacks, adopted many fighting techniques and cultural traditions from the native Adyge tribes. Relations between
the two peoples, often united against the hated tsarist administration, were generally good.

The Russian government forced the weakened Ottoman Empire to give up all
claims to the region in the Treaty of Adrianople in 1829. The treaty was only
a formality as rebellions, skirmishing, and reprisals continued for several more
decades. In 1857 the Russian military established a fort at Maykop in Adyge
territory.

The Muslim peoples of the eastern Caucasus region rebelled under Shamyl
in 1859, and although the Adyge were not directly involved in the war, they

did take advantage of the Russians' weakness to raid and harass the Russian forts in the west Caucasus region. An influx of freed serfs seeking lands led to more violent confrontations between the Adyge and the new arrivals following the abolition of serfdom in Russia in 1861. In 1864 the Russians, after years of sporadic fighting, finally conquered the Circassian peoples. The defeated Circassians, including the Adyge, were given a choice between settling on the plains among the growing Russian population under Russian military control or emigrating to Turkish territory. Some 400,000 tribespeople, rejecting Christian domination, fled or were expelled to Turkish territory. Those who survived the trek to Turkish territory were either assimilated or moved on to settle in Syria, Jordan, Palestine, and Lebanon. Russians, Ukrainians,* and Armenians* were settled in the depopulated Adyge lands.

Slavic migration to the region, spurred by the discovery of oil at Maykop in 1900, resulted in the formation of an urbanized, industrial proletariat in the region. Relegated to a marginal existence in the rural areas, the Adyge proved an enduring problem for the Russian military and civil authorities of the vast Kuban territory.

Openly sympathetic to the Muslim Turks when war began in 1914, the Adyge enthusiastically welcomed the news that revolution had overthrown the hated tsarist government in February 1917. Adyge appeals to the new government for religious freedom, political autonomy, and the reunification of the Circassian lands received no response. Responding to calls for Muslim solidarity, the Adyge sent delegates to an all-Muslim conference in September 1917, which supported demands for the religious and political rights of the Muslim peoples of the Caucasus region.

Vehemently opposed to the antireligious stance of the new Bolshevik government, installed after a coup in October 1917, the Muslim leaders of the Caucasus region organized an autonomous state called North Caucasia. In January 1918 Soviet rule was established at Maykop, but the region remained chaotic. Threatened by both sides in the Russian civil war, the Bolsheviks and the anti-Bolshevik White forces, the Muslim leaders declared North Caucasia independent of Russia on 11 May 1918. The news was greeted with great enthusiasm in Adygea. A rival government, set up by the Kuban Cossacks, also laid claim to Adygea as part of the Kuban Republic.

The breakaway Republic of North Caucasia was overrun by the White forces of General Deniken in January 1919. The Whites' vehement opposition to the secession of the region from Russia pushed the Adyge and other Muslim tribes into an alliance with the opposing Reds. Promised independence in a Soviet federation of states, most of the Adyge went over to the Bolshevik forces. In January 1920 the Red Army drove the last White units from the region. In 1922 a part of the traditional Adyge homeland was established as an autonomous district under the Soviet's nationalities policy with Krasnodar as its capital. Most mosques and all religious schools were closed by the government.

Soviet repression, particularly of religion, provoked sporadic rebellions, particularly serious in 1929 and 1937. In 1936, in an effort to diffuse Adyge nationalism, the Soviet government upgraded Adygea's status to that of an autonomous region with redrawn borders and a new capital at Maykop.

Thinking to capitalize on the Circassians' grievances, the Nazi Germans, after taking the Kuban region during the Caucasus campaign of 1942, offered the Adyge an alliance and promoted anticommunist solidarity. The Germans held Adygea from August 1942 to January 1943; however, the Adyge view that the Germans represented just another in a long series of invaders spared them the brutal deportations suffered by neighboring Muslim peoples following the return of the Soviet authorities.

The reform of Soviet society under Mikhail Gorbachev in the late 1980s allowed the Adyge to voice decades of frustrations and grievances. The three Circassian peoples, the Adyge, the Cherkess or Circassians, and the Kabards, separated under tsarist and Soviet rule, demanded unification and the dissolution of the hybrid territories that the Cherkess and Kabards had been forced to share with the Turkic Karachai and Balkar peoples for most of this century. Demands for a separate Circassian republic within the Russian Federation accelerated with the disintegration of the Soviet state in August 1991.

The three Circassian peoples, joined to the other Muslim Caucasian peoples in traditional alliances and historic associations, in late 1994 condemned the Russian military attack on the separatist government in Chechenia. The Russian advance, mirroring that of the nineteenth century, has inflamed nationalist and anti-Russian sentiment in the Circassian regions.

SELECTED BIBLIOGRAPHY

Bennigsen, Alexandre, and S. Enders Wimbush. *Muslims of the Soviet Empire: A Guide.* 1986.

Goldenberg, Suzanne. *Pride of Small Nations.* 1994.

Olson, James S. *An Ethnohistorical Dictionary of the Russian and Soviet Empires.* 1994.

Pushkarev, Sergei. *Self-Government and Freedom in Russia.* 1988.

Wixman, Ronald. *The Peoples of the USSR: An Ethnographic Handbook.* 1984.

AGULS

Aguil Shui; Aghul Shuy; Aghuls;
Aguly; Agulskiy

POPULATION: Approximately (2000 e) 24,000 Aguls in Europe, mostly in the Dagestan Republic of the Russian Federation.

THE AGUL HOMELAND: The Agul homeland lies in the Dagestan Republic of southeastern European Russia, one of the most isolated regions in Europe. The rural Agul homeland remains a center of animal husbandry, sheep and goats in the highlands and cattle in the lowlands. Some Agul have settled in the Derbent region of Dagestan. Their mountains impede communications, even between Agul communities. Contact is possible only from spring to autumn, when the narrow mountain passes are negotiable. This isolation has been a major factor in the development of dialectical differences between the various Agul communities.

The Agul canyons form a nearly inaccessible valley isolated from the world by four forbidding spurs of the Caucasus Mountains, the Aguldere, Gushandere, Magudere, and Khyukdere. Before the building of the Tpig-Kasumkent Highway, the Aguls were almost completely isolated. The Agul homeland is watered by two rivers, the Tshirakh-Tshay and Kurakh-Tshay. Administratively, the Agul homeland is situated in the Agul Rayon (county) of the Dagestan Republic of the Russian Federation, which is divided into eight subdivisions. The Agul capital and cultural center is the largest of the Agul towns, Tpig.

FLAG: The flag used by the Aguls is the Dagestani national flag, a horizontal tricolor of green, pale blue, and red.

PEOPLE: The Aguls are a small Caucasian nation, part of the larger group of nations called the Dagestanis or the peoples of Dagestan. The Aguls have little sense of group ethnicity due to their isolated communities, the nature of their traditional economies, and their social structure. The Agul, until recently, identified more with one of the four subgroups, based on where they live, than with the larger Agul nation. This local loyalty began to change only following the overthrow of Russia's communist government. Although the Agul population underwent a decline between the censuses of 1933 and 1959 due to assimilation by the neighboring Lezgins, that trend reversed in the 1970s as many Aguls, formerly counted as ethnic Legzin, changed their ethnic designation. Between 1970 and 1979 the number of people claiming Agul ethnicity grew by nearly 50%.

The four primary Agul subgroups are the Aguldere, Kurkhdere, Khushandere, and Khpuikdere. The largest of the groups is the Aguldere. Within these subgroups, the Aguls are further divided by a patriarchal clan system in which young Aguls are encouraged to marry first or second cousins. The pattern of communal landholding strengthens the extended family unit and the prevailing clan system.

The Aguls speak a Caucasian language belonging to the Lezgian-Samur or southeastern group of Dagestani languages. The language is close to Lezgin, which has replaced Russian as the literary language since 1991. Four Agul dialects are distinguishable, Agul, Kere, Gekxun, and Koshan. An estimated 98% use Agul as their mother tongue. In the last two decades the Agul region has been influenced by the increasingly strident voice of Muslim religious fundamentalism.

NATION: The Aguls are a native Caucasian nation, thought to have inhabited the region since before recorded history. The oldest reference to the Aguls is found in an Armenian source from the seventh century A.D. The Lezgins,* living just to the south, have traditionally been the Aguls' contact with the outside world. The two peoples have had a long trading relationship with the Lezgins buying the Aguls' wool, fleece, and cheeses.

The Aguls' geographical isolation failed to protect their small nation from invaders. In the seventh century Arabs overran the region but failed to take the mountain strongholds. In the thirteenth and fourteenth centuries, the Golden Horde and Tamerlane's forces fought their way into the high mountain valleys. In the fifteenth century the Turks* of the Ottoman Empire began to extend nominal authority in the Dagestan region.

The Aguls were historically controlled by the Laks* and then the Tabasarans.* The communities of Aguls in the Aguldere region established their own territorial and political unity, a free community that was eventually incorporated into the Kasikumukh Khanate in the seventeenth and eighteenth centuries. Other Agul communities, not self-governing, were subjected by local feudal rulers such as the Tabasaran *qadis*, who levied tribute or taxes but generally left the Aguls to look after themselves in their isolated mountain villages. Owing to the political disunion, the Aguls did not develop a state structure, which retarded their development as a distinct nation.

The system of local administration was mostly at village level. Problems were decided by a village elder, the *begaoul*, and his advisers. The elders were elected by a village assembly, the *dzhamat*. In the nineteenth century, after the imposition of Russian rule, when market forces began to make themselves felt, the village elders tended to be elected from among the richest in the village rather than from among the wisest or most distinguished.

Until the fifteenth century the Aguls were primarily animists with their own folk religion, although Zoroastrianism, Christianity, and Judaism were gaining adherents in the region. In the fifteenth century Persian traders introduced Islam into the Agul communities. According to Agul oral tradition, a part of their nation adhered to Judaism and a part to Christianity before the conversion to Islam. By the nineteenth century all the Agul communities had been converted to Sunni Islam.

In 1813, under the terms of the Treaty of Gulistan, the Agul territories were incorporated into the Russian Empire. The majority of the Agul communities were included in the Kürin Khanate, which was disbanded and became the Russian-administered Kürin district. The class structure, the superiority of the Agul nobility and clergy, was retained under Russian rule, while the establishment of a common territory created a basis for the evolution of the Agul nation.

The Russian administration of the Agul homeland was not finally established until the defeat of Iman Shamyl and the end of the Murid Wars in the region in 1859. Shamyl had rallied all the Dagestani peoples against the Christian Russians* by calling for holy war against the invaders of the Dagestani homelands.

The Russian Revolution in 1917 brought chaos and war to the region. The Aguls, officially listed as Lezgins in Russian census figures, sent delegates to an all-Muslim government, which was erected in the region following the Bolshevik takeover of Russia in late 1917. The Muslim government, finally defeated in 1920, was replaced by the new Soviet administration.

The Soviets created the Mountain Autonomous Republic, with Arabic as the official language of government and education. The Aguls, along with the other highland Dagestani peoples, opposed the policy and rebelled. In 1921 the authorities created the Dagestan Autonomous Soviet Socialist Republic and, in 1925, launched an antireligious campaign. Mosques were turned into storehouses, the clergy were dispersed or killed, and a new cult of Soviet prophets became official policy. The Azeri language was declared the official language of the region. In 1928 the Soviets declared that Dargin, Avar, Lezgin, and Azeri were all official languages in Dagestan. The government also decided to include the Aguls in the larger Lezgin ethnic group.

The Soviet policies of cultural manipulation only increased Agul resentment of Russian domination. The Aguls resisted Russification of their culture and refused to accept the disappearance of their small nation within the Lezgin culture. Agul resistance increased when the Soviet authorities attempted to relocate them to the lowland towns and collective farms.

In order to strengthen their hold on the region, the Soviet authorities had first to do away with the territorial isolation of the Aguls. This was accomplished in 1936 with the construction of the Tpig-Kasumkent Highway. The importance of the road to Soviet policy in the region was immediately apparent through Soviet collectivization. In 1935 the Agul clans still held their lands in the traditional manner. By 1937 there were over twenty collectives, which constituted 89% of the Agul population. Although collectivized, the Aguls retained their traditional occupations, caring for herds of sheep and cattle. Land cultivation was for personal necessities; however, arable land and the distortions of the Soviet system forced many Agul men to spend winters working in Baku or Derbent.

The completion of the Tpig-Kasumkent Highway also aided the development of state-run health and educational systems. In 1936 the first hospital in the Agul homeland opened in Tpig. Between 1937, when no public educational facilities were available, and 1952, the Aguls gained a secondary school, seven middle schools, and one primary school. Until 1953, when Russian was declared the official language, local administration and education were carried out in the Lezgin language.

In the 1950s and 1960s industrialization was brought to Dagestan. This increased the number of Aguls seeking work in the towns and cities. Urbanization, although it has not threatened the survival of the small Agul nation, has brought major changes to the material culture. Every year brings an increase in the consumption of factory-made goods and consumer products. Among younger Aguls there is a disdainful attitude toward the old tradition; however, the old ways have retained a venerable place in Agul society, and the old customs still persist. Because of their continuing geographic isolation and their resentment of attempts to Russianize education, Agul educational levels are among the lowest in the Russian Federation and therefore among the lowest in Europe.

In mid-1998, as violence increased in Dagestan, talk of secession from Russia became more open. Dagestan's nationalities minister, Magomedsalikh Gusaev, an ethnic Agul, commented that if the violence gets out of hand, he would again be an Agul and would return to his homeland to fight. Tradition still remains paramount, with many officials repeating that they don't want to fight, but if any of their relatives are killed, they will have no choice.

SELECTED BIBLIOGRAPHY

Bennigsen, Alexandre, and S. Enders Wimbush. *Muslims of the Soviet Empire: A Guide.* 1986.

Olson, James S. *An Ethnohistorical Dictionary of the Russian and Soviet Empires.* 1994.

Salkeld, Audrey, and Jose Bermudez. *On the Edge of Europe: Mountaineering in the Caucasus.* 1994.

Weekes, Richard V. *Muslim Peoples.* 1984.

Wixman, Ronald. *The Peoples of the USSR: An Ethnographic Handbook.* 1984.

AJARS

Ajarians; Adjars; Adzhars; Achars;
Ajhareli; Ach'areli

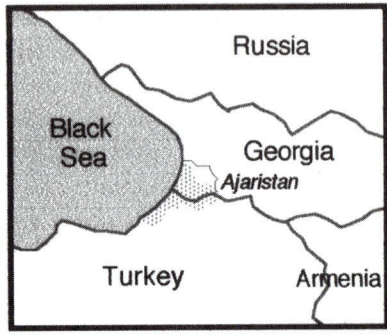

POPULATION: Approximately (2000 e) 260,000 Ajars in Europe, mostly in Georgia, and another 95,000, called Laz, in adjacent areas of Turkey.

THE AJAR HOMELAND: The Ajar homeland lies in southwestern Georgia, just north of the international border with Turkey. It is predominantly mountainous, with some river valleys and a lowland coastal area. Mountain ranges in the republic include the Meskhet'is K'edi, running southwest to northeast, and the Shavshet'is K'edi, bordering the south. The mountainous areas of Ajaria are mostly densely forested. A narrow coastal plain on the Black Sea has a pleasant, subtropical climate and is the heartland of the Ajar nation. Ajaria's economy is primarily based on agriculture, while industrial activity is centered in Bat'umi, which has an oil refinery supplied by an oil pipeline from Baku, Azerbaijan.

The Ajar homeland forms an autonomous republic within the Republic of Georgia. *Ajar Republic (Ajaristan)*: 1,160 sq.mi.–3,005 sq.km. (2000 e) 391,000— Ajars 65%, Georgians* 14%, Russians* 6%, Armenians* 6%, Greeks* 2%. The Ajar capital and major cultural center, Batumi, (2000 e) 142,000, lies on the Black Sea near the Turkish border.

FLAG: The Ajar national flag is a horizontal bicolor of green and red, the red twice the width of the green, bearing a white crescent moon, points up, and a white five-pointed star centered on the red.

PEOPLE: The Ajars or Ajarians are a South Caucasian people who call themselves Ach'areli or Ajareli. Mostly of Georgian ancestry, the Ajars have been counted as ethnic Georgians in Soviet and Georgian censuses since 1926. Ethnically, the Ajars are Georgians, and their language is a Gurian dialect of Georgian laced with Turkish borrowings called Guruli. The literary language of the Ajar nation is standard Georgian. The majority of the Ajars are bilingual, speaking both their own Georgian dialect and Turkish. The Ajar nation is traditionally divided into the Ajars in the south and east and the Kabuletians in the north and west. The Ajars are not considered a separate ethnic group by the Georgian government, although they do have distinct religious and cultural traditions. The Ajars, traditionally oriented toward Turkey, have attempted to win greater autonomy within Georgia by peaceful means.

Religion has historically and emotionally divided the Ajar nation from the Georgians. The majority adhere to the Hanafite rite of Sunni Islam and remain devoted to their Muslim faith. The Ajar homeland formed part of the Turkish Ottoman Empire until the Russo-Turkish War of 1877–78 divided the region, bringing the majority under Russian rule but leaving a sizable minority in Turkey.

NATION: The Ajar homeland, known to the ancient world as Colchis, flourished with the Greek colonization of the coastal region between the sixth and fourth centuries B.C. Celebrated in the Greek legends of *Jason and the Argonauts* and *Medea*, Colchis remained part of the Greek world for centuries. In the first century B.C. Colchis formed an important part of the Greek kingdom of Pontus.

Colchis, conquered by the Romans in 62 B.C. and known as Iberia, became a prosperous, Latinized province that eventually adopted the new Christian religion in the fourth century. The Christian Ajars formed part of the Roman kingdom of Lazica in the fourth century. Following the decline of Roman power, the region was contested by the Byzantine and Persian Empires until the seventh century, when the Arab conquest of the Persian Empire brought a new power and a new religion to the region. Ajaria later became part of the Christian Armenian kingdom and in the ninth century nominally formed part of the expanding Georgian kingdom.

Over the following centuries the region was conquered many times. The Seljuks overran the region in the eleventh century, the Mongols in the thirteenth century, the forces of Timur (Tamerlane) in the fourteenth century, and in the fifteenth century the Ottoman Turks* conquered the area. The Ajars' ancestors, concentrated in the coastal plain and protected by high mountains, remained semi-independent until the Turkish conquest in the seventeenth century. Called Laz by the Turks, the Ajars prospered under Turkish rule. Over the next two centuries a majority adopted the Turks' Islamic culture and religion, their homeland forming an important part of the administrative district called Lazistan.

The rich region, with the important port of Batumi, was one of the prizes awarded to Russia by the Congress of Berlin at the end of the Russo-Turkish War of 1877–79. The region remained a frontier district between the Russian and Ottoman Empires. Undeterred by the frequent Ajar uprisings and disturbances in the region, the Russians developed Batumi as a major Black Sea port and fostered the growth of subtropical agriculture in the region. In the late nineteenth and early twentieth centuries, the port of Batumi grew rapidly with an influx of Slavs and Georgians and was linked by railways and pipelines to the important centers of Baku and Tbilisi.

The devoutly Muslim Ajars, restive under Christian rule, rose during the 1905 Russian Revolution and attacked the estates of the Georgian and Russian landlords who dominated their homeland. Subdued by imperial troops, Ajar resentment of the privileges enjoyed by their Christian overlords continued to grow, reinforced by their pro-Turkish sentiment as tensions mounted prior to World War I. The Ajar homeland formed part of the front line when war began in August 1914. Ajar nationalists in December 1914 rebelled in support of a Turkish invasion of the region. The entire Ajar nation suffered repression and restrictions when the Russian military defeated the invading Turks.

The outbreak of revolution in Russia in February 1917 threw the region into chaos as the local civil government collapsed. Armed bands of Russian soldiers and Ajar, Georgian, and Armenian nationalists roamed the area at will until Turkish troops took control of the region in April 1918 with the active assistance of the Ajar nationalists. With Turkish encouragement the nationalists declared Ajaristan independent of Russia on 18 April 1918, calling their new state the Southwestern Caucasian Republic. An Ajar national council, the Showra, formally claimed the Muslim majority districts of Batumi, Kars, Akhaltsikh, Skhalkalaki, Sharur, and Nakichevan, areas also claimed by newly independent republics of Georgia and Armenia.

British troops occupied Batumi in December 1918. The British authorities promised to protect the new republic until its fate could be decided by the Paris Peace Conference. However, in April 1919, pressured by the governments of Georgia and Armenia, the British forcibly disbanded the Showra and in June 1920 evacuated all British troops from the area. Quickly overcoming armed Ajar resistance, Georgian forces took Batumi and the north, while the Armenians incorporated Kars and the south into their new state.

The Red Army, victorious in the civil war, turned on independent Georgia in early 1921. Amid the ensuing disorder the Ajars declared their homeland independent of Georgia and requested Turkish military aid. In March Turkish troops occupied the region and over vehement Ajar protests attempted to annex the region to Turkey. Pressed by the Soviet government, the Turks finally withdrew in May but retained control of Kars and the southern districts. Soviet Ajaristan, given the status of an autonomous republic in 1922, was incorporated into Soviet Georgia, although the Georgians disputed Ajar autonomy, claiming the Ajars as Muslim Georgians.

In 1926 the Ajars rose in rebellion against the Soviets' anti-Muslim religious campaign and the forced collectivization of Ajar agriculture. After crushing the Ajar rebellion, Joseph Stalin ordered large numbers of Ajars deported to Central Asia. The Ajars were declassified as a distinct nationality and from that time on were officially considered a Georgian subgroup.

Counted as ethnic Georgians in Soviet censuses since 1926, the loyalty of the

Muslim Ajars remained suspect. Stalin drew up a plan for their deportation during World War II, but the plan was postponed and finally abandoned at Stalin's death in 1953. Spared by the Soviet leader's death, the Ajars experienced a modest national revival that strengthened Ajar resistance to attempts by the government of Soviet Georgia to eliminate their autonomy and to promote assimilation during the 1960s and 1970s.

In the wake of the failed Soviet coup in August 1991 the Georgians regained their independence under a nationalist, ethnocentric government that fanned ethnic and religious tensions in the new Georgian state in January 1992. In spite of the overtures of the new Georgian government, the attitude of the radical Georgian nationalists that the Ajars represent a threat to the Christian Georgian state has come to dominate the Ajars' relations with the Georgians.

Officially designated an autonomous republic within Georgia in 1992, the region remains effectively independent in all but foreign and monetary policy. The only area of Georgia not to have experienced violent confrontations since Georgia regained its independence, the Ajar homeland, Ajaria or Ajaristan, is increasingly going its own way. The Georgian government, already at odds with the Abkhaz* and Ossetians,* has been careful not to inflame Ajar nationalism.

Russia maintains a naval base near Batumi, and Russian soldiers patrol Ajaristan's border with Turkey. Russia's interest in the port of Batumi has not lessened since the collapse of the Soviet Union, so that Russian support for Ajar separatism remains a threat to Georgia's hold on the Ajar homeland. In 1993 the Ajar leader, Aslan Abashidze, declared Russia the protector of the Ajars' national interests.

The Georgian president Eduard Shevardnadze in November 1994 endorsed the statute of a free economic zone in Ajaristan. The zone, centered on Batumi, would give the Ajars greater access to foreign investment and would set up a rival to the Trabzon free economic zone, just across the frontier in Turkey. The region, quiet and calm by Caucasus standards, has become one of the most prosperous on the eastern shore of the Black Sea.

In September 1996 the Ajar nationalist political party, Revival Union, in partnership with the Citizen's Union of Georgia, the ruling party in the national parliament, easily won the regional elections. The party, led by Aslan Abashidze, took 81.9% of the vote in the region. The Ajars, political analysts claim, are more interested in economic and political stability than the other national minorities in Georgia, which is why Abashidze has increasingly separated the small region from the rest of Georgia.

SELECTED BIBLIOGRAPHY

Allen, W. E. *A History of the Georgian People*. 1978.
Boyette, William. *Soviet Georgia*. 1988.
Caplan, Richard, ed. *Europe's New Nationalism: States and Minorities in Conflict*. 1996.
Olson, James S. *An Ethnohistorical Dictionary of the Russian and Soviet Empires*. 1994.
Wixman, Ronald. *The Peoples of the USSR: An Ethnographic Handbook*. 1984.

ALANDERS

Ålanders; Aland Islanders

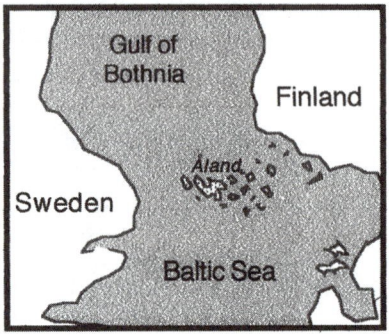

POPULATION: Approximately (2000 e) 65,000 Alanders in Europe, mostly in the Aland Islands and mainland Finland, but with some 35,000 in Sweden. Aland nationalists claim an Alander population of over 75,000 in Scandinavia.

THE ALANDER HOMELAND: The Alander homeland is an archipelago lying at the mouth of the Gulf of Bothnia between Sweden and Finland. Known as Åland or Ålandsöerna in Swedish, the islands are called Ahvenanmaa, the Land of Streams, in Finnish. The archipelago comprises 6,544 islands and islets in the Baltic Sea fifteen miles west of the Finnish mainland and fifteen miles east of Sweden. The islands, only some 700 of which are inhabited, take their name from the largest and most important island of the group, Åland or Ahvenanmaa.

The Alanders accepted a statute of autonomy in 1951, which has been widened in new legislation since. *Autonomous Province of Aland Islands* (Ahvenanmaa in Finnish): 581 sq.mi.–1,505 sq.km. (2000 e) 25,000—Alanders 96%, Finns* 3%. The Aland capital and major cultural center is Mariehamm, called Maarianhamina in Finnish, (2000 e) 11,000, a port city on the largest of the islands, Åland.

FLAG: The Aland national flag, the official flag of the autonomous state, is a blue field bearing a red Scandinavian cross outlined in yellow.

PEOPLE: The Alanders, overwhelmingly of Swedish descent, are now a separate Scandinavian nation whose unique culture incorporates both Swedish and Finnish influences. The population of the islands, following a sharp decline from nearly 30,000 in the 1950s, mostly due to immigration to Sweden, has stabilized over the last decade. The Alanders, like the other Scandinavian nations, are predominantly Protestants, most belonging to the Evangelical Lutheran Church. The Alanders are mostly engaged in the fishing, shipping, and tourism industries, and farming is important on the larger islands. The islanders, with their long seafaring history, control much of Finland's large merchant fleet.

The Alanders, following a long dispute between Sweden and Finland, have been recognized as a separate Scandinavian nation by the Nordic Council, a regional grouping of the Scandinavian states. They participate in several international organizations as a distinct Scandinavian nation.

NATION: The islands have been inhabited from prehistoric times. The islands' original inhabitants were absorbed by Finnish peoples migrating from the east in the eighth century A.D. The pagan Finns were often subject to raids by the Vikings of the Scandinavian region. During the age of the Vikings the Alanders became exposed to both Eastern and Western influences. Vikings from Sweden used the islands, colonized by mainland Swedes in the sixth century, as a base for their journeys of pillage and trade into Russia as far south as the Black Sea.

The Swedish kingdom began to expand in the twelfth century, first to the nearby territories of Finland and the Åland Islands. The Christian Swedes* launched a crusade to conquer and Christianize the pagan Finns in 1154. The islands, colonized by the victorious Swedes, became thoroughly Swedish in culture and language and remained an integral part of the Swedish kingdom for over 600 years. In the sixteenth century, along with the rest of Scandinavia, the Alanders adopted the Protestant Reformation.

The strategically important islands, contested by Sweden and Russia during the eighteenth-century wars, remained an area of conflict. The Russians* under Peter the Great seized the archipelago in 1714 but returned the islands to Swedish rule in 1721. During the Napoleonic Wars the archipelago was ceded, along with Swedish Finland, to the Russian Empire in 1809. The Alanders protested the cession, but ecclesiastically the islands belonged to the diocese of Abo (Turku) in Finland and were claimed by the Russians as part of Finnish territory.

The Swedish-speaking Alanders resisted Russian rule, and the islands were subject to international disputes and treaties throughout the nineteenth century. The Russian government militarized and fortified the islands. Shelled by an Anglo-French fleet in 1854 during the Crimean War, the islands' fortifications were later destroyed, and remilitarization was forbidden under the terms of the 1856 Treaty of Paris.

The energetic Alanders, stifled by the unpopular and repressive Russian bureaucracy, looked beyond their islands to sustain themselves. A huge Alander merchant fleet dominated the nineteenth-century European-Australian grain trade and engendered a tradition of independence and self-reliance, an important part of the Alander national character.

Opposition to Russian rule fanned the growth of nationalism in the islands. Affected by the wave of nationalist sentiment that swept Europe in the late nineteenth century, the islanders developed a particular Alander self-awareness.

Alander resentment erupted in open conflict during the 1905 Russian Revolution, the rebellion quickly crushed by troops hastily dispatched from the Finnish mainland.

Following the outbreak of war in 1914, Aland's strategic military importance again became the subject of debate. With British and French* consent, the Russians refortified the islands in 1915. The remilitarization of their islands spurred the growth of nationalism and pro-Swedish sentiment during the war. Agitation for autonomy grew as the war dragged on, and the near-feudal Russian Empire began to collapse.

Finland, independent of Russia in 1917, claimed the islands as part of its national territory. Asserting their right to self-determination, the Alanders declared their autonomy and voted to secede from Finland and to unite with Sweden. In January 1918 the Swedish government recognized Finnish independence without reservation about the islands. The Swedish government gave no open support to the Aland separatists, but the Swedish public displayed considerable interest, especially when open revolt seemed inevitable.

The Finnish democrats, involved in a bloody civil war with Red factions, ignored the islanders' demands. As the civil war dragged on, the Swedish military occupied the islands but were quickly withdrawn by the Swedish government. German troops, sent by the Allies to intervene in the Russian and Finnish civil wars, next occupied the islands. The Swedish public demanded that their government take action, and for a time it seemed that war would break out between Sweden and Finland in early 1920, with the dispute complicated by Soviet territorial claims to the islands. The Finnish government, victorious in the civil war, sent troops to occupy the islands, and the leaders of the Aland secessionist movement were arrested.

In July 1920 the League of Nations looked into the dispute, which Finland claimed was a domestic affair. In September of that year the dispute was referred to the league, and a committee was dispatched to visit Sweden, Finland, and the archipelago. In June 1921 the decision on the claims of Sweden, Finland, and the new Soviet Union favored Finland, which received sovereignty. The agreement provided for an autonomous Aland state in union with the Finnish Republic. The autonomy statute provided for full protection of the Alanders' political, linguistic, and cultural rights, the right to private property, and the right to fly the distinctive national flag raised by the Aland nationalists in 1920. The islands were to remain neutral and unfortified, with their autonomy guaranteed by the League of Nations.

After World War I, the last of the great Aland sailing ships were laid up, and the era of Aland dominance of the Australian grain trade ended. The islanders turned to sheep farming and trade between Finland and Sweden. The Finnish government, respecting the islands' autonomy, generally left the Alanders to look after themselves.

In the late 1930s, as relations between Finland and the Soviet Union deteriorated, the Finnish government sought to remilitarize Aland, but in May 1939 the Soviet Union blocked League of Nation's approval for refortification. Finland and the Soviet Union fought a bitter war in 1939–40, following which they signed a new demilitarization agreement on the Aland Islands. The agreement was renewed following the end of World War II.

At the end of World War II, the Alanders again began a movement for separation, but as Finland settled in a democratic system, the movement lost momentum. In 1951, under Soviet pressure, the Finnish parliament renounced the 1921 League of Nations guarantee of autonomy, but at the same time the Finnish government accorded the Alanders added rights of self-government. A new autonomy statute went into effect on 1 January 1952.

In the 1960s and 1970s traditional pro-Swedish sentiment persisted in the islands, and immigration to Sweden caused a population decline. The Aland economy, based on tourism, was buoyed by the duty-free goods sold on ships moving between Aland and the mainland ports in Finland and Sweden. The tourist income gave the Alanders one of the highest incomes in the region in the 1980s. Increased prosperity and closer ties among the Scandinavian nations stabilized the islands' economy and population. Since 1970 the Alanders have had separate representation in the Nordic Council, the grouping of Scandinavian nations.

Aland nationalism, dormant for decades under liberal Finnish authority, again became an issue in the late 1980s, stimulated by the disintegration of the Soviet Union and Finland's application to join the European Union. The Alanders, already enjoying most of the trappings of independence, took a step closer in March 1991 with the endorsement of a proposal to introduce their own currency, the Aland *daler*. A revised autonomy statute, effective on 1 January 1993, provides for greater economic and legislative freedom.

Finland's entry in the European Union has raised fears that membership will affect the island's demilitarized status and affect the duty-free tourism that contributes 70% of the Alanders' national income. The Alanders negotiated and won special concessions from the European Union. For tax purposes Aland counts as a country outside the union, allowing the Alanders to go on selling duty-free goods after 1999, when duty-free sales became illegal in the rest of the union. The deal also allows the Alanders to block other Europeans from buying properties or setting up industries in the islands. The negotiated concessions, finalized in November 1994, brought the Alanders a step closer to full independence within the European Union.

SELECTED BIBLIOGRAPHY

Hamalainen, P. K. *In Time of Storm: Revolution, Civil War and the Ethnolinguistic Issue in Finland.* 1979.

Hannikainen, Lauri, and Frank Horn, eds. *Autonomy and Demilitarisation in International Law: The Aland Islands in a Changing Europe.* 1996.

Matts, Dreijer. *History of the Aland People: From the Stone Age to Gustavus Wasa.* 1986.

Mead, W. R. *A Historic Geography of Scandinavia.* 1981.

ALBANIANS

Shiptars; Shqipetars

POPULATION: Approximately (2000 e) 6,200,000 Albanians in Europe. Major concentrations are 3,050,000 in Albania, 2,100,000 in Serbia (prior to the early 1999 expulsion of nearly the entire Albanian population), 460,000 in Macedonia, 75,000 in Turkey, 60,000 in Greece, 50,000 in Montenegro, and 20,000 in Italy.

THE ALBANIAN HOMELAND: The Albanian homeland lies in the southern Balkans on the eastern shore of the Adriatic Sea, just forty-seven miles east of Italy. In the north are rugged mountains, an extension of the Dinaric Alps, which extend through Albania and Kosovo, called Kosova in Albanian. In the central uplands strong erosive forces have created bare rock surfaces, deeply cut valleys, and a scarcity of fertile land. The highlands contain several lakes, the largest being Ohrid and Prespa. In the north, just west of the North Albanian Alps, lies Lake Scutari, which forms part of the border with Montenegro. The coastal region along the Adriatic Sea is the only fertile region with a Mediterranean climate and a long growing season.

The Albanian republic, proclaimed in 1912, is the poorest and least developed state in Europe, mostly the result of the policies of a radical communist government installed after World War II. *Republic of Albania (Republika e Shqipërisë/Shqiperia "Country of the Eagle")*: 11,100 sq.mi.–28,749 sq.km. (2000 e) 3,385,000—Albanians 90%, Greeks* 8%, Macedonians,* Montenegrins.* The Albanian capital and major cultural center, Tirana, Tiranë in the Albanian language, (2000 e) 267,000, lies eighteen miles inland from the Adriatic Sea. The capital and major cultural center of the Kosovar Albanians, Pristina, had a population of about 250,000 prior to the outbreak of fighting in the region in early

1999. The most important center of the Albanian region of Macedonia is Tetovo, (2000 e) 214,000.

FLAG: The Albanian national flag, the official flag of the Republic of Albania, is a red field charged with the Albanian symbol, the Eagle of Scanderbeg.

PEOPLE: Albanians are among the most ancient ethnic groups in Southeastern Europe, calling themselves Shiptars or Shqipetars (Sons of the Eagle). They are thought to be descended from ancient Illyrian and Thracian peoples who settled the Balkan Peninsula long before the Greeks. Albanians are divided by the Shkumbin River into the two major cultural and dialectal subgroups: the Ghegs in the north and the Tosks in the south. The Ghegs, who make up about two-thirds of the total, are less intermarried with non-Albanians than the Tosks, who throughout history were more often subjected to foreign rule and other foreign influences. In the past, the Ghegs were organized in clans, and the Tosks in a semifeudal society, but the communists largely erased both types of organization. Before World War II the Ghegs dominated Albanian politics, but after the war many Tosks came to power because the new communist government drew most of its support from Tosks. The largest segment of Europe's Albanian population lives within the borders of the Republic of Albania, but sizable Albanian populations also live in adjacent parts of neighboring states, the Kosovo region of Yugoslavia, called Kosova by the Albanians, and the northwestern districts of Macedonia.

The majority of the Albanians are peasant farmers, although a very high birthrate, possibly Europe's highest, has accelerated urbanization in recent decades. Housing construction in the 1990s did not keep pace with the Albanians' high rates of birth and the rapid process of urbanization. As a result, many large towns and cities are overcrowded, and the number of shanty dwellings continues to grow. Education and social welfare remain among the least developed in Europe, while the Republic of Albania remains the continent's poorest state.

Most Albanians are Muslims, with Orthodox and Roman Catholic minorities. In Albania about 65% of the population is Muslim, making the republic Europe's only predominantly Islamic state. Orthodox Christians, living mostly in southern Albania, make up about 20% of the population, and Roman Catholics, mainly in the north, make up about 13%. The Kosovar and Macedonian Albanians are predominantly Muslims, around 70%, with Orthodox Christian minorities. Religious divisions in Albania are not significant, and religious tolerance is such that members of the same family sometimes belong to different religions.

The Albanian language forms the only surviving dialect of the Thraco-Illyrian branch of the Indo-European languages. Unrelated to neighboring languages, the Albanian language seems to validate the Albanian claim to be the Balkan Peninsula's original inhabitants. In the course of time the language has borrowed many words from younger languages, particularly Greek and Latin. The language is spoken in two major dialects, Gheg in the north and Tosk in the south, but both groups can understand each other. Both Gheg and Tosk are further divided into a number of subdialects, including Kosove or Ship, the Gheg dialect spoken in the Kosovo region of Yugoslavia. A southern Gheg dialect was used as the official language from 1909 until World War II. In 1945 a new official dialect, based on Tosk, was adopted as the national language, largely because support for the communist regime was stronger in the Tosk-speaking south.

NATION: Considered the original inhabitants of the Balkan Peninsula, the Albanians have inhabited the region since before the rise of the ancient Greeks. Illyrian culture is believed to have evolved from the Stone Age and to have flourished in the region toward the beginning of the Bronze Age, about 2000 B.C. The Illyrians were not a uniform body of people but a conglomeration of many tribes that inhabited the western part of the Balkans. Ancient Illyria and Epirus were known to the ancient peoples of the Mediterranean. During the ancient Greek period, from the eighth to the sixth centuries B.C., the coastal regions were colonized by Greek city-states, while the interior remained an independent kingdom, which reached its peak of power in the third and fourth centuries B.C.

The kingdom of Illyria controlled much of the Balkan Peninsula when it came into conflict with the expanding Roman state. The depredations carried out by the large Illyrian navy on Roman shipping resulted in a declaration of war by the Roman Senate on the Illyrian queen, Teuta. In 227 B.C., after two years of war, Queen Teuta finally sued for peace. A prize, known for its lucrative mines, the Albanian homeland was fought over by stronger neighboring states, particularly Macedon and Rome. The last Illyrian king, Gentius, after his defeat, was brought to Rome as a captive, and his kingdom came under nominal Roman rule in A.D. 167. Latinized under Roman rule, the coastal region, called Illyricum, was known for its wealth and culture.

Roman rule extended over most of Albania for about six centuries, and in the middle of the first century A.D. Christianity was introduced to the coastal clans and quickly gained adherents in the mountainous interior. The first Albanian bishopric was established at Dyrrhachium, the Roman name for Epidamnus, in A.D. 58. The Illyrians in the Roman Empire excelled in the military. In the third and fourth centuries several military leaders of Illyrian origin became Roman emperors.

Following the division of the Roman Empire in A.D. 395, Albania passed to the eastern or Byzantine Empire, and several Albanians became Byzantine emperors. In the fourth century the region was overrun by Ostrogoths but was reconquered by Byzantine emperor Justinian I in 535. While nominally under weak Byzantine rule, much of the Albanian homeland came under the control of invaders, the Serbs* in northern Albania in the seventh century and the Bulgarians,* who annexed southern Albania in the ninth century. The arrival of large numbers of Slavs gradually pushed the earlier Illyrians into the mountainous southwest of the Balkan Peninsula. In 1014 southern Albania was retaken by the Byzantines, who held the region until it passed, in 1204, to the despotate of Epirus.

Byzantine control of the Albanian territories was disputed by Venice, which established coastal colonies in the eleventh century, and the Normans.* The Normans' efforts to undermine Byzantine rule continued with the Neapolitan Angevins, and in 1272 Charles I of Naples was proclaimed king of Albania. In 1347 the Serbs under Stephan Dushan conquered most of the Albanian tribes, prompting a mass migration of Albanians to Greece. Following Stephan Dushan's death in 1355, the Albanians were mostly ruled by native chieftains until the arrival of the Ottoman Turks* in the fifteenth century.

The Turkish threat forced the Christian peoples of the region to unite. The Serbs, the most powerful of the Christian nations, rallied the region to face the Ottoman onslaught. On 20 June 1389 a force of Serbs, Albanians, and Bosnians* met the Turkish army on the elevated plain known as Kosovo, the Field of Blackbirds. The Christian defeat shattered the alliance and began five centuries of Muslim Turkish rule in the Balkan Peninsula.

The Albanian tribes, supported by Venice and Naples and led by their national hero, George Castriota, called Scanderbeg, in the fifteenth century united to resist the Turkish conquest of their homeland. In 1461, under his eagle banner, the basis for the modern Albanian flag, Scanderbeg forced the Turkish sultan to enter a ten-year truce. Two years later, Scanderbeg broke the truce when Pope Pius II called for a new crusade against the Turks. The pope's death in 1464 left Scanderbeg without allies. He withdrew his army to mountain strongholds, where he died in 1468. With Scanderbeg's death Albanian resistance gradually collapsed, and by 1478 most of the Albanian territories had come under Ottoman rule. Scanderbeg's fight against the mightiest military power of the time became an icon for the Albanian nation, solidifying their national consciousness, and served as an inspiration for their later fight for independence.

Ottoman power in Albania lasted longer and influenced the Albanians more than any of the small nation's many conquerors. The Turkish conquest of Albania, just as the Renaissance was taking hold in the West, cut the region off from the humanistic achievements of the era. Sporadic rebellions, often inspired by the Albanians' Christian faith, pushed the Ottomans to begin a systematic drive to convert the Albanians to Islam at the end of the sixteenth century. By the end of the seventeenth century about two-thirds of the Albanian population had adopted the Turks' Islamic religion, often to escape the heavy taxes imposed on Christians.

Conversion to Islam by the majority of the Albanians placed them in a more favorable position in the Ottoman Empire. Their conversion to Islam and their position as landlords and administrators sparked an enmity with the Orthodox Serbs and Greeks that continues to the present. The sporadic Christian uprisings were generally focused on the Albanian landholding and merchant classes rather than their Turkish overlords. Many Muslim Albanians gained high office in the Ottoman Empire despite the numerous uprisings and revolts against the Ottoman rule by local Albanian chieftains.

The decline of Ottoman power gave rise to numerous local warlords. In 1787 an Albanian chieftain, Ali Pasha, was made governor of Yanina, now Ioanina in Greece, where his power grew until he ruled as a semi-independent despot over most of Albania and Epirus. During the Napoleonic Wars, Ali Pasha negotiated an alliance with Great Britain and warred on the French along the Adriatic coast. Valuing Ali Pasha's services, the Turkish sultan allowed him great autonomy, but when he ordered the assassination of an opponent, the sultan had him deposed. He refused to comply, keeping large numbers of Ottoman troops engaged, troops urgently needed to fight the Greeks, who had begun their bid for independence. Ali Pasha was finally assassinated, and his head was exhibited at Constantinople, an affront never forgiven by many of the fierce Albanian tribes.

In the late nineteenth century the tottering Ottoman Empire was beset by the nationalist aspirations of the subject peoples. The Albanians in 1878 sent delegates to a nationalist congress in the Kosovar town of Prizren. The first openly nationalist organization was formed, the League of Prizren. The aims of the league were to unify the Albanian lands, then divided between four Ottoman vilayets or provinces, in one autonomous Albania within the empire and to spearhead the movement to develop the Albanian language and culture. In 1881 the league was suppressed by the Ottoman authorities.

The first of two short wars for control of the European territories of the tottering Ottoman Empire, fought in 1912 and 1913 between the Balkan states, gave the Albanians the opportunity to proclaim their independence on 28 November 1912. During the Second Balkan War in 1913 the Serbs, seeking an outlet to the Adriatic Sea, occupied Albania but were opposed by the Great Powers, which forced them to withdraw from Albania proper, although they retained control of Kosovo. An international commission dominated by the Great Powers traced the borders of the new Albanian state in 1913 but destroyed the dream of a united Albanian nation-state by assigning large tracts of traditional Albanian territory to Montenegro, Serbia, and Greece.

The Great Powers selected a German army officer, Prince William of Wied, to be the ruler of Albania, but civil war in the country undermined his position. Soon after the outbreak of World War I, in September 1914, he was overthrown, but he refused to abdicate. His departure threw the country into chaos, which grew more serious as the armies of neighboring states invaded Albanian territory. During the war Serbs, Montenegrins, Greeks, and Italians* invaded Albania. In 1916 Bulgarians and Austrians* entered the region, which remained a battleground until the end of the war. The disappearance of Albania was averted largely through the efforts of U.S. president Woodrow Wilson, who vetoed a plan, supported by Britain, France, and Italy, to partition Albania among its neighbors.

The Congress of Lushnje in 1920 reasserted Albania's independence while renewing claims to the Albanian-populated territories controlled by neighboring states. A boundary dispute, involving Albanian-populated territories, with neighboring Yugoslavia was settled by the League of Nations in 1921. Between 1918 and 1940 the Yugoslav government settled thousands of ethnic Serbs in the Albanian-populated Kosovo region.

The immediate postwar era was marked by opposing forces in the Albanian homeland. The first was liberal and oriented to the West, led by an American-educated Orthodox bishop, Fan S. Noli. The opposing force, the landed gentry and tribal chieftains, tied to the old Ottoman power structure, was led by Ahmed Zogu. A popular uprising installed Bishop Noli as prime minister in June 1924, but within six months he was overthrown by Zogu, with aid from neighboring Yugoslavia. Albania was proclaimed a republic under the presidency of Ahmed Zogu in 1925, and three years later Zogu had himself proclaimed king as King Zog I. Under his rule Albania became a virtual protectorate of fascist Italy. Thousands of Albanians emigrated to escape grinding poverty, and the first communist organizations were formed.

In April 1939, shortly before the start of World War II, the Italians occupied the kingdom and united it to the Italian state. During the war, the Kosovo region, separated from defeated Yugoslavia, was added to Italian Albania. The long-running Albanian dispute with Greece regarding their respective minorities provided Italy with a pretext to invade Greece in 1940. The Albanian government, controlled by Italy, declared war on the Allies in 1940, but later, guerrilla groups formed to fight the fascists, particularly following the occupation of the region by German forces in 1943. The new Albanian entity lasted until the German evacuation of the region in November 1944. The strongest of the guerrilla bands, led by Enver Hoxha, was a radically leftist group supported by the Soviet Union and partisans in Yugoslavia, which seized power on 29 November 1944.

The Kosovar Albanians, freed from Slav domination during the war, sought to drive the Serb minority from the region. The fighting and massacres eventually claimed over 50,000 lives, including many Kosovar Albanians who died resisting the Serb authorities in 1945–46.

A communist-dominated legislature proclaimed Hoxha premier of the new communist Albanian state in 1946. Thousands of noncommunist Albanians fled abroad, many to Italy. Hoxha's government nationalized land and industry and ended the traditional subjugation of women. Hoxha's government was aided by Yugoslavia from 1944 to 1948, then by the Soviet Union from 1948 to 1961, and finally by communist China. In spite of modernization, aspects of the clan system survived, especially in the highlands, but men there have considerably less authority than they enjoyed in the past.

By 1968, when the Albanian government withdrew from the Warsaw Pact, Albania had become the most isolated and closed country in Europe. Albania's isolation increased when its alliance with China ended in 1977, following Albanian government accusations against the Chinese leadership for abandoning orthodox communist principles. Alienated from both East and West, Albania became a bastion of antiquated Stalinism. The Hoxha regime relied on oppression to retain power in Albania. Periodic purges eliminated all opposition and maintained a climate of fear. In 1967, charging that religion was holding the country back, the Albanian government banned all religion and closed all churches and mosques.

The Kosovar Albanians, suffering high unemployment and abject poverty in Serb-dominated Yugoslavia, joined in antigovernment rioting in 1968. To diffuse the escalating dispute, Yugoslavia's leader, Joseph Broz Tito, in 1974 granted Kosovo an autonomy statute broadly comparable to that of the various Yugoslav republics, although the Republic of Serbia retained overall control. Despite greater autonomy, the Albanians remained dissatisfied, and renewed rioting broke out, especially severe in 1976 and 1981.

Following Hoxha's death in 1985, the Albanian government sought to maintain communist control while gradually introducing economic reforms. Workers and students, the former supporters of communist rule, demanded greater freedoms. By the time communism began to collapse in Europe in 1989, agitation against the government was widespread. In December 1990 the government legalized opposition political parties, signaling the end of the communist domination of power. In 1991 a new interim constitution was adopted that created a multiparty parliamentary democracy and guaranteed basic freedoms. The democratic opposition won a decisive victory in elections, and a new government was installed that moved to immediately end Albania's long isolation.

The changes taking place in Albania resonated in Kosovo. Renewed tensions between the Albanian majority and the Serb minority in Kosovo provoked a Serbian nationalist backlash in March 1989. The Serbian government effectively ended the autonomy granted the Albanians in 1974. Thousands of ethnic Albanians lost their jobs in local governments and in schools and universities closed by the Serb authorities. In late 1989, under Serbian military rule, the Kosovar Albanians began a peaceful campaign to win equal rights within Yugoslavia.

The disintegration of Yugoslavia in 1991 spurred the Kosovar Albanians to attempt to break the Serbian military hold on the province. The campaign included setting up schools and a clandestine university to teach in the Albanian language. Periodic repression by the increasingly radicalized Serbian authorities and the appearance in 1997 of an armed separatist organization brought increasing violence to the region. By late 1998 over one-tenth of the Albanian population of Yugoslavia had been driven from their homes, and the threat of a wider war, involving Serbia, Albania, and Macedonia, with its restive Albanian minority, became a real possibility. Many of the volunteers fighting with the Kosovo Liberation Army (KLA) in Kosovo are ethnic Albanians from Macedonia and Albania.

In postcommunist Albania, economic chaos followed the tentative reforms of the former command economy. Many Albanians put their meager savings in so-called pyramid schemes. These moneymaking pyramids so permeated Albanian society that their collapse in March 1997 pulled down the Albanian government and touched off a national uprising and widespread violence that left 1,500 dead.

The election of a coalition government in Macedonia, consisting of Macedonian nationalists and pro-Western democrats, but also including ultranationalist groups, in October 1998 further alienated the large Albanian minority of Macedonia. The Albanians in Macedonian are increasingly calling for secession of their territory and amalgamation with Albania and Kosovo.

The Kosovar Albanians met, under British and French sponsorship, with representatives of the Serbian government in France in February 1998. The talks, put forward as a way to avert an ever-widening war in Kosovo, were to hammer out a system of government for the province that would satisfy both the Kosovar separatists and the Serbian government. The Kosovar Albanians accepted the February agreement, but it was rejected by the Serbian government.

In March 1999, following increased ethnic cleansing, the expulsion of the Kosovar Albanian population by Serbian military union finally brought an international response. Forces of the North Atlantic Treaty Organization (NATO) launched an aerial bombardment of Serbian military targets even as the expulsions of the Kosovar Albanians accelerated. The bombings, which continued for over two months, greatly damaged Serbia's large military, but the hundreds of thousands of Kosovar Albanian refugees fleeing Kosovar for sanctuary in Albania greatly strained the resources of the country, Europe's poorest.

The Albanians' close cooperation with the North Atlantic Treaty Organization (NATO) during the Kosovo conflict brought their country into closer economic and political ties to the European Union (EU), the United States, and other Western countries. The economic benefits of closer cooperation may finally stabilize the Albanian economy and aid the long and painful process of breaking with their Communist past.

SELECTED BIBLIOGRAPHY

Dragnich, Alexander N., and Slavko Todorovich. *The Saga of Kosovo: Focus on Serbian-Albanian Relationships*. 1985.

Hall, Derek. *Albania and the Albanians*. 1994.

Jacques, Edwin E. *The Albanians: An Ethnic History from Prehistoric Times to the Present*. 1995.

Kaplan, Robert D. *Balkan Ghosts*. 1993.

Vickers, Miranda. *Albanians: A Modern History*. 1995.

ALSATIANS

Elsassers; Alsatians and Lorrainers;
Elsassers und Lotharingens

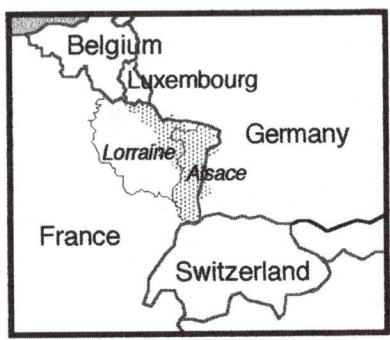

POPULATION: Approximately (2000 e) 2,123,000 Alsatians in Europe, mostly in the Alsace Region of France. The closely related inhabitants of the neighboring Moselle Department of Lorraine, the Lorrainers, are traditionally considered part of the Alsatian national group.

THE ALSATIAN HOMELAND: The Alsatian homeland lies in northeastern France, east of the Vosges Mountains. Most of the region lies in the valley of the Rhine River, which forms the frontier between France and Germany. The region, forming the Bas-Rhin, Haut-Rhin, and Moselle departments and the Territory of Belfort, is now included in the planning regions of Alsace, Lorraine, and Franche-Comté, but there is little real autonomy. The economy of the region depends as much on Germany, where many of those who work in Alsace live, as on France. The Alsatians speak of going to France when they leave their region.

Since the 1970s a growing movement, supported by cultural associations and municipalities, has sought greater autonomy, the unification of the Alsatian lands, and protection and recognition of the unique Alsatian dialects and culture. *Historic Region of Alsace-Lorraine (Elsass-Lotharingen)*: 5,842 sq.mi.–15,134 sq.km. (2000 e) 2,430,000—Alsatians and Lorrainers 75%, other French* 20%, Germans* 4%. The Alsatian capital and major cultural center is Strasbourg (Strassburg in the Alsatian dialects), (2000 e) 241,000. The Lorrainers' most important cultural center is Metz, (2000 e) 120,000.

FLAGs: The Alsatian national flag, the flag of the Alsatian autonomy movement, is a horizontal bicolor of red over white. The flag of the Lorrainers is the same red and white bicolor charged with the arms of Lorraine, a gold field with a red band charged with three silver alerions (heraldic eagles without beaks or claws).

PEOPLE: The Alsatians, descendants of early Germanic peoples, are historically related to the Luxembourgers* and the Swabians* of neighboring parts of Germany. Culturally, the Alsatians have retained their unique, traditional culture, which incorporates both Germanic and French influences. Culturally and linguistically, the Alsatians see themselves as neither French nor German but as a separate European nation.

Traditionally, the Alsatians are 90% German-speaking, with a small, culturally Alsatian, but traditionally French-speaking, minority. The Alsatians are now effectively bilingual, speaking both French and one of the German vernaculars collectively called Alsatian (Elsaessisch) or Elsasserdeutch. Alsatian includes a Franconian dialect spoken in northern Alsace and Lorraine and an Alemannic dialect in the southern districts of Alsace. The Alsatian dialects are akin to the Rhenish and Alemannic dialects spoken by the neighboring Swabians and Rhinelanders* and by the Swiss-Germans* in Switzerland but differ considerably from standard, spoken German. The linguistic division of Alsace approximates the region's religious division, the Roman Catholic Franconian majority in the north and the large Protestant Alemannic minority concentrated in the south.

NATION: Various Germanic tribes occupied the Roman frontier district west of the Rhine River as Roman power declined in the fourth and fifth centuries. An early Frankish duchy, Alsace was eventually absorbed by Charlemagne's Frankish Empire. Following Charlemagne's death in 814, control of the empire fell to squabbling heirs. The division of the empire among Charlemagne's three grandsons, formalized by the Treaty of Verdun in 843, was written in the earliest recorded examples of the French and German languages. By the terms of the treaty Alsace formed part of the middle kingdom of Lotharingia, named for Charlemagne's eldest son, Lothair, who inherited a long strip of territory extending from the Low Countries to Rome. Further division among Lothair's sons eventually divided the region into several distinct territories, including the separate duchy called Lotharingia, or Lorraine.

The Alsatian lands, incorporated by the Holy Roman Empire in 870, were gradually partitioned and by the fourteenth century formed a number of tiny lordships, bishoprics, and independent municipalities, while some southern districts came under Hapsburg rule. A noted center of secular and ecclesiastical learning, the Alsatians produced many noted medieval scholars, including Martin Waldseemuller, the person who proposed naming the New World after Amerigo Vespucci in 1507.

The region, which formed part of the Holy Roman Empire, was a prosperous agricultural and wine-producing area, predominantly German-speaking. Many of the free cities and small states formed military alliances with the Swiss Confederation. In the later Middle Ages the duchy of Lorraine came under strong French cultural and political influence.

The French kingdom began to subjugate the numerous small states on its borders at the end of the Thirty Years' War. By the terms of the 1648 Treaty of Westphalia, all the Hapsburg lands in Alsace were annexed to France. Mulhouse and a few smallholdings allied to the Swiss were not annexed until the French Revolution. Under French rule, Alsace retained considerable autonomy with its own legislature or *parlement* at Colmar. Lorraine remained a separate duchy until 1734. Religious freedom prevailed until the revolution, as the Edict of Nantes, which was revoked in France in 1685, remained in effect in Alsace.

Under Napoleon's highly centralized government Alsace lost its former autonomy, and the historic provinces disappeared into small administrative departments in 1789. The region's German-speaking inhabitants were subjected to intense assimilation pressures but clung tenaciously to their distinct dialects and culture.

The unification of Germany, the goal of the most powerful of the numerous German states, Prussia, threatened France's hegemony in Europe and escalated the cultural and linguistic tensions in Alsace. German nationalists laid claim to Alsace and part of Lorraine as historically German-speaking lands.

Alsace and Lorraine were quickly overrun by German troops when war between Prussia and France broke out in July 1870. The Franco-Prussian War ended in a German victory in May 1871. The term "Alsace-Lorraine" was first used in 1871, when, by the terms of the Treaty of Frankfurt concluding the Franco-Prussian War, the former provinces, which had been under French rule since the middle of the seventeenth century, were annexed by Germany. A small part of Alsace, Belfort and its surrounding area, was left to France, partly as a gesture of respect to the Belfort garrison, which had fought bravely during a siege lasting 108 days. Called Elsass-Lotharingen, the Alsatian homeland was held in common by all the states of the German federation. Thousands of Alsatians emigrated rather than submit to German rule.

The Alsatians resisted official German efforts to eradicate their unique culture and dialects and developed a strong anti-German sentiment. Resistance to the Germanization of the region fostered a growing sense of the separate Alsatian culture and spurred the growth of Alsatian nationalism. Autonomist and separatist organizations, often with the support of the French government, were active in the region up to World War I. In 1911 the German government granted limited autonomy to the region to counter rising nationalist sentiment. Anti-German rioting broke out at Zabern (Saverne) in November 1913 after Alsatian conscripts for the German military were repeatedly insulted by German officers. The rioting spread to the cities, where Alsatian leaders demanded political and cultural autonomy. Following the serious nationalist rioting in 1913, new restrictions were imposed on the region. The cultural and linguistic restrictions heightened Alsatian resentment of German rule and exacerbated tensions between France and Germany.

Alsatian discontent with German rule and France's refusal to accept the loss of the region or to refrain from meddling in Alsace-Lorraine fueled an ongoing crisis between France and Germany. Both states, with rapidly growing arms industries, coveted the rich iron mines of Lorraine. The Alsatian question added to the distrust and tensions that eventually led to the outbreak of World War I in 1914.

During World War I, while sentiment in the region was markedly pro-French, thousands of Alsatian conscripts were sent to the eastern front. Thousands more assisted the Allies against their German masters. By the Treaty of Versailles, signed on 28 June 1919, Alsace and German Lorraine, the Alsatian homeland, were ceded to France by defeated Germany. At the end of the war only one-quarter of the region's inhabitants were able to speak French.

A nationalist minority, hoping for independence from both Germany and France, began a campaign of agitation against the returning French administration. Nationalists pointed out that the French annexation of Alsace-Lorraine violated the principle of self-determination of European minorities contained in U.S. president Woodrow Wilson's Fourteen Points, the conditions he believed were necessary to ensure continued peace in Europe. The return of French authority, although initially welcomed by the majority of the Alsatians, proved as harsh and restrictive as the Germans. The French government in 1919 promised not to interfere with traditions, customs, language, or local rights but soon began a program of Gallicization of the region.

The Alsatians were again subjected to intense assimilation pressures despite government assurances of cultural and linguistic autonomy. Many supporters of French rule joined the nationalists in demanding self-determination for the region. A minority supported complete independence following the decline of the early enthusiasm for reunion with France. Separatist sentiment, fanned by the suppression of Alsatian newspapers, cultural institutions, schools, and local government, provoked massive demonstrations led by the nationalists.

The heavily Roman Catholic Alsatians also resented French government efforts to reduce church influence in the region during the 1920s. The administration's efforts to end the Concordat of 1801, which gave Alsace a special relationship with the Vatican, provided considerable impetus to the separatist movement. The concordat was terminated in the rest of France in 1905.

The region by 1925 had been stripped of all the autonomy promised by the French government in 1919. In May 1926 the various nationalist organizations united in the Heimatbund, the Home League, which pressed for cultural and political autonomy and for the supremacy of the Alsatian dialects. The government's response to increased nationalist activities culminated in the trial of twenty-two nationalists at Colmar in 1928.

In spite of the French government's attempts to crush the movement, Alsatian nationalism retained widespread support up to World War II. However, with the fall of France in 1940, the majority of the Alsatians opposed the region's annexation to the Third Reich, even though the region was treated as a recovered part of Germany rather than as a conquered territory. The Alsatians' stubborn resistance and growing discontent soon led to harsh measures by the Nazi administration. Thousands of reluctant Alsatian conscripts were drafted into the German military. There were very few volunteers among the more than 100,000 Alsatians sent to fight on the Russian front. Many Alsatian nationalists were arrested and sent to concentration camps.

Alsatian historians claim that the German occupation of the region from 1940 to 1944 did more for the French language in Alsace-Lorraine than any other event. German restrictions on the French language and Alsatian culture were so harsh that the former assimilation efforts of the French government were mostly forgotten. The German authorities outlawed all traces of French culture in the region, even banning the wearing of berets.

Generally hailed as liberators, French and American troops occupied Alsace in 1944, and the region officially reverted to French rule when the war in Europe ended. As in 1919–20, the French government stressed assimilation in an effort to eliminate the "Alsatian Question," which had plagued Franco–German relations since 1870. In 1945 the French government banned the use of the Alsatian dialects in the area's schools and posted signs throughout the region reading, "It is chic to speak French."

Alsatian nationalist sentiment declined with rising prosperity and the beginnings of European integration and Franco–German cooperation in the 1950s. A national revival, a decade later, spurred by the collapse of the important steel industry, accelerated as a united Europe became a viable reality. In 1949 President Charles DeGaulle and Chancellor Konrad Adenauer chose Strasbourg as the symbol of Franco–German reconciliation. The city, with its bilingual population and distinct Franco–German culture, became the home of the twenty-three-nation Council of Europe. In 1958 Strasbourg was chosen as the site of the future parliament of a united, federal Europe.

The decline of the iron and steel industries, particularly in Lorraine, led to agitation, mass demonstrations, and violent confrontations in the region in 1978–79 and 1984–85. The agitation took on a definite ethnic edge as Alsatians and Lorrainers accused the French government of neglecting the region while financing the regeneration of aging industries in the French heartland.

In 1980, under socialist rule, the highly centralized French government began to devolve some autonomous powers to twenty-two newly created planning regions that loosely mirrored France's historic regions. In spite of Alsatian demands for unification, the new regions included historic Alsace, but Alsatian Lorraine remained part of the larger Lorraine region, and the Territory of Belfort was included in the region of Franché-Comte.

In 1990 only about half the Alsatians and Lorrainers spoke their Alsatian dialects as their first language, a drop from about 90% in 1922. Over 1 million speak the Alsatian dialects as their first language, using the dialects in daily life. Although the vast majority of the Alsatians are loyal to France, they continue to speak of France as they speak of Germany, the region beyond their borders. In February 1991 the municipal authorities of Strasbourg decreed that the Alsatian dialect should be revived on all street signs. The move was widely denounced in the rest of France as a "Teutonic takeover," reviving memories of the Nazi occupation.

The continuing process of European unification has given the Alsatians a new focus, a Europeanized Alsace, a bilingual and bicultural federal state at the heart of united Europe. In a 1993 French referendum on the European integration, the Alsatians had the highest number of votes in favor. Large German investment in the region has spurred the renewal of German-language education and a return of the Alsatian culture and traditions. The assimilation of the Alsatians into French culture has reversed, with new emphasis on their distinct dialects and culture. Opinion polls in 1998 found that the Alsatians expressed loyalty to their commune, Alsace or Lorraine, Europe, and then France, in that order.

In the 1990s foreign firms, mostly German and American, provide 36% of the jobs in the Alsatian regions, with another 30,000 Alsatians crossing the border to jobs in Germany. Unemployment, high in the rest of France, has not been a major problem in the Alsatian region.

Talk of moving the European parliament to Brussels or Luxembourg is enough to arouse Alsatian nationalism and renewed demands for an autonomous, neutral Alsatian enclave between France and Germany. Alsatian national pride has become closely tied to Strasbourg's status as a European capital.

Considered too French by the Germans and too German by the French and having been forced to change nationality four times in the twentieth-century, the fervently pro-European Alsatians look to a continental federation that will allow them to finally be themselves, a distinct European nation.

SELECTED BIBLIOGRAPHY

Craig, John E. *Scholarship and Nation Building: The Universities of Strasbourg and Alsatian Society, 1871–1939.* 1989.

Duijker, Hubrecht. *Alsace.* 1995.

Kahn, Bonnie M. *My Father Spoke French: Nationalism and Legitimacy in Alsace, 1871–1914.* 1990.

Vassberg, Liliane M. *Alsatian Acts of Identity.* 1993.

Ziethen, Karl-Heinz. *Journey through Alsace.* 1996.

ANDALUSIANS

Andalucians; Andaluz

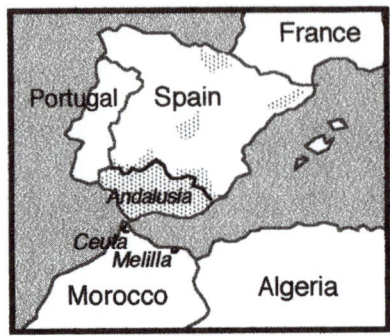

POPULATION: Approximately (2000 e) 9,458,000 Andalusians in Europe, concentrated in the Andalusia region of Spain, but with sizable communities in other parts of Spain and in France, Switzerland, Luxembourg, and Germany.

THE ANDALUSIAN HOMELAND: The Andalusian homeland lies in the southern part of the Iberian Peninsula in Southwestern Europe at the mouth of the Mediterranean Sea opposite North Africa. The region is traversed by mountain ranges, including the Sierra Morena and the Sierra Nevada. The highest peaks, in the Sierra Nevada, are Mulhacén, 11,407 feet (3,477 m.), and Picacho de Veleta, 11,125 feet (3,391 m.). Andalusia is watered by the Guadalquivir and its tributaries, and the Guadalimar, Gaudiato, and Genil Rivers. Geographically, Andalusia is divided into two zones, Upper Andalusia, the valley of the upper Guadalquivir, and Lower Andalusia, the valley of the lower Guadalquivir. The region is celebrated for its fertility and is often called the "granary of Spain" for its fertility and subtropical climate.

Andalusia forms an autonomous region of the Spanish kingdom comprising eight provinces, Almeria, Cadiz, Cordoba, Granada, Huelva, Jaen, Malaga, and Seville. *Autonomous Region of Andalusia (Andalucía)*: 33,694 sq.mi.–87,267 sq.km. (2000 e) 6,987,000—Andalusians 88%, Roms* (Gypsies) 10%, other Spaniards.* The Andalusian capital and major cultural center is Seville, called Sevilla in Spanish, (2000 e) 652,000 (metropolitan area 1,114,000), the capital of the autonomous region.

FLAG: The Andalusian national flag, the official flag of the autonomous region, has three horizontal stripes of green, white, and green.

PEOPLE: The Andalusians are a distinct Iberian people, the descendants of the region's many conquerors and immigrants, the Iberians, Phoenicians, Moors, Roms, Goths, Vandals, and Castilians. The Moorish and Castilian strains predominate, while the large Rom population, called Gitanos, has had great influence on the Andalusian character, language, music, and culture. The poorest of the nations of Spain, emigration has long been the solution to the region's high unemployment and lack of opportunities, which has established a large Andalusian diaspora across the regions of Spain and in other parts of Europe and the Americas. The Andalusian culture, characterized by Flamenco music and dance, bullfights, and their Moorish heritage, is often seen by non-Spaniards as typical culture of Spain. Moorish influence, so strong in the character, language, and customs of the Andalusians, may partly account for the hostility other segments of the Spanish population feel toward them.

The language of the Andalusians, called Andaluz, which nationalists claim is a separate Romance language, is a dialect of Castilian Spanish spoken in a number of subdialects that correspond to the region's historic provinces. Castilian speakers counter that the dialect, rather than forming a separate language, is simply a slovenly articulated Castilian.

NATION: Andalusia is thought to have been first settled 1,500 years before the time of Christ by the early Iberians. In the latter half of the second millennium B.C., the region formed the kingdom of Taressus, the biblical Tarshish.

Phoenicians founded colonies along the coast, including Gadir, later called Cadiz, around 1100 B.C. The Phoenicians' descendants, the Carthaginians, destroyed Taressus and established themselves as the dominant power in the region in 480 B.C. The Romans, victorious over the Carthaginians in the Punic Wars, took control of the region in 209–206 B.C. Called Baetica by the Romans, the land was parceled out in large agricultural estates, a legacy that persists to the present.

The decline of Roman power in the fifth century A.D. was followed by invasions of Germanic Goths and Vandals. The English word "vandal," meaning senseless and wanton destruction, originated with the Vandal conquest of the Roman province. The Vandals crossed the narrow strait into North Africa, but the name remained as Vandalusia.

In 711 Muslim Berbers, called Moors, defeated the Goths and settled Vandalusia from North Africa. The region, called Al-Andalus, flourished under the Muslim Ommiad dynasty, which ruled from 756 to 1031. The Moors created a brilliant civilization where religious tolerance, cultural autonomy, science, and literature flourished. Large Christian, Jewish, and Muslim communities existed side by side. Many non-Muslims attained wealth and power under the enlightened rule of the Moors. Cordoba, the Moorish capital, was one of the largest and most advanced cities of the known world. While other European capitals remained backward and filthy, Cordoba was known for its beauty and architecture and boasted over two miles of streets mounted with street lamps. Agriculture, trade, and universities sustained Europe's most advanced culture.

By the thirteenth century the region had been divided into a number of separate kingdoms based on Seville, Cordoba, Jaen, and Granada. In 1212 Castilian Christians from the north conquered Lower Andalusia and gradually extended their authority over several of the small kingdoms. The Inquisition, introduced to the region in 1478, led the persecution of the large Jewish and Moorish populations that came under Christian Spanish rule.

Upper Andalusia, constituting the last of the Moorish kingdoms, Granada, fell to the victorious Christians in 1492, bringing an end to the brilliant Moorish civilization of Spain. At the camp outside the walls of Granada the monarchs of Catholic Spain agreed to sponsor Christopher Columbus' expedition in search of the Indies. Jewels and gold from the looted Moorish towns helped to finance the expedition. The Inquisition ruthlessly persecuted the more sophisticated non-Christian populations of Al-Andalus. The Jews, formerly a respected segment of the population of Al-Andalus, were the first targets of Spanish Christian intolerance. Their extensive properties were confiscated, and they were finally forcibly driven from Spanish territory in 1492, many taking refuge in the more tolerant Ottoman Empire.

The Christian reconquest of Andalusia brought about an immediate decline in the standard of living in the region. Magnificent monuments and religious structures were destroyed or converted to Christian churches, libraries were destroyed, and Christian intolerance of the Islamic and Jewish faiths was introduced. Religious tolerance, practiced under Moorish rule, gave way to persecution of the Moors, Jews, and Roms and ended the golden age of Andalusia.

In 1568 the Moors, called Moriscos by the Spaniards, rebelled and appealed to the Turks* for aid but were quickly put down. The Spanish solution to the problem of the large Moorish populations in Andalusia was the same as with the Jews, expulsion. The Moors' properties, including vast rice and cereal plantations, were confiscated, and in 1609 the Moors were expelled from Spain. The expulsion of the Jews and the Moors led to a sharp decline in trade and agriculture.

Andalusia partially recovered with the exploration of the New World and the subsequent rise of the commercial centers of Seville and Cadiz. The Andalusian monopoly on trade with the Americas made the area wealthy and a meeting place between cultures. At Ronda the rules for the *corrida*, or bullfight, were first drawn up. Due to Andalusia's position as the gateway to the New World, the Andalusian dialect, rather than the Castilian spoken in Madrid, spread to much of Latin America and became the basis for the dialects spoken throughout much of present Latin America.

The region, split into numerous large estates, became progressively less productive and fostered a tradition of rural poverty and illiteracy. In 1833 the province of Andalusia was split into provinces to dilute the traditional Andalusian regionalism and to centralize all power in the Spanish capital, Madrid. Although celebrated for its fertility, the control welded by the large landowners and backward farming methods made Andalusia one of the poorest regions of Spain. In the large rural region the lack of education in Castilian and the retention of folk traditions perpetuated a separate Andalusian dialect and culture.

A period of relative prosperity began in the latter half of the nineteenth century. Flourishing vineyards, agriculture, and mines spurred the growth of the local economy. The period of prosperity ended about 1900, when vine diseases and a drop in mining output left Andalusia as a poor, backward, and underdeveloped region, with large estates, many owned by absentee landlords, continuing to dominate the region. Early in the twentieth century the region became a center of the anarchist movement.

In August 1932, led by reactionary elements, the Andalusians rebelled against the central government but were quickly crushed by Spanish troops. The rebellion, the forerunner of the Spanish civil war, left much devastation. In 1936, when the civil war broke out, much of Andalusia was held by the Nationalist rebels, although eastern Andalusia was held by the Loyalists until March 1939. The civil war left behind prejudices and hatreds that persist in the region to the present.

The victory of Francisco Franco's Nationalists in 1939 was followed by the imposition of a strict dictatorial regime, although Andalusia was the scene of several serious anti-Franco demonstrations between 1939 and the outbreak of World War II. Under Franco's fascist rule, the Andalusians were under intense pressure to accept Castilian speech and culture as the government stressed the lessening of regional differences.

In the 1940s and 1950s Andalusia remained neglected, underdeveloped, and backward, while the Spanish state developed the richer northern regions into the state's industrial heartland. Emigration, long an outlet for poor Andalusians, accelerated in the 1950s and 1960s as the Andalusians left their homeland to settle in the industrialized north, in the homelands of the Basques* and Catalans.* There they were dubbed "Franco's Legions."

A growing antifascist movement in the late 1960s triggered a new awareness of the Andalusians' distinct dialect and culture. Activities and events in the region showed the emergence of a national awareness in Andalusia, a totally new political and cultural phenomenon. With the return of democracy, in 1975, at Franco's death, an active autonomy movement emerged. The poor level of economic development in the region was a major contributing factor in the rising nationalist demands. The Andalusians looked back on periods of greatness, giving them the basis for the subcultural nationalist movement of the 1970s and 1980s. The Andalusian Socialist Party emerged as the leading regionalist party in the 1970s.

In 1979–80 strikes and demonstrations in support of regional autonomy swept the region. In October 1980 a referendum was organized in Andalusia, with 89% of the voters favoring home rule. Self-government for the Andalusians put an end to over three centuries of centralized rule from Madrid.

The Andalusians were particularly hard hit during the worldwide recession of the 1980s. The region's farmers suffered the worst drought of the century, although the growth of tourism somewhat offset the agricultural losses. In the 1990s the region continued to suffer from backward and inefficient farming methods. In spite of the great natural wealth of the region and the phenomenal growth of tourism, the Andalusians remain among the poorest people of Europe, and many Andalusians have begun to question the booming tourist industry, which has brought unbridled construction to the southern coast.

In the late 1980s several regionalist political parties emerged, including the Partido Andalucista (PA), the Andalusian Party, and an openly separatist organization, Liberación Andaluza. In early 1989 the PA demanded the recognition of Andaluz as a separate language, insisting that the language has evolved to a point where it is distinct enough from spoken Castilian to be a separate language. Nationalists also insisted that the dialects spoken throughout Latin America are, in fact, dialects of the Andaluz language, not of Castilian Spanish.

In the 1990s Andalusians living outside their homeland, particularly in other parts of Spain, maintain their culture through strong cultural associations. The antipathy they feel from other peoples has helped the Andalusians to maintain their separate identity. In the early 1990s the first encyclopedia of Andalusian culture was presented at the World Exposition in Seville.

SELECTED BIBLIOGRAPHY

Douglass, Carrie B. *Bulls, Bullfighting, and Spanish Identities*. 1997.

Fletch, R. A. *Moorish Spain*. 1998.

Kean, George. *Andalucia*. 1993.

Kern, Robert W. *The Regions of Spain: A Reference Guide to History and Culture*. 1995.

Mead, Rowland. *Andalucia Handbook*. 1997.

ANDORRANS

Andoreños; Andorenyos

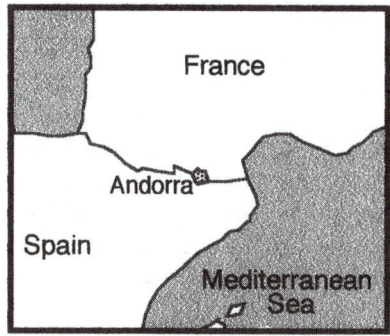

POPULATION: Approximately (2000 e) 25,000 Andorrans in Europe, the majority in Andorra, and with smaller numbers in Spain and France.

THE ANDORRAN HOMELAND: The Andorran homeland lies on the south slope of the eastern Pyrenees Mountains on the border between France and Spain. The region consists of gorges, narrow valleys, and high mountain peaks. The high mountain valleys, with generally poor soil, support large flocks of sheep and cattle. The region's dense forests and spectacular scenery have made Andorra a summer and winter vacation destination.

The small state, functionally independent since 1278, joined the United Nations in 1993. *Principality of Andorra (Principat d'Andorra)*: 180 sq.mi.– 482 sq.km. (2000 e) 66,000—Spaniards* 61%, Andorrans 30%, French* 6%. The Andorran cultural center is the capital of the principality, Andorra La Vella (2000 e) 21,000.

FLAG: The Andorran national flag, the flag of the Andorran state, is a vertical tricolor of blue, yellow, and red, bearing the Andorran national emblem, a quartered shield.

PEOPLE: The Andorrans are a Romance people, originally of Catalan descent, whose separate history has its beginnings during the Carolingian era. Through the centuries of relative isolation in the high mountain valleys, the Andorrans have developed a unique culture and continue to cling to their distinct identity.

The majority of the inhabitants of the country are non-Andorrans, mostly Spanish citizens; however, the major language is Catalan, which is also spoken in the neighboring regions of Spain. Catalan is spoken by an estimated 62% of the country's inhabitants, and most are bilingual in Spanish, which is spoken by about 60% of the inhabitants. A smaller number, around 10% of the population, are able to speak French.

NATION: The valleys of Andorra have been inhabited for thousands of years. Archaeologists have discovered pottery and jewelry dating from the Neolithic period, between 5,000 and 8,000 years ago. Historians speculate that the original inhabitants of the valleys were related to the Basque people of northern Spain and southwestern France and that the name "Andorra" is of Basque derivation.

The valleys were subsequently repopulated during the Celt tribal migrations and colonized by Iberians from the south. At the time of the Punic Wars, the valleys were, according to the historian Polybius, inhabited by a small tribal group called the Andosinos.

Andorra formed part of the Roman Empire, although the high mountain valleys were remote from the centers of Roman power. When Roman power waned, Andorra became a gateway for the northern barbarian tribes to pass from the Roman provinces of Gaul to the Iberian provinces to the south. Several of these tribes left traces of their passing, including the Alans, the Visigoths, and the Vandals.

The small nation, predominantly Christian by the eighth century, was divided into six parishes. The parishes were first mentioned in records of the church in the Acts of Consecration of the Cathedral of Seu d'Urgell in A.D. 839. The arrival of the Moors, who came north through Spain from North Africa, threatened the valleys. The inhabitants of the mountain valleys welcomed the liberation of their country by Charlemagne. According to local legend, Charlemagne was quartered in the village of El Puy d'Olivesa during his campaign to drive the Moors from the Pyrenees.

The origins of the Andorran nation lie in the Carolingian period. The most important historic document of the Andorrans is the Carta de Funcacio d'Andorra, a charter for the country written by Charlemagne and given to his son, Louis the Pious, which established Andorra's independence. In A.D. 843 Emperor Charles II, the son of Louis the Pious, made the count of Urgell the overlord of Andorra.

In 1133 the count of Urgell ceded the Andorran valleys to the bishop of Urgell; however, the rights passed from the counts of Urgell to the counts of Foix through inheritance. The struggle for control, which began in 1159, was prolonged conflict between the counts of Foix and the bishops of La Seu d'Urgell (Urgell). Although an agreement signed that year recognized the bishop's authority while ceding certain rights to the counts of Foix, the dispute lasted until 1278, when Roger Bernard, count of Foix, and Father d'Urtx, the bishop of Urgell, signed a peace treaty forced on them by the king of Aragon. The treaty established joint suzerainty and recognized the Andorrans' constitution as the law of the nation.

This treaty and another signed eleven years later established the Andorrans' independence but stipulated that an annual tribute, called the *questia*, be paid, alternating each year, to the counts of Foix and the bishops of Urgell. The agreement, called the *Pareage*, remained the basis of Andorra's constitution and political independence for over seven centuries. The twin heads of state were called coprinces, and the country was officially called the Principality of Andorra.

The French rights to the joint suzerainty of Andorra passed through the counts of Foix and the House of Albret to Henry IV in 1589. From the French kings the Andorran rights eventually passed to the presidents of France.

In 1419 the Andorrans petitioned the coprinces for permission to establish a local parliament, which would consider local issues. The coprinces granted permission, and the Council of the Land was established. The members were elected by the heads of families, which, in practice, meant males over the age of twenty-five. There were also four representatives from each of the six communes, resulting in a membership of twenty-four.

The Andorrans have always maintained a virtual independence, paying a nominal tribute to France and Spain, 960 francs to the French president, and 460 pesetas to the bishops of La Seu d'Urgell. The semifeudal status of the Andorran homeland was based on its ancient agrarian communal organization. The French franc and the Spanish peseta are both legal currencies, and the Andorrans are prepared for the introduction of the European Union currency, the euro, in the early twenty-first century.

In the late sixteenth century Henry II of Foix became Henry IV of France, and the title to Andorra passed into the royal domain. King Louis XIII, the son of Henry IV, confirmed the Andorrans' rights to independence. However, in 1793 the French monarchy was overthrown, and for the next fifteen years the Andorrans were without the protection of the French government. The Andorrans feared that their Spanish overlord would take this opportunity to revoke their independence and make their homeland a subordinate territory, but when Napoleon became emperor of France, he issued an imperial decree reestablishing the overlordship and protection of the French government. The document, signed on 26 March 1806, reaffirmed the Andorrans' cherished independence. When France became a republic in 1870, the role of overlord became part of the duties and powers of the French president.

Following a brief period of turmoil in 1933, which ended with the arrival of squads of French gendarmes, the established government was reformed. All men over the age of twenty-four were allowed to vote, and all men over age thirty could hold office. In 1970 women were granted the right to vote and hold office, and in 1971 the age requirements were lowered to twenty-one for the right to vote.

The evolution of Andorran democracy included the addition of a seventh parish in 1978, made up of part of the rapidly urbanizing region around the Andorran capital. Two years later the government of Andorra was created. It was established as the executive branch of government, bringing Andorra closer to the democratic principles of the expanding European Union.

The valleys of Andorra, while remaining somewhat isolated in the high Pyrenees, grew prosperous as a center of duty-free trade and Alpine tourism. The Andorrans, once poor shepherds and farmers, had become a prosperous nation of traders, bankers, and hosts to over 10 million visitors a year.

The joint sovereignty of the Spanish and French coprinces lasted from 1278 to 1993. In 1993 Andorra's voters chose to end a feudal system that had been in place for 715 years. They adopted a parliamentary system of government on 14 March 1993. The new system of government effectively ended Andorra's semi-independent status and allowed the Andorrans to join the United Nations and other international organizations as an equal member. Andorra's new representative to the United Nations, speaking in Catalan, used that language for the first time as the representative of a sovereign state in the world body.

SELECTED BIBLIOGRAPHY

Azevedo, Milton M., ed. *Contemporary Catalonia in Spain and Europe.* 1991.

Cameron, Peter. *Andorra.* 1997.

Carrick, Noel. *Andorra.* 1988.

Duursma, Jorri. *Self-Determination, Statehood, and International Relations of Micro-States: The Cases of Liechtenstein, San Marino, Monaco, Andorra, and the Vatican City.* 1994.

Taylor, Barry, ed. *Andorra.* 1993.

ARMENIANS

POPULATION: Approximately (2000 e) 4,650,000 Armenians in Europe, 3,300,000 in Armenia, and another 1,350,000 in the neighboring states of Azerbaijan and Georgia and in Russia. An estimated 70,000 Armenians remain in Turkey. The Armenian diaspora is estimated to number between 7 and 9 million.

THE ARMENIAN HOMELAND: The historic Armenian homeland lies in the Transcaucasus region of Southeastern Europe and the northwestern part of Anatolia. The area is now divided between the Republic of Armenia, Southern or Iranian Armenia, Western or Turkish Armenia, which forms part of the Republic of Turkey, and Eastern Armenia, more commonly known as Nagorno-Karabakh. Artsakh in the Armenian language, which forms an enclave within the Republic of Azerbaijan. The region is centered in the mountainous Transcaucasus region southeast of the Black Sea and southwest of the Caspian Sea and consists mostly of a rugged plateau. The highest point in historic Armenia is Mt. Ararat, the ancient symbol of the Armenian nation, which is now included in Turkish territory.

Armenia formed a member republic of the USSR until the collapse of the Soviet state. In 1991 the Armenians declared their homeland an independent republic. *Republic of Armenia (Haikakan Hanrapetoutioun)*: 11,506 sq.mi.– 29,808 sq.km. (2000 e) 3,472,000—Armenians 95%, Kurds 1.7%, Russians* 1.5%, Azeris* (Azerbaijani), Roms* (Gypsies), Ukrainians.* The Armenian capital and most important cultural center, Yerevan, has a population of (2000 e) 1,345,000 and a metropolitan area population of 1,790,000.

FLAGs: The traditional Armenian national flag, the official flag of the Republic of Armenia, is a horizontal tricolor of red, blue, and orange. The flag of the Artsakh Armenians is the traditional red, blue, and orange tricolor with the addition of a white step triangle on the fly.

PEOPLE: The Armenians, an ancient people first mentioned in the seventh century B.C., form a separate branch of the Caucasian peoples. Among the most ancient of the peoples of the Caucasus, the Armenians have clung to their distinct culture and language through nearly 3,000 years of their history. Their culture, closely tied to their Orthodox religion, has survived massacres, deportations, and persecutions. The Armenians call all non-Armenians Odars, meaning strangers or outsiders. The majority of the population is Christian, belonging to an independent Armenian Orthodox Church headed by the Armenian Katholikos based at Echmiadzin, a holy city near Yerevan. A small minority, called Khemsils, adopted the Islamic religion during the centuries of Turkish rule but remains Armenian in culture and history.

The Armenian language is the only surviving example of the Thraco-Phrygian group of the Indo-European languages. The language, written in a separate alphabet called Mesrobian, was invented by the Armenian saint St. Mesrob, a monk and scholar, traditionally in the year A.D. 410. The language is spoken in two major dialects, Western or Turkish Armenian and Eastern or Yerevan Armenian, the official language of the Armenian republic. Because of the presence of many words borrowed in ancient times from Iranian, it was long believed to be an Iranian dialect, but modern scholarship has firmly established it as an independent branch of the Indo-European language group, although it has diverged in striking ways from the parent language. Armenian literature appeared by the fifth century, and the written language of the era, called Grabar or Classical Armenian, with various changes, remained the literary language of the Armenians until the nineteenth century. Meanwhile, the spoken language developed independently, with many distinct dialects, not all mutually intelligible.

Turkish Armenia, populated by over 2 million ethnic Armenians in 1890, is now mostly inhabited by Muslim Turks and Kurds. The Armenian diaspora, estimated to number between 7 and 9 million, includes large populations in the United States and Canada, Russia, Iran, Syria, Lebanon, Romania, Bulgaria, Greece, France, Cyprus, Egypt, and in the neighboring states of Georgia and Azerbaijan.

NATION: According to Armenian tradition, Noah's Ark, after weathering the great flood, landed on Mt. Ararat, the sacred symbol of Armenian nationhood, now in Turkish territory. The Armenians claim descent from Noah through Haik, thus their name for their homeland, Haikakan or Hayastan. Known to the world as a separate people since very ancient times, the ancestors of the Armenians are thought to have settled in the Transcaucasus region before 800 B.C. By the sixth century B.C. the Armenians had formed a homogeneous nation, known as Utartu by the ancient Assyrians. Traditionally, the foundation of the Armenian nation is set in the year 624 B.C. From 518 to 330 B.C. the region formed a satrapy of the Persian Empire until the arrival of the Greeks* of Alexander the Great.

The Armenians declared the independence of their kingdom in 189 B.C. under a native dynasty. War between the Armenian kingdom and the growing Roman Empire finally ended in defeat for the Armenians. The Armenian homeland was declared a protectorate after Trajan's conquest of the area 114–117 B.C.

The Armenian nation was the first to adopt Christianity as the national religion in A.D. 303. Their distinct national church was established in 491, when the Armenian Church separated from the Greek rite. The fourth and fifth centuries saw a level of religion-inspired learning and cultural achievement unknown in other parts of Europe.

The collapse of Roman power left the Christian Armenian nation vulnerable to invaders. Sovereign Armenian states, with varying borders and always prey to more powerful neighbors, existed for brief periods, the most notable an independent Armenian kingdom from 886 to 1046. Persians, Byzantines, White Huns, Khazars, and, in the seventh and eighth centuries, Muslim Arabs threatened or overran the Armenian homeland. The Armenian nation, often subjugated and their lands devastated, nevertheless survived, while most ancient peoples disappeared into history.

In the thirteenth century the invading Mongols decimated the population. The survivors of the massacres fled to the southwest, to Cilicia in present southeastern Turkey, where they established Little Armenia, which was destroyed by the Egyptian Mamelukes in 1373. Tamerlane, one of the successors to the Mongols' far-flung empire, invaded Armenia in the late fourteenth century, his forces again massacring a majority of the Christian population.

The Armenian homeland fell to the advancing Ottoman Turks in the fifteenth century, although Turkish control of the region was disputed by the Persians. Even though subject to cruel restrictions and special taxes as Christians under Muslim rule, the industrious Armenians acquired a vital economic role in the workings of the Ottoman Empire, some even rising to high office in the Ottoman government.

The Persian conquest of eastern Armenia in 1639 effectively partitioned the nation. Suffering persecution and discrimination under Muslim rule, the Armenians welcomed the advance of the Christian Russians in the Transcaucasus in the late eighteenth and early nineteenth centuries. In 1828 the Russians took control of eastern Armenia from Persia, setting off a wave of pro-Russian sentiment among the harshly treated Armenian population under Ottoman rule. Russian interest in the region set off a period of Turkish repression and persecution of the Armenian Christians that worsened in the latter half of the nineteenth century. The focal points of Armenian life, due to the Muslim repression, lay outside the nation's heartland, in the great centers of diaspora Armenian culture, Constantinople, Tiflis (Tbilisi), and Van. The major European nations, uncomfortable with the persecution of Christians, demanded reforms in 1878 and again in 1883, but the demands only increased the Turkish distrust of their Christian subjects.

A small number of educated Armenians founded the Armenian national movement in the relatively more liberal Russian Armenia in 1840. National sentiment, fueling a cultural revival in the mid-nineteenth century, rapidly spread throughout the Armenian populations in Russia, Turkey, and Persia.

Determined to crush the perceived Christian threat to the Ottoman Empire, the Turkish authorities, beginning in 1890, officially encouraged attacks on defenseless Armenian towns and villages, leading to horrible massacres by rampaging Turks and Kurds. An 1896 attack by Armenian nationalists on the Ottoman Bank cost the Armenians over 50,000 lives in official reprisals. Nationalists in the late 1890s formed the Armenian Revolutionary Federation, the Dashnaktsutium, which soon had cells in most towns and villages in both Russian and Turkish Armenia. The nationalists openly opposed Turkish oppression and the Russian policy of assimilation.

The official policy of the Russification of the Armenian population in Russian Armenia increased in parallel with the growth of Armenian national sentiment. In 1903 all the holdings of the Armenian Church in Russia were confiscated and turned over to the Russian Orthodox Church. The outraged Armenians joined in the revolutionary activities that swept the Russian Empire in 1905. As part of the concessions promised by the government to end the revolution, all church property was returned to the Armenian Church, and the 1903 decree was retracted.

The divided Armenian homeland became a battleground when war broke out in 1914. The Armenian population under Ottoman rule mostly favored the enemy Russians, seen as the protectors of their kin in the Russian Empire. The Armenian majority in the town of Van, in Turkish Armenia, rebelled on 13 April 1915. The rebels quickly captured the important fort and held off the Ottoman military until relieved by Russian troops on 19 May.

Ottoman Turkey, allied to the Central Powers, continued to view its Christian minorities with suspicion. Claiming that the over 2 million Armenians in the empire were aiding the Russian enemy, Ottoman officials ordered non-Muslim populations removed from all points of military concentrations and lines of communications. The orders, carried out with incredible cruelty, were interpreted as sanctioning the virtual annihilation of the Armenian minority. Forced from their homes at gunpoint, hundreds of thousands of Armenians were driven into the Syrian Desert to perish from hunger, thirst, and violence. Armenian men were systematically murdered, and the women were raped and, with the surviving children, were sold into slavery. The deserted Armenian towns and villages were annihilated, with particular attention devoted to the destruction of churches. Over half a million scattered survivors fled to sanctuary in Russian Armenia or escaped abroad. An estimated 1 million people died in the century's first genocide, 1915–16.

Revolution in Russia in 1917 freed Russian Armenia to seek protection within an independent federation made up of Armenia and the neighboring secessionist states of Georgia and Azerbaijan. Tensions between the partners, particularly between Christian Armenia and Muslim Azerbaijan, ended the attempt to form a strong federation even as new threats appeared to menace Armenia's fragile independence. The Armenian authorities, with the collapse of the Transcaucasian Federation, declared Armenia a separate, independent state on 28 May 1918. The new state laid claim to the traditional Armenian lands, including the Armenian-populated parts of newly independent Azerbaijan and the largely depopulated provinces of Turkish Armenia.

Armenian troops moved west into the Ottoman provinces, hailed as liberators by the surviving Armenians and the numerous Greeks living along the Black Sea coast. Looting of Muslim properties and massacres, in retaliation for the earlier Turkish massacres, became widespread before the government in Yerevan could restore order. In May 1919, taking advantage of Turkey's defeat by the Allied powers, Armenia formally annexed Turkish Armenia; however, much of the area remained outside Armenian control. The Armenian republic in 1918, covering an area of over 68,000 square miles, officially had a population of over 2 million, 65% Christian and 33% Muslim.

Cilicia, in southeastern Turkey, with a large Armenian population, was taken by Allied forces in 1918. In 1919 French troops took control of the Cilicia region, and due to the majority non-Turkish population the region was separated from Turkey and was given as a mandate to France by the new League of Nations in 1920.

The beleaguered Armenian government sought British and French protection, but without success. The delegates sent by the Armenian government to the Paris Peace Conference in 1919 put forward territorial claims to former Russian Armenia, plus the former Turkish provinces of Van, Bitlis, Diyarbakir, Kharput, Sivas, Erzurum, Trebizond, and Cilicia in the south. The Turks rejected the Armenian claims to former Ottoman territory claims completely. The Allies, over Turkish objections, made provision for recognizing an independent "Greater Armenia" in the 1920 Treaty of Sevres, which formally ended hostilities with Turkey. However, the Allies refused to accede to all of the Armenians' territorial demands, which were thought excessive. The new state's western border, as defined by the treaty, was delimited personally by U.S. president Woodrow Wilson.

The Armenian republic, soon threatened by the advancing Red Army and a resurgent, nationalist Turkey, appealed to the Allies for protection. In April 1920 at the San Remo Conference of Allied powers, the Allies urged the United States to accept Armenia as a mandate under the new League of Nations. The U.S. Senate, having kept the United States out of the League of Nations, voted fifty-two to twenty-three against the mandate proposal. The vote sealed the fate of the beleaguered state.

The Soviet government, emerging victorious from the Russian civil war, and Turkey, under its new nationalist leader Ataturk, by tacit agreement planned the demise of the bothersome Armenian republic. The Red Army in the east and the Turks in the west launched a simultaneous attack on the republic in September 1920. In November Turkish troops, abetted by the Soviets, overran the poorly defended former Ottoman provinces in western Armenia. The Turkish conquest of western Armenia ended with near-obliteration of the Armenian presence in the region. The renewed massacres of the remaining Armenian population forced the survivors to flee to the eastern districts of the besieged republic. In March 1921 the Red Army finally defeated the starving, ill-equipped, and seriously overcrowded remnant of the Republic of Armenia. In the south Turkish troops expelled the French forces from the Cilicia Mandate. The Turkish conquest of Cilicia forced thousands of Armenians to flee across the border into French territory in Syria, the last large refugee Armenian population to be driven from their homelands.

The fallen republic, partitioned between the Turkish and Soviet states, ceased to exist. In the Turkish zone the new nationalist government sponsored Muslim settlement to the depopulated region. In the east the Soviets joined Armenia to Soviet Georgia and Azerbaijan in a new Transcaucasian Federation. The federation was admitted to the Soviet Union as a constituent republic on 30 December 1922. The federation was abolished, and Armenia became a separate republic within the union in 1936.

In 1953, on behalf of the Armenian people, the Soviet government formally renounced all claims to Turkish Armenia. After World War II the Soviet government, despite decades of purges that had eliminated the Armenian political and cultural leadership, urged diaspora Armenians to return to the world's only Armenian state. Over 200,000 Armenians returned from exile, preferring to live among their own people, even under Soviet rule.

Armenian nationalism, sustained by the large disapora, reemerged in the 1970s, led by the pro-Western Dashnaks. Militant groups demanded that Turkey admit to the crime of genocide and as partial compensation cede Turkish Armenia to a reconstituted Armenian state. Armenian terrorist groups struck at Turkish targets around the world, particularly Turkish diplomatic missions in Europe and the Middle East. More moderate nationalist groups lobbied Western support from offices in Europe, the United States, and the Middle East.

Nationalism in Soviet Armenia grew rapidly in the more relaxed atmosphere fostered by the Soviet leader Mikhail Gorbachev after 1987. Renewed Armenian territorial claims to Nagorno-Karabakh, an Armenian majority enclave within the neighboring Soviet republic of Azerbaijan, became a major nationalist issue. Nationalists formed the Karabakh Committee, demanding that the region, called Artsakh in Armenian, be returned to Armenian administration. Nationalist crowds, estimated at over 1 million, demonstrated in Yerevan.

The Karabakh Committee openly demanded greater economic, political, and cultural freedom in Armenia. The nationalists insisted on a veto on all development projects in the republic, freedom to fly the Armenian national flag, the right to open consulates in countries with large Armenian populations, and the creation of a separate Armenian detachment to the Red Army, so that young Armenians could perform their military service on home soil. The most politically charged nationalist demand, the unification of the Armenian-populated areas of the Soviet Union, starting with Nagorno-Karabakh, led to an open and bitter dispute with neighboring Azerbaijan.

The Armenian demands sparked a parallel nationalist upsurge among the Muslim Azeris, leading to attacks on the Armenian districts of Azerbaijan's largest cities. In February 1988 Azeri mobs tore into the Armenian quarter in the industrial city of Sumgait, killing over thirty Armenians and injuring hundreds. In an effort to quell the growing ethnic violence the Red Army sent troops to occupy both Armenia and Azerbaijan, but the mob violence continued. Over 200,000 Armenian refugees fleeing the growing violence in Azerbaijan poured across the Armenian border, only to be engulfed in a new disaster. The most destructive earthquake to hit the region in over 1,000 years struck on 7 December 1988.

Leaders of the Karabakh Committee, critical of the Soviet rescue effort and blaming poor planning and construction techniques for the massive death toll of over 55,000, were arrested at the height of the disaster and charged with spreading false information and slandering the Soviet state. New Armenian protests erupted, leading to clashes between demonstrators and the army and police. Army units, withdrawn from Azerbaijan to aid the earthquake rescue effort, freed the Azeri mobs to renew their attacks. Even after the enormously destructive earthquake, trains full of Armenian refugees continued to arrive in Yerevan.

On 26 March 1989 the citizens of the Soviet Union, for the first time in over seven decades, voted in free, multicandidate elections for a new Chamber of Deputies. The Armenians, defying the occupation troops of the Red Army and an official ban on demonstrations, took to the streets to protest the elections, while their proposed candidates, members of the Karabakh Committee, were in prison in Moscow. A mass boycott negated the results of the elections in Armenia, where most refused to vote while their entire nationalist leadership remained in jail or in hiding.

In January 1990 sporadic skirmishing turned into full-scale war in Nagorno-Karabakh and neighboring areas. In May 1990 the Armenian parliament suspended the spring draft of military conscripts following massive antidraft demonstrations in Yerevan. The Armenian National Movement, a coalition of several separate nationalist organizations, grew out of the Karabakh Committee and rapidly gained support in the republic, even among longtime Armenian communists. Nationalists quickly took over local governments and soon controlled the major organs of the republic.

The republic, battered by an Azeri economic blockade that crippled the economy and brought earthquake construction to a halt, suffered shortages of food and other essentials. The blockade further inflamed Armenian nationalism as the advantages of Soviet citizenship withered away. On 30 April 1991, for the first time in the dispute, Soviet troops openly sided with the still communist-controlled Azerbaijan against the nationalist-controlled Armenia. In May, following a two-week campaign by Azeri and Soviet troops along the Azeri-Armenian border, thousands of Armenians were forced to flee, further eroding support for the maintenance of the tottering Soviet Union.

The new government on 23 August 1990 declared Armenia a sovereign state. The declaration extended citizenship rights to the Armenian diaspora, particularly to the inhabitants of the enclave of Nagorno-Karabakh. The nationalist government appealed to the Soviet government for negotiations on peaceful secession from the Soviet Union. The declaration declared Armenian territorial control to Artsakh, the disputed enclave of Nagorno-Karabakh in Azerbaijan.

In the wake of the failed military coup in Moscow in August 1991 the Armenian government organized a referendum on independence on 21 September. The Armenians voted 95% in favor of immediate independence. On 23 September 1991 the Armenian president, Levon Ter-Petrossian, formally declared the republic's independence as the Republic of Armenia, Haikakan Hanrapetoutioun.

The republic, strongly supported by the Armenian diaspora, faced massive economic and political problems as the change from communism to capitalism was further complicated by an economic blockade by neighboring Azerbaijan. The dispute over Nagorno-Karabakh fueled a continuing war involving the local Armenians and Azeri troops. In December 1991 the Armenian inhabitants of Nagorno-Karabakh voted in a referendum for independence from Azerbaijan, further escalating the war between the newly independent republics.

Azeri forces besieged Nagorno-Karabakh in November 1992, forcing the residents of the enclave's capital to live in underground shelters for several months. The enclave's only lifeline was a dangerous helicopter route to Armenia. The military forces of Karabakh, backed by troops of the Republic of Armenia, to break the siege went on the offensive, finally opening a land corridor between the enclave and the republic in late 1992. By April 1993 the Armenian forces had occupied nearly 20% of the national territory of Azerbaijan.

The Armenians, surrounded on three sides by Muslim states, see themselves as the standard-bearers of Western civilization in the region. The new republic's ties to the large diaspora reinforce the Armenians' view of themselves as an outpost of Western culture, although in the late 1990s ties to the neighboring Iranians and the Russians strengthened.

The Armenian republic and Azerbaijan finally agreed to a cease-fire, which became effective in May 1994, leaving large areas of Azeri territory under Armenian occupation. The cease-fire has generally held in spite of continuing tensions and a state of war between the two former Soviet states. In August 1997 the government announced that a border crossing would soon be opened between Armenia and Turkey, which had formerly refused diplomatic ties and border crossings due to the Nagorno-Karabakh conflict.

The election of an ardent nationalist, Robert Kocharian, as president in March 1998 was accompanied by a very strong showing for the former Communist Party leader, Karen Demirchian. The revival of the communists, once reviled in

Armenia, has alarmed nationalists and their supporters among the large overseas Armenian populations, particularly those in North America and Western Europe.

The Armenian nation has survived adversity since the dawn of history, sometimes as an independent nation-state but more often as an oppressed minority within larger territory held by more powerful neighbors. The government of the Republic of Armenia, with the strong support of the Armenian diaspora, is seeking an honorable place for the Armenian people within the confines of a democratic, peaceful Europe.

In late October 1999, armed gunmen attacked the Armenian parliament, killing the prime minister and other politicians. They held other members of parliament hostage before surrendering a day later in exchange for airing their grievances on television, where they accused the Armenian government of massive corruption and blamed the country's leaders for the poverty of the Armenian nation.

SELECTED BIBLIOGRAPHY

Coppieters, Bruno, ed. *Contested Borders in the Caucasus.* 1996.

Libaridian, Gerald J., ed. *Armenia at the Crossroads.* 1991.

O'Ballance, Edgar. *Wars in the Caucasus, 1990–1995.* 1997.

Sunny, Ronald Grigor. *Looking toward Ararat: Armenia in Modern History.* 1993.

Walker, Christopher. *Armenia: The Survival of a Nation.* 1990.

AUSTRIANS

Österreichers

POPULATION: Approximately (2000 e) 6,920,000 Austrians in Europe, primarily in the Republic of Austria, forming the majority in the provinces of Burgenland, Carinthia, Lower Austria, Salzburg, Styria, Upper Austria, and Vienna.

THE AUSTRIAN HOMELAND: The Austrian homeland is a landlocked region in the heart of Europe. Most of the area is mountainous, except for northern Austria, which lies in the valley of the river Danube, and the Vienna Basin. These lowlands are the major farming region of the Austrian territories. Southern Austria contains ranges of the Alps, which rise to their highest at Grossglockner, at 12,457 feet (3,797 m.). Woods and meadows cover much of the territory, estimated at about 39% of the total area of the Austrian republic. The forests include a variety of trees, giving Austria the highest proportion of forest of any other European state. Of the total land area, about 17% is considered suitable for cultivation. Meadowlands and pastures make up about 24% of the total land area, and market gardens and vineyards account for slightly more than 1%. About half of Austrian farms are under ten hectares (twenty-five acres) in size.

With the famous Alps and a wealth of cultural and recreational facilities, Austria is one of the world's top tourist destinations. A premier winter sports area, the country also has summer music festivals (including the famous Salzburg Festival), lake resorts (especially in Carinthia), medicinal spas, and many museums and other attractions. In the 1990s about 20 million people from other countries visited Austria annually. An important part of the Austrian national economy, tourism generated about $15 billion annually in revenue for the country in the 1990s.

Austria produces an agricultural abundance in the river valleys, giving the Austrians one of the highest standards of living in Europe. *Republic of Austria (Republik Österreich)*: 32,375 sq.mi.–83,851 sq.km. (2000 e) 7,849,000—Austrians 88%, Tyroleans* 8%, Vorarlbergers* 4.5%, Slovenians,* Croatians,* Hungarians.* The Austrian capital and major cultural center, Vienna, Wien in German, (2000 e) 1,522,000 (metropolitan area 1,904,000), is the national capital of the Republic of Austria.

FLAG: The Austrian national flag, the flag of the Austrian republic, has three horizontal stripes of red, white, and red.

PEOPLE: The Austrians, situated in Central Europe and with a history of conquest and reconquest by varying tribes and factions, are a nation of mixed ancestry. Germanic in language and culture, the Austrians have mixed with, and incorporated, cultural traits from many of their former subject peoples, Hungarians, Slavs, and Latins. The development of a specifically Austrian national consciousness, suppressed during the Nazi era, began to flower only during the 1960s. The question now is, will that consciousness be strong enough to withstand the homogenizing affects of Austrian membership in the European Union?

The culture of the Austrians is famed for its music, art, and architecture, along with an extensive literature that began take form in the nineteenth century. Vienna, once cut off from its natural hinterland, is once again a vibrant European capital and one of the major cities of the expanding European Union.

The Austrians speak German, with 99% of the Austrians using German as their first language. The standard German, as spoken in Germany, is understood and spoken throughout the Austrian homeland; however, regional dialects remain vibrant, and the Austrians, in daily life, use a dialect closer to Bavarian German than the German of Berlin or Frankfurt.

The Austrians remain strongly Roman Catholic, with 78% members of the church. There are smaller numbers of Protestant Austrians, about 5% of the population, and even smaller minorities of Jews and Muslims.

NATION: The Austrian homeland has been inhabited since about 80,000 B.C. In the early Iron Age, it was settled first by Illyrians and later by Celts from Western Europe. The region is located at the crossroads of Europe, Vienna is at the gate of the Danubian Plain, and the Brenner Pass links Northern Europe to Italy and the Mediterranean. From earliest history the Austrian homeland has been a highway and a battlefield.

Celts and Suebi occupied the region, and then the Romans took control between 15 B.C. and A.D. 10. Under Roman rule the region was divided between the provinces of Rhaetia, Noricum, and Upper Pannonia. Christianity, coming north from Italy, became the dominant religion in the region by A.D. 200.

Following the decline of Roman power, in the fifth century, Huns, Ostrogoths, Lombards,* and Bavarians* overran the region and destroyed the Roman culture and order. Slavs, migrating from the east, moved into the devastated region in the late sixth century. By the year 600 the Slavs had occupied modern Styria, Carinthia, and Lower Austria. The next threat, the Avars,* also came from the east, sweeping all before them. Although a number of tribes settled in the region, none held power for long until the arrival of the Franks.

In 788 the Frankish Empire of Charlemagne conquered the area and set up the Eastern March in present Upper and Lower Austria to halt the advance of the Avars. Under Charlemagne's empire, Germanic colonization was encouraged, and Christianity was spread to all areas. Following Charlemagne's death his empire was weakened and overrun by Moravians.*

The Magyars, the ancestors of the Hungarians, a nomadic people migrating slowly from the east, advanced easily along the Danube River valley until they were finally defeated by the German king Otto I at Augsburg in 955 in the Battle of the Lechfeld. Otto I revived the Eastern March (Österreich) and gave the more influential title of margrave to its administrator; these moves marked the emergence of Austria as a political entity.

Otto II bestowed the region, as a separate fief, on Leopold of Babenberg, the founder of the first Austrian dynasty. The Babenbergs moved their residence, and therefore the center of Austrian lands, to Vienna. In the eleventh and twelfth centuries the region grew prosperous during the height of Austrian feudalism. The era also witnessed the marked development of urban centers as the Danube was converted to one of Europe's great trade routes. Emperor Frederick I raised Austria to the status of a duchy in 1156, and in 1192 Styria also passed to Babenberg rule. The Babenbergs controlled the region until Duke Freidrich died childless in 1246, leaving the Austrian homeland once again open to warring tribes.

Following the death of the last Babenburg ruler, King Ottocar II of Bohemia gained control of Austria, Styria, Carinthia, and Carniola. Fearing his power, the German princes elected Rudolf of Hapsburg German emperor in 1273. Rudolf asserted his royal prerogative to reclaim the four Austrian duchies from Ottocar and to incorporate them into their growing domains. In 1278 Ottocar was defeated and slain in battle by Rudolf's forces. By 1283 most of the former domain of Ottocar had come under the rule of Rudolf's son, Albert I.

The Hapsburg dynasty was to rule for 650 years. New territories were acquired, as much by royal marriage as war, which resulted in the Hapsburgs, after 1438, becoming emperors of the Holy Roman Empire. The Hapsburg Empire ruled much of Central Europe, including Switzerland, Hungary, and Bohemia as well as the Netherlands and Spain and its far-flung overseas possessions. During the long reign of Frederick III, Austria was raised to an archduchy in 1453 and was engaged in protracted wars with the French for dominance in Europe. The lasting union of Austria, Bohemia, and Hungary, established in 1526, under the same crown, laid the foundations of the Austrian Empire.

In 1556 the Hapsburg Empire was divided into Austrian and Spanish halves. In spite of their vast territorial possessions, the Hapsburgs always considered the German-speaking core of the empire as the true Austria and the heart of the Hapsburg lands. The weakening and instability of the Austrian heartland, due to the diminished value of the Austrian trade routes and mines, allowed the Protestant Reformation to advance during the sixteenth century. In opposition the Hapsburgs nurtured the Catholic Counter-Reformation in the empire.

The wars of the seventeenth century brought new territory under Austrian domination and finally ended the Turkish threat to the empire. In 1619 rebels deposed the Hapsburg ruler, Ferdinand, setting off a serious conflict in the region. The internal Austrian conflict grew into a European war, the Thirty Years' War, fought mainly on German soil. The Hapsburgs were defeated in battle, and the Peace of Westphalia in 1648 weakened Hapsburg control over the Holy Roman Empire by reducing the empire to a loose union of independent states. The Austrian provinces, virtually untouched by the holocaust of the Thirty Years' War, emerged as the core of the renewed Hapsburg Empire, while the Holy Roman Empire faded into a shadow existence.

Emperor Charles VI, whose dynastic wars drained the empire in the late eighteenth century, secured as his successor a woman, his daughter, Maria Theresa. She turned Austria into a modern state, but a series of devastating wars with Prussia for dominance in German Europe again weakened the empire. Maria Theresa's son, Joseph II, motivated by the ideas of the Enlightenment, abolished serfdom, improved civil and criminal procedures, and decreed religious toleration and freedom of the press. He also reformed the Roman Catholic Church by removing its control over secular matters and tried to centralize imperial administration. His reforms aroused widespread opposition. At the time of his death, Hungary and the Low Countries were in full revolt, and there was unrest in the Austrian hereditary lands and among the Czechs.* Joseph's brother and successor, Leopold II, revoked most of the reforms and was forced to recognize Hungary as a separate unit of the Hapsburg lands. Even so, Joseph's reign had regenerated the Austrian monarchy and opened it up to European trends.

Throughout the eighteenth and nineteenth centuries, Vienna was a world center of culture, particularly in music and literature. Austrian fine art usually is considered with the art of the southern Germans, the Bavarians, and the Swabians.* A distinctive Austrian style, however, is manifested in the refined baroque architecture and sculpture of the seventeenth and eighteenth centuries, notably in Vienna, Salzburg, and Melk. Austrian musicians led Europe, and their compositions are among the greatest creations of European music.

Austria was drawn into war with revolutionary France and Napoleon I. The treaties signed between Austria and France in 1797 and 1806 ended the Holy Roman Empire. In 1804 Francis II took the title Francis I, emperor of Austria. At the end of the Napoleonic Wars, the Congress of Vienna, 1814–15, called to reorganize war-torn Europe, awarded Austria territories in Italy and the Balkan Peninsula. The wars and their aftermath halted the Austrians' progress toward a modern society.

The Austrians' power was further undermined by the 1848 revolution, both in the Austrian heartland and in Hungary. Austria lost most of its Italian territories in the 1850s and lost control of the German Federation when Prussia defeated the empire in 1866, the Austro-Prussian War. After the Prussian victory, Austria was expelled from the German Confederation and lost Venetia to the new Italian kingdom. A reorientation toward Eastern Europe and a reorganization of the government of the empire became inevitable. In 1867 a compromise established a dual state with Hungary, the Austro-Hungarian Empire. The vast, multiethnic empire, ruled by an Austrian-Hungarian elite, increasingly became an anachronism in the age of nationalism in the late nineteenth century.

The 12 million German-speaking Austrians in 1910 ruled an empire of over 50 million inhabitants, the second largest country of Europe after Russia. The "Dual-Monarchy" was 77% Roman Catholic, 9% Protestant, 9% Greek Orthodox, 4% Jewish, and 1% Muslim. Hapsburg opposition to reforms or autonomy for the non-Austrian and non-Hungarian peoples of the empire spurred the growth of nationalism among the other nations in the late nineteenth century.

The Serbs* actively opposed Austrian control of Bosnia-Herzegovina, which was annexed in 1908, ultimately leading to war in Europe. On 28 June 1914 the heir to the Austro-Hungarian throne, Archduke Francis Ferdinand, and his wife were assassinated in the Bosnian capital of Sarajevo by Gavrilo Princip, a Serbian nationalist. After receiving German assurances of support, the Austro-Hungarian foreign office sent a harsh ultimatum to the Serbian government, holding it responsible for the assassination and requiring its total acceptance of Austria-Hungary's demands within three days. Despite a conciliatory reply that accepted all but two of the demands and mediation efforts by the European powers, Austria-Hungary declared war on Serbia on 28 July. Germany's declaration of war on Russia and France in early August transformed the conflict into World War I.

During the spring and summer of 1918 Austro-Hungarian forces were defeated on every military front; shortages of food and other necessities triggered strikes and demonstrations at home and mutinies in the army and navy. Recognizing that the collapse of the monarchy was inevitable, the nationalist groups within the empire organized national councils that acted like separate governments. The South Slav peoples, meeting in Zagreb on 7 October 1918, advocated union with Serbia, and on 28 October the Czechs proclaimed an independent republic in Prague. The Hungarian government announced its complete separation from Austria on 3 November. That same day the Austrians and Hungarians each signed an armistice with the Allies. On 12 November Charles relinquished all part in the administration of the state and left Austria.

Following the abdication of the last Hapsburg emperor, a peaceful socialist revolution proclaimed the Austrian heartland a republic and a part of Greater Germany. However, the treaties imposed by the Allies prohibited any political or economic union, *Anschluss*, with Germany. Reorientation toward Germany was blocked by the insistence of France, Italy, and Czechoslovakia on the treaty clauses against union. Many German-speaking Austrians fled the newly independent states that emerged from the collapse of the empire to live in the Austrian lands, the core provinces that made up the new Republic of Austria.

In the postwar period starvation and diseases took a heavy toll on the Austrians, particularly in overcrowded Vienna. These ills were followed by currency inflation, chronic unemployment, and economic chaos. Various political parties on the left and right vied for power in the new republic during the 1920s. Strikes and demonstratons became normal in Vienna and other Austrian cities.

By 1930 National Socialism, feeding on renewed anti-Semitism, gained many adherents and gradually absorbed the pro-German political organizations. In 1932 Engelbert Dolfuss became chancellor, and, although opposed to *Anschluss* and National Socialism, the Nazis, Dolfuss increasingly imposed a fascist-style authoritarianism. In 1934 a totalitarian state was created, and the Nazis and other political organizations were outlawed. In July 1934, Dolfuss was assassinated by Nazis, but they failed to seize the Austrian government. German pressure on the Austrians increased, and the Nazis were again legalized and in 1938 received cabinet posts. A last-minute attempt to prevent *Anschluss* by holding a plebiscite on Austrian independence bought a German ultimatum. The Austrian government yielded and in March 1938, German troops occupied the Austrian homeland. Hitler made a triumphal entry into Vienna amid the adulation of an enormous crowd of Austrians. In 1940 the Austrian homeland was fully incorporated into the Nazi German state.

The Austrians fought alongside the Germans in World War II, suffering bombings and shortages as the war continued. The large Jewish population was mostly massacred during the Holocaust, in which many Austrians participated. In 1943 the Allied leaders agreed to reestablish a separate Austrian state at the end of the war. In 1945 the Austrians surrendered to invading American troops. Like Germany, the Austrian homeland was partitioned into four zones of occupation, controlled, respectively, by the United States, France, Great Britain, and the USSR.

Austria was recognized within its prewar borders in 1946, but Soviet objections delayed the formal peace treaty. The most significant event in the postwar era was the restoration of Austrian sovereignty in May 1955, after long negotiations that had begun in 1947. The main issue between the USSR, on one side, and the United States, Great Britain, and France, on the other, was the future of Germany. The Soviets would not give up their strategic position in Austria unless Germany was "neutralized." Finally, in exchange for Soviet concessions, Austria promised "not to join any military alliances or permit any military bases on its territory." The four Allies and Austria signed the State Treaty on 15 May 1955, formally reestablishing the Austrian republic, which proclaimed its permanent neutrality. Economically aided by their former enemies, the Austrians repaired the war damage, and by 1961 the country was a neutral, prosperous, and peaceful state on the border between the two Cold War blocs.

In spite of its professed neutrality, the Austrian republic in 1993 applied for membership in the European Union, and in 1994 the Austrians voted in favor of membership. On 1 January 1995 Austria became a full member state of the union; however, opposition to Austrian participation in an integrated Europe remained strong in some sectors. By late 1996 the right-wing Freedom Party had increased in popularity. An outspoken opponent of immigration and the EU, the party won support among working-class Austrians by arguing that both posed dangerous threats to Austrian jobs. The Freedom Party also tapped into a growing dissatisfaction among Austrians over budgetary cuts designed to meet EU criteria for participation in a common European currency in 1999.

In national elections in mid-1999, the right-wing Freedom Party, associated by many outside Austria with the neo-Nazi movement, won 27% of the vote, bringing with it the possibility of participating in the Austrian government for the first time. The electoral victory, denounced by many Austrians and others within the European Union, also alarmed the Israeli government, which threatened to break diplomatic relations with Austria if the Freedom Party was brought into the government. The large number of votes for a party associated with the darker side of Austria's past reflects the failure of the Austrians to cleanly break with their Nazi past. The percentage of Austrians belonging to the Nazi movement was even higher than that of the Germans.

SELECTED BIBLIOGRAPHY

Brook-Shepherd, Gordon. *The Austrians: A Thousand-Year Odyssey.* 1997.

Greene, Carol. *Austria.* 1986.

Luther, Kurt Richard, and Peter G. J. Pulzer, eds. *Austria 1945–95: Fifty Years of the Second Republic.* 1998.

Philpott, Don et al. *Austria.* 1993.

Sked, Alan. *The Decline and Fall of the Habsburg Empire, 1815–1918.* 1989.

AVARS

Maarlulal; Magarulal; Avarskiy;
Avaros; Dagestanis

POPULATION: Approximately (2000 e) 622,000 Avars in Europe, 574,000 in Russia, the majority in Dagestan, with smaller numbers in Chechenia and Kalmykia, and 48,000 in Azerbaijan. An estimated 43,000 ethnic Avars live in Turkey and the Middle East.

THE AVAR HOMELAND: The Avar homeland is in the mountainous highlands of the Dagestan Republic of southeastern European Russia. They are concentrated in west-central Dagestan and extend across the international border into northern Azerbaijan and southeastern Chechenia. The Avars inhabit the valleys of the Avar-Koisu and Andi-Koisu Rivers and their tributaries. The region, which includes the high peaks of the eastern Caucasus Mountains, was nearly inaccessible until the early twentieth century.

Avaristan, the Avar homeland, has no official status. Avar nationalists claim that traditional Avaristan extends south into Azerbaijan and west into Chechenia. The 48,000 Avars in the Belakan region of northern Azerbaijan have been working for the unification of Belakan with Avaristan. The Avar capital and major cultural center is Khunsakh.

FLAG: The Avar national flag, the flag of the national movement, is a green field bearing a white crescent moon and three four-pointed stars.

PEOPLE: The Avars are the largest of the Dagestani peoples of the Dagestan Republic of southern European Russia. The Avars, historically and linguistically united, actually encompass a complex mix of related, though quite distinct, ethnic communities. The Avaro-Andi-Dido Peoples is a generic reference to the seventeen peoples who are considered part of the Avar nation, each speaking its own dialect. Those considered part of the Avar nation include the Avars,

Andis, Akhwakhs, Botligs, Godoberis, Bagulals, Karatas, Tindis, and Chamalals, who are all Avar peoples. The Dido group includes the Didos, the Khwarshia, Bezhetas, Khunzals, and Ginugs. A separate group, the Archis, are considered distinct and not part of the Avar or Dido groups; however, all seventeen of the Avar ethnic groups are descended from the proto-Avar tribes that originally settled the region.

The Avars speak a Caucasian language that forms part of the northeast branch of the Caucasian languages. Four mutually unintelligible Avar dialects are spoken, Khunzakh, Antsukh, Charoda, and Gidatl-Andalalay-Karkh. The other peoples of the Avar, Dido, and Archi groups speak related languages but use the Khunzakh Avar dialect as their literary language. The Khunzakh dialect is also the lingua franca, the common language, for a large part of southern Dagestan. Because the town of Khunzakh has historically been the political and cultural center of the Avars, as well as the entire region, the Khunsakh dialect is the dominant one and the foundation for the Avar literary language, which is written in the Russians' Cyrillic alphabet.

The majority of the Avars live in the river valleys, where they have traditionally dominated commerce and trade. The modern Avars' connection to the historic Avars who dominated much of Russia and Eastern Europe until defeated by Charlemagne is doubted by some scholars, even though Avar nationalists claim direct descent.

The Avars are fervently Sunni Muslim, the majority adhering to the Shafi rite or school. Although under Soviet pressure for over seventy years to renounce their religion, since 1991 the Avars have experienced a marked religious revival. The Avar peoples, particularly those in the more isolated mountains, have nurtured many pagan beliefs that have been adapted to their Islamic faith. The traditional religion of the Avars was based on pagan gods and beliefs. Islam became widespread among the Avars in the fifteenth century.

NATION: The first historic mention of the Avars was by Pliny the Elder in the first century A.D., when Avaria or Avaristan was known as Serir. The Avars were recorded in the fourth and fifth centuries as a mounted, nomadic people who dominated the steppe lands of Central Asia. Displaced by more powerful tribes, the Avars in the sixth century pushed west, their formidable army increasing rapidly by incorporating conquered peoples. They invaded the area of Russia north of the Black Sea, an area previously held by the Huns, where many settled.

Thought to be related to the Mongols, the Avars in A.D. 461 conquered the Uygurs, a Turkic tribe, and with the Uygurs formed a confederation on the steppe lands of the Volga Basin. In the middle of the sixth century the confederation was almost annihilated by the Turks.* The survivors, mostly Uygurs led by Avar chiefs, took the name of Avars but then split into two groups. One group remained in Eastern Europe, the ancestors of the modern Avars; the other moved westward, eventually reaching the Danube River. The members of the second group settled in Dacia, now in Romania, and inaugurated an era of conquest and domination of a vast area. At the end of the sixth century the domain of the Dacian Avars extended from the Volga River to the Baltic Sea, and they exacted enormous tribute from the Byzantine Empire.

In 626 the Avars invaded Byzantine territory and lay siege to the Byzantine capital, Constantinople. Although unsuccessful, they extended their dominion over the Bulgars* and Slavs formerly controlled by Byzantium. To the west the Avars controlled the Hungarian Plain and moved into territory that formed part of Charlemagne's Frankish Empire. During this period the Avars were probably the greatest military power in Europe, and they tremendously influenced the later development of the continent by driving most of the western Slavs into the areas they have occupied since. In 796 Charlemagne's forces defeated the Avars. By the ninth century they had virtually disappeared from history in Western Europe. According to Avar traditions, remnants of the defeated nomads moved south to refuge in the Caucasus Mountains.

Since the seventh century Avaria has suffered foreign invasions. In their isolated valleys and mountain strongholds, the Avars resisted all invaders of their homeland. In the first half of the eighth century, Arabs, led by Abu Muslim, according to Avar tradition, invaded Avaria and brought the Islamic religion with them. The consolidation of Islam was inhibited by the simultaneous advance of Christianity from the west, but the weakening of the Christian Georgians,* following the invasion of the region by the forces of Tamerlane, allowed Islam to prevail.

In 1241 the Mongol Golden Horde overran the region, but by the fourteenth century independent states, particularly the Avar Khanate, began to break the hold of the Golden Horde on the eastern Caucasus region. In the fifteenth century, the region was the center of a fierce struggle for control by the Ottoman Turks and the Persians. Under Turkish influence in the seventeenth century the majority of the Avars adopted the Islamic religion. The consolidation of Islam in Avaristan in the eighteenth century resulted in a series of religious wars with the Christians of Georgia.

The Avar Khanate, a tributary state of the Ottoman Empire, extended its power by incorporating neighboring peoples and territories in the fifteenth and sixteenth centuries. The ruler of the consolidated Avar state took the title of khan. The khanate rose to the height of its power in the seventeenth and eighteenth centuries. Even at the apex of its political power, the khanate was divided by tribal and clan loyalties. The power of the Avar khans, although acknowledged across an extensive territory, was mostly felt in the accessible valleys. The peoples of the high mountains were mostly left to their own devices during the period of Avar domination, from the fifteenth to the eighteenth centuries. The Avar khans wielded powers in the name of the Ottoman Sultans.

The Russians, moving south into the Caucasus, established a protectorate over the Avar Khanate in 1803. The remaining Avar territories and those of the subgroups came under Russian rule in 1806. After the Napoleonic Wars, the Russian government tried to extend its authority to the Caucasus. Growing Russian influence in their homeland pushed the Avars to rebel in 1821. In response, the Russian authorities abolished the protectorate and imposed direct control. The Caucasian War, from 1816 to 1856, is the most celebrated period in the history of the Avars.

The government authorities alienated the Avars as large numbers of ethnic Slav settlers poured into the rich valleys of Avaria. The Dagestani peoples were united by an Avar Muslim leader, Iman Shamyl, who declared Dagestan independent of Russia in 1834. The Muslim holy book, the Koran, was made the law of the new state, and older animistic beliefs were discouraged. Shamil's declaration began over two decades of war between the Caucasian peoples and the Russian Imperial Army. After 1856, at the end of the Crimean War, the Russian government was able to concentrate troops against the Muslims. The Shamil Revolt finally collapsed in 1858, but Avar hatred of the Russians continued to color their relations with the Russian authorities. In 1864 the Russian authorities changed the Avar Khanate into the Avar district. Effective Russian rule was imposed only in the 1870s.

Government pressure to Russianize followed the imposition of strict Russian rule in the late 1860s. The Avars lost much of their most productive lands to Slavic settlers, and the majority lived in abject poverty in the isolated mountains. Avar resistance to Russian rule continued, mostly by Avars who moved from their valleys into the high mountains beyond the reach of the Russian administration. Many Avar warriors continued to fight the Russians until finally defeated in 1877.

The Avars were mostly untouched by World War I, although pro-Turkish sentiment was widespread. The Russian Revolution, which overthrew the monarchy in February 1917, was slow to be felt in the region. When news of the event arrived, the majority of the Avars thought their nation would finally be free of hated Russian rule and that old wrongs would be righted, including the return of their confiscated lands.

The Muslim leaders of the northern Caucasus convened a congress at Vedens, Shamil's old capital, on 27 October 1917. They elected a national committee of sheiks, officers, and merchants to govern as the Russian civil government collapsed. In November 1917 they declared *gazava*, holy war, against the Slavs. In December the new Muslim army captured several important Russian cities, which were looted. Pressed by Cossack troops, the Muslim leaders declared the independence of the Republic of North Caucasia on 11 May 1918. The following month, the new republic signed a treaty with Turkey and was recognized by the Central Powers, Germany and Austria-Hungary.

During the Russian Revolution, various Caucasian peoples, promised autonomy by the Bolsheviks, often actively supported the Bolsheviks. The promise of autonomy made by Lenin was more attractive to the Avars than the Russian nationalism of the anti-Bolshevik White forces. The defeat of the Whites in 1919 brought a bloody suppression of the Cossack settlements in the Avar region. The Red Army commissars assigned to the suppression of the Cossacks were often assisted by Avar and other Caucasian volunteers.

The North Caucasian republic collapsed with the final Red victory in the Russian civil war in 1920. Soviet power was officially established in Dagestan on 20 January 1920 but was immediately faced with severe problems. An autonomous Mountain Republic was erected to replace the independent North Caucasia. In August and September 1920 the Dagestani peoples, not having received the promised autonomy, rebelled against their new Soviet masters but were defeated and brutally punished. The Mountain Republic lasted only twenty months due to ethnic tensions, which eventually forced the Soviets to partition the region along ethnic grounds. A Dagestan Autonomous Soviet Socialist Republic was established on 20 January 1921. Later, in 1920–21, an anti-Bolshevik uprising, mainly supported by Avars, was brutally crushed. Soviet policy, particularly collectivization, provoked a renewed rebellion in Avaristan in 1930. The rebellion, centered in the highland Ando-Dido villages, was crushed with widespread destruction. Imposed collectivization enabled the Soviet authorities to eradicate their last opponents in the Avar communities.

From the early 1960s until the mid-1970s, government policy in the region pressed for resettlement of mountain peoples to the lowland plains. The resettlements involved all Caucasian ethnic groups, but the Avars in particular. The policy was accompanied by an aggressive propaganda campaign in favor of "voluntary" migration and a virtual end to the financing of public services in the mountainous areas. The forced migration to the plains led to the domination of both urban society and the rural lowlands by the Avar nation.

The loss of isolation, the growth of industrialization and urbanization, and the rise in educational standards resulted in marked changes in Avar culture. Elements of European urban culture, particularly the material culture, penetrated even the most remote corners of the Avar homeland. The Sovietization of Avar society led to severe social problems, particularly alcoholism and divisions between the older and younger generations.

Following the collapse of the Soviet Union, Dagestan was declared a member state of the new Russian Federation, but ethnic tensions have been increasing since 1991. The Avars, as the largest of the Dagestani peoples, have been pushing for greater sovereignty for Avaristan. An Avar nationalist organization, the People's Front Iman Shamil, was formed to lead the fight for greater Avar independence and the unification of the Avar nation. On 11 July 1994 troops of Azerbaijan clashed with armed Avars in northwest Azerbaijan after the seizure of arms. The armed Avars were reportedly linked with separatist Avars active on both sides of the Russian-Azeri border.

SELECTED BIBLIOGRAPHY

Abtorkhanov, Abdurahman, and Marie Bennigsen Broxup. *The North Caucasian Barrier: The Russian Advance towards the Muslim World.* 1992.
Funch, Lars, and Helen Krag. *The North Caucasus: Minorities at a Crossroads.* 1994.

Gammer, Moshe. *Muslim Resistance to the Tsar: Shamil and the Conquest of Chechnia and Dagestan.* 1994.

Goldenberg, Suzanne. *Pride of Small Nations: The Caucasus and Post-Soviet Disorder.* 1994.

Smith, Sebastian. *Allah's Mountains.* 1997.

AZERIS

Azerbaijanis; Azerbaydzhanis;
Azeri Turks

POPULATION: Approximately (2000 e) 7,332,000 Azeris in Europe, 6,665,000 Azeris in Azerbaijan and large numbers in neighboring states, 315,000 in Georgia, 342,000 in Russia, 540,000 in Turkey, 10,000 in Armenia, and over 5,000 in Ukraine. There are large Azeri populations in Central Asia, smaller numbers in Afghanistan and Iraq, and an estimated 15 to 20 million Azeris inhabit the region called Iranian Azerbaijan.

THE AZERI HOMELAND: The Azeri homeland lies in the Transcaucasus region of southeastern Europe, a mountainous region sloping down to the Caspian Sea on the east and bordering Georgia and the Dagestan Republic of Russia on the north, Armenia on the west, and the Aras (Araks) River on the south, the river forming the international border between the Republic of Azerbaijan and Iranian Azerbaijan. A small region, Nakhichevan, is separated from Azerbaijan proper by Armenian territory and forms an enclave lying between the western border of the Republic of Armenia and the northwestern frontier of Iran.

Azerbaijan, formerly a member republic of the USSR, became an independent republic in 1991. *Republic of Azerbaijan (Azerbaijchan Respublikasy)*: 33,436 sq.mi.–86,621 sq.km. (2000 e) 7,723,000—Azeris 87.8%, Dagestanis 3.2%, Russians* 2.4%, Armenians* 2.3%, Talysh* 1.8%, Kurds 1.4%. The Azeri capital and most important cultural center, Baku (2000 e) 1,835,000 (metropolitan area 2,220,000), lies on the Abseron (Apsheron) Peninsula, which juts into the Caspian Sea in the east of the country.

FLAG: The Azeri national flag, the official flag of the Republic of Azerbaijan, is a horizontal tricolor of pale blue, red, and green, bearing a white crescent moon and eight-pointed star centered on the red stripe.

PEOPLE: The Azeris are a Turkic people, the descendants of early Caucasian peoples with later Persian and Turkic admixtures. The Azeris are divided into five major divisions, the Ayrumy, Afshary, Karapapakhi, Padary, and Shakhseveny. In the past, the clan-type family structure was common among the Azeris. The clan, the *hoj*, was usually named after a common ancestor. Clan members shared pastureland and were bound to provide mutual aid to each other. They frequently acted as a unified entity in business dealings. It was also common for up to forty members of an extended family to live together in large dwellings called *gazma*. Landless peasants, the *tavyrga*, made up the lowest social class.

The Azeris speak a Turkic language belonging to the Southwestern or Orguz branch of the Turkic language family. There are two main subgroups of Azeri, Azerbaijani North, spoken mostly in Azerbaijan, and Azerbaijani South, spoken in Iran. The main differences are in the sounds and basic grammatical structure of the dialects. Azeri has a written tradition that dates back to the fourteenth century. Azeri serves as the somewhat hybrid, yet common, language of eastern Transcaucasus, southern Dagestan, and northwestern Iran.

Officially about 70% of the Azeris in Europe adhere to the Shi'a branch of Islam, the predominant sect in neighboring Iran, while some 20% practice the Hanafite rite of Sunni Islam, primarily in the northern districts of the republic; however, the number of practicing adherents is considerably lower than the official figures. Among the Azeri Muslims, religious practices are less restrictive of women's activities than in most of the other Muslim countries. The majority of Azeri women have jobs outside the home, and a few have attained leadership positions. However, some evidence of the traditional, restrictive female role remains.

The Azeri population of the former Soviet Union and Iran, although separated by political borders for nearly two centuries, retains strong cultural and linguistic ties. Some Azeri nationalists continue to work for the union of the two Azerbaijans in one sovereign Azerbaijani republic. Considered the most sophisticated of the Muslim peoples of the former Soviet Union, the Azeris have also reestablished their old ties to the Turks.*

NATION: An ancient Caucasian region inhabited by early Caucasian tribes, the Azeri homeland is thought to have been settled by the ancient Medes in the eighth century B.C. The region formed part of successive Persian Empires and is traditionally the birthplace of Zoroaster, the founder of Persia's pre-Islamic religion. A Persian governor, Atropates, appointed by Alexander the Great, established an independent Mede kingdom in the region in 328 B.C. Known as Atropatene or Media Atropatene, the region, lying on the major invasion route between Asia and Europe, was often conquered by migrating armies.

Claimed by the Parthians and later by Persia, continuous Persian control was not firmly established until the third century B.C. Except for a brief period of Byzantine control in the early seventh century A.D., the area remained Persian until the Muslim Arabs' conquest. The region was ruled by the Muslim Empire, the Caliphate, until the eleventh century, when the region fell to migrating Seljuk Turks. The conquerors adopted the Islamic religion of the inhabitants, but the Turkish language and culture of the Seljuks eventually replaced the earlier Persian and Arab cultures.

For centuries the Azeri homeland formed a frontier district at the confluence of the competing Turkish and Persian Empires. The Persian Safavid dynasty, established in 1499, from its beginnings in Iranian Azerbaijan, restored internal order in the Persian Empire. Under Safavid rule the Shiite sect was established as the state religion. Wars between Safavid Persia and the Turkish Ottoman Empire marked the next centuries in the region. Between 1578 and 1603 the Azeri homeland again fell to Turkish rule; however, in the seventeenth century Azerbaijan was once again under firm Persian control. As Safavid power waned, Russia and the Ottoman Turks vied for power in the region.

The Russian Empire, expanding south into the Caucasus region, annexed the northern Azeri territories piecemeal from a weakened Persia between 1805 and 1813. Southern Azerbaijan remained under Persian rule as a separate satrapy with its capital at Tabriz. Russian attempts at further expansion to the south were mostly unsuccessful.

Baku, a small and dusty Muslim town in newly annexed Russian Azerbaijan, following the discovery of oil, became the first and, at the time, the greatest petroleum-producing center in the world. Azerbaijan's oil industry, then the largest in Europe, was established in 1872. Baku's oil fields, tremendously important to the industrializing Russian Empire, brought an influx of Slavic oil and industrial workers. The wealth generated by oil brought an unprecedented rate of growth and development and made millionaires of the first investors, including the Nobel brothers, later known for the prizes awarded to the world leaders in various fields. These new millionaires financed a massive array of public institutions, schools, and buildings in Baku. In 1907 Baku boasted not only the first opera house in the Muslim world but also the first Muslim opera, Uzeir Ghajibekov's *Leila and Majnun*.

The sudden economic importance of the area exposed the Azeris to urbanization, Western education, and technology with the accompanying growth of national consciousness. Resentment of Slavic privileges sparked an Azeri cultural and religious revival in the late nineteenth century. The Azeri population in Persia, affected by the nationalism spreading across the border from Russian Azerbaijan, although less developed than their northern kin, also began to espouse nationalism as a reaction against the corrupt and feudal rule of the Persian state. The Russian government often cooperated with the Persian authorities to combat the growing nationalism.

Serious nationalist-religious rioting rocked Russian Azerbaijan in 1901 and 1904, escalating into a popular revolt during the revolution that swept all of Russia in 1905. During the revolution the Azeri nationalists controlled Baku and the surrounding areas until routed by tsarist troops. Nationalist unrest spread to Persian Azerbaijan during the same period, inciting serious Azeri revolts against

Persian rule during the 1906 revolution and again in 1909. The second revolution in Persia in 1909 gave the Russian government the opportunity to occupy Persian Azerbaijan, but the troops were later withdrawn.

The Azeri national movement led to the formation of specifically Azeri political parties. The most important, Hemmat (Endeavor), the Muslim Marxist Party, formed in Russian Azerbaijan in 1904 and participated in the 1906 revolution in Persian Azerbaijan. Severe anti-Russian rioting swept Russian Azerbaijan in 1907. During the repression that followed, Mussavat and the other political parties were forced underground, while the rioters were put down by Cossack troops. The nationalist political party, Mussavat (Equality), was founded in 1911 with supporters in both Russian and Persian Azerbaijan. Nationalist sentiment, based on the idea of a united Azeri homeland and promoted by the newly formed political parties, spread rapidly in both areas.

Effectively freed from Russian rule by the Russian Revolution in early 1917, the Azeris, fearing Turkish and Persian designs on the region and with their homeland increasingly destabilized by Russian soldiers returning from the Turkish front, agreed to join neighboring Georgia and Armenia to form a Transcaucasian federation. The federation cut all ties to the collapsing Russian Empire following the Bolshevik coup that overthrew the democratic Russian provisional government in October 1917. The federation, weakened by severe ethnic and religious differences, particularly between the Muslim Azeris and the Christian Armenians, was further threatened by fighting between nationalists and Russian soldiers, many supporting the radical Bolsheviks. The soldiers, taking advantage of the collapse of civil government, occupied Baku and other strategic points in the region. The tensions and fighting between the Azeris and the Armenians in the federation culminated in the massacre of some 12,000 Azeris in Baku by radical Armenians and Bolshevik troops in March 1918.

The federation was finally dissolved, and the three states were proclaimed separate republics. The Republic of Azerbaijan, led by nationalists of the Mussavat Party, proclaimed its independence on 28 May 1918. The capital of the new country was established at Ganja, as Baku, the Azeri metropolis, remained under the control of Bolshevik forces. In June 1918 the Azeris signed a treaty with Turkey and won recognition by Great Britain and other nations. In the summer of 1918 Muslim rioters killed an estimated 4,000 Armenians, the killings stopping only when British troops occupied the port and oil facilities in Baku in July. Turkish troops supported the Azeris in their reconquest of Baku on 15 September 1918, and two days later the government was transferred to the city. Attacks on the Christian Armenians began again, and over 8,500 Armenian residents of Baku were killed.

The Azeris, caught up in the vicious Russian civil war, frantically sought Allied assistance as the Bolshevik threat neared. In November 1918 the Azeri government appealed directly to President Wilson of the United States for help with the Allies, particularly the British, whose troops had occupied Baku and the oil fields. Pressured by the Allies, the Azeris formed an alliance with the anti-Bolshevik White Russian forces. The alliance, in the most part, was unsuccessful, as the Whites were unsympathetic to non-Russian national aspirations. In August 1919 the British, trusting that Azeri independence was assured by the recent Soviet declaration concerning the rights of national minorities, withdrew their troops from Baku, leaving the Azeris at the mercy of the advancing Red Army.

The Soviet defeat of the anti-Bolshevik Whites brought the Red Army to Azerbaijan's northern border in early 1920. Betrayed by their former allies, the Turks, the new state was caught in a two-front war. The Soviet authorities, ignoring their earlier assurances to the Azeri government, massed troops on the border. The Red Army overran the northern districts of the republic, while the Turks occupied the south in April 1920. On 20 April 1920 the Red Army occupied Baku, and the Azeri national government collapsed, its leaders imprisoned, shot, or fled abroad. The Soviet victors set their soldiers loose on the city of Baku for twenty-four hours, looting, raping, and murdering. The Red troops were allowed to "amuse" themselves with the city's large number of class enemies, the middle- and upper-class inhabitants, Azeri, Armenian, or Russian. Hundreds died in the orgy of violence.

The victorious Bolsheviks declared Azerbaijan a Soviet republic on 1 May 1920, and oil from Azerbaijan's rich fields began to flow to Soviet Russia. The republic, along with Armenia and Georgia, also under Soviet control, was again joined in a Transcaucasian federation, which joined the Union of Soviet Socialist Republics as a constituent republic on 30 December 1922. In 1936 the federation was disbanded, and the three republics were made separate constituent republics within the union.

Azeri nationalism, during the purges and oppression of the 1920s and 1930s, shifted to Iranian Azerbaijan, where many Mussavat leaders had taken refuge. In concert with the nationalists in Tabriz, the exiled Azeri leadership continued to work for a free, united Azeri nation. In 1938 Iranian Azerbaijan was reorganized into two separate provinces in an attempt to dilute growing Azeri nationalist sentiment. During World War II, an Azeri separatist government was established in Iranian Azerbaijan, which fomented Azeri nationalism in the Soviet Union. The Azeri republic in Iran collapsed in 1946, following Soviet leader Joseph Stalin's withdrawal of Soviet troops as part of a new oil deal with the Iranian government.

Improved medicine and food production fostered a rapid growth of population from the 1930s. The demographic explosion undermined Stalin's plan to colonize and assimilate the republic into a Soviet nationality. The population of the republic grew a startling 26% between 1939 and 1959, giving the Muslim Azeris an overwhelming majority. The demographic explosion worried the authorities in Moscow, as it paralleled a drop in the Slavic birthrate in the region. Soviet government attempts to introduce family planning, seen by the Azeris as yet another attack on their persecuted religion, led to new confrontations in the 1960s and 1970s. The confidence of the post-Stalin era manifested itself in a renewed interest in the culture, language, and their Muslim religion.

The prohibition on contacts between Soviet Azeris and Iranian Azeris became increasingly hard to enforce as the use of radios became widespread, allowing the Azeris in the Soviet Union to lend some covert aid to their kin suffering under the oppressive rule of the Iranian government. In Iran the Azeris provided the middle class in the stratified society, dominating the bazaars and providing two-thirds of the army officers and many of Iran's intellectuals, writers, and teachers.

The fall of the shah of Iran's government in 1979 spurred Azeri nationalism in opposition to the excesses of the new revolutionary clique. Azeri opposition to the Islamic Revolution fueled nationalist rioting in Tabriz and other large cities. In 1983 the Democratic Party of Azerbaijan and the leftist Tudeh Party were officially dissolved by Iran's Islamic government. In a massive crackdown hundreds of party members and suspected Azeri nationalists, including many women, were imprisoned, while others fled across the border into Soviet Azerbaijan.

In the years since the revolution in Iran, Azeri-language radio broadcasts from the Soviet Union were jammed, while broadcasts, in Azeri, from the Islamic Republic of Iran attempted to stir up Islamic fundamentalist zeal in Soviet Azerbaijan. The Soviet Azeris, after decades of official atheism, were less stirred by religious fundamentalism than the demands of the increasingly open economy and the perceived Armenian threat. The vast majority of the republic's urbanized population found little attraction in the radical, restrictive doctrines of the Islamic Republic, although kinship ties remained firm. Azeris wishing to visit relatives across the border were subjected to lengthy paperwork and scrutiny.

The liberation of Soviet society, the result of the introduction of glasnost and perestroika by Mikhail Gorbachev in 1987, loosed long-simmering ethnic and nationalist tensions in the region. Economic stagnation, mostly due to the region's petroleum fields being neglected in favor of the Siberian oil fields, became a serious problem for the Azeri republican government. Production dropped from 21.5 tons in 1965 to just 3.7 tons in 1988.

A resurgent Azeri nationalism, spurred by Armenian nationalist claims to Nagorno-Karabakh, an Armenian-populated enclave added to Soviet Azerbaijan by Stalin in 1923, sparked mass demonstrations, strikes, and protests. In February 1988 anti-Armenian rioting erupted in the important industrial city of Sumgait north of Baku. Azeri mobs attacked the Armenian quarters of the city, killing between thirty-two and seventy-eight (the official and Armenian estimates) and leaving hundreds injured. Over 10,000 Armenians fled the city.

On 12 July 1988 the local legislature of the autonomous region of Nagorno-Karabakh voted to secede from Azerbaijan. The Soviet government rejected the move, but in September, following renewed ethnic violence, Nagorno-Karabakh was placed under curfew, and Soviet troops moved into the region. In an effort to control the publicity surrounding the Soviet Union's worst outbreak of ethnic violence since the civil war period, the Soviet authorities closed Azerbaijan to foreign journalists.

In November 1988 the ethnic clashes began again, particularly in Baku and the large industrial cities in the east of the republic. As the violence spread, thousands of Armenians fled west to Armenia, bringing stories of atrocities and horrors that further fueled the growing rift between the two Soviet republics. Soviet troops occupied Azerbaijan to prevent wholesale massacres of Armenians. The ethnic confrontations added to the nationalist fervor, with mass Azeri demonstrations in Baku and other cities.

In December 1988 most of the Soviet government troops were withdrawn from Azerbaijan to aid with the rescue effort following a massive earthquake in neighboring Armenia. The newly formed Azeri Popular Front (APF) called for new demonstrations and the establishment of an independent Azeri republic. The APF, openly nationalist, threatened war if Nagorno-Karabakh was turned over to Armenia and in August 1989 called a general strike that effectively blockaded Armenia, which received 87% of its goods and fuel through Azerbaijan. By the end of September the Azeri Popular Front virtually controlled the republic, having moved more quickly from obscurity to power than any similar organization in the Soviet Union.

In November 1989 a more radical faction won control of the APF, with demands for the unification of the Azeri nation. Protest rallies on the Iranian border demanded an open frontier with Iranian Azerbaijan. Unsatisfied with the government response, demonstrations broke out, quickly spreading to the Azeri heartland on the Caspian Sea. Azeri demonstrators on the Iranian border tore down the border posts and the frontier fence that divide the two halves of the Azeri homeland, while leaders called for independence for a reunited "Greater Azerbaijan." In January 1990 nationalists erected barricades around Baku and demanded immediate independence.

On 19 January 1990 Soviet troops smashed through the barricades and occupied Baku. Officially, eighty-three people died in the occupation, but nationalists claimed that the number of martyrs exceeded 500. The use of violence ended the de facto power of the APF but united most of the diverse Azeri factions, the nationalists, the republican government, and even the Azeri Communist Party. Anti-Armenian sentiment quickly became anti-Russian and anti-Soviet as even the most virulently anti-Armenian groups began to see the Soviet government as the real enemy. The Soviet authorities installed a new government, led by Ayaz Mutalibov, but in order to cling to power, he quickly began to outdo the nationalists in supporting Azeri nationalism.

The Communist Party, all but discredited in the republic, lost much of its membership to the nationalists, who represented the only force able to speak for the majority of the Azeri nation. Despite the continued occupation by the Red Army, over 1 million Azeris turned out to publicly mourn, on 2 May 1990, the martyrs killed when the Soviet troops attacked Baku. In a further act of defiance thousands took to the streets to commemorate the seventy-seventh anniversary of Azeri independence declared on 28 May 1918.

The failed Soviet coup of August 1991 against the continuing reforms of Mikhail Gorbachev shook the republican government. The subsequent breakup of the Soviet state pushed the communist Azeri government to embrace popular nationalism in order to retain power. On 30 August 1991 the government declared Azerbaijan independent of the collapsing Soviet Empire. In October the government nationalized all military equipment and recalled 140,000 Azeri conscripts serving with the Soviet forces.

The continuing conflict with newly independent Armenia over Nagorno-Karabakh presented the new state with its most pressing problem. When negotiations failed, the Soviet troops in Nagorno-Karabakh withdrew, and violence escalated. Nagorno-Karabakh's autonomy was abolished by Azerbaijani Supreme Soviet on 26 November 1991. In response, the local legislature of Nagorno-Karabakh voted to separate from Azerbaijan and on 31 December 1991 declared independence as the Republic of Artsakh.

Heidar Aliyev, named head of the Azeri Communist Party in 1969 and a full member of the Soviet Politburo in 1982, replaced Mutalibov as head of Azerbaijan's independent government in 1991. Antigovernment feeling continued to mount as Armenian victories pushed Azeri troops back from the western border. In June 1992 APF chairman Aliyev Abul'faz Elchibey was elected president with 55% of the popular vote. Elchibey soon lost popularity, however, because of his inability to improve the economy or end the war in Nagorno-Karabakh. The APF government, unable to stem the military defeats, saw the Armenians occupy the western districts of the republic and displace up to 1 million Azeris. The National Council voted to transfer Elchibey's powers to Aliyev, the long-time Communist Party leader who had been elected chairman of the council earlier that month. A republic-wide referendum supported Elchibey's removal, and in October 1993 Aliyev was elected president with 98.8% of the popular vote in a virtually uncontested election. In November 1995 the Aliyev government was reelected by Azeri voters longing for stability.

Under new government policies oil wealth again began to flow, but for ordinary Azeris, the benefits have barely started to arrive. The Aliyev government has brought inflation under control and has begun a tentative privatization, but democratic institutions have suffered. The Aliyev government has become less eager to appease Russia and refuses Russian demands to military bases or a say in the terms of the exploitation of the rich Caspian Sea oil fields. Closer ties to the United States, the European Union, and even Israel are being actively pursued.

The most pressing of Azerbaijan's problems remains the status of Nagorno-Karabakh. The Karabakh Armenians, with the aid and support of the Republic of Armenia, continue to hold about 20% of the country's territory while up to 1 million Azeri refugees languish in camps in the east of the country. Both sides have generally observed a Russian-mediated cease-fire in place since May 1994, but the prospects for a negotiated settlement remain dim.

Heidar Aliyev's Soviet-style personality cult is reinforced by a heavy-handed intimidation and the self-censorship of the tame national press. On 28 May 1997, on the anniversary of the proclamation of the Azeri republic in 1918, President Aliyev announced the end of all student deferments to military service and stated that the defense of the country and the restoration of the country's territorial integrity are more important than education. On 2 July 1997 the president announced a new official state holiday to be celebrated on 15 June. Called National Salvation Day, the holiday is to commemorate his taking power in Azerbaijan in 1993.

Azerbaijan's gross domestic product has contracted about 60% since 1991, and the downward trend began to reverse only in 1997, due to the expanding oil production. Foreign oil companies are vying for part of Azerbaijan's massive oil reserves. Western governments, mostly ignoring the abuses and dictatorial aspects of the Aliyev government, continue to court the Azeri government. In November 1997, in a ceremony attended by both American and Russian officials, the Azeris officially started oil production in the Caspian Sea. The offshore oil reserves, thought to rival those of the Middle East, have become a divisive issue for the new states and Iran that border the Caspian Sea, particularly the conflicting claims to the Caspian oil fields by the Azeris and Turkmenistan on the eastern shore. The oil reserves, seen by the Azeris as insurance for a better future, have become something of a national treasure.

SELECTED BIBLIOGRAPHY

Altstadt, Audrey L. *The Azerbaijani Turks: Power and Identity under Russian Rule*. 1992.
Atatbaki, Touraj. *Azerbaijan: Ethnicity and Autonomy in Iran after the Second World War*. 1995.
Roberts, Elizabeth. *Georgia, Armenia, and Azerbaijan (Former Soviet States)*. 1992.
Swietochowski, Thadeusz. *Russian Azerbaidzhan 1905–1920: The Shaping of National Identity in a Muslim Community*. 1985.
Swietochowski, Thadeusz. *Russia and Azerbaijan*. 1995.

AZOREANS

Açoreanos

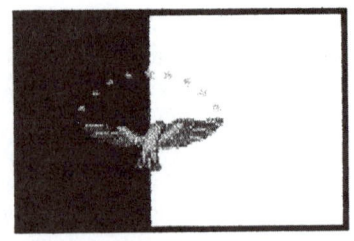

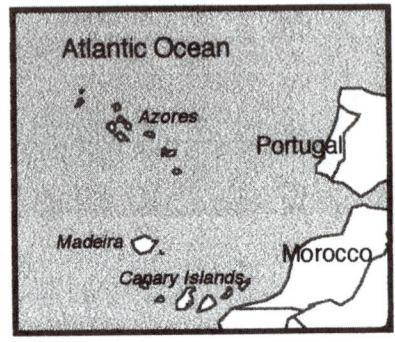

POPULATION: Approximately (2000 e) 300,000 Azoreans in Europe, the majority in the Azores, but with a substantial numbers living in mainland Portugal.

THE AZOREAN HOMELAND: The Azores lie in the eastern Atlantic Ocean 745 miles (1,200 kilometers) west of the Portuguese mainland. The islands, rising from the Mid-Atlantic Ridge in the North Atlantic Ocean, are mostly mountainous, being, with the exception of Santa Maria, of fairly recent volcanic origin. The islands are still thought by many to be the remnants of ancient Atlantis. The fertile volcanic soil yields abundant harvests of grains and fruits and supports vineyards.

The nine islands and several islets of the archipelago are geographically divided into three groups. The northwest group is made up of Flores and Corvo, the central group is Terceira, São Jorge, Pico, Faial, and Graciosa, and the eastern group is São Miguel and Santa Maria. Most of the islands have steep topography, with the highest point, on Pico, at 7,713 feet (2,351 m.).

The islands were granted autonomy as a special region within the Portuguese state in 1976. The three groups of islands correspond to the three administrative districts of Ponta Delgada, Angra do Heroísmo, and Horta. *Autonomous Region of the Azores*: 905 sq.mi.–2,344 sq.km. (2000 e) 229,000—Azoreans 96%, other Portuguese.* The Azorean capital and cultural center, the capital of the autonomous region, is Ponta Delgada, (2000 e) 21,000, on São Miguel.

FLAGs: The Azorean national flag, the official flag of the islands, is a vertical bicolor, the third nearest the hoist dark blue, the remainder white. Overlying the color division is a golden hawk, *açor* in Portuguese, its spread wings surmounted by nine gold stars arranged in an arc, wing to wing. The same blue and white flag but with the *açor*'s wings spread downward around nine stars as a map of the islands, is the flag of the largest nationalist organization, the Front for the Liberation of the Azores (FLA).

PEOPLE: The Azoreans are an Atlantic island people, descended from fifteenth-century colonists from Europe, mostly Portuguese and Flemish.* The combination of the fair Flemish and the Iberian Portuguese was the foundation of the Azorean nation. Later admixtures included African slaves brought in to work the sugar plantation and Arabs and Berbers from northwestern Africa.

The Azorean language, the language of daily life, is a dialect of Portuguese that incorporates borrowings from Flemish, English, and African languages. Nationalists claim that the Azorean dialect is so different from mainland Portuguese that it constitutes a separate Romance language.

Large Azorean immigrant populations live in the United States, Canada, and Brazil, and emigration to mainland Europe continues as the poor economy offers few opportunities to young Azoreans. The immigrant populations have maintained their ties to the islands and are often more nationalistic than the islanders themselves.

NATION: The actual date of the discovery of the islands is lost in history, but their existence was known in Europe as early as the fourteenth century, since the islands appear on a map drawn in 1351. The uninhabited islands, rediscovered by Diego de Sevilla, sailing for the Portuguese king in 1427, were visited by Gonzalo Velho Cabral between 1431 and 1444.

The islands received colonists from Portugal beginning in 1445. For centuries the archipelago was called the Flemish Islands, stemming from the gift of the island of Faial to Isabela of Burgundy in 1466. Her Flemish subjects, dispatched to establish farming communities on Faial, later spread to all of the islands. The capital of Faial, Horta, was named for a Flemish leader called Horter.

The remote islands, used as a place of exile by the Portuguese government, later developed as important stops on the sea routes between Europe and the New World. The first Azoreans emigrated during the colonial period, the forerunners of an exodus that continued for centuries. The large immigrant Azorean populations fostered ties to the United States and other American republics that were often stronger than the island's ties to metropolitan Portugal.

The islanders often played a considerable part in Portuguese history. They fiercely resisted the accession of the Spanish heir, Philip II, to the Portuguese throne in 1580–83 and suffered under the so-called Spanish captivity from 1580 to 1640. The Azoreans later supported the claimant Dom Pedro against Dom Miguel, who seized the Portuguese throne in 1832.

Azorean emigration to North America has been a major factor in Azorean history, economy, and culture. Beginning in the nineteenth century, when island residents joined the crews of American whaling ships, large numbers of Azoreans have emigrated to work and live in both the United States and Canada. By the 1990s more Azoreans resided in North America than in the archipelago.

Administered as a colonial possession until the 1930s, the islands remained neglected, overcrowded, and underdeveloped. High unemployment and the pressure of a rapidly growing population escalated the need for the Azoreans' traditional escape, emigration. In 1940 the islands had a population of 484,278, according to official census figures, far too large a population to be supported by the agricultural output of the region.

Immigrant communities, retaining strong emotional ties to their island homeland, were the first to develop a sense of Azorean national awareness. Although they often lived alongside immigrant Portuguese communities in the Americas, they retained their dialect and customs, their distinct group consciousness reinforced by continuing emigration from the home islands.

During World War II, the neutral Portuguese government granted the Allies access to bases in the islands in 1943. A military and economic agreement signed in 1951 established joint American and Portuguese military facilities in the islands, particularly Lajes Air Base on Terceira, a joint Portuguese-American North American Treaty Organization (NATO) base. The agreement, renewed many times since, financially benefits the Portuguese government but has conveyed few advantages to the Azoreans. Resentment of the continued colonialism kindled the first stirrings of national sentiment within the islands.

Political instability in mainland Portugal continued to hamper modernization of the islands in the early twentieth century. Although the islands were known as the breadbasket of Portugal, farming methods remained rooted in the nineteenth century. Modern conveniences and technology were slow to reach the remote islands. Only in the 1970s were electricity and tap water made available on the more remote of the islands.

The devoutly Catholic and conservative Azoreans, alarmed by the popular revolution that installed a leftist government in Lisbon in 1974, quickly organized to resist the new government's nationalization of banks, industries, farms, and fisheries. Nationalists mobilized the population against the revolutionary excesses of the new government in Lisbon.

The Portuguese government's announced intention to free the last of Portugal's colonial empire incited a rapid growth of support for the nationalists. Several nationalist organizations formed as separatist demonstrations rocked the islands. By the summer of 1975 the Azoreans had driven every leftist official from the islands and had burned the headquarters of the Communist Party in Ponta Delgada. Considering their islands a colony, although officially, they formed an integral part of the Portuguese republic, Azorean nationalists prepared for independence from Portugal.

Disappointed at the Portuguese government's refusal to grant the Azores the same right to self-determination as the African colonies, nationalists gained widespread popular support. In January 1976 the local government reported that a poll of islanders indicated that 45% favored immediate independence, while 55% favored varying degrees of autonomy, fearing that premature independence would aggravate the island's chronic economic problems and its lack of trained technicians and administrators.

Popular support for independence declined following a grant of autonomy by a newly installed democratic Portuguese government in 1976. Rejecting independence, for now, the regional government negotiated new agreements bringing major development funds and a larger share of the money earned from the island's American military bases. Although autonomy satisfied the majority of the Azoreans, separatist demonstrations continued sporadically until 1980.

The island's leaders, including the nationalist leader, João Mota Amaral, although putting aside the issue of independence until the islands were prepared economically and politically, set about winning more autonomy from Lisbon. The aims of the Azores regional government were to slow immigration and promote local development not dependent on funds sent from Azorean communities in the United States. An estimated 1.5 million Azoreans and their descendants live in the United States and Canada.

In the early 1980s the regional government had brought local unemployment down to less than 2%, compared with mainland Portugal's 12%, and prices of commodities, such as gasoline, were held at about half the price on the mainland. With relative economic prosperity, the population stabilized in the early 1980s, for the first time since the 1950s. Outward emigration was offset by Azoreans returning to the islands from the Americas.

Portugal's entry in the European Economic Community in 1986 and rising prosperity in the islands, although incomes are still only one-third of community levels, animated a resurgent nationalist movement in the late 1980s. Disputes over the use of the Azorean flag and anthem and the disposition of Azorean properties confiscated in 1975 have become major nationalist issues. The Lisbon government views the Azoreans' preference for their own flag and anthem as evidence of continuing separatist sentiment in the islands. In 1991 Azorean nationalist leaders claimed that 74% of the Azoreans favored independence within the context of a united, federal Europe. The nationalists often receive the backing of local government officials, as support for secession is a useful tool when the Azoreans wish to pressure Lisbon, even though advocating secession is a grave offense in Portugal.

SELECTED BIBLIOGRAPHY

Bragança-Cunha, Vicente. *Revolutionary Portugal.* 1987.
Ludtke, Jen. *Atlantic Peaks: An Ethnographic Guide to the Portuguese-Speaking Islands.* 1989.
Rogers, Francis M. *Atlantic Islanders of the Azores and Madeira.* 1979.
Symington, Martin, ed. *Portugal: With Madeira and the Azores.* 1997.
Williams, Jerry R. *And Yet They Come: Portuguese Immigration from the Azores to the United States.* 1982.

BALKARS

Taulu; Malkars; Malkaris;
Mallqarlis; Balkalar; Balkary; Five
Mountain Tatars

POPULATION: Approximately (2000 e) 95,000 Balkars in Europe, the majority in the Kabardino-Balkaria Republic in the Caucasus, in the southern European region of the Russian Federation. Outside Europe there are small Balkar populations in the Central Asian republics of Kazakhstan and Kyrgyzstan.

THE BALKAR HOMELAND: The Balkar homeland lies in southern European Russia, a rugged area in northern foothills of the western Caucasus Mountains traversed by the valleys of the upper Baksan, Cherek, Chegem, and Malka Rivers and their tributaries. Balkaria, known as the Five Mountains, is an alpine region of high river valleys and towering peaks, some of the highest in the Caucasus. The region contains many of the "five-thousanders," the highest peaks of the Caucasus, many with glaciers on their crests. The high valleys, where the majority of the population resides, is mostly wooded with fertile, often terraced farmlands and alpine meadows. Most of the valleys are agricultural, with herding and mining in the higher elevations.

In 1992 the Balkars proclaimed the autonomous Republic of Balkaria as a separate member state of the Russian Federation, but the Russian government has not recognized the state. *Republic of Balkaria (Malkar Respublika/Malqar)*: 950 sq.mi.–2,461 sq.km. (2000 e) 158,000—Balkars 57%, Karachais* 16%, Russians* 14%, Kabards* 10%. The Balkar capital and cultural center, Tirni-hauz, called Tirni-Auds in Balkar, (2000 e) 32,000, lies in the valley of the Baksan River.

FLAG: The Balkar national flag is a pale blue field with a centered design of two white mountains and bearing narrow white stripes near the top and bottom.

PEOPLE: Historical ethnologists searching for Balkar origins believe that they are descendants of a complex fusion of Huns, Karachais, Kypchak, Khazar, Bulgarian, Alan, and Caucasic peoples and are among the most ancient nationalities of the Caucasus region. The roots of Balkar history and culture are intimately intertwined with the history and culture of many Caucasian peoples as well as the numerous Turkic national groups. Traditionally, the Balkar nation formed when the Kipchak Turks fled to the Caucasus Mountains to escape from invading Mongols in the thirteenth century. In the mountains the Kipchaks mixed with local Alans to eventually form the Balkars. Among the Turkic peoples the Balkars are thought to be the group living highest in a mountain region.

Since ancient times, Balkars and Karachais have been engaged in alpine, distant pasture of *yailag* cattle and sheep herding. In the summers, they drive their cattle and sheep herds to the mountain pastures called *zhailik*.

The Karachai and Balkar constitute the two parts of a single nation, but since the fourteenth and fifteenth centuries they have become territorially isolated. The two peoples refer to themselves as Taulu. The Balkars are a people of mixed Turkic and Caucasian background, speaking dialects of the Karachai-Balkar language of the Kypchak Turkic language group. Although categorized as a Turkic language, its linguistic roots are both Persian and Turkic.

The Balkars are overwhelmingly Sunni Muslim but retain strong elements of their indigenous animist traditions and are only sporadically devout. Their conversion to Islam in the nineteenth century is considered marginal, and the religion has been adapted to their earlier beliefs and traditions.

NATION: Early Turkic tribes are thought to have migrated to the North Caucasus region by the end of the fourth century B.C. The Turkic tribes encountered the indigenous Caucasian peoples, with close contacts and relationships developing. In the third century B.C. the Turkic tribes began to penetrate the South Caucasus through the Derbent Passage in Dagestan and through the passes in the present Kuban region. The fusion of the Turkic and Caucasian tribes resulted in a settled agricultural and cattle-breeding community.

The Balkars were first mentioned by Arabian sources of the tenth century A.D. as the Taulu-as, the Mountain-as, a tribe living in the far regions of Georgia. Many ethnographers and scientists believe the Balkars were already settled in their present homeland by the tenth century. The conqueror Timur, or Tamerlane, who invaded the region in 1395–96, called the inhabitants "As," the same name presently used for the Balkars and Karachais by their immediate neighbors, the Ossetians.*

Other scientists believe the Balkars and Karachai originated in the Crimea and migrated to their present homeland in the fifteenth century. The first contact between the Balkars and the Russians is detailed in letters written by visitors to the region in 1629. Ten years later a Russian expedition explored the region and in 1643 passed through Balkaria.

The Balkars lived as pastoral nomads dependent on sheep breeding, along with herds of cattle and horses. The products of their herds dressed, fed, and housed the people, while extra goods were traded to neighboring peoples for fabrics, crockery, salt, and other necessities. A highly developed mining industry provided metals, coal, and other raw materials. Since arable lands were scarce, terraces were used for agriculture on the mountain slopes, watered by ingeniously designed irrigation systems.

The Balkars maintained friendly cultural and economic relations with all the neighboring peoples. These contacts frequently resulted in numerous mixed marriages and interethnic kinship ties. The historic Balkar culture absorbed many features of the Caucasian peoples living in the neighboring valleys.

The region, often overrun by migrating tribes, was the scene of much ethnic conflict. To escape marauding tribes, the Balkars gradually migrated to higher altitudes in the mountains, where they adopted less nomadic forms of farming and herding. Invasions and migrations, particularly in the fourteenth and fifteenth centuries, forced the Balkars and Karachais to gradually became territorially isolated.

In the sixteenth century the Balkars became vassals of the Kabard princes. Over the next century Turkish influence in the region grew, and the nomadic Balkar tribes were brought under direct Ottoman Turkish rule in 1733.

Islam was first introduced to the Balkars by the Crimean Tatars* and then by Nogai* nomads from the Kuban Basin in the eighteenth century. At the beginning of the eighteenth century, the Balkars had already adopted Arabic as their literary language. The Balkar conversion to Islam accelerated during the Shamil rebellion against Russian rule between 1834 and 1858.

Russians moved into the territory of the declining Ottoman Empire in the eighteenth century and reached Balkaria in 1774. In 1827 Balkaria was under firm Russian control, and two years later the Russians succeeded in forcing the Turks to cede the Caucasian territories to the Russian Empire. Thousands of Balkars moved south to Turkish territory. Those who remained under Russian rule took up arms against the tsarist authorities at every opportunity. Large-scale immigration of ethnic Russians took more and more of the Balkars' pastoral lands for farming, and the Balkars' former nomadic lifestyle changed more and more toward farming and settled stock raising.

The Muslim peoples of the empire, their loyalty suspect, were exempted from military duty when war began in 1914. Even though a majority of the Muslim peoples openly favored Muslim Turkey, the Russian government, desperate for manpower, began conscripting Muslims in 1916. The Muslim work units, sent to the front, came into contact with new revolutionary and nationalist ideas that took hold as Russia slipped into chaos.

The Karachai-Balkar conscripts deserted the front to return home after the revolution of February 1917. As civil government collapsed, a Karachai-Balkar national committee took control of the region. The national committee gave its support to Russia's new provisional government, which vaguely promised autonomy for Russia's minority peoples.

The Muslim peoples of the North Caucasus attempted to unite in a cooperative independence following the Bolshevik coup in October 1917 but faced tremendous problems of increasing disorder and pressure from rival political groups, including local Bolsheviks. The collapse of White resistance opened the way for the Red Army in August 1920. A detachment of the Ninth Soviet Army invaded Karachai-Balkaria in support of an uprising of local communists. The victorious Soviets overthrew the national committee government of "bourgeois nationalist exploiters" and divided the territory.

In 1921 the Balkar district was established under Soviet power. In the next year, it became part of the new Kabardino-Balkar autonomous Province, which in 1936 was made an autonomous republic of the Russian Federation.

Nazi Germany turned on its Soviet ally in June 1941, and a German offensive drove into the Caucasus in mid-1942. Welcomed by many Balkars as liberators from hated Soviet rule, the Germans won thousands of recruits to their Turkish League, an anticommunist military unit under Nazi command. Nationalists convened a Karachai-Balkar national committee and formed a national government under Kadi Kairamukov.

The new government moved to restore the region's traditional social and religious structure, opening closed mosques and decollectivizing rural life. Horrified by German brutality, the Karachai-Balkar government increasingly distanced itself from German sponsorship and attempted to create a neutral state allied to Turkey. By early 1943 over a dozen guerrilla bands had taken up arms against the German occupation force.

The Karachai-Balkar state collapsed with the Soviet reconquest in October 1943. Joseph Stalin, the Soviet leader, accused the two nations of treason and participation in Nazi atrocities, and in November 1943 the 75,000 Karachai were shipped east in closed cattle cars. In March 1944 the 46,000 Balkars followed. Among the crimes allegedly committed by the Balkar nation was having sent a white horse to Hitler. The Soviet guards dumped the deportees in the Central Asian wastes without provisions or shelter. Thousands died of exposure, hunger, and disease. The Balkars disappeared as a distinct Soviet ethnic group.

The survivors, officially rehabilitated in 1956, returned to their Caucasian homes to remain under close KGB security until the Soviet liberalization in the late 1980s. The Balkars turned to education and by the 1970s had one of the highest ratios of higher education in the former Soviet Union. Renewed contact between the two peoples of the small nation, forbidden for over three decades, spurred a dramatic resurgence of Karachai-Balkar culture and a renewed nationalism in the late 1980s.

The Soviet collapse in August 1991 stimulated demands for separation from the hybrid regions they had been forced into under communist rule. In 1992 the Karachai and Balkar unilaterally withdrew their territories from the joint republics, a move that the Russian authorities have not recognized. Demands for the official unification of the long-divided nation have so far been ignored by the Russian authorities, which has raised tensions in the region, one of the least assimilated areas of the North Caucasus.

During the 1990s, as the Balkars' ethnic identity has grown stronger, demands for recognition of their separation from the joint Kabard-Balkar republic have grown, but with only 9% of the republic's population, their political power is limited. Pan-Turkic nationalism, with stronger ties to other Turkic peoples, has become a growing factor in the region.

In November 1996 a Council of the Balkar People declared the secession of Balkaria from the joint Kabardino-Balkaria Republic and the establishment of a sovereign Balkar republic within the Russian Federation. The parliament of the Kabardino-Balkaria republic, which had previously agreed to the formation of the Balkar council, outlawed it and any outgrowths. In Moscow the move was denounced as a menace to stability in the region.

The government, alarmed by separatism in Balkaria, has granted more state aid and development funds for the region. The funds, part of a bill passed in 1994 to complete the rehabilitation of the Balkars, has mostly been used to build roads and improve communications in the formerly isolated region.

SELECTED BIBLIOGRAPHY

Ahmed, S. Z. *Twilight on the Caucasus.* 1997.
Nekrich, Alexander M. *The Punished Peoples.* 1978.
Olson, James S. *An Ethnohistorical Dictionary of the Russian and Soviet Empires.* 1994.
Ro'I, Yaacov, ed. *Muslim Eurasia: Conflicting Legacies.* 1995.
Smith, Sebastian. *Allah's Mountains: Politics and War in the Russian Caucasus.* 1998.

BASHKORTS

Bashkurds; Bashkyrs; Bashkirs;
Bashgurds; Bashqurts

POPULATION: Approximately (2000 e) 2,310,000 Bashkorts in Europe, all but a few in the Russian Federation. Official government estimates place the Bashkort population in the Russian Federation at around 1,600,000, a figure that, according to Bashkort nationalists, does not include the ethnic Bashkorts who for political or other reasons had registered as ethnic Tatars* or Russians* in successive Soviet censuses.

THE BASHKORT HOMELAND: The Bashkort homeland lies in eastern European Russia between the Volga River and the Ural Mountains. The region, mostly a flat plateau or steppe just west of the Ural Mountains, forms the dividing line between the European and Asian continents and between European Russia and Siberia. From the republic's highest point at Mt. Yamantau, 5,381 feet (1,640 m.), elevations generally decrease to the south and west, as uplands give way to plains and lowlands.The region is heavily forested, some 40%, in the east and in the Ural foothills. The western districts of the Bashkort homeland form part of the important Ural industrial and mining region. To the south, part of the traditional Bashkort lands are now included in Orenburg Oblast, which borders on Kazakhstan.

The region formed an autonomous republic within Russia until the disintegration of the Soviet Union in 1991, when the republic became a member state of the newly independent Russian Federation. *Republic of Bashkortostan (Bashkortostan Respublikasi)*. A member state of the Russian Federation. 55,443 sq.mi.–143,635 sq.km. (2000 e) 4,146,000—Russians 36%, Bashkorts 27%, Tatars 24%, Chavash* 4%, Maris* 3%. The population of the Bashkortostan Republic includes representatives of 106 distinct national groups. The Bashkort capital and cultural center, Ufa, the capital of the republic, population (2000 e) 1,102,000, is a major industrial center some 725 miles east of Moscow.

FLAG: The Bashkort national flag, the official flag of the Bashkortostan Republic, is a horizontal tricolor of pale blue, white, and green bearing a centered gold circle surrounding a seven-petaled *kurai*, a reed that grows only in the Bashkort homeland. The seven petals stand for the seven tribes or clans of the Bashkort nation.

PEOPLE: The Bashkorts, called Bashkirs by the Russians, are a Turkic people of mixed background, although the majority are European in physical appearance. The word "Bashkort" comes from the Turkic term for "head wolf" and refers to a heroic ancestor of the Bashkorts. The Bashkort nationality developed from a mixture of Finno-Ugric tribes and a variety of Turkic tribes, although their origins are still somewhat unclear. They were recognized as a distinct people by the ninth century, when they migrated to the territory between the Volga, Kama, Tobol, and Ural Rivers, where most Bashkorts still live. Traditionally, the Bashkort nation comprises seven clans, the Kypchak, Yurmat, Myng, Usergan, Katai, Tabin, and Burzyan. Two smaller, related groups, the Teptyars, Tatars who settled among the Bashkorts following the Russian conquest of Kazan, and the Nogaybaks or Christian Bashkorts, have recently been reclassified as ethnic Bashkorts. The clans are further divided into numerous subclans and extended family groups. The Bashkort nation is closely related to the neighboring Tatar nation to the west.

The Bashkort language is a Turko-Tatar language closely related to the language of the neighboring Tatar language. The two languages are mutually intelligible. The language, a Uralian language of the West Turkic language group, is spoken in three major dialects, Kuvakan (Mountain Bashkort), Yurmaty (Steppe Bashkort), and Burzhan (Western Bashkort). Bashkort is the mother tongue of only about three-quarters of the ethnic Bashkorts in the Russian Federation, with the remainder speaking Tatar or Russian as their first language. Bashkort became a separate literary language only in 1919. Before the Soviet period, the Bashkorts, used the so-called Turki language as their literary language, switching to the related Tatar language in the early twentieth century. Both languages used an Arabic script as their written language. In 1939–40 the Soviet authorities imposed the Cyrillic script on the Bashkort language.

The susceptibility of the Bashkorts to assimilation is partly due to education. The only Bashkort-language schools available to the Bashkort children are those within the boundaries of the Bashkortostan Republic. The large number of Bashkorts living outside the republic, estimated at more than half the total, are dominated by Tatar or Russian schools, media, and culture. Similarly, the rural dwellers have preserved their national identity almost intact, while the growing urban population has adopted much of the culture of European Russia. Since the collapse of the Soviet Union, cultural clubs promoting the Bashkort language and culture have sprung up both in Bashkortostan and in the territories of the Bashkort diaspora.

The Bashkort population began to urbanize in the 1950s. By 1980 some 36% of the total lived in urban areas, the percentage reaching some 43% in 1998. Until the 1980s the urban Bashkorts had been highly susceptible to assimilation. In 1959 only 62% of the Bashkorts considered Bashkort their first language. About 35% spoke Tatar as their mother tongue, with the remainder speaking Russian. The decline of the language has slowly reversed since the national and cultural revival that has taken hold since the late 1980s, and speaking Bashkort has become a matter of pride. Since 1991 many Bashkorts who had been assimilating into Tatar or Russian culture have registered as ethnic Bashkorts in local censuses.

According to official census figures the Bashkort nation, which numbered some 1,500,000 in 1897, reached its prerevolutionary numbers only in 1989. The figure for 1926 placed the Bashkort total at just 1 million, which in 1959 had dropped to 955,000. During the 1960s and 1970s, in spite of increasing assimilation, the overall numbers increased, and in 1970 there were an estimated 1,240,000 Bashkorts in the Soviet Union. In 1980 the number had increased to 1,380,000 in official estimates, and in 1989 the official census counted 1,345,000 Bashkorts, but unofficially their numbers were considered to have passed the 1897 figure. Bashkort nationalists claim an ethnic population of some 2.5 million in the Russian Federation and the other states of the former Soviet Union.

The majority of the Bashkorts are Sunni Muslims, one of the largest of the Muslim nations in the Russian Federation. They had originally adopted Islam in the tenth century, but many were forced by the Russians to convert to Orthodox Christianity between the sixteenth and eighteenth centuries. By the nineteenth century the majority of the converts had reconverted to Islam. Polygamy, allowed by the Muslim religion, was outlawed during the Soviet era; however, some Bashkort men still have more than one wife, particularly men of high social status. An estimated 3% of the Bashkort population are now Christian. Foreign Christian sects have been active in the region since 1991, some claiming that the number of Christian Bashkorts had risen to around 7% of the total population by 1999.

NATION: Nomadic herders in the southern Ural Mountains, the first records that mention the Bashkorts, in the ninth and tenth centuries, list them as a people under the nominal rule of the Volga Bulgar state of the Chavash. The name "Bashkort" has been known since the ninth century and was used by Turkic peoples of Central Asian and south Siberian origin living in the territory just west of the Ural Mountains. The first written reference to the Bashkorts appeared in the tenth century. Slavic monks, venturing into the pagan lands to the east, converted the Bashkorts to Christianity, traditionally in the year A.D. 922. By the eleventh century most of the Bashkorts had abandoned Christianity for the Islamic religion brought north by traders from Central Asia.

The Golden Horde, Mongol and Turkic warriors of the Mongols' vast empire, overran the region in the thirteenth century. The Bashkort tribes were absorbed by the different hordes following the breakup of the Golden Horde. The Bashkort lands later came under the rule of the Tatar khanate of Kazan, established as Mongol power declined in the fourteenth century. The period of Tatar rule drew the two Turkic peoples closer both linguistically and culturally.

A long series of wars with the growing Russian state ended with the Tatar khanate's conquest in 1552. Soon after the fall of the conquest, the tsarist authorities began to actively colonize the region, displacing the Bashkorts from their traditional lands. The conquered Bashkort lands, settled by Slavic colonists and controlled by a string of Russian forts, formed the new frontier districts of the expanding Russian Empire. The Muslim Bashkorts sought Turkish and Crimean Tatar assistance in reasserting their independence in the late 1500s and early 1600s.

In 1708 the Muslim Bashkorts rebelled and attacked the 3,000 Cossack and Russian settlements on their traditional lands, killing or capturing over 13,000 colonists. The widespread Bashkort revolt quickly spread from the Urals to the other subject peoples of the Volga River basin, thus threatening Russian rule in the east until enough troops arrived to defeat the rebels in 1711. The most serious revolt occurred in 1773, led by the Bashkort national hero Salavat Yulay. Bashkort rebellions became so frequent that in the late eighteenth century smiths were forbidden to practice their trade to prevent the fabrication of weapons. To counter the endemic Bashkort revolts the government established Cossack military colonies in the southern Bashkort lands. The Cossack colonists took the name of an important military fort, calling themselves the Orenburg Cossacks.

In the late eighteenth and early nineteenth centuries, there was a great influx of Tatars, Russians, and other national groups into the Bashkorts' traditional territory. The newcomers began buying or seizing the remaining pastoral land, which severely damaged the Bashkort economy. Many were forced to labor in the mines and the new factories built in the region. The majority turned to agriculture to survive when their nomadic way of life ended, and some even moved into the growing Russian towns to find work.

The abolition of serfdom in 1861 brought a massive influx of freed serfs seeking land. The migration, seen as a threat to the Bashkorts' survival, fanned the growth of Bashkort nationalism in the late nineteenth century. They again rebelled when news of the 1905 Russian Revolution reached the area. Nationalists demanded the return of 5.4 million acres of stolen land, while more radical groups attacked Russian settlements and estates and assassinated tsarist officials, including the governor-general of Ufa, before the Orenburg Cossacks quelled the revolt.

Largely untouched by World War I, the nationalists rapidly organized as revolution swept the empire in February 1917. Bashkort leaders formed the Bashkir National Movement, which called a national congress at Orenburg on 19 July 1917. The congress adopted an interim program favoring autonomy within a democratic Russian state and the expulsion of Slav colonists from the traditional Bashkort lands in Ufa and Orenburg Provinces. Bashkort army units at the front deserted en masse and made their way home, where they formed the nucleus of the Bashkir National Army.

The threat posed by the Bolshevik coup in October 1917 forced the reluctant Bashkorts into an alliance with their old enemies, the Orenburg Cossacks, who represented the White forces in the region. The Bashkort Revolutionary Committee (Bashrevkom), in spite of White opposition to the secession of any part of Holy Russia, declared their homeland independent of the collapsing empire on 29 November 1917, claiming as national territory the traditional Bashkort lands in the provinces of Ufa and Orenburg. The claim to Orenburg ended the uneasy alliance with the Orenburg Cossacks, who fought and defeated the Bashkorts for control of the southern province. On 4 February 1918 Bolshevik military forces attacked the newly proclaimed republic, and heavy fighting ensued.

In the summer of 1918 Czech and Slovak prisoners of war held in Russia formed the Czech Legion, one of the strongest fighting forces in the region. The legion, intent on getting back to their homeland via Siberia, swept the Bolshevik forces from the region in their march to the east. In September 1918 a state conference of the anti-Bolshevik and nationalist groups in the area was held at Ufa. The Whites' insistence that Russia remain intact and their poor treatment of minority groups soon led to splits within the ranks of the allies. Thousands of Bashkorts fled from the Cossack-controlled lands in Orenburg Province.

Exposed to the persecutions of both the Whites under Admiral Kolchak and the Orenburg Cossacks under Hetman Dutov, the Bashkorts were often at odds with their allies, particularly over the Bashkorts' demands for self-government. Spurned by the Whites as separatists, the Bashkort leadership, believing a Bolshevik promise of independence within a Soviet federation of sovereign states, switched sides and went over to the Reds in March 1919.

The Bashkort leaders prepared to send ambassadors to Moscow to represent the new Bashkurd Republic but were dismayed at their treatment. The Bolshevik authorities treated the Bashkort nation as a conquered people rather than as an ally. In the summer of 1919 the region was again overrun by Kolchak's Whites, and Soviet authority was not reestablished until August. A Bashkort autonomous region was erected, the first created for a non-Russian nationality within the new Soviet state. In spite of their earlier promises the Soviet authorities suppressed all manifestations of Bashkort nationalism, and Bashkort institutions were eliminated, including the Bashrevkom and their Muslim religious hierarchy.

Betrayed by Bolshevik promises, the Bashkorts turned on their new allies. The Bashkort leaders proclaimed the reestablishment of the Bashkurd Republic, but with its capital at Sterlitamak, as Ufa remained under firm Bolshevik control. At first the angry Bashkort troops were victorious, but the Red Army, following its victory over the Whites, was able to concentrate large numbers of troops in the region. The starving rebels finally surrendered in early 1922. The northern part of their traditional lands, called Little Bashkiria, the province of Ufa, became the first autonomous republic erected for a national group within the Soviet

Russian Federation on 23 March 1922. The Bashkorts, under Soviet rule, enjoyed relatively less freedom than under the tsars. The Soviet government set up in the region in 1922 lacked even one ethnic Bashkort.

The Bashkort nation lost about one-third of its pre–World War I population in the suppression of their republic, the civil war, and the imposition of Soviet rule. Crop failure and famine in 1920–21 added to the massive death toll. During the Soviet period many aspects of traditional Bashkir culture disappeared; however, Soviet rule, while oppressive, did bring some cultural and educational benefits. Improved health care and the spread of literacy were the most immediate benefits. The use of the Bashkort language, which became a literary language only in 1919, was widely used in education and the lower rungs of the local administration. The language was written in the Arabic script until 1927, and from 1927 to 1940 it used the Latin script. The Soviet authorities in 1939–40 imposed the Russian language's Cyrillic alphabet.

Many Bashkorts remained nomadic until the forced collectivization of the region in the early 1930s. Many died resisting the end of their traditional way of life. The Bashkorts were forced to settle in permanent villages or were moved to towns where new industries and large Slavic populations were also being resettled. Many found work in the mines or on collective farms.

Oil was discovered at Ishimbay in 1932, but an even greater field was found at Oktyabriskiy in 1944 during World War II. Five new oil fields opened in the 1960s, making Bashkiria the leading oil producer in the Soviet Union. In the 1970s coal and natural gas production became important to the region. Despite the great natural wealth of their homeland, the Bashkort leaders claimed that they received little benefit from the exploitation of their traditional lands.

Suppressed for over fifty years, a Bashkort cultural revival began in the late 1970s, spurred by a renewal of interest in their Islamic religion. Led by Soviet intellectuals of Bashkort origin, the nation experienced a national revival that glorified their past, emphasized their language, whose use had been declining since the 1920s, and revived their rich folk traditions. The growing cultural movement coincided with the liberalization of Soviet society in the late 1980s, stimulating a resurgence of dormant Bashkort nationalism.

Bashkort pressure on the local Soviet government won significant cultural and linguistic concessions and, in 1990, a declaration of state sovereignty. In the wake of the disintegration of the Soviet Union demands for independence gained public support in the republic. Negotiations with the new Russian government yielded new economic policies and more local control over the republic's oil reserves.

In November 1991 the republican government reversed previous policy and announced its aim of eventual independence and in February 1992 changed the official name of the republic to Bashkortostan. In early 1993 Bashkort nationalists renewed their old claims to Greater Bashkortostan, including Orenburg Oblast, which would give Bashkortostan and the other republics in the Volga

River basin an outlet and a land border with the Republic of Kazakhstan on the south.

The Bashkortostan leadership in August 1994 negotiated extensive political and economic autonomy within the Russian Federation. The agreements, which allow the republican government to retain a larger share of the oil revenue from the Bashkort fields, have given the Bashkorts within the republic greater financial security, but those outside the republic's borders will not benefit. The republic has also asserted its right to enter into agreements with foreign governments, including an economic and political agreement signed with the Republic of Iraq in March 1995. Later in 1995 the first All-World Conference of Bashkorts was held in Ufa and included delegates from the widespread Bashkort diaspora.

The first serious clash between the Bashkort leadership and the federal authorities since the power-sharing agreement was signed in 1994 erupted in October 1997. The conflict grew out of the Bashkort assertion that presidential candidates in the Bashkortostan Republic must speak Bashkort, which many Russians claim violates the Russian constitution.

The uneasy ethnic balance in the Bashkort homeland is an important issue for the regional Bashkort government. In November 1998 the Bashkort republican government expelled six Pakistanis for preaching Islamic fanaticism and fanning ethnic tensions. In June 1998 the president of Bashkortostan, Murtaza Rakhimov, had himself reelected after refusing to put on the ballot two opposition candidates who had been declared legitimate by the Supreme Court in Moscow. The increasingly independent government, in order to remain in power, has become more authoritarian as powers devolved from the federal government in Moscow.

SELECTED BIBLIOGRAPHY

Akiner, Shirin. *Islamic Peoples of the Soviet Union.* 1987.

Frank, Allen J. *Islamic Historiography and "Bulghar" Identity among the Tatars and Bashkirs of Russia.* 1998.

Jacobsen, Karen. *The Russian Federation.* 1994.

Kirkow, Peter. *Russia's Provinces: Authoritarian Transformation versus Local Autonomy.* 1997.

Warhola, James W. *Politicized Ethnicity in the Russian Federation: Dilemmas of State Formation.* 1996.

BASQUES

Euskal; Eskauldunak; Vascos

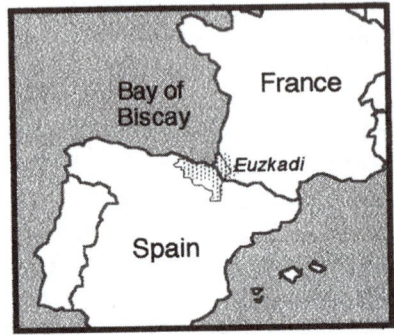

POPULATION: Approximately (2000 e) 2,338,000 Basques in Europe, mostly in northern Spain and southwestern France. Outside Europe, Basque communities numbering an estimated 500,000 live in the Americas.

THE BASQUE HOMELAND: The Basque homeland lies in southwestern France and northern Spain, straddling the Franco-Spanish border on the Bay of Biscay at the western end of the Pyrenees Mountains. The region is mostly mountainous with the forested foothills of the Pyrenees in the east and part of the Cantabrian Mountains in the west. In the south is the valley of the upper Ebro River and its tributaries, a region famed for its orchards. The coastal plain along the Bay of Biscay extends into France and the northern districts of the Basque homeland.

The region, called Euzkadi in the Basque language, forms two regions of the Spanish state, Pais Vasco (Euzkadi) and Navarra (Nafarroa), and three districts of the French department of Pyrénées-Atlantiques collectively called Iparralde in the Basque language, Basse Navarre (Benaparroa), Labourd (Lapourdi), and Soule (Zuberos). *Autonomous Basque Country (Pais Vasco/Euzkadi)*: 2,803 sq.mi.–7,260 sq.km. (2000 e) 2,102,000. *Autonomous Region of Navarra (Nafarroa)*: 4,024 sq.mi.–10,422 sq.km. (2000 e) 522,000. *Pays Basque (Iparralde)*: 1,270 (2000 e) 621,000. *Euzkadi* (2000 e) 3,245,000—Basques 71%, other Spaniards,* other French.* The Basque capital is Vitoria, Gasteiz in the Basque language, (2000 e) 203,000, the capital of the autonomous Basque Country in Spain. Other important Basque cultural centers are Guernica, called Guernika in Basque, (2000 e) 21,000, the traditional site of the Basque assemblies; Bilbao (Bilbo), (2000 e) 363,000 (metropolitan area 1,061,000), the region's largest city; San Sebastian (Donostia), (2000 e) 190,000, the former summer residence of Spanish monarchs; Pamplona (Iruñea), (2000 e) 176,000, the capital of Navarra; Bayonne (Baiona), (2000 e) 41,000 and Biarritz (Miarritze), (2000 e) 28,000 (Bayonne-Biarritz metropolitan area 148,000), the major urban area of French Euzkadi.

FLAG: The Basque national flag, the official flag of the Pais Vasco in Spain, is a red field bearing a centered white cross backed by a green saltire.

PEOPLE: The Basques are a unique national group, being of unknown origin and almost certainly the oldest surviving ethnic group in Europe. Even the Basque blood type differs from the blood types of other Europeans. The origins of the Basques are still theoretical, with some experts claiming they are the descendants of early Iberian tribes, the pre-Celtic inhabitants of the region, while others connect them with wandering Caucasian nomads, and a third group claims they are a lost tribe of Israel. Many of the Basques are fair, often blond and with light eyes.

Among the outstanding characteristics of the Basques are their independent spirit, love of freedom, and respect for individual liberty; a favorite Basque motto is "Neither slave nor tyrant." These qualities are reflected in their ancient laws, called *fors* in France and *fueros* in Spain, which traditionally governed every area of their lives and were strictly adhered to. These laws were maintained by democratically elected assemblies, the juntas, and great care was taken to secure honesty at the polls. It was not uncommon for a fisherman to preside over meetings in which Spanish noblemen were seated.

Genetically and culturally, the Basque population has been relatively isolated and distinct, perhaps since Paleolithic times. The Basques have guarded their ancient customs and traditions in the isolation of their homeland, although they have been prominent in the histories of both Spain and France. Subgroups include the mainly Spanish-speaking Navarese in the east and the French-speaking Gascons and Bearnese in the north. The majority of the Basques are devoutly Roman Catholic, with a small Protestant minority, mostly among the Gascons and Bearnese in France.

The language of the Basques, Euzkarra, is the sole surviving example of the languages that preceded the spread of the Indo-European languages. No relationship between Basque and any other language has been definitely established. The languge is written in the Roman alphabet and is spoken in eight regional dialects, Guipuzcoan, High Navarese Septentrional, High Navarese Meridional, Biscayan, Alavan in Spanish Euzkadi, Labourdin-Low Navarese, Souletin in French Euzkadi, and a number of subdialects; the ninth dialect, Batua, is a created variety used as the Basque literary language. The dialects are mutually intelligible, but there are significant differences between the dialects spoken in Spain and those spoken in France. The Basques are mostly bilingual, speaking either Spanish or French in addition to their own language. Their language is one of the few non-Indo-European languages spoken in Europe.

NATION: Prior to the Roman conquest of Gaul and Spain, the Basque tribes, loosely organized, extended farther north and south of their present homeland at the western end of the Pyrenees. Thought to predate the ancient Celts, the Basques were first mentioned as a people in Roman chronicles as a nation difficult to subdue, even though the region remained under nominal Roman rule until the fifth century A.D. The core tribes of the Basque nation resisted Romanization and were only nominally under Roman authority.

Christianity, introduced between the third and fifth centuries, was slow to penetrate the Basque heartland, but once converted, the Basques became fervent Christians. By the tenth century most Basques were devout Catholics. Although devout, the Basques retained a certain tradition of independence from both the Spanish and French church hierarchy.

During the barbarian invasions that followed the Roman collapse in the fifth century, Germanic Vandals and Visigoths passed through the Basque lands destroying the last vestiges of Roman authority, but they failed to conquer the Basque strongholds in the Pyrenees Mountains. They withstood the Franks, and in the sixth century, taking advantage of turmoil in the Frankish kingdom, the Basques expanded northward to take control of Vasconia, later called Gascony. Chronically at war with the Franks, Moors, and Visigoths, the Basque territories were closely associated with the Aquitaine, to the north.

The Germanic Franks overran Gascony and Navarre in the eighth century, while the Basques in the west successfully resisted the invaders. In 824 the western Basques returned to expel the Franks from the area south of the mountains, where they erected the kingdom of Navarre. Muslim Moors attacked the kingdom in the early tenth century and burned the capital, Pamplona, but by 937 the Basques had taken the offensive and later played a prominent role in the Christian reconquest of northern Spain.

In the eleventh century, powerful nobles established a commercial association between the region and Castile, a Spanish kingdom, largely due to the Castilians' desire to use Basque ports. By the thirteenth century, the Castilian Spaniards were attempting to incorporate all of the Iberian Peninsula under their rule. Basque and Castile representatives met in Guernica under an oak tree to pass laws and approve extensive personal rights for the Basques. These laws became the basis of the *fueros*, or traditional laws. The oak tree, known as the Guernikako arbola, became a symbol of Basque self-rule. The tree was destroyed in the 1800s, but the symbol survives today in a tree grown from an acorn believed to be from the original oak.

Castile, the most powerful of the Iberian kingdoms, conquered the western Basque provinces between 1200 and 1390, and with the conquest of Navarre in 1512, the Basques lost their last independent territory. Traditionally, many Basques were fishermen and sailors, and in 1492 a majority of the crews sailing for Christopher Columbus came from the Basque region of Spain. When the united Spanish kingdom was established late in the fifteenth century, the Basque provinces preserved their customs, laws, and diplomatic relations with other countries with slight variation until 1876, when the provinces were absorbed by Spain.

The northern Basques, incorporated in the French kingdom in 1601, were granted limited autonomy, a status they enjoyed until the French Revolution in 1789. The border between France and Spain, established in the Pyrenees and confirmed by a 1659 treaty, has remained unchanged to the present, although the frontier had little meaning for the Basques, who passed freely through the high passes in the Pyrenees Mountains.

The centralization of the French and Spanish kingdoms reduced Basque autonomy, but by the eighteenth century the prosperity of the region had declined. Population growth created increased demand for land during the eighteenth century. Land prices rose, and many *baserritarrak*, family farmsteads, had to be sold when the *etxekojaun*, the eldest son and customary heir, could not pay his siblings for his inheritance as required by custom. Since farmsteads were linked to others of the area in a cooperative social organization known as an *auroa*, rural Basque life disintegrated, and many Basques emigrated, particularly to the Spanish colonies in the Americas. Other Basques, mostly sheep herders from France, migrated to the western territories of the United States.

Resistance to attempts by the highly centralized Spanish and French governments to abrogate their ancient rights stimulated the growth of Basque nationalism in the 1850s and 1860s. The Basque national and cultural revival accelerated in the late nineteenth century, reversing centuries of assimilation and bringing the first demands for Basque reunification and self-determination. In 1873–74, during the Carlist Wars in Spain, the Basques resisted the Spanish republican forces, and in 1876 the *Fueros* were abolished in the Spanish Basque region. To regain their autonomy, the Basques habitially supported political movements directed against the central authorities in Madrid and Paris, and by the 1890s a strong Basque nationalist movement had emerged on both sides of the international border.

Political turmoil in the Spanish state in the 1920s and 1930s strengthened the Basque national movement. In 1931, as virtual civil war paralyzed the Spanish government, the Basques of the three western provinces voted for secession. The Republic of Euzkadi, declared independent on 14 June 1931, was rapidly overrun and suppressed by Spanish troops sent by the government in Madrid. Granted autonomy by a new leftist government in 1936, at the outbreak of the Spanish civil war, the Basques supported the Loyalist government against the fascist rebels, the Nationalists, and their German and Italian allies.

The Spanish civil war brought devastation to the region and divided the Basques, with some supporting the fascist rebels. The town of Guernica, the site of the sacred oak tree, the symbol of Basque liberty, was deliberately destroyed by Nazi bombers in 1937. The destruction of the Basques' spiritual capital, commemorated by a famous painting by Pablo Picasso, marked the end of Basque autonomy and the imposition of harsh fascist rule under the Franco dictatorship. Thousands of Basques fled to France as the victorious fascists banned the Basque language, suppressed the culture, and instituted a policy of forced assimilation into Castilian Spanish culture.

The Basque region, industrialized by the Franco regime, eager to exploit its natural resources, by the early 1950s had attained a standard of living comparable to that of the Benelux countries. Rapid economic development attracted thousands of migrants from Spain's backward south, their presence abetting the government's efforts to stamp out the Basque language and culture.

In 1952 a nationalist group, Euzkadi ta Azkatazuna (Basque Homeland and Liberty), known by its initials ETA, launched a resistance campaign. In France a related group, Iparretarrak (Those of the North), became active. Spanish government pressure drove ETA underground, and in 1968, joined by their counterparts in French Euzkadi, ETA turned to violence and terrorism. In the early 1970s Basque nationalists often took sanctuary in the French Basque country, where the French government refused to extradite Basques wanted for political crimes in Franco's Spain. Under the slogan "Zazpiak bat," (the seven are one), referring to the seven Basque regions, the nationalists won the support of a large segment of the Basque population of Spain and France.

The Spanish dictatorship ended with Francisco Franco's death in 1975, and the Spanish kingdom rapidly democratized under a restored Bourbon monarchy. In 1978 the Basques were able to celebrate their National Day for the first time since 1937. The Basque language, after four decades of suppression, was spoken by only 20% of Spain's Basques as compared with 60% among Basques in France. The language in the late 1970s and early 1980s experienced a dramatic resurgence as part of the Basques' cultural renaissance.

The Basque provinces received a grant of autonomy in 1980, and a moderate nationalist regional government took control with 70% support in local elections. The region of Navarre, Navarra in Spanish, granted separate autonomous status, has strengthened ties to Euzkadi since 1988. The autonomous status of the Basques dramatically decreased support for the violent separatist organizations, with a corresponding rise in support for moderate nationalist political parties. The sacred oak of Guernica, grown from a branch of the original, again became the symbol of Basque sovereignty.

The Basque militants in both Spain and France, vowing to settle for nothing less than full independence, continued their campaign of terror in the 1980s and 1990s. Since 1984 the Spanish and French governments have cooperated closely in a concerted antiterrorist crusade. Horrified by indiscriminate violence, the vast majority of the Basques have rejected violence and support moderate nationalist parties seeking greater independence within united Europe. A poll among the French Basques in 1990 showed that only 20% of the total Basque population considered themselves to be French.

In 1993 moderate nationalists in control of the regional government in the Basque country put forward a plan for greater autonomy, which included closer official ties between Spanish and French Basques and separate representation within the European Union. The plan was rejected by the French and Spanish governments, but efforts to bring peace to the region began in earnest.

ETA members in July 1997 kidnapped and murdered a young local politician in the Spanish Basque country. The murder proved to be a turning point as the majority of the Basques joined millions of other Spaniards in demonstrations against ETA violence. Crowds in the larger Basque cities attacked offices of Herri Batasuna, the legal, political wing of ETA. In 1998 a cease-fire was agreed to by the Spanish government and ETA, although supporters of Basque sovereignty continue to try for greater political support in the region.

SELECTED BIBLIOGRAPHY

Allard, William Albert, and Robert Laxalt. *A Time We Knew: Images of Yesterday in the Basque Homeland.* 1990.

Corversi, Daniele. *The Basques, the Catalans and Spain: Alternate Routes to Political Mobilisation.* 1997.

Heiberg, Marianne. *The Making of the Basque Nation.* 1989.

Payne, Stanley G. *Basque Nationalism.* 1975.

Zirakzadeh, Cyrus E. *A Rebellious People: Basques, Protests, and Politics.* 1991.

BAVARIANS

Bayrisch; Bayerns

POPULATION: Approximately (2000 e) 10,512,000 Bavarians in Europe, the majority in Germany, but with small Bavarian populations in Austria and Italy.

THE BAVARIAN HOMELAND: The Bavarian homeland occupies a mountainous region in Central Europe, traversed by the Danube River and its tributaries. The region is made up of rich, softly rolling hills traversed by several important rivers, rising to the Bavarian Alps in the south. The Bavarian Alps contain Germany's highest mountain, the Zugspitze, at 9,729 feet (2,963 m.). Between the Alps and the Bohemian Forest lies the Franconian Jura Plateau, traversed by the Danube River, Europe's longest river.

Bavaria forms an autonomous state of the Federal Republic of Germany. *State of Bavaria (Land Bayern)*: 27,239 sq.mi.–70,549 sq.km. (2000 e) 11,626,000—Bavarians 83%, other Germans* 13%, Turks* 4%. The Bavarian capital and major cultural center is Munich (München), (2000 e) 1,219,00 (metropolitan area 2,046,000), an important industrial and cultural city lying on the Isar River in southern Bavaria.

FLAG: The Bavarian national flag, the official state flag, is a lozenge pattern of pale blue and white.

PEOPLE: The Bavarians are a German people comprising three distinct groups that reflect the regional distribution of the early Germanic tribes, the Bavarians in the south, the Bavarian Swabians* in the west, and the Franconians in the north. Until the nineteenth century the Swabian and Franconian regions were separate and had distinct histories.

The Bavarian language, a dialect of High German, is more closely related to the German dialects spoken in neighboring Austria and Switzerland than to the standard German spoken throughout Germany. Only an estimated 40% of the Bavarian language is intelligible to speakers of standard German. The language is spoken in three dialects. North Bavarian is spoken in the region north of Regensburg and Nuremberg and east to the Czech border. Central Bavarian is spoken in the Alps and is also spoken by some Austrians* in Lower Austria and Salzburg provinces of the Austrian republic. South Bavarian is spoken in the Bavarian Alps, by the Tyroleans* in Austria, in Austrian Styria, and is called Heanzian in Austrian Burgenland and Carinthia. There are small pockets of Bavarian speakers in northern Italy and in the Gottschee in Slovenia.

The Bavarians are the most nationalistic of the German peoples. Their national pride is based on over 1,000 years of separate history and culture. Regionalism and nationalism remain a strong feature of the Bavarian nation. Although the Swabians and Franconians in northern and western Bavaria have separate histories, they remain staunchly Bavarian.

The majority of the Bavarians, about 70%, are Roman Catholic, with a Protestant minority, about 26% of the population. Religion in Bavaria has remained regional, with the Bavarians and Swabians in the south mostly Roman Catholic and the Franconians in the north mostly Protestant, but with a large Catholic minority.

NATION: Most of the Bavarian homeland was conquered by the Romans in the first century B.C. The Bavarii, one of the Germanic tribes just north of Roman territory, as a result of periodic overpopulation and land hunger, combined with pressure from remote tribes and the attraction for the wealth of the peaceful Roman provinces to the south, began to raid Roman settlements at various times beginning in A.D. 166. The Roman frontiers broke down completely during the fourth century, and the Germanic tribes crossed into the defenseless Roman provinces. The tribes, Bavarians, Swabians, and Franconians, settled in distinctive regions. The borders of Bavaria varied considerably during its long history, with the Swabian and Franconian territories often included in neighboring states.

The Slavs and the Avars moved into the region from the east and southeast at about the same time the Germanic tribes invaded the northwest. By the mid-sixth century the Bavarians had occupied the plains and the central Alps. The Slavic peoples were split into northern and southern groups by Avars and Bavarians contending for control of the Danube River valley.

Bavaria, named for the Bavarii tribe, formed a region tributary to the Franks in the sixth century and in 787–88 came under the rule of Charlemagne's Frankish Empire. Converted to Christianity in the eighth century, the Bavarians developed one of the five stem duchies of the Holy Roman Empire and one of the most powerful of the German states. In 911 a native dynasty again took power in the region. From the ninth to the eleventh centuries, the Bavarian dukes were often at the center of rebellions against the power of the emperors of the Holy Roman Empire.

Due to its central location in Europe, the Bavarian homeland was often invaded by foreign armies. The Bavarian state, traditionally allied to neighboring

Austria, became militarily strong and the most powerful of the southern German states. The Bavarian territories were often divided and subdivided among various rulers.

Under Saxon rule in the twelfth century, the Bavarian Österreich (East Mark) separated in 1156 to become a distinct duchy, called Austria in English. In 1180 the Saxon lands were further divided by Frederick Barbarossa, who gave Bavaria to the house of Wittelsbach, which was to rule Bavaria until 1918.

The Reformation in the sixteenth century was opposed by the majority of the Bavarians, who fought in the Thirty Years' War on the Catholic side. In the south the Bavarians remained staunchly Roman Catholic, but the related Franconians to the north eventually accepted the Protestant Reformation. The majority of the Bavarians remained staunchly Roman Catholic and were consequently ravaged by Protestant forces during the Thirty Years' War between 1618 and 1648.

Allied to France in the early nineteenth century, Napoleon awarded Bavaria additional territories in Swabia and Franconia and in 1806 raised the Bavarian ruler, Maximilian I, to the rank of king. The Bavarian king later deserted Napoleon and participated in the Congress of Vienna as the head of an allied nation. The congress awarded Bavaria additional territory. The Bavarians participated in the Congress of Vienna, 1814–15, as a victor nation and joined the loose German Confederacy erected by the congress.

The Bavarian kings, known for extravagant living and architectural fantasies, were increasingly out of touch with the Bavarian people. King Louis I, who ruled Bavaria from 1825 to 1848, had a famous affair with actress Lola Montez. King Louis II, 1864–86, was the patron of composer Richard Wagner. The brother of King Louis, Otto I, incurably insane after 1872, nevertheless succeeded Louis in 1886, when the king, too, was judged insane. Otto died under mysterious circumstances in 1913. King Louis III, who succeeded Otto, was dethroned following the German defeat in November 1918.

Politically and culturally closer to Vienna than to Berlin, Bavaria joined Austria to fight the hated Prussians in 1866 and with defeat paid a large indemnity and joined the Prussian-dominated German Empire in 1871, effectively ending Bavaria's independence. Pan-German nationalism, fostered throughout the empire, spread to Bavaria but without replacing Bavarian national sentiment. Bavarian nationalists remained adamantly opposed to the domination of the empire by Protestant Prussia. The Bavarians fought alongside the Prussians during the Franco-Prussian War of 1870–71 but refused to accept further integration into the Prussian-dominated German Empire.

Bavarian armies fought for the empire as war engulfed Europe in 1914 and shared Germany's defeat in November 1918. As revolution swept Germany, revolutionaries deposed the Bavarian king and declared the kingdom a republic. By mid-November the major functions of government had come under the control of the socialists led by Kurt Eisner, who declared Bavaria independent of

Germany on 22 November 1918. Six days later the Bavarian government closed its legation in Berlin and severed all ties to the German government.

Eisner, a Jewish socialist, viewed as the one man produced by Germany's revolution who compared with his Russian counterparts, was assassinated by an embittered monarchist while on his way to open parliament on 21 February 1919. Without Eisner's leadership the socialist government faltered, its weakness a pretext for a communist coup. The coup ended Bavarian negotiations with U.S. president Woodrow Wilson, contacted in an attempt to win recognition of independent Bavaria.

The communists, inspired by Soviet Russia, declared the Soviet Republic of Bavaria on 7 April 1919. German troops, called in by the deposed socialists, invaded the state and defeated the communists in May. A new Bavarian government, firmly under the control of Pan-German nationalists, joined the recently inaugurated German federation.

Bavarian nationalism, anti-Semitic and anti-Prussian, proved fertile ground for radical and reactionary political movements. In November 1923 monarchists attempted to seize the government, intent on secession and the restoration of the kingdom. A small, radical political group, the Nationalist Socialist Party, called Nazis, preempted the planned coup and attempted its own takeover of the Bavarian government, the so-called Beerhall Putch. For his part in the failed coup the group's leader, Adolf Hitler, received a five-year prison sentence. In the Bavarian prison he wrote *Mein Kampf*, his plan for world domination. After serving less than a year, Hitler was released and continued to build the Nazi Party.

In German elections in 1932, the Nazis had become the largest party in all the German states except Bavaria, which was dominated by the Roman Catholic Bavarian People's Party. The Nazis, with their only strong support in Bavaria's Protestant north, took control of the Bavarian government. On 7 March 1933 the Nazis dispatched SS and SA troops to Bavaria on the pretext that the Bavarian government was unable to maintain order. The Bavarian premier was overthrown, and to forestall a separatist plot the Nazis took over all facets of government and closed all Bavarian legations in other countries. A Catholic separatist plot, discovered in 1934, gave the Nazis a reason to ruthlessly eliminate all remaining Bavarian opposition.

Initially enthusiastic for war in 1939, which was presented as an anticommunist campaign, Bavarian support for the war declined rapidly as Allied bombers reduced many cities to rubble. Bavaria was the scene of a famous anti-Nazi underground group, the White Rose. Several of the group's young members were beheaded in 1943. A resurgent nationalist movement attempted to win Allied support for separate independence at the end of the war, but the Bavarians ultimately settled for major autonomy within a reconstituted federal Germany.

The poorest of the states in 1949, when the new Federal Republic of Germany was proclaimed, Bavaria's economic miracle began with industries relocating from communist East Germany. In the 1950s and 1960s the so-called German Miracle was interpreted in Bavaria as a Bavarian miracle. By 1972 Bavaria had become the richest of the German federation's states.

European integration and German reunification in 1990 have rekindled Bavarian nationalism. Nationalists compare Bavaria's inclusion in united Europe, as part of Germany, to the still-controversial accession of the state to Bismarck's Germany in 1871. For many Bavarian nationalists the German government has become an unwanted tier of government above Bavaria's cherished autonomy. Nationalists continue to press for greater direct Bavarian participation in united Europe, while an increasingly vocal minority argues for the "European Option," Bavarian independence within a European federation.

In 1998–99 Bavarians increasingly opposed the change of the German federal capital from Bonn to Berlin, fearing a return to Prussian centralizing. The Bavarians see Europe and the European Union (EU) as their main focus, while many officials in Berlin look to the traditional markets and areas of interest in Eastern Europe.

SELECTED BIBLIOGRAPHY

Dorondo, D. R. *Bavaria and German Federalism: Reich to Republic, 1918–33, 1945–49.* 1992.

James, Peter. *The Politics of Bavaria—An Exception to the Rule: The Special Position of the Free State of Bavaria in the New Germany.* 1995.

Kershaw, Ian. *Popular Opinion and Political Dissent in the Third Reich, Bavaria, 1933–1945.* 1985.

Nohbauer, Hans F. *Bavaria.* 1995.

Shlaes, Amity. *Germany: The Empire Within.* 1991.

BELARUSSIANS

Byelorussians; Belorussians;
Bietarrussiyans; Belarusians

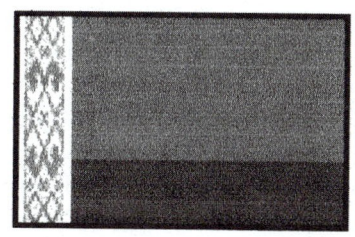

POPULATION: Approximately (2000 e) 11,650,000 Belarussians in Europe, 8,170,000 in Belarus and another 3,450,000 in adjacent areas of Russia, Ukraine, Poland, Lithuania, and Latvia. Smaller numbers live in Western Europe.

THE BELARUSSIAN HOMELAND: The Belarussian homeland occupies the western extremities of the East European Plain in Eastern Europe. Most of the region is hilly lowlands drained by several large rivers, including the Dnieper Lowlands in the southeast, the Central Berezina Plain in the center, and the Polotsk Lowland in the north. Forests cover about 30% of the area, and lumbering is important to the Belarussians' economy. The flat plains of Belarus are crossed by several large rivers such as the Dnieper, Neman, and the Zapadnaia (Western) Dvina. Belarus has Europe's largest tract of swamp, the Pripat Marshes, in the south. The southern parts of the Belarussian homeland are still affected by the Chernobyl nuclear disaster of 1986, which spread nuclear radiation over a wide area of southern Belarus. Belarussians also inhabit parts of Smolensk, Pskov, and Bryansk Oblasts of Russia, the Chernikov region of Ukraine, the Dvinsk (Daugavpils) region of Latvia, and the Bialystok region of Poland.

The Republic of Belarus was declared independent of the disintegrating Soviet Union in 1991. *Republic of Belarus (Respublika Belarus)*: 80,134 sq.mi.– 207,601 sq.km. (2000 e) 10,420,000—Belarussians (Belarusy) 78.4%, Russians* 10.6%, Poles* 4.4%, Ukrainians* 3.1%, Roms* (Gypsies) 1.1%, Jews 1.0%, Tatars,* Lithuanians.* The Belarussian capital and major culture center is Minsk, called Miensk in the Belarussian language, (2000 e) 1,711,000, located in the center of the country.

FLAG: The Belarussian state flag is a horizontal bicolor of red over green, the green half the width of the red, bearing a white vertical stripe at the hoist charged with the traditional Belarussian design in red.

PEOPLE: The Belarussians, calling themselves Belarusy, are a Slavic people, the smallest of the three main divisions of the Eastern Slavs. The Belarussians emerged as a separate nation in the thirteenth century and were called *byleo* (white) for the color of their traditional costumes. Considered the purest of the Slav nations, the blond Belarussians more closely resemble the Baltic and Scandinavian peoples than their Russian neighbors.

The Belarussians speak an East Slavic language of the Slavic group of Indo-European languages that utilizes many borrowings from Russian and Polish. The language, standardized only after the Russian Revolution, was developed from several dialects spoken in the region. The use of the language has been increasing since the revolution, with only 71.9% considering it their mother language in 1926; by 1959, 84.2% considered it their first language; and in 1992 an estimated 89% considered Belarussian their mother tongue. The Belarussian language is spoken in three major dialects, Northeast Belarussian, Southwest Belarussian, and Central Belarussian. The language is written in the Cyrillic alphabet. Linguistically, Belarussian lies between Russian and Ukrainian and has transitional dialects to both. In 1990 Belarussian was designated the official state language. In 1995, after a national referendum on the subject, Russian also was elevated to a state language. More than 90% of the population has native fluency in Russian, which was promoted by the state during the Soviet period. Belarussian is commonly spoken in rural areas, but in urban centers it is rarely heard.

The majority of the Belarussians belong to the Orthodox Church, about 60% of the total Belarussian population. An estimated 18% of the Belarussians are Roman Catholics, mostly in the western provinces, Poland, and western Ukraine. A small Protestant minority lives in the north of the region, in the northern Belarussian provinces and in Latvia.

NATION: The present Belarussian homeland was populated by Slavs during the great Slav migrations of the fifth and eighth centuries. The migrating Slav tribes displaced the region's original Finnic peoples and divided the area into tribal territories. The largest of the tribes, the Kryvichy, occupied the northern districts. In the center the Dreulane became the predominant tribe, in the south the Drehavichy, and in the east, the Radzimichy. The northwestern part of the territory was occupied by a Baltic tribe, the Yatviags. These tribes had become distinct political entities by the sixth century A.D. The Kryvichy tribe in the north founded the principalities of Polotsk and Smolensk and the Pskov republic. The Dreulane united into the principality of Turau. The two tribal principalities became the first states of the territory of modern Belarus.

The Belarussian Plains formed the northern part of the first great Slav state, Kievan Rus', in the ninth century. Following the conversion of the Kievans in 988, Christianity spread north to the Belarussian principalities, although some historians believe that Christianity came to Belarus much earlier from Scandinavia. Allied to Kiev, or at times fighting it for control of the region, the Polotsk principality reached its greatest territorial extent, wealth, and power in the eleventh century.

Development as a separate people began in the tenth century, when the Slavs in the northwestern region began referring to themselves as Belarusy, or white Rus, after the distinctive white clothing worn by both men and women. Although they used the name White Rus for the entire people, the newly Christian Belarusy remained split into several petty principalities, tributary states to Kievan Rus or dependencies of the powerful Novogorod republic, to the northwest, after it broke away from Kievan rule in 1136. The separation from the main body of the East Slavs was completed when all the East Slavs, except the White Rus, came under the rule of the Mongol-Tatar Golden Horde in the thirteenth century.

Coming from the northwest, the Catholic Lithuanians* under their prince, Ryngold, began to take control of the petty Belarussian principalities. His successors extended their growing federation, called Great Lithuania, to control Polotsk, Vitebsk, Smolensk, and Turau in the fourteenth century, often by marrying their children into the Belarussian princely families. Prince Gediminas, who took the Lithuanian throne in 1316, limited the power of the members of the federation, making the principality of Great Lithuania a true monarchy. Protected by the vast swamps in the south of the country, the Belarussian territories mostly remained free of Tatar incursions.

The area, called Byelorussia or Belorussia (White Russia), prospered as part of the medieval Lithuanian Empire, while the other East Slavs languished under Mongol rule. The Belarussian's Slav language became the dominant language of the multiethnic Lithuanian Empire. The middle of the fifteenth century saw a great flowering of Belarussian arts and culture, the apex of a golden age that flourished to the end of the sixteenth century. Large Jewish populations, fleeing persecution in the west, settled in the region in the sixteenth century, forming an urban middle class of bankers, merchants, and traders.

Bitter rivalries between the empire's Catholic and Orthodox aristocracies and nearly constant wars with the expanding power of Moscow weakened the Lithuanian Empire in the early sixteenth century. The Belarussians lost importance in the Empire after the merger of Lithuania and Catholic Poland in 1569. Many of the upper classes adopted the predominant Polish language and culture, relegating Belarussian to the position of a peasant dialect. Following a series of revolts, in 1697, the Poles forbade the use of the Belarussian language in official circumstances, and in 1699 they forbade the election of Orthodox citizens to local governments.

Almost totally lacking in natural barriers, the flat plains of Belarus were repeatedly overrun during the wars fought in the region between the sixteenth and eighteenth centuries. The region ultimately came under Russian rule during the Polish partitions of 1772, 1793, and 1795. The official policy of assimilation to Russian culture eventually achieved the conversion of the majority, particularly in the eastern provinces, from Catholicism to Orthodox Christianity, but was less successful culturally. To further its aim of assimilation, in 1839 the Russian government banned the Belarussian Uniate Church, which had become a bastion of Belarussian culture and traditions. The formerly prosperous region declined under Russian rule. Widespread poverty, especially among the Jews, fueled the massive immigration in the early nineteenth century, mostly to North America. The Russian government finally banned the Belarussian language and forbade the use of the name "Belarusy" or "White Russian" in the 1840s.

Serfdom, extensively practiced in the Belarussian region, was officially abolished in the Russian Empire in 1861, and the freed serfs were promised lands of their own. In 1863 the former serfs of Byelorussia, still without the promised lands, led a rebellion that quickly attracted support among the region's upper classes and the free peasant farmers. The revolt, brutally suppressed by tsarist troops, virtually ended all economic activity in the Belarussian provinces. The grinding poverty and the harsh conditions sent a new wave of immigrants to the New World between the 1880s and the turn of the century.

Russian suppression of the Belarussian culture and language nearly achieved the desired assimilation. By the late nineteenth century most of the Belarussians had no clear identity, considering themselves ethnic Russians or Poles, the distinction determined by religion. In 1888 an estimated 82% of the population was illiterate, retarding the ethnic revival that swept most of Europe in the latter half of the nineteenth century. Only in the 1890s did a national revival begin to take hold, much later than the cultural revival of neighboring nations. The revival, more modest than in most of Europe, was held back by the backward condition of the region.

The growth of revolutionary ideas after the turn of the century added to the growth of the Belarussian national movement. Nationalists formed the Byelorussian Revolutionary Hramada in 1902. A year later the organization was renamed the Byelorussian Socialist Hramada. Following the 1905 revolution, the tsarist government granted some concessions, including some freedoms of language and publishing previously forbidden the Belarussians.

The nascent Belarussian national movement, active particularly among the Catholic minority, was overtaken by the outbreak of World War I in 1914. Over the next three years thousands of Belarussians perished, mostly from hunger and disease. Poorly equipped Belarussian military units suffered massive losses. The massacre of nearly an entire generation of young Belarussian men added to the growing discontent with the war and with the tsarist autocracy. The Germans overran western Belarus, while the Russians retained control of Minsk and the eastern provinces.

The Belarussians of the eastern provinces enthusiastically joined the revolution that overthrew the hated Russian autocracy in February 1917. A new government organized by the nationalists gained importance with the onset of the revolution, quickly organizing to fill the vacuum left by the collapsing civil administration. The new Belarussian government laid claim, on ethnic and historic grounds, to territory also claimed by Russians, Ukrainians,* and Latvians.*

In March 1917 the Hramada dominated the new Byelorussian National Committee and demanded autonomy within a newly proclaimed democratic Russia. A Belarussian parliament, the Rada, was convened in July–August to debate the region's future relations with the Russian government. The debate was made more urgent by the German and Polish occupation of the western Belarussian provinces and the occupation, in the east, of some territory by soldiers of the Russian provisional government.

The Bolshevik coup in October 1917 set off a power struggle in the region between the Belarussian nationalists, led by the Hramada, and the local Bolshevik forces. On 14 November the numerous Bolsheviks took control of Minsk and the eastern provinces. The nationalists, driven from the capital, convened the All-Byelorussian National Congress in December. The delegates to the congress on 17 December 1917 declared Byelorussia an autonomous state and later voted by a majority for immediate independence. Before they could consolidate their power, German troops invaded the infant state in February 1918, taking control of the territory held by the nationalists and quickly driving the Bolsheviks from the territory.

The Bolshevik government of Russia, desperate for peace in the west while threatened by the White forces in the growing Russian civil war, signed a treaty with the Central Powers that left most of the former western provinces of the Russian Empire to German and Austrian control. The Treaty of Breast-Litovsk, signed in western Byelorussia between the Central Powers and the new Soviet government in March, confirmed German control of much of Byelorussia. The nationalists of the Hramada emerged from hiding and, with German protection and support, reconvened the Rada. The delegates again voted overwhelmingly for independence from Russia. The Rada declared Byelorussia independent on 25 March 1918 as the Byelorussian National Republic. The new republic quickly severed all remaining ties to Russia and was recognized by many national governments.

Territorial disputes marred the new government's relations with neighboring states. The republic laid claim to the regions historically inhabited by the Belarussian nation, including the the western Russian oblasts of Smolensk, Bryansk, and Kalinin and the southern districts of Pskov Oblast, the Dvinsk (Daugavpils) region of Latvia, and the Bialystok region, also claimed by Poland. The Poles occupied the Bialystok region and on 28 November 1918 held a plebiscite for incorporating the region into the Polish state despite the protests of the Belarussian government to the Allies at the Paris Peace Conference. With no effective fighting force to oppose the Poles, as the Germans had prohibited armed groups in the region, the Belarussians could not militarily oppose the Polish annexation of the western districts. The withdrawal of German forces in December 1918, following the armistice that ended World War I in November, left the new republic virtually defenseless as the Russian civil war spread to the region. In January 1919 the Red Army occupied the eastern districts, creating a Byelorussian Soviet Republic at Smolensk as a rival to the nationalist government in Minsk.

Newly independent Poland in April 1919 declared war on Soviet Russia.

Polish troops stopped the advancing Bolsheviks and occupied the western Belarussian provinces but refused to recognize Belarussian independence. The Poles offered the Belarussians major autonomy in a "Greater Poland" and gained the support of many nationalists by driving the Soviets from the eastern provinces. The Soviets, embroiled in a massive civil war, were unable to hold the region against the Poles and their Belarussian allies, but with their victory over the Whites in 1920, Red Army troops were freed for service on the Polish front. In July 1920 the Bolsheviks went on the offensive. The Belarussian nationalists, caught between the Poles in the west and the Soviets in the east, lost all remaining political power in the region. The Soviet promises of independence within a federation of Soviet states, which had some support in the region, were set aside following the brutal suppression of a Belarussian nationalist uprising against communist rule in Slutsk Province in 1920.

The Treaty of Riga, signed on 18 March 1921 by Poland and the Soviet Union, partitioned Byelorussia between the Polish and Soviet states. The Polish government annexed the mostly Roman Catholic western districts with a population of 4 million. In 1922 the eastern provinces under Bolshevik control were organized as a separate Soviet republic that joined the new Soviet Union as a constituent state. Between 3% and 5% of the population died of starvation following the forced collectivization of agriculture in the Soviet zone.

The purges of the Stalinist era, especially severe in 1929–30 and 1933–34, destroyed all remaining national and cultural leadership. The Soviet government in 1933 charged that nationalists had formed a Byelorussian National Center with its aim the secession of the republic from the Soviet Union, a right guaranteed in the Soviet constitution but never allowed. The entire Belarussian republican government, including the president of the Soviet Central Committee, was purged for advocating a united Belarussian republic, to include both the Soviet and Polish zones, in 1937. The victims of the Stalinist purges, numbering in the thousands, were buried in mass graves and later were claimed, by the Soviet government, as the remains of the victims of Nazi atrocities.

The western Belarussians, under Polish rule, although free of the fear and panic of the Soviet purges, were also deprived of their rights and language. Belarussian schools were closed, and the Belarussian language was forbidden in Catholic churches. In 1927 the Polish government cracked down on all specifically Belarussian organizations and arrested a number of national leaders. A program of assimilating the Belarussian population into Polish culture became the official government policy.

The Ribbentrop-Molotov pact between Nazi Germany and the Soviet Union divided the small countries between the two powers into spheres of influence on 23 August 1939. The pact allowed the Soviets to occupy eastern Poland and to unite all of the Belarussians in an expanded Byelorussian Soviet Socialist Republic. With ruthless efficiency anti-Soviet Belarussians were eliminated in the newly annexed western provinces. Thousands, including many Roman Catholic priests and nuns, were deported or quickly executed.

A minority of Belarussians welcomed the German invasion of the Soviet

Union in June 1941. The Germans and their allies were hailed as liberators from Soviet rule. Despite the harsh Nazi occupation Belarussian nationalists were encouraged to collaborate in an anticommunist crusade. Those nationalists convened the Byelorussian Central Council and the Second All-Byelorussian National Congress at Minsk in 1944. A Byelorussian National Guard, created as a national army, helped to massacre the republic's large Jewish population. Many of the traditionally anti-Semitic Belarussians served as guards at concentration camps.

A Belarussian national uprising began with the Nazi defeat in 1944. Poorly armed partisan units fought the victorious return of the Red Army to Belarus. Guerrilla units continued to operate in the republic, especially in the Pripat swamps, well into the 1950s. Thousands of Belarussians fled to the West.

A battleground during the war, the Belarussian homeland suffered the worst devastation of any region in Europe. An estimated quarter of the prewar Belarussian population died in the war, the postwar uprising, and the deportations of the "ideologically contaminated" survivors that accompanied the reimposition of Soviet rule and the imposition of communist regimes in Poland and Latvia.

The Soviet leader Joseph Stalin, intent on the assimilation of the Belarussians, instituted a policy of intense Russification, the language once again banned and the culture suppressed. In an effort to placate the surviving Belarussian nationalist sentiment, the Soviet constitution was amended to allow Byelorussia and Ukraine to maintain separate armed forces and diplomatic representation but was implemented only one time, to secure United Nations seats for the two Soviet republics in 1945.

A modest national revival, a reaction to Stalin's excesses, began at his death in 1953 and gradually gained momentum, particularly in the Roman Catholic west, until it was stifled by renewed suppression in the 1970s and early 1980s. The introduction of reforms in 1987 by Soviet leader Mikhail Gorbachev allowed the expression of ideas and sentiments unthinkable under former Soviet leaders. Unofficial political groups began to form, but the changes that occurred, in rapid succession, in the neighboring Baltic republics were resisted by the old-line communists, who continued to control the republican government in Minsk. The national movement gained support due to the poor government response to the 1986 Chernobyl nuclear disaster, which affected thousands of Belarussians living near the path of the radioactive contamination. The nuclear disaster, the worst in modern history, released radiation into the air, contaminating areas in Ukraine and Byelorussia, which received 70% of the radiation.

In May 1988 news of the discovery of mass graves at Kurpaty, in the outskirts of Minsk, further galvanized the growing anticommunist feeling in the republic. The graves held the remains of between 100,000 and 300,000 Belarussians systematically murdered by the NKVD, the predecessor of the KGB, between 1937 and 1941. Formerly attributed to Nazi atrocities, the discovery that the Soviets had committed the murders added fuel to the antigovernment movement taking hold in the most obedient of Soviet republics.

Adradzhen'ne (Rebirth or Renewal), the Belarussian Popular Front, modeled on the Baltic movements, was formed in 1989 despite official opposition and harassment by the secret police, the KGB. Official opposition to perestroika in the republic forced the Popular Front to hold its first congress in Vilnius, the capital of neighboring Lithuania. Partly in resentment of Belarussian officials to endorse the changes that were rapidly reshaping the Baltics, the Popular Front adopted an openly nationalist platform, demanding a separate budget for the republic, control of the local economy, cultural and economic autonomy, the right to fly the long-banned national flag, and an open accounting of the Stalinist-era crimes against the Belarussian nation.

The Soviet Union's first "multicandidate elections" since 1917 were held on 26 March 1989. Many communist officials in Byelorussia, through devious means, ran unopposed. Where there was a choice, local candidates viewed as pro-change easily won, while even some officials running unopposed failed to receive the 50% of the vote needed to retain their positions, including the Communist Party chief of the republic. The elections galvanized the nationalist opposition, and by February 1990 Adradzhen'ne had over 100,000 members, a tenth of the republic's population. On 17 July 1990 the Belarus government, pressed by the growing national movement, issued a declaration of state sovereignty.

The Belarussians, fearful of premature independence, voted by an overwhelming 83% to retain the Soviet Union in a referendum organized in early 1991. In the wake of the aborted coup against Gorbachev in August 1991, the Belarussian leaders reluctantly declared the republic's independence from the Soviet Union on 25 August 1991. The republic, a separate member of the United Nations since 1945, was recognized as an independent state by the United States and most of Western Europe in late 1991.

Nationalist organizations that were increasingly winning support at the expense of the republic's neocommunist leadership were mostly driven underground in the mid-1990s. Intent on creating the first truly independent Belarussian state, the nationalists must first wrest political control from the old communist hierarchy that survived and continues to govern the republic under the guise of a national government.

The Belarussian homeland, once one of the more advanced regions of the Soviet Union, in the first seven years of independence slipped to the levels of the poorest regions of Europe. Among the causes were poor management, clinging to the old Soviet forms, and looking to Russia before making any decisions. The severe economic decline has accelerated the republic's economic and military integration with Russia. The Belarussian government subordinated its military policy to that of Russia's in December 1993 and in January 1994 subordinated its economic policies to those of Russia.

On 23 June 1994 Belarussians voted to follow the rest of the former Soviet republics in establishing an office of president. Six candidates, including the prime minister, participated in the poll. On 11 July 1994 Alexander Lukashenka, a former collective farm director, won the elections and became the first elected president with 80.1% of the vote. Lukashenka's favorite themes, anticorruption and closer ties to Russia, appealed to the weary voters of the republic. Buffeted by a continuing economic crisis and mounting crime, the voters turned to the man who promised to restore their former prosperity. Since his election, President Lukashenka has severely undermined democracy in the republic. In parliamentary elections in November 1995, many opposition candidates were elected on their opposition to a return to Soviet economy and growing Russian domination. The parliamentary elections set the stage for serious conflicts between the parliament and president.

The historic white-red-white national flag, which was adopted as the official state flag upon the declaration of Belarus' independence in 1991, was replaced as the result of a 1995 referendum whose legitimacy is still questioned. The new state flag, almost identical to the Soviet-era flag, is not accepted by the nationalist groups or the democratic opposition.

The majority of the Belarussian people, long accustomed to seeing themselves as part of the Russian sphere of influence, support Lukashenka's aims of closer relations with Russia. A new constitution and a revamped parliament aid Lukashenka's dictatorial government. The oppression of democratic forces in the country brought protests from within and from outside the country. Since the spring of 1996 a number of rallies and demonstrations against the president's policies have begun to unite the fragmented democratic groups.

The country, strategically placed in the middle of Eastern Europe, is the least democratic of the former communist states. The republic's chief problem is its autocratic, erratic president, Alexander Lukashenka. Although he was democratically elected, he quickly destroyed the country's fragile democracy and established one-man rule. In March 1997 the government moved to severely curb human rights in the country, including bans on the political opposition and groups with foreign affiliations. The freedoms of the Belarus people have deteriorated severely under the regime of President Lukashenka. Three opposition newspapers, banned in Belarus, are printed in neighboring Lithuania.

In May 1997 Belarus and Russia signed a union charter drawing the two countries closer to full integration. Nationalists in Belarus, increasingly run as a Stalinist dictatorship, demonstrated against the agreement. In spite of growing opposition, the Belarus government has clung to a Soviet-style economy and has rapidly slipped back into the totalitarian ways of the past. On 25 December 1998 the presidents of Russia and Belarus announced plans for a common policy on economic, foreign, and military matters. Demonstrating by opponents of closer ties to the Russians were attacked by state police, and several were hospitalized.

While most of East and Central Europe has made gains, both economically and socially, during the 1990s, Belarus has drifted into a separate catagory as an unreformed authoritarian state. Alexander Lukashenka, seemingly deaf to the Belarussian democrats, the European Union (EU), and other governments and international organizations, instituted strict rule, rewrote the constitution, extended his term in office, dismissed the parliament, appointed a new constitutional court, silenced the media, suppressed the opposition, and gave greater powers to an unreformed KGB. He has made himself, in all but name, the dictator of the Belarussian nation.

In the late 1990s, President Alexander Lukashenka converted Belarus into a neo-Stalinist state, where opposition newspapers have been closed and anti-government leaders routinely disappear. Demonstrations against the government's Stalinist style and against plans to unite Belarus with Russia rocked Minsk and other large cities in October 1999. The demonstrators, waving the nationalist white, red, white flag, clashed with police and soldiers before being dispersed. The nationalists, increasingly calling for real democracy and a new Belarus government, have found aid and support among the large Belarussian diaspora in Europe and the Americas.

SELECTED BIBLIOGRAPHY

Applebaum, Anne. *Ukraine, Moldova, Belarus: Between East and West.* 1995.
Keep, John. *Last of the Empires: A History of the Soviet Union 1945–1991.* 1995.
Marples, David R. *Belarus: From Soviet Rule to Nuclear Catastrophe.* 1996.
Zaprudnik, Jan. *Belarus at a Crossroads of History.* 1993.
Zaprudnik, Jan. *Historical Dictionary of Belarus.* 1998.

BOSNIANS

Bosniaks; Bosnian Muslims; Bosnans

POPULATION: Approximately (2000 e) 1,900,000 Bosnians in Europe, the majority in the Republic of Bosnia and Herzegovina, but with an estimated 700,000 refugees now scattered around the world. The total number of Bosnians includes smaller populations living in neighboring areas in the Balkans, 90,000 in Montenegro, and 60,000 in Kosovo.

THE BOSNIAN HOMELAND: The Bosnian homeland lies in the central part of the Republic of Bosnia and Herzegovina. The homeland is a hilly region of high valleys rising to the mountains of the Dinaric Alps in the west, which run parallel to the Adriatic coast. About half the region is forested, with only one-quarter under cultivation. The federation has about twelve miles (twenty k.) of coastline along the Adriatic Sea.

The Bosnian population is concentrated in the river valleys of the Bosna, Drina, and Vrbos Rivers. Prior to the outbreak of war, in 1992, the Bosnians, called Bosnian Muslims, lived in ethnically mixed regions across the republic. However, ethnic cleansing and the expulsions of whole populations by Serbs* and Croats* have consolidated the Bosnian population in the central districts of the republic.

The Bosnian homeland since 1995 has formed part of the Muslim-Croat Federation, one of the two statelets that make up the Republic of Bosnia and Herzegovina. *Republic of Bosnia and Herzegovina (Respublika Bosna i Hercegovina)*: 19,741 sq.mi.–51,142 sq.km. (2000 e) 3,120,000—Bosnians 36%, Serbs 34%, Croats 21%, Roms* (Gypsy) 5%, Montenegrins* 1%, Albanians,* Jews. The Bosnian capital and major cultural center is Sarajevo, (2000 e) 405,000, which was badly damaged during the Bosnian War.

FLAG: The Bosnian national flag is a white field with narrow green strips top and bottom, charged with a centered, white crescent moon outlined in green. The state flag of Bosnia and Herzegovina is a diagonal bicolor of yellow over pale blue, with ten white fleur-de-lis on the blue half along the color divide.

PEOPLE: The Bosnian Muslims, now popularly called Bosniaks or simply Bosnians, are a South Slav people ethnically and historically related to the neighboring Croats and Serbs. The Bosnians are distinguished by their Muslim religion, their unique background, and recent history. Until the post–World War II era, the Muslims of Bosnia-Herzegovina usually identified themselves as Serbs or Croats, depending on their geographic location.

Highly secularized and well educated, the Bosnian population has traditionally formed an urban middle class in Sarajevo and the other large urban areas. Since the ethnic cleansing that accompanied the war, the majority of the rural Bosnians have also sought refuge in Sarajevo, Tuzla, Zenica, and other large towns under Bosnian government control. In the 1991 census the Muslims accounted for 44% of the population. Since the war began in 1992, hundreds of thousands of Bosnians have been forcibly expelled from areas overrun by the Serbs or Croats. Many sought refuge abroad and now live in 127 countries worldwide.

The Bosnians speak a dialect of Serbo-Croatian that they have begun to call Bosnian or Serbo-Bosnian. The Bosnian dialect of Serbo-Croatian, which is written in the Latin alphabet, uses many Arabo-Turkish forms and words absent from the dialects spoken by the Croats and Serbs of Bosnia.

NATION: Originally inhabited by the early Illyrian peoples, Bosnia was part of the Roman Empire during the first centuries of the Christian era. Christianity spread to the region, but most of the population adopted the Eastern rites, later to be called Orthodox Christianity. The Roman Empire split into eastern and western halves in A.D. 395, with the Balkan territories contested by the eastern empire, Byzantium, and Rome's successors in the West.

Nomadic Slavic tribes, migrating from the north, settled the mountain valleys of the Dinaric Alps in the sixth and seventh centuries. Coming under nominal Byzantine rule, the Slavs gradually absorbed the region's earlier inhabitants. The majority gradually adopted much of the Byzantine culture and converted to Orthodox Christianity. The Slavs formed a number of small counties and duchies too weak to oppose the powerful Byzantines. Two neighboring kingdoms, Serbia and Croatia, were established in the ninth century. They rose to prominence among the small Slav states in the region. The two kingdoms were often at war over the division of authority and territory in the region.

In the tenth century many of the Christian Slavs of the high mountain valleys of the Dinaric Alps converted to a dualistic creed attributed to Bogomil, a Bulgarian priest. The creed, intensely nationalistic and political as well as religious, opposed Slavic serfdom, church authority, and Byzantine cultural influences. The Slav believers in the creed, known as Bogomils, suffered severe and violent persecutions as religious heretics.

Ruled by Croatian kings from 958, a separate Bosnian state formed in the twelfth century as a vassal of the Kingdom of Hungary. In 1180 a local ruler, Kulin, declared himself the *ban*, the governor, under nominal Hungarian rule and established the Bosnian state in the center and north of the present Bosnia and Herzegovina. In the same year Kulin openly declared his adherence to the Bogomil sect.

The population of medieval Bosnia, although professing Christianity, adhered to not one but three different beliefs, Roman Catholicism, Eastern Orthodoxy, and the local schismatic Bogomil sect. All three belief systems were organizationally weak, and religious leaders were largely uneducated. None of the three could count on steady and exclusive state patronage. The weakness of the religious systems contributed to the later conversion of many Bosnians to Islam.

Neighboring Herzegovina, an independent principality dominated by the Huns from the tenth century, came under Serbian rule in the fourteenth century. The region, influenced by the Venetian territories along the coast, remained a separate duchy until the thirteenth century, when it came under the rule of the *bans* of Bosnia.

The Bosnian region, after a period of Serbian rule, became a strong Christian lordship with territory extending to the Adriatic Sea under the leadership of Ban Stephen Kotromanic, 1322–53. A later governor, Stephen Tvrtko, took the title of king of Bosnia and Serbia in 1376. The Bosnian kingdom joined an alliance of Balkan Christian nations in a vain attempt to block the northward advance of the Muslim Ottoman Turks. In 1389 at Kosovo Polje, the Field of Blackbirds, the Slavs were defeated in one of medieval Europe's largest battles. Legends tell of blackbirds feasting on the corpses of thousands of dead for weeks after the battle. More fierce battles lay ahead as the Turks were held at bay for another seventy years. The Bosnian kingdom, weakened by war and religious strife between the Bogomils, Roman Catholics, and Orthodox Christians, split into several small, weak states in the fifteenth century, including Herzegovina, which became an independent duchy. In 1463 Bosnia and, in 1482, Herzegovina fell to the expanding Turkish Ottoman Empire.

The Bogomils, hated and persecuted by their Christian neighbors, succumbed to Turkish pressure and largely converted to the Turks' Islamic religion. As Muslims under Ottoman rule, they formed a favored minority. Augmented by a Turkish military aristocracy that confiscated the lands of annihilated Christian nobles, the Muslims controlled large estates worked by mostly Christian serfs, the *rayas*, who were treated little better than slaves. Although the serfs were forbidden weapons, insurrections against harsh Muslim rule were frequent.

Sporadic peasant rebellions during the nineteenth century culminated in a widespread Slavic uprising against weakening Turkish rule in 1875, a major factor in the Russo-Turkish War of 1877–78. The Congress of Berlin, convened to revise the treaty forced on the defeated Ottoman Turks by Russia, assigned the Turkish territories south of Croatia and west of newly independent Serbia to the Austro-Hungarian Empire. The Slav rebellion was finally crushed by the Austrian military occupation of the region in 1878.

The Pan-Slav nationalist dream of a great South Slav state united under the leadership of Orthodox Serbia was supported and promoted from Serbia and financed by Russia, the self-appointed guardian of the Eastern Orthodox peoples. The Muslim Slavs saw no place for themselves in this proposed new Orthodox order, and many embraced the Austro-Hungarian authorities as protectors. Some Bosnian Muslims emigrated to Turkey and other parts of the Ottoman Empire, fleeing Austrian military conscription and a politically uncertain future, but the majority stayed, taking advantage of the educational and economic opportunities brought in by the new rulers. Under Austrian rule, the Muslim Bosnians and the Roman Catholic Croat communities grew more modern and prosperous than their Orthodox rivals.

Serbian nationalists in Bosnia, meanwhile, were plotting to overthrow Austro-Hungarian rule not only in Bosnia but also in the neighboring South Slavic lands of Croatia and Slovenia. The annexation of Bosnia and Herzegovina in 1908 aroused Serbian nationalists, who saw the Austrian annexation as thwarting their dream of resurrecting the medieval Serbian empire.

On 28 June 1914 a Bosnian Serb, Gavrilo Princip, an ardent Serbian nationalist, assassinated Archduke Francis Ferdinand, the heir to the Austro-Hungarian throne in Sarajevo. Francis Ferdinand was an advocate of a triple monarchy to include a Slav state alongside Austria and Hungary. The proposal to add a third crown to the dual empire had won the enmity of the powerful Pan-Serbian nationalists, who viewed a Slav state in the empire as an impediment to the Serb dream of dominating the South Slav nations of the Balkan Peninsula. The Austrian reaction led to war with Serbia, and the conflict rapidly spread to engulf Europe and eventually most of the world.

The Bosnian homeland, the object of competing Croatian and Serbian claims during World War I, was one of the more difficult points to settle for the delegates of the Croats, Slovenes, Serbs, and Montenegrins at the meeting of South Slav leaders on the island of Corfu in 1917. The leaders, determined to forge a South Slav state out of the Balkan Peninsula territories, finally declared a union of all South Slav peoples and agreed to the principle of unity once the Central Powers had been defeated. The South Slav territories of defeated Austria and Hungary, Slovenia, Croatia, and Bosnia and Herzegovina were joined to the independent states of Serbia and Montenegro to form a separate South Slav kingdom in 1918.

The Bosnians suffered persecution and discrimination in the years after the end of World War I. On 26 October 1918 Bosnia and Herzegovina were annexed by Serbia and remained part of Serbia within the new Kingdom of the Serbs, Croats, and Slovenes, called Yugoslavia from 1929. As the original name indicates, there was to be no special provision made for people who considered themselves neither Serbs nor Croats, and in the interwar years Bosnia's Muslim Slavs were pressured to register themselves as one or the other. Insofar as the Muslims counted on the political scene, it was as a weak population of despised non-Christians caught between Serb and Croat nationalist ambitions.

Overrun by the fascist German and Italian armies in 1941, the Yugoslav state was quickly defeated and divided by the victors. A German-sponsored Croat republic, including Bosnia and Herzegovina, declared its independence of Yugoslavia. The Bosnians, called Muslim Croats by the fascist Croat government, generally supported the Croats against the hated Orthodox Serbs. Ideological and religious violence, especially severe in ethnically mixed Bosnia, led to widespread atrocities and massacres perpetrated by all sides. Following the German withdrawal in 1944, several thousand Bosnians were murdered in savage Serbian reprisals.

A local communist leader, Josip Broz Tito, organized a partisan army in Bosnia in 1942. Opposed by the fascist Croats and Muslims and the Serb nationalists and royalists, led by Draja Mikhailovich, a civil war raged in Bosnia in parallel to the wider World War II. Mikhailovich's anticommunist group, mostly nationalistic, ethnic Serbs, often clashed with Tito's communist resistance, which increasingly won the support and material aid of the Allied governments.

The postwar Yugoslav state, under a communist government led by wartime partisan leader Tito, was reconstructed as a federation of socialist states under a new 1946 communist constitution. The constitution, promulgated on 31 January 1946 and modeled on the constitution of the Soviet Union, replaced the Yugoslav monarchy with a federation of six republics and two autonomous provinces within the Serbian republic. Bosnia-Herzegovina was the only constituent republic of the new federation not created within discernible ethnic borders but included large Muslim, Serb, and Croat populations, plus minorities of Albanians, Jews, and Montenegrins. The Bosnians prospered under the pragmatic national communism practiced in Tito's Yugoslavia.

The 1948 Yugoslav census listed the population of the republic as Serb, Croat, and undetermined Muslim, while the census of 1953 listed the Bosnian Muslims as undetermined Yugoslavs. Not recognized as a separate nationality until 1969, the Bosnians were counted as a separate Yugoslav people, called Muslims, only in the 1981 Yugoslav census. The Bosnians, having identified themselves only by their religion, or as Serbian or Croatian Muslims, up to World War II, in the decades after the war slowly developed a distinct national identity around their traditional Muslim beliefs and their secular, urbanized culture.

Tito, an ethnic Croat, held the disparate nations together in the Yugoslav federation by allowing cultural autonomy and more rights and freedoms than were usual for the postwar communist dictatorships of the Cold War period. In 1974 a new constitution allowed for greater republican autonomy and recognized the Muslims as a nationality. Ethnic relations in Bosnia remained fairly peaceful, with intermarriage between Muslims, Catholics, and Orthodox very common. Despite the fairly good relations between the national groups, some 600,000 ethnic Serbs left the republic for Serbia between 1945 and 1986.

Tito died in May 1980, fatally weakening the federal institutions. Tito's position as the leader of the Yugoslav state was turned over to a rotating presidency of the leaders of the republics and autonomous provinces. Without Tito's strong hand the various nationalities began to move in separate directions, straining the fabric of the multiethnic federation. The one strong federal institution that remained, the military, came increasingly under the domination of the Orthodox Serbs.

The collapse of communism across Eastern Europe in 1989 aroused the old nationalisms buried under decades of communist suppression. Political parties quickly formed in the republic, mostly along ethnic lines. The Muslim Party of Democratic Action (SDA) represented the majority Bosnian Muslim population. On 15 October 1990 the parliament of Bosnia and Herzegovina declared the republic's sovereignty.

Free elections in Bosnia on 18 November 1990 resulted in a governing coalition of the three ethnically based parties generally corresponding to the three major ethnic groups. Muslims and Croats in the governing coalition favored independence for Bosnia-Herzegovina, while most Bosnian Serbs rejected independence amid calls for union with neighboring Serbia.

Squeezed between the increasingly combative Croat and Serb states, the Bosnian coalition government carefully maintained a neutral stance, but the war between Croats and Serbs in Croatia fatally damaged the fragile balance of nationalities in Bosnia. In early May 1991 violence spilled over into the republic, raising tensions alarmingly. The secession of neighboring Croatia from Yugoslavia in June 1991 provoked Bosnian Serb claims, backed by the Yugoslav government in Belgrade, to much of the territory of Bosnia-Herzegovina.

In August 1991, as the war in neighboring Croatia wound down, the Serbs stepped up pressure on Bosnia-Herzegovina. The Bosnian Serbs, led by the Serbian Democratic Party and supported by the Yugoslav government in Belgrade, gained control of most of northern Bosnia in August 1991. In September the Serbs declared three large, mainly Serb-populated areas autonomous regions and prepared for unification with Serbia. Armed clashes erupted between Serbs and Bosnian Muslims in several areas.

Serbian territorial claims to Bosnia territory pushed the Bosnian government, supported by the Muslims and Croats, to hold a referendum on independence in October 1991. The referendum, boycotted by the ethnic Serbs, favored independence for Bosnia-Herzegovina.

On 24 December 1991 the governments of four Yugoslav republics, Bosnia-Herzegovina, Croatia, Macedonia, and Slovenia, requested recognition as sovereign states from the European Community. However, on 9 January 1991 European Community leaders announced that the risk of ethnic conflict was too great for Bosnia-Herzegovina to qualify for recognition, effectively leaving the region isolated and vulnerable.

The United States and the major European states pressed for the continuation of a looser Yugoslav confederation. The assembly representing the Bosnian Serb population declared an autonomous republic and announced that Bosnia-Herzegovina's government no longer represented the Serb portion of the population in international forums. Sporadic fighting soon broke out between Muslims and Serb irregulars, units of the Yugoslav army, and Croat irregulars.

The most ethnically mixed of the former Yugoslav republics, the major national groups in the region had a very high incidence of intermarriage, 16% of the population were the product of mixed marriages, and the various national groups mixed freely until war began in the republic in April 1992. The ethnic hatred that swept the republic tore families apart and separated the formerly tolerant population into three suspicious ethnic armies.

Following international recognition of Croatian and Slovene independence in January 1992 and news that Macedonia's secession was imminent, the elected Bosnian government found itself faced with an impossible choice. The prospect of remaining part of a rump Yugoslavia dominated by advocates of "Greater Serbia" was clearly unacceptable to the majority of Bosnia's population, while Bosnian independence was anathema to Serb nationalists both within Bosnia and in Serbia.

On 29 February 1992, with 63% of eligible voters taking part, including some ethnic Serbs, 99.4% opted for full independence. The referendum, one of the conditions demanded by the international community before Bosnia's independence would be recognized, was boycotted by the majority of the Bosnian Serb community. On 3 March 1992 the government formally declared the independence of the Republic of Bosnia and Herzegovina. The Bosnian Serbs, rejecting the independence referendum, moved their parliamentary representatives from the Bosnian capital to the ski resort of Pale, outside Sarajevo. The new Bosnian Serb parliament at Pale declared the autonomy of the areas under Serb control.

On 18 March leaders of the three major ethnic groups signed an agreement, under European Union threats of withholding recognition, that provided for the division of the republic into three autonomous units. The agreement was signed, even though all agreed that it would be extremely difficult, if not impossible, to implement because very few areas of the republic were exclusively Muslim, Croat, or Serb. The Bosnian Serbs declared the independence of their region on 27 March. On 6 April ministers representing the European Union recognized the independence of the republic. Fighting between the different national groups intensified week by week.

A mass demonstration by citizens of Sarajevo's three major communities, including moderate Serbs who favored Bosnian independence, took to the city's streets on 5 April 1992. Yugoslav National Army snipers and Serb nationalist militants hidden on surrounding rooftops opened fire on the crowd, killing and wounding scores of unarmed citizens. The following day, Yugoslav army units began to shell Sarajevo from prepared positions on the hillsides overlooking the city, and columns of troops and tanks crossed the Drina River from Serbia into eastern Bosnia. Initially armed only with police sidearms and hunting rifles, later with captured and smuggled weapons, the Bosnian forces, including Muslims, Croats, and Serbs, tried to defend their newly independent country against the onslaught of radical nationalism.

On 22 May 1992, Bosnia-Herzegovina, already recognized by many states, was admitted as a full member of the United Nations (UN). An arms embargo, imposed on all of the former Yugoslavia by the UN in 1991, in effect barred the internationally recognized Bosnian government from acquiring the means to exercise its right to self-defense as guaranteed under the UN Charter. The Serb forces, armed and supported by the Yugslav Army (JNA), were well armed and quickly overran many districts.

Islamic volunteers entered Bosnia. Called *mujahideen*, the volunteers formed the Muwafag and the Muwafaqah brigades, which fought alongside the Bosnian Muslim forces. The presence of foreign volunteers fed the propaganda put out by the Serbian and Croatian press that the Bosnians were intent on turning the country into an Islamic state modeled on Iran.

Badly crippled by an arms embargo imposed by the West, the Bosnians fell back under concerted attacks. The Bosnian Serbs and the Yugoslav army quickly defeated the poorly armed republican forces and overran much of Bosnia's national territory. Employing a new and brutal weapon called ethnic cleansing, the murder, rape, and expulsion of entire populations, the triumphant Serbian forces surrounded Sarajevo and several other enclaves held by the mostly Muslim forces of the Bosnian government.

The fragile Bosnian-Croat alliance collapsed in March 1993. Severe fighting between Muslims and Croats spread across the south and west, devastating ancient monuments and cities, including the traditionally Muslim and Croat city of Mostar, the capital of Herzegovina. The war devastated the economy, and by 1995 the Bosnian unemployment rate had risen as high as 75%.

The Bosnian War, a three-sided conflict between the Bosnian Muslims, the Bosnian Croats, and the Bosnian Serbs, aided by the truncated Yugoslavia (Serbia and Montenegro), quickly escalated into the most brutal conflict to take place in Europe since World War II. The international community, reluctant to get involved in the conflict, failed to react strongly to the ethnic cleansing, reports of mass rape, concentration camps, and massacres. Refusing direct involvement, many governments called on the United Nations to act.

Representatives of the United Nations and the European Union, Cyrus Vance and Lord Owen, presented a peace proposal for Bosnia-Herzegovina on 2 January 1993. The proposal included the reorganization of the republic into ten provinces, the establishment of safe corridors for the movement of civilians and humanitarian aid, a large measure of autonomy for the provinces under a decentralized state, and cease-fire and demilitarization arrangements.

In late April the Bosnian Serb Assembly rejected the proposed territorial arrangements in the Vance-Owen peace plan for Bosnia, which had been endorsed by Bosnian Croats and Muslims. Many interpreted the Bosnian Serb decision as a calculated gamble that the West's response to the crisis would remain tentative and that there would be no direct international military intervention. However, under strong pressure from Serbia, the Bosnian Serbs signed the Vance-Owen plan in May, but then the Serbian parliament in Pale refused to endorse the agreement and submitted the final decision to a referendum. The Bosnian Serbs rejected the plan and with a 96% majority voted for the independence of the Bosnian Serb-held areas.

After a year of war, in April 1993 the Bosnians and Croats accepted a UN peace plan that would divide the country into two areas, a Muslim-Croat federation and a Serbian republic. The plan, formalized in March 1994, reduced the warring factions from three to two and created a projected federation of Bosnia and Herzegovina. The plan, rejected by the Bosnian Serbs, remained as the principal bargaining position taken up by the Western powers. Several subsequent peace plans floundered on the inability of the combatants to agree on an equitable division of territory between the three national groups.

The Bosnian state, devastated by continuing war, was overwhelmed by some 200,000 dead and 2 million refugees, most "ethnically cleansed" from their villages in areas held by the Bosnian Serbs. The UN, supported by troops from many member nations, attempted to secure a fragile peace but, failing that, took over the job of trying to keep transportation routes open and the flow of desperately needed food and medicine moving to where it was needed.

Bosnian Serb troops, disregarding the UN and the North Atlantic Treaty Organization (NATO), overran the UN-protected enclaves of Srebernica and Zepa in eastern Bosnia in July 1995. Reported massacres of Bosnians and continued attacks on the other so-called protected zones, particularly a brutal attack on a market in Sarajevo, finally provoked a massive NATO air attack on the Bosnian Serbs on 30 August. Pressed militarily by the NATO attacks, the Serbs began to lose territory in western Bosnia to renewed attacks by the Bosnian government forces and their Croat allies. As a result of the war, between 100,000 and 250,000 people were reported killed, and about 200,000 were wounded. The overwhelming majority were Bosnians.

The August 1995 NATO attacks on Bosnian Serb military targets set the stage for a United States-brokered peace plan. On 21 November 1995 in Dayton, Ohio, the former Yugoslavia's three warring parties signed a peace agreement that brought to a halt over three years of interethnic civil strife in Bosnia and Herzegovina. The Dayton Agreement divided Bosnia and Herzegovina roughly equally between the Muslim and Croat Federation (51%) and the Bosnian Serb Republic of Srpska (49%) while maintaining Bosnia's currently recognized borders.

An international peacekeeping force (IFOR) of 60,000 troops began to enter Bosnia in late 1995 to implement and monitor the military aspects of the agreement and was scheduled to depart the country within one year. Under the new constitution initialed in Dayton the name of the country will be changed from Republic of Bosnia and Herzegovina to simply Bosnia and Herzegovina and will be made up of the Muslim and Croat Federation and the Bosnian Serb entity. As a result of successful government offensives, Serbian control of territory in the republic had shrunk to about half the total territory by early 1996.

Despite the general compliance with the military aspects of the peace agreement, little progress was made toward implementing those aspects relating to human rights, such as freedom of movement and the right of displaced people and refugees to return to their homes. About 1.5 million Bosnians driven from their homes remain refugees.

The country, with the first relative peace since 1992, began the task of re-construction. By mid-1997 some 300,000 of the 2.1 million displaced persons had returned to their homes, but fewer than 30,000 had returned to territory controlled by a different ethnic group. The country, experts estimate, will need around $20 billion to resettle the refugees and the displaced and to reconstruct the major war damage.

According to Bosnian leaders, survival of the Bosnian nation is now just as important as the survival of the internationally recognized state of Bosnia-Herzegovina. Should fighting again break out in the republic, Bosnian leaders fear that the survival of the nation, not just the country, will be at stake.

SELECTED BIBLIOGRAPHY

Donia, Robert J., and John V. A. Fine, Jr. *Bosnia and Herzegovina: A Tradition Betrayed.* 1994.

Friedman, Francine. *The Bosnian Muslims: Denial of a Nation.* 1996.

Greenberg, Keith Elliott, and John Isaac. *Bosnia: Civil War in Europe.* 1996.

Malcolm, Noel. *Bosnia: A Short History.* 1994.

Manuel, David. *Bosnia: Hope in the Ashes.* 1997.

BRETONS

Bretonants; Brezhoneg

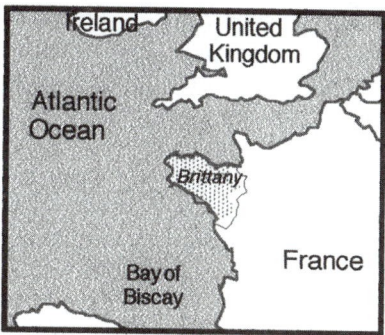

POPULATION: Approximately (2000 e) 2,825,000 Bretons in Europe, most in the historic Brittany region in western France. Breton communities also live in Paris and other regions of France. Outside Europe there are sizable Breton communities in Canada and the United States.

THE BRETON HOMELAND: The Breton homeland occupies a large peninsula in the Atlantic Ocean, between the English Channel on the north and the Bay of Biscay on the south. Most of the region lies north of the Loire River in northwestern France but includes the mouth and delta of the river. Brittany is traditionally divided into two distinct areas, Amor, the coastal regions, and Argoat, the hinterland. The coast of Brittany, particularly at the western tip, is irregular and rocky, with a number of natural harbors and numerous islands.

The peninsula, one of the three that traditionally have been held by Celts, is the most southerly. To the north, across the narrow English Channel, are the peninsulas inhabited by the related Cornish* and Welsh* nations. Politically, the Breton homeland, called Bretagne in French, is divided between two French regions, consisting of five departments. One of the rallying points of Breton nationalism is the unification of their homeland in a single administrative unit. *Historical Region of Brittany (Breizh)*. 13,643 sq.mi.–35,344 sq.km. (2000 e) 3,890,000—Bretons 72%, other French.* The Breton capital and major cultural center, Rennes, called Roazhon in Breton, (2000 e) 205,000, lies at the junction of the Ille and Vilaine Rivers 193 miles (311 km.) west of Paris.

FLAG: The Breton national flag has nine horizontal stripes of black and white charged with a white canton on the upper hoist bearing eleven black ermines.

PEOPLE: The Bretons are a Celtic people, the only Celtic-speaking nation in continental Europe. Closely related to the Celtic peoples of the British Isles, the Bretons are the descendants of fifth-century migrants from southwestern Britain. In their new homeland the Bretons developed an extraordinary wealth of folklore and music. The Bretons are described as being as dreamy and passionate as the Irish,* as whimsical as the Welsh,* yet as hardworking as the Scots.*

The Breton language belongs to the Brythonic branch of the Celtic group of Indo-European languages. The language, spoken in western Brittany but also dispersed in eastern Brittany, is spoken in four distinct dialects, Leonais, Tregorrois, Vannetais, and Cornouaillais. Increasingly, young Bretons are learning the language in schools, and speaking the language in daily life has become a matter of national pride. Developed between the fourth and sixth centuries by Welsh and Cornish exiles fleeing invaders, it differs from the Welsh and Cornish of their homelands in its use of nasals and loanwords from the French. The French language is now the first language of the region, although Breton, predominant in the western departments, is rapidly being reestablished as Brittany's national language.

THE NATION: The Celtic peoples of Britannia, divided by tribal and clan loyalties, developed a remarkable civilization in the islands. Originating on the Western European mainland, the Celts, armed with iron weapons, spread across most of Europe. Western European folklore is derived mainly from the Celts.

Subjugated by the Romans in the first century B.C., the western Celts became an urbanized and, later, a Christian population. The Romans under Julius Caesar invaded the Breton Peninsula in 56 B.C., and it subsequently became the Roman province of Gallia Lugdunensis. The gradual decline of Roman power, leading to the abandonment of Britannia and the withdrawal of the Roman garrisons in A.D. 410, left the island open to invasion. Angles, Saxons, and Jutes, Germanic peoples from Northern Europe, overran the island, driving the Celts into the western peninsulas, Cornwall and Wales, and eventually across the narrow channel to the peninsula called Armorica. Celtic refugees arrived in such numbers in the fifth and sixth centuries that the peninsula became known as Little Britannia, Britannia Minor, and, later, Brittany. The Britons (later called Bretons) gradually converted the native Celts of the peninsula, then mainly pagans, to Christianity.

During the seventh and eighth centuries a number of petty principalities developed in Brittany. These principalities became subject to Charlemagne early in the ninth century, but in 846, led by Nomenè, who had united the clans against invaders, the Bretons revolted against Charlemagne's grandson, Charles the Bald, and won independence. In the latter part of the tenth century the Bretons acknowledged the rule of the Norman dukes. Geoffrey, count of Rennes, proclaimed himself duke of Bretagne in 922. Later, they repulsed incursions by the Normans,* who went on to conquer England in 1066. Threats by the counts of Anjou to the east were also successfully defeated.

The dukedom became, through marriage, a possession of Geoffrey Plantagenet, son of Henry II, king of England, in 1171. In 1196 the duchy passed to Arthur I, who was presumably murdered by the English during an attempt to take control of the duchy. The title was recognized by the French king in 1213, but the extinction of the ruling house led to war. France and England contested control of Brittany, and the two kingdoms backed rival claimants to the ducal title during the War of the Breton Succession, which devastated the peninsula from 1341 to 1365. Long coveted by the French kings, the Bretons maintained their independence for many centuries as the inhabitants of a powerful duchy.

Anne of Brittany, heiress to the duchy in the fifteenth century, was wooed by most of Europe until her marriage to Charles VIII of France in 1491, the basis of later French claims to the duchy. In 1532 the French kingdom took control of Brittany, ending Brittany's golden age and over five centuries of independence. The French kingdom annexed the duchy outright in 1589. Brittany became a French province, one of the last territories incorporated into the French kingdom. The province of Brittany retained considerable autonomy, with its own *parlement* at Rennes from 1590 to the French Revolution in 1789.

An early center of revolutionary activity, the conservative Bretons soon turned against the revolutionary excesses, antireligious doctrines, and the centralization of all political power in Paris. In 1793 the Vendeé uprising spread to most of Brittany, where it became a popular uprising, spurred by Breton nationalism. The immediate causes of the uprising were the banning of religion and the introduction of universal conscription. The uprising, called the War of the Vendeé, continued sporadically until the rebels were decisively routed in 1796. One of the rebel leaders, General Cadonal, executed in 1804 on Napoleon's orders, is considered the first martyr to Breton nationalism.

The Bretons, having lost all administrative and cultural autonomy during the French Revolution and the Napoleonic reorganization of the French state, mobilized to protect their culture and language. The first Breton dictionary, published in 1821, led to a proliferation of poetry, novels, and history written in the Breton language. In 1829 the first pro-autonomy organization was formed, the Association Breton. Fired by the cultural revival and the nationalism of their Celtic cousins, the Irish, the Bretons began to espouse nationalism in the 1870s, the movement starting a reversal of the assimilation pursued by successive French governments. In the 1880s the French government made education compulsory in the French language, and all publications in Breton were banned.

The first avowedly separatist group was formed in 1911, called Strollad Broadel Breiz, advocating severing all ties to the alien French government and the creation of a sovereign Breton state. In spite of German overtures, when World War I began three years later, the Bretons remained loyal to France. Another Breton national hero is France Laurent, a young soldier executed during the war for not obeying an order given in French, a language he did not understand. After the war, at the Paris Peace Conference in 1919, the Bretons presented U.S. president Woodrow Wilson, who advocated self-determination for Europe's minority peoples, a petition signed by over 800 prominent Bretons calling for a sovereign Brittany.

Breton nationalism grew dramatically during the turmoil and economic depression of the 1930s. In 1931 nationalists formed Given Ha Du (Black and White), modeled on the Irish Sinn Fein and named for the national colors. The organization carried out several violent attacks, including the bombing in 1932 of the statue in Rennes commemorating Breton union with France. In 1936 several nationalist groups formed the Front Breton, but as tensions increased in Europe, the French government outlawed the organization as subversive.

The Germans during the World War II occupation of France attempted to use Breton national sentiment by placing the region under separate administration and allowing broad cultural and linguistic rights. In spite of the German concessions, Nazi doctrine held little attraction for the majority of the conservative, devoutly Catholic Bretons. The French Vichy government, allied to the Nazis, separated the area of Nantes and created a separate region over the protests and opposition of the Bretons.

The German concession to Breton-language education, publishing, and broadcasting was immediately withdrawn by the returning French authorities at the end of the war. Some 800 Bretons were shot for supposedly collaborating with the Germans. In 1947 the French minister of education, Marcel Nagelen, decreed, that "the task of teachers in the Breton speaking regions is identical with that of teachers in Algeria: Assimilate the population at any price." Children speaking Breton at school were punished.

The postwar suppression of the Breton language and culture provoked a Breton revival in the 1950s, with a parallel growth of nationalism over the next decade. The revival of the language and culture, including the standardization of Breton grammar, led to a renewed interest among the population. Numerous cultural, nationalist, and separatist groups emerged, the most militant employing violence and terrorism to press their cause of Breton independence. The separatist organizations, often employing terrorist tactics, found willing recruits among the young.

In the 1970s, as the Breton region continued to decline, not sharing in the postwar French boom, many young Bretons were forced to leave the region to find work. Among the general population young, urban, French-speaking Bretons began to embrace the language as the first language of the family. The Bretonization of French-speaking Bretons became fashionable. In the late 1970s the emigration from the region began to reverse as many young Bretons refused to leave their homeland. The 1976 census showed more Bretons returning than leaving for the first time in the twentieth century. In 1977 the French government officially adopted a policy of recognition and tolerance of the Breton language.

Formerly a region of rural subsistence farming, Brittany emerged as a major industrial and food-exporting region in the 1970s as trade increased with Britain and Ireland following their inclusion in the European Community in 1973. By 1975 only 21% of the Bretons were engaged in agriculture.

The activities of a number of Breton separatist organizations increased during the 1970s, including the bombing of historic Versailles Palace near Paris. Several of the organizations, socialist- and Marxist-oriented, received military training by the Irish Republican Army (IRA). The largest of the groups, the Breton Republican Army (BRA) and the Breton Liberation Front (BLF), often included government functionaries and Catholic priests.

In 1981, 2.5 million people claimed Breton nationality in France. The decentralization of the French government, beginning the same year, returned some powers to local authorities, including powers the Bretons had not exercised since the twelfth century. However, the creation of regions loosely based on the historic provinces gave rise to yet another Breton nationalist grievance. The Nantes region, historically an integral part of Brittany, became part of a neighboring region, its separation loudly denounced by Bretons. By the mid-1980s most of the Breton nationalists had renounced violence.

In 1987 the effort to rescue the Breton language from extinction accelerated. After several generations of Bretons were punished for speaking their native language, younger Bretons took up the struggle to save Breton as the spoken language of the Breton nation. The French government finally allowed bilingual road signs and commercial advertising. An estimated 600,000 of the 2.7 million Bretons in 1988 spoke Breton as their first language.

In the 1980s and 1990s ecology, economy, and linguistic concerns have become nationalist issues. The nonviolent Breton nationalists have wide support for their campaign to win greater autonomy for a reunited Brittany. Resurgent Breton nationalism, supported by a network of flourishing language schools, cultural centers, and the Breton media, remains a potent force in the region. The Bretons, having won the struggle to save their nation from extinction, now focus on finding a place for Brittany within united Europe.

The Breton revival received a new blow in July 1999, when the French government rejected the European Union (EU) directives on the wider use of local languages. However, the inauguration of the first all-Breton television channel in March 2000 somewhat offset the government's refusal to support spoken languages other than the state's official French language. The new television channel became part of the wider Celtic celebration held in Lorient, in southern Brittany, in August 1999. The Celtic festival, attended by over 400,000 in 1999, has become one of Europe's largest and most popular events.

SELECTED BIBLIOGRAPHY

Barbour, Phillipe. *Brittany.* 1998.

Brustein, William. *The Social Origins of Political Regionalism: France 1849–1981.* 1982.

Ford, Caroline. *Creating the Nation in Provincial France: Religion and Political Identity in Brittany.* 1993.

Gallioui, Patrick, and Michael Jones. *The Bretons.* 1991.

Morris, Elisabeth. *Brittany.* 1993.

BULGARIANS

Bulgars; Bulgar Slavs

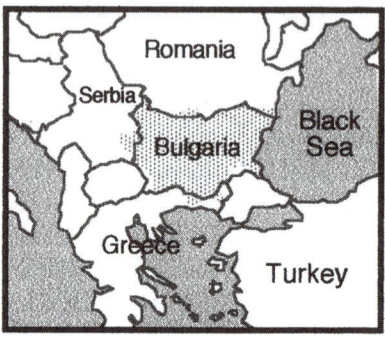

POPULATION: Approximately (2000 e) 8,520,000 Bulgarians in Europe, 7,230,000 in Bulgaria, with smaller numbers in Yugoslavia, Romania, Moldova, Ukraine, Turkey, and Russia.

THE BULGARIAN HOMELAND: The Bulgarian homeland consists of plateaus, plains, and river valleys divided by mountains, which cover more than half the national territory. In the north the Danubian Plain rises to the Balkan Mountains, locally called the Stara Planina. To the south the Thracian Plain and the Maritsa River valley are enclosed by the Rhodope and Strandzha Mountains. To the east lies the Black Sea. The chief rivers are the Danube, which forms the northern border of Bulgaria, and the Maritsa, which flows east into Turkey. The Struma and Mesta in the southwest flow into Greece. Forests cover some 35% of the homeland, with more than half under cultivation or used as pasture. In the north the region is flat plains suitable for crops, with alpine meadows and forested mountains in the center of the country. In the south, with its Mediterranean-like climate, crops and plants are similar to those of Greece or Turkey.

The Bulgarian homeland has formed an independent state since 1908. *Republic of Bulgaria*. 42,822 sq.mi.–110,910 sq.km. (2000 e) 8,483,000—Bulgarians 86%, Turks* 8%, Roms* (Gypsies) 3%, Macedonians* 2%. The Bulgarian capital and major cultural center, Sofia, Sofiya in the Bulgarian language, (2000 e) 1,241,000, has been the capital of Bulgaria since 1879.

FLAG: The Bulgarian national flag, the official flag of the Bulgarian republic, is a horizontal tricolor of white, green, and red.

PEOPLE: The Bulgarians are a South Slav nation, historically incorporating early Slav and Turkic peoples. Thought to have originated in the Volga River basin of European Russia, the Bulgars had a long history before mingling with the Slav inhabitants of the region they conquered after crossing the Danube. The fusion of the two peoples is the basis of the unique Bulgar culture. Formerly a majority rural people, the Bulgars increasingly urbanized after World War II, and in the late 1990s over 70% of the Bulgarians live in urban areas.

The language of the Bulgarians is classified as a South Slav language and is one of the oldest written languages in Europe. Together with the language of the Macedonians, it forms the eastern branch of the South Slavic branch of the Slavic language group. The language, written in the Cyrillic alphabet, developed from early Bulgarian, which influenced all the oldest Slavic languages, especially Russian, in the early Middle Ages. Modern Bulgarian came into use in the fifteenth century, but the modern literary language, which is quite different from Old Bulgarian, was adopted only during the nineteenth century. Modern Bulgarian's two major dialect groups are the eastern and western dialects, each subdivided into north and south varieties. The modern literary language is based on the northeastern Bulgarian dialects. The language has many borrowings from Greek, old Slavonic, Turkish, and Russian. Since World War II, many West European words were adopted, especially those connected with technology.

The Bulgarians are overwhelmingly Orthodox Christians, an estimated 90% adhering to the Bulgarian Orthodox Church in the late 1990s. Orthodox monasteries played a large part in preserving the Bulgarian identity during the centuries of Muslim Turkish domination. A minority, called Pomaks, are Bulgarian in speech and culture but were converted to Islam during the Ottoman domination of the region.

NATION: Before the Christian Era, Greeks colonized the coastal regions, and Romans eventually conquered the regions known as Thrace and Moesia. The Greeks and Romans left substantial imprints on the culture of the inhabitants of the region. Overrun by Asian tribes, many of the inhabitants of the region around the Sea of Azov fled north to the eastern European Plain, where they came under the rule of the Huns. In the middle of the fifth century, after the death of Atilla, the great Hun Empire disintegrated, and several Turkic kingdoms emerged, including a kingdom called the kingdom of Great Bulgaria. This kingdom broke up following the death of its ruler, Kubrat Han, and the Bulgars became two separate groups. One group, led by the khan's youngest son, Asparuh Han, moved west and mixed extensively with the migrating Slavic tribes.

The Slavic and Turkic tribes settled in the Balkan Peninsula between about the fourth and sixth centuries A.D. One branch of the people known as Bulgars, who had established a large state near the Volga River on the east side of the Black Sea, invaded the Balkan Peninsula in the seventh century. The Bulgars, a Ural-Altaic people of mixed Turkic stock (the name "Bulgar" derives from an old Turkic word meaning "of mixed nationality"), settled in the northern Balkan Peninsula and adopted much of the Slavic culture of the more numerous, defeated Slavs who had settled the region a century before.

The western Bulgars established the Bulgarian kingdom in A.D. 681, the first organized state in the Balkans. They set up a state between the Danube River and the Balkan Mountains, an area that was then claimed by the Byzantine Empire. Byzantine armies failed repeatedly to dislodge the invaders during the eighth and early ninth centuries. By the end of the ninth century the Bulgarians had annexed considerable additional territory and laid the foundations for a strong state under Khan Krum, who reigned from 803 to 814. In 809 the Bulgarians captured Sofia from the Byzantines. The Krum armies inflicted a devastating defeat on an invading Byzantine force in 811 and, assuming the offensive, nearly succeeded in 813 in taking Constantinople, the capital of the Byzantine Empire. The Bulgarian defeat of Byzantine forces in 811 allowed the Bulgarian state to expand its territory eastward to the Black Sea, south to include Macedonia, and northwest to present-day Belgrade. The Bulgarians withdrew from central Byzantium only after receiving promises of yearly tribute.

By the ninth century the Bulgars had fully merged with the Slavs, including adopting the Slavs' language. An area of intense rivalry between Byzantium and Rome, in 865 King Boris accepted baptism, and soon after, the Bulgars joined the Greek Orthodox Church of Constantinople. The Bulgars consolidated a distinct Christian, Slavic culture that expanded and grew powerful. The first Bulgarian Empire reached its height under Simeon the Great, who ruled between 893 and 927 and took the title tsar. A brilliant administrator and military leader, Simeon introduced Byzantine Greek culture into his kingdom, encouraged education, expanded Bulgaria's border, defeated the Hungarians, and conducted a series of successful wars against the Byzantines.

In the tenth century the Bulgarian state fell to attacks by a reinvigorated Byzantium and in 1018 was annexed by Emperor Basil II. In the twelfth century Byzantine power in the region was weakened by invasions of migrating tribes, the Petchenegs and Cumans. Led by noble brothers, Asen and Peter, the Bulgarians revolted against Byzantine rule in 1185, and in 1186 the second Bulgarian Empire was established when Ivan I was crowned tsar. The powerful empire under Ivan II extended its authority over most of the Balkan Peninsula, except Greece, but it soon collapsed, and in 1330 Bulgaria became a tributary to Serbia.

The Bulgars, weakened by Serbian domination and internal strife, were unable to resist the powerful Ottoman Turks, who moved north to conquer the Balkan territories. Following the Battles of Kosovo, in 1389, and Nikopol, in 1396, the Turks turned on Byzantium. In 1453 the Ottoman Turks captured Constantinople, and soon the entire Bulgarian homeland was absorbed into the Ottoman Empire. Four centuries of Muslim Turkish rule, oppressive and anti-Christian, sparked repeated rebellions and uprisings in the region.

By the eighteenth century the Ottoman Empire's hold on the Balkans had weakened, allowing a Bulgarian cultural revival. In the next century Western political ideas gradually combined with the reborn national consciousness to form a strong Bulgarian separatist movement. The movement was complicated by internal frictions over aims and methods and the attitudes of the major European powers toward Bulgaria.

Between 1864 and 1869 the administration of Midhat Pasha briefly made Bulgaria the Ottoman Empire's model province, but a just administration had come too late; Bulgarian nationalism was already a strong force in the region. The national movement, supported by Russia, the self-proclaimed protector of the Slavic nations, gained widespread support.

In 1876 a premature uprising, led by Stefan Stambulov, broke out in the region. The subsequent Turkish reprisals, called the Bulgarian massacres or atrocities, during which over 30,000 men, women, and children were killed, served as an excuse for Russian intervention and expansion toward the Mediterranean. The Russo-Turkish War, 1877–78, was ended by the Treaty of San Stefano, which created a large Bulgarian state under Russian protection. To avert the expansion of Russian influence in the region, a European congress was called to revise the treaty. The Congress of Berlin made northern Bulgaria a tributary principality under nominal Turkish rule, while southern Bulgaria, called Eastern Rumelia, and Macedonia, claimed as Bulgarian territory, remained under direct Ottoman rule.

Between 1878 and full independence in 1908, Bulgaria passed through a period of peaceful modernization with expansion in industry, science, education, and the arts. However, modernization and industrialization sowed the seeds of class conflict, nurturing strong socialist and agrarian opposition parties in the decades that followed independence.

Alexander of Battenberg, elected the first prince of Bulgaria, bowing to popular pressure, annexed Eastern Rumelia in 1885. His successor, Prince Ferdinand of Saxe-Coburg-Gotha, taking advantage of the revolution that shook the Ottoman Empire in 1908, declared Bulgaria independent with himself as tsar. Irredentist claims to territories with large Bulgarian populations still under Turkish rule continued to fire Bulgarian nationalist aspirations. The issue of the Turkish territories inhabited by the Macedonians, claimed by the Bulgarians as ethnic kin, became an important nationalist issue. The "Macedonian Question," rival claims by Bulgaria, Greece, and Serbia, hovered over European relations from 1878 to World War I.

The outbreak of the Italo-Turkish War for the possession of North African territories in 1911 encouraged the Balkan states to try to increase their national territories at the expense of the tottering Ottoman Empire. In 1912 the Bulgarian government formed an alliance with neighboring Serbia. In a secret protocol, brokered by Russia, the allies agreed to joint military action and the division of prospective conquests. The outbreak of the first Balkan War in October 1912, with Greece and Montenegro joining the allies, was followed by the rapid expulsion of Turkish troops from all of the European territories except the Constantinople area. The Bulgarians received extensive territories in Thrace and Macedonia.

The Serbians, denied access to the Adriatic Sea by the Great Powers' support for an independent Albania, demanded of Bulgaria a greater share of the Macedonian territories. The Bulgarians refused and launched an attack on Serbia, only to be attacked in turn by the armies of Serbia, Greece, Romania, and Ottoman Turkey. The humiliating Bulgarian defeat in the second Balkan War led to the loss of the recent gains as each enemy state took territory, again reducing the Bulgarian state almost to its prewar borders. The Bulgarians' territorial aspirations added to the war fever that eventually engulfed Europe and much of the world.

Hoping to recover lost territories in Macedonia, in 1915 the Bulgarians entered World War I on the side of Austria-Hungary and Germany. At first victorious, the Bulgarians occupied large parts of the Balkan Peninsula, but by 1917 the tide of war had turned. At the end of the war in 1918, Bulgaria again lost territory, including its outlet to the Aegean Sea to Greece and most of its Macedonian territories to Yugoslavia.

After the war an agrarian reform government, led by Aleksandur Stamboliski, failed to unite the country. In 1923 the military took control, leading to a series of unstable factions and forms of government that severely hampered Bulgaria's development. In 1935 King Boris II established a personal dictatorship.

The Bulgarian government saw an opportunity to finally satisfy its territorial aspirations when war again broke out in Europe in 1939. In 1940 the Axis powers forced Romania to return territory taken in 1913, and in 1941 Bulgaria became a full member of the Axis alliance. Bulgarian troops occupied the Macedonian and adjoining territories of Yugoslavia and Greece, while the Bulgarian government declared war on Great Britain and the United States, but not on the Soviet Union. On the mysterious death of Boris III in 1943, the infant Simeon II succeeded to the Bulgarian throne.

With defeat looming for the Axis, the Soviet Union in 1944 declared war on Bulgaria and Soviet troops overran the country. Pro-Soviet opposition forces seized control of the government, and prewar boundaries were restored. A coalition government, after only a short period of rule, was overthrown, and a communist government installed. In 1946 Bulgaria was proclaimed a socialist republic. Industry was nationalized and farming collectivized, with resistance ruthlessly eliminated. All political parties, except the communists and their allies, were outlawed in 1948. The restriction of human rights and close adherence to Soviet Cold War policy marked the 1950s and 1960s. During the entire Cold War era, Bulgaria was the closest East European imitator of Soviet internal and foreign policy.

Until 1947 Bulgaria was predominantly agricultural, with virtually no heavy industry. The new communist government nationalized all industrial enterprises and operated under a series of five-year economic plans, modeled after the Soviet system, with financial aid from the USSR. Heavy industry was the government's highest priority. For a time in the 1950s and 1960s the Bulgarians enjoyed one of the most prosperous economies of the Soviet bloc. Under the leadership of Todor Zhivkov, secretary of the Communist Party from 1954, the country's premier from 1964 to 1971, and head of state from 1971 to late 1989, the Bulgarians suffered under one of the most restrictive regimes in Europe.

Tensions between Bulgarian nationalists and the large Turkish minority led to violence and the emigration of thousands of Turks during the 1980s. Others were forced to change family names to Bulgarian names and to adopt Bulgarian traditions. Pomaks, ethnic Bulgarian Muslims, were denied visas or physically restrained when they tried to join the exodus of Muslims to Turkey.

In the late 1980s reforms in the Soviet Union pushed Bulgaria's government to introduce a multiparty political system in 1990. A noncommunist government was elected in 1991 in the first free elections in forty-four years. Since 1991 the Bulgarians have faced severe problems in trying to reform the old communist command economy into a modern economy based on private enterprise. The economy continued to deteriorate, and in late 1996 the country entered a deep economic crisis, with near-hyperinflation and a rash of bankruptcies in the banking system.

In mid-1997 a newly elected pro-reform government undertook measures to stabilize the economy and to fight the deep-seated corruption prevalent in many of the country's large enterprises. The new government, with the widespread support of the population, has begun to break up the conglomerates that dominated Bulgaria's postcommunist economy. The government from January 1999 pegged the currency to the euro, further strengthening economic ties between the Bulgarian state and the European Union.

SELECTED BIBLIOGRAPHY

Atanasoff, Christ. *The Bulgarians.* 1977.

Crampton, R. J. *A Concise History of Bulgaria.* 1997

Hall, Richard C. *Bulgaria's Road to the First World War.* 1996.

Melone, Albert P. *Creating Parliamentary Government: The Transition to Democracy in Bulgaria.* 1998.

Wentwick, Andrew. *Bulgaria.* 1998.

BURGUNDIANS

Bourgignons; Bourgognes

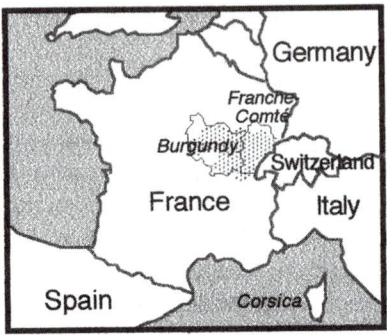

POPULATION: Approximately (2000 e) 2,582,000 Burgundians in Europe, 2,377,000 in the historic region of Burgundy, and with smaller communities in Paris and other parts of France and in Switzerland.

THE BURGUNDIAN HOMELAND: The Burgundian homeland lies in east-central France, a mostly hilly region around the valleys of the Saône and the Rhône, which forms the southern boundary of the historic region. In the east the land rises to the Jura Mountains, which form the international frontier between France and Switzerland, and in the north are the Vosges Mountains. The mountainous districts have dense pine forests and extensive grazing lands. A rich agricultural area, Burgundy is especially famous for wines of the Chablis region, the uplands of the Côte d'Or, and the valleys of the Saône and Rhône River valleys.

The historic region of Burgundy comprises six French departments divided among three planning regions: the department of Ain, which forms part of the Rhône-Alpes region, Doubs, Haute-Saône, and Jura of the Franche-Comté region, and Côte d'Or, Saône-et-Loire, and part of Yonne departments of the present Bourgogne region. 14,929 sq.mi.–38,666 sq.km. (2000 e) 2,502,000—Burgundians 91%, Swiss* (Romands*) 3%, other French.* The Burgundian capital and major cultural center is Dijon, (2000 e) 152,000, the historic capital of Burgundy. Other important Burgundian cultural centers are Besançon, (2000 e) 118,000, the historic capital of Franche-Comté or the Free County of Burgundy.

FLAG: The Burgundian national flag, the flag of the region of Burgundy, has blue and yellow diagonal stripes within a border of red.

PEOPLE: The Burgundians are a French nation, the descendants of the early

Germanic Burgundii who occupied the region in the fifth century A.D. The culture of the region, more oriented to Dijon and Geneva than to Paris, retains many traditions and customs unique to the Burgundians. Poverty and unequal land distribution forced many Burgundians to leave their homeland for Paris or other parts of France in the nineteenth and early twentieth centuries. Over the centuries the boundaries of the Burgundian homeland have changed greatly, but the Burgundians retain a sense of identity that transcends political borders.

The Germanic Burgundian language died out long ago, and the modern Burgundians speak standard French along with two regional dialects, Bourgignon and Franc-Comtois, which differ considerably from the spoken French of Paris. The Burgundian dialects are further divided into a number of subdialects that mostly reflect the boundaries of the regional departments.

NATION: Originally occupied by various Celtic tribes, the region came under Roman rule following the Gallic Wars of Julius Caesar in the first century B.C. Under Roman rule the region prospered, and the city of Autun evolved as a major Roman cultural center. In the fourth century Roman power collapsed, and the region was overrun by invading Germanic tribes.

In 480 the Germanic Burgundii conquered the region and expelled the other Germanic peoples. Mixing with the Romanized population, the Burgundii accepted Christianity, established their *Lex Burgundionum*, and established the first kingdom of Burgundy. At its height, the Burgundian kingdom included most of southeastern France and western Switzerland.

The Franks conquered the Burgundian kingdom in 534 and annexed the region to the growing Frankish kingdom. Throughout the Mergovingian period Burgundy was subject to numerous partitions, although Burgundy survived as a political concept. At Charlemagne's death the Frankish empire was divided among his heirs, and two new Burgundian kingdoms were founded, Cisjurane Burgundy, or Provence, and Transjurane Burgundy in the north. In 933 the two kingdoms were united in the Second Kingdom of Burgundy, also called the Kingdom of Arles. A smaller area, roughly equivalent to present Burgundy, was created as a separate duchy of Burgundy by the Holy Roman Emperor Charles II in 877.

The golden age of Burgundy began in 1364, when John II of France gave Burgundy to his son, Philip the Bold, as a fief, beginning the Valois-Bourgogne dynasty. Philip and his successors, by conquest, treaty, or marriage, acquired vast territories, including most of the present Netherlands, Belgium, Luxembourg, and extensive regions in France and southwestern Germany.

In the fifteenth century, the Burgundians, through their partisans in France, dominated French politics. At that time Burgundy was the greatest European power and dominated the continent in trade, industry, and agriculture. The Burgundian court was a center of European culture and art.

The wars of the ambitious Charles the Bold proved ruinous for the Burgundians. Opposed by the French and the Swiss, the Burgundians were defeated in several major battles in 1476–77, and Charles was killed. His daughter, Mary of Burgundy, married Emperor Maximilian I, bringing most of the Burgundian territories, excluding the original French duchy, under Hapsburg rule. The duchy of Burgundy was seized and annexed to France. Although divided between two empires, the Burgundians maintained their distinct identity and culture, which ignored the political frontiers that traversed their homeland.

In 1556 the Burgundian territories of the Holy Roman Empire came under the control of the Spanish Hapsburgs. Although some of the region's fortified towns were occupied by the French during the sixteenth-century wars of religion, the area was devastated by both Catholic and Protestant forces. In 1668 the French conquered the region of Franche-Comté, also called the Free County of Burgundy, and in 1674 finally obtained its cession from the Spaniards.*

The two Burgundian regions, Burgundy and Franche-Comté, remained French provinces with regional *parlements* until the French Revolution. In 1790 the regions were dissolved and replaced by departments in an effort to eliminate the strong regionalist feelings that permeated the French regions. All political and bureaucratic functions were centralized in Paris, ending centuries of autonomous rule in the Burgundian regions. Under Napoleon the government gave land tenure to the peasants and encouraged the growth of a middle class. Regionalist sentiment gave way to enthusiastic support for Napoleon's dream of a united Europe under French domination, but with Napoleon's final defeat regionalist sentiment again became a strong feature of local Burgundian society.

In the late nineteenth century the construction of railroads and better transportation ended the relative isolation of the Burgundians. Limited opportunities in their homeland drove the brightest and most talented to Paris, where all power in France was centralized. Resentment of the need to leave their homeland to succeed in the arts, professions, or academic life raised resentments and fed a growing regionalist movement demanding greater say over decisions involving the Burgundian homeland. After World War I, the economic decline that set up in 1918 accelerated, with young Burgundians forced to move to other, more prosperous parts of France.

In the 1930s radical political groups gained followings in the region, which reflected the chaotic situation in France. Populist regional leaders were opposed by conservative groups intent on maintaining France's centralized government. In the late 1930s opposition to the growing power of Nazi Germany united the Burgundians behind the French government. In May-June 1940 the French government was ignominiously defeated by the invading forces of Nazi Germany. The Burgundians, under German occupation, were among the most active in the resistance, using the rugged area in eastern Burgundy to maintain contacts with exile and anti-Nazi groups based in neutral Switzerland.

Burgundian identity had nearly disappeared when student demonstrations against France's outdated educational system triggered widespread unrest among striking workers and farmers. In Dijon and other Burgundian cities the traditional Burgundian flag was displayed during demonstrations and marches and on barricades in the late 1960s. Regionalist sentiment, spurred by anger at France's overly centralized and inefficient central government, grew throughout the 1970s.

A socialist government, elected in 1981, devolved some limited powers to the reconstituted French regions, including Burgundy and Franche Comté. Demands for the unification of the historic Burgundian territories were ignored. In the 1980s and 1990s the Burgundians have championed greater European integration with its possibility of regaining their historical identity within a Europe no longer dominated by the outdated nation-states of the nineteenth century.

SELECTED BIBLIOGRAPHY

Coates, Clive. *Burgundy.* 1997.

Cobban, Alfred. *A History of Modern France.* 1967.

Hanson, Anthony. *Burgundy.* 1995.

Markoff, John. *The Abolition of Feudalism: Peasants, Lords, and Legislators in the French Revolution.* 1996.

Price, Roger. *A Concise History of France.* 1993.

CANARIANS

Canarios; Canary Islanders

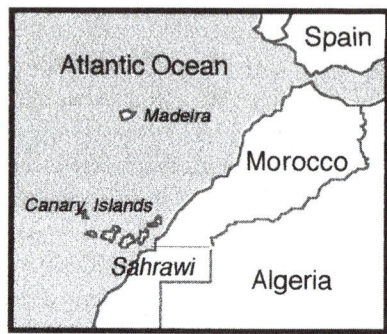

POPULATION: Approximately (2000 e) 1,750,000 Canarians in Europe, the majority in the Canary Islands, but with substantial numbers living in mainland Spain. Outside Europe there are sizable Canarian communities in Latin America and in the American state of Louisiana.

THE CANARIAN HOMELAND: The Canarian homeland, the Canary Islands, is an archipelago of thirteen islands, that lies just off the coast of southern Morocco, 823 miles (1,324 km.) southwest of the Spanish mainland. The islands constitute an autonomous region of Spain and are divided into two provinces, Santa Cruz de Tenerife, which comprises Tenerife, La Palma, Gomera, and Hierro, and Las Palmas, with Grand Canary, Fuenteventura, Lanzarote, Alegranza, Graciosa, and Isla de Lobos. The last three islands are uninhabited.

The islands are of volcanic origin and are mostly mountainous with some fertile valleys. The proximity to Africa has greatly influenced the flora of the islands, which has both African and Mediterranean strains. Farming and fishing are the principal industries. The volcanic soil of the Canaries is extremely fertile, and the islands are a major source of winter vegetables and tropical fruits. The islands have no rivers, however, and severe droughts are common; artificial irrigation is therefore a necessity in most cultivable areas. Tourism is also important, and the islands are a popular winter resort area.

The Canary Islands have formed an autonomous region of the Kingdom of Spain since 1983. *Autonomous Region of the Canary Islands (Islas Canarias)*. 2,796 sq.mi.–7,242 sq.km. (2000 e) 1,463,000—Canarian 90%, other Spanish,* other European. The capitals and a major cultural centers of the islands are Santa Cruz de Tenerife, on Tenerife, (2000 e) 192,000, and the island's major port, Las Palmas de Gran Canaria, on Grand Canary, (2000 e) 338,000.

FLAG: The Canarian national flag, the official flag of the autonomous region, is a vertical tricolor of white, pale blue, and yellow. The same white, pale blue, and yellow flag, with the addition of seven green stars on the center stripe, is the flag of the largest nationalist organization, the Movement for the Autonomy and Independence of the Canary Archipelago (MAIAC).

PEOPLE: The Canarians, mostly descendants of colonists from mainland Spain in the fifteenth century, can mostly trace their roots to Andalusia. Among rural Canarians there is a high incidence of fair hair and fair eyes, considered a holdover from the archipelago's original Berber inhabitants. The Canarians often refer to people from the Spanish mainland as Goths.

Isolated from the Spanish mainland, the islanders developed a distinctive culture, including a separate dialect called Canario, which some experts consider a subdialect of the Andalusian dialect of Spanish. Over the centuries many Canarians settled in Latin America, and the lilting Canarian dialect is very similar to that spoken in Cuba and elsewhere in the Caribbean. In the New World, the Canarian dialect became known as Isleno. The Canarians, considered the most conservative of the Spanish peoples, are overwhelmingly Roman Catholic.

NATION: The islands, thought to mark the western limit of the world in ancient times, received their name from the Latin word for dog, *canis*, due to the fierce dogs encountered in the islands by ancient maritime peoples. Known as the Fortunate Islands, the archipelago was known to the ancient peoples of the Mediterranean.

Fair Berbers from North Africa, the Guanche, believed to have arrived in the islands with Phoenician colonists from ancient Carthage, were transported as workers or slaves. The Guanche regressed to a tribal existence when contact with the mainland ceased following the Roman destruction of Carthage in 146 B.C. The Roman writer Pliny mentions an expedition to the islands around 40 B.C. Later, Arabs and Europeans occasionally visited the islands, but they were mostly ignored.

Virtually forgotten as Europe entered the Dark Ages, the Portuguese rediscovered and claimed the islands in 1341. Repulsed by the fierce Guanche warriors, the Portuguese abandoned efforts to colonize the islands. In 1344 a papal bull awarded the islands to the Spanish kingdom of Castile. In 1402 a Norman adventurer, Jean de Betencourt, supported by Castile, took control of Lanzarote. Two years later he proclaimed himself king of the islands.

The object of a Portuguese expedition in 1425, the islands were again confirmed as Castilian territory by papal decree in 1479. Colonists from Andalusia, newly reconquered from the Moors, settled the islands. By the Treaty of Alcacovas, signed in 1480, the Portuguese government recognized the islands as Spanish territory. In 1496 the Berber Guanches were conquered, and Spanish authority was extended to all the islands. The Guanches, either assimilated or exterminated, soon disappeared completely from the islands.

The islands became an important station on the sea routes that the Spanish established to the New World in the early 1500s. Often attacked by pirates and privateers preying on Spanish shipping, the islands remained remote and isolated from mainland Spain. Sailing for England, Sir Francis Drake attacked the Canarian port towns in 1595, followed by a Dutch attack in 1599.

From the seventeenth century, the islanders supplied wine in exchange for fish brought by New England sailors, a trade that sustained the islands following the establishment of more direct sea routes to Spain's American colonies. The Spanish government lost interest in the islands following the independence in the early nineteenth century of the majority of Spain's colonies in the New World.

Neglected by the Spanish government, only locally produced wine provided the islanders with incomes until grape blight ruined the vineyards in 1853. The Canarian vineyards were replaced by cocinal until aniline dyes came into use. Sugarcane then replaced cocinal as the islands' economic mainstay. Unable to rely on the Spanish government, the Canarian culture and way of life developed a strong tradition of self-sufficiency little affected by the trends and influences of the Spanish mainland.

In the early 1900s a sense of their distinctive culture and lifestyle was born amid agitation for an end to their humiliating colonial status. On 21 September 1927 the islands were formally incorporated into the Spanish state. Provincial status, a disappointment to the Canarians, did little to alleviate the problems created by centuries of neglect and underdevelopment.

Francisco Franco, sent to the islands as captain-general in 1932, greatly resented his posting to the remote province, virtual exile for an ambitious officer. Franco's indignation influenced his later decision to lead the Spanish fascists in revolt and civil war.

The islands, virtually unaffected by the civil war that swept mainland Spain from 1936 to 1939, remained remote and isolated. The Canarians began to think of their islands as separate from mainland Spain. During the 1950s the idea of a Canarian identity grew with increased education and the growth of nationalism in nearby Morocco. Tourism, beginning at the same time, brought much needed income and development and gradually ended the islands' insularity.

In the 1960s, as national liberation swept the rest of Africa, a national movement formed among the Canarians, claiming that the Spanish government continued to treat the islands as a colony. In the late 1960s several small groups formed demanding autonomy for the islands but were soon outlawed by the dictatorial Franco government. Several of the small groups combined to form the first avowedly separatist organization, the Movement for the Autonomy and Independence of the Canary Archipelago (MAIAC). The MAIAC was recognized as a legitimate African liberation movement by the Organization of African Unity (OAU) in 1968. Considered by the OAU as an African territory still under foreign rule, many African states and organizations championed the decolonization and independence of the islands. In 1975 the MAIAC announced Libyan support after its secretary-general, Antonio Cubillo, paid a visit to Tripoli. The MAIAC increasingly turned to terrorism to win independence for the islands.

A MAIAC separatist bombing at Las Palmas Airport on Grand Canary Island on 27 March 1977 forced a Pan American 747, en route from Los Angeles and New York, to divert to the overcrowded Los Rodeos Airport on Tenerife. A runway collision between the American jet and a Dutch 747 resulted in the deaths of 583 people, the worst disaster in aviation history. The disaster horrified the Canarians and caused a dramatic loss of support for the separatists.

Democracy returned to Spain at Franco's death in 1975, allowing the formation of regional, even openly nationalist political parties. In 1979 the Canarians elected an openly separatist deputy to represent them in the new democratic legislature in Madrid. Granted autonomy in 1983, the islands have experienced a rapid development of a territorial identity and a resurgence of national sentiment as the memories of the 1977 disaster faded. In 1982 the OAU again claimed the islands as an African territory still under foreign colonization.

Spain's entry into the European Economic Community in 1986 raised new issues, as the islanders feel they suffer for decisions made far away in Brussels, while their concerns must be channeled through an often unsympathetic national government in Madrid. Nationalists, with increasing support, advocate independence and bilateral ties to both Spain and the European federation. Supported by the income from over 1 million tourists a year, the Canarians became increasingly assured and less willing to accept decisions made far from their islands.

The Canarians experienced a resurgence of culture and national pride during the 1980s and have become increasingly more assertive in protecting their culture, dialect, and the fragile environment of their islands. In a further move to reclaim a separate Canarian culture, the regional parliament in April 1991 outlawed bullfights, the cruel and cherished symbol of mainland Spanish culture.

Moderate, pro-autonomy politicians have won support in the islands, and Canarian nationalist parties have become important partners in national coalition governments in Madrid. Canarian participation in the Spanish government in the 1990s has eased the calls for greater autonomy or independence.

SELECTED BIBLIOGRAPHY
Gravette, Andy. *Canary Islands.* 1996.
Lenning, Camille. *Notes from the Canary Islands.* 1996.
Mercer, John. *The Canary Islands: Their Prehistory, Conquest, and Survival.* 1994.
Stone, Olivia M. *Tenerife and Its Six Satellites, or the Canary Islands Past and Present.* 1976.
Yeoward, W. *Canary Islands.* 1981.

CARPATHO-RUSYNS

Carpatho-Russians; Carpatho-
Ukrainians; Ruthenians; Ruthenes;
Rusyns; Rusnaks; Lemkos;
Uhro-Rusyns

POPULATION: Approximately (2000 e) 1,500,000 Carpatho-Rusyns in Europe, the majority, 1,200,000 in Ukraine, and another 130,000 in Slovakia and 80,000, called Lemkos or Lemkians, in Poland. There are smaller numbers in Romania, Yugoslavia, Hungary, the Czech Republic, and Croatia. One Carpatho-Rusyn nationalist group claims a national population of some 5 million in Central and Eastern Europe. Outside Europe the largest Carpatho-Rusyn populations live in the United States, Canada, and Australia.

THE CARPATHO-RUSYN HOMELAND: The Carpatho-Rusyn homeland, Carpathian Rus', historically called Ruthenia, Carpatho-Ukraine, or Subcarpathian Rus', lies in the heart of Europe, along the northern and southern slopes of the Carpathian Mountains where the borders of Ukraine, Slovakia, and Poland meet. The Carpatho-Rusyn heartland, historically known as Subcarpathian Rus' or Carpathian Rus', lies in southwestern Ukraine, occupying part of the Carpathian Mountains with long, fertile valleys leading into Slovakia. The mountainous region is heavily forested, with most Carpatho-Rusyns engaged in industries connected with forest products. In the limited area available for cultivation, wheat, rye, oats, and tobacco are grown.

Three-quarters of the Carpatho-Rusyns in Europe live within the borders of Zakarpats'ka Oblast of the Ukraine, the historic heartland of the region. In Slovakia the Carpatho-Rusyns live in the Presov region of Eastern Slovakia Province. On the northern slopes of the Carpathians, the Carpatho-Rusyns had traditionally lived in southeastern Poland, a region known as the Lemko Region but now called Beskid Niski. After World War II, the Lemko Rusyns were deported from the Carpathians to Silesia in western Poland or the northern Polish provinces. Several thousand have returned to their homeland, but the majority of the Lemkians remain scattered around Poland. There are several Carpatho-Rusyn towns just south of the Tisza River, in the Maramures region of Romania, and a few villages in northeastern Hungary.

Outside the historic homeland, Carpatho-Rusyns live in the Vojvodina region of Yugoslavia and the Syrmia (Srem) region of Croatia. In the Czech Republic, Carpatho-Rusyns are concentrated in northern Moravia and in Prague, where many fled just after World War II. The largest community outside the homeland is in the United States, to which, between the 1880s and 1914, some 225,000 Carpatho-Rusyns emigrated. Smaller numbers of Carpatho-Rusyns immigrated to Canada and Argentina in the 1920s and to Australia in the 1970s and 1980s.

Most of the region forms an oblast or province of Ukraine. *Zakarpats'ka Oblast (Transcarpathia).* 4,942 sq.mi.–12,803 sq.km. (2000 e) 1,273,000— Carpatho-Rusyns 69%, Hungarians* 14%, Ukrainians* 9%, Slovaks* 8%, Romanians,* Russians,* Germans.* The Carpatho-Rusyn capital and cultural center, Uzhgorod, called Uzhorod in Ukrainian, (2000 e) 126,000, is situated on a tributary of the upper Tisza River.

FLAG: The Carpatho-Rusyn national flag, the flag of the national movement, is a horizontal tricolor of red, white, and blue. The flag of the Lemko Rusyns is a horizontal tricolor of pale blue, yellow, and green. There is also in use a horizontal bicolor of pale blue over yellow emblazoned with the Carpathian bear symbol.

PEOPLE: The Carpatho-Rusyns are believed to have descended from Slavic migrants who settled the region in the fifth and sixth centuries. The name "Rusyn," an early designation for all East Slavs, persisted in the isolated valleys of the Carpathians. A long tradition of not mixing with neighboring peoples has safeguarded the unique Carpatho-Rusyn culture and dialect.

The separate Carpatho-Rusyn Greek Catholic (Uniate) Church is closely identified with Carpatho-Rusyn culture and national sentiment. Like their language and culture, the Carpatho-Rusyn churches share elements from both the Eastern and Western Christian traditions. Religion has traditionally been an important element in the lives of the Carpatho-Rusyns, and they have often been perceived as synonymous with the traditional Byzantine rite churches; an estimated 38% are Orthodox, and 17% are Byzantine rite Catholic (Uniate). In the last decade a growing number have joined Jehovah's Witnesses, evangelical sects, and the Baptists.

The national name, "Rusyn," connects them to the east, as Rus' was the name given the inhabitants and territory of the medieval East Slav state based in Kiev. The many names used by the Carpatho-Rusyns or the names they have been called by others, Carpatho-Russian, Carpatho-Ukrainian, Rusnak, Ruthene, Ruthenian, and Uhro-Rusyn, all relate to their traditional ties to the historic East Slav Rus'. In spite of the confusion over a national name, the nation itself prefers Carpatho-Rusyn, or simply Rusyn. In Poland the Carpatho-Rusyns call themselves Lemkos, but they, too, before the twentieth century, called themselves Rusyns. Since 1991 many in Poland have begun to use the term "Lemko Rusyn."

The Carpatho-Rusyn dialects are classified as East Slavic and are closely related to Ukrainian but have been heavily influenced by Polish, Slovak, and Hungarian borrowings. The Carpatho-Rusyns speak four separate dialects, Lemko, Hutsul, Boiko, and Transcarpathian. The first three also designate the major divisions of the Carpatho-Rusyn nation. Influence from both East and West, together with numerous inclusions from Church Slavonic liturgical language and dialectal words unique to the Carpatho-Rusyns, distinguish the Carpatho-Rusyn language from the other East Slavic languages. However, unlike the neighboring East Slavic languages, Polish and Slovak, the Carpatho-Rusyns use the Cyrillic alphabet. In addition to dialectical and local divisions, the Carpatho-Rusyns are divided geographically between the *dolyshniany*, the lowlanders, and the *verkhovyntsi*, or highlanders.

NATION: Slavic migrants, coming from the east, settled among the earlier Ruthene tribes in the high valleys of the Carpathian Mountains in the fifth and sixth centuries. The early tribes believed, like other Slavs, in several gods related to the forces of nature. The most powerful of the pagan gods was Perun, whose name is still preserved in the Carpatho-Rusyn language as a curse.

Traditionally, Chistianity was brought to the Carpatho-Rusyns by the so-called Apostles to the Slavs, Cyril and Methodius, two monks from Byzantium. Some scholars believe that the Carpatho-Rusyns, already Christian, settled the region after the conversion of Kievan Rus'. The Carpatho-Rusyns' Carpathian homeland, in the tenth and eleventh centuries, formed part of Kievan Rus', the first great Slav state.

The Carpatho-Rusyns remained within the Eastern Orthodox sphere, nominally under the authority of the patriarch of Constantinople, when the Christian Church was divided after 1054. Religion distinguished the Carpatho-Rusyns from their Slovak, Hungarian, and Polish neighbors who were mostly Roman Catholic or Protestant. They were also distinguished from their fellow Eastern rite neighbors, the Ukrainians, Belarussians,* and Russians, by certain practices and rituals borrowed from their Latin rite neighbors, particularly liturgical music.

The Magyars of Hungary conquered most of the region in the eleventh century, with the Carpathians becoming a battleground for rival Hungarian and Polish states. The non-Slav Magyar cultural influences further distanced the Carpatho-Rusyn culture from the other Slav cultures to the east. The Lemko Region north of the Carpathians was divided until the mid-fourteenth century between Galicia and Poland. From the 1340s the entire Lemko region came under Polish rule.

Following the Protestant Reformation and the Catholic Counter-Reformation, the governments and local aristocracy of the region began in the late sixteenth century to try to bring the Orthodox Carpatho-Rusyns closer to the official Roman Catholic state religion of the two states that controlled their homeland, the Hungarian kingdom and Poland-Lithuania. The Byzantine rite Uniate Church accepted the authority off Rome in 1596, and several bishops of the Carpatho-Rusyn population in northeastern Hungary organized the separate Carpatho-Rusyn Uniate Church in 1646.

The Carpatho-Rusyn homeland remained divided, with the Lemko region taken by Austria during the Polish partition of 1772. The Carpatho-Rusyns, without the territorial recognition accorded the other minority peoples of the Austrian Empire in the eighteenth century, remained divided among several counties in northeastern Hungary, the Presov region of Hungarian Slovakia, and the adjoining areas of Austrian Galicia. The majority, denied all cultural rights and under intense assimilation pressures, lived as illiterate peasants held in near-feudal conditions on large Hungarian estates. Without a clear ethnic identity, most identified with their church, around which Carpatho-Rusyn life revolved.

Initially led by a small, church-educated elite, a national and cultural revival spread through the Carpatho-Rusyn lands in the late nineteenth century. The growing self-awareness highlighted the misery of the Carpatho-Rusyns' daily life. To escape grinding poverty, cultural repression, and pressure on their exploited lands, the Carpatho-Rusyns turned to emigration. Thousands left, mostly for the Americas, with mass emigration beginning in the 1880s and continuing until the outbreak of World War I in 1914 blocked the immigrant routes.

One of Europe's poorest and most backward peoples, the Carpatho-Rusyns served in the Austrian armies. Nationalist sentiment grew rapidly during World War I, developing as an anti-Hungarian mass movement. In May 1917 Carpatho-Rusyn leaders demanded the creation of a separate Carpatho-Rusyn state within the Austro-Hungarian Empire.

The nationalists mobilized as revolution overtook the defeated empire in October 1918. A Carpatho-Rusyn provisional government sent a delegation to the 1919 Paris Peace Conference to demand recognition under Point 10 of U.S. president Wilson's Fourteen Points, self-determination for the peoples of the Austro-Hungarian Empire. Carpatho-Rusyn independence, emphatically opposed by the region's large Hungarian minority, was finally put aside when the nationalist leader, Gregory Zsatkovich, accepted an alternative proposed by the Allies, the status of a trust territory, with broad autonomy, within the newly formed Czecho-Slovak state. Over nationalist protests, the Presov region and Subcarpathian Rus' south of the Carpathians became part of Czechoslovakia, except for about twenty towns and villages south of the Tisza River, which were incorporated into Romania. The Lemko region was added to newly independent Poland. A few Carpatho-Rusyns towns in the far south of former Hungarian territory became part of the new South Slav state later called Yugoslavia.

The Czechoslovak government created a new province, called Ruthenia, on 8 May 1919, with Gregory Zsatkovich as the first governor. The union of the Transcarpathian region with Czechoslovakia was recognized by the Paris Peace Conference in its Treaty of St. Germain, on the condition that Ruthenia be given broad autonomy. The Carpatho-Rusyns of the Presov region, under Slovak authority, and the Lemko Rusyns of Poland attempted to unite with the new Ruthenia but were blocked by the Czechoslovak and Polish governments. Zsatkovich resigned in 1920 to protest the abrogation of the autonomy agreement. Czechoslovakia's highly centralized government took control of most administrative functions and placed ethnic Czechs in most Carpatho-Rusyn government positions.

The Czech government, threatened by Hungary and Germany in 1938, sought to bind the Carpatho-Rusyns' loyalty by finally granting the long-promised autonomy. When Czechoslovakia was betrayed by its allies at Munich and under the terms of the Munich Pact was transformed into a federal state in October 1938, Ruthenia received fully self-governing status. The Ruthenian government was first headed by Andrej Brodij and then by the pro-Ukrainian Avhustyn Voloshyn (August Voloshin). Six months later, the dismemberment of Czechoslovakia by the fascist powers gave the Carpatho-Rusyns an opportunity. The nationalists mobilized to expel all Czech officials and to form a government under Voloshin. On 15 March 1939 the state, called Carpatho-Ukraine, declared its independence. The Carpatho-Rusyn government collapsed following an invasion by Hungarian troops, and on 16 March the Hungarian government annexed the region.

Following the Soviet occupation of the region in October 1944, a pro-communist Transcarpathian National Council was formed as the Hungarian civil government collapsed. At the end of 1945, under intense Soviet pressure, the Czechoslovak government formally ceded the region to the Soviet Union. In early 1946 the Carpatho-Rusyns lost their self-governing status, and the region was administered as an oblast of Soviet Ukraine. In the neighboring Presov region in 1945 the Carpatho-Rusyns set up a national council and demanded self-rule but were blocked by the restored Czechoslovak government. In 1948 the communists took power in Czechoslovakia, and in 1949 the national council was disbanded, and its leaders jailed.

The new communist government in Poland, in an effort to end the problem of the Carpatho-Rusyn minority, in 1946–47 deported the Lemkians from their border homeland, sending about 80% to the Soviet Ukraine and the remainder to the former German lands taken by Poland after the war in the west. Following the deportation, the Polish government denied the existence of a distinct Carpatho-Rusyn national group in the country.

One of the most immediate results of Soviet rule was the implementation of a government policy of Ukrainianization. Similar programs were instituted in neighboring, communist-dominated Poland and Czechoslovakia. The idea of a distinct Carpatho-Rusyn nationality was outlawed, and only Ukrainian identity was recognized. The Carpatho-Rusyns suffered decades of religious, cultural, and political oppression under Soviet rule. A national revival began to emerge as a powerful force with the Soviet liberalization in the late 1980s.

When the Soviet Union disintegrated, and Ukraine became an independent country, the Carpatho-Rusyns of Transcarpathia called for a return to their historic status as an autonomous province. In a referendum on Ukrainian independence carried out on 1 December 1991, over 78% of Transcarpathia's inhabitants voted for self-government within the newly independent Ukraine. When the Ukrainian government failed to fulfill the obligations of the December 1991 referendum, Carpatho-Rusyn leaders formed a provisional government for the Republic of Subcarpathian Rus' in May 1993. Since the summer of 1994, the struggle for autonomy has taken place within the chambers of the fifty-one-member Transcarpathian National Council, the local parliament. In 1992 the first openly separatist political organization was formed by nationalists advocating secession from Ukraine.

The collapse of communist governments in the neighboring states also raised demands among their Carpatho-Rusyn populations. Newly formed organizations put forward demands for cultural autonomy in Slovakia, Poland, Hungary, Yugoslavia, and the Czech Republic. The major aim of these organizations is to have the Carpatho-Rusyns recognized as a distinct nationality and to codify a literary language for instruction in schools and for use in the press, radio, theater, and other cultural events. In March 1991 all these organizations, along with groups from Ukraine and the United States, formed the World Congress of Rusyns, which meets periodically to formulate common goals for the entire nation.

The result of these increased contacts among the politically divided Carpatho-Rusyns has, for the first time, allowed joint programs and close cooperation in cultural, scholarly, and economic endeavors, regardless of the country in which they live. The increasing economic and political chaos in independent Ukraine has pushed the Carpatho-Rusyns to look west, not east to Kiev. Weakening economic and political ties to the rest of Ukraine have forced the inhabitants of the region to establishment a separate economic region, with its own rules and trade links. Some Carpatho-Rusyn leaders have called for the creation of a free economic zone across national boundaries that would devise its own economic policies.

At the turn of the century the Carpatho-Rusyns have moved closer to their Hungarian and Slovak neighbors, even to setting their clocks and watches to Central European time, an hour behind the time in Kiev. However, as those countries integrate into the European Union, they could begin restricting the free movement of the Carpatho-Rusyns across international borders. Should neighboring states, at European Union insistance, begin demanding visas for visiting Ukrainians, the already fragile economy of their homeland would collapse. The unemployment rate is among the highest in Ukraine and in some areas two-thirds of workers are on "unpaid leave." Every day, an estimated 20,000 Carpatho-Rusyns cross the borders to buy food and clothes to sell back home, often in return for smuggled petrol and cigarettes, which are cheaper in Ukraine. As many as 100,000 Carpatho-Rusyns work on building sites and farms across the borders, mostly in Carpatho-Rusyn areas of Slovakia and Hungary, earning up to six times what they could earn in the Ukraine.

SELECTED BIBLIOGRAPHY

Bonkalo, Alexander. *The Rusyns*. 1990.

Magocsi, Paul R. *Our People: Carpatho-Rusyns and Their Descendants in North America*. 1994.

Nemec, F., and V. Moudry. *The Soviet Seizure of Subcarpathian Ruthenia*. 1980.

Pekar, Athanasius B. *Our Past and Present: Historical Outlines of the Byzantine Ruthenian Metropolitan Province*. 1974.

Shandor, Vincent. *Carpatho-Ukraine in the Twentieth Century: A Political and Legal History*. 1998.

CATALANS

Catalonians; Valencians;
Valencianos; Balearic Islanders;
Mallorquins

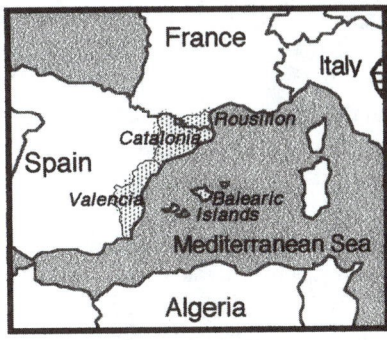

POPULATION: Approximately (2000 e) 9,855,000 Catalans in Europe, 6,238,000 Catalans in Catalonia (Catalunya) in northeastern Spain and southern France, 2,854,000, called Valencians or Valencianos, in the Valencia region, and 521,000, called Balearic Islanders or Mallorquins, in the Balearic Islands of Spain, and 242,000 in the Roussillon region, also called Catalunya Nord, in France. Other large Catalan populations are in other parts of Spain and France and in Germany. A smaller number live in northern Sardinia.

THE CATALAN HOMELAND: The Catalan homeland lies on the Mediterranean Sea in Southwestern Europe, comprising a mainland region in Spain and France, and the Balearic Islands in the western Mediterranean Sea. The region, called Catalunya in Catalan, is traversed by the eastern spur of the Pyrenees Mountains, which form the international border between France and Spain. Spanish Catalonia, called Països Catalans, consists of the autonomous regions of Catalonia, Valencia, and the Balearic Islands. The French region, Roussillon, is made up of the Department of Pyrénées Orientales.

The region is mostly rugged and mountainous, broken by fertile inland valleys and coastal plains. The northern region of Catalonia is watered by the Ebro, Llobregat, and Ter Rivers; in the south, in Valencia, the major rivers are the Segura, Turia, Júcar, and Mijares Rivers. The pleasant climate and abundant beaches have made the region one of Europe's major resort areas. In Valencia numerous salt lagoons lie along the coast. The Balearic Islands include the major island of Majorca and the smaller islands of Menorca, Ibiza, Formentera, and Cabrera and eleven islets.

Spanish Catalonia was granted autonomy within the Spanish state in 1980.

French Catalonia, joined to the region of Languedoc, was created as a planning region, with very limited autonomy, in 1981. *Autonomous Region of Catalonia (Catalunya)*: 12,238 sq.mi.–31,930 sq.km. (2000 e) 6,084,000. *Autonomous Region of Valencia*: 8,998 sq.km.–23,305 sq.km. (2000 e) 3,912,000. *Autonomous Region of the Balearic Islands (Baleares)*: 1,936 sq.km.–5,014 sq.mi. (2000 e) 728,000. *Roussillon (Catalonie/Catalunya Nord)*: 1,589 sq.mi.–4,116 sq.km. 366,000. *Països Catalans*: (2000 e) 11,090,000—Catalan (Catalan, Valencian, Balearic Islanders) 76%, other Spaniards,* other French.* The Catalan capital and major cultural center, Barcelona, (2000 e) 1,613,000 (metropolitan area 4,432,000), is an important commercial center and port on the Mediterranean. The Valencian and Balearic capitals, Valencia, (2000 e) 759,000 (1,732,000), and Palma de Majorca, called Ciutat Mallorca in Catalan, (2000 e) 334,000, are other important cultural centers. The capital and cultural center of Roussillon, or Northern Catalonia (Catalunya Nord), is Perpignan, (2000 e) 112,000, called Perpinyà in Catalan.

FLAG: The Catalan national flag, the official flag of the regions of Catalonia and French Catalonia, has nine yellow and red horizontal stripes. The yellow and red flag, with the addition of a yellow triangle bearing a five-pointed red star, or a blue triangle bearing a white star, at the hoist, is the flag of the Catalan nationalist movement. The official flags of the Valencian and Balearic Islands autonomous regions are variations on the Catalan flag.

PEOPLE: The Catalans are a Romance people, a mixture of early Pyreneean and Mediterranean strains. Known for their energy and intelligence and for their clannish defense of their language and culture, they have created one of Europe's most dynamic regions. The Catalans form the largest non-Castilian nation in Spain and one of the largest of the nonstate nations in Europe.

The Catalan language is a separate Romance language closer to Italian or the dialects of the Occitans* in southern France than to Spanish. The language is spoken in three major dialects in Catalonia, Catalan-Roussillonese or Northern Catalan, Central Catalan, and Northwestern Catalan, with several subdialects. The other major dialects are Valencian, spoken in Valencia, and Balearic, also called Mallorqui or Insular Catalan, in the Balearic Islands, which includes several subdialects. The Valencian and Balearic dialects are 90% to 95% comprehensive to speakers of Catalan dialects. Catalan and its major dialects more closely reflect its Latin roots than most modern Romance languages. For years some philologists held that Catalan was merely a dialectal offshoot of Occitan, spoken in southern France, and that during the Middle Ages it had raised itself for a time to the dignity of a literary language. Subsequent research led other scholars to claim the complete independence of Catalan as a language. Catalan and the Occitan dialects are not mutually intelligible.

Catalan culture, famous for art and architecture, has its roots in the Catalan Renaissance of the Middle Ages, not in the mixture of Gothic and Moorish influences that prevails in the rest of Spain. The distinctive Catalan culture, suppressed during the decades of the Franco dictatorship, has recovered strength since Spain's adoption of a democratic system in the late 1970s.

NATION: Originally inhabited by small, independent Iberian tribes, the Mediterranean coast was colonized by the Greeks around 600 B.C. In the third century B.C. the Carthaginians, under General Hamilcar Barca and Hannibal, invaded the region. Absorbed by the Roman Empire in 218 B.C., the inhabitants adopted Latin culture and speech. Under Roman rule the region became a wealthy province with its capital at present Tarragona.

The region flourished until the collapse of Roman power in the fifth century A.D. The weakness of the Romans left the region open to invasion by the Germanic Goths from the north, who overran the region in 470 A.D. The Goths called the region Gothalonia, later changed to Catalonia, and the region formed part of the Gothic kingdom established in northern Spain.

Muslim Moors, extending their empire to the north, conquered Catalonia in A.D. 711–14 but lost the northern districts to the Frankish king, later Holy Roman Emperor, Charlemagne in 795. The northern region was organized as the Spanish March of Charlemagne's empire in 801, with its capital at Barcelona, while the islands and Valencia, created as a separate Moorish kingdom in the eleventh century, remained under Moorish rule. Frankish counts ruled Catalonia, effectively making the region an independent domain.

In the ninth century the Catalan heartland became an independent county, the County of Barcelona or Catalonia. Catalonia merged with the kingdom of Aragon in 1132, although the Catalans retained their own laws, language, and government. The expanding Aragonese kingdom conquered Valencia and the Balearic Islands from the Moors in the thirteenth and fourteenth centuries and resettled the newly conquered regions with Catalan settlers. The growing Catalan Empire expanded its ties to the eastern Mediterranean, competing with the republics of Genoa and Pisa for control of Mediterranean trade. From 1230 to the fifteenth century a Catalan trading empire stretched as far east as the Balkan Peninsula, with extensive territories in the Mediterranean and north of the Pyrenees. Catalan wealth generated a golden age accompanied by a great flowering of medieval Catalan arts and culture that continued into the Renaissance.

Valencia, in the south, upon the dissolution of the caliphate of Cordoba in the early eleventh century, became an independent Moorish kingdom. Toward the close of the century the region came under the rule of the Almoravids, who were supplanted by the Christian hero El Cid in 1094. His death in 1099 forced his wife to give way to the Moors. In 1238 the city of Valencia again came under Christian control when it was taken by King James I of Aragon, who soon became master of the region as well. Although ruled by the kings of Aragon, Valencia remained autonomous until 1319, when it was united with Aragon and Catalonia.

Aragonese attempts to curtail Catalonia's autonomous rights incited a Catalan rebellion and led to civil war in the kingdom from 1460 to 1472. The war's devastation marked the beginning of a long decline that accelerated following the unification of the kingdoms of Aragon and Castile in 1479 and the centralizing of all government functions. The Catalans began a long struggle to preserve their culture and language.

The Catalans rebelled, with French help, against the Spanish government of Philip IV during the Thirty Years' War. The rebellion lasted from 1640 to 1659, when the French virtually ruled the region. French influence in Catalonia contributed to the development of a distinct Catalan culture. By the terms of the Treaty of the Pyrenees, France took control of northern Catalonia, Roussillon, and Cerdagne and established the northern boundary of Spanish territory at the Pyrenees. The Catalans sided with Archduke Charles of Austria against Philip V, the first Bourbon king of Spain, during the War of the Spanish Succession. In 1705 the Generalitat, the legislative assembly, met for the first time to coordinate the Catalan rebellion intended to win Catalan independence from Spain. After a long campaign Barcelona was conquered by the forces of Philip V in 1714. In reprisal for the rebellion, Philip deprived the Catalans of all their traditional privileges. In 1716 the Spanish government banned the Catalan language and attempted to eradicate Catalan culture in the Spanish domains. Many Catalans emigrated to Spain's American colonies.

The suppressed Catalan culture and language began to revive with the spread of education and publishing in the 1830s, the revival leading to a resurgence of nationalism. A rebellion at Barcelona in 1842 provoked renewed government efforts to stamp out the Catalan culture. The Catalan culture revival resumed in the 1870s and over the next decades produced some of Europe's greatest artists, architects, and writers. In the late nineteenth century, as part of the Catalan revival, nationalism gained support in the region. In 1902 the first nationalist organizations demanded a separate administration and budget for Catalonia. Amid continuing turmoil in the Spanish state, the Catalans called a general strike, leading to another revolt in 1909. Nationalism gained support in the Balearic Islands and Valencia, with some groups seeking local privileges, while others sought the reunification of the entire Catalan-speaking region in Spain and France.

Spain remained neutral during World War I, but between 1917 and 1919 separatist agitation swept the Catalan homeland. In 1919 the Catalan Union, the major nationalist organization, met in Barcelona and drafted a program for home rule. They sent a delegation to the Paris Peace Conference attempting to present a petition to U.S. president Woodrow Wilson, hoping for support under his proposal for self-determination for Europe's minorities. The Spanish government, by diplomatic means, was able to block the petition and to circumvent the issue of home rule for Catalonia.

A serious separatist uprising swept the region again in 1923, and in 1926 Catalan leaders were arrested in France while agitating for support in French Catalonia. On 9 June 1931, while the Madrid government was in disarray, the

Catalans convened the Generalitat for the first time in over 200 years. They formed an autonomous government, first under Francesc Macia, then under Louis Companys. The Catalan government received the recognition of the new republican government in Madrid on 25 September 1931.

The Spanish government's continued interference in the affairs of Catalonia caused increased tensions between Barcelona and Madrid. On 4 October 1934 the Catalan government declared the autonomous state independent of Spain, with Louis Companys as the first president. The government in Madrid responded by sending troops into Barcelona. All the Catalan leaders, including Louis Companys, were arrested, and all statutes of autonomy were rescinded.

The election of a leftist Spanish government in 1936 led to the restoration of the Catalans' autonomy. Catalonia was granted broad self-determination with its own language, flag, anthem, president, and parliament, the Generalitat. To preserve their autonomy, the majority of the Catalans sided with the Loyalists against Franco's fascist forces as civil war spread across Spain from 1936 to 1939. Aided by Germany and Italy, the Spanish fascists conquered Catalonia in early 1939. The entire Catalan government and officials of the Generalitat were executed. Over 200,000 Catalans fled into exile. The triumphant Franco banned all manifestations of Catalan culture, including severe penalties for publishing or teaching in the Catalan language.

Rapid industrial growth, particularly along the Mediterranean coast, in the 1950s and 1960s drew in a massive influx of peasant immigrants from Spain's backward south. Dubbed "Franco's Legions" by the Catalans, the immigrants served the Spanish government in two ways, by providing a low-cost industrial workforce and by spreading the traditional Spanish culture approved by Franco's dictatorial government. Underground nationalist organizations became active, while Catalan writers, politicians, and educators were persecuted.

Franco's death in 1975, followed by the rapid democratization of Spain, allowed the Catalan culture to resurface. In 1978 the new democratic Spanish government granted limited autonomy to Catalonia. Promoted by a proliferation of autonomist, nationalist, and separatist organizations, the Catalan culture and language quickly revived and replaced the Castilian language and culture the Franco regime had attempted to impose on Catalonia.

Catalonia was granted full autonomy on 11 January 1980, but with less actual power than the autonomy statute of 1932. Valencia and the Balearic Islands became separate autonomous regions in 1982. The Catalans elected a government dominated by moderate nationalists determined to win the maximum independence within Spain. After over four decades of suppression, only about half the population could speak Catalan, although only 16% were totally illiterate in the Catalan language. Following the restoration of the language, speaking and using Catalan and its regional varieties became a matter of pride.

Following Spain's entry into the European Community in 1986, Catalan nationalism has focused on independence within a united Europe and the reunification of the Catalan regions in Spain and France. In 1988 the Catalan language, spoken by more Europeans than many official state languages, became an official language of the European Community.

Nationalist leaders claim that Catalonia, Spain's richest and most advanced region, is now more closely linked to the rest of Europe than to the rest of Spain. As the member states of the European Union draw closer economically and politically, the hold of the Spanish government over Catalonia is weakening. In February 1994 negotiations between Catalan leaders and members of the Spanish government centered on the Catalans' desire to take up the status the region enjoyed before 1714, independence under the Spanish king but not subject to the Spanish government.

In October 1998 the Catalan parliament passed a resolution confirming the right of the Catalan people to self-determination. The resolution, proposed by the Catalan Independence Party, was supported by a broad spectrum of Catalan political parties. The Catalan regional government is expected to use the resolution to press for greater autonomy from the Spanish government.

To many Catalans autonomy is only the first step to an independent Catalonia within the framework of a united Europe, while some already refer to the rest of the country as Spain, as if they already formed a separate European state. Catalonia is Spain's most important industrial region, and its loss would be disastrous for the Spanish state, but with new markets the Catalans could survive as a viable nation-state. Many seek the unification of the Països Catalans within the framework of the European Union (EU).

SELECTED BIBLIOGRAPHY

Abulafia, David. *A Mediterranean Emporium: The Catalan Kingdom of Majorca.* 1994.

Azevedo, Milton M., ed. *Contemporary Catalonia in Spain and Europe.* 1991.

Balcells, Albert et al. *Catalan Nationalism: Past and Present.* 1996.

Keating, Michael. *Nations against the State: The New Politics of Nationalism in Quebec, Catalonia and Scotland.* 1996.

Medrano, Juan Diez. *Divided Nations: Class, Politics, and Nationalism in the Basque Country and Catalonia.* 1995.

CHAVASH

Tavas; Chävash; Chuvash; Volga
Bulgars; Bolgars

POPULATION: Approximately (2000 e) 2,255,000 Chavash in Europe, mostly in the Volga River basin of eastern European Russia. Less than half live in the Chavash Republic of the Russian Federation, with large Chavash populations in neighboring republics and regions, in Ukraine. Outside Europe there are numerous Chavash communities as far east as western Siberia and in the Central Asian republics of Kazakhstan, Kyrgyzstan, and Uzbekistan.

THE CHAVASH HOMELAND: The Chavash homeland mostly lies on the right bank of the middle Volga River, a wooded steppe between the Sura and Sviyaga Rivers, which are tributaries of the Volga. The rivers, as well as 400 lakes, are known as the pearls of the Chavash. Much of the homeland consists of the low hills and ravines of the Chavash Plateau, which forms the northern end of the Privolzhskaya Upland on the right bank of the Volga. The Chavash left bank of the Volga is a plain with sandy knolls, peat bogs, and swamps. Forests of pine, spruce, birch, oak, and linden cover nearly a third of the republic, and forestry is an important industry. However, agriculture remains the mainstay of the Chavash region, with grains, potatoes, hemp, tobacco, and hops as regional products. The Chavash Republic accounts for about 80% of the hops grown in the Russian Federation. Industry, which developed after World War II, has led to increasing urbanization, particularly in Cheboksary and its suburbs.

The Chavash leadership declared the sovereignty of the republic on 26 October 1990, and in 1991 Chavashia became a member state of the newly independent Russian Federation. *Chavash Republic (Chävash Jen)*: A member state of the Russian Federation. 7,066 sq.mi.–18,301 sq.km. (2000 e) 1,447,000— Chavash (Chuvash) 71%, Russians* 24%, Tatars* 3%, Mordvins* 2%. The Chavash capital and major cultural center is Cheboksary, (2000 e) 457,000, situated on the Volga River eighty miles west of Kazan.

FLAG: The Chavash flag, the official flag of the republic, is a yellow field with a narrow crimson stripe on the bottom and bears a stylized "Tree of Life" and three stylized crimson suns in the center.

PEOPLE: The Chavash, called Chuvash by the Russians, call themselves Chavash or Tavas. They are the descendants of Finno-Ugric tribes that mixed with the medieval Bulgars (Bolgars), a powerful nation of the Volga River basin. Later admixtures of Turkic and Finnic peoples formed the unique Chavash culture. Traditionally agriculturists, now about half the Chavash live in urban areas in the central part of the Volga River basin.

Considered a Turkic-Tatar people, the Chavash form a transition nation between the Orthodox Russians and the Finnic peoples, on one hand, and Turkic Muslim Tatars and Bashkorts,* on the other. The Chavash derive a strong identity from their Bulgar past, which makes their national identity somewhat immune to assimilation by other peoples.

The majority are Orthodox Christians; however, their religion and culture have been influenced by the proximity of Muslim peoples. The traditional religion of the Chavash involved the worshiping of images and spirits, but under Tatar rule, a segment of the Chavash converted to Islam. In the eighteenth century the Chavash nominally accepted Orthodox Christianity under Russian influence, but Russian religious practices never became widespread. Many reconverted to Islam in the nineteenth and early twentieth centuries. In the 1990s the majority were Orthodox Christians, with an important Sunni Muslim minority. Since the collapse of the USSR in 1991, Chavash folk culture and their traditional religious beliefs have revived, reinforcing their identity as a nation.

The Chavash language, though of basic Turkic structure, is not considered to belong to any of the four Turkic language groups but forms a separate Bolgar branch of the West Altaic language group. The language is a complicated mixture of Turkic, Finnic, Mongol, Russian, Farsi, and Arabic roots. The mostly Orthodox Chavash comprise two major divisions that correspond to the major dialects, Anatri (Lower Chavash) and Viryal (Upper Chavash). An estimated 82% use Chavash as their first language, and 80% are able to speak Russian as a second language. The old Chavash literary language used the Russian script, but a new writing system was created by I. Ya. Yakolev and existed until 1933, when it was substituted by a modified Cyrillic alphabet. The literary language is based on the Anatri dialect.

Large Chavash populations live in the Volga Basin republics of Tatarstan and Bashkortostan and the oblasts (provinces) of Ulyanovsk, Penza, Samara, Saratov, and Orenburg. Even though more than half the Chavash live outside the republic, they have proved less susceptible to assimilation than many larger national groups and have preserved their unique culture intact. The strong link between the Chavash culture and national identity has sustained the Chavash nation for hundreds of years.

NATION: In the middle of the fifth century, after the death of Attila, the great Hun Empire began to disintegrate. Several new kingdoms emerged, including the Kingdom of Great Bulgaria. This kingdom was short-lived, and upon the death of its ruler, Kurbat Han, the Bulgars split into two sections. One part, under the leadership of the khan's youngest son, Asparuh Han, moved west and mixed extensively with the Slavs to form the later Bulgarians.* The other, led by the two eldest sons, Batbay Han and Kutrag Han, mixed extensively with the Khazar and Alan tribes and remained in the eastern reaches of the European Plain. A portion of the eastern Bulgars in the eighth century moved to the Volga Basin, where they settled among the Turkic and Finnic tribes and, in the ninth and tenth centuries, established the medieval Volga Bulgar state. Descended from the Finno-Ugric tribes of the middle Volga area and the Bulgar tribes of the Kama and Volga Rivers, the Chavash were identifiable as a separate people in the tenth century.

The Chavash, called Black Bulgar or Volga Bulgar, developed an advanced, urban society in the region. The largest towns of the state, Bolgar and Buljar, were among the largest urban communities in Europe, surpassing London, Paris, Kiev, or Novgorod. Converted to Islam in the tenth century, the Black Bulgars created an extensive, early medieval state that eventually controlled many neighboring Finnic and Turkic peoples.

The flourishing state, conquered by the Mongols in 1236, never recovered, and the Black Bulgars later came under the rule of the Tatar Khanate of Kazan, a successor state established as Mongol power declined in the 1440s. Tatar raids on Chavash communities forced the southern Chavash to migrate northward out of their traditional homeland, abandoning their southern districts almost entirely from the fourteenth to the late sixteenth centuries.

Orthodox monks, venturing into the unknown east in the fourteenth century, converted the majority of the Muslim Chavash to Christianity by 1500. Following their conversion, almost all traces of their earlier Islamic society disappeared. At the same time the Chavash mostly abandoned their former seminomadic life of cattle herding for more settled agricultural communities.

In 1551 the Chavash joined with the Russians and helped them to defeat the Tatars. The Russian conquest of Kazan, the center of the Tatar Empire in 1552, brought the Chavash under direct Russian rule. Russian attempts to assimilate the Chavash undermined the common bond of the Orthodox religion and provoked a strong anti-Russian movement among the Chavash population. In 1555 the Russians established a capital for the Chavash at Cheboksary and five years later created the position of the *namestnik*, the local Muscovite governor. After an initial period of prosperity, the living conditions of the Chavash deteriorated under the Russian tsars, and much of the Chavash peasantry was forced to live as serfs on Russian estates.

Severe famine during a time of political chaos in Moscow sparked rebellions in the region in the seventeenth century. The Chavash, allied to the neighboring Maris* and Mordvins, attempted to throw off Russian rule in 1601–3. Savage reprisals against the entire population accompanied the defeat of the rebels by Russian troops, but the Chavash again rebelled, along with the other Volga nations, under the leadership of Stenka Razin in 1667–71.

By 1750 the Chavash lands had been included in the large Russian provinces of Kazan and Simbirsk. The division of the Chavash in two provinces led to protests and stimulated a modest national revival. During this period, from the eighteenth to the early nineteenth centuries, many Muslim Chavash were forced to adopt Orthodox Christianity.

The consolidation of the Chavash nationality was advanced by the spread of literacy in the early nineteenth century. The first Chavash grammar was published in 1769. A more complete grammar and dictionary appeared in 1836. In 1868 the first Chavash secondary school was opened in Simbirsk, and in 1871 the first Chavash grammar was published using the Russians' Cyrillic alphabet. A Chavash alphabet, created in 1872, remained unaltered until the Soviet period in 1938.

An impoverished rural minority dominated by Russian landlords, the Chavash stubbornly clung to their language and culture. Serfdom, prevalent in most of Russia, failed in the region as the Chavash traditionally located their villages in remote ravines to elude tsarist officials. Chavash resistance to Russian rule manifested itself in periodic disturbances, crop damage, illegal timber cutting, and the looting of Russian property.

Russian attempts to force the Chavash into serfdom or to conscript Chavash men for military duty led to several confrontations with the authorities between 1827 and 1860. Disturbances escalated following an influx of Russian peasants freed from serfdom in the provinces to the west in 1861. Due to the domination of the region by Russian landlords, Chavashia remained economically backward, and illiteracy was widespread.

At least half of the Chavash rose during the 1905 Russian Revolution, attacking Slavic colonies, burning estates, and skirmishing with troops sent to restore order. Chavash guerrillas from hidden villages continued to harass the authorities for over two years, until finally routed out of hiding in 1907. Up to World War I the Chavash remained primarily agricultural, with little development of the potentially important timber industry.

The Chavash, living far from the front lines, felt little of the immediate effects of World War I until conscription of minorities began in 1916. The Chavash resisted conscription, and skirmishes broke out with tsarist troops. When revolution overtook the conflict in February 1917, most of the Chavash soldiers deserted and returned home, bringing with them new ideas, including a new national sentiment that rapidly took root in the region.

The Chavash leaders convened a national congress to take over as civil government collapsed in the region. The congress sent delegates to a conference of all the non-Russian peoples of the Volga-Ural region convened in late 1917 to discuss the Bolshevik coup and the future of the nations in the region. A majority of the Chavash supported inclusion of their homeland in an independent regional federation of states, the expulsion of the Slavic settlers, and the return of all lands to the Chavash. A minority favored a separate Chavash state or a federation only with the Orthodox Maris and Mordvins.

In February 1918 Bolshevik troops overran Chavashia before the Chavash had a chance to decide their own future. Devastated by heavy fighting between 1918 and 1920, the Chavash homeland witnessed some of the largest battles of the Russian civil war. Thousands of Chavash died in the fighting and from hunger and disease.

The victorious Bolsheviks initially promised freedom of religion and cultural autonomy, but Chavash leaders advocating autonomy were quickly eliminated. However, the Chavash continued to make demands on the new government, including the incorporation of the town of Simbirsk, later called Ulyanovsk, into their region. On 24 June 1920 the Soviet government created a Chuvash autonomous region; however, all administrative posts in the newly created region were held by ethnic Russians. To diffuse growing Chavash anti-Soviet sentiment, the region was raised to the status of an autonomous republic within the Russian Federation on 21 April 1925. In 1926 the government changed the republic's boundaries to include a proletarian district that did not share the Chavash's bourgeois nationalist attitudes.

The Chavash homeland was forcibly collectivized during the dictatorship of Joseph Stalin in the 1930s. The program, carried out with great brutality, was accompanied by purges of the Chavash cultural and political leadership for anti-Soviet bourgeois nationalism. Suspected of pro-Finnish sentiment during the Finno-Russian War of 1939–40, the Chavash were subjected to new oppression, including the forced adaptation of their language to the Russians' Cyrillic alphabet.

The Chavash, constituting over 80% of their republic's population in 1965, experienced a modest cultural revival over the next decade, partly in response to increased Slavic immigration to the republic. The cultural revival, particularly important in publishing and cultural studies, reinforced the Chavash resistance to the government's assimilation pressures in the 1960s and 1970s. A renewed interest in their unique history and an emphasis on the purification and de-Russification of the Chavash language took hold in the late 1960s.

In an influx of Slavic populations in the 1970s, many worked in the flourishing oil and natural gas refineries. By the 1980s Chavashia had several rail shops and electronics, chemicals, and food-processing industries; however, the majority of the Chavash remained rural and agricultural. Only one city in the Chavash homeland, Cheboksary, had a population of over 100,000 in 1980.

The Chavash population, which grew rapidly in the 1970s and 1980s, increased the number of Chavash living outside the Chavash republic. In 1979 only 52% of the Chavash population lived within the republican borders. The Chavash national revival, which spread to all Chavash populations, took the reunification of their nation in one administrative unit as an important national issue. The revival took on nationalist overtones following the introduction of liberal reforms in the late 1980s and became openly nationalist with the disintegration of the Soviet Union in 1991.

Since 1991, nationalist and cultural groups belonging to Tavas, a popular front organization, have pressed for the de-Russification of their language, the adoption of the Latin alphabet, and the creation of a Chavash university. Growing nationalist sentiment forced the local government to declare the republic's sovereignty and to change the name from the Russian to the Chavash version. In late 1991 the Chavash government unilaterally proclaimed the upgrading of the republic's status to that of a republic within the newly democratic Russian Federation.

On 21 January 1994 Nikolai Fedorov, a constitutional lawyer, was inaugurated as the first president of the Chavash Republic. Federov, a former Russian justice minister who resigned in 1993 to protest the use of force in Chechenia, has had a stormy relationship with the Chavash legislature, which is dominated by leftist political parties. In January 1995 Federov signed a decree allowing citizens of the republic to refuse to participate in military activities in Chechenia.

On 27 May 1996 the president of the Chavash Republic, Nikolai Fedorov, and the president of the Russian Federation, Boris Yeltsin, signed a treaty on the delimitation of the powers and jurisdictions between the Chavash state and those of the Russian Federation. In the late 1990s Fedorov and other officials of the Chavash government have increasingly criticized the Russian government and its economic policies.

Chavash nationalism focuses on the consolidation of their traditional lands and the incorporation of all Chavash-populated territories in one state. Although the majority of the Chavash in the Russian Federation now live outside the Chavash Republic, the Chavash remain distinctly less susceptible to Russification than other nations in the Volga River region. The Chavash, unlike the Russians in the region, remain mostly rural and agricultural.

SELECTED BIBLIOGRAPHY

D'Encausse, Helene C. *The Great Challenge: Nationalities and the Bolshevik State, 1917–1930.* 1991.

Pushkarev, Sergei. *Self-Government and Freedom in Russia.* 1988.

Rywkin, Michael. *Russian Colonial Expansion to 1917.* 1988.

Shnirelman, Victor A. *Who Gets the Past?: Competition for Ancestors among Non-Russian Intellectuals in Russia.* 1995.

Smal-Stocki, Roman. *The Captive Nations: Nationalism and the Non-Russian Nations and Peoples of the Soviet Union.* 1960.

CHECHENS

Nokh; Nakh; Nakchuo; Nokhchi;
Nokhchii; Chechenians

POPULATION: Approximately (2000 e) 1,020,000 Chechens in Europe, the majority in the North Caucasus region of the Russian Federation, primarily in Chechenia, but also in neighboring Dagestan and Ingushetia and other Russian republics and regions, including a sizable population in Moscow. Smaller Chechen populations live in Azerbaijan, Ukraine, and in Central Asia.

THE CHECHEN HOMELAND: The Chechen homeland occupies the northern slopes of the middle Caucasus Mountains and extends into the floodplain of the Terek River in southern European Russia. The region is mostly rugged and mountainous, with steppe and sandy plains to the north, particularly in the valley of the Terek River. The Terek and Sunzha River valleys of western Chechnya are the republic's agricultural centers. Fertile soil covers the lowlands and valleys, while dry steppe vegetation characterizes the northern plains. The highest peak in Chechnya is Mt. Tebulosmta at 14,741 feet (4493 m.). Chechenia is the site of the Grozni oil fields, one of Russia's major sources of petroleum.

Chechenia's status remains undecided; officially, it forms a member state of the Russian Federation, although Russian government authority ceased to function in the republic in 1996. The republic borders Dagestan on the east, Stavropol Krai on the north, North Ossetia on the west, and the Republic of Georgia on the south. *Chechen Republic of Ichkeria (Nokhchyïchuo)*: 6,210 sq.mi.– 16,088 sq.km. (2000 e) 1,011,000—Chechens 79%, Russians* 11%, Ossetians* 2%, Ingush* 1%, Ukrainians,* Kuban Cossacks,* Dagestanis. The Chechen capital and major cultural center is Syelzha Ghaala, called Grozni or Grozny in Russian, which had a population of 411,000 in 1994 at the outbreak of fighting in the republic.

FLAG: The Chechen national flag, the flag of the breakaway republic, is a green field with three horizontal stripes of white, red, and white on the lower half and the Chechen national symbol, a leopard under a full moon within a stylized yellow circle, centered near the top.

PEOPLE: The Chechens, who call themselves Nakh or Nakchuo, are a Caucasian nation comprising 128 lowland and highland clans called *teips*. The mountain clans, traditionally the most powerful, are bound by strict traditions of hospitality and vendetta. Chechen society is strongly patriarchal, and the Council of Elders, drawn from the elders of each clan, remains very influential. The Chechens are mainly Sunni Muslims, adhering to the Shafi rite.

The Chechens and their neighbors, the Ingush, constitute the Veinakh or Vainakh ethnic group. They have lived in the same region of the North Caucasus for over 1,000 years, except for the years spent in exile. The Chechens have retained an extremely high birthrate despite the urbanization of 40% of the Chechen population in recent years.

The Chechen language, a dialect of the Vienakh or Vainakh, the northeastern branch of the Caucasian languages, developed as a literary language in the nineteenth century and is spoken by 98% of the Chechens as their mother tongue. The language is spoken in six major dialects and is the most widely spoken of the North Caucasian languages. The majority of the Chechens are bilingual in Russian. In 1992 a new Latin-based alphabet was adopted, and in 1997 the Chechen parliament enacted a law making Chechen the only official language in the republic.

NATION: The Chechens, thought to be descended from ancient Scythian tribes, have lived in the Ciscaucasia region since before 600 B.C. Their homeland, straddling the main invasion route between Europe and Asia, knew many invaders, the Caucasian tribes evolving a warrior tradition necessary to hold their lands against numerous would-be conquerors. From about 200 B.C. to A.D. 200 they were under the domination of the Sarmathians, although Roman influence entered the region from the Roman-held region just to the south. The region was controlled by the Huns from around 400 A.D. and was ruled by the Khazars from 650 to 750. Influenced by the Romans and later the Byzantines, most of the fierce mountain tribes had adopted Christianity by A.D. 1000. The Chechens were part of the multiethnic empire of the Alans (Ossetians) from the eighth century until its destruction by the Mongols.

The Mongols conquered the region in 1241, laying waste the Chechen lowlands. Withdrawing to mountain strongholds, the Chechens fought the invaders for over fifty years, finally throwing off Mongol rule in 1300. Over the next centuries the Chechens resisted Persian and Turkish attempts to dominate the region. They developed a warrior culture and were often at war with neighboring peoples. A mountain-dwelling people organized in clans, the Chechens first descended to the plains in the fifteenth and sixteenth centuries.

Slavic Cossacks, the spearhead of Russian expansion, began to explore the region in the sixteenth century and in 1598 reached the Terek River in Chechen territory. The Chechens, converted to Islam coming from Dagestan about 1650, resisted incursions by the Christian Russians. Slowly extending their influence as Persian and Turkish power declined, the Russians finally pushed south in the late eighteenth century.

In 1785 Sheikh Mansur, now a lengendary folk hero, led an uprising against the Russian conquerors. Mansur was captured by Russian forces in 1791 and died several years later. For much of the nineteenth century the Chechens resisted Russian efforts to extend their frontiers to the south. Grozni, founded in 1818 as a frontier fort, established a Russian foothold in the center of Chechen territory, where the Russians met the fiercest resistance to their conquest of the Caucasus.

The most ardent opponents of Russian rule, the Chechens, under their political and religious leader Iman Shamil (Shamyl), fought an effective guerrilla war against the Russians from 1834 to 1859, when the Russians formally annexed the Chechen homeland. Tens of thousands of Muslim warriors died in the final Russian conquest of the region. The surviving Chechens, driven from their fertile lowlands along the Terek River, lived in abject poverty in the high Caucasus. Hatred of the Slavs, particularly the Terek Cossacks,* settled on their confiscated lands, provoked repeated revolts, especially severe in 1863, 1867, and 1877. In 1865 the Russians deported 39,000 Chechens to Ottoman Turkish territory.

The Chechen homeland in the North Caucasus was covered in beech and oak forests, giving the Chechens cover and income. But since the Chechens were particularly skilled at forest fighting, the Russian authorities completely deforested the Caucasian foothills.

The region was given added importance following the discovery of oil near Grozni in 1893. By 1900 the Grozni fields were the second greatest oil-producing region in tsarist Russia and were the target of Chechen rioters during the 1905 Russian Revolution. The uprising in the region, severely put down by Cossack troops, ended when thousands of Chechens were deported to Russia's Siberian provinces.

Openly sympathetic to Muslim Turkey during World War I, the Chechens rejoiced as revolution spread across Russia in February 1917. Believing the revolution would redress old injustices and return their lost lands, the Chechen leaders sent petitions to the new democratic Russian government detailing their grievances. Ignored by Russia's beleaguered provisional government, the Chechens mobilized and launched an offensive against the Terek Cossack settlements on their traditional lands in the Terek River basin. In September 1917 a Chechen government took control of the local government and expelled all Slavic officials.

The Bolshevik coup in October 1917 ended Chechen attempts to win autonomy within Russia. On 27 October 1917 the first Congress of the Union of the North Caucasus was held at Vedens, Shamil's old capital. Alarmed by the antireligious Bolshevik proclamations, the Chechens formed an alliance with their old enemies, the Terek Cossacks, but old grievances soon ended the alliance.

Proclaiming a holy war, a *gazava*, the Muslim warriors drove the Cossacks from Grozni, and a Chechen congress elected a national committee of sheiks, officers, and merchants to govern the region. The national committee declared Chechenia independent on 2 December 1917. They established a theocratic democracy headed by the Chechen emir Sheikh Ilzum Hadji, which at first was allied to the anti-Bolshevik forces in southern Russia.

Allied to the other Muslim peoples of the region, particularly the Dagestani peoples, the Chechens organized a republic called North Caucasia, which was proclaimed on 11 May 1918. In June 1918 the new state concluded a treaty with Turkey. The first capital of the new state, Vladikavkaz, called Dzaudzhikau, was captured in August 1918 by Cossack troops. The capital was moved to Nazra and later to Temir Khan Shura. Severe fighting broke out between the Muslims and the troops of the Whites, the Russians fighting the Bolsheviks, the Reds.

Seeking allies, the Muslims, led by the Chechens, believing Bolshevik promises of independence, switched sides in the civil war. In November 1918 the Bolsheviks overran the Terek lowlands and began to redistribute confiscated lands to their Chechen allies. In January 1919 the White Volunteer Army of General Anton Deniken invaded the region, and, despite a valiant resistance, the Chechens were defeated in the spring. The Chechens appealed directly to the Allied nations, but while the Volunteers were exterminating Muslims in the region, the British, the only nation with forces in the region, refused to intervene against their White allies.

The Bolshevik forces, the Red Army, finally forced the Whites from the region in January 1920. The Chechens' communist allies attempted to take direct control of the region and to incorporate it into the new Soviet Russian state as a so-called autonomous Mountain Republic. The Chechens turned on their Red allies and fought a vicious two-month war. They were finally defeated in March 1920. The Mountain Republic lasted only twenty months, after which ethnic tensions caused its division into separate ethnic regions. The Chechen autonomous region was erected in November 1922.

The region, one of the last to be conquered by the Reds, remained a center of Muslim anticommunist activity. The government's antireligious stance provoked a widespread revolt in 1927. In 1934 Chechenia was joined with Ingushetia to form a larger region, which became an autonomous republic in 1936. To avoid further disturbances in the region, the Chechens' entire political and cultural leadership was purged, killed, or deported in 1937; however, a serious revolt again swept the region in 1939–40.

A World War II German drive on the Caucasus oil fields reached the border of the rebellious region in 1942. The Nazi advance prompted a renewed Chechen revolt as many joined the Nazis' anticommunist campaign, while other Chechens formed anti-Nazi partisan groups. In January 1943 the Red Army again occupied Chechenia.

In 1944, accused of treason by Joseph Stalin, the entire Chechen nation, including the families of soldiers in the Red Army, were ordered punished.

Driven from their homes at gunpoint and loaded on cattle cars, the 408,000 Chechens suffered a brutal deportation to Central Asia. Tens of thousands of Chechens died in the deportation and from hunger and disease in the areas where they were dumped in Central Asia and Siberia. Chechen soldiers in the Red Army, when they returned to their homes, were rounded up and were also shipped east.

Officially rehabilitated and allowed to return to the Caucasus in 1957, the surviving Chechens arrived back in their homeland to find their homes occupied by Slavs and all traces of their culture eradicated. In 1958 severe Chechen rioting paralyzed the region, forcing the Soviet authorities to act on the Chechen grievances. Given some rights, the Chechens and the neighboring Ingush were joined in a joint autonomous republic.

In the 1960s and 1970s the Chechen leadership suffered periodic purges, while their Muslim religion remained the target of suppression and persecution. An estimated half of the Chechen men in the mid-1970s belonged to underground brotherhoods called *tariqat*. The Muslim Chechen population urbanized without assimilating into the predominantly Russian urban culture. By 1979, 40% of the Chechen nation lived in urban areas.

The liberalizing of Soviet life in the late 1980s allowed the Chechens to organize more openly. A popular front against communist rule was formed in 1988, and by 1990 there was an active pro-independence movement, motivated partly by a desire to secure control over Chechenia's lucrative oil industry.

The attempted coup against Soviet president Mikhail Gorbachev in August 1991 triggered a popular uprising in Chechenia. Led by the United Congress of Chechen People (UCCP), the Chechens took control of the republican government and expelled the communist government in Grozny. Major-General Dzhokar Dudayev exploited clan rivalries to take control of the government and to proclaim himself president following a resounding victory in elections held in October. On 2 November 1991 Dudayev declared Chechenia an independent state, but the Russian government refused to accept an independent Chechen republic. The Russian government imposed economic sanctions, which seriously affected Chechen living standards and contributed to Dudayev's unpopularity in the republic.

Popular unrest increased against Dudayev's government, and in March 1992 a military coup was attempted during widespread demonstrations. In June the Ingush decided to separate their region from Chechenia and reached an agreement with Moscow on its new status within the Russian Federation. All Russian troops stationed in Chechenia were withdrawn, leaving behind a large quantity of arms.

In 1993 opposition to Dudayev's government increased, with many clans openly in revolt; however, the expulsion of hundreds of Chechen traders and illegal residents from Moscow united the Chechens in fury against the Russians. In August 1994 opposition forces, with Russian government support, attempted to overthrow Dudayev. In mid-August Dudayev ordered a general mobilization to combat the Chechen opposition and their Russian backers. In September fighting between the Chechen government forces and the Russian-backed opposition broke out, and in December Russian troops moved into Chechenia. Fighting spread across the republic, creating over 200,000 refugees. Sustained aerial bombing and artillery bombardments caused thousands of civilian deaths. Grozny was almost completely destroyed before it fell to Russian troops in February 1995. Many Chechens became disillusioned with their unrecognized independence and were apprehensive about the future of their small nation but still refused to bow to Russian domination. General Dudayev was killed in a rocket attack and was replaced by Aslan Maskhadov.

While some Chechens were willing to support a negotiated settlement to end the war, the rebels continued to fight, claiming that they would settle for nothing less than complete independence from Russia. In August 1996 a major Chechen offensive to retake Grozny was successful. Later that month Russian president Yeltsin's national security adviser, Aleksandr Lebed, brokered a peace agreement with Chechen leaders in which both sides agreed to postpone a decision on Chechnya's status until 2001.

In June 1997 President Maskhadov announced measures to enhance the role of Islamic institutions in the republic. The government is to set up an Islamic state bank and replace civil courts with Sharia courts and plans to change the Latin alphabet, adopted in 1991, to Arabic script. In July 1997 President Boris Yeltsin offered a power-sharing agreement similar to that between the Russian Federation and Tatarstan.

Chechenia's secular constitution was set aside, and Islamic Sharia law was declared the official law in the state in February 1999. The adoption of Sharia law will impact on education, non-Muslims in the state, and the status of women. At the turn of the century, Chechenia is far more independent than many in Russia wished to admit but far less independent than most Chechens desired.

SELECTED BIBLIOGRAPHY

Baddeley, John F. *Russian Conquest of the Caucasus.* 1997.

Gall, Carlotta et al. *Chechnya: Calamity in the Caucasus.* 1998.

Gammer, Moshe. *Muslim Resistance to the Tsar: Shamil and the Conquest of Chechnia and Dagestan.* 1994.

O'Ballance, Edgar. *Wars in the Caucasus, 1990–1995.* 1997.

Smith, Sebastian. *Allah's Mountains.* 1997.

CHERKESS

Adyges; Circassians; Central
Circassians; Cherkessians

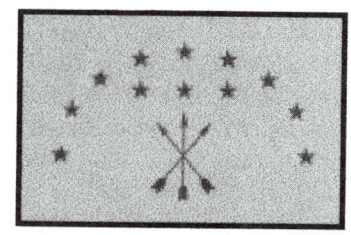

POPULATION: Approximately (2000 e) 76,000 Cherkess in Europe, mostly in the northwestern Cherkess region of the Karachai-Cherkess Republic, a member state of the Russian Federation. There are large numbers of Circassians, including Cherkess, in Turkey, Syria, Jordan, Lebanon, and Israel.

THE CHERKESS HOMELAND: The Cherkess homeland lies in the foothills of the western spur of the Greater Caucasus Mountains in southern European Russia, mostly occupying the valley of the upper Kuban River, a region of open grassland, rich soil, and numerous rivers carrying Caucasus snowmelt to the important Kuban River and on to the sea. Much of the region is wooded foothills surrounding the lowland steppe of the Kuban valley. The rivers of Cherkessia drain to the Black Sea, not the Caspian, a simple geographical fact that early distinguished the Cherkess from other Caucasian peoples.

Cherkessia, suitable for agriculture, has long attracted many Russian and Ukrainian settlers. The Cherkess region, which borders the homeland of the Karachais* on the south, is the most urbanized part of the Karachai-Cherkessia Republic.

Officially, Cherkessia remains part of the Republic of Karachai-Cherkessia; the Cherkess Republic, proclaimed in 1992, has not been recognized by the Russian government. *Cherkess Republic (Cherkess Respublike)*: 1,623 sq.mi.– 4,204 sq.km. (2000 e) 315,000—Russians* 36%, Kuban Cossacks* 28%, Cherkess (Circassians) 24%, Ukrainians* 9%. The Cherkess capital and major cultural center is Cherkessk, (2000 e)128,000, on the Kuban River.

FLAG: The flag of the Cherkess, the flag of their unrecognized republic, is a yellow field bearing three crossed, red arrows surmounted by three red stars under an arc of nine red stars.

PEOPLE: The Cherkess are a Northern Caucasian people, one of the three divisions of the Circassian peoples, which also include the Adgye* and Kabards.* There has long been a debate as to the classification of the Cherkess, but the modern classification includes only the Circassian group called Cherkess that inhabit the northern districts of the Karachai-Cherkess Republic.

The Cherkess call themselves Adyge, as do the Adyge nation farther west, which indicates their relationship with the other Circassian peoples. However, the Cherkess identity is formed by tribal and clan loyalties, as they also identify themselves by clans or subgroups. The most important of the Cherkess subgroups are the Abadzeg, Beslenei, Bzhedug, Gatjukai, Jererukoi, Kemgoi, Kheak, Nadkhokaudzh, Shapug, and Temirgoi.

In their traditional social organization, Cherkess princes and nobles controlled the herds and soil. The mass of people were organized in a complex system of subordinate ranks and clans. Slavery was maintained until recent times, and women occupied a low position in Circassian society.

The Cherkess language is a Kiakh language of the Abzhazo-Adygheian group of Caucasian languages. The language, often called Central Circassian, is very close to Kabardian and similar to Adyge. The majority of the Cherkess speak Russian as their second language, and a smaller number speak Karachai.

The Muslim Cherkess mostly follow the Hanafi school of Sunni Islam. The religion, coming relatively late to the Cherkess, traditionally has been less militant and more tolerant than the Islam practiced by the Caucasian peoples farther to the east. Among the Cherkess the Adat or custom laws—the Adyge-Habze— have remained extremely powerful.

NATION: The Cherkess homeland is distinguished by its rivers, which flow west to the Black Sea, so that from earliest times they have had peripheral contact with the peoples of the Mediterranean. Known to the ancient Greeks as Zyukhoy, the Cherkess probably settled the region of the north Caucasus before the sixth century B.C. Greek and Roman writers described tribes in the northwest Caucasus famed for their horse breeding and horsemanship. Possibly the earliest representative of the Caucasian peoples, the Circassians populated a wide area north of the Caucasus Mountains that figured prominently in the legends of ancient Greece.

The handsome Cherkess, valued as slaves, developed a warrior society as protection against the region's frequent invaders and raids by slavers. Cherkess women were considered especially beautiful and were valued in Turkish and Arabian harems. Cherkess men often hired out as mercenaries to powerful rulers.

Greek monks introduced Christianity to the warlike tribes in the sixth century A.D. A common Christian religion facilitated the Cherkess' establishment of ties to the Byzantines to the south and to opening trade routes to the early Slav state, Kievan Rus, in the north. By the late ninth century regular trade and diplomatic ties existed with the Slavs. The Circassian tribes adopted Christianity, while retaining many of their former pagan beliefs, during the eleventh and twelfth centuries.

The newly Christianized tribes became known for their skill in commercial trading. The Cherkess carried on an extensive trade with Byzantium, receiving goods unavailable in their homeland in exchange for horses, furs, honey, and filigreed jewelry.

The Mongol invasion of the region in 1241–42 ended contacts with Byzantium and forced some Circassians to move east toward the Terek River. Those Circassians who stayed in the west became known as the Cherkess. The devastation of rule by the Mongol Golden Horde greatly disrupted the consolidation of a single Circassian nation. Weakened by the Mongol conquest, the tribes came under the rule of Christian Georgia by the end of the thirteenth century. By the fifteenth century, the Cherkess had resumed trade with the West through Genoese merchants established in the coastal towns.

Circassian Kabard princes, from the fifteenth to the seventeenth centuries, dominated much of the North Caucasus as tributaries of the Turkish Ottoman Empire. Early in the sixteenth century the Ottoman Turks and the Crimean Tatars* introduced Islam to the region. The majority of the Cherkess clans, influenced by the Turks and Tatars, adopted the Islamic religion in the seventeenth century.

The Muslim Cherkess in the sixteenth and seventeenth centuries were in a perpetual state of war with the Tatar Khanate of Crimea and with the Turkic peoples of the region, the Karachais, Kumyks,* and Nogais.* The western Caucasus Mountains are relatively low and gentle, not allowing the Cherkess to retreat to mountain strongholds like the peoples farther east. For protection, the Cherkess, like other Circassians, alternatively sought alliances with Ottoman Turkey and the expanding Russian Empire. The Circassian peoples sent three diplomatic missions to Muscovy in the 1550s, which resulted in what the Circassians called an "alliance" but which the Russians termed a "voluntary union" with Russia.

The Christian Russians, extending their frontiers to the south, came into conflict with the Ottoman Turks, setting off a series of wars that continued sporadically for centuries. Russian settlers, following the Cossacks into the region, began to settle in the region claimed as traditional Circassian lands. The Russo-Turkish Wars, mostly fought on Circassian territory, sealed the fate of the Cherkess. In 1790 Russian forces defeated the Ottoman troops of Batal Pasha on the upper Kuban River. In 1804 the Russians founded Balalpashinsk, later renamed Cherkessk, in the middle of Cherkess territory. From the fort the Russians carried out vicious reprisals against the Cherkess who resisted Russian rule. In 1829 the Turks, in the Treaty of Adrianople, gave up all claims to the Circassian territories.

Rebellions and reprisals continued in the region in the 1840s and 1850s. In 1864 the Russians, after years of fighting, triumphed over the Circassian warriors. Some 400,000 Circassians, rejecting Christian domination, fled or were expelled to Turkish territory. Many died on the long journey. Of those who survived, some were assimilated, and some went farther south to settle in Syria, Jordan, Palestine, and Lebanon. Russians, Ukrainians, and Armenians* were settled in the depopulated Cherkess lands. By the beginning of the twentieth century only an estimated 20,000 Cherkess remained in the region. Relegated to a marginal existence in the rural areas, the Cherkess proved an enduring problem for the Russian military and civil authorities.

Openly sympathetic to the Muslim Turks when war began in 1914, the Cherkess enthusiastically welcomed the news that revolution had overthrown the hated tsarist government in February 1917. Cherkess appeals to the new government for religious freedom, political autonomy, and the reunification of the Circassian lands received no response. Responding to calls for Muslim solidarity, the Cherkess sent delegates to an all-Muslim conference in September 1917, seeking Muslim support for their demands.

The region was the scene of severe fighting during the Russian civil war, with the Cherkess alternately attacked or courted by both Whites and Reds. White opposition to autonomy for the Caucasian nations prompted many Cherkess to join the Reds, believing the Soviet promise of sovereignty within a federation of Soviet states. In January 1920 the Red Army drove the last of the White forces from Cherkessia and joined the region to the newly created Mountain Republic, which lasted only twenty months.

The victorious Bolsheviks subjected the region to a seemingly endless round of administrative changes designed to keep the Cherkess separated from the other Circassian peoples and always outnumbered by ethnic Slavs. Soviet linguists devised three separate written languages for the Cherkess, Adyge, and Kabards in an effort to further divide the three small nations. In January 1922 the Soviets established the Cherkess Autonomous Oblast.

Soviet repression, particularly of religion, included the closing of all religious schools in 1922. During the 1920s the Soviet authorities consolidated the Circassian peoples into two distinct groups, the Cherkess and the Kabards. Late in the 1930s the ethnic lines were again redrawn, with the Circassians being divided into three groups, the Adyge in the west, the Cherkess in the center, and the Kabards in the east. Each of the regions was separated by Slav-populated territory.

Thinking to capitalize on Cherkess grievances, the Nazi Germans, after taking the area during the Caucasus campaign of 1942, offered an alliance and promoted anticommunist solidarity. The Cherkess view that the Germans represented just another in a long series of invaders spared them the brutal deportations suffered by neighboring Muslim peoples following the return of the Soviet authorities.

Regional and ethnic tensions, suppressed for decades, emerged with the easing of Soviet restraints in the late 1980s. The three Circassian peoples, separated under tsarist and Soviet rule, demanded unification and the dissolution of the hybrid territories that the Cherkess and Kabards have been forced to share with the Turkic Karachai and Balkar peoples for most of this century. Demands for a separate Circassian republic within the Russian Federation accelerated with the disintegration of the Soviet state in August 1991.

Growing tensions between the Cherkess and Karachais mounted following the breakup of the Soviet Union. Demonstrators in Cherkessk demanded the withdrawal of the Cherkess from the parliament they share with the Karachai. In March 1992 the local republican governments signed a new federal treaty regulating relations with Moscow, but Cherkess nationalists continue to demand a separate federal republic, reunification of the Circassian lands, and redress for past injustices.

The Cherkess, joined to the other Muslim Caucasian peoples in traditional alliances and historic associations, in late 1994 condemned the Russian military attack on the separatist government in Chechenia. The Russian advance, mirroring that of the nineteenth century, has inflamed nationalist and anti-Russian sentiment in the Circassian territories.

One of the smaller of the Caucasian nations, the Cherkess look back on a long history, and their sense of identity is equal to that of many larger nations. During the 1990s the appearance of a number of Pan-Circassian groups seems to point to the establishment of closer ties to the other Circassian peoples, ties that were broken during the years of Soviet domination.

SELECTED BIBLIOGRAPHY

Abtorkhanov, Abdurahman, and Marie Bennigsen Broxup. *The North Caucasus Barrier: The Russian Advance towards the Muslim World.* 1992.

Diuk, Nadia, and Adrian Karatnycky. *The Hidden Nations: The People Challenge the Soviet Union.* 1990.

Mufti, Shauket. *Heros and Emperors in Circassian History.* 1972.

Traho, R. *The Circassian History.* 1994.

Wixman, Ronald. *The Peoples of the USSR: An Ethnographic Handbook.* 1984.

CORNISH

Kerne; Cornishmen

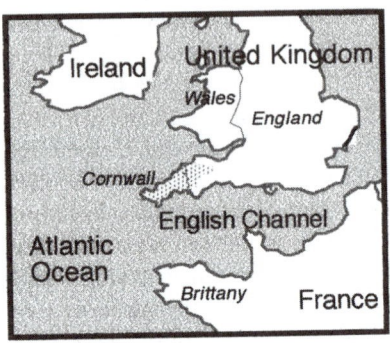

POPULATION: Approximately (2000 e) 590,000 Cornish in Europe, most in the Cornwall region of southwestern England in the United Kingdom. Large Cornish populations, the product of Cornish emigration, live in the United States, Canada, Australia, and New Zealand.

THE CORNISH HOMELAND: The Cornish homeland occupies a peninsula some 75 miles (120 km.) long and 45 miles (72 km.) wide at its base, terminating in the rugged promontory of Land's End. The region lies west of the Tamar River in southeastern England with the English Channel and Atlantic Ocean on its seaward side. Most of the region is a low plateau, which slopes from the rocky northern coast to the south and reaches its highest point at Brown Willy, 1,375 feet (419 m.). The peninsula, marked by a rocky, indented coast, is England's only area of subtropical vegetation. The deeply indented coasts, with their fine harbors, are lined with rocky cliffs. In the scenic river valleys are some of England's most productive fruit, vegetable, and dairy farms. In the uplands lush pastures support herds of sheep and cattle. The many fine harbors support a thriving fishing industry.

Officially, Cornwall includes the Isles of Scilly, 140 small islands in the Atlantic Ocean west of Land's End. Cornwall forms a county of England and a separate hereditary duchy, the title held by the heir to the British throne. *County of Cornwall and Isles of Scilly (Mebyon Kernow)*: 1,418 sq.mi.–3,546 sq.km. (2000 e) 472,000—Cornish 89%, other English* 10%. The Cornish capital and major cultural center is Truro, (2000 e) 16,000. The largest city in Cornwall is Cambronn (Camborne-Redruth) (2000 e) 49,000, and the other important cultural center is Bodmin, (2000 e) 12,000, the former capital.

FLAG: The Cornish national flag, the flag of the national movement and the unofficial flag of the county, is a black field charged with a centered white cross, the cross of St. Pirin, Cornwall's patron saint.

PEOPLE: The Cornish are a Celtic people, the descendants of the pre-Roman Celtic population of the British Isles and Western Europe. The Cornish are related to the other Celtic peoples of Europe, the Bretons,* Irish,* Scots,* Manx,* Welsh,* and the Galicians* of northwestern Spain.

The Cornish language, Kernewek, which died out in the eighteenth century, since the 1960s has been successfully revived as the national language. The language belongs to the Brythonic branch of the Celtic languages and is closely related to the Breton language of Brittany, across the English Channel in northwestern France. Among younger Cornish, learning and speaking the language have become a matter of pride.

The Cornish culture, which has survived in the isolation of their peninsula, is closely tied to the traditional Cornish occupation, tin mining. The working of the mines in the region goes back for over thirty-five centuries. The majority of the Cornish belong to the Protestant Methodist faith, which has also become closely identified with the Cornish culture.

NATION: The origins of the Celts has been traced to southwestern Germany and northeastern France in the second millennium B.C. to a group of tribes speaking Indo-European dialects. Armed with weapons made of iron and mounted on horses, the Celts spread rapidly across the continent to control all of Europe, from Spain and Ireland to the Black Sea. Celtic tribes moved into the British Isles during the Iron Age.

The Brythonic Celts migrated to the island of Britain from the European mainland in the first century B.C., later than the Celtic migrations to Ireland, Scotland, and the Isle of Man. The earlier Celtic migrants spoke Goidelic Celtic, while the later migrants, the ancestors of the Cornish, Welsh, and Bretons, spoke Brythonic Celtic, a linguistic division that has persisted to the present.

Conquered by the Romans in the first century A.D., the Celts of Britannia assimilated into Roman life, becoming an urban, sophisticated population comfortable with the multiethnic Roman Empire. The Romans gradually abandoned Britannia in the fifth century. The withdrawal of the Roman garrison led to local squabbles, which further weakened the island's defenses. Germanic peoples from northern Europe invaded, and many of the Romanized Celts fled west, leaving the eastern districts to the newcomers, the Angles, Saxons, and Jutes.

Many of the refugees settled the western peninsulas, presently Cornwall and Wales, and even crossed the narrow channel to settle the peninsula later called Little Britannia or Brittany. The southern peninsula in Britain, called corn, the old Celtic word for "horn," referred to the horn-shaped peninsula and came to signify the Celts on the horn or Cornwall. In the eighth century Celtic Dumnonia, later called Devon, fell to the invading Anglo-Saxons, leaving the peninsula isolated beyond the Tamar River. Cornwall became closely associated with the Arthurian legend, the mass of popular medieval lore that originated with the tales of a Celtic warrior who fought twelve victorious battles against the Saxon invaders. The region's tin mines, known to the ancient Greeks and Phoenicians, sustained Cornwall's independence until its conquest by Saxon King Athelstan in 936. In the eleventh century the Saxons extended their rule throughout the peninsula.

Following the invasion of England by the Normans* in 1066, the Celts of Cornwall vigorously resisted Norman influence. In recognition of its separate character and history, Cornwall became a separate duchy in 1337, an appendage of the royal heir in England. The duchy has traditionally descended to the eldest son of the British monarch.

The Cornish fiercely resisted assimilation, although English gradually replaced Cornish as the language of daily life in the seventeenth century. Fervently Roman Catholic, the Cornish were slow to accept the Protestant Reformation. Ten thousand marched to protect their Roman Catholic faith in the sixteenth century, but two centuries later they abandoned Catholicism to embrace Wesleyan teachings. The Cornish converted en masse to the new Protestant Methodist sect, which became closely identified with their unique culture.

Scorned as backward peasants and punished for speaking their Celtic language, the Cornish struck back the only way they could: they turned to the ancient Cornish traditions of piracy and smuggling. Cornish "wreckers" lured English ships onto the rocky coast, then legally salvaged the cargoes. The practice became so widespread that the Cornish coast came to be called the graveyard of ships in the seventeenth and eighteenth centuries.

Tin mining, closely tied to Cornish culture and the mainstay of the local economy, collapsed in 1866. Over 7,000 destitute Cornish families emigrated, mostly to Canada, the United States, Australia, and New Zealand. Between 1860 and 1900 over one-tenth of the population left the region. The unprofitable mines continued as the only important source of income until the worldwide depression of the 1930s ended even the minimum of mining activity in Cornwall, which increased unemployment and the hardships of the depression.

Demand for tin during World War II allowed the reopening of many of the mines, bringing a modest economic upturn that continued as Britain's access to colonial resources disappeared after the war. In the 1960s tourism replaced mining as Cornwall's economic mainstay. The visitors, drawn to Cornwall's subtropical climate and unique culture, are called *emmets* by the locals, a Cornish word for the insects they resemble as they swarm across the Cornish peninsula.

The Cornish, even before the reculturation that began after World War II, maintained that the land beyond the Tamar River was a separate country, Celtic Cornwall. Tourists at the border were given instructions telling they were entering a foreign country. Much of that attitude remains with trips across the Tamar referred to as "going up to England."

Cornish nationalism, spurred by increased inter-Celtic contact since the early 1960s, focused on the Cornish language, whose last native speaker died in 1777. A revived interest in their language, beginning in the 1920s, prompted a revival of the Cornish culture. The successful revival of Kernewek and the revitalization of the traditional Cornish culture fueled the growth of Cornish nationalism in the 1960s and 1970s. Nationalists demanded the same status within the United Kingdom accorded the other Celtic nations, Wales and Scotland. So successful was the national revival that in the late 1980s Kernewek became the fastest growing of all the Celtic languages. Cornish leaders pressed for a regional council and the teaching of the Cornish language in the region's schools.

The United Kingdom's entry into the European Economic Community opened a nationalist debate on Cornwall's future, the subject given added urgency by the closing of all but a few of Cornwall's 600 mines by 1990. The last tin mine in Cornwall closed in March 1998.

The region, one of the most neglected in England, is increasingly restive. The crisis in tin mining, beginning in 1995, gradually closed the last five mines, making unemployment in the region up to 35% in some areas. With the end of tin mining, the Cornish feel that they are losing a basic part of their culture and identity. Economic hardships have reinforced the local pride in being Cornish, but many are not overly proud of being British. Cornish miners are again looking for overseas mining jobs as their forebears did in the past.

Economic and cultural grievances have added to the rising Cornish nationalism, the more militant asserting that the European Union begins beyond the Tamar River until the Cornish are recognized as a separate European people with their own state under their black and white St. Pirin flag. Groups such as Cornish Solidarity work for the equality of the Cornish nation within a federal United Kingdom. Plans for separate legislatures in Scotland and Wales have raised new demands for a separate Cornish administration and an autonomous Cornish state within the United Kingdom.

The Cornish consider the closing of the last mine not only an economic disaster but a cultural disaster. In March 1998 the last Cornish tin mine was closed, but in November of that year it was purchased by an investment company. In March 1999 the mine was reopened with 250 mine workers. Mining, although an integral part of Cornish history, is now nearly extinct and has lost its importance to the Cornish culture.

SELECTED BIBLIOGRAPHY

Filbee, Majorie. *Celtic Cornwall*. 1996.
Guthrie, A. *Cornwall in the Age of Steam*. 1995.
Henwood, George. *Cornwall's Mines and Miners*. 1981.
Oblinger, Carl. *Cornwall: The People and Culture of an Industrial Camelot*. 1984.
Strong, Richard. *Cornwall*. 1998.

CORSICANS

Corsu; Corce; Corse; Corsos

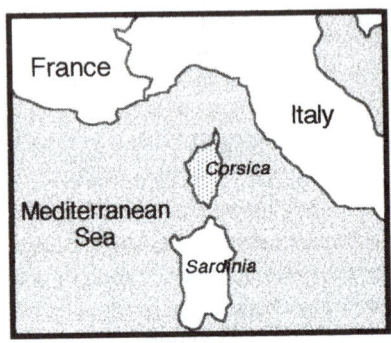

POPULATION: Approximately (2000 e) 390,000 Corsicans in Europe, the majority living on the island of Corsica in the Mediterranean, but with over one-third living in mainland France.

THE CORSICAN HOMELAND: The Corsican homeland lies in the Mediterranean Sea southeast of mainland France, between the Italian mainland on the north and the Italian island of Sardinia on the south. Corsica is a mountainous island 115 miles long from Cape Corse in the north to Bonifacio in the south. Much of the region is wild, mostly covered in thick undergrowth called *maquis* in French. The flowers of the *maquis* produce a fragrance that is carried far out to sea, giving the island the name "the scented isle." The east coast of the island is unbroken by harbors or bays, and the coastal plain of Aleria is dotted with lagoons and swamps. The west coast is very irregular and indented with the Gulf of Ajaccio its largest inlet. The island's Mediterranean climate makes tourism and agriculture the major industries.

The island, called Corse in French, since 1975 has formed a region of France, divided into two departments. *Region of Corsica (Corsu)*: 3,367 sq.mi.–8,772 sq.km. (2000 e) 231,000—Corsicans 55%, French* 30%, Italians* 5%. The Corsican capital and major cultural center is Corte (Corti in the Corsican language), (2000 e) 15,000. The island's major cities are Ajaccio (Aiacciu), (2000 e) 64,000, and Bastia, (2000 e) 38,000.

FLAG: The Corsican national flag, the flag of the national movement, is a white field bearing a centered black Moor's head in profile.

PEOPLE: The Corsicans are a Romance people, their Latin heritage modified by the influences brought to the island by its many conquerors. Related to the mainland Italians and to the Sards of Sardinia, the Corsicans have developed a unique Mediterranean culture. The islanders are known for the vendettas, the bitter prolonged feuds that, until recent decades, were passed down from one generation to the next. The *maquis* provided a perfect hideout for bandits, and blood feuds were a traditional occupation until suppressed by the French government. The clan system, formerly the basis of Corsican society, has also declined under French rule.

The Corsicans speak a Tuscan dialect of Italian with a strong admixture of non-Italian borrowing, particularly French. The Corsican nationalists claim the language is a separate Romance language spoken in four dialects, Sartenais, Vico-Ajaccio, Northern Corsican, and Venaco. The language has been recognized as a separate language by the French government. The Corsicans are bilingual in French, but many are fluent only in Corsican. There is a movement for bilingual education on the island. Corsicans remain conservative and devoutly Roman Catholic. Their faith, which has sustained them through centuries of rule by outsiders, is an integral part of their unique Mediterranean culture.

NATION: The island was originally settled by Etruscans, the mysterious pre-Roman people of northern Italy, but has a long history of domination by various Mediterranean empires. Phoenicians from present Lebanon held the island, followed by their offspring, the Carthaginians from North Africa. Ionian Greek settlements existed on Corsica as early as 550 B.C. The Romans took control of the island from the Carthaginians during the Punic Wars, in 259 B.C., and from the third century B.C. to the fifth century A.D., the Romans ruled the island. Latinized by Roman settlers, the islanders were prosperous and contented.

The collapse of Roman power left the island virtually defenseless. Devastated by the Germanic Vandals who crossed from the mainland, the island briefly came under the rule of the Byzantines in A.D. 534, but they were unable to hold Corsica against successive invasions of Germanic tribes from the mainland. The island fell to the invading Goths, was taken by the Lombards* in 725, and eventually came under the control of the Germanic Franks.

Threatened by the Muslim Saracens in the eighth century, the Franks ceded the island to the Holy See. Between 800 and 1034 the island was held or constantly threatened by Arabic Saracens. Pope Gregory VII in 1047 gave the island to the maritime republic of Pisa. In 1132 Pisa's rival, Genoa, induced Pope Innocent II to divide jurisdiction between Pisa and Genoa. After a long and bloody struggle, the Pisans were defeated, and Genoese rule was extended to most of the island in 1312. The Genoese expelled the last of the Pisan troops in 1347.

Genoese rule proved harsh and unpopular. In the fifteenth century the actual administration of the island was taken over by the Genoese Bank of San Gregorio. From 1458 to 1558 the French controlled the island, bringing more modern administration before returning the island to Genoese rule. In 1729 the unhappy Corsicans launched a decades-long rebellion. The revolt after 1755 was led by Pasquale Paoli, whose military successes achieved virtual independence for the island. Paoli created a Corsican government and opened a university to train the administrators needed by the new state. Corsican success and Genoa's inability to break the rebellion continued as a stalemate. Genoa finally sold the island to France in 1768, just in time for Corsica's most famous son, Napoleon Bonaparte, to be born a French citizen in 1769.

The French colonial administration dissolved all Corsican institutions and in 1770 forcibly closed the Corsican university, which is still a nationalist issue. Sporadic revolts against French rule continued up to the French Revolution. The Corsicans rebelled against the French after the 1789 revolution and in 1793 drove the last French officials from the island. The rebel leaders requested British assistance and in 1794 organized a plebiscite that confirmed Corsican appeals for union with Great Britain. Recovered by Napoleon's troops in 1796, the island fell to the British in 1814 during the Napoleonic Wars, but despite Corsican protests the 1815 Congress of Vienna returned the island to French rule.

Banditry, blood feuds, and attacks on French authorities continued to disrupt the island's administration, the *maquis* providing refuge for bandits and dissidents as it had for centuries. Clan rule, the major loyalty of the islanders, declined slowly under French administration, while a strong Bonapartist tradition and anti-Genoese sentiment helped to assure Corsican loyalty to France during most of the nineteenth century.

French rule brought the island education, in French, and relative order, but the economy was left mainly agricultural. The French language became predominant in the cities, but efforts to assimilate the Corsicans mostly failed. Neglected and underdeveloped, the island's inhabitants found it necessary to leave for the French mainland to find work. Resentment of this forced emigration coalesced national sentiment on the island in the 1920s. The first autonomist organization formed in 1927. Banditry was not fully eradicated until the 1930s.

Italian troops occupied the island after the fall of France in 1940 and initiated a program to Italianize the islanders. A Corsican uprising in 1943, aided by Free French forces, drove the Italians from the island. The triumphant Corsicans, preparing for independence, felt gravely disappointed by the reimposition of French rule. In 1945 the Corsican nationalists lost spirit, and the movement became dormant. Despair spurred a massive postwar exodus to the mainland, finally forcing the French authorities to accelerate development, mainly in tourism. Development of the island's tourist facilities continued under several French administrations.

The emergence of the modern national movement stems from a failed insurrection in 1958, during the French colonial war in Algeria. The uprising was partly the result of the French policy of settling evacuated colonists and loyal Algerians, some 17,000 between 1958 and 1963, on the island. The insurrection failed, but it sparked the rebirth of Corsican nationalism. Numerous nationalist groups formed over the next two decades. Several groups turned to violence and terrorism, mostly directed at tourist installations owned by foreigners, including the French. In 1975 Libya began monetary and training support for the largest of the nationalist organizations, the Front for the Liberation of Corsica (FLNC).

In 1980 the socialists won the French general elections, and the Corsicans looked for the decentralization promised during the election campaign. Terrorism waned, and Corsican leaders entered into negotiations with the new socialist government, demanding education in the Corsican language, the reopening of the Corsican university, closed since 1770, and the teaching of specifically Corsican history. In 1982 the French government passed a statute giving the island greater powers than the mainland regions. Corsica became the first French region to elect its own government under the decentralization scheme.

Unsatisfied with the limited autonomy offered by the French government, the FLNC and other groups resumed their activities. Terrorist incidents grew from 111 in 1974 to 238 in 1976 and a record 805 in 1982. The majority of the incidents involved the destruction of tourist homes or complexes owned by non-Corsicans. In January 1983 the government began a crackdown on nationalist activities and banned several organizations. In March 1986 the Corsican nationalists took their campaign to mainland France, with a series of bomb attacks across southern France.

Corsica remains virtually without industrial development, and unemployment would be much higher except for continuing immigration to the mainland. A lack of transportation and airports is among the main Corsican grievances. Since 1988 the majority of the Corsicans have supported more moderate political parties with a subsequent loss of support for the violent separatist organizations.

In 1991 French senators rejected key portions of a bill that would recognize the Corsicans as a separate nation. Despite opposition in the French General Assembly, a new statute was finally passed recognizing the Corsicans as a distinct people, only to have the statute overturned by the Constitutional Court. A 1991 poll of the islanders resulted in overwhelming support for some form of autonomy, with one-third favoring immediate independence from France.

A report released by the French government in September 1998 stated that the island is run by Mafia-like gangs that intimidate the authorities, carry out vendetta killings, and are involved in shady financial dealings. The report also denounced decades of French government attempts to buy off nationalists with public works and financial aid, most of which never reached its planned destination. The number of murders is three times that of the French mainland, and the number of violent crimes continues to climb. The Corsicans, although they often rankle under French rule, have benefited economically. By 1998 the French government subsidies amounted to about $4,600 per Corsican per year.

SELECTED BIBLIOGRAPHY

Carrington, Dorothy. *The Dream-Hunters of Corsica*. 1996.
Chiari, Joseph. *Corsica, Columbus's Isle*. 1960.
Taylor, Theo. *Corsica*. 1994.
Thrasher, Peter A. *Pasquale Paoli: An Enlightened Hero, 1725–1807*. 1970
Wilson, Stephen. *Feuding, Conflict and Banditry in 19th Century Corsica*. 1988.

CRIMEAN TATARS

Krym-Tatars; Krym-Turks; Crim
Tatar; Krymskije; Attars

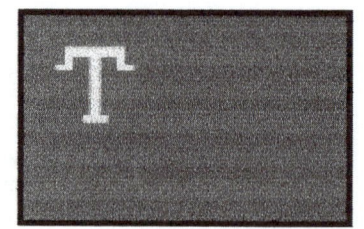

POPULATION: Approximately (2000 e) 332,000 Crimean Tatars in Europe and another 210,000 in Central Asia, mostly in Kazakhstan and Uzbekistan. There are smaller Crimean Tatar populations in Romania and Bulgaria.

THE CRIMEAN TATAR HOMELAND: The Crimean Tatar homeland lies in southern Ukraine, a large peninsula jutting into the Black Sea and connected to the mainland by the narrow Isthmus of Perekop. The northern part of the peninsula is steppe, drained by occasional streams. In the south the Crimean or Yaila Mountains protect the Black Sea littoral, the Crimean Riviera, with a fine, subtropical climate. The eastern tip of the Crimean region is the Kerch Peninsula, which is separated from the Russian mainland by the Kerch Strait, a narrow opening that connects the Black Sea to the Sea of Azov. The peninsula, with its pleasant climate, was a favorite resort of tsarist aristocracy and later Soviet hierarchy.

Officially, the Crimean Peninsula forms an autonomous republic in Ukraine, but the region's future is disputed by the Ukrainian government, the peninsula's Russian majority, and the indigenous population, the Crimean Tatars. *Republic of Crimea (Respublika Krim)*: 10,425 sq.mi.–27,001 sq.km. (2000 e) 2,623,000—Russians* 63%, Ukrainians* 24%, Crimean Tatars 10%, Greeks* 2%, Germans* 1%. The traditional Crimean Tatar capital and major cultural center is Bakhchysarai (called Bakchisarai in the Crimean Tatar language), (2000 e) 23,000. The peninsula's largest cities are Sevastopol, called Akhtiar by the Tatars, (2000 e) 409,000 and Simferopol (Akmechet), (2000 e) 387,000.

FLAG: The Crimean Tatar national flag, the flag of the national movement, is a light blue field bearing the *tarak tamga*, a yellow device resembling a scale, on the upper hoist.

PEOPLE: The Crimean Tatars, the indigenous nation of the Crimea Peninsula and the mainland area formerly known as Taurida, are a Turkic people belonging to the southern branch of the Turkic peoples, the Orguz. In Soviet censuses the Crimean Tatars were included with the larger group of Tatars* of the Volga region, but the culture and language of the Crimean Tatars are quite different.

The Crimean Tatar language is a Turkic language belonging to the Kipchak or Western Turkic group of languages. Since 1939 the language has been written in the Cyrillic alphabet. The language is spoken in three major dialects, Northern or Steppe Crimean, Central Crimean, and Southern Crimean.

The Crimean Tatars comprise three distinct divisions united by culture and history, the Tatars, the descendants of the peninsula's original inhabitants, the Krymchaks, numbering some 60,000, formerly the inhabitants of the adjacent mainland, and the Karaites, numbering about 30,000, who speak a distinctive dialect and practice an archaic form of Judaism.

NATION: The Cimmerians were the first known inhabitants of the peninsula, with evidence that they lived in the region as early as the eighth century B.C. Scythians overran the area in the seventh century B.C. and settled the interior steppe lands. Greeks began to colonize the coastal areas in the sixth century B.C., and in 438 B.C. most of the Crimea came under the rule of the Spartocids, a Thracian dynasty of Greek culture. The peninsula later formed part of the Greek kingdom of the Cimmerian Bosporus ruled by the Spartocids.

In the first century A.D., the peninsula became a Roman protectorate and remained part of the Roman Empire for over two centuries. In the third century barbarian tribes invaded the peninsula, the Goths and later the Huns. From the seventh to the eleventh centuries the Khazars controlled the region. The Khazars introduced Judaism as their state religion, which remains the religion of the Karaites. The Khazars were followed by the Cumans, who held the region from the eleventh to the thirteenth centuries. The many peoples who conquered and settled the peninsula left behind an ethnically and religiously diverse population.

The Crimean Tatars first emerged as a distinct national group in the thirteenth and fourteenth centuries. At the time, the coastal cities were controlled by Greeks, Armenians,* Jews, Italians,* and French* merchants. The steppe lands north of the Crimean Mountains were inhabited by nomadic tribes that were Turkic in terms of language and Islamic in religion.

The Byzantines ruled the multiethnic Crimea when the Turkic and Mongol hordes overran the region in 1239. Turkic tribes, remnants of the invaders, settled the peninsula and mixed with the earlier Turkic peoples. The Turkic tribes took control of the coastal cities and extended their authority across the peninsula. Following the disintegration of the Mongol-Turkic Golden Horde, the local Turkic peoples, called Tatars, erected a separate Tatar khanate in 1475 with Haci Giray as the first khan of the independent state.

The khanate, although eventually it became nominally tributary to the Turkish Ottoman Empire, expanded to control much of southern Russia, Ukraine, and eastern Poland. The khanate formed a buffer between the Ottoman Empire and the expanding Muscovite and Polish-Lithuanian states. The presence of a militarily strong Crimean Tatar khanate prevented the Europeans from expanding southward into the steppes.

The Tatars established trading links to most of the Mediterranean and beyond through the contacts and ties of the large Genoese and Greek populations of their southern port cities. In the early eighteenth century the related Krymchaks settled the adjoining mainland region known as Tauria. The Crimean Tatar state developed an advanced administrative bureaucracy, a codified legal system, and hierarchical political institutions.

The decline of the Ottoman Empire allowed the Russians to push south. Muscovite troops first invaded the Crimea in the 1680s, and in 1696 Peter the Great captured Azov, on the mainland, giving the Russians access to the Black Sea. The khanate, rich on trade, developed a brilliant and sophisticated civilization even as its outer provinces fell to the expanding Russian Empire. In 1736 invading Russians conquered all except the Tatar heartland, the Crimean Peninsula and mainland Tauria. The Russian empress Catherine the Great forced the Ottoman Empire to recognize the independence of the khanate, which she annexed in 1783. The annexation opened the way for the Russian conquest of the remaining territories in 1792–93, without risking war with the still-powerful Turks. Due to centuries of slave raids and incursions by the Tatars, there was a deep Slavic hostility toward them.

An estimated 1 million Tatars fled the Russian onslaught to refuge in Turkish territory, leaving large parts of the newly annexed region virtually depopulated. Government-sponsored settlement brought an influx of Slavs to settle the mainland Tauria. Over the next century, an official policy of assimilation was pressed by the local authorities. Tatar architecture was destroyed, and ancient cultural monuments disappeared. The government encouraged large-scale Slavic immigration and Tatar emigration to Turkish territory.

The remaining Tatars, mostly in Crimea, accused of collaborating with the Turks during the Crimean War of 1853–56, suffered another great population decline as the authorities deported 100,000 to Russia's interior provinces, and over twice that number fled to Ottoman territory before the authorities stopped all emigration in 1862. By 1897 the devastated Tatar nation accounted for only 34% of the population of Taurida Province, which comprised the Crimean Peninsula and mainland Tauria.

The Russian government after 1860 enrolled Tatar children in Russian schools. Eventually, a Tatar intelligensia emerged, separate from the traditional Muslim hierarchy. Education, which led to modernization, spurred the growth of national consciousness and led to demands for greater rights within the Russian Empire.

The opening of a Tatar press in 1883 stimulated a Tatar cultural revival and the growth of Tatar nationalism. Suppressed in 1891, many nationalists fled to Turkey. In 1909 Tatar students in Constantinople formed Vatan, a nationalist organization dedicated to the creation of an independent Crimean Tatar state. Openly favoring the Turks during World War I, the nationalists mobilized. By the time revolution swept Russia in February 1917, Vatan had underground cells in most Tatar towns and villages.

A Tatar congress convened in September 1917 rejected the Bolshevik coup in October, which was seen as just another form of Slavic oppression. Threatened by local Bolsheviks, nationalist leaders declared Taurida independent on 10 December 1917. Fighting soon broke out between Tatar nationalists and the pro-Bolshevik soldiers and sailors who took control of Sevastopol, and in January 1918 the poorly equipped Tatars suffered defeat.

In March 1918 German troops took control of the region, and the Tatar leaders emerged from hiding to organize an independent state on the Crimean Peninsula. On 16 May 1918 they declared the Crimean Democratic Republic independent of both the Russian factions as civil war swept across the disintegrating Russian Empire. Defeated by the Soviet Red Army in 1919, the peninsula was quickly occupied, and Tatar nationalist leaders were executed. In 1921 the new Soviet government, unable to fully suppress Tatar nationalism, decided to allow the Tatars, like the other large Soviet nationalities, to have their own national republic.

Soviet collectivization of the peninsula led to widespread starvation in 1921. Food was confiscated for shipment to central Russia, while more than 100,000 Tatars starved to death, and tens of thousands fled to Turkey or Romania. During the collectivization of 1928–29, thousands of Crimean Tatar peasants were deported or slaughtered. The government campaign led to another famine in 1931–33. No other Soviet nationality suffered the decline imposed on the Crimean Tatars; between 1917 and 1933 half the Crimean Tatar population had been killed or deported.

Occupied by German forces in 1941, the Tatars attempted to protect their Jewish Karaite minority while collaborating the least of all the Soviet peoples in the occupation zones, including the ethnic Russians. However, the Soviet leader Joseph Stalin accused the entire Crimean Tatar nation of treason. On the night of 18 May 1944 the entire Crimean Tatar population was rounded up by the Red Army, and between 200,000 and 300,000 suffered a brutal deportation east in sealed cattle cars. The Tatars claim that 110,000 died as a result of the deportation, which they denounce as genocide.

The Soviet authorities obliterated all historical, linguistic, and cultural traces of the Crimean Tatar nation. Place-names were changed, and the history of the Crimean Tatars was rewritten, portraying them as no more than nomadic brigands. The Soviet government made a gift of the peninsula to the Ukrainian Soviet Socialist Republic on the 300th anniversary of Ukraine's union with Russia in 1954.

Only after Stalin's death in 1953 did life begin to improve for the Crimean

Tatars. Restrictions on the movement of the Tatars was lifted, and Tatar organizations began to organize. Not rehabilitated with the other nations deported by Stalin in 1956–57, the Crimean Tatars launched a campaign to win official recognition of their right to return to their homeland. The Tatars staged demonstrations and protests and attempted to bring the issue before the United Nations and other international organizations. Delegations sent to the Kremlin to present their case to successive Soviet leaders were simply ignored or imprisoned. Finally, on 8 September 1967, the Crimean Tatars were officially rehabilitated, but permission to return to their homeland was not granted.

From the 1960s to the 1980s the revival of the culture accelerated with the participation of Tatar newspapers, publishing houses, and organizations. A Soviet government commission appointed in 1987 finally addressed the issue. By 1989 over 150,000 had returned to the Crimea. The liberalizing of Soviet society in the late 1980s allowed the nationalist movement to organize. In 1990, after forty-six years in exile, the right to return to their homeland was finally granted. On 28 June 1991 a Crimean Tatar congress proclaimed their historic right to the peninsula as the "national territory of the Crimean Tatar nation."

The disintegration of the Soviet Union, resulting in the establishment of an independent Ukrainian state, opened a bitter conflict over the fate of the region and dealt a blow to the Crimean Tatars' right to a national homeland. Russian claims to the Crimea, particularly to the large former Soviet naval fleet at Sevastopol, quickly strained relations between Russia and Ukraine. Both governments attempted to use the Crimean Tatars in the dispute while carefully avoiding the issue of the Tatars' ancient claim to the peninsula.

The returning Crimean Tatars, numbering over 250,000 by 1993, found themselves relegated to marginal lands or the shantytowns around their former capital and other cities. The harsh conditions of the lives of the returnees have given new impetus to the national movement. In July 1993 a number of nationalist organizations joined to demand the resurrection of the independent Crimean Tatar state and reiterated the Tatar claim to the entire peninsula, a claim that Crimean Tatar nationalist leaders point out predates either the Russian or Ukrainian claims on the region.

In January 1994, in an effort to enlist Crimean Tatar support in the ongoing dispute with the Russians, the Ukrainian government increased tenfold its allocation for construction projects to house the returning Crimean Tatars; however, the government continued to demolish Tatar refugee settlements. In February 1995 the leaders of the Tatars demanded a quota for the Crimean Tatars in the Ukrainian parliament to overcome their dispersed demographics in gaining representation. Although ethnic clashes are rare, some tensions continue to exist between the Crimean Tatars and the ethnic Russians who dominate the region.

The three claims to the peninsula, Russian, Ukrainian, and Crimean Tatar, could lead to violence in the region; however, the Tatar leader, Mustafa Cemioglu, is a firm believer in nonviolence and was a close friend of Andrey Sakharov. The Tatars remain loosely allied with the Ukrainian authorities in opposition to the Russian majority in the region. Their claims for special status have still to be addressed, and thousands of returning Crimean Tatars have still not received Ukrainian citizenship.

SELECTED BIBLIOGRAPHY

Allworth, Edward A. *The Tatars of the Crimea: Return to the Homeland.* 1998.
Allworth, Edward A., ed. *Tatars of the Crimea: Their Struggle for Survival.* 1988.
Fisher, Alan W. *The Crimean Tatars.* 1978.
Gibbs, Peter. *Crimean Blunder.* 1960.
Kirimli, Hakan. *National Movements and National Identity among the Crimean Tatars (1905–1916).* 1996.

CROATS

Hrvatski; Croatians

POPULATION: Approximately (2000 e) 5,450,000 Croats in Europe, the majority, 3,678,000 in Croatia. Croat populations outside the republic include the 750,000 in adjacent parts of Bosnia and Herzegovina and smaller groups in Yugoslavia, Macedonia, Romania, Greece, Slovakia, Germany, Sweden, and other European countries. There are also large Croat populations in the United States, Canada, and Australia. Croat sources count 10 million Croats worldwide.

THE CROAT HOMELAND: The Croat homeland lies in the northern Balkan Peninsula in South-Central Europe. Topographically, the country can be divided into three regions. The barren, rocky mountains of Dalmatia are part of the Dinaric Alps and extend through the center of Croatia. The rolling hills of the Zagorje region that is located north of Zagreb and the Pannonian Plain, which is flat plain and is bordered by the Drava River in the north, and the Danube and Sava Rivers to the east and south are the most productive regions of the country. Croatia includes a string of islands lying in the Adriatic Sea along the subtropical Dalmatian coast. The country's principal rivers are the Drava and Sava.

Part of the Croat homeland is included in the neighboring Republic of Bosnia and Herzegovina, primarily in the southwest Herzegovina region. Attempts to unite with Croatia during the Bosnian War were never recognized. The peace agreement, signed in 1995, precludes the union of the Bosnian Croat territories and the Republic of Croatia. According to the terms of the Dayton peace accord, the separate Croatian state of Herzeg-Bosnia was supposed to disappear, but it remains effectively in existence.

The Croatian republic was declared independent of Yugoslavia in 1991 and

was internationally recognized in 1992. *Republic of Croatia (Republike Hrvat-
ske)*: 21,829 sq.mi.–56,537 sq.km. (2000 e) 4,859,000—Croats 80%, Serbs*
10%, Hungarians* 3%, Italians* 2%, Bosnians* 1%. The Croat capital and major
cultural center is Zagreb, (2000 e) 965,000 (metropolitan area 1,213,000).

FLAG: The Croatian national flag, the official flag of the Republic of Croatia,
is a horizontal tricolor of red, white, and blue bearing a centered shield of
twenty-five red and white squares surmounted by a crown of five crests representing the historic regions of Croatia, Slavonia, Dalmatia, Dubrovnik, and
Istria.

PEOPLE: The Croats are a South Slav people whose name comes from an
old Slavic word meaning mountaineer. Ethnically related to the neighboring
South Slav peoples, the Croats' claim to national identity is based on their
separate history and their Roman Catholic faith. Traditionally oriented to Western Europe, since the breakup of the Roman Empire in the fourth century, Croats
continue to see themselves as the frontier of the Western world. According to
Croat tradition, the Orthodox and Muslim East begins beyond their eastern and
southern borders. The Croat nation includes the Croats in the Croat heartland
around Zagreb, the Slavonians in the eastern region of Slavonia, and the Dalmatians, who live west of the Dinaric Alps along the coast of the Adriatic Sea.
Until the nineteenth century the Dalmatians spoke a Romance language related
to Italian.

The Croats speak Croatian, formerly considered a western dialect, written in
the Latin alphabet, of the Serbo-Croatian language. Since the independence of
Croatia in 1991, the Croats have claimed Croatian as a separate South Slav
language, the official language of their new state. Following the commencement
of war with Serbia, many Croats sought to differentiate Croatian from Serbian,
resurrecting archaic Croatian words and stressing the existing difference in
script. Croatian is written in the Latin alphabet, while Serbian utilizes the Cyrillic alphabet used by a number of other Slavic languages. Croats also reject
the 1954 Novi Sad Agreement, which declared Serbo-Croatian to be one language with two scripts.

NATION: Little was known of the northern Balkan Peninsula until the imposition of Roman rule in 39–34 B.C. The region's population, under Roman
rule, became Latin in culture and language. The area, particularly the districts
along the Adriatic Sea coastline, were favorites of many illustrious Romans.
Forming part of Illyricum, the Illyrian provinces, the region prospered under
Roman rule with fine cities and a wealthy, cultured population.

The Balkan Peninsula, after centuries of Roman rule, formed the border established at the division of the Roman Empire in A.D. 395, the beginning of the
historic religious and cultural divisions of the Balkan region. While most of the
Balkan nations were assigned to the Eastern or Byzantine Empire, the Illyrian
provinces remained part of the western empire, the Latin Empire of Rome. The
division divided the Balkan Peninsula into a western region focused on Latin
Rome and an eastern region focused on Greek Constantinople.

The flourishing region, called Pannonia, remained under Roman rule until the fifth-century invasions by barbarian tribes, Huns, Ostrogoths, and Visigoths. Pannonia was conquered by the Avars,* a Mongolian people, in the sixth century A.D. During the seventh century, the Slavic Croats conquered the Avars; subsequently, the Croats were conquered by the Franks. The Slavs were converted to Christianity by Latin and Greek missionaries, already feeling the religious and political strains between Rome and Constantinople.

During the next centuries parts of the region were included in Charlemagne's empire as a region tributary to the Franks. Venetians* finally gained a foothold in the coastal Dalmatian districts in the 900s. A Croat kingdom, created in 924 under Tomislav, formed a dynastic union with the Hungarian kingdom in 1102 after a period of political anarchy. Under Hungarian influence the Croats remained oriented to the western half of Europe, where Roman Catholicism and the Latin alphabet predominated. The Turks took control of the Croat-populated Herzegovina in 1482 and conquered the eastern region of Slavonia in the sixteenth century. Although divided between three foreign empires, Austria, Venice, and the Ottoman Empire, the majority of the Croats escaped the centuries of Turkish rule that so influenced the development of the other South Slav peoples.

The Hungarian Kingdom, including the Croat heartlands, became part of the Hapsburg Empire that ruled from Vienna after 1687. Slavonia, with its large Croat population, was ceded by the Turks to Austria in 1699. Other parts of Croatia came under Hapsburg rule during the reign of Maria Theresa after 1740, although most of Dalmatia remained under Venetian control, and the city of Ragusa, later called Dubrovnik, was a semi-independent republic. In 1797 the Venetians ceded their part of Dalmatia to Austria.

The major South Slav language, called Serbo-Croatian, spoken in Croatia, Serbia, Montenegro, and Bosnia-Herzegovina, remained a collection of regional dialects in the nineteenth century. Although Serb and Croat intellectuals ultimately agreed on a standard literary form, partly under the heady influence of Pan-Slavism and the South Slav Illyrian movement following the Napoleonic Wars, the standard was not, in fact, used as such.

Croatian resistance to Hungarian rule accompanied a cultural and national revival in the mid-nineteenth century. Early Croatian nationalism focused on the creation of a separate South Slav kingdom equal to Austria and Hungary within the Austro-Hungarian Empire. The Croat national movement soon split into two factions, one favoring an exclusively Croatian nationalism and another calling for the unification of all the South Slavs. In 1878 the Bosnian Croat territory in Herzegovina was transferred from the Ottoman Turks to Austria-Hungary.

Prior to World War I, strong Hungarian opposition to the South Slav demands provoked serious nationalist disturbances, particularly in 1903. Frustrated in their attempts to win equality within the empire, Croat nationalists in 1912 began to advocate outright independence. The national movement gained support up to the outbreak of World War I, which began with the assassination of the imperial heir in neighboring Bosnia in 1914.

South Slav representatives from the Austro-Hungarian lands of Croatia and Slovenia met with the South Slav leaders of the independent states of Serbia and Montenegro on the Greek island of Corfu during the war in June 1917. The meeting, with Allied encouragement, put forward a plan for an independent South Slav state with substantial autonomy for each of the national groups. In 1918, with the collapse of the Austro-Hungarian Empire and the end of the war, the South Slav peoples of the Balkan Peninsula formed the Kingdom of the Serbs, Croats, and Slovenes.*

Serious conflicts between the Catholic Croats and the majority Orthodox Serbs over Croat demands for the autonomy provided for in the 1917 Corfu Manifesto began soon after independence. Tensions between the two largest peoples in the kingdom plagued the new state from its inception. The throne, held by the former Serbian dynasty, and the government, disproportionally Serb in character, gradually alienated even the most ardent South Slav nationalists among the Croats. Calls for Croatian autonomy, led by the largest political party in the Croat districts, the Croat Peasant Party, and supported by the Roman Catholic clergy, followed the adoption of a centralized constitution.

The leader of the Croatian Peasant Party, Stjepan Radic, and several other Croat leaders were assassinated in the parliament by a Montenegrin Serb in 1928. The outraged Croats withdrew from the central government on 1 October 1928. They set up a separate Croat parliament at Zagreb and prepared to secede from the Yugoslav kingdom. Croat demands for separation from the kingdom were blocked by the imposition of a dictatorship. King Alexander suspended the constitution in 1929 and imposed a dictatorship. The name of the country was changed to the Kingdom of Yugoslavia.

Radical organizations gained followers as the crisis deepened, and the world-wide depression brought ever more economic hardships. The Croats became divided between the Ustase, supported by Italy and led by Anton Pavelic, openly fascist and separatist, and a moderate faction, led by Dr. Matchek, which favored Croat autonomy within an antifascist Yugoslavia.

The more radical Croat organizations in the early 1930s resorted to terrorism to undermine the unstable kingdom. In 1934 a Croat assassinated King Alexander while on a state visit to France. The assassination, carried out with the complicity of Macedonian nationalists, plunged the country into a renewed crisis. Moderate Croat political parties, fearing the growth of fascism, reached an autonomy agreement with the Yugoslav government in August 1939. The autonomy agreement was loudly denounced by the Ustase, which was supported by the fascist governments of Germany, Italy, and Hungary.

The outbreak of war in Europe began a protracted political crisis in which Germany and Italy pressed for Yugoslav support, and the Allies sought Yugoslav cooperation against the fascists. The Yugoslav government vacillated, and the Yugoslav army finally overthrew the government, vowed to resist the Axis, and thus triggered the invasion of April 1941. Italian, Hungarian, and German troops quickly overran the country.

Backed by his fascist allies in the occupation armies, the Ustase leader, Anton Pavelic, declared Croatia independent of Yugoslavia on 10 April 1941. The new state included within its borders the neighboring region of Bosnia and Herzegovina, with large Croat, Muslim, Serb, and Gypsy populations. The Bosnian Muslims, called Croatian Muslims, were courted as allies against the Orthodox Serbs. The Croatian government adopted anti-Semitic laws and persecuted the state's Jewish, Serbian, and Gypsy minorities. Many Croats, believing that the Axis would win or simply motivated by hate of the Orthodox Serbs, joined the government's anticommunist and anti-Serbian campaigns. Others, opposed to fascism, joined the royalists or the communist-led partisans headed by an ethnic Croat, Josip Broz (Tito).

In June 1941 the Pavelic government adopted a policy for dealing with the large Serb minority within Croatia. A third was to be expelled, a third forcibly converted to Catholicism, and a third exterminated. The policy set off a vicious civil war in the state, a war within the larger conflict of World War II. Massacres, atrocities, and genocide committed by Croats, Serbs, and Muslims left between 300,000 and 700,000 dead by the end of the war in 1945.

On 19 November 1945 the Anti-Fascist National Liberation Council (AVNOJ), which was a provisional government led by Marshal Tito, took power. The new government abolished the monarchy and established the Federative People's Republic of Yugoslavia, which consisted of Slovenia, Croatia, Bosnia and Herzegovina, and Serbia with its semiautonomous provinces. Tito, having defeated the nationalist and anticommunist forces, became Yugoslavia's first postwar communist leader and imposed a strict, centralized regime. In January 1946 a new constitution, modeled on that of the Soviet Union, was adopted, and all opposition parties were officially abolished. Although an ethnic Croat, Tito opposed any form of political autonomy and promoted the centralization of the country.

A postwar Croat cultural revival culminated in renewed calls for autonomy in the 1960s. The language issue became an important rallying point for Croatian nationalists determined to establish Croatian as a literary language separate from Serbo-Croatian. The period from 1965 to 1971 saw a great flowering of culture, the so-called Croatian Spring. The Croatian republic, one of the wealthier in Yugoslavia, earned 40% of Yugoslavia's foreign earnings but received only 5% to 7% from the government. The resentment over Croatia's foreign earnings' going to prestige projects in the poorer republics added to the growing nationalist fervor. The language and economic conflicts led to a serious nationalist crisis in Croatia. In December 1971 the entire Croat leadership was dismissed, and the army was purged of Croatian officers. Thirty-two thousand Croats were arrested, and 400 Croatian government and student leaders were tried and imprisoned. The crisis ended when a new 1971 Yugoslav constitution gave the constituent republics broad powers and turned Yugoslavia into looser confederation of ethnic states.

Tito's death in 1980 and the collapse of communism in 1989 fatally weakened the federation. In the first multiparty elections in nearly fifty years, the communist reformers lost to parties favoring national sovereignty for the Croats. Faced by Serbian intransigence, the new nationalist government rapidly moved the republic toward secession. Croatian nationalism was vehemently opposed by the Serbian-dominated and neocommunist Yugoslav federal government and by Croatia's own Serb minority. Serbian insurgents in the districts with large Serb populations, particularly in the southwestern Krajina and the eastern Slavonia regions, organized autonomous districts.

During the spring of 1991 while delicate negotiations were taking place between the republican governments over the future of Yugoslavia, armed Serbian guerrillas took over village after village. The Yugoslav National Army (JNA), led by an officer corps that was 80% Serbian, then entered the rebellious regions under the pretext of preventing ethnic violence. Long before the final breakup of Yugoslavia, the federal army had already occupied up to one-quarter of Croatian national territory. In neighboring Bosnia and Herzegovina, the Croat minority clamored for union with Croatia.

The Yugoslav government and military leadership flatly rejected proposals for a looser federation or union of sovereign Yugoslav states. The Croatians responded to Serbian refusals with a plebiscite in which the vast majority voted to authorize the Croatian parliament to declare independence at the end of June 1991 in the event that the ongoing negotiations proved futile. The Croat government, supported by the referendum that showed overwhelming support, declared Croatia independent of Yugoslavia on 25 June 1991.

Local Serb militias, with increasing support from the JNA, attacked across the new state. The Croatian military, poorly armed and crippled by an arms embargo imposed by the United Nations (UN), fell back as the Serbs took control of the Krajina region adjoining Bosnia, which nearly severed the southern Dalmatia region from contact with Zagreb and the north. Fighting also broke out in the eastern Slavonia region adjoining Serbia with its mixed population of Croats and Serbs.

In July 1991, as fighting intensified, Croat president Franjo Tudjman announced that legislation had been prepared to offer home rule to the Serbs of the self-proclaimed "Autonomous Republic of Krajina." On 8 October 1991, when negotiations broke down, Tudjman severed relations with rump Yugoslavia and declared the Yugoslav army an invading force. The victorious Serbs, intent on reunion with Serbia in a "Greater Serbia," on 9 December declared all the Serb-held regions a newly constituted Serbian Republic of Krajina, covering about a third of Croatia's territory. In the course of their war against the Croats, local Serbian militias and the Yugoslav armed forces seized wide stretches of territory where Croatians formed a majority. In such regions they began a systematic effort to terrorize and expel the Croatian population.

The so-called Homeland War, leaving over 10,000 dead and over 600,000 refugees, was tentatively brought to an end in early 1992 with United Nations intervention. However, a tentative truce left Slavonia and Krajina in Serb hands. In January 1995 the rearmed and reorganized Croatian military forces launched a ten-day offensive in Krajina that allowed Croat control of key installations. In July 1995 the Croatian army, in a lightning campaign, rolled over the Serb enclave of Krajina, sending 180,000 Serb refugees fleeing.

In May 1993 a conflict erupted between Croats and Muslims in newly independent Bosnia. The fighting was associated with brutal ethnic cleansing and resulted in thousands of casualties. Centered on the historic city of Mostar, which was badly damaged, the vicious fighting continued until the signing of peace agreement in March 1994. The Bosnians (Bosnian Muslims) and the Bosnian Croats agreed to create a joint federation to battle the Serbs and to ally the new federation with neighboring Croatia.

In April 1997 elections were held in Eastern Slavonia, which had been under Serb control since the war in 1991. The region was reintegrated into the Croat republic with autonomy for the local Serb population. The return of the Serbs who fled the fighting in Slavonia and Krajina and the status of the Serb minority that fought against the Croatian government forces are problems that remain to be resolved.

On 15 June 1997 Franjo Tudjman, the self-proclaimed "Father of the Nation," was elected for another five-year term as president with 61% of the vote. The election was denounced by European Union (EU) and other observers as below minimum democratic standards. The Tudjman regime, in spite of its desire to draw Croatia into the European Union and other Western alliances, has become increasingly authoritarian.

SELECTED BIBLIOGRAPHY

Glenny, Misha. *The Fall of Yugoslavia: The Third Balkan War*. 1992.

McAdams, Michael C. *Croatia: Myth and Reality*. 1994.

Stallearts, Robert, and Jeannine Laurens. *Historical Dictionary of the Republic of Croatia*. 1995.

Tanner, Marcus. *Croatia: A Nation Forged in War*. 1997.

Vladovich, Simon. *Croatia: The Making of a Nation*. 1994.

CZECHS

Bohemians; Ceské

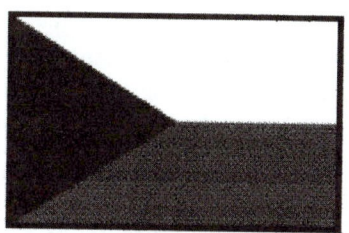

POPULATION: Approximately (2000 e) 10,550,000 Czechs in Europe, the majority, 8,498,000, in the Czech Republic, but with Czech populations in Slovakia, Bulgaria, Ukraine, Yugoslavia, Slovenia, Austria, Germany, and other European states.

THE CZECH HOMELAND: The Czech homeland is a landlocked region lying in the heart of Europe, a hilly area of flat plateaus and rolling plains, called the Czech Highlands, surrounded by low mountains, the Bohemian Forest in the southwest, the Erzgebirge in the northwest, and the Sudetic (Sudety) Mountains in the northeast. The chief rivers are the Labe (Elbe) and the Vltava (Moldau). The Czech Highlands extend east to become part of the Bohemian-Moravian Highlands, which form the border between Bohemia and Moravia. Central Bohemia consists of fertile lowlands that produce crops of fruit, grains, sugar beets, flax, and the famous hops that feed the beer breweries of Plzen (Pilsen).

Bohemia, the Czech homeland, formed part of the Republic of Czechoslovakia until the division of the country into two states, the Czech Republic and Slovakia on 1 January 1993. *Czech Republic (Ceská Republika)*: 30,449 sq.mi.– 78,883 sq.km. (2000 e) 10,481,000—Czechs 81%, Moravians* 13%, Slovaks* 3%, Poles,* Germans,* Roms* (Gypsies). The Czech capital and major cultural center is Prague, called Praha in the Czech language, (2000 e) 1,213,000, an important European cultural and commercial center.

FLAG: The Czech national flag, the official flag of the republic, is white over red with a blue triangle at the hoist.

PEOPLE: The Czechs, formerly called Bohemians, are a Western Slav people related to the Poles, Slovaks, Kashubs,* and the Sorbs* of Germany. The Slavic

Czech culture, influenced by German and Austrian traditions and customs, is oriented to the West. About 69% of the Czechs live in Bohemia's numerous urban areas. During the communist period, living standards in Czechoslovakia were among the highest in the communist states. The reintroduction of a market economy in the early 1990s led to a sharp decline in living standards, but the economy in the late 1990s had recovered, and most Czechs live comfortably. Certain sectors of the population, single mothers, the elderly, and adults with low education and skill levels, have been particularly hard hit by the process of economic transition from a communist command economy to a market economy.

The largest religious denomination is Roman Catholic, and there is a large Protestant minority. However, the largest segment of the population is considered atheist, a consequence of decades of antireligious tradition under communist governments.

The Czech language, often called Bohemian, spoken in a number of dialects, is the second in importance of the Western Slav languages after Polish. It has a long literary tradition centered on Prague, and the Czech literary language is based on the dialect spoken in the city and its immediate region. The language is spoken in six distinct dialects, including Czecho-Moravian, and is inherently intelligible to speakers of Slovak, the language spoken in Slovakia, which separated from the Czech Republic in 1993. Except for the growth of vocabulary, the Czech language has not changed significantly since the sixteenth century.

NATION: Bohemia takes its name from the Boii, possibly of Celtic origin, who inhabited the region in ancient times. The region formed part of the area called Germania by the Romans, a frontier area lying north of the Alps, the limit of Roman control. With the decline of Roman power in the fifth century A.D., the region was overrun by Huns and Vandals moving into the Roman provinces.

The region later called Bohemia was inhabited by Celtic and Germanic tribes before the Slav tribes from Eastern Europe arrived in the fifth century. Soon after the Slav migration, the tribes were conquered by the Avars,* a people from the east. Traditionally, in 623 a Frankish merchant named Samo united the Slav tribes. He first organized the Slavic tribes into a protective league against the Avars and led the Slavs to victory. Samo ruled over the Slavic kingdom, centered in Bohemia, until his death in 658, when the state broke up.

In the eighth century the Premsyl dynasty of the legendary Cechove tribe was established in Bohemia. Its founder, a peasant named Premsyl, was chosen as husband by Princess Libussa. Their successors united the Bohemian tribes into a single duchy. By the early ninth century, the Bohemian territories had become tributary to the Frankish Empire of Charlemagne, who ruled from Aachen in western Germany.

In 870 A.D., the western Slavic tribes revolted against the German emperor and formed a protective alliance, later called the Great Moravian Empire. Germans and Jews, merchants and adventurers, settled in the cities, forming a powerful commercial class. Greek missionaries, St. Cyril and St. Methodius, converted the western Slavs to Christianity, traditionally in 863. Borivoj, the Czech ruler, converted to Christianity around 867 A.D. The Moravian Empire fell apart in the early tenth century under attacks by Germans, Magyars, and Huns.

St. Wenceslaus, Vaclav in the Czech language, the first great Bohemian ruler, in the 920s negotiated a peace with the Germans. The Czechs had angered the Germans by aiding the Wends, later called the Sorbs. Wenceslaus completed the Christianization of Bohemia, but his religion and his treaty with the Germans alienated many of the Czech nobles. In 929 Wenceslaus was assassinated by his brother, Boleslav, who was forced to acknowledge the authority of the Holy Roman Empire.

Under the rule of the Premsylide dynasty, Bohemia expanded in 1029 to include Moravia, parts of Silesia, Slovakia, and territory in Poland. In the twelfth century Bohemia was raised to the rank of electorate and in 1212 became a hereditary kingdom within the Holy Roman Empire. German influence increased with the growth of towns and increasing trade. At the height of its power in the thirteenth century the Bohemian kingdom expanded into traditionally Austrian and Hungarian lands until its defeat in 1278.

The Bohemians revived in the fourteenth century and under the rule of Charles I, who ruled from 1347 to 1378, entered a golden age of culture, art, and power. Under Charles, who was crowned Holy Roman Emperor in 1355, Prague became a major European center of learning and culture. Extensive building projects were undertaken, the most significant of which was the founding of Charles University in 1348, the first university in Central Europe.

The golden age ended when the religious wars erupted in Europe. Based on the teaching of the Bohemian religious reformer Jan Hus, the Hussite movement attacked the authority and corruption of the Roman Catholic hierarchy. Hus was tried for heresy and burned at the stake in 1415. His death triggered a series of religious wars in Bohemia, which ended only in 1446. In 1458 a leader of the moderate Hussites, George of Podebrad, was elected king of Bohemia, becoming the first Protestant king to be elected in Europe. Under his rule the majority of the Czech nobility converted to Protestantism. The Czech nobles profited from the disorders in Bohemia and in 1487 secured vast privileges, reducing the peasant majority to virtual serfdom. The Reformation and Renaissance saw a revival of religious writing and the development of liberal ideals and thinking. Publishing in the Czech language, begun with the Bible, was followed by works on history, science, and medicine.

With the election of the Austrian Ferdinand of Hapsburg as king of Bohemia in 1526, when the ruling house died out, Bohemia became an integral part of the Hapsburg Empire. Under his rule the Bohemians were gradually deprived of their self-rule. Ferdinand also introduced the Jesuits in order to return Bohemia to Roman Catholicism; however, Rudolph II was forced to grant freedom of religion in 1609. In 1618 a revolt by the Czech Protestant nobility began the Thirty Years' War. The Czechs elected a new ruler, Frederick the Winter King, but lost their remaining independence with the defeat of Frederick and the Protestant forces at the Battle of White Mountain in 1620. Those who remained in the Czech lands were forced to convert to Catholicism and to give up their own language and culture in favor of German. In 1627 Bohemia was formally declared a Hapsburg crownland. The war, fought from 1618 to 1648, brought the wholesale destruction of Czech literary and artistic works followed by the repression of Czech national life. Many Czechs fled abroad to escape oppressive taxes, religious persecution, forced Germanization, and absentee landlords.

German culture dominated the Czech homeland for the next two centuries. In the eighteenth century the Czech lands were completely incorporated in the Austrian Empire. The suppression in 1749 of a separate chancellery at Prague and the introduction of German as the sole official language completed the Germanization process. Under Empress Maria Theresa and Emperor Joseph II, the Czechs were subjected to a program of intense Germanization. The Czech language was gradually reduced to a peasant dialect mostly spoken in rural areas.

Cultural oppression continued into the nineteenth century, but at the same time a national revival took hold, with new interest in their separate traditions, language, and history. Led by Protestant intellectuals, a great revival of the Czech language and culture spread through the Czech lands as a rejection of the Germanization pressed by the Hapsburg authorities.

The Czechs led the movement for the equal rights of the Slavs of the Austrian Empire. During the Revolution of 1848 the Czechs convened a congress of Slavic leaders in Prague, but by early 1849 absolute Austrian domination had been restored, and Moravia was made a separate Austrian crownland. The establishment of the Dual Monarchy in 1867, which gave the Hungarians rights within the empire equal to those of the Austrians, gravely disappointed the Czechs. In spite of some concessions in 1879, when Czech delegates entered the parliament at Vienna, the Czechs of the empire remained unsatisfied that a third kingdom, a Slav state, had not been created within the dual empire.

Stirred by immigrant Czechs in the United States and Canada, support for autonomy within the empire grew in the early twentieth century. A Czech National Council formed by exiles in the United States began to coordinate efforts with exile Slovak and Moravian groups. The Czech leader, Thomas Masaryk, joined by Slovak leader Milan Stefanik and supported by the U.S. government, began to press for independence for the region.

The defeat of Austria in October 1918 opened the way for Czech independence. On 28 October 1918 the Czech leaders declared Bohemia and Moravia independent of Austria. The union of the Czech lands, Bohemia and Moravia, and Slovakia was officially proclaimed on 14 November 1918. The September 1919 Treaty of St. Germain between the Allies and Austria paved the way for official recognition of the new state of Czechoslovakia. Of the new nations that emerged in Europe following the defeat of the Central Powers, all began with democratic governments, but only Czechoslovakia remained a democratic state, as the others succumbed to totalitarian regimes.

The most cosmopolitan of the Slavic nations between the wars, Czechoslovakia gained fame as the home of many influential writers and playwrights. Bustling Prague became one of the centers of the European post–World War I revival. Economically the most favored of the former Hapsburg territories, Czechoslovakia looked forward to a bright future.

While Czech cultural life flourished, Czechoslovak political life between the wars was marked by minority demands for autonomy, particularly the Slovaks and the Sudeten Germans, who were supported by Nazi Germany after 1933. Demands for union with Germany by the Sudeten Germans led to a serious crisis between Prague and Berlin in 1938.

In September 1938 Czechoslovakia was betrayed by its allies, Britain and France. As part of the Munich Agreement between the European powers, Czechoslovakia was forced to cede the Sudetenland, the German majority areas, to Nazi Germany. The agreement, meant to resolve the German–Czech crisis and ensure peace in Europe, actually prolonged the crisis. Slovakia and Ruthenia, given autonomy in 1938, increasingly opposed Czech domination of the state. On 14 March 1939 the autonomous Slovak state declared its independence, and the following day Nazi Germany annexed the Czech lands of Bohemia and Moravia as a German protectorate.

Except for the brutalities of the German occupation, including the extermination of nearly all of the formerly large Jewish population, the Czech lands suffered little physical damage and emerged from the war with its industrial base and economy mostly intact. At the end of the war in April 1944, Soviet troops overran eastern Czechoslovakia, while American and Allied troops moved into the Czech lands in the west. In March 1945 Edward Benes, who was elected president of Czechoslovakia in 1935, agreed to form a National Front government with Klement Gottwald, leader of the Communist Party of Czechoslovakia (CPCz).

On 5 May 1945 the Czechs rebelled against the German occupiers. Accompanied by members of the National Front coalition government, the Allies finally took control of Prague on 12 May 1945. The fall of Prague marked the end of Allied military operations in Europe. At the Potsdam Conference of 1945 the expulsion of some 3 million ethnic Germans from the Czech lands was approved, and ethnic Czechs moved into the depopulated regions.

The communists emerged as the strongest party in the elections of 1946 and became the leading political force in the coalition government. In 1946 Gottwald was elected prime minister. In February 1948 in a coup d'état, the communists seized the government. In June 1948 President Benes resigned and was succeeded by Gottwald. Gottwald embarked on a campaign of repression, and new legislature provided for the nationalization of nearly every part of the economy. The 1950s were a period of harsh repression for the Czech nation.

In 1960 a new constitution was established, modeled on that of the Soviet Union, which established a unitary state of the Czech and Slovak nations. The country's name was changed to the Czechoslovak Socialist Republic. During the 1960s Czechoslovakia's intellectuals called for more freedom of expression and many Slovaks renewed their efforts to gain recognition for Slovak rights equal to those enjoyed by the Czechs. In January 1968 the Slovak Alexander Dubcek became first secretary of the Czechoslovak Communist Party and introduced a program of liberal reforms called the "Prague Spring." The reforms included freedom of the press as well as increased contact with noncommunist countries.

Leaders of the Soviet Union and other Warsaw Pact nations feared Dubcek's program would weaken communist control in Czechoslovakia and undermine neighboring communist states. Warsaw Pact troops from Soviet Union, Bulgaria, East Germany, Hungary, and Poland invaded on 20 August 1968. One-third of the membership of the Communist Party was expelled. Over 40,000 Czechs fled the invasion and the repression that followed. A new federal system was introduced on 1 January 1969 providing for autonomous Czech and Slovak regional governments, but real power remained firmly in the hands of the Communist Party. In April 1969 Dubcek was replaced, which resulted in further anti-Soviet protests.

In May 1970 a new twenty-year Treaty of Friendship was signed with the Soviet Union. In 1973, amid continuing repression, the communist government offered an amnesty to those who had fled in 1968. Many leading Czech intellectuals returned, but the government's repressive policies remained unchanged. More than 700 leading Czech and Slovak intellectuals and former party members signed a human rights declaration in 1977. The manifesto, called Charter 77, prompted a renewed crackdown on dissident groups in the country.

During the 1980s economic stagnation threatened Czechoslovakia's position as one of the more advanced of the communist states and fed a growing popular unrest. However, a lack of anonymity, particularly in rural areas, meant very little criticism of the communist regime. In August 1988 only some 10,000 demonstrators braved severe repression to take part in a protest that marked the twentieth anniversary of the Warsaw Pact invasion of 1968.

Czech reactions to the new spirit of glasnost coming from the communist Jerusalem, Moscow, were cautious and defensive. The government ordered a wave of arrests of dissidents in 1988 and 1989. The Czechoslovak government initially aligned itself with the German Democratic Republic in opposition to the reforms. However, during November 1989 large demonstrations took place in all of the country's major cities, culminating in the resignation of the Communist Party leadership in December. The so-called Velvet Revolution had swept the communist government from power virtually without bloodshed.

The Czechoslovak government, pressed by mass demonstrations and demands for change, initiated talks with the main Czech opposition group, Civic Forum. Civic Forum's newly found influence over the political process led to the appointment of dissident playwright Vaclav Havel as president, while the country set about introducing a pluralistic political system and market economy. In the east, the increasingly nationalistic Slovaks demanded autonomy, and even in the eastern Czech lands, in Moravia and Silesia, mass demonstrations in favor of autonomy swept Brno and other cities.

Despite the firm opposition of President Havel, negotiations opened between representatives of the Czechs and Slovaks in November 1991. The talks broke down within weeks, and both sides retired to await the June 1992 national election. The two parts of the country voted for nationalist parties, and a complete split between the Czech lands and Slovakia was quickly accepted as the only viable option. The formal division into the Czech Republic and Slovakia took place with the formal declarations of independence of the two republics on 1 January 1993. The so-called Velvet Divorce had brought two new states into being in Europe.

The Czechs looked to the West for expertise and aid. The Czech economy, freed of the less prosperous Slovak economy, became one of the strongest in the former communist block and was dubbed the Czech Miracle. Only in mid-1997 did the economy begin to show signs of weakening.

The Czech government, dominated by reformers and former dissidents, moved the Czech Republic into line to join the North Atlantic Treaty Organization (NATO) and the European Union. After decades of communist repression, the Czechs see their future security linked to a network of alliances with the most powerful states in the West. The Czech Republic has been invited to join NATO, and negotiations to join the European Union began in 1998.

SELECTED BIBLIOGRAPHY

Dedek, Oldrich, ed. *The Break-Up of Czechoslovakia.* 1996.
Hochman, Jiri. *Historical Dictionary of the Czech Republic.* 1997.
Otfinoski, Steven. *The Czech Republic.* 1997.
Rees, H. Louis. *The Czechs during World War I: The Path to Independence.* 1992.
Skrabanek, Robert L. *We're Czechs.* 1995.

DANES

Danish; Dansk; Dänisch

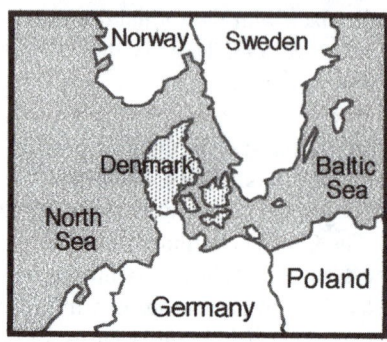

POPULATION: Approximately (2000 e) 5,129,000 Danes in Europe, concentrated in the Kingdom of Denmark, but with smaller populations in Germany, where 50,000 Danes live, Norway, and Sweden. Other large Danish or Danish heritage populations are in Greenland, some 8,000, and the United States and Canada, numbering over 200,000.

THE DANISH HOMELAND: The Danish homeland lies in Northern Europe, comprising the Jutland Peninsula and more than 400 islands in the Baltic Sea. The most important of the islands are Sjaelland, Fyn, Falster, Lolland, Langeland, and Bornholm. The smallest, but most densely populated, of the Scandinavian states, most of Denmark is low, flat lands with no important rivers and few lakes, but its shoreline, especially in the north and west, is indented by numerous lagoons and fjords, the most important of which is the Limfjorden, extending across northern Jutland from the North Sea to the Kattegat, which divides Denmark from Sweden. The surface of the Danish mainland is generally low, with the average elevation about 100 feet (thirty m.) above sea level. About two-thirds of Danish territory is fertile pasture and farmland, but only about 8% of the population is engaged in agriculture.

The Danish kingdom, one of the most ancient on the continent, once dominated most of Northern Europe. The kingdom lost power and territory since the seventeenth century, with the Danish homeland now comprising only the original homeland of the Danes. *Kingdom of Denmark (Kongeriget Danmark)*: 16,629 sq.mi.–43,069 sq.km. (2000 e) 5,143,000—Danes 96%, Turks,* Germans.* The Danish capital and major cultural center is Copenhagen, (2000 e)

465,000. Greater Copenhagen, the metropolitan area, has a population (2000 e) of 1,371,000.

FLAG: The Danish national flag, the Dannebrog, the official flag of the kingdom, is a red field with a white Scandinavian cross. It may be the oldest national flag in continuous use.

PEOPLE: The Danes are a Scandinavian nation, descendants of the early Vikings, related to the other Scandinavian nations, the Swedes,* the Norwegians,* the Icelanders,* the Faeroese,* and the Alanders.* Like the other Scandinavian peoples, the Danes are a tall, fair people with pale skin and light eyes. Although Copenhagen is the only large city, the Danes are highly urbanized, with 85% of the population living in urban areas.

The Danish language, called Dansk, is an East Scandinavian language of the North Germanic group of languages. Modern Danish developed from Middle Danish from about the beginning of the sixteenth century. The language is spoken in three major dialects, Western Danish on the Jutland Peninsula, Central Danish in Copenhagen and Sjaelland, and Eastern Danish, close to the dialect of the Scanians,* in Bornholm, the most easterly of the Danish islands, lying in the Baltic Sea. Native speakers of Danish include about 50,000 in adjacent areas of Germany, from 12,000 to 15,000 in Norway, and about 8,000 in the Danish dependency of Greenland.

The majority of the Danes, some 91%, belong to the Protestant Lutheran Church, with a small Roman Catholic minority, about 1%. In spite of the predominance of Lutheranism, the Danes were among the first in Europe to allow complete freedom of religion.

NATION: Little is known of the history of the region before the era of the Vikings, and knowledge of Danish antiquity is derived largely from archaeological research. The Danes, a Scandinavian branch of the Teutons, settled the Jutland Peninsula in the fifth and sixth centuries A.D. Originally, the Danes lived in small, autonomous communities as farmers, fishermen, and hunters. Local leaders soon assumed increased authority and gained dominance over neighboring communities. They sought to gain wealth by overseas conquests. At the beginning of the Viking Age they were the best sailors and shipbuilders in the known world. Called Vikings or Norse, the Danes participated in raids on England, France, and the Low Countries from the eighth to the eleventh centuries. Among the reasons for the Vikings to leave their homeland were overpopulation, internal disputes, a quest of goods and trade, and a thirst for adventure, an integral part of Viking culture.

The conquests of the Vikings included, in the ninth and tenth centuries, most of England. In the 860s the Vikings, known in English history as the Danes, launched a full-scale invasion of the island. They were checked by local forces but gained control of a region called the Danelaw, where their leaders divided the lands among the soldiers for settlement. The Danelaw eventually fell, but a new Danish invasion in the tenth century overran most of England. Under King

Harold Bluetooth in the tenth century, political consolidation increased, and the Christianization of the Danes was begun. Harold's son, Sweyn I, conquered most of England in 1013–14. His son, Canute, from 1018 to 1035, united Denmark, Scania, Norway, and England in a single kingdom and completed the Christianization of the Danes. The Scandinavian dynasty established by Canute of the Danes died out in 1042, and Denmark was wracked by internal divisions and civil war.

The Viking Age ended with the introduction of Christianity by German missionaries in the tenth and eleventh centuries and the rise of the three great Scandinavian kingdoms, Denmark, Norway, and Sweden. To the south the emergence of European states capable of defending themselves against further Viking invasions hastened the end of the Viking adventures.

Growing discord between the Danish crown and the powerful nobility led to a power struggle. In 1282 the Danish nobles forced King Erik V to grant the first written constitution, sometimes referred to as the Danish Magna Carta. By the terms of this charter, the Danish crown was made subordinate to law, and the assembly of lords, called the Danehof, became an integral part of the administration of the Danish state. The reduced Danish kingdom in the thirteenth century included Denmark, Scania, now in southern Sweden, and Schlesvig, part of Germany's Schleswig-Holstein state.

In the mid-fourteenth century, under King Waldemar IV, Danish power was again paramount in Northern Europe but waned following the war and the humiliating Treaty of Stralsund between the kingdom and Hanseatic League in 1370. The league dominated Denmark and established a trade monopoly in Scandinavia. In 1380 the Danes and the Norwegians were joined in a union under one king. Along with Norway, Iceland and the Fareoe Islands became part of the kingdom. Queen Margaret in 1397 achieved the union of the crowns of the Danish, Norwegian, and Swedish kingdoms in the Union of Kalmar. The Swedes soon escaped effective Danish rule, however, and in 1523 the Swedes revolted, and the union between Denmark and Sweden was dissolved.

During the reign of Christian III the Protestant Reformation was established in the kingdom. Lutheranism was established as the state religion. The end of religious dissension added to the golden age of Danish intellectual life in the fifteenth and sixteenth centuries, a period called the Danish Renaissance.

The historic division between the Danish nobles and king hampered the Danish struggle for control of the Baltic. The Danes, involved in wars with Sweden and other states, gradually lost their supreme position in Scandinavia. In 1658 the Swedes took control of Scania, which had formed a historic part of the Danish kingdom for hundreds of years. The Scanians revolted several times but eventually accepted Swedish domination. The wars weakened the nobility by reducing their numbers and strengthened the power of the king, who controlled the army. In the late seventeenth century the kings gained absolute power. The Danes maintained an overseas empire consisting of Norway, Iceland, Greenland, and, from 1672, the Danish West Indies.

In the eighteenth century the Danes began the colonization of Greenland and expanded their trade with East Asia. Trading companies were established in the West Indies, and the poorer classes began to immigrate to escape poverty and oppression. In 1788 constraints on the liberties of the peasants were finally abolished, serfdom was ended, and peasant ownership of land was encouraged.

The Danes attempted to remain neutral during the French Revolution and Napoleonic Wars, but with the bombardment of Copenhagen by the English in 1807, they agreed to an alliance with the French.* The kingdom shared France's defeat and in 1815, at the Congress of Vienna, was deprived of Norway and Helgoland.

In 1848 plans for a liberal centralized constitution brought Denmark into conflict with Prussia over the duchies of Schlesvig and Holstein, which had German-speaking majorities. The controversy led to the first Prusso-Danish War in 1848–49. The defeated Danes agreed to give the duchies special status, but the conflict continued, and a second war broke out in 1864. Defeated by Prussia and the Austrians,* the Danes lost Schlesvig and Holstein, constituting nearly one-third of the kingdom's territory.

The loss of the duchies to Prussia was offset by rapid economic and social changes that transformed the Danes, in the second half of the nineteenth century, from a poor peasant nation into a region cultivated by the most prosperous farmers in Europe. This was achieved mostly by persuading the Danes to concentrate on dairy farming. The economic advances were paralleled by the spread of education, particularly the folk high schools.

Denmark remained neutral during World War I and in 1917 sold the Danish West Indies, renamed the Virgin Islands, to the United States. Reforms enacted in 1915 established many of the basic features of the present government system. Universal suffrage went into effect in 1918. However, government reforms and strict neutrality failed to safeguard the Danes from the effects of the world war. The Danes recognized the Icelanders' declaration of independence, and Germany's defeat in 1918 led to demands by the Danish minority in northern Schlesvig for union with Denmark. In 1920, following a plebiscite, the region and its Danish population were returned to the kingdom. In the years after the war progressive welfare measures were introduced, and taxation was equalized. The Danes by the 1930s had achieved one of the highest standards of living in the world.

The Social Democrats, who controlled the government, signed a ten-year non-aggression pact with Nazi Germany in 1939, but the neutral kingdom was invaded and occupied by German forces in April 1940. At first treated as a model protectorate, the Danes' refusal to accept Nazi domination brought harsher measures. Nearly alone among the European nations, the Danes refused to surrender their small Jewish population and, using their fishing fleet, smuggled nearly 8,000 people to safety in neutral Sweden. The Nazi authorities tended to treat the Danes as fellow Germanics, but the growth of a Danish underground and attacks on German forces resulted in increasing repression. In August 1943 the

Germans established martial law and the Danes were treated as an enemy people until their liberation by the Allies in May 1945.

At the end of the war, the Danes, after years of German occupation, led in the creation of a cooperative organization in Scandinavia, the Nordic Council. The council, made up of all the Scandinavian countries, eliminated trade barriers and coordinated Scandinavia's response to world events.

Rapid economic recovery after the war was aided by the growth of manufacturing. The social welfare schemes begun before the German occupation were continued, and Denmark made remarkable strides in the 1950s. In 1953 the Danes adopted a new, liberal constitution that established norms of social welfare widely copied by other countries.

In 1972 the Danish government signed a treaty of accession to the European Community, later called the European Union, and in 1973 formally joined the organization. A slim majority of Danish voters in 1992 rejected the Maastricht Treaty on closer European ties, but in 1993 they ratified the treaty by 50.7%. Sweden's entry into the European Union in 1995 changed the Danes' position within the union from the periphery to a more central region. The Danes, veterans of European politics, became the leaders of the Nordic bloc following Sweden and Finland's entry in the union. Although Denmark forms part of the European Union, Danish nationalism remains a potent force. Many Danes have tall flagstaffs in their front gardens from which they fly the Dannebrog flag.

The kingdom, which includes the self-governing dependencies of the Faeroe Islands and Greenland, is one of the most prosperous in Europe. The production of oil and natural gas by 1991–92 was sufficient for the country's needs. Economically and socially stable, the Danes support the monarchy, which includes the oldest ruling dynasty in Europe.

The dependencies, in spite of generous Danish government subsidies, in the late 1990s were moving toward a looser association. The Faeroese proposed in mid-1998 full autonomy under the Danish crown for twenty-five years, leading to full independence at that time.

SELECTED BIBLIOGRAPHY

Borish, Steven M., and Vagn Skovgaard-Petersen. *The Land of the Living: The Danish Folk High Schools and Denmark's Non-Violent Path to Modernization.* 1991.

Flyvbjerg, Bent, and Steven Sampson. *Rationality and Power: Democracy in Practice.* 1998.

Hansen, Ole Steen. *Denmark.* 1998.

Kjrgaard, Thorkild, ed. *The Danish Revolution, 1500–1800: An Ecohistorical Interpretation.* 1994.

Pundik, Herbert. *In Denmark It Could Not Happen: The Flight of the Jews to Sweden in 1943.* 1998.

DARGINS

Dargwa; Dargan; Dargintsy;
Khiurkilinskii

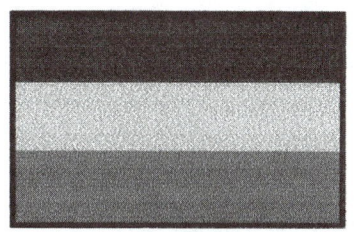

POPULATION: Approximately (2000 e) 337,000 Dargins in Europe, most living in the Dagestan Republic of the Russian Federation.

THE DARGIN HOMELAND: The Dargin homeland, called Darganstan, lies in the mountainous southern districts of the Dagestan Republic in southern European Russia. The region, which includes the high peaks of the eastern Caucasus Mountains, was nearly inaccessible until the early twentieth century except for the Dargin-populated areas of the plains near the Caspian Sea. The majority of the Dargins still live in the high mountain valleys, having resisted repeated Soviet efforts to relocate them to lowland collective farms. Dargin economic life revolves around animal husbandry, sheep and goats in the highlands and cattle in the lowlands, gold, and silversmithing, pottery, weaving, and rug making.

The Dargin region, mostly concentrated in the Sergokala and Dakhadajev Rayons of the Dagestan Republic, forms an unofficial area called Darginstan or Darganstan. The Dargin capital and major cultural center is the small city of Alusha.

FLAG: The flag used by the Dargins is the Dagestani national flag, a horizontal tricolor of green, pale blue, and red.

PEOPLE: The Dargins are a Dagestani people who call themselves Dargwa or Dargan. The majority are mountain dwellers, but with a substantial number of clans living in the lowlands of eastern Dagestan. The Dargins make up 10% of the population of the capital of the Dagestan Republic, Makhachchkala, (2000 e) 362,000. The Dargins are divided into three subgroups, the Dargins, Kubachins, and Kaitaks or Kaitags. The Kubachins number only several thousand

and are concentrated in the town of Kubachi in central Dagestan. The Kaitaks, numbering about 27,000, live in the highlands and are divided into two distinct groups, the southern Kaitaks and the northern Kaitaks.

The Dargin language is a northeastern Caucasian language and is spoken in three mutually unintelligible dialects. The Khurkili or Urakhi dialect is spoken in the highlands, and in the eastern plains the Dargins speak the Tsudakhar dialect, but the majority speak the Alusha dialect, which is used around their capital city and is the basis of the Dargins' written language. Most Dargins are also bilingual in either Avar or Kumyk, the languages used before the 1920s, when the highland Dargins were being gradually assimilated into the Avar community and the Dargins of the Alusha region were influenced by the Kumyks.* The Kaitaks and Kubachis speak distinct dialects but are assimilated into the larger Dargin nation.

Historians believe that the Dargins are an indigenous Caucasian people, and most are Sunni Muslims belonging to the Shafi theological school. A small minority are Shiite Muslims. They have been increasingly influenced by strident religious fundamentalism that is closely identified with local nationalisms. The traditional religion of the Dargins was based on pagan gods and superstitious beliefs. Islam became the majority belief among the Dargins only in the late eighteenth and early nineteenth centuries.

NATION: The Caucasus forms a bridge between Europe and Asia, which has been used by invading armies since the dawn of time. Many of the conquerors left remnants of their peoples in the mountains, with each valley becoming home to a distinctive national group. Nominally ruled by Sarmathians, Romans, Persians, Khazars, and others, the tribes never united but remained separate and often warred among themselves. Each tribe retained its own language, culture, and gods.

Conquered by invading Arabs in A.D. 728, the mountain tribes were introduced to the Arabs' unifying religious and social system, Islam. A flourishing Muslim civilization developed in the lowlands, centered on Derbent, a major center of the Muslim Empire known as the Caliphate. However, the highland peoples mostly retained their traditional beliefs, even while Islam, Zoroastrianism, Judaism, and Christianity were finding converts.

The Mongol Golden Horde devastated the lowlands in the early thirteenth century, forcing the Dargins and other tribes to withdraw to traditional mountain strongholds. In the fourteenth century, the Kaitaks, now considered a subgroup of the Dargins, established political control over most of the Dargin clans and a large number of Laks* and Kumyks. The Kaitaks' authority remained powerful in the region for nearly four centuries.

Persians extended their rule to the coastal lowlands in the fourteenth century, beginning a long rivalry between the Persian and Turkish Empires that eventually facilitated the Russian conquest of the Caucasus. Persian traders spread Islam through the southern Dargin clans in the fifteenth century, and the Tatars* of the Golden Horde converted the northern clans in the sixteenth and seventeenth centuries. The occupation of Darganstan by the Ottoman Turks in the sixteenth century consolidated the hold of Islam in the region.

In 1723 the Russians* took control of the plains of northern Dagestan, and a weakened Persia ceded the mountainous south in 1813. The Dargins, allied to the other Dagestani tribes, fiercely resisted Russian rule. Fired by religious fervor, they followed the political and religious leader, the Iman Shamil or Shamil, in a long holy war against the Russians. Effective guerrilla tactics in the high mountains halted the Russian advance for over two decades. Thousands died in the final Russian conquest of the region in 1859–60. The last of the fierce Dargin warriors did not submit to Russian rule until 1877, and a profound anti-Russian sentiment still permeates Dargin culture.

The Dargins openly supported the Muslim Turks against their Russian masters when war began in 1914. Wild celebrations greeted the news that revolution had broken out in Russia in February 1917. Effectively independent as civil administration collapsed, the Dargins, like the neighboring tribes, attacked Slavic settlements and took control of their historic territories. The Bolshevik takeover of the Russian government in October 1917 created chaos in the region as local Bolsheviks attempted to take power.

The Muslim peoples formed a separate republic in March 1918 and attempted a cooperative defense as the Russian civil war spread south. The anti-Bolshevik forces, the Whites, took control of the region in January 1919, but forced conscription of Muslims incited strong resistance. Promised local autonomy, the Dagestani peoples mostly went over to the Reds. The last of the defeated Whites withdrew from Darganstan in January 1920.

Regional leaders, representing a number of tribes, disappointed at their treatment by the Soviet authorities, demanded the promised autonomy. Rebuffed by the Soviets, the tribes rebelled and held out until finally subdued in May 1921, at a cost of over 5,000 Soviet casualties. A hypothetically autonomous Dagestani republic, created in early 1921, joined the new Soviet Russian Federation.

In 1925 the Soviet government launched an antireligious campaign in the region, closing mosques and Islamic schools, eliminating the use of Arabic, and executing many Dargin imans, or Islamic teachers. Azerbaijani, the language of the Azeris* to the south, was made the official language of Dagestan in 1925, but later, in 1928, Dargin, along with Avar, Lezgin, and Azerbaijani, was made an official language.

The policies of cultural manipulation and the rewriting of history by the Soviet authorities only increased Dargin resentment of the dominant Russians. They resisted the anonymous Soviet culture imposed on their culture and refused to participate in government programs to relocate the Dargin clans of the highlands into lowland collectives. The Dargin resistance helped them to retain their traditional culture, but Dargin educational levels by the 1960s were among the lowest in the Soviet Union. A religious and cultural revival in the 1970s, which spread through the thousands of illegal, underground mosques, marked a renewed Dargin resistance to official Soviet atheism in the 1970s. The majority of Dargin men in the 1980s belonged to illicit Muslim brotherhoods known as *tariqat*.

The liberalization of Soviet society, introduced by Mikhail Gorbachev in the late 1980s, allowed the expression of opinions and ideals outlawed for decades. Religious and nationalist sentiment emerged as powerful forces among the Dargin clans. Formerly dominated by the Laks or Lezgins,* the Dargins began to assert their distinct national identity. The aborted Soviet coup, followed by the rapid disintegration of the Soviet Union in August 1991, gave new impetus to the Dargin national revival. The Dargin leaders organized the first specifically Dargin nationalist organization in their history. Called Tsadesh (Unity), the group attempted to counter the ambitions of other national groups in Dagestan and organized the Dargins to vote in the first noncommunist elections in the region.

A Dagestani majority in the local parliament in November 1991 unilaterally declared Dagestan a full member republic of the Russian Federation while adopting a measure that indirectly endorsed the eventual independence of the republic. Since 1991 one of the most difficult tasks of the national movement has become the region's national unity. The Dagestan federation mirrors the Russian Federation, with many national groups seeking separate autonomous states. Many Dargins support the formation of a separate Darganstan.

The Russian military assault on neighboring Chechenia in December 1994 stirred nationalist and anti-Russian sentiment in the region. Fighting broke out between Avar and Dargin irregulars and government troops crossing their territory en route to Chechenia. The skirmishing raised Russian fears that Dagestan could pose the next nationalist crisis in the fragile Russian Federation.

The Dargins, along with the Avars, hold many official jobs in the Dagestan Republic, far more than their share of the population would warrant. Dargin officials allegedly favor their own national group, so that the Dargins are seen by some rival groups as privileged. The strong anti-Russian elements of Dargin nationalism have intensified as Russia's economic slide brings hardships to the Dargin homeland. Some Dargin leaders in 1998 talked openly of secession, membership in a loose, independent federation, and the political unification with neighboring peoples. Should Dagestan splinter along ethnic lines, some Dargins have suggested the most favorable outcome would be a federation of the Dargin, Kumyk, and Avar territories in a separate state structure.

SELECTED BIBLIOGRAPHY
Baddeley, John F. *Russian Conquest of the Caucasus.* 1997.
Krag, Helen, and Lars Funch. *The North Caucasus: Minorities at a Crossroads.* 1994.
Minorsky, Vladimir. *Studies in Caucasian History.* 1953.
Olson, James S. *An Ethnohistorical Dictionary of the Russian and Soviet Empires.* 1994.
Wixman, Ronald. *The Peoples of the USSR: An Ethnographic Handbook.* 1984.

DON COSSACKS

Kazaki Donu; Kazaky

POPULATION: Approximately (2000 e) 2,250,000 Don Cossacks in Europe, mostly living in the Rostov-na-Donu region of southern European Russia.

THE DON COSSACK HOMELAND: The Don occupies the basin of the Don River in southern European Russia, a major agricultural region with a narrow outlet, the Gulf of Taganrog, on the Sea of Azov and the Black Sea. The region, mostly low fertile plains along the Don and its tributaries, produces wheat, corn, barley, wines, and melons. The territory of the Don Cosssacks forms one of three Cossack territories in southern European Russia. To the southwest is the territory of the Kuban Cossacks,* and to the south are the Terek Cossacks.* The region borders the homeland of the Kalmyks* on the east and steppe lands and the Volga River basin on the country of the Ukrainians* on the west.

The Don, formerly the Territory of the Don Cossacks, later the Republic of the Don, forms Rostov Oblast (province) of the Russian Federation. *Rostov-na-Donu Oblast (Territory of the Don Cossacks)*: 38,919 sq.mi.–100,826 sq.km. (2000 e) 4,366,000—Don Cossacks 46%, Russians* 34%, Ukrainians 17%. The Don Cossack capital and major cultural center is Novocherkassk, (2000 e) 190,000, founded as their new capital in 1805. The region's largest city is Rostov-na-Donau, (2000 e) 1,056,000 (metropolitan area 1,237,000), an important industrial city.

FLAG: The Don Cossack national flag, the flag of the former Republic of the Don, is a horizontal tricolor of blue, yellow, and red.

PEOPLE: The origins of the Cossacks go back to the Tatars, who controlled the steppe lands of Ukraine and southern Russia in the thirteenth century as part of the Golden Horde. With the breakup of the Mongol-Tatar Empire many Tatars came to terms with the Russians and formed defensive service on the expanding Russian borders. From the mid-fifteenth century Russians, Ukrainians, and Poles fleeing oppression, debts, or punishment joined the bands. The runaways formed defensive groups, borrowing traits and structure from the Tatars and developing their military skills through brigandage and mercenary service. The Cossack communities were formed along most of the rivers that flowed into the Black and Caspian Seas. They began to call themselves Cossacks, free warriors, and often mixed with neighboring warrior nations, developing linguistic and cultural characteristics that distinguished them from each other.

The Don Cossacks, the largest of the Cossack nations, are of Russian and "Eastern," probably Kalmyk, ancestry and evolved as a separate people in the sixteenth and seventeenth centuries. The Don Cossack claim to separate cultural and ethnic identity, not recognized by the Russian government, is based on their unique history, mode of life, geographic location, and their language, a Cossack dialect of mixed Russian, Ukrainian, Kalmyk, and Tatar elements.

NATION: The fertile basin of the Don River has attracted migrants and conquerors since ancient times. Settled by nomadic Slavs around A.D. 880, the region formed a tributary state of Kievan Rus, the first great Slav Empire. In the early thirteenth century Mongols and Tatars of the Golden Horde overran the Don River area, and ethnic Tatars settled in the depopulated lowlands between 1241 and 1300.

The Don River valley was vacant and controlled by no country in 1520 but was roamed by nomads and Tatar raiders. Bands of Russians, fleeing oppression and serfdom, began to form in the region, joined by Lithuanians,* Ukrainians, Finns,* and Turks.* The number of Slavs fleeing to the Don region increased rapidly during the reigns of Ivan the Terrible and his successors in the late sixteenth and the early seventeenth centuries. In 1570 Ivan the Terrible began to employ Don Cossacks to escort caravans and, later, to raid Tatar camps and recapture Slavs taken as slaves.

The Don Cossacks were originally divided by the river into upper and lower groups, but they gradually united into a single nation. Virtually independent, they lived by plunder and by selling their military prowess. A Don Cossack assembly, called the *krug*, was formed to deliberate on important matters, and, in a structure borrowed from the Tatars, it elected a *hetman* or *ataman*, a leader or chief. The Cossack communities of the Don were tolerant of people of other faiths, except for the Jews, and accepted into their hordes Buddhists, Old Believers, Muslims, and pagans. The Don Cossacks pledged personal loyalty to the tsar in 1614 and received official recognition as a self-governing community in 1623.

The Cossack communities of the Don freely mixed with the neighboring peoples, particularly the Kalmyks and Tatars. Isolated in the wild country between the Russians and the Muslim lands to the south, they developed a distinctive culture and language, which incorporated Russian, Ukrainian, Kalmyk, and Tatar elements.

At the end of the seventeenth century, the Russian frontier had moved closer to the Don Cossack homeland, with newer settlers taking up agriculture. The Cossacks, living in autonomous communities under elected chiefs called *atamans*, were allowed to govern themselves in return for military service, but until 1690 their leaders forbade farming. With agriculture came personal landholdings in place of the formerly communal lands, with the Don Cossacks developing as a privileged, landowning class employing newly arrived peasants and poorer Cossacks as agricultural workers.

The Don Cossacks fiercely resisted periodic attempts by the Russian bureaucracy to impose direct government control. Sporadic revolts against the government gradually eroded the Cossacks' privileges, and in 1708 they lost the right to elect their own *atamans*. The region, formally ceded to Russia by the Ottoman Empire in 1739, was organized as an autonomous military district, the Territory of the Don Cossacks, in 1790. By 1800 the majority of the Don Cossacks were reconciled to Russian rule. To centralize the administration of the Territory of the Don Cossacks, a new capital was founded at Novocherkassk in 1805.

Fifty thousand Cossack soldiers fought for the Russian Empire during the Napoleonic Wars, with 20,000 dead. A tsarist decree of 1835 established the Don Cossacks as a military caste with special privileges, their loyalty to the tsar ensured by specific gendarme units garrisoned at Taganrog. Male Don Cossacks were obliged to serve as long as they could sit a horse or shoulder a rifle.

The Don Cossacks, better educated than ordinary Russians, prospered on the proceeds from their rich farmlands. Most Cossack communities held the land in common and rented parcels to Russian and Ukrainian peasants. An influx of freed serfs and urban workers to the expanding industrial cities in the 1860s impelled the Don leaders to establish a modern civil government in the region. The Cossacks, after three centuries of guarding Russia's now secure frontiers, became a mobile military force used within the country. From 1886 the Don Cossacks were dispatched to crush rebellions in other parts of the vast empire, the feared "fist" of the tsar. In the latter part of the nineteenth and the early part of the twentieth centuries, the tzarist government used Cossack troops to perpetrate pogroms against the Jews.

In the years before World War I, the Azov-Black Sea oil fields and the growing industries brought a great migration of non-Cossack industrial workers to the region. The influx caused increasing friction between the Don Cossack population and the newcomers, who introduced revolutionary ideas. Industrial strikes and disturbances during the 1905 Russian Revolution were quickly put down by Don Cossack troops loyal to the tsar.

Elite Don Cossack military units, sent to the front in 1914 and decimated in heavy fighting, greatly resented their new duties as they were pulled back to police an increasingly restive civilian population but remained largely immune to revolutionary influences. Freed of their oath of loyalty by the overthrow of the tsar in February 1917, the Don Cossacks formed a military government under their own *ataman*, the first to be elected since 1708. The Don, virtually independent as Russia collapsed, remained calm and peaceful, the peace overseen by the Don Cossack military units. General Alexis Kaledin, who became *ataman* on 30 June 1917, established the Don Military Government as the only recognized authority in the region.

The Don Cossack government supported the provisional government, but the new Bolshevik government in Petrograd, after taking power in October 1917, quickly proclaimed the expropriation of the extensive Cossack lands. In December 1917 the Don Cossacks declared war on the new Bolsheviks. The region's leaders, refusing to recognize Russia's Bolshevik government, on 10 January 1918 declared the sovereignty of the Republic of the Don until Russia could be reunited under a government acceptable to the Don Cossacks. The Don Cossacks were the first nation to openly revolt against the Bolsheviks. On 10 January 1918 in Novocherkassk the Don Cossack leaders formally declared the complete independence of the Republic of the Don. The new state had a population of 3,750,000, the majority Don Cossacks.

General Kaledin committed suicide following a defeat by the new Red Army in February 1918. Another defeat on 1 March 1918 was followed by the occupation of the Don Cossack republic by Bolshevik troops, but they were quickly driven out by German troops as a result of the Treaty of Brest-Livostok between the Central Powers and Soviet Russia. On 21 April 1918 a new provisional government was proclaimed, and by May the Don Cossack government, reestablished in Novocherkassk, declared the republic neutral in the continued fighting of World War I.

Mostly allied to the anti-Bolshevik White forces as civil war spread across Russia, a minority of the Don Cossacks joined the Bolsheviks and fought their kin in the White forces. The Don Cossacks represented one of the Whites' most powerful military units, but strains soon appeared over the Whites' vehement opposition to the secession of any part of Russia. A Don Cossack delegation sent to the 1919 Paris Peace Conference failed to win recognition of the republic or to sway the Allies' support of the White position on secession.

Close to victory over the Red Army in October and November 1919, the White offensive first began to falter and finally to collapse. Refugees flooded into the republic, bringing turmoil, disease, and hunger. Rostov, a city of 200,000 in 1914, had a population of 1.5 million in early 1920. Its frantic appeals to the Allies ignored, the beleaguered Don Cossack state finally fell to the advancing Red Army in late 1920. Thousands fled the advance of the Red Army, many making their way to Western Europe.

The Soviet authorities, determined to end the Cossack threat to their control, ended all traditional Cossack privileges, prohibited military training, banned the use of the Cossack language, and forbade all references to Cossack culture or history. The Don Cossack population, decimated by war and purges, suffered further losses to the famine that accompanied the forced collectivization of the Don Cossack lands in 1932–33. Thousands died in purges initiated during Joseph Stalin's dictatorship.

The Nazis, following the invasion of their Soviet ally in 1941, proclaimed the Cossacks descendants of Germanic Ostrogoths and not subhuman Slavs, therefore acceptable allies. Thousands of Don Cossacks joined the Nazis' anti-communist campaign, often facing Cossack soldiers in the Red Army in battle. Some 40,000 Cossacks, including 11,000 women and children, surrendered to the Allies in Austria at the end of the war. The Allies ignored their pleas and forcibly repatriated them to face Stalin's wrath. By the early 1950s nearly all traces of Cossack culture in the Don region had been eradicated or suppressed.

A national and cultural revival sprang from an aborted uprising in 1962. Riots broke out in Novocherkassk over the price of basic necessities but soon became antigovernment demonstrations accompanied by old Cossack slogans. The region was placed under a state of siege, and, according to Cossack sources, more than 5,000 died during the insurrection. The shock of the violent onslaught triggered a Don Cossack cultural reawakening, accompanied by the publication of the first Cossack-language dictionary and many reference books on Cossack history, culture, language, and nationalist aspirations. The majority of the Don Cossack cultural material was published by exile Cossack groups in the West.

The Don Cossack reculturation has grown dramatically since the late 1980s. Discarding bureaucratic neckties for the traditional Don Cossack uniforms, the Don Cossacks are resurrecting their long-banned heritage. A Don Cossack national movement, with its roots in the prerevolutionary autonomous state, had demanded recognition of the Don Cossacks as a separate people and creation of a separate Don Cossack republic within the Russian Federation. Claiming that the Don Cossacks form a majority in the Rostov region, nationalists have demanded the replacement of the provincial government with the traditional *hetman* boards of government.

Many Don Cossacks have participated in places like Moldova, Azerbaijan, Armenia, and Siberia, where Russians now form a minority. The Cossacks claim that Russia will benefit from the Cossack revival and proposed the revival of specialized Cossack military service, the restoration of Orthodoxy as the official Cossack religion, and special representation for the Cossack nations in the highest levels of the government of the Russian Federation.

At first the goals of the Cossack associations were cultural and historical in nature—to preserve Cossack traditions and promote historical accuracy of Cossack lifestyles. Don Cossacks then began to demand local self-administration and the return of traditional lands. The Don Cossacks reestablished their traditional Great Circle, the council or *krug*, and selected Mikhail Sholokov as their *hetman*. Sholokov is the son of the Don Cossack writer Mikhail Aleksandrovich Sholokov, who won international fame for epic novels of his homeland, *The Silent Don, And Quiet Flows the Don*, and other works.

The Russian government, like the former Soviet government, continues to claim the Cossack nations as ethnic Russians, a claim increasingly disputed by the Don Cossacks. While political scientists, linguists, and ethnologists continue to debate whether the Cossacks constitute a separate national group or are a subgroup of the Russians, for the first time in nearly seventy years the Don Cossacks began making their presence felt once again.

Several Don Cossack associations sought to form an autonomous republic within Russia, and they demanded that Cossacks be considered a separate ethnic group. In mid-1992 a decree signed by Russian president Boris Yeltsin rehabilitated the Cossacks. The decree granted them the status of an ethnic group and gave them the right to receive land free of charge. The decree also called for the use of Cossack forces to protect Russia's borders; however, some Don Cossacks refused to serve outside their traditional homeland.

In 1997 the Russian government estimated the Don Cossack population of Rostov Oblast at 28% of the total, a figure disputed by both the regional government and Don Cossack organizations. Although the Don Cossacks have not been counted as a separate national group since before World War I, in 1998 regional and Don Cossack officials claimed that nearly half the population of Rostov Oblast is of Don Cossack heritage.

SELECTED BIBLIOGRAPHY

Gajecky, George. *Cossack Administration of the Hetmanate.* 1978.

Groushko, Mike. *Cossack: Warrior Riders of the Steppes.* 1993.

Longworth, Philip. *The Cossacks.* 1970.

McNeal, Robert H. *Tsar and Cossack: Eighteen Fifty-Five to Nineteen Fourteen.* 1987.

Shott, Paul. *Geography and Cultural Portrait of the Volga-Don Region.* 1986.

DUTCH

Nederlanders; Netherlanders;
Hollanders

POPULATION: Approximately (2000 e) 14,076,000 Dutch in Europe, concentrated in the Kingdom of the Netherlands, but with substantial populations in Germany and Belgium. Other large Dutch populations are in Canada, the United States, Australia, and the Netherlands Antilles.

THE DUTCH HOMELAND: The Dutch homeland forms part of the Northern European Plain, with nearly one-quarter of the total area below sea level and protected along part of the coast by dikes. The north-central area was formerly a large shallow inlet of the North Sea, the Zuider Zee. The lands reclaimed from the sea are called *polders*. There are numerous islands, the most important of which are Walcheren, North Beveland and South Beveland, and the West Frisian Islands. The maritime provinces, more than any other area of Europe, are an artificial creation made by the toil of the Dutch nation. In the south the region is plains and the deltas of the Neder Rijn and Maas Rivers. The Dutch homeland is one of the most densely populated areas of the European continent.

One of the Low Countries, the Netherlands had no unified history before the sixteenth century. The Dutch declared their independence from Spain in 1581 and were finally recognized by the Spanish* as a sovereign state in 1648. The Netherlands are often called Holland, after the historic region of Holland, which now makes up two modern provinces. *Kingdom of the Netherlands (Koninkrijk der Nederlanden)*: 16,033 sq.mi.–41,525 sq.km. (2000 e) 15,554,000—Dutch 95%, Indonesians 2%, Turks* 1%, Arabs. The Dutch administrative capital and major cultural center is Amsterdam, (2000 e) 681,000 (metropolitan area 1,896,000). The royal capital and the seat of government is The Hague ('s Gravenhage in Dutch), (2000 e) 445,000 (metropolitan area 811,000).

FLAG: The Dutch national flag, one of Europe's oldest, dating from 1630, is a horizontal tricolor of red, white, and blue.

PEOPLE: The Dutch are a western Germanic people, the descendants of the ancient Batavi, Frisians,* Franks, and Saxons. United by their opposition to foreign rulers, the various peoples of the northern Low Countries began to unite in the sixteenth century. Known for their relentless fight to reclaim the lowlands from the sea, the Dutch are regarded as hardworking, devout, and a bit dour, yet the Dutch kingdom is among the most tolerant and liberal in the world. The Dutch nation is heavily urbanized, with about 89% living in urban areas.

The Dutch language is a Low German language that forms a separate branch of the West Germanic language along with Afrikaans and Flemish. The language is spoken in a number of regional dialects that are all inherently intelligible. The language of the Flemish, just to the south in Belgium, is a variant of the Dutch language. Low Saxon dialects, related to the dialects spoken in adjacent areas of Germany, are spoken by about 1.5 million Dutch in the northeastern province.

Most of the Dutch population is Christian, with the Roman Catholics as the largest denomination at 36%. Protestant groups count for 27% of the population. Although Roman Catholicism remains the predominant religion in many areas, Protestantism and the Protestant Reformation have shaped the Dutch national history and culture.

NATION: The region left of the Rhine River formed part of the Roman province of Lower Germany and was inhabited by the Batavi, who settled the region in the first century B.C. On the right bank of the river the territory belonged to the Frisians. The Romans penetrated the lowlands mainly to control the several mouths of the Rhine, which were then farther north than at present. The Batavi formed regiments under the Romans until A.D. 70, when a revolt spread through the region. Under Roman rule, general peace and prosperity prevailed for more than 250 years.

Roman power began to wane about A.D. 300, and indigenous Germanic tribes pushed into the area from the east. In the fifth century, as Roman power collapsed, the region was overrun by Huns and Franks. The Franks eventually subjugated the Frisians and the Saxons, and by the mid-fifth century the Low Countries formed a major part of the kingdom of the Franks. Under Frankish rule Christianity became widespread. The Frankish kingdom expanded in the late fifth century east and south to include most of modern France and southern Germany, developing into the Holy Roman Empire of Charlemagne. The counts of Holland emerged as the most powerful medieval rulers of the Rhine delta area.

The provinces of Holland, Zeeland, Gelderland, and Brabant passed to the dukes of Burgundy, which gained control of nearly all the Low Countries. Although the Dutch cities, under Burgundian rule, were slower to develop than those in Flanders and Brabant to the south, by the fourteenth century they had begun to rival them in power and wealth. Nearly all the Dutch cities belonged to the Hanseatic League and enjoyed large measures of self-government. In 1477 Mary of Burgundy, to gain Dutch support against France, granted the Great Privilege, which restored the liberties that her father and grandfather had abrogated. Her later marriage to Maximilian I of Austria established the Hapsburgs in the Low Countries.

In 1555 the Hapsburg emperor Charles V assigned the Low Countries to his son, Philip II of Spain. Oppressive Spanish rule, particularly in the northern provinces, where Protestantism was making inroads, was particularly resented by the inhabitants of the prosperous region. King Philip's attempts, through Cardinal Granvelle and later through Fernando Alvarez de Toledo, duke of Alba, to introduce the Spanish Inquisition and to reduce the Low Countries to a Spanish province met with resistance from all classes of the population, both Catholic and Protestant.

Open revolt against Spanish rule broke out in 1568 under the leadership of William the Silent, prince of Orange. The Dutch of the northern provinces expelled the Spanish garrisons and took control of the area north of the Rhine River. The Pacification of Ghent, signed in 1576, united all the Low Countries against Spanish rule. The Spanish eventually regained control of the southern provinces, where Catholicism was reestablished, but the river systems protected the northern Dutch provinces. The seven northern provinces, Holland, Zeeland, Gelderland, Utrecht, Overijssel, Friesland, and Groningen, called the United Provinces, formed the Union of Utrecht in 1579 and in 1581 declared their independence from Spain. By 1600 the seven provinces had been cleared of Spanish troops. After eighty years of nearly constant war, including the fighting of the Thirty Years' War, the independence of the Netherlands was recognized by Spain in 1648. The Spanish also ceded parts of Brabant and Limburg to Dutch control.

While struggling to win their independence and still involved in the religious conflicts between Protestants and Catholics, the Dutch laid the foundations of a great empire, and by the mid-seventeenth century the Dutch were the leading commercial nation in Europe. A golden age of art and culture made Amsterdam and the other Dutch cities among the finest on the continent. The Dutch, having thrown off Catholic Spanish oppression, opened their provinces to refugees from all over Europe. Spanish and Portuguese Jews and French* Huguenots fleeing religious persecution settled in the Netherlands and greatly contributed to the immense prosperity of the United Provinces.

To protect their independence and their growing commercial empire, the Dutch fought numerous wars with the English* in 1652–54, 1665–67, and 1672–74 and with the French in 1672–78, 1689–97, and 1702–13. During the war against the French in 1672, the Dutch opened the dikes, letting the sea in and flooding the country, creating a virtually impenetrable barrier. The rulers of the Netherlands, William and Mary of Orange, became corulers of England in 1689.

Dutch power began to decline after 1715, accelerated by conflicts between republicans and monarchists. In 1747 the republicans lost power, and William

IV of Orange became the hereditary ruler. The Netherlands sided with the Americans during the American Revolution and as a result lost several colonies to Great Britain by the terms of the Treaty of Paris in 1783. When the French overran the Netherlands during the French Revolutionary Wars in 1794–95, there was much popular approval. William V was forced to flee, and the Batavian Republic was created under French protection. In 1806 Louis Napoleon was made king of Holland by his brother, but four years later he was deposed, and France annexed the Netherlands. Although French rule was increasingly resented, the legal, financial, and educational reforms introduced during the period spurred a great national revival.

The Congress of Vienna, called to reorganize Europe at the end of the Napoleonic Wars in 1815, united the Netherlands and the former Austrian Netherlands, the Belgian provinces, under the rule of William I, son of William V of Orange. In 1830 the southern provinces, whose language, religion, and culture differed from those of the Dutch, rebelled against Dutch rule and declared their independence. A formal agreement between the Belgians and the Dutch was signed in 1839, and in 1840 William I was forced to abdicate. In 1848, during the reign of William II, important cultural and economic reforms were introduced. The seeds of reform were contained in the 1848 constitution, that became the basis of the present Dutch democracy.

In the last half of the nineteenth century, the Dutch experienced a period of commercial expansion and internal advancement that greatly reduced the differences between the various social classes. Industrialization progressed rapidly after 1860. Under popular Queen Wilhelmina progressive social welfare legislature was adopted, making the Dutch one of the socially advanced nations in Europe.

The Dutch remained neutral during World War I, but in May 1940, following the outbreak of World War II, the neutrality of the Netherlands was violated, and the country, without warning, was invaded, and the important city of Rotterdam was wantonly destroyed. The queen and the government fled to London, while thousands of soldiers escaped to fight as part of the Allied forces. Underground activities led to mass executions, deportations, and a reign of terror. Of the 112,000 Dutch Jews, 104,000 were deported to death camps in Poland. The German collapse in May 1945 was followed by the immediate return of the Dutch government amid joyous celebrations across the country.

Discarding their prewar neutrality, the Dutch became a founding member of the United Nations and in 1947 formed a close alliance with the Belgians and Luxembourgers.* The Benelux Alliance became the foundation of the later European Community and Common Market. In 1957 the Netherlands became a founding member of the European Community, later called the European Union. The Dutch, one of the staunchest supporters of closer European integration, pressed for the widening of the community to eventually include most of Europe. Fearing overpopulation, the government encouraged emigration in the 1950s and

1960s, and some half million Dutch left the Netherlands, mostly for the United States and Canada.

On 1 February 1953, the spring tide severely flooded the delta region in the southwest Netherlands, and about 1,800 people died. The Delta Plan, launched in 1958 and completed in 1986, was coordinated to prevent future flooding of this kind. Under the plan, the Dutch shortened their coastline by about 435 miles (700 km.); developed a system of dikes; and built bridges, dams, locks, and a major canal. The dikes created numerous freshwater lakes and united some islands.

In the 1960s and 1970s the Dutch prospered as trade barriers in Europe came down. Their country, one of the most peaceful in Europe, became one of the most industrialized in Europe. Although the flourishing Dutch economy is based on private enterprise, the government introduced many model social welfare programs. Again, as during the sixteenth and seventeenth centuries, the Dutch allowed refugees from around the world to settle in their already crowded country.

The density of the population, which restricts the amount of land available to agriculture, has led to many innovative advances. Agriculture employs only 5% of the population, but scientific methods are used, and yields are among the highest in Europe. Ecological concerns are an important part of any undertaking in the region. With so much of the Dutch homeland lying below sea level, the threat of the polar ice caps melting due to global warming and a rise in sea level is not taken lightly. Advanced social schemes and a liberal worldview are the hallmarks of the modern Dutch nation. In 1993 the Netherlands became the first governmental body to regulate euthanasia, or mercy killings, in special cases.

In the 1990s the Dutch remain devoted to the idea of a united, peaceful Europe, on which their continued prosperity depends. More than many other European nations, the Dutch are aware of the fragility of their homeland. According to an old Dutch saying, "God created the world, but the Dutch created Holland."

SELECTED BIBLIOGRAPHY
Israel, Jonathan I. *The Dutch Republic: Its Rise, Greatness, and Fall 1477–1806.* 1995.
Kossmann, E. H., ed. *The Low Countries, 1780–1940.* 1978.
Price, J. L. *Holland and the Dutch Republic in the Seventeenth Century: The Politics of Particularism.* 1994.
Seth, Ronald. *The Netherlands.* 1997.
Van Gelderen, Martin, ed. *The Dutch Revolt.* 1993.

ENGLISH

Englanders; British

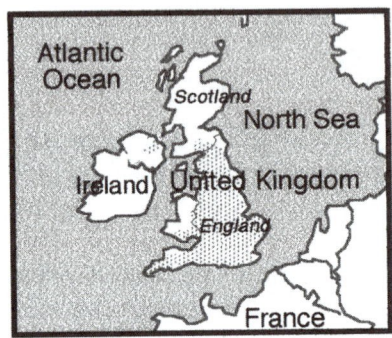

POPULATION: Approximately (2000 e) 47,640,000 English in Europe, the majority in England, but with large populations in Scotland, Wales, Northern Ireland, and Ireland. Other large English populations live in Canada, the United States, New Zealand, Australia, and South Africa.

THE ENGLISH HOMELAND: The English homeland lies in the south and southwestern parts of the island of Great Britain. England has some highland areas, including the Cumbrian Mountains, also called the Lake District, including the highest point in the country, Scafell Pike, 3,210 feet (978 m.), and the Pennine range in the north, but the remainder of the country is mostly fertile lowlands. The northern and western portions are generally mountainous. The coast is heavily indented, especially in the west, which has a milder climate than the rest of Northern Europe due to the Gulf Stream and ample rainfall. Most of the indentations are excellent natural harbors, easily accessible to deepwater shipping, a factor that has been decisive in the economic development and imperial expansion of the English. The major rivers are the Severn and the Thames. Moors and heathlands occur in many upland areas, in all covering about one-quarter of England.

The original vegetation in much of the English homeland was deciduous forest, with oaks as the predominant tree. But centuries ago human activity greatly reduced the forests and modified the landscape, leaving only small patches of the original woodlands. Most of the English countryside is farmed or used to pasture livestock.

The Kingdom of England forms a political unit of the United Kingdom of Great Britain and Northern Ireland, which is separated from continental Europe by the English Channel, the Strait of Dover, and the North Sea. The English homeland forms the largest part of the territory of the island of Great Britain, and shares the island with the territories of the Northumbrians* and Scots* in the north and the Welsh* and Cornish* in the west. *Kingdom of England*: 50,333 sq.mi.–130,362 sq.km. (2000 e) 46,148,000—English 94% (including Northumbrians and Cornish), Pakistanis 2%, Indians 1%, West Indians 1%. The English capital and major cultural center is London, (2000 e) 6,214,000 (metropolitan area 12,843,000), the capital of England and of the Kingdom of Great Britain and Northern Ireland.

FLAG: The English national flag, the official flag of the kingdom, is a white field bearing a centered red cross, the Cross of St. George, the patron saint of England.

PEOPLE: The English are a Germanic people, the dominant nation of the British Isles and one of the major nations of Europe. The great majority of the English are descended from early Celtic and Iberian peoples and the later invaders of the islands, including the Romans, Saxons,* Danes,* and Normans.* The descendants of a mixture of different European nations, the English culture and language have been influenced by the many invaders of the island, and each of the invaders from continental Europe left its mark on the culture and the language of the island. The population density of the English homeland is one of the highest in the world and is highly urbanized, with an estimated 77% living in urban areas in 2000. Among the prime traditions of the English are a fierce pride in their traditional freedoms, a unity against adversity, and an ability to bring opposing factions together in compromise. Pride in being English is another strong trait, even though the English show considerable diversity in traditions, habits, manners, and speech.

The English homeland, established as an independent monarchy many centuries ago, in time achieved political control over the rest of the island, all the British Isles, and vast sections of the world, becoming the nucleus of one of the greatest empires in history, which lasted until the mid-twentieth century. Called the British Empire, the reality was almost exclusive control by the most powerful people of the British Isles, the English, with auxiliary roles played by the Scots, Irish,* and Welsh.

The English language, carried to the far corners of the earth by English adventurers and colonists, is now the most important of the world's languages and is spoken as a first language by some 350 million people and as a second language by another 150 million. The language belongs to the Anglo-Frisian branch of the Low German languages of the West Germanic group. Spoken in over a dozen regional dialects and many more subdialects in England, the language is also spoken by a majority of the population of the British Islands. Standard English, as spoken in the United Kingdom, is based on the London dialect, which became predominant in the fourteenth century. It has been estimated that the present English vocabulary consists of more than 1 million words, including slang and dialect expressions and technical and scientific terms, many of which came into use after the middle of the twentieth century. The English vocabulary is the most extensive in the world, although some languages, such as the Chinese dialects, have a word-building capacity equal to that of English. Extensive, constant borrowing from every major language, particularly Latin, Greek, French, and the Scandinavian languages, accounts for the great number of words in the English vocabulary.

The Church of England, a Protestant Episcopal denomination, is the state church and the nominal church of nearly three-fifths of the population. The denomination next in importance is the Roman Catholic Church, which has about 6 million members in England. Among the numerous Protestant denominations are the Methodist, Baptist, Unitarian, Congregationalist, and Society of Friends.

NATION: The New Stone Age, during which the practice of agriculture was begun, was marked by the arrival of the Iberians, or Long Skulls, who came from the European mainland about 3000 B.C. The island was the site of an ancient Neolithic society called the Beaker folk, established by 2500 B.C., which left its mark in the form of mound-tombs and henge monuments, particularly the famous monument at Stonehenge. These monuments attest to their social and economic organization as well as their technical and intellectual abilities.

The first lasting influence on English culture was the Brythonic-speaking Celts, who crossed from continental Europe in several migrations in the first century B.C. The Celts spread across the island, living in autonomous communities. With their iron weapons and two-wheeled chariots, the Celts dominated and absorbed the indigenous populations. Their religious elite, the Druids, came to dominate Celtic society.

The Romans under Julius Caesar attempted to invade the island in 55 and 54 B.C. but were repulsed by the fierce Celtic warriors. Roman rule was not imposed on the Celts of Britannia until the attack by the legions of Emperor Claudius in A.D. 43. The last of the Celtic kingdoms was subdued following the uprising led by Boudicca, queen of the Iceni, in A.D. 60.

The Romans built a system of roads that for the first time pulled the island's various communities together. Britannia developed as an important mining and military province. Roman culture was adopted by the urban Celts, who used the Latin language, and later some accepted the Christian religion. Magnificent cities and Romanized towns, connected by the Roman road system and protected by Roman soldiers, rivaled any in the Roman Empire. In the north the Romans eventually, in A.D. 123, built the defensive wall called Hadrian's Wall to protect the rich province from its northern neighbors, the Picts.

By the early fifth century, Roman Britannia was in considerable turmoil. Hadrian's Wall had been abandoned, and the Roman legions were being withdrawn to meet barbarian threats elsewhere in the empire. In 410 in an appeal to Rome for military aid, the Britons were refused, and Roman officials were subsequently evacuated. Without the defenses of the Roman legions, Irish and Picts attacked from the north and west, and Anglo-Saxons from the east and south.

After nearly four centuries of occupation the Romans left little that was permanent: a superb network of roads, the best England would have for 1,400 years; a number of urban centers; and Christianity.

The Anglo-Saxons and Jutes, raiding from continental Europe, invaded and colonized the area as Roman civil government collapsed, traditionally establishing their presence in England in 449. Thousands of refugees fled the Germanic onslaught, falling back on the western peninsulas, Wales and Cornwall, and crossing to Brittany in Gaul. Those Britons who remained quickly went back to their pre-Roman lifestyle. Roman towns were no longer habitable, so they moved back to the Celtic hill forts and refortified them. Christianity became a binding force, the last link to a more civilized world.

Of all the migrating Germanic peoples, those who imposed their identity most indelibly on the lands they conquered were the Anglo-Saxons. Unlike other migrating peoples who absorbed earlier populations, the Anglo-Saxons mostly displaced the native Celtic population and changed the ethnic map of the British Isles forever. Although some scholars claim that the modern English are as much Celtic as Teutonic in ancestry, English place-names and the English language show almost a complete lack of Celtic influence. The Celts driven westward were given a contemptuous name by the Anglo-Saxons—"Welsh," meaning simply "foreigners." The loose alliance of Germanic tribes, called by the Romans the Anglii, Saxones, Frisii, and Jutae, collectively used the name "Englisc," a term that has survived almost unmodified. The term "Anglo-Saxon" was invented by the invading Normans as the name of the people they conquered.

The loose alliances of the invading Germanic tribes gradually coalesced into a number of small kingdoms, the so-called Heptarchy. Missionary efforts to Christianize the kingdoms resumed in the sixth century. Warlords, nominally Christian, ruled small, unstable kingdoms and continued some Roman traditions of government. Gradually, the kingdom of Wessex gained dominance among the Anglo-Saxon kingdoms.

Late in the eighth century, Vikings, called Danes in English history, began raiding the coastal regions, their raids growing in violence and severity. Anglo-Saxon unity was first successfully encouraged by Wessex king Alfred the Great, who finally defeated the Danes in 878. Alfred's victory effectively confined the Viking invaders to a region in the east called the Danelaw, where the Viking leaders distributed land to soldiers for settlement. Alfred's successors finally conquered the Danelaw and united England, but new Danish invasions in the late tenth century resulted in a defeat for the English, and by 1016 the Dane Canute ruled all of England as part of his Danish kingdom. Canute's Scandinavian dynasty died out in 1042, and the Wessex line, under Edward the Confessor, regained the English throne.

The disputed succession after the death of King Edward resulted in a new invasion from continental Europe, which led to the defeat of the Saxon English in 1066. The Normans, descendants of Vikings who had settled on the northern

French coast, established a centralized, feudal state. The Norman domination of England mixed elements of the Saxon and Celtic past with the Norman and French* and created a new culture. The Norman conquest of England ended the Anglo-Saxon period, which had emphasized the rights of free farmers. Military feudalism, brought from Normandy, was extended to all parts of the conquered kingdom. Norman French became the state language and remained so until the fifteenth century. Latin was used as the scholarly literary language.

Under Norman rule the farmers were reduced to near serfdom and were dominated by a hierarchy of Norman nobility. The Norman nobles came to hold autonomous power over estates granted by the Norman king. The freemen of the early Anglo-Saxon kingdoms had been responsible to their kings and were superior to the serfs; however, under Norman rule, the majority of the freemen were forced into serfdom or to dependence on the aristocracy.

The English kingdom acquired territory in France and in the late twelfth century conquered Ireland. However, the Norman homeland, Normandy, was lost to English rule in 1204. The rapid growth of towns was aided by charters sold them by the king, who needed money for conquests and religious crusades. An increasing conflict between the king and the nobles led to the signing of the Magna Carta in 1215 by King John. Later in the thirteenth century a parliamentary system was established, and the centralized royal courts and legal system were reformed.

The decline of feudalism, starting in the later fourteenth century, led to the rise of cities and the development of an English middle class. A national secular culture began to emerge, and the English language, a mixture of Anglo-Saxon and Norman-French elements, was adopted by the educated classes. The English, however, had distinct limitations due to the size of their island homeland and the limited type and amount of natural resources available. To fill their needs they developed into a nation of traders and seamen.

The Hundred Years' War between England and France, fought from 1337 to 1453, resulted in the loss of most of England's continental territories but reinforced the English national consciousness. English, after centuries of struggle for survival, reemerged as the court language in 1413. The Black Death, which first struck in English territory in 1348, finally brought an end to feudalism and serfdom even while the growth of the English towns gave rise to new commercial and artisan classes. The dynastic wars between the Houses of Lancaster and York, which plunged England into turmoil and political anarchy, were finally ended with the accession of Henry VII of the Tudor family in 1485.

The reign of the Tudors was one of the most glorious in English history. Henry VII restored political order in the kingdom and fostered the financial solvency of the crown. Henry VIII inherited a more powerful kingdom, a strong centralized government, and a full exchequer. One measure of Tudor power was the introduction by Henry VIII of the Protestant Reformation and establishment of the Church of England in 1534 with the English monarch as head of the church. As part of the Reformation in England, the orders of monks and friars were suppressed, and their properties were secularized.

England, under the rule of Elizabeth Tudor, Elizabeth I, entered a period of great maritime and colonial expansion in the late sixteenth century. The Elizabethan era, the English Renaissance, flowered under her rule, particularly in literature. Under Elizabeth's rule England changed from indebted state divided by religious strife to become one of Europe's great nations, its power sustained by a powerful navy. Elizabeth died childless after forty-five years on the English throne.

A long conflict with Spain, partly commercial rivalry and partly religious, culminated in the Battle of the Spanish Armada in 1588, although the war continued for another fifteen years. The defeat of the Spanish Armada led to commercial advantages. Supremacy at sea not only gained the English an empire but put the insular nation in touch with peoples the world over. New ideas and inventions returned to the island with English travelers and seamen, leading to rapid changes in the island society. Limited local workforces contributed to the invention of industrial machines and the earliest manifestations of what would later be known as the Industrial Revolution.

The Stuart line came to power in 1603 at Elizabeth's death, effectively uniting the thrones of England and Scotland. The efforts of the early Stuart kings to revive feudal dues were one factor in the religious and constitutional upheaval called the Puritan Revolution. The struggle of parliament to control the monarchy led to civil war in 1642. A parliamentary victory led to the eventual execution of King Charles I in 1648. The overthrow of the Stuart monarchy was followed by the establishment of a commonwealth under Oliver Cromwell from 1649 to the restoration of the Stuart line in 1660. The restoration was a popular reaction against Puritanism. In 1688 parliamentary supremacy was confirmed by the Glorious Revolution.

Religious and political dissidents, unable to gain influence in England, began to emigrate to the new American colonies. There dissidence finally led to the American War of Independence and the loss of the southern American colonies in the late eighteenth century, the greatest loss of territory to the growing British Empire.

The Act of Union in 1707 united Scotland with England and Wales in the Kingdom of Great Britain. The union, ending strife on England's northern border, allowed the English to concentrate on trade, where they outstripped the Dutch,* and on their growing colonial empire, which set off a long rivalry with the French. In 1801 legislative union with Ireland was enacted, changing the kingdom to the United Kingdom of Great Britain and Ireland.

English society from the late seventeenth century to the late eighteenth century remained remarkably stable, despite enormous economic and social changes. Wealth and power remained in the hands of the aristocracy, the landed gentry, and the commercial classes in the growing cities and towns. The majority of the English population, agricultural and industrial workers, semi-illiterate and landless, lived under a paternalistic system dominated by the wealthy classes. Parliament, dominated by the aristocrats and gentry, concerned itself primarily with foreign affairs and private legislation on behalf of the ruling classes.

After 1760 the effects of industrialization rapidly changed English society. Social unrest grew among the working classes of the new industrial cities, mostly lying in the north of England. Miserable working conditions and widespread unemployment accompanied the Industrial Revolution. A new industrial middle class began to demand rights and parliamentary representation but did not extend their newly won rights to the working class. Fear of revolutionary unrest spurred the passage of the first of a long series of labor legislation in the 1830s and 1840s. In 1846 the last barriers to free trade were repealed.

Improved and expanded educational opportunities raised the working classes from misery. Political activity by workers organized into trade unions, courted by rival political parties, resulted in the enfranchisement of the working classes in legislation passed in 1867 and 1884. Full parliamentary democracy was achieved peacefully.

In spite of great changes in the social structure of the kingdom, much of the old England remained until World War I. The aristocracy was still the bastion of social and political power, and the working classes, although enfranchised, had received only a small portion of their economic demands. From 1906 to 1914 numerous new bills were passed that expanded the economic and welfare rights of the working classes.

World War I, which pitted Great Britain and its allies against Germany and its allies, decimated a generation of aristocratic officers, which greatly diminished the hold of the aristocracy over England's wealth. At the end of the war new attitudes and more militant trade unions promised a more equal distribution of the national wealth, but the Great Depression, which began in 1929, devastated the industrial areas and made farming unprofitable. Progressive social legislation was slowed by the depression and the hegemony of the Conservative Party. In 1932 the British government abandoned the policy of free trade.

In September 1939 Great Britain declared war on Germany and its allies. Following the fall of France in 1940, England was faced with invasion. The English rallied to face the German onslaught until the German threat was eliminated by German defeat in the air war, the Battle of Britain, in 1940–41. England served as a base for the Allied invasion of Normandy in June 1944, the beginning of the end of the war.

Increased education and the leveling effects of two world wars finally broke the rigid class system and opened opportunities to people of the lower classes. Under the Labour Party, welfare legislation between 1945 and 1951 brought numerous benefits to the English public. Although the Conservative Party gained control of elections in 1951, ending the development of the welfare state, medical care, secondary education, pensions, and employment benefits were already among the services available to all English citizens.

Industrial growth continued in England in the 1960s and 1970s, but England, shorn of its former colonial empire, lost its leadership role to other states, particularly the United States. A so-called special relationship between the United Kingdom, particularly England, and the United States marked a growing coincidence of world outlook and foreign policy among the countries of the English-speaking world. At the same time, the United Kingdom moved closer to continental Europe politically with its accession to the European Community in 1972.

The growth of nationalist movements in the non-English parts of the United Kingdom, particularly in Scotland and Wales, began to have an effect on the English in the 1980s. A feeling that the English had carried the burden of the state since its inception, only to be faced with nationalism and separatism on its periphery, triggered a modest reculturation in the late 1980s and early 1990s. English nationalism, long submerged in the British nationality, began to re-emerge with demands for recognition of their special position within the United Kingdom.

The decline of heavy industry has greatly exacerbated the problems of the former industrial cities, particularly in the north of England. The southern counties have mostly converted to service industries and are thriving, while the English counties in the northeast and northwest remain the poorest, with higher unemployment and fewer services. The regional disparities have spurred the growth of regionalism and demands for the decentralization of the English government.

SELECTED BIBLIOGRAPHY

Elton, Geoffrey. *The English.* 1994.
Ernest, Frank. *England: A Concise History.* 1980.
Jones, Edwin. *The English Nation: The Great Myth.* 1998.
Lace, William W. *England.* 1997.
Thompson, David. *England in the Nineteenth Century: 1815–1914.* 1991.

ESTONIANS

Esths; Ests; Tallogoeg; Maames

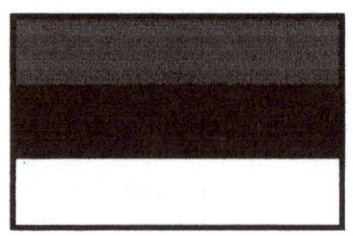

POPULATION: Approximately (2000 e) 1,025,000 Estonians in Europe, including 940,000 in Estonia, 55,000 in Russia, and smaller groups in Latvia, Finland, and Sweden. Other large Estonian populations live in the United States, Canada, and Western Europe.

THE ESTONIAN HOMELAND: The Estonian homeland lies in Northeastern Europe on the Baltic Sea, a region of broad, flat plains that make up a northern extension of the East European Plateau. The country, with only slight variations in elevation and no heights of land, has over 1,400 lakes, including the large lakes Peipus and Pskov in the east, which it shares with Russia. About one-fourth of the homeland is forested. In the southwest the Estonian coast is the northern shore of the Gulf of Riga. Estonia's national territory includes four large islands and some 1,500 smaller islands in the Baltic Sea. The four large islands are Saaremaa, Hiumaa, Muhu, and Vormsi. The major rivers are the Pärnu, Kasari, and the Narva.

The Estonians' neighbors include the Russians* to the east, the Latvians* to the south, and across the narrow Gulf of Finland, the Finns.* The Estonians declared their independence of the disintegrating Soviet Union in 1991. *Republic of Estonia (Eesti Vabariik)*: 17,413 sq.mi.–45,099 sq.km. (2000 e) 1,471,000—Estonians 64%, Russians 29%, Ukrainians* 2%, Belrussians* 1%, Finns 1%, Livonians.* The Estonian capital and major cultural capital is Tallinn, (2000 e) 442,000 (metropolitan area 563,000), which is also the Estonians' major port.

FLAG: The Estonian national flag, the official flag of the Republic of Estonia, is a horizontal tricolor of pale blue, black, and white.

PEOPLE: The Estonians are a Finnic people closely related to the neighboring

Finns. Physically, religiously, and socially, the Estonians are closer to the Finns and the Scandinavian peoples than to the Slav peoples to the east. At Estonian independence in 1991, some 8% of the total world Estonian population lived outside the republic, mostly in adjacent areas of Russia, which numbered about 90,000 people. Since independence over 30,000 ethnic Estonians have left Russia to live in Estonia. Others have come back to the country from as far away as the United States, Australia, and South America. The Estonians are highly urbanized, with about 73% of the population living in urban areas.

The majority of the Estonians are Lutheran, with a small minority, the Setu in the southeast, belonging to the Orthodox Church. Their Lutheran religion, which is the majority religion of the Scandinavian nations, the Finns, Swedes,* Norwegians,* and Danes,* has helped the Estonians to establish strong cultural ties to the other nations of the Baltic region.

The Estonian language, a Finno-Ugrian language closely related to Finnish, is spoken in five major dialects, Tallinn, Tartu, Mulgi, Voru, and Setu, and is written in the Roman alphabet. The dialects are divided into three geographic groups, northeastern coastal, north, and south. The standard language is based on the central dialect of north Estonian, which has assimilated most of the spoken dialects and is the dialect spoken in Tallinn. Two dialects spoken in the south, Voru and Setu, and the dialect spoken in the islands differ considerably from standard Estonian.

NATION: The oldest traces of human habitation in the region have been traced to the middle of the eighth millennium B.C. Around 3000 B.C. Finno-Ugrian tribes migrating from the east settled in the region and absorbed the earlier inhabitants. Around the year A.D. 100 the Roman historian Tacitus mentioned the Aestii as a tribal people living along the Baltic Sea. The nomadic Finno-Ugrian tribes, originating in the Volga River basin, had migrated to Northeastern Europe before the Christian Era. They settled a huge area but were later pushed west to the shores of the Baltic Sea by the Slav migrations of the sixth to the eighth centuries.

The marshy lands and forests along the eastern shore of the Baltic Sea formed the homeland of the isolated Finnic tribes. At the end of the twelfth century, armed German religious expansion began to pressure the tribes from the south. The Danes conquered the region in 1219, founded Tallinn and other towns, and began the conversion of the pagan Estonians. The Estonians revolted against Danish rule in 1343–45, the St. George's Night Uprising, the first serious Estonian attempt to throw off foreign rule. They expelled the Danes, but their victory was short-lived, as the German knights of the Livonian Order, part of the Teutonic Order, invaded and conquered free Estonia in 1346. The German knights divided Estonia into some 600 feudal manors and formed a class of landed gentry with large estates worked by Estonian peasants.

The Protestant Reformation came to Estonia from Germany in 1523. The rapid conversion of the German-populated towns increased the tensions between the German masters and their Estonian serfs, who mostly remained Roman Catholic until much later. The first book published in the Estonian language, in 1525, was religious but was later destroyed as heretical. A decade later, in 1535, the first catechism was published in the Estonian language.

The Swedes took control of northern Estonia in 1558 during the Livonian War. At the dissolution of the Livonian Order in 1561, the Poles* annexed the southern region, Livonia, although a large part of the Livonian region was taken from the Poles by Swedish king Gustavus Adolphus in 1626. In 1645 the important Estonian island of Saaremaa also came under Swedish control. Under the less stringent rule of Sweden the power of the German aristocracy was somewhat curbed and limited legal protection extended to the Estonian serfs. In 1632 the first university was founded, and some education in the Estonian language was begun. In the 1670s and 1680s the Swedes introduced reforms that improved the lot of the general population but embittered the local German nobility.

Sweden's expansion to the east brought the Scandinavian kingdom into open conflict with the growing Russian Empire. The conflict culminated in the Great Northern War, which began in 1700. By the terms of the Treaty of Nystad in 1721, Sweden ceded Estonia to victorious Russia. Like the Swedes before them, the Russians allowed the German minority to retain its privileged position and restored the privileges of the nobility. The German language remained the language of government, while the Estonian language was relegated to the position of a peasant dialect. By the 1740s classical serfdom was firmly in place, and peasants were treated as property of the manor. The Junkers or Baltic Barons, the descendants of the Teutonic Order, remained the dominant national group in Russian Estonia until 1918.

Social reforms adopted by the provincial governments of Estonia and Livonia in 1816 and 1819 gradually freed the peasants from serfdom. Teaching in Estonian and German quickly raised the educational level of the peasantry. Laws passed in 1849 and 1856 ensured a certain amount of land would be made available to the peasants, and in 1866 the German manors lost control over the peasants' governing bodies. The new land laws, which enabled peasants to acquire leased land as personal holdings, marked a radical change in the social structure.

The gradual spread of education spurred the growth of Estonian national consciousness in the mid-nineteenth century. Nationalism grew as an anti-German mass movement, inspired by their near-feudal subjugation by the Baltic German nobility. The publication of the Estonians' epic poem, *Kalevipoeg*, the story of their ancient and powerful hero, and the first of the now-famous folk festivals in the 1860s accelerated the Estonian national. Industrialization, particularly textiles, led to the growth of urban areas and the rise of an Estonian middle class and proletariat. Tallinn, called Reval, already more than 50% Estonian in 1870, was over 70% Estonian by the end of the century. Education expanded rapidly with urbanization.

In the late 1800s official Russian nationalism was strengthened in order to tie the peripheral provinces to the center. Alexander III, who came to the throne of Russia in 1881, greatly reduced the feudal privileges of the Baltic German aristocracy but also suppressed the activities of the Estonian awakening. Russian became the language of government and education, censorship became stricter, and conversion to Russian Orthodoxy was encouraged.

The policy of Russification ended in 1897, and the Estonian national movement gained strength. A new generation of educated, urbanized Estonians quickly restored the nationalist ideals. In 1904 Estonians, for the first time, gained control of a major city by constituting a majority in the municipal council of Tallinn. The activism of the 1905 Russian Revolution accelerated the spread of nationalist ideas. Following the suppression of the revolution, reforms were introduced that allowed legal and political opposition and trade unions. In 1909 the Estonian National Museum was founded.

Nationalist sentiment spread rapidly following the outbreak of World War I in 1914. The aspiration for autonomy disposed most Estonians to support the revolution that overthrew the tsar in February 1917. Granted autonomy in April, the Estonians were still organizing when they lost control of their homeland to Workers and Soldiers Soviets following the Bolshevik takeover in nearby Petrograd in October 1917.

The Bolsheviks desperately needed peace on their western border, but in February 1918 the peace talks between Soviet Russia and Germany broke down. The Russian forces and the Bolsheviks who controlled Estonia fled as the German forces again advanced. The Estonian nationalists emerged from hiding to defeat the remaining Bolsheviks and declare Estonia independent on 24 February 1918. The new state, although recognized by the major world powers in May 1918, was quickly overrun, and a German military government was established.

An Estonian provisional government assumed control following the collapse of Germany in November 1918. The Soviets established a Worker's Commune of Estonia in Narva, and by the beginning of 1919 two-thirds of Estonia was under Soviet control. Aided by the presence of a British fleet in the Baltic and by volunteers from Finland and Scandinavia, the Estonians counterattacked and in a three-week campaign drove most of the Soviet forces from the country. In June and July 1919 the Estonians were successful against a Baltic German force that attempted to seize control of the new state. On 2 February 1920 the Tartu Peace Treaty was signed, and the Soviet government recognized the new Republic of Estonia.

Right-wing political parties gained strength during the 1920s at the expense of the centrists. The illegal Estonian Communist Party attempted a coup on 1 December 1924, aided by the Soviet government, but was defeated. Following the failure of the coup, the communist movement lost support as the more reactionary parties gained support. In spite of the political uncertainties, the Estonians prospered, and their standard of living soon equaled that of prosperous Finland just to the north.

The small Estonian nation attempted to steer a course between its powerful Soviet neighbor and a resurgent Nazi Germany during the 1930s. Destabilized by the worldwide depression, authoritarian rule was instituted in the republic. Isolated from the West, the Estonians turned to Germany to offset Soviet pressure; however, in December 1938 the Estonian government declared Estonia a neutral state amid the growing continental crisis.

In August 1939 Nazi Germany and the Soviet Union signed a secret protocol, the Molotov-Ribbentrop Pact, which divided Europe into spheres of interest. After months of increasing tensions Soviet troops massed on Estonia's eastern border, their presence a forceful argument to back the Soviet demand for a more compliant Estonian government. Unable to resist, elections were organized in which only Soviet-supported candidates were permitted to run. A puppet pro-Soviet regime was installed in Tallinn, which formerly requested admission to the Soviet Union on 6 June 1940. The Red Army quickly occupied the tiny republic and deported to Siberia and Central Asia over 70,000 Estonians deemed anticommunists or anti-Stalin. On one night alone, that of 14–15 June 1941, over 60,000 Estonians were deported. Further deportations were precluded by the Nazi invasion of its Soviet ally on 22 June.

Estonia was quickly overrun by the advancing Nazi forces. To many Estonians the Nazis appeared as liberators from the Soviet oppression. The Germans* conscripted 45,000 Estonian soldiers, while many more volunteered, eager to avenge the Red Terror of 1940–41. The German population of Estonia, 1.5% of the total in 1939, was evacuated to Germany. Although many Estonians supported Germany's drive against the hated Soviets, their hopes that the Germans would support the restoration of the Estonian republic were quickly dimmed. Estonia became part of the Ostland Province of the Reich. Anti-Semitic Estonians found a place in the Nazi concentration camps and in special units.

In February 1944 the Red Army again posed a threat to German-occupied Estonia. Over 40,000 Estonians joined the army in a general mobilization and, together with the Germans, stopped the Soviet forces at the Narva River in northeastern Estonia. In August the Red Army invaded southern Estonia, driving the Estonian and German forces before it. The Soviets reached Tallinn on 22 September, and by the end of November the country was again under firm Soviet rule. Over 70,00 Estonians fled, mainly to Germany and Sweden. In all some 100,000 Estonians reached the West before the Soviets closed the escape routes. Another 80,000 Estonians were deported between 1945 and 1949, including most of the country's farmers, finally breaking the Estonian resistance to Soviet collectivization.

The Soviets replaced the 350,000 Estonians killed, fled, or deported since 1939 with reliable ethnic Russians. The percentage of the republic's Estonian population fell from 94% of the total in 1945 to just 72% in 1953. Before Soviet annexation in 1940, Russians constituted only about 8.5% of the total.

The limited liberalization of Soviet life in the 1950s aided the economic growth of Estonia, even though the Russian minority in the republic retained

ultimate control. Light industry and advances in agriculture gave the tiny republic one of the highest standards of living in the Soviet Union, although still
dismal in comparison to neighboring Finland. In the late 1950s those deportees
who had survived were allowed to return from exile, and more Estonians were
taken into the communist hierarchy in the republic. The first contacts with exile
Estonian groups were established, and traveling was allowed to a limited extent.
By the 1960s the Estonians had achieved the highest standard of living in the
Soviet Union. Called Soviet Scandinavia, Estonia led the Soviet Union in per
capita income, but the continuing Slavic influx and the suppression of their
culture rekindled Estonian nationalism, which had the strong support of the large
ethnic Estonian populations in Europe and North America. The economic
achievements paled as the Soviet stagnation spread, and by the mid-1980s there
were increasing shortages of food, industrial goods, and services.

Estonian nationalism grew rapidly in the more liberal atmosphere introduced
into the Soviet Union by Mikhail Gorbachev in 1987. The first large political
organization in the Soviet Union, outside the Communist Party, was formed in
Estonia on 13 April 1988, the Estonian Popular Front. Compromised politicians
were forced to resign, and Estonian demands for autonomy began to be voiced
in public demonstrations. Pressured by the mass nationalist movement, the Estonian Supreme Soviet passed a sovereignty declaration on 16 November 1988,
which acknowledged the supremacy of Estonian laws within the republic.

Nationalists claimed that their nation had never voluntarily joined the Soviet
Union and therefore could restore its sovereignty under international law. On
24 December 1989 the Soviet government declared invalid the secret protocols
of the Hitler–Stalin pact that had led to the Soviet takeover of Estonia. On 30
March the new Supreme Council declared Soviet power to be illegal in Estonia
and proclaimed a transition period for the restoration of the independent republic. The symbols of the Soviet era were abolished, the Estonian national flag
was made the official flag of the republic, and the former name, the Republic
of Estonia, was restored. In a referendum on 3 March 1991, 77.8% of the republic's population, including about a third of the immigrant Slav population,
supported independence.

In the wake of the 19 August 1991 coup against Mikhail Gorbachev in the
USSR, the Estonian government moved to sever all ties to the Soviet government. On 20 August the Supreme Council passed a resolution on national independence and appealed for international recognition, leading the way to the
rapid disintegration of the Soviet Union.

The Estonians, free of the Soviet command economy, successfully reoriented
their trade toward the West, with two-thirds going to Western markets by the
late 1990s. The Estonian government's free trade policies and democratic institutions have pushed Estonians to the front of the line of nations seeking entry
to the big Western clubs, the North Atlantic Treaty Organization (NATO) and
the European Union (EU). In July 1997 Estonia was among the small group of
former communist states named by the EU as prospective new members.

The problem of Estonia's large Russian population remains an obstacle to better relations with its huge neighbor. In 1992 laws were passed that greatly restricted Estonian citizenship. The laws, based on a 1939 law, granted automatic citizenship to all residents who had lived in Estonia before 1940 and their descendants, regardless of ethnicity. Other inhabitants are required to meet a residency requirement and to pass a proficiency exam in the Estonian language. The residency requirement was extended from two to five years in 1995. In September 1997 leading Russian politicians reiterated their dissatisfaction with Estonia's citizenship laws and demanded that all inhabitants of the republic resident in 1991 be granted citizenship. Many Estonians resent the continuing Russian presence in their homeland and resist demands to extend citizenship to the people they see as their former oppressors.

A team of young reformers who took control of the economy after independence quickly reformed the Soviet command economy. As a result of the economic reforms, the Estonians by late 1998 had the highest economic growth among the former communist states of Europe, with a 11.4% growth in gross domestic product. The Estonians' economic success is based on trade with the EU, which accounts for over 65% of total trade and has allowed the Estonians to become one of the nations slated for EU membership early in the twenty-first century.

SELECTED BIBLIOGRAPHY
Hiden, John, and Patrick Salmon. *The Baltic Nations and Europe: Estonia, Latvia and Lithuania in the Twentieth Century.* 1995.
Lieven, Anatol. *The Baltic Revolution: Estonia, Latvia, Lithuania.* 1994.
Raun, Toivo U. *Estonia and the Estonians.* 1991.
Taagepera, Rein. *Estonia: Return to Independence.* 1993.
Von Rauch, Georg., ed. *The Baltic States: The Years of Independence: Estonia, Latvia, Lithuania, 1917–1940.* 1996.

FAEROESE

Faeroe Islanders

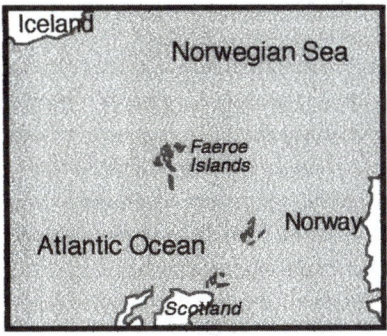

POPULATION: Approximately (2000 e) 54,000 Faeroese in Europe, most in the Faeroe Islands, but with a large population living in mainland Denmark.

THE FAEROESE HOMELAND: The Faeroese homeland, the Faeroe Islands, is an archipelago of twenty-one islands, seventeen inhabited, lying in the North Atlantic Ocean between Iceland and the Shetland Islands, 250 (402 km.) miles north of mainland Scotland and 357 miles (575 km.) west of Norway. The largest of the islands are Stromo, Streymoy in the Faeroese language, and Ostero (Østerø). The islands, historically called the Sheep Islands, high and rugged and with sparse vegetation, depend mostly on fishing and some farming, whaling, and sheep herding. Fishing, closely tied to the Faeroese culture and history, accounts for 95% of the islands' economy as only 6% of the land is suitable for agriculture. The islands are traversed by a number of fjords and have deeply indented coastlines. Mainly treeless because of continual high winds, many of the islands have been planted with sturdy conifers, maples, and mountain ash. Despite frequent storms and fog, the climate is relatively mild due to the warm North Atlantic Drift. The longest summer day is twenty-three hours, and the shortest winter day is four hours, giving the islands a very short growing season.

The Faeroe Islands form an autonomous state within the Kingdom of Denmark. *Faeroe Islands (Förøyar)*: 540 sq.mi.–1.398 sq.km. (2000 e) 44,000—Faeroese 95%, Danes* 5%. The Faeroese capital and major cultural center is Thorshavn, Tórshavn in Faeroese, (2000 e)17,000, situated on the largest of the islands, Stromo. The capital is an ice-free port.

FLAG: The Faeroese flag, the official flag of the autonomous state, is a white field bearing a red Scandinavian cross outlined in pale blue.

PEOPLE: The Faeroese are a separate Scandinavian nation, the descendants of early Viking colonists and the original Celtic inhabitants. The Faeroese culture developed in relative isolation, retaining many traits and traditions that have disappeared elsewhere in Scandinavia. The majority of the Faeroese are the descendants of medieval Norwegians* who settled the region in the fourteenth and fifteenth centuries. The Faeroese take great pride in their language and culture, particularly in holdovers such as boats made by hand, one of the few places on earth where this skill is still practiced.

The Faeroese speak a separate Scandinavian language based on the Old Norse brought to the islands by the Norwegian Vikings. The language is related to the language of the Icelanders* but is not inherently intelligible with Icelandic.

The Faeroese are overwhelmingly Lutheran and remain one of the more religious of the Scandinavian peoples. Their Protestant religion, like their traditional occupation, fishing, has become an integral part of the Faeroese culture.

NATION: The Faeroe Islands, inhabited in ancient times by Celts from mainland Europe, were the home of Irish hermit monks who came to the island around A.D. 700. The islands were colonized by Norwegian Vikings between the eighth and tenth centuries. Traditionally, the Vikings came to the islands around the year 800. In 1035 the islands became part of the Norwegian kingdom. Christianity came to the islands from the Norwegian mainland in the eleventh century.

In the fourteenth century the islands were devastated by the Black Death, the plague that ravaged all of Europe. The Norwegian kingdom's government augmented the surviving population with renewed immigration from the mainland in the fourteenth and fifteenth centuries. The new settlers from the Scandinavian mainland adapted their language and culture to that of the surviving Faeroese, which differed little from the mainland in the Middle Ages.

With Norway, the islands passed to Danish rule in 1386. Under Danish rule the isolated Faeroese retained their language and culture; however, they accepted the Reformation and the Lutheran doctrine brought to the islands by Danish reformers in 1540. The inhabitants of the remote islands, virtually ignored by the Danish government, developed a strong tradition of self-reliance. Sparsely populated and underdeveloped, the islands became almost wholly dependent on fishing. However, in the eighteenth century the islanders discovered a new use for their large fishing fleet. The islands became a notorious center for smuggling goods between the British Isles and Scandinavia.

At the end of the Napoleonic Wars in 1814, the Swedish kingdom took control of Norway, but the Faeroes, long considered an integral part of Norway, remained under Danish rule, ending nearly 1000 years of association with the Norwegians. The Danes made the Faeroe Islands a separate Danish county and introduced a written language, although Danish became the chief language of the islands.

Between 1814 and 1856 all island trade came under the control of a Danish royal monopoly, which the islanders circumvented by returning to their traditional smuggling activities. When the monopoly was ended in 1856, the Faeroese turned to fishing, but farming remained the main economic activity during most of the nineteenth century.

The decline of the Faeroese language became a major issue of the Faeroese cultural revival of the 1880s. In the 1890s demands for autonomy within the Danish kingdom began among the educated classes. The development of a distinct alphabet, based on that of the Icelanders to the northwest, spurred the development of an extensive Faeroese literature. Faeroese nationalism, growing out of the cultural revival, led to demands for political autonomy. In 1912, as a concession to growing Faeroese nationalism, the Faeroese language was made the second official language of the islands with equal status to that of Danish.

Faeroese self-awareness, a renewed appreciation of their unique culture and history, advanced rapidly during World War I, when the islands were briefly granted autonomy. In the first decade after the war the Faeroese experienced a rapid population growth, but for the first time the islanders rejected emigration to the Danish mainland and began to colonize the formerly uninhabited islands of the group. The advanced social legislation of Denmark, extended to the islands, brought increased social services and welfare to the islands.

The British occupied the Faeroes following the fall of Denmark to the Nazis in 1940. Allowed to govern themselves, the islanders provided three-quarters of the fish consumed in Britain during the war. The effort cost the Faeroese over one-third of their fishing fleet and the lives of hundreds of fishermen. Many Faeroese women married British servicemen stationed in the islands during the war and left to live in Britain, strengthening the ties between the Faeroese and the British Isles.

At the end of the war and the return of Danish administrators, there was growing sentiment for full independence. Nationalists pressed for the islands to follow Iceland, which had declared its independence of Denmark in 1944. Following a plebiscite, the Faeroese parliament, the Lagting, declared the islands independent on 18 September 1946, and the Lagting ratified the proclamation by a vote of twelve to eleven. The inhabitants of Sudhuroy, the third largest of the islands, announced their continued union with Denmark. The Danish authorities then declared the ballot inconclusive and temporarily dissolved the Lagting. A subsequent poll gave the proponents of continued union a slight plurality, and a parliamentary delegation was invited to Copenhagen for further discussions. Faced with continuing separatist sentiment, the Danish government granted extensive autonomy in 1948. The Faeroese took over all aspects of the island's administration except for defense and foreign relations.

The modernizing of the fishing fleet and the expansion of local processing in the 1950s and 1960s gradually raised the standard of living to mainland levels. The prosperous Faeroese, their language firmly established as the predominant language, became increasingly confident and assertive. In 1953 the Faeroese sent two delegates to the Danish parliament, but increasing nationalist demands brought separate Faeroese representation in Scandinavian economic and cultural councils and recognition as a separate Scandinavian nation. By 1970 the Faeroese were overwhelmingly using the Faeroese language, completing a program begun during the nationalist revival begun some ninety years before.

Denmark's entry in the European Economic Community in 1973 increased the competition for the diminishing fish stocks by the large fishing fleets of the other member states. Threats to their one important industry and therefore their culture reopened the autonomy versus independence debate in the late 1970s. The massive overextension of the fishing fleet in the prosperous 1980s led to an industry collapse in 1992. Accompanied by a severe recession and high unemployment, the collapse of the fishing industry affected the island's autonomous financial institutions. In January 1993, for the second time in many years, the Faeroese government faced the prospect of compromising its independence by accepting a loan from the Danish government.

The economic crisis left many Faeroese angry with fishing quotas and austerity measures imposed by the European Union and the Danish government. The revitalized national movement has again begun to call for full independence. The Faeroese are already recognized as a separate Scandinavian people, and many nationalists are determined to win official recognition as a separate, independent European people.

The Faeroese became skilled at driving hard bargains in dealing with the Danes. In 1998 the Faeroese opened negotiations with the Danish government with the intention of becoming a sovereign nation under the Danish crown for twenty-five years. Iceland in 1917 received that status and a quarter century later became an independent state.

The discovery of oil and gas in the waters around the islands promises to reverse the economic downturn of the 1990s and to again make the Faeroese rich. However, for the immediate future, the Faeroese want to continue receiving the subsidies from Copenhagen, worth at least $147 million a year in 1998–99, which is needed to keep the islands' schools, hospitals, and social services up to the high Scandinavian standards.

SELECTED BIBLIOGRAPHY

Gaffin, Dennis. *In Place: Spatial and Social Order in a Faeroe Islands Community.* 1996.

Levine, Charlotte. *Danish Dependencies.* 1989.

Rutherford, G. K. *The Physical Environment of the Faeroe Islands.* 1982.

Williamson, Kenneth. *The Atlantic Islands.* 1952.

Young, G.V.C. *Isle of Man and the Faeroe Islands: Two Similar Countries.* 1981

FINNS

Suomi; Suomalaiset; Fins; Finnish

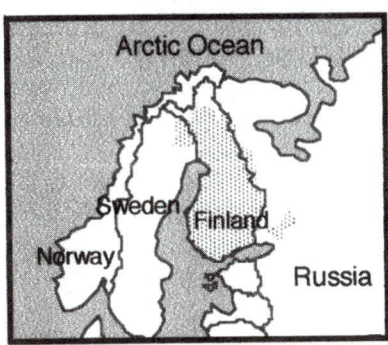

POPULATION: Approximately (2000 e) 5,128,000 Finns in Europe, including 4,782,000 in Finland, 302,000 in Sweden, and smaller numbers in Norway and Estonia. Large Finnish populations outside Europe are mostly concentrated in the United States and Canada.

THE FINNISH HOMELAND: The Finnish homeland lies in Northeastern Europe, a tableland of few hills or mountains and average heights of between 400 and 600 feet (120 to 180 m.) The region has innumerable lakes, more than 55,000, which make up nearly one-tenth of the total territory. The largest of the lakes are Oulujärvi, Saimaa, Näsijärvi, Keitele, and Pielinen, all in the south and center, and Inari in the north, many connected by rivers and canals. One-quarter of the Finnish territory lies above the Arctic Circle, including the highest point in Finland, Haltiatunturi at 4,343 feet (1,324 m.). The country has a long coastline on the Gulfs of Bothnia and Finland with several excellent ports. Only about 9% of the territory is suitable for agriculture, and over 60% is covered in forests.

The Republic of Finland was declared an independent state on 6 December 1917 following the collapse of tsarist Russia. *Republic of Finland (Suomen Tasavalta)*: 130,128 sq.mi.–337,032 sq.km. (2000 e) 5,143,000—Finns 93%, Swedes* 6%, Samis,* Alanders.* The Finnish capital and major cultural center is Helsinki, (2000 e) 501,000, metropolitan area 1,346,000, lying on a peninsula on the southern coast on the Gulf of Finland.

FLAG: The Finnish national flag, the official flag of the republic, is a white field with a pale blue Scandinavian cross.

PEOPLE: The Finns are a Finno-Ugric people whose origins lie in the Volga

River basin of European Russia, which is still home to related peoples, the Maris* and Mordvinians.* More closely related to the Finns are the Karels* and Veps* of northwestern Russia, the Estonians* and Livonians* of the Baltic States, and the Samis of far Northern Europe. Over 300,000 Finns live in Sweden, with smaller numbers in Norway, about 13,000, and Estonia, 6,000. Finns and descendants of Finnish immigrants number over 250,000 in the United States and Canada.

Like their Scandinavian neighbors the Finns tend to be tall and fair yet still show traces of their origins. Traditionally, the Finns worked in the timber industry or farmed, but by the late twentieth century, the majority of Finns are involved in manufacturing, high-technology industries, and the service industries. By the 1990s over 80% of the Finns lived in urban areas.

The Finnish language belongs to the Balto-Finnic branch of the Finno-Ugric languages and with the language of the Magyars,* Hungarian, is considered the most important of the language group. Finnish is spoken in seven major dialects and subdialects, but other languages often described as Finnish, Karelian and Olonetsian, are distinct languages of the same family. Some 300,000 Finns are bilingual in Swedish.

The established church in Finland is the Evangelical Lutheran, with 89% of the Finns as members, which was brought to the region by the Swedes. The church, which has become an important part of Finnish culture, was formerly the measure of identity, as Orthodox Finns were classified as ethnic Karels under Russian rule. Orthodox Finns now make up 1.1% of the population, and the Orthodox Church of Finland is an official state church. About 7% of Finns belong to no organized religion.

NATION: The region of present-day Finland became habitable about 8000 B.C., following the retreat of the glaciers. The first peoples to move north were Neolithic peoples, who are identified, according to the *Kalevala*, the great Finnish folk epic, as the people of the mythical land of Pohjola who fought against the Kalevala people, the Finns. However, archaeological and linguistic discoveries of the prehistory of Finland are fragmentary.

Traditionally, the ancestors of the Finns migrated westward and northward from their ancient home in the Volga River basin during the second millennium B.C., arriving on the southern shore of the Baltic Sea during the first millennium. About the beginning of the Christian Era, the early Finnic tribes crossed from present Estonia to settle along the northern coast of the Gulf of Finland, driving the native Samis to the north. Some research suggests that the Finns arrived in the area much earlier, which questions the traditional Finnish history.

The Finnic tribes included the Suomalaiset, who settled southwestern Finland and eventually gave their name to the country. The Tavastians settled inland from southern Finland, while the Karels moved farther east to the Karelian Isthmus and the region of Lake Ladoga. On the southern coast of the Gulf of Finland were the Estonians and Livonians, and north of the Finnic tribes were the Samis, who resisted assimilation. The Finnic tribes, with few ties beyond the clan or tribal level, were increasingly threatened by the more advanced Scandinavian peoples to the west and the Slavic peoples to the east.

The conversion of the Finnish tribes to Christianity was initiated from both the Orthodox East and Roman Catholic Sweden. In the twelfth century, traditionally in the year A.D. 1154, the Finns were conquered by the more powerful Swedes under their king Eric IX. Forced to adopt Christianity, which had already been making inroads in the region, the Finns began to see themselves as a single people rather than as disparate tribes. According to tradition, Nicholas Breakspear, an English* cardinal who became Pope Adrian IV, encouraged the Swedish king Eric to conquer the Finns. His goal was not only to convert the heathen tribes but to gain economic and political ends. King Eric defeated the Finnish tribes but was unable to hold the region. An English clergyman, Henry, who had been bishop of Uppsala in Sweden, remained in Finland. He was killed within a year and subsequently became the patron saint of all the Finns. In 1216 the pope confirmed Swedish title to conquered territories in Finland. A crusade launched in 1249 firmly established Swedish rule in much of the territory.

Finland became an administrative province of the Swedish kingdom in 1362, and the Finns were given the same rights within the Swedish kingdom as the Swedes. In the sixteenth century the Swedes made Finland a grand duchy as a royal appendage. During the seventeenth century, under Charles IX the entire administration of the Finnish territories was concentrated in Stockholm. Crop failures and famine in the late 1690s caused the death of between one-quarter and one-third of the Finnish population.

Swedish rule over the Finns lasted for more than 600 years, making the Finns an essentially European people, tied by religion, culture, economics, and politics to the West. The Finns, while adopting much of the Swedish culture, maintained their own culture and language, which is complex, but remained as a peasant dialect in rural areas. The centuries of Swedish rule saw the Finns' increasing involvement in European politics as their homeland was often a battleground between the West and Russia. Over the centuries, the Russians* exerted a powerful pressure on the Finnish homeland. Many wars were fought by the Swedes and Finns against Russian expansion on their eastern border.

In 1721, by the Treaty of Nystad, which ended the twenty-one-year Northern War, Peter I of Russia acquired the province of Vyborg, Viipuri in Finnish, and in 1743 acquired other territory in Finland. In 1808 during the Napoleonic Wars, Sweden was forced to cede the Grand Duchy of Finland to Russia, which became an autonomous state with the Russian tsar as grand duke in 1809. The tsar guaranteed the continuing validity of the Swedish constitutional laws and allowed the Finns to develop their own democratic system of government with little interference from the Russian government. As a further conciliatory gesture to his new Finnish subjects, in 1812 the tsar restored to Finland Viipuri and the other territories taken from Swedish control in the eighteenth century. For most of the nineteenth century the Finns were exempted from conscription into the Russian army.

In spite of the safeguards, the Finns often felt the autocratic rule of the tsar. The Finnish Diet, established under Swedish rule, was dismissed in 1809 and was not reconvened for more than fifty years. The government of the grand duchy became an uneasy balance of Finnish traditions of self-government and Russian autocracy, but as long as the Russians respected the balance, the Finns remained loyal. The period of Russian rule was a period of peaceful internal development as the country, for the first time in centuries, was free of war.

Early in the nineteenth century the Finns were a subject nation seemingly without a culture or history of their own. Inspired by cultural and political leaders, Finnish national consciousness began to awaken, bringing recognition of the uniqueness of their nation and its culture after 1820. In 1863 the Lantdag, the Finnish parliament, which had not met since 1809, was reconstituted. In the same year the Finnish language was accepted as an official language in the grand duchy with equal status to Swedish. The folktales of the Finns and Karels, the basis of the *Kalevala*, were complied in a monumental epic, which became the national heritage of both peoples and an inspiration to the growing Finnish national movement.

Toward the end of the century a shift in Russian policy curtailed the growing national movement. The intensive Russification policy, begun in 1899, aroused strong resistance among the Finns, including the assassination of the governor-general in 1904 and a serious general strike in 1905. In 1902 the Finnish language was given official status, and under the terms of an agreement signed in 1906 the Finns were granted a unicameral legislature, and universal suffrage was introduced. Another wave of Russification swept the Finnish homeland in 1908, culminating in laws passed in 1912 that gave Russians the same rights in Finland as the indigenous Finnish population.

The Finns were little affected by World War I until the Bolsheviks took control of the Russian government in October 1917. The Finns on 6 December 1917 declared their independence of Russia, but their transition to independence was not to be easy. Civil war broke out between the Finnish Reds, sympathizers of Soviet Russia, and the Whites, Finnish nationalists led by Marshal Carl Gustav Emil Mannerheim and aided by German troops. The Whites emerged victorious, and in 1919 the country became a republic under a democratic parliamentary government. In 1920 the Soviet Union recognized Finland's independence.

Many problems faced the Finns, among them famine, widespread unemployment, and a stagnant economy. Agrarian and social reforms passed by the new government did much to heal the wounds of the civil war, but deep scars remained, giving rise to radical rightist and leftist organizations and increasing political instability. The Communist Party, outlawed in 1923, remained active until suppressed by new laws in 1930. The right-wing Lapua Movement, which emerged from anticommunist disturbances in 1929, was also suppressed following an unsuccessful coup d'état in 1932. The extremist groups lost popularity, and the Finns were active in the League of Nations and other organizations.

Finland's pre–World War II population of 3.5 million was no threat to the

mighty Soviet Union, but Stalin suspected that Finnish territory, located strategically close to Leningrad, could be used as a base for German aggression.
The Soviet and Finnish governments held talks from the spring of 1938 to the
summer of 1939, but the Finns refused Soviet demands for military bases on
their territory, while giving the Soviets assurances that the Germans would never
be allowed to use neutral Finnish territory to attack the Soviet Union.

The Soviet–Nazi pact of August 1939, which effectively divided much of
Europe into Nazi and Soviet spheres of interest, revolutionized European politics. The secret protocol gave the Soviets a sphere that included Finland, the
Baltic states, and parts of Eastern Europe. Following the stunningly quick
German victory over the Poles* in September 1939, the Soviets moved to take
control of the Baltic States. The alarmed Finns, while accepting Soviet offers
of negotiations, declared the country's neutrality but mobilized their military
forces. Soviet demands included the cession of territory near Leningrad in
exchange for Soviet territory in Karelia, but Finland's first line of defense, called
the Mannerheim Line, lay in the area demanded by Moscow, and the Soviet
demands were rejected.

Isolated diplomatically, the Finns continued their refusal to give in to the
Soviet demands. On 30 November 1939 the Red Army attacked without a declaration of war. Unlike the other threatened peoples, the Estonians, Latvians,*
and Lithuanians,* who were unable to resist, the Finns, fought back desperately
and won some astounding victories. The Soviets underestimated the Finns, who
withstood massive Soviet attacks in the bitter winter of 1939–40, although a
renewed Soviet offensive in February 1940 finally began to wear down the
outnumbered and exhausted Finnish defenders. To stave off total defeat, the
Finnish government quickly agreed to Soviet terms and signed the Peace of
Moscow on 13 March 1940. By the terms of the agreement the Finns ceded
territories along the Soviet border, including their second largest city, Viipuri.
The ceded territories contained about one-eighth of Finland's population, most
of whom fled west to Finnish-held territory. Finland's losses in the Winter War
were 25,000 dead and 35,000 wounded.

Foreigners had observed the Soviet Red Army's performance in Finland, with
most opinions discounting their abilities. Four months after the conclusion of
the Winter War, Adolf Hitler launched a surprise attack on his Soviet ally,
greatly widening the area of fighting in World War II. The Finns again declared
their neutrality, but in June 1941 they were again at war with the Soviets, often
fighting alongside the Germans, although the Finns considered theirs a separate,
defensive war and refused to join German assaults on Leningrad and Murmansk.
The United Kingdom declared war on Finland, but the United States did not.

The Paris Peace Treaty, signed in 1947, obliged the Finns to pay war reparations of $300 million and to cede to the victorious Soviets the Karelian Isth-
mus, with Viipuri and other border territories. Despite great difficulties, the
Finns completed the reparations payments in 1952, the only nation to fully pay
the war reparations demanded.

In 1948 the Finns signed a treaty of mutual assistance with the USSR and pursued a policy of political neutrality during the long years of the Cold War. The diametrical change in Finnish policy after World War II, replacing the traditional hostility to the Soviets with a policy of mutual friendship, guaranteed Finland's survival as an independent state. The relationship between the Finns and the Soviet Union was derogatorily labled "Finlandization" by many Western observers; however, the Finns' position was not subservient, and the Finns also strengthened their ties to the other Scandinavian states and became an associate member of the European Free Trade Association (EFTA) in 1961.

In 1987 the Finns celebrated the seventieth anniversary of national independence. The intense social conflicts of the first decades of independence had been resolved, and Finland had developed into a prosperous, modern welfare state. By the mid-1980s the Finns had achieved the world's lowest infant mortality rate, but the Finns' most outstanding achievement has been their survival against great odds—against a harsh climate, cultural and physical isolation, and stronger neighbors.

Following the collapse of the Soviet Union in 1991, Finland and Russia nullified the 1948 treaty and signed a new pact in January 1992.

To ensure their continued security and prosperity, the Finns abandoned their traditional neutrality to join the European Union (EU) on 1 January 1995. The Finns, with their 800-mile (1,300 km.) border with shaky Russia, see security as their most pressing need. Membership in the EU, including participation in the single currency, inaugurated on 1 January 1999, remains the mainstay of Finnish policy.

SELECTED BIBLIOGRAPHY

Engle, Eloise, and Lauri Paananen. *The Winter War: The Soviet Attack on Finland 1939–1940.* 1992.

Jakobson, Max. *Finland in the New Europe.* 1998.

Kirby, D. G. *Finland in the Twentieth Century.* 1979.

Maude, George. *Finland.* 1995.

Tiilikainen, Teija. *Historical Dictionary of Europe and Finland: Defining the Political Identity of Finland in Western Europe.* 1998.

FLEMISH

Vlaamsch; Vlaams; Flemings;
Flamands

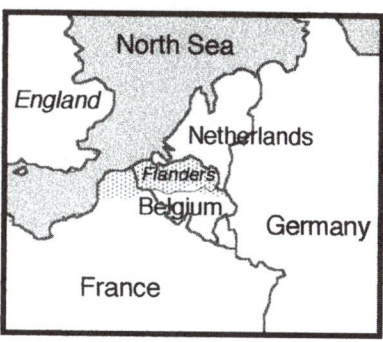

POPULATION: Approximately (2000 e) 6,092,000 Flemish in Europe, 5,771,000 in Belgium, and 371,000 in Westhoek (French Flanders).

THE FLEMISH HOMELAND: The Flemish homeland occupies a broad, flat plain in northern Belgium, bordering the North Sea on the west, where Flanders has a thirty-nine-mile (sixty-three km.) coastline. Behind the coastline lie the coastal plains, with some of the low-lying areas below sea level. Called *polders*, they are protected from the sea by dikes or seawalls. In southern and western Flanders the land is mostly low plateau. The original birch forests and heathlands have largely been replaced by plantations of evergreen trees. The major river, the Schelde, and a canal system connect the major port of Antwerp and other inland cities to the North Sea.

Flanders forms an autonomous region of Belgium. Flemish nationalists also claim the Brussels metropolitan area, which is an enclave within Flanders but forms a separate autonomous region, and French Flanders, Westhoek in Flemish, the northwestern districts of the French region of Nord-Pas-de-Calais. *Region of Flanders (Vlaanderen)*: 5,217 sq.mi.–13,512 sq.km. (2000 e) 5,763,000- Flemish 86%, Walloons* 11%, Italians* 1%, Portuguese,* Spanish,* Turks.* The Flemish capital and major cultural center, Brussels, called Brussel in Flemish, forms an enclave within the Flemish autonomous region, (2000 e) 948,000 (metropolitan region 2,399,000). The major cultural center of Westhoek or French Flanders is Dunkirk (Dunquerque) 70,000 (209,000).

FLAG: The Flemish national flag, the official flag of the autonomous region, is a yellow field bearing the rampant Black Lion of Flanders centered.

PEOPLE: The Flemish, also called Flemings, are a Germanic people closely related to the Dutch* of the Netherlands. However, the Flemish majority remains staunchly Roman Catholic, while Protestant religions prevail in the Netherlands. Formerly a rural people, the Flemish were dominated since Belgian independence in the nineteenth century by the more sophisticated, French-speaking Walloons. This domination finally ended in the 1960s, when the aging heavy industries of Wallonia lost importance, while the Flemish ports gained as gateways for much of Northern Europe. The Flemish nationalist movement grew from the initial demands for the cultural equality that their new economic importance in Belgium warranted. Until the mid-twentieth century the Flemish majority remained rural; only since World War II has a large Flemish urban population developed. The heirs of the Flemish Renaissance, the Flemish culture is one of the richest in Europe.

The Flemish language, belonging to the West Germanic language group, is a low German dialect closely related to Dutch. In its spoken form, Flemish diverged from Dutch in the sixteenth century but remains nearly identical in its written form. The language, long suppressed in favor of French, is the focal point of modern Flemish nationalism. In the city and suburbs of Brussels, both French and Dutch are officially recognized, although French speakers are the larger group in the Brussels metropolitan area.

NATION: Ancient Flanders, part of the Roman province of Belgica, named for the Celtic Belgae tribe conquered by the Romans in 57 B.C., became thoroughly Latinized in culture and language. Invaded by Huns and Salic Franks in the fourth century A.D. as Roman power waned, the Germanic conquerors drove the Latins south to a line approximating the present linguistic division of Belgium. The region formed a major part of the new kingdom of the Franks, which began to expand in the late 400s. The Franks eventually established a vast empire and gained control of most of modern France and southern Germany.

The empire established by the Franks reached its apex under Charles the Great, better known as Charlemagne. The empire began to decline at Charlemagne's death in 814 and was divided by three heirs in 843. Baldwin Bras-de-Fer, a son-in-law of Emperor Charles II, became the first count of Flanders in 862, forming a fief of the French kingdom. Under Baldwin I and Baldwin II, the basis was laid for the industrial and commercial greatness of the region by the establishment of the wool and silk industries at Ghent and the inauguration of annual fairs at Brugge, Ieper, and other towns.

In the eleventh century, the Flemish lands became a vassal of the Holy Roman Empire as well as the French crown. The County of Flanders, with its capital at Lille, enjoyed virtual independence and at its greatest extent controlled Flanders, Westhoek, Artois, and part of Picardy. The county, with power equivalent to that of a kingdom, wielded considerable influence in the political affairs of Western Europe.

In conjunction with the northern Italian cities, the French-speaking Flemish cities led the European Renaissance, a movement little affecting the rural,

Flemish-speaking peasantry. The Flemish cities, called communes, gained broad privileges and liberties, which reflected their growing prosperity and importance.

In 1191 the direct line of the counts of Flanders died out, and the counts of Hainault, in present Wallonia, also became the Flemish counts, perpetuating the predominance of the French language among the upper classes. The power of the county was weakened by the departure of its count, Baldwin IX, on the Fourth Crusade. He was later proclaimed the emperor of Constantinople as Baldwin I in 1204.

In the struggle for control of Flanders, the counts gradually lost Artois, Picardy, and other territories to the French crown. The region in the thirteenth and fourteenth centuries was the scene of serious political and economic tensions, which often caused bloody rivalries among classes, trade guilds, and independent cities. The turbulence was worsened by a continuing rivalry between the pro-French and pro-Flemish groups. On 11 July 1302 the Flemish won the Battle of the Golden Spurs against the forces of the French king. The date, 11 July, is now the official holiday of the Flemish nation. However, civil war in 1322 again left Flanders little more than a French province. In 1384 the entire region passed to the dukes of Burgundy, and Flemish privileges were suppressed but were partially restored in 1477. Under Burgundian rule Flemish commerce and Flemish art reached their flower in a great golden age.

In 1500, then the richest and most populous area of Europe, Flanders came under the rule of the Austrian Hapsburgs and in 1555 passed to the Spanish Hapsburgs and became part of the Spanish Netherlands. The religious differences between the southern and northern provinces led to a serious division in the Low Countries. In 1566 Protestant activists destroyed statues in Catholic churches across the region, setting off nearly eighty years of sectarian violence.

The Roman Catholic south remained under Spanish rule when the Protestant Dutch rebelled and won their independence in 1579. The Flemish, although they split from the Dutch when the northern provinces accepted the Reformation, again united with the Dutch and Walloons to fight first Spanish and later Austrian domination in the seventeenth and eighteenth centuries. The Flemish joined the Dutch in a widespread revolt against Spanish rule in 1576, but by 1584 the Spanish had recovered control of Flanders and imposed an oppressive rule. The expanding French kingdom took control of western Flanders, including the historic capital, Lille, between 1668 and 1678. In 1714 the Flemish homeland again passed to the Austrian Hapsburgs.

The military forces of revolutionary France occupied the Flemish provinces in 1792. Austria ceded the provinces to France in 1797, and Napoleonic France annexed the region in 1801. At the conclusion of the Napoleonic Wars in 1815, the Low Countries were reunited in the Kingdom of the Netherlands.

Rejecting the domination of the kingdom by the Protestant Dutch, the predominantly Roman Catholic southern provinces in Flanders and Wallonia rebelled in 1830 and formed the separate Kingdom of Belgium under the protection of the major European powers. The new kingdom remained a French-speaking state, with Flemish relegated to the position of a peasant dialect. Most of the nineteenth century industrialization of Belgium took place in the southern Walloon provinces, leaving the Flemish as a rural, agricultural nation dominated by the richer, more sophisticated Walloons. The adoption of French as the official language effectively barred Flemish-speakers from most government positions.

Flemish resentment of Walloon domination stimulated a cultural and linguistic revival. The first works published in modern Flemish appeared in 1837. The revival spread to the Flemish minority in France, and the first cultural organization in Westhoek formed in 1852. A strong sense of Flemish grievance grew throughout the nineteenth century. Although Flemish became an official language in 1898, the dissatisfied Flemish leaders demanded full cultural and linguistic equality with the Walloons in 1900.

Overrun by German troops in 1914, the occupation authorities, to win Flemish support, granted the linguistic and cultural rights long denied by the Belgian government. Heavy fighting devastated the province of West Flanders and French Flanders. The region's strategic location, as it had since the Middle Ages, made Flanders a natural battleground. A faction of the Flemish national movement formed a Council of Flanders in February 1917 and, with German encouragement, declared Flanders independent of Belgium on 11 November 1917. The republic collapsed with the German surrender in 1918, and its leaders faced charges of high treason when the Belgian government returned.

At the end of the war, linguistic and economic controversies again caused friction between the Flemish and the dominant Walloons. Flemish extremist groups, many from the first Flemish university, opened at Ghent in 1930, emerged during the turbulent interwar period. Some of the groups, drawn to the Nazi propaganda promoting the unity of Europe's Germanic peoples, collaborated following the German occupation in May 1940, some even joining Nazi fighting units. The German occupation authorities raised the Flemish language to the status of an official language along with French.

The rapid postwar reconstruction of Europe greatly increased the economic importance of the Flemish port cities. By the early 1960s Flanders had surpassed Wallonia as Belgium's economically predominant region. Material prosperity prompted demands for Flemish cultural and linguistic equality. Mass rallies erupted across Flanders in 1961–62. In November 1962 the government adopted Flemish as the sole official language of the Flemish provinces. In 1963 a law was passed establishing three official languages within Belgium: Flemish was recognized as the official language in the north, French in the south, and German along the eastern border. Universities, banks, political parties, and other official institutions split along linguistic lines. In the late 1960s and early 1970s the Flemish national movement gained broad support among the Flemish population of Belgium and France.

The economic and cultural rivalry between the Flemish and Walloons made weak coalition governments the norm in Belgium. Governments rose and fell on the linguistic issue, with major political parties split into Flemish and Walloon factions. The traditional grievances of the Flemish population, developed during the nineteenth and early twentieth centuries, continue to spur the national movement, which works for an independent Flanders within Europe, which would include Brussels, the so-called Flemish Jerusalem.

In 1970 the first changes were made to the Belgian constitution that established a federal state. The Egmont Pact, adopted in 1977, created autonomous governments in Flanders and Wallonia and later in bilingual Brussels. The devolution of powers over taxation, culture, and education gradually shifted power from the federal government to the powerful autonomous regions through reforms to the constitution in 1980, 1988, and 1993. The status of Brussels, a French-speaking center surrounded by Flemish-speaking suburbs, remains a major nationalist issue. Demand for even greater devolution of government powers, agreed to in February 1993, created a federation and has left the Belgian government responsible for little more than finance, foreign policy, and defense. When these limited federal powers are surrendered to a united European federation, Belgium will effectively cease to exist except as a geographic area. In parliamentary elections held in May 1995, a coalition was returned to power, signaling the completion of the conversion to a more decentralized form of government.

Flemish nationalists on 29 November 1997 proclaimed a provisional government of the Republic of Flanders with Gert Geens as the first president. The proclamation, made to draw attention to the Flemish demands for independence within the European Union, was followed by unofficial parliamentary elections held in February 1998.

SELECTED BIBLIOGRAPHY

Deprez, Kas, ed. *Language and Intergroup Relations in Flanders and the Netherlands.* 1989.

Hermans, T. J. *The Flemish Movement: A Documentary History 1780–1980.* 1991.

Nicholas, David. *Trade, Urbanization, and the Family: Studies in the History of Medieval Flanders.* 1996.

Pateman, Robert. *Belgium.* 1996.

Strikwerda, Carl. *A House Divided; Catholics, Socialists, and Flemish Nationalists in Nineteenth-Century Belgium.* 1997.

FRENCH

Français

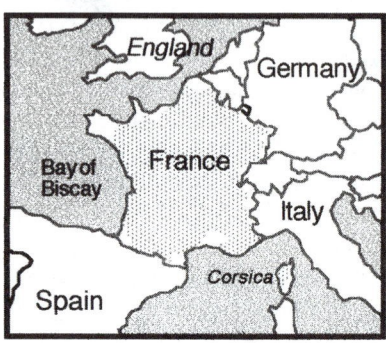

POPULATION: Approximately (2000 e) 52,117,000 French in Europe, concentrated in France, but with smaller numbers in Italy, Spain, Belgium, and Switzerland. Other large French populations live in the United States, Canada, Israel, Monaco, South America, the Caribbean, the Indian Ocean, the South Pacific, and other areas.

THE FRENCH HOMELAND: The French homeland, France, is the largest state in Western Europe, with extremely varied terrain and scenery within natural land frontiers, the mountains on its borders. The Pyrenees Mountains in the south separate France from Spain, the Jura Mountains form part of the border with Switzerland, the Vosges Mountains overlook the Rhine Valley in the northeast, and the Alps lie along the borders with Switzerland and Italy. The only important highland area entirely within French territory is the Massif Central in southern France, a south-central plateau, and contiguous to the plateau is a vast region of rolling plains. In the northwest the English Channel separates France from Great Britain, in the west the Bay of Biscay forms a long coastline, and in the south lies the Mediterranean. The chief rivers are the Seine and its tributaries, flowing into the English Channel, the Loire, Garonne, and Adour, which flow into the Bay of Biscay, and the Rhone, with its tributary the Saône, flowing south to the Mediterranean.

France is one of the most powerful countries in the world, a parliamentary republic since the French Revolution in the late eighteenth century. *Republic of France (Répulic Française)*: 212,918 sq.mi.–551,458 sq.km. (2000 e) 58,329,000—French 92%, Bretons* 4%, Arabs 3%, Alsatians* 3%, Occitans* 2%, Berbers, Catalans,* Germans,* Portuguese,* Algerians,* Moroccans,* Italians,* Turks,* Flemish.* The French capital and major cultural center is Paris, (2000 e) 2,148,000 (metropolitan area, 10,702,000).

FLAG: The French national flag, the official flag of the republic, is a vertical tricolor of blue, white, and red.

PEOPLE: The French are a basically Latin people of mixed Germanic, Mediterranean, and other European strains. French culture, based on the earlier Roman influences, is one of the most renowned in Europe and has been a world culture for centuries following the establishment of an extensive world empire from the sixteenth century. The culture of the French has profoundly influenced that of the entire Western world, particularly in the areas of art, letters, and fashion. Although the French homeland has never been a single cultural unit, the French heartland first attained cultural preeminence in Europe during the Middle Ages. About 74% of the French population is classified as urban.

The French language, like the French culture, is a world language spoken around the globe. The largest of the Gallo-Romance languages of the Romance group of Indo-European languages, French is spoken in France in at least thirteen distinct regional dialects. An estimated 125 million people in the world speak French, including those using French as their second language. In the sixteenth and seventeenth centuries French replaced Latin as a common language for international, especially diplomatic communication in Europe, and it continues to be used for that purpose.

The vast majority of the French nation are Christians, mostly Roman Catholics, 89%, with other Christian sects making up 7% of the population, and non-Christians making up the rest. Protestants and Jews make up about 2% and 1% of the French population, respectively. Although nominally Roman Catholic, the French majority are highly secular, with religion playing a lesser role in public life than in centuries past.

NATION: Celts, called Gauls, occupied the region from at least the seventh century B.C. and became the dominant group. The varied topography and the vastness of the territory imposed varied lifestyles in different tribal groups. The Celtic language of the region was a language called Gaulish, which was spoken in many different dialects. Although some of the earliest anthropological and archaeological remains in Europe have been found in France, little is known of the Celtic peoples who inhabited the region.

Contact with Mediterranean culture began when the Greeks explored the western Mediterranean Sea in the seventh century B.C. and traded with the interior via the Rhone Valley. Greek and Phoenicians colonized the Mediterranean coast around 600 B.C. The most important, Massilia, developed an extensive trade up the Rhone Valley and in the Mediterranean area. The Massilian Greeks were aided by the Romans in their conflict with Carthage, and the region was gradually annexed to Rome from the second century B.C. to the annexation of Massila in 49 B.C. A Roman settlement farther inland at Narbonne became the center of a flourishing Roman province. Gallia Narbonensis, the southeastern part of Gaul, was formed as a Roman province in 121 B.C.

Gaul, called Gallia Celtica or Gallia Proper by the Romans, included most of modern France and Belgium and parts of Switzerland, Germany, and the Netherlands. The Roman legions, led by Julius Caesar, conquered most of Gaul between 58 and 51 B.C. The Roman authorities divided Gaul into three parts according to the Celtic peoples inhabiting the regions, Aquitania in the southwest, Gallia Lugdunensis in the west and center, and Belgica in the northeast. The main center of Roman administration was Lugdunum, modern Lyon. The entire region was reorganized by Emperors Augustus and Tiberius as administrative areas of Narbonensis, Aquitania, Lugdunensis, Belgica, and the military districts of Germania Inferior and Germania Superior. Over five centuries of Roman rule the Gauls developed a distinct Gallo-Roman civilization and adopted the Roman language and Roman law. Christianity, introduced in the first century A.D., spread rapidly, particularly to the large and prosperous Roman cities.

In the third century A.D., as the Roman Empire began its decline, Roman Gaul was afflicted by a variety of ills: political instability, a dwindling supply of slaves, plague, rising inflation, and its complement of economic insecurity, mounting pressure from the Germanic tribes along the frontier, and a general breakdown of law and order. Powerful landlords fled from the defenseless cities to fortified villas, and corruption flourished as Roman rule weakened. The privileged classes were exempted from taxes and increasingly took power from the Roman authorities. Temporary respite was gained in the time of the emperor Diocletian, whose military and fiscal reorganization was carried out, in part, from an imperial residence in Gaul at Trier. Christianity, which had been introduced as a persecuted sect in the second century, flourished under imperial protection in this period of personal insecurity and political disorder. By the fifth century, even the Gallo-Roman aristocracy was converting; men from old senatorial families moved rather easily into episcopal positions.

Throughout the fourth century small groups of Germanic tribesmen had been settling in Gaul with the permission of the Roman authorities. The arrival of small groups of Germans became an invasion in 406, when Vandals, Suevi, and Alans broke through the frontier and moved rapidly across Gaul and on into Spain. The Romanized Gauls gradually lost the power to defend their fertile homeland from invasions by the Germanic tribes, particularly the Franks, Visigoths, and Burgundians.* In 412 the Visigoths entered southern Gaul from Italy, and about 440 the Burgundians settled in eastern Gaul. In 451 Germans, Romans, and Gauls united to defeat a new horde of invaders, the Huns under Attila.

In 486, ten years after the traditional date given for the fall of Rome, the Franks, under Clovis I, defeated the last Roman governor, Syagrius. Clovis, the Frankish leader, married to a Burgundian princess, became a Christian in 496 and had himself crowned ruler of all the Franks. He conquered southern Gaul from the Visigoths and made the German tribes to the east vassals following his victory over the Alemanni in 496. Clovis accepted Christianity and founded the dynasty of the Merovingians, but he failed to provide for the unity of Gaul when he divided his kingdom among his four sons at his death. The Frankish kingdom expanded under the Merovingians to include Burgundy and Provence.

Effective rule of the Frankish lands passed to the Carolingians in the seventh century, while the kingdom continued under weak Merovingian kings. The territory declined, many areas were depopulated, and commerce suffered. In the eighth century, the only remnant of Gallo-Roman civilization, the church, was seriously threatened by the Muslim Saracens, who invaded Gaul. In 732 Charles Martel decisively defeated the Saracens, and his son, Pipin the Short, dethroned the last Merovingian in 751 and proclaimed himself king of the Franks.

Pipin's son and heir, called Charlemagne, was crowned in Rome by Pope Leo II and received the title emperor of the Romans. There had not been a Roman emperor in the western provinces since the late fifth century. Charlemagne established a vast administrative system, divided into some 250 counties, for governing his vast empire. Charlemagne was the sole ruler of the Franks for more than four decades, until his death in 814. Under Charlemagne's rule the Frankish kingdom expanded to rule parts of modern Spain, Italy, Germany, and the Low Countries.

Charlemagne's son, Louis, sought to provide for an orderly succession by decreeing in 817 that his eldest son, Lothair, would inherit the empire and that his two younger sons, Pepin of Aquitaine and Louis II, called Louis the German, would hold subordinate kingdoms within the empire. The emperor then had a fourth son, Charles, by his second wife, who was determined that her son should share the royal inheritance. The sons fought bitterly among themselves and sometimes against their father as well. One temporary settlement among three of the brothers is of particular historical interest. By the Treaty of Verdun in 843, Lothair was to get the imperial title plus a long strip of territory stretching from the North Sea at the mouth of the Rhine all the way down to and including Rome. Louis the German received the lands east of the Rhine, and Charles the Bald those west of the Rhone, the Seine, the Meuse, and the Schelde (Escaut). Louis' territory was a forerunner of modern Germany, Charles' a forerunner of modern France, and Lothair's a forerunner of the lands in between that have been so often fought over by France and Germany in modern times. Although this particular division did not prove lasting, the separation of Francia Occidentalis (the West Frankish Kingdom, or France) from Francia Orientalis (the East Frankish Kingdom, or Germany) became permanent at this time.

During the medieval period central authority was merely nominal, with the French lands divided into several separate territories. The authority of the French kings was increasingly usurped by feudal lords. When the Carolingian line died out in 987, the nobles chose Hugh Capet as king. Originally, the Capetians were dukes of Francia, a small territory around Paris, and their authority was virtually nonexistent in the rest of France. The Capetians gradually expanded their powers, defeated robber barons, and held against the great feudal lords. France, as a distinct kingdom, traditionally dates from the small Duchy of Francia, the crown of which was seized by Hugh Capet in 987. His state evolved into the first kingdom in Europe.

In 911 the Norsemen, who had been raiding the coastal regions for over a century, took control of the northwest, which was called Normandy after its new masters. The Norse leader, Rollo, was named the first duke of Normandy. In 1066, under Duke William, the Normans* crossed the English Channel in force to invade and conquer England. Although Normandy and England were ruled by the Normans, English rule was eventually extended to large areas of present France. A resurgent French kingdom gradually won back the territories, including Normandy in 1204. The last English-held areas were taken by the French in 1453.

Under the rule of Louis XI the power of the feudal lords was destroyed, and almost all of present France was bought under the authority of the French kings. In the sixteenth century the Italian Renaissance greatly influenced French culture, even while the Protestant Reformation was gaining a following among all classes. In 1560 religious conflict broke out in the first of a series of civil wars that devastated France.

In the seventeenth century the French kingdom regained its power and prosperity while steadily centralizing most authority in the king. The powerful nobles were humbled, and the rights of the Protestants were eroded. Territorial gains under the rule of Louis XIV included Alsace, Franche-Comté, and Lorraine; however, the power, prestige, and overseas possessions of the French were decreased by the English victory in the Seven Years' War.

Louis XV inherited a unified kingdom, but a kingdom still with remnants of its earlier feudalism. The power of the king was curtailed by a bewildering multitude of charters and special privileges held by noble families, trade guilds, monopolies, communes, and provinces. The heavy taxes demanded by the state were raised inefficiently, raising resentment among all classes, although the more privileged were exempt from specific taxes. Operating under a system of special privileges, the wealthiest state in Europe was perennially on the verge of bankruptcy. French backing of the American Revolution increased the huge public debt.

Attempts at economic reform led to an avalanche of grievances and finally to demands for a constitution. A Paris mob revolted and on 14 July 1789 stormed the Bastille prison. The outbreak of violence marked the first entry of the lower classes into French political life. Mobilized by food shortages and fears of an aristocratic conspiracy, rural estates and country houses were sacked, while increasing labor troubles brought violence to the cities. On 5 October 1789 a Paris mob marched on the royal palace at Versailles, beginning the end of the monarchy in France. Thousands fled abroad to escape the spreading violence.

In 1799, during the French Revolutionary War, Napoleon Bonaparte took power. Following a series of brilliant military campaigns, he was finally defeated by an alliance of European powers in 1815. The French Revolution, though it seemed to have been nullified by Napoleon's defeat in 1815, had far-reaching results for the French nation. The middle-class capitalists were established as the dominant power in the state, feudalism was finally ended, social justice had been introduced with the Code Napoléon, and the French capital, Paris, became the center of European liberal thought. However, the revolution and the Napoleonic Wars destroyed the ancient structure of Europe, hastened the growth of nationalism, and began an era of modern, total warfare.

Attempts to reverse the revolutionary gains led to upheavals in 1830 and 1848. In 1848, during the upheavals in Paris, Louis Napoleon Bonaparte, the nephew of Napoleon I, became president of the Second Republic. Four years later, by a coup d'état, he became emperor as Napoleon III. The Second Empire was a period of colonial expansion and material prosperity, but the period was also marked by Napoleon's autocratic style and a series of unrewarding wars. His rule ended in the disaster of the Franco-Prussian War, which forced the defeated French to cede Alsace and Lorraine to Germany. The Third Republic was founded with the fall of Napoleon III in 1871, and a republican constitution was adopted in 1875.

In the years before World War I, the French increased their vast colonial empire in Asia and Africa, bringing France into conflict with Great Britain and Germany. Eventually, France allied with Great Britain and Russia to balance the German, Austrian, and Italian alliance. In World War I the French bore the brunt of the war damage, but the French also claimed the majority share of the victory. Severe terms dictated to defeated Germany were one of the reasons for the rise of Nazism and eventually World War II, causing great loss of life and much damage to the French economy. The role of French collaborators with the German occupation forces still remains a very sensitive issue.

In 1946 France adopted a new constitution, establishing the Fourth Republic, but political instability and devastating colonial wars slowed the postwar recovery. Several colonial possessions were lost in the 1940s and 1950s. The crisis brought on by the war for Algerian independence brought an end to the Fourth Republic. In 1958 Charles de Gaulle was elected president, and he introduced a new constitution, giving the president extra powers and inaugurating the Fifth Republic.

Since the 1960s the French have made rapid economic progress, becoming one of the most prosperous nations in the European Union. One of the major social problems that emerged from the French economic expansion was the presence among the French of large numbers of immigrants from North Africa and Southern Europe, many concentrated in poor, peripheral areas around the major cities. In 1993 the government set tight rules for entry into the country and made it easier for the government to expel foreigners.

A socialist government, voted into government in June 1997, gave the French a briskly growing economy, a thirty-five-hour workweek (due in 2000), dropping unemployment, and closer integration with the rest of Western Europe. The socialist-led coalition of Lionel Jospin includes, besides the socialists, some communists, Greens, and other leftist groups and has retained its popularity, but rifts within the coalition are becoming more severe, with clouds gathering over the French homeland on the threshold of the twenty-first century.

Socially, the French homeland since World War II has become a multiethnic and multireligious society; however, in the late 1990s, according to an official study in July 1998, four out of every ten admit to being "racist" or "fairly racist," almost twice the number of the more openly racist Germans, British, or Italians.

SELECTED BIBLIOGRAPHY

Kaplan, Steven Laurence. *Farewell, Revolution: The Historians' Feud, France 1789/1989.* 1995.

Kramer, Steven Philip. *Does France Still Count?: The French Role in the New Europe.* 1994.

Markoff, John. *The Abolition of Feudalism: Peasants, Lords, and Legislators in the French Revolution.* 1996.

Price, Roger. *A Concise History of France.* 1993.

Shirer, William L. *The Collapse of the Third Republic: An Inquiry into the Fall of France.* 1994.

FRISIANS

Frysk; Friesisch; Fries

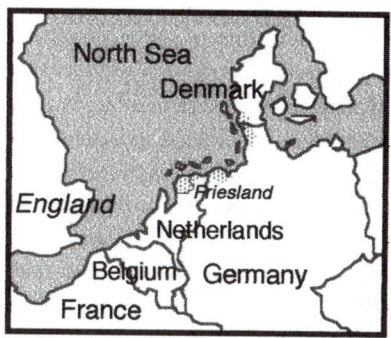

POPULATION: Approximately (2000 e) 865,000 Frisians in Europe, 411,000 in Friesland in the Netherlands, another 303,000 in other parts of the Netherlands, and 151,000 in Denmark and Germany. An estimated 35,000 Frisians live in the United States and Canada.

THE FRISIAN HOMELAND: The Frisian homeland lies in Northern Europe, a region of flat plains and polders, lands in the northern Netherlands reclaimed from the North Sea between A.D. 1200 and 1600. The Dutch province includes a string of offshore islands along the northern coast, the West Frisian Islands. East Friesland in Germany, including the East Frisian Islands, is separated from Dutch Friesland by the Dollart, an inlet of the North Sea formed by the Ems River estuary. North Friesland, including the North Frisian Islands, lies on the western part of Denmark's Jutland Peninsula, on both sides of the Danish–German border. Dutch Friesland is the least populated region of the Netherlands, one of the most densely populated states in Europe.

Most of the region has fertile lands along the coast with sandy heath and fenlands in the interior. Located in the low region of the Netherlands, much of Friesland lies below sea level; many of its towns and cities were originally established on earthen mounds called terpen, which were constructed to provide raised areas above the marshlands. The province's poorly drained soils are best suited for pasture, and Friesland is well known in Europe for its cattle.

Western Friesland forms a province of the Kingdom of the Netherlands. East Friesland and North Friesland have no official status other than distinctive cultural and linguistic regions recognized by the German and Danish governments. *Province of Friesland (Fryslân)*: 1,464 sq.mi.–3,792 sq.km. (2000 e) 609,000—

Frisians 89%, other Dutch.* The Frisian capital and major city is Leeuwarden, Ljouwert in Frisian, (2000 e) 86,000, a city noted for its gold and silver manufactures. The cultural centers of the East Frisians are Emden, a seaport in Germany with a population of (2000 e) 51,000, and Norden, (2000 e) 25,000. The cultural center of the North Frisians is the town of Husum, Hüsem in Frisian, (2000 e) 24,000.

FLAGS: The Frisian flag, the official flag of the province and recognized by the Frisian communities in Germany and Denmark, is a blue field divided by three white diagonal stripes charged with seven red devices representing water lilies. The flag of the East Frisians in Germany is a horizontal tricolor of black, red, and pale blue. The flag of the North Frisians in Denmark is a yellow field bearing a blue Scandinavian cross outlined in red.

PEOPLE: The Frisians are a Germanic people with historical and linguistic ties to the English,* Dutch, and Germans.* Closely related to the ancient Anglo-Saxons, the Frisians have maintained their unique culture from the time of Roman control in Northern Europe, over 2,500 years. The Frisians once controlled the whole of the North Sea coast, and isolated Frisian minorities still live in the East Friesland region and the East Frisian Islands of Germany and the North Friesland region and the North Frisian Islands of Denmark. The Dutch Frisians claim they molded the first dikes, which were later copied by the Dutch across the Zuider Zee.

The Frisians speak a language of the Anglo-Frisian branch of the West Germanic languages, the closest of the continental Germanic languages to English, particularly close to the northern English dialects, Lallans in Scotland and Northumbrian in Northumbria. The language is considered, linguistically, to be a bridge language between English and Dutch. The eastern Frisian dialects, East Frisian and North Frisian, are not inherently intelligible with West Frisian spoken in the Netherlands. At least nine distinct dialects are spoken by the Frisians, although some, such as Fering, spoken on the island of Fohr, Solring on Sylt, and Halunder on Helgoland, are not called Frisian. Since the mid-1980s, as part of the ethnocultural revival, the number of schools teaching in Frisian has significantly increased.

The Frisian majority are Protestant, mostly belonging to the Dutch Reformed Church in the Netherlands and the Lutheran Church in Germany and Denmark. Minorities belong to the Mennonite sect and the Roman Catholic Church.

NATION: Migrating Germanic tribes settled the shores of the North Sea following the breakup of Celtic Europe in the fourth century B.C. The Germanic Frisians eventually controlled the coastal region from present Bremen in Germany, to Brugge in Belgium. The Frisians conquered and settled the offshore islands lying in the North Sea. In the first century B.C. the Frisians stopped the northward advance of Roman power. While holding off Roman incursions, the Frisians, called Frisii by the Romans, maintained their independence and sent raiding parties into the Roman territories to the south. The fierce Frisian warriors became the scourge of the settled peoples on the borders of the Roman Empire in the first centuries of the Christian Era.

Later Germanic tribes, taking advantage of the collapse of Roman power, attempted to conquer the Frisians but were unable to subdue the warlike nation. Germanic Angles and Saxons moved into the region in the fifth century, establishing strong linguistic and cultural ties to the Frisians before they eventually moved on to cross the channel and conquer England.

The Salic Franks invaded the Frisian homeland in the eighth century and gradually brought Friesland under Frankish control, completing the conquest during Charlemagne's reign. Friesland formed the northern portion of the middle kingdom, Lotharingia, at the division of the empire by Charlemagne's heirs in 843. The region passed to the eastern kingdom of Louis the German in 870 and ultimately became a fief of Holland. Subject to Viking raids between the eighth and tenth centuries, the Frisians, to protect themselves, reverted to their earlier warrior culture, striking fear in their more settled neighbors.

The region in the Middle Ages extended from the Scheldt River in the south to the Weser River in the east. In 1248 William of Holland restored the Frisians' ancient rights, but they again revolted six years later. The Frisians were defeated and absorbed into the province of Holland. Although nominally a part of Holland, the Frisians did not submit to a regional ruler but continued to obey their local headmen.

In 1433 Holland came under the rule of the House of Burgundy, but the authority of the Burgundian dukes was not recognized by the independent-minded Frisians. In 1498 Emperor Maximilian I bestowed Friesland on Albert, duke of Saxony, whose son, unable to control the wild Frisians, finally sold the Frisian homeland back to the emperor in 1515. Western Friesland, along with the Low Countries, passed to the Spanish Hapsburgs and was finally pacified by Spanish troops led by Maximilian's grandson, Charles V, in 1523. East Friesland, created a separate duchy in 1454, was not included in the transfer, and its history became separate.

The Frisians joined the United Provinces in 1579, an alliance of the northern Protestant provinces opposed to Catholic Spanish rule. In 1581 the seven northern provinces of the Low Countries formed an independent Dutch kingdom. Friesland, as part of the Dutch kingdom, retained considerable autonomy with a separate Frisian stadtholder appointed by the Frisian people. In 1748 the Frisian stadtholder, Prince William of Orange, became the sole stadtholder of all the Dutch provinces. Since that time the Dutch Frisians have remained loyal to the House of Orange, if not always to the Dutch state.

Geographically separated from the Dutch by the waters of the Zuider Zee and dispersed across a number of islands, the isolated Frisians retained their language and culture, which the Frisian Parliament jealously guarded. In February 1782 the parliament of Friesland became one of the first official organs of a foreign government to extend recognition to the fledgling United States.

The pastoral Frisians remained a mainly rural people but developed a strong culture with an extensive literature. The Frisian metropolis, Leeuwarden, called Ljonwert by the Frisians, developed as the center of the modern Frisian culture and helped to maintain ties to the Frisian diaspora in Northern Europe.

The French forces led by Napoleon overran Friesland in 1794–95 and later formed part of the French-controlled Batavian Republic. Annexed, along with the rest of the Netherlands, by France in 1810, the Frisian territories remained staunchly loyal to the Dutch monarchy. Following French defeat in 1815, the Frisians again welcomed their participation in the kingdom of the Netherlands under their beloved House of Orange.

The Dutch language gradually replaced Frisian as the language of government and education in the nineteenth century and became the first language of the growing urban areas. A Frisian national revival beginning in the 1880s transformed the Frisian language into a modern literary language and slowly reversed the Frisian assimilation into Dutch culture. In the early twentieth century the general cultural revival continued, with Frisian becoming the language of the towns and cities as the rural Frisians urbanized. During World War I, Frisian nationals formed the Frisian National Party, called In Fryske Aksyjeploesch in Frisian, to press for the maintenance and wider use of the Frisian language.

Friesland's relative isolation ended with the construction of dikes and a highway linking the peninsula to the Dutch heartland in the 1932. In 1933 the major enclosing dam was completed, calming the Zuider Zee and allowing the opening of a four-lane highway from the other Dutch provinces. The end of Friesland's geographic isolation brought the Frisian heartland into closer dependence on the Dutch economy but gave new impetus to the efforts of Frisian cultural and national groups to protect their language and culture. In the interwar period the Dutch government maintained firm control of the region, especially when the Nazis of neighboring Germany began to make overtures to the Germanic peoples of Europe.

The Frisian homeland was overrun by German troops during World War II, but German overtures, including promises of self-rule, failed to sway the Frisians' loyalty to the exiled House of Orange. At the end of the war Frisian nationalists accelerated the advancement of the cultural movement that had begun at the turn of the century, but with major Dutch concessions on the culture and use of the Frisian language most Frisians were content with Dutch rule. During the 1950s and 1960s the Dutch Frisians renewed their ties to the German and Danish Frisian minorities. In 1956 the Frisian Council was formed with the participation of the various Frisian groups in the Netherlands, Germany, and Denmark.

Postwar Dutch governments encouraged the Frisian cultural movement. Intensely loyal to the House of Orange, the Frisians have not developed the militant nationalism of many smaller European nations. Following minor nationalist disturbances in the 1960s and 1970s, the Dutch government moved to defuse rising nationalism by granting broad linguistic and cultural autonomy, with the

Frisian language accepted in the local courts, administration, and the Frisian parliament. The use of the Frisian language in radio and television broadcasting increased dramatically. In 1981, with government approval, the teaching of Frisian became obligatory in the province's 600 schools.

The Frisians look back on 2,000 years of separate history and are intensely proud of their separate culture and history. They enjoy a large measure of self-government, with their own national flag, anthem, and parliament. Calling themselves the Scots* of the Netherlands, the Frisians maintain a prosperous economy, with 80% of their lands devoted to cattle, sheep, and hogs. In 1989, to further the use of their language, the Frisian parliament passed legislation changing all town, street, and commercial signs from Dutch to Frisian.

The unification of Europe has stimulated some sentiment for independence within a united Europe, but the majority are satisfied with the status quo. The relations between the Frisian minority and the Dutch government, considered the best of its kind in Europe, have attracted attention from other small nations within Europe and beyond. Free of the tensions and quarrels that preoccupy other small European national groups, the Frisian culture has flourished, and nationalist organizations turn their attention to other issues, such as the environment and threats to the Frisian coast and the wildlife of the Frisian tidal flats.

SELECTED BIBLIOGRAPHY

Mahmood, Cynthia Keppley. *Frisian and Free: Study of an Ethnic Minority in the Netherlands.* 1989.

Markey, Thomas L. *Frisian.* 1994.

Mellink, A. F. *Friesland.* 1995.

Seth, Ronald. *The Netherlands.* 1997.

Tash, Robert C. *Dutch Pluralism: A Model in Tolerance for Developing Countries.* 1990.

FRIULIS

Friuli; Friûl; Friulians

POPULATION: Approximately (2000 e) 762,000 Friulis in Europe, mostly in Italy, but with smaller populations in Slovenia, some 7,000, and Croatia. Another 700,000 Friulis, considered an integral part of the Friuli nation, live in other parts of the world, mostly in the Americas.

THE FRIULI HOMELAND: The Friuli homeland occupies a mountainous region in the Carnic and Julian Alps and a lowland region bordering the Gulf of Venice and the Gulf of Trieste on the Adriatic Sea in northeastern Italy and western Slovenia. The northern mountainous region, which receives the highest rainfall in Italy, has some elevations exceeding 8,990 feet (2,740 m.). In the east Fruilia includes a fertile plain. The coastal plain supports extensive agriculture, producing wheat, corn, and other vegetables and fruits, particularly grapes for wine.

Friuli has no official status; the Friuli homeland forms the provinces of Gorizia, Pordenone, and Udine of the autonomous region of Friuli-Venezia Giulia, the Portoguaro district of Venice province of the Veneto Region in Italy, and the western districts of several Slovenian provinces. *Friuli region of Italy (Friûl)*: 3,190 sq.mi.–8,264 sq.km. (2000 e) 1,057,000—Friulis 71%, Slovenes* 11%, Sauris 1%, other Italians.* The Friuli capital and major cultural center is Udine, called Udin in Friuli, (2000 e) 102,000 (urban area 155,000), which lies sixty-one miles (ninety-eight km.) northeast of Venice. The region's second city, Gorizia (Gurizze), (2000 e) 41,000, the capital of the region under Austrian rule, is also an important cultural center. The town of Nova Gorica, (2000 e) 15,000, in Slovenia, formerly part of the city of Gorizia, is the center of the Slovene Friulis.

FLAG: The Friuli national flag is a blue field charged with the Friuli national symbol, a yellow eagle with red beak and claws.

PEOPLE: The Friulis are an ancient people thought to predate the Etruscans and Romans in northeastern Italy. The Friulis consider the large emigrant population, the Fôgalâr, numbering over 700,000, as an integral part of their nation. The Friulis are the largest of the Rhaeto-Romantic peoples of northern Italy and Switzerland, which includes the Ladins* and the Romansch.* The Sauris, a closely related people, inhabit the mountainous north of the region, and are often counted as ethnic Friulis. The majority of the Friulis are Roman Catholics, and the influence of leftist political parties in Italy alarms many moderate Friulis, which has increased support for the growing autonomy movement.

The Friuli language, Furlan, is a Rhaeto-Romantic language of the Italo-Romance group of languages. The language has been influenced by Venetian and retains a strong Celtic substratum. Furlan is spoken in three major dialects, East Central Furlan, Western Furlan, and Carnico. The majority of the Friulis are bilingual in Italian, although many of the Italians, Slovenes, and others in the region speak Friuli as a second or third language. Friuli is being cultivated as a literary language, although the use of a standardized form of the language is relatively recent and is still debated by scholars and linguists. The language, not recognized as a minority language by the Italian government, is taught in schools on a voluntary basis and depends on the availability of Furlan teachers.

NATION: The Friuli, believed to have inhabited the area north of the Adriatic Sea before the rise of the Etruscans and Romans, are thought to have originally formed part of the Celtic peoples. Roman rule, established in the coastal plain, extended to all of Friulia in the first century B.C. The Roman culture and language, over centuries, replaced the Celtic language and culture of the region. The region and the Friuli nation took its name from the Roman city of Forum Iulii, the modern town of Cividale.

Germanic Longobards (Lombards*) conquered Friulia in 568 following the collapse of Roman power. Under Lombard rule Friulia formed a separate duchy, and in 801, called the March of Friuli, the region came under the rule of Charlemagne's Frankish Empire. The region was later divided into East Friulia and West Friulia, the two areas eventually becoming the counties of Gorizia and Friuli.

In the eleventh century West Friulia, the county of Friuli, and its capital of Udine passed to Aquileia. In the Middle Ages the Friulis' free city-states participated in the great European awakening, the Renaissance. The cities formed a protective league, a union that greatly aided the perpetuation of the separate Friuli language and culture. In 1420 Venice took Friuli, and in 1500, when the line of counts became extinct, Gorizia passed to the Austrian Hapsburgs. The name Friuli lost all political meaning.

The imposition of foreign rule greatly influenced the development of the Friuli culture and language. The language in the region ruled by Venice absorbed many Venetian dialect words and forms, while in the east, under Hapsburg rule, the region became essentially Slovene-speaking, although Furlan, the Friuli language, remained the second language of a large part of the population. The population of Gorizia retained a large degree of autonomy, as the Hapsburg crownland of Görz and Gradisca, until the eighteenth century.

Reunited when Austria gained control of Venice in 1797, the legality of Hapsburg rule in western Friuli was reaffirmed by further treaties in 1814–15 at the end of the Napoleonic Wars. However, at the conclusion of the Austro-Prussian War in 1866, Austria was forced to cede western Friuli, called Udine Province, to the new Italian kingdom, bringing almost the entire Friuli population under Italian rule, with the exception of the Friuli minority in the Austrian port city of Trieste and its hinderland.

Subjected to intense government pressure to adopt standardized Italian language and culture during the nineteenth century, the Friulis mobilized to resist. Friuli opposition to assimilation inspired a national revival in the late nineteenth century. The growth of nationalism led to demands for autonomy within the Italian kingdom. The unrest spread to the Friuli population of the Austrian crownland of Görz and Gradisca with its mixed population of Friuli, Slovene, and Austrian inhabitants.

Italy remained neutral when war began in Europe in 1914, but Allied promises of increased territory persuaded the Italians to enter the war in 1915. Heavy fighting devastated the Friuli districts that formed the fluctuating front lines between the Italian and Austrian troops. Italy lost over 600,000 soldiers before taking Gorizia and eastern Friuli. The Italian government, with Allied approval, annexed the captured regions in 1919.

The Italian fascists of Benito Mussolini took control of the Italian government in 1922. The fascist doctrine stressed Italian nationalism and a uniform Italian culture and language. The Friuli minority, their language outlawed and under intense official pressure, were forced to Italianize all family and place-names and abandon the ancient customs and traditions not approved by the authorities. As repression increased, many Friuli fled to sanctuary among the related Romansh in southeastern Switzerland.

The Friuli homeland was again devastated during World War II in battles between Italian and Yugoslav forces. The Friulis faced even greater danger from the postwar territorial claims to their region. Communist Yugoslavia laid claim to eastern Friulia, with its large Slovene minority, while Italy claimed Istria, with its Italian and Friuli minorities. A 1947 agreement partitioned the region with all of eastern Friulia, except Gorizia, assigned to Yugoslavia, while an independent Free Territory of Trieste, under United Nations protection, with a mixed population, was created in the southeast. While Gorizia remained Italian, the Yugoslav authorities built Nova Gorica in the eastern suburbs of the city, effectively partitioning the Gorizia urban area.

The competing national claims to their homeland inspired the growth of modern Friuli nationalism. In 1948 Friuli nationalists formed the Moviment Friuli, a nationalist organization dedicated to winning autonomy for the Friuli nation.

Demands for autonomy grew after 1954 and the incorporation of the province of Trieste, with its large, Italian-speaking population, into the largely Friuli-speaking region to form the new region of Friuli-Venezia Giulia. Protests against Friulia's inclusion in the "hybrid region" fueled the spread of nationalist sentiment. In 1963 the Italian government granted the region limited autonomy in recognition of its distinct culture and language.

In the 1960s the Friulis began a second national revival, with the young especially embracing the Friuli culture, language, and history. The Friuli language, called Furlan, became a rallying point for the autonomy movement in the 1960s and 1970s. The Friuli nationalists drew on their history, the free cities of the Middle Ages, as justification for their demands for autonomy for the Friuli nation. In 1975 the Italian and Yugoslav government formally recognized their international border, which runs through the Friuli nation. The ineffective government response to the devastating earthquake that hit the region in 1976 turned disaster into a renewed sense of Friulian national consciousness.

Affected by the nationalism sweeping all of northern Italy in the late 1980s, the movement became increasingly nationalistic. In concert with other northern Italian peoples, the Friuli increasingly look to a united Europe as their salvation. Disgusted with Italy's corruption and the huge, inefficient administration, nationalists point to the organized crime that plagues the Italian state and has recently moved into the Friuli heartland. Mafia-related crimes in the region increased 300% in 1990–91 alone. The inequities of the bloated Italian bureaucracy infuriate even the most moderate Friulis, who cite examples such as the fifteen men employed to shunt goods wagons at the Udine rail center, while 15,000 do the same work in the southern city of Reggio Calabria.

The independence of Slovenia, on Friulia's eastern border, and the dramatic increase of regional and national movements across northern Italy have fueled Friuli demands for greater independence and recognition as a separate European people. In 1992 over 100,000 Friuli signed a petition calling for separation from Friuli-Venezia Giulia and the creation of a separate, autonomous Friuli region. In local elections in June 1992, Friuli nationalists became the largest political order in the Friuli region.

SELECTED BIBLIOGRAPHY
Facaros, Dane, and Michael Pauls. *Northeast Italy.* 1990.
Geipel, Robert. *Long Term Consequences of Disasters: The Reconstruction of Friuli, Italy, in Its International Context, 1976–1988.* 1991.
Holmes, Douglas R. *Cultural Disenchantments: Worker Peasantries in Northeast Italy.* 1988.
Muir, Edward. *Mad Blood Stirring: Vendetta and Factions in Friuli during the Renaissance.* 1993.
Smith, Denis M. *The Making of Italy 1796–1870.* 1988.

GAGAUZ

Gagauzi; Gagaus

POPULATION: Approximately (2000 e) 225,000 Gagauz in Europe, with 172,000 in Moldova and 35,000 in adjacent areas of Ukraine. Smaller numbers live in Bulgaria, about 5,000, Ukraine, Russia, Romania, Greece, Turkey, and in Central Asia.

THE GAGAUZ HOMELAND: The Gagauz homeland occupies the valleys of the Prut and Jalpug Rivers south of the Roman fortification called Upper Trajan's Wall in southeastern Moldova and southern Ukraine. The region, partly lying in the Bugeac Plain, is mostly agricultural land, particularly suited to the production of white wine, which is the Gagauz national drink.

The Gagauz districts of Moldova, Komrat, Cadir-Lunga, Kangaz, Tarkliya, and Vulkanesti form the Gagauz Republic, an autonomous state within the Republic of Moldova. The Gagauz homeland also includes part of the district of Zaporozh'e of Odessa Oblast in Ukraine. *Republic of Gagauzia (Gagauz-Yeri)*: 1,320 sq.mi.–3,419 sq.km. (2000 e) 244,000—Gagauz 71%, Moldovans* 20%, Russians* 5%, Ukrainians* 2%, Bulgarians* 2%. The Gagauz capital and major cultural center is Comrat, called Komrat by the Gagauz, (2000 e) 35,000. The city of Cagul (Kagul), (2000 e) 45,000, is also an important cultural center.

FLAG: The Gagauz national flag, the official flag of the autonomous republic, is a blue field bearing three yellow stars near the hoist and white and red stripes at the bottom.

PEOPLE: The early history of the Gagauz nation is unclear, and there are a number of hypotheses for their origins. Some scholars believe that the Gagauz derive from the Turkic Orguz, Uzy, and Kumans who roamed the south Russian steppes until the Mongol invasion of the thirteenth century, when they migrated to the Dobrudja region of eastern Bulgaria. Another hypothesis claims that the Gagauz are the descendants of forcibly Turkified Bulgarians who adopted the Turkish language but retained their Orthodox religion. The most common belief is that their ancestors fled the continuous Russian-Ottoman Wars in the Balkans in the eighteenth century. Culturally and linguistically, the Gagauz are a Turkic people related to the Turks.* The small nation, divided in 1945, when the eastern district of their territory was transferred to Ukraine, has developed a strong sense of their separate identity.

According to tradition, the Gagauz were settled in Bessarabia during the reign of Russian empress Catherine II, on condition that they convert to the Orthodox religion. Today, of all the Turkic peoples, the Gagauz and the Chavash* are the only predominantly Christian Turkic nations in Europe.

Wine production, the major economic activity, is closely tied to the Gagauz culture, which revolves around the yearly growing and production periods. Wine festivals and religious observances, part of their Orthodox faith, are closely tied to the Gagauz culture. Culturally, they resemble the Bulgarians, but with some traits borrowed from the neighboring Moldovans and Ukrainians.

The Gagauz speak a Turkic language that belongs to the Orguz-Bulgar sub-group of South Turkic languages of the Uralic-Altaic language group. The language is spoken in two dialects, the central and southern, with the former the basis of the literary language. Gagauz is unique among the Turkic languages for both the large number of Russian, Bulgarian, Ukrainian, Moldovan, and Romanian loanwords and the tenacity and persistence of the Gagauz people to maintain their unique language. In the late 1990s, 92% considered Gagauz their mother language, but 73% also spoke Russian. However, only 4% spoke Moldovan (Romanian).

NATION: According to Gagauz tradition, their ancestors, a tribe called the Kay-Ka'us, formed a small state in the Dobruja region of northeastern Bulgaria in 1296 with its capital at Karvuna (Kavarna). In the thirteenth century the Kay-Ka'us converted to the Orthodox Christianity brought to their state by Bulgarian monks. Conquered by the Ottoman Turks in 1398, the people, called Gagauz by the Turks, adopted the Turkish language and culture but refused to abandon Christianity for the Turks' Islamic religion. The Gagauz, over the next centuries, lived as a despised minority, often persecuted by the Turks for their refusal to accept Islam and by the neighboring Bulgars for their Turkish speech.

In the eighteenth century the Gagauz fled to the Russian Empire to escape a concerted Turkish attempt to force their conversion to Islam. The refugees moved north in small groups, often accompanied by Christian Bulgarians. The first Gagauz arrived in the contested region of Bessarabia in 1750. During the Russo-Turkish War, 1806–12, the majority of the Gagauz took the opportunity to leave Turkish-ruled Bulgaria and settle in Russian-held territory. Bessarabia, ceded to Russia by Turkey in 1812, was later opened to almost unlimited immigration in an effort to dilute the Romanian majority. The remainder of the Gagauz refugees settled in the rural southern districts of Russian Bessarabia between 1812 and 1846.

The small Gagauz nation, reunited in their new homeland in Bessarabia, experienced a dramatic revival of their culture and religion. The production of their famous white wines became an integral part of their culture. A nationalist movement developed from the cultural movement as tsarist rule became progressively onerous, with intense pressure on the Orthodox Gagauz to assimilate. Although the small Christian nation had always looked on the Christian Russians as protectors against the Muslim Turks, in 1848 the Gagauz rebelled against the arbitrary rule of the tsarist bureaucracy. Cossacks, sent against the Gagauz rebels, ended the uprising with great brutality.

At the end of the Crimean War in 1856, the region was ceded to the Romanian principality of Moldavia. The Congress of Berlin, convened in 1878, recognized united Romania as an independent state, but the Romanians* were forced to cede southern Bessarabia to Russia in return for territory on the Black Sea. The Gagauz, again under tsarist rule, remained calm until the upheavals of 1905.

Revolution swept Russia following the empire's defeat by Japan and other setbacks. Serious disturbances in Gagauzia broke out during the 1905 Russian Revolution but gradually quieted after concessions and promises of increased rights. In December 1905 their authority restored, the local tsarist authorities moved to punish the disturbances, setting off a widespread Gagauz uprising. The rebels drove all tsarist officials from the region and formed a provisional government. On 18 January 1906 the Gagauz leaders declared their homeland the independent republic of Gagauz Khalki. The tiny republic lasted just two weeks before being suppressed by Cossacks and Russian police. The Gagauz, although defeated, again rebelled, along with the Moldovans, in March and April 1907. The renewed rebellion brought brutal reprisals.

Gagauzia became a battleground during World War I, particularly after Romania joined the Allies in 1916. Many Gagauz, caught up in the fighting, died of disease and hunger. Tsarist Russia collapsed in revolution in 1917, with many Gagauz supporting a movement for autonomy within a revived, democratic Russia. They sent delegates to a Moldovan council, which, after the Bolshevik coup in October, declared Moldova independent of Russia on 23 December 1917. Before the Gagauz could implement their autonomy within Moldova, their homeland was invaded by Ukrainian nationalists and later by Bolshevik troops. The Moldovan government, seeking protection from the invading Bolsheviks, voted to unite with neighboring Romania. In November 1918 Moldova, including Gagauzia, joined the Romanian kingdom.

The Gagauz lands were colonized by Romanian Boyars, landlords moving north into the new province. The region was treated as an agricultural colony, while the Gagauz were pressured to assimilate into Romanian culture. The 1920s and 1930s were marked by massive corruption and a fall in the Gagauz standard of living. The Romanian authorities refused to build roads in the region during the interwar period, fearing the roads could be used by the Red Army should a new war break out, a decision that made marketing the Gagauz wines and agricultural products very difficult.

In 1939, after years of tensions between the Soviet Union and Romania, the region was invaded by the Red Army. In 1940 Gagauzia, along with Moldova, was ceded to the USSR, but in June 1941 Romanian troops, allied to the invading Germans,* reoccupied the region. The Romanian authorities, determined to assimilate the Gagauz, forbade the use and publication of their language, the wearing of their national costumes, or the holding of their national holidays, which mostly celebrated their wines.

The Soviet reconquest of the region in 1944 was quickly followed by the collectivization of the Gagauz vineyards and farms. In 1945 the eastern districts of their homeland were transferred to Ukraine. Under Soviet rule, the Gagauz were allowed to use their language, but publication was permitted only if using the Russian Cyrillic alphabet. The Gagauz, too weak to resist but refusing to assimilate to either Russian or Moldovan culture, withdrew into isolation, preferring to tend their collectivized, yet prosperous, vineyards and farms while leaving the painful issue of politics to others.

The Gagauz during the years of the Cold War mostly remained on the land, working as peasant farmers on Soviet collectives. Their refusal to assimilate or urbanize was emphasized by a very high birthrate. Between the 1950s and 1970s the Gagauz population grew dramatically.

In 1982 a few young Gagauz began to sponsor poetry readings and other cultural events that gradually gathered force in an overall cultural revival. They began to question why their wines, sold in expensive foreign-currency Soviet shops, brought them little in the way of income, or why there were no Gagauz-language schools in Soviet Moldova.

Gagauz nationalism remained the preoccupation of a few intellectuals until late 1988, when Moldovan language demands sparked a rapid spread of Gagauz national sentiment. In addition to their own language, they were obliged to learn Russian but, under a new Moldovan language law, would be obliged to learn yet another language, Moldovan (Romanian).

The language issue loosed a torrent of grievances: unpaved roads, inadequate drinking water, a total lack of Gagauz schools and kindergartens, and the need for technical and agricultural schools. Of the forty-one regions of Moldova, the Gagauz regions ranked thirty-fifth to forty-first in standard of living.

A national congress convened in May 1989 demanded autonomy for the Gagauz districts or Moldova and the reunification with Ukrainian Gagauzia. Ignored by the Moldavian authorities, the Gagauz leaders unilaterally declared the region an autonomous republic within Soviet Moldova in November. During the October 1990 elections, the Moldovan authorities moved to disband the Gagauz government and to retake control of the Gagauz districts, setting off a severe nationalist crisis in the region. The Gagauz nationalists, successful in the local elections, proclaimed Gagauz independent of Moldavia, but not of the Soviet Union, on 11 August 1990.

Soviet Moldavia, renamed the Republic of Moldova, became independent following the collapse of the Soviet Union in August 1991. The Moldovan authorities attempted to end the Gagauz secession and to bring the region under the authority of the new republican government, but by early 1992 the Moldovan government's authority in the region had practically ceased to exist. Fearing the ethnic violence that had broken out in a number of former Soviet republics, the Gagauz accepted a March 1992 offer of autonomy within Moldova, but with the stipulation that should Moldova decide to reunite with neighboring Romania, Gagauzia would be allowed to secede peacefully.

The Gagauz nationalists carefully monitor the events taking place in Moldova that will affect the future of their nation. In January 1993 the Moldovan parliament narrowly rejected a proposal to hold a nationwide referendum on reunification with Romania. In elections held in early 1994, the Moldovan nationalists won greater support than those favoring Romania, which aided relations between the Gagauz and the Moldovan government. In May 1994 Moldova's draft constitution provided for a special legal status and for broad powers of self-government for the Gagauz nation. The Act Providing for the Special Status of Gagauzia/Gagauz-Yeri was adopted by the Moldovan parliament on 23 December 1994, the first time a territorial autonomy had been established for a national minority in postcommunist Central and Eastern Europe.

The end of Soviet rule has allowed the Gagauz to establish ties to other Turkish communities. Gagauz leaders have visited Turkey and the new republics in Central Asia seeking cultural and political ties. The Turks have sent economic assistance and language teachers and have even established a satellite link to allow the Gagauz to receive Turkish television.

SELECTED BIBLIOGRAPHY

Bruchis, Michael. *Nations—Nationalities—People: A Study of the Nationalities Policy of the Communist Party in Soviet Moldavia.* 1984.

Dima, Nicholas. *Bessarabia and Bukovina: The Soviet-Romanian Territorial Dispute.* 1982.

Gribincea, Mihai. *Agricultural Collectivization in Moldavia: Bessarabia during Stalinism 1944–1950.* 1996.

Lerman, Zvi, ed. *Land Reform and Farm Restructuring in Moldova: Progress and Prospects.* 1998.

Van Meurs, Wim P. *The Bessarabian Question in Communist Historiography: Nationalist and Communist Politics and History-Writing.* 1994.

GALICIANS

Galegos; Gallegos; Galizanos

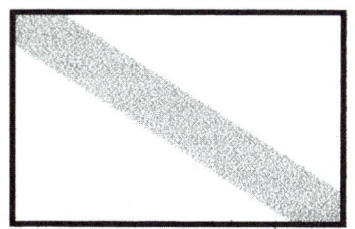

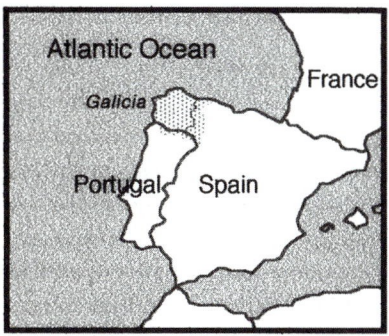

POPULATION: Approximately (2000 e) 3,585,000 Galicians in Europe, 3,437,000 in Spain, and the remainder in Portugal, France, and Germany. There are large Galician populations, estimated to number 1.5 million, in the Americas, particularly in Uruguay, Argentina, Brazil, and Chile.

THE GALICIAN HOMELAND: The Galician homeland occupies the mountainous northwestern corner of the Iberian Peninsula, just north of Portugal. The region, mostly lying in the Galician Uplands, has a rugged coastline on the Atlantic Ocean on the west and on the Bay of Biscay on the north. The *rías* are fjordlike inlets cutting deep into the coastline and giving Galicia a number of good, protected harbors on the Atlantic Ocean and the Bay of Biscay. Most of the region is devoted to agriculture, while timber and fishing are also important industries. The major river is the Miño, called Minho in Portuguese, which forms the international border between Spain and Portugal.

Galicia forms an autonomous region of the Kingdom of Spain made up of the provinces of La Coruña, Lugo, Orense, and Pontevedra. *Region of Galicia (Galizia)*: 11,365 sq.mi.–29,435 sq.km. (2000 e) 2,729,000—Galician 94%, Portuguese* 2%, other Spanish. The Galician capital and major cultural center is the ancient city of Santiago de Compostela, (2000 e) 94,000, a center of religious pilgrimages. The region's largest cities, Vigo, (2000 e) 301,000, and La Coruña, called A Coruña in Galician, (2000 e) 246,000, are also important cultural centers.

FLAGs: The Galician national flag, the official flag of the region, is a white field crossed by a diagonal stripe of pale blue, upper hoist to lower fly. The

Galician national flag, with the addition of a centered, five-pointed, red star, is the banner of the Galician national movement.

PEOPLE: Named for the Celtic Gallaeci, the Galicians are the descendants of early Celts and later Germanic Visigoths and are the only Iberian people not of Latin origin. Although the Celtic language is long extinct, Celtic cultural traditions are evident in the traditional bagpipes, dances, and music, and many of the Galicians are fair, with blond or red hair and light eyes.

The Galician language is a Romance language more closely related to Portuguese than to Castilian Spanish and is spoken in four major dialects corresponding to the region's four provinces. An intermediate language between Portuguese and Spanish, it is closer to Portuguese, with about 85% intelligibility. The language is spoken in adjacent areas of Portugal and in the Spanish regions of Leon and Asturias.

All but few of the Galicians are Roman Catholics, and their capital, Santiago de Compostela, is one of the great Catholic pilgrimage centers of Europe. Among the most religiously conservative of the peoples of Spain, the yearly religious calendar continues to modulate the rhythm of daily life.

NATION: The region was early inhabited by the Celtic Gallaeci tribe, who left large stone monuments in the rocky highlands. The Romans conquered the Gallaeci in the early part of the first century A.D. and included the region in the Roman province of Hispania Tarraconensis. The Celts, except those in the more mountainous regions, mostly adopted the Romans' Latin language and culture. Christianity, introduced by missionaries from Italy, began to make converts in the region around A.D. 100.

The decline of Roman power in the fourth and fifth centuries left the region nearly defenseless. A Germanic tribe, the Suevi, invaded the region and established an independent kingdom in 411 A.D. In 585 the Suevi kingdom was overrun by invading Visigoths, who settled the region and mixed with the earlier Suevi and Celts. Traditionally, the Visigoths adopted Christianity in 587. A substantial Germanic population settled in the region during the Visigothic period.

Muslim Moors from North Africa overran most of Visigothic Spain in 711–12. Christian knights held the Moors to the lowlands in the northwest while forming the Christian kingdom of Asturias in the mountains. The Christians eventually began to expand, reconquering lands from the Moors and retaking control of all of Galicia. The reconquered areas united with the kingdom of Leon in 866. Leon, including Galicia, in turn, united with the kingdom of Castile, newly liberated from Moorish rule in 1037. In 1157 Leon again became an independent kingdom but reunited with Castile in 1230.

A unique medieval culture developed in isolated Galicia, uniting Celtic, Germanic, Latin, and Iberian elements. The Galician language, originally a dialect of Portuguese, diverged in the fourteenth century to become the foremost literary language of the Iberian Peninsula. The Galicians developed a lyrical, poetic literature. The devoutly Roman Catholic Galicians, the caretakers of the important medieval shrine of St. James at Santiago de Compostela, maintained contact with all of Europe through a constant stream of religious pilgrims visiting the shrine. Santiago developed as the center of the vibrant Galician culture and the object of religious pilgrims from all over Europe.

Opposition to the centralizing tendencies of the Castilian kingdom prodded the Galicians to follow the Portuguese in an attempt to leave the Spanish kingdom in 1640. Crushed by Castilian troops, the Galicians embarked on a long cultural and economic decline. By the eighteenth century the Galician language had degenerated to a peasant dialect, and the upper classes had adopted Castilian speech and culture. The Galician tradition of splitting lands among heirs resulted in a backward, fragmented agriculture that forced many to emigrate, mostly to South America. The French attack on Spain in 1808 allowed the Galicians to regain nominal independence, but the region again came under Castilian rule under the restored Bourbon monarchy at the end of the Napoleonic Wars.

In the mid-nineteenth century the Galicians entered a period of cultural vibrancy, accompanied by a literary revival. The Galician language, formerly a peasant dialect, again became the first language of the majority and gradually replaced Castilian as the language of the upper classes.

The region's severe economic problems, mostly blamed on the highly centralized government in Madrid, provoked widespread resentment and fueled a movement to revive the Galician culture and nation in the 1880s and 1890s. Among the demands put forth were cultural and economic autonomy and the reopening of the Galician Cortes or parliament, which had functioned, but with little real power, until the early nineteenth century. The region's poverty and lack of opportunity fed a continuing stream of emigrants to the New World, largely to Brazil, where they rapidly assimilated into Portuguese-speaking Brazilian society.

In the early years of the twentieth century, Galicia was one of the most conservative and traditional areas of Spain. Economically backward, Galicia was mostly ignored by the government in Madrid, which concentrated on the industrialization of other areas of the country. In 1931 the Galicians demanded autonomy from Spain's new republican government, and in 1932 they established a Galician parliament and pressed for greater linguistic autonomy. Serious nationalist demonstrations rocked the region between 1932 and 1936, until the nationalist resurgence was overtaken by the outbreak of the Spanish civil war.

The leader of the rebel fascist forces, Francisco Franco, born in El Ferrol, looked to his native Galicia for support, but the majority of his countrymen joined the antifascist forces. Following Franco's 1939 victory the Galicians suffered punishments, their culture was suppressed, and edicts were issued forbidding the speaking, teaching, or publishing of books or newspapers in the Galician language. Only one book was published in the Galician language between 1936 and 1945.

The Galician culture and language began to revive in the 1950s despite the official restrictions. Publishing in the Galician language began tentatively with poetry, and later publications included fiction, the sciences, philosophy, and economics. Renowned poets and writers, such as Rosalia de Castro and Antonio Castelao, fostered the rebirth of the Galician language. The postwar revival increased friction with the Franco authorities and spurred the growth of Galician nationalism. Openly nationalist organizations, beginning in the 1960s, gained widespread support in Galicia, which had benefited little from the rapid modernization of Spain in the 1960s and 1970s. By 1975 the average income in Galicia was only half the Spanish average.

In early 1975 under the slogan "Galizia Ciebe" (Galician for Free Galicia), nationalism exploded with an outbreak of violence and demonstrations. Several nationalist organizations called for immediate independence. In August 1975 the elderly dictator Francisco Franco unleashed a reign of terror accompanied by mass arrests, unexplained deaths and disappearances, and widespread torture. Franco's death in November 1975 brought an end to the terror as liberated Spain rapidly embraced democracy under a restored Bourbon monarchy.

The new democratic Spanish state granted autonomy to the Galicians in 1980. The small nation experienced a dramatic cultural and national revival, and by the late 1980s, 90% of the Galician population spoke the Galician language. Growing ties to other Celtic nations in France and the United Kingdom have resulted in cultural exchanges and strong support for the Galicians' campaign to win greater freedom. Small, militant nationalist groups turned to violence in 1988, even though the majority of the conservative Galicians continued to support the more moderate nationalist policies that they hope will eventually establish their small nation within a united, democratic Europe.

Autonomy has been popular with the Galicians but has done little to help the economy, even though maintaining the Galician regional government is expensive. The region's cities remain upper- and middle-class, while the rural population continues to farm small, unprofitable holdings. Urbanization of the population, begun in the 1960s, accelerated in the 1990s, even as the population of the region continued to fall due to continuing emigration. Being a relatively underdeveloped region, Galicia has not attracted the large number of Spanish-speaking migrants in contrast to wealthier Catalonia and the Basque Country. In 1998 an estimated 94% of the population used Galician in their daily life, while only 5% of the population of the region had no understanding of the Galician language.

SELECTED BIBLIOGRAPHY

Coyle, Dominick J. *Minorities in Revolt.* 1982.
Kern, Robert. *The Regions of Spain: A Reference Guide to History and Culture.* 1995.
Slater, Bert. *Across the Rivers of Portugal: A Journey on Foot from Northern Spain to Southern Portugal.* 1991.
Truscott, Sandra, and Maria Garcia. *A Dictionary of Contemporary Spain.* 1998.
Wilgram, E. *Northern Spain.* 1976.

GEORGIANS

Kartveli; Kartuli; Kartvelians;
Gruziny; Gurcu

POPULATION: Approximately (2000 e) 4,211,000 Georgians in Europe, 3,990,000 in Georgia and another 220,000 in adjacent areas of Russia, Armenia, and Azerbaijan, and up to 200,000, called Laz, in northeastern Turkey.

THE GEORGIAN HOMELAND: The Georgian homeland lies in Southeastern Europe, a mountainous region on the southern slopes of the Caucasus Mountains with a narrow coastal plain on the Black Sea. Essentially part of an isthmus between the Black and Caspian Seas, Georgia is bounded on the north by the Greater Caucasus Ranges, which includes Mt. Kazbek, 16,558 ft. (5,047m.), one of the highest points in Europe. On the south lie the Lesses Caucasus Ranges and the Armenian Highlands. Between the mountain ranges lie a number of river valleys, particularly the valleys of the Rioni and upper Kura Rivers, and fertile plains, including lowland areas lying to either side of the Surami range, which bisects the country along a northeast-southwest axis.

Briefly independent from 1918 to 1921, Georgia later formed a union republic of the USSR and again became an independent republic with the collapse of the Soviet Union in 1991. *Republic of Georgia (Sak'art'velos Respublika)*: 26,911 sq.mi.–69,717 sq.km. (2000 e) 5,641,000—Georgians 70%, Armenians* 7%, Azeris* 6%, Russians* 4%, Ossetians* 3%, Greeks* 2%, Abkhaz* 2%, Ukrainians.* The Georgian capital and major cultural center is Tbilisi (2000 e) 1,271,000 (metropolitan area 1,550,000), an ancient city founded in the fifth century A.D.

FLAG: The Georgian national flag, the official flag of the Republic of Georgia, is a scarlet field bearing a bicolor canton on the upper hoist, black over white.

PEOPLE: The Georgians are an ancient Caucasian people known for their beauty and longevity. Scholars believe the Georgians are the descendants of the earliest indigenous inhabitants of the Caucasus region. The Georgian nation unites a number of closely related Kartalian peoples, all speaking dialects of the Georgian language. The largest group, the Georgians, knows as Kartalians or Gruzians, inhabit the central part of the country. The Imeritians live west of the Surami Mountains and around the city of Kutaisi. The Gurians inhabit the river lowlands in western Georgia. The Mingrelians inhabit the Black Sea lowlands. The Svanetians live in the high valleys of the Inguri and Tskhenis Tskhali Rivers. The Kabuletians and Ajars* inhabit the Tskhali Valley and the Black Sea Coast in the southwest. Over 90% of the world's Georgians live in the Republic of Georgia. Very few have emigrated beyond the borders of their homeland, although a few Georgian émigré enclaves exist in Western Europe and North America. Because of the existence of numerous minority groups within Georgia, however, the percentage of Georgians as part of the country's total population stands at around 70%.

The Georgian language, the official language of the republic, belongs to the southern or Kartvelian branch of the Caucasian-language family. Although Georgia has known many conquerors, the language displays unique qualities that cannot be attributed to any outside influence. The alphabet, written in a beautiful script dating to the fourth century or before, has undergone several modifications or reforms but remains, like the language itself, a cherished part of Georgia's culture. Many Georgians also speak Russian, the dominant language of the former Soviet Union.

The majority of the Georgians belong to the independent Georgian Church under the authority of the Catholicos at Tbilisi. The church is very closely tied to Georgia's culture and history as a separate Christian nation.

NATION: The Georgian homeland, possibly the earliest home of the Caucasian race, has been known since ancient times. Because of its strategic location between Europe and Asia, the region was frequently invaded by foreign armies, the lands devastated, and the Georgian peoples subjugated to foreign rule. During the Bronze Age large tribal confederations were formed in the region, forming the basis for the first Georgian states, Colchis, in the sixth century B.C. in western Georgia and Kartli (Iberia) in the inland regions in the fourth century B.C. Mtskheta, ancient capital of the Kartli or eastern Georgians, existed as early as the third century B.C., but by the late fifth century A.D. a new capital had been established at Tbilisi.

In the last centuries of the pre-Christian Era, Georgia, in the form of the kingdom of Kartli-Iberia, was strongly influenced by Greece to the west and Persia to the east. After the Roman Empire completed its conquest of the Caucasus region in 66 B.C., both Colchis and Kartli became Roman vassals in 64 B.C. Colchis became a Roman province, called Iberia, and the kingdom was a Roman ally for some 400 years.

Even before A.D. 337, when Christianity was made the official religion in the

Kingdom of Kartli and subsequently in the entire territory of Georgia, an alphabet had been developed, and a written language had appeared. Between the fifth and seventh centuries, the Georgian states were deeply involved in the rivalry between Byzantium and Persia.

Included in the Armenian kingdom in the sixth century, Georgia later split into several rival states but reunited under the Bagratid dynasty in 571. Weakened by the Arab invasion of 645, the Georgian lands again increasingly came under Armenian influence. In 813 Armenian prince Ashot I began 1,000 years of rule in Georgia by the Georgian branch of the Bagratid dynasty. King David IV, called the Builder, in the twelfth century initiated a golden age by driving the Turks from the country and expanding Georgian cultural and political influence southward into Armenia and eastward to the Caspian Sea. That era of unparalleled power and prestige for the Georgian monarchy concluded with the great literary flowering of Queen Tamar's reign (1184–1212).

In 1236 the Mongol hordes invaded Georgia, beginning a century of fragmentation and decline. A brief resurgence of Georgian power in the fourteenth century ended when the Turkic conqueror Timur (Tamerlane) destroyed Tbilisi in 1386. The capture of Constantinople by the Ottoman Turks in 1453 began three centuries of domination by the Ottoman and Persian Empires, which divided Georgia into spheres of influence in 1553. By the eighteenth century, however, the Bagratid line again had achieved substantial independence under nominal Persian rule.

In this period of renewed unity, trade increased, and feudal institutions lost influence in Georgia. In 1773 King Herekle I began efforts to gain Russian protection against the Turks, who were threatening to retake his kingdom. In 1783 Herekle placed his small kingdom under Russian protection by signing the Treaty of Georgievsk. The Persians sacked Tbilisi in 1795, and Herekle again sought the protection of Orthodox Russia. The last Georgian king, Peter XIII, abdicated in 1801, placing central Georgia under Russian protection. Contrary to the expectations of the Georgian aristocracy and other national leaders, the autonomous protectorate was not long honored by the tsar. The southward advance of the Russian Empire eventually brought all the Georgian lands under Russian rule, Imeretia in 1810, Svanetia in 1858, Abkhazia in 1864, and Mingrelia in 1866.

The economy of the region stabilized, however, under the rule of its northern neighbor, and Russian and European ideas came to influence the educated class of Georgians. A large and powerful Russified aristocracy, accounting for one of every seven Georgians, gained fame for its wealth and extravagance. Forbidden their language, their cherished church absorbed by the empire's official Russian Orthodox Church, a new generation of educated Georgians reacted by supporting a modest cultural revival that began to take hold in the 1840s. Literature and cultural life revived in spite of the oppressive Russian censorship. The cultural revival evolved a strong nationalist sentiment in the 1880s and 1890s.

The Georgians initially supported the Russian government when war began in 1914, particularly after Ottoman Turkey, to the south, became a member of the Central Powers and the Caucasus region became a major battleground. By late 1916 economic conditions and the arrival of thousands of war refugees had raised social discontent throughout the Caucasus region, with radical groups gaining support.

The Georgians enthusiastically joined the revolution that finally ended tsarist rule in Russia in early 1917. The more moderate Menchevik faction took control of Georgia as the tsarist civil administration collapsed and proclaimed Georgia's sovereignty. Seeking safety for their small state, the Georgian leaders joined their new republic to a Transcaucasian Federation in partnership with neighboring Armenia and Azerbaijan. Tensions between the member states soon ended the attempt at cooperative sovereignty. On 26 May 1918 Georgia was declared a separate independent state.

The new Red Army, emerging victorious from Russia's civil war in 1920, quickly advanced south, reconquering the secessionist states. By early 1921 Georgia stood alone with the Red Army massed on its borders. In February 1921, less than nine months after Moscow had signed a treaty accepting the sovereignty of the Georgian republic, the Red Army secretly crossed into Georgia from Azerbaijan and quashed the young state. The Georgians surrendered in April 1921.

Under the personal direction of the Soviet leader, Joseph Stalin, a Georgian whose real name was Josef Dzhugashvili, Soviet Georgia was established as one of three nations, along with Armenia and Azerbaijan, making up the Soviet-created Republic of Transcaucasia in 1922. Violent resistance to Soviet power continued until 1924, when a last uprising was crushed by Bolshevik authorities. As many as 4,000 rebels were executed, and countless others were imprisoned. The Soviet Republic of Transcaucasia prevailed until 1936, when it was divided, and Georgia was declared a full union republic of the Soviet Union.

During Stalin's dictatorship, Georgia might have been expected to enjoy a special status within the Union of Soviet Socialist Republics, but the more Stalin came to identify himself as a Russian nationalist, the less he seemed willing to show any favoritism to his fellow Georgians. Instead, the incredible horrors of the purges of the 1930s, carried out among Georgian political leaders and the intelligentsia, took as high a toll in Georgia as elsewhere.

In the 1930s forced urbanization and industrialization, as well as drastic reductions in illiteracy and the preferential treatment of Georgians at the expense of ethnic minorities in the republic, set the stage for later ethnic animosities. During the 1940s and 1950s the influence of traditional village life decreased significantly for a large part of the Georgian population. In 1951 the Soviet Georgian government, exercising its right under the Soviet constitution, submitted a formal notice of Georgia's intention to secede from the union. An infuriated Stalin instituted a harsh repression that eased only with his death in 1953.

A modest Georgian national revival took hold during the 1970s, led by Zviad

Gamsakhurdia, the son of a recognized national poet, who began to organize dissident Georgian nationalists. In 1972 Moscow named a relative moderate, Eduard Shevardnadze, to the post of first secretary of the Georgian Communist Party. Shevardnadze's policies were generally accepted until 1978, when mass demonstrations shook the republic as the Georgians protested the government's efforts to make Russian an official language in Georgia. Shevardnadze left Georgia to become minister of foreign affairs under Mikhail Gorbachev in 1985.

Radical Georgian nationalism reemerged with the relaxation of Soviet rule in the late 1980s. Gorbachev's reforms, introduced in 1987, fanned nationalist demands by the Georgians and by the non-Georgian national groups in the republic. Calls by the Ossetian and Abkhazian minorities for secession from Georgia sparked a Georgian nationalist backlash. A peaceful demonstration in Tbilisi was attacked by Soviet soldiers on 9 April 1989, leaving twenty dead and many more injured. The attack on the peaceful marchers, carried out with sharpened shovels and poison gas, provoked a great outpouring of nationalism in the republic. By August 1989 the Georgian Supreme Soviet, despite the dominant role of the Communist Party, had voted to declare Georgia's sovereignty.

Zviad Gamsakhurdia, a charismatic Georgian intellectual, with useful credentials as a Soviet dissident, emerged as a popular national hero and political leader. The son of a recognized national poet, Gamsakhurdia never made a significant mark as an original writer, but he came to national attention as an outspoken opponent of Georgian communist officialdom, having earlier served time in prison for his underground activities. Gamsakhurdia galvanized the support of a roundtable coalition of informal political groups. In the elections of October 1990, Gamsakhurdia's Roundtable/Free Georgia coalition won an overwhelming victory in the Georgian Supreme Soviet, taking 54% of the vote.

Viewing himself as a moral savior of the Georgian nation, Gamsakhurdia backed ethnocentric, anti-Muslim government policies that further alienated the republic's non-Georgian national groups. Gamsakhurdia fanned opposition within Georgia proper as well as in the autonomous republics and regions. The chaos increased as the Georgian economy suffered from high rates of inflation and chronic shortages of food and fuel.

The Georgian parliament formally declared independence in April 1991. The rapidly increasing political instability, violence, and economic hardships quickly eroded Gamsakhurdia's support despite the clear plurality in the May 1991 elections. In December 1991, following the collapse of the Soviet Union, open rebellion broke out, and in January 1992 rebel forces violently ousted Gamsakhurdia from power. Gamsakhurdia finally fled in early 1992 to his home region of Mingrelia and eventually abroad. The rebel coalition quickly sought new elections to add legitimacy to the political situation. In a step that would have been unthinkable just a year earlier Eduard Shevardnadze was invited back to head a new interim State Council.

Shevardnadze's credentials as an associate of Mikhail Gorbachev helped the return of Western recognition and aid. However, the uneasy calm that settled over the country was soon disrupted. Rebel troops still loyal to Gamsakhurdia took control of several areas in the western regions of Mingrelia and Abkhazia. Adding to Shevardnadze's problems, the chauvinist directives of the former president had added fuel to the deepening conflicts over South Ossetia, Abkhazia, Ajaristan, and other border regions. In the autumn of 1993 the fall of Sukhumi to Abkhazian separatist forces signaled the crumbling of the Georgian army, and the return of Gamsakhurdia to lead his rebel supporters threatened to split Georgia.

By mid-1995 Georgia's gross domestic product was a mere 17% of what it had been in 1989. The economic decline represented the largest drop of any former Soviet republic or Warsaw Pact country. Supported by the West, Shevardnadze slowly imposed economic and political stability on the central Georgian regions, leaving the problem of the autonomous areas for the future. In elections held on 5 November 1995 Shevardnadze was chosen from a field of six candidates to take office as president of Georgia.

President Shevardnadze, despite numerous handicaps, has proved to be a democratic and impressive president and has helped keep the Georgian homeland relatively stable despite continuing ethnic conflicts and instability in the region. Under Shevardnadze's policies the Georgian government has increasingly oriented itself toward the West while seeking to maintain a necessary balance with its powerful northern neighbor, Russia.

By the end of 1997, according to some estimates, between 800,000 and 1 million people, approximately 20% of the total population, had left Georgia over the previous five years. The emigrants, leaving largely for economic reasons, were mostly workers and university graduates under thirty-five years of age.

SELECTED BIBLIOGRAPHY

Aves, Jonathan. *Paths to National Independence in Georgia, 1987–1990.* 1992.
Gachechiladze, R. G. *The New Georgia: Space, Society, Politics.* 1995.
Nasmyth, Peter. *Georgia: A Rebel in the Caucasus.* 1992.
Spilling, Michael. *Georgia.* 1997.
Suny, Ronald Grigor. *The Making of the Georgian Nation.* 1994.

GERMANS

Deutsch

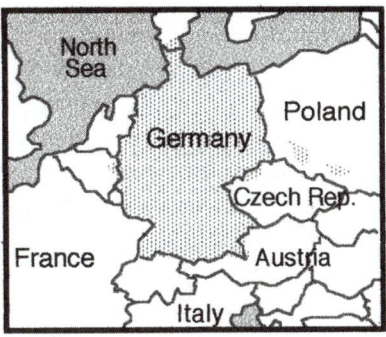

POPULATION: Approximately (2000 e) 83,885,000 Germans in Europe, the majority in Germany, but with substantial German populations in Belgium, Czech Republic, Hungary, Poland, Slovenia, and Romania. Other large German concentrations are in the United States and Canada, South America, particularly Argentina, Brazil, and Chile, Australia, and southern Africa.

THE GERMAN HOMELAND: The German homeland lies in Central Europe on the Baltic and North Seas. In the north is the generally flat North German Plain; in the northeast and center are the central highlands, which include the Harz Mountains, the Thuringian Forest, the Ore Mountains, and the Bohemian Forest. The south is mountainous and includes the Bavarian Alps and the Black Forest. Germany is crossed by numerous rivers, the most important being the Elbe, Rhine, Oder, Weser, Saale, Spree, Ems, and Main, all flowing north toward the Baltic and North Seas, and the Danube, which flows east toward the Black Sea.

Germany, due to its central position in Europe, adjoins many of Europe's states. In the north the German homeland borders Denmark; in the northwest, the Netherlands, Belgium, and Luxembourg; and in the southwest, France. To the south Germany borders Switzerland and Austria and to the east, the Czech Republic and Poland.

The German homeland, divided between East and West after World War II, was reunited on 3 October 1990. The Federal Republic of Germany is divided into sixteen states roughly based on the historic divisions of the region. *Federal Republic of Germany (Bundesrepublik Deutschland)*: 137,735 sq.mi.–356,734 sq.km. (2000 e) 81,045,000—German 95%, Turks* 3%, Italians,* Croats,*

Greeks,* Spaniards,* Dutch.* The German capital and major cultural center is Berlin, in the east of the country, (2000 e) 3,436,000 (metropolitan area 4,845,000), which forms a separate *lander* or state of the federal republic. Bonn, (2000 e) 294,000, a university city on the Rhine River, was the capital of West Germany and retained several ministries and the Bundesrat, the federal council, after the governmental move to Berlin.

FLAG: The German national flag, the official flag of the republic, is a horizontal tricolor of black, red, and gold.

PEOPLE: The Germans are an ancient ethnic group, the basic stock in the composition of the peoples of Germany, Scandinavia, Austria, Switzerland, northern Italy, the Netherlands, Belgium, Luxembourg, north and central France, lowland Scotland, and England. Scholars believe that the Germans retained little ethnic solidarity beyond the seventh century B.C. Originally, the German tribes inhabited northern Germany, southern Sweden, Denmark, and the shores of the Baltic Sea. From this ancient heartland they expanded in great migrations to the south, southwest, and west. The earliest mention of the Germans is in the writings of a Greek navigator of the fourth century B.C., but their real appearance in history began with their contact, in the first century B.C., with the Romans. The Germans include a number of important national groups, including the Bavarians,* Rhinelanders,* Saxons,* and Swabians.*

The standard language of the Germans, called Deutsch or Hochdeutsch (High German), is spoken as the first or second language by all the German peoples in Europe except some of the Volga Germans* in Russia. It comprises two main groups of dialects, High German, which includes standard literary German, and Low German. Together the two dialect groups form a continuum from Switzerland north to the Baltic Sea and includes such diverse groups as the Swiss-Germans,* Austrians,* Bavarians,* Swabians,* and Saxons.* The dialects of German reflect the historic and geographic divisions of Central Europe. There is no generally accepted standard of pronunciation, and many of the dialects are not inherently intelligible. Local dialects can usually be understood by speakers of nearby dialects, but not necessarily by speakers of faraway dialects. Standard German is based on the Upper German dialect of the upper Rhine region.

Regional loyalties remain strong, particularly in the southern German states. The historic divisions often reflect religious divisions, with the northern Germans mostly Protestant, and the southern Germans, especially the Bavarians and Swabians, predominantly Roman Catholic.

NATION: The Teutonic peoples at the end of the second century B.C. began to expand to the west and south, displacing the earlier Celtic inhabitants. The Teutonic expansion was confined to the region east of the Rhine and north of the Danube by the Roman conquests of the borderlands from the first century B.C. to the first century A.D. From the late first century to the third century A.D., the Romans held the *Agri Decumates*, protected against attacks by Germanic tribes by a line of forts from present Cologne to Regensburg.

The decline of Roman power allowed the Germanic peoples to penetrate former Roman territory in the fourth and fifth centuries. The German tribes, in a series of great migrations, overran most of the Roman provinces, while Slavic tribes moved into the former German lands east of the river Elbe. By the sixth century the Franks, one of the more powerful of the tribal groups, controlled most of west and south Germany and much of present France.

The beginning of a German state is traced to the Frankish chieftain Clovis, who defeated the Romans and united the Germanic Franks in the fifth century. He established the Mergovingian dynasty that controlled a kingdom that included most of Gaul and southwestern Germany. The inhabitants of his newly established kingdom, believers in a heretical offshoot of Christianity known as Arianism, were ordered to adopt orthodox Christianity. In 751 the Carolingians, established by Pepin the Short, replaced the Mergovingians as the ruling house. His son, called Charlemagne, conquered the Saxons and Lombards* and extended the Frankish territories east to the Elbe. He was crowned emperor by Pope Leo on Christmas Day in the year 800. The Holy Roman Empire historically became known as the First Reich.

The Carolingian Empire was based on the social structure of the late Roman Empire but was beset by tribal dissension. The official language of the court and the church was Latin, but the Franks in Gaul adopted the vernacular that became French, and the Franks and the subject Germanic tribes in the east continued to speak various languages that preceded modern German.

The empire did not long survive Charlemagne's death in 814. In the first division of the Frankish territories among Charlemagne's heirs in 843, the kingdom of East Francia, under Louis the German, emerged as the nucleus of the German nation. In 918 a century of Saxon domination was begun by Emperor Henry I. The German lands were included in the Holy Roman Empire, which came into being in 962, but even at the height of the German emperors' influence the region remained divided into numerous secular and ecclesiastical feudal states, which increased their powers during the frequent papal-imperial struggles. The growth of feudalism led to the emergence of a number of powerful duchies, which increased their powers at the expense of the central authority.

The secular lords gradually made their fiefs hereditary. The greatest of them were the rulers of five stem (tribal) duchies of Franconia, Swabia, Bavaria, Saxony, and Lorraine. Lesser warriors joined princely retinues out of tribal loyalty and in exchange for smaller grants of land and other gifts. Common people lost the right to bear arms. They worked the fields of warriors and churchmen in return for protection and a share of the crops. Thus, the Carolingian governmental system blended with the German tradition of free tribesmen to form a society in which a military nobility was supported by an agricultural peasantry of freemen and serfs.

In the twelfth century the Hohenstaufen family was established as the ruling dynasty in the empire. The power of empire under Hohenstaufen rule played a part in later German history and inspired myths of German greatness. Under the Hohenstaufen emperors the power of the duchies was weakened, and until the dissolution of the Holy Roman Empire, Germany remained a patchwork of innumerable small states, duchies, principalities, and free cities. By ancient German tradition, the kings were elected. Because no noble family wanted to be subject to another family or to a strong king, weak kings were often chosen. These conditions delayed for centuries the consolidation of a strong German state and led to the formation of a number of German national groups.

Campaigns against the Slavs in the twelfth and thirteenth centuries awakened German interest in the territories to the east, although the appearance of rival rulers in the early thirteenth century left the German lands in a state of anarchy. The accession of the first ruler of the Hapsburg line, Rudolph I, in 1273 began the great German expansion to the east, but neither he nor his heirs were able to establish a centralized monarchy. In the thirteenth century Prussia was conquered by the Teutonic Knights, and the margraviate of Brandenburg and the domain of the Teutonic Knights were established.

The feudal system in the German lands supported a number of great lords, theoretically vassals of the king, but, in fact, usurped the royal rights to build castles and administer justice. The vast majority of the Germans lived on rural manors belonging to nobles or churchmen. By the late Middle Ages, the great stem duchies had been broken up and new principalities created. Three princely families, the Hapsburgs, Wittelsbachs, and Luxemburgs, struggled for the imperial crown. Albert of Austria, who ruled until 1493, made the imperial crown hereditary in the Hapsburg line.

The cities became the home to merchants, artisans, and uprooted peasants settled as free citizens under the authority of local rules. The cities also sheltered Jews, who were not allowed to own land. The cities, which often supported the emperors against the nobles, formed into leagues for their common defense and economic interests. The formation of the most powerful of the leagues, the Hanseatic League and the Swabian League, led to the tremendous prosperity of German commerce and banking in the fifteenth and sixteenth centuries.

The weakness of the emperors was most evident during the Protestant Reformation. The Roman Catholic emperors were unable to enforce religious policies or to prevent powerful nobles from embracing the Reformation. The religious issue further divided the population, and economic unrest became tied to religion. Protestant gains helped to stimulate the Catholic Counter-Reformation, which hardened the religious and political divisions in the empire. A religious settlement was reached only after the Thirty Years' War, which devastated the German lands from 1618 to 1648 and dealt a final blow to German unity. Through the Peace of Westphalia, depopulated, miserable Germany was reduced to a loose confederation of petty princes under the nominal rule of the emperor.

The most powerful German state to emerge from the wars of the seventeenth and eighteenth centuries was Prussia, ruled by the Hohenzollern dynasty. Prussian forces under Frederick II successfully challenged the military might of the Austrians and made Prussia a major European power. The influence of the

French Revolution and the Napoleonic Wars finally swept away the obsolescent Holy Roman Empire and forced the German states, particularly Prussia, to adopt long-postponed social, economic, and political reforms. The Germans' humiliation by Napoleon's forces stimulated nationalist sentiments and calls for German unification. The Congress of Vienna at the end of the Napoleonic Wars in 1814–15 redrew the map of Germany, eliminating many petty states and expanding others, notably, Prussia and Bavaria. The many German states were loosely linked in the German Confederation set up by the congress.

The conservative, Catholic Austrians gained virtual control of the German Confederation, frustrating German nationalist ambitions. German nationalists, fed by romantic, historic legends of former German greatness, became a major force during the revolutions of 1848, but the revolutionaries were eventually defeated, having failed to obtain their goal, the unification of the German homeland. The Kingdom of Prussia, humiliated by Austria in the 1850 Treaty of Olmütz, used the Zollverein, a customs union of north German states, to consolidate its power.

In 1862 Otto von Bismarck took charge of Prussian foreign policy with the aim of expelling the Austrians from the German Confederation and to consolidate Prussian power in Germany. Bismarck's rule inaugurated the Second Reich in Germany. Increasing tensions led to war between Prussia and Austria in 1866, and defeated Austria was excluded from the new Prussian-led North German Confederation. Bismarck deliberately encouraged a growing rift between Prussia and France in order to bring the states of southern Germany into a national union. On 19 July 1870 France declared war on Prussia. Partly due to the belief that the French* were the aggressors, the southern German states acceded to the North German Confederation, just as Bismarck had planned, and joined Prussia in war with the French. The German forces invaded France and besieged Paris, which finally surrendered on 28 January 1871 after several months of famine. The German Empire was formally established on 18 January 1871 in the Hall of Mirrors at Versailles, with William I, the king of Prussia, proclaimed German emperor by the assembled German princes.

A conservative constitution, largely the work of Bismarck, united Germany under a government of blood and iron, with authoritarian, semifeudal Prussia the dominant state. The Industrial Revolution, which came late to Germany, rapidly urbanized the population as the empire transformed itself into Europe's foremost industrial power. In the late nineteenth century the Germans began to acquire colonial possessions, bringing them increasingly into conflict with the French and British.

Germany supported Austria's policies in the Balkans, which eventually dragged most of Europe into war in 1914. The German government, having declared war on the Russians* and convinced that Russia's ally, France, was about to attack on the west, struck at France through neutral Belgium and Luxembourg. The violation of Belgian neutrality brought the British into the war. A two-front war, in spite of German advances, eventually turned the war against the Germans. The sinking of American ships in 1915–16 brought the United States into the war. Exhausted to the point of collapse, the German Empire was forced to accept the Allied armistice terms and in 1919, the harsh peace terms of the Treaty of Versailles. Emperor William II abdicated and fled during the outbreak of a left-wing revolution that swept the rulers of the various German states from their thrones.

The Germans, having overthrown the imperial government, expected a negotiated and honorable peace, but the Allies pushed for punishment and reparations. The Versailles Treaty, although understandable from the Allies' post-hostilities attitudes, did not ensure lasting peace in Europe. The Germans were neither crushed completely nor encouraged to return to the European community of nations. In Weimar in 1919 a national assembly wrote a new democratic constitution for the new German republic, but the prospects of the new republic were dim. For most Germans the government bore the stigma of military defeat and was overshadowed by the Versailles Treaty, which most Germans regarded as temporary.

The economic and political chaos in the aftermath of the war brought mass unemployment and currency inflation. The continuing crisis severely weakened the middle class and strengthened extremist political parties, including the Nationalist Socialists, later known as the Nazis. The stabilization of the country in the middle and late 1920s, both politically and economically, was reversed by the worldwide depression beginning in 1929, which brought back high unemployment, business failures, and renewed political tensions. Nazi and communist gains made governing the country nearly impossible. In January 1933, in an effort to avert a military takeover, Adolf Hitler, the leader of the National Socialists, was made chancellor of Germany.

A former army corporal, Hitler hated aristocrats, capitalists, communists, and liberals, as well as Jews, Roms* (Gypsies), and other so-called non-Aryans. Hitler promised to build a 1,000-year Third Reich, the successor to the Holy Roman and Hohenzollern Empires. As chancellor, Hitler organized every aspect of German life, in particular subjecting the population to the barbaric and destructive propaganda that constituted the Nazi doctrine. The powers of the state governments were abolished, and in 1934 the National Socialists were made the sole legal political party. Science, the arts, and the intelligentsia adopted the Nazi doctrine without effective protest, and many Germans welcomed what they considered the rebirth of a strong Germany. Nazi propaganda prepared the Germans for war, while the government prepared plans for the conquest of Europe. The anti-Semitic Nuremberg Laws deprived Germany's large Jewish population of their citizenship and began a persecution that ultimately became the Holocaust, the murder of some 6 million Jews in the German-occupied territories during World War II.

On 1 September 1939 Hitler unleashed his military forces on neighboring Poland, and war again spread across Europe. Slave-labor systems were organized, and the German people were mobilized for total war. The early successes of the Nazi war machine led to a ruthless Nazi tyranny as state after state fell to the German forces. The rise of Allied power eventually reversed the German victories, and Germany itself became an occupied state. Its cities lay in ruins, and an entire generation of young Germans had perished in a mad command to save the Nazi Third Reich. In May 1945 the Germans accepted an unconditional surrender.

Germany was divided into four occupation zones, while territories in the east were transferred to Poland and the Soviet Union. The Allied occupation armies of the United States, Great Britain, France, and the Soviet Union, failed to agree and separate governments were erected in the occupation zones. In the Soviet Union a police state was created, and government was dominated by the communists. The onset of the Cold War, in which Germany became the major battleground, allowed the guilt for the Germans' Nazi past to rapidly recede.

In 1952 the Federal Republic of Germany, known as West Germany, joined the Western Allies and in 1955 became a sovereign state. In the East the communist dictatorship was replaced by a civilian communist government closely allied to the Soviet Union. Soviet troops ruthlessly crushed a workers' uprising in East Germany in 1953. The division of Germany between East and West was symbolized by the construction of the Berlin Wall by the communist authorities in 1961 in an effort to stop the flow of refugees fleeing to the West.

West Germany experienced rapid economic growth in the 1950s and 1960s, the so-called German Miracle. Fully integrated into the political and economic alliances of the West, the West Germans joined the European Economic Community in 1958, which brought the country into a close alliance with France, Germany's historic rival. In 1972 West Germany signed a treaty of cooperation with the German Democratic Republic (GDR), which somewhat eased the Cold War tensions between the two Germanys. During the 1980s West Germany played an increasingly important economic and political role in the European Community.

In the late 1980s, reforms in the Soviet Union led to widespread unrest in East Germany. The beginning of the collapse of communism in 1989 brought rapid changes in East Germany. The political crisis in the East was followed by the opening of the Berlin Wall, which sparked talk of reunification. On 3 October 1990, under the leadership of Chancellor Helmut Kohl, the two German states were formally reunited under a democratic government, but, in reality, the richer West Germans economically colonized the East, causing increasing resentment among the former East Germans. In spite of the enormous cost of absorbing the former communist state into the Federal Republic, Germany is one of the world's greatest economic powers.

In the late 1990s the eastern Germans are rapidly catching up with the western Germans, called *Wessis*. The telephone system in the east is already better than that in the west, and the road and rail systems will soon be better than in the west. The rapid improvement of life for the eastern Germans has, however, done little to heal the rift between the two halves of the German nation. The *Wessis* grumble that since unity over DM1 trillon ($551 billion) has been transferred from the rich west to the poor, former communist east, but in spite of the massive financial support, the Germans of the eastern states are still twice as likely to be unemployed, their productivity is over one-third lower than that of the *Wessis*, and exports remain weak. The eastern Germans reply that they work longer hours, are more flexible, and have less bureaucratic hindrances. The divisions between the two halves of the German nation seem set to remain well into the new century.

SELECTED BIBLIOGRAPHY

Ardagh, John, and Katharina Ardagh. *Germany and the Germans: The United Germany in the Mid-1990s.* 1996.

Craig, Gordon A. *The Germans.* 1991.

Elias, Norbert, ed. *The Germans: Power Struggles and the Development of Habitus in the Nineteenth and Twentieth Centuries.* 1996.

Gedmin, Jeffrey. *The Germans: Portrait of a New Nation.* 1995.

Todd, Malcolm, ed. *The Early Germans.* 1995.

GIBRALTARIANS

Yanitos

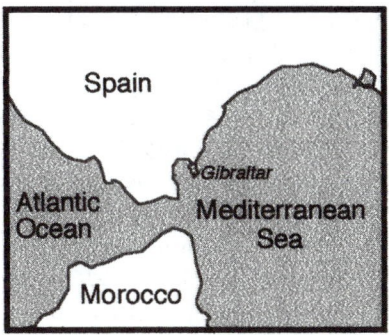

POPULATION: Approximately (2000 e) 35,000 Gibraltarians in Europe, mostly in Gibraltar and Great Britain.

THE GIBRALTARIAN HOMELAND: The Gibraltarian homeland lies in Southwestern Europe, a peninsula 2.5 miles long surrounding the Rock of Gibraltar, an enclave on Spain's southern coast. The Rock of Gibraltar, once considered one of the Pillars of Hercules, lies at the western entrance to the Mediterranean Sea. The Rock of Gibraltar is composed of limestone and rises abruptly from the sea in the east with a more gradual slope on the west. The maximum elevation is 1,396 feet (426 m.). Cacti, aloes, capers, and wild asparagus grow in the crevices, and certain parts contain grassy glens with native fauna, including the Barbary ape, the only wild monkey of Europe. Among the numerous natural caves, St. Michael's, with an entrance 1,100 feet (335 m.) above sea level, is the largest. The rock is connected to the Spanish* mainland by a narrow, sandy spit, which constitutes a neutral zone between Gibraltarian and Spanish territory.

Gibraltar is a self-governing British colony. *Colony of Gibraltar (Calpe)*: 2.3 sq.mi.–6 sq.km. (2000 e) 29,500—Gibraltarians 68.5%, other British, Spanish, Moroccans.* The Gibraltarian capital and major cultural center is the city of Gibraltar, (2000 e) 29,500, which is coextensive with the colony, including the British air and naval bases.

FLAG: The Gibraltarian national flag is a horizontal bicolor of white over red, proportions two by one, charged with the red, three-towered castle of Gibraltar, from which is suspended a golden key.

PEOPLE: The Gibraltarians are a distinct European people, including in their background Italians,* Maltese,* British, Spanish, and Portuguese.* Most Gibraltarians are of Italian or Maltese heritage, although the ethnic divisions of the Gibraltarians have been blurred by extensive intermarriage and the formation of a distinct Gibraltarian nationality. The majority of the Gibraltarians speak English, along with a variant of Andalusian Spanish called Yanito. The majority of the Gibraltarians are Roman Catholic (75%), with important Protestant (8%), Muslim (6%), and Jewish (2%) minorities. National self-awareness, a recent phenomenon, is based on Gibraltar's unique history and culture, a blend of British and Mediterranean traditions.

NATION: The two large promontories at the eastern end of the Strait of Gibraltar, the Rock of Gibraltar and Jebel Musa at Ceuta in Africa, known in ancient times as the Pillars of Hercules, were believed by the ancient Mediterranean peoples to mark the edge of the world. The peninsula guarding the entrance to the Mediterranean and the shortest route from North Africa to Europe has attracted conquerors since boats first ventured into the Mediterranean Sea. The peninsula, with its easily defensible rock, was conquered or controlled by Phoenicians, Carthaginians, Romans, Vandals, Visigoths, and Moors.

Gibraltar's name is derived from Jebel-al-Tarik, Mount of Tarik, named for the Moorish leader who crossed from Africa to capture southern Spain in 711. Fortified by the Moors, Gibraltar served as the southern defense of the opulent Muslim state of Al-Andalus, based on Cordoba, later called Andalusia by the Spaniards.

In 1309 the rock was captured by the Castilians but was retaken by the Moors in 1333 and held until the Christian conquest of Moorish Spain in 1462. The peninsula was annexed to the Spanish crown in 1502. Gibraltar was fortified in the late sixteenth century and became a Spanish stronghold, which controlled the entrance to the Mediterranean Sea.

During the War of the Spanish Succession, which eventually involved most of the European powers, the peninsula was captured by English and Dutch troops in 1704. The English commander took possession in the name of Queen Anne. Nine years later the Peace of Utrecht confirmed British possession of Gibraltar in 1713 over strong Spanish objections. Heavily fortified by the British authorities, the British naval base was several times unsuccessfully besieged by Spanish forces.

During the American Revolution, Spanish troops, assisted by the French,* imposed a stringent three-year blockade of the colony. On 14 September 1782 the British destroyed the floating batteries of the French and Spanish besiegers. In February 1783 the signing of a preliminary peace finally ended the long siege. In 1830 Gibraltar was named a crown colony. Spain made several attempts to recover the peninsula during the nineteenth century, which clouded British–Spanish relations during most of the century.

Gibraltar was officially designated a British Crown Colony in 1830 in spite of Spanish objections. The impregnable fortress, Britain's major Mediterranean base, developed as a flourishing trading center that attracted immigrants from

Italy, Malta, and other parts of Mediterranean Europe. The Spanish population of the colony dwindled, while the immigrant population, schooled in English, gradually developed as a distinct Mediterranean people.

The base at Gibraltar became one of Britain's most important military and naval bases. Numerous caverns and galleries, extending two to three miles in length and of sufficient width for vehicles, were cut through solid rock, providing sheltered communications from one part of the garrison to another. The citadel and naval base protected Allied shipping during both world wars. During World War II, Spain's dictator, Francisco Franco, a neutral ally of Nazi Germany, resisted Hitler's calls to take control of the British enclave. Franco feared that the British would retaliate by taking control of the important Canary Islands.

The Spanish government sought to regain control of the peninsula, considered an integral part of the Spanish state, after World War II. Despite Spain's protests that the move contravened the 1713 Treaty of Utrecht, Britain granted autonomy to the Gibraltarians in 1964, giving them their own elected government and control of the colony's booming economy. The Spanish government proposed an Anglo-Spanish condominium under joint rule as a transition government leading to eventual Spanish sovereignty. The British government refused to cede the colony to Spain against the wishes of the inhabitants. In 1967 the British authorities agreed to a referendum, but only 44 out of the 12,762 voters chose Spain and the Franco dictatorship.

A new constitution granted in 1969 created a Gibraltarian legislature, the House of Assembly, with substantial powers. In retaliation the Spanish government closed the border and forbade Spanish citizens to cross to jobs in the colony. Almost wholly dependent on the Spanish mainland for food, the blockade forced the British authorities to mount an extensive program to provision the colony by sea and air. The blockade hardened the Gibraltarians' attitude to Spanish claims. The Gibraltarian government, to counter the blockade, allowed a substantial number of laborers, mainly from Italy and Malta, to settle in the colony.

In the 1970s the colony lost its military importance as the nuclear age precluded its strategic importance but, as a naval base guarding the entrance to the Mediterranean, Gibraltar retained its importance. The colony's economy, formerly dependent on military spending, diversified into banking and international trade.

The Spanish state's return to democracy in 1975 greatly decreased tensions between Spain and Great Britain. The border between Gibraltar and Spain was reopened to foot traffic in 1983 and to vehicles in 1985. Following Spain's entry into the European Economic Community in 1986, the Spanish government again raised the question of sovereignty. In 1988 the Gibraltarians again voted to retain their ties to the United Kingdom.

Rising prosperity in the 1980s and 1990s, based on banking and trade, has given the colony's inhabitants new confidence. The results of an August 1991 poll showed that a majority desire to be known as Gibraltarians, a separate

European people. For the first time the poll showed a majority of Gibraltarians wished for independence, with support for retaining ties to Britain at 47%, down from 62% in 1988. In late 1991 the British government confirmed Gibraltar's right to independence, the only hindrance being Spain's continuing territorial claims to the Rock of Gibraltar.

The Spanish and British government continued talks, often within the auspices of the European Economic Community, later the European Union, during the 1990s. The British have adamantly maintained that the Gibraltarians themselves must decide on their future. The Gibraltarian parliament, the House of Assembly, has the final word on any change of sovereignty and seems intent on remaining British or, failing that, not becoming Spanish.

SELECTED BIBLIOGRAPHY
Harvey, Maurice, and Richard Van Emden. *Gibraltar.* 1996.
Jackson, William G. *The Rock of the Gibraltarians: A History of Gibraltar.* 1991.
Lutz, William. *Gibraltar.* 1987.
Morris, Dennis S., and Robert Henry Haigh. *Britain, Spain, and Gibraltar, 1945–90: The Eternal Triangle.* 1992.
Shields, Graham J. *Gibraltar.* 1996.

GREEKS

Hellenes; Grecs; Graecae

POPULATION: Approximately (2000 e) 11,616,000 Greeks in Europe, the majority in Greece, and with substantial numbers in Cyprus, 588,000, Germany, 315,000, Georgia, Poland, Albania, Ukraine, Russia, Sweden, and Italy. Large Greek populations outside Europe live in the United States, Canada, Australia, South America, and southern Africa.

THE GREEK HOMELAND: The Greek homeland lies in Southeastern Europe, occupying the southernmost part of the Balkan Peninsula and numerous islands. Most of the region forms a peninsula of irregular shape, with many deep indentations in the coastline and two large peninsulas projecting from it, Chalcidice, with its three long projections, and the Peloponnisos, joined to the mainland by the Isthmus of Corinth. Most of the Greek homeland is mountainous and arid, with only about 23% arable. The heavily indented Greek coastline is 9,385 miles long. Over 2,000 islands in the Aegean and Ionian Seas make up nearly one-fifth of the country's territory, although only 169 are inhabited.

Prior to the collapse of the Ottoman Empire at the end of World War I, the Greek homeland extended to western Anatolia in Asia Minor. Other large Greek populations inhabited the large cities of the empire, particularly Constantinople/Istanbul.

The region, inhabited since very ancient times, was once covered by forests, but much of Greece's original vegetation has been destroyed. Some areas are now bare of plants, and others are covered by *maquis*, a thorny shrub. About 75% of Greek territory is nonarable, with mountains in all areas.

Greece, called Hellas by the Greeks, won its independence from the Turkish Ottoman Empire in 1829 and was recognized as an independent state by the major European powers in 1832. *Hellenic Republic (Elliniki Dimokratia)*: 50,944 sq.mi.–131,945 sq.km. (2000 e) 10,536,000- Greeks 96%, Macedonians* 2%, Turks* 1%, Albanians.* The Greek capital and major cultural center is Athens (2000 e) 3,091,000 (metropolitan area 5,435,000), an ancient city that has grown rapidly during the twentieth century.

FLAG: The Greek national flag, the official flag of the republic, has nine horizontal stripes of blue and white with a blue canton on the upper hoist bearing a centered white cross.

PEOPLE: The Greeks are an ancient people, forming a separate branch of the Indo-European peoples. Over the thousands of years of Greek history they have absorbed many cultural traits and traditions from the region's many conquerors, particularly the Turks. Greek culture, particularly music, art, cuisine, and architecture, show definite Turkish influence, although relations between the Greeks and Turks are often turbulent.

The Greek language, which forms the Greek branch of the Indo-European languages, is derived from the standard Greek (Koine) of the Hellenistic world. Spoken in several dialects, the Dimotike dialect is the spoken literary dialect and is now the official dialect of the Greek state. The vernacular modern Greek and the language of popular literature is called Demotike, as opposed to Katharevousa, a more formal, modern Greek, also known as purist Greek. Demotike became the official language of Greece by an act of parliament in 1976. It is used in government, by newspapers and magazines, and in educational institutions. Great differences exist between the language of the educated classes and that used by the majority of the people. The *Iliad* and the *Odyssey* are the earliest known European poems; they are believed to have been written by Homer around 800 B.C.

The majority of the Greeks, about 98%, belong to the Greek Orthodox Church, the religion of the Greek state and the large Greek diaspora. A small minority, notably the Pomaks, are Sunni Muslims and mostly live in northern Greece.

NATION: Evidence of occupation in the region dates back to the Paleolithic period, although little is known of Greek history until the Indo-European invasions, about 2000 B.C. The earliest civilizations, Mycenae and Tiryns on the mainland and the Minoan on Crete, developed during the Bronze Age. By the mid-eleventh century B.C. invasions by peoples traditionally considered part of the Greek nation had spread early Greek culture throughout the eastern Mediterranean, particularly the Aegean Sea region, including the shores of Asia Minor, which became part of the Greek world.

The Greek Peninsula has been culturally linked with the Aegean Islands and the western coast of Asia Minor since ancient times. The many natural harbors along the coasts of mainland Greece and the close-lying islands led to the development of a homogeneous, maritime civilization, but cultural homogeneity did not induce political unity. Numerous mountain ranges and deep valleys cut the peninsula into small economic and political units, each little larger than a city and its surrounding territory.

Gradually, in the late Bronze Age, the mainland Greek culture absorbed the earlier civilization, based on the island of Crete. The Achaeans, originally invaders from the Danube Basin, by 1400 B.C. became the dominant power with their center around Mycenae. The Trojan War, described by Homer in the *Iliad*, began about, or shortly after, 1200 B.C. and was probably one of a series of wars waged in the region during the thirteenth and twelfth centuries B.C.

The Dorians left their mountainous homeland in Epirus and pushed south to conquer the Peloponnisos and Crete. Using iron weapons to conquer or expel the previous inhabitants, the invaders overthrew the Achaean kings and settled the southern and eastern part of the peninsula. Sparta and Corinth became the chief Dorian cities. Many of the Achaeans took refuge in the northern Peloponnisos, a district later called Acheaa. Other Greek peoples resisted the Dorians but were subjugated and were made serfs, called helots. Others fled the onslaught and settled on the coast of Asia Minor. In the next centuries the increased colonization of the Asia Minor coast made the area a political and cultural part of the Greek homeland.

Between the eighth and sixth centuries B.C. the Greek city-states sent out colonies that founded new Greek cities on the shores of the Black Sea, Sicily and southern Italy (Magna Graecia), southern France, North Africa, and eastern Spain. These new city-states had a great influence on the Greek heartland, where the city-states were developing in quarrelsome isolation. Due to their political independence, the Greek city-states developed distinct political systems. Democracy, with limited citizenship and slave-holding, developed in a number of city-states, particularly Athens. Ancient Greece never achieved political unity, although Sparta and Athens became the predominant states in shifting and loosely organized leagues.

The Greek city-states of Asia Minor were conquered by Croesus, king of Lydia, in the mid-sixth century B.C. Croesus was a mild ruler, sympathetic to the Hellenes and an ally of the Spartans. The economic, political, and intellectual life of the Asia Minor Greeks was greatly stimulated by Lydian rule. In 546 B.C. Croesus was overthrown by Cyrus the Great, king of Persia, and, except for the island of Samos, Cyrus incorporated the cities in Asia and the coastal islands into the Persian Empire.

War with Persia in the first half of the fifth century virtually ended with a major Greek victory in 479 B.C., although the Persian Wars continued for another three decades. Out of the war came a surge of Greek civilization, with a great flowering of the arts and medicine that left its imprint on all successive civilizations. As a result of its brilliant leadership during the Persian Wars, Athens became the most influential state in Greece. War between Athens and Sparta, the Great Peloponnesian War of 431 to 404 B.C., further eroded Greek unity and paved the way for the Macedonian conquest of the warring city-states, although the Greek culture continued to develop.

The Macedonian king Philip II, after taking the throne of Macedonia in 359 B.C., on the northern frontier of the Greek world, initiated a policy of expansion. An admirer of Greek culture, he was also aware of its greatest weakness, its political disunity. He consolidated the Macedonian Empire in the Balkans and Asia Minor, but his son, Alexander, called the Great, expanded the empire to its greatest extent and spread Greek civilization throughout the known world east to India. At Alexander's death his empire was torn apart by jealous generals, while the Greek heartland reverted to quarreling city-states, some opposing Macedonian rule, others siding with the Hellenized Macedonians.

Incessant wars continued to weaken the Greeks, while to the west the Romans continued to increase their power and territory. In 146 B.C. the remnants of the Greek city-states fell to Roman rule, and Greece was divided into Roman provinces. Under the Roman Empire in the first centuries of the Christian Era, a Greek renaissance took hold, particularly during the reign of the emperor Hadrian. The Greek rebirth was checked by the Goths, who in A.D. 267–68 overran the peninsula, captured Athens, and destroyed the rebuilt Greek cities. Although the Greek heartland became a Roman backwater, Greek civilization continued to flourish farther east with its center at Constantinople.

The Greeks became the predominant people in the Eastern or Byzantine Empire from the division of the Roman Empire in 395 A.D. The Eastern or Byzantine Empire, which was thoroughly Greek, spread Greek civilization and influence throughout the Balkans, the Middle East, and the Black Sea region. In the eleventh century inroads by invading Turks began the decline of the empire. In 1204 the Fourth Crusade, European knights sent to fight Muslim control of the Holy Land, turned on Christian Constantinople. The fall of the Byzantine capital led to the temporary disintegration of the empire. Venetian, Italian, French, and Flemish nobles took control of the Greek provinces. The restored Byzantine Empire after 1261 recovered only part of the Greek territories; others remained under the control of Italian and French rulers.

In 1453 the Greek metropolis Constantinople fell to the Turks, who continued moving west to conquer most of the Greek provinces in 1456. Within a century the Turks changed from a nomadic horde to the heirs of the most ancient empire in Europe, the Greeks' Byzantine Empire. Under Ottoman Turkish rule, Greece was merely one of many exploited territories. The Turks allowed religious observances, but otherwise their rule was grasping and oppressive. Although, particularly in its later stages, Turkish rule was corrupt and brutal, many Greek families held important positions in the Ottoman Empire, and Greek merchants dominated commerce in Constantinople and the port cities of Asia Minor, but the Greek heartland remained an underdeveloped, ignored, and poverty-stricken region.

The Venetians* held Crete until 1669 and the Ionian Islands until 1797. During its numerous wars with the expanding empire of the Turks, Venice also held Athens, Euboea, and a number of ports and islands for periods up to 1718.

The influence of the French Revolution and the Turkish reserves in its wars with Christian Russia stimulated the growth of Greek nationalism in the late eighteenth century. In 1821 Alexander and Demetrios Ypsilanti led a widespread rebellion against Ottoman rule. Most European governments favored the Greeks in the widening war, and volunteers and aid flowed in. Pressure by the Europeans and war with Russia finally forced the Turks to recognize the independence of the Greek state in 1829. In 1832 the major European powers granted recognition, and the Greeks accepted the Europeans' choice of a Bavarian prince as king.

Greek claims to areas inhabited by ethnic Greeks in Cyprus, Asia Minor, and southeastern Europe continued to mark relations with neighboring countries. In 1864 the Greeks gained control of the Ionian Islands and in 1881 extended their authority to Thessaly and part of Epirus, although in 1878 Great Britain took control of Cyprus, with its large Greek population. Nationalist agitation in favor of a Cretan rebellion against Turkish rule led to war with the Ottoman Empire in 1896–97, in which Greece was defeated. Pressure by the European powers eventually led to the independence of Crete, which united with Greece in 1913. Greece entered the Balkan Wars, 1912–13, gaining territory in Macedonia, part of Thrace, and several islands.

The British, when war broke out in 1914, annexed Cyprus, while the Greek state remained neutral. An agreement to allow the Allies to land troops at Salonica (Thessaloníki) brought down the government, but in 1917 the Greeks fully entered the war on the side of the Allies. Following the Ottoman defeat, the Greeks received the Bulgarian coast on the Aegean and the remnants of the European Ottoman territories except the Zone of the Straits, which included Constantinople. Smyrna (Izmir) and territories in western Asia Minor were placed under Greek administration pending a plebiscite of the population, but the Turks refused to accept the loss of the Asia Minor territories. Encouraged by the Allies, the Greeks invaded in 1921 but were defeated by the resurgent Turks. A peace agreement restored the European territories east of the Maritsa River to Turkey and provided for an exchange of populations. An estimated 1.5 million Greeks left Turkish territory to resettle in Greece.

In 1924 the monarchy was dissolved, and a republic was proclaimed, but political instability and economic chaos led to violent political strife, coups, and countercoups. In 1935 the monarchy was restored, but within a year a dictatorship was created under the premier, John Metaxas. When war broke out in Europe, Metaxas kept Greece neutral, but the Italians,* after a farcical ultimatum, invaded. The Greek forces, aided by the British, resisted the invasion and drove the Italians back into southern Albania. The intervention of German forces turned the tide, and Greece fell to the Nazis in April and May 1941.

In 1943, while the country remained occupied and divided, a sporadic civil war began between pro-communist and pro-monarchy partisan groups, which continued following the German withdrawal in 1944. At the end of the war the Greeks voted to restore the monarchy, but the country remained in anarchy. In the north the communists, aided by neighboring communist states, proclaimed a rival government. Aided by the British and Americans, the Greek government slowly drove the rival communists back. The war, marked by extreme cruelty and brutality on both sides, finally ended with the communist defeat in 1950.

In spite of several disastrous earthquakes and incompetent governments and still in need of foreign aid and support, Greece began to recover both politically and economically in the 1950s. Greece joined the North Atlantic Treaty Organization (NATO) in 1951 and signed an alliance with Turkey in 1954. But tensions over Cyprus, with its large Greek population, which desired union with Greece, soured relations with Turkey and Great Britain. The dispute was settled in 1959, and Cyprus became an independent republic in 1960.

In the mid-1960s the conservative government, which had overseen the rapid economic gains, was defeated by the Center Union, led by George Papandreou. King Constantine, who took the Greek throne in 1964, forced Papandreou to resign, setting the stage for a period of political maneuvering and instability that ended in a military coup on 21 April 1967. The king tried to reverse the consolidation of the harsh military junta but failed and fled to Italy on 13 December 1967.

Greek army officers serving in the National Guard of Cyprus staged a coup on the island and proclaimed union with Greece on 15 July 1974. The Turks, citing the independence agreement of 1960, invaded Cyprus a week later. The Cyprus crisis brought Greece and Turkey close to war and precipitated the collapse of the Greek military junta, which was implicated in the Cypriot coup. Democratic government was returned to Greece, and in 1975 the Greeks voted to abolish the monarchy. In 1981, in an effort to reinforce Greece's fragile democracy, the French* pushed for Greece's inclusion in the European Economic Community (EEC).

In spite of rapid economic growth and substantial aid from the European Union, formerly the EEC, Greece remains in the 1990s the poorest nation in the union. Due to its chronic financial shortfalls, Greece was the only applicant that was unable to qualify for the advent of a common currency in 1999.

SELECTED BIBLIOGRAPHY

Brewster, Harry. *Classical Anatolia: The Glory of Hellenism.* 1993.
Cartledge, Paul. *The Greeks: A Portrait of Self and Others.* 1993.
Grant, Michael. *Rise of the Greeks.* 1997.
Shuter, Jane, and Pat Taylor. *The Ancient Greeks.* 1997.
Vernant, Jean Pierre, ed. *The Greeks.* 1995.

GUERNSEIANS

Guernesíais

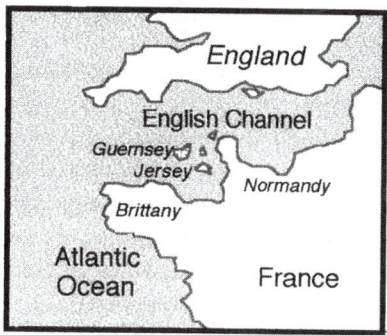

POPULATION: Approximately (2000 e) 84,000 Guernseians in Europe, 67,200 living in Guernsey and its dependencies and most of the others in England.

THE GUERNSEYITE HOMELAND: The Guernseyite homeland forms part of the Channel Islands, which lie off the coast of Normandy in the English Channel. Guernsey is the westernmost of the islands, lying just forty-six miles southwest of Cherbourg. The bailiwick includes all of the Channel Islands except Jersey. The major islands are Guernsey, which has a population of (2000 e) 57,800, Alderney, and Sark. Guernsey covers twenty-four sq.mi. (sixty-two sq.km.), Alderney has eight sq.mi. (twenty sq.km.), and Sark has two sq.mi. (five sq.km.). The northern part of Guernsey is flat and low, and the southern part rises to a plateau about 300 feet (ninety m.) above sea level.

The Bailiwick of Guernsey, which forms a crown dependency independent of the British government, is made up of the major island of Guernsey and the dependencies of Alderney, Herm, Great Sark, Little Sark, Brechou, Jetou, and Lihou. *Bailiwick of Guernsey*: thirty-four sq.mi.–eighty-eight sq.km. (2000 e) 64,200—Guernseians 87%, English* 10%, Normans* 2%. The Guernseyite capital and major cultural center is St. Peter Port, (2000 e) 17,400.

FLAG: The Guernseyite national flag, the official flag of the bailiwick, is a white field with a centered red cross bearing a gold Norman cross centered.

PEOPLE: The Guernseians, Guernesíais in the local dialect, are the descendants of refugees from ancient Gaul, medieval Norman settlers, and a later admixture of mainland English and refugees from the religious wars in nearby France. The majority of the population claim Norman ancestry, but on Alderney the English form a majority. The customs and traditions of their Norman ancestors are still maintained. The majority of the Guernseians are Roman Catholic, with a substantial Protestant minority.

Although English has replaced French as the official language of the state, a group of closely related Norman dialects is still used in daily life. Although each of the languages is a form of the Norman patois, they vary from island to island. The dialects, which are older than modern French, are not part of the formal educational system, but increasingly, language classes and schools are reviving the language. The Guernseians fear that without these efforts their unique culture and language will disappear within fifty years. Aurignais, the dialect formerly spoken on Alderney, has already died out, the victim of the German evacuation of the island during World War II.

NATION: The islands were inhabited by Celts from the mainland in prehistoric times. Structures such as cromlechs and menhirs indicate that an organized tribal society dominated the islands, but a central authority was never developed. The islands formed part of the province of Gaul under Roman rule. With the decline of Roman power the islands fell to invading Franks, Germanic tribesmen moving into the former Roman provinces in the fifth century A.D.

Christianity came to the islands in the sixth century, introduced by the islands' patron saints, St. Helier and St. Sampson. The conversion of the population began the development of a culture distinct from that of the mainland.

In the ninth century the islands were conquered by the Norsemen, later known as Normans, who came to the islands from the region they had conquered on the mainland. In 1066 the Normans crossed the English Channel, still called the Norman Channel in the islands, and conquered England. Guernsey and the other Channel Islands were attached to the Norman kings of England. In 1204 Philip II of France annexed Normandy, but the islands, known as the Norman Islands, remained under English authority, the only part of historic Normandy to remain part of the English kingdom.

The French, claiming the islands as historic parts of Normandy, attempted to take control of the islands in the fourteenth century, but the English defeated the invasion, and Guernsey, along with the other islands, remained English fiefs. The English crown's claims to the islands were recognized by the French in the Treaty of Bretigny in 1360.

Despite their ties to the English monarchy, the islanders retained their Norman law, dialects, and culture. The islands, historically self-governing, remained subjects of the English monarchy but were not subject to the English parliament. Their personal union with the English crown reinforced their long histories of independence and local self-government.

The feudal customs retained on Guernsey and the smaller islands were part of the traditional agricultural society. The famous Guernsey breed of cattle was developed in the eighteenth century, and dairy farming became a mainstay of the economy. To the present the breed is kept pure by law, which forbids the import of other breeds.

In the late nineteenth century Guernsey became a popular Victorian resort and retirement center. The island's subtropical climate, unique foreign culture, and beautiful scenery drew many English visitors and immigrants. The writer Victor Hugo, exiled from France, lived in St. Peter Port from 1855 to 1870. By the turn of the century, Guernsey had developed as one of the premier resorts of the British Isles.

The Guernseians, during World War I remained loyal to the British monarch, and many volunteered to fight in the British military. The islands were used as staging areas for British troops fighting on the continent.

The fall of France to the Nazi invaders in 1940 forced the British to evacuate the islands as undefendable. Left virtually defenseless, Guernsey and the other islands were occupied by German troops, the only British territory to fall to the Nazi tyranny. During five years of occupation, the Germans were unable to sway the Guernseyites' loyalty to Britain. Severe reprisals, including sinking barges filled with prisoners, became common as the sabotage and anti-German actions increased. The population nearly starved as foodstuffs were confiscated by the occupation authorities. In 1945 the islands were liberated by British troops.

In the postwar period the islands quickly recovered. The mild, sunny climate attracted new residents from Britain, bringing a substantial English minority to the population. During the 1950s and 1960s the islands flourished with tourism and early crops for the British market, mainly vegetables and fruits. In 1958 Guernsey began to issue its own currency and stamps.

In the 1960s low taxes made Guernsey a major offshore tax haven and banking center. The traditional enmity between the Guernseians and Jerseians* accelerated as rivalry as financial centers grew. The Guernseians claim to dislike the inhabitants of Jersey even more than they dislike the mainland British.

In 1968 the British government appointed a commission to consider the relations of the Channel Islands with the British crown. The islanders lobbied for the status quo, preferring to remain a self-governing state, but with the British government taking responsibility for defense and foreign affairs.

Until the 1970s tomato cultivation remained the major industry, but by the 1980s the Guernseians had diversified into other industries such as precision instruments, kiwi fruit, flowers, and butterflies for collectors. Guernsey's income tax has remained a flat 20% for over four decades, a much lower percentage than that of the British mainland. In the 1980s the Guernseians became alarmed at the growth of population, and immigration was severely restricted, even for millionaires, with only a few being allowed to settle in the islands each year.

The status of the bailiwick came into question following Great Britain's entry into the European Economic Community (EEC) in 1973, but the islanders preferred to maintain their present status. The Guernseians remain attached to the British crown in personal union but are not subject to acts of parliament unless specifically mentioned. The British government is responsible for defense and foreign affairs; otherwise, Guernsey is an independent state. In the 1990s several groups formed specifically to encourage and protect Guernsey's distinct culture and dialects. The largest of the groups, L'Assembllaïe d'Guernesíais, gained widespread support.

The islands are not only a fiscal paradise but to the Guernseians are also an earthly paradise. There is almost no crime, pollution, or unemployment. The citizens of the bailiwick can still invoke "clameur de hars," invoking the help and protection of the feudal lord by reciting the old Norman plea.

SELECTED BIBLIOGRAPHY

Bell, Brian, ed. *Channel Islands.* 1996.

Bunting, Madeleine. *Model Occupation: The Channel Islands under German Rule.* 1998.

Burns, Bob, ed. *Guernsey: An Island Community of the Atlantic Iron Age.* 1996.

Greenwood, David. *Guernsey, Alderney, Sark and Herm.* 1998.

Ogier, D. M. *Reformation and Society in Guernsey.* 1997.

HUNGARIANS

Magyars

POPULATION: Approximately (2000 e) 12,948,000 Hungarians in Europe, 9,471,000 in Hungary, 2,105,000 in Romania, 648,000 in Slovakia, 457,000 in Yugoslavia, 185,000 in Ukraine, and smaller populations in Austria, Slovenia, Germany, and Poland. Other large Hungarian populations live in the United States, Canada, Israel, Australia, and New Zealand.

THE HUNGARIAN HOMELAND: The Hungarian homeland is a landlocked region in Central Europe, historically including Hungary, southern Slovakia, western Romania, and northern Yugoslavia. The land is mostly low-lying and is drained by two rivers, the Danube and the Tisza. The Danube River separates northwestern Hungary from Slovakia, then flows south through Budapest, dividing the Hungarian homeland into two general regions, a low rolling steppe, the Great Hungarian Plain, also called the Nagyalföld or Great Alfold, east of the river and extending to the Carpathians and the Transylvanian Alps of Romania, and Transdanubia, a hilly region including the basin of Lake Balathon, west of the river.

In the aftermath of World War II a communist government was installed in Budapest, but four decades later, in 1989, the Hungarians adopted a new constitution and in 1990 held free elections. The former Hungarian People's Republic was replaced by the democratic Republic of Hungary. *Republic of Hungary (Magyar Népköztársaság)*: 35,919 sq.mi.–93,030 sq.km. (2000 e) 10,310,000—Hungarians (Magyars) 90%, Roms* (Gypsies) 4%, Germans* 2%, Ukrainians,* Slovaks.* The Hungarian capital and major cultural center is Budapest, (2000 e) 2,003,900 (metropolitan area 2,621,000), consolidated from the cities of Buda and Pest and surrounding towns in 1873.

FLAG: The Hungarian national flag, the official flag of the republic, is a horizontal tricolor of red, white, and green.

PEOPLE: The Hungarians, who call themselves Magyars, are a Finno-Ugric people who migrated to Central Europe from western Siberia in the eighth and ninth centuries. Centuries of contact with the Latin Romanians,* the Slavs, and the Germanic Austrians* have greatly influenced the Hungarians' culture and traditions. The Hungarian national group in Europe inhabits many areas outside the borders of the Hungarian Republic, mostly in regions annexed by neighboring states after World War I. About half the population live in rural areas; although official figures give an urban population of 63%, many of the largest towns are merely rural agglomerations.

The Hungarian language, also called Magyar, is the most important of the Ugric languages of the Finno-Ugric language group. The language has been influenced by a number of other languages, including Turkish, the Slavic languages, German, Latin, and French. Magyar is spoken in seven major dialects, several outside the borders of Hungary, particularly in Romania.

Christianized in the tenth and eleventh centuries, the Hungarians remain mostly Roman Catholic, 64%, with a large Protestant minority of 23% and smaller Jewish and Orthodox minorities. The chief Protestant groups are the Hungarian (Calvinist) Reformed Church and the Hungarian Lutheran Church. The Orthodox and Unitarian Churches also have adherents among the scattered Hungarian population in Europe. After four decades of communist rule over 10% of the Hungarian population profess no religious beliefs.

NATION: The Magyar tribes, pagan Finno-Ugric peoples, began to migrate from the region east of the Ural Mountains into the Russian steppes in the seventh century. Pushed by hostile tribes, they later moved west to the area between the Don and lower Dnieper Rivers, where they came under the sway of the Bulgar-Turkish peoples. They called themselves Magyar, thought to refer to one of the tribes, but others began to use a Slavic form of a Turkish word, *on ogur*, meaning ten arrows, which may have referred to the number of Magyar tribes. The term eventually came into popular use as Hungarian and Hungary.

The Hungarians first arrived in the area of the Carpathian Basin in the ninth century, traditionally in 895 or 896. The Magyars defeated the Avars* and occupied the valleys of the mid-Danube and the Tisza, the crossroads in the geographic center of Europe. The Hungarians absorbed the earlier inhabitants but continued to move westward until defeated by Holy Roman Emperor Otto I in 955. Their expansion halted, the Hungarian tribes began to solidify and set defensible borders. Following peace with the Holy Roman Empire, Western culture and Christianity began to penetrate the region.

The first Hungarian king, St. Stephen of the Arpad dynasty, who ruled from 1001 to 1038, completed the conversion of the Magyars to Christianity. Hungary became a powerful kingdom, defeating and absorbing the Cumans and Petchenegs, who began to invade Hungarian territory in the eleventh century. The rise of a class of powerful nobles, the magnates, who won wide privileges at the expense of the lesser nobles, the majority peasants, and the towns, increased tensions in the kingdom in the thirteenth century. In 1222 the lesser nobles forced King Andrew II to grant the Golden Bull, the so-called Magna Carta of Hungary, which effectively limited the king's authority.

Under Andrew's son, Bela IV, the kingdom barely survived. Mongol invaders defeated Bela in 1242 and occupied the kingdom for a year. Hungary fell into anarchy, and when the Arpad dynasty died out in 1301, the magnates seized the opportunity to increase their power. In 1308 Charles Robert of Anjou was elected king as Charles I, the first of the Angevin line. His autocratic rule somewhat checked the power of the magnates and furthered the development of urban areas. Under his son, Louis I, called the Great, the kingdom reached its greatest territorial extension and became one of the largest realms of Europe. After his death a series of foreign rulers weakened the kingdom, while the Turks began their incursions into Central Europe. Transylvania became virtually independent under the Zapolya family.

The first of the Hapsburg rulers, Albert III, died in 1439, leaving a bitter contest for the Hungarian throne. The Hungarian heartland was saved from Ottoman domination during this chaotic period by the military leadership of Janos Hunyadi. Still the national hero of the Hungarians, Hunyadi is best known for breaking the Turkish siege of Belgrade in 1456.

A peasant uprising, crushed in 1514, was followed by defeat by the Ottoman Turks at the Battle of Mohacs in 1526. King Louis II and more than 20,000 of his men perished in the battle, which marked the end of Hungarian power in Central Europe. In the long wars that followed, Hungary was divided into three parts, the western, where the Austrians were influential, the central plains under Turkish domination, and Transylvania, ruled by noble families as nominal vassals of the Ottoman Empire.

The Reformation gained widespread support in Hungary until the Counter-Reformation, led by Cardinal Pazmany in Hungary, brought the kingdom back to Roman Catholicism. The principle of religious tolerance among the Christian churches was established and maintained for many centuries. The treatment of the large Hungarian Jewish population was less tolerant and often gave way to prejudice and persecution.

Hungarian opposition to increasing Austrian domination included extreme measures, such as the Hungarians who aided the Turks during the 1683 siege of Vienna. However, the Austrians, under Emperor Leopold I, made gains against Turkish-held territory. Budapest was liberated in 1686, and by the Treaty of Karlowitz, in 1699, the Ottoman Empire ceded most of Hungary proper and Transylvania to Austrian authority. The office of palatine (regent) of Hungary, traditionally held by members of the great Hungarian families, was held from 1790 to 1849 by members of the Hapsburg family.

Hungarian nationalism, spurred by the French Revolution, erupted in the Revolution of 1848. War broke out between the Hungarians and Austrians in April 1849, and Hungary was declared an independent republic under the presidency of the revolutionary leader Louis Kossuth. Russian aid to the Austrians and an uprising against Kossuth's nationalist government by the non-Hungarian Slavs and Romanian minorities of the kingdom brought about the collapse of the government. The Hungarian surrender in August 1849 was followed by severe reprisals and the abolition of all Hungarian autonomy within the Austrian Empire.

Austria's defeat by Prussia in 1866 obliged the imperial government to seek an accommodation with the Hungarians. The *Ausgleich* of 1867 created a dual monarchy, the Austro-Hungarian Empire, under the Hapsburg dynasty. The Hungrian kingdom, besides Hungary proper, also included Transylvania, Slovakia, Ruthenia, Croatia, and the Banat. The constitution of the dual monarchy granted the Hungarians full sovereignty in the conduct of their internal affairs and equal status with the Austrians in the conduct of national defense, foreign affairs, and certain financial matters. On 8 June 1867 Franz Joseph, the Austrian monarch, was crowned king of Hungary. Some conflicts remained between the Hungarians and Austrians, but a common interest in keeping the other national groups in the empire under control united the two nations.

War in Europe began with the assassination of the Austro-Hungarian heir by a Serb student in 1914. Hungarian political leaders supported the imperial war effort largely because they feared that a victory by the Russians* would lead to the defection of Hungary's large Slavic populations and the dismemberment of the kingdom. As the conflict continued, however, war losses and food shortages produced widespread dissatisfaction and a growing antiwar sentiment. The defeated empire finally collapsed in November 1918. By the terms of the peace treaties the kingdom lost about one-third of its territory and population. The Hungarians lost Transylvania to Romania, Croatia and the Banat to the new South Slav kingdom, and Slovakia and Ruthenia to the new Czechoslovak republic. All the lost territories had large Hungarian-speaking populations.

The remnant of the Hungarian kingdom was made a republic under Michael Karolyi, but stability remained elusive. A Bolshevik revolt led by Bela Kun seized power in March 1919. The subsequent Red Terror was followed by the White Terror, which came after Romanian intervention and defeat of Kun's Bolshevik forces in July. Following the Romanian withdrawal, the Hungarians voted to restore the monarchy, with Admiral Nicholas Horthy as regent. Hungarian nationalism during the interwar period was shaped by efforts to recover their lost territories. Frustrated by powerful rivals, the Hungarian government turned to fascist Italy and eventually signed an alliance with Nazi Germany.

Drawn into World War II as an ally of the Axis powers, Hungary was allowed to annex most of its lost territories in Czechoslovakia, Yugoslavia, and Romania. The fascist government instituted anti-Semitic laws and other doctrines popular with their Nazi allies. German troops entered Hungary in March 1944 and installed, with the backing of many Hungarians, a puppet government controlled from Berlin. The Nazi campaign against the Jews was extended to Hungary, and 600,000 Hungarian Jews were sent to the death camps. In October 1944

Soviet troops invaded the country. Facing collapse, the Hungarians signed an armistice in January 1945, but fighting between German and Soviet troops devastated the country. The Soviet victory was followed by a return to Hungary's 1937 borders, national elections, and the establishment of a republic in 1946.

Early in 1948 a communist coup d'état gained full control of the state, and Hungary was proclaimed a people's republic in 1949. Industry was nationalized, and collectivization was ruthlessly applied. Persecution of the Roman Catholic Church, peasant resentment of collectivization, and a continuing economic crisis led to a political crisis in 1953, with a temporary easing of collectivization and nationalizations. In 1955 hard-liners again took control. Popular discontent with the government mounted throughout 1956, while students demonstrated against compulsory courses in the Russian language and in Marxist-Leninist theory. On 23 October 1956 a popular anticommunist uprising broke out in Budapest. A new coalition government installed under Imre Nagy withdrew Hungary from the Warsaw Pact and appealed to the United Nations for aid. However, a rival communist government asked the USSR for support. In severe and brutal fighting, Soviet tanks quickly ended the Hungarian Revolution. Hundreds were executed, thousands more were imprisoned, and 200,000 Hungarians fled the country to exile in the West.

The communist government, following a purge of former Stalinists in 1962, attempted to win popular support and to improve relations with neighboring countries, particularly Romania and Yugoslavia. The strict controls imposed after the 1956 uprising were relaxed somewhat beginning in 1967. Hungarian troops participated in the 1968 invasion of Czechoslovakia, but the same year saw major economic reforms that allowed market forces and profit to influence the government's economic decisions. By the mid-1980s the Hungarians were one of the most prosperous nations of the Warsaw Pact, but by Western standards they remained poor and backward.

The reforms instituted by Mikhail Gorbachev in the Soviet Union brought rapid change to the Hungarians in the late 1980s. In 1989 the Hungarian parliament passed reform legislation that created the democratic Republic of Hungary and radically shifted the country away from its communist past. In October the Communist Party was officially dissolved. The last Soviet troops left Hungary on 19 June 1991.

The reform government of Hungary, faced with hard economic reforms and territorial disputes with the neighboring states, quickly lost popularity as liberal policies failed to reform Hungarian society quickly enough to satisfy the Hungarian public. In an effort to better relations with the national minorities, the government in 1993 passed a law recognizing the Roms as a national minority. Jews were recognized as a religious minority but continue to seek the status of a national minority.

In recent years tensions have mounted between the Hungarian minorities and the governments of Slovakia and Romania. In July 1994 the Hungarian government took a step toward reconciliation when territorial claims on Slovakian and

Romanian territory were dropped in return for a guarantee of safety for ethnic Hungarians living in those countries. The Slovak government passed a law allowing the use of Hungarian as an official language in areas of Sloavkia where at least 20% of the residents speak Hungarian. However, this was retracted by a subsequent law, passed by the Slovak parliament in November 1995, that made Slovak the only language that can be used in the civil service, on road signs, and in advertisements. Along with efforts to improve relations with neighboring states, the Hungarian government also issued an official apology for the Hungarians' role in the deaths of 600,000 Hungarian Jews during the Holocaust.

Economic hardships, the result of the reform of the communist command economy, were reflected in local elections as the reformers were ousted. In 1994 the Hungarian Socialist Party, composed of ex-communists who had renounced their past, won a majority in new elections. The party set up a coalition government and vowed to pursue Hungary's entry into the North Atlantic Treaty Organization (NATO) and the European Union. After four years of leftist government, the Hungarians in May 1998 voted in a right-wing coalition. In early 1999 the Hungarian republic became a full member of NATO and participated, although with divided public opinion, on the NATO attacks on neighboring Serbia.

To the south, the Vojvodina Magyars in Serbia, numbering about 350,000, have become a particular concern during the Balkan crisis of 1999. Like the Albanians of Kosovo, the Hungarians were also stripped of their autonomy in 1989, but they are more integrated and many have married Serbs. Hungarian leaders in Serbia have been careful not to provoke the Milosevic government, but in Hungary several extremist political parties have proposed redrawing the map to put at least a third of Vojvodina back in Hungary. The extreme nationalist organizations in Hungary, with some collaboration from nationalists in Vojvodina, call for greater autonomy and even separation, while the official Hungarian government line is that Vojvodina should resume its former autonomous status as part of a final, pan-Balkan, peace settlement.

SELECTED BIBLIOGRAPHY

Hill, Raymond. *Hungary*. 1997.
Hoensch, Jorg K., and Kim Traynor. *A History of Modern Hungary: 1867–1994*. 1996.
Steins, Richard. *Hungary: Crossroads of Europe*. 1997.
Sugar, Peter F. *A History of Hungary*. 1994.
Teleky, Richard. *Hungarian Rhapsodies: Essays on Ethnicity, Identity, and Culture*. 1997.

ICELANDERS

Islanders; Icelandics

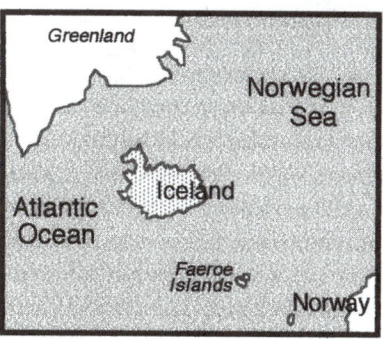

POPULATION: Approximately (2000 e) 257,800 Icelanders in Europe, mostly in Iceland, but with small populations in other parts of Scandinavia.

THE ICELANDER HOMELAND: The Icelandic homeland is a large island between the North Atlantic and Arctic Oceans, 155 miles (249 km.) southeast of Greenland and 570 miles (917 km.) west of Norway. Roughly oval, Iceland's long coastline is indented by many fjords, especially in the west and north. The island is of recent volcanic origin, and three-quarters of the surface is wasteland made up of glaciers, lakes, more than 100 active volcanoes, and a vast lava desert. The climate is moderated by the Gulf Stream, and there are abundant geysers and hot springs used for expensive heat in homes and offices. Only 1% of the land is used to grow crops, and the habitable areas are limited, but 23% of the land is used for grazing sheep and cattle, making Iceland self-sufficient in meat and dairy products. The bulk of the Icelandic population lives along the coast, particularly in the southwest. The Icelanders' homeland is often called "the land of fire and ice" due to the severe winters and the continuing volcanic activity. Iceland has few natural resources, but the seas around Iceland are rich in fish stocks and provide the major economic activity. Fishing and fish processing constitute the major industry. The Icelandic fishing fleet is one of the world's largest and most modern, and the fishing industry employs 13% of the workforce, while accounting for about three-quarters of the country's exports.

Iceland formed part of the Danish kingdom until World War II, and in 1944 the Icelanders proclaimed their homeland an independent republic. *Republic of Iceland (Lyoveldio Island)*: 39,702 sq.mi.–102,828 sq.km. (2000 e) 267,900—

Icelandic 94%, Danes* 2%. The Icelandic capital and major cultural center is Reykjavik, (2000 e) 103,000, the only large city.

FLAG: The Icelanders' national flag, the official flag of the republic, is a blue field bearing a red Scandinavian cross outlined in white.

PEOPLE: The Icelanders are a Scandinavian nation, the descendants of Norse settlers of the ninth century. Most came from Norway, bringing with them many Scots* and Irish* slaves, so that the present Icelander population is extremely homogeneous, being almost entirely of Scandinavian and Celtic origin. The early Icelandic culture developed in a unique seafaring world removed from the influences of the warring Scandinavian mainland. The island's isolation led to the development of a distinct culture and language, with many traditions and customs unlike those of the other Scandinavian peoples. The Icelanders do not have family names and are properly addressed by their first names. Their second name combines their father's first name, plus-*son* for males or-*dóttir* for females.

The Icelanders' language, called Icelandic, is a West Scandinavian language with no appreciable dialectal differences. Descended from Old Norse, the language developed from the body of oral mythological poetry brought by the first settlers and developed as a literary language between the twelfth and fourteenth centuries. Modern Icelandic is virtually identical to the language of the early Norse sagas, while the present form of the language is considered to date from 1540, when the New Testament was translated into Icelandic.

The majority of the Icelanders are Protestants, mostly belonging to the Evangelical Lutheran Church, which accounts for 94% of the population. About 3% of the Icelanders belong to other Lutheran groups, and about 1% are Roman Catholics.

NATION: Iceland may have been the Ultima Thule of the ancient world. Traditionally, Norse settlers from the Norwegian mainland, many fleeing the campaigns of Norwegian king Harold I, settled the island between 850 and 875 A.D. According to the *Landnamabok*, Norse settlers, led by a Norwegian chieftain, Ingolfur Arnarson, came to the island in 874. A general assembly, called the Althing, was established in 930, becoming the world's oldest parliament.

Christianity, introduced around the year 1000, became an integral part of the Icelandic culture. The colonization of the island and the many Norse myths the colonists brought with them provided themes for the remarkable thirteenth-century literature. In spite of the development of a sophisticated culture, the Icelanders remained politically divided.

The Icelandic Norse society developed as a feudal state, and the civil wars of rival chieftains allowed the Norwegians* to intervene in the twelfth and thirteenth centuries. Attempts to establish Norwegian rule failed until King Haakon IV of Norway incorporated Iceland into the Roman Catholic archdiocese of Trondheim on the Norwegian mainland. In 1262 the Icelanders acknowledged the authority of the Norwegian kingdom. Norwegian rule imposed order on the

Icelandic clans, but high taxes and the imposed Norwegian legal system caused much discontent. Foreign domination brought with it a long decline of the nation.

In 1380 the island, along with Norway, passed to Danish rule. The Danes, concerned only with the economic aspects of the island, showed even less interest than the Norwegians in the welfare of the Icelanders. The imposition of the Protestant Reformation between 1539 and 1551 stimulated a rebirth of culture and intellectual activity. Their new Lutheran religion replaced Catholicism as an integral part of the Icelandic culture.

The seventeenth and eighteenth centuries were very difficult for the Icelanders. English, Spanish, and Algerian pirates raided the coastal towns, ruining the island's trade. The creation in 1602 of a private Danish trading company with exclusive right to trade with Iceland brought economic ruin to the islanders. The private monopoly was finally revoked in 1771 and transferred to the Danish crown, and in 1786 trade was allowed with all Danish and Norwegian merchants, but foreign traders were still excluded. Prices for necessities, such as grains, lumber, and metal goods, remained exorbitant, while the Icelandic products, mostly fish and wool, were undervalued, as their prices were set by the same merchants.

During the eighteenth century, Icelanders reached the lowest point of their national existence. Around the year 930 an estimated 60,000 to 90,000 people lived on the island, but by the early years of the 1700s, when the first national census was taken, the Icelander population was down to 50,000. A series of disasters, including a severe smallpox epidemic in 1707–9, famines, emigration, and the eruption of the volcano Laki in 1783, which killed more than 9,000 people, further reduced the population to about 35,000. The Danish government seriously considered evacuating all the remaining Icelanders to Denmark.

In the eighteenth century Icelander national fortunes reached a turning point. Shortly after the middle of the century an enterprising Icelandic official established several cottage industries in Reykjavik, then a mere collection of huts. Although his efforts failed, he provided inspiration for other attempts that gradually improved the dismal conditions of the Icelanders. The first tangible sign of this was the modification of the Danish trade monopoly in 1787, which allowed trade between the Icelanders and any Danish subject.

The nineteenth century was a period of national and cultural revival. The Althing, abolished by the Danish authorities in 1800, was reestablished in 1843. The trade monopoly and the exclusion of foreign traders were lifted in 1854, beginning a period of rapid economic growth. The waves of revolution on the European mainland brought about the end of absolutism in Denmark, and soon the Icelanders began to clamor for their national rights. In response to the rise of Icelandic nationalism, the Danes granted a constitution and limited home rule in 1874.

The growth of the Icelanders' fishing fleet brought economic stability to the island from the 1880s. Although part of the neutral Danish kingdom, the large fishing fleet helped to feed the Allies while bringing greater prosperity to Iceland. The nationalist ideals that helped reshape Europe at the end of the war in 1918 galvanized the Icelandic nationalist movement. In 1918 Iceland was declared a sovereign kingdom in personal union with the Danish crown.

The Althing, following the German occupation of Denmark in 1940, assumed control of Iceland's foreign affairs. A British military force was landed to defend the island, and in 1941 American troops were dispatched to Iceland. The treaty of union with the Danes ended in 1943, and in early 1944 an overwhelming majority, 97%, voted to end the personal union with Denmark, and on 17 June 1944 Iceland was proclaimed an independent state.

Beginning in the 1940s, a large-scale movement from the rural districts to the coastal towns and cities occurred. The growth of the coastal population added new burdens that were met with advanced social schemes and far-reaching educational and welfare systems. By the 1990s over 90% of the Icelanders lived in urban areas.

The Icelanders, determined to play an important part in European affairs, joined the United Nations and granted the United States the right to use the American-built airport at Keflavik for military and commercial flights in 1946. Although the Icelanders possessed neither a navy nor an army, they joined the North Atlantic Treaty Organization (NATO) in 1949.

Threats to their major industry, fishing, brought the Icelanders into conflict with the British and other European states with large fishing fleets. In 1958 the Icelanders extended the limits of their territorial waters from 4 to 12 miles (6 to 19 km.). At times the controversy led to exchanges of fire between Icelandic coast guard vessels and British destroyers. The conflict was resolved when the British accepted the new territorial limits in 1961. Renewed threats to their fishing grounds were met by extending the territorial limits to 50 miles (80 km.) in 1972 and to 200 miles (322 km.) in 1975.

The Icelanders, with a standard of living among the highest in the world, joined the European Free Trade Association in 1970 but by the late 1990s had not followed the majority of Scandinavia into the European Union (EU). Icelandic membership in the Nordic Council, made up of the Scandinavian states, and association membership in the EU in 1992 have helped to maintain economic stability during the turbulence of the 1980s and 1990s. Politically, the Icelanders are among the more progressive nations in Europe. Vigdís Finnbogadóttir became the first woman elected as a European chief of state in 1980. She began her fourth term of office in 1992. In the late 1990s one of the major debates that continue to animate politics is whether or not to join the European Union, but opening their fishing grounds to other European fleets remains an obstacle.

SELECTED BIBLIOGRAPHY
Francke, Klaus D., ed. *Iceland*. 1994.

Halfdanarson, Gudmundur. *Historical Dictionary of Iceland.* 1997.
P'alsson, Gisli. *From Sagas to Society: Comparative Approaches to Early Iceland.* 1992.
Picano, Felice. *Iceland.* 1998.
Roberts, David, and Jon Krakauer. *Iceland: Land of the Sagas.* 1998.

INGRIANS

Inkeri; Inkeroiset; Ingers;
Inkeriläinen; Inkerin Suomalainen

POPULATION: Approximately (2000 e) 360,000 Ingrians in Europe, 90,000 in Russia, and another 20,000 in Estonia and 250,000 in Finland.

THE INGRIAN HOMELAND: The Ingrian homeland lies in northwestern Russia, mostly a flat plain between Lake Ladoga and the Gulf of Finland along the shores of the Neva River and on the east bank of the Gulf of Finland just north of the St. Petersburg metropolitan area. Lake Ladoga, called Laatokka by the Ingrians, the largest lake in Europe, has abundant fish harvests but is frozen from October to April.

Ingria has had no official status since 1938; the region now forms a nonpolitical district of St. Petersburg Oblast of the Russian Federation. *Region of Ingria (Inkeri)*: 1,546 sq.mi.–4,005 sq.km. (2000 e) 172,000—Russians* 49%, Ingrians 47%, Finns* 3%. The unofficial capital of Ingria is Zelenogorsk, called Terÿoki by the Ingrians, (2000 e) 33,000. The other major cultural center is Lomonosov, called Kaaresta by the Ingrians, (2000 e) 44,000.

FLAG: The Ingrian national flag, the flag of the former Ingrian republic, North Ingermanland, is a yellow field charged with a blue Scandinavian cross outlined in red.

PEOPLE: The Ingrians or Ingers, who call themselves and their homeland Inkeri, are a Finnic people, the remnant of a much larger pre–World War II Ingrian population. Estimates of the total Ingrian populations in the region, including the Izhor on the south shore of the Gulf of Finland, vary greatly, as many have registered as ethnic Russians since World War II. The Ingrians are divided into two distinct groups, the Izors, the original inhabitants of the region, and the Finnish Ingrians, seventeenth-century immigrants from present Finland.

Soviet census figures for 1989 included 70,000 Ingrians in St. Petersburg Oblast, 18,000 in Karelia and only a few hundred Izhor. The Izors until the 1990s were nearing extinction, but the reculturation of the Finnish peoples living in Russia has reversed the assimilation into the surrounding Russian population. Nationalists claim an Ingrian population in the region of over 200,000 and another 400,000 outside Russia, mostly in Finland.

The Ingrian language, Inkerin, is closely related to Finnish and is partially intelligible to the other Finnish peoples of northwestern Russia, the Karels,* the Veps,* and the Votes. Although the spoken form of the language is different, the Ingrian literary language is identical to Finnish. The language, like Finnish, is written in the Latin alphabet and is spoken in four major dialects that gradually merge into Karelian. The majority of the Ingrians and Finns are Protestant Lutherans with an Orthodox minority.

NATION: Finnish tribes from the Volga River basin settled most of Northwestern Europe in the eighth century. The tribes gradually separated into a number of separate nations speaking similar languages and with many cultural traits in common. The Ingers or Inkeri, later called the Ingrians, occupied the region around the Gulf of Finland. Formerly nomadic, the Ingrians settled as farmers and fishermen in the flatlands around the gulf and Lake Ladoga to the north. During the tenth and eleventh centuries some groups broke off from the Ingrians to settle farther south along the Izhora River and eventually were called Izhors. In the thirteenth century Scandinavian monks introduced Christianity to the pagan Ingrians.

In the Middle Ages the Ingrians were under the rule of the Slav Republic of Great Novgorod. The Ingrians, with their prosperous farms and fishing activities, prospered from the trade routes that crossed their homeland. The Novgorodians, more interested in trade than in empire, mostly left the Ingrians to govern themselves.

In 1478 Russians from Muscovy or Moscow overthrew the prosperous Novgorodian republic. The fall of Novgorod left the Ingrian homeland open to invaders. Russians, Swedes, and Teutonic Knights contested control of the region, leaving devastation in their wake. In 1617 the Swedes under Gustavus II conquered the region. During the century of Swedish rule, the Ingrians adopted many Swedish cultural traits and the Swedes' Lutheran religion. Thousands of immigrants from Swedish Finland settled in the provinces around the Gulf of Finland.

During the Northern War between Sweden and Russia, the major Swedish fort on the Neva River fell to the forces of Peter II in 1702. The next year Peter, called the Great, began to lay out a new city on the site, St. Petersburg, Russia's new capital and its window on the West. The construction of Russia's new capital brought a massive influx of Slav workers and the city's expansion, slowly pushing the native Ingrians west along the north and south shores of the gulf. Despite the loss of many of their ancient lands, the Ingrians prospered by supplying the growing capital with timber, grains, and vegetables.

The Russian government's policy that stressed the assimilation of minorities succeeded in the expanding urban area in the eighteenth and nineteenth centuries but met strong resistance among the large rural Ingrian population. Influenced by the neighboring Finns and Estonians, a cultural revival began to take hold in the 1880s. The revival spawned a modest national movement that gained support following the disturbances and violence of the 1905 revolution.

In the wake of the February revolution in 1917, the 500,000 Ingrians petitioned the new Russian government for autonomy within a democratic Russia. More militant nationalists proposed the creation of an independent Ingria around the Gulf of Finland, which would link Finland and Estonia. The city of Petrograd (St. Petersburg), in the proposal, would enjoy autonomous status within the new state.

The Bolsheviks, after taking power in Petrograd in October 1917, promised the Ingrians autonomy within the new Soviet state, but they soon faced harsh suppression. The many Ingrians who had supported the Bolsheviks, betrayed by the Soviet promise of autonomy, mostly joined the nationalists in opposition to Bolshevik rule. Rebellion spread across the region, with Ingrian rebels taking control of the territory between the new Finnish border, Lake Ladoga, the northern shore of the Gulf of Finland, and the outskirts of Petrograd. The Bolsheviks, hard-pressed by the demands of the escalating Russian civil war, were unable to spare troops to deal with the Ingrian rebels until late 1919. Threatened by units of the Red Army, the Ingrian leaders declared the independence of their homeland, often called North Ingermanland, on 23 January 1920 while sending frantic pleas for aid to newly independent Finland. The Finns, in the final months of war with the Soviets in the north, could not respond to the appeals, but in late 1920 they negotiated Finnish control of western Ingria, called Ingerinta by the Finns.

The Soviet government created a national district, called Kuivaisi or Toksova, for the remaining 115,000 Ingrians in 1928. Around 18,000 people were deported from northern Ingria to eastern Karelia, Central Asia, and elsewhere in order to frighten others into accepting collective farms. The Soviet authorities accused the Lutheran hierarchy of anti-Soviet activities, and all churches and religious societies were forcibly closed in 1932. A further 7,000 were deported in 1935, and over 20,000 were shipped to Siberia and Central Asia in 1936. Accused of anti-Soviet activities as relations worsened between the Soviet state and Finland in the late 1930s, the entire Ingrian national leadership was purged in 1937. Further punishments included mass deportations and the burning of all Ingrian books. In 1938 the Soviet authorities dissolved the Ingrian national district, which was incorporated into Leningrad Oblast.

The Soviet Union in 1939 demanded that Finland cede its eastern provinces to Soviet control. The Finnish government refused, relying on the defensive forts called the Mannerheim Line, which had been constructed across Finnish Ingria. The Red Army during the Winter War quickly overran the Mannerheim Line and conquered the region. Forced to give up the territories following the brief war in 1940, the defiant Finns joined the German assault on the Soviet Union two years later. Finnish troops liberated Ingria in June and July 1941, but the Finns refused to join the German siege of Leningrad, claiming that theirs was a separate war.

The return of the victorious Red Army in 1944 forced the majority of the Ingrians to flee west to Finnish territory. The Ingrians joined a flood of 400,000 Finns, Ingrians, Karels, and others who fled the return of Soviet authority. Thousands of Ingrians, unable to escape, faced deportation to slave labor camps in 1944–45. The Soviet authorities demanded of Finland that all former Soviet citizens be repatriated. Over 55,000 Ingrians were forced to return to the Soviet Union and were scattered across European Russia. Some years after the war even those children of Ingrian descent adopted by Finnish families were reclaimed by the Soviet Union. During the 1950s over 16,000 of the 140,000 Ingrians were forcibly resettled to Soviet Estonia.

In the 1970s small groups began to form in an effort to keep alive the culture and language of the Ingrians in Finland. In the late 1980s the small Ingrian population in the Soviet Union began to demand the revision of their history, falsified by Soviet historians, particularly the period of their revolt against the Bolsheviks during the Russian civil war. Many Ingrians, having registered as ethnic Russians during the years of oppression, began to rediscover their past. The loosening of rigid Soviet rule allowed the Ingrians in Russia to reestablish ties to Ingrian populations in the West, particularly the Ingrian population in Finland. Language schools, opened with Finnish aid, and thousands of books donated by sympathetic Finnish citizens have begun to reverse decades of forced assimilation.

An Ingrian congress held in Tallinn, Estonia, in April 1990 and a second congress convened at Zelenogorsk following the collapse of the Soviet Union in September 1991 endorsed the Ingrians' right to self-determination. In November 1992 the Ingrians demanded official recognition of their suffering over seven decades of Soviet domination. The Ingrian nation became a member of the unofficial United Nations, the Unrepresented Nations and Peoples Organization (UNPO). The Russian government officially rehabilitated the Ingrians in 1993 but has refused to grant nationality status as a separate ethnic group or as an indigenous people.

In 1997 Russian geographers estimated that about 1% of the population of St. Petersburg Oblast, or some 70,000 people, are of Ingrian or Finnish descent. Nationalist and cultural organizations claim that the Ingrian population is much higher, but until the many Ingrians who registered as ethnic Russians over the last decades feel safe enough to register as ethnic Ingrians, the real Ingrian population of the region will remain a matter of dispute.

SELECTED BIBLIOGRAPHY

Engle, Eloise, and Lauri Paananen. *The Winter War: The Soviet Attack on Finland 1939–40*. 1992.

Lehto, Manja Irmeli. *Ingrian Finnish: Dialect Preservation and Change*. 1996.

Maude, George. *Historical Dictionary of Finland.* 1995.
Nenola, Aili. *Studies in Ingrian Laments.* 1994.
Paasi, Anssi. *Territories, Boundaries and Consciousness: The Changing Geographies of the Finnish-Russian Boundary.* 1997.

INGUSH

Ingus; Galgai; Galghay; Lamur; Kist;
Nakchuo

POPULATION: Approximately (2000 e) 289,000 Ingush in Europe, concentrated in the Republic of Ingushetia and neighboring regions of the Russian
Federation.

THE INGUSH HOMELAND: The Ingush homeland lies in the Northern Caucasus between Chechenia and North Ossetia in southern European Russia. The
Fortanga River is traditionally the dividing line between the Ingush and Chechen
homelands. In the north are the Terek lowlands, where most of the population is
located and which are the main focus of Ingush economic activity. In the south
Ingushetia occupies the slopes and northern foothills of the Caucasus Mountains,
which rise to peaks as high as 14,737 feet (4,492 m.). The main rivers are the
Sunzha, a tributary of the Terek, and the Assa, which flows into the Sunzha.

The Republic of Ingushetia, also called the Galgai Republic, formed part of
the Chechen-Ingush Republic until 1992, when the region was made a separate
republic within the Russian Federation. *Republic of Ingushetia*: 1,242 sq.mi.–
3,218 sq.km. (2000 e) 331,000—Ingush 80%, Chechens* 9%, Russians* 6%,
Ossetians* 4%. The Ingush capital and major cultural center is Nazran, (2000
e) 37,000, the traditional capital of the Ingush nation. Vladikavkaz, the capital
of the neighboring republic of North Ossetia, was long considered the major
cultural center of the Ingush, but the majority of the Ingush population was
expelled in 1992.

FLAG: The Ingush national flag, the official flag of the republic, is a white
field with narrow, green, horizontal stripes at the top and bottom, charged with
the Ingush national symbol centered, a purple circle with three extensions or
points.

PEOPLE: The Ingush are a Caucasian people closely related to the neighboring Chechens, and both nations identify themselves as the Nakchuo people. The Ingush call themselves Galgai or members of the Galgai tribe of the Nakh nation. The main differences between the Ingush and Chechens stem from their different experiences with Russian colonization. The Ingush are descendants of the western Nakh tribes, mostly the Galgai and Feappi clan federations, which were less hostile to Russian conquest than the eastern Chechen tribes.

The Ingush language is a dialect that, with Chechen, constitutes the northeastern or Vienakh group of Caucasian languages. The language is partially intelligible to Chechen speakers. A spoken dialect until the Russian Revolution, Ingush became a literary language in 1923, using the Cyrillic alphabet, and is now spoken by 97% of the Ingush as their first language.

Nearly the entire Ingush nation is Sunni Muslim, mostly of the Hanafi sect. Between the ninth and sixteenth centuries many of the Ingush adopted the Orthodox Christian faith of the Georgians,* and many Ingush, unlike their Chechen kin, remained Christian until the nineteenth century.

NATION: The Ingush are thought to have inhabited the North Caucasus from the seventh century B.C. and claim descent from the region's early Scythian tribes. The Caucasus Mountain region, often used as an invasion route between Asia and Europe, became the only refuge for the early tribal peoples who sheltered in the high, inaccessible valleys. The tribes early on developed a warrior society in response to the region's many invaders. Influenced by the Roman culture in the lands to the south, the tribes adopted the Christian religion in the sixth century, but without giving up their warlike culture and traditions.

In the thirteenth century the Mongols overran the lowlands but were unable to take the mountain strongholds of the Caucasian tribes. In the fifteenth century Persians and Turks fought for predominance in the strategic region. In the seventeenth century the Ingush, driven into the mountains by the Mongol invasion, returned to settle their ancestral lands along the Terek River, where they formed close cultural and military ties to the neighboring Chechens. For centuries the Ingush were not distinguished from the larger Chechen population and were often called Western Chechens. Under the influence of the Ottoman Turks many of the Ingush accepted the Islamic religion late in the seventeenth century, but a large minority retained their Christian beliefs well into the nineteenth century.

Increasing Russian interest in the potentially rich area sent Cossack explorers and soldiers to the North Caucasus in the sixteenth century. The Cossacks constructed a string of forts as they moved south, bases for further expansion. In 1784 Vladikavkaz was founded as a fort on the edge of Ingush territory, beginning the Russian expansion in the region. The region was annexed to the Russian Empire in 1810. The Ingush rose to drive the invaders from their territory in 1818 but failed to take the Cossack forts. The Russian authorities forced many Ingush to settle in the region around Nazran, where they could be more easily controlled.

Joining the region's other Muslim peoples, some of the Ingush clans participated in a great holy war against the Russians from 1847 to 1860, particularly during an Ingush uprising at Nazran in 1858, but the majority, less militantly anti-Russian than the Chechens, took little part in the long Caucasian war. Although many clans remained neutral in the conflict, their treatment by the tsarist authorities was just as harsh as that meted out to other, more hostile groups. Frequent rebellions and grinding poverty devastated the Ingush culture. By the turn of the century most of the Ingush lived as poor herders in the high valleys, close to the strongholds the Russian military dared not enter.

The Ingush supported their fellow Muslims, the Turks,* when war began in 1914 but took little active part in the fighting. With the overthrow of the hated tsarist regime in February 1917, the Ingush believed that at last old wrongs would be righted. Their petitions and pleas ignored, the Ingush swept out of their mountain strongholds to attack the lowland Cossack, Russian, and Ossetian settlements on what they considered their traditional lands. In September 1917 Ingush delegates participated in the newly created autonomous government of North Caucasia, and the Ingush warriors declared *gazava*, holy war, on the Terek Cossacks.* The Bolshevik coup in October 1917 forced the Muslims into an uneasy anti-Bolshevik alliance with the Cossacks, but the alliance soon ended in violent confrontations. In December 1917 the Ingush captured Vladikavkaz but were again driven from the lowlands in the confused fighting and shifting alliances of 1918.

On 11 May 1918 the Muslims of the region declared the independence of the Republic of North Caucasia. The Ingush transferred their capital to Nazran after the Cossacks, aided by the anti-Bolshevik Whites, retook Vladikavkaz in August 1918. Believing the Soviet promise of independence in a Soviet federation, the Ingush, along with the Chechens, went over to the Reds. With the aid of the Bolshevik forces, the Ingush captured and looted Vladikavkaz in November.

In spite of earlier promises of independence within a federation of Soviet states, the communist authorities attempted to incorporate the Ingush lands into their new Soviet republic. The Ingush, allied to the Chechens, turned on their former allies but were finally defeated in a vicious, two-month war in 1920. The Ingush homeland was included in the new Mountain Republic, but ethnic conflicts soon led to the breakup of the republic into smaller national units. A dispute between the Ingush and the Ossetians over the city of Vladikavkaz, which represented the only major urban center of both peoples and the only source of educational institutions and industry led to conflict. In 1924 the authorities set up a separate Ingush region, without Vladikavkaz, which united with Chechenia to form an autonomous republic ten years later.

Most of the Ingush homeland was joined to neighboring Chechenia in 1934 to form the Chechen-Ingush Autonomous Oblast. The autonomous oblast was raised to the status of an autonomous republic in 1936. In 1937 the Ingush joined a mass Muslim uprising in the region but again suffered defeat and reprisals.

The Russian and Soviet treatment of their nation persuaded some Ingush to support the German invasion of the region during World War II, for which Joseph Stalin accused the entire Ingush nation of treason. In January 1944 Soviet soldiers herded the entire Ingush population into Nazran and forced them onto cattle cars for deportation to the east. They were dumped at scattered locations across the steppe lands of northern Kazakhstan, where their language and culture were supposed to die out. Between one-quarter and one-half the entire population perished from the brutal treatment or from disease and hunger in the camps set up on the cold and windy steppes. The dissolved Ingush national region was divided, part given over to the neighboring republic, North Ossetia.

Suffering oppression by special KGB units, the Ingush survived their exile by clinging to their religion, culture, and language. In 1957 the deported Caucasian peoples received an official rehabilitation, allowing them to return to their homes in the officially designated Ingush homeland. Ingush leaders demanded the return of the Prigorodnyy Rayon, a district along the Terek River that had been transferred to North Ossetia during their exile. Rioting broke out in the region in 1958 as Russians and Ossetians refused to vacate the properties in Ingushetia that they had occupied since 1944. The Christian settlers began attacking the returnees, and three days of violence left many dead and wounded before police could reestablish order. The bitter return sparked the beginning of the modern national movement.

A very high birthrate raised the Ingush population from 74,000, before their exile, to 158,000 in 1970. The birthrate, attributed to their Muslim religion, remains very high to the present.

In 1970 the Ingush again put forward claims to their former lands in North Ossetia. They demonstrated in the disputed district of Prigorodny but were driven out by Osset police and Russian soldiers. Religion became a part of the Ingush-Ossetian conflict, as the majority of the Ossetians are Orthodox Christians. The influence of Islam in Ingush daily life, not as curtailed as it was under Stalin's long dictatorship, grew rapidly during the 1970s. In 1975 the Soviet authorities estimated that half the Ingush men belonged to forbidden Sufi brotherhoods. The brotherhoods were considered hotbeds of dissent and nationalist ideals.

The collapse of the Soviet Union in 1991 fueled a dramatic growth of Ingush nationalism and stimulated demands for the return of the Prigorodny region, which was transferred to North Ossetia in 1944. Some Ingush groups laid claim to half the city of Vladikavkaz, the capital of North Ossetia, but traditionally the Ingush cultural capital.

The neighboring Chechens declared their independence of Russia, but the Ingush refused all Chechen overtures, fearing Chechen domination. In January 1992 Ingushetia officially separated from Chechenia, and on 4 June 1992 the Russian parliament approved the creation of a separate Ingush republic.

Rising demands for the return of the Prigorodny Rayon, the territory transferred to Ossetia in 1944, became the primary nationalist issue. In October 1992 fighting broke out in the disputed region. In November Ossetians, aided by

Russian troops, drove 60,000 Ingush from Vladikavkaz and the northern districts of North Ossetia into squalid refugee camps in Ingushetia and left over 300 dead. The involvement of the government troops ended the Ingush support for the Moscow government. In July 1993 the Ingush parliament voted to hold a referendum on the republic's ties to the Russian Federation, and in early 1994, on the fiftieth anniversary of their deportation, nationalists confirmed support for the eventual independence of the Ingush nation.

In 1997 the Russian government revoked the status of free economic zone, which had been granted to Ingushetia on an experimental basis in 1993. The authorities justified the decision as ending a status that had deprived the federal budget of sorely needed revenue. The decision came as a bitter blow to the Ingush, who are among the poorest of Russian citizens. Their homeland has virtually no industrial infrastructure and has the highest unemployment of any region in Russia.

In early 1997 returning Ingush refugees to North Ossetia were attacked or threatened, raising Ingush nationalist sentiment both within Ingushetia and in the conflict areas of North Ossetia. A joint action program was signed in Moscow in later 1997 by representatives of the Ingush, the Ossetians, and the Russian government, aimed at overcoming the consequences of the ethnic conflict between the Ingush and Ossetians. In spite of official efforts to end the conflict, the territorial dispute between the two Caucasian nations continued in 1999.

SELECTED BIBLIOGRAPHY

Conquest, Robert. *The Nation Killers: The Soviet Deportation of Nationalities.* 1970.
Coppieters, Bruno, ed. *Contested Borders in the Caucasus.* 1996.
Human Rights Watch Staff. *Russia: The Ingush-Ossetian Conflict.* 1996.
Nekrich, Alexander. *The Punished Peoples.* 1978.
O'Ballance, Edgar. *Wars in the Caucasus, 1990–1995.* 1997.

IRISH

Erse; Gaelic

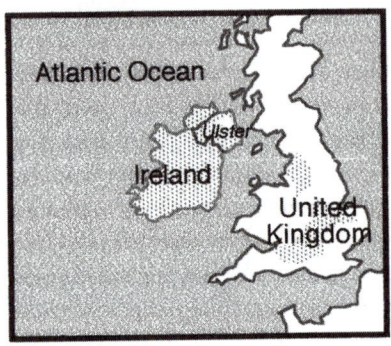

POPULATION: Approximately (2000 e) 5,895,000 Irish in Europe, 3,375,000 in the Irish Republic, and 1,770,000 in the United Kingdom, including 750,000 in Northern Ireland. Estimates of the number of Irish and people of Irish descent in the United Kingdom run as high as 8 million. Other large Irish populations are in the United States, Canada, Australia, and New Zealand. The total population of the Irish diaspora is estimated at many times the population of Ireland itself.

THE IRISH HOMELAND: The Irish homeland is an island in the North Atlantic Ocean. Ireland is the second largest of the British Isles, lying west of Great Britain, from which it is separated by the North Channel, the Irish Sea, and St. George's Channel. Most of the island consists of a central plain or lowland occupying the central and eastern sections, with many bogs and lakes (loughs) and groups of hills in the north, west, and south. The principal rivers of Ireland are the Erne and the Shannon, which are actually chains of lakes joined by stretches of river. The eastern coast of the island is fairly regular with few deep indentations; however, the western coast is deeply indented, and the irregular coastline has many good harbors, bays, and estuaries. Carrantouhill, rising to 3,414 feet (1,041 m.) above sea level and located in the southwest, is the highest point on the island. The rains, heavier in the west, are responsible for the brilliant green foliage, which gives the island the name "Emerald Isle."

Ireland is made up of two distinct political entities, the Republic of Ireland and Northern Ireland, which is a division of the United Kingdom of Great Britain and Northern Ireland. In the 1920s the island's four traditional provinces were divided, with Connaught, Leinster, Munster, and three counties of Ulster uniting in the Irish Free State, later the Irish Republic, and six counties of Ulster remaining under British rule as Northern Ireland. *Ireland*: 32,584 sq.mi.–84,392 sq.km. *Republic of Ireland (Eire)*: 27,132 sq.mi.–70,271 sq.km. (2000 e) 3,589,000—Irish 94%, Anglo-Irish 5%. *Northern Ireland (Ulster)*: 5,452 sq.mi.– 14,121 sq.km. (2000 e) 1,571,000—Scots-Irish (Protestant) 53%, Irish (Roman Catholic) 46%, other British. The capital city and major cultural center of Ireland is Dublin, called Baile Atha Cliath in the Gaelic language, (2000 e) 479,000 (metropolitan area 1,184,000). The capital and major cultural center of Northern Ireland is Belfast, Béal Feirste in Gaelic, (2000 e) 295,000 (metropolitan area 726,000).

FLAG: The Irish national flag, the official flag of the Irish Republic, is a vertical tricolor of green, white, and orange.

PEOPLE: The Irish are a Celtic people, descendants of immigrants thought to have settled the island from about 400 B.C. Related to the Scots,* Bretons,* Welsh,* Cornish,* and Galicians,* the Irish are one of Europe's most important Celtic nations. Dreamy and passionate, the Irish have produced some of the greatest writers of the nineteenth and twentieth centuries. Although known for fair hair, particularly red hair, and light eyes, many Irish are dark-haired, the result of the many invaders and migrants who have come to the island. About 62% of the Irish population lives in urban areas.

Gaelic or Irish Gaelic is the oldest of the Goidelic group of Celtic languages. Ancient written examples exist in the ogham inscriptions on about 370 gravestones scattered through southwestern Ireland and Wales. Dating from the fifth to the eighth centuries, the inscriptions consist almost entirely of proper names. The Celtic language of the Irish was supplanted by English in the eighteenth and nineteenth centuries and is now spoken by about 13% of the total Irish population, although efforts are being made to increase its use in daily life on both sides of the border. At the beginning of the twentieth century an estimated 50% of Ireland's population spoke Gaelic. The language is spoken in five distinct dialects, Munster, Connacht, Donegal, Leinster, and Ulster. English, the national language of both Ireland and Northern Ireland, spoken with a characteristic lilt, is divided into two dialects in Ireland, South Hiberno English and North Hiberno English.

The vast majority of the Irish are Roman Catholics, an estimated 97% of the population of the Irish Republic and 46% of the population of Northern Ireland, with a small Protestant minority in the republic and a large Protestant population in Northern Ireland. The birthrate of the Catholic Irish is higher than the average in Europe, with the Irish portion of the population of Northern Ireland growing more rapidly than the Protestant majority.

NATION: In the centuries before the Christian Era a number of small Celtic tribes invaded the island and established their distinctive culture while absorbing the island's earlier inhabitants. Ancient Irish legends tell of four successive tribes that invaded the country in ancient times, the Firbolgs, the Fomors, the Tuatha de Danann, and the Nemedians. These tribes are believed to have been eventually subdued by the Milesians, later called Scots. The Romans, who controlled England for 400 years, never came to Ireland, and little is known with certainty of the island before the fourth century A.D.

The Gaelic sagas and myths tell of the origins of the Irish and of the ultimate triumph, in the fourth century, of the Gaels. The Gaels' rich culture and pagan traditions were absorbed, rather than replaced, by the gradual adoption of Christianity under the influence of St. Patrick in the fifth century. Although Christianity had been previously introduced in some parts of the island, Patrick encountered great obstacles, and the new faith was not fully established until a century after his death around A.D. 461.

Isolated from the collapse of Roman power in Europe, the learning of past centuries was preserved by Irish monks in great libraries while the rest of Europe descended into the Dark Ages. Ireland's learning, craftsmanship, and Christian devotion were renowned. The richness of the Irish culture was augmented by contacts as far away as Iberia, North Africa, and the Middle East. Irish missionaries traveled to England and the European mainland, where they founded many monasteries and seats of religion and learning.

Celts and non-Celts were organized into clans, or tribes, which owed allegiance to one of five provincial kingdoms, Ulster, Munster, Connaught, Leinster, and Meath. These kings were nominal vassals of the high king of all Ireland at Tara. Until the introduction of Christianity, traditionally by St. Patrick in the fifth century, the clans warred among themselves, but despite civil strife, literacy and culture were greatly respected.

Viking raids, beginning in the eighth century, mostly ended the brilliant Irish civilization. Never united under a strong central authority, the Irish clans fell to the invading Norsemen, who settled the coastal areas and created new kingdoms. In 1014 at Clontarf, Brian Boru, who had become high king by conquest, defeated the Norse invaders. There followed a period of 150 years during which the island was free of foreign interference.

In the twelfth century Pope Adrian IV granted overlordship of Ireland to the Norman king of England, Henry II. The Anglo-Norman conquest of Ireland, 1169–71, began a struggle that continued for nearly 800 years. The English conquerors seized much of the land, dispossessed the native Irish, and exploited the country's resources, beginning the difficult landlord–tenant problem that plagued the Irish until modern times. The invasion destroyed the traditional Irish land laws but failed to effectively establish English law in their place. By the sixteenth century the Irish, including the Anglo-Irish nobility, had sunk into desperate poverty. The Protestant Reformation, adopted by the English,* but not by the Irish, gave the conflict between the disinherited Irish and their English masters a bitter religious element.

During the reign of Elizabeth I the English crushed three serious Irish rebellions against oppressive Protestant rule by soldiers turned loose to rape, pillage, and murder. To further punish the Irish rebels, much land in the northern province, Ulster, was confiscated, and Protestant settlers were brought to the region from Scotland. Another rebellion, brutally crushed by the English dictator Oliver Cromwell in 1651, cost 600,000 lives and ended with thousands of Irish, again mostly in Ulster, being dispossessed and driven from their lands. English Protestants were settled on the confiscated lands. Over the next century many more Protestants were settled in Ulster, which took on a distinctive Protestant character. Subsequent government policy in all of Ireland favored the Protestant minority.

The Roman Catholic Irish supported Catholic James I of England following the revolution of 1688, but James was defeated at the Battle of the Boyne in Ireland in 1690. New restrictions and laws were imposed on the Irish, both Roman Catholic and Protestant. Bitter rebellions and savage repression continued through the eighteenth and nineteenth centuries. Thousands of Irish left the island, often serving in the armies of Roman Catholic countries, particularly France and Spain, fighting the English. Protestant domination was maintained by a corrupt Irish parliament controlled by the agents of English absentee landlords. Thousands of Irish, both Roman Catholic and Protestant, emigrated to the colonies in North America.

The American Revolution provided an excuse for the raising of Protestant volunteers as a defensive military unit as Irish nationalism took hold. The volunteers, led by Henry Grattan, demanded and obtained trade concessions and an independent parliament, which remained restricted to Protestants only. In 1798 the Irish, under nationalist Wolfe Tone and the United Irishmen, including both Catholics and Protestants, rebelled unsuccessfully. As a result of the rebellion the Irish parliament was abolished. The growth of Irish nationalism during the nineteenth century made the Protestant population of the island even more pro-British.

The Irish language, Gaelic, declined rapidly during the nineteenth and early twentieth centuries. English, the language of education, became the predominant language of the majority of the Irish population.

Largely through the efforts of Daniel O'Connell, the most odious restrictions placed on the Roman Catholics were removed by the Catholic Emancipation Act of 1829. The Irish representative in the British Parliament, from that date, represented both the Protestants and the Roman Catholics of Ireland and kept the Irish question a major political issue throughout the next seventy-five years. They were supported in Ireland by an increasingly restive and nationalistic population.

The Irish land question, aggravated by the large number of absentee landlords, grew constantly more serious with the rapid growth of the population. When the potato blight struck the island in the 1840s, the population of the island was approximately 8.5 million. Between 1846 and 1851 around 1 million Irish died of hunger and disease, and by 1854 an estimated 1.6 million embittered Irish had emigrated, mostly to the United States but also to Canada, Australia, and

New Zealand. The Irish emigrant population in the United States continued the bitter opposition to the British government and organized the Fenian Movement, a revolutionary group dedicated to the separation of Ireland from Great Britain.

In the second half of the nineteenth century the religious divide widened. The Irish were forced to pay tithes to support the Protestant Church of Ireland until the church was disestablished in 1869. By the 1870s Irish sentiment favored self-determination and an end to British domination. The nationalists, led by Charles Steward Parnell, formed the Home Rule Movement to work for Irish autonomy. Irish nationalism was supported by the literary and cultural revival of the late nineteenth century. The Home Rule Movement, resisted by the British government, was gradually supplanted by the Sinn Fein, dedicated to the complete separation of Ireland from the United Kingdom.

After the turn of the century, the British government belatedly moved to grant home rule to quell the sporadic violence and demonstrations, but the majority of the Protestant population, alienated by the growth of Irish nationalism, were opposed. After the outbreak of World War I, serious rioting broke out across the country, and groups of Roman Catholics and Protestants, in spite of bans, succeeded in importing arms. On 14 July 1914 the Protestants declared a provisional government with the power to call up volunteers, the Ulster Volunteers, to fight for Great Britain. In the south, the Irish Volunteers were organized as a Catholic military unit. The threat of civil war over the question of Irish independence was imminent, but the crisis was temporarily averted by the outbreak of World War I, and both groups joined the war effort.

In the spring of 1916 the Irish Catholics, led by the Sinn Fein Movement, rebelled against British rule. The Easter Rebellion was defeated, with the participation of the Protestant Ulster Volunteers, but the movement continued as guerrilla warfare, largely led by Irish nationalist Michael Collins. On 21 January 1919 Irish nationalist leaders declared the independence of Ireland but were suppressed. The Protestants of Ulster, fearing domination by the Roman Catholic majority, vehemently opposed separation from the United Kingdom. In 1920 the British government attempted to restore order with a group of paramilitaries, the Black and Tan, who terrorized the country, setting off months of ferocious warfare and strengthening the Irish will to resist.

In 1920 the six northern counties with Protestant majorities accepted the Home Rule Bill, separating most of Ulster from the rest of Ireland. In December 1920 the Government of Ireland Act established separate parliaments in Dublin and Belfast. A Council of Ireland representing the two Irelands was to attempt to effect common action. The British prime minister, David Lloyd George, in 1921 began negotiations with the leader of Sinn Fein, Eamon de Valera. The result was the establishment of the Irish Free State in the remaining twenty-six counties. Religion became an integral part of both Irish and Northern Irish ideology.

Many Irish nationalists refused to accept the division of the Irish homeland, and Sinn Fein split into moderates and republican groups. A period of terrorism and civil war followed, but the boundary between the Free State and Northern Ireland was fixed after long negotiations in 1925. The Irish Republican Army (IRA) refused to accept the treaty that recognized the separate government in Northern Ireland. The moderate nationalists finally prevailed, and in 1937 Ireland was established as a sovereign state within the British Commonwealth of Nations. Attempts at unification continued until 1938, when elections in Northern Ireland resulted in an overwhelming victory for the Protestant Unionists. Under the Unionist government the Catholic minority in Ulster suffered discrimination in education, employment, and religion.

Southern Ireland remained neutral during World War II, even though some 600,000 Irish volunteers served with the British forces. Northern Ireland, particularly Belfast, suffered heavily in German bombing raids. The outlawed IRA continued with sporadic bombings and shootings to agitate for the end of the partition of Ireland. After World War II, emigration, mostly to Britain and the United States and Canada, led to a decline in population.

In 1948 the Irish prime minister, John A. Costello, demanded final independence and the unification of Ireland and the six counties of Ulster. Unification, resisted by the British government and the Protestant majority in the north, remained the goal, but on Easter Monday, 18 April 1949, the anniversary of the 1916 Easter Rebellion, the Irish government withdrew Ireland from the Commonwealth, and a republic was proclaimed. The following month the British parliament confirmed the status of Northern Ireland as part of the United Kingdom. The new Irish republican government claimed jurisdiction over the six northern counties, but the British government asserted its right to incorporate the six counties into the United Kingdom. The Protestants of Northern Ireland rejected ties to the Irish Republic and declared their continuing loyalty to the British government.

Relations between the Republic and Northern Ireland steadily improved during the 1950s, but as late as 1961 there were raids across the border by members of the IRA. During the early 1960s Northern Ireland had one of the lowest crime rates in the United Kingdom, although official discrimination continued against the Catholic minority. The Catholics, watching American civil rights demonstrations on television, began to demonstrate for Catholic civil rights in Ulster in 1966.

In 1969 violence broke out between Catholics and Protestants in Ulster with street fighting and communal riots. The British government intervened militarily, but the two communities became armed camps. The IRA and other nationalist organizations turned to terrorism, with their aim a united, socialist Ireland. The Provisional IRA, its military wing, fought pitched battles with British troops and Protestant paramilitary units. By 1972 the British had 21,000 troops in Northern Ireland. Home rule for Northern Ireland, attempted in the 1970s, was ended by extremists on both sides.

The Irish Republic joined the European Economic Community (EEC) on 1 January 1973, along with Northern Ireland, as part of the United Kingdom. A referendum held in the Republic ended the special constitutional status of the Roman Catholic Church. Irish membership in the continental alliance aided the growth of the economy in the Republic, where unemployment fell, and the benefits of economic growth were felt across the country. The Irish living in Northern Ireland, where in some areas unemployment had climbed to 50% by 1985, continued to suffer discrimination.

The sectarian violence in Northern Ireland, Europe's longest conflict, left in its wake 2,400 dead and over 20,000 injured by the mid-1980s. Called Ulster by the Protestants and Northern Ireland by the Catholics, the region remained under British military occupation; however, not all the Roman Catholics in the north favored unification with Ireland, where standards of living were lower, and bans on abortion and divorce remained in effect. In 1985 34% of Northern Ireland's Catholics wished to remain in the United Kingdom, 47% favored unification, and 19% were undecided. Protestant groups have vowed to fight to the death rather than to submit to rule from Dublin.

Rapid economic growth and changing attitudes to women's role in Irish society were demonstrated by the election of Mary Robinson as president in November 1990. She was the first woman to hold so high an office in the Republic of Ireland. However, when the Irish government signed the Treaty of European Union at Maastricht, the Netherlands, in December 1991, it was only after securing a special provision that guaranteed that the Republic's abortion laws would not be affected by future European Union policies. The provision was strongly opposed by many women's groups. In the November 1992 election, Irish voters approved measures guaranteeing access to information about abortion and legalized foreign travel to obtain an abortion but rejected a constitutional amendment that would have broadened the availability of abortion within the republic. These changes were overturned by a July 1993 Irish Supreme Court decision, which upheld a ban on the distribution of overseas abortion information by a Dublin clinic.

In December 1993 the Irish and British governments agreed to a peace plan for Northern Ireland. In 1994 the IRA and Sinn Fein, its political wing, agreed to a cease-fire, and in February 1995 the Irish and British governments established a framework for negotiating the status of Northern Ireland. The document recognized Northern Ireland's right to self-determination, expanded its autonomy and representation in the British government, and proposed the creation of a joint Irish and Northern Irish parliament. However, the two sides failed to agree on the disarming of the IRA, which resumed its terrorist activities in February 1996.

To an extent unknown in the rest of Western Europe, religion determines a person's way of life in Northern Ireland. While violence seems to run in cycles, job and housing discrimination against the Roman Catholic minority remained a constant throughout the years of the so-called Troubles. Although the Protestant minority in the south is small, they tend to be well integrated and content. Liberalization of the antiquated abortion and divorce laws gradually brought the

Irish Republic into line with the rest of the European Union (EU) in the mid-1990s. In February 1997 a law legalizing divorce under certain circumstances went into effect.

The Irish, with the fastest growing economy in the EU, in the 1990s became a center of high technology and the headquarters for many foreign companies wishing to do business in the union. The young and highly educated population helped the country move into the ranks of the richer European nations. Emigration, formerly the only alternative to unemployment and a lack of opportunity, was slowly reversed, with many Irish emigrants returning to Ireland to work in the booming computer and electronic industries.

SELECTED BIBLIOGRAPHY

Ardagh, John. *Ireland and the Irish: Portrait of a Changing Society.* 1995.

Harkness, David. *Ireland in the Twentieth Century: Divided Island.* 1996.

Hennessey, Thomas. *Dividing Ireland: World War One and Partition.* 1998.

O'Brien, Jacqueline, and Peter Harbison. *Ancient Ireland: From Prehistory to the Middle Ages.* 1996.

Thomas, Colin, and Avril Thomas. *Historical Dictionary of Ireland.* 1997.

ISTRIANS

Istra; Istriots

POPULATION: Approximately (2000 e) 412,000 Istrians in Europe, mostly in Croatia, estimated at 245,000, and Slovenia, with 77,000.

THE ISTRIAN HOMELAND: The Istrian homeland occupies a heavily wooded, mountainous peninsula projecting into the Adriatic Sea between the Gulfs of Trieste and Rijeka just south of the Karst Plateau in southwestern Slovenia and northwestern Croatia. The peninsula is about sixty miles (ninety-seven km.) from its base near Trieste to its southern point. The region is heavily forested and predominantly agricultural; however, tourism and trade through its port cities have increased in importance since 1991. Istria is known for its gently rolling scenery, pleasant climate, good wines, coastal tourist resorts, and beautiful beaches.

Istria has no official status; the region forms the Istria district of Croatia and the Koper district of Slovenia. *Region of Istria (Istra)*: 1,545 sq.mi.–4,005 sq.km. (2000 e) 381,000—Istrians 91%, Italians* 8%, Friulis,* other Croats,* other Slovenes.* The Istrian capital and major cultural center is Pulj, also known as Pula, (2000 e) 67,000, at the southern tip of the peninsula in Croatia. The major Istrian cultural center in Slovenian Istria is the capital of the region, Koper, called Capodistria in Italian, (2000 e) 24,000.

FLAG: The Istrian national flag, the traditional flag of the region and the flag of the national movement, is a horizontal tricolor of yellow, red, and blue.

PEOPLE: The Istrians, who refer to themselves as an Istro-Romanic people, are a distinct nation that has developed over centuries of mixed Slav, Germanic, and Latin elements. Their homeland has a long history as a crossroads of cultures and languages, while the strong sense of a separate Istrian identity has developed mostly since World War II. The Istrian culture, an amalgam of many influences, embraces not only the Istrians but also the Italian and Friuli minorities. Extensive intermarriage, particularly in the decades since the 1950s, has added greatly to the development of a separate Istrian identity. The Istrians are mostly Roman Catholic, but with smaller Protestant and Muslim minorities.

The Istrians mostly speak Croat and Slovene, but historically they spoke Istriot, a Romance language of the Italo-Romance group of Italo-Western languages. The language survives but is spoken by only about 1,000 people as their first language, mostly in the towns of Rovinj and Vodnjan. Another language, called Istro-Romanian, more closely related to Romanian, is spoken by fewer than 1,000 in a few villages in the northeastern part of the peninsula. Many Istrians, estimated at over 100,000, also speak the Istrian dialect of the language spoken by the Venetians* of northeastern Italy.

NATION: Settlements developed in the region during the Bronze Age, with the region taking its name from the Illyrian tribe called the Histri. The first mention of the region occurred in the third century B.C., in the writings of the Greek poets Callimachus and Lycophron, the story of Jason and the Golden Fleece. According to legend, the Cholcheans chasing Jason and the stolen golden fleece, unable to recover the treasure, feared returning home, so they settled among the Histri and founded a city, called the City of Refugees, in their language, Polai, later called Pula.

The region fell to the invading Romans in 177 B.C. Over several centuries of Roman rule, the Istrians adopted the Roman culture and language. In 46–45 B.C. the region became a Roman colony, with a great spurt in development and construction. Roman towns, complete with elegant buildings, villas, theaters, and public areas, dotted the lush Istrian landscape. The colony backed the losing side in the civil war that divided the empire from 42 to 31 B.C. The victor, Octavian, ordered the capital, Pula, destroyed, and Roman legions were set loose on the peninsula, destroying most of the towns and villages. But due to its advantageous geographical situation, the region soon recovered and was rebuilt. Caesar Augustus transformed Pula into an imperial city, and over several centuries monumental examples of Roman architecture were constructed, including the sixth largest amphitheater in the Roman world, seating 23,000 people.

Barbarian tribes from the north, taking advantage of the collapse of Roman power in A.D. 476, invaded the peninsula. Huns and Ostrogoths overran the region, and several decades of anarchy ensued before the rule of the Eastern Roman Empire at Byzantium was established. Migrating Slav tribes, the ancestors of the Croats and Slovenes, settled the peninsula and accepted nominal Byzantine rule in the sixth century. The Slavic settlers settled among the Latin population and soon adopted much of the Latin culture that still dominated.

The peninsula was divided between several neighboring states following the collapse of Byzantine authority in 752. Dominated by a series of local overlords, the major powers in Europe, Venice and the Frankish kingdom, vied for authority in the region. In 788 most of the region was included in the March of

Istria, part of Charlemagne's empire. The southern coast formed part of the Venetian state. In the tenth century the duchy of Bavaria gained control of most of the peninsula, which was again split, in the thirteenth century, between Venice, the dukes of Carinthia, the patriarchs of Aquileia, and the counts of Gorizia.

In 1347 the northeastern part of Istria passed to the Hapsburg family, and in 1420 the southwestern districts came under the direct rule of the Venetians. The northern part, under Hapsburg rule, formed a separate crownland of the Austrian Empire. The southern districts passed to Austria under the terms of the Treaty of Campoformio in 1797. Under Austrian rule the peninsula formed part of a region of mixed Italian, South Slav, and Austrian population.

Austria, at war with Napoleonic France, lost the peninsula to French rule in 1805. The new French administration added the peninsula to the Illyrian provinces but allowed a measure of autonomy. In 1813 the peninsula was returned to Austrian rule. The Istrians, after centuries of foreign rule, began to realize that they had more in common with their immediate neighbors, Slav, Italian, or Austrian, than with populations outside their peninsula.

In the late nineteenth century the large Italian-speaking population became the subject of irredentist claims by the newly united Italian kingdom, and a movement to unite the peninsula with Italy gained support. In 1915, to entice Italy into the war, the Allies promised Istria and other Italian-speaking Austrian territories to Italy.

In the wake of Austria's defeat in World War I, in 1918 a strong movement for separate Istrian independence won widespread support. The prospect of dividing the interdependent region whose peoples had coexisted for centuries stimulated the Istrian national movement. In October 1918 the regional parliament at Trieste, the capital of the Austrian crownland, voted to erect an autonomous Republic of Venezia-Giulia under the protection of the new League of Nations, an Italo-Croat-Slovene state to include Trieste and its territory, the Julian region, and the Istrian Peninsula.

The fate of the Istrians remained unsettled until 1920, when the entire region was placed under Italian administration. The area's economic and political importance declined rapidly under Italian rule, particularly following the fascist takeover of Italy in 1922. The fascists instituted programs designed to homogenize the many regional cultures and to eradicate the non-Italian influences. In 1926 the government banned the Slav languages and many of the South Slav traditions. All family names were ordered changed to names agreeable to the fascist authorities.

The outbreak of World War II exacerbated the peninsula's simmering ethnic and regional tensions. Pro-fascist, pro-Allied, Istrian nationalist, and Yugoslav-supported pro-communists clashed with rival groups and the Italian army. The peninsula became a battleground. In the spring of 1945, following the German withdrawal, Tito's Yugoslav partisans occupied the peninsula. Thousands of Istrians, both Italian and Slav, real or imagined fascists, anticommunists, and others opposed to communist Yugoslav rule, were rounded up and executed. In an orgy of revenge the partisans tossed the bodies of men, women, and children from the Istrian cliffs into the Adriatic Sea. The Yugoslav communist authorities expelled over 300,000 Italian Istrians between 1945 and 1951.

Yugoslavia received most of Istria in the postwar territorial transfers in 1946; however, the west of the peninsula, due to the ongoing territorial dispute, became part of the new Free City of Trieste under United Nations auspices in 1947. In 1954 the state of Trieste was divided by Italy and Yugoslavia. The city of Trieste and its environs became part of Italy, and the southern zone went to Yugoslavia, divided between the Yugoslav republics of Slovenia and Croatia. Istrian opposition to the division between the two Yugoslav republics was one of the reasons that the Treaty of Osimo was not ratified by Yugoslavia and Italy until 1975.

The collapse of the communist Yugoslav state in 1991 again divided Istria, this time between the independent republics of Slovenia and Croatia. The new Croatian government, under a resolute nationalist administration began to limit local government autonomy and passed new laws that threatened Istrian culture. With excellent interethnic relations in the peninsula, the Croat Istrians rejected the virulent nationalism emanating from Zagreb and began to campaign for closer ties to the neighboring Istrian Slovenes and the Italians.

In 1990, even before the disintegration of Yugoslavia, the Istrians had formed the Istrian Democratic Diet (Dieta Democratica Istriana, DDI), a trilingual, triethnic forum that advocated autonomy for the peninsula. Nationalists put forward plans for a transnational autonomy of two sovereign provinces, one in Croatia with its capital at Pula, the other in Slovenia with its capital at Koper. The Croatian Istrians in February 1993 firmly rejected Croatia's aggressive nationalism. The Istrian party, the DDI, won 72% of the vote as opposed to the Croat national party's 16%. The DDI won on a platform of liberal tolerance and the creation of a multiethnic region away from the chaos and violence of the former Yugoslavia. The Italian-speaking Istrians, many of whom fled communist rule after World War II, formed the Istrian Union in Trieste to press for their right to return to their homes in Istria. The Italians, with good relations with the Slavic Istrians, have been supported by local Istrian groups.

An ongoing border dispute between Slovenia and Croatia over the Istrian Bay of Pirin is fueling Istrian nationalism and demands for a separate transborder Istrian region. However, the bitter territorial dispute has been put aside, an agreement on outside arbitration was agreed to in 1997, and the Slovenian and Croatian governments are united in their opposition to the growing Istrian national movement.

SELECTED BIBLIOGRAPHY

Bendery, Jill, and Evan Kraft, eds. *Independent Slovenia: Origins, Movements, Prospects.* 1996.

Macan, Tripimir. *A Short History of Croatia.* 1992.

McAdams, Michael C. *Croatia: Myth and Reality.* 1997.

Novak, Bogan C. *Trieste 1941 to 1954: The Ethnic Politics and Ideological Struggle.* 1970.

Plut-Pregelj, Leopoldina. *Historical Dictionary of Slovenia.* 1996.

ITALIANS

Italianos

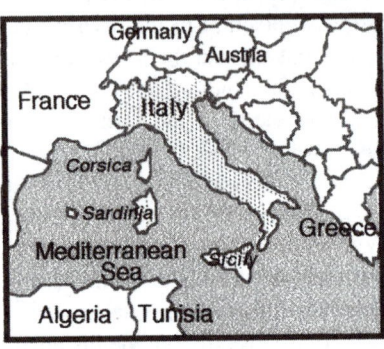

POPULATION: Approximately (2000 e) 57,125,000 Italians in Europe, 54,690,000 in Italy, and with large populations in France, about 1 million, Croatia, 330,000, Belgium, Germany, and the United Kingdom. Large Italian populations outside Europe are in Argentina, Brazil, Canada, Australia, the United States, and Uruguay.

THE ITALIAN HOMELAND: The Italian homeland lies in Southern Europe, a long peninsula jutting into the Mediterranean Sea and separated from the rest of Europe by the Alps on the north. More than half of the Italian homeland consists of the Italian Peninsula, a long projection of the continental European mainland. Shaped like a boot, the peninsula extends generally southeast into the Mediterranean Sea. The Alps overlook the northern plains, which are drained by the Po River, Italy's most fertile and densely populated region. The Apennines is a long mountain range that forms the backbone of the peninsula. Southwestern Italy is volcanic, with a string of volcanoes stretching from Vesuvius, near Naples, to Mt. Etna in Sicily. The large islands of Sicily and Sardinia lie in the Mediterranean west of the peninsula. The industrial north, largely integrated with the rest of Europe, contrasts greatly with the agrarian and poorer south.

Italy remained politically divided until the middle of the nineteenth century, and regional loyalties remain strong and vibrant. The Italian Republic consists of twenty regional governments, based on Italy's historic geography and with some autonomy, divided into ninety-four provinces. *Republic of Italy (Republica Italiana)*: 116,320 sq.mi.–301,270 sq.km. (2000 e) 58,083,000—Italians (including Ligurians,* Lombards,* Piedmontese,* Venetians,* and Sicilians*)

94%, Sards* 3%, Tyroleans,* French,* Greeks,* Albanians,* Slovenians,* Ladins.* The Italian capital and major cultural center is Rome, Roma in Italian, (2000 e) 2,724,000, in the center of the peninsula.

FLAG: The Italian flag, the official flag of the republic, is a vertical tricolor of green, white, and red.

PEOPLE: The Italians are a Latin people, a mixture of Germanic and Mediterranean peoples, the heirs of a long and glorious history. The political and cultural divisions of the Italian peoples remain sharp to the present, with regional dialects and cultures vying for the loyalty of the distinct Italian national groups. In spite of a carefree and nonchalant attitude, the Italians are a hardworking and frugal nation and are among the most ardent supporters of European integration. The Italian population is about 71% urban, with urban populations mostly concentrated in the northern regions. Italy can be generally divided into the more urban north and the mostly rural south. The dividing line, which runs across the peninsula from the port of Ancona, is called the "Ancona Wall" by Italians.

The dominant religion of the Italians is Roman Catholicism, the faith of about 84% of the population. However, the church's role in Italy is declining, with only about 25% attending services regularly. A law ratified in 1985 abolished the role of the Roman Catholic Church as the official state church and ended mandatory religious instruction in Italian schools.

Standard Italian, an Italo-Romance language based on a Tuscan dialect, is the national language and is spoken throughout the country, but wide regional, dialectical differences remain. Some experts estimate that only about half the Italian population uses standard Italian as the first language. Piedmontese, Sicilian, Venetian, and Lombard are distinct enough to be considered separate languages. Neapolitan, spoken in southern Italy, is often unintelligible to speakers of standard Italian.

NATION: The history of the Italian Peninsula before the fifth century B.C. is mostly speculation, except for those regions in southern Italy and Sicily where the Greeks had established colonies. The earliest known inhabitants of the peninsula were probably of Ligurian stock.

The Etruscans, probably originally from Asia Minor, established themselves in central Italy around 800 B.C. They reduced the Ligurians to the status of slaves or serfs while establishing a brilliant and civilized empire. In the fourth century B.C. the Celts, called Gauls by the Romans, invaded the peninsula and drove the Etruscans from the Po Valley. In the south the Etruscan expansion was checked by the Samnites, who had adopted much Greek culture. The Latins, living along the coast of central Italy, were never fully subjugated by the Etruscans. They and their neighbors, the Sabines, traditionally formed the ancestors of the Romans.

Evidence unearthed by archaeologists in 1988 shows Rome as a dynamic, highly civilized society as early as the sixth and seventh centuries B.C. Rome emerged as the major power in Italy in the fifth century B.C., dominating the more civilized Etruscans to the north and the Greeks to the south. The Roman

Empire, of which Italy formed the core, eventually expanded to include most of Western Europe, the Balkans, Asia Minor, the Middle East, and North Africa. By the beginning of the Christian Era all of Italy had been thoroughly Latinized, and Roman citizenship had been extended to all free Italians.

The growth of Christianity in Italy in the second century A.D. divided the population. For the first centuries the church was a martyr's church, and its adherents and persecution were legal, motivated by the Christians' refusal to worship the state and the emperor. In A.D. 313, Constantin I issued the Edict of Milan, which began a period of toleration of the growing Christian sect. The bishop of Rome became the leading figure in the church hierarchy, which remained separate from the Roman state.

The decline of Rome's power in the fourth century A.D. left the empire open to invaders. The overthrow of the last Roman emperor, Romulus Augustulus, by Germanic mercenaries serving the weakened Roman state in 476 is traditionally the end of the Roman Empire. The assumption of rule in Italy by a tribal chief, Odoacer, as king of Rome changed little, as Rome had long been prey to the barbarian soldiers, and the emperors had been mere puppets. The Roman administration of Italy continued to function under Odoacer's rule. The Roman emperors of the East, residing at Byzantium, who had never renounced their claim to Italy, backed Theodoric, king of the Ostrogoths, who murdered Odoacer and began a long and beneficial rule in Italy. Theodoric, like Odoacer, maintained the Roman institutions.

In the sixth century the Byzantines reconquered Italy, but in most of the peninsula their rule was soon displaced by that of the Lombards, who established a new kingdom in 569. The papacy became the chief bulwark of Latin civilization during the Germanic conquests. Gregory I, without assistance from Byzantium, saved Rome and the Patrimony of St. Peter from the Lombard conquest, laying the basis of the Papal States in central Italy.

The rivalry between the Lombards and the Franks for control of Italy ended Lombard hegemony. In 800 Charlemagne, after defeating the Lombard king, was crowned emperor of the West by the pope at Rome. Following the division of Charlemagne's Frankish Empire, local power became increasingly strong in Italy. A series of weak rulers and the increasing degradation of the papacy in the ninth and tenth centuries left Italy divided among petty, feuding princes and prelates. The German king Otto I invaded Italy at the request of the pope and was crowned king of Italy. In 962 he was crowned emperor by the pope. The union of Italy and Germany was the beginning of the Holy Roman Empire.

In the eleventh and twelfth centuries the prevailing chaos in Italy was increased by the quarrel between the emperors and the popes. The independence of many local rulers and the gradual freeing of the cities prevented feudalism from gaining a strong foothold in central and northern Italy. Trade with the Muslim world made merchants and towns the middlemen for much of Western Europe. The rise of the city-states in northern Italy was aided by the survival of Roman institutions and the example of the commune of Rome, under the rule of the popes. Leagues of cities were strong enough to defy the emperor, while the conflict between the papacy and the emperors continued to divide the cities and prevented any union strong enough to extend control over any substantial part of Italy.

Gradually, local ruling families and the powerful republican city-states began to extend their authority at the expense of weaker neighbors. Numerous small states emerged, along with two great merchant republics, Venice and Genoa. Constant wars between the states, generally fought by mercenaries, did less harm than the Black Death, which ravaged Italy in the fourteenth century. The material prosperity of northern Italy facilitated the great cultural flowering known as the Renaissance, which permanently changed the direction and character of Western civilization. The Renaissance reached its zenith in the late fifteenth century, even while Italy's political independence was threatened by the rise of imperialistic states in France, Spain, and Austria.

The invasion of northern Italy by the French in 1494 marked the beginning of the Italian Wars, which ended in 1559 with most of Italy under Spanish rule or influence. Italian statesmen, particularly Niccolò Machiavelli, one of the outstanding figures of the Renaissance, realized that only unity could save Italy from foreign subjugation, but unity was never achieved. Pope Julius II consolidated the Papal States under his rule, but his Holy League, an alliance to drive out the French, failed to unite the petty Italian states. Political weakness was accompanied by a period of economic decline. The center of European trade shifted away from the Mediterranean, further eroding the Italians' influence in European affairs.

The French Revolution rekindled Italian nationalism, and the Napoleonic Wars swept away the political landscape of eighteenth-century Italy. Napoleon Bonaparte, who first triumphed against the Sardinians and Austrians in 1796–97, was at first welcomed by most Italians. Napoleon redrew the political map of Italy several times. The Cispadane and the Transpadane Republics, established by Napoleon in 1796, were united a year later as the Cisalpine Republic, which comprised Lombardy and Emilia-Romagna. The Cisalpine Republic became the Italian Republic in 1802 and in 1805, with the addition of Venetia, became the Kingdom of Italy with Napoleon as king. Between 1795 and 1812 nearly all of northern and central Italy was annexed by France. Napoleon's failure to unite Italy or to give the Italians self-government disappointed many of his earlier supporters and spurred the growth of Italian nationalism.

The Congress of Vienna, convened to redraw the map of Europe at the end of the Napoleonic Wars, generally restored the pre-Napoleonic borders and the old ruling families. Austrian influence in northern Italy became paramount, but efforts to suppress the growing Italian nationalism failed. The Risorgimento, as the movement for unification was known, embraced many distinct groups and aims, republican, monarchist, and religious. Unification was ultimately achieved under the House of Savoy, the ruling house of the Kingdom of Sardinia, which was centered on Piedmont. Italian unification, largely through the efforts of the

Sardinian premier, Camillo Benso, conti de Cavour, and Guiseppe Garibaldi began in Northern Italy. Cavour, the force behind King Victor Emmanuel II of Sardinia, is credited with being the man who finally accomplished Italian unity under the House of Savoy in 1860–61. Garibaldi, at the head of 1,000 irregulars called Red Shirts, conquered southern Italy, which he relinquished to united Italy. The French protectorate over the Papal States delayed the unification of Rome and central Italy with the expanded kingdom until 1870. Italian irredentism, the movement for the annexation to Italy of territories, called Italia irredenta, inhabited by large, Italian-speaking populations but retained by Austria after 1866, gained support.

From 1861 until the 1920s Italy was ruled under the liberal constitution adopted by the Sardinian kingdom in 1848. The late nineteenth century and the early years of the twentieth century were marked by moderate social and political reforms and industrialization. Periodic unrest and economic stagnation led to mass emigration to the Americas, particularly from southern Italy.

During World War I the Italians at first remained neutral, but following Allied promises of territorial gains, particularly in Italia irredenta, Italy entered the war in 1915 on the Allied side. Though suffering serious setbacks, the Italians finally won a great victory at Vittorio Veneto, which was followed by the collapse of Austria-Hungary. At the Paris Peace Conference in 1919 the Italians obtained South Tyrol, Trieste, Istria, part of Carniola, and several Dalmatian islands, but the territorial gains were far less than the Allies had promised.

Italian discontent fed the growth of Italian fascism. From 1919 to 1922 Italy was torn by social and political strife, inflation, and economic problems, aggravated by the belief that Italy had won the war but lost the peace. A period of instability followed the collapse of the government in 1922. Many landowners feared the seizure of their estates by peasants; the middle class and the industrialists feared a Soviet-style republic; and conservative Roman Catholics worried that radical political organizations threatened the religious order.

On 24 October 1922 the fascist leader Benito Mussolini, emboldened by the support of the conservatives and former soldiers, demanded that the government be entrusted to his party and threatened to seize power by force if his conditions were refused. He directed his march on Rome on 27 October 1922 and was named premier by the king. He headed a coalition government in 1923 that included Liberals, Nationalists, and Catholics, as well as fascists. After the violence of the 1924 elections Mussolini moved to suspend constitutional government and proceeded in stages to establish a dictatorship.

Mussolini increasingly imposed strict controls on chaotic Italy while promising the restoration of order and the return of the political greatness of ancient Rome, but the fascist economic program mostly failed as the worldwide depression spread after 1929. Mussolini turned more and more to the military and his imperialistic dreams, conquering Ethiopia in 1935–36 and drawing closer to Nazi Germany and to Japan. In 1936–39, the Italians intervened in the Spanish civil war and in 1939 conquered and annexed Albania.

When World War II broke out in September 1939, Mussolini took the position that he was under no obligation to aid the Germans,* and Italy initially remained neutral. However, German successes during the first year of the war led Mussolini to reverse his policy. In June 1940 the Italian government declared war on collapsing France and on the United Kingdom. In attacks on North Africa and in Greece, the Italians were unsuccessful, until German troops came to their aid. In 1941 the Italians declared war on Russia and the United States. By mid-1943 Italy had lost its African colonies, American troops were moving north from Sicily, many cities and ports were being heavily bombed, and the Italian population was suffering from Allied attacks and from growing hunger. Mussolini was finally dismissed by the king, the Fascist Party was dissolved, and a new Italian government declared war on Germany. Mussolini was later killed by partisans in the north. In May 1945 the Germans, who had occupied northern Italy, surrendered.

Postwar Italy was beset by many problems, with economic problems widespread and the problem of the unpopular monarchy dividing the population. King Victor Emmanuel II abdicated on 28 April 1946 in favor of his son, Humbert II. Nearly 25 million voters, who for the first time included women, voted in the general elections of early June 1946, resulting in 54.3% favoring the end of the monarchy. On 10 June 1946 the Italian homeland became a de facto republic. Three days later King Humbert abdicated and left the country.

Since the late 1960s Italy has experienced dramatic social, economic, political, and religious developments. In 1968 students demanding educational reforms clashed with police on university campuses in Rome and other cities, and workers called general strikes to urge an overhaul of the social security system. Feminist issues became more important as a divorce law was adopted in 1973, and abortion was legalized in 1978.

The Italians have enjoyed growth in industry and growing prosperity since World War II, partly due to Italy's membership in the European Economic Community (EEC). The so-called Italian Miracle, the rapid postwar economic growth, was mostly confined to northern Italy, while the south remained backward in spite of government aid programs. This forced many southerners to leave the poor south to find jobs in the north or abroad. In 1950 Italy was a mainly agricultural society, but by the 1970s the country had become a leading industrial power. However, political instability continued with severe social problems, corruption at high levels of society, and a succession of weak coalition governments.

In the June 1975 regional elections the communists won 33% of the vote and pressed the government to support a long-term alliance between communism and Roman Catholicism. In parliamentary elections in June 1976 the communists made more gains, winning 35% of the vote; the Christian Democrats won 39%. A wave of left-wing political violence began in the late 1970s with kidnappings and assassinations and continued into the 1980s.

The northern regions in the 1980s, disillusioned with Rome's bloated bureaucracy and with the massive funds transferred to the corrupt and backward south, began to agitate for autonomy and the expulsion of foreigners, both from outside and from southern Italy. The northern rebellion, which took on cultural and political colorings, threatens to split Italy into two or more sovereign states.

In the 1990s growing corruption scandals brought demands for political reforms. In 1992 Italian voters ended the long rule of the Christian Democrats, who ran the country from the end of World War II. In 1993 Italian voters approved reforms in a referendum, and new political groupings emerged. A right-wing coalition was formed in 1994, but like its predecessors it, too, fell. The election in 1996 was won by the left-wing Olive Tree alliance. A center-right coalition managed to pull Italy into the single European currency in 1998 in spite of ongoing fiscal difficulties, but in later local elections, the opposition did well, including the Christian Democrats; however, an ex-Communist, Massimo D'Alema, in October 1998 became Italy's new prime minister.

On the threshold of the twenty-first century, the Italian population is aging fast, while the Italians' fertility rate is thought to be Europe's lowest. Once known for big weddings, big families, and many children, the Italians now produce fewer births than deaths, and the Italian population in Europe is falling.

SELECTED BIBLIOGRAPHY

Ginsborg, Paul. *A History of Contemporary Italy: Society and Politics, 1943–1988.* 1990.
Hearder, Harry. *Italy in the Age of the Risorgimento, 1790–1870.* 1983.
Hine, David. *Governing Italy: The Politics of Bargained Government.* 1992.
Pollard, John F. *The Fascist Experience in Italy.* 1998.
Robson, Mark. *Italy: Liberalism and Fascism 1870–1945.* 1992.

JERSIANS

Jèrriais

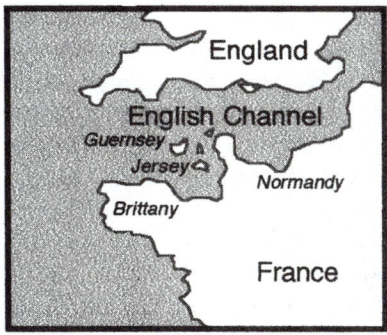

POPULATION: Approximately (2000 e) 102,000 Jersians in Europe, mostly in Jersey, but with a large Jersian population in the United Kingdom.

THE JERSIAN HOMELAND: Jersey is an island lying in the English Channel twelve miles (nineteen km.) west of the Cotentin Peninsula of Normandy in France and southeast of Guernsey. The island, eleven miles long by five miles wide, is the largest of the Channel Islands archipelago, which the Jersians often call the Norman Islands. The mild, subtropical climate, moderate rainfall, and beautiful scenery have contributed to Jersey's popularity as a vacation destination.

The soil is generally good, and large quantities of vegetables are grown, particularly tomatoes and early vegetables and fruits for the British market. Cattle raising and dairying, with its own breed of Jersey cattle, are important to the economy.

Jersey forms a bailiwick, a self-governing dependency of the British crown. The Jersey state is not subject to the British government or parliament unless specifically mentioned in legislation. *Bailiwick of Jersey*. 45 sq.mi.–117 sq.km. (2000 e) 86,900—Jersians 85%, English* 7%, Normans* 4%, other British. The Jersian capital and major cultural center is St. Helier, (2000 e) 28,000.

FLAG: The Jersian national flag, the official flag of the Jersey state, is a white field bearing a red paltaire, and often with a red shield with three gold lions surmounted by a gold crown.

PEOPLE: The Jersians, calling themselves Jèrriais, are the descendants of early Norman colonists with admixtures of later French religious refugees and migrants from Great Britain. The culture of the islanders is a unique blend of

Norman, French, and British, although the majority of the population claim Norman ancestry. The majority of the Jersians are Roman Catholic, with a small Protestant minority.

Although French is the official language of the state, a Norman dialect quite distinct from French is the language of daily life. The dialect, which is older than modern French, is not part of the formal educational system, but increasingly, language classes and schools are reviving the language. The Jersians fear that without these efforts their unique culture and language will disappear within fifty years.

NATION: The island of Jersey has been inhabited since ancient times. Ancient stone structures such as cromlechs and menhirs are evidence of early occupation. Included in the Roman province of Gaul, the Celts, called Gauls by the Romans, formed the first large population to occupy the island. Following the collapse of Roman power in the fifth century, the island fell to invading Franks, Germanic tribes moving into the former Roman provinces.

Christianity was brought to the island in the sixth century. Traditionally, the island's patron saint, St. Helier, led the conversion of the pagan islanders. The conversion to Christianity marked the beginning of the development of a distinct culture on the island.

Vikings, called Norsemen, took control of the island in the eighth century. Later known as Normans, the Norsemen came to the island from the large mainland French territory they had earlier conquered. In A.D. 933 Jersey became a dependency of the Duchy of Normandy, and with the Norman conquest of England, in 1066, Jersey was joined to the new Norman monarchy of England. The French seized mainland Normandy in 1117, but the Norman Islands, protected by England's fleet, remained with the Norman-dominated English kingdom. The union with England was made permanent in 1154.

The French, claiming the islands as historic parts of Normandy, attempted to take control of the island in the fourteenth century, but the English defeated the invasion, and Jersey, along with the other islands, remained an English fief. The English crown's claims to the islands were finally recognized by the French in the Treaty of Bretigny in 1360, but whenever French and English relations soured, French claims to the Channel Islands were pressed. The English used the island as a base to recover Normandy in 1417, but the mainland territories were again lost to French control in 1450. The Jersians remained loyal to the English monarch despite French efforts to regain control of the island during the 1500s. From 1617 justice and civil rights were handled by a bailiff through the Royal Court.

Although Jersey maintained ties to the English monarchy, the islanders retained their Norman law, dialects, and culture. The island, historically self-governing, remained subject to the English monarchy but were not subject to the English parliament. The Jersians' personal union with the English crown reinforced their long history of independence and local self-government. The feudal customs retained on Jersey and the smaller islands were part of the traditional agricultural society. The famous Jersey breed of cattle was developed in the eighteenth century, and dairy farming became a mainstay of the economy. To the present the breed is kept pure by law, which forbids the import of other breeds. The island's legislative powers were separated in 1771, and responsibility was taken by the States of Jersey, an elected body presided over by the bailiff, appointed by the crown.

Protestant refugees from religious persecution in France fled to the island in the sixteenth century. The new arrivals easily assimilated into the Norman culture of the island, but many retained their Protestant religion. The French Revolution sent another wave of French refugees to the island.

An early bailiff of Jersey, Sir George Carteret, in 1664 was rewarded for his support of the Royalists in the English civil war with a grant of land in North America. His holdings later became the state of New Jersey.

Jersey became a popular Victorian resort and retirement center in the late nineteenth century with its fine climate and foreign culture. The island's subtropical climate, unique foreign culture, and beautiful scenery drew many English visitors and immigrants. English immigrants, attracted to the mild climate and relative ease of life, settled in Jersey permanently, but the government of Jersey carefully controlled the number of new residents.

The islanders remained loyal to Britain during World War I, and many Jersians volunteered to fight in the British military. Jersey was used as a staging area for British troops embarking for nearby France. In the postwar era, Jersey was a favorite British resort and retirement center.

Soon after the beginning of World War II in 1940, France fell to the invading Germans, bringing enemy troops to the coast opposite the island. Unable to defend the island, the British evacuated all military troops but were unable to evacuate the entire civilian population. German troops occupied Jersey on 30 June 1940. The Channel Islands were the only British territory to be occupied by enemy troops during the war. Although many of the Jersians were evacuated to the British mainland before the arrival of the Germans, thousands who stayed were deported to forced labor in Germany. Many others nearly starved as the products of the island were taken to feed the German military.

The German surrender in 1944 allowed the Jersey government to return from exile in Britain. During the 1950s the island quickly recovered its earlier prosperity. In the 1960s the island, with its low taxes and lack of inheritance tax, became one of Europe's major offshore banking centers. The mild, sunny climate attracted new residents from Britain, bringing a substantial English minority to the population. The island's economy flourished with tourism and early crops for the British market, mainly vegetables and fruits.

In 1958 Jersey began to issue its own currency and stamps, two of the trappings of an independent state, which raised new questions about the ultimate status of the island. In 1968 the British government convened a special commission to study the relationship of the island to the United Kingdom. Proposals to join Jersey and Guernsey in a cooperative sovereignty were quickly rejected as the traditional enmity between the Jersians and Guernsians* accelerated as rivalry as financial centers grew. The Jersians claim to dislike the Guernseians even more than they dislike the mainland British. The islanders lobbied for the status quo, preferring to remain a self-governing state, but with the British government taking responsibility for defense and foreign affairs.

Jersey's development as an offshore banking center accelerated following the United Kingdom's entry into the European Economic Community (EEC) in 1973. The island's banking system held some $1.36 billion in 1973, but by 1983 the total had climbed to $24.5 billion, about 80% in foreign currencies. Thousands of foreign firms registered in St. Helier and are managed by Jerseyites. By 1990 financial services accounted for 28% of the economy, tourism accounted for 37%, and the income brought in by wealthy immigrants accounted for some 20%. The Jersey government has declared a budget surplus every year since World War II.

The census return in late August 1989 showed that the island's population had swollen to 82,536. The news was greeted with near hysteria, as it revealed that the psychologically important 80,000 had been breached. The growth of the population has aggravated the chronic housing shortage, and development is encroaching on the island's green zones. New immigration limits were set in 1990, but the government came under intense pressure to stop immigration completely.

The growth of the population, plus the danger to their unique culture and language, led to the growth of national and culture organizations in the 1980s. The largest of the groups, L'Assembliée d'Jèrriais, works to extend the use of their Norman dialect in daily life and to preserve their endangered culture. Less moderate Jersians advocate full independence for the island with ties to the European Union (EU) similar to those they now have with the British crown.

The island seeks to be a conduit for non-European funds into the EU. Its special political and economic status continues within the new European reality, but with respect for the movement of peoples and services. For all practical purposes Jersey is not part of the EU and is treated as an outside country.

SELECTED BIBLIOGRAPHY

Bell, Brian, ed. *Channel Islands*. 1996.
Bunting, Madeleine. *Model Occupation: The Channel Islands under German Rule*. 1998.
Hillsdon, Sonia. *Jersey*. 1997.
Maugham, R.C.F. *Jersey under the Jackboot*. 1992.
Mawer, Fred. *Channel Islands*. 1998.

KABARDS

Kabardians; Kabardinians;
Keberdeï; Kabartai; Kabardintsy

POPULATION: Approximately (2000 e) 412,000 Kabards in Europe, concentrated in the Kabardia region of the Kabardino-Balkar Republic in southern European Russia. The largest Kabard population outside Europe is the estimated 200,000 in Turkey.

THE KABARDIN HOMELAND: The Kabardin homeland lies in the central region of the north slopes of the Caucasus Mountains, the highest part of the Greater Caucasus. Kabardia, called Kabarda or Qeberdej by the Kabards, is a lightly settled and very mountainous region with the inhabited regions concentrated in the narrow gorges of the streams flowing into the Terek River. Industrialized in the 1920s and 1930s, the region is one of the most advanced in the Caucasus region of the Russian Federation.

Kabarda or Kabardia, united with the neighboring region of Balkaria, was made an autonomous area in 1922, soon after the Soviet victory in the Russian civil war. In 1936 its status was raised to that of an autonomous republic. In 1991 Kabardino-Balkaria became a member state of the newly proclaimed Russian Federation. In 1992 the Kabards and Balkars agreed to the division of the republic into two new republics, but the Russian government has refused to recognize the new republics. *Republic of Kabardia (Respublike Kabarda/ Qeberdej)*: 3,876 sq.mi.–10,038 sq.km. (2000 e) 644,000—Kabards 61%, Russians* and Terek Cossacks* 24%, Ukrainians* 9%, Ossetians* 3%, Balkars* 2%. The Kabard capital and major cultural center is Nalchik, called Nalshyk by the Kabards, (2000 e) 254,000.

FLAG: The Kabardin national flag, the flag adopted by the proposed republic in 1992, has seven green and white stripes with a light blue canton on the upper hoist bearing four yellow stars in the form of a diamond.

PEOPLE: The Kabards are a Circassian people, one of the three divisions of the Circassians living in the Southern European part of the Russian Federation. The largest of the Circassian nations, the Kabards developed a separate identity in the nineteenth century, an identity that transcended the identities of its subgroups. In the 1920s the Soviet government officially recognized the Kabards as a distinct nationality. The Kabards feel superior to surrounding peoples, and this conviction has contributed to the maintenance of the Kabard ethnic identity, as there is a powerful tradition against marrying outside the national group. Over 90% of the total Kabard population in Russia lives within the borders of the Kabardino-Balkar Republic.

The language of the Kabards, called Upper or Eastern Circassian, is a North Caucasian language of the Abkhazo-Adygheian group, which also includes the languages of the Abaza,* Abkhaz,* Adyghe,* and Cherkess.* Due to the isolation of the Kabard subgroups, the language is spoken in eight dialects, the most important of which are Greater Kabard, Mozdok, Beslan, and Kuban. The Kabard literary language is based on the Greater Kabard dialect, which is spoken around Nalchik. About 97% speak Kabard as their first language, while Russian is often spoken as a second language.

The Kabards are Sunni Muslims, but they were the last of the Circassian nations to be converted, and their ties to Russian Orthodoxy and the Russian culture in general remain strong. A minority of the Kabards, particularly those living around the city of Mozdok in the neighboring Republic of North Ossetia, remained Christian and adhere to the Armenian Gregorian rite.

NATION: Scholars believe the Kabards descended from a group of Caucasian tribes that originated in the Kuban River basin. Known to the ancient Greeks as Zyukhoy, the Circassians probably settled the region of the North Caucasus before the sixth century B.C. Possibly the earliest representative of the Caucasian peoples, the Circassians populated a wide area north of the Caucasus Mountains that figured prominently in the legends of ancient Greece. The handsome Circassians, valued as slaves, developed a warrior society as protection against the region's frequent invaders and raids by slavers.

Greek monks introduced Christianity to the warlike tribes in the sixth century A.D., but the majority of the Circassian tribes were converted in the eleventh and twelfth centuries. A common Christian religion facilitated the Circassians' establishment of ties to the Byzantines to the south and to opening trade routes to the early Slav state, Kievan Rus, in the north. The Circassians became widely known for their skill as traders.

At the beginning of the twelfth century, the Circassian tribes began a slow migration from the Kuban to the east. The Mongol invasion in 1241–42 accelerated the eastward migration and weakened the tribes, which came under the authority of the Christian Georgians.* To escape Georgian rule, some of the tribes moved farther east, arriving on the left bank of the Terek River by the fourteenth century. There they mixed with the local Alans and eventually became known as Kabards.

In the fifteenth century the territory on the left bank of the Terek River was known as Greater Kabardia, while the territory on the right bank was known as Littler Kabardia. Those Kabards who stayed west of the river became known as Cherkess. Early in the sixteenth century the Ottoman Turks* and their vassals, the Crimean Tatars,* extended their authority into the Caucasus region. The Kabards, formerly the dominant nation in the region, resented Tatar control, and in 1557 Kabard prince Temryuk petitioned the Russian tsar Ivan IV for protection. In 1561 Kabardia became a Russian protectorate, and the alliance was cemented by Ivan's marriage to a Kabard princess. The Russians between 1563 and 1567 established military forts along the Terek River but left the feudal Kabard nobility to dominate the northern Caucasus region until the eighteenth century.

The Russian domination of Kabardia was opposed by the Turks and the Persians. In 1739 the Treaty of Belgrade established Kabardia as a neutral buffer state between the Ottoman territories and the expanding Russian Empire, and the territory was annexed by Russia in 1774. Only the Kabardin nobility, noted for wealth and extravagance, integrated into tsarist society. Some of the Kabard clans, influenced by the Turks, adopted the Islamic religion in the seventeenth century. By the early 1800s the majority of the Kabards had adopted the Sunni Islam of the Hanafi rite.

In the mid-nineteenth century, when Shamil led many of the Caucasian nations in a revolt against Russian rule, the Kabards mostly remained neutral. After the Russians had defeated the rebels in the 1860s, around 400,000 Caucasian Muslims left for Turkish territory. A mass exodus of Kabards greatly reduced their population in Russia. The Kabards in the Russian Empire numbered only about 90,000 at the turn of the twentieth century.

Many Kabards were openly sympathetic to the Muslim Turks when war broke out in 1914. The overthrow of the tsar in the third year of the war was greeted with enthusiasm. Kabard leaders appealed to the new government for religious freedom, political autonomy, and the reunification of the Circassian lands but were ignored. Vehemently opposed to the policies of the Bolsheviks, who took control of the Russian government in October 1917, the Muslims of the region organized an autonomous state called North Caucasia. Threatened by both the Bolsheviks and the anti-Bolshevik White forces, the Muslim leaders declared North Caucasia independent of Russia on 11 May 1918, but the new state collapsed less than a year later, when the Whites took control of the region. The Red Army drove the last of the White forces from Kabardia in early 1920, and Soviet rule was established.

The Caucasian peoples accepted a proposal for an autonomous Mountain Republic, with Muslim Sharia law as its basis. In January 1921 the multiethnic state was erected, including the homelands of the Ingush,* Kabards, Balkars, Karachais,* Chechens,* and Ossetians. Ethnic and territorial conflicts quickly arose, and the republic was dissolved. In January 1922 Kabardia was organized as part of an autonomous province, which also included Balkaria. The Kabards, unlike other Muslim groups, did not actively resist the imposition of Soviet rule. The Kabard homeland was industrialized, and Slavs were encouraged to settle in the region. Kabard children were taught in Russian, although the Kabards continued to use their own language as their first language. Soviet efforts to eradicate religion was not as serious in Kabardia as it was in other Caucasian regions, as the Kabards, converted to Islam later than neighboring peoples, were not as intensely Muslim and were considered by the Russian, and the later Soviet, authorities as one of the most loyal of the Caucasian nations.

During World War II, the Nazi Germans,* after taking the area during the Caucasus campaign of 1942, offered an alliance to the small Muslim nations and promoted anticommunist solidarity. The Germans closed the hated collective farms and allowed mosques to function. The Kabards' generally pro-Russian tradition and the view that the Germans represented just another in a long series of invaders spared them the brutal deportations suffered by the Balkars and other Muslim peoples following the return of the Soviet authorities in 1943–44.

Ethnic tensions, particularly between the Kabards and the Balkars, emerged with the easing of Soviet authority in the late 1980s. The Kabards, forced to share their republic with the Turkic Balkars for most of this century, demanded a separate Kabard republic. Ties to the other Circassian peoples, the Adyge and Cherkess, discouraged under tsarist and Soviet rule, were reestablished with calls for the unification of the Circassian peoples.

Demands for change accelerated following the collapse of the Soviet Union in 1991. Nationalist sentiment and growing conflicts between the Kabards and the Balkars led to the partition of the parliament of Kabardino-Balkar into its constituent parts in February 1992. In March 1992 the local republican governments signed a new federal treaty regulating relations with Moscow, but Kabard demands for a separate republic within the Russian Federation were not recognized by the new Russian government.

The Kabards, never having developed any sense of Pan-Islamic identity, have been careful to remain outside the many ethnic and regional conflicts in the Caucasus region in the 1990s. The growing conflict with the neighboring Balkars, who claim they are dominated by the more numerous Kabards, has ignited dormant Kabard nationalism in the 1990s. The Kabards increasingly demand a separate Kabard republic within the Russian Federation.

SELECTED BIBLIOGRAPHY

Bondarevsky, G. L. *The Caucasus: Archives of the Central Administration 1802–1862.* 1996.

Goldenberg, Suzanne. *Pride of Small Nations: The Caucasus and Post-Soviet Disorder.* 1994.

Olson, James S., ed. *An Ethnohistorical Dictionary of the Russian and Soviet Empires.* 1994.

Ro'I, Yaacov. *Muslim Eurasia: Conflicting Legacies.* 1995.

Smith, Sebastian. *Allah's Mountains.* 1997.

KALMYKS

Kalmucks; Kalmuks; Khal'mgs;
Qalmaqs; Volga Oirots

POPULATION: Approximately (2000 e) 212,000 Kalmyks in Europe, concentrated in the Kalmyk Republic, a member state of the Russian Federation.

THE KALMYK HOMELAND: The Kalmyk homeland lies in southern European Russia, an area of plains and barren steppe south of the Volga River and west of the Caspian Sea. Most of Kalmykia is a sparsely populated barren steppe or plain, an arid semidesert between the Don and Volga Rivers. Only a few areas are suitable for cultivation, mostly east of the dry desert and hills that lie in the west, but in the north there are loamy soils and grasslands. Streams flow briefly in the spring, forming the extensive estuaries of the Caspian Depression, a lowland region on the border between Europe and Asia. The republic has no railroads except one line that runs south along the Caspian shore from Astrakhan. In spite of the arid nature of the region, Kalmykia is primarily agricultural.

Kalmykia, formerly an autonomous republic, since 1992 has been a member state of the Russian Federation. *Kalmyk Republic (Khal'mg Tangch)*: 29,305 sq.mi.–75,919 sq.km. (2000 e) 323,000—Kalmyks 53%, Russians* 26%, Don Cossacks* 8%, Kazakhs 5%, Dargins* 4%, Kumyks* 2%. The Kalmyk capital and major cultural center is Elista, (2000 e) 97,000, formerly called Stepnoi.

FLAG: The Kalmyk national flag, the official flag of the republic, has a yellow field with a pale blue circle centered bearing a white water flower.

PEOPLE: The Kalmyks are a branch of the Oirot people of Mongolia, western China, and southeastern Siberia. The descendants of Mongol nomads, the Kalmyks are the only large Buddhist nation in Europe. The name Kalmyk comes from a Turkish word for "remnant," as the Kalmyks are the descendants of those Mongols left behind when the majority left the region in 1771. A long association with the Don Cossacks has greatly influenced Kalmyk social life, which developed a strong tribal-military tradition. Since 1991 thousands of ethnic Kalmyks returned to their homeland from other parts of the former Soviet Union. Oral historic poetry is an important part of Kalmyk culture, traditionally recited by local poets accompanied by a two-stringed lute called a *dombr*. At public gatherings and parties and on holidays poetry, storytelling, and singing are an important part of the festivities.

The language spoken by the Kalmyks is a language of Oirot-Khalka branch of the Mongol language group. The language, which has diverged from other Mongol languages, is spoken in two major dialects in Europe, Torgut (Torgout) and Derbent (Dörböt), which correspond to the geographic divisions. The Torgut live in southern and eastern Kalmykia, and the Derbent Kalmyk inhabit the northern and western districts. A third division, numerically small, is the Khosheut Kalmyks, the remains of a much larger group that mostly left the region in 1771. The language was written in the Mongol alphabet until 1931 but was forcibly switched to the Cyrillic alphabet, although there is an active campaign to change the language to the Latin or the original Mongol alphabet. Over a third of the Kalmyks speak only their own language, but the majority are bilingual, also speaking the Russian language.

The Tibetan branch of Buddhism, Lamaism, is the major religion of the Kalmyks. Many traces of their earlier pre-Buddhist shamanism is evident in their unique rituals. The Tibetan language is the language used in religious services. The Kalmyks are the only nation in Europe with a Buddhist majority. The Orthodox minority are mostly the descendants of Kalmyks converted to Christianity before the Russian Revolution.

NATION: The Kalmyks were among the last Asian migrants to penetrate European territory. A branch of the Oirot Mongols left their homeland in the Altai Mountains of Central Asia in 1636, fleeing the disintegration of the Mongol Empire and growing political and economic pressure by Chinese, Kazakh, and Mongols. The Oirot clans moved west, displacing the native Nogais* as they went. The clans, according to Kalmyk tradition, after migrating for thirty-two years, eventually settled in the lower Volga River basin. The region, which had formed part of the Astrakhan Khanate, had been incorporated into the Russian Empire in 1556. In 1608 the Kalmyk leaders asked the Russian tsar, Vasilii Shuiskii, for protection against the ravages of the Tatars* and Nogais.

The Oirot clans established an independent khanate, a confederation of tribes ruled by *noyons* (princes) under the ultimate authority of the khan. In 1646 the confederation signed a treaty of allegiance to the Russian tsar, Peter I, who charged them with guarding Russia's new eastern frontier. Russian protection saved the small nation, and from 1664 to 1771 the Kalmyk homeland formed a frontier khanate that pledged allegiance to the Russian tsars.

In the eighteenth century the Mongols adopted the Lamaism brought to the region by missionary monks from Mongolia. As adherents of Tibetan Lamaism the Dalai Lama in distant Tibet, the spiritual leader of their religion, appointed the confederation's khans.

News that their ethnic cousins, the Oirots, still living in Chinese territory, were suffering intense persecution by the Chinese authorities rallied the clans in 1769–70. Catherine II, Russia's ruler, in the winter of 1771 put aside the 1646 allegiance treaty and attempted to impose direct Russian rule on the clans. Refusing to submit to Christian domination and determined to rescue the Oirots of China, the clans east of the Volga River, led by Khan Ubushi, suddenly undertook a harrowing journey to return to their original homeland over 2,000 miles to the east. Of the 300,000 that departed only one-third survived the passage. The majority succumbed to cold, heat, hunger, and attacks by Russians, Bashkorts,* and Kazakhs.* The Volga River did not freeze in the winter of 1771, trapping the 13,000 families living on the west bank. Unable to cross the raging river, some 60,000 were forced to stay behind. The Russian government dissolved the khanate and placed the remaining clans under the authority of Astrakhan Province.

Those who stayed in their homeland between the Don and Volga Rivers formed close political and cultural ties to the Don Cossacks. The Kalmyks took on many of the military attributes of the Cossacks while retaining their own culture and social structure. Kalmyk society was dominated by the White Bone, the *noyons* and aristocracy, while the majority of the Kalmyk population formed the Black Bone, the commoners. In return for military service and an oath of loyalty to the Russian tsar, the Kalmyks enjoyed broad powers of self-government, from 1803 overseen by a Guardian of the Kalmyk People appointed by the Russian monarch. The Kalmyks became divided into two major linguistic and geographic groups, the Torgot and the Derbent.

The government-sponsored settlement of the Kalmyk lands by ethnic Russians in the nineteenth century began the process of bringing the Kalmyk clans under closer Russian authority. In 1806 the authorities limited the Kalmyk pasturelands to a region between the Caspian Sea and thirty kilometers from the Volga River. The tsarist decree severely limited the Kalmyks' nomadic way of life. The Kalmyk herds declined from 2.5 million head in 1803, to 1 million in 1863, and to only 450,000 at the turn of the twentieth century. Many impoverished Kalmyks were forced off the land to find work as fishermen and salt miners. Only in 1892 was serfdom abolished in Kalmykia.

Numbering over 200,000 when war began in 1914, the small nation's warriors formed elite military units. Released from their oath of loyalty by the overthrow of the tsar in February 1917, the Kalmyk soldiers returned home. A Kalmyk congress, convened in March, authorized the formation of a national army from the returning military units and renewed an old alliance with the Don Cossacks. In the wake of the Bolshevik coup in October 1917, the Kalmyks rebelled as Russia collapsed in chaos. Most of the Kalmyk clans supported the anti-Bolshevik Southeastern League, an organization of Cossacks and other non-Russian peoples of the North Caucasus region, although the Kalmyks were divided into pro- and anti-Bolshevik groups.

The Kalmyk congress, dominated by the White Bone, voted for secession as the Bolshevik threat increased. On 12 June 1918 the congress declared Kalmykia independent of Russia. Devastated by heavy fighting during the Russian civil war, thousands of Kalmyks died in battle or of hunger and disease. The advancing Red Army occupied Kalmykia in 1920, where a Kalmyk Autonomous District was created. The communists eliminated the White Bone aristocrats and nationalized the Kalmyk herds. Between 1922 and 1925, Kalmyks living in other parts of Russia were transferred to the autonomous district.

In the late 1920s collectivization of the Kalmyk herds was begun. The Kalmyks resisted Joseph Stalin's orders, and he ordered that all opposition be ruthlessly crushed. Thousands of Kalmyks died in the process, while others joined antigovernment resistance groups. The last Kalmyk guerrilla bands were liquidated in 1926. Purges and antireligious campaigns destroyed the Kalmyks' cultural, political, and religious hierarchy. In 1932 most buildings of Mongol architecture, including temples, schools, and public buildings, were ordered destroyed, along with their contents.

For a brief period during the 1930s, the Soviet authorities promoted contacts between the Mongol peoples of the Soviet Empire. In January 1931 a cultural conference of the Mongol peoples was held in Moscow, but within a few years concern about the growth of Pan-Mongol nationalism and Japanese support of the Mongol peoples led to forbidding of further contacts between the Kalmyks and the other Mongol peoples farther east. In 1933 the autonomous district was raised to the status of an autonomous republic.

The fervently Buddhist and anticommunist Kalmyks, their monasteries and temples destroyed during the Stalinist purges, often welcomed the German invaders who reached Kalmykia in 1942. Promoted as German allies, many Kalmyks enthusiastically joined the German's anticommunist crusade. Émigré Prince N. Tundutov, the Kalmyk leader during the Russian civil war, arrived in Elista as head of a new Kalmyk government. The authorities allowed the reopening of shrines and monasteries. A Kalmyk army, the Kalmyk Banner Organization, fought as German allies, often against Kalmyks fighting with the Red Army.

The Red Army returned in February 1943. Stalin accused the entire Kalmyk nation of treason and ordered their deportation. Often with only minutes' notice, the Kalmyk population, including the families of soldiers fighting in the Red Army, was herded into closed cattle cars and shipped east. Only three Kalmyk families escaped the brutal deportation. Thousands perished from hunger and thirst on the twenty-two-day journey. Dumped at rail sidings in the Siberian waste, many more died of disease, exposure, and malnutrition. By 1950 over half the prewar Kalmyk population of 140,000 had perished.

The Kalmyks were officially rehabilitated in 1956, three years after Stalin's death. The survivors gradually made their way back to the North Caucasus, the first 6,000 survivors arriving in their former homeland in early 1957. In 1958 their homeland was officially reestablished as an autonomous republic within the Russian Federation, but under strict surveillance and with a large ethnic Russian presence to ensure stability in the region. The Kalmyk population reached its 1926 level only in the late 1960s. The Kalmyk population grew rapidly during the 1970s and 1980s, reaching a total of 174,000 in 1989.

Soviet economic and agricultural planning is blamed for the sorry state of the Kalmyks' homeland. Ill-conceived irrigation projects and overgrazing have left over half the region as infertile desert, with another third in a marginal state. Too many sheep were grazed in the region in the 1950s; plus they were the wrong type of sheep. Soviet planners brought in sheep from the Caucasus Mountains. The sheep, famed for their wool, had very sharp hooves, which were perfect for the flinty mountainsides but were a disaster for the fertile, yet fragile, grasslands of Kalmykia.

The reforms introduced by Mikhail Gorbachev in 1987 fueled a Kalmyk religious and cultural revival. Renewed ties with the Kalmyk exile community in the United States and Europe reinforced calls for religious freedom. The exile community, served by five Buddhist temples, numbered only about 1,500, while the over 200,000 Kalmyks in the Soviet Union had only one active temple. Kalmyk scholars, especially at Kalmyk University in Elista, protested the genocide of the Stalin era and the falsification of Kalmyk history by Soviet historians. Inspired by the new freedoms, Kalmyk nationalism became a popular movement in the republic, inspired by the revival of their Buddhist religion. In August 1990 the first *khural* (congress) since World War II convened in Elista and included delegates from the exile White Bone community. The congress adopted a nationalist platform endorsing the Kalmyk right to self-determination.

The collapse of the Soviet Union in August 1991 provoked a strong nationalist reaction, particularly demands for control of the extensive mineral wealth of their republic. In February and March 1992 the Kalmyks changed the name of the republic to Khal'mg Tangch and unilaterally upgraded the republic's legal status within the Russian Federation. One of the conditions demanded for approving the new Russian Federation was Kalmyk control of their subsoil resources.

In April 1992 a young Kalmyk millionaire, Kirsan Ilyumzhinov, won the republican presidential elections with a vow to convert Kalmykia into a neutral, Buddhist state. Lapel pins featuring the likeness of the Dalai Lama are as common as the former hammer and sickle. His religious views and his peaceful campaign for Tibetan rights have made him the icon of Kalmyk nationalism.

The Kalmyk culture and language revived rapidly following the collapse of the Soviet Union. By 1992 five prayer houses had been opened in the region. The Institute for the Rebirth of the Kalmyk Language and Buddhism was established in Elista, and Buddhist holidays were again celebrated. Kalmyk University, founded in Elista in 1970, became a center of the Kalmyk renaissance during the 1990s.

The Kalmyk leader Kirsan Ilyumzhinov in November 1998 set off a crisis in Russia when he demanded greater autonomy for his small nation. He threatened to withhold tax revenues, claiming that while the Kalmyks pay heavy taxes to the federal government, they get nothing in return. More radical nationalists pressed for secession from the Russian Federation. The crisis deepened as other discontented ethnic groups gave the Kalmyks their support in their confrontation with the federal government. President Boris Yeltsin called an extraordinary meeting of his advisers to combat the Kalmyks' challenge, fearing that secessionist sentiment could easily spread to other regions.

The Kalmyks, after decades of Soviet domination, have quickly recovered their culture and language. Their old Mongol script, abolished in 1924, is again being taught in Kalmyk schools. Traditional musical instruments are again being made with skins and wood brought from Mongolia, and students are being sent to China and Mongolia to learn to play them. There is talk of bringing sheep and cattle from Xinjiang to restore the breeds that arrived with the first Kalmyk settlers.

SELECTED BIBLIOGRAPHY

Brower, Daniel R., and Lazzerini, Edward J., eds. *Russia's Orient: Imperial Borderlands and Peoples.* 1997.

Khodarkovsky, Michael. *Where Two Worlds Met: The Russian State and the Kalmyk Nomads, 1600–1771.* 1992.

McAuley, Alistair, ed. *Soviet Federalism, Nationalism and Economic Decentralization.* 1991.

Nekrich, Alexander. *The Punished Peoples.* 1978.

Rubel, P. *The Kalmyk Mongols.* 1997.

KARACHAIS

Karachays; Karachevs; Qarachaili;
Kiarchal

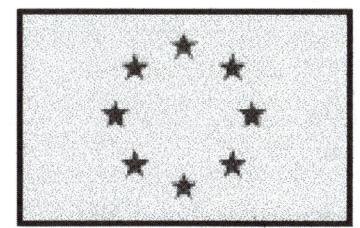

POPULATION: Approximately (2000 e) 159,000 Karachais in Europe, mostly living in the Karachai region of the Karachai-Cherkess Republic, a member state of the Russian Federation.

THE KARACHAI HOMELAND: The Karachai homeland lies in southern European Russia, a rugged area of foothills and canyons in the western Caucasus Mountains. The region, with several peaks over 10,000 feet (3,050 m.), is mountainous, except the regions traversed by the valleys of the upper Kuban River and its tributaries, the Taberda, Zelenchuk, and Aksut. Karachais' highland valleys are called the Dombai. Karachai also has some of the largest glaciers and snowfields in the Caucasus, although the area abounds in woodlands.

The region has no official status; the region forms the southern districts, known as Karachai, of the Karachai-Cherkess Republic. The division of the republic has not been recognized by the Russian government. *Karachai Republic (Qarachai Respublika)*: 3,821 sq.mi.–9,896 sq.km. (2000 e) 184,000—Karachais 80%, Nogais* 10%, Russians* and Cossacks 6%, Cherkess* 2%, Ukrainians* 1%. The Karachai capital and major cultural center is Mikoyan Shakhar, called Karachayevsk by the Russians, (2000 e) 33,000, the capital of the former Karachayev Autonomous Oblast.

FLAG: The Karachai national flag, the flag of the unrecognized republic, is a yellow field bearing a centered circle of eight small, red, five-pointed stars.

PEOPLE: The Karachais are a Turkic people who have traditionally inhabited the Dombai since time immemorial. The origin of their name is disputed, with some scholars believing that it means "people living near a mighty river," since "kara" means strong or mighty, while "chay" is water, drink, or river. Others think the name comes from Karcha, the legendary ancestor of all the Karachais. Some believe that the Karachais are descended from the Kuban Bulgars and Kipchak tribes driven into the Caucasus Mountains by the Mongols in the thirteenth century. They were joined by many Alans, and the union of the peoples formed the Karachai nation.

Cattle breeding generally dominates Karachai life, along with sheep and horse breeding and some farming. In the summer, they take their herds to mountain pastures, returning in winter to keep the herds in forested fields or valley pastures.

The Karachais, until World War II, did not have a well-developed sense of nationhood due to the geographic isolation that divides them, with patriarchal clan loyalty more important than their sense of being Karachais. The four clan groups are the Adurkhay, Budian, Nawruz, and Trama, and loyalty to one of the clans remains a prominent feature of Karachai society. Each family is still led by a family council, which consists of the men of the oldest generation and the eldest woman. The senior woman plays a significant role in keeping the family pride and honor, as hospitality is extremely important to Karachai relationships.

Sunni Islam of the Hanafi school is the official religion of the Karachais, and each village has its own mosque, but they remain less devout than some neighboring peoples and have not experienced the fervent Islamic revivals that other Muslim peoples have undergone in recent years. Karachai women enjoy greater independence than among most Muslim peoples, and the traditional dietary restrictions, including the eating of pork, are not generally observed. Many traditional pagan beliefs have been intermingled with their religious rituals. The Karachais believe in evil spirits, and pagan sacrifices and rituals are often performed.

NATION: The origins of the Karachais are unknown, with many theories, but according to Karachai legend, they are descended from the ancient inhabitants of the Dombai, and archaeologists have found bronze and iron tools and gold ornaments dating back to the first millennium B.C. The culture of the region, known as the Koban culture, is still mostly a mystery, with little known of the region before the coming of the steppe and nomad tribes that intermingled with the local inhabitants.

The Alans controlled the area from the first to the fourteenth centuries, while Bulgars and Kipchaks also migrated to the region. The mixture of the Kipchaks, Bulgars, and Alans in the twelfth century is considered the beginning of the distinct Karachai nation. Traditionally, Kipchak tribes from the Crimean Peninsula, driven from that territory during upheavals in the fourteenth century, migrating south along the shore of the Black Sea, mixed extensively with the earlier Cherkess and finally settled in the mountains, where they merged with the local tribes.

The Karachai clans became vassals of the Kabards* in the sixteenth century. Islam was introduced by the Kabards, and the Karachais attribute their conversion to Ishak Efendi, an eighteenth-century Kabard mullah. In the seventeenth century the Ottoman Turks began to exert influence in the region. In 1733 the Karachai homeland came under direct Turkish rule.

Russians expanded into the territory of the declining Ottoman Empire in the eighteenth century and reached the Dombai in 1774. The Russians took control of the Karachai region in 1828 and in 1829 succeeded in forcing the Ottoman Turks to cede the Caucasian territories. Resistance to Christian Russian rule erupted in a long and savage guerrilla war that continued until 1864. Thousands of Karachai-Balkars moved south to Turkish territory. Those who remained under Russian rule took up arms against the tsarist authorities at every opportunity.

The Muslims of the Russian Empire, their loyalty suspect, were exempted from military duty when war began in 1914. Even though a majority of the Muslim peoples openly favored Muslim Turkey, the Russian government, desperate for manpower, began conscripting Muslims in 1916. The Muslim work units, sent to the front, came into contact with new revolutionary and nationalist ideas that took hold as Russia slipped into chaos. The Karachai and Balkar conscripts deserted the front to return home after the revolution of February 1917. As civil government collapsed, a Karachai-Balkar national committee took control of Karachai and Balkaria. The national committee gave its support to Russia's new provisional government, which vaguely promised autonomy for Russia's minority peoples.

The Islamic peoples of the North Caucasus attempted to unite in a cooperative independence in opposition to the antireligious stance of the Bolsheviks, who took power in revolutionary Russia in October 1917. Threatened by local Bolsheviks and rival political groups, the Karachai-Balkar leaders declared Karachai-Balkaria independent of Russia on 18 May 1918. Forced into an alliance with the White forces fighting the Bolsheviks in the expanding Russian civil war, the Karachais withdrew to mountain strongholds when the White resistance collapsed in 1920.

A detachment of the Ninth Soviet Army invaded the region in support of an uprising by local Bolsheviks, mostly ethnic Russians living in the territory. The invading Soviets overthrew the separatist government, which they called "bourgeois nationalist exploiters." The new Soviet government, bent on destroying any sense of North Caucasus unity or resistance, separated the related Karachais and Balkars as part of their divide-and-conquer strategy.

The religious life of the Karachais also came under attack, with most mosques and religious schools forcibly closed during the collectivization of the region. Karachai resistance to collectivization in 1930 led to open rebellion, which was brutally crushed, and over 3,000 rebels were executed. Continued opposition to Soviet collectivization and the Soviet antireligious programs was countered by a purge of over 1,500 Karachai Communist Party members for "counterrevolutionary" activities.

During World War II, following the Nazi attack on their Soviet ally in June 1941, a German offensive drove into the Caucasus in mid-1942. The invaders were welcomed by many Karachais as liberators from hated Soviet rule, and thousands of volunteers joined the Turkish League, an anticommunist military unit fighting as an ally of the Germans. Encouraged by the occupation forces, Karachai nationalists convened a national committee and formed a national government under Kadi Kairamukov. Supported by the Germans, the national committee declared the region, including Balkaria, independent of the Soviet Union on 11 August 1942. The new government moved to restore the region's traditional social and religious structure, opening closed mosques and decollectivizing rural life. Horrified by German brutality, the republican government increasingly distanced itself from German sponsorship and attempted to create a neutral state allied to Turkey. By early 1943 over a dozen guerrilla bands had taken up arms against the German occupation force.

The sovereign Karachai-Balkar state collapsed with the Soviet reconquest of the North Caucasus in October 1943. Joseph Stalin, the Soviet dictator, accused the entire Karachai nation of treason and participation in Nazi atrocities. In November 1943, 75,000 Karachai were shipped east in closed cattle cars. The Soviet guards dumped the deportees in the Central Asian wastes, often without provisions or shelter. Thousands of Karachais perished from exposure, hunger, and disease. The survivors, officially rehabilitated in 1956, returned to their Caucasian homes. In 1957 the Karachai-Cherkess Autonomous Oblast was reestablished. All contacts between the Karachai and Balkar, except cultural, were forbidden.

Under the Soviet liberalization of the late 1980s the Karachais began to mobilize. The leaders of the autonomous province they shared with the Cherkess, following the disintegration of the Soviet Union in 1991, unilaterally declared the region a full republic of the newly constituted Russian Federation. The change in the region's status, recognized by the government in Moscow, allowed the numerically superior Karachais to dominate the new republic. Renewed contact with the closely related Balkars, forbidden for over three decades, aided the cultural and national revival of the small nation.

The Soviet collapse also stimulated demands for separation from the hybrid region they had been forced into under communist rule. In 1992 the Karachai leaders unilaterally withdrew their territory from the joint republic, a move that the Russian authorities have not recognized. Demands for the official unification of Karachai and Balkaria have so far been ignored by the Russian authorities, which has raised tensions in the region, one of the least assimilated areas of the North Caucasus.

The Russian, Cossack, and Cherkess population of the republic demanded the return of the Karachai-Cherkess Republic to the administrative control of Stavropol Oblast in 1997. The demand, which would place the Karachais once again under the Russian-dominated provincial government, has been vigorously resisted.

SELECTED BIBLIOGRAPHY

Akiner, Shirin. *Islamic Peoples of the Soviet Union.* 1986.

Conquest, Robert. *The Nation Killers.* 1970.

Nekrich, Alexander. *The Punished Peoples.* 1978.

Olson, James S. *An Ethnohistorical Dictionary of the Russian and Soviet Empires.* 1994.

Smith, Sebastian. *Allah's Mountains.* 1997.

KARELS

Karelians; Karjala; Korela;
Karyalainen; Karjaliset; Karjalazhet

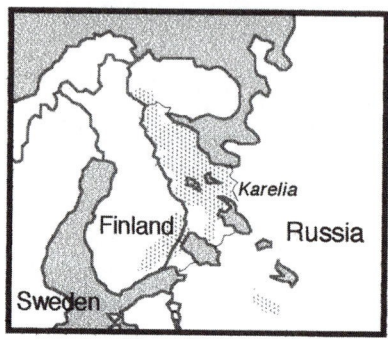

POPULATION: Approximately (2000 e) 504,000 Karels in Europe, concentrated in the Karelian Republic in Russia, but with a large Karel population in Finland. Other Karel populations are in the Russian regions of Tver, St. Petersburg, Arkhangelsk, Moscow, and Kemerov.

THE KARELIAN HOMELAND: The Karel homeland lies in northwestern European Russia, extending from the Finnish border east to the White Sea. Most of the region forms part of the Karelian Plateau, a broad, flat, and swampy plain with mountains in the west. The western districts of the plateau are sparsely populated and heavily wooded. Karelia is rich in minerals and water resources, with over 50,000 lakes. In the north the traditional Karel lands extend to the Kola Peninsula. Much of Karelia is state forest, about 60%, and the numerous lakes, including Ladoga, Onega, Vygozero, Topozero, and Segozero, make up almost 20% of the area.

The traditional territory of the Karels is now divided. The largest part forms the Republic of Karelia, a member state of the Russian Federation. Historic Karelia also includes Western Karelia, transferred to Leningrad (St. Petersburg) Oblast in 1946, and Northern Karelia, which was transferred to Murmansk Oblast in 1938. *Republic of Karelia (Karjala)*: 66,567 sq.mi.–172,466 sq.km. (2000 e) 809,000—Russians* 55%, Karels 26%, Belarussians* 6%, Finns* 6%, Ukrainians* 2%, Veps* 2%, Ingians* 2%. The Karelian capital and major cultural center is Petrozavodsk, called Petroskoi in Karelian, (2000 e) 290,000. The major cultural centers of Western Karelia and Northern Karelia are Vyborg (Viipuri), (2000 e) 84,000, and Kandalaksha (Kaananlahti) 56,000.

FLAG: The Karelian national flag, the traditional flag of the Karelian nation, is a pale green field bearing a black Scandinavian cross outlined in red.

PEOPLE: The Karels are a Finnic nation, descendants of a collection of tribal peoples who migrated from the Volga River region, probably between 100 B.C. and A.D. 100, although some scholars place the migrations many centuries earlier. The Karels, closely related to the Finns, are the descendants of the Finnish peoples most influenced by contact with the Slavs. The actual number of ethnic Karels in the Russian Federation is a matter of dispute. Official records count about 140,000 Karels, but during the Soviet era many Karels registered as ethnic Russians to escape oppression. During the Soviet era many Karels assimilated into the Russian nationality, and by 1989, 56% of urban ethnic Karelians and 35% of rural ethnic Karelians considered Russian their first language. A movement to restore the Karelian language and culture developed in the late Soviet period, and by the late 1990s thousands of Karels had again assumed the Karelian nationality.

Over the centuries the Karelians have become dispersed over a wide territory and now constitute several distinct subgroups. The largest are the North Karels in Karelia, the South Karels in the Tver, Novgorod, and St. Petersburg Oblasts, the Olonets in northwestern Karelia, between Lakes Ladoga and Onega, and the Ludics in the central and southern districts of Karelia. In the 1960s the Karels of Tver, Novgorod, and St. Petersburg (Leningrad) Oblasts numbered between 90,000 and 100,000 but were not included in subsequent official records. The Valdai Karels of the Novgorod region and the Tikhvin Karels of the St. Petersburg region were considered assimilated, but during the 1990s a reculturation is taking hold, and Karels who speak Russian as their first language are taking a new interest in their culture and language.

The language of the Karels, which is identical in its written form to Finnish, is spoken in three distinct dialects, all of which have been influenced by Russian. Karels in the southern districts are called Livviki and speak the Livvi dialect. The Karels in the center, the Karels proper, speak Karjala, and the Lyydidi, who inhabit districts in the south and southwest, speak the Lyydiki dialect. Unlike most ethnic minorities in the former USSR, the Karels had been allowed to retain the Latin alphabet.

The Russian influence on Karel society is most pronounced in religion. The Karels are mostly Russian Orthodox, while the Finns and Ingrians to the west are Protestant Lutherans. The historic boundary between Finland and Karelia reflected the religious boundary between the two Finnish nations until the twentieth century.

NATION: Nomadic tribal peoples from the Volga River basin west of the Ural Mountains settled the forested Karelian Plateau, probably in the eighth century, driving the earlier Samis* or Lapps farther to the north. Mentioned in Scandinavian writings of the eighth century and European and Russian chronicles of the ninth century, the Karels were known as a separate northern people living in the forests between the Baltic and White Seas and around Lakes Ladoga and Onega. The Karel tribes never unified but mostly lived in autonomous groups with few ties beyond the clan level.

From the ninth to the twelfth centuries, the southern clans were under the authority of the Kievan Rus' principality. In 1216 the pope confirmed Swedish title to much of Finland and also to mission territories in the east and north. In 1323 a treaty divided Karelia between the Swedes and the Novgorodians. The eastern Karels mostly came under the rule of the Slav Republic of Novgorod, and many adopted Orthodox Christianity. Traditionally, the Karels worked as farmers, fishermen, or timber cutters.

The Swedes,* expanding their empire to the east, conquered Finland, but the fierce Karels stopped the Swedish advance for a time. Eventually, in the fifteenth century the Swedes gained control of Western Karelia, but Slavs from the Republic of Great Novgorod maintained control of Eastern Karelia. The Karels were freed by the Russian conquest of Novgorod in 1478 and formed a separate confederation, which developed into a strong medieval state with a vigorous culture. The Karelian folktales and songs of this period are the source of the Finnish national epic, the *Kalevala*, considered the national heritage of both peoples. The influence of the Slavs extended to religion, and most Karels adopted the Slavs' Orthodox religion.

The Swedes finally conquered the Karel state in 1617 but kept the newly conquered region separate from Western Karelia. Thousands of Karels, evicted from their lands or fleeing the imposition of feudal taxes and the Lutheran faith, left the northwestern shores of Lake Ladoga to migrate to North Karelia, and another large group moved south to the Valdai hills in central Russia. The Karel emigration from their war-torn homeland had already begun in the late sixteenth century but became extensive in the first half of the seventeenth century. An estimated 25,000 to 30,000 people left the region. The Russian government supported the Karelian exodus, giving financial assistance and freeing them temporarily from taxes.

During the Northern War in 1716, the Russians took control of Karelia from the Swedes, the annexation formalized by the Treaty of Nystad in 1721. Western Karelia, along with Finland and the Aland Islands, were ceded by Sweden to Russia during the Napoleonic Wars, at the conclusion of yet another Swedish-Russian War in 1809. The two Karelian regions remained divided by Russia's internal political borders. Eastern Karelia, poor and underdeveloped, became known as a place of exile for tsarist political prisoners and common criminals.

The Finnic people's experience at the hands of both the Swedes and the Russians had stimulated a sense of nationalism. Influenced by the Finns, the Karels experienced a national and cultural revival in the late nineteenth century. In 1899 the tsarist authorities clamped down and imposed new restrictions on education and publishing in the Karel language. Finnish nationalist literature, smuggled across the border, supported the growth of an underground nationalist movement. The Russian authorities countered with increased assimilation pressure.

During World War I, Karel soldiers fought in the Russian army, but in February 1917 the overthrow of the tsarist autocracy threw Karelia into chaos, with prisoners and political exiles suddenly freed to roam the region. Karel military units, deserting the front, took control of Karelia as civil government collapsed. Protected by British troops landed to support the Whites, the Karel forces opposed the Bolsheviks in the spreading Russian civil war. The Karel leaders declared their homeland an autonomous state in May 1919.

The independence of Finland, the White defeat in Russia, and the withdrawal of all foreign troops from the new Soviet Union left Karelia to the mercy of the Red Army in 1920. A Karel congress in March 1920 voted for independence, but occupation by the Red Army ended the movement. The region became the refuge for Red Finns, defeated in the Finnish civil war. In early 1921 the Karels rebelled and drove the Soviets from the region. On 21 April 1921 the rebels proclaimed the independence of the Republic of Eastern Karelia (Itä Karjala) and created a democratic government that invited participation by the area's many national groups. The Finns, exhausted by war and attempting to maintain peace with their giant Soviet neighbor, were unable to respond to the Karels' frantic appeals for aid. Reconquered by the Red Army in 1922, the Soviets dissolved the independent republic. Karelia was organized as an autonomous province and in 1923 was raised to the status of an autonomous republic within the Russian Federation. In 1935 the leadership of the autonomous republic was accused of nationalist tendencies and was purged, most ending in labor camps in Siberia.

In the late 1930s the Stalinist government of the Soviet Union became increasingly aggressive with the small republics that had seceded during the Russian civil war, Finland, Estonia, Latvia, and Lithuania. In late 1939 the Soviet government demanded the cession of Western Karelia from Finland as part of a plan to reunite the Karels under Soviet rule. The ensuing conflict, the Winter War, ended with Finnish defeat in 1940. The Soviets added Finnish Karelia to the Karelo-Finnish Soviet Socialist Republic, which joined the Soviet Union as the twelfth constituent republic. Tens of thousands of Karels and Finns fled west to escape Soviet domination, with the remaining population punished for aiding the Finns during the brief war. The 1939 Soviet census counted 253,000 Karels, but by 1959 that number had dropped to 167,000 as ethnic Karels sought to hide their nationality by registering as ethnic Russians.

The Finns, unreconciled to the loss of Western Karelia, joined the German assault on the Soviet state in June 1941. Finnish troops liberated all of Karelia but, claiming that theirs was a separate conflict, refused to join further German offensives, particularly the German attack on Leningrad. Defeated in 1944, the Finnish troops withdrew, accompanied by over 400,000 Karels and Finns fleeing the Soviet advance. The Soviet authorities again divided the Karel lands in

1945–46, transferring the western districts to Leningrad Oblast and returning Northern Karelia to Murmansk Oblast. On the grounds that the Karels formed only a minority in the republic, the Soviet government downgraded Karelia's status to an autonomous republic in 1956.

In the late 1980s Mikhail Gorbachev introduced reforms to the creaking Soviet system. In May 1988 the administration officially acknowledged the campaign of terrorism launched against the Karels by Joseph Stalin. Renewed contacts with the Finns and the large Karel exile population spurred a rapid growth of national sentiment. Pressed by the multiethnic Karel national movement, the region's government became the first in the Soviet Union to declare sovereignty, on 9 August 1990. In June 1991 the first Karel congress in seventy years, at Olonets on Lake Ladoga, brought together representatives of the exile Karel population, representative of the autonomous republic, and delegates from the Tver Karels. A fifty-member executive committee was elected to introduce a bill proposing sovereign Karel territories, where the Karel language and culture could be preserved.

The nationalist mobilization accelerated after the disintegration of the Soviet Union in August 1991. In February 1992 republican leaders warned Moscow that the demands for independence could spin out of control if the Russian government refused to grant greater autonomy. In November 1992 representatives of the Karels demanded legal recognition as a "repressed nation" that suffered disportionately during seventy years of Soviet communist rule. Democracy in Russia has allowed the Karels to reestablish close cultural ties to neighboring Finland, which has begun to finance cultural and economic development in Karelia.

Karel cultural and nationalist groups in the 1990s campaigned for the partition of Karelia to provide for a Karel majority homeland while denying accusations that they wish to unite with neighboring Finland. The large exile population in Finland supports the exile Karels' right to return to their homeland, particularly the region of Western Karelia ceded to the Soviet Union in 1940. Karel nationalists look to wealthy Finland, while their own homeland is dismal and poor, even by low Russian standards. The Karels have finally been freed of communist rule but now fear their homeland will become a backward dependency of the Russian Federation. Nationalists vow that Karelia won't return to the status of a colonial outpost of a new Russian Empire.

The language issue also continues to cause friction, as Finnish, not Karel, is the second official language of the republic. There is now a serious campaign to revive the Karel language and culture. The campaign has been directed by the Union of the Karelian People (Karjalan Rahvahan Liitto). A dictionary of the Karelian language in several volumes is being compiled in Finland.

SELECTED BIBLIOGRAPHY

Allison, Roy. *Finland's Relation with the Soviet Union 1944–84*. 1985.

Engle, Eloise, and Lauri Paananen. *The Winter War: The Soviet Attack on Finland 1939–1944*. 1992.

Maude, George. *Historical Dictionary of Finland*. 1995.

Mouritzen, Hans. *Bordering Russia: Theory and Prospects for Europe's Baltic Rim.* 1998.

Rozzardo, Rene. *Cultural Policy and Regional Identity in Finland: North Karelia between Tradition and Modernity.* 1987.

KASHUBS

Kashubians; Kaszébé; Kaszubes;
Kaszubi; Kaszubians; Kaschuben;
Cassubians

POPULATION: Approximately (2000 e) 250,000 Kashubians in Europe, concentrated in Gulf of Gdansk region of northeastern Poland. The largest concentrations outside Europe are in the United States and Canada, with smaller numbers in Brazil, Argentina, and Australia.

THE KASHUBIAN HOMELAND: The Kashubian homeland lies in the lowlands of northeastern Poland, mostly in the delta of the Vistula River and the coastal plains around the Gulf of Gdansk. Traditionally, Kashubia occupies a triangular-shaped area directly south of the Baltic Sea and between the Odra (Oder) and the Wisla (Vistula) Rivers. The region, west and northwest of Gdansk, is included in the Polish provinces of Bydgoszcz, Gdansk, and Slupsk, comprising all or parts of the districts of Puck, Wejherowo, Kartuzy, Koscierznya, Bytow, Chojnice, Czluchow, Lebork, Starogard Gdanski, and Tuchola. Kashubia is one of the most scenic parts of Poland, with sandy beaches, the picturesque and unusually narrow Hel Peninsula, and the numerous lakes found in the Kashubian Lake District, the so-called Kashubian Switzerland to the south. Historically, the Kashubian region is divided into a western and eastern part with the border running along the Slupia River in the north and south to the town of Szczecinek.

The region of Kashubia (Kaszuby), also called Region Kaszubski, has no official status in Poland but constitutes a historic region and is considered the homeland by the Kashubian nation. The region has a large Polish majority. The Kashub capital and major cultural center is Kartuzy, (2000 e) 12,000, which was named for the Carthusian monks from Chartreuse in France, who built a monastery and a settlement there in the fourteenth century.

FLAG: The Kashubian national flag, the unofficial flag of the Kashubian region, is a horizontal bicolor of black over yellow.

PEOPLE: The Kashubs or Kashubians are called Kaszubi by Poles but call themselves Kasz'b'. Traditionally, the Kashubs are the last remnants of the ancient Slavic Pomeranians, whose name in the West Slavic dialects, Pomorze, means along the sea. Traditionally, the Kashubs' main occupation was fishing, which was managed by teams, usually composed of members of a single family, called the *mazoperia*. The leader of each unit, the *szyper*, was the most trusted and experienced member of the unit. Before each fishing expedition, special prayers were offered to the Madonna of Swarzewo, the patroness of Kashubian fishermen. The modern Kashubs are mostly fishermen, both along the Baltic Sea and in the lake region. A minority are industrial workers in the large cities of Gdansk, Gdynia, and Slupsk. The culture of the Kashubs has been influenced by the region's many rulers, particularly the Germans* and Swedes.* The culture, which has enjoyed new interest in the last decade, includes a distinct musical tradition. The traditional Kashubian *kapela*, a band of musicians, has been revived as part of the overall cultural revival of the 1990s. Roman Catholicism, the religion of the Kashubs, is an integral part of their culture.

The Kashubian language is a West Slavic language related to Polish and is often called the Pomeranian dialect of Polish, but the language is distinct and has been heavily Germanized. The number of speakers is thought to surpass 200,000, although the language of daily life is primarily the Pomeranian variant of Polish. Kashubian is spoken in two distinct dialects, Kashubian Proper and Slovincian, and there are transitional dialects between Kashubian Proper, Slovencian, and Polish. Since the late 1980s efforts have been made to revive the language. The Kashubian language differs greatly from literary Polish and, with Polish and Sorbian, spoken in Saxony in Germany, belongs to the Lechitian subgroup of West Slavic languages.

NATION: The ancestors of the Slavs are thought to have been Neolithic tribes that occupied the Polesie marshes in western Ukraine centuries before the Christian Era. By the sixth century Slavic tribes, including the Kashubs, had settled the coast of the Baltic Sea and occupied the inland territories. Sedentary fishermen and farmers, the Kashubs adopted a loosely democratic social organization.

In the tenth century, the Polians (dwellers of the fields), later known as Poles,* led by their chief, Boleslaus I, conquered the Slavic tribes that inhabited Pomerania. The Poles' conversion to Christianity brought missionaries to work among the conquered tribes. In the eleventh century the Kashubs of Pomerania threw off Polish rule and created an independent duchy. In the twelfth century, the Poles again overran Pomerania, bringing with them their Christian religion, which was adopted by the conquered Kashubs. At the death of Boleslaus III in 1138, the Polish kingdom broke up, and the Kashubs regained their independence in 1227.

Pomerelia, as eastern Pomerania, the Kashubian homeland, came to be known, was retaken by the Poles in 1295. Germans, called Teutonic Knights, gained a foothold in the region, and in 1308 the 10,000 inhabitants of Gdansk, mostly Kashubs, were massacred and replaced with ethnic Germans. By 1309 all of Kashubia had fallen to the German knights. The Poles defeated the Germans at Tannenberg in 1410 and began the reconquest of the region around the Gulf of Gdansk. In 1454 the entire Kashubian territory was incorporated into the Polish kingdom. The western Kashubs, over several centuries of German influence, became partly Germanized in culture and language, but the eastern Kashubs, under Polish rule, retained their Slavic language and culture.

In 1466 the city of Gdansk, with its large German population, was granted the status of an autonomous city under Polish protection. The Kashubs, the original inhabitants, were reduced to a small minority by the beginning of the sixteenth century. The city, called Danzig by the Germans, became one of the leading cities of the Hanseatic League. In 1576 the city withstood a long Polish siege and preserved its special privileges.

Kashubia, although overrun by foreign armies several times during the wars of the fifteenth and sixteenth centuries, remained an integral part of the Polish kingdom. Mostly peasant farmers and fishermen, the Kashubs had been reduced to virtual serfdom by the sixteenth century under both Polish and Swedish rule. Many began to assimilate into the Polish culture and language, particularly those living in the large city of Gdansk, where both the Kashubs and the Poles were less numerous than the German population.

The Poles lost Kashubia to Prussia during the first partition of the kingdom in 1772. The region formed part of the Prussian province of West Prussia with Gdansk as its capital. Under Prussian rule the Kashubs were subjected to a program of intense Germanization. Danzig, with its surrounding area, became a German stronghold and cultural center. At the end of the Napoleonic Wars, the Congress of Vienna created a small Polish kingdom, including Kashubia, in personal union with Russia under the tsar.

The Kashubs participated in the Polish national revival, which began in the 1820s. The revival, which helped to unite the various regional Polish groups, began as an anti-German and anti-Russian mass movement. Thousands of Kashubs joined the general uprising against Russian rule in 1830, and with Polish defeat in 1831, their homeland, except for the region under Prussian rule, became an integral part of the Russian Empire. Further violence broke out in Prussian Poland in 1848 and in Russian Poland in 1863.

Political instability added to the grinding poverty in Kashubia. Poor, sandy soil made farming difficult, and the returns from fishing were always unpredictable. Many Kashubs chose to leave their homeland and emigrate to Canada and the United States. The largest wave of immigration took place between 1859 and 1898. Kashubian colonies were established in North America, where the customs, traditions, and language were preserved alongside their new culture and their new language, English.

Germany's defeat in World War I allowed the Poles to resurrect their independent state. The 1919 peace treaty gave Poland part of eastern Kashubia, but the German-populated Danzig and its surrounding Kashubian hinterland, in spite of Polish claims, were made a separate free city under the protection of the new League of Nations. The city-state joined the Polish Customs Union and served as Poland's primary outlet to the sea, but the Poles, preferring their own port, constructed a new port at Gdynia, a small Kashubian village north of Danzig. In 1930 the city of Danzig, which was 95% German-speaking, had a population of 259,000, while the Free State of Danzig had a population of 407,000, including many Kashubs.

The rise of the Nazis in Germany during the 1930s was paralleled by the increase in Nazi activity in Danzig. In November 1937 the Nazis obtained a two-thirds majority in the Danzig legislature. The Poles and Kashubs living in the state suffered increased aggression as totalitarian rule was extended. In March 1939 Nazi Germany made extensive demands on Poland regarding Danzig and Pomerania, but Poland's alliance with France and the United Kingdom induced the German government to back down.

On 1 September 1939, without a declaration of war, the Germans invaded Poland. The Kashubs suffered tremendous losses of life and property in the war, with many, particularly those able to speak German, sent to labor camps in Germany. The last German troops were expelled from Poland in 1945 by Soviet troops. With the conclusion of peace, the Soviet authorities encouraged the Poles to expel the German population of the Gdansk region, which included many Germanized Kashubs, but Kashubia was once again reunited.

Poland became a communist state allied to the Soviet Union during the Cold War of the 1950s through the 1980s. In spite of authoritarian government and economic hardships, since 1945 the authorities promoted research, preservation, and promotion of the Kashubian culture. Dance troops and *kapelas* were organized to preserve the distinct Kashubian musical heritage.

The end of communism in Poland began in the shipyards of Gdansk with workers unions in the 1980s. In 1989 an accord between the unions and the government opened the way for democratic government in Poland. The Kashubs, long considered assimilated by the Polish majority, began to reassert their distinct culture and identity in the 1990s. Organizations such as Kaszubskiego (Kashub Nation), and Zrzeszenie Kaszubsko-Pomorskie (ZKP), the Kashubian-Pomeranian Association, based in Gdansk, are leading the revival of the ancient Kashubian nation.

SELECTED BIBLIOGRAPHY

Guuenwald, Myron E. *Pomeranians: The Persistent Pioneers.* 1987.
Iglicka, Krystyna, and Keith Sword, eds. *The Challenge of East-West Migration to Poland.* 1998.
Millard, Frances. *The Anatomy of the New Poland: Post-Communist Politics in Its First Phase.* 1994.
Starski, Stanislaw. *Class Struggle in Classless Poland.* 1982.
Wandycz, Piotr. S. *The Lands of Partitioned Poland, 1795–1918.* 1993.

KOMIS

Komi Mort; Komi Zyranes; Zyrians

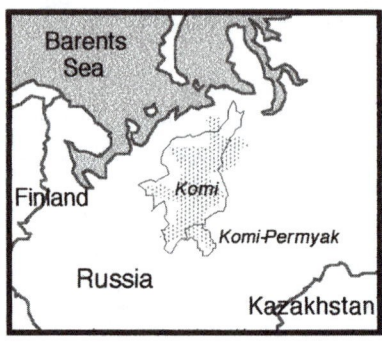

POPULATION: Approximately (2000 e) 567,000 Komis in Europe, concentrated in the Komi Republic of the Russia Federation and with smaller Komi populations in the autonomous Komi-Permyak district in Perm' Oblast, and in neighboring regions.

THE KOMI HOMELAND: The Komi homeland occupies the basins of the Pechora, Vychegda, and Kama Rivers and the upper reaches of the Mezen River, a region partly above the Arctic Circle in northern European Russia. The Arctic Circle crosses the northern part of the republic, and permafrost covers more than 10% of of the territory. Most of the region is level ground, with permanently frozen tundra in the north. The Timan Mountains cut throught the region from the northeast to the southeast, and the Northern and Polar Ural Mountains rise in the east. The highest peak in the region and in the Ural Mountains as a whole is Mt. Narodnaia, 6,217 feet (1,895 m.). Over two-thirds of the homeland is covered by evergreen forests, although there are some agriculture and herding, mostly cattle and reindeer. There are major coalfields in the Pechora Basin, which yield both heating and coking coal.

The majority of the territory of the Komi homeland, often called Zyria, forms a member state of the Russian Federation. *Komi Republic (Komi Mu)*: 160,579 sq.mi.–415,900 sq.km. (2000 e) 1,258,000—Russians* 54%, Komis 31%, Ukrainians* 10%, Belarussians* 3%, Nenets. The Komi capital and major cultural center is the city of Syktyvkar, (2000 e) 242,000, called Ust-Sysolsk from 1780 to 1930. A smaller portion of the traditional Komi homeland forms an autonomous district in Perm' Oblast. *Komi-Permyak Autonomous Okrug (Permyakia)*: 12,703 sq.mi.–32,901 sq.km. (2000 e) 166,000—Komi-Permyaks 71%,

Russians 22%, Ukrainians 6%, Belarussians 1%. The capital and major cultural center of the Komi-Permyaks is Kudymkar, (2000 e) 39,000.

FLAG: The Komi national flag, the official flag of the Komi Republic, is a horizontal tricolor of blue, green, and white.

PEOPLE: The Komis are the largest of the two divisions of the Permian peoples, which also includes the Udmurts.* The Permians are a major branch of the Finno-Ugric peoples. Although they all consider themselves to be one nation, there are three distinct Komi groups, the Komis, the Komi-Permyaks, and the Izhmi. The Komi-Permyaks are further divided into two major groups, the Yazvinians and the Zyuzdinians. The Komis are the most advanced of the northern peoples of the Russian Federation.

The Komis, calling themselves Komi-More or Komi-Zyrane, the most northerly of the Finnic peoples, inhabit the upper Vychegda and Pechora River basins, with other groups scattered in neighboring regions and as far east as western Siberia. An estimated 15,000 Komis live in the Nenets region above the Arctic Circle, which was administratively separated from the Komi homeland in 1929. The majority of the Komis work in farming and timber and as traders or as cattle or reindeer herders. The language of the Komis is a Finno-Permian language of the Permian group of Finno-Ugric languages. Komi is spoken in three major dialects, Pechora, Udor, and Verkhne-Vyshegod. Another dialect, Yazva, often included as a dialect of Komi, is more accurately a transition dialect to Komi-Permyak. The Komi reculturation is evident in language figures. In 1989 the Komis living in the republic who reported Russian as their first language amounted to 42.8%; by 1994 this percentage had dropped to 26.3% of the total.

The Komi-Permyaks inhabit the region just southeast of the Komis. Calling themselves Komi-Voityr or Komi Otir, they separated from the Komis around A.D. 500. The language of the Komi-Permyaks, closely related to Komi, is spoken in two primary dialects, the northern or Kosinsko-Kama, and the southern or Inven. The third division of the Komis, called the Izhmi, who call themselves Izva Tas, live northeast of the Komis, inhabiting the region between the Pechora and the Izhma Rivers, although several thousand live farther east in the Yamalo-Nenets and Tyumen regions. The Izhmi, many living above the Arctic Circle, have mixed with the Nenets* and have taken on some of the Nenets' religious and cultural traits.

The Komis are mostly Russian Orthodox, but their religious traditions remain laced with the shamanistic traditions of their pre-Christian heritage. A substantial number of the Komi Orthodox population are Old Believers, who adopted their religious beliefs from the Russian Old Believers who settled in the region to escape persecution by the Orthodox authorities.

NATION: The Permian peoples are descended from ancestors who originally inhabited the middle and upper Kama River area. The ancestors of the closely related Udmurts occupied the nearby basin of the Viatka River. During the first millennium before the Christian Era, the Komis and Udmurts split into two major groups. Around A.D. 500 the Komi group split, with some of the clans migrating from the upper Kama River region to the Vychegda Basin. The migrants, settling in the colder north, mixed with local peoples and began the development of a separate nation. Those clans left behind in the Kama Basin became known as Komi-Permyaks.

The Komis came under the rule of the Slavic republic known as Great Novgorod in the thirteenth century. Formerly practicing a form of ancestor worship, the Komis converted to the Orthodox Christianity introduced to the clans by St. Stephen in the 1360s and 1370s. St. Stephen of Perm, the Komis' patron saint, called the "Enlightener of the Komi," is revered for opening the Komi homeland to the world outside. He converted many to Orthodox Christianity but also constructed an alphabet for the Komi language and translated parts of the Bible.

The Russians of the rival Muscovite duchy began to penetrate Novgorodian territory in 1450 and finally conquered Novgorod between 1471 and 1478. Although more blond and Nordic than the Russians, the Komis were subjected to prejudice and a harsh colonial regime. The Russians suppressed the Komi languages and culture and forced assimilation but encouraged their Orthodox faith, although Old Believers often suffered. In the mid-sixteenth century, to escape harsh Russian rule, many Komi clans again migrated, moving deeper into the upper Vychegda and Pechora River basins.

In the eighteenth century, the authorities opened the southern Komi districts to Slavic colonization, while setting aside the forest and Arctic zones as a place of exile for criminals and tsarist political prisoners. The abolition of serfdom in Russia in 1861 led to a massive influx of freed serfs into the region. Major trade routes developed across the Komi homeland from Archangel to the Viatka-Kama Basin and on to Siberia, and the Komis earned a reputation as shrewd traders in the isolated settlements north of the Arctic Circle. By the nineteenth century industries were established in the region. The Komis took to reindeer breeding late in the nineteenth century, mostly among the clans living in the northern reaches of the homeland.

Komi resentment of the Slav colonists, who appropriated the best lands, led to violent confrontations in the 1870s and 1880s. Their treatment by the growing Russian population in their territory triggered a national revival. A Komi cultural movement in the late nineteenth century emphasized their language, particularly the distinguished tradition of oral epics and folk literature. The revival began to reverse centuries of forced assimilation. A parallel movement, heavily influenced by the attitudes and ideals of the large population of political exiles in the region, evolved a Komi national sentiment, antigovernment and anti-Russian.

The outbreak of World War I reinforced the growing antitsarist movement. Many young Komis took refuge in the forests to escape conscription. The overthrow of the tsar in February 1917 raised Komi expectations that the abuses and wrongs of the past would finally be addressed. A Komi congress in the summer of 1917 voted for autonomy in a new democratic Russia and sent a formal petition to the provisional government.

The Bolshevik coup in October 1917 swept away the remaining Russian authority in the region. Left virtually independent, the Komi leaders began to organize the institutions of self-rule, but early in 1918 Bolshevik troops of the new Soviet government invaded the region. Allied Anglo-American interventionist forces landed at Arkhangelsk and drove the Bolsheviks from the Komi region in May and June 1918. The interventionists encouraged the Komis to organize a national state to combat Bolshevik influence in the region. Aided by the numerous freed political prisoners and members of the foreign interventionist forces, the Komis created a number of cultural and governmental institutions. In 1919 the interventionist forces withdrew from the region, opening the way for the Soviet reoccupation of the Komi state.

To disseminate information over the large territory, a new Komi alphabet was devised to fit the Komis' Permian language by the new Soviet authorities. The alphabet, using mixed Latin and Cyrillic characters, was used in printing after 1920, but in 1938 the authorities eliminated the distinctive Komi alphabet, and the Russian Cyrillic script was substituted.

The Soviet authorities created an autonomous province, as part of the early nationalities policies, for the Komis in 1921. The province was raised to the status of an autonomous republic within the Russian Federation in 1936. A Komi-Permyak district was organized in 1925 and was created as an autonomous district in 1929. The Slav population of the region, only 7% of the total in 1926, with the Komis accounting for 92%, expanded rapidly during the Stalinist years. The Pechora Basin was sparsely inhabited until high-quality coal was discovered in the 1930s, when the region was quickly incorporated into the Gulag system of slave labor camps. Northern Zyria, a region so forbidding that it had been rejected as a place of exile by Tsar Nicholas I, by the mid-1930s had a population of over 100,000, mostly prisoners.

The Komi homeland gained new importance during World War II as threatened industries and populations shifted east and north from the provinces overrun by the Germans. In 1943 the Vorkuta-Kotlas Railway was completed across the region, entirely built by slave labor. The opening of the rail link allowed the exploitation of the oil fields discovered in Pechora and Ukhta regions and began a period of spectacular growth. The population of the Komi region quadrupled between 1939 and 1949. By the end of World War II, the Komi population formed only a large minority in their homeland.

Purges ordered by Joseph Stalin during the late 1940s and early 1950s mostly eliminated the cultural and political leadership of the Komis. Ethnic Slavs filled nearly all the positions in the local government Communist Party hierarchies. In the 1960s the region became more important economically as the extensive minerals began to be exploited. Rapid regional industrialization forced many Komis to settle in cities and urban areas where they could find work in the new mills, factories, and mines.

The Soviet reforms introduced by Mikhail Gorbachev in the late 1980s had an immediate impact on the region. The relaxation of strict controls provoked massive strikes by the region's coal miners to punctuate demands for higher pay and better working conditions in 1989–90. The strikes and the disturbances by miners, already handsomely paid by Komi standards, loosed a torrent of Komi grievances and demands that Komi mistreatment be addressed by the republic's Chamber of Deputies. Economic demands gave way to political demands, including calls for the reunification of the Komi lands divided by Stalin between 1925 and 1929. On 29 August 1990 the leaders of the republic declared Komi a sovereign state.

The disintegration of the Soviet state in August 1991 fueled a dramatic increase in the Komi's national awareness. The republican government in November 1991 unilaterally declared Komi a constituent republic of the renewed Russian Federation, and reiterated an earlier demand for the reunification of the Komi homeland in one state.

Several Komi national organizations, formed mostly since 1991, have increasingly demanded local control of the region's vast mineral resources and a larger share of the revenues earned for local development projects. Economic demands have grown since the economic collapse of the Russian economy in 1998. The coal reserves in the Komi homeland would give the region a valuable commodity to trade for basic needs.

Since 1993 the Komi nationalists have waged a nonviolent war of symbols in the region. Denouncing the new Russian flag as a symbol of colonialism and as offensive as the former red banner of the communists, nationalists routinely tear down the Russian flag and raise the banner of Komi nationalism in its place. The Komi flag, representing the nationalists' aspirations and demands for unification, has come to symbolize the Komis' contention that their natural resources would sustain their small nation through the hard economic times ahead.

The Komi rebirth, which began during the late Soviet era, accelerated in the post-Soviet period. During the Soviet period some Komi traditions were lost, but a literary culture developed. Komi literature had been published in the eighteenth and nineteenth centuries, but alphabet reforms and mass education during the Soviet period generated a literary renaissance, which continues to the present as part of the Komi renaissance. Organized movements to revive the Komi languages, traditions, and religious practices developed in the late Soviet period but have become a mass cultural movement since 1991.

SELECTED BIBLIOGRAPHY

Allworth, Edward. *Soviet Nationality Problems.* 1971.
Duik, Nadia, and Adrian Karatnychky. *The Hidden Nations: The People Challenge the Soviet Union.* 1990.
Kozlov, Viktor. *The Peoples of the Soviet Union.* 1988.
Olson, James S. *An Ethnohistorical Dictionary of the Russian and Soviet Empires.* 1994.
Wixman, Ronald. *The Peoples of the USSR: An Ethnographic Handbook.* 1984.

KUBAN COSSACKS

Kazaki Kuban; Kazaky Kuban

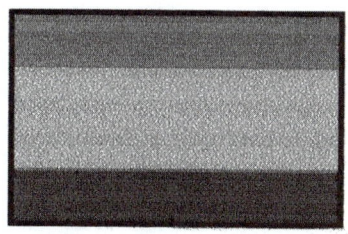

POPULATION: Approximately (2000 e) 1,730,000 Kuban Cossacks in Europe, concentrated in the Kuban, officially Krasnodar Kray, but with large Kuban Cossack communities in other parts of southern Russia and also in France, Germany, and Scandinavia. Outside Europe the largest Kuban Cossack communities are located in the United States, Canada, and Australia.

THE KUBAN COSSACK HOMELAND: The Kuban Cossack homeland occupies the Kuban Steppe and the valley of the Kuban River on the eastern shore of the Black Sea in southern European Russia. The northern districts of the Kuban are plains, but in the south the Caucasus Mountains extend across one-third of the territory. In the high Caucasus glaciers creep down into the high valleys. The Kuban River and its tributaries make up the region's principal river system and run through one of the most important agricultural areas in Russia. The region, forming the Krasnodar Kray or Territory, is one of the so-called Cossack provinces, which also includes Rostov Oblast, the homeland of the Don Cossacks,* and Stavropol Kray, the homeland of the Terek Cossacks.*

The Kuban, including the fertile Kuban River lowlands, is historically part of the North Caucasus region of Russia and is separated from the Crimean Peninsula by the Kerch Strait. In the south the region lies in the mountains and foothills of the Greater Caucasus Mountains. Although much of the region is fertile and cultivated, the districts along the Sea of Azov in the north are mostly marshlands.

The historic homeland was organized as Krasnodar Territory 1937. *Krasnodar Territory*: 32,278 sq.mi.–83,600 sq.km. (2000 e) 4,823,000—Russians* 36%, Kuban Cossacks 32%, Ukrainians* 21%, Adyge* 2.5%, Armenians* 1%,

Greeks* 1%, Belarussians,* Germans,* Georgians,* Azeris.* The Kuban Cossack capital and major cultural center is Krasnodar, called Ekaterinodar by the Cossacks, (2000 e) 641,000, which was founded as a Cossack fort in 1794.

FLAG: The Kuban Cossack national flag, the flag of the former Kuban Cossack republic, is a tricolor of blue, raspberry red, and green, the red twice the width of the other stripes.

PEOPLE: The Kuban Cossacks are a Slavic people of mixed Russian, Ukrainian, and Circassian background traditionally divided into two groups, the Chermomortsy, descendants of Zaporozhye Cossacks and Ukrainian settlers concentrated in the lower reaches of the Kuban River, and Lineitsy (First Liners), descendants of Don Cossacks, Circassians, and Russian colonists in the middle and upper reaches of the Kuban Basin. The Kuban Cossack claim to separate national status is based on their history, way of life, culture, and language. Nationalists claim that at least one-quarter of the regional population has Cossack ancestry, although official figures put the Kuban Cossack regional population at about one-seventh of the total.

The Kuban Cossacks speak a Cossack language of mixed Russian and Ukrainian influences, although the dialect spoken in the upper Kuban Basin has considerably less Ukrainian influence and has absorbed many Circassian words. There are an estimated twenty Cossack dialects spoken in the Russian Federation. The culture and dialects spoken by the Kuban Cossacks have been strongly influenced by their long association with the neighboring Circassian peoples, particularly the Adyge. Many of the customs and traditions of the Kuban Cossacks have their origins in Circassian culture.

NATION: The territory of the Kuban Cossacks was originally inhabited by fierce Circassian tribes that blocked further Slavic expansion to the south. Although nominally a part of the first great Slav State, Kievan Rus', the Kuban was overrun by the Golden Horde in 1241 and later formed part of the successor state to the Golden Horde, the khanate of the Crimean Tatars.*

The Russians began to penetrate the area in 1774 and ultimately annexed the territory to the expanding Russian Empire in 1783. Many of the Zaporozhye Cossacks, defeated and officially dissolved following an uprising in the Ukraine in 1775, fled across the Danube River into Turkish-controlled territory. Those who stayed in Russian territory were allowed to settle along the Black Sea between the Dniepr and Bug Rivers and evolved into the Black Sea Cossacks. At the end of the Russo-Turkish War of 1787–91, the tsarist authorities grew suspicious of the ties between the Black Sea Cossacks and the Zaporozhe Cossacks across the Danube. Forcibly relocated to the Kuban, newly annexed as part of the Crimean Tatar territory, the Black Sea Cossacks came to be called the Kuban Cossacks. In 1828 most of the remaining Zaporozhe Cossacks left Turkish territory to join the Kuban Cossacks in their new homeland on the steppes of the North Caucasus.

Called *Chermomortsy*, the Black Sea People, the Kuban Cossacks governed themselves in exchange for a vow of loyalty to the tsar and military service as the guardians of Russia's new southern frontier. Don Cossacks, from the Don River Basin to the north, settled the interior of the territory in the 1830s and became known as *Lineitsy*, the First Liners. Collectively rechristened the Kuban Cossacks in 1860, the Kuban Horde formed the largest Cossack community in southern Russia.

The Muslim Circassian tribes farther to the south, finally defeated in 1864, mostly fled or were expelled to Turkish territory. Their confiscated lands became Kuban Cossack lands, held in common by the villages and clans with many Circassians taken into the horde. Thousands of freed Russian and Ukrainian serfs migrated south to the fertile region following the abolition of serfdom in 1861. The Kuban Cossack communes absorbed many of the former serfs, while others settled on the Cossacks' communal lands as tenant farmers.

The new Russian and Ukrainian migrants greatly resented Cossack privileges, with increasing tension in the region in the late nineteenth century. The Kuban Cossacks traded military service for freedom from taxes and direct Russian control, giving them control of the Kuban territory. Under the tsars they formed elite military units with special statutes of self-government. Whenever their privileges were threatened, the Kuban Cossacks rebelled. In the latter part of the nineteenth and the early part of the twentieth centuries, the tsarist government used Cossack troops to perpetrate pogroms against the Jews. Cossack troops were used on a large scale in the suppression of the Russian Revolution of 1905; they refused to be used for the same purpose in the Revolution of 1917.

Personally loyal to the tsar, not to the Russian state, the Kuban Cossacks formed front-line military units when war began in 1914. The Kuban Cossack units suffered heavy casualties that fueled growing unrest among the military clans. Their oath of loyalty invalidated by the overthrow of the tsar in February 1917, the Kuban Cossacks deserted the front in large numbers to return to their homeland to protect it from a threatened Turkish advance from the south.

Kuban Cossack leaders convened a parliament, the Rada, in March 1917, creating a Kuban military government to replace the local tsarist administration. On 17 July 1917 the Rada declared the Kuban a sovereign state within the new democratic Russia. The Kuban Cossacks joined the anti-Bolshevik White forces following the Bolshevik coup in October 1917.

At first the Kuban Cossacks wholeheartedly supported the White cause, but confrontations between Kuban nationalists and the White leadership, who opposed the breakup of the Russian Empire, soon soured relations. The *Chernomortsy* favored full independence but faced strong resistance from many of the *Lineitsy*, committed to Russian unity, and the *Ingorodnie*, the Slavic tenant farmers won over by Bolshevik promises to redistribute the Cossack communal lands. The Kuban government insisted on forming a Kuban National Army, separate from the hierarchy of the White military forces of General Anton Deniken, which were based in the Kuban. The Kuban separatists gained support as the Russian Empire collapsed, and chaos spread across the region.

On 16 February 1918 the Kuban Rada, dominated by the *Chermomortsy*, declared the independence of the Kuban as the Kuban People's Republic. The new state had a population of 3.5 million, 53% Russian, 47% Kuban Cossack, 10% Adyge. A delegation from the Kuban government traveled to Paris to attend the Paris Peace Conference in 1919 in an effort to win Allied recognition. In the fall of 1919 Deniken arrested the Kuban's leaders and executed eleven of them before moving his headquarters out of the breakaway state he claimed was dominated by nationalists.

The White defeat in 1920 was followed by the rapid occupation of the Kuban by the Red Army and the formation of a Kuban-Black Sea Soviet Republic. Widespread famine swept the Kuban in 1921–22, leaving many dead in its wake. Many of the Kuban Cossacks fled abroad or joined guerrilla bands that harassed the Soviet authorities until finally eradicated in 1924. The Soviet authorities revoked all traditional Cossack privileges, including military Training. The authorities reclassified the Kuban Cossacks from Ukrainian-speakers to Russian-speakers, with enforced use of Russian in place of the Kubans' unique Ukrainian-Russian-Circassian dialect.

Collectivization in 1931–32 was followed by yet another famine in 1933, partly caused by the confiscation of all grains, including seeds and fodder, by the Soviet government. Thousands of Kuban Cossacks starved, their fate ignored by the Soviet authorities. The government of Joseph Stalin is accused of planning the famine in areas where Soviet rule was opposed. In 1936 some Cossack privileges were returned, and they were again allowed to serve in the country's military. The Krasnodar Territory was created in 1937, but the Cossack name of the region, Kuban, remained forbidden.

In 1941 Hitler turned on his Soviet ally, and German troops invaded the Soviet Union. The Germans, advancing on the Maikop oil fields in the southern Kuban in late 1942, decreed that the Kuban Cossacks were descended from Germanic Ostrogoths, not subhuman Slavs, and therefore constituted acceptable allies. Thousands of Cossacks joined the anticommunist crusade of the Nazi Germans. In October 1942 an autonomous Kuban government under Ataman Domanov was created and was policed by a Kuban Cossack militia. At the end of the war over 40,000 Cossacks, with their families, surrendered to the Allies in Austria. However, at Stalin's insistence, the Allies forcibly repatriated the Cossacks to face Stalin's punishment. Thousands were sent to labor camps in Siberia, executed, or imprisoned.

A cultural revival in the 1960s began with the publication of the first Cossack dictionary and works on Kuban Cossack history and culture that exile groups smuggled into the Soviet Union. The revival raised demands for recognition of the Kuban Cossacks as a separate ethnic and cultural group in the Soviet Union. The resurgence of their culture and traditions incited a parallel nationalist revival, and Kuban Cossack nationalism emerged as a potent force following the liberalization of Soviet society in the late 1980s with demands for a revival of their role as the protectors of Russia's borders. Several powerful Kuban Cossack associations formed in the region. At first the goals of the Cossack associations were cultural and historical in nature, to preserve Cossack traditions and promote historical accuracy of Cossack lifestyles. Kuban Cossack leaders later began to demand local self-administration and the return of traditional lands.

Kuban Cossack nationalists, with the support of the Ukrainian minority, are gaining support for demands that the Kuban be granted republican status within the Russian Federation. More radical nationalists claim that their separate history and culture are the basis of a viable national state, while even more nationalistic groups advocate the creation of a greater Cossackia of some 20 million inhabitants to incorporate the traditionally Cossack lands between Kazakhstan, Ukraine, and the Caucasus Mountains. The growing divisions within the Kuban Cossack revival have not blunted the power of the culture that has emerged after seven decades of suppression.

Thousands of Cossack volunteers traveled to Moldova to fight on the side of the self-proclaimed, Russaian-dominated Trans-Dniester Republic, and many others served with the Serbians* during the fighting in the former Yugoslavia. Several Kuban Cossack associations sought to form a semiautonomous republic within Russia, and they demanded that Cossacks be considered a separate ethnic group. In mid-1992 a decree signed by Russian president Boris Yeltsin rehabilitated the Cossacks. The decree granted them the status of an ethnic group and gave them the right to receive land free of charge. The decree also called for the use of Cossack forces to protect Russia's borders.

The Kuban Cossacks in August 1996 celebrated 300 years of the Kuban Cossack Army, the *Voisko*, with a huge gathering in Krasnodar with traditional music and a remembrance of their heritage. Many of the Cossacks attended in traditional uniforms complete with swords. The crowd listened to speeches and waved the Kuban Cossack flag as speakers called for the resurrection of the tradition of self-government and unity.

At the beginning of 1996 the government of the region negotiated broad powers that include the right to regulate migration to the region, to pass its own legislation on land, and to officially rehabilitate the Kuban Cossacks. In September 1997 the governor of Krasnodar Kray set up a regional Kuban Cossack militia, while legislation adopted by the provincial legislature is turning the region into an outpost governed by its own laws, many of which run counter to federal legislation.

SELECTED BIBLIOGRAPHY
Glaskow, Wasili G. *History of the Cossacks.* 1968.
Groushko, Mike. *Cossack: Warrior Riders of the Steppes.* 1993.
McNeal, Robert H. *Tsar and Cossack: 1855–1914.* 1987.
Newland, Samuel J. *Cossacks and the German Army, 1941–1945.* 1991.
Sienkiewica, Henry K. *With Fire and Sword.* 1991.

KUMYKS

Kumuks; Kumiks; Kumihs;
Qumuqs

POPULATION: Approximately (2000 e) 287,000 Kumyks in Europe, concentrated in the northern districts of the Dagestan Republic, a member state of the Russian Federation, in southern European Russia. Smaller numbers live in neighboring regions.

THE HOMELAND: The Kumyk homeland is primarily in the lowlands of the northeast Caucasus Mountains between the Terek and Samur Rivers. Because there is no easily accessible pass over the Caucasus Mountains, the coastal plain bordering the Caspian Sea has historically been an important north-south passage. The mountains just to the south of the Kumyk homeland are still extremely isolated, notably in winter. The region, called Kumykstan by the Kumyks, comprises seven districts of lowland Dagestan, Khasavyurt, Babayurt, Kizilyurt, Buinaksk, Karabudakhkent, Kaiakent, and Kaitak.

The region called Kumykstan has no official status, although the majority of the Kumyks have expressed their desire to separate their homeland from the multiethnic Dagestan Republic. The capital and major cultural center of the Kumyks is Buynaksk, called Temir-Khan-Shura by the Kumyks, (2000 e) 68,000. Makhachkala, the capital of Dagestan, (2000 e) 348,000, is located in traditional Kumyk territory and has a large Kumyk population.

FLAG: The Kumyk national flag, the proposed flag of the Kumyk Republic, is a horizontal bicolor of red over green with a pale blue trapezoid at the hoist. Over the joining of the three colors is a white circle, outlined in gold, bearing a gold crescent moon and five-pointed star. Around the edge of the circle are the symbols of the three Kumyk groups, in gold.

PEOPLE: The Kumyks originated with Turkic nomads migrating to northern

Dagestan from Central Asia. There they mixed extensively with the native Caucasian peoples, although traditionally they remained in the northern steppe lands as nomadic or seminomadic horse and stock herders, with some engaged in trading or farming. The Kumyks are divided into three traditional groups based on dialect and location. The northern Kumyks inhabit the Kumyk Steppe. The central Kumyks, the most influential of the three, inhabit the region around Buynaksk and Makhachkala. The southern Kumyks are highlanders, living in the Caucasian foothills.

Once the dominant people of the Caspian lowlands, the Kumyks have become a minority in their homeland owing to the migration of mountain peoples, principally Avars,* Laks,* and Dargins.* The destruction of mountain villages and farmlands by the former Soviet authorities forced the migration of the mountain peoples. The situation of the pastoral peoples such as the Kumyks has deteriorated seriously during the twentieth century, with many settling in the cities as industrial workers. Although the Kumyks were somewhat dispersed during the Soviet era, 82% of the Kumyk population in Russia continues to live in their ancient homeland.

The Kumyk language is a Turkic language, a Ponto-Caspian dialect, part of the Oghuz group of the Kypchak or West Turkic division of the Turkic language group. The language is spoken in three major dialects, Khasavyurt in the north, Buinaksk in the central districts, and Kaitak (Khaikent) in the south. Because of centuries of ethnic mixing, the language has incorporated many Caucasian borrowings and is intelligible to the Azeris,* who inhabit the region south of Kumykstan. The Kumyk language has become the lingua franca of much of central Dagestan.

The Sunni Muslim religion and their identity as a Turkic people in a region dominated by Caucasian nations have reinforced the Kumyks' culture and sense of identity. Although the rate of urbanization is high, they have maintained a strong ethnic identity and rarely marry outside their national group. The Kumyk culture emphasizes family ties and their Muslim religion, even though their religious observances are less fervent than those of their Caucasian neighbors, and there is a Shi'a Muslim minority.

NATION: The origin of the Kumyks is not clear, although Kumyk tradition sets the origins of their nation with the migrations of Turkic and Mongol peoples west across the steppes of Central Asia to the region around the Caspian Sea in the fifth century A.D. The Turkic Khazars by the year 650 had established a stable state in the region, with trading routes across the Caucasus. In spite of stable trading relations, the Caucasus Mountains, which separated the Khazar Empire from the Persian lands, became the scene of repeated and devastating wars in the eighth and ninth centuries. By the tenth century, some Turkic tribes had migrated to the area west of the Caspian Sea, where they mixed extensively with the indigenous Caucasian peoples. Between the eleventh and thirteenth centuries, the Kumyks consolidated their sense of nationhood and strengthened their hold on the lowland steppes. During the fifteenth and sixteenth centuries the Kumyks established an independent state, the Shamkhalat of Tarki, which controlled large areas inhabited by non-Kumyk Caucasians. Because the Kumyks controlled the lowland winter pastures used by the Caucasian mountain herders, their language was adopted as a second language by large numbers of their Caucasian subjects.

The expansion of the Russians* into the steppe lands weakened Kumyk power in the sixteenth century. To counter Russian influence, the Kumyks declared their loyalty to the Safavid dynasty of Persia, which controlled the Caucasus highlands just south of Kumyk territory. The Kumyks were caught between the great powers during the wars for control of the Caucasus in the seventeenth and eighteenth centuries. When Peter the Great conquered Derbent in 1722 and defeated the Persians, the Kumyks lost their independence.

The Kumyks managed to retain a degree of autonomy over the next century, but Russian influence divided the Kumyk clans. In the early 1830s Shamil, imam of Dagestan, called for strict observance of Sharia, Islamic law, and for *gazawat*, holy war against the Christian invaders. The northern clans joined the anti-Russian Shamil movement, while the central clans sided with the Russians, and the southern clans maintained their neutrality. When the Russians finally crushed the Shamil rebellion, the Kumyks, along with the other Caucasian nations, were brought under strict Russian control. In 1867 the Russian authorities dissolved the Shamkhalat, and the Kumyk homeland came under direct Russian control.

The industrialization of the region, particularly the Caspian port cities, in the latter half of the nineteenth century drew in large numbers of Kumyks, who formed an urban labor class. Many of the urbanized Kumyks were involved in the revolutionary movement. The overthrow of the Russian tsar in 1917 was followed by the takeover of Russia by the radical Bolsheviks. Although most Kumyks preferred Pan-Turkic or Islamic nationalism, the Bolsheviks found much support among urban Kumyks in the region's industrial towns.

The civil war that followed devastated the Kumyk homeland. Villages and towns were destroyed, and the population dispersed. In 1920 the Red Army, victorious in the civil war, took control of the region. The new Soviet authorities in 1921 proclaimed the Dagestan Autonomous Soviet Socialist Republic, formed from the tsarist region of Dagestan plus the Kumyk region of Terskaia. Over the next year the borders of the republic were extended northward to include the lowland territories of the Kumyks and Nogais.*

In 1928–29, the Soviet program of collectivization started, Kumyk farming and pasturelands were confiscated, the clans were disarmed, and Muslim Sharia law was abolished. The Kumyk leadership, accused of bourgeois nationalism and Pan-Turkic policies, was annihilated or deported. Government functionaries sent from Moscow filled all posts in local government. The situation in Kumykstan stabilized only in 1936, when the government formalized the structure of the Dagestan autonomous republic.

During World War II, the German army drove south toward the oil fields in the North Caucasus. The Kumyk homeland was occupied in 1942. *Kalkhozes,* collective farms, were closed, mosques were reopened in areas under German control, and promises of self-determination were given to those Kumyks who were willing to listen. The majority, viewing the Germans as just another in a long line of invaders, refused to cooperate and saved the Kumyk nation the brutal deportations suffered by other nations in the Caucasus region.

The postwar industrialization of the region drew many Kumyks into the growing cities in the 1950s and 1960s. Because of their population concentration in Dagestan's central districts, the urban and rural Kumyks were able to stay in close communication, which reinforced their traditional culture and values. Soviet policies forced many of the mountain peoples to move down to the lowlands, where they were more easily controlled. By the 1970s the Kumyks were sharing their traditional lands with Caucasian mountaineers. The agricultural practices and attitudes of the Caucasian peoples clashed with those of the rural Kumyks. The tensions between the two groups accelerated during the reforms instituted in the Soviet Union in the late 1980s. Dominating the Caspian lowlands, the Kumyks resented the massive migration to their homeland. The forced resettlement of mountain peoples to Kumyk territory destroyed the traditional settlement patterns and deprived the Kumyks of half their arable land by the time the Soviet Union disintegrated in 1991.

In 1990 the newly formed Kumyk national movement, Tenglik (Equality), also known as the Kumyk People's Movement, announced its intention to form a Kumyk national state out of seven districts of Dagestan. According to Kumyk leaders, their nation is underrepresented in the republican structures and is economically deprived. In November 1990 the Congress of People's Deputies of Dagestan voted to create a Kumyk republic within Dagestan, but the Kumyk representatives considered the offered level of autonomy insufficient.

In October 1991 Tenglik mobilized virtually the whole of the Kumyk nation in protest against the dominant position of the Avars in regions with Kumyk majorities, as well as to express their dissatisfaction with the ongoing resettlement of mountain peoples in traditional Kumyk territories. In 1994 the Kumyk National Congress was formed. It is less radical than Tenglik and is believed to be an initiative of the Dagestani government to counterbalance the radical nationalists of Tenglik. The Kumyks, who claim the Khazars as their ancestors, are increasingly unhappy being part of the multiethnic Dagestan Republic. Their homeland is potentially rich, but the Kumyks remain among the poorest of the nations in the Russian Federation.

SELECTED BIBLIOGRAPHY

Abtorkhanov, Abdurahman, and Marie Bennigsen Broxup. *The North Caucasus Barrier: The Russian Advance towards the Muslim World.* 1992.

Beddeley, John F. *Russian Conquest of the Caucasus.* 1997.

Gammer, Moshe. *Muslim Resistance to the Tsar: Shamil and the Conquest of Chechenia and Dagestan.* 1994.

Olson, James S. *An Ethnohistorical Dictionary of the Russian and Soviet Empires.* 1994.

LADINS

Ladinos; Dolomitos; Nones; Ladini

POPULATION: Approximately (2000 e) 36,000 Ladins in Europe, concentrated in the Dolomite Alps region of northeastern Italy.

THE LADIN HOMELAND: The Ladin homeland lies in the Dolomite Alps in northern Italy, occupying high Alpine valleys between the Piave and Isarco Rivers just south of the Austrian border. The region is famous for its strikingly bold outline of the Dolomites, named for the stone of which it is formed. The Marmolada, at 10,965 feet (3,342 m.), the highest peak in the region, is the object of special affection among the Ladin population. The majority of the Ladin population lives in the Val di Badia and Val di Gardena of Bolzano Province, with other groups in the provinces of Trento, the Val di Fiemme, and Belluno, the parishes of Val Moena, Cortina d'Ampezzo, Pieve-di-Livinallongo, Colle-Santa-Lucia, Cles, and Val di Non.

The Ladin homeland, called Ladinia, has no official status. The region claimed by Ladins as the heartland of their small nation forms the Cadore district of Belluno Province and Val Gardena district of Bolzano Province. *Ladinia (Patrje Ladine)*: 920 sq.mi.–2,382 sq.km. (2000 e) 57,000—Ladins 55%, Tyroleans* 35%, other Italians.* The Ladin capital and major cultural center is Cortina d'Ampezzo, called Cortina de Cadore in Ladin, (2000 e) 8,000, a major winter tourist resort. Another important cultural center is San Martino in Badia, called San Martin de Tor Val Badia in the Ladin language, the largest town of the Badia Valley.

FLAG: The Ladin national flag, the flag of the national movement, is a horizontal tricolor of pale blue, white, and green.

PEOPLE: The Ladins are a Rhaeto-Romantic nation living in the high valleys of the Dolomite Alps. They traditionally trace their ancestry to the ancient Celtic tribes conquered and Latinized by the Romans. The Ladins are the smallest of the three Rhaeto-Romantic nations that inhabit the eastern Alps. The related nations are the Romansch* of southeastern Switzerland and the Friulis,* who inhabit the region just southeast of Ladinia. The Ladins are mostly Roman Catholics, with a small, but important, Protestant minority.

The Rhaeto-Romantic language spoken by the Ladins is derived from ancient Latin. Due to the relative isolation of their high Alpine valleys, a number of dialects of the language are spoken, the most important being Atesino, Cadorino, Fassano, Gardena, Nones (Parlata Trentina), Badiotto, Marebbano, Livinallese, and Ampezzo. A Venetian-influenced dialect called Zoldino is spoken in the southern valleys. The literary language, written since 1700, which is taught in area schools, is based on Fassano, spoken in the Val di Fassa, and is the basis of a thriving local literature.

NATION: In 44 B.C., after the campaigns of Julius Caesar, the Roman Empire in Europe remained divided by a vast mountain chain inhabited by a diverse collection of indigenous Celtic tribes. The Retic and Noric tribes in the eastern Alps independently resisted integration into the Roman Empire. Their mountain homeland effectively divided Italy from Caesar's conquests in Germania. Emperor Augustus, between 25 and 15 B.C., directed several military campaigns against the tribes. Some tribes were decimated, while others were sold as slaves and deported to far-flung corners of the Roman Empire. Finally subjected, the various peoples were forcibly united into the new Roman province called Rhaetia by Drusus and Tiberius, stepsons of the Roman emperor Augustus.

The colonization of the region by the Romans, with an influx of soldiers, merchants, officials, and colonists, spread the Latin language into the new province. The structure of the Latin was modified by the original inhabitants, who wove it into their existing language structures. The Ladin language evolved over several centuries to become a separate language about A.D 450.

After three centuries of relative peace and stability in the region, the Roman Empire began to disintegrate. The Alpine peoples once again were under attack, this time from successive invasions of Goths, Franks, Bavarians,* and Lombards.* Many of the small tribes suffered the ultimate defeat and disappeared completely. The Lombards and other invaders settled in the lowlands south of the Alps and spread into the mountains, displacing or absorbing all but a few of the Rhaetian peoples. Most of the Ladin homeland formed part of a Lombard county until the eighth century, when the expanding empire of the Germanic Franks took control of the Lombard territories.

The Germanization of the Alps was assisted by a period of glacial retreat between the tenth and twelfth centuries, which raised the vegetation limits by as much as 6,561 feet (2,000 m.), allowing more extensive colonization of the valleys and an easier passage through the high Alpine passes. Under Germanic rule the Ladins formed a small minority overlooked in their isolated Alpine valleys, where they were able to maintain their own cultures and dialects.

In the eleventh century the western Ladin valleys came under the rule of the bishops of Brixen and Trent. In 1420 the Cadore and Zoldo regions in the east came under Venetian rule. The Austrian Hapsburgs extended their influence into the area in the fourteenth century. In 1797 the Austrians* took control of Venice, and the eastern Ladin valleys came under Austrian rule. Hapsburg rule was extended to the western Ladin valleys following the secularization of the bishoprics of Brixen and Trent in 1802.

For centuries the Ladins lived under the cultural and linguistic domination of the neighboring Tyroleans and Venetians,* their Alpine culture taking on many borrowed traits and customs, and their dialects absorbing many foreign words and styles. In the multiethnic Hapsburg Empire the Ladins formed one of many different ethnic groups, and pressure to assimilate eased. In 1866 the Austrians ceded the Veneto to Italy, again partitioning the small Ladin nation.

The era of European national revival in the latter half of the nineteenth century was felt throughout the vast, multiethnic Austro-Hungarian Empire. The movement, as interpreted by the Ladins, provoked a renewed interest in their unique history, culture, and dialects. The cultural revival in the 1880s and 1890s began to reverse centuries of assimilation. The standardization of the language, based on the Fassano dialect, strengthened the ties between the Ladin inhabitants of the isolated Alpine valleys. The Ladin national movement focused on the reunification of the divided Ladin territories in Italy and Austria.

Ladinia in 1900 remained divided between the Austrian region of South Tyrol and the Italian province of Belluno. The large Italian and the small Ladin population of South Tyrol were the object of Italian irredentist claims. Promised the South Tyrol and other Austrian territories with large Italian populations by the Allies after the outbreak of war in Europe in 1914, the Italians finally entered the war in 1915. The fighting between the Italians and Austrians swept through the Ladins' Alpine valleys and settled down to a war of attrition on the line of defense, the Piave River, in 1917–18.

Tyrolean opposition to the Italian claims fueled a nationalist movement that had some support from the Ladins, even though unification under Italian rule became the theme of Italian propaganda directed at the Ladin population in Austria. In October 1918 the Tyroleans convened an assembly of all of the region's peoples, which approved a plan for a federation of autonomous cantons based on the Swiss model. On 24 April 1919, the Tyroleans declared the independence of their homeland, which included western Ladinia, but were blocked by the Allies. The Italian kingdom, based on the Allied promises, annexed the South Tyrol.

In a conciliatory gesture soon after annexation, the Italian government made Italian, German, and Ladin the official languages of the annexed territory. Italian guarantees of cultural and linguistic freedom lasted only until the fascists took power in Rome in 1922. The fascist authorities closed all Ladin cultural institutions, schools, and publications and in forbade the use of the Ladin language. Standard Italian was the only language allowed in education, in the courts, and in local administration. In 1926 the authorities decreed that all family and place-names must conform to Italian guidelines.

During World War II, following Italy's surrender in 1943, German troops occupied the Alpine regions, which were united under one administration. The Ladins' brief administrative reunification, under German rule between 1943 and the end of World War II initiated the growth of modern Ladin nationalism. After the war, the Ladins attempted to win Allied support for the creation of an independent state modeled on Liechtenstein and under the protection of the new United Nations. The Allies, occupied with the reconstruction of Europe, refused to accept their petitions. In the 1950s and 1960s, while their homeland became a favorite winter tourist destination, influenced by the larger Tyrolean nationalist movement, the Ladins pressed for linguistic, economic, and cultural autonomy in a united Ladin district within Italy.

Ladin nationalism experienced a resurgence in the 1980s as Europe began to unite in a proposed federation of independent states. The European ideal, theoretically able to accommodate an independent Ladinia that is economically integrated with the rest of the union, has spurred the growth of nationalism since 1988. The Ladin nationalists claim that their movement is not separatist but works for the equality of their small nation with the other nations of a united Europe.

After centuries of resisting assimilation, the Ladins are still fighting for the survival of their small nation. They are no longer threatened by armed invasion but by rural depopulation and the cultural transformation associated with mass tourism. Organizations such as Inant Adum and the Uniun Generela di Ladins in the 1980s and 1990s have organized to safeguard the culture and language of the Ladin nation.

SELECTED BIBLIOGRAPHY

Barfield, Lawrence. *Northern Italy before Rome.* 1991.

Facaros, Dana. *Northeast Italy.* 1990.

Hofmann, Paul. *South Tyrol and the Dolomites.* 1995

Holmes, Douglas R. *Cultural Disenchantments: Worker Peasantries in Northeast Italy.* 1989.

Toscano, Mario. *Alto Adige, South Tyrol: Italy's Frontier with the German World.* 1991.

LAKS

Laqs; Kazilkumyks; Kazi Kumukh;
Laksians

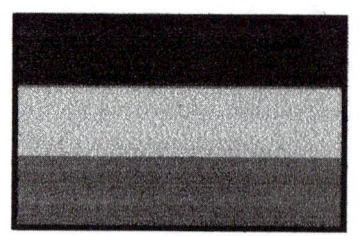

POPULATION: Approximately (2000 e) 133,000 Laks in Europe, concentrated in the Dagestan Republic of the Russian Federation. About 3,000 ethnic Laks live in Azerbaijan to the south of their traditional territory.

THE LAK HOMELAND: The Lak homeland lies in the south-central region of the Dagestan Republic in the high valleys of the Caucasus Mountains. One of the most isolated regions in the Russian Federation, the region is rugged, with isolated valleys where the Laks farm and tend herds of cattle or sheep. Due to its isolation, the Lak region was nearly inaccessible until the twentieth century, when roads were built by the Soviet authorities. Under Soviet rule some of the Laks were forcibly resettled in the lowlands to the north, where they could be controlled. The high mountains impede communication, even between Lak communities. Easy contact is possible only from the spring to the autumn when the narrow mountain passes are open.

The Laks call their homeland Lakstan, but the region has no official status in the Dagestan Republic. Lakstan is administratively divided between the Kuli, Lak, and New Lak Rayons of the republic. The Lak capital and major cultural center is the largest of the Lak towns, Vachi.

FLAG: The flag used by the Laks is the Dagestani national flag, a horizontal tricolor of green, pale blue, and red.

PEOPLE: The Laks are a Caucasian nation living in the high Caucasus Mountains with their homeland wedged between the territory of the Avars* and that of the Dargins.* Although the Soviet government attempted to relocate the Laks to urban areas, they prefer their traditional rural villages. Considered the most conservative of the Caucasian nations, the Lak sense of identity intensified during the decades of Soviet rule. Unlike other Dagestani nations, the Laks have no tribal or clan divisions. Because of their historical experience, the Laks enjoy high prestige among the other Dagestani peoples.

The Laks' upland region is mostly devoted to sheep herding. Formerly the sheep provided the majority of the Laks' needs, food, clothing, and shelter. Wool and meat were traded to neighboring peoples for necessities the Laks couldn't produce.

The Caucasian language of the Laks is closely related to Dargin, although they are mutually unintelligible. The two languages form a branch, called Lak-Dargwa, of the Northeast Caucasian language family. The language, called Lak or Laki, is spoken in five major dialects, Kumukh, Vikhli, Vitskh, Ashtikuli, and Balkar-Calakan. The Lak literary language is based on the Kumukh dialect and is written in the Cyrillic alphabet. A high percentage of the Laks, estimated at over 95%, still use the language on a daily basis.

Fervently devoted to their Sunni Muslim values and beliefs, today the Laks attend mosque regularly, observing Ramadan, praying daily, circumcising male children, and conducting regular Muslim ceremonies for official occasions, marriages, births, and funerals. The majority of the Laks adhere to the Shafi theological school.

NATION: The Laks are believed to be the descendants of the ancient Gumik tribe that inhabited the eastern Caucasus and was mentioned by early visitors to the region. Their homeland, straddling the invasion route between Europe and Asia, was often overrun by foreign armies, forcing the tribes to take refuge in strongholds in the mountains. The geographic isolation failed to protect their homeland from invaders but provided refuge in the high mountain valleys.

In the seventh century Muslim Arabs overran the region but failed to take the Laks' fortified mountain villages. Arab traders first introduced Islam to Lakstan in the eighth century, but conversion of the Laks to the new religion was slower than for other Dagestani peoples and would take many hundreds of years.

In the thirteenth and fourteenth centuries, the Golden Horde and Tamerlane's Turkic and Mongol forces fought their way into the high mountain valleys. The Laks emerged as a powerful regional group in Dagestan during the fourteenth century. Their principality, known as the Kazikumukh Khanate, became a semi-independent state on the southern border of the territory of the Golden Horde. The Lak warriors established control over areas inhabited by neighboring peoples, and in the fifteenth century they extended their boundaries to the lowlands of the northeast, bringing them into conflict with the Kumyks.*

In their high valleys, the Laks were primarily animists with their own folk religion, although outside religions, Zoroastrianism, Christianity, and Judaism, were gaining converts. Persian traders from the south again brought Islam to the isolated Lak villages in the fifteenth century. Over the next two centuries, Mongols, coming from the north, forcibly converted many of the pagan and

Christian Laks to the Islamic faith. By the middle of the nineteenth century, the Lak nation had been converted to Islam, both religiously and culturally, adopting the Sunni Muslim values and beliefs.

The Lak territories came under Russian rule under the terms of the Treaty of Gulistan between Russia and Persia in 1813. The arrival of Russian administrators and colonists, who took control of the best lands, alienated the Laks, who became one of the most anti-Russian of the Dagestani peoples. The Laks maintained a degree of political autonomy but gave their loyalty to an Avar religious and secular leader, Iman Shamil, who led a widespread rebellion against Russian rule in 1834. The Shamil revolt collapsed in 1858, but by that time the Laks hated everything Russian. In 1865 the Russian authorities abolished the Lak khanate and brought Lak territory under direct Russian administration.

During the late nineteenth and twentieth centuries, the policies of the colonial administration further alienated the Laks and intensified their sense of ethnic identity. Russian settlers seized large areas of Lak territory and brought commercialized forms of agriculture and animal husbandry. The Russians who came to the region, backed by the Russian state, were impossible for the Laks to oppose, although uprisings were frequent. A policy of assimilation was pressed under tsarist rule, which was fiercely resisted by the isolated Lak communities.

The outbreak of World War I in 1914 divided the Lak communities. Many supported their fellow Muslims, the Turks, while others, fearing Russian reprisals, remained loyal to the Russian government. The overthrow of the Russian monarchy in February 1917 was followed by the slow collapse of the Russian civil administration in the Dagestan region. The Muslim peoples of the Caucasus united in a breakaway state called North Caucasia, but their homeland became a battleground in the expanding Russian civil war.

In 1920 the Red Army drove the last of the anti-Bolshevik forces from the region. The new Soviet government established the Mountain Autonomous Republic, with Arabic as the official language, but the Laks opposed the use of Arabic other than for religious services. They resisted, and in 1921 the Mountain Republic was divided, and the Soviets created the Dagestan Autonomous Soviet Socialist Republic but divided Lakstan among several administrative subdivisions.

In the late 1920s the Soviet administration conducted an intense anti-Islamic campaign that included widespread violence, including the imprisonment and execution of local Lak religious leaders. Mosques and religious schools were forcibly closed, and the Soviet state's official atheism was imposed.

The government also worked to Sovietize the Lak economy. Traditionally, the Laks had owned their lands and herds communally. The Soviet officials in the region assumed that the process of converting the Lak communal traditions to communist norms would proceed quickly. Attempts to collectivize the land and herds were met by fierce Lak resistance. Selling their produce to government collectives impoverished the Lak communities.

Because of the state-controlled local economy and the government's heavy-handed attempts to change the Lak culture and religious beliefs, the sense of identity of the small nation intensified over the years. Government policy made Russian the only language of instruction in 1938, and in the 1960s state policy prohibited the teaching of Lak in public schools. The Laks became distinctly anticommunist, anti-Soviet, anti-Christian, and anti-Russian. By the 1980s an estimated half of all Lak male adults belonged to underground Muslim brotherhoods, the Tariqats.

In the 1950s and 1960s, industrialization was intensified in Dagestan. The number of Laks seeking work in the towns and cities increased rapidly. Urbanization, although it has not threatened the survival of the Lak nation, has brought many changes to their material and cultural life. Every year brings an increase in the consumption of factory-made goods and consumer products. Many younger Laks are disdainful of the old traditions; however, those traditions have retained a venerable place in Lak society, and the old customs persist. The loss of isolation, the growth of industrialization and urbanization, and the rise in educational standards resulted in marked changes in Lak culture. Elements of European urban culture, particularly the material culture, penetrated even the most remote corners of the Lak homeland. The Sovietization of Lak society led to severe social problems, particularly alcoholism and divisions between the older and younger generations.

Following the collapse of the Soviet Union, Dagestan was declared a member state of the new Russian Federation, but ethnic tensions have been increasing since 1991. The Lak homeland has been widely recognized as the religious center of Islam for the Dagestani Muslim nations. Their historic unity in the Kazikumukh Khanate is cited by Lak nationalists as the basis for an autonomous Lakstan.

SELECTED BIBLIOGRAPHY

Chenciner, Robert. *Daghestan: Tradition and Survival.* 1997.

Dawisha, Karen, and Bruce Parrott, eds. *Conflict, Cleavage, and Change in Central Asia and the Caucasus.* 1997.

Gammer, Moshe. *Muslim Resistance to the Tsar: Shamil and the Conquest of Chechnia and Dagestan.* 1994.

Mesbahi, Mohiaddin. *Central Asia and the Caucasus after the Soviet Union: Domestic and International Dynamics.* 1994.

Smith, Sebastian. *Allah's Mountains.* 1997.

LATVIANS

Latviesi; Letts; Latyshi

POPULATION: Approximately (2000 e) 1,632,000 Latvians in Europe, including 1,420,000 in Latvia and 100,000 scattered throughout Russia and Belarus, especially in the cities of St. Petersburg and Moscow.

THE LATVIAN HOMELAND: The Latvian homeland occupies a region of flat plains in Northeastern Europe on the eastern shore of the Baltic Sea. The republic is divided into four historic regions, Kurzeme in western Latvia, Zemgale in southern Latvia, Vidzeme in the north, and Latgale in eastern Latvia. Most of Latvia is situated on a flat coastal plain with no part above 1,000 ft. (305 m.). The fertile lowlands rise inland to a hilly region of forests and lakes in the east. About 20% of the country is forested and is drained by many rivers, the largest the Western Dvina or Daugava, which flows into Latvia from Russia. The northern half of the Latvian coastline is indented by the Gulf of Riga, a large inlet of the Baltic Sea.

Latvia was an independent republic from 1919 to 1940. Annexed by the Soviet Union in 1940, the Latvians regained their independent republic in 1991. The republic is divided into twenty-six rayons or counties and seven independent municipalities. *Republic of Latvia (Latvijas Republika)*: 24,595 sq.km.–63,701 sq.km. (2000 e) 2,583,000—Latvians 56%, Russians* 31%, Belarussians* 4%, Ukrainians* 3%, Poles* 2%, Lithuanians* 1%, Estonians.* The Latvian capital and major cultural center is Riga, (2000 e) 876,000 (metropolitan area 1,041,000), a major Baltic seaport.

FLAG: The Latvian national flag, the official flag of the republic, is a maroon field divided by a centered, horizontal white stripe half the width of the maroon stripes.

PEOPLE: The Latvians are a Baltic people and, with the Lithuanians, make up the Baltic branch of the European peoples. Generally tall and fair, the Latvians and their culture resemble of the Scandinavians and their culture farther to the west. The Latvians are highly urban, approximately 72%. The Latvians are divided into two major cultural and religious divisions, the mostly Lutheran Latvians and the Roman Catholic Latgalians. The Roman Catholic Latgalians, numbering over 500,000, are the only one of the ancient tribes that has retained an ethnic identity. The Latgalians, who call themselves Latgolisi, are considered a transitional people between the Latvians and the Lithuanians. The majority of the Latgalians live in southeastern Latvia near the Lithuanian and Russian frontiers.

The Latvian language is one of only two in the Baltic language group, along with Lithuanian. The language, which has absorbed more Slav influences than neighboring Lithuanian, has many features in common with the ancient Indo-European languages. Spoken in two major dialects, Central or Western Latvian and Eastern Latvian, also called Augszemnieks or Latgalian, the language is written in the Roman alphabet. Central Latvian is the basis of the Latvian literary language. Latgalian, which nearly died out in eastern Latvia, has had a vigorous revival since 1988. The two dialects are similar but have separate literary traditions. Latvian and Lithuanian are not mutually intelligible, but speakers of both languages can understand Latgalian.

NATION: The region on the eastern shore of the Baltic Sea has been populated since the end of the last glacial era, about 10,000 B.C. Finnic tribes migrating from the east settled the area around 3000 B.C. The settlers, the ancestors of the Finns,* Estonians, and Livonians,* took control of the flat plains. Around 1,000 years later, the Baltic tribes moved into the region and are regarded as the ancestors of the present-day Latvians and Lithuanians.

The Baltic tribes first appear in the written records of the Roman historian Cornelius Tacitus in approximately 100 B.C. Tacitus referred to the Baltic tribes as farmers living on the coasts of the Amber Sea. Around the same time the Balts split into tribal groups, the Latgalians, Zemgalians, Kurzemians (Couronians), and Selonians. The tribes, straddling the major trade route between Scandinavia and the Mediterranean, developed as traders and maintained contacts with many distant nations. Traditionally, the four Latvian tribes were established in their present homelands as early as A.D. 800. Until the twelfth century the marshes and forestlands along the eastern coast of the Baltic Sea protected the tribes. Their pagan religion, which revered the spirits in all living things, was a system of beliefs based on nature.

Germans,* on the pretext of converting the pagan Balts, invaded the region in the twelfth century. The crusading knights, intent on spreading Christianity and their feudal traditions, founded Riga in 1201 and spread German influence across the region. By the 1270s the crusaders had established a feudal state dominated by the German Knights of the Livonian Order. Regular economic and cultural ties were established with neighboring areas of Europe. In 1282

Riga became part of the Hanseatic League, a vast network of trading cities around the Baltic Sea. The city rapidly assumed a central role in the growing east-west trade. The fertile Latvian lands were parceled out to individual knights in large feudal holdings, and the Latvian tribes were reduced to a class of peasant serfs. The imposition of the German feudal system stimulated the unification of the various Latvian tribal peoples.

The Baltic Germans were still in control of Latvia in the sixteenth century, when the Protestant Reformation swept Europe. The Reformation had a significant impact on the region, except in the eastern region of Latgalia, which was part of Catholic Poland. The Lutheran creed appealed to the Latvian serfs oppressed by the small German Catholic aristocracy. Peasant uprisings against the Baltic German landlords spread rapidly, often spurred by religious zeal. In 1554 the Master of Order, Walter von Plettenberg, fearing a wider uprising, declared Protestantism the official religion. The decision weakened the medieval state and allowed the expanding Russians to gain influence. The Livonian Wars, fought from 1558 to 1583, were partly due to Moscow's desire for a warm-water port on the Baltic Sea. To prevent a Russian conquest, the German aristocrats dissolved the Teutonic Order, except in Kurzeme and Riga, and in 1561 placed their vast estates under the protection of the Lithuanian-Polish state. Catholicism was again proclaimed the state religion. The privileges of the German lords were preserved on both banks of the Daugava, and the Latvian serfs became even more closely tied to the land.

The Swedes* wrested most of Livonia from Poland between 1621 and 1626. Swedish rule reinforced Lutheranism as the predominant religion and promoted the use of the Latvian language in religion. The first Roman Catholic catechism was published in Latvian in 1585, with a Lutheran version appearing the next year. Due to the more liberal Swedish laws, the rights of the German feudal lords were somewhat curtailed, and serfdom was abolished. The Latvian farmers were given representation in the Swedish parliament and could lodge complaints directly to the king. Schools were established in the rural areas, and the first books in Latvian were printed.

In 1700 the army of tsarist Russia confronted the Swedes for the purpose of winning access to the ice-free ports on the Baltic Sea. In 1710 the northern provinces of Latvia, Vidzeme, and Riga came under Russian rule. By the Treaty of Nystad in 1721 Sweden ceded Livonia, while Poland retained control of Latgalia, Zemgalia, and Courland. In the Polish partition of 1772 Latgalia passed to Russian rule, and in 1795 Zemgalia and Courland also passed to Russian rule.

The imposition of Russian authority was welcomed by the Baltic Germans, whose privileges were quickly restored. Russian Orthodoxy was imposed as the state religion, and the Lutheran faith was suppressed. The Latvian language was forbidden in the region's schools, and traditional or national holidays were restricted. Only after the period of change from feudalism to industrialism began at the end of the eighteenth century did circumstances begin to change for the average Latvian. The abolishment of serfdom between 1817 and 1819 stimulated the growth of industry, which absorbed the excess workers of the expanding population.

The formation of the modern Latvian nation began only at the beginning of the nineteenth century, much later than in most of Europe. Education, becoming more widespread, stimulated the unity of the nation and resulted in the formation of a nationalist Latvian elite. Reforms that allowed peasants to acquire land differentiated them from the rest of the Russian Empire. The rise of a Latvian urban middle class between the 1840s and 1860s began to challenge both the Russians and the Baltic German aristocracy.

In the 1880s the tsarist government instituted a program of Russification, threatening the autonomy of the Baltic German-dominated province and the newly emerged Latvian national movement. In 1885 Russian replaced German as the official language of the region. Latvian worker movements, organized in the 1890s, espoused a radical form of nationalism.

Heavy fighting spread across Latvia soon after war was declared in Europe in 1914. German troops occupied most of Latvia south of the Daugava River. One-fifth of Latvia's population of 2.5 million became refugees. Much of Latvia's industry was transferred to the Russian interior. As the war dragged on, radical and nationalist political organizations gained support.

Latvia became effectively independent following the 1917 Russian Revolution, and nationalists in unoccupied Latvia proclaimed a sovereign state in November 1917, soon after the Bolshevik coup in Petrograd. Many Latvians, believing in the Bolshevik promises of freedom for Latvia, voted 72% in favor of the Bolsheviks in elections in unoccupied Latvia, with a Bolshevik government proclaimed in December to rival the previously proclaimed nationalist government. German troops occupied all of Latvia in February 1918, suppressing both governments. Radical, pro-Soviet groups took control of Latvia as the Germans withdrew but were soon ousted by nationalists supported by a British naval squadron in the Baltic Sea. A democratic Latvian government declared Latvia independent of Russia on 18 November 1918. After the declaration of independence, the fight against Bolshevik troops, as well as against German forces and Russian monarchists, lasted for two years. The first free elections were finally held in 1920.

Cut off from Soviet raw materials, industrialized Latvia quickly reverted from an industrial economy to an essentially agrarian economy. New property rights laws aided the success of the economy based on agriculture and light manufacturing. The prosperous republic, in spite of impressive cultural and economic achievements, failed to achieve political stability. The situation was aggravated in the 1930s by Latvia's position between the hostile Soviet Union and a rearmed and aggressive Nazi Germany. The threat of civil war hung over the republic as antidemocratic groups formed that were hostile to the Russian, German, or Jewish minorities.

Latvia's president, Karlis Ulmanis, in 1934, in an attempt to strengthen the government, suspended the parliament, assumed dictatorial powers, and banned all political activity. The slogan of the Ulmanis government, "Latvia for the Latvians," highlighted the exclusion of the Baltic German and other minorities from the new government. In 1935 Latvia's multinational population consisted of Latvians 61%, Latgalians 16%, Russians 12%, Jews 4.5%, Germans 4%, and smaller Polish, Belarussian, and Lithuanian minorities.

The Soviet Union and Nazi Germany signed a secret protocol on 23 August 1939, effectively dividing much of Europe into spheres of influence. With Soviet troops massed on the border, the neutral Latvian nationalist government was replaced with a pro-communist regime. On 17 June 1940 Soviet troops occupied the country, and the puppet government applied for membership in the Soviet Union. Annexed on 22 July 1940, over 35,000 Latvians, particularly from Roman Catholic Latgalia, were deported before the deportations were stopped when Latvia was overrun when the Nazi forces attacked their Soviet ally in 1941.

Thousands eagerly joined the Nazis' anticommunist crusade, some even participating in the massacre of Latvia's Jewish minority. At the end of the war, thousands refused repatriation to Soviet Latvia and gradually settled in the United States, Canada, and Western Europe. An estimated 130,000 fled the advance of the Red Army to reach the West. The Red Army executed thousands of anticommunists and deported between 100,000 and 120,000 between 1945 and 1953. To maintain Latvia's productivity the Stalinist Soviet government replaced the Latvians with more reliable Slavs, who found work in the new Soviet heavy industries. An estimated 300,000 Latvians died during the war, and by 1949 the Latvian portion of the population, 75% of the total in 1940, had fallen to just 56%.

During the so-called thaw of the 1950s following Stalin's death in 1953, the survivors of the Gulag and the deportations of 1940–41 and the postwar persecutions began to return to the republic. An estimated 20% had survived the ordeal. In spite of the massive influx of non-Latvians, the Latvian culture began to slowly revive, aided by the return of a portion of the prewar intelligentsia. When attempts to gain more independence for the Latvian Soviet Socialist Republic failed, a new wave of deportations followed in 1959.

In the late 1980s in the more relaxed atmosphere initiated by Mikhail Gorbachev, nationalist organizations proliferated, many demanding the reversal of the illegal 1940 annexation. The fight for the survival of the Latvian language was a rallying point for many in the country, and in a petition, 354,000 residents demanded that Latvian be once again officially named the state language. On 5 May 1989 the language law was passed, and Latvian became the state language.

Campaigning for democracy and independence did not begin in earnest until October 1988 with the formation of the Popular Front of Latvia (Latvijas) (LTF). At elections to the Supreme Soviet in March 1990, the LTF won a convincing victory with the support of the majority of the Latvian population. A new Latvian parliament proclaimed the restoration of Latvia's former independence on 4 May 1990 and demanded negotiations on peaceful secession from the USSR.

The continuing immigration of non-Latvians into the republic, seen by the

Latvians as slow genocide, became a rallying cry for national movement. More radical nationalist groups called for the expulsion of all immigrants who had no ties, family or business, to the prewar Latvian republic. The moderate nationalists preferred cooperation, and many ethnic Slavs supported the Latvians' drive for sovereignty. The attempted coup against Gorbachev in Moscow in August 1991 presented the Latvians with an unprecedented opportunity. The Latvian parliament proclaimed Latvia's independence from the Soviet Union on 21 August 1991.

Other than a crumbling post-Soviet economy, the Latvians' major challenge is to reach a workable accommodation with its large non-Latvian populations. Relations with the Russian Federation have been soured by the argument over the status of ethnic Russians resident in the republic. They have been subjected to discrimination, and the majority are not allowed to vote in general elections. On 5 May 1992 the language laws were put into full force, with employment, citizenship, and passports dependent on proficiency in the Latvian language. Hundreds of thousands of non-Latvians were classed as noncitizens.

The Latvian language, according to linguists, had reached the second stage of language extinction by the mid-1980s. Since independence the language has again flourished, and the threat of extinction has receded. However, less than one-quarter of the non-Latvians living in the republic spoke the language six years after independence.

A new citizenship law that allows for the naturalization of non-Latvians took effect in June 1994. It offered Latvian citizenship to 50,000 people in 1995 and an additional 180,000 between 1996 and 1999. Preference is given to those who lived in Latvia prior to 1940 or had a Latvian spouse or parent. The law set quotas for citizenship applications after 2000, and this provision was criticized by Russia as well as some European nations and international organizations. In July 1994 the Latvian parliament officially removed the quota system.

The Latvians, along with the neighboring Baltic peoples, have sought membership in the large European economic and military alliances, the European Union (EU) and the North Atlantic Treaty Organization (NATO). On 27 October 1995 Latvia submitted its application for full EU membership. In 1997 the EU, citing the treatment of non-Latvian residents and government failure to fully implement a market economy, did not invite Latvia to join talks for the first expansion of the union into Eastern Europe.

SELECTED BIBLIOGRAPHY

Hiden, John, and Patrick Salmon. *The Baltic Nations and Europe: Estonia, Latvia and Lithuania in the Twentieth Century*. 1995.

Karklins, Rasma. *Ethnopolitics and Transition to Democracy: The Collaspe of the USSR and Latvia*. 1994.

Lieven, Anatol. *The Baltic Revolution: Estonia, Latvia, Lithuania and the Path to Independence*. 1994.

Penkis, Janis J., and Andrejs Penikis. *Latvia: Independence Renewed*. 1997.

Plakans, Andrejs. *The Latvians: A Short History*. 1995.

LEZGINS

Lezghi; Lezgi; Lesghians; Kurins;
Akhtas; Akhtins

POPULATION: Approximately (2000 e) 458,000 Lezgins in Europe, 277,000 in the Dagestan Republic of southern European Russia, and 174,000 in the adjacent districts of northern Azerbaijan. Lezgin nationalists claim a national population of 1.2 million in Russia and Azerbaijan. Other Lezgin populations live in Central Asia, Turkey, and Georgia.

THE LEZGIN HOMELAND: The Lezgin homeland lies along the Samur River in southeastern Dagestan and northeastern Azerbaijan. The river forms part of the international boundary between the Dagestan Republic of the Russian Federation and the Republic of Azerbaijan. Most of the region lies in the eastern Caucasus and is very mountainous, but a small portion is included in the Caspian Sea lowlands around the mouth of the Samur River. The Lezgins call their divided homeland Lezgistan. Most Lezgins live in the high, rugged mountain areas where there are deep, isolated canyons and gorges. The summers are hot and dry, while winters are windy and brutally cold. Some live near the Caspian Sea, where the winters are dry and mild.

There is no easily accessible pass over the Caucasus Mountains, so that most Lezgins are isolated, notably, in winter. The Lezgin landscape changes from high mountains to flat plains along the Caspian Sea, a fertile plain that historically has been an important north-south passage between Europe and Asia. The rugged landscape of Lezgistan makes agriculture possible only in the lowlands and the high river valleys. Most of the region is highland pasture with sheep and goats in the highlands and cattle in the lowlands.

Never united in a single political entity, Lezgistan remains divided and forms the Kurakh, Kasumkent, Magaramkent, Akhty, and Dokuzpara Rayons of Dagestan in the Russian Federation and the Kuba and Kusar Rayons of the Republic of Azerbaijan. The Lezgin capital and major cultural center is the town of Mamash, (2000 e) 11,000. Other important Lezgin cultural centers are Derbent in Dagestan and Kuba and Sheki in Azerbaijan.

FLAG: The Lezgin national flag, the flag of the national movement, is a horizontal bicolor of green over blue bearing a centered circle of yellow over pale blue outlined in white and with a centered black eagle in flight.

PEOPLE: The Lezgins are a Caucasian people, one of the indigenous nations of the Caucasus Mountain region of Southeastern Europe. The Lezgins traditionally lived in free societies, consisting of groups or clans led by a male elder responsible for making all major decisions for the group. The clans, called *turkum*, remain to the present, but with modernization and outward migration, the *turkum* have become less important, although the Lezgins generally marry within their own clans. The elder women are very influential in such traditions. The custom of paying *kalim*, the bride-price, is still followed by some, but it is now more symbolic than a required payment. Because of their geographic isolation and their resistance to state authority, Lezgin educational levels remain among the lowest in the region.

While the Lezgins are primarily Sunni Muslims, there is a substantial Shi'a Muslim minority in Azerbaijan. Many of their former animist beliefs have been mingled with their Islamic practices. During the spring, as well as during planting and harvesting seasons, several ancient rituals are still practiced. The bones of animals are believed to have magical and healing powers.

The language spoken by the Lezgins belongs to the Samurian group of northeastern Caucasian languages. The relative isolation of the Lezgin communities fostered the development of seven dialects, the most important of which are Kiuri or Kurin, spoken by the majority of Lezgins and the basis of the literary language, Akhty, spoken on both sides of the international border in the high Caucasus region, and Kuba, which is spoken mostly in Azerbaijan. The three dialects reflect the division of the Lezgins into three subgroups, the Kurin, the Kuba, and the Akhty or Sumar. Most Lezgins speak Azeri as their second language.

Lezgin national organizations estimate the actual Lezgin population in Azerbaijan at between 600,000 and 700,000, much higher than the official estimates. The disparity arises from the number of ethnic Lezgins who registered as ethnic Azeris* during the Soviet period and continue to claim Azeri nationality to escape job and education discrimination in Azerbaijan.

NATION: For thousands of years invaders from Europe and Asia crossed or conquered Lezgistan, driving the early clans into mountain strongholds in the high Caucasus. The clans formed loose federations for defensive purposes. The Lezgins are believed by historians to have their origins in the amalgamation of three ancient tribal federations that spoke similar dialects and shared many cultural traits, the Akhty, Alty, and Dokuz Para.

Invading Arabs conquered the lowlands in A.D. 728, introducing their new

Islamic religion with its unifying religious and social system. A flourishing Muslim civilization developed in the coastal plains centered on Derbent, on the edge of Lezgin territory. The city became a major political and cultural center of the Muslim Empire known as the Caliphate. The influence of Muslim society converted most of the lowland clans, but the highland clans continued to resist all invaders and to cling to their own folk religions.

The Mongols devastated the Lezgin lowlands in the early thirteenth century, forcing most of the clans to withdraw to traditional mountain strongholds. Persians extended their rule to the coastal lowlands in the fourteenth century, beginning a long rivalry between the Persian and Turkish Empires that eventually facilitated the Russian conquest of the Caucasus. Until the fifteenth century the majority of the Lezgin clans remained animists, but other religions were making inroads. Persian traders introduced Islam to the highland clans in the south, while the Golden Horde brought Islam to the northern clans in the sixteenth and seventeenth centuries. The Ottoman Turks* occupied the region in the sixteenth century, and under their rule Islam became the major religion.

The Lezgins, unlike other Dagestani peoples, maintained loyalty based on tribal and clan federations and never formed their own principality or state. The Lezgin tribes in the south came under the authority of the Kuba Khanate, while the northern clans were ruled by the Derbent Khanate. The Laks* took control of the Lezgin territories for a time in the eighteenth century, but real authority mostly remained with the local Lezgin leaders.

In 1723 the Russians took control of the plains of northern Dagestan, and a weakened Persia ceded the rugged, mountainous south in 1813. The Russians created a new political entity in the Lezgin territories, the Kiurin Khanate, which was later dissolved and made the Kiurin district. The Lezgins fiercely resisted Christian Russian rule. Stirred to religious and nationalist fervor, they followed the religious leader of the Avars,* Iman Shamil, in a long holy war against the Russians. Effective guerrilla tactics in the high mountains halted the Russian advance for over two decades. Thousands died in the final Russian conquest of Lezginstan in 1859–60. The last of the fierce Lezgin warriors did not submit to Russian rule until 1877. A profound sense of hatred of the Russians continues to permeate Lezgin culture. The term "Lezgin" was applied to a number of separate peoples until the early twentieth century.

The Lezgin clans were assimilating into the larger Azeri culture until the World War I and the revolution that followed. The Lezgin clans openly supported Muslim Turks when war began in 1914, and they celebrated the news that revolution had broken out in Russia in February 1917. Effectively independent as civil administration collapsed, a Muslim conference of all the Dagestani peoples elected Mullah Gotinsky as their political and religious leader in May 1917. The Bolshevik takeover of the Russian government in October 1917 created chaos in the region as local Bolsheviks attempted to take power. The Muslim peoples joined with the Terek Cossacks* to declare an independent Terek-Dagestan republic on 20 October 1917, but the new state, undermined by ethnic, religious, and territorial disputes, collapsed in December 1917. The Muslim peoples formed a separate state in March 1918 and attempted a cooperative defense as the Russian civil war spread south. The anti-Bolshevik forces, the Whites, took control of the region in January 1919, but forced conscription of Muslims incited strong resistance. Promised autonomy, the Muslims mostly went over to the Reds. The last of the White forces withdrew in January 1920.

The Soviet authorities created the Mountain Autonomous Republic, with Arabic as the official language. The Lezgins, along with many other Muslim highlanders, were opposed to the Soviet policy and rebelled. The government then created a separate Dagestan for the highland peoples of the eastern Caucasus. In 1925 the Soviets began an anti-Islamic campaign, which included closing mosques and religious schools, eliminating the use of Arabic, and the execution or deportation of local Lezgin religious leaders, the imams. Azeri was declared the official language of the region, but in 1928 Lezgin was made an official language in Dagestan, and a Latin alphabet was devised. Ten years later the Lezgins were forced to adopt the Russians' Cyrillic alphabet. Over the next decades, the Russian language was imposed on administration, education, and intergroup communications.

The manipulations of the Soviet authorities increased Lezgin resentment of Russian and Soviet domination. The Lezgin clans resisted attempts to move them from their mountain villages to lowland towns and collective farms and as a result remained largely rural until the 1970s. The move to the nearby towns and cities, forced on them by the need to find work, increased the popular resentment of the Soviet authorities. Government attempts to suppress their religion, relocate them away from their homelands, and manipulate their language created a powerful unity among the Lezgin clans.

The reforms begun by Mikhail Gorbachev, perestroika and glasnost, allowed the Lezgins to finally give voice to their decades of grievances. In the early 1990s, following the collapse of the Soviet Union, their homeland was divided between the successor states, the Russian Federation and the Republic of Azerbaijan. The disintegration of the USSR transformed an internal boundary into an international border, threatening the unity of the Lezgin nation. The international border running through their territory spurred the growth of Lezgin nationalism, with demands for unification and independence from both Russia and Azerbaijan.

The Lezgin national movement, Sadval (Unity), was founded in July 1990 in Derbent. The national movement's stated aims are to promote democracy, unification, and independence. In 1992, when the Russian Federation and Azerbaijan agreed to a formal boundary at the Samur River, thousands of Lezgins on both sides of the border demonstrated. Other organizations, particularly the All-National Congress of Lezgins, called for the immediate creation of an independent Lezgistan in 1991–92.

In April 1995 a new political party, Alpan, was founded by the Dagestani Lezgins with its primary objective the unification of the Lezgin territories in

Azerbaijan with the Dagestani Lezgin territories. The Lezgins accuse the Azeri government of suppressing the rights of the Lezgin population, while observers believe that the Russian government is encouraging Lezgin nationalism to increase pressure on the Azeris over oil quotas and pipelines. The Lezgin National Council was formed in 1992 to coordinate Lezgin efforts for a united homeland.

The mobilization of the Lezgins in Dagestan started with the collapse of the Soviet Union, but those in Azerbaijan joined their kin later, a result of forced conscription during the Azeri war with the Armenians* and the settlement of Meskhtekians* on land claimed as Lezgin territory. Lezgin nationalism remains stronger in Russia than in Azerbaijan, where large numbers of Lezgins have settled in the Azeri capital, Baku. In Azerbaijan confrontations between Lezgins and the Azeri authorities evolved from government attempts to conscript young Lezgins into the armed forces and attempts to impose Turkic culture on their Caucasian nation.

In March 1993 the Azeri police fired on a Lezgin demonstration of over 70,000 people, killing at least six demonstrators. A change of government in Azerbaijan, bringing pro-Russian ex-communists to power, resulted in the closing of the Lezgian nationalist offices in Moscow. Further demonstrations led to violence in 1994–95. A considerable degree of ethnic cohesion was formed during the mass demonstrations against conscription in Azerbaijan. In 1995 the new Azeri government banned the nationalist Sadval movement in Azerbaijan.

In 1996 a special hearing before the Russian state Duma's Committee on Nationality Affairs was held to examine the status of the estimated 1.2 million Lezgins living along the Azeri-Russian border. Lezgin leaders testified that the Azeri government had conducted a campaign of repression directed at the Lezgins living on the Azeri side of the border. The Lezgins have demanded the transfer of Azerbaijan's northernmost district to Russia's Dagestan Republic as well as the right to dual citizenship and the right to unrestricted travel between communities on both sides of the international border.

SELECTED BIBLIOGRAPHY
Bremmer, Ian, and Ray Taras, eds. *Nations and Politics in the Soviet Successor States.* 1993.
Broxup, Marie Bennigsen, and Abdurahman Abtorkhanov. *The North Caucasus Barrier: The Russian Advance towards the Muslim World.* 1992.
Gammer, Moshe. *Muslim Resistance to the Tsar: Shamil and the Conquest of Chechenia and Dagestan.* 1994.
Tutuncu, Mehmet. *Caucasus: War and Peace.* 1998.
Wixman, Ronald. *The Peoples of the USSR: An Ethnographic Handbook.* 1984.

LIECHTENSTEINERS

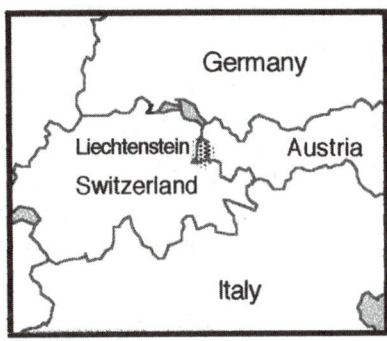

POPULATION: Approximately (2000 e) 34,000 Liechtensteiners in Europe, concentrated in the Principality of Liechstenstein.

THE LIECHTENSTEINER HOMELAND: The Liechtensteiner homeland lies on the Rhine River between Switzerland on the west and Austria on the east. The Rhine River, which forms the western border, drains, along with its tributaries, the greater part of the region. The other principal river is the Samina. The small region is mostly agricultural in the Rhine Valley, which makes up about one-third of the country. The rest is of Liechtenstein is rugged, consisting of foothills of the Alps, with a spur of the Rhaetian Alps rising to over 8,400 feet (2,560 m.).

The principality was recognized as a sovereign state in the nineteenth century. *Principality of Liechtenstein (Furstentum Liechtenstein)*: 62 sq.mi.–161 sq.km. (2000 e) 29,800—Liechtensteiners 95%, Italians* 5%. The Liechtensteiner capital and major cultural center is Vaduz, (2000 e) 5,000, lying on the upper Rhine River about fifty miles (80 km.) southeast of Zurich, Switzerland.

FLAG: The Liechtensteiner national flag, the official flag of the principality, is a horizontal bicolor of dark blue over red bearing a gold crown on the upper hoist.

PEOPLE: The Liechtensteiners are a German nation of the Alemannic Germans, related to the Swiss Germans,* the Alsatians,* Vorarlbergers,* and the Swabians.* They developed as a separate European nation in the eighteenth and nineteenth centuries, particularly after the principality's sovereignty was recognized in 1866. The majority of the Liechtensteiners are employed in industry, with less than 2% of the labor force engaged in agriculture. Roman Catholicism is the religion of 87% of the Liechtensteiners, while 8% adhere to various Protestant sects.

The German spoken by the Liechtensteiners is an Alemannic dialect of High German, which is about 40% inherently intelligible with standard German. The dialect is close to the spoken dialects of the German-speaking cantons of neighboring Switzerland. The Alemannic or Allemannisch dialects differ from most other German dialects in not having undergone the second *lautverschiebung*, the second vowel shift. The Liechtensteiners are bilingual, speaking also standard German, which is the official language of the principality.

NATION: The Germanic peoples first made contact with the major European power, Rome, in the first century B.C. The Alemanni, one of the chief Germanic tribes, originated as a splinter group of the Suebi or Swabians and grew as a confederation of tribes. First mentioned in A.D. 213, the Alemanni unsuccessfully assaulted the Roman wall between the Elbe and the Danube. In the third century A.D. they settled in upper Italy as Roman power weakened. By the fifth century they occupied territories on both sides of the Rhine River south of its junction with the Main River, present Alsace, Swabia, Vorarlberg, and northeastern Switzerland.

The Alemanni's western expansion brought them into conflict with the Franks, and they were defeated in 496. In 505 the Frankish king, Clovis I, forced the Alemanni back into Rhaetia, and in 536 they passed under Frankish rule. By the seventh century the Alemanni had accepted Christianity and settled in farming and trading communities along the region's major rivers. The local rulers retained much power under the rule of the Frankish kings, particularly Charlemagne, who consolidated the Frankish Empire.

The isolated region, without interest to invaders, remained a refuge from the frequent European wars of the fourteenth and fifteenth centuries. In 1499 in war between the Swiss and the Holy Roman Emperor Maximilian I, the region was overrun, and the town of Vaduz was heavily damaged but was later rebuilt.

In 1608, in recognition of faithful services, Karl of Liechtenstein, an Austrian nobleman, was raised to the rank of prince. Johann Adam of Liechtenstein purchased the barony of Schellenberg in 1699 and the county of Vaduz in 1712. In 1719, in order to obtain a seat in the powerful Council of Princes, Schellenberg and Vaduz were united to form a separate principality as an immediate fief of the Holy Roman Empire. The Liechtenstein family, who also owned huge estates, many times the size of the principality, in other parts of the Austrian Empire, rarely visited their small country but were active in the service of the Austrian Hapsburg monarchy.

The tiny principality was a member of the Napoleonic Federation of the Rhine in 1806 and German Confederation from 1815 to 1866. Technically allied to Austria during the Austro-Prussian War of 1866, it was overlooked in the peace treaty and therefore remained technically at war with Prussia. From 1866 to 1918 Liechtenstein formed part of the Austrian Customs Union, but with Austria's defeat in World War I, the principality increasingly oriented itself toward neutral, prosperous Switzerland.

In 1924 the Liechtensteiners were accepted into the Swiss Customs Union. The customs treaty with Switzerland formed a common economic region between the two nations. The border between Switzerland and Liechtenstein is open, and Swiss customs agents guard the border between Liechtenstein and Austria. The Swiss franc remains the legal currency of the principality.

Neutral, like the neighboring Swiss, during World War II, the Liechtensteiners emerged from the war with their country undamaged. Protected from economic difficulties by a postal, customs, and monetary union with Switzerland, the principality grew prosperous in postwar Europe. With low taxes and generous incentives, the country attracted many international businesses and in 1972 signed association agreements with the European Economic Community (EEC). By the early 1990s up to one-third of the population of the principality was made up of foreign workers employed in Liechtenstein's growing number of industries.

The Liechtensteiners are among the most prosperous nations in Europe, with incomes equal to those the neighboring Swiss or Austrians.* Unemployment, at about 1% of the total workforce, is among the lowest in Europe. To widen their contacts beyond Switzerland, the Liechtensteiners joined the Council of Europe in 1978, the United Nations (UN) in 1990, the European Free Trade Association (EFTA) in 1991, and the European Economic Area (EFA) in 1995. The only claim against a foreign state is with the Czech Republic, which confiscated estates owned by the Liechtenstein family after World War I.

SELECTED BIBLIOGRAPHY

Bentley, James. *The House of Liechtenstein: The Centuries of European History.* 1988.

Duursma, Jorri. *Fragmentation and the International Relations of Micro-States: Self-Determination and Statehood.* 1996.

Duursma, Jorri. *Self-Determination, Statehood, and International Relations of Micro-States: The Cases of Liechtenstein, San Marino, Monaco, Andorra, and Vatican City.* 1994.

Gèunther, Erich. *Liechtenstein.* 1991.

Meier, Regula A. *Liechtenstein.* 1993.

LIGURIANS

Ligures; Liguris

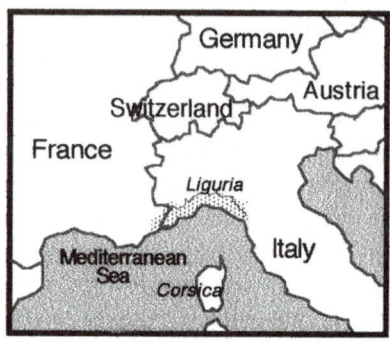

POPULATION: Approximately (2000 e) 1,859,000 Ligurians in Europe, 1,371,000 in the Liguria Region of Italy, with other populations in the neighboring Italian regions of Piedmont, Emilia-Romagna, and Tuscany and in France and Monaco.

THE LIGURIAN HOMELAND: The Ligurian homeland lies in the southwestern part of northern Italy on the Ligurian Sea. The region forms an arch from the mouth of the Roia River to the Magra River, embracing the southern slopes of the Ligurian Alps and the Apennines around the Gulf of Genoa. Most of the region is mountainous or hilly but penetrated by numerous valleys. Woodlands cover over half the region, making Liguria the most heavily wooded of Italian regions. Protected by their mountains, the Ligurians live in a region of mild, Mediterranean climate that is often called the Italian Riviera.

The ancient region of Liguria was reestablished in 1948, and the Region of Liguria was granted limited autonomy in 1970. *Region of Liguria*: 2,089 sq.mi.– 5,410 sq.km. (2000 e) 1,724,000—Ligurians 82%, French* 8%, other Italians.* The Ligurian capital and major cultural center is Genoa, (2000 e) 677,000 (metropolitan area 922,000), one of Italy's most important ports.

FLAG: The Ligurian national flag, based on the flag of the former Republic of Genoa, is a white field with a centered red cross and bearing a likeness of St. George and the Dragon on the upper hoist.

PEOPLE: The Ligurians are an ancient people, the descendants of the region's pre-Roman population and later migrants. The culture and traditions of the Ligurians were formed during the centuries of the Republic of Genoa, one of the most powerful maritime states of medieval Europe. Heavily influenced by the nearby French, the culture and dialect differ greatly from those of the Italian heartland in Rome and the central regions of Italy. The Ligurians are mostly Roman Catholic, with a small Protestant minority. In Liguria, more than any other region in Italy, the distribution of the population is determined by the topology. An estimated 90% of the Ligurian population live in the coastal towns, with a subsequent depopulation of the hilly and mountainous inland areas.

The dialect spoken by the Ligurians is a Gallo-Romance language, often referred to as a Celto-Romance dialect, of the Romance group of languages. The language has two major dialects: Genoese or Genovese, which is spoken around the capital, Genoa, and with variations is spoken in the towns of Caloforte and Calasetta and several small islands in Sardinia and in Corsica; and the Monégasque dialect, also called Ventimigliese, spoken along the coast west of San Remo and across the border in France and Monaco. The language is not inherently intelligible to speakers of standard Italian, although all Ligurians are bilingual in standard Italian. In most areas Ligurian remains the language of daily life.

NATION: The ancient Ligurii, who gave their name to the modern region, occupied the Mediterranean coast from the Rhone to the Arno. A people of pre-Indo-European stock, the Ligurians controlled the inland regions of the Po Valley to the foothills of the Alps and settled the Mediterranean coast by the sixth century B.C. In the fourth century B.C. the Ligurian tribes were driven from the highland regions by the Celtic migrations, while Greeks,* Phoenicians, and Carthaginians colonized the Ligurian coast.

The tribes west of the Rhone River were gradually subdued by the Romans during the second century B.C. The Ligurian town of Genua was first mentioned in Roman records in 218 B.C. and flourished under Roman rule and developed as the major trading center of Roman Liguria, which stretched west to present Nice and north to Turin. The decline of Roman power in the fourth and fifth centuries A.D. gradually reduced the area protected by Roman troops. Visigoths overran the Roman province, and in 539 the Germanic Burgundians* conquered Liguria. In 679 the Lombards* extended the boundaries of their kingdom to include Liguria.

In the tenth century the city of Genoa developed as a free commune governed by consuls. Its maritime power increased with the growth of trade around the Mediterranean Sea. Allied to Pisa, the Genoans drove the Arabs from Corsica and Sardinia, but rivalry over Sardinia resulted in the rupture of the alliance. A long series of wars ensued, which finally ended with Pisa's defeat at the naval battle of Meloria in 1284. In return for Genoa's assistance against the Venetians,* the Genoans were awarded by the Byzantines with special trading privileges and colonies at Chios, Lesbos, and Samos in Greece and at Kaffa and Azov on the Black Sea.

The center of the far-flung Ligurian mercantile empire, Genoa developed as a major European financial center. The Crusades furthered the prosperity of the region, which was based on the new trade routes to the eastern Mediterranean.

Prosperity facilitated the development of the great cultural flowering of the Renaissance.

The Genoese republic in the fourteenth century was weakened by factional strife between the Guelphs and Ghibellines, representing the nobility and the growing middle class. In 1339 the first doge was elected, who would serve for his lifetime. Although Genoa, from the late thirteenth through the sixteenth centuries, gained control of the various territories of the Ligurian coast, it gradually lost its overseas colonies. The republic became the object of a French and Milanese rivalry and eventually came under nominal French rule. The power of the republic was revived under the military leader Andrea Doria, who expelled the French and wrote a new republican constitution in 1528.

The decline of the republic accelerated as the French, Spaniards,* and Austrians* vied for influence in Liguria. A popular uprising in the region drove the Austrians from the region in 1746, but in 1768 the Genoese, unable to control the Corsicans,* were forced to sell the island, their last colony, to France. In 1797 French military pressure forced the formation of the Ligurian Republic, which was annexed to Napoleonic France in 1805. The annexation of the republic ended over 1,000 years of Ligurian independence. At the end of the Napoleonic Wars, the Congress of Vienna was convened in 1815 to remap the continent of Europe. Liguria, over the protests of the region's leaders, was given to the kingdom of Sardinia. During the Risorgimento the Sardinian kingdom expanded to include almost all of Italy. In 1861, Victor Emmanuel II of Sardinia was proclaimed king of Italy.

The unification of Italy was followed by a period of national consolidation. To overcome the language problem of dozens of different dialects spoken in the national territory of Italy, a Tuscan dialect was selected as the new national language. The dialect in 1871 was spoken by only 10% of the Italian population and was written by just 1%. The adoption of a standard language failed to impose national unity, and loyalty to regional dialects and cultures endured. The Ligurian language began to give way to the standardized Italian dialect only with the arrival of radio broadcasts in the 1930s.

Until the rise of the fascist dictatorship in the 1920s, the Ligurians enjoyed the fruits of the liberal constitution adopted by the Sardinian kingdom in 1848. After World War I, political and social unrest increased, furthering the growth of fascism. In 1922 the fascist leader, Benito Mussolini, promising the restoration of order, was made premier by the king.

The fascists, although unpopular with the Ligurian middle class, gained support among the workers and the rural population. In the 1930s there were frequent conflicts between fascists and communists, especially in industrial Genoa. Under government edicts, the Ligurian language was prohibited, and only standard Italian was allowed. Migrants from the poor, backward south were resettled in the region in unpopular government-sponsored schemes.

When World War II broke out, the Ligurians, although initially supportive, soon lost enthusiasm as fighting broke out on their border with France. In 1943 the Italian government surrendered, but northern Italy, including Liguria, was occupied by German troops, and the Ligurians were treated as a conquered nation. Liberated by American troops, the Ligurians in 1946 began to agitate for regional autonomy, including the teaching and official use of their distinct dialect. In 1947 the government promised autonomy, but a year later only very limited self-government was granted. In the postwar period the northern Italian industrial triangle centered on Turin, Genoa, and Milan experienced a booming economy and led the so-called postwar Italian Economic Miracle.

The Ligurians' standard of living reached the levels of the more prosperous European nations, but at a cost. The depopulation of the upland areas as well as the excessive concentration of industrial plants in certain districts became serious problems. Badly planned urban growth and the construction of the tourist industry in the region, which is often called the Italian Riviera, caused further damage and was frequently motivated by speculation.

In the 1960s the Ligurians, like the other nations of northern Italy, pressed for greater autonomy. The movement was triggered by resentment of the amount of their wealth used for projects in Italy's poor and corrupt southern regions. Autonomy was finally granted in 1970 but fell far short of the self-government demanded by Ligurian activists. An appreciation of their glorious history fueled the regional movement in the 1970s and 1980s.

The Ligurians, traditionally oriented to the Mediterranean trade routes, have enthusiastically supported Italy's integration in the European Union (EU). A Europe without borders would allow the Ligurians to reestablish their historical ties to inland regions by serving as the natural outlet for much of Southern Europe. By 1998 an estimated two-thirds of the active population was employed in the service industries related to the region's port cities.

Resentment of the corruption and political instability in Rome continues to add to calls for autonomy or even independence within the European Union (EU). Many Ligurians support the Northern League, which advocates the secession of the northern Italian regions and the formation of a confederation to be called Padania. In September 1996 Umberto Bossi, leader of the Northern League, declared the "federal republic of Padania" independent from the rest of Italy. The so-called republic consists of a region stretching from the Po River to Italy's northern border and includes Liguria. Although opinion polls showed little support for outright secession in Liguria, analysts agree that the autonomy movement has tapped into a growing discontent among Ligurians.

SELECTED BIBLIOGRAPHY

Coyle, Dominick J. *Minorities in Revolt.* 1983.
Facaros, Dana. *Northwest Italy.* 1991.
Hearder, Harry. *Italy in the Age of the Risorgimento, 1790–1870.* 1983.
Hume, David D. *Towns of the Renaissance: Travelers in Northern Italy.* 1998.
Whaley, Daniel Philip. *The Italian City Republics.* 1988.

LITHUANIANS

Liths

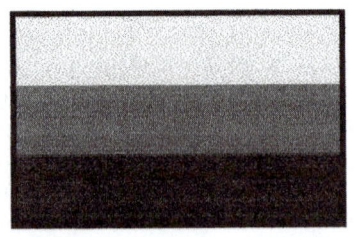

POPULATION: Approximately (2000 e) 3,275,000 Lithuanians in Europe, mostly in Lithuania, but with about 200,000 in the Russian Federation and 70,000 in Latvia and Belarus.

THE LITHUANIAN HOMELAND: The Lithuanian homeland lies in Northeastern Europe, on the eastern shore of the Baltic Sea. Lithuania has very few natural resources other than agricultural land, which makes up about two-thirds of the land area, and forests, about one-quarter of the land. Lying on the rim of the Russian Plain, the country has only two elevated regions, separated by the Lithuanian Lowlands, a hilly country of lakes and bogs in the east and the Samogitian hills in the west. Neither of the upland regions reaches over 1,000 feet. Over 2,800 lakes are included in Lithuania's national territory.

Lithuania formed an independent republic between the world wars but was forcibly annexed by the Soviet Union in 1940. Following the disintegration of the USSR in 1991, Lithuania regained its independence. *Republic of Lithuania (Lietuvos Respublika)*: 25,174 sq.mi.–65,201 sq.km. (2000 e) 3,754,000—Lithuanians 81%, Russians* 8%, Poles* 7%, Belarussians* 2%, Jews, Latvians,* Tatars.* The Lithuanian capital and major cultural center is Vilnius, (2000 e) 602,000, which was in Polish territory from 1920 to 1939.

FLAG: The Lithuanian national flag, the official flag of the republic, is a horizontal tricolor of yellow, green, and red.

PEOPLE: The Lithuanians are a Baltic people closely related to the Latvians, the other nation that, with the Lithuanians, makes up the Baltic group of the Indo-European peoples. The largest of the Baltic nations, the Lithuanians are also the most rural, with about one-third living in rural areas. Traditionally, the

Lithuanian nation is divided into four major subgroups, the Aukstaiciai in the northeast, Zemaiciai in the west, Dzukai in the southeast, and the Suvalkieciai in the south. About 72% of the Lithuanians live in urban areas.

Although the Lithuanians were one of the last nations in Europe to adopt Roman Catholicism, the church eventually came to play a central role in its national culture. A small minority, about 4%, formerly living under Prussian rule, are Lutherans, and there is a smaller Orthodox minority, mostly in the urban areas.

The Lithuanian language, along with Latvian, forms the Baltic branch of the European languages. The language is related to ancient Sanskrit and retains many archaic elements, particularly the sound system and morphological peculiarities that have disappeared from the other Indo-European languages. Each of the four major groups speaks a distinct dialect, with the Aukstaiciai dialect the basis of the literary language. The language is considered notably pure in its retention of archaic Indo-European forms.

NATION: From their original homeland far to the east, the Baltic tribes are believed to have arrived in Northeastern Europe around 2,000 B.C. Pushed west by the great Slav migrations of the eighth and ninth centuries A.D., the tribes eventually settled along the eastern shore of the Baltic Sea. Their fierce resistance halted the westward expansion of the Slav tribes. The Lithuanians were first mentioned in written records in a medieval Prussian manuscript, the Quedinburg Annals, in 1009, although centuries earlier the Roman historian Tacitus wrote of the tribes along the Baltic shore as an agricultural people trading in amber.

Under the rule of Grand Duke Gediminas, who is recognized as the founder of modern Lithuania in the early fourteenth century, the territory of the Lithuanian state began to expand, eventually stretching from the Baltic Sea to the Black Sea. In the mid-thirteenth century, Duke Mindaugas united the lands inhabited by the Lithuanians, Samogitians, Yotvingians, and Couranians into the Grand Duchy of Lithuania. In 1251 Mindaugas adopted Christianity and was acknowledged as the head of the united Lithuanian state two years later.

Duke Jagiello in 1385, surrounded by German crusaders on the north and west and Muscovites and Tatars on the east, married a Polish princess and joined Lithuania to Poland in a dynastic union. Jagiello agreed to accept Catholicism and baptized the remaining pagan tribes, traditionally in 1387. The conversion of the Lithuanians invalidated claims by the German crusaders and temporarily ended the support by the pope for their campaign. Peace between the Lithuanians and the Teutonic Knights allowed the Christian peoples of Northeastern Europe to unite to face a new threat. Under a descendant of Gediminas, the Lithuanians led a great Christian army against Timur (Tamerlane) in Ukraine in 1399. The battle ended without a clear victor but so weakened Timur's forces that he eventually returned to Asia.

Following the indecisive conflict with the Tatars, the German knights returned to the offensive. In spite of Lithuanian appeals to the pope that the Germans sought land, not converts, in Christian Lithuania, the war intensified. The power of the medieval Lithuanian state, in alliance with Poland, finally defeated the crusading German Teutonic Knights at the Battle of Tannenberg in 1410. After the decisive defeat Lithuania became the most powerful state in Northeastern Europe. The Lithuanian state evolved a sophisticated, advanced society, and the conditions of the groups on the lower rungs of society were generally good.

Lithuania and Poland, beginning in 1501, were ruled by one sovereign. The Poles in 1569 raised the recurrent question of the unification of Poland and Lithuania. The two states, joined in a dynastic union since 1385, were beset by wars with Moscow and attacks by Swedes* in Livonia and by Crimean Tatars* in southern Ukraine. In Lublin, Poland, the state union was signed, and the two states merged into one. The culture of the more numerous Poles became predominant, and the Lithuanian upper classes gradually became Polish in language and culture.

The mid-sixteenth century saw a rapid development of agriculture, the growth of towns, and the spread of ideas of humanism and the Reformation. The earliest book written in Lithuanian was a Roman Catholic catechism published in 1547. Book printing expanded the dissemination of knowledge and facilitated the emergence of Vilnius University in 1579. The liberal Lithuanian code of law, the Statutes of Lithuania, stimulated the development of popular culture.

In the early seventeenth century wars with the Russians and Swedes dominated the region. The Lithuanians and Poles eventually drove the invaders from their empire, but the wars had critically weakened the state. Between 1772 and 1795 Poland-Lithuania was partitioned by Austria, Prussia, and Russia, with most of the Lithuanian territories coming under the authority of the Russian Empire. Attempts to throw off Russian rule spurred uprisings in 1794 and 1830–31. In 1832 the Russian authorities closed Vilnius University and pressed assimilation.

The Lithuanians in the mid-nineteenth century began to embrace nationalism as a mass movement. The abolition of serfdom in 1861 stimulated the development of a market economy. As Lithuanian farmers grew stronger, an increasing number gained education. Rejecting Russification, the Lithuanians joined the Poles in open rebellion in 1863. In 1864 the authorities banned the printing of Lithuanian books in the traditional Latin alphabet. To the west, in German-controlled Memel (Klaipeda), called Lithuania Minor by the nationalists, Lithuanian publications were published, then smuggled into Russian-ruled Lithuania. The national movement, suppressed in Russia, continued among the Lithuanian minority in neighboring German East Prussia. The first Lithuanian newspaper was founded in Memel in 1883. In 1894 all Roman Catholics were excluded from local government positions.

During World War I, German troops occupied Lithuania in 1915. In September 1917, after the February revolution in Russia, the Germans allowed a nationalist conference to convene in Vilnius. The conference demanded the restoration of an independent Lithuanian state and elected the Lithuanian Council, chaired by Antanas Smetona. In the wake of the Bolshevik takeover of Russia in October 1917, the Lithuanian Council, with German support, declared an independent kingdom on 16 February 1918 and designated Duke William of Wurttemburg as their king. When the war turned against their German allies, the Lithuanians renounced the monarchy and proclaimed Lithuania a republic on 30 November 1918.

Local Bolshevik groups overthrew the new nationalist government in December 1918, but the Lithuanian Bolsheviks soon lost support due to the continuing attacks on the Catholic religion. A force of Lithuanians, Poles, and German Free Corps, supported by the Allies, drove the Soviet government from power in Lithuania in January 1919. The Lithuanian forces occupied the region claimed as national territory, including the important cities of Vilnius and Gardinas (Grodno), also claimed by Lithuania's newly independent neighbors, Poland and Belarus. The new state was quickly embroiled in a crisis brought on by territorial disputes.

Invaded by Polish troops in October 1920, the Lithuanian army fell back, losing the historically and economically important Vilnius and Gardinas to the victorious Poles. The Lithuanian government, transferred from Vilnius to the city of Kaunas, continued to claim their ancient capital, Vilnius, inciting renewed fighting in 1922. The territorial dispute, taken to the new League of Nations, was finally settled in Poland's favor. The disgruntled Lithuanians then expelled the French forces that had occupied Memel at the end of the war and annexed the city.

Lithuania's independence remained precarious due to its position between the Soviet Union and the turmoil in postwar Germany. On 17 December 1926 a military coup overthrew the government. The leader of the Nationalist Party, Antanas Smetona, became president and introduced an authoritarian regime. The state's stability, undermined by the ongoing territorial dispute with Poland, worsened in the 1930s as pressure increased from both the Stalinist Soviet Union and a resurgent Nazi Germany. In March 1939 Nazi Germany forced Lithuania to surrender the Memel (Klaipeda) region, which was annexed to the expanding Nazi Empire.

A secret nonaggression pact between Germany and the Soviet Union in August 1939 placed Lithuania in the so-called Soviet sphere. Soviet troops massed on the eastern border, forcing the Lithuanian government to resign and hand power to a pro-Soviet clique that requested incorporation of Lithuania in the Soviet Union. The next day 100,000 Soviet troops occupied the country. On 3 August 1940 Lithuania was proclaimed a member state of the USSR. The Soviets held Lithuania for about one year; then, only days before the Germans invaded in June 1941 and occupied the region, the Soviet government began deporting large numbers of Lithuanians deemed anticommunist or anti-Stalin.

Over 100,000 Lithuanians took up arms, many joining the Nazi forces that occupied Lithuania. Many Lithuanians were rounded up and taken to forced labor camps in Germany. Others volunteered for duty with the Nazi forces. The

Nazis and their local Lithuanian collaborators implemented the anti-Jewish laws of the Third Reich and eventually massacred about 200,000 Lithuanian Jews. Some of the Lithuanian recruits participated in the Jewish Holocaust outside Lithuania, serving as guards at concentration camps or in special units.

The Red Army drove the last German units from Lithuania in 1944. Special Soviet screening commissions investigated the past and political views of every inhabitant over the age of twelve. Formal charges fell into two categories, war criminal or enemy of the people. Official statistics state that over 120,000 Lithuanians were deported during the period 1945–52, but many Lithuanian sources estimated the number to be as high as 300,000. The deportees included a majority of the republic's surviving national, cultural, and religious leaders.

Lithuanian nationalism, kept alive by underground and exile groups in Western Europe and the United States, grew dramatically in the late 1980s, quickly pushing far beyond the modest reforms instituted by the Soviet leader Mikhail Gorbachev in 1987. In mid-1988 the Lithuanian reform movement, called Sajudis, was formed and proclaimed a program of democratic and national rights. The popular front group won nationwide popularity with its calls for the reestablishment of independent Lithuania.

Sajudis candidates won elections to the Lithuanian Supreme Soviet in February 1990. On 11 March 1990 its chairman, Vytautas Landsbergis, proclaimed the restoration of Lithuanian independence. The Soviet government immediately demanded revocation of the act and applied political and economic sanctions against the republic. The defiant nationalists refused to back down despite a crippling oil embargo and threatened military action. The oil embargo, put in place in April, was lifted in June following the Lithuanians' agreement to suspend the independence declaration while negotiations were undertaken. To clearly demonstrate popular support for independence, the Lithuanian government organized a national referendum. On 9 February, over 90% of those who voted, 76% of all eligible voters, backed Landsbergis and his bid for independence.

The attempted coup against Gorbachev on 19 August 1991 dramatically ended the standoff. The Lithuanian government banned the Communist Party and ordered the confiscation of its properties. On 6 September 1991 President Landsbergis reinstated the March 1990 declaration, formally proclaiming Lithuania independent of the disintegrating Soviet Union. The long-running border dispute between Lithuania and Poland over the Vilnius region was finally settled with the signing of a friendship and cooperation treaty in January 1992.

Lithuanian voters in October 1992, alarmed by the rapidly deteriorating economy, chose ex-communist candidates over the nationalists who had led the state to independence. In December in presidential elections, the ex-Communist Party chief of the 1980s was elected to replace Vytautas Landsbergis. In February 1993, following new elections, a former Sajudis leader became the head of state. The instability of the government continued into the late 1990s, with resignations, dismissals, and scandals involving official corruption.

The precarious economic position and the government's hesitation on implementing the reforms demanded for entry led to Lithuania's exclusion from the list of candidate countries issued by the European Union (EU) in 1997. The Lithuanian government, still wary of its Russian neighbors, is intent on membership in the EU and the Western military alliance, the North Atlantic Treaty Organization (NATO), but in spite of the aid and support of the large Lithuanian diaspora, mostly in the United States, the country's economic situation continues to hinder its progress toward the Lithuanians' goal of financial and military security within the Western alliances.

In early January 1997 the United States overtook Germany as Lithuania's largest foreign investor. Germany remains the second largest investor, while Sweden has become the third. The investment patterns highlight the Lithuanians' growing trade with the West and their decreasing ties to the states of the former Soviet Union.

In September 1997 in Vilnius, Lithuanian president Algirdas Brazauskas hosted the presidents of ten countries in the region between the Baltic and Black Seas. The meeting, which should help the countries integrate into the West and smooth their relations with each other and with Moscow, marked the Lithuanians' new confidence as the economy began to turn around, and political stability began to benefit the entire population.

A retired American bureaucrat of Lithuanian ancestry won the January 1998 presidential elections by a narrow margin. Valdas Adamkus, who spent most of his life fighting Nazi and Soviet occupations of Lithuania before becoming an official in the U.S. Environmental Protection Agency, faces a slowly reforming economy and little foreign business interest in Lithuania. Unlike the Brazauskas government, which looked to Moscow, the Adamkus government will likely pull the Lithuanians closer to Washington and Brussels.

The Lithuanians, in spite of democratic government, growing material comfort, and increasing integration in Europe, remain burdened by the past. The rapidity and trauma of social change, crumbling social welfare systems, and the postcommunist phenomenon of unemployment have contributed to increasing alcoholism and depression. Among the European nations, in 1999 the Lithuanians have the highest suicide rate.

SELECTED BIBLIOGRAPHY

Chicoine, Stephen, and Brent K. Ashabranner. *Lithuania: The Nation That Would Be Free.* 1995.

Krickus, Richard J. *Showdown: The Lithuanian Rebellion and the Breakup of the Soviet Empire.* 1997.

Smith, Graham, ed. *The Baltic States: The National Self-Determination of Estonia, Latvia, and Lithuania.* 1996.

Suziedelis, Saulius. *Historical Dictionary of Lithuania.* 1997.

Zalys, Vytautas, ed. *Lithuania in European Politics: The Years of the First Republic, 1918–1940.* 1998.

LIVONIANS

Livs; Livians; Livods; Livlis

POPULATION: Approximately (2000 e) 100,000 Livonians in Europe, concentrated in northwestern Latvia and southwestern Estonia.

THE LIVONIAN HOMELAND: The Livonian homeland lies on the eastern shore of the Baltic Sea around the Gulf of Riga in Latvia and Estonia. In Latvia the region is included in the historic regions of Kurzeme on the western shore of the Gulf of Riga and western Vidzeme on the eastern shore of the gulf. In Estonia the Livonian homeland includes the coastal region south of the city of Parnu. Much of the region is lowland swamps and forests, which helped to protect the isolated Livonian communities.

Livonia has no official status, although a small part of the Livonian homeland, approximately a fifty-mile-long (eighty km.) strip of land in extreme northwestern Latvia, was officially designated the Livonian Coast special region. The Livonian capital and major cultural center is Mazirbe, called Ire by the Livonians, in northern Latvia. The city of Ventpils (2000 e) 48,000 at the southern edge of the Livonian homeland is also a major Livonian cultural center. In Estonia the most important Livonian cultural center is the town of Massiaru.

FLAG: The Livonian national flag, recognized by Livonians in both Latvia and Estonia, is a horizontal tricolor of green, white, and pale blue. The white stripe is half the width of the green and blue stripes.

PEOPLE: The Livonians are a Finno-Ugric people related to the Estonians* and Finns,* although culturally they are close to the Latvians.* The Livonian population is concentrated in Latvia, both east and west of the Gulf of Riga, and with smaller numbers in southeastern Estonia and on the Estonian island of Saaremaa. The total number of Livonians in the region is uncertain, as most

Livonians have traditionally registered as ethnic Latvians or Estonians. Officially, only those who still speak the Livonian language are counted as ethnic Livonians. Traditionally, the Livonians are divided into two groups, the Raandali, the "people of the seashore," west of the Gulf of Riga, and the Kalamied, "fishermen," on the eastern shore of the Gulf of Riga straddling the border between Latvia and Estonia. Like their Latvian and Estonian neighbors, the Livonians are mostly Protestant Lutherans.

The Livonian nation, considered assimilated by the Soviet authorities since the 1960s, has reemerged since the disintegration of the Soviet Union and the independence of Latvia and Estonia. Although only a small number are able to speak the Livonian language, the traditional Livonian cultural traits and customs remain an integral part of the regional culture.

The Livonian language is a Balto-Finnic language related to Estonian and Finnish, formerly spoken in two distinct dialects, Western Livonian in Kurzeme and Eastern Livonian in Vidzeme. The western dialect, also called Raandalist, is spoken on a daily basis by less than 50 people and is used by between 400 and 1,000 frequently, although an estimated 1,700 in eight villages west of Kolka (Kolkasrags) in Kurzeme have some knowledge of it. Eastern Livonian became extinct in the late nineteenth century. A written form of the language was codified only in 1935.

NATION: The Livonians claim to have inhabited their present homeland for over 5,000 years. The descendants of Finno-Ugric tribes that migrated to the northern Baltic Sea region in pre-Christian times, the Finnic tribes were pushed into the coastal regions by the Slav migrations of the sixth and seventh centuries A.D. Historic Livonia traditionally consisted of the region east of the Gulf of Riga from the Daugava River into present Estonia and in the northern districts of Kurzeme west of the Gulf of Riga.

German merchants landed at the mouth of the Daugava River in the twelfth century, establishing trading posts and Catholic missions. In 1201 Bishop Albert founded the town of Riga on Livonian territory, and a year later the Livonian Knights, also called the Livonian Order, were formed to serve the bishop in Christianizing the Livonians. The knights, a military-religious order, conquered the Livonian tribes and took control of the territory. The Livonian defeat began 700 years of foreign domination. Latvian tribes began to settle in the depopulated Livonian territories. According to Henric the Lett's chronicles, at the beginning of the thirteenth century Livonians lived on the shores of the Gulf of Riga, on lower reaches of the Daugava River, and on the Gauja and Salaca Rivers.

The Livonian state dominated by the Germanic knights was a militarily strong state that threatened Lithuania and Novgorod in the thirteenth and fourteenth centuries. The knights divided the territory into numerous feudal manors and reduced the Livonians to a class of peasant serfs. Peasant uprisings were frequent, with reprisals that sustained an enduring hatred of their German masters. In 1554 the Master of Order, the head of the Livonian Order, Walter von Plettenberg, fearing a wider uprising, declared Protestantism the official religion. The decision weakened the feudal state and allowed the expanding Russians to gain influence. The Livonian Wars, fought from 1558 to 1583, were partly due to Moscow's desire for a warm-water port on the Baltic Sea.

To prevent a Russian conquest of the region, the Germans dissolved the Teutonic Order, except in Kurzeme and Riga, and placed their vast estates under the protection of the powerful Roman Catholic Lithuanian-Polish state in 1561. Catholicism was again proclaimed the state religion. Following the dissolution of the Livonian Order, the Livonian homeland was contested by the Poles,* Russians,* and Swedes.* The Swedish kingdom, which had controlled northern Estonia from 1521, wrested most of Livonia from Poland between 1621 and 1626. Swedish rule reinforced Lutheranism as the predominant religion of the Livonians.

The rivalry between Sweden and Russia for domination in the Baltic region culminated in the Northern War, which devastated the region between 1700 and 1721. By the terms of the Treaty of Nystad most of the region passed to Russian rule. In 1783 Livonia was constituted a Russian province. Under Russian rule, the German "Baltic Barons" retained their power, and German was the official language of the region.

In the eighteenth and nineteenth centuries, the Livonians began to assimilate into the larger neighboring cultures. The language gave way to Latvian in the south and Estonian in the north, although Livonian culture, much influenced by the Latvians, remained dominant throughout the region. In the nineteenth century the Livonians east of the Gulf of Riga adopted Latvian as their mother tongue, and the eastern dialect of Livonian virtually disappeared. In 1817–19 the Livonian serfs were emancipated, but by that time the Livonian language had nearly disappeared. In 1835 only 2,074 considered Livonian their first language.

During World War I, the Russian authorities ordered thousands of Livonians living along the Baltic Sea to leave their villages and to move inland. Their coastal villages were deserted and patrolled by troops guarding the coastal defense installations. After the war many of the dispersed Livonians remained where they had settled, mostly in the nearby Latvian cities.

The independence of Latvia and Estonia following the Russian Revolution further endangered the Livonian nation. In 1918 their homeland was divided between the two new states, which sparked a period of national awakening. Sustained by the development of the newly independent Estonians and Finns, the Livonians began to recuperate their disappearing language and culture. The Latvian government supported the revival, and from 1923 the Livonian language was taught in area schools, textbooks were compiled, a newspaper was issued, and books in the Livonian language were published. A nationalist organization, the Livonian Union, was formed to promote the culture and intercede with local and national governments on behalf of the Livonian people. In 1939, with support from the Estonian and Finnish governments, the Livonian Community Center was built at Mazirbe.

Soviet troops occupied Latvia and Estonia in 1940 and quickly eliminated all resistance. Many Livonians were deported along with their Latvian neighbors. The Germans overran the region in 1941, with young Livonians among the conscripts or volunteers for the Germans' anticommunist crusade. Livonians were once again forced to abandon their homes as war swept across the region. Following German defeat in 1944, the Soviet authorities returned, and new deportations eliminated the Livonian cultural and political leadership. According to the regulations covering the coastal zones, the Livonians were not allowed to go to sea, even for fishing. In 1955 Soviet military bases were built between the coastal villages. All elements of the Livonians' national culture were banned, and the Livonian Union was dissolved. Livonian organizations among the emigrant population, particularly in the United States, became the center of Livonian culture.

In Soviet censuses the Livonians, fearing official attention, registered as ethnic Latvians or Estonians. In the Soviet census of 1959 only 200 claimed Livonian nationality. In the 1970 census no Livonians were counted in the region. In the 1979 census several hundred people of Livonian descent in Latvia wished to identify themselves as Livonians but were ignored. In the late 1980s only thirty-five people could still speak Livonian, only fifteen of them fluently.

The disintegration of the Soviet Union in 1991 and the subsequent independence of Latvia and Estonia began the modern reculturation of the Livonians. Overseas Livonians supported the revival with monetary and cultural aid. The Livonian Cultural Society, later renamed the Livonian Union, was founded in Latvia, where the Livonian language was again taught in area schools. Famous singing choirs, based in Riga and Ventpils, developed as the spiritual centers of the reviving Livonian nation.

Young Livonians, in order to safeguard the future of their nation, began to learn the language and to sing in the Livonian choirs. On 4 February 1991 the Latvian government approved the creation of a special cultural region, the Livonian Coast, in a territory about fifty miles (eighty km.) long, on the extreme northwestern shore of Latvia, which is inhabited by the last speakers of the Livonian language. In 1996 the University of Latvia's Foreign Languages Faculty began offering Livonian language studies. Great interest in Livonian culture has been shown by Finnish and Estonian researchers keen to learn more about a related culture, and the Livonian language is now taught in Finnish and Estonian universities.

SELECTED BIBLIOGRAPHY
Dreifelds, Juris. *Latvia in Transition.* 1996.
Penkis, Janis J., and Andrejs Penikis. *Latvia: Independence Renewed.* 1997.
Plakans, Andrejs. *Historical Dictionary of Latvia.* 1997.
Raun, Toivo U. *Estonia and the Estonians.* 1991.
Von Rauch, Georg, ed. *The Baltic States: The Years of Independence, Estonia, Latvia, Lithuania.* 1996.

LOMBARDS

Lombardi; Lombardos

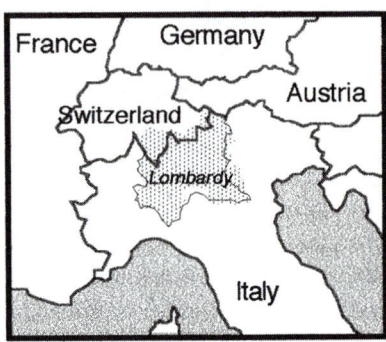

POPULATION: Approximately (2000 e) 8,721,000 Lombards in Europe, 8,145,000 in Italy, 564,000 in the Ticino and Graübunden cantons of Switzerland, and the remainder mostly in France and Germany.

THE LOMBARD HOMELAND: The Lombard homeland lies between the Lepontine and Rhaetian Alps in Ticino and Graübunden and the Po River in northern Italy. Three distinct natural zones are easily distinguishable in Lombardy, mountain, foothill, and plain. Most of the region occupies the broad Lombard Plain in the Po River valley, rising in the north to the Alpine foothills and the lake region, which includes the lakes Como, Garda, Maggiore, and Lugano. The Alps, with numerous Alpine peaks and glaciers, rise to their highest points at Monte Leone in the Lepontine Alps, 11,654 feet (3,552 m.), on the Swiss-Italian border, and Piz Bernina in the Rhaetian Alps, 13,284 feet (4,049 m). The major rivers are the Ticino, Lambro, Adda, Mincio, and Oglio, most being the outlets of the various large lakes. There is a large network of canals for irrigation purposes. The rich Po Valley, where irrigated agriculture has been practiced since Roman times, is one of the most fertile regions in Europe, with abundant crops of rice, cereals, fruits, and livestock. It is also the primary industrial region of Italy, producing textiles, iron and steel, automobiles, and chemicals.

Historical Lombardy forms a semiautonomous region of the Italian Republic and the Ticino Canton and the southern districts of Graübunden Canton of Switzerland. *Region of Lombardy (Lombardia)*: 9,202 sq.mi.–23,833 sq.mi. (2000 e) 8,954,000—Lombards 77%, other Italians* and non-Italians. The Lombard capital and major cultural center is Milan (Milano), (2000 e) 1,406,000 (metropolitan area 4,758,000), the industrial and financial capital of Italy. Bellinzona,

(2000 e) 18,000 is the capital of Ticino, but Lugano (2000 e) 26,000 (metropolitan area 104,000) is the most important cultural center in the region.

FLAGs: The Lombard national flag, the official flag of the region, is a white field charged with a centered red cross. The flag of the Lombards of Ticino Canton in Switzerland is a square bicolor of red over blue.

PEOPLE: The Lombards are a distinct Italian nation descended from the early Latin population and the later Germanic Langobard or Lombard tribes. The Lombards' history and culture, distinct from those in central and southern Italy, have strengthened the Lombards' sense of identity, with a parallel growth of nationalism in the late twentieth century. Innovative, energetic, and pro-European, the Lombards are the most advanced of the Italian peoples. The majority of the Lombards are nominally Roman Catholic, with a small, but influential, Protestant minority in northern Lombardy and in Graübunden Canton in Switzerland.

The Lombard language belongs to the Gallo-Romance group of the Romance language group and is spoken in ten regional dialects. Milanese, Eastern Lombard, Western Lombard, Alpine Lombard, Latin Fiamazzo, Latin Anaunico, and Bergamasco are spoken in Lombardy, Novarese Lombard is spoken in eastern Piedmont, Trentino Western is spoken in Trentino-Alto Adige Region, and Ticinese in Switzerland. The group of dialects that make up the Lombard language vary greatly from region to region, but all have much in common and are understood by the majority of the population. Lombard, called Lombardo, is very different from standard Italian.

NATION: An ancient region, the fertile northern plains came under the rule of the Etruscans as early as 500 B.C. The Romans, extending their authority to the north, absorbed the Etruscan cities one by one in the third century B.C. Added to the Roman province of Cisalpine Gaul, the northern cities developed as centers of Roman culture and art and continued to flourish for a time after the division of the empire in A.D. 395. The rapid decline of Roman power left the wealthy region nearly defenseless as the garrisons withdrew.

The Lombards, or Langobards, originated in the lower Elbe valley in present Germany. They were mentioned by Tacitus in the first century A.D. as one of the many tribes collectively known as the Suebi or Swabians.* Tacitus noted that they were small in number and hemmed in by more powerful Germanic tribes but that they found safety not in submission but in war. They played little role in the Germanic invasions of the Roman Empire, moving into northern Austria only in the wake of other tribes about 486, long after the Romans had departed.

Early in the sixth century, they moved into Pannonia, where they established themselves as a powerful presence. In 547 Emperor Justinian of the Eastern Roman Empire allowed them to settle permanently in Pannonia and Noricum, modern eastern Austria and Hungary. The Lombards, under their kings Wacho and Audoin, became allies of the empire and assisted imperial forces against the Ostrogoths and Franks. During the wars they helped Justinian to reconquer the fertile Po valley from the Goths. When they came under pressure from the advancing Avars,* they migrated southwest to settle on the plains of the Po River in 568. They erected a small kingdom centered on Pavia and extended their rule to much of northern Italy while adopting the culture and language of the surviving Latin population.

After the death of the Lombard king Alboin in 572, the kingdom soon divided into thirty-six duchies in a loose federation, and the region fell into chaos from 575 to 584. Finally, the Lombard nobility gathered to elect a new king to wear the Lombard Iron Crown and to unite the Lombard lands against the threats by the expanding Franks and the growing power of the papacy. In the early seventh century the Lombard kingdom replaced the autonomous duchies. The Lombards gradually converted to Christianity, although the Lombard kings initially resisted conversion.

Lombard power reached its peak during the reign of King Liutprand in the early eighth century, but after his death the popes enlisted the Franks to defeat them. In 755 Pepin the Short, the king of the Franks, invaded Lombardy at the direct invitation of the pope. Lombard rule was finally destroyed by Pepin's son, Charlemagne, in 773. In the next year he was crowned with the Lombard Iron Crown, and the Lombard kingdom disappeared.

Following the breakup of Charlemagne's empire in 843, power in the region gradually passed from the feudal lords to the urban communes. The Lombard cities formed a defensive alliance in 1167, the Lombard League. In 1176 the Lombards defeated the forces of the Holy Roman Empire and forced the emperor to recognize their status as free cities in 1183. Mostly ruled by branches of the Sforza and Visconti families, patrons of Leonardo da Vinci, the cultural revival of the northern Italian cities initiated the Renaissance.

In the late fourteenth century Milan became one of the most powerful states in Italy, with most of Lombardy sharing its fortunes. The region flourished but soon became involved in the Italian Wars as France and Spain fought for dominance in divided Italy. Wars between the city-states and vicious family rivalries accelerated the rise of Milan and the loss of territories to Venice and other powers in the fifteenth and sixteenth centuries. The Swiss intervened in the wars and conquered Milan but were eventually defeated, although they retained control of the northern districts of Milan on the Ticino River.

The dominant Lombard power, the Duchy of Milan, came under Spanish rule in 1535 and passed to the Austrian branch of the Hapsburgs in 1713. Taken from Austria by Napoleon in 1796, the Lombards were mostly under French rule until Austrian authority was reestablished in 1815. The Lombardo-Venetian kingdom, set up under Austrian rule, was garrisoned by Austrian troops.

The area of Lombardy conquered by the Swiss in the sixteenth century was ruled jointly by Schwyz and Uri cantons until 1798 and became a separate canton within the Swiss Confederation in 1803. Since the Lombards in Switzerland enjoyed a large measure of self-government, there was little sentiment for reunion with the Lombard heartland in chaotic Italy.

The territorial exchanges and the imposition of differing laws, languages, and political systems sparked a Lombard national movement that culminated in widespread disturbances in 1848. The region formed part of the so-called Lombardo-Venetian Kingdom of the Austrian Empire until its liberation by French troops in 1859. In 1861 Lombardy joined the Risorgimento, the union of the numerous Italian states in a united Italian state, the Kingdom of Italy.

The numerous Italian peoples, united between 1861 and 1870, spoke dozens of regional dialects, many mutually unintelligible. The new Italian government chose a Tuscan dialect as a national language, a dialect spoken by only 10% of the population and written by just 1%. The adoption of a standard language failed to impose national unity on the diverse Italian peoples loyal to their regions, dialects, and cultures. The Lombard language, like many others, began to give way to standard Italian only with the arrival of radio broadcasts in the 1930s.

Lombard industrialization, accelerated after unification, evolved an urbanized, middle-class culture unlike that in most of agrarian Italy. The fascist government in the 1920s and 1930s began to settle poor, culturally and linguistically distinct southern Italians in Lombardy to staff the booming factories.

The Lombard industries, vitally important to Italy during World War II, suffered massive bombing and destruction. The final Allied offensive in Italy began in April 1945, and by the end of the month the German armies in northern Italy had been completely smashed. Mussolini, his mistress, and several of his high-ranking colleagues were captured by partisans at a small town near Lake Como. The entire group was summarily tried and, on 28 April, executed. The Lombards, blaming the southern fascists for the devastation of the war, inflicted brutal vengeance on Mussolini's followers after the German surrender on 2 May. More than 1,000 fascists were shot in Milan alone.

The Lombards recovered quickly in the postwar era. Their region became the center of the "Italian Miracle," the rapid industrial expansion of the 1950s. Millions of poor southerners from Italy's underdeveloped Mezzogiorno migrated north to the expanding Lombard industrial cities. The influx further strengthened standard Italian as a lingua franca used by southern workers and Lombard supervisors. Lombardy's postwar growth raised Lombard living standards to the equal of those of any region in Europe but increased tensions between the Lombards and the culturally and linguistically distinct southern Italian immigrants.

The unification of Europe, widely supported in Lombardy, began to raise questions and resentment in the 1970s. In 1978 Umberto Bossi published a tract advocating Lombard secession from Italy. The tract was widely denounced as the work of a lunatic. Undeterred, Bossi organized the Lombard League in 1981. Anti-Rome and anti-immigrant, meaning both foreigners and the southern Italians, the league's nationalist message struck a chord in Lombardy, which pays more taxes to the Italian state than the entire area south of Rome. Growing dissatisfaction with Rome's huge and hugely inefficient bureaucracy and with the Lombard taxes lavished on southern Italy only to line the pockets of corrupt officials and organized crime bosses fueled the growth of Lombard nationalism. The movement raised the Lombard League's portion of the vote from only 8% in 1988 to 20% in 1989 and to between 37% and 46% in local elections since 1992.

In the 1990s the idea of a federation of independent states within a united Europe, to be called Padania, gained support across northern Italy. The proposed federation, to include the Lombards, Piedmontese,* Venetians,* Ligurians,* and other nations in northern Italy, remains the goal of many of the pro-European Lombards. Italy's ongoing corruption scandals, affecting hundreds of politicians and officials of the traditional political parties, have outraged many Lombards who see themselves as Europeans first and Italians second. The pull of Europe, the idea of an independent Lombardy that is able to participate as an equal in a united Europe, continues to fuel the growth of nationalism and the growing support for the reversal of the Risorgimento that would make Italy once more just a geographical expression.

In 1995 the Northern League, the major political force supporting autonomy for the northern regions, changed its name to Northern League-Federal Italy. In September 1996 Umberto Bossi, leader of the Northern League, declared the "federal republic of Padania" independent from the rest of Italy. The so-called republic consists of a region stretching from the Po River to Italy's northern border. The declaration was not to take effect for up to twelve months to enable a Northern League provisional government, formed earlier in the year, to negotiate a treaty of separation with the Italian government. While the Northern League was founded on a federalist platform, Bossi had redefined the party's goals and had begun calling for the region's secession. Although opinion polls showed little support for secession, analysts said that the movement tapped into a growing discontent among Lombards. In response to such concerns, the Italian parliament had been working to pass constitutional reforms aimed at giving local leaders a stronger voice in national government and changing the country's tax structure.

The Swiss Lombards, in the 1990s, have reestablished their historic ties to the Italian Lombards to the south, particularly after the dominant Swiss Germans* outvoted the other Swiss nations and rejected closer ties between Switzerland and the European Union (EU). The rise of the People's Party in the Swiss German cantons, a far-right political party that plays to the Swiss Germans anti-European Union and anti-immigrant attitudes, has further alarmed the pro-European Lombards of southeastern Switzerland.

SELECTED BIBLIOGRAPHY

Butler, William F. *Lombard Communes*. 1969.
Carello, Adrian N. *The Northern Question: Italy's Participation in the European Economic Community and the Mezzogiorno's Underdevelopment*. 1989.
Greenfield, Kent R. *Economics and Liberalism in The Risorgimento: A Study of Nationalism in Lombardy 1814–1848*. 1965.
Hine, David. *Governing Italy: The Politics of Bargained Pluralism*. 1992.
Williams, William K. *The Communes of Lombardy from the Sixth to the Tenth Centuries*. 1995.

LUXEMBOURGERS

Luxembourgeois; Luxemburgian;
Luxembourgish; Letzburgisch;
Letzeburgesch

POPULATION: Approximately (2000 e) 310,000 Luxembourgers in Europe, 289,000 in Luxembourg, and 15,000 in Belgium. Other small Luxembourger populations are in France and Germany.

THE LUXEMBOURGER HOMELAND: The Luxembourger homeland is divided into a mountainous north, belonging to the upland region that includes the Ardenne in Belgium and Luxembourg and the Eifel highlands in Germany. This area includes the region's highest point, at 565 feet (1,854 m.) above sea level. The southern two-thirds of Luxembourg is a rolling plateau region, the Bon Pays. This region is rich and fertile, particularly in the Moselle and Sauer River valleys in the east. The grand duchy is drained by the Sauer and Alzette Rivers, both tributaries of the Moselle, which forms part of the eastern border. Forests cover about one-fifth of Luxembourg, mainly in the north. Farms make up about 25% of the region, and pasture covers another 20%.

Traditionally, Luxembourg became an independent state in A.D. 963 and was raised to the status of a duchy in 1354, making it one of the oldest countries in Europe. *Grand Duchy of Luxembourg (Grand-Duché de Luxembourg)*: 999 sq.mi.–2,587 sq.km. (2000 e) 408,000—Luxembourgers 71%, Portuguese* 10%, Italians* 5%, French* 3%, Belgians 3%, Germans* 2%. The Luxembourger capital and major cultural center is the city of Luxembourg, also called Luxembourg City or Luxembourg-Ville, (2000 e) 76,000, built on rocky heights with steep cliffs on three sides.

FLAG: The Luxembourger national flag, the official flag of the state, is a horizontal tricolor of red, white, and pale blue.

PEOPLE: The Luxembourgers are a Germanic people of mixed German and

French background, but with a distinct national consciousness and a long and distinct history as a European nation. Ethnically, the Luxembourgers belong to the Alemannic subgroup of the Germans, but with substantial Dutch* and French influence in their culture and traditions. Although the nation is small in population, the Luxembourgers have played a part in European history that belies their numbers. The population is about 95% Roman Catholic, with a small Protestant minority estimated at 1% of the total.

The language of the Luxembourgers, commonly called Letzeburgish, is a Moselle variety of Frankish-German origin, although it is not inherently intelligible with standard German. The language is as distinct from standard German as is Dutch. The language is the mother tongue of the Luxembourgers and is also spoken by a minority in the Belgian province of Luxembourg to the west. Smaller numbers speak the language in the Bitburg region of Germany and in Thionville, France. Letzeburgish is taught in the schools and is the language of government and business; however, the majority of the Luxembourgers are mostly multilingual, speaking French, German, and increasingly, English, as well as their own dialect.

NATION: The present-day homeland of the Luxembourgers is located in the heartland of the ancient Civitas Trevirorum, the land of the Gaulish tribe of the Treveri. Part of the region known to the Romans as Germania, the Treveri tribe came under Roman rule around 50 B.C. After the conquest of Gaul by Julius Caesar, the nearby city of Trier, the ancient Augusta Trevorum, became a major center of Roman culture. The mingling of peoples in the region gave rise to a brilliant Germanic-Celtic-Roman culture in the region in the third and fourth centuries.

In the fourth century the Franks overran the region. The Latinized Gauls and Celts were absorbed or displaced, and the region became Germanic in language and culture. The Frankish Empire of Charlemagne broke up at his death in A.D. 843, when his sons divided the territories among themselves. Luxembourg was included in the middle kingdom of Lotharingia, later called Lorraine, but the region soon broke up into semi-independent territories. Luxembourg became a sovereign state within the Holy Roman Empire in 963, when Sigefroid, the count of Ardennes and the founder of the Luxembourg dynasty, had a castle built on the site of present Luxembourg city. The House of Luxembourg, beginning with Henry VII in 1308, produced four German emperors. In 1354 Emperor Charles IV elevated the County of Luxembourg to the rank of a duchy.

The duchy came under the rule of the Burgundians* in 1451 but later, in the early sixteenth century, passed to Hapsburg rule, first the Spanish Hapsburgs and then the Austrian Hapsburgs as part of the Netherlands, often called the Low Countries. The southern districts of the duchy, including Montmédy, Thionville, and Longwy, were ceded to France in the Peace of the Pyrenees in 1659. In 1684 King Louis XIV seized the duchy, but in 1697, along with the other Low Countries, it passed to Spanish rule. In 1714 it passed to Austrian rule. In 1794 the troops of revolutionary France occupied the duchy, which was annexed to the First French Republic.

The Congress of Vienna in 1815, convened to remap the continent at the end of the Napoleonic Wars, established Luxembourg as a grand duchy in personal union with the Kingdom of the Netherlands. The grand duke was also the king of the Netherlands. Following the Belgian revolt in 1839 the southern provinces formed a separate Belgian state, which claimed the entire grand duchy but gained control only of the majority French-speaking western districts of Luxembourg. The grand duchy continued in personal union with the Netherlands, but also as a member of the German Confederation with a Prussian garrison in the fortress in Luxembourg city. In 1848 the grand duchy became an autonomous state under a new constitution.

The personal union between the Luxembourgers and the Dutch lasted until 1890. During this period the political independence, national identity, and autonomy of the Luxembourgers were strengthened, and strong democratic institutions were developed. The status of the small state was again questioned when the German Confederation was dissolved in 1866. William III of the Netherlands agreed to sell the grand duchy to France, which nearly led to war between France and Prussia. At the London Conference the European powers declared the grand duchy a neutral state. On 11 May 1867 the great powers signed the treaty that reaffirmed Luxembourg's territorial integrity and political autonomy. The major European powers agreed to guarantee and protect the neutrality of the Grand Duchy of Luxembourg. Its fortress, often called the Gibraltar of the North, was dismantled, and the Prussian garrison was withdrawn. In 1890, when Wilhelmina became queen of the Netherlands, the Luxembourgers ended the dynastic union, and the title of grand duke passed to a collateral line.

In 1914 German troops violated the Luxembourgers' neutrality and occupied the grand duchy for the duration of World War I. The German occupation, which ended in 1918, pushed the Luxembourgers to look outside their small state for political and economic security. In 1922 Luxembourg formed an economic union with Belgium. Germany once again invaded the small state in May 1940 during the World War II. The Luxembourg government fled into exile in London, and Luxembourg troops fought with the Allies against the Nazi occupiers. Allied troops liberated Luxembourg in September 1944. The Luxembourgers counted the third highest percentage of human losses in World War II, after the Soviet Union and Poland. The Battle of the Bulge, 1944–45, was to a great extent fought on Luxembourg territory.

Putting aside their traditional neutrality, which had been violated during both world wars, the Luxembourgers participated in the European Recovery Program and entered the United Nations and the North Atlantic Treaty Organization (NATO). In 1947 they joined the Dutch and Belgians in a new customs union. A treaty signed in 1958 provided for a full economic union of the three Low Countries, and in 1960 the Benelux Economic Union went into effect. The

Benelux Union became the basis of the expanded European Economic Community (EEC), later renamed the European Union (EU).

In the 1990s the Luxembourgers are among the most fervent supporters of closer European cooperation and eventual political union. Their position between France and Germany, which led to much destruction in the past, is now an opportunity to prosper in the continental economic and political union. The Luxembourgers are prosperous and democratic, and although they support closer European integration, they are fond of their constitutional monarch and are proud of the history of their small nation.

SELECTED BIBLIOGRAPHY

Barteau, Harry C. *Grand Duchy of Luxembourg*. 1996.

Lepthien, Emilie U. *Luxembourg*. 1989.

Newton, Gerald, ed. *Luxembourg and Letzebuergesch: Language and Communication at the Crossroads of Europe*. 1996.

Sheehan, Patricia. *Luxembourg*. 1997.

Thomas, George. *The National Profile of the Low Countries*. 1989.

MACEDONIANS

Macedonian Slavs; Makedonians;
Makedoniyans

POPULATION: Approximately (2000 e) 2,250,000 Macedonians in Europe, 1,461,000 in Macedonia, 182,000 in Bulgaria, 100,000 in Greece, and another 150,000 in adjacent areas of Yugoslavia and Albania. Macedonian nationalists claim Macedonian populations of over 1 million in Greece and 500,000 in Bulgaria.

THE MACEDONIAN HOMELAND: The mountainous Macedonian homeland lies in the southern Balkan Peninsula in Southeastern Europe. The region is largely mountainous or hilly and extends from the Aegean Sea north to comprise the vast valleys of the Vadar, Struma, and Mesta Rivers. Much of the region is forested, especially the mountains, with farmland, including pasture, making up about one-third of the total. In the southwest, two large lakes, Ohrid and Prespa, form part of the international borders between Macedonia, Albania, and Greece.

The historic Macedonian homeland is divided into three regions, Vadar Macedonia, now the Republic of Macedonia, Aegean Macedonia in Greece, and Pirin Macedonia in Bulgaria. The Republic of Macedonia, also known as the Former Yugoslav Republic of Macedonia (FYROM), declared its independence of Yugoslavia in September 1991. *Republic of Macedonia (Republika Makedonija)*: 9,928 sq.mi.–25,714 sq.km. (2000 e) 2,181,000—Macedonians 66%, Albanians* 23%, Turks* 4%, Roms* (Gypsies) 2%, Serbs* 2%, Muslims 1.5%, Greeks,* Bulgarians,* Vlachs, Croats,* Jews. The Macedonian capital and major cultural center is Skopje, (2000 e) 572,000, which was made capital of Yugoslav Macedonia in 1945. The cultural center of the Bulgarian Macedonians is the town of Petrich, called Pirin by the Macedonians, (2000 e) 36,000.

FLAGS: The Macedonian national flag, the official flag of the republic, is a red field with a centered yellow sun and eight yellow rays extending to the edges. The flag used by some nationalist groups, the official flag of the republic until 1995, is a red field charged with a centered, sixteen-point gold star, the Star of Vergina associated with Alexander the Great.

PEOPLE: The Macedonians are a South Slav people, a mixture of South Slav, Bulgarian Slav, and Greek strains. The Macedonians, divided between Serbia, Greece, and Bulgaria in 1912–13, remain divided. Until the latter part of the nineteenth century, the Macedonians had little sense of being a separate nation, calling themselves Bulgarians, Serbs, or Greek Slavs. The number of Macedonians outside the republic is very difficult to estimate as the Greek government denies the existence of a Macedonian population in Greek Macedonia, and the Bulgarian government does not count the Macedonian population in Pirin Macedonia separately in national censuses. About 60% of the Macedonians in the republic live in urban areas.

The Macedonian language belongs to the eastern branch of the South Slav languages. The language was developed after World War II and is written in the Cyrillic alphabet with the addition of two letters not utilized by any other Slav language. The major dialects are Northern Macedonian, Southeastern Macedonian, and Western Macedonian, which has two subdialects. Standard Macedonian was developed from the Western Macedonian spoken in the southwestern districts and has a large number of borrowings from Turkish and Greek. In Greece the language is called simply Slavic. The Bulgarian government classifies the language as a southwestern Bulgarian dialect. Many Serbs continue to claim that Macedonian is a south Serbian dialect.

The majority of the Macedonians belong to the independent Macedonian Orthodox Church, with minorities adhering to Orthodox sects or Sunni Islam. The Macedonian Orthodox Church, which was promoted as part of the government-supported campaign to nurture a separate Macedonian identity after World War II, became increasingly identified with Macedonian nationalism in the late 1980s.

NATION: The Balkan Peninsula has been a crossroads for thousands of years, invaded and traversed by many different peoples. The historic region of Macedonia roughly corresponds to the ancient Macedonian kingdom founded in the seventh century B.C. Under King Philip II, who ruled in the fourth century B.C., the Macedonian kingdom began to expand at the expense of weaker nations. His son, Alexander III, called Alexander the Great, conquered the entire Greek world and most of the known world, with territories as far east as India.

In 148 B.C. the Macedonian heartland became a province of the growing Roman Empire. In A.D. 395 the empire divided into east and west, with Macedonia included in the Eastern or Byzantine half. Migrating Slavs in the sixth and seventh centuries occupied most of the region, eventually pushing south to the Aegean Sea. They eventually acknowledged Byzantine rule and adopted the Orthodox Christianity of the Byzantine Empire.

In the ninth century the Bulgarian kingdom conquered Macedonia from the

Byzantines. A western Bulgarian kingdom emerged in the region at the breakup of Bulgaria in the tenth century. The kingdom, with its capital at Okhrida (Ohrid), is considered by nationalists as the first Macedonian Slav state. According to tradition, the first Slavonic university in the Balkans was founded at Okhrida in the year 893. With the decline of Byzantine power in the Balkans, Macedonia was the center of both Serb and Bulgarian kingdoms. Variously under Serb or Bulgarian control, in 1394 Macedonia finally came under the control of the Ottoman Turks.

The imposition of the Turks' Islamic religion triggered a migration from the region of Orthodox Slavs, who took refuge in areas controlled by Christian states. They were mostly replaced by Turks from Anatolia, ethnic Albanians, and Ladino Jews expelled from the Spanish kingdom. The Muslim Albanian population in the north and west of Ottoman Macedonia formed a favored class of landowners and administrators. The Slav population by the nineteenth century had lost its separate ethnic identity. They considered themselves either as ethnic Bulgarians or, to a lesser extent, as ethnic Serbs or Slav-language Macedonian Greeks. The growth of the Bulgarian national movement, which claimed Macedonia as part of Bulgaria's national territory, triggered rival claims on ethnic and historical grounds by Serbia and Greece.

At the end of the nineteenth century, it became apparent that the end of the Ottoman Empire was inevitable. Greece, Serbia, and Bulgaria during the 1880s increased their efforts to assimilate the Macedonian Slavs and gain influence in the Turks' remaining European territories. The so-called Macedonian Question was one of the most serious diplomatic problems that confronted Europe. Not until 1885, when relations between Bulgaria and Serbia became strained over the Macedonian Question, did the idea of a separate Macedonian identity begin to gain support among the local Slavs. In the 1890s nationalist organizations were formed to work for the separation of Macedonia from the Ottoman Empire. Some of the groups were backed by Bulgaria, Serbia, or Greece, but the Macedonian Revolutionary Organization (IMRO), founded in 1893, rejected claims by neighboring states and worked for independence.

Guerrilla fighters of the IMRO rebelled against the Turkish authorities at Salonika in 1902. The ill-equipped rebels overran northern Macedonia and on 2 August 1903 declared the province independent of the Ottoman Empire. Threatened by a Turkish army of 40,000, the Macedonian rebels, numbering 15,000, held the Turks at bay in a vicious seven-week war. A political compromise placed Macedonia under the control of a five-power European force. In 1908 the Europeans returned the turbulent province to Turkish rule. A renewed Macedonian rebellion was crushed with incredible cruelty.

In 1912 Serbia, Greece, and Bulgaria united in the First Balkan War. Victorious over the Ottoman forces, the three states took control of all the remaining Ottoman territory in Europe, except for the Constantinople area, but territorial conflicts immediately arose, setting off the Second Balkan War in 1913. By the terms of the Treaty of Bucharest, Bulgaria lost most of its Macedonian lands.

Serbia annexed Vadar Macedonia, and Greece took Aegean Macedonia, leaving a disgruntled Bulgaria with the small Pirin Macedonia territory.

Greek persecution of its Macedonian minority in the early 1920s forced thousands to flee, with many more expelled from Aegean Macedonia to make way for ethnic Greeks evacuated from Asia Minor between 1922 and 1924. Macedonian demands for reunification and independence brought Greece and Bulgaria close to war in 1925, provoked serious nationalist violence in Bulgarian Macedonia in 1933–35, and sparked a widespread nationalist Macedonian uprising in northern Greece in 1935. In Yugoslavia Vardar Macedonia constituted the county of Vardarska, and Macedonians were called Southern Serbs, and an oppressive authority promoted assimilation. The IMRO, supported by the Bulgarians, remained an active terrorist organization in southern Yugoslavia. In 1934 King Alexander of Yugoslavia was assassinated in Marseilles by Croatians, with the active assistance of Macedonian nationalists of the IMRO.

Bulgaria joined the Axis in 1941, primarily to regain the Macedonian territory. Bulgarians occupied and annexed Yugoslav and Greek Macedonia. German troops occupied Macedonia in 1944 and actively supported the Macedonian nationalists. On 8 September 1944 local leaders declared the independence of a united Macedonian republic, but the evacuation of the German troops in November left the self-proclaimed republic virtually defenseless. Greek and Yugoslav troops overran the republic soon after. The occupation of Bulgaria by advancing Soviet forces in 1944 ended the Bulgarians' attempt to regain permanent control of Macedonia.

The promise of an autonomous Macedonian republic rallied many to Tito's communist Yugoslav partisans during the war. He promised to unite Vadar, Aegean, and Pirin Macedonia in a separate state within a communist South Slav Federation, a promise he was never able to keep. Vadar Macedonia was established as a separate Yugoslav republic. In 1948 Tito, the Yugoslav communist leader, split with Moscow. All contact between Yugoslavia and Moscow's ally, Bulgaria, was immediately severed, including the ties between the local Macedonians.

Thousands of ethnic Slavs fled from Greek Macedonian territory during the Greek civil war that raged from the end of World War II until the Yugoslav-backed communist rebels were finally routed in 1950. Following the Greek civil war, an estimated 80,000 to 100,000 Slavs left Greek Macedonia, many to Yugoslav Macedonia, while other immigrants left Europe.

The Bulgarian communist government counted the Macedonian population separately in the 1956 census. At that time 187,729 were counted as ethnic Macedonians in Bulgaria, about 95% living in Pirin Macedonia. The Bulgarian government again denied the existence of a separate Macedonian identity in 1958, raising tensions in the area that eased only with the normalization of relations between Bulgaria and Yugoslavia in the 1970s. According to the 1965 Bulgarian census, there were only 8,750 Macedonians in the country, and in 1975 there were none.

The creation of a standard Macedonian language, clearly distinct from Bulgarian, and the reinterpreted history of the region gave the Yugoslav Macedonians an ethnic identity equal to that of the other Yugoslav peoples. Religion, which forms an integral part of Balkan identities, was used by the government in a unique partnership between church and state in a communist country. The establishment of a separate Macedonian Orthodox Church in 1958 served the purpose of developing the Macedonian national consciousness. The Macedonians made impressive educational and economic gains under communist rule.

The Yugoslav policy of promoting a separate Macedonian identity antagonized not only Bulgaria, but also Greece, which controlled the southern part of historic Macedonia and feared claims to its territory by Macedonian nationalists. The Greeks had always refused to recognize the Slavs living in Greece as Macedonians. The government refers to them as Slavophone or Slavic Greeks. The Greek stance on its Slav minority has remained consistent since the annexation of Aegean Macedonia in 1913.

The collapse of communism in Yugoslavia in 1989 resulted in the holding of free elections in the constituent republics in 1990. The new government elected in Skopje, dominated by Macedonian nationalists and led by Kiro Gligorov, attempted to curb the activities of the more militant groups that published claims to Aegean and Pirin Macedonia. The adoption of the name the Republic of Macedonia and the design of a new flag based on an ancient Macedonian symbol led the Greek government to accuse the new state of irredentist claims. In August 1991 the Greek government closed the border, cutting off Macedonia from its major trade, and imposed a crippling oil embargo. As Yugoslavia disintegrated, a nationalist coalition organized a referendum on Macedonian independence that resulted in 95% voting for independence. Even though the Serbian and Albanian minorities had boycotted the referendum, Gligorov declared Macedonia independent of Yugoslavia on 17 September 1991 amid widespread fears that the war and ethnic fighting extending across much of former Yugoslavia would spread to Macedonia.

The Macedonian constitution was amended in January 1992 to fall in line with European Community (EC) criteria for recognition. The amended constitution stated that Macedonia had no territorial claims on other countries and renounced interference in the affairs of neighboring states. Greece, an EC member state, blocked recognition of Macedonia because of the Macedonian refusal to change the name of the republic or to adopt a different flag. The landlocked republic, already suffering the loss of trade with Yugoslavia, which had been placed under United Nations sanctions, was brought to the brink of collapse by the Greek embargo. Although criticized by other European states for selling oil to Serbia while slowly strangling tiny Macedonia, the Greek government remained adamant.

Under the provisional name Former Yugoslav Republic of Macedonia (FYROM), Macedonia was finally admitted to the United Nations on 8 April 1993 over the strident objections of the Greek and Yugoslav governments. The Greek government in

September 1995 finally recognized the republic, ending a four-year quarrel over the republic's name and flag. Greek recognition ended the economic blockade and released European Union financial aid, which the Greeks had blocked. The Macedonian government, in turn, redesigned its flag and changed two articles of the constitution that the Greeks claimed hinted at territorial claims to Aegean Macedonia.

In June 1997 representatives of Macedonia, Greece, and the United Nations again met in an effort to find a permanent name for the republic acceptable to both Macedonia and Greece. The Greek government continues to insist that the republic be called the Former Yugoslav Republic of Macedonia because Macedonia alone implies territorial claims on Greek Macedonia in spite of Macedonian government denials of irredentist claims on Greek or Bulgarian territory.

When the Macedonians broke away from disintegrating Yugoslavia in 1991, they luckily survived without the ethnic fighting suffered by the Bosnians* and Croats; however, by 1997 tensions between the Macedonian Slav majority and the Albanian minority had become a serious threat to the stability of the state. In July 1997 violence between the two groups broke out in the town of Gostivar over the flying of the Albanian flag. The violent suppression of a nationalist movement in Kosovo, the Albanian-majority province of Serbia just north of the Macedonian border, in 1998 raised fears that the fighting would spill over into Macedonian territory. In elections in late October 1998 the communists and their descendants were not included in the new government. Macedonian nationalists and their pro-Western democratic allies have won the elections in a coalition, including elements of the ultranationalists. They have pledged to include the ethnic Albanian minority in all levels of government, which could lessen the growing ethnic tensions in Macedonia.

In early 1999 thousands of Kosovar Albanians fleeing ethnic cleansing by the Serbs fled across the border into Macedonia. Following the collapse of diplomatic efforts, North Atlantic Treaty Organization (NATO) planes began attacking Serbia, while the Serbs steppped up their efforts to drive the Albanians from Kosovo. By mid-1999, nearly 400,000 ethnic Albanians had crossed into Macedonia, seriously threatening the delicate ethnic balance in the state.

By September 1999 most of the Kosovar Albanians had left the country, but tensions between Macedonia's own Albanian minority and the majority Macedonians remained. The Macedonian government's close cooperation with the Western military operation that ended the oppression in neighboring Kosovo raised Macedonian hopes of eventual membership in the important Western military and economic alliances.

SELECTED BIBLIOGRAPHY

Danforth, Loring M. *The Macedonian Conflict: Ethnic Nationalism in a Transnational World.* 1995.

Georgieva, Valentina, and Sasha Konechni. *Historical Dictionary of the Republic of Macedonia.* 1998.

Karakasidou, Anastasia N. *Fields of Wheat, Hills of Blood: Passages to Nationhood in Greek Macedonia, 1870–1990.* 1997.

Privichevich, S. *Macedonia: Its People and History.* 1982.

Shea, John. *Macedonia and Greece: The Struggle to Define a New Balkan Nation.* 1997.

MADEIRANS

Madeira Islanders

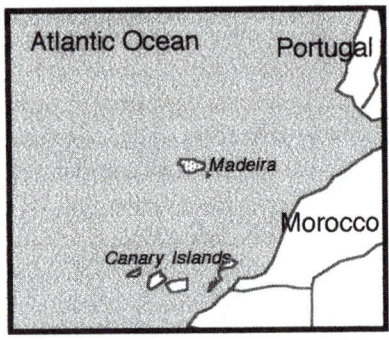

POPULATION: Approximately (2000 e) 354,000 Madeirans in Europe, the majority in the autonomous Portuguese region of Madeira, but with substantial Madeiran populations in mainland Portugal, France, Germany, and Luxembourg. Outside Europe large Madeiran populations live in the United States, Canada, South Africa, and Brazil.

THE MADEIRAN HOMELAND: The Madeiran homeland is an island group in the Atlantic Ocean 440 miles (708 km.) west of Morocco and 530 miles (852 km.) southwest of the Portuguese mainland. The archipelago comprises the large island of Madeira, the smaller island of Porto Santo, and two groups of barren, uninhabited islets, the Desertas and Selvagens. The islands, of volcanic origin, are mountainous, with deep, green valleys and high basalt cliffs along parts of the shore. The equitable climate, marred only by the occasional *leste*, a dry, hot Saharan wind, makes the islands a major tourist destination.

Madeira has formed an autonomous region of the Republic of Portugal since 1976. *Autonomous Region of Madeira*: 314 sq.mi.–813 sq.km. (2000 e) 252,000—Madeirans 92%, other Portuguese.* Most Madeirans live on Madeira, while the second island of the group, Porto Santo, has a population of about 5,000. The Madeiran capital and major cultural center is Funchal, (2000 e) 48,000, the archipelago's largest city and major port.

FLAGs: The Madeiran national flag, the official flag of the autonomous region, has three vertical stripes of blue, yellow, blue with a centered cross of the Order of Christ, a square white cross outlined in red, in the center. The same blue, yellow, blue flag, but with five blue shields, each with five white guinas (roundels), in the form of a centered cross, is the flag of the largest nationalist organization, the Madeira Archipelago Liberation Front (FLAMA).

PEOPLE: The Madeirans are an island people, descendants of early Portuguese settlers, with later admixtures of African slaves brought in to work the sugar plantations and Berbers and Arabs from the Moroccan mainland. Emigration, particularly in the twentieth century, has resulted in a large immigrant population, estimated at over 1 million, primarily in South America and South Africa. The immigrants contribute to the Madeiran economy and are the most nationalistic and most ardent supporters of the Madeiran national movement. An insular, conservative nation, the Madeirans are overwhelmingly Roman Catholic.

The dialect of Portuguese spoken in the archipelago is the Madeira-Azores dialect, quite different from the Portuguese of mainland Portugal, which is based on the Extremenho dialect spoken around Lisbon and Coimbra. The dialect is further divided into two subdialects, Madeiran and Azorean. The Madeiran dialect has incorporated many words from Arabic, Berber, and African languages.

NATION: The islands, lying in the eastern Atlantic Ocean, were known to the Romans as the Purple Islands due to their habitual haze. They were lost to all but legend following the coming of the Dark Ages to Europe. A Portuguese navigator, João Goncalvo Zarco, sailing under orders from Prince Henry the Navigator, sighted the island of Porto Santo and claimed the uninhabited islands for Portugal in 1420. The name of the largest island, called Madeira, the Portuguese word for "wood" in reference to its extensive forest cover, became the name for the entire archipelago.

Portuguese colonists established a settlement at Funchal in 1421, Portugal's first overseas colony. By 1425 several other Portuguese settlements had been established in the islands. The extensive forests were burned to create cultivable land. According to Madeiran legends, the fires raged for seven years.

Madeira is believed to have been the location of the world's first sugarcane plantation. The introduction of sugarcane cultivation in 1452 transformed Madeira, as sugar is a crop that requires a large workforce. The islanders bought black African and Moorish slaves in the slave markets of nearby Morocco to work on the sugar and tropical fruit plantations. The Portuguese, without the strong racial prejudices common in other parts of Europe, freely mixed with the large slave population.

The archipelago, lying on the sea routes between Europe, Africa, and the Americas, prospered in the sixteenth and seventeenth centuries. During the colonial period, the Madeirans, drawn by tales of riches, emigrated to the new Portuguese colonies, particularly Brazil. The emigrants began a tradition of leaving the islands in search of work or fortune that continued for centuries.

The islands were occupied by the British during the Napoleonic Wars, 1801–14. While the British controlled the islands, a number of British families settled in the islands, most to engage in the lucrative wine trade. The production of the famous Madeira wine began when a shipment of red wine, sent to the East Indies, was returned unsold. On opening the cask the owner discovered that the heat of the warm hold had considerably enhanced the flavor. The production of the unique Madeira wine has involved heat since that time and has become one of the Madeirans' major industries.

Thousands of Madeirans left the neglected, overpopulated, and underdeveloped islands in the nineteenth century, some to settle as far from their homeland as Hawaii, where they introduced the musical instrument called the ukulele. Tourism, particularly from Britain, brought some much needed income in the early twentieth century. The island of Madeira was a favorite holiday destination of Winston Churchill.

In the twentieth century the economic mainstays of tourism, sugar, wine, and lace-making provided for only a fraction of the burgeoning population. In the 1950s banana production replaced sugar as the major export crop. By the early 1960s emigration reduced Madeira's population by an average of 2.5% to 3% a year.

A cultural and linguistic revival beginning in the 1960s, partly in response to the need to leave their beloved islands to find work, quickly evolved a strong nationalist faction following the leftist revolution in Portugal in 1974. Portugal's revolutionary government moved quickly to dismantle the costly remnants of the Portuguese Empire, granting independence to remaining overseas possessions. Nationalists, led by the Madeira Archipelago Liberation Front (FLAMA), created a provisional government in anticipation of independence for Portugal's oldest overseas possession. Disappointed by the government's refusal to grant independence to Madeira along with the other overseas territories, thousands of Madeirans joined demonstrations in Funchal and other towns demanding immediate independence for the archipelago.

Political conditions in Lisbon stabilized under a new centrist government in 1975, and mass support for Madeiran separation waned over fears that the islands would suffer economically and lacked trained administrators. Although many nationalists agreed that premature independence might prove a disaster, the national organizations pressed for association status or other forms of independence. In 1976 the Madeirans accepted a government offer of broad economic and political autonomy, seen by the more militant nationalists as an interim step to the eventual independence of the islands.

The islands' rising prosperity, accelerating after Portugal's entry into the European Economic Community in 1986, has given the Madeirans a new confidence. Madeira's membership in the European Community again raised the question of independence within a united Europe. Emigration, once a necessity, has reversed, and the population is again growing slowly. Many Madeirans found work in the expanding financial and banking industries spawned by the islands' emergence as a major offshore European financial center, tax haven, and free port.

The Madeiran national movement, with the support of the large immigrant

Madeiran population, focuses on ending the state's semicolonial status and seeks full national sovereignty within the European Union (EU). In October 1990 the president of the regional government met with nationalist leaders to discuss the independence issue and to forestall threatened separatist activities. Since then the autonomous government has moved closer to the nationalists, and their cooperation has benefited the autonomous island state. In September 1993 during a heated dispute with the Lisbon government, the governor, Social Democrat Alberto Joan Jardim, threatened to throw his government's support behind the separatists. In 1994 Portuguese intelligence officers spying on Madeiran leaders were exposed, further harming relations between the Madeiran and Portuguese governments.

Portuguese law makes advocating secession a grave offense, and nationalist organizations are banned under the terms of the Portuguese constitution, forcing the Madeiran nationalists to seek broad support as legal political parties. In the islands the nationalists have begun to integrate into local politics, making the Portuguese prohibitions on secession and nationalism irrelevant in light of the growing relationship between the nationalists and the autonomous Madeiran government.

SELECTED BIBLIOGRAPHY
Bragança-Cunha, Vicente. *Revolutionary Portugal*. 1976.
Duncan, Thomas Bently. *Atlantic Islands: Madeira, the Azores, and the Cape Verdes in Seventeenth-Century Commerce and Navigation*. 1972.
Ludtke, Jen. *Atlantic Peeks: An Ethnographic Guide to the Portuguese-Speaking Islands*. 1989.
Mailer, Phillip. *The Impossible Revolution*. 1977.
Rogers, Francis M. *Atlantic Islanders of the Azores and Madeiras*. 1979.

MALTESE

Maltans

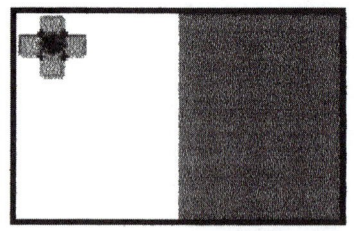

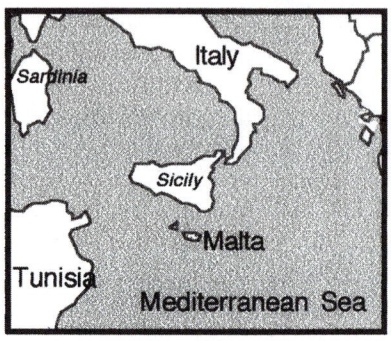

POPULATION: Approximately (2000 e) 405,000 Maltese in Europe, 347,000 in Malta, in the central Mediterranean, with smaller groups in Italy, about 30,000, and the United Kingdom, 22,000. Outside Europe there are Maltese communities in Tunisia, the United States, Canada, and Australia.

THE MALTESE HOMELAND: The Maltese homeland is a small archipelago lying south of Sicily in the Mediterranean Sea. The island group consists of two main islands, Malta and Gozo a third, much smaller island, Comino, and two tiny islets. The islands have heavily indented coasts, and low hills cover the interiors. The Maltese islands consist of low-lying coralline limestone plateaus surrounded by impermeable clay slopes. The porous limestone of Malta allows rainwater to seep down to underground caves, so the land is mainly dry. On Gozo clay covers much of the island, so the land is much less dry and more fertile. Farmland covers about 40% of the total territory of the islands. The highest point in the islands is about 785 feet (239 m.) above sea level.

Because Malta has no permanent rivers or lakes, and precipitation is limited, the natural water level has become a serious problem. The government of Malta has implemented a program to desalinate seawater, and by the late 1990s up to 70% of Malta's water comes from the country's desalination plants.

The islands, under British rule from 1814 to 1964, were granted independence in 1964 and became a republic in 1974. *Republic of Malta (Repubblika Ta' Malta)*: 122 sq.mi.–316 sq.km. (2000 e) 379,000—Maltese 96%, British 2%, Italians,* Arabs, French.* The Maltese capital and major city is Valetta, (2000 e) 10,000 (metropolitan area 103,000), named for Jean Parisot de La Valette, grand master of the Knights of Malta in the sixteenth century.

FLAG: The Maltese national flag, the official flag of the republic, is a vertical bicolor of white and red with a small St. George's cross on the upper hoist. The colors are those of the Knights of Malts. The George Cross, added in 1943 to the upper hoist, commemorates the heroism of the Maltese nation in World War II.

PEOPLE: The Maltese are a Mediterranean people of mixed background, reflecting the many conquerors and colonizers of their strategic islands. Their ancestry includes Carthaginians, Greeks,* Romans, Normans,* Arabs, Italians, and British. The unique situation of the islands, in a narrow strait between Sicily and the African mainland, has added many distinct cultural traits to their island culture. An estimated 99% of the Maltese are Roman Catholics.

The language of the Maltese descended from Maghrebi Arabic but has borrowed heavily from Italian, so that the language, although classified as an Arabic language, has developed a Latin-based syntax and phonology and is written in the Roman script. The language is spoken in seven dialects, Standard Maltese, Port Maltese, Rural West Maltese, Rural East Maltese, Rural Central Maltese, Zurrieq, and Gozo. Maltese became a written language only in the twentieth century. English, the language used during the British administration of the island, is also widely spoken and is the republic's second official language. Italian is also widely spoken in the islands.

NATION: Megalithic remains are evidence that the islands have been inhabited since the dawn of Mediterranean history. The Temple of Ggantija on the island of Gozo dates from around 3600 B.C. On the island of Malta, there are also Neolithic remains, but little is known of the island's early inhabitants.

The islands' history revolved around their location and the excellent natural harbor on Malta. Control of the islands was necessary to any military power seeking domination in the Mediterranean Sea. The harbor provided a sheltered base for naval fleets, while the islands themselves, located at the crossroads of the ancient world, enabled colonizing powers to exercise control over shipping in the vast Mediterranean Sea.

Due to their proximity to the coast of North Africa, the islands were of interest to the early Phoenicians, who colonized the island as a way station to their colonies farther west about 850 B.C. The Phoenicians were followed by the Greeks, who occupied the islands they called Melita in 736 B.C., and later, the offspring of the Phoenicians in North Africa, the Carthaginians, controlled the islands. During the Second Punic War, between Carthage and Rome, the Romans in 218 B.C. took control of the islands. Christianity was brought to the islands by missionaries, who included St. Paul, who was shipwrecked there in A.D. 60 and spent three months in the islands.

Malta, again called Melita, became part of the Greek-speaking Eastern Roman or Byzantine Empire at the division of the Roman territories in 395 A.D. The islands remained under Byzantine control until 870, when Arabs, called Saracens, from North Africa overran the islands. The Norman king of Sicily, Roger I, ejected the Muslims from Malta and restored Christian rule in 1090. The islands formed part of the Sicilian kingdom, which developed a brilliant, tolerant culture in the early Middle Ages. By the fifteenth century the islands had achieved a measure of home rule under an administration called the Universita.

A succession of feudal lords ruled Malta until the early sixteenth century. In 1530 the islands were given by the emperor of the Holy Roman Empire, Charles V, to the Knights Hospitalers, also called the Order of St. John, a religious order created to aid pilgrims to the Holy Land following the Crusades. The order, often called the Knights of St. John of Jerusalem, was later called the Knights of Malta. Although their origins were as custodians of a hospital for Christian pilgrims in Jerusalem, they developed as a military order. The knights held the islands against a determined Turkish siege in 1565 and continued to rule the islands for more than two centuries. The Knights constructed vast fortifications, castles, palaces, and churches on the islands.

Napoleon Bonaparte during his Egyptian campaign in 1798, seeing the strategic value of the islands, took control of Malta, and the Knights were compelled to leave. Unwilling to be ruled by the French, the Maltese rose against French rule and requested British protection. The British ousted the French in 1800, and British possession was confirmed by the Treaty of Paris in 1814. Under British rule, the islands were fortified and became a strategic military base. For most of the nineteenth century the islands were ruled by a British military governor, while increasingly the Maltese demanded self-government.

During World War I, Malta was an important naval base, which was the islands' major employer and extremely important to the Maltese economy. At the end of the war sentiment for home rule grew, and in 1921 the islands were given a new constitution and dominion status in the British Empire. The constitution of 1921 was revoked in 1936, and Malta reverted to the status of a crown colony. A limited constitution was inaugurated in 1939.

The outbreak of World War II made Malta one of Britain's most important military and naval bases. The islands, particularly the large urban area around the port facilities and the naval base, were repeatedly bombed by Italian and German aircraft, but the British garrison and the Maltese population resisted. In 1942 King George VI awarded the George Cross to the entire Maltese nation for their loyalty and bravery.

At the end of World War II, the Maltese demanded greater self-government. A new constitution, similar to that of 1921, was promulgated in 1947. In 1953 Malta became an important base for the North Atlantic Treaty Organization (NATO) under British administration. The 1947 constitution was revoked in 1959, and Malta was ruled by a British governor until 1962, when the first elections were held under a new constitution of 1961. On 21 September 1964 Malta was granted independence and in 1974 became a republic. Britain's military agreement with the Maltese government expired, and Malta ceased to function as a British military base. The withdrawal of the last British sailors on 1 April 1979 ended 179 years of British military presence on the island.

The end of the British military presence caused economic upheaval, as the military base was one of Malta's major employers. High unemployment led to some unrest and strengthened the more radical members of the socialist government. The socialist Labor Party government, which ruled Malta from 1971 to 1987, strengthened ties to radical regimes in nearby North Africa, particularly that of Libya. In 1980 the Maltese declared their country a neutral state during the ongoing Cold War.

The Maltese voted in a more conservative government in 1987, which promoted a more pro-European stance. In the 1990s the Maltese government applied to join the European Union (EU), but the application was set aside when the socialist Labor Party won elections in 1996.

The Maltese homeland lacks natural resources, and most Maltese work in the former naval dockyards, which are now used for commercial shipbuilding and repair, and in manufacturing and the vital tourist industry. The region produces only 20% of its food, and raw materials for manufacturing are imported, so that Malta's economy has become closely integrated with that of the Union EU. In September 1998 a new government, led by Eddie Fenech Adami of the Nationalist Party, renewed Malta's application to join the EU. The application, first put forward in 1990, had been withdrawn by a socialist government elected in 1996 but ousted following a snap election.

SELECTED BIBLIOGRAPHY
Balm, Roger. *Malta.* 1996.
Berg, Warren G. *Historical Dictionary of Malta.* 1995.
Boswell, David Mark, and Brian Beeley. *Malta.* 1997.
Hoppen, Alison. *The Fortification of Malta by the Order of St. John, 1530–1798.* 1979.
Sire, H.J.A. *The Knights of Malta.* 1994.

MANX

Mannin

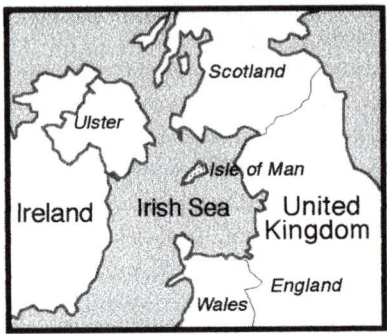

POPULATION: Approximately (2000 e) 89,000 Manx in Europe, with 66,000 living on the Isle of Man and the others mainly living on the British mainland.

THE MANX HOMELAND: The Manx homeland is a small island lying in the Irish Sea, nearly equidistant from Ireland, Scotland, England, and Wales. The island, thirty-three miles (fifty-three km.) long and from six to twelve miles (ten to nineteen km.) wide, is ringed by tall cliffs indented by numerous bays. Most of the surface of the island is covered with wooded glens, and the rounded hills rise to over 2,034 feet (620 m.) at the highest point on the island, the Snaefell. The Calf of Man is a detached rocky islet off the southwest coast. Traditionally, the island's name, Ellan Vannin in Manx Gaelic, comes from the magical Celtic sea god Manainn MacLir, who could summon at will a mantle of sea mist to make the island invisible to enemies.

In the north of the island there is a flat plain with lazy rivers and streams that cross fertile farmlands behind long, sandy beaches. Some of the river valleys have rich pastures, and livestock is raised extensively. The island has a mild climate, and subtropical plants and crops are grown without protection. About 40% of the island is uninhabited, and the population is concentrated in several urban areas, particularly the Douglas-Onchan area, which accounts for about half the total population.

The Island of Man forms a self-governing state, which is a dependency of the British Crown with its own parliament, laws, currency, and taxation. *Isle of Man (Ellan Mannin)*: 221 sq.km.–572 sq.km. (2000 e) 74,500—Manx 89%, other British 8%, Irish* 1%. The Manx capital and major cultural center is Douglas, (2000 e) 23,000, a major British resort.

FLAG: The Manx national flag, the official flag of the autonomous state, is a red field bearing three white legs, armored and spurred, detailed in gray and yellow.

PEOPLE: The Manx are a Celtic people, descendants of the island's early Celtic inhabitants, later Celts driven from the mainland by invasions of Anglo-Saxons, and with later admixtures of Scandinavians, Scots,* and Welsh.* The Manx culture and language developed over many centuries in the relative isolation of the island from the nearby mainland regions. The culture, including many traits and traditions that have disappeared from the other Celtic cultures, has revived in the since the 1960s and is once again flourishing on the island. The Manx are mostly Protestant, the majority belonging to the Methodist sect.

Throughout the centuries the Isle of Man has developed a way of life and a culture all its own. Many of the events that shaped the nearby islands, such as the Roman and Norman invasions of Britain, passed it by, leaving its Celtic culture intact. The arrival of the Vikings, however, did leave a lasting mark on the small Celtic nation. After a period of turbulence, the Celts and the Vikings merged as one nation under a unique system of government brought to the island by the Scandinavians, the Tynwald.

The Celtic language of the Manx, of the Goedelic branch of the Celtic languages, was virtually extinct by the 1950s but has been revived as part of the Manx cultural resurgence. English remains the first language of the island, but it has become a matter of pride for the Manx to learn and use their ancient language. The language of the Isle of Man is classed as a dialect of Scottish Gaelic, with strong Norse influence. It began to decline in the nineteenth century, and in the early twentieth century it was rapidly replaced by English. The first written records in the language are of the seventeenth century, and Manx literature, apart from ballads and carols, is negligible.

NATION: Traces of Neolithic times abound on the island. There are ancient crosses and other stone monuments, a round tower, an ancient fort, and several castles. Celtic clans are thought to have migrated from mainland Britain around 500 B.C. The island was ruled by a Welsh line of kings from the sixth to the ninth centuries and remained a Celtic kingdom, while most of Celtic Britain fell to the Germanic Angles, Saxons, and Jutes. The Isle of Man, a Celtic stronghold, was reinforced by refugees fleeing the Germanic invasion of the nearby mainland territories.

In A.D. 798 the Celtic inhabitants of the islands experienced the first of many terrifying Viking raids. Norse raiders eventually overthrew the Celtic monarchy in 800. Norse settlers from Scandinavia settled the island and mixed with the earlier Celtic inhabitants, adding many Norse words to their Celtic language. The island became a dependency of the kingdom of the Norwegians.*

Magnus, the Norwegian king, sold the island to Alexander III of Scotland in 1266, but the Manx, unhappy under Scottish rule, placed their island under the protection of the English king Edward I in 1290. The island's mixture of Celtic and Scandinavian influences evolved a distinct culture by the fifteenth century, with traditions and customs quite unlike those of the neighboring islands.

In 1405 King Henry IV gave the island to the Stanley family. The Stanleys, later the earls of Derby and Salisbury, ruled the Isle of Man for over three centuries. The island's economy revolved around smuggling between Ireland, Scotland, Wales, and England. Many Manx fortunes stemmed from this illegal trade. The island passed to the duke of Athol in 1736. In an effort to stop the Manx smuggling of goods into England, the British crown purchased the island in 1765 for £70,000. While the purchase was designed to save the British treasury approximately £100,000 per annum, it deprived the Manx of their main source of income.

The Isle of Man in 1828 was placed under the authority of the British crown as a crown dependency and possession, but with self-government for the Manx nation. A statute formalizing the arrangement was passed in 1866 confirming local autonomy, and the Manx were given the right to choose representatives to the House of Keys, the lower house of their 1,000-year-old parliament, the Tynwald, the upper house of which is the Legislative Council. The Manx would remain subject to the British monarch, but not the British parliament.

English in the eighteenth and nineteenth centuries gradually took over as the language of Manx daily life. By 1871 only one-quarter of the population could still speak Manx. The island's mild climate, beautiful scenery, and unique culture attracted many visitors, the island becoming one of the premier resorts of Victorian Britain, which reinforced the use of English. By 1900 only 5,000 could still speak their Celtic language. Opposition to the arrival of thousands of English tourists sparked periodic demands for independence, but no serious negotiations were undertaken, as the authorities considered the island too small for viable nationhood.

During World War I, the Manx supplied many volunteers to the Allied cause, but after the war, influenced by the Irish, nationalism began to gather support, and the Manx began to take measures to save their ancient culture from extinction. In World War II many Manx again fought, but there was more sentiment for neutrality, as in nearby Ireland. After World War II the island again prospered as a major British resort. Younger Manx, fearing that tourism guaranteed the extinction of their ancient culture, began a campaign to save the Manx culture and language. In 1961 only 165 people spoke the Manx language, the numbers beginning to grow as younger Manx took pride in learning and using the language. The Manx renewed ties and contacts with the other Celtic peoples of Europe, the annual Celtic festivals and congresses sustaining a growing cultural and national revival. In 1968 the Executive Council decreed that the British Union Jack would not fly from public buildings on official holidays, only the Manx flag, even on British royal birthdays.

In 1973, when the United Kingdom joined the European Economic Community (EEC), the Manx signed a separate associate agreement, which initiated a dramatic economic surge. Offshore banking and financial services flourished with favorable tax laws and less restrictive banking rules than on the neighboring islands. The financial services industry brought much income to the island, but tourism, with over 500,000 visitors a year, remained the island's major support.

The prosperity of the island attracted many new residents from the British mainland.

From 1980 the population grew rapidly, raising house prices to a level higher than those of London, far beyond the reach of the average Manx. The invasion of newcomers sparked renewed Manx nationalism accompanied by a campaign of arson against holiday homes owned by foreigners in 1989–90. Pressed by the nationalist agitation, the island's government passed laws restricting immigration from the mainland and giving special protection to the Manx culture and language. In 1992 the government introduced the Manx language in the school curriculum, and the nearly extinct Manx language began to revive dramatically.

The Manx retain and are proud of their 1,000 years of political stability and parliamentary government. The laws passed by the Tynwald must receive royal assent, then every 5 July, known as Mid-Summer Day or Tynwald Day, the laws are read from Tynwald Hill, first in Manx, then in English. The British monarch, as Lord of Man, appoints the lieutenant governor of the island. The Manx are not bound by acts of the British parliament unless they are specifically mentioned.

The unification of Western Europe in the European Economic Community, now the European Union, has given Manx nationalism a new focus. The Manx nationalists now look to the union, theoretically able to accommodate smaller nations, not to Great Britain as their future. A nationalist campaign favors transferring the island's sovereignty from the British crown to a similar relationship with the European Union.

SELECTED BIBLIOGRAPHY
Killip, Christopher. *Isle of Man: A Book about the Manx.* 1980.
Kinvig, R. H. *The Isle of Man: A Social, Cultural, and Political History.* 1976.
Moore, A. W. *A History of the Isle of Man.* 1986.
Robinson, V., and D. McCarroll, eds. *The Isle of Man: Celebrating a Sense of Place.* 1990.
Young, G.V.C. *Isle of Man and the Faeroe Islands: Two Similar Countries.* 1981.

MARIS

Chermiss; Chermis; Marians

POPULATION: Approximately (2000 e) 768,000 Maris in Europe, concentrated in the Republic of Mari El, a member state of the Russian Federation, but with Mari populations in the republics of Bashkortostan, Udmurtia, and Tatarstan, as well as the regions of Kirov, Perm, Nizhe-Novgorod, and Sverdlovsk.

THE MARI HOMELAND: The Mari homeland is mostly rolling steppe north of the Volga River, heavily forested with fir and pine. The gently rolling plains are crossed by more than 4,000 miles (7,000 km.) of rivers, which include the Vetluga, the Rutka, the Ilet', the Ulakhan-Botuobuya, the Nemda, and the Buy. Coniferous forests cover about half the territory of the traditional Mari homeland. The region, stretching across the middle Volga valley, with few good roads and only one railroad, a branch line from Kazan to Yoshkar-Ola, is mostly rural and agricultural, with an extensive forest industry, and grain, dairy, and livestock farms. The chief products of the area are timber, corn, rye, flax, and potatoes. The Mari region is known for its numerous lakes and peat bogs, and about half the total area is forested.

The region, organized as an autonomous oblast in 1920, was raised to the status of an autonomous republic within the Soviet Russian Federation in 1936 and became a member state of the new Russian Federation in 1991. *Republic of Mari El (Respublika Mariy El)*: 8,958 sq.mi.–23,201 sq.km. (2000 e) 771,000—Maris 48%, Russians* 42%, Tatars* 6%, Chavash* 1%, Udmurts 1%. The Mari capital and major cultural center is Yoshkar-Ola, called Joschkar-Ola by the Maris, (2000 e) 267,000, founded in 1578 as a Russian outpost.

FLAGS: The Mari national flag, the official flag of the republic, is a horizontal tricolor of pale blue, white, and red, the white stripe twice the width of the other stripes, and bearing the Mari national symbol over the name of the republic on the white stripe. The flag of the nationalist movement is horizontal tricolor of pale blue, white, and red, the white twice the width of the other stripes and bearing a narrow, horizontal, purple stripe across the center.

PEOPLE: The Maris are a Finnic people, belonging to the Volga branch of the Finno-Ugric nations, believed by many historians to be the Volga region's earliest inhabitants. They are divided into three basic divisions, each distinguished by a distinct dialect and cultural traits. The Kuryk Maris, known also as Mountain Maris, Forest Maris, or Highland Maris, inhabit the right bank of the Volga River and are the largest of the three groups. The second group is the Olyk Maris, also called Meadow Maris or Lowland Maris, who live on the left bank of the Volga. The smallest of the three groups, the Upo Mari or Eastern Maris, dwell in Bashkortostan, Tatarstan, and the Sverdlovsk Oblast. About 62% of the Maris live in urban areas.

The Finnic language of the Maris, also called Finno-Cheremisic, belongs to the Finnic branch of the Finno-Ugric language group. The language, which has been influenced by Russian and Turkic languages, is divided into two major dialects, Highland Mari, also known as Hill Mari, and Lowland Mari, called Woods or Lugovo Mari. High Mari is spoken by fewer than 100,000, and its speakers have difficulty reading Low Mari, the majority dialect, because of lexical differences. A subdialect of Lowland Mari, called Eastern Mari, is spoken by the Upo Maris. There are two literary languages, one based on the Lowland and Eastern dialects and another based on the Highland dialect. An estimated 90% of the Maris speak their own dialects, while only 65% are able to speak Russian, even though over half the ethnic Maris live outside the boundaries of their republic.

For centuries the spiritual life of the Maris was closely connected to the nature of their forested homeland. The traditional beliefs developed into a nationalistic animist sect called Kugu Sorta, which remains very influential among the Mari population. Even the Orthodox Maris retain many pagan beliefs and traditions. Sacred ceremonies are accompanied by performing ancient hymns, historic ballads, and prayers said to the accompaniment of traditional Mari instruments, the *gusli*, similar to a banjo, *sahuvir* or bagpipes, and *tumire*, drums.

NATION: The Maris, believed the first inhabitants of the vast Volga River basin, traditionally roamed the steppe lands between the Volga Basin and the Ural Mountains to the east. They are believed to have formed as a distinct nation in the Volga and Vyatka valleys during the first millennium A.D. First mentioned in sixth-century records as seminomadic tribes in the Volga region, the Maris never developed a state system but lived under the political control of stronger neighboring nations as a group of related, but disunited, tribes or clans.

In the eighth century the Turkic Khazars established a nominal authority in the Volga Basin. The Maris, under Khazar rule, practiced slash-and-burn agriculture, hunting and fishing, and limited trade with neighboring peoples. By the mid-ninth century the Volga Bulgars, the ancestors of the Chavash, took control of the region. The Bulgars ruled the Mari territories until the mid-twelfth century, leaving a marked cultural and political impression on the scattered Mari tribes. The Bulgar state fell to the Golden Horde in 1236, and the Maris came under the rule of the Tatars, who settled the Volga Basin.

Significant Russian cultural and economic contact with the Maris began as early as the twelfth century, but Russian influence remained nominal until Slavic Cossacks and Orthodox missionaries began to penetrate the Tatar khanate in the fifteenth century. Under the influence of the Slavs a Mari minority converted to Orthodox Christianity. In 1552 the Russians, led by Ivan the Terrible, conquered Kazan and initiated the Slav colonization of the Volga River basin. The Maris, although more blond and Nordic than the Russians, were subjected to a harsh colonial regime and relegated to virtual slavery on the vast estates of absentee Russian landlords. The Upo Maris began to migrate to the east in the sixteenth century, with more leaving the region in the seventeenth and eighteenth centuries, by which time they had evolved a distinct identity. Some converted to Islam under the influence of the Bashkorts* and Tatars to the east, while others incorporated elements of Islam into their traditional beliefs.

Pressure to adopt Orthodox Christianity became especially intense in the early 1800s, when Russians began to worry about the number of distinct nationalities living in the empire. The Maris' resistance to Christianity resulted in severe persecution and intense assimilation pressures led by the Orthodox missionaries. Official efforts to eradicate their languages and culture provoked several serious revolts in the seventeenth and eighteenth centuries. To divide Mari resistance, the tsarist authorities partitioned their lands among several Russian provinces and banned the Mari language and culture. Believing that Christianity and education were closely related, the missionaries worked to develop a literary language for the Maris, which was produced in 1803, and that same year a catechism was published in Kuryk Mari. Many of the Kuryk Maris converted to Christianity, but the Olyk and Upo Maris resisted and clung to their animist faith.

Living in conditions of cruelty, ignorance, and poverty, a majority of the Maris clung to the traditional shamanistic beliefs that played a large part in the maintenance of their separate identity. The Mari effort to preserve their animist beliefs stimulated a strong religious and nationalist resurgence, a mass anti-Russian movement, in the latter half of the nineteenth century. In the 1870s, when a number of Mari leaders began to openly resist Russification and conversion to Christianity, the various Mari religious beliefs were formalized as part of a nationalistic religious sect called Kugu Sorta (Great Candle), intensely anti-Russian and anti-Orthodox. Kugu Sorta was especially influential among the Olyk and Upo Maris.

The Maris, 90% illiterate, rose during the 1905 Russian Revolution to attack and burn Russian estates and settlements on their traditional lands. Following a number of skirmishes with government troops, the Mari rebels moved into the thick forests and former guerrilla bands called the Forest Brethren. The government troops sent against them finally overcame the last rebel bands in 1906.

Thousands of young Mari conscripts, sent to the front during World War I, deserted and returned home following the spread of the news of the revolution in St. Petersburg in February 1917. The Mari soldiers formed the nucleus of a national army that formed to protect the Mari people as civil government collapsed, and armed bands roamed the Volga region. Freed from Russian domination, the Maris established the organs of self-rule that oversaw the setting up of hospitals and the organization of literacy classes and Mari-language schools, *Likeezes*.

In the summer of 1917 the Mari convened a national congress and voted in favor of a federation of non-Russian states in the Volga-Ural region and the expulsion of the region's Slav settlers. On 24 January 1918 the federation, the Idel-Ural Federation, made up of several Finnic and Turkic nations in the Volga Basin, declared independence from Russia. Before the Volga nations could organize, Bolshevik troops invaded in February 1918, rapidly overrunning Mari El, Mari territory. In July 1918 the Maris rebelled against the excesses of the Red Army and the bureaucratic Soviets. Crushed by the Red soldiers, the authorities ordered the detention of the Maris' small, educated elite. Branded class enemies, all of the Maris' potential leaders were deported or liquidated.

On 4 November 1920 the Soviets created a nominally autonomous region for the surviving Maris. In 1920–21, tens of thousands perished in the famine that followed the massive destruction of the civil war and the inept introduction of communism. Over one-third of the 1914 Mari population had died by the end of 1921. The collectivization of Mari agriculture began in the late 1920s and was completed, over Mari protests and resistance, in the early 1930s. Under Soviet rule the Mari language was again allowed and became one of the official languages of the autonomous republic created in 1936. The Soviet government later launched a drive to industrialize the region, and Russian was introduced as the only official language in education and government in the late 1930s. In spite of official Soviet suppression the Mari made great strides in education and culture.

The small Mari republic was increasingly industrialized and urbanized during World War II as whole factories and Slav populations were transferred to the region from western Russia. By 1945 the Maris formed a minority in their homeland, which had a mixed population of Maris, Slavs, and other Soviet nationalities. Resentment of their minority status sparked a cultural reawakening in the 1960s. Younger Maris took a new interest in their history, their language, and their unique religion as Russian pressure to adopt the ideal of Soviet culture intensified.

The number of Mari industrial workers grew from 5.5% of the workforce in 1926 to 25% of the total in 1940. The growth of an urban workforce brought increasing Russianization, and many Maris began to adopt Russian as their primary language. In 1959 an estimated 95% of the Maris spoke Mari. Thirty years later, in 1989, the total using Mari as their first language had fallen to 81%.

The Mari revival, taking on nationalistic overtones in the 1970s, grew into a mass movement following the Gorbachev reforms that liberalized Soviet life after 1987. Unofficial nationalist organizations, organized in 1989, pressured the republican government to change the republic's name and to declare Mari El a sovereign state on 22 October 1990, with three official languages, Lowland Mari, Highland Mari, and Russian. The republic's government unilaterally declared Mari El a full republic within the reorganized Russian Federation following the disintegration of the Soviet Union in August 1991. At the end of 1991 a presidential system was introduced in the republic, and free elections for the local legislature were inaugurated.

The democratization of Russia allowed the Maris to again assert their national identity. The number of Maris who had registered as ethnic Russians for political or economic reasons decreased rapidly as many changed their official identity back to Mari. The percentage of Maris in their national republic grew from 43% in 1989, to an estimated 48% in 1999. The percentage of those claiming Russian identity fell during the same period from 47% to 42%.

In spite of hundreds of years of Russian efforts to assimilate the Maris, they have maintained a cohesive sense of their distinct identity. In the late 1990s over 80% use Mari as their first language, and less than two-thirds of all Maris understood the Russian language. Their animistic religion, which venerates the Maris' past, remains a strong influence among all the Maris, but particularly among the Olyk and Upo Maris. Nationalism, which has grown rapidly during the 1990s, is based on resentment of the Russian population settled in their homeland during the twentieth century, but separatism has not become an issue.

The leadership of the Republic of Mari El in June 1997 announced a new economic status for the republic. The status, equivalent to offshore status, would give investors tax breaks and other incentives to invest in the republic. The tiny republic, with few national resources, has received little foreign investment since the collapse of the Soviet system.

SELECTED BIBLIOGRAPHY

Caplan, Richard, ed. *Europe's New Nationalism: States and Minorities in Conflict*. 1996.

Hilderley, Jeri. *Mari*. 1990.

Kozlov, Viktor. *The Peoples of the Soviet Union*. 1988.

Pushkarev, Sergei. *Self-Government and Freedom in Russia*. 1988.

Warhola, James W. *Politicized Ethnicity in the Russian Federation: Dilemmas of State Formation*. 1996.

MESKHTEKIANS

Meshetians; Meskhtekis; Yerlis

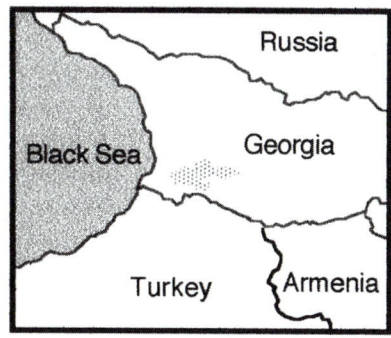

POPULATION: Approximately (2000 e) 100,000 Meskhtekians in Europe, out of an ethnic population of 265,000. The majority of the Meskhtekians live in Azerbaijan, Georgia, and the North Caucasus region of southeastern European Russia. Other large Meskhtekian populations remain outside Europe in southern Kazakhstan and Central Asia, in Uzbekistan, Kyrgyzstan, and Tajikistan, where they were deported in 1944.

THE MESKHTEKIAN HOMELAND: The Meskhtekian homeland lies in southeastern Georgia and northern Armenia. Traditionally known as Meskhi, the region occupies a highland region in the Meskhtekian Range on the Georgian-Armenian border, including a part of the autonomous republic of Ajaristan in Georgia, just north of the Turkish border. The region is very mountainous and lies mostly in the Meskhtekian Range of the Lesser Caucasus.

The homeland of the Meskhtekians, called Meskhtekistan, has no official status. The region claimed by Meskhtekian nationalists lies in southwestern Georgia and northwestern Armenia, mostly in the Akhaltsikhe, Akhalkalaki, Borzomi, and Chulo districts of Georgia and the Gukasan district of Armenia. Traditionally, the capital and major cultural center of the region is Akhaltsikhe in Georgia, (2000 e) 34,000, which was formerly the capital of Turkish Armenia.

FLAG: The Meskhtekian national flag, the flag of the national movement, is a horizontal tricolor of white, red, and black bearing a vertical green stripe at the hoist charged with a white crescent moon.

PEOPLE: The Meskhtekians are one of the world's newest nations, a contemporary example of ethnogenesis. There was no Meskhtekian ethnic group in the Soviet Union until the 1950s and 1960s. The small nation, which formed following their deportation from their homeland in the Caucasus Mountains, overcame differences in religion, dialect, and culture to form a distinct national group. They are the remnants and descendants of various Muslim groups deported from the Turkish border region by Joseph Stalin. Although primarily a Shi'a Muslim nation, a minority adheres to the Sunni branch of Islam.

United by hardships, common experiences, and their Muslim religion, the diverse peoples formed a separate nation in exile, including the development of a national language, a hybrid dialect combining the Laz dialect of Georgian and admixtures from several Turkish languages. A lingua franca used for intergroup communication developed as a viable national language. The new dialect, which is close to that of the Ajars,* has become the national language.

NATION: The region, in the Lesser Caucasus Mountains, was known to the ancient Greeks, who colonized the coastal plains. The mountains east of the Black Sea have traditionally been a refuge for refugees fleeing wars and invasions. In the high, isolated valleys, the inhabitants developed numerous dialects and cultures. In the early Christian Era, the mountains came under nominal Roman rule. The region later formed part of the early Georgian kingdom in the ninth century and was under the authority of the Kingdom of Armenia from A.D. 846 to 1046.

The Turks of the Ottoman Empire took control of the Meskhetia region in the fifteenth century. The chief town of the area, Akhaltsikhe, was made the capital of a Turkish pashalik in the sixteenth century and the center of the Caucasian slave trade. By the seventeenth century the inhabitants of the mountainous region, mostly ethnic Georgian and Armenian Christians, had converted to Islam and had adopted many Turkish cultural traits.

Meskhetia was annexed by the expanding Russian Empire in 1828–29, beginning decades of Russian efforts to force the small Muslim groups of the Meskhtekian Range to revert to their earlier Christian religion. In spite of the common oppressor, the small groups remained separate, uniting only when threatened by Christian violence or attacks on the Shi'a Muslim groups by the majority Sunni Muslim population.

In 1905 serious unrest broke out among the Muslim peoples of the region. The Russians' brutal methods in crushing the disturbances reinforced the pro-Turkish sentiment shared by the diverse groups. Their homeland formed part of the front line when war began in 1914. As the war dragged on, the Muslims suffered increasing persecution for their pro-Turkish sentiments. Briefly occupied by Turkish troops after the Russian Revolution in 1917, the Muslims again became the brunt of anti-Turkish Georgian and Armenian nationalism when the region became part of the new Transcaucasian republics in 1918.

Soviet rule, established in 1921 following the conquest of Georgia and Armenia, was especially harsh for the Muslim peoples, whose loyalty to the new Soviet state was suspect. During World War II, the German forces fought their way into the Caucasus in pursuit of the region's oil reserves, often finding allies among the oppressed Muslim nationalities of the northern Caucasus. Stalin in

1943–44 accused many of the small Muslim nations of the Caucasus of treason, refusing to differentiate among those who had remained loyal and those who had joined the Nazis' anticommunist crusade. He ordered entire nations deported to the wastes of Kazakhstan and Central Asia. Although neighboring Turkey remained carefully neutral during the war, Stalin still regarded Russia's ancient adversary as an enemy state. The small Muslim groups of the Meskhtekian highlands, far south of the German advance in the southern Caucasus, were also charged with treason and suffered deportation in November 1944.

The question of the Meskhtekians belongs squarely in Soviet history. The small Muslim peoples of southern Georgia, collectively called the Meskheti, were charged with treason and deported. In 1944 around 130,000 Muslims from the Meskhetia region were secretly driven from their homes and herded onto rail cars. The deportees included a diverse group, both culturally and religiously. The largest in number were the Meskhi Turks, Sunni Muslims who lived in the Kura River valley of Georgia. They also included Karapapakh Turks, Shi'a Muslims from northern Armenia, Armenian Sunni Muslims called Kemsils, two groups of Kurds, one Sunni Muslim and the other Shi'a Muslim, from southern Georgia and Ajaristan, and smaller numbers of Azeri-speaking Turkmens, Abkhaz,* and Ajars.

Many of the deportees died of hunger, thirst, and cold on the long journey east. Their Soviet guards dumped them at rail sidings across a vast region, often without food, water, or shelter. Meskhtekian soldiers fighting with the Red Army, numbering over 4,000, began to return to their homes in the Meskhtekian hills in 1945, only to face immediate arrest and deportation. The Meskhtekians claim that 50,000 of their people died as a direct result of the deportations and the deprivations suffered in exile. In exile they were required to report every two weeks, like prisoners on parole.

At the end of World War II the disparate groups were living in abject poverty in widely scattered communities in Kazakhstan and the Central Asian republics. Their suffering and losses made them only more anti-Soviet and anticommunist and even more religious. Putting aside their religious and dialectical differences, they began to solidify as a separate people. They took the name Meskhtekian as a collective name for the many small groups that were merging into the new national group. Not included in the rehabilitation of the deported peoples in 1956, they were forgotten in the Soviet Union, and their existence was unknown in the West.

The scattered groups strengthened their ties in the 1960s, coordinating petitions, appeals, and agitation for the right to return to their Caucasian homeland. Delegates from the dispersed Meskhtekian groups attended a national congress in Tashkent, Uzbekistan, in 1964. The congress voted to form the Meskhtekian National Movement (MNM) and to send representatives to Moscow and Tbilisi to plead their case. Officially rehabilitated and restored to full rights as Soviet citizens, the Meskhtekians were released from KGB control in 1968, the last of the deported nations to be rehabilitated. The Meskhtekians stepped up their

464 MESKHTEKIANS

campaign to win the right to return to their homeland. Details of the secret Meskhtekian deportation began to leak out to the West in 1969, bringing some international support, particularly among Western human rights groups. Free from police control for the first time in over two decades, many Meskhtekians moved from their scattered settlements to the Fergana valley in Uzbekistan, the site of the largest Meskhtekian exile community. The growing prosperity of the energetic exiles, who advanced more rapidly than their Uzbek neighbors, raised ethnic and religious tensions that worsened with the Soviet liberalization of the late 1980s.

In an incident arising out of the cost of a basket of strawberries, a new tragedy struck the small nation. An Uzbek nationalist demonstration in June 1989 turned into a pogrom as the Sunni Muslim demonstrators turned on the mostly Shi'a Muslim Meskhtekians. Enraged Uzbeks hunted the terrified exiles through a week of violence, rape, and murder. Over 100 Meskhtekians died, and over 500 were injured before the Soviet military evacuated 74,000 Meskhtekians to guarded camps outside the Uzbek cities. Told they would be returned to their Georgian homeland within two weeks, the majority of the refugees still languish in the camps. Considered foreigners in newly independent Uzbekistan, as unwanted aliens they can obtain neither work nor housing.

The government of Georgia, also independent following the Soviet disintegration of 1991, under a radical Christian and nationalist administration refused to discuss the return of a troublesome Muslim minority. A more moderate Georgian government, installed in January 1992, has received Meskhtekian delegations but, beset by problems on every side, has not allowed the Meskhtekians, except for some 300, to return home from their long exile. Their homeland is now inhabited by peoples settled in the depopulated region during the Stalin era, with only a handful of Meskhtekians allowed to resettle in the region. Some Meskhtekians have settled in other parts of the Caucasus or in Azerbaijan, where the ethnically related Azeris* have given them land in districts with large non-Turkic populations.

The Meskhtekian nation, one of Europe's newest, has increasingly pled their case at the United Nations, to the governments of the European Union and North America. The Meskhtekian nationalists are mostly organized by two nationalist organizations that are somewhat opposed in their methods and aims, Khsna and Vatan.

SELECTED BIBLIOGRAPHY
Caplan, Richard, ed. *Europe's New Nationalism: States and Minorities in Conflict.* 1996.
Coppieters, Bruno. *Contested Borders in the Caucasus.* 1996.
Dawisha, Karen, and Bruce Parrot, eds. *Conflict, Cleavage, and Change in Central Asia and the Caucasus.* 1997.
Ro'I, Yaacov. *Muslim Eurasia.* 1995.
Sheehy, Ann. *The Crimean Tatars, Volga Germans and Meskhtekians: Soviet Treatment of Some National Minorities.* 1980.

MOLDOVANS

Moldavians

POPULATION: Approximately (2000 e) 3,804,000 Moldovans in Europe, 2,832,000 in Moldova and another 600,000 to 1 million in adjacent areas of Ukraine, with other communities in the Russian Federation and Romania.

THE MOLDOVAN HOMELAND: The Moldovan homeland lies in Eastern Europe, occupying the southwestern part of the East European Plain, in the valleys of the Prut and Dniestr Rivers. The homeland was divided in 1944, with the traditionally Moldovan regions of Northern Bukovina and the Bugeac (Budshak), the coastal area on the Black Sea, transferred to the control of the Soviet Ukraine. The country is generally rolling hills that slope from the northwest to the southeast and is dissected by many streams and deep river valleys. The Moldovan Uplands or Kodry are located in the center of the country, which also contains the broad flat valleys along the western bank of the Dniester (Dnestr) River, the Dnestr Uplands. In the south, the Moldovan republic is separated from the Black Sea by the so-called Budshak, which is Turkish for angle, the part of the plains between the Dniester and Danube Rivers that was transferred to Ukraine.

The area, separated from the Romanian region of Moldavia in 1812, has changed hands several times, being ruled by the Russians* or Soviets for 132 years, Romanians* for 57 years, and twice declaring independence, during the Russian Revolution and on 27 August 1991. The Moldovan heartland now forms an independent republic, while the Moldovan territory transferred to Ukraine makes up the oblast of Chernivtsi and the southern districts of the oblast of Odesa. The Moldovan republic joined the United Nations in 1992. *Republic of Moldova (Republica Moldova)*: 13,012 sq.mi.–33,701 sq.km. (2000 e)

4,479,000—Moldovans 65%, Ukrainians* 14%, Russians 13%, Gagauz* 3.5%, Jews 1.5%, Bulgarians* 1.5%, Germans,* Belarussians.* The Moldovan capital and major cultural center is Chisinau, formerly called Kishinev, (2000 e) 684,000. Other important Moldovan cultural centers are Chernivtsi, called Cernauti by the Moldovans, (2000 e) 266,000, and Izmayil, Ismail to the Moldovans, (2000 e) 95,000, the major cities in the territory transferred to Ukraine in 1944.

FLAG: The Moldovan national flag, the official flag of the republic, is a vertical tricolor of pale blue, yellow, and red bearing a centered gold eagle and shield charged with the national symbols, a Roman eagle in gold outlined in black, with a red beak and talons, and a yellow scepter in its left talon; on its breast is a shield divided horizontally red over blue with a stylized ox head, star, rose, and crescent, all in black-outlined yellow.

PEOPLE: The Moldovans are a Romanian people, one of the three divisions of the Romanian peoples. Separated from the Romanians in 1812, the Moldovans have evolved dialectical and cultural differences but remain basically Romanian in language and culture. The name "Moldovan" is now used to designate the people of Romanian language living in the historic Bessarabia region in the territory of the former Soviet Union, including an estimated 165,000 Romanians not of Moldovan origin.

The descendants of early Latin peoples and the Bessi Slavs, who gave their name to the region as Bessarabia, the Moldovans speak a Moldavian dialect of Romanian with a considerable Slavic admixture. Soviet linguists claimed that the Moldovan language diverged from standard Romanian in the sixteenth century. The language is the most easterly of the Romance languages, and there is little dialectal variation in the spoken form in Moldova. Under Russian and Soviet rule, the Moldovan dialect was written in the Cyrillic alphabet, but since the late 1980s the Latin alphabet has increasingly been used. The proposed official change from the Cyrillic to the Latin alphabet in the Moldovan Republic, which was initially postponed from 1994 to 1997, has still to be fully implemented.

NATION: The Romanians claim their ancestry includes the original inhabitants of the region, called Getae by the Greeks and Daci by the Romans, and the Latin colonists who settled in the region between 106 B.C. and A.D. 238. The Daci or Dacians, subdued by the Romans under the emperor Trajan, were Latinized and mixed with the Roman colonists.

The decline of Roman power left the region open to invasion. Overrun by Gothic tribes around 250 A.D. the Roman province was finally abandoned when the Roman colonists withdrew to south of the Danube in 270. The Romans' Latin language and the fortifications called Trajan's Walls are the only lasting legacies of Roman rule. A succession of invaders followed the Goths, each leaving an imprint on the regional population. Named for the Slavic Bessi tribe that settled the area during the great Slav migrations of the seventh century, Bessarabia constituted part of the huge territory conquered by the Slavic tribes.

The Moldova region formed part of the first great Slav state, Kievan Rus, from the ninth to the eleventh centuries, laying the basis for of the later Russian claims to the area.

Conquered by the Mongols, who invaded the area in 1242, the region was devastated. Bessarabia began to recover only under the rule of Stephen the Great, the creator of the first Moldovan principality in 1359, with its historic nucleus in northern Bukovina, now the Ukrainian oblast of Chernivtsi. The principality fell to the Ottoman Turks* and Crimean Tatars* in 1513, the conquest marking the northern limit of Turkish rule. The Ottoman bureaucracy ruled through local officials, mostly leaving the Moldovans to look after their own affairs. The Austrians wrested control of the western district, Bukovina, from Turkey in 1774. Bukovina, with its large Moldovan population, was added to Austrian Galicia as a separate district.

An expanding Russia contested Turkish control of the Moldovan principality from 1711, finally annexing the northern region, Bessarabia, following the Russo-Turkish War of 1806–12. The newly annexed territory, 86% Romanian-speaking, was subjected to intense Russification and opened to settlement by non-Romanian colonists in order to dilute the Romanian-speaking majority. Thousands of Gagauz, Bulgarians, Ukrainians, Russians, and Poles* settled in the region.

In 1818 Moldova was given the status of an autonomous area, and Romanian was given the status of the second national language, after Russian; however, step by step the Moldovans lost their privileges. In 1828 the autonomous status of the region was revoked, and Moldovans occupying posts in the administration were replaced by Russians. The Russian legal and administrative system was introduced, and most Romanian-language schools were closed.

Anti-Russian sentiment incited the growth of nationalism in Bessarabia in the 1840s. The national movement was crushed during the severe disturbances that erupted in 1848, only to surface again in the 1870s and 1880s with the support of the neighboring Romanian kingdom. The Romanians, seeking to recover lands they claimed were part of the historic Romanian homeland, supported the growth of Moldovan nationalism as an anti-Russian movement.

The western region of Bessarabia, Bukovina, was made a separate Austrian crownland in 1849, following severe disturbances the year before. As part of the Roman Catholic Hapsburg Empire, Bukovina became the most advanced and prosperous of the Moldovan territories. Moldovan nationalist organizations, suppressed in Russian Bessarabia, were allowed to function in Austrian Bukovina, but only as anti-Russian movements. Moldovan political newspapers and anti-Russian pamphlets were smuggled from Austrian Bukovina into Bessarabia.

The Russian government's attempts to channel Moldovan nationalist sentiment into the region's traditional anti-Semitism led to horrible pogroms, particularly awful during the attack on Kishinev's Jewish quarters in 1903. However, anti-Semitism proved only a temporary distraction, and Moldovan nationalists continued to gather strength, culminating in widespread disturbances during the

Russian Revolution of 1905 and a futile Moldovan revolt in March and April 1907. The revolt, brutally crushed by tsarist troops, drove the movement underground.

The tsarist government during World War I collapsed in revolution in February 1917, leaving Bessarabia effectively independent. In May 1917 the Moldovan nationalists formed a government but supported Russia's new democratic government. The Moldovans demanded political, linguistic, and ecclesiastical autonomy for the province and for the estimated 1 million Moldovans in neighboring provinces of Ukraine. Following the October 1917 Bolshevik coup, the alarmed nationalists declared the region's autonomy and formed the Sfatul Tarii (Council of the Land), inviting participation by all of Bessarabia's national groups. On 7 December 1917 the Moldovans rose against the imposition of Bolshevik rule, and on 12 December the council proclaimed autonomy. No demand for union with Romania was put forward, as the Moldovans believed there was more hope of securing free and full development within a restored federal, democratic Russia than as part of backward, feudal Romania. The council decreed the use of the Moldovan language, with the Latin alphabet, and newspapers and other publications began to publish using the Roman script in place of Russia's Cyrillic alphabet.

Pressed by Ukrainian nationalists seeking to annex the region and under a growing Bolshevik military threat, the Sfatul Tarii declared the independence of the Democratic Republic of Moldova, including Bukovina, which remained under Austrian rule. The new republic, menaced by the advancing Red Army, finally voted for union with neighboring Romania in April 1918. Romanian troops crossed the Prut River and halted the Bolshevik advance at the Dniester. In November 1918 the region held by Romanian and Moldovan troops was formally joined to the Romanian kingdom.

The collapse of defeated Austria-Hungary in November 1918 left Bukovina without a government. The Ukrainians, dominant in the north of the region, voted for union with the Ukrainians, but the Moldovans in the south refused to become part of a Ukrainian state. The Treaty of Saint Germain, signed in 1919 by Austria and the Allies, gave only the southern districts of Bukovina to Romania, but the subsequent Treaty of Sèvres transferred the entire Bukovina territory, including the Ukrainian-populated northern districts, to Romania.

The Moldovan territories were virtually colonized by Romanian Boyars moving north into former Russian and Austrian territories. The Boyars, landlords given large tracts of land in the new territories by the Romanian monarchy, relegated the Moldovans of the region to a condition little better than serfdom. Initial enthusiasm for union with Romania quickly gave way to indignation and disgust with the corrupt, feudal Romanian system. In 1919 the Moldovan protests and demonstrations were cruelly put down by Romanian troops.

The new Soviet government of Russia refused to recognize the separation of Moldova or the Romanian annexation of the region. The region east of the

Dniester, conquered by the Red Army in 1918, was organized as an autonomous Moldovan republic within Ukraine in 1924, with Tiraspol as its capital.

The Romanian provinces of Bessarabia and Bukovina were treated as a semiagricultural colonies virtually ruled by the powerful Romanian Boyars, leading to much dissatisfaction with Romanian rule in the 1920s and 1930s. The region, more developed than most of Romania in 1918, became one of the more backward and the most corrupt regions in Romania within a decade of the Romanian annexation. The union of Moldova and Romania from 1918 to 1940 was an economic disaster for the Moldovans.

The Molotov-Ribbentrop Pact, signed on 23 August 1939, a nonaggression agreement that virtually divided Eastern Europe into Nazi and Soviet spheres of influence, placed Moldova within the Soviet sphere. The pact, assuring Nazi noninterference in Soviet actions, allowed the Soviet government to send troops into Bessarabia and the northern part of Bukovina. The territories taken from Romania were formally ceded by the weak Romanian government in June 1940. Added to Soviet Moldova north of the Dniester River, an enlarged Moldovan republic was admitted to the Soviet Union as a union republic, while thousands of Moldovans were deported.

The Romanians joined the Axis, partly to recover the lost territories, and in June 1941 Romanian troops joined the German attack on the Soviet Union and quickly overran Moldova. The Romanian government promoted the Romanian language and culture in the region to counter two decades of Soviet rule. In 1940, when the territories were formally ceded to the Soviet Union, an estimated 65% of all Moldovan men and 85% of women were illiterate. By 1941, when the Romanians returned as conquerors, even the small Romanian-speaking intelligentsia had been devastated by a year of Soviet rule. The Moldova region, part of the so-called Pale of Settlement in tsarist Russia, had a very large population on the eve of the Romanian-German invasion, estimated to number about 250,000. The Jewish population of the territories was mostly massacred by the Romanian fascists and their Nazi German allies between 1941 and 1944, often with the support of the local Moldovan population.

In 1944 the Axis was defeated, and Soviet troops invaded the region. Moldova was forcibly collectivized, and many Moldovans from other regions of the Soviet Union were resettled within the republic. The returning Soviet authorities forbade all contact with Romania, and a separate Moldovan culture and language were imposed, which stressed the region's historic Slavic influences and excised the Latin Romanian elements. Northern Bukovina and the Black Sea districts of eastern Bessarabia, areas with large non-Moldovan populations, were transferred to the Soviet Ukraine. In all, an estimated 80,000 Moldovans were deported in three mass movements between 1940 and 1949. In the 1950s and 1960s relations and contacts between the Moldovans and the related Romanians were often prohibited.

The Soviet program to separate the Moldovans from the Romanians had by the early 1970s succeeded too well. The Moldovan nationalism fostered by the Soviet government after World War II had slowly moved from government policy to a popular Moldovan movement, often with anti-Soviet overtones. Moldovan nationalism quickly gained support as the Gorbachev reforms, introduced in 1987, reduced the pressure to conform to the Soviet ideals of nationhood and brotherly unity. In early 1988 the Moldovan popular front, the Frontul Popular al Moldovei, was formed and held its first congress in May of that year.

Nationalism in the region rapidly gained strength, and in March and April 1989 thousands took to the streets to protest the Russification of their language and culture. The many demonstrators demanded the return of the Latin alphabet and that the Moldovan language be made the official language of the republic. A plan was put forward to replace Russian and the Cyrillic alphabet with Moldovan (Romanian) and the Latin alphabet within five years. The proposed changes to the language laws were met with strikes and demonstrations by the large Slavic population, particularly in the heavily Slav region east of the Dniester River.

A Moldovan nationalist government, elected in February 1990, continued to stress the predominance of the Romanian language. Proposals to restrict the use of Russian exacerbated tensions between the Moldovan majority and the Slav minority. The Moldovan government passed a proclamation of state sovereignty on 23 June 1990, and in September the Slavs, who controlled the region east of the Dniester, unilaterally proclaimed the autonomy of the Transdniestria region, with its Moldovan minority, under an unreformed communist regime.

Moldova was effectively independent following the abortive coup and the subsequent disintegration of the Soviet Union in August 1991, and the Moldovan government formally declared independence on 27 August. The declaration, greeted with mass rallies and enthusiasm by the Moldovans, was rejected by the Slavic population concentrated north of the Dniester River, who feared that Moldova would unite with neighboring Romania. Some Moldovan national groups demanded that the new government begin immediate negotiations with neighboring Ukraine to recover the territories transferred to Ukraine by Stalin in 1944.

The demands of the Slav-majority districts north of the Dniester River for separation of the region from newly independent Moldova escalated ethnic tensions. The Russian Fourteenth Army, which had formerly policed the southwestern Soviet Union, supported the secession of Slav Transdniestria from Moldova. In December 1991 armed conflict broke out, pitting the secessionists, backed by the Soviet Fourteenth Army, against the new Moldovan Army. By June 1992 over 700 people had died in the fighting, and 50,000 people had fled the escalating conflict. On 21 June 1992, following a series of meetings with the participation of Moldova, Russia, Romania, Ukraine, and the Dniestrian leaders, the Transdniestria region was accorded a special status within Moldova.

In January 1993 the Moldovan parliament narrowly defeated a proposition to hold a referendum on reunification with Romania. In elections held in early

1994, the Moldovan nationalists won greater support than those favoring unification with Romania. In a subsequent referendum, 19% of the voters favored continued independence over union with Romania. The Moldovan government in March 1994 rescinded the language law that began the alienation of the non-Moldovan national groups in the republic in 1989. In May 1996 Moldovan and Russian officials agreed to establish a joint commission on procedures and deadlines for withdrawing the former Soviet and now Russian Fourteenth Army from eastern Moldova. The accord, protested by the Dniester separatists, calls for the phased withdrawal to Russia of the mostly ethnic Russian military units.

The Moldovan government, firmly rejecting any suggestion that Moldova and Romania may merge, has applied for both European Union and North Atlantic Treaty Organization (NATO) membership and has joined many international organizations. Romania, the first country to extend diplomatic recognition, having had second thoughts on Moldovan independence, maintained only low-level representation in Chisinau until 1994. Since 1996 relations between the two Romanian nations have been arranged to suit their status as independent states.

In presidential elections in November 1996, the chairman of the parliament, Petru Lucinschi was elected. In February 1991 a pro-Luchinschi political group, the Movement for a Democratic and Prosperous Moldova, was formed as a centrist party, with affinities to both the moderate Left and Right. The move to centrist politics should aid the Moldovan government's campaign to negotiate the final autonomy agreements with both the Slavs of the Transdniestria region and the Gagauz.

The Moldovans, in the 1990s, have experienced great difficulty in transforming their Soviet command economy to a market economy, although the export of their wines had been a success until the collapse of the Russian economy in 1998, the Moldovans remain the poorest, after the Albanians,* in Europe. The Moldovan economy, worth only about $1.6 billion a year, is hardly bigger than than of a small American city and is shrinking.

The Moldovans have opted for the status of a separate national group, but few know what it means to be Moldovan and the majority are half-hearted patriots. Even fewer would like to see their small state knitted back into Romania. The small minority that advocates the Moldovan's inclusion a greater Romania have attracted only small numbers of supporters.

SELECTED BIBLIOGRAPHY

Bruchis, Michael. *The Republic of Moldova: From the Collapse of the Soviet Empire to the Restoration of the Russian Empire.* 1997.

Dima, Nicholas. *Bessarabia and Bukovina: The Soviet-Romanian Territorial Dispute.* 1983.

Dima, Nicholas. *From Moldavia to Moldova: The Soviet-Romanian Territorial Dispute.* 1991.

Dyer, Donald L. *Studies in Moldovan: The History, Culture, Language and Contemporary Politics of the People of Moldova.* 1996.

Van Meurs, Wim P. *The Bessarabian Question in Communist Historiography: Nationalist and Communist Politics and History-Writing.* 1994.

MONÉGASQUES

Munegascs

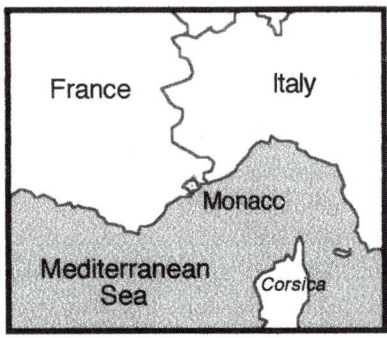

POPULATION: Approximately (2000 e) 5,800 Monégasques in Europe, most living in the Principality of Monaco, but with small numbers living in Paris and other parts of France.

THE MONÉGASQUE HOMELAND: The Monégasque homeland forms an enclave within the Alpes-Maritime department of southeastern France, between Nice and the Italian border. The enclave surrounds a natural harbor and is made up of three communes, La Condamine, the business district, Monte Carlo, the resort district with a famous casino, and Monaco-Ville, the capital, atop the promontory called the Rock of Monaco. Monaco's beautiful location and mild climate have made it one of Europe's best-known resorts. The principality is Europe's second smallest independent state, after Vatican City.

The Principality of Monaco is an independent city-state, which has been under French protection since 1861. *Principality of Monaco (Principanté de Monaco)*: 1.95 sq.mi.–5.1 sq.km. (2000 e) 32,000—French* 47%, Monégasques 17%, Italians* and Ligurians* 16%, Occitanians* 15%. The Monégasque capital and major cultural center is the city of Monaco, which encompasses the entire principality, with its capital at Monaco-Ville, (2000 e) 2,500.

FLAG: The Monégasque national flag, the official flag of the principality, is a horizontal bicolor of red over white.

PEOPLE: The Monégasques are a Mediterranean people closely related to the neighboring Ligurians of Italy, but with a substantial French admixture. The inhabitants of the principality, although ethnically and linguistically Ligurians, have a separate history and a culture more French than Italian. They now form a minority in the state, which has a French majority, but Monégasque citizenship is difficult to obtain. The Monégasques are not admitted to the gaming tables at the famous casino at Monte Carlo. An estimated 95% of the inhabitants of the principality are Roman Catholics.

The Monégasque language is a dialect of the Ligurian language, which is closer to French than to standard Italian. The dialect spoken in the principality, called Monégasque or Munegasc, was nearly extinct by the 1970s, but compulsory teaching of the dialect in Monaco's schools has revived it. The majority of the inhabitants of Monaco also speak French, the official language of Monaco, and substantial numbers also speak the Provençal dialect of the Occitanians of southern France.

NATION: The promontory later called the Rock of Monaco has provided shelter to populations since ancient times. Traces of prehistoric occupation have been found, but the first known inhabitants of the region were the Ligures, a mountain people who inhabited a wide region of present northern Italy and southeastern France. Many historians believe the name Monaco came from the Monoïkos, a Ligurian tribe that inhabited the area in the sixth century B.C. In antiquity, the region was colonized by Phoenicians and Greeks, and the port was associated with the cult of the Greek hero Herakles. The modern port of Monaco is called the Port of Hercules.

Between 25 and 15 B.C., the Roman emperor Augustus directed several military campaigns that extended Roman rule to the region. The region formed part of the Roman province of Liguria, and the Ligurian inhabitants became Latinized under centuries of Roman authority. The decline of Roman power left the region open to invasions by barbarian tribes from beyond the empire's borders. In the fifth century the Visigoths overran the region, beginning a period of chaos as the region was regularly sacked by different tribes. In the seventh century the Lombards* added the region to their expanding kingdom.

At the end of the twelfth century the Count of Provence drove the Arab Saracens from the coast, and the region slowly became repopulated. The rise of Genoa to the east as a powerful city-state was brought about by Genoese expansion at the expense of weaker neighbors. In 1215 Fulco des Castello, of the Genoese Grimaldi family, laid the first stone of a stronghold on the promontory after obtaining sovereignty for all the lands surrounding the Rock of Monaco from the emperor Henry VI.

The rock and the excellent harbor became the object of the ongoing struggle between the two parties disputing power in the Republic of Genoa, the Ghibellines, supporters of the emperors, and the Guelfs, faithful followers of the pope. The Guelfs and their allies, the Grimaldis, were expelled from Genoa in 1296 and took refuge in Provence. According to tradition, François Grimaldi on 8 January 1297 penetrated and captured the stronghold of Monaco disguised as a Franciscan monk. The Grimaldis lost control of Monaco in 1301, but thirty years later, Charles I reconquered the stronghold and founded the principality. He extended the boundaries to include Menton and Roquebrune and became the first lord of Monaco.

The sovereignty of Monaco was recognized by the king of France and the duke of Savoy in 1489, but the Genoese continued to claim the region. After a siege of more than 100 days, the Genoese were finally repelled by the garrison of Lucien I. In 1512 the French king, Louis XII, recognized the independence of Monaco. The small state was under Spanish protection from 1524 to 1641. Honoré II took the title of prince in 1612, which was recognized by the European powers as a hereditary title. After ten years of negotiations, Honoré II and Louis XIII of France signed the Treaty of Péronne, which recognized the sovereignty of Monaco and granted the prince and his descendants equality with the highest French nobles. From 1641 to 1793 Monaco was a protectorate of the French kingdom.

In the early eighteenth century, Monaco's ruler, Antoine I, built extensive fortifications in the principality to protect Monaco from invasion by the Savoyards,* who had occupied Provence. In 1731 the male line of the Grimaldis became extinct, but the French husband of Princess Louise-Hippolyte of the Goyon-Matignon family took the name Grimaldi and acceded to the throne under the name of Jacques I.

The principality was annexed to revolutionary France on 15 February 1793 under the name Fort Hercule. The Grimaldis' palace was sacked, and its treasures disappeared. The Grimaldis were forced to flee, although members of the family were guillotined in 1794. At the end of the Napoleonic Wars, the first Treaty of Paris, in 1814, restored Monaco and its princes. The second Treaty of Paris, in 1815, placed Monaco under the protection of the Kingdom of Sardinia, which was unpopular with the Monégasque population.

During the European revolutionary upheavals of 1848, the inhabitants of Menton and Roquebrune proclaimed their communes independent of Monaco and placed themselves under the direct protection of Sardinia, which, in turn, ceded them to France in 1860. On 2 February 1861, in exchange for French recognition of Monaco's independence, the prince formally ceded Menton and Roquebrune to France, thereby formally losing 80% of the principality's territory. In 1863 gambling, illegal in France, was first introduced, and in 1865 the Monégasque state issued its first postage stamp. Four years later all forms of direct taxation were abolished in Monaco. The principality became a constitutional monarchy on 5 January 1911, and by the terms of a 1918 treaty, the succession to the throne must be approved by the French government.

Prince Rainier III succeeded his father, Prince Louis II, on 9 May 1949. In 1956 he married an American film star, Grace Kelly, following a much-publicized romance. The publicity surrounding the couple made the almost unknown state familiar to people around the world, particularly in Kelly's home country, the United States. Princess Grace died in a tragic automobile accident on 14 September 1982.

In 1962 the French government demanded that Monaco cease being a tax haven for French corporations and businessmen. The demand was rejected, but to modernize the administration, the Monégasque government in 1962 adopted a new constitution, and in May 1963 Prince Rainier signed a fiscal and customs agreement with France. The new constitution greatly reduced the power of the sovereign.

The principality, long considered too small to qualify, was admitted to the United Nations as a member state on 28 May 1993 and obtained its own telephone country code in 1996. In 1997 the Monégasques celebrated seven centuries of the reign of the Grimaldi dynasty.

SELECTED BIBLIOGRAPHY

Black, Loraine. *Monaco*. 1988.

Duursma, Jorri. *Self-determination, Statehood, and International Relations of Micro-States: The Cases of Liechtenstein, San Marino, Monaco, Andorra, and the Vatican City*. 1994

Edwards, Anne. *The Grimaldis of Monaco*. 1992.

Glatt, John. *The Royal House of Monaco: Dynasty of Glamour, Tragedy and Scandal*. 1998.

Hudson, Grace L. *Monaco*. 1991.

MONTENEGRINS

Crnogorci; Chernogortsy

POPULATION: Approximately (2000 e) 643,000 Montenegrins in Europe, 445,000 in Montenegro, and with other communities in Serbia, Bosnia and Herzegovina, and Albania.

THE MONTENEGRIN HOMELAND: The Montenegrin homeland, called Crna Gora or Black Mountain in the Serbian language, occupies a rugged, mountainous region of the western Balkan Peninsula. Situated at the southern end of the Dinaric Alps and including part of the North Albanian Alps, Montenegro is nearly entirely mountainous and difficult to access. The most famous peak is Mt. Lovcen at 5,738 feet (1,749 m.). The mountain, called the "black mountain" for its basaltic rock, is the mountain from which the region's name is derived. The well-forested region is traversed by high, fertile valleys and has a short coastline on the Adriatic Sea. Most of the highlands are used as pasture for sheep and goats, with only about 6% of the land under cultivation.

The tiny state was recognized as an independent principality in 1878. Following World War I, the Montenegrins voted for the union of the South Slav lands, later called Yugoslavia, which broke up in 1991, leaving the Serbs* and Montenegrins to form a new Yugoslav state comprising two constituent republics. *Republic of Montenegro (Republika Crna Gora)*: 5,333 sq.mi.–13,812 sq.km. (2000 e) 648,000—Montenegrins 69%, Sanjakis* (Sanjak Muslims) 15%, Serbs* 9%, Albanians* 7%. The Montenegrin capital and major cultural center is Podgorica, (2000 e) 159,000, called Titograd from 1980 to 1992. The other important Montenegrin cultural center is Cetinje, (2000 e) 23,000, the former royal capital.

FLAGS: The Montenegrin national flag, the official flag of the republic, is a horizontal tricolor of red, blue, and white. The flag of the nationalist movement, the former royal flag, is a red field with a narrow white border bearing a centered, white Montenegrin cross.

PEOPLE: The Montenegrins are a robust mountain nation with a long warrior tradition. The smallest of the South Slav nations, the Montenegrins are ethnically Serbs, and although they share strong cultural ties, including their Orthodox faith, their history is distinct, and they consider themselves a separate nation. The Montenegrin culture, developed in the isolation of their mountain homeland, diverged from the Serbian culture in the fourteenth century. For centuries Montenegrin society was composed of patrilineally related, extended families organized into clans. The clan system lasted well into the twentieth century, and personal tenacity and combat skills are still the most valued male virtues. Women have traditionally tended the fields, maintained the home, and raised the next generation of Montenegrin warriors. Practices such as bride theft and blood brotherhood were formerly widespread, and blood vengeance has survived to the present.

The language of the Montenegrins is a dialect of the Serbian branch of the Serbo-Croatian language, which, like Serbian, is written in the Cyrillic alphabet. The Montenegrin dialect, called Ijekavian, which evolved from the upland variations of Serbian, is closer to old Serbian and lacks the Turkish admixture of the dialect spoken in Serbia. The language issue has become a rallying point for Montenegrin nationalists since 1992.

The Montenegrins are mostly Orthodox Christians, with a small Roman Catholic minority, mostly along the coast. The Montenegrin Orthodox Church, closely tied to their culture and history, officially separated from the larger Serbian Orthodox Church in 1993. A minority of Montengrins converted to Islam between the seventeenth and nineteenth centuries.

NATION: Inhabited by Illyrian tribes, the highland region east of the Adriatic Sea formed part of the Roman, then Byzantine Empires before the migration of Slavic tribes to the region in the seventh and eighth centuries. The Slavs adopted Christianity and accepted nominal Byzantine authority. In the twelfth century, the highlands formed part of a small Serbian kingdom, which was centered in the less accessible and more easily defensible mountains. The Venetians, in control of the coastal plain, called the highland region Black Mountain, Crna Gora in the Slavic dialect. The mountain tribes of the region in the early fourteenth century were united in the Zeta principality, which formed part of the medieval Serbian Empire.

The Montenegrins' history as a separate nation began in the mid-fourteenth century. The Serbian Empire collapsed in 1355, leaving the highland principality effectively independent. The Ottoman Turks, taking advantage of the regional turmoil, advanced northward and defeated a combined Christian force at the Battle of Kossovo in 1389, beginning five centuries of Turkish domination of the southern Balkans. The tiny principality of Zeta, called Montenegro, fielded a small, determined band of warriors, who defeated Turkish attempts to conquer their mountain state. The region became a refuge for Serbian nobles fleeing direct Turkish rule after 1459. Isolated from their Slavic kin, the Montenegrins, the only independent Balkan nation, evolved a warrior society, with a culture quite distinct from that of Turkish-dominated Serbia.

In 1515 the last secular prince resigned, and the prince-bishop of Cetinje became the ruler of the small state, his office combining both the secular and religious leadership of the Montenegrins. First an elective office, the episcopate became hereditary in 1697, the hereditary secular and religious titles traditionally passing from uncle to nephew within the Petrovich dynasty established in the sixteenth century. In 1702–3, under Prince-Bishop Danilo I, during the so-called Montenegrin Vespers, the Orthodox Montenegrins massacred many of their countrymen who had adopted the Turks' Islamic religion. Danilo in 1715 requested and received Russian assistance against the Turks, beginning an alliance that would last until World War I. In 1796 the Montenegrins, with Russian help, defeated an invading Turkish army, and in 1799 the Ottoman authorities recognized the independence of the tiny mountain state. The reigning prince-bishop made an annual pilgrimage to St. Petersburg to reaffirm the alliance of his small state with the mighty Russian Empire.

In the 1800s the Montenegrin rulers began to consolidate power among the unruly Montenegrin clans. Feuding tribal chiefs surrendered power to Prince-Bishop Peter II in 1830, beginning the national revival of the decaying state. The state remained a practical theocracy until 1852, when Prince-Bishop Danilo II secularized the state, giving the religious duties to the bishop of Cetinje, retaining for himself secular power as prince of Montenegro. The first Montenegrin constitution was drawn up in 1868. The tiny state, allied to resurgent Serbia, again fought the Turks and at the Congress of Berlin in 1878 was recognized as an independent state with increased territory, including a narrow outlet to the Adriatic Sea. In 1905 Prince Nicholas decreed the end of autocratic government, granted a liberal constitution, and established a parliamentary government. In 1910 Nicholas proclaimed himself king of the Montenegrins. Allied to Serbia, the Montenegrins fought the Turks in the Balkan Wars, 1912–13, and for their assistance shared the conquered territory of Sanjak with Serbia in 1913.

In 1914 the Montenegrins joined the Serbs in their conflict with Austria, the conflict that spread to become World War I. The Austrian occupation of Montenegro in 1915 strengthened the faction that favored the creation of a united South Slav state in the Balkan Peninsula. In 1917 Montenegrin delegates signed the Pact of Corfu, agreeing to merge the small kingdom into a South Slav federation at the end of the war. The opposing political forces were deeply divided between the Greens, including the king and several powerful clans, who supported an independent Montenegrin state, and the Whites, who advocated unification with Serbia. The Whites triumphed following the surrender of the Central Powers in November 1918, and on 2 December 1918, the Pan-Slav nationalists deposed the Petrovich dynasty and joined Montenegro to the new Kingdom of the Serbs, Croats, and Slovenes. The surrender of Montenegrin sovereignty divided the clans, the crisis worsened by the takeover of their cherished autonomous church by the Serbian Orthodox hierarchy in 1920. A rebellion of the Green clans dissatisfied with the status of the former kingdom, little better than that of a Serb province, kept the area in turmoil until their defeat in 1921. The same year King Nicholas, who had done so much to modernize Montenegro, died in exile. Between 1922 and 1926 sporadic revolts erupted among the anti-Serbian Green clans.

In censuses taken during the interwar period the Montenegrins were classified as ethnic Serbs. The mountaineers, with their long warrior tradition, played a significant role in the defense forces of the interwar Kingdom of Yugoslavia. Up to World War II, the Serbs claimed the Montenegrins were only a branch of the Serbian nation. A number of clans remained unreconciled to Serb domination and again rose as Yugoslavia collapsed under German and Italian attack in 1941. The clan leaders on 13 July 1941 declared Montenegro an independent, neutral kingdom under the deposed Petrovich dynasty. Before the clan leaders could mobilize the kingdom, Italian troops occupied the state. The majority of the former Greens joined the royalist partisans fighting the fascists. The royalist partisans also fought against the rival communist partisans led by Josip Broz Tito, which drew many Montenegrin recruits from the so-called White clans.

Montenegro, with the addition of territory on the Dalmatian coast, became a separate republic in Tito's communist Yugoslav federation in 1946, the smallest and poorest of the six republics. Montenegrins were disproportionately represented in the Communist Party of Yugoslavia (CPY) and in the federal government after the war. Although a large number of Montenegrins were expelled from the party for pro-Soviet sympathies after Yugoslavia broke with the Soviet Union in 1948, Montenegrins remained overrepresented in the Yugoslav bureaucracy and military hierarchy, which translated into increased development funds for their small republic. The rapid development of mines, ports, and industries urbanized the traditionally rural Montenegrins. The urban population of the republic grew by 40% between 1948 and 1953.

Montenegrin nationalism, dormant since 1945, reemerged in 1966–67 as part of a campaign to resurrect their separate Orthodox Church. The relative prosperity of the 1970s, based on mining and tourism, gave the Montenegrins a new confidence. In 1980 at Tito's death, nationalism again gained support as the republics of the Yugoslav federation began to take on greater autonomy, but a government crackdown in Montenegro stifled the dissident movement in 1982–84. Fueled by economic and ethnic tensions, street demonstrations broke out in the republic in October 1988, with students and workers united in calling for the ouster of the Montenegrin communist leaders.

The collapse of communism in 1989 again divided the Montenegrin clans. In free elections in December 1990 the ex-communists won, ending dissident clans' efforts to move Montenegro away from Serbian domination. In June 1991 the Yugoslav federation collapsed, and the ex-communists in control of Serbia and Montenegro joined in opposing the breakaway republics and in creating a new

Yugoslav federation of the two states. Montenegrin soldiers joined in the Serbian attack on Croatia.

Montenegrin dissatisfaction with Serb domination grew into a strong nationalist movement; however, in a March 1992 referendum 66% of the voters, including many residents of Serbia, voted to remain in the truncated Yugoslav state. Since 1992 Montenegrin nationalists have regained support against the misguided Serb nationalism that dragged Montenegro into war and the status of an international pariah. Increasingly strident Serb nationalists deny that the Montenegrins are a separate nation and call them Mountain Serbs, which is resented by the Montenegrins. Calls for Serbian annexation of the state by ultranationalist Serbian groups have strengthened Montenegrin nationalists who work for secession from the rump Yugoslav state but have also raised fears of yet another Balkan war in their mountain homeland.

On 15 January 1998 the inauguration of the new Montenegrin president, who opposes Serbian domination, was marked by violent confrontations between his supporters and supporters of the former president, an ally of President Slobodan Milosevic of Serbia. The Montenegrin nationalists also clashed with ethnic Serbians in Podgorica. The clashes, which continued sporadically, raised the specter of the post–World War I civil war between the Greens and Whites in the tiny republic.

In March 1999, North Atlantic Treaty Organization (NATO) forces intervened in the Serbian suppression of the Albanians of the province of Kosovo. While Allied planes bombed Yugoslav military targets in Serbia and Montenegro, the pro-Western Montenegrin government declared the country neutral in the conflict and refused to accept the Serbians' declaration of war and the imposition of martial law. Clashes broke out between the Montenegrin police and Yugoslav military units in the region, particularly after the Montenegrin government refused to turn over young Montenegrin conscripts who refused to report for military duty. By mid-April an estimated 70,000 Albanian refugees had crossed the border into Montenegro, where they were given shelter, but with increased tensions with the Serbian minority in the region and the Yugoslav military, which was accused of extending ethnic cleansing to Albanian villages in Montenegro.

At the end of the Kosovo conflict, as the Albanian refugees returned home, the Montenegrins moved to distance themselves from Serbia while maintaining a looser Yugoslav federation. Although a growing number support a complete break with Yugoslavia and independence for Montenegro, fears of another secessionist conflict holds them back. In August 1999, the Montenegrin government approved a plan to dismantle the Yugoslav federation and to recast Montenegro's relations with Serbia as a loose federation of sovereign states. The increasing tensions with the Serbs, at the turn of the century, brought threats by the Montenegrins to hold a referendum on independence.

SELECTED BIBLIOGRAPHY

Banac, Ivo. *The National Question in Yugoslavia: Origins, History, Politics.* 1984.
Denton, William. *Montenegro: Its People and Their History.* 1977.
Glenny, Misha. *The Fall of Yugoslavia: The Third Balkan War.* 1992.
Magas, Branka. *The Destruction of Yugoslavia.* 1993.
Stevenson, Francis S. *History of Montenegro.* 1971.

MORAVIANS

Moravans; Czecho-Moravians

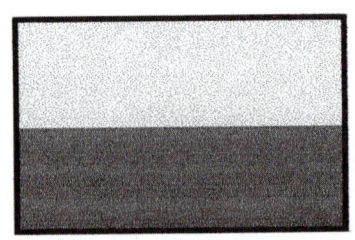

POPULATION: Approximately (2000 e) 1,528,000 Moravians in Europe, with 1,389,000 in the Moravia region of the Czech Republic and large concentrations in Prague and other parts of the republic.

THE MORAVIAN HOMELAND: The Moravian homeland, which includes the small Silesia region, is mostly a high plain characterized by rolling hills crossed by several mountain ranges, particularly the Bohemian-Moravian Highlands and in the north the Sudetic Mountains, which extend into Moravia from Bohemia to the west. In the east, the Little and White Carpathians separate Moravia from Slovakia. Central Moravia is a large valley drained by the Danube and the Morava Rivers and their tributaries.

Moravia is a historic region of central Europe that formed a separate crownland under the rule of the Austrians* and later made a region of Czechoslovakia and the Czech Republic. The historic region is divided into two administrative regions, North Moravia and South Moravia. *Region of Moravia (Kraje Morava)*: 10,066 sq.mi.–26,070 sq.km. (2000 e) 3,847,000—Czechs* 44%, Moravians (including Silesians) 37%, Slovaks* 5%, Poles* 1%, Germans* and Austrians 1%, Roms* (Gypsies), Ukrainians.* The Moravian capital and major cultural center is Brno, (2000 e) 391,000, which was the capital of the Austrian crownland of Moravia prior to World War I. The cultural center of the Silesians is the city of Opava, (2000 e) 64,000.

FLAG: The Moravian national flag, the unofficial flag of the Moravian regions of the Czech Republic, is a horizontal bicolor of yellow over red.

PEOPLE: The Moravians are a Western Slav people closely related to the neighboring Czechs. Culturally, the Moravians have incorporated more Austrian influences than the Czechs and have maintained their distinct traditions and dialect. While the Czechs are famous for their beer, the Moravians are traditionally vintners, and wine is the national drink. About 65% of the Moravians dwell in urban areas. In recent government censuses and official figures the Moravians are usually counted as ethnic Czechs. The Silesians, numbering about 45,000 in northern Moravia, are closely identified with their Moravian neighbors but see themselves as a separate people traditionally more religious than the Moravians or Czechs. The majority of the Moravians are Roman Catholic, with a small Protestant minority.

The Moravians and Silesians speak dialects of Czech called Czecho-Moravian, which has been influenced by German and Polish. The Moravian dialect shows only slight phonetic and syntactic differences. Moravian has a somewhat more archaic sound system. The Silesian dialect is comprehensible to both Poles and Moravians, and some Silesian dialects are transitional to both. Standard Czech, based on the dialect spoken in Prague, is quite distinct but is spoken by all but a few in the region.

NATION: The earliest known inhabitants of the region, the Celtic Boii and Cotini tribes, were displaced by Germanic tribes in the first century B.C. Forming part of the area called Germania by the Romans, Moravia formed a frontier district lying north of the Roman provinces. Following the decline of Roman power, the region was overrun by peoples moving into the former Roman lands, the Huns and the Vandals. In the fifth century, Slavic tribes, moving from the east, settled the region. By the end of the sixth century the Slavs had taken control of Moravia. Subjugated by the Avars,* the Slavs broke free under the leadership of Samo in the seventh century and established the first Western Slav state, which disintegrated with his death around the year A.D. 660.

The Moravians, first mentioned in historical annals written in 822, gradually united and by the ninth century controlled Bohemia, Moravia, Silesia, southern Poland, and northern Hungary. The Moravian Empire, called Greater Moravia, meaning distant Moravia, was centered on Staré Mesto, which lies east of present Brno. The Moravian ruler Duke Rotislav appealed to the pope for teachers, and German missionaries, Cyril and Methodius, were sent to the region in 863. The Moravians adopted Christianity and placed themselves under the authority of the Roman Catholic Church. Germans and Jews, merchants and adventurers, settled in the cities, forming a powerful commercial class. Greater Moravia reached its peak in the late ninth century but later declined under attacks from Hungarians* and Poles. In 902 the Moravians defeated the Magyars (Hungarians), but by 908 the empire had been vanquished by the Magyars and disappeared from history. In 955 Emperor Otto I defeated the Hungarians, and Moravia became a march of the Holy Roman Empire.

The Czechs, to the west in Bohemia, expanded their territories to include Moravia in 1029. Bohemia became a hereditary kingdom within the Holy Roman Empire in the thirteenth century, while Moravia, although under Czech rule, retained its separate diet, its parliament, and administration. At the height of its power, the Bohemian kingdom included traditionally Austrian and Hungarian territories, but defeat by Rudolph of Hapsburg in 1278 brought Moravia under Hapsburg rule.

With the election of the Austrian Ferdinand as king of Bohemia in 1526, Bohemia and Moravia became integral parts of the Hapsburg Empire. The Moravian towns and cities, from the thirteenth century, underwent thorough Germanization. By the sixteenth century nearly the entire upper and middle classes in Moravia were German by culture and language. The German-speaking cities were surrounded by rural countryside that remained Slavic in language and culture.

The Reformation and Renaissance saw a revival of religious writing and the development of liberal ideals and thinking. The Moravian Church is one of the very few Protestant churches that antedate the Reformation. It had been in existence for sixty years when Martin Luther posted his famous thesis in 1517. Publishing in the Czech language, begun with the Bible, was followed by works on history, science, and medicine. Religious strife between Protestant and Catholic nobles foreshadowed the later wars of religion. During the Hussite Wars in the fifteenth century the Moravian homeland was again separated from the Czech lands.

From 1608 to 1611, when Bohemia was ruled by Emperor Rudolph II, Moravia was ruled by his brother, Matthias. The disposition of the Hapsburg ruler by Czech and Moravian nobles in 1618 inaugurated the Thirty Years' War, which devastated the region. The Czechs and Moravians lost their remaining independence with the defeat of the Protestant forces at the Battle of White Mountain in 1620. The war, fought from 1618 to 1648, bought the wholesale destruction of literary and artistic works followed by the repression of Moravian national life.

By the eighteenth century the Czech lands were completely incorporated in the Austrian Empire. Under Empress Maria Theresa and Emperor Joseph II, the Czechs and Moravians were subjected to a program of intense Germanization. The majority of the Czech and Moravian cultural leaders worked abroad, and their native language was gradually reduced to little more than a peasant dialect. The oppression of the Czech culture and language in Bohemia and Moravia continued into the nineteenth century, but at the same time a national revival took hold, with new interest in their Slavic traditions, language, and history. Brno became the center of the Moravian cultural revival, which developed as an anti-Austrian mass movement in the region and as a rejection of the Germanization of the region that was the official policy of the Hapsburg authorities.

The Czechs and Moravians led the movement for the equal rights of the Slavs of the Austrian Empire. During the Revolution of 1848, the Czechs convened a congress of Slavic leaders in Prague, but by early 1849 absolute Austrian domination had been restored. In 1849 Moravia was separated from Bohemia and was raised to the status of a separate Austrian crownland.

The establishment of the Dual Monarchy of Austria and Hungary in 1867, which gave the Hungarians rights within the empire equal to those of the Austrians, gravely disappointed the Slavs of Bohemia and Moravia. In spite of some concessions to the Slavs in 1879, when Czech and Moravian delegates entered the parliament at Vienna, the Slavs of the empire remained unsatisfied that a third Slav kingdom had not been created within the dual empire.

Supported by activist immigrants in the United States, support for the autonomy of the Slav provinces within the Austro-Hungarian Empire grew in the first years of the twentieth century. A Czech National Council, including Moravian groups, was formed by exiles in the United States and began to coordinate with exile Slovaks. The Czech leader Thomas Masaryk pressed for the independence of Bohemia and Moravia from the empire after World War I began in 1914.

The defeat of Austro-Hungary in October 1918 opened the way for independence. On 28 October 1918 nationalist leaders declared Bohemia and Moravia independent of Austria. The union of Bohemia, Moravia, and Slovakia was officially proclaimed on 14 November 1918. The Czechs, the dominant national group in the newly independent Czechoslovakia, quickly took control of most ministries and set the tone of government. The constitution of 1920, although liberal and democratic, set up a highly centralized state and failed to address the increasingly serious question of the national minorities. The German upper and middle classes continued to dominate Moravia. Moravian resentment of Czech hegemony and the antireligious stance of the Prague government grew as Europe lurched from crisis to crisis during the 1920s and 1930s. In 1927 Moravia, along with the small section of Silesia that belonged to Czechoslovakia, was constituted as the separate province of Moravia and Silesia.

While Czech cultural life flourished, Czech political life between the wars was marked by minority demands for autonomy, particularly the Slovaks and the Sudeten Germans, including those in northern and southern Moravia, who were supported by Nazi Germany after 1933. The German minority continued to play a large part in the affair of Moravia between the wars.

Demands for union with Germany by the Sudeten Germans led to a serious crisis between Prague and Berlin in 1938. In September 1938 Czechoslovakia, as part of the Munich Agreement between the European powers, was forced to cede the Sudetenland, the German majority areas, to Nazi Germany. The agreement, meant to resolve the German–Czech crisis and ensure lasting peace in Europe, prolonged the crisis. On 14 March 1939 the autonomous Slovak state declared its independence, and the following day Nazi Germany annexed Bohemia and Moravia as a German protectorate.

Soviet troops in April 1944 overran the region from the east, while American and Allied troops moved into the Czech lands in the west. In March 1945 Edward Benes, who was elected president of Czechoslovakia in 1935, agreed to form a National Front government with Klement Gottwald, leader of the Communist Party of Czechoslovakia (CPCz). On 5 May 1945 the Czechs rebelled against the German occupiers. Accompanied by members of the National Front coalition government, the Allies finally took control of Prague on 12 May

1945. The fall of Prague marked the end of Allied military operations in Europe. At the Potsdam Conference of 1945 the expulsion of some three million ethnic Germans from Bohemia and Moravia was approved.

The Communist Party emerged as the strongest political party in the country in the elections of 1946. In February 1948 the communists seized the Czechoslovak government. The new communist administration began a campaign of repression of noncommunists. The powers held by the provinces were centralized in Prague, and most levels of government were staffed with loyalists. In 1949 the province of Moravia and Silesia was replaced by four new regions. In 1960 a new constitution was adopted, modeled on that of the Soviet Union, which established a unitary state including Moravia, which was split into two new regions. During the 1960s Slovak demands of communal rights triggered a parallel movement in Moravia.

In January 1968 the Slovak Alexander Dubcek became first secretary of the Czechoslovak Communist Party and introduced a program of liberal reforms, the so-called Prague Spring. The reforms included freedom of the press as well as increased contact with noncommunist countries. While the Czechs tended to emphasize democratic reform, the Slovaks and the Moravians emphasized national advances. Leaders of the Soviet Union and other East European nations feared Dubcek's program would weaken communist control in Czechoslovakia.

Under the terms of the Warsaw Pact, troops from Soviet Union, Bulgaria, East Germany, and Hungary, as well as Poland, invaded Czechoslovakia on 20 August 1968. One-third of the membership of the Communist party were expelled. Over 40,000 people fled the invasion and the repression that followed. The Red Army remained when the other national armies withdrew later the same year. On 1 January 1969 a communist-dominated federal system was introduced, but demands for a separate Moravian state were ignored.

The communist government of Czechoslovakia offered an amnesty to those who had fled in 1968, and many Moravian intellectuals returned to their homeland, but the government's repressive policies remained unchanged. During the 1980s economic stagnation fed popular unrest, but the unrest was countered by increasingly repressive government measures.

The new spirit of openness emanating from the Soviet Union was met in Czechoslovakia by a wave of arrests in 1988 and 1989. Pro-democratic groups organized in Brno, Ostrava, and other Moravian cities were forcibly closed. The Czechoslovak government initially aligned itself with the hard-line communist governments in opposition to political and economic reform. In November 1989 large demonstrations broke out across the country, which culminated in the resignation of the government in December. The so-called Velvet Revolution overthrew the communist government virtually without bloodshed. In 1989 and 1990 mass demonstrations were held in Brno and other Moravian cities with crowds, waving the red and yellow Moravian flag, demanding autonomy for their ancient homeland.

Multiparty elections for a new national assembly in June 1990 were won by pro-democratic parties. In Moravia, following the first taste of freedom, nationalism became an important issue. Mass demonstrations in favor of Moravian autonomy swept Brno and other cities but waned as the country moved toward the division of its Czech and Slovak halves. On 1 January 1993 Czechoslovakia split into the Czech Republic and Slovakia, with Moravia making up one of the two parts of the new Czech Republic, Bohemia and Moravia. The Czech lands, more advanced economically than Slovakia, looked to the West for expertise and aid. The Czech economy, freed of the less prosperous Slovak economy, became one of the strongest in the former communist bloc and was dubbed the Czech Miracle. Only in mid-1997 did the economy begin to show signs of weakening, leading to renewed Moravian demands for economic and political autonomy.

The Czech government, dominated by reformers and former dissidents, moved the Czech Republic into line to join the Northern Atlantic Treaty Organization (NATO) and the European Union. After decades of communist repression, the Czechs and Moravians see their future security linked to a network of alliances with the most powerful states in the West. The Czech Republic has been invited to join NATO and the continental federation, the European Union (EU).

To the Moravians, membership in the European Union would give them a greater voice in their own affairs, as European regions have increasingly demanded greater powers. Although the Moravians have rejected separatism, nationalism, the idea that their unique culture and dialect should be preserved and nurtured, has won widespread support.

SELECTED BIBLIOGRAPHY

Hochman, Jiri. *Historical Dictionary of the Czech Republic.* 1997.
Krejci, Oskar. *History of Elections in Bohemia and Moravia.* 1995.
Rees, H. Louis. *The Czechs during World War I: The Path to Independence.* 1992.
Turk, Irene Toganzzini, and N. C. Tognazzini. *The Czech Book.* 1990.
Wiskeman, Elizabeth. *Czechs and Germans: A Study of the Struggles in the Historic Provinces of Bohemia and Moravia.* 1983.

MORDVINS

Mordvinians; Mordovians; Mordva;
Erzya; Moksha

POPULATION: Approximately (2000 e) 1,848,000 Mordvins in Europe, concentrated in the Mordvinia Republic in the Volga Basin of Russia. Other large Mordvin communities live in the Penza, Orenburg, Nizhniy Novgorod, Kuybyshev, Ulyanovsk, and Saratov Oblasts and the republics of Bashkortostan, Tatarstan, and Chuvashia. An estimated 120,000 Mordvins live in Russian Siberia and the Central Asian repubics.

THE MORDVIN HOMELAND: The Mordvin homeland occupies the Volga uplands, the Oka-Don lowlands, and the wooded Mordvin Steppe in the Volga River basin of European Russia. The region is mostly steppe land in the Oka-Don Plain in the northwestern districts and the highland area of the Volga Upland in the southwest. Most of the region is densely forested steppe, with forests covering about one-quarter of the homeland, making lumbering the main industry. Crossed by the Moksha River, part of the Mordvin homeland is included in the so-called Black Earth region of central Russia and produces abundant crops of rye, wheat, millet, oats, corn, tobacco, and livestock.

Mordvinia, the Mordvin homeland, traditionally stretches across a broad territory from Nizhny Novgorod and Razan in the west to the Ural Mountains in the east. The largest concentration of the Mordvin population, the Mordvin heartland, is included in the Republic of Mordvinia, which is a member state of the Russian Federation. The republic has less than one-third of the total Mordvin national population in Russia. *Republic of Mordvinia (Respublika Mordva)*: 10,116 sq.mi.–26,207 sq.km. (2000 e) 961,000—Russians* 52%, Mordvins 43%, Tatars* 3%, Chavash* 1%. The Mordvin capital and major cultural center is Saransk, (2000 e) 356,000, founded as a Russian fort in 1641.

FLAG: The Mordvin national flag, the official flag of the republic, is a horizontal tricolor of red, white, and blue, the white twice the width of the other colors and bearing a centered Mordvin cross.

PEOPLE: The Mordvins are a Finno-Ugric people, the descendants of the pre-Slav population of the Volga River basin. They are scattered in clusters among the Russian-speaking population of the southern Volga region. Often tall and Nordic, the Mordvins, until the disintegration of the Soviet Union, had been assmilating into Russian culture. Nationalists claim a Mordvin national population of over 2 million in Russia. The majority of Mordvin believers belong to the Russian Orthodox Church. Although Christianity is common in the region, ancient forms of nature worship are still practiced. The chief divinity of the non-Christian Mordvin faith is Shkay, a sun god. The moon, trees, water, frost, and thunder are also deified. Altars, on which animals are sacrificed, are sometimes built in homes.

There are five main groups of Mordvins, the two largest of which are the Moksha and Erzya. The Moksha live particularly in the western districts of the Morvinian Republic and in the Penza and Orenburg Oblasts and in Tatarstan. The Ezyra live in the northern districts of Mordvinia, in Tatarstan and Baskhortostan, and in several neighboring regions. The Tengushev Mordvins live in southern Mordvinia and constitute a transitional group between the Erzya and the Moksha. The Teryukhan are Mordvins living near the city of Nizhniy Novgorod who have adopted Russian as their first language, although they remain Mordvin in culture. The fifth group of Mordvins are the Karatai, who live in Tatarstan and have adopted Tatar as their first language. Other groups that have been discovering their Mordvin identity since 1991, the Tengushen, who are ethnically Erzya but speak Moksha, Meshcheryaks, who speak Russian and live in Russian majority regions, and Mishars, ethnic Mordvins who adopted the Tatar language and converted to Sunni Islam.

The Mordvin language is actually two distinct languages, Erzya, spoken by the eastern Mordvins, and Moksha, spoken primarily in the west and north. The two languages make up the Mordvinic branch of the Finno-Ugric languages. The languages, although similar, are mutually unintelligible, and Russian is often used as a means of intergroup communication. Only about 70% of the Mordvins consider one of the Mordvin languages as their first language, with about 25% speaking Russian as their mother tongue. Both languages have literary status, with literary Erzya based on the dialect of the town of Kozlovka in the Atyashevo district of Mordvinia. The languages are written in the Cyrillic alphabet.

NATION: The Gothic historian Jordanes in the sixth century mentioned the Mordvins as tillers and herdsmen living in villages between the Oka and Volga Rivers. Many Mordvin groups had economic and political ties to the early Slavs. An early Mordvin state, between the Volga, Don, and Sura Rivers, became a dependency of the Bulgar Chavash state in the Volga Basin in the late eighth century.

Ethnologists believe that between the seventh and twelfth centuries, as agriculture took hold among the Mordvins, their patriarchal and clan-based social system gave way to a more village-oriented political and social system. The city of Nizhniy Novgorod was the Mordvin capital prior to its conquest by troops from three Russian principalities, Suzdal, Ryazan, and Murom, in 1172. The Russian princes of Ryazan and Nizhni Novgorod subjugated the remaining Mordvin tribes in the early thirteenth century.

In 1236 the Mordvin lands fell to the invading Mongols and Tatars of the Golden Horde, and the expanding Muscovite state conquered the western Mordvin territories between 1392 and 1521. Many Mordvins joined their Russian neighbors in resistance to Mongol and Tatar rule. The eastern Mordvin tribes came under the rule of the Tatar successor state, the Khanate of Kazan, which fell to Russian rule in 1552. The Mordvins, whose traditional religion revolved around ancestor worship, were forcibly converted to Orthodox Christianity between the sixteenth and eighteenth centuries. The upper levels of Mordvin society quickly assimilated into the Russian culture, and education was largely in Russian. Traditional Mordvin culture was preserved among the rural population in their village communes.

During the late sixteenth and seventeenth centuries, the Russians built a strong line of military fortifications and settlements in the southeastern districts of Mordvinia to provide a defensive line against nomadic tribes. At the same time, thousands of ethnic Russians colonized the region, reducing the Mordvins to the status of a conquered people. In the early seventeenth century the Mordvins joined the neighboring Chavash and Maris* in a widespread revolt against Russian rule. The Russians finally crushed the rebellion in 1613, and thousands of Mordvins fled across the Urals to Siberia to escape reprisals and forced conversion to Christianity. Others moved east of the Sura and Volga Rivers, where Russian authority was weaker. The Mordvins, occupying a large area of fertile lands west of the Volga River, were gradually reduced to servitude on large Russian estates. The harsh Slav rule and serfdom provoked sporadic Mordvin rebellions. In 1641, to better control the tribes, the Russians constructed Saransk as a fort in the center of Mordvin territory. The Mordvins again rebelled in 1670, 1743–45, and 1773–75, but Russian rule only grew harsher with each uprising.

Russian rule, although harsh and oppressive, stimulated the growth of education and the creation of a small, educated class. The earliest Mordvin writing, using the Roman alphabet, dates from the late seventeenth century.

The Mordvin economy remained overwhelmingly agricultural well into the twentieth century. Russian colonization, accelerating with the freeing of the serfs in 1861, pushed the Mordvins into scattered ethnic pockets surrounded by Slavs. Mordvin assimilation into Russian culture accelerated even as nationalism began to affect the small, educated elite, particularly following the improvement of communications brought about by the completion of the Moscow-Kazan Railroad across their homeland in the 1890s. During the revolutionary disturbances in 1905 the Mordvins rose, attacking Russian estates and settlements and skirmishing with Russian police and troops. The rebels retreated into the thick forests and continued to harass the authorities until 1907.

Mordvin nationalism grew rapidly after the outbreak of war in 1914, mainly among disgruntled soldiers. A coalition of nationalists and moderate Russian political parties took power in the region as civil government collapsed following the overthrow of the tsarist government in February 1917. While the region was under the influence of more moderate Mensheviks and Social Revolutionaries, a Mordvin congress sent delegates to a meeting of the region's non-Russian nations in Kazan to decide on the region's future. The majority of the Mordvins favored inclusion in a federation of states in the Volga-Ural region or in a smaller federation with the Christian nations, the Mordvins, Maris, and Chuvash. The Mordvin debate on the future of their homeland within a democratic Russia ended with the Bolshevik coup in October 1917. In November, before the Mordvins could organize effectively, Bolshevik forces took control of the region. Mordvin resistance ended after several weeks of fighting, and by December 1917 the Soviets had firmly established their control.

The Soviet authorities, in an effort to win Mordvin support, distributed the lands of the great Russian estates to individual farmers in 1918, just before the Russian civil war spilled into the region. Devastated by war, famine, and disease, over one-third of the Mordvin population of 1914 had perished by 1921. The Soviets, emerging victorious from the civil war, created a theoretically autonomous territory for the Mordvins in 1921, but the forced collectivization of the lands distributed to the Mordvins in 1918 sparked renewed disturbances and violence in the region. In 1925 the authorities established autonomous districts and village councils for the Mordvins outside the autonomous territory. In 1928 the Mordvin national area was created with Saransk as its capital.

The Mordvins, despite the oppressive Soviet rule, made rapid advances in education and culture. The Soviets created a literary language using the Cyrillic alphabet for the Erzya dialect in 1922 and for the Moksha dialect in 1926. There was some resistance to collectivization on the part of the Mordvin kulaks, free farmers, in the late 1920s, but they were mostly liquidated or deported.

The arbitrary borders of the Mordvin autonomous republic, created in 1934, left a majority of the Mordvin population outside the boundaries in the neighboring Russian provinces. The majority, denied even the cultural autonomy allowed those within the autonomous republic, became the target of Soviet assimilation efforts. During World War II, when the Soviet government relocated most Russian industry away from the front, the Mordvin lands underwent dramatic population and demographic changes. By 1970 only 78% of the total Mordvin population considered Mordvin their first language, and the number claiming Mordvin nationality continued to decline in the 1970s and 1980s.

The liberalization of Soviet society in the late 1980s started a slow reversal of decades of Mordvin assimilation. The collapse of communism, followed by the disintegration of the Soviet Union in 1991, stimulated a Mordvin national and cultural revival. Nationalist organizations, organized among the scattered

Mordvin population, began to press for the redrawing of the republic's borders to incorporate the Mordvin-populated districts of the neighboring provinces of Nizhniy Novgorod, Simbirsk, and Penza.

In April 1993 the pro-reform president of the republic, in office since 1991, was toppled by the conservative, communist-dominated republican parliament in what amounted to a coup. The reformers, including the growing national movement, now constitute the major challenge to the neocommunist republican government. Until the coup, supporters of full independence, within a Volga federation of states, made up only a small minority in the national movement. Since 1993 the nationalist majority's support for economic and political autonomy in Russia has come increasingly under pressure from the so far small, but growing, militant wing of the movement, which demands reunification of the Mordvin lands in a sovereign Mordvin state.

SELECTED BIBLIOGRAPHY
Colton, Timothy J. *Growing Pains: Russian Democracy and the Election of 1993.* 1998.
Din, Shams. *Perestroika and the Nationalities Quest in the Soviet Union.* 1991.
Kirkow, Peter. *Russia's Provinces: Authoritarian Transformation versus Local Autonomy.* 1998.
Kozlov, Viktor. *The Peoples of the Soviet Union.* 1988.
Milner-Gulland, R. R., ed. *Cultural Atlas of Russia and the Former Soviet Union.* 1998.

NOGAIS

Nogays; Nogai Tatars

POPULATION: Approximately (2000 e) 128,000 Nogais in Europe, 76,000 in the North Caucasus region of Russia, and 50,000 in Bulgaria, Romania, Ukraine, and Turkey.

THE NOGAI HOMELAND: The Nogai homeland lies in the vast sandy, semi-arid Nogai Steppe west of the Caspian Sea between the Terek and Kuma Rivers in the Nogai, Babayurt, Tarum, and Kizlar districts of the Republic of Dagestan, the Achikulak and Neftekumsky districts of Stavropol Krai, and the Shelovsk district of the Chechen Republic. Most of the region is high, flat pasturelands rising from the coastal plain on the Caspian Sea, with part of the steppe covered with desertlike vegetation. The Nogais are traditionally cattle and sheep herders, although farming has become more widespread in recent decades. One Nogai community lives farther west, in the Sholkovsky district of Karachay-Cherkessia.

The region inhabited by the Nogais has no official status but remains divided between several administrative regions. Nogai nationalists seek a separate, sovereign homeland in the region, but their aspirations have not been recognized by the government of the Russian Federation. The Nogai capital and major cultural center is Kizlyar, (2000 e) 47,000, the center of the Kara Nogais. The other important Nogai centers are Babayurt, (2000 e) 23,000, in central Dagestan, and the town of Terekin-Mekteb in the northern Nogai Steppe.

FLAG: The Nogai national flag, the flag of the Nogai National Movement, is a pale blue field bearing a centered green, winged dog or wolf, outlined in yellow.

PEOPLE: The Nogais are a Turkic people related to the Kumyks* and are of

Central Asian origin, being descended from the peoples of the Golden Horde. Traditionally, the Nogais are divided into three hordes that cross tribal and clan lines, the White Nogais in the west, the Central Nogais in the center, and the Kara or Black Nogais in the east. They are further divided into four major tribes, Bujak, Edisan, Jambulak, and Edishkul, and five minor tribes, Mansur, Kypchak, Karamurza, Tokhtam, and Novruz. Another group of Nogais lives in the Astrakhan region and is divided into four clan groups, Yurt, Kundrovets, Karagash, and Utar-Alabugaty. Nogai identification with their tribe is often more powerful than their identity as Nogais, although the recent growth of nationalism is changing their attitudes. The Nogai culture has been influenced by contacts with neighboring Turkic and Caucasian peoples and with the Russians.* The Nogais mostly adhere to the Hanafi school of Sunni Islam.

The Nogai language belongs to the Kipchak or Northwestern group of the Turkic languages and is one of the least studied of the Turkic languages. The language is divided into three major dialects, Black Nogai, Achikuluk or Central Nogai, and the Aknogai (White Nogai) dialect spoken in the Kuban region. The dialectical differences are the result of long geographical separation. Until 1957 the teaching of Nogai was widespread in the Nogai homeland, but now teaching is mostly restricted to the northern region of Dagestan. Secondary education in the Nogai language is available only in the Nogai district of Dagestan, which has a Nogai majority.

NATION: The Nogais are thought to have originated in the steppe lands of Central Asia, with later mixing with the peoples of the Kipchak tribal confederacies. They were conquered by the expanding Mongol-Tatar Empire, the Golden Horde, probably in the early thirteenth century, and moved west with the other subject peoples. Traditionally, the Nogais claim descent from one man, Nogai or Nogay, grandson of Genghis Khan, who controlled the Nogai Horde in the late thirteenth century. He was killed either in 1294 or 1300, and the horde disintegrated, but the sense of Nogai ethnic identity remained, and his name remained to denote the vagrant nomadic peoples of the steppe lands by the Sea of Azov. In early Russian manuscripts the Nogais were referred to as the North Caucasian Tatars.

The nomadic tribes roamed the vast steppes between the Danube River and the Caspian Sea until the sixteenth century, when Tsar Ivan IV of Russia conquered Astrakhan and Kazan, bringing most of the Nogai territories under Russian rule. The Nogai Horde split into two groups; one, known as the Great Horde in the lower Volga region, came under nominal Russian domination in 1557; and the other, the Little Horde, occupied the right bank of the Kuban River, the area east of the Sea of Azov, and southern Ukraine. The hordes were known as fierce opponents to Russian expansion.

The two Nogai hordes reunited in the seventeenth century after the Little Horde was driven south by an invasion of warlike Kalmyks* in 1634. Other clans of the Great Horde, to escape the Kalmyks, moved north into the lower Volga region around Astrakhan. The united Nogais then came under the political control of the Crimean Tatars.* In the seventeenth century, some of the Nogai chiefs entered into an alliance with Moscow and sometimes fought as Russian allies against the Kabards,* Kalmyks, and the nations of Dagestan. They took part in the expeditions of Peter I in the 1600s and 1700s.

In 1723 the Russians took formal control of the Nogai homeland in the North Caucasus, their rule formally recognized by the Ottoman Turks in 1724. The Nogais managed to exercise a degree of autonomy over the next century, but in 1859, when the Russians finally pacified the mountainous areas to the south, all the peoples of the region were brought under closer Russian authority. During the 1860s, when significant Russian expansion into their territory began, there was a large-scale emigration of Nogais to Turkey, the Crimea, and Romania.

The numerous Nogai tribes remained nomadic but were united by shared political and economic interests. In the early nineteenth century the majority of the tribes settled the Nogai Steppe region of North Caucasia. There they began to lose their former tribal structures and to mix across tribal and clan lines. Throughout their history, horse breeding remained the primary activity. Horses were transport, battles were fought by mounted cavalry, horse milk was the main drink, and horsemeat was the main staple. From the seventeenth century horses were sold annually to agents of the Russian government. The Kara Nogais in the east continued as nomads, but the Kuban or White Nogais to the west left their nomadic life to settle along the Greater and Smaller Zelenchuk Rivers and Lower Uruk and Laba Rivers beginning in the late eighteenth century. There they took up farming, although horse breeding also remained important.

Openly supportive of the Muslim Turks when war began in 1914, the Nogais celebrated the news that revolution had broken out in Russia in February 1917. Effectively independent as civil administration collapsed, a Muslim conference elected Mullah Gotinsky as their political and religious leader in May 1917. The Bolshevik takeover of the Russian government in October 1917 created chaos in the region as local Bolsheviks attempted to take power. The Muslim peoples joined with the Terek Cossacks* to declare an independent Terek-Dagestan republic on 20 October 1917, but the new state, undermined by ethnic, religious, and territorial disputes, collapsed in December 1917.

The Muslim peoples of Dagestan formed a separate republic in March 1918 and attempted a cooperative defense as the Russian civil war spread south. The anti-Bolshevik forces, the Whites, took control of the region in January 1919, but forced conscription of Muslims incited strong resistance. Promised autonomy, the Nogais mostly went over to the Reds. The last of the Whites withdrew in January 1920. The regional leaders, disappointed at their treatment by the Soviet authorities, demanded the promised regional autonomy. Rebuffed by the Soviets, the Muslim peoples rebelled and held out until finally subdued in May 1921, at a cost of over 5,000 Soviet casualties.

A standardized Nogai language was created, based on the Kara dialect, on the grounds that it was the language of the working masses. The Nogai written language, based on the Arabic alphabet, was changed in 1928 to the Latin alphabet, and the first spelling book was published in 1929. Schoolbooks, several dictionaries, and an orthographic manual followed. In 1936 in an effort to further standardize the language, a new literary language was developed, but in 1938 the Cyrillic alphabet was introduced as a means of introducing the Russian language.

The Nogai regions of Kizlar, Tarumovsky, and Nogaisky were added to Dagestan in 1922, while other Nogai districts were added to neighboring regions. In spite of being administratively divided, the Nogai clan and tribal system ignored administrative boundaries, and many government policies, such as education, were extended to all the Nogai districts. In 1938 all the land north of the Terek River was transferred to Astrakhan Oblast, which included a large Nogai community. Between 1931 and 1941 the Narimanovsk district comprised the Tatar-Nogai National Territory, but all administrative autonomy was ended with the dissolution of the territory.

Until 1957 the Nogai language was taught everywhere in the Nogai Steppe region for the first five years of schooling, but the administrative changes put in place in that year divided the Nogais into three administrative regions, which implemented different educational policies. The Nogai territory west of the Kizlar district was transferred to Chechenia. In Stavropol Territory and Chechenia, Nogai-language teaching was ended, with Nogai-language schools continuing only in the northern districts of Dagestan.

After World War II, several waves of immigration swept over the Nogai territories. In the first, in the 1960s, Caucasians were moved to the lowland steppes from their mountain regions by the Soviet authorities. Massive resettlement of peoples occurred again in the 1970s and 1980s. Relations between the Nogais and the new settlers have raised ethnic tensions in the region. The relations between the Nogais and the newly settled Dargins* are especially tense as the Dargins have also engaged in horse breeding in competition with the Nogais.

No attention was paid to modernizing the Nogai region. Roads were primitive, and communications almost nonexistent. In many villages water supplies were deficient. The result of underdevelopment and an influx of non-Nogai migrants was that many Nogais began to leave their historic districts to move to cities, where they joined Nogai organizations. By 1970 only 20% of their historic territory was in use by Nogais. The Astrakhan and Crimean Nogais were being assimilated.

The threat to their homeland in the 1970s began a movement for self-determination. The movement strengthened in the late 1980s, particularly following the relaxation of Soviet rule after 1987. In the 1989 census thousands of ethnic Nogais, formerly counted as other ethnic groups, registered as members of the Nogai nationality. Two newspapers in the Nogai language were begun, but due to poor road conditions and poorly managed communications their distribution is not wide. The first fledgling Nogai political groups were dismissed as extremists, but the movement toward autonomy, particularly calling for the autonomy they enjoyed before 1957, included petitions to the authorities in Moscow.

The Nogai national movement, Birlik or Unity, existed since 1957 as a cultural organization, but was transformed into a political movement in December 1989, when it came out in favor of an autonomous Nogai republic to include parts of Dagestan, Stavropol, and Chechenia. The goal of Birlik has been to undo the division of their historic homeland among three different administrative entities in which the Nogais form small minorities.

In the 1990s the Nogais have mobilized to save their small nation from extinction. Administratively divided and with education in their language limited, they were nearly assimilated in the 1970s, but a reversal of that trend and the reculturation of the Nogais in the years since the disintegration of the Soviet Union have revived the language and culture and brought the Nogais back from the edge of extinction.

SELECTED BIBLIOGRAPHY
Beddeley, John F. *Russian Conquest of the Caucasus.* 1997.
Gleason, Gregory. *Federalism and Nationalism: The Struggle for Republican Rights in the USSR.* 1990.
Warhola, James W. *Politicized Ethnicity in the Russian Federation.* 1996.
Wixman, Ronald. *The Peoples of the USSR: An Ethnographic Handbook.* 1984.
Wurm, Stefan. *Turkic Peoples of the USSR.* 1954.

NORMANS

Normands; Normandians

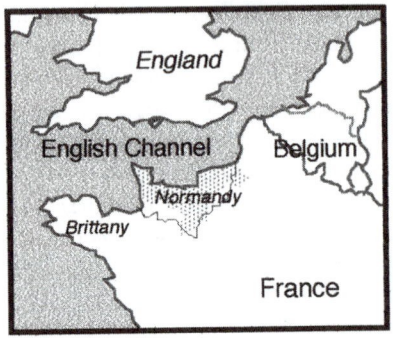

POPULATION: Approximately (2000 e) 4,031,000 Normans in Europe, mostly concentrated in the Normandy Region of France, but with large communities in Paris and other large French cities. Outside Europe there are large Norman populations in Canada and the United States.

THE NORMAN HOMELAND: The Norman homeland lies in northwestern France, a region of coastal plains rising to the hills of Normandy in the southeast and including the Cotentin Peninsula and the Norman coast on the English Channel, locally called the Norman Channel. The region is well watered and is traversed by the Seine, Orne, and Eure Rivers. Most of Normandy is flat farmland, forests, and gentle hills, including the western spur of the Massif Armoricain. Normandy is an agricultural region known for its dairy industry. The coast has a number of excellent harbors, particularly Le Harve and Cherbourg.

The historical region of Normandy has no official status but forms two planning regions of the French republic, Basse-Normandie and Haute-Normandie. *Region of Normandy (Normandie)*: 11,521 sq.mi.–29,840 sq.km. (2000 e) 3,157,000—Normans 91%, other French* 8%, English* 1%. The Norman capital and major cultural center is Rouen, (2000 e) 98,000 (metropolitan area 443,000) the major city of the region since the tenth century.

FLAGs: The Norman national flag, the flag of the national movement, is a red field bearing a red Scandinavian cross, outlined in yellow. The flag of the regionalist movement of Normandy is a red field bearing two yellow lions, called Norman Lions, the same lions featured on many of the personal flags of the British royal family and on flags used in the Channel Islands.

PEOPLE: The Normans are a French-speaking nation, the descendants of

Germanic Franks and later Norse Vikings. The Normans, true to their Scandinavian heritage, are generally taller, fairer, and more often light-eyed than the other French peoples. The largely rural Normans, in spite of the urbanization of the 1960s and 1970s, have been plagued by rural depopulation since World War II. Although the majority of the Normans are believers, with a large Roman Catholic majority and a Protestant minority, they tend to be less intensely religious and more skeptical than is usual in France.

The Normans have retained a distinctive culture and dialect, which predates modern French and displays many Norse and English words and forms. They are bilingual in the standard French of Paris, but the language of daily life remains the Norman dialect, which is spoken is several subdialects that correspond to the historic districts of Normandy. The Norman dialect still retains many words of Scandinavian origin, although in greatly changed form. The largest class of words inherited from their Viking ancestors is that of proper names of persons and places. The Norman dialect played a significant role both in French literature and in the development of Middle English and English literature.

NATION: The coastal region facing Britannia across the narrow channel formed part of Roman Gaul for centuries but suffered economically and politically following the Roman withdrawal from Britannia in A.D. 410. Invading Germanic Franks, moving into the crumbling Roman Empire, settled in the region in 486. In the sixth century the region was brought under the authority of the Frankish kingdom. The area's only large population centers evolved around the coastal ports and in the valley of the Seine River, while rural lords held most the land in small feudal holdings.

Vikings, called Norsemen, began to raid the coastal regions in the early ninth century and from 841 controlled most of the coastal districts. The Norsemen established large colonies on the English Channel and pushed inland against French resistance. Unable to defeat the fierce Vikings, the French king, Charles the Simple, finally accepted Norse control of the region. In 911 the French king recognized Rollo, the Norse chief, as the first duke of Normandy. The Norsemen, later called Normans, accepted Christianity and the French language as the price for French acceptance. In adopting French as a medium of communication, the Normans retained for purposes of literary expression many Scandinavian words.

The Normans gradually lost contact with Scandinavia but did not lose the Norse craving for adventure and conquest. On the pretext of expelling the Byzantine Greeks and Arabs from Roman Catholic lands, the Normans conquered southern Italy and Sicily between 1057 and 1091. Another Norman army, under Duke William of Normandy, crossed the channel to conquer Saxon England in 1066. The dukes of Normandy ruled both England and Normandy until the French conquest of the mainland Norman territories in 1204. The Norman king of England renounced title to Normandy in 1259, but his descendants returned to the mainland to reconquer Normandy in 1346. Returned to the French by treaty in 1360, Normandy again came under English rule in 1417–18 during the Hundred Years' War, which evolved from Norman claims on both sides of the English Channel. A young Frenchwoman, Joan of Arc, burned at the stake in Rouen by the English in 1431 during the long war, became the patron saint of Normandy. In 1450 the defeated English abandoned mainland Normandy, retaining only the Norman Islands, later renamed the Channel Islands.

A Norman legislature, the *parlement*, was established at Rouen in 1499 as a focus for Norman loyalty, but King Louis XIV suppressed the provincial estates of Normandy. The legislature exercised considerable regional power until the French Revolution in 1789 and the dissolution of all provincial autonomy. Divested of all traditional privileges, the Normans turned against the French Revolution they had enthusiastically welcomed in 1789–90. In 1791 the French revolutionary government abolished the province and replaced it with five administrative departments. Open rebellion broke out in Normandy in 1793. The Norman rebels took the name Chouans, meaning "owls" in the Norman dialect, and used owl hoots as signals and communication. The Chouans fought a bitter guerrilla war against the revolutionary forces but were ultimately defeated with great loss of life. The crushing of the Chouan revolt is still referred to by Normans as the first modern genocide.

Napoleon Bonaparte, coming to power in the aftermath of revolution and war, split France's historic regions into small departments to undermine local loyalties. Under Napoleon's reorganization of the French state all power was centralized in Paris, where it remained until the late twentieth century. The Normans again rebelled against the loss of all rights in 1815, forcing Napoleon to divert troops from the decisive final battle at Waterloo.

In the nineteenth and early twentieth centuries, Normandy remained pastoral and underdeveloped. With all state functions centralized in Paris, Normans had to leave their homeland in order to excel in the arts, literature, government, or education. Resentment of the need to emigrate and the threat to their culture incited the beginning of a modest Norman national movement, one of the few in Western Europe not based on language in the late nineteenth century.

Prior to World War II, nationalist and radical political parties proliferated in Normandy, stimulated by the region's economic backwardness. In 1939 workers in Paris earned an average of 40% more than their Norman counterparts. The region, although economically backward, remained an important region in France's trade with the British Isles.

Normandy was occupied by Nazi German troops in 1940 and became part of the front line facing Britain across the channel. A concerted German campaign during the war to win Norman support by stressing common Nordic origins of the German and Norman peoples met with little success, and the vast majority remained loyal to the French state. The first region of continental Europe to be liberated from Nazi occupation in June 1944, Normandy sustained massive damage during the Allied invasion, which began on the Norman beaches.

Normandy had recovered from the damage done by the war by the early 1950s and experienced a modest prosperity based on cross-channel trade. A regionalist movement, claiming that Paris appropriated Normandy's finest resources and most talented people, gained support after France's entry in the European Economic Community (EEC) in 1960 shifted French trade to the east and away from Normandy and the channel. The Normans, but not the French government, supported Britain's and Ireland's bid to join the EEC, finally realized in 1973. The increasing integration of Europe has given new impetus to the growing Norman national movement. Few Normans see the sense of applying to Paris, to the east, for trade agreements with Normandy's natural trading partners, Britain and Ireland, to the west.

A socialist government, elected in France in 1981, granted some regional powers to a planning region based roughly on France's historic regions, but limited autonomy only brought demands for greater home rule. The national movement focused on the unification of the historic Norman territories and demands for greater economic and cultural autonomy. The survival of the declining Norman dialect has become a major nationalist issue in the 1990s. For the small, but growing, number of pro-European Norman nationalists, the survival of the Norman culture, economy, and dialect depends on achieving Norman sovereignty in a united Europe of the regions.

SELECTED BIBLIOGRAPHY

Caracalla, J. P., ed. *Normandy.* 1991.

Chrisp, Peter. *The Normans.* 1995.

Christiansen, Eric. *History of the Normans.* 1998.

Douglas, David C. *William the Conqueror: The Norman Impact on England.* 1964.

Jewett, S. *The Story of the Normans.* 1990.

NORTHUMBRIANS

Geordies

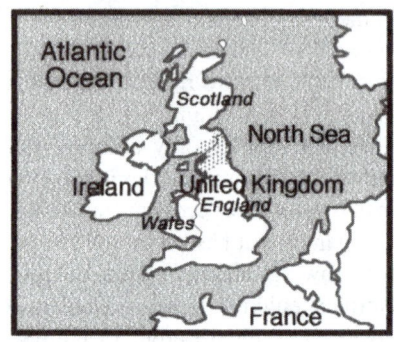

POPULATION: Approximately (2000 e) 3,496,000 Northumbrians in Europe, mostly in the northern counties of England, but with sizable concentrations in London and other large British cities.

THE NORTHUMBRIAN HOMELAND: The Northumbrian homeland, commonly called the North, occupies a region of rolling hills and lakes between the Irish and North Seas in northern England, just south of the Scottish border. The region is level along the North Sea but is hilly in the interior, with the Cheviot hills on the northern border and the Pennine Chain in the south. Inland are highland moors, which alternate with fertile valleys. The most important river is the Tyne and its tributaries, which flow into the North Sea.

Northumbria has been designated a European region, but in England the region remains divided between the metropolitan county of Tyne and Wear and the nonmetropolitan counties of Cleveland, Cumbria, Durham, and Northumberland. *Region of Northumbria*: 5,944 sq.mi.–15,401 sq.km. (2000 e) 3,054,000—Northumbrians 90%, Scots* 5%, other English.* The Northumbrian capital and major cultural center is Newcastle upon Tyne, (2000 e) 265,000 (metropolitan area 1,308,000), named for a castle built on the site by Robert II, duke of Normandy, in the eleventh century.

FLAG: The Northumbrian flag is a horizontal bicolor of red over green charged with a centered, broad yellow cross.

PEOPLE: The Northumbrians, commonly called Geordies, particularly in the Tyneside region, are also sometimes called Northern English. The Geordie character and culture, incorporating both English and Scottish influences, retain many traits and traditions that disappeared in other parts of England. The culture of the North developed around the ancient coal mines; mining dictated the way and rhythm of life for centuries. The Northumbrians increasingly consider themselves a distinct British people and a separate European nation equal to the other distinct nations of the British Isles.

The Northumbrians speak a dialect that developed from medieval Northumbrian, a language not influenced by the introduction of Norman French to the South in the eleventh century. The dialect is spoken in seven subdialects that roughly correspond to the historic counties that make up the region, Geordie, Cumberland, Central Cumberland, Durham, Northumberland, Newcastle Northumberland, and Tyneside Northumberland. Although standard English is the official language and the language of the media and education, the Geordie dialects remain the language of daily life across the region.

NATION: The Celtic Ottadeni of the region between the seas came under Roman rule in the first century A.D. Their Latinized homeland formed the northern frontier of Roman Britannia. In an effort to protect the northern districts from attacks by Picts and Celts, the Romans constructed the long defensive structure known as Hadrian's Wall between A.D. 120 and 123. The modern city of Newcastle began as a station, called Pons Aelii, on the wall. The region, prosperous under Roman rule, declined rapidly with the collapse of Roman power and the withdrawal of the Roman garrisons from Britannia in 410.

About the middle of the sixth century the Angles, a people related to the Saxons, overran most of Caledonia south of the Firth of Forth and east of Strathclyde. Together with the extensive Angle holdings in the north of what is now England, this region became the kingdom of Northumbria.

The inhabitants of the region accepted Christianity in 627, which introduced Christian themes to the Northumbrian Renaissance. Mediterranean Christianity from Rome met Celtic Christianity in Northumbria. Celtic Christianity was brought from Ireland to Scotland by St. Columba and then to Northumbria by St. Aidan, who founded the monastery of Lindisfarne in 635. The Celtic church differed from the Roman in the way the monks tonsured their heads, in its reckoning of the date of Easter, and, most important, in its organization, which reflected the Celtic clans rather than the highly centralized tradition of Rome. In 664 the Northumbrian king, Oswy, chose to adhere to the Roman tradition, bringing the Northumbrians closer to the southern English. The meeting in Northumbria of Celtic and Mediterranean traditions produced a flowering of literature and art unequaled in Western Europe. In the sixth and seventh centuries, from 547 to 735, Northumbria experienced a golden age, a great flowering of the arts, literature, and scholarship. Parallel to the cultural golden age was almost constant political discord.

The coastal districts of Northumbria came under Viking attack in the ninth century, and the southern part of the kingdom was conquered in 867. The Viking invasion ended Northumbria's preeminent position in England and virtually destroyed the culture of the region. The Angles, maintaining a small kingdom north of the Tees River, accepted the authority of the king of Wessex in 920 and became part of the united English kingdom.

The conquest of England in 1066 by the Normans* from mainland Europe introduced a more centralized form of government in England. The North was divided into counties administered by Norman nobles, and the traditional liberties of the Anglo-Saxon inhabitants were greatly curtailed. Reaction to authoritarian Norman rule, especially among the Anglo-Saxon majority, led to the reestablishment of political and personal freedom with the signing of the Magna Carta in 1215 and the creation of an English parliament in 1295.

Northumbria, forming the English border with the separate Kingdom of Scotland, suffered during centuries of border wars until the two kingdoms united under the rule of the House of Stuart in 1603. Peace on the border allowed the Industrial Revolution to spread to the North, with the rapid development of large industrial enterprises, ports, and mines, largely based on the region's important coal deposits, the world's oldest coalfield and the center of Northumbrian economic and cultural life.

Far from the center of government, the North experienced serious unrest in the early nineteenth century with Geordie industrial workers demanding the same rights as those enjoyed by the more prosperous classes in the South. Rapid industrial expansion converted the region into a powerhouse of English industry, spurred by the expansion of the overseas British Empire. The profits from the industrialization of Northumbria, however, mostly went to the industrialists and the government based in London.

The region was vital to the British war effort during World War I, but the long conflict seriously drained the region's wealth and manpower. Severe economic problems in the 1920s converted the declining northern counties into a bastion of unionism and antigovernmental sentiment and a center of support for the new Labor Party. Economically devastated by the depression of the 1930s, the region revived during World War II as its industries turned out war goods. A Labor government elected in 1945 nationalized the mining industry and in 1948 introduced the British welfare system that helped to eliminate regional economic and social differences. In 1950 the Northumbrian incomes finally drew equal to those of the prosperous South.

The Northumbrian region began a long decline following the election of a Conservative government in 1951, exacerbated by the increasing centralization of political power in London and the southeastern counties. Chronic unemployment, decaying cities, and aging industries raised social tensions and sparked a renewal of a regionalist movement and a resurgence of separate Geordie identity. The growing regional movement demanded a fairer distribution of development and investment for the perennially depressed northern counties.

The United Kingdom's entry into the European Economic Community in 1973 further concentrated investment and development in the prosperous counties around London, the center of continental trade. By 1985 incomes in the

North had fallen to 3% below the national average, while incomes in the southeast climbed to 5% above the average, and the gap continued to widen, exacerbating regional differences.

Demands for autonomy and devolution of political power by the Scots, Welsh,* and Cornish* in the United Kingdom reverberated in the Geordie North. Proposals for regional government, more responsive to local needs, have met with repeated rejections in London. Geordie regionalism grew rapidly during the 1980s amid increasing unrest and growing unemployment, up to 30% in some areas. In 1991 severe rioting swept the region, highlighting the massive political and economic problems of the North. The longest economic decline since the depression of the 1930s, blamed on the Conservative government, has raised demands for economic independence. The region, with strong support for devolution of power, increasingly looks to Europe, with a nationalist minority advocating independence within a federal United Kingdom or even within a united, federal Europe. Following the overthrow of communism in Eastern Europe, Northumbria was often called the only remaining one-party state in Europe, a state ruled by a political party, the Conservatives, that has never won an election in the region.

The election of a Labor government in the United Kingdom in 1997 somewhat eased regionalist tensions in the northern counties, but expectations are high, and the Geordies are determined to bring their region into the European mainstream. The region, a Labor stronghold, helped the party to power and expects to gain by doing so.

The British government plan, announced in July 1997, for devolution of power to the Welsh and Scots raised new demands for devolution of power to the North, northern England or Northumbria. Eighteen years of Conservative government, which ended in May 1997, was a sustained assault on local administration, and the United Kingdom became highly centralized. The North, staunchly anti-Conservative, celebrated when Labor gained hold of the government, but many Northumbrians were highly incensed when only Scotland and Wales were singled out for devolution. Even London has been promised its own local government, but the other English regions have been ignored.

In November 1997 regional leaders in Northumbria issued a symbolic declaration of sovereignty and began a campaign to press their case for political devolution such as offered to Wales and Scotland. The Northumbrians claim their culture and dialect are unique in England, as unique as those of the Welsh or Scots. Economically, the region is prospering for the first time since the coal boom of the last century. Greater economic opportunities are giving the Geordies a new confidence.

SELECTED BIBLIOGRAPHY

Forester, G.C.F., ed. *Northern History: A Review of the History of the North of England.* 1966.

Fraser, C.M., and K. Emsley. *Northumbria.* 1989.

Higham, N.J. *The Kingdom of Northumbria:* A.D. *350–1100.* 1993.

Mason, Roger. *The North.* 1986.

Willpenny, David. *Northumbria and Hadrian's Wall.* 1997.

NORWEGIANS

Nordmenn; Norsk

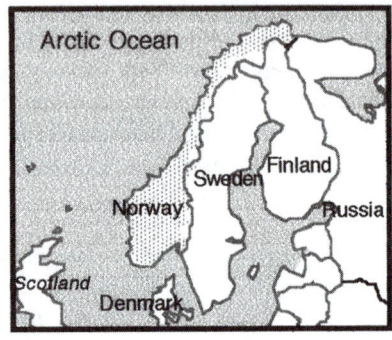

POPULATION: Approximately (2000 e) 4,452,000 Norwegians in Europe, 4,279,000 in Norway, with small communities in Sweden and Denmark.

THE NORWEGIAN HOMELAND: The Norwegian homeland forms the western part of the mountainous Scandinavian Peninsula and extends farther north than any other European territory to North Cape on the Arctic Ocean, some 300 miles north of the Arctic Circle. Nearly one-third of Norway's territory lies north of the Arctic Circle. The region has one of the most indented coastlines in the world and includes over 150 offshore islands. The fjords, the deep inlets along the coast, were formed by glaciers during the Ice Age. Ice has also sculpted the inland mountains. The fertile lowlands in the south are the most densely populated, while for three months of every year the sun does not set in the northern districts. Forests and woodlands cover 27% of the Norwegian territory, although at higher altitudes large areas of the rugged mountains are bare rock. In the far north and at high elevations are tundra regions. The Norwegian tundra is a treeless heath, with vegetation consisting mainly of hardy dwarf shrubs and wildflowers.

Norway was ruled by the Danes* from 1380 to 1814, then by the Swedes,* becoming an independent kingdom only in 1905. *Kingdom of Norway (Kongeriket Norge)*: 154,790 sq.mi.–400,906 sq.km. (2000 e) 4,407,000—Norwegians 97%, Samis* (Lapps) 1%, Finns,* Swedes. Norway has the lowest population density in continental Europe, with about thirty-seven persons per square mile (fourteen per sq.k.). The Norwegian capital and major cultural center is Oslo, (2000 e) 457,000 (metropolitan area 734,000). About one-quarter of the total Norwegian population lives in the vicinity of Oslo.

FLAG: The Norwegian national flag, the official flag of the kingdom, is a red field with a blue Scandinavian cross outlined in white.

PEOPLE: The Norwegians are a Scandinavian people closely related to the neighboring Danes and Swedes. The descendants of Germanic tribes called Vikings or Norsemen, the Norwegians have a long tradition of seafaring and historically terrorized and raided many parts of Europe. The Norwegians are ethnically quite homogeneous, with the majority tall and fair, with light hair and eyes. Their culture, more than that of most Europeans, has been shaped by the environment of their homeland. Although Oslo is the Norwegians' only large city, the Norwegian population is highly urbanized, with 73% living in urban areas. Nearly all the Norwegians are Protestant Lutherans, making up 88% of the population. Other Protestant sects and a small Roman Catholic minority account for the remainder. Although a high percentage of Norwegians officially belongs to the Lutheran Church, many are nonpracticing members.

The language of the Norwegians is actually slightly different dialects, Riksmaal, the Oslo dialect of Danish, which was the official language until the twentieth century, and Landsmaal, which is a standardization of Norwegian dialects and became popular as part of the nineteenth-century national movement. During the nineteenth century, the spoken Danish in Norway developed into a language called Dano-Norwegian, which was heavily Danish in structure and vocabulary, but with particular Norwegian pronunciation. In the mid-nineteenth century, in response to a desire for a new national language, the Landsmaal or country speech, based on Norwegian dialects and free of Danish forms, was developed. Both Norwegian dialects are taught in the country's schools, and the two languages have equal validity in law.

NATION: The history of the Norwegians before the Viking era is indistinguishable from that of the rest of Scandinavia. According to archaeological research, Norway was inhabited as early as 14,000 years ago by a hunting people with a Paleolithic culture derived from that of Western and Central Europe. Later, colonies of Germanic farming people from Denmark and Sweden were established in the region. These settlers spoke a Germanic language that became the mother tongue of the later Scandinavian languages. In the first historical records of Scandinavia, in the eighth century A.D., some twenty-nine small kingdoms existed in Norway.

Harold I, of the Yngling or Scilfing dynasty, which claimed descent from the old Norse gods, began to expand his small kingdom in the ninth century, eventually uniting the region and conquering the Shetland and Orkney Islands, but failed to achieve permanent unity among the Viking clans. During his reign the Viking raids on various parts of Europe reached their peak, including the establishment of a political entity in France by the Norsemen, later called Normans.* At Harold's death in 933, his kingdom was divided by his sons but was reunited when Haakon I defeated his brothers in 935. Vikings, traditionally led by Leif Eriksson, are believed to have discovered the Americas four centuries before Christopher Columbus.

Christianity, brought to the region by Irish* monks, gained a foothold under the rule of Olaf I and became the established religion under Olaf II in the eleventh century. King Olaf II was driven from the kingdom by King Canute of England and Denmark, in alliance with discontented Norwegian nobles; however, his son, Magnus I, was restored to the throne in 1035. In 1042 Harold Hardrada, Harold Stern Council, led a revolt and overthrew Magnus and, as Harold III, became king in 1047.

King Harold greatly affected the history of the English.* In 1066 he accompanied Tostig, the exiled ruler of the Northumbrians,* on an invasion of northern England. At the same time, William of Normandy was preparing an invasion of southern England. The hard-pressed English king moved north and defeated the Norse invasion at Stamford Bridge on 25 September 1066. During the battle both Harold III of Norway and Tostig were killed, but the way had been prepared for a Norman victory in the south. The English moved south to oppose the Norman landing at Pevensey, but their exhausted troops were routed, opening the way for the Norman domination of England.

In the thirteenth century medieval Norway reached its greatest power and enjoyed a great flowering of culture and scholarship. The peace and prosperity of the kingdom ended when Norway's separate development was halted by the accession to the throne of Magnus VII, who was also king of Sweden. His rule was unpopular with the Norwegians, and he eventually was compelled to abdicate in favor of his son, Haakon VI, the husband of Margaret of Denmark. Margaret subsequently united the crowns of Norway, Denmark, and Sweden and in 1397 united the three kingdoms in the Union of Kalmar. Although the union was a dynastic one, Norway virtually ceased to exist and was ruled by Danish governors from 1380 until 1814. Norwegian prosperity and culture declined steadily after the union. Lutheranism, the official religion of Denmark, was extended to the Norwegian territories.

Under Danish rule the Norwegians enjoyed considerable economic autonomy, although the Danes maintained strict control, the Norwegians were allowed to maintain their own military and naval forces. In 1814 the Danes, who had sided with Napoleon, were forced to cede Norway to the Swedish kingdom. The Norwegians, rejecting Swedish rule, attempted to set up a separate kingdom under the Danish prince Christian, but a Swedish army invaded, obliging the Norwegians to capitulate. However, the Swedes recognized Norway as a separate kingdom, in personal union with the Swedish crown, with its own constitution and parliament.

In spite of some Swedish concessions to growing Norwegian nationalism, relations between the two peoples remained tense throughout the nineteenth century. The liberal movement in Norwegian politics, accompanying the surge of nationalism, became more pronounced after the revolutions of 1848 in the major countries of Europe. Political nationalism was bolstered by intellectual and cultural nationalism. Norwegian folktales and folk songs were collected and arranged and became extremely popular. Norwegian dictionaries, histories, and grammars were compiled. In the late nineteenth and early twentieth centuries, there was a mass migration to the United States and Canada by Norwegians seeking better economic opportunities or freedom from Swedish laws.

In the 1890s the Norwegians demanded a separate consular service and a separate flag. Although the demands were justified by the spectacular growth of Norwegian shipping, they were refused by the Swedish king, Oscar II. Finally, in 1905 the Norwegian parliament, the Sorting, declared the dissolution of the union with Sweden and the disposition of Oskar II as king of Norway. In a plebiscite in August 1905 the Norwegians voted overwhelmingly for separation from Sweden. The Swedes acquiesced, and the second son of the Danish king was elected king of Norway as Haakon VII.

The new Norwegian government, dominated by liberals, became one of the most advanced in Europe with such policies as unemployment insurance benefits, liberal laws concerning divorce and illegitimacy, and old-age pensions. In 1913 Norwegian women achieved the right to vote in national elections, and women continue to play a prominent role in political life.

The Norwegians, dependent on their large fleet, remained carefully neutral during World War I. After the beginning of World War I in 1914 the sovereigns of Sweden, Norway, and Denmark agreed to maintain the neutrality of the Scandinavian countries and to cooperate for their mutual interest. The policy of neutrality and friendship thus established continued to be the joint policy of all three nations after the war ended.

Undamaged in the continental conflict, the Norwegian economy grew rapidly in the 1920s and 1930s. Progressive social welfare legislation was passed, including old-age pensions, aid to the disabled, and unemployment insurance. The Norwegians again sought to remain neutral when war again broke out in Europe in 1939, but in April 1940 German troops invaded, and, despite valiant resistance, the country fell. King Haakon and many Norwegians fled to London, where a Norwegian exile government was established. The Norwegian shipping fleet was of vital importance to the Allied war effort. In spite of the efforts of the Norwegian fascist leader, Vidkun Quisling, to promote the unity of the Nordic peoples, the Norwegians remained defiant of the occupation army. The German forces in Norway surrendered in May 1945.

Although nearly half the Norwegian fleet was sunk during the war, the Norwegians quickly recovered following the end of the war in 1945. The postwar economic recovery was rapid with abundant hydroelectric resources to provide for the industrialization of the country. Forgoing their former neutrality, the Norwegians joined the United Nations and in 1949 became a member of the North Atlantic Treaty Organization (NATO). By the late 1950s the Norwegians had became one of the most prosperous of the European nations.

In the 1950s and 1960s the Norwegians continued to prosper. In 1960, together with six other European nations, the Norwegians formed the European Free Trade Association (EFTA), a loose economic alliance that included many of the states that had not joined the rival European Economic Community (EEC).

The discovery of oil and natural gas in the North Sea gave the Norwegians the confidence to reject EEC membership in a referendum in 1972.

Increasing prosperity, fueled by oil exports, in the 1980s and 1990s gave the Norwegians one of the highest standards of living in the world. In May 1994 the European Parliament endorsed membership for the Norwegians in the European Union (EU). However, in November 1994, in spite of government encouragement, the Norwegians again voted 52% to 48% against membership in the continental economic and political alliance. Although more and more dependent on petroleum exports, the Norwegians remain one of Europe's most successful nations.

The Norwegian prime minister, Kjell Magne Bondevik, in early 1998 created a "Values Commission" to help the Norwegians reflect on their values as the millennium neared. Even with high rates of out-of-wedlock births, divorces, and disintegrating families, the Norwegians have fared a bit better than the other Scandinavian nations, but the trends were still worrying, and the back-to-basics initiative of the government found widespread approval.

Opposition to membership in the EU remains high among the Norwegians. A 1998 poll found that 65% of the Norwegian population opposed EU membership for Norway. Through a mechanism called the European Economic Area the Norwegians already participate in the economic integration of Europe, but as the world's second largest exporter of oil and natural gas, they can afford to remain outside the continental system.

SELECTED BIBLIOGRAPHY

Cohen, Maynard M. *A Stand against Tyranny: Norway's Physicians and the Nazis.* 1997.
Hintz, Martin. *Norway.* 1982.
Kagda, Sakina, and Rudolf Steiner. *Norway.* 1996.
Vanberg, Bent. *Of Norwegian Ways.* 1992.
Zickgraf, Ralph. *Norway.* 1997.

OCCITANS

Occitanians; Occitens

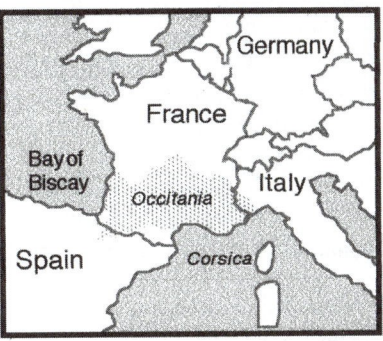

POPULATION: Approximately (2000 e) 12,200,000 Occitans in Europe, with 10,840,000 in the Occitania region of France and other large concentrations in Paris and northern France. A small group, called Aranese, live in the Aran valley of northern Spain, and some 300,000 called Transalpin Occitans live in adjacent areas of northwestern Italy. Some 5,000 Monégasques* are of Occitan background.

THE OCCITANIAN HOMELAND: The Occitanian homeland, Occitania or the Pays d'Oc, lies in southern France, comprising the historic regions of Auvergne, Bourbonnais, Béarn, Dauphiné, Foix, Gascony, Guyenne, Languedoc, Limousin, Marche, Provence, and Venaissin. The region is largely mountainous and includes the large plateau region, the Massif Central, in the center, the Alps in the east and in Italian Occitania, and the Pyrenees in the south. The valleys of the Garonne and the coastal lowlands in the west and the coastal plains of the Mediterranean and the valley of the Rhone in the southeast are the most densely populated.

Occitania has no official status in France. Historic Occitania forms the French planning regions of Aquitaine, Auvergne, Languedoc-Rousillon, Limousin, Provence-Alps-Côte d'Azur, Midi-Pyrénées, and the southern departments of Rhone Alps Region. *Occitania (Occitanie)*: 83,371 sq.mi.–215,987 sq.km. (2000 e) 14,871,000—Occitans 71%, other French* 14%, North Africans 10%, Spanish* 1%. Occitanian cultural centers are mostly the regional capitals, the most important being Marseilles (Marselha in the Occitan language) 861,000 (metropolitan area 1,140,000); Nice (Niça) 343,000 (462,000); Toulouse (Tolosa) 339,000 (666,000); Montpellier (Montpelhier) 213,000; Bordeaux (Bordèu)

202,000 (701,000); Toulon (Tolon) 176,000 (437,000); Grenoble 152,000 (476,000); Aix-en-Provence (Ais-de-Provença) 152,000; Limoges (Limòtge) 144,000; Clermont-Ferrand (Clarmont d'Auvernha) 142,000 (265,000); Nîmes (Nismes) 125,000; Perpignan (Perpinyà) 122,000; Avignon (Avinhon) 107,000 (180,000); Pau 86,000 (148,000).

FLAG: The Occitan flag, the flag of the national movement, is a red field charged with a red Cross of Toulouse outlined in yellow.

PEOPLE: The Occitans are the descendants of the Latin peoples of Roman Gaul, more closely related to the Catalans* of northeastern Spain and the Piedmontese* and Ligurians* of northwestern Italy than to the Germanic descendants of the Franks in northern France. The Occitans, unlike the northern French, are a Mediterranean people, having mixed very little with the Franks, and tend to be shorter and darker than the inhabitants of Paris and northern France. The Occitans, who mostly identify with regional identities, have only recently begun to view themselves as a united national group. The inhabitants of southern France often refer to the northern French as Franks, referring to their Germanic origin.

The Occitan language, often called Langue d'Oc, is considered the closest to the original Latin of the modern Romance languages and is the oldest of the Romance languages still in use. The language has never been standardized and is characterized by a group of related Oc dialects, all of which are called Occitan and are spoken by only about 10% of the Occitanian population. The most important of the dialects are Auvergnat, Gascon, Languedocien, Limousin, and Provençal. Auvergnat or Auvernhas is spoken in the central Augergne region in two subdialects, Haut-Auvergnat and Bas-Auvergnat. Gascon is spoken in the southwest and includes four subdialects, Landais in the west, Béarnais in Béarn, Ariégeois in Foix, and Aranese in the Aran valley in the Spanish Pyrenees. Languedocien or Lengadoucian is spoken in the southern region of Languedoc and the central and western region of Guyenne and includes four subdialects, Bas-Languedocien, Languedocien Moyen, Haut-Languedocien, and Guyennais. Limousin or Lemosin is spoken in Limousin and Marche and comprises two subdialects, Haut-Limousin and Bas-Limousin. The most widely spoken of the dialects is Provençal, with over 250,000 fluent speakers and over 1 million with some knowledge of the language. Provençal is spoken in the southeast, in Provence, Dauphine, and Venaissin in five subdialects, Niçard or Niçois in the Nice region, Maritime Provençal around Marseilles, Toulon, and in the department of Var, Gavot in Dauphine, Rhodanien or Nimois west of the Rhone River around Nîmes, Dauphinois or Dromois in southern Dauphine, and Tranalpin in the adjacent districts of Piedmont in northwestern Italy. The dialects are structurally separate languages with none of the dialects universally accepted as the standard literary language, although all are mutually intelligible. An estimated 55% of the population of southern France speak the Occitan dialects, 70% understand them, and 85% are in favor of saving the dialects as regional languages.

All Occitans speak French as their first or second language. Occitan has a vocabulary of 160,000 words, 130,000 more than modern French.

   NATION: The Mediterranean lowlands of the southeast were known to the
ancient civilizations and were colonized by Greeks* as early as the sixth century
B.C. The flourishing Greek port cities fell to Roman rule in the second century
B.C., forming part of the first Roman possession outside Italy. Julius Caesar
conquered the interior districts in a series of wars called the Gallic Wars from
58 to 51 B.C. The Romans called the region Gaul, the Latin name for the area's
Celtic inhabitants. Roman Gaul developed as a prosperous center of Roman
commerce, art, and culture.

   The decline of Roman power left the region open to invasion, and Germanic
tribes, Visigoths, Vandals, Burgundians,* and Franks, overran Gaul in the fifth
century A.D. The most powerful of the Germanic tribes, the Franks, settled northern Gaul in the sixth century. The region, retaining many Roman institutions
and traditions, remained more advanced than the Frankish north. The countship
of Toulouse, founded in 788, and the kingdom of Provence, erected in 879,
evolved as the major states in the politically divided area. The Occitan states
carried on an extensive trade with North Africa, enjoying luxuries and inventions
unheard of in most of Europe.

   Occitania experienced a great cultural flowering in the eleventh and twelfth
centuries, when the whole area south of a line running from Bordeaux to Grenoble spoke Oc dialects. From its inception in Limousin, the budding troubadour
culture spread across the region, carried by wandering troubadours, who turned
the Oc dialects into a standardized Romance language. The Occitans developed
an eminent literature during the Middle Ages, which included the poems of the
troubadours. The language extended significantly farther north than its present
speech region, and its standard literary dialect bridged many local dialects. The
cultural awakening, a forerunner of the Renaissance, developed an extensive
Occitan literature, marked by new forms and a striking lyric poetry.

   The Occitan cultural flowering coincided with the spread of an eastern religious sect, the Cathars or Cathari. The troubadour culture and the Cathari beliefs
became closely intertwined in the brilliant medieval Occitan civilization, which
combined Roman heritage, sophisticated Arab imports, and Christian concepts.

   The Cathari sect, originating in the Balkans, gained converts in the region
from the eleventh century. The converts, called Albigenses, after Albi, one of
the major Cathar cities, were branded heretics by the Catholic Church. The
Cathars were not heretics or even Christians but adherents of a dualistic system
believing in good and evil, body and soul, and so on. The Albigenses, very
aesthetic in contrast to the local Roman Catholic clergy, gained many converts.
Supported by many powerful nobles, the Cathar sect became a virtual state
religion in many of the Occitan states. In the west, the English* took control of
Gascony and other areas in Aquitaine.

   The Cathars gained the wrath of the Catholic Church by criticizing its wealth and vast landholdings. In spiritual questions the Cathars attacked the very foundations of Christianity by denying the value of the sacraments. The Catholic pope sent missionaries to Occitania to stop the rapid spread of the Cathar heresy and issued increasingly stringent instructions for dealing with heretics and nonbelievers. Efforts to bring the heretics back to the church having failed, the pope, encouraged by the French, proclaimed a crusade against the Cathars in 1208. The French kingdom to the north of the Oc states answered the pope's call, seeing in the wealthy south a chance for conquest, expansion, and plunder. Cathar nobles, backed by Catholic Aragon, united to resist the French invasion. The Albigensian Crusade of 1209–29 quickly became a political war with the Occitan states as the battleground.

French knights, under the guise of stamping out heresy, plundered and devastated Occitania, driving thousands of refugees, both Catholic and Cathar, across the borders into Spain and Italy. Horrible massacres of Occitan populations marked the French acquisition of the Oc lands. Pope Gregory IX in 1233 established a system of legal investigation in the conquered Albigensian centers, the beginning of the infamous Inquisition.

In 1229 Languedoc was partly annexed by France, and in 1271 the county of Toulouse was incorporated into the French kingdom, while other areas retained some independence until after the Hundred Years' War in the fifteenth century, which again devastated much of the region. Under blows from the Inquisition and the revitalized Catholic Church, the Albigensian sect disappeared within a century. The Occitan language, suppressed in favor of the Oïl French spoken in Paris, was relegated to a folk language spoken in rural areas and was finally banned in 1539 by the Edict of Villers-Cotterets, which made French the only official language. The Wars of Religion, from 1562 to 1598, again devastated the region, with massacres of Protestants echoing the earlier Cathar massacres.

Under the rule of the French kingdom, Occitania was divided into provinces, which retained some local autonomy until the French revolution swept away the local *parlements* in Toulouse, Aix-en-Provence, Grenoble, and other provincial capitals. Until the revolution, the Occitan provinces remained outside the French Tariff Union as "provinces considered foreign." For centuries after the Albigensian crusade, Occitania remained the poorest region of France, although the vitality of the Occitan culture and language was evidenced by their refusal to die under massive French government pressure. After the revolution, Napoleon divided France into numerous departments in an effort to blunt regional loyalties.

The Occitans, during the revolutionary upheaval in 1851 began to revive their culture and language with demands for a federal system in France. An Occitan cultural organization, Felibrige, formed by the famed Occitan poet Frédéric Mistral in 1854, stimulated a resurgence and a new interest in the Occitan history, language, and culture. The cultural movement stimulated demands for cultural and political autonomy in highly centralized France. Between 1851 and 1871

Occitan nationalists campaigned for a federal system to replace the system of dictating all government from Paris. Mistral, in attempting to standardize the Occitan language, produced a monumental two-volume dictionary plus a collection of Occitan poetry that won him the Nobel Prize in 1904.

The Occitan dialects remained the language of daily life until the early twentieth century, with many writers, as part of the Occitan revival, using the language despite French cultural pressure. The Occitan movement lost support during World War I, and by the 1930s standard French had replaced Occitan as the language of daily life.

During World War II, Occitania formed part of unoccupied France, under the authority of the fascist French regime at Vichy in northern Occitania. The Germans sought to garner support by emphasizing the Latin heritage of the region, but with little success. Liberated by American troops, the Occitans remained pro-American in the postwar era, while the attitude of the Parisian French and the French government became increasingly anti-American as France lost it place as a major world power.

The Institute of Occitan Studies was formed in 1945, taking on itself the daunting task of defending and expanding the Occitan language and culture. The legalization of the Occitan language in 1951 stimulated the rebirth of the Occitan movement. In the 1960s local politicians, aware that the Occitans had a weak sense of national identity, at first turned to ecological and other regional issues, but a regionalist movement soon emerged. Regionalist political groups, Lutte Occitane and VVAP (Volem Viure al Pais), grew from local action committees formed to resist pressures from the central government. The generations born in the 1960s and 1970s learned to speak Occitan as a matter of pride and were able to communicate with their grandparents in their own language. By the 1970s autonomist and nationalist sentiment in the region had begun to politicize the Occitan population.

The integration of Europe in the 1970s and 1980s gave the movement focus. Occitan nationalists claim that the region, like the Mezzogiorno in Italy, is at once colonized, neglected, and underdeveloped. With the socialist victory in France in 1981, some powers were returned to the regions, but a regional Occitan assembly, as demanded by Occitan nationalists, was rejected by the French government. Massive Muslim immigration from the former French colonies in North Africa has become a major issue in the region, with rising support for racist, reactionary political groups, indicating dissatisfaction with the French government. An ongoing feature of the Occitan revival has been the conflict between Pan-Occitan nationalists and regionalists loyal to Occitania's various distinct regions. The strength of the renaissance of the neighboring and closely related Catalans has, in the 1980s and 1990s, boosted Occitan confidence.

In the 1980s militants and academics successfully forced the government to introduce Occitan into regional schools, and by 1991 an estimated 6 million people had some knowledge of the various Occitan dialects. Increasingly, inhabitants of the southern regions of France use the name Occitania. In 1993 the

Council General of Midi-Pyrénées, which includes Toulouse, proposed changing the name of the region to Central Occitania but was opposed by the French government. In the same year, in a move to preserve regional heritage and culture, the French government instructed state schools in the region to start teaching Occitan.

The Occitans still recall that they were forcibly joined to France through the devastation of their troubador culture in the Albigensian crusade and the Hundred Years' War. The national movement in the 1990s looks back on the massacres and horrors visited on their nation by "foreign invaders" from northern France in the thirteenth century. Modern Occitan nationalists seek independence within a united Europe and see the Albigenses as the first Occitan nationalists.

SELECTED BIBLIOGRAPHY

Baldit, J. P. *Occitania.* 1982.
Brustein, William. *The Social Origins of Political Regionalism: France, 1849–1981.* 1982.
Lambert, Malcomb. *The Cathars.* 1998.
Roche, Alfonse. *Provençal Regionalism.* 1954.
Sanger, Andrew, and Joe Cornish. *Regions of France: Languedoc and Roussillon.* 1997.

OSSETIANS

Ossets; Ossetins; Osetians; Osetiny;
Digors; Ir; Iristi; Ironi

POPULATION: Approximately (2000 e) 722,000 Ossetians in Europe, with 652,000 concentrated in the North Ossetia (Alania) Republic of southern Russia and South Ossetia and neighboring regions of north-central Georgia. Other Ossetian communities live in the Kabardino-Balkar Republic, Stavropol Krai, Moscow, Chechenia, Rostov Oblast, Krasnodar Krai, and Dagestan Republic of the Russian Federation and in the Central Asian republics and in Azerbaijan.

THE OSSETIAN HOMELAND: The Ossetian homeland lies in southern European Russia and north-central Georgia, occupying the northern and southern slopes of the central Caucasus Mountains and the Mozdok and Ossetian lowlands drained by the Terek River and its tributaries to the north. The northern slopes of the Caucasus Mountains make up the rugged terrain of the Ossetian homeland, where the highest peak is Mt. Dzhimara, 15,682 feet (4,780 m.). The main ridge of the Caucasus provides a natural boundary between the two parts of the homeland, North Ossetia or Alania and South Ossetia. The Ossetian homeland straddles one of the world's most forbidding mountain ranges, so there is tremendous environmental diversity according to the altitude. Mountains give way to lowlands in the central and southern parts of the homeland, and forests cover over one-quarter of Ossetia. The principal rivers of the region are the Terek, the Urukh, the Ardon, the Fiagdon, and the Gizel'don, all of which are fed by ice and snow from the high mountains. The Ossetian republic is connected with South Ossetia in Georgia by the Ossetian Military Road, which leads over the Caucasus through the Mamison Pass near Mt. Kazbek, one of the highest of the Caucasian peaks.

Ossetia, the Ossetian homeland, has no official status but forms two distinct political entities, the Republic of North Ossetia, often called Alania or Iryston in the Ossetian language, a member state of the Russian Federation, and South Ossetia, formerly an autonomous province within the Republic of Georgia. *Republic of North Ossetia (Alania)*: 3,089 sq.mi.–8,001 sq.km. (2000 e) 705,000—Ossetians 56%, Russians* 30%, Ukrainians* 7%, Ingush* 5%, Kabards.* *South Ossetia*: 1,506 sq.mi.–3,901 sq.km. (2000 e) 116,000—Ossetians 63%, Georgians* 34%, Russians 2%. The Ossetian capital and major cultural center is Vladikavkaz, called Dzaujikau by the Ossetians, (2000 e) 337,000, the capital of North Ossetia. The city of Tskinvali, (2000 e) 44,000, is the capital of South Ossetia and the major Ossetian cultural center south of the Caucasus Mountains.

FLAGs: The Ossetian flag, the official flag of North Ossetia, is a horizontal tricolor of white, purple, and yellow. The flag of the South Ossetians is a horizontal tricolor of white, red, and yellow bearing a centered white, crouching snow leopard.

PEOPLE: The Ossetians, calling themselves Iristi and their homeland Iryston, are the most northerly of the Iranian peoples. The descendants of the medieval Alans, the Ossetians were driven into the Caucasus Mountains by waves of invaders. Intermarriage and centuries of contact with neighboring peoples have greatly influenced the Ossetian culture and language. Formerly, Ossetian traditions included such practices as clan warfare, bride-stealing, and vendettas. There are three culturally and linguistically distinct divisions of the Ossetians, the Irons, Tuallags, and Digors. The largest group, the Iron or Ir, reside mainly in North Ossetia, the Tuallag or Tual predominate in South Ossetia, and the Digor are in the northwest, who were converted to Sunni Islam in the seventeenth and eighteenth centuries.

The language of the Ossetians is an Iranian language somewhat modified by borrowings from their Caucasian and Turkic neighbors. Dialectical differences originally followed tribal divisions, but one dialect, called Iron, has been recognized as the basis of standard Ossetian. Ossetian is spoken in three dialects, Iron, Digor, and Tual or Tuallag. Iron is spoken in the eastern districts of North Ossetia, Digor is spoken in the Digor Valley of western North Ossetia, and Tual is mostly spoken south of the mountains in Georgia. Most Ossetians speak Russian as a second language.

There is a profound religious division in the Ossetian nation, which affects their culture and relations with other nations. The Irons and Tuals are mostly Orthodox Christians, while the Digors are mostly Sunni Muslims and have been affected by the spread of radical Islamic doctrines. Both the Christianity and Islam practiced by the Ossetians incorporate many of their ancient pagan traditions and practices.

NATION: The Ossetians trace their ancestry back to the ancient Scythians, but this is disputed by some historians. They are descended from a division of the Sarmatians, the Alans, who were pushed out of the Terek River lowlands and into the Caucasus foothills by invading Huns in the fourth century A.D. Waves of invaders pushed the Alans farther back into the mountain gorges. The high passes of the Caucasus Mountains that united the scattered Alan tribes, also called Ossetes, also served as major invasion routes between Europe and Asia.

The Ossetians organized a state structure between the tenth and thirteenth centuries but maintained only a precarious independence against the region's numerous invaders, the Huns, Khazars, Arabs, Seljuk Turks,* and Georgians. The Ossetians north of the mountains were constantly at war with the neighboring Kabards. In the twelfth century Georgia's Queen Tamara persuaded the Ossetian population to adopt Christianity, the religion of the Georgian state.

The Mongols overran Georgia and the Caucasus in the thirteenth century. The Ossetian homeland was devastated by the reckless destruction of the conquerors. The majority of the Ossetians fled the lowlands to sanctuaries in the defensible mountains. In the fourteenth century the recovering Ossetians won religious freedom under the rule of the Mongol successor, the Golden Horde. The Digors, whose territory lay closest to Kabardia, were culturally influenced and were converted to Islam by the Kabards.

The entire Caucasus was the center of a fierce struggle for dominance by the Turkish Ottoman Empire and the Persians in the fifteenth century. The expanding Russian state to the north, taking advantage of the chaos created by the Muslim rivals, began to penetrate the region in the sixteenth century. Christian Russian influence, particularly in the Ossetian region north of the mountains, brought the Christian Ossetians some protection against the depredations of the warlike Muslim tribes of the Caucasus Mountains; however, during the seventeenth century, the northern Ossetian clans were subject to Kabard princelings.

The Ossetians came under nominal Russian influence in 1774. The mostly Christian Ossetians welcomed the Russians since they offered protection against the Kabards and permitted the Ossetians to repopulate the plains to the north. After the Russian annexation, thousands of Ossetians descended from the mountains to the plains, where they established most of the towns and cities in the region. The key fortress of Vladikavkaz, founded in 1784, became a center of Russian expansion in the Caucasus. Resistance to Russian rule replaced the earlier good relations as tsarist bureaucrats attempted to take control of all aspects of Ossetian life. In 1794 the Ossetians rebelled, and following their defeat the Russians annexed their territories between 1801 and 1806.

The Ossetians, through their early good relations with the Slavs, became the most advanced people in the Caucasus, favored by the tsarist authorities over their Muslim neighbors and as important Christian allies in the region. In 1889 the Ossetian Military Road was hacked through the 9,000-foot Mamison Pass, facilitating contact between the northern and southern clans of the Ossetian nation.

The neighboring Muslim peoples, generally sympathetic to Muslim Turkey when war began in 1914, viewed the Orthodox Ossetians as Russian agents, with violence and tensions increasing as the war dragged on. The Ossetians, to protect themselves amid the spreading chaos, formed an alliance with the Terek

Cossacks* to the north, the dominant military power in the region. The coming of the Russian Revolution in February 1917 escalated the confusion in the Caucasus. In April 1917 the Ossetians called a national congress to establish organs of self-rule within a new democratic Russian state.

Frightened by the Bolshevik coup in October 1917, the Ossetian national congress supported the creation of a joint Christian-Muslim government in the region. The alliance collapsed in December 1917, when fighting broke out between the Muslim tribes and the Cossacks in the Terek River valley. In January 1918 a new council brought together the anti-Bolshevik groups in the region, the Ossetians, the Terek Cossacks, some Muslim groups, and delegates from the major Russian political organizations.

Bolshevik officials declared Ossetia an autonomous Soviet republic in March 1918, but their authority was limited. The spreading Russian civil war spilled into the region in mid-1918. Bolshevik troops allied to the Muslim Chechens and Ingush overran Russian Ossetia in November 1918. Ingush warriors captured and looted Vladikavkaz. Under the direction of the Bolshevik leader Comrade Ordzhonikidze the Bolsheviks and Muslims unleashed a reign of terror with Ossetian, Terek Cossack, and anti-Bolshevik Russians arrested and executed.

The Bolsheviks in January 1920 created the Mountain Autonomous Republic, which included most of the territory of the Caucasus Mountain region. In 1922 the southern part of Ossetia was made part of Georgia, and the Georgian Soviet government established an autonomous South Ossetian region to win Ossetian loyalty. Regional and ethnic disputes caused the breakup of the mountain republic, and North Ossetia was created as a separate autonomous region in 1924, but the majority of government posts were held by ethnic Russians. In 1925 the leaders of North and South Ossetia unsuccessfully attempted to unite the Ossetian homeland. The autonomous region was raised to the status of an autonomous republic within the Russian Federation in 1936.

During World War II, German columns invaded the Caucasus region and occupied North Ossetia in 1942. The Ossetians remained unmoved by the overtures of the Nazi authorities, but once the Germans were driven back, the Muslim Digors received the same treatment as the other Muslims in the region and were deported to Central Asia on the orders of Joseph Stalin. In 1944 Stalin, whose mother was Ossetian, after deporting the Muslim Digors, arbitrarily enlarged the North Ossetian republic with the addition of districts separated from Stavropol Krai and the western district of Ingushetia, the Ingush homeland.

In the postwar period literary and artistic expressions of Ossetian culture were encouraged by the Soviet government. After 1954 the writing system of the South Ossetians, which had been based on Georgian, was changed to the Cyrillic alphabet used in North Ossetia. The Digors, rehabilitated in 1956, began to return to their homeland in 1957, although Ossetian communities remain scattered throughout Central Asia.

The Soviet liberalization of the late 1980s sparked a rapid and dramatic rise of nationalism among the divided Ossetian peoples. In 1988 the Ossetians in

Georgia demanded secession and unification with North Ossetia, the demands setting off violent clashes between Ossetians and Georgians in South Ossetia. Thousands of Ossetian refugees fled across the mountains to North Ossetia, their plight fanning nascent nationalism in Russian Ossetia. On 11 December 1990 the nationalist Georgian government rescinded South Ossetia's autonomy and renamed the region Shida Khartli, Inner Georgia. The following day, 12 December 1990, the region's nationalist leaders declared the independence of the South Ossetian Democratic Republic, which was not recognized by the governments of Georgia or Russia. In April 1992 South Ossetia's autonomous status was reestablished within Georgia, but independence remained a volatile issue.

The disintegration of the Soviet Union allowed long-suppressed grievances to be aired. The Ingush renewed their old claim to territory transferred to North Ossetia in 1944 and laid claim to the city of Vladikavkaz. In May 1992, after separating from Chechenia, the Ingush demanded the return of their traditional territory, but Ossetian nationalists reacted by driving the Ingush inhabitants of Vladikavkaz from the city and attacking Ingush villages in the disputed districts. Over 50,000 Ingush refugees fled across the border into Ingushetia, but the dispute remained unsettled. Sporadic fighting in the region has left hundreds of dead and injured.

The conflicts with the Georgians in the south and the Ingush in the west have fueled the growth of Ossetian nationalism, but the majority work for autonomy, not full independence, fearing the loss of Russian protection in the volatile region they have inhabited since ancient times. The Ossetians, although needing Russian protection in the mostly Muslim region, continue to work for the unification of their small nation in a single political entity. In the spring of 1995 the Ossetians changed the name North Ossetia to Alania to emphasize their historical connection to the ancient Alans.

In 1997 a state of emergency was again declared in South Ossetia following the lapse of the state of emergency first declared in 1990. Many of the tens of thousands of Ossetian refugees who fled the fighting in 1990–91 have returned to the region, but ethnic tensions in the region remain a serious problem for the Georgian government.

SELECTED BIBLIOGRAPHY

Olson, James S. *An Ethnohistorical Dictionary of the Russian and Soviet Empires.* 1994.
Pereira, Michael. *Across the Caucasus.* 1973.
Pushkarev, Sergei. *Self-Government and Freedom in Russia.* 1988.
Rywkin, Michael. *Russian Colonial Expansion to 1917.* 1988.
Weekes, Richard V. *Muslim Peoples: A World Ethnographic Survey.* 1984.

PIEDMONTESE

Piemonti; Piemontese

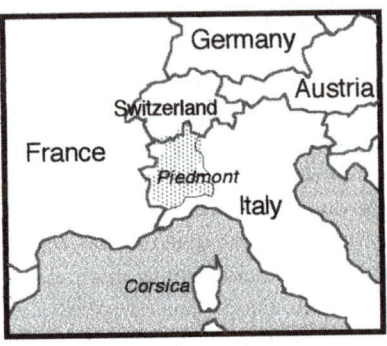

POPULATION: Approximately (2000 e) 3,750,000 Piedmontese in Europe, concentrated in the northwestern Piedmont region of Italy.

THE PIEDMONTESE HOMELAND: The Piedmontese homeland occupies the upper part of the Po valley, a fertile upland plain drained by the Po River and its tributaries. The region is nearly surrounded by mountains, the Cotian and Maritime Alps on the west, the Graian and Pennine Alps on the north, and the Apennines in the south. In the west, high Alpine valleys lead into the Alps, which comprise many high peaks including Punta Argentera, at 10,817 feet (3,297 m.), and Mount Viso, at 12,602 feet (3,841 m.). In the south, Piedmont is separated from the Mediterranean Sea by the homeland of the Ligurians.*

Piedmont forms a semiautonomous region of the Italian Republic that was established in 1948 and received limited autonomy in 1970. *Region of Piedmont (Piemonte)*: 9,807 sq.mi.–25,399 sq.km. (2000 e) 4,281,000—Piedmontese 77%, Occitans* 7%, other Italians* 12%. The Piedmontese capital and major cultural center is Turin, called Torino in Piedmontese and Italian, (2000 e) 958,000 (metropolitan area 1,721,000), the former capital of the Kingdom of Sardinia and the first capital of united Italy.

FLAG: The Piedmontese national flag, the official flag of the region, is a red field divided by a centered white cross and bearing an inverted blue crown on the top half.

PEOPLE: The Piedmontese are an Italian people of mixed Italian, French,* and Occitan ancestry. The culture of the Piedmontese is quite different from the standard Italian culture of central and southern Italy, being a basically Alpine culture with considerable Italian, French, and Occitan influences. The long, separate history of the Piedmontese sets them apart from other Italians, as do their culture and dialect. The majority are Roman Catholics, with a small, but influential, Protestant minority.

The language spoken in Piedmont, along with standard Italian, is Piedmontese, which is distinct enough from standard Italian to be considered a separate Romance language. The language, with considerable French and Occitan borrowings, is spoken in two dialects, High Piedmontese and Low Piedmontese, and remains the language of daily life for most of the Piedmontese population. The language, called a Gallo-Italic language, displays a close affinity to French in the pronunciation and truncated terminations.

NATION: The region, originally settled by early Celtic peoples, came under Roman rule between 177 and 121 B.C. Called Pedemontium by the Romans, meaning at the foot of the mountains, the province formed part of Cisalpine Gaul. The mountainous regions remained outside Roman control until 25 to 15 B.C., when the Celtic tribes were defeated, and the Roman provinces in Italy and Gaul were united. The region formed a prosperous part of the Roman Empire for over five centuries.

The collapse of Roman power in the fifth century left the region open to invasions by tribes from outside the empire. Huns overran and ravaged the region in A.D. 452, and in the sixth century Longobards (Lombards*), a Germanic tribe, conquered the fertile Po River basin. The Lombards incorporated Piedmont into their kingdom in 568, and modern Piedmont developed from the western districts of Turin and Ivera of the Lombard kingdom.

Conquered by Charlemagne in 774, the Franks absorbed Piedmont into the Frankish Empire, later the Holy Roman Empire. In the eleventh century parts of the region passed by marriage to the Savoyards.* Free communes emerged as alternative power centers in the twelfth century, while other districts remained under the rule of feudal lords, the most powerful being the counts (later dukes) of Savoy and the marquises of Saluzzo and Montferrat. In the fifteenth century the Savoyard state emerged as the most powerful regional force, its territories straddling the mountains that traditionally divided the Italian and French territories of Southern Europe.

The bilingual Savoy duchy, dominated by the French-speaking Savoyards, was occupied by French troops in 1536. Later restored, the duchy moved its capital from Chambéry to Turin, although the language and tone of the court remained French until the eighteenth century. The region was often a battlefield in the European wars, with Savoy traditionally allied to the French. In 1720 the duke of Savoy acquired the island of Sardinia and renamed the state, taking the title king of Sardinia. In 1848 the Sardinian kingdom acquired additional territories, including the remaining Piedmontese territories.

The Sardinian kingdom became a center of the Risorgimento in the 1850s, the movement to unite the numerous Italian states under the rule of the kingdom's House of Savoy. Napoleon III, for his help in uniting Italy, demanded the cession of the culturally French regions of the kingdom, Savoy, Nice, and

Menton, which were ceded to France in 1860. Turin was named the capital of the newly united Italian kingdom in 1861; however, a Tuscan dialect spoken around Florence was adopted as the new national language over unwavering Piedmontese opposition. The Tuscan dialect, spoken by less than 10% and written by only 1% of Italy's population, was considered more representative of the majority of the spoken dialects in Italy than the distinct Piedmontese language.

The Italian kingdom finally wrested Rome and the central provinces from papal rule in 1870, and the authorities transferred the capital of the kingdom to the more central city. The Italian government's move to Rome dealt a severe blow to the Piedmontese and has never been forgiven. The loss of prestige and power undermined Piedmontese enthusiasm for Italian unification. A movement formed in the 1870s to protect the Piedmontese dialect from Italianization incited a literary revival and over the next decades spurred a cultural revival. The Piedmontese revival coincided with the development of a large industrial middle class that further divided the region from agrarian central and southern Italy.

Fascism gained strength in Italy after World War I, but its base lay in Rome and the poor, backward south. Nationalists and communists gained support in industrial Piedmont, the rival ideologies leading to frequent violent clashes, particularly in Turin. The fascist Italian government, allied to the Axis powers in the late 1930s, won enthusiastic Piedmontese backing with promises to recover the territories lost to France in 1860. The region's initial enthusiasm declined rapidly after fighting broke out on the nearby French border in June 1940. The Italian government surrendered to the Allies in 1943, and the Germans* quickly occupied the northern Italian regions, treating their former allies as a conquered people.

Liberated from German rule in 1945, the Piedmontese began agitation for autonomy, the movement gaining support following the 1946 Italian referendum that eliminated the beloved monarchy that had ruled Piedmont for over 900 years. In 1948 a separate Piedmont region was created, but all decisions remained with the bureaucrats in Rome.

Piedmont's industries boomed in the 1950s and 1960s, attracting hundreds of thousands of workers for Italy's underdeveloped southern regions. Forced to communicate, both the workers and their Piedmontese supervisors replaced their mutually incomprehensible dialects with standard Italian in the workplace. In 1950 approximately 60% of the Piedmontese spoke only the Piedmontese dialect, the percentage dropping rapidly with the influx of southerners and the spread of mass media over the next two decades. Fearing unrest in the northern regions that led Italy's postwar economic recovery, the government promised self-rule but after numerous delays finally granted only semiautonomous status in 1970.

The Italian economic miracle, confined to the northern regions, raised the Piedmontese levels of industrial production and incomes to the equal of neighboring European regions but greatly increased Piedmontese frustrations with the massive and inefficient Italian state. Resentment of their taxes being squandered on the corrupt and backward south grew from the increasing integration of the northern regions into mainstream Europe in the 1970s.

A Piedmontese nationalist movement emerged in the 1980s, closely allied to other such movements evolving across the prosperous northern regions, particularly in neighboring Lombardy. By 1992 the alliance of northern Italian nationalist, autonomist, and separatist groups, the Northern League, had become a major political force. The Europeanization of Piedmont has fueled a strong desire to participate in the continental federation, the European Union, without the encumbrance of the huge and inefficient Italian bureaucracy or the poor, crime-ridden southern regions.

In 1990 the majority of the Piedmontese described themselves as bilingual. Only 36% spoke Italian only, but just 17% continued to use Piedmontese as the only language of daily life. The revival of the 1970s and 1980s has reinforced the Piedmontese literary tradition and the vibrant middle-class culture of the region.

In the 1990s the northern Italian regions have increasingly demanded greater economic and cultural autonomy. The frustration with the creaking Italian state has manifested itself in increasing support for a separate federation of independent states in northern Italy, which nationalists call Padania. The Piedmontese, looking forward to European integration, see themselves as the only nation in Italy able to compete as equals with the most advanced regions of the European Union (EU). The per capita income in Piedmont is over 30% higher than the Italian national average.

SELECTED BIBLIOGRAPHY

Carello, Adrian N. *The Northern Question: Italy's Participation in the European Economic Community and the Mezzogiorno's Underdevelopment.* 1989.

Cunsolo, Ronald S. *Italian Nationalism from Its Origins to World War II.* 1990.

Facaros, Dana. *Northwest Italy.* 1991.

Hine, David. *Governing Italy: The Politics of Bargained Pluralism.* 1992.

Smith, Denis M. *The Making of Italy 1796–1870.* 1988.

POLES

Polsky; Polish

POPULATION: Approximately (2000 e) 44,880,000 Poles in Europe, 37,820,000 in Poland, 1,153,000 in Ukraine, 414,000 in Belarus, 265,000 in Lithuania, 245,000 in Germany, and sizable communities in Russia, Czech Republic, Slovakia, Latvia, Austria, Hungary, and Romania. Outside Europe the largest Polish populations are in the United States, Canada, Kazakhstan, and Australia.

THE POLISH HOMELAND: The Polish homeland lies in Central Europe south from the Baltic Sea. Most of the region is flat lowlands, part of the North European Plain with few natural barriers. The only upland regions are in the south, the Malopolska hills, the Sudeten Mountains, and the Carpathian Mountains, which rise to 8,197 feet (2,499 m.) at the highest peak, Rysy. The major rivers, the Vistula, Oder, Warta, and the Western Bug, are major transportation routes connected to the Baltic Sea. There are many lakes, particularly in the northeast. About half of the land is arable, and about 28% is forested.

Poland disappeared as an independent state in the late eighteenth century but regained its independence in 1918, although its boundaries have varied considerably during the twentieth century. *Republic of Poland (Rzeczpospolita Polska)*: 120,756 sq.mi.–312,758 sq.km. (2000 e) 38,592,000—Poles 98%, Ukrainians* 1%, Germans,* Kashubians,* Belarussians,* Czechs.* The Polish capital and major cultural center is Warsaw, (2000 e) 1,648,000 (metropolitan area 2,389,000), on both banks of the Vistula River.

FLAG: The Polish national flag, the flag of the republic, is a horizontal bicolor of white over red.

PEOPLE: The Poles are a West Slav nation, the largest of the West Slav peoples. They belong to the Lechitian branch of the West Slavs, which also includes the Kashubians and Sorbs.* Influenced by centuries of domination by more powerful neighboring nations, the Prussians, Austrians,* and Russians,* the Polish culture and language exhibit many borrowings, including a marked Germanic influence, particularly in the western and southern provinces. The overwhelming number of Polish believers are Roman Catholic, officially about 95%, although many are nonpracticing, and the Catholic Church has retained a strong influence on the culture of the Poles. Roman Catholicism has played an important role in the history of the Poles and serves as a cornerstone of Polish identity. About 62% of the Poles live in urban areas. The Polish heartland, Poland, now contains very little ethnic diversity, with about 98% of the country's inhabitants being ethnic Poles. Before World War II there were about 3 million Jewish Poles; however, more than 90% were killed during the Nazi occupation, often with Polish help. The survivors mostly left Poland for Israel or the West, and in the late 1990s less than 10,000 remain in Poland.

The Polish language, called Polska, is a Lechitic language of the West Slavic group of languages spoken in four major dialects, Mazovian, Malopolska, Wielkopolska-Kujawy, and Silesian. The language is written in the Roman alphabet augmented by the use of diacritical marks. It is extremely rich phonetically, having ten vowels and thirty-five consonants. The vocabulary is basically Slavic but has been enriched by borrowings from German, French, English, Italian, Belarussian, Russian, and Ukrainian. The language of the Kashubians is often treated as a dialect of Polish, although it evolved as a separate West Slavic language.

NATION: The flat plains between the Sudeten and Carpathian Mountains and the Baltic Sea were originally populated by Celtic peoples. In the first century A.D. Goths from Scandinavia moved across the plains, beginning a long history of invasions. In the fifth century diverse Slav tribes, moving from the east, overran and settled the region. The Polians or Polanie, the Dwellers of the Fields, in the ninth and tenth centuries extended their authority over the other Slavic tribes and united the region around present Poznan under the Piast dynasty. The name Polska or Poland was first used in the eleventh century.

The history of the Polish nation traditionally dates from 966, when the Piast ruler Mieszko I adopted Latin Christianity. The Poles expanded their territory in wars with Germans, Hungarians,* Czechs, Kashubians, Danes,* and Ukrainians. The Polish kingdom was established in 1025 under the Piast dynasty, but following the death of Boleslaw III in 1138 the kingdom was divided between his sons and subsequently disintegrated into a number of warring principalities.

The Mongols invaded the region in 1240–41, ravaging the countryside. At the same time the neighboring dominions of the Prussians had been subjugated by the Teutonic Knights, and German colonists, encouraged by the Polish princes, began to settle in the Polish lands. During the period of German colonization, large numbers of Jews, fleeing persecution in Western Europe, found refuge in the region.

The reunification of Poland was begun by Ladislaus I, who ruled from 1320 to 1333. Enlightened policies, including protection of the Jews, brought massive Jewish immigration from other countries where persecutions continued. The union by marriage of the Poles and the Lithuanians* began in 1386, bringing the two nations into dynastic union under the Jagiello dynasty. During the period of disunity, the German Teutonic Knights gained a foothold in the north, and their power was broken only by their defeat by combined Polish and Lithuanian forces at Tannenberg in 1410.

Although involved in frequent wars, the Polish-Lithuanian Empire eventually stretched from the Baltic to the Black Sea. In 1526 the Poles took control of territory that included the city of Warsaw, which was made the Polish capital sixty years later. In 1569 the Polish and Lithuanian states were administratively unified. The fifteenth and sixteenth centuries saw a great cultural flowering, a golden age of scholarship, literature, and the arts, but also the growing power of the Polish nobility and gentry.

From 1572, when the Jagiello dynasty died out, the Polish crown became elective, and the nobility had effective control of the kingdom. Contested elections, factional disputes, and frequent insurrections prevented a strong dynasty from evolving in Poland and kept the kingdom weak and divided. The nobility and gentry enjoyed a certain democratic freedom, but the peasantry was reduced to serfdom, and conditions continued to worsen for the Polish majority. The middle class, which controlled commerce, was mostly German or Jewish.

Wars with Russians and Swedes* in the sixteenth and seventeenth centuries, led to the loss of much territory. In 1655 the Swedes overran much of Poland, while the Russians invaded from the east. Inspired by the heroic defense of the monastery at Czestochowa, the Poles managed to regroup and save their country from complete dismemberment. King John III, John Sobieski, who reigned from 1674 to 1696, temporarily restored the prestige of Poland, but at his death the kingdom virtually ceased to function as an independent state, its fate increasingly determined by its powerful neighbors, Russia, Prussia, and Austria.

In the early eighteenth century shifting alliances involved the Poles in the Northern War, and dynastic disputes led to the War of the Polish Succession. The Polish economy, still primarily agricultural, declined, and orderly administration was made impossible by feuding among the great landed families and the involvement of the neighboring states. In 1772, fearing that all of Poland would come under Russian domination, the German emperor, Frederick II, proposed to Catherine I of Russia that Poland be partitioned, the plan later enlarged to include Austria. Three successive partitions, in 1772, 1793, and 1795, resulted in the complete disappearance of the Polish state.

A national revival begun in the early nineteenth century among the Polish intellectual class in Germany quickly spread to Austrian and Russian Polish territories. A nationalist revolt in 1830–31, known as the November Revolution, in Russian Poland was at first successful, but the Polish army was eventually defeated, and Congress Poland lost its autonomy and was integrated into the Russian Empire. Thousands of Poles emigrated, particularly to the United States,

Canada, and to Paris, which became the center of Polish nationalist activities. Rebellions broke out in 1848 in Prussian and Austrian Poland, and in 1863 the Poles in Russian Poland rebelled. After crushing the revolt, the Russians reduced the Polish territories to mere administrative provinces and began an intensive program of Russification.

The late nineteenth century saw the breakup of the great estates, which were divided into peasant freeholds, and the industrialization of the cities, particularly the manufacture of textiles and iron goods. The policies of Russification and Germanization, official government programs in Russia and Prussia, left only the Poles in Austrian territory with some autonomy.

The outbreak of World War I spurred renewed Polish nationalist activity, with the early efforts mostly directed against Russia. Polish legions, led by Joseph Pilsudski, fought for two years alongside the Germans and Austrians, who had occupied Russian Poland. In November 1916 the German and Austrian governments declared Poland an independent kingdom; however, the Germans retained control over the Polish government. Pilsudski resigned and was imprisoned, and from then on the Polish national movement was centered on Paris and became actively anti-German.

The defeat of the Germans and Austrians and the collapse of tsarist Russia allowed the Poles to regain their independence, which was proclaimed on 9 November 1918. Pilsudksi returned as chief of state. The 1919 Treaty of Versailles gave the new Polish state access to the Baltic Sea via the Polish Corridor, which divided German territories in West and East Prussia. The Polish-Russian border, as proposed by the Paris Peace Conference, would have given the formerly Polish districts with large Belarussian and Ukrainian populations to the new Soviet Union, but the Poles insisted on the restoration of their 1772 borders. War with Soviet Russia followed, and the Poles drove the Russians back from Warsaw and secured part of the claimed territory. About one-third of the population of the new Polish state was made up of non-Poles, who often suffered discrimination and unequal treatment.

A liberal constitution was adopted in 1921, and industrialization progressed; however, the condition of the peasantry remained poor, and the landed gentry retained much of their former power and properties. Political instability continued until a 1926 military coup that suspended constitutional government and gave Pilsudski dictatorial powers. After his death in 1935, a new constitution made the parliament a tool of the governing clique, called the Colonels. During the 1930 the Polish government attempted to maintain a pragmatic balance of power among the country's powerful neighbors, Nazi Germany and the Soviet Union. The economic depression of the period led to widespread unemployment accompanied by increasing anti-Semitism.

In early 1939, backed by the French and British governments, the Polish government rejected a German demand for Danzig (Gdansk). On 23 August 1939 Nazi Germany and the Soviet Union signed a nonaggression pact, which included a secret clause for the partition of Poland between the two new allies.

On 1 September the Germans invaded Poland, precipitating World War II. In spite of guarantees from their British and French allies, the Poles received little effective assistance, and on 17 September Soviet troops attacked on the east. After the Nazis turned on their Soviet allies and invaded the Soviet Union in 1941, all of Poland came under German rule.

Poland suffered tremendous material damage and loss of life during the war. The Nazi authorities eliminated nearly the entire Jewish population, and millions of Poles died or were deported to forced labor in Germany. Many Poles, traditionally anti-Semitic, participated in the massacres of Jews, including working at the infamous death camps established on Polish territory. Other Poles, including members of the government-in-exile, fought with distinction with the Allies or joined partisan groups fighting the Germans inside Poland.

When Soviet troops entered Poland in 1944, a pro-Soviet government was established at Lublin. A Polish uprising from August to October 1944 was brutally crushed by German troops, while Soviet troops remained inactive outside Warsaw. The last German troops were expelled from Poland in early 1945. The postwar reorganization of territory gave the Poles former German territory in Silesia and Prussia, while the Soviet Union annexed the eastern districts of Poland. The expulsion of the German population was sanctioned, and German property was mostly confiscated. Under Soviet auspices a communist government was established following controlled elections in 1947. Polish foreign policy became identical to that of the Soviet Union and relations with the Vatican were severed. The Catholic Church became the object of oppression, and many prelates were imprisoned, church properties were confiscated, and church schools were closed.

The harsh conditions of life under the communist government led to widespread rioting in 1956, which forced the government to reconsider many policies. A new government under Wladyslaw Gomulka denounced the Stalinist terror and removed many Stalinists from official positions. Agricultural collectivization was halted, leaving most farmland in the hands of individual farmers. After a brief period of liberalization, Gomulka again tightened the party's hold on Poland in the early 1960s.

In December 1970 increasing food prices led to riots by workers in the Baltic port cities, particularly Gdansk. Gomulka was replaced, but by the mid-1970s a severe recession necessitated more price increases that led to strikes and the arrests of hundreds of protesters. The bishop of Krakow, Karol Wojtyla, became Pope John Paul II in 1978, and his first official visit to Poland, in June 1979, drew several crowds of over 1 million people. Emboldened by the pope's visit, antigovernment protests increased.

The continued food shortages and the expensiveness of housing caused new strikes in 1980, first at the Lenin Shipyards in Gdansk. The striking workers, led by Lech Walesa, formed an illegal labor union, Solidarity, which was later recognized and became tremendously popular, and the strikes continued. Martial law was declared in December 1981, Solidarity was banned, and many leaders were arrested. Solidarity and its leaders, particularly Walesa, remained a powerful force throughout the 1980s as the Polish economy failed to improve.

In 1989 Solidarity was again granted legal status and participated in negotiations that led to free elections. Solidarity, converted into a political party, won a majority in parliament, and Lech Walesa was named president. In January 1990 the new government introduced a radical program to convert Poland's command economy to a market-led economy. The transition proved harder than anticipated, and popular discontent grew as political instability increased. From 1990 through 1992 Poland had four prime ministers. In presidential elections in 1995, Walesa was defeated by an ex-communist, Aleksander Kwasniewski. However, Kwasniewski continued to follow the reform policies and to maintain Poland's applications to join the important Western political and military alliances, the European Union (EU) and the North Atlantic Treaty Organization (NATO), which the Poles officially joined in early 1999.

The Polish economy, following a sharp decline with the introduction of a free market system in the early 1990s, began to recover in 1996. Between 1996 and 1999 the Poles began to see the fruits of economic reform; however, their goal, integration into the European Union, was complicated by the number of Poles engaged in farming. The largest part of the EU budget goes to farm subsidies, making the incorporation of the Polish homeland into the union an expensive proposition.

SELECTED BIBLIOGRAPHY

Hintz, Martin. *Poland.* 1998.

Millard, Frances. *The Anatomy of the New Poland: Post-Communist Politics in Its First Phase.* 1994.

Quinn, Frederick. *Democracy at Dawn: Notes from Poland and Points East.* 1998.

Wandycz, Piotr. S. *The Lands of Partitioned Poland, 1795–1918.* 1993.

Zamoyski, Adam. *The Polish Way: A Thousand-Year History of the Poles and Their Culture.* 1993.

PORTUGUESE

Portuguesas

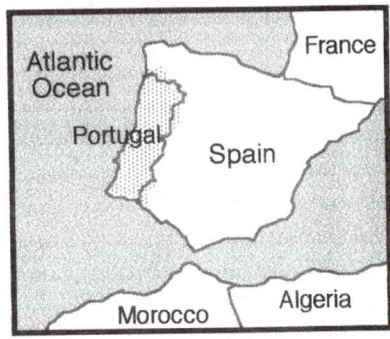

POPULATION: Approximately (2000 e) 11,872,000 Portuguese in Europe, 10,301,000 in Portugal, 754,000 in France, and smaller numbers in Switzerland, Germany, Belgium, Luxembourg, and Spain. Large Portuguese communities outside Europe include an estimated 1 million in South America, mostly in Brazil, Uruguay, and Paraguay, over 600,000 in South Africa, 350,000 in the United States, and 90,000 in Canada.

THE PORTUGUESE HOMELAND: The Portuguese homeland lies in Southwestern Europe on the western side of the Iberian Peninsula with a 500-mile (805-kilometer) coastline on the Atlantic Ocean. The frontiers of the homeland are defined by mountains and rivers, and Portugal is roughly divided by the Tagus River. The territory north of the Tagus is mountainous, cool, and rainy, while south of the river the terrain is mostly drier, rolling plains. The land rises from the fertile coastal plains on the Atlantic Ocean to the western edge of the huge plateau, the Meseta, which occupies most of the Iberian Peninsula. The highest range is the Estrela Mountains in central Portugal, rising to almost 6,562 feet (2,000 m.). The country is crossed by rivers rising in Spain and flowing to the Atlantic that provide the only good harbors at their mouths.

Portugal became a separate kingdom, independent of Spain, in 1143. The monarchy was ended in 1910 and Portugal became a republic. *Republic of Portugal (República Portugesa)*: 35,383 sq.mi.–91,642 sq.km. (2000 e) 10,510,000— Portuguese 98%, Africans, Brazilians. The Portuguese capital and major cultural center is Lisbon, Lisboa in the Portuguese language, (2000 e) 675,000 (metropolitan area 2,562,000), a major seaport on the Tagus River.

FLAG: The Portuguese national flag, the official flag of the republic, is a vertical bicolor of red and green, the red stripe twice the width of the green. The national arms, framed by a yellow artillery sphere, appears over the color division.

PEOPLE: The Portuguese are a Latin nation whose ancestry combines a number of distinct ethnic elements, principally Iberians, Romans, Visigoths, and, later, Moors. The modern Portuguese claim descent from the ancient Lusitanians, the pre-Roman inhabitants of the region. The Portuguese culture and language, based on early Latin traditions and dialects, have been influenced by centuries of contact with North Africa and the mixing of Portuguese colonists with the subject peoples in Africa, Latin America, and Asia. The culture is closely related to that of the neighboring Spaniards* and has been influenced by the three primary cultures that dominated the Iberian Peninsula, the Latin, the Visigoth, and the Moorish. The Portuguese population is overwhelmingly Roman Catholic, with an estimated 97% considering themselves believers. A majority of the population lives in rural villages, with just 37% of the population living in urban areas.

The language of the Portuguese is a Western language of the Romance language group spoken in four distinct dialects, Beira, Galician, Estremenho, and Madeira-Azores, the last spoken by the Madeirans* and Azoreans.* Standard Portuguese, the literary language, is based on the Estremenho dialect spoken around Lisbon and Coimbra. Originally, Portuguese developed among the Galicians,* then spread south throughout present-day Portugal. Like Spanish, the language contains a very large number of words of Arabic origin along with a great many words of French or Greek origin. The language of the former extensive Portuguese Empire, it is spoken by 165 million in Brazil and by millions more in Africa and Asia.

NATION: Celtic tribes, the forerunners of the Lusitani or Lusitanians in central Portugal and the Conii in the south, are thought to have occupied the region by 1000 B.C. Part of the large network of Celtic tribes that predated the Roman expansion, the Lusitanians had their stronghold in the Serra da Estrela. The Lusitanian Celtic culture was characterized by disunity, with tribal or clan loyalty superseded only when the tribes faced a common foe.

Under Viraitus in the second century B.C. and Sertorius in the first century B.C., the Lusitanians, despite defeats, stoutly resisted Roman incursions into their territory. The Conii, in the southern Algarve, submitted more readily. Julius Caesar and Augustus completed the Roman conquest, and the Roman province of Lusitania flourished. Roman ways and speech were adopted, and commerce with other parts of the vast Roman Empire evolved a sophisticated Romanized culture in the region.

At the beginning of the fifth century A.D., when Roman power collapsed, the whole Iberian Peninsula was overrun by Germanic invaders. The Visigoths took control of the southern districts, while the Suevi established a kingdom that included the northern territories of modern Portugal. In the later sixth century the Visigoths absorbed the Suevi kingdom. During the sixth and seventh centuries, the Algarve remained under the rule of the Byzantines of the Eastern Roman Empire.

In A.D. 711 the Visigoths were defeated by Moors invading from North Africa. The Muslim culture and science had a great impact on the region, particularly in the south. Religious toleration was practiced under Moorish rule, but a large minority of the Christian population converted to the Moors' Islamic religion.

The long period of the Christian reconquest of the Iberian Peninsula lay the foundations of the Portuguese nation. Up to the Middle Ages, the history of Portugal was that of the Iberian Peninsula. The kings of Asturias drove the Moors from the northern area of Galicia in the eighth century, and the Castilians invaded Beira and took control of Coimbra in 1064. Alfonso VI of Castile obtained French* aid in his wars against the Moors, and Henry of Burgundy married Alfonso's illegitimate daughter and was granted the county of Portugal in 1095. The territories reconquered from the Moors were organized into a feudal county, composed of Spanish fiefs. Portugal and the Portuguese derive their names from the northernmost fief, the Comitatus Portaculenis, which extended around the old Roman seaport of Portus Cale, the present Oporto.

On the death of Alfonso I in 1109, Count Henry and later his widow, Teresa, refused to continue feudal allegiance to the Spanish kingdom of Leon. In 1139 Henry's son, Alsonso Henriques, declared Portugal independent of the Spanish kingdom of Castile and Leon and took the title Alsonso I, king of Portugal. Portuguese independence was recognized by the Spaniards in 1143. The pope recognized Portugal's independence in 1179.

Alfonso I, aided by the Knights Templars and other military orders sworn to fight the Moors, extended the Portuguese border as far south as the Tagus River. His son, Sancho I, who ruled from 1185 to 1211, encouraged Christians to settle in the newly conquered southern districts. King Alsonso III, who reigned from 1248 to 1279, completed the conquest of the southern Algarve and established his capital at Lisbon.

The last of the legitimate descendants of Henry of Burgundy, Ferdinand I, was followed by his illegitimate half brother, John I, who secured the Portuguese throne in 1385. His branch of the Burgundian line became known as the House of Aviz. King John's reign was one of the most notable in Portuguese history. He successfully defended the kingdom against the Castilian Spaniards in 1385 and in 1386 permanently allied his nation to the English* by the Treaty of Windsor.

The Aviz dynasty of Portugal maintained a brilliant court and promoted the Portuguese culture and exploration. Under the aegis of Prince Henry the Navigator, the Portuguese ventured out into the unknown seas, discovering Madeira and the Azores and in 1415 taking control of the first colonial territory in Africa, the Moroccan town of Ceuta. Portugal flourished as a maritime and colonial power, and Portuguese explorers in the fifteenth and sixteenth centuries, opened the African coast to European trade, discovered the Cape of Good Hope route to India and the East Indies, and secured a trade monopoly in the newly contacted regions of Asia. Lisbon grew as the center of Portugal's trade with Africa and Asia. Portugal and Spain divided the non-Christian world between them.

In the late fifteenth century, as had other Portuguese kings before him, Emanuel dreamed of uniting the Iberian Peninsula under his rule and successively married two daughters of King Ferdinand V and Queen Isabella I. Under pressure from his Spanish relations, he followed Spanish example by expelling the Jews and Muslims in 1497, thus depriving Portugal of much of its commercial middle class. His son, John III, again influenced by the Spaniards, in 1536 introduced the Inquisition into Portugal to enforce religious conformity. By the time he died in 1557, the Portuguese had begun to decline as a political and commercial nation. The Aviz dynasty died out in 1580, and Philip II of Spain, the nephew of the last Portuguese king, claimed the throne, and the period known as the Spanish or Sixty Years' Captivity began.

Spain's wars against the English in the sixteenth century cut off Portuguese trade with Northern Europe, and the Portuguese were compelled to participate in Spain's wars, including the Thirty Years' War. The Dutch* attacked the Portuguese overseas territories during the war, and although they were eventually driven from Brazil, most of Portugal's vast empire was lost. Gradually reduced to the status of a Spanish province, Spanish rule provoked widespread discontent. After unsuccessful revolts in 1634 and 1637, Portuguese revolutionaries, aided by the French, finally won independence from Spain in 1640, but the Portuguese never regained their position as a major European nation.

Gold from Brazil stabilized the weak Portuguese economy in the early eighteenth century but allowed the Portuguese kings to rule without dependence on the parliament, the Cortes, which was last called in 1677. Absolutism reached its height in the mid-eighteenth century, when the marquis de Pombal was the de facto ruler of the kingdom. He attempted to introduce aspects of the Enlightenment in education and to revitalize agriculture and commerce, but his policies disturbed the entrenched interests of the church and the nobility. Most of his reforms were rescinded during the late eighteenth and early nineteenth centuries.

Portugal's traditional alliance with England brought the kingdom into war with Napoleonic France. In 1807 French forces invaded the country, and the royal family fled to Brazil and made Rio de Janeiro the seat of the Portuguese government. Portugal was devastated during the Peninsular War, which ended with the French defeat in 1811. The Portuguese king, John VI, returned to Portugal only after a liberal revolution in 1820. He accepted a liberal constitution in 1822, but feuding among his sons led to civil war and the loss of Portugal's Latin American colonies in Brazil. The later nineteenth century was marked by coups, revolutions, and dictatorship, but the Portuguese hold on large African territories, particularly in Mozambique and Angola, was secured.

In an attempt to end the inefficiency and corruption that characterized public life, Charles I in 1906 established a dictatorship under a conservative leader, João Franco, but in 1908, Charles and his heir were assassinated. Manuel II succeeded to the Portuguese throne; however, in 1910 a republican revolution overthrew the monarchy and established a republic. The change in rule failed to cure Portugal's chronic economic problems, while anticlerical measures aroused the hostility of the Catholic Church.

During World War I, the Portuguese were at first neutral but in 1916 entered the war against Germany and Austria. The economy deteriorated, and in the postwar period insurrections of both the Right and the Left made conditions in the country even worse. In May 1926 an army coup deposed the fortieth ministry since the proclamation of the republic. Within a few days of their success the military leaders selected General António de Fragoso Carmona to head the new government. In 1928 Carmona was elected president in an election in which he was the sole candidate. In the same year he appointed António de Oliveira Salazar, a professor of economics at the University of Coimbra, as minister of finance. Salazar was given extraordinary powers in order to put Portuguese finances on a sound basis. In 1926 a military coup overthrew the government. A new corporate constitution, adopted in 1933 under António de Oliveira Salazar, established what would become the longest dictatorship in Western European history.

Portugal remained neutral during World War II but was friendly toward the Allies. After the war, determined to end their isolation, the Portuguese joined the North Atlantic Treaty Organization (NATO) in 1949 and became a member of the United Nations (UN) in 1955; however, under Salazar's rule modernization tended to be neglected in favor of maintaining the status quo, with the result that the Portuguese increasingly fell behind the other European nations during the 1950s and 1960s.

Portugal lost its colonies in India to an invasion of Indian troops in 1961, and armed insurrections in its African colonies threatened the remainder of its once-extensive colonial empire. In 1968 Salazar suffered a stroke and was replaced by Marcello Caetano as prime minister. Under his regime development plans were put into place in Portugal and the overseas territories, and repression was somewhat eased. The official liberalization was so timid that the democratic opposition rejected it as counterproductive, and the economy continued to decline as the growing African wars ate up 40% of the country's annual budget.

In early 1974 dissatisfaction with the unending African wars, compulsory military service, and growing economic problems resulted in widespread unrest. On 25 April 1974 a group of military officers toppled the government, but the movement quickly came under the domination of Marxists. To free Portugal of the drain of its long colonial wars, Angola, Mozambique, São Tomé and Principe, and Cape Verde were granted independence, while Indonesian troops invaded and took control of Portuguese East Timor. Most banks and industries were nationalized, and a massive agrarian reform program was instituted. The return of troops and settlers to Portugal from the newly independent African nations aggravated the homeland's problems of unemployment and political unrest.

Free elections were held in 1978, and several moderate governments followed, each trying to stabilize the country politically and economically. From 1983 to 1985 a coalition government under Marco Soares began to make headway against the chaos and poverty that remained as a legacy of Salazar's long dictatorship. In 1986 Portugal, along with Spain, was admitted to the expanding continental political and economic union, the European Economic Community (EEC), later changed to the European Union (EU). Development funds from the EU and favorable domestic policies raised the Portuguese standard of living, although they remain among the poorest of the Western Europeans.

In July 1996 the Portuguese republic and six of its former colonies formed the Commonwealth of Portuguese-Speaking Countries (CPLP). The Portuguese Commonwealth seeks to preserve the Portuguese language, coordinate diplomatic efforts, and improve cooperation among the member states. The group's members are Angola, Brazil, Cape Verde, Guinea-Bissau, Mozambique, Portugal, and São Tomé and Príncipe.

Portuguese voters in 1999 rejected an initiative to devolve political power to newly created regions. One of the reasons for rejecting regional councils is the historical Portuguese fear of the more numerous Spaniards of the Iberian Peninsula. Should the northern Portuguese be given more political power, they may draw closer to the culturally and linguistically related Galicians of Spain, a move that could be reinforced by the EU policies of promoting cross-border regionalism.

SELECTED BIBLIOGRAPHY

Bragança-Cunha, Vicente. *Revolutionary Portugal.* 1987.
Ferreira, H. G., and M. W. Marshall. *Portugal's Revolution: Ten Years On.* 1986.
Hobbs, Hoyt, and Joy Adzigian. *Portugal.* 1996.
Kaplan, Marion. *The Portuguese.* 1998.
King, John, and Julia Wilkinson. *Portugal.* 1997.

RHINELANDERS

Rheinlanders; Rheinfränkisch

POPULATION: Approximately (2000 e) 13,765,000 Rhinelanders in Europe, 11,500,000 in the Rhineland region of Germany, and other large Rhinelander communities in Berlin and other parts of Germany. Outside Europe there are large Rhinelander populations in Canada, the United States, and Brazil.

THE RHINELANDER HOMELAND: The Rhinelander homeland lies in Northwestern Europe, mostly in the valley of the Rhine River, primarily on the west bank of the river but with small areas on the east. The region is drained by the Rhine, Moselle, and Wupper Rivers and the lower course of the Ruhr. The only upland area lies in the Rhenish Slate Mountains in the south. The northern districts include part of the industrialized Ruhr district, and the south has some of Europe's most celebrated wine-producing districts.

The area has no official status, and the historic Rhineland region is split between the German states of North Rhine-Westphalia, Rhineland-Palatinate, Saarland, and Hesse. *Rhineland (Rheinland)*: 9,454 sq.km.–24,485 sq.km. (2000 e) 13,763,000—Rhinelanders 83%, other Germans* 11%, Turks* 4%. The Rhinelander capital and major cultural center is Cologne, Köln in German, (2000 e) 951,000 (metropolitan area 1,893,000), the historic capital of the region. Other important cultural centers are Düsseldorf, (2000 e) 574,000 (1,321,000), the capital of North Rhine-Westphalia, Wiesbaden, (2000 e) 260,000 (923,000), the capital of Hesse, and Bonn, (2000 e) 295,000 (592,000), the post–World War II capital of West Germany.

FLAG: The Rhenish national flag, the flag of the post-World War I national movement, is a horizontal tricolor of green, white, and red. The flag was subsequently adopted as the official flag of the German state of North Rhine-Westphalia.

PEOPLE: The Rhinelanders are a German people of Franconian descent, traditionally oriented to the French* and the West, not to Berlin and the East. The Rhenish culture is distinct from the Prussian-influenced culture of Berlin and has been shaped by liberal ideas and historic ties to the West since the Roman conquest of the region. The Rhenish homeland contains some of the most densely populated regions of Europe. The Rhinelanders are divided religiously, with about two-thirds Roman Catholic and about one-third Protestant, mostly in the northern districts.

The language of the Rhinelanders is German, mainly the dialect called Rheinfränisch, which is spoken extensively in the Rhine Valley. The language, not inherently intelligible with other German dialects, is actually a group of dialects spoken in geographically distinct areas of the region and descended from medieval Franconian. The Rhinelanders are bilingual, with standard German spoken in all areas, although the identity of the Rhinelanders is readily recognized due to their characteristic pronunciation.

NATION: Celtic tribes inhabited the fertile territory along the Rhine River, but the first organized government of the region was under the Romans, who conquered and colonized the region from the first century A.D. Many of the present Rhenish cities are of Roman origin. Latinized in culture and language, the inhabitants of the region developed a sophisticated, advanced culture that lasted for nearly four centuries.

In the fifth century Roman control faltered, and the region fell to invading Franks, Germanic tribes from outside the Roman Empire. By the sixth century the Franks controlled the Rhineland, much of western Germany, and northern France. In the eighth and ninth centuries the Rhineland formed the heartland of the Frankish realm under Charlemagne, whose capital was at Aachen. In 843 Charlemagne's heirs divided his empire into three parts, with the Rhineland included in the middle kingdom, Lotharingia or Lorraine.

In the tenth century the Rhenish territories were included in the Holy Roman Empire, which reached its peak of power and influence in the mid-eleventh century. Following the breakup of the duchy of Lower Lorraine in the eleventh century, the Rhineland split into more than 100 ecclesiastic and secular fiefs and free imperial cities. In 1356 the several Rhenish rulers, the archbishops of Mainz, Trier, Cologne, and the Count Palatinate of Rhine, became electors of the empire.

The region remained a Roman Catholic stronghold during the Protestant Reformation and the religious wars in the sixteenth century. Politically divided into a number of petty states, the region was often a battleground for competing powers and religions. The devastation of the period left most Rhinelanders looking toward Paris and the West as new and liberal ideas began to be felt in Europe. In the east, Brandenburg and its successor, Prussia, came to represent to the Rhinelanders the harsh militaristic and Protestant influences in Germany.

The expanding Prussian kingdom first gained control of small territories in the Rhine region in 1614. The feudal system, which disappeared from much of Europe by the eighteenth century, remained a force in many of the small Rhenish states. During the eighteenth and nineteenth centuries hundreds of thousands of Rhinelanders emigrated to escape the feudal backwardness and poverty of the region, most going to North America.

During the French Revolution thousands of fugitives took refuge in the region, but with the rise of Napoleon the area became a target of French expansion. Following the French conquest, Napoleon abolished most of the small states, and in 1803 he annexed all of the Rhineland west of the Rhine River to France, the first time all of ancient Gaul had been under one government since the fall of the Roman Empire. Napoleon's reorganization of the Rhineland eliminated the numerous petty states but prepared the way for Prussian control, gained by the victorious Prussians through the Peace of Vienna in 1815 at the end of the Napoleonic Wars.

The Westernized, mainly Roman Catholic Rhinelanders greatly resented the harsh, conservative, Protestant Prussians, while the industrialization of the Ruhr in the late nineteenth century made Prussia the strongest power in Europe. A great increase in population accompanied the industrialization, leading to much emigration to America of the excess. The Rhineland, despite rule by reactionary Prussia, remained one of the centers of liberal German thought, spiritually and culturally closer to Paris than to Berlin.

Rhenish chafing under "foreign" Prussian rule came to a head during the revolutionary upheavals in Europe in 1848–49. Democratic and Rhenish separatist groups fought pitched battles with Prussian troops. The Rhenish revolution was finally put down with brutal reprisals and increased oppression in the region. In 1866 the French supported the creation of an independent buffer state in the Rhineland, which the Prussians supported in exchange for French neutrality during Prussia's war with the Austrians.* The Prussian failure to live up to its promises further soured Franco-Prussian relations and was one of the causes of the Franco-Prussian War in 1870.

Rhenish nationalism evolved as an anti-Prussian mass movement in the late nineteenth century. Nationalists in the region supported the idea of the separation of the Rhineland, called Rhine Province, from Protestant Prussia. Prussian rule remained very unpopular in the region, being both authoritarian and anti-Catholic.

During World War I, the Rhineland's industries were very important to the German war effort. The collapse of the German Empire, militarily defeated in November 1918, was followed by revolution. A Rhenish separatist movement formed in Koblenz and Aachen, with disturbances breaking out in the Rhenish cities by separatists and radicals opposed to the National Congress of Soldiers and Workers Councils meeting in Berlin in December 1918 to form a new German government. On 4 December 1918 in Cologne, a meeting of the Catholic Center Party adopted a resolution in favor of a Rhenish-Westphalian Republic as part of a renewed German state. The separatists had the support of much of the Catholic population of the region. The Catholics hoped to end the privileged position the Protestants had enjoyed under Prussian rule.

The French and Belgian governments, seeking a neutral space between their borders and those of Germany, supported the erection of an independent Rhenish buffer state at the Paris Peace Conference in 1919, but they were opposed by American president Woodrow Wilson and other Allied leaders. Germany ceded small districts to Belgium, and in the south the Saar Territory was formed under French military rule with the output of the important Saar mines turned over to the French for compensation for the coal mines destroyed by the Germans in French Lorraine.

Communists took control of many industrial areas, and chaos ruled throughout the region. A meeting of Rhenish leaders in Cologne adopted a resolution in favor of secession from Germany. On 1 June 1919 the independence of the Rhenish Republic was proclaimed with its capital at Koblenz. A Rhenish government was formed under the leadership of Hans Dorten, but by the terms of the Treaty of Versailles between Germany and the Allies, Allied troops occupied the Rhineland, and the Dorten government collapsed. British and Belgian troops occupied the northern districts, and American troops occupied the south.

The Saar Territory in January 1920 was given the status of a sovereign state under French military occupation and the League of Nations. By the terms of the treaty, the Saarland's future would be decided by plebiscite in 1935, with the choices of inclusion in Germany, union with France, or separate independence.

In March 1920 a communist "Red Army" of 50,000 to 80,000 took over the major industrial centers but was driven underground by German Freikorps dispatched by the German government. Instability in the region and default on the German reparations were used as an excuse for the French and Belgian governments to send troops to occupy the region in January 1923.

The French, unable to persuade the other Allies for annexation or the creation of a Rhenish buffer state, supported a Rhenish rebellion to achieve French aims, a buffer between French territory and Germany. On 21 October 1923 separatist uprisings broke out in Düsseldorf, Bonn, Koblenz, Wiesbaden, and Mainz. The separatists, including Konrad Adenauer, a member of the provincial diet from 1917 to 1933 and the post–World War II German leader, proclaimed the independence of the Rhineland Republic (Rheinische Republik) with its capital at Aachen on 22 October. The new republic was created as a federation of three states, North State, South State, and Ruhr State.

Rioting by communists, fighting between Rhenish separatists and the German government's Freikorps, the opposition of the United States and the United Kingdom, and the assassination of the Rhenish president on 31 January 1924 finally brought on the collapse of the republic. Many Rhenish nationalists fled to France, and in 1925 Germany and the Allies signed the Locarno Pact, which regulated the administration of the Rhineland under Allied occupation and reaffirmed the demilitarization of the region. Support for Rhenish nationalism faded with the return of constitutional government.

In 1930 the last Allied troops in the region, the French, withdrew, but under the terms of the Locarno Pact the Rhineland was to remain demilitarized. The rise of National Socialism, the Nazis, in the early 1930s was accompanied by agitation for the reoccupation of the Rhineland. In January 1935 a plebiscite was held in the Saarland after a massive propaganda campaign by the Nazis. The result was 90.7% in favor of reunion with Germany. Soon after the plebiscite, the German government purchased the Saar mines from France, and they were exploited for the German rearmament effort.

The heavy industries of the Rhineland were crucial to the Nazis' plans for rearmament and for the later conquest of Europe. On 8 March 1936 Adolf Hitler denounced the Locarno Pact, and on the same day German troops crossed the Rhine and occupied the region. All important Catholic, socialist, nationalist, and communist leaders were removed from official posts, and the many anti-Nazi organizations and political parties were forcibly abolished. Despite the suppression of all opposition, the region, particularly Cologne, remained an anti-Nazi stronghold for several years.

The German fortifications in the Rhineland, called the Siegfried Line, an extensive system of defenses, were penetrated by the Allies during World War II only after very heavy fighting. The region was heavily bombed, particularly the industrial cities of the Ruhr. Aachen was the first important German city to fall to the Allies in October 1944. In 1945 French troops occupied the districts of Trier and Koblenz, while British troops occupied Cologne, Düsseldorf, and Aachen districts. The French government again proposed the separation of the Rhineland from Germany but was stopped by the British and Americans, who opposed the breakup of Germany into a number of small states.

In 1946 the region was reorganized, with the consolidation and creation of new states in the region. The state of Rhineland-Palatinate was formed from the merger of the Rhenish Palatinate, Rhenish Hesse, the southern districts of the former Prussian Rhine Province (including Koblenz and Trier), and a small district of the former Prussian province of Hesse-Nassau. North Rhine-Westphalia was formed through the union of the former Prussian province of Westphalia, the northern districts of Prussia's Rhine Province, and the state of Lippe. The Saarland, again under French occupation, was made a self-governing state under the auspices of the United Nations. The new states had little national or historical unity or political cohesion.

Konrad Adenauer, the former Rhenish nationalist leader, was elected chancellor of the Federal Republic of Germany in 1949. Adenauer, mayor of Cologne until dismissed by the Nazis in 1933, had twice been imprisoned. He was the cofounder of the Christian Democratic Union in 1945 and was the party's president from 1946 and 1966. He was reelected chancellor in 1953, 1957, and 1961.

In spite of the division into several states, the Rhinelanders retained a cultural and historical unity in the region. The Rhenish Catholic vote remained important, and in the 1960s and 1970s the Rhinelanders were among the most avid supporters of European unity, as the Rhine River links the economically inseparable areas of eastern France, the Rhineland, and the Low Countries.

In the 1990s the Rhineland is split between a prosperous south and an economically ailing north, a consequence of the postwar period, when the leaders of the industrial Ruhr actively discouraged industries moving from East Germany from settling in the area. The industries generally went to the southern districts, which are now among the most prosperous in Germany. In the state of Lower Saxony, the Rhinelanders have a separate regional league with responsibility for traffic, cultural affairs, and welfare.

The integration of Europe in the European Union (EU), a political and economic federation, has again stimulated interest in Rhenish autonomy. The region, closely tied economically and historically with neighboring French, Belgian, and Dutch* regions, remains oriented toward Paris and Brussels, not to Berlin and the east. The transfer of the German capital from Bonn in the Rhineland to the historic capital of Berlin has raised Rhenish fears that Germany is once again moving its attentions to the east.

SELECTED BIBLIOGRAPHY

Ardagh, John, and Katharina Ardagh. *Germany and the Germans: The United Germany in the Mid-1990s.* 1996.

Bunn, T. Davis. *Rhineland Inheritance.* 1993.

Craig, Gordon A. *The Germans.* 1991.

Medlicott, W. N. *The Rhineland Crisis and the Ending of Sanctions, March 2–July 30, 1936.* 1978.

Sperber, Jonathan. *Rhineland Radicals: The Democratic Movement and the Revolution of 1848–1849.* 1991.

ROMANDS

Romandes; Suisse Romands

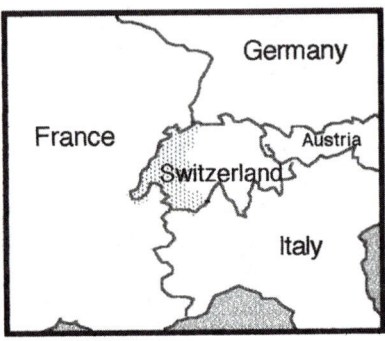

POPULATION: Approximately (2000 e) 1,428,000 Romands in Europe, 1,291,000 in the Romande region of Switzerland, and the remainder in other regions of Switzerland and in France, particularly Paris.

THE ROMAND HOMELAND: The Romand homeland, called Romandy, lies in western Switzerland, occupying the western part of the Swiss Plateau and bounded by the Jura Mountains on the west and the Pennine Alps in the south. The Jura, from the Celtic word for forest, are much lower and smaller than the Alps and are the birthplace of the renowned Swiss watchmaking industry. Romandy includes the lake regions around Lake Geneva, Lac Léman, Lake of Neuchâtel, Lake Morat, Lake La Gruyère, and Lake Bienne [Bielersee]. Much of the region comprises fertile uplands and grassy meadows of the western Swiss Plateau, which has the majority of the population. Forests cover the foothills and lower peaks of the mountains and help to reduce the risk of avalanche during the snowy winter months.

Romandy, popularly called Swiss Romandy, has no official status; the region forms the majority, French-speaking cantons of Fribourg, Geneva, Jura, Neuchâtel, and Vaud and the western districts of Valais and Bern cantons. *Swiss Romandy (Romande)*: 3,934 sq.mi.–10,189 sq.km. (2000 e) 1,535,000—Romands 82%, other Swiss* 14%, Portuguese,* Spaniards,* Turks.* The Romand capital and major cultural center is Geneva, Genève in French, (2000 e) 165,000 (metropolitan area 443,000), the capital of Geneva Canton. The other major Romand cultural center is Lausanne 123,000 (319,000), the capital of Vaud Canton.

FLAG: The Romand national flag is a vertical tricolor of blue, white, and red, bearing three white stars on the blue stripe, two stars divided vertically white and blue at the juncture of the blue and white stripes and a single blue star centered on the white stripe.

PEOPLE: The Romands are a distinct Romance people whose national identity has been shaped by Protestantism and their long, separate history rather than by ethnic or linguistic considerations. Ethnically, the Romands are related to the Burgundians* and Savoyards* in the adjacent areas of France. The Roman national identity is that of a French-speaking, Protestant nation, but not as part of the French nation. The descendants of ancient Latinized Celtic tribes, the Romands have only recently become politically mobilized, one of the latest in Europe to define their national identity as a distinct European nation. The majority, estimated at over 75%, are Protestants, with a minority, about 23%, Roman Catholic.

The language of the Romands is French, with the majority speaking both the standard French based on the Paris dialect and the local Romand or Jurassic dialects, which differ considerably from standard French. An estimated one-third of the total Swiss population is able to speak French, although the Romands account for less than 20% of the total.

NATION: Celtic tribes, Allobroges, Sequani, and Helvetii or Helvetians, inhabited the region around the highland lakes by the sixth century B.C. Part of the Celtic culture that extended across the European continent, the Celts remained tribal and never developed a state structure. Disunited, the tribes fought valiantly, but the region fell to Roman rule in 58–57 B.C. The Celts adopted the Roman culture and language, and the Latinized Celtic towns became centers of Roman culture.

Barbarian tribes overran the lake region with the decline of Roman power in the fifth century. Invading Germanic Burgundians devastated the Roman towns in A.D. 442–43. The Burgundians settled, and Geneva became the seat of a Burgundian kingdom. Another Germanic tribe, the Franks, conquered the area in 534–36 and joined it to their kingdom, the forerunner of the Holy Roman Empire.

Romandy formed an important and prosperous part of Charlemagne's empire. At the division of the empire among Charlemagne's heirs in 843, Romandy was included in the middle kingdom of Lotharingia and later, from 888 to 1032, the region was included in the successor kingdom known as Transjurane Burgundy. In 1033 the Holy Roman Empire gained control of the Romandy area. Politically divided, the region included the ecclesiastical states of Lausanne and Geneva, Hapsburg territory in Fribourg and other areas, and French-speaking districts controlled by the German-speaking Bernese.

In 1285 the citizens of Geneva placed themselves under the protection of the rulers of Savoy and by 1387 enjoyed wide powers of self-rule. Savoyard control of the bishops of Geneva nearly succeeded in subjugating the region. In 1481

Fribourg became the first of the Romand states to join the expanding Swiss Confederation. In 1533 Geneva formed an alliance with two Swiss cantons, Fribourg and Bern, to resist Savoyard pressure.

In 1536 Geneva, where the French theologian John Calvin had just settled, revolted against the duchy of Savoy and refused to acknowledge the authority of its Roman Catholic bishop. Calvin organized his church democratically, incorporating ideas of representative government. From 1541 to 1564 Geneva became the stronghold of the Calvinist brand of Protestantism. The citizens expelled the Savoyard bishop, and many turned to the new doctrine, the Protestant Reformation.

The German-speaking Bernese conquered Vaud in 1536, facilitating the eastward expansion of the Protestant Reformation to the other Romand states. In 1538 the Genevans expelled the Protestant leader John Calvin, but in 1541 the majority accepted Calvin's doctrine. Calvin established a theocratic state at Geneva that developed as a leading political and intellectual center of Protestant Europe. Geneva's preeminence grew with the arrival of thousands of Protestant Huguenot refugees fleeing persecution and massacres in Roman Catholic France.

The Romand states, both inside and outside the Swiss Confederation, were protected by a network of political and defensive alliances. The Romands, both Protestant and Catholic, prospered, and the old ruling classes were gradually replaced by patrician elites more concerned with commerce than politics or religion. Carefully avoiding involvement in the sporadic wars that convulsed the surrounding regions, the Romands in the eighteenth century grew rich on trade and services.

Buffeted by the chaos and upheavals that followed the French Revolution in 1789, the Romand states became a refuge for those fleeing the revolutionary excesses in France. Occupied by French troops in 1798, the states were forcibly joined to Napoleon's Helvetic Republic. In 1803 the Swiss Confederation was partly restored, including the new French-speaking canton of Vaud and the important city of Lausanne. Following Napoleon's final defeat in 1815, Geneva, Neuchâtel, and Valais joined the Swiss Confederation. In 1848, following a nearly bloodless civil war between the Protestant and Catholic cantons, the Swiss adopted a new constitution that guaranteed cantonal autonomy.

The Swiss Confederation carefully avoided involvement in the European wars of the nineteenth and twentieth centuries while developing as one of Europe's major banking centers, including secret financial ties to the Nazis during World War II. The confederation remained a prosperous, multinational, and multireligious island of tolerance in the center of turbulent Europe.

Switzerland's strict neutrality precluded membership in the League of Nations, the later United Nations, or any international organization; however, Geneva became the headquarters for many international organizations, including the League of Nations and many branches of the United Nations. In 1959 a referendum favored an exception, and Switzerland joined the European Free Trade Association (EFTA). In February 1971 women were, for the first time, allowed to vote in federal elections, and women have greatly affected subsequent elections in the region.

Modern Romand nationalism grew from the movement of the French-speaking western districts in the Jura Mountains to separate from the predominantly German-speaking Bern Canton. In 1978 the majority French-speaking districts of northwestern Bern voted to form a new canton called Jura, but the separatists failed to win enough votes in the mixed districts around Lake Bienne (Biel). The controversy opened a bitter rift between the French and German cantons of Switzerland. Nationalist organizations called not just for the separation of Jura but for the separation of the French-speaking Romandy from Switzerland.

The Cold War in Europe pushed the traditionally neutral Swiss into closer cooperation with Switzerland's European neighbors. In May 1992 the Swiss government formally applied for membership in the European Economic Community (EEC). A referendum in December 1992 on membership on a joint EEC-EFTA trading area was rejected, primarily due to opposition in the German-speaking cantons. To the chagrin of the pro-European Romands, Switzerland was left out of the continental trading system, while a growing rift separated Switzerland's two largest groups, the Romands and the Swiss-Germans.* The Romands, angered at the continuing domination of Switzerland by the more numerous Swiss Germans, became markedly more nationalistic, even removing the cross representing their allegiance to Switzerland from their national flag.

The increasing split between the two largest national groups in Switzerland has exacerbated the Romand perception that the Swiss-Germans are increasingly usurping Swiss identity and shunting the Romands to the margins of Swiss political life. The so-called fried potato ditch, the *Rösti-Graben*, has become more than just the imaginary line dividing the two peoples. For centuries Swiss identity has been defined in negative terms, not German, not French, not Italian, and not part of any international organization. The changing reality in Europe is also changing Romand perceptions of themselves, and they have now begun to redefine their identity as a separate European nation.

In February 1998 the Swiss-German canton of Zurich announced plans to start compulsory English in cantonal schools from an early age. The initiative of the cantonal government, which seems to be gaining favor in other parts of German-speaking Switzerland, threatens the teaching of French in the region and infuriated Romand leaders, who denounced the moves as threats to Switzerland's unity.

SELECTED BIBLIOGRAPHY
Bullen, Susan. *The Alps and Their People*. 1994.
Hilowitz, J. E. *Switzerland in Perspective*. 1991.
Lundman, B. J. *Nations and Peoples of Europe*. 1984.
Mayer, K. B. *The Population of Switzerland*. 1982.
Steinberg, Jonathan. *Why Switzerland?* 1996.

ROMANIANS

Rumanians; Daco-Rumanians

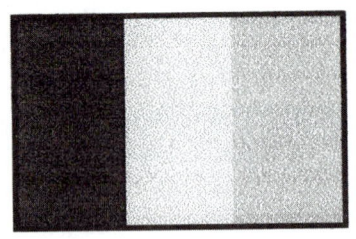

POPULATION: Approximately (2000 e) 23,723,000 Romanians in Europe, 20,610,000 in Romania, and other large Romanian communities in Ukraine, Russia, Hungary, and Moldova. Outside Europe there are Romanian populations in Central Asia, Israel, the United States, and Canada.

THE ROMANIAN HOMELAND: The Romanian homeland is rolling plains, the Walachian Plains and the eastern part of the Great Hungarian Plain, divided by mountains, the southeastern end of the Carpathians, which united in the center of Romania with the Transylvanian Alps. The country's major rivers are the Danube, which forms the southern boundary, and its tributaries, the Seret, Ialomita, Arges, Olt, Jiu, and Timis. The rivers water the extensive fertile plains in Walachia and Transylvania, which forms the eastern extension of the Great Hungarian Plain.

Romania's eastern regions, Walachia and Moldavia, united and took the name Romania, meaning "land of the Romans," in 1861. The country was recognized as an independent state in 1878 and was enlarged by the acquisition of former Hapsburg territory after World War I. *Republic of Romania (Republica Romania)*: 91,699 sq.mi.–237,500 sq.km. (2000 e) 23,148,000—Romanians 89%, Hungarians* 9%, Roms* (Gypsies), Saxons* (Germans), Ukrainians,* Slovaks.* The Romanian capital and major cultural center is Bucharest, called Bucharesti in Romanian, (2000 e) 2,341,000, which constitutes a separate provincial district.

FLAG: The Romanian national flag, the official flag of the republic, is a vertical tricolor of blue, yellow, and red.

PEOPLE: The Romanians are a Latin nation whose culture combines Roman heritage with later Germanic, Slavic, Rom, and Hungarian influences on both the culture and language. Although the Romanian nation was united after World War I, there remain sharp cultural and dialectical differences between the "Old Kingdom" Romanians of Moldavia and Walachia and the "New Province" Romanians of Transylvania, Bukovina, and Banat, territories incorporated into the Romanian state in 1918–20. The "Old Kingdom" Romanians were influenced by contact with Turks* and Slavs, while those in the west were included in the Hapsburg Empire of Austro-Hungary and remain more Western-oriented. The majority of the Romanians belong to the Romanian Orthodox Church, with sizable Roman Catholic and Protestant minorities, mostly in the western regions. About 55% of the Romanians live in urban areas.

The language of the Romanians is a Romance language of the Italic subgroup that is spoken in four major dialects, Moldavian, Muntenian or Walachian, Transylvanian, and Banat. The first two, Moldavian and Muntenian, are spoken in the east and have absorbed many Turkish and Slavic words and usages. They form the basis of standard Romanian, the official language of the republic. The dialects spoken in the west, Transylvanian and Banat, are closer to the other Italic languages as they developed without the Turkic influences of standard Romanian. Romanian has absorbed many Slavic words and forms from the neighboring Slavic nations, along with borrowings from Turkish, Greek, and Albanian.

NATION: The region was originally inhabited by peoples of Thracian stock. Called Getae by the Greeks and Daci or Dacians by the Romans, they were a tribal people with an advanced culture on the edges of the Roman Empire. The Dacians invaded Roman territory and were subsequently paid tribute by the Romans to keep the frontier peaceful. Roman emperor Trajan invaded Dacia in A.D. 102 and again in 105. Trajan established a number of Roman colonies, and Dacia became a Roman province.

In the third century the region was overrun by Germanic Goths, and Emperor Aurelian was forced to evacuate the Roman colonists in 270, leaving behind the Romanized Dacians, who perpetuated the Latin language and culture in the region. Successively overrun by Huns, Avars,* Bulgars,* and Magyars (Hungarians), the region broke up into feudal holdings. After a period of Mongol domination, in the thirteenth century, the history of the Romanian nation became that of the two Romanian principalities that emerged under native dynasties, Moldavia and Walachia, and of Transylvania in the west, which was often a dependency of the Hungarians and later of the Hapsburgs.

The Romanian homeland came under the influence of the Turkish Ottoman Empire and the Holy Roman Empire in the fifteenth century. The princes of Walachia in 1417 and Moldavia in 1504 became tributary to the Turkish sultans while retaining considerable independence. Hungary's defeat by the Ottoman Turks in 1526 led to the creation of a separate Transylvanian principality under nominal Turkish rule.

The Protestant Reformation gained converts in Transylvania, particularly among Roman Catholics. Transylvania became the cradle of Unitarianism and experienced a golden age as the bulwark of Protestantism in Eastern Europe. The religious and cultural influences further divided the Romanians of Transylvania and the western provinces from the Orthodox population of Moldavia and Walachia.

The prince of Walachia, Michael the Brave, defied both the Ottoman and Holy Roman Empires and at his death in 1601 controlled Walachia, Moldavia, and Transylvania, but his empire soon fell apart, and the Romanian regions again came under Turkish rule. In 1699 the Turks ceded Transylvania to the Austrians.* An ill-fated alliance between the Romanian princes and the Russians* in 1711 against the Turks led to Turkish domination and the disposition of the princes. Until 1821 the Turkish sultans appointed governors, called *hospodars*, usually chosen from the Greeks* resident in the Phanar district of Constantinople. The Phanariot Greek governors reduced the Romanians, with the exception of the landowning gentry, the boyars, to a mass of shepherds and peasant serfs. The period of Phanariot rule was one of the most oppressive and corrupt in the history of the Romanians. Exploitation of the large peasant class caused mass starvation and emigration.

At the end of the eighteenth century Russia and Austria-Hungary, which ruled a large Romanian population in Transylvania, gained considerable influence in Moldavia and Walachia. In 1821, when the Greeks under Alexander Ypsilanti revolted against Turkish rule, the Romanians of Moldavia, who hated the Greek administrators even more than the more distant Turks, aided the Ottoman Turkish forces to expel the Greeks. Tudor Vladimirescu, a Romanian officer in the Russian army, led a nationalist revolt in 1821, which resulted in the replacement of Phanariot rule with that of the native Romanian princes in Moldavia and Walachia. Russia, however, gained concessions in the principalities following the Russo-Turkish Wars. During the Russo-Turkish War of 1828–29, the Russians occupied both principalities. Although technically, Walachia and Moldavia remained under nominal Turkish rule, they became virtual Russian protectorates, and the eastern Romanians came under strong Slavic influence.

Under Russian pressure new constitutions were adopted in Moldavia in 1832 and Walachia in 1831, giving the boyars, the great landholding families, more extensive powers. At the same time a national revival was taking hold among the Romanians, a mass nationalist movement, antiboyar, anti-Russian, and anti-Turk. In 1848 Romanians in both principalities rebelled but were crushed by a joint Turkish and Russian force. Russian troops remained in the principalities until 1854, when they were withdrawn during the Crimean War and were replaced by a neutral Austrian force.

The Congress of Vienna in 1856 established the two principalities under Turkish suzerainty under the guarantee of the major European powers. In 1859 Alexander John Cuza was elected prince of both Moldavia and Walachia, which prepared the way for the union of the principalities as Romania in 1861. Cuza freed the serfs from their feudal bondage in 1864 and distributed some lands confiscated from religious orders, but his despotic rule was unpopular, and he was deposed in 1866. His successor, the German prince Carol of the House of Hohenzollern-Sigmaringen, approved a liberal constitution giving the Romanians greater freedoms and abolishing many of the feudal powers of the boyars.

In 1877 the Romanians joined Russia in war on the Turks, and in 1878 Romania was recognized as a fully independent state. In 1881 Romania was proclaimed a kingdom under King Carol I but continued to be torn by violence and turmoil, mostly due to the government's refusal to enact land reform, the corruption of government officials, and the interference of foreign governments. There was no attempt to curb the Romanians' traditional anti-Semitism, and the exploited peasants were encouraged to vent their frustrations against the Jews, particularly the Jewish agents of the absentee boyar landlords. A serious revolt broke out in 1907 and was directed at both the Jews and the boyars.

The Romanians remained neutral during the First Balkan War in 1912 but entered the Second Balkan War a year later and gained territory won from Bulgaria. When World War I broke out in 1914, the Romanian government proclaimed the kingdom's neutrality, but Romanian irredentism in the Austro-Hungarian Empire, particularly in Transylvania, persuaded the Romanians to declare war on the Central Powers in 1916. Knocked out of the war by an invasion of Austrian and German troops, the Romanians later rallied and ended the war as a victorious state. Shortly after the end of the war, the Romanian government annexed Bessarabia from Russia, Bukovina from Austria, and Transylvania and the Banat from Hungary.

New land laws passed in 1917 did much to break up the great estates and won favor with the Romanian majority, but the large, non-Romanian minorities were a constant source of friction. The Romanian government during the interwar period negotiated alliances primarily to retain the postwar territorial acquisitions. Although the Romanians enjoyed some prosperity, conflicts with the large, non-Romanian populations in the territories annexed after the war added to a growing instability in the region.

After 1929 the Romanians were engulfed in the general world economic crisis. Large-scale unemployment and political unrest led to the rapid growth of radical organizations. Romanian politics remained chaotic and violent. During the 1930s the monarchist party became very unpopular, but the legal opposition was divided and ineffectual. Radical groups emerged, including anti-Semitic and fascist groups such as the National Christian Party, which was linked to the violently anti-Semitic Iron Guard, a terrorist organization. By the late 1930s the Romanian kingdom had developed close ties to the fascist Axis states, Germany, Italy, and Hungary. Between the wars there was considerable tension between the Westernized "new province" Romanians of the territories taken from Hungary and the "old kingdom" Romanians of the heartland.

The country remained neutral when war broke out in Europe in September 1939, but in 1940 it became a neutral partner of the Axis. The government was powerless to resist territorial claims backed by Germany, losing Bessarabia and North Bukovina to the Soviet Union, Dobruja to Bulgaria, the Banat, part of

Transylvania, and Crisana-Marmures to Hungary. In 1940 the Iron Guard rebelled against the territorial losses. The king was deposed and replaced, and Ion Antonescu became dictator. In June 1941 the Romanians joined the German invasion of the Soviet Union. During the war half of Romania's Jewish population of 750,000 was killed in pogroms and in Axis extermination camps.

In August 1944 Soviet troops invaded Romania, which became a Soviet ally during the Cold War that followed the end of World War II. Politically and economically, the country became dependent on the Soviet Union, and on 30 December 1947 King Michael was forced to abdicate, and Romania was proclaimed a people's republic with a constitution similar to that of the USSR. In 1948 and 1949 all Romanian cultural and political institutions were reorganized along Soviet lines. The process of Sovietization included frequent purges of dissidents and anti-Soviet elements.

A new constitution adopted in 1952 was patterned on that of the Soviet state. The nationalization of industry and the collectivization of agriculture were carried out over stiff resistance by the small middle class and the peasant farmers. After the death of Soviet leader Joseph Stalin in 1953, Romania gradually drew away from close dependence on the USSR, and the Romanians asserted the country's right to develop its own variety of socialism.

In 1965 Nicolae Ceauşescu succeeded as head of the Romanian Worker's Party, which was renamed the Romanian Communist Party. Ceauşescu adopted a new constitution and changed the name of the republic to the Socialist Republic of Romania to mark its alleged attainment of a higher level of socialist achievement. During the late 1960s the Romanian government increasingly followed a foreign policy independent of the Soviet Union, gaining some support from the West, but the economic hardships and repression continued. The government promoted a personality cult around Ceauşescu and his family, accompanied by heavy censoring of the press and restricted personal liberties for ordinary Romanians. During the 1970s and 1980s industrialization was pressed at the expense of agriculture, which employed the majority of the Romanians. In 1981, with severe economic problems overwhelming the state, the government instituted an austerity program that resulted in shortages of food, electricity, and consumer goods.

Widespread unrest finally erupted in western Romania. Ceauşescu's brutal suppression of antigovernment demonstrations finally turned the army against him. Ceauşescu and his wife, Elena, fled Bucharest on 22 December 1989, but the two were soon captured. Charged with murder and embezzlement of government funds, they were tried in secret and were executed on 25 December. Hundreds died in the violence that swept the country following the overthrow of the Ceauşescu regime. In 1990 a provisional government was created to take control of the collapsing communist state, and the first free elections were held since 1937, but violence among political factions continued into the 1990s. The new government revoked many of Ceauşescu's repressive policies and imprisoned some of the leaders of his regime.

In 1992 a new constitution was approved that replaced Romania's communist legislation with democratic ideals. Elections held under the new constitution resulted in the reelection of the reformed communists, renamed the Party of Social Democracy in 1993. The government, suffering a lack of expertise, faced many problems in its efforts to reform the former command economy. The Romanians, already among the poorest in Europe, suffered from the dislocations that accompanied the institution of a market economy. In 1994 the Romanian government began to negotiate entry into the European Union (EU).

Although the barely reformed communists were ousted from government in 1996, fractious coalition governments have done little to reform the Romanian economy or political system. Economic gains in the middle 1990s gave way to renewed economic crisis in 1998, a trend that seems to mark the Romanian economy on the threshold of the twenty-first century.

In March 1999, when the North Atlantic Treaty Organization (NATO) planes attacked neighboring Yugoslavia, the Romanians supported the attack and drew closer to both the EU and NATO. The Romanian government's desire to integrate the country into the important European alliances dictated many of the positions adopted during the late 1990s.

SELECTED BIBLIOGRAPHY

Castellan, Georges. *A History of the Romanians.* 1989.
Ganeri, Anita. *Romania.* 1994.
Georgescu, Vlad, and Matei Calinescu. *The Romanians: A History.* 1991.
Kellogg, Frederick. *The Road to Romanian Independence.* 1995.
Treptow, Kurt W., and Marcel D. Popa. *Historical Dictionary of Romania.* 1996.

ROMANSH

Grischa; Rhaetians; Romansch;
Romanche

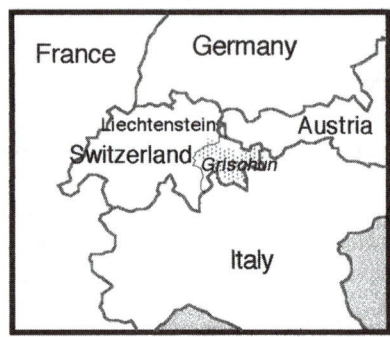

POPULATION: Approximately (2000 e): 71,000 Romansh in Europe, concentrated in the Grisons (Graubünden) Canton of Switzerland.

THE ROMANSH HOMELAND: The Romansh homeland lies in the Rhaetian and Leopontine Alps in southeastern Switzerland. The region has Alpine peaks, glaciers, forested highlands, and fertile valleys, including the famed Engadin valley of the Inn River, the valley of the Upper Rhine, and the Rheinwald valley on the Lower Rhine River. The Grisons Canton, called Graubünden in German, is the largest and least populated of the Swiss cantons. The Romansh population is concentrated in the valleys of the central districts of the canton.

The homeland of the Romansh is included in the Swiss canton of Grisons or Graubünden, an autonomous division of the Swiss Confederation. *Canton of Grisons (Grischun)*: 2,745 sq.mi.–7,111 sq.km. (2000 e) 174,000—Romansh 39%, Swiss-Germans* 37%, Italian Swiss 22%. The Romansh capital and major cultural center is Chur, called Cuera in the Romansh language, (2000 e) 33,000, the capital of the canton. Another important cultural center is Saint-Moritz, called San Maurezzan in Romansh, (2000 e) 7,000, site of the Winter Olympic games in 1928 and 1948.

FLAG: The Romansh national flag, the official flag of the canton, is a square banner divided horizontally, the lower half bearing a black mountain goat on white, the upper half, divided vertically, with blue and gold squares on the upper fly and black and white vertical stripes on the upper hoist.

PEOPLE: The Romansh, calling themselves Grischa, are a Rhaeto-Romantic people, one of the group of Rhaeto-Romantic nations that inhabit the eastern Alps and include the Ladins* and Fruilis.* The descendants of Latinized Alpine tribes, the Romansh are one of the four recognized nations within Switzerland.

The Romansh language belongs to the Rhaeto-Romantic branch of the Romance language group. It is spoken in three major dialects, Lower Engadine or Grisons, Upper Engadine, and Oberland. The language is the direct descendant of the Roman language brought to the region by the Roman legions.

A conservative Alpine people, the Romansh have preserved their unique culture in the high mountain valleys. The majority of the Romansh are Protestant, as are many of the canton's non-Romansh inhabitants.

NATION: The Alpine region was populated by the Celtic expansion in ancient times. The Celtic Suanetes dominated the high Alpine valleys when the region was conquered and annexed by the Romans in 15 B.C. Incorporated into the Roman province of Rhaetia, the region had practically no economic importance, but militarily Roman control of the high mountain passes was important for communications and trade between Italy and the northern Roman provinces. Christianity, brought to the region by the Romans, was codified by the establishment of a bishopric at Chur in the early fifth century.

The Latinized Celts, later called the Romansh, fought to preserve their Latin language, laws, and culture against the Germanic tribes that invaded the crumbling Roman Empire in the latter fifth century. Overrun by Ostrogoths in A.D. 493 and by the Franks in 537, the region eventually came under the authority of the Frankish kingdom, the forerunner of the Holy Roman Empire.

In the ninth century the bishops of Chur, a free imperial city of the Holy Roman Empire, began to attain prominence in the region. The bishops—after 1170, prince-bishops—allied themselves to the rising power of the Hapsburgs. Their power, however, was checked and gradually reduced by leagues of free communes and feudal lords that formed in the region between 1367 and 1436. The League of God's House, the Graubünden or Gray League, formed an alliance and joined the Swiss Confederation. The leagues made the Grisons a regional military power. In 1512 the leagues conquered the Valtellina region from Milan and ruled the region, richer and more populous than their Alpine homeland, as a subject territory.

The majority of the population of the leagues, including the Romansh, accepted the Protestant Reformation in 1524–26, but their Catholic subjects in the Valtellina staunchly resisted the Reformation. The Grisons, unlike the other Swiss cantons, did not remain neutral during the Thirty Years' War, which began in 1620, when the Valtellina Catholics rose and massacred their Protestant masters. The ensuing conflict eventually drew in most of the European powers. Restored to league rule in 1639, the Valtellina remained a subject territory until its incorporation into the French-dominated Cisalpine Republic by Napoleon in 1797. Two years later Grisons, more popularly known by its German name, Graubünden or Gray League, was forced to join Napoleon's Helvetic Republic. In 1803 Grisons joined the restored Swiss Confederation with German and Italian, but not Romansh, as official cantonal languages.

Mass emigration of the rural population, mainly to the Americas during the drought and depression after 1815, greatly reduced the number of German-speakers in the canton, giving the native Romansh more access to local authority.

The bitter controversy in the early nineteenth century over Switzerland's political system emphasized religious and cultural differences and marked the beginning of a particular Romansh nationalism. The conflict, settled in the nearly bloodless civil war of 1847–48, resulted in a new Swiss constitution that guaranteed cantonal autonomy in a loose confederal political system.

The Romansh, protected by Switzerland's armed neutrality during World War I, launched a peaceful campaign to end their domination by the German-speaking Swiss population and to win equal linguistic and cultural rights. The campaign, led by an active and persistent national movement, continued for over two decades. In 1937 the Swiss government finally accepted the Romansh language as one of the confederation's four official languages. Added protection for Romansh group, linguistic, and cultural rights became part of the constitution.

Their national identity protected by cantonal autonomy and guaranteed by the Swiss constitution, few Romansh felt culturally or linguistically threatened in multinational and multireligious Switzerland. The small national movement received little support and remained on the fringes of political life until the late 1980s and the growing debate over Switzerland's relations with a uniting Europe.

The growth of pro-European sentiment in the canton paralleled the emergence of a new awareness of their right to recognition as a separate European people. In May 1992 the Swiss government formally applied for membership in the European Community, a move widely supported by the Romansh. In December 1992 the Romansh, like the other non-Swiss-German national groups, voted for closer ties with the European Community, but the vote, due to the opposition in the German-speaking cantons, was narrowly defeated, and Switzerland remained outside the continental economic system.

The integration of the European continent has animated the long-dormant Romansh national movement in the 1990s. The movement's leaders stress that the national movement is a pro-European movement and is not directed against the Swiss Confederation that has sheltered the Romansh nation for nearly two centuries. The growing pro-European faction of the national movement foresees Romansh sovereignty transferred from the Swiss Confederation to a united and secure federal Europe that would protect the independence of one of Europe's smallest, but most ancient, of nations.

SELECTED BIBLIOGRAPHY

Mayer, K. B. *The Population of Switzerland.* 1982.
Murray, J. L. *History of Switzerland.* 1985.
Robertson, Ian. *Switzerland.* 1987.
Snyder, Louis L. *Global Mini-Nationalisms: Autonomy or Independence.* 1982.
Steinberg, Jonathan. *Why Switzerland?* 1996.

ROMS

Gypsies; Romani; Roma

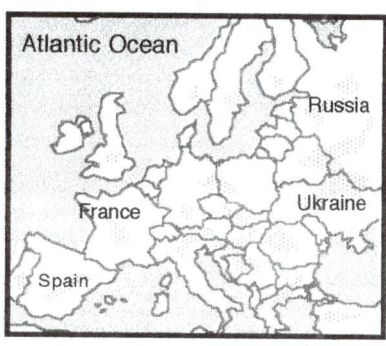

POPULATION: Approximately (2000 e) 8 to 10 million Roms in Europe, about four-fifths of the total in Eastern Europe and the former Soviet Union. Accurate estimates are difficult to obtain, as many governments count only nomadic Roms, others misrepresent Rom population figures, and some governments even deny the existence of Rom populations in their countries. Only about a half million maintain the Roms' traditional, nomadic way of life.

In 1999, the Council of Europe and the International Romani Union estimated the number of Roms in each European country, with the largest Rom populations in Romania with 1.8 million, Bulgaria and Spain with 600,000 each, Hungary with 450,000, Slovakia with 420,000, Russia with 400,000, Yugoslavia 300,000, Czech Republic 300,000, Macedonia 250,000, France 150,000, Greece 120,000, Germany 100,000, Britain 100,000, Italy 100,000, Albania 85,000, Ukraine 75,000, Poland 50,000.

THE ROM HOMELAND: The Roms are dispersed throughout the world, with the largest concentrations in Europe, particularly the countries of Central and Eastern Europe. In the majority of European states the Roms have few or no rights or official status.

FLAG: The Rom flag, recognized by all Rom communities, is a horizontal bicolor of blue over pale green charged with a centered red wheel with six or more spokes.

PEOPLE: The Roms, popularly called Gypsies, a medieval corruption of the name Egyptian, are a transnational European group with communities in virtually every European state. The Roms call themselves Gajo, Rom, or Romani and refer to all others as Gadje. The European Roms comprise three major divisions, the Roms, the Sinti, and the Kale, each with numerous subdivisions. The most important of the European Rom groups are the Gitano in Spain and Portugal; the Manouche in France; Sinte in Germany and Italy; Roms in Eastern Europe and the former Soviet Union; Romnichals in the British Isles; Boyash or Bayash in Romania; and the Xoraxaya in European Turkey. The Roms have adopted local languages and religions while retaining their separate cultures and languages. Intermarriage with Gadje has been limited, but some mingling over the centuries has given the Rom populations a wide range of physical appearances, from very dark to very fair.

The Rom language, called Romany or Romani, is spoken in seventeen major and minor dialects, many mutually unintelligible. The language belongs to the Indo-Iranian language family and is closely related to the languages of the northwestern Indian subcontinent. The Romany dialects and subdialects vary greatly from region to region, as local language borrowings have been absorbed.

In religion the Roms have adapted to local traditions, so that the European Roms display a wide variety of religious beliefs. The majority of the Roms are Christian, with Orthodox, Roman Catholic, and Protestant groups, but with others adhering to Islam or other belief systems.

NATION: According to Rom legends, their original homeland lay in the present province of Sind in southeastern Pakistan. Some Rom nomads are thought to have migrated west between 500 and 600 B.C., but the main migration arrived in Iran in the first millennium A.D. The migration is thought to have begun with refugees fleeing the Muslim conquest of Sind in A.D. 711–12. During their time in Iran the nomads split into three groups, the Gitanos, Kalderash, and the Manush.

Rom bands were first reported as moving into Eastern Europe from Asia Minor in the fourteenth century, and by the fifteenth century they first appeared in Western Europe. Many of the Roms settled as sedentary farmers and tradesmen, but others, less fortunate in the attitudes of local governments, were hounded from place to place. Smithing and metalworking developed as the primary occupations, valuable skills to sell to the settled populations. The name "Gypsy" began with the name Egyptian, on the mistaken idea that the Roms originated in a mythical Little Egypt, although some Roms entered Southern Europe from North Africa, having passed through Egypt. The name, corrupted to Gypsy, was eventually applied to all the European Roms.

By the mid-fifteenth century hostility to the Roms was widespread, and anti-Gypsy laws affected all Roms in Europe. Their eastern origins evolved many myths associated with the Roms, and a magical aura grew around the Roms that persists to the present. Rom women were often famous and sought-after fortunetellers. By the sixteenth century, the Roms in Europe were reduced to despised noncitizens. Their darker skin, different languages, and lack of an organized religion provoked widespread prejudices and opposition by the three pillars of European society, church, state, and the trade guilds. The Roms were barred from many established churches as legends associated the Roms with the crucifixion of Jesus, child stealing, and cannibalism.

The conquest of Southeastern Europe by the Ottoman Turks* forced many Roms to migrate to Western Europe, while others fled west to escape enslavement by feudal lords. By the fifteenth century most European states had passed stringent anti-Gypsy laws. The most abhorrent allowed enslavement or death, with bounties paid for Gypsies, dead or alive. Tales associating the Roms with the Crucifixion were used to justify the persecutions, expulsions, and suffering that followed the Roms throughout Europe. In the sixteenth and seventeenth centuries the first Rom prisoners were forcibly transported to the New World, often as slaves. The Roms in the Middle East and North Africa, where nomadic peoples were common, fared better than their kin in Europe.

European governments in the eighteenth and nineteenth centuries often treated the Roms very like the Jews, subject to special taxes, restrictions, official discrimination, and religious persecution. Only in the late nineteenth century did some European states rescind the more odious anti-Gypsy laws. Immigration to North America became one of the few options for the persecuted Roms of Europe. Only in the late 1800s were some of the most repressive laws rescinded in several Eastern European states; however, new restrictions and discrimination became common in Western Europe following World War I. As late as 1927 a group of nine Roms stood trial in Slovakia, charged with cannibalism.

German law had already legalized many anti-Gypsy restrictions when the Nazis came to power in 1933. The Nazis refused to accept the Roms as an Aryan nation, even though their language is of Aryan origin. Considered, like the Jews, to be of Asiatic origin, official Nazi persecution of the Roms escalated during the 1930s. In 1936 the first group of 400 Roms was imprisoned at the Nazi concentration camp at Dachau. Genealogical investigations, initiated in December 1938, followed a decree labeling the Roms as a menace to German society. Even persons with one-eighth Gypsy blood became subject to the increasingly harsh strictures.

Although the Germans had nothing to gain by persecuting the Roms, the treatment of Rom populations worsened radically following the outbreak of war in September 1939. In 1940 many thousands of German Roms were transported to concentration and work camps in occupied Poland. By the summer of 1942 the Nazi hierarchy had decided to exterminate Europe's Roms. On 16 December 1942 Heinrich Himmler signed a decree sending the remaining German Roms to the extermination camp at Auschwitz. Germany's allies, Italy, Vichy France, Romania, Slovakia, and Croatia, issued similar decrees. The Gypsy Holocaust claimed some 2 million lives during World War II, most dying in massacres or of hunger and disease, but 500,000 Roms perished in the Nazi death camps. At the end of the war not one Rom was called to witness at the German war crimes trials at Nuremberg in 1945–46. West Germany denied compensation to the surviving Roms, and throughout Europe many Roms were declared stateless.

In the postwar years the Roms began to organize closer intergroup contacts within the various European countries and to develop ways to protect Europe's remaining Rom population. In the early 1950s Rom leaders pleaded at the United Nations for the establishment of a Rom "Israel," an independent homeland to be called Romanistan, the Land of the Roms. The Rom petition did not receive a sympathetic hearing, and discrimination in many areas continued. Governments, often well intentioned, forced nomadic groups to settle, often in urban or rural slums, where unemployment, violence, and crime added to the generally poor public opinion of the Roms in many regions.

Until the 1960s there were few contacts between the various dispersed groups across Europe, but Rom nationalism asserted itself in spite of official opposition in many countries. In the early 1970s Rom leaders from many areas formed the World Romani Congress (WRC). In April 1971 the WRC brought together representatives of Roms from fourteen countries, representing over 3 million Roms. In 1976 the first International Rom Congress, held in India, brought together the representatives of the global Rom populations. In 1978 a second congress was held in Geneva, Switzerland. Each year the European Roms gather in the southern French town of Saintes-Maries-de-la-Mer.

Still surrounded by mystery, myth, and superstition, the Roms have again become the targets of ethnic hatreds released by the overthrow cf Communism in Eastern Europe and the Soviet Union. The frustrations and economic hardships of converting command economies to free markets are all too often turned on the most defenseless minority, the Roms. Attacks on Roms were particularly severe in Romania and the states of the former Soviet Union in the early 1990s.

Rom nationalists believe that the anticommunist revolution of 1989–91 may have opened their last opportunity to join the world community. In October 1991 a conference of European Gypsies at Rome put forward a new proposal for the recognition of the Roms as a transnational European community, a nation without a state but with the same guaranteed cultural, economic, and political rights everywhere in a united, federal European Union (EU).

Although many of the European countries in the late 1990s with the largest Rom populations are doing all they can to ensure that the EU sees them as potential members, the Roms living in these countries continue to suffer discrimination. In the Czech Republic, usually seen as a tolerant and peaceful state, the 300,000 Roms are denied jobs and are increasingly under attack. In two cities in the west of the country there have been proposals to seal off Rom neighborhoods from the rest of the communities. The proposals have roused not only human rights groups but many politicians and ordinary citizens. The provisions of the Czech Republic's citizenship law include stiff requirements that prevent some of the Roms from qualifying as citizens.

The end of hostilities in Yugoslavia, in mid-1999, particularly the return of hundreds of thousands of Kosovars* to the Serbian province of Kosovo, sent a wave of up to 80,000 Roms fleeing the region. The returning Albanians accused the entire Rom population of collaborating with the Serbs in driving the ethnic

Albanians from the area even though only a minority were involved in the ethnic cleansing. Many of the Roms sought refuge in neighboring countries, but others attempted to emigrate, legally or illegally, to Italy and other countries farther west.

SELECTED BIBLIOGRAPHY

Fraser, Angus. *The Gypsies.* 1994.
Kenrick, Donald, and Grattan Puxon. *Destiny of Europe's Gypsies.* 1990.
Liegeois, J. *Roma Gypsies: A European Minority.* 1995.
Moreau, Roger. *The Rom: Walking in the Paths of the Gypsies.* 1997.
Taylor, Gillian. *Historical Dictionary of the Gypsies (Romanies).* 1998.

RUSSIANS

Russkis; Russkies

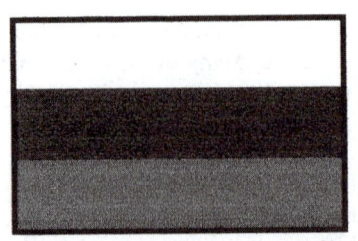

POPULATION: Approximately (2000 e) 112,847,00 Russians in Europe, 96,204 in European Russia, 15,880,000 in other European states of the former Soviet Union, and 365,000 in Germany, 65,000 in Poland, 18,000 in Bulgaria, and smaller numbers in other European countries. Outside Europe there are 25,893,000 Russians in the eastern regions of the Russian Federation, Siberia, and the Far East and an estimated 6,500,000 in the countries of Central Asia. Other large Russian populations live in the United States, Israel, Canada, and China.

THE RUSSIAN HOMELAND: The Russian homeland in Europe is the largest territory on the European continent and extends from the Arctic to the Black Seas and east to the Ural Mountains, which officially divide Europe from Asia. Much of the region lies in the East European Plain, often called the Russian Plain, which extends east to the Urals and south to the Caucasus Mountains. The southern border of European Russia lies in the geologically young, seismically active Caucasus Mountains, which extend between the Black and Caspian Seas and include European Russia's highest point at Mt. El'brus, 18,510 feet (5,642 m.). The Russian plains, called steppes, are grassy in the south and wooded in the north. In the west the oblast of Kaliningrad is separated from the rest of Russia by Belarussian and Lithuanian territory.

The European regions of Russia form the heartland of the Russian Federation, formally created on 31 March 1992 between the federal government in Moscow and nineteen republics inside what had been the Russian Soviet Federated Socialist Republic (RSFSR), one of the fifteen republics of the Union of Soviet Socialist Republics (USSR). *Russian Federation (Rossiyskaya Federatsiya)*:

European Russia only—1,592,812 sq.mi.–4,125,364 sq.km. (2000 e) 123,568,000—Russians 83%, Tatars* 5%, Ukrainians* 3%, Bashkorts* 2%, Dagestanis 2%, Mordvinians* 1%, Belarussians* 1%. The Russian capital and major cultural center is Moscow, called Moskva in Russian, (2000 e) 8,513,000 (metropolitan area 13,591,000), the ancient capital of Russia. Other important cultural centers are Sankt-Petersburg (St. Petersburg) 4,690,000 (6,376,000), the former imperial capital, and Nizhniy Novgorod 1,345,000 (2,106,000), formerly called Gorki.

FLAG: The Russian national flag, the official flag of the federation, is a horizontal tricolor of white, blue, and red.

PEOPLE: The Russians are the largest of the European national groups and one of two, along with the Turks,* that populate large areas outside Europe. The Russian population is decreasing due to a drastic drop in birthrates and the increase in mortality. Even with the large number of ethnic Russians returning to European Russia from the other states of the former Soviet Union, the population of the Russian Federation is shrinking, which is considered a demographic disaster by Russian nationalists. The low birthrate and the very high mortality—the average life span for a Russian man is fifty-eight years—has resulted in a rapidly shrinking national population.

The culture of the Russians combines both Oriental and Occidental influences in a basically European tradition, but the Russian culture embraces many divergent groups that consider themselves ethnic Russians, while over the centuries a number of smaller national groups have emerged within the larger Russian community. The Russians were the core ethnic group around which imperial Russia and the later Soviet Union were formed. Russian Orthodox Christianity, adopted from the neighboring Byzantine Empire in the tenth century, is the primary religion, with an estimated one-quarter of the population considering themselves believers. Even among nonbelievers, the church is respected as the repository of Russian culture and history.

The Russian language, the most important of the East Slav language group, is spoken in two major dialects, North Russian and South Russian, and dozens of regional and geographical subdialects. The language of many renowned writers, Tolstoy, Dostoevsky, Chekov, Pushkin, and Solzhenitsyn, Russian has great importance in world literature. The official language of the Russian Federation, Russian is also the lingua franca used for intergroup communications in most of the states of the former Soviet Union.

NATION: Archaeological evidence shows that European Russia was inhabited before the Paleolithic age. Written history indicates that early Greek traders conducted extensive commerce with Scythian tribes around the shores of the Black Sea and the Crimean Peninsula region. In the third century B.C. the Scythian tribes were displaced by Sarmatians, who, in turn, were overrun by waves of Germanic Goths in the third century A.D. Huns from Asia overran the region, scattering the Goths, but were conquered by the Turkic Avars* in the sixth century.

In the ninth century Eastern Slavs, thought to have originated in present Poland, began to settle Ukraine, Belarus, and the Novgorod and Smolensk regions of Russia. Many of the Slav clans came under the rule of the Khazar nation to the south. Kiev became the primary Eastern Slav cultural and commercial center and was known as the "Mother of Cities."

The Eastern Slavs became renowned traders, and the rivers and waterways extending throughout the territory facilitated the establishment of Slav trading posts. Water transport allowed the Slavs to move goods from the Baltic to the Black Seas. Colonization also followed the rivers, with new Slav settlements spreading from the region of the historic Valdai hills in northwestern Russia. Traditionally, the warring tribes in 860 cleared the Dniepr lowlands and attacked Constantinople. The political organization of the Eastern Slavs was largely tribal, with no unified system through which the constant tribal conflicts could be resolved. They voluntarily chose a foreign prince in 862, Rurik, a Viking leader, as the ruler of the consolidated tribes. Under Rurik and his successors Eastern Slav territory was expanded northeast and northwest. Prince Oleg in the early tenth century from Kiev led his forces against the Byzantines and in 911 signed a treaty with the Byzantine Empire.

In 980 Vladimir, later St. Vladimir, took the throne. Under his leadership distant Slavic tribes were brought under Kievan rule, and he waged successful wars against the Lithuanians,* Bulgars,* and the Greeks* of the Crimea. In 989, in order to wed Anna, the sister of the Byzantine emperor, Vladimir was baptized and made orthodoxy the state religion. Following Vladimir's conversion and marriage, Byzantine culture predominated in the state, greatly influencing East Slav architecture, music, and art. The schism between the Eastern Orthodox and the Western Catholic churches in 1054 deepened the Byzantine influence. The confederation of Kievan Rus' principalities reached its peak of power in the middle of the eleventh century. Between 1054 and 1073 the Russkaia Pravda, the first Russian law, was written even as the confederation was divided, and new centers rose to challenge Kiev's supremacy.

In 1125 Yuri Dolgoruki became the ruler of a much-reduced Kievan Rus'. During his reign Novgorod, which controlled northern Russia to the Urals, became an independent republic. He founded Moscow in 1156 as a fortified village. In 1169 Kiev was sacked by the forces of the prince of Vladimir-Suzdal, and the capital of the grand duchy was moved from Kiev to Vladimir. The decline of Kiev was due, in part, to a loss of trade following the sack of Constantinople by the Crusaders in 1204 and the consequent migration of the Kievans to the north. Novgorod became a flourishing trade center and rose to a dominant position.

The Mongols invaded the Eastern Slav lands in 1223, and over the next decades the Eastern Slavs were divided. The town of Moscow in the principality of Vladimir occupied a favorable geographical position in the center of the Russian lands and astride the principal trade routes. Daniel, the son of Alexander Nevsky, who defeated the Swedes* on the Neva River, founded the principality of Moscow in 1271 as a vassal state of the Mongol-Tatar Golden Horde. The next two centuries saw the rise of Moscow as a provincial capital and the center of the Orthodox Church. Gradually, Moscow became the center of the most powerful of the Russian principalities under the hegemony of the Golden Horde. The rulers of Moscow took the title of grand duke as the state expanded. Between 1430 and 1466 the Golden Horde, weakened by internal wars and outside pressures, disintegrated, leaving the Grand Duchy of Moscow to dominate Russia.

Constantinople fell to the Ottoman Turks in 1453, and the Orthodox Church thereafter considered Moscow the "third Rome," the successor to Constantinople and the new center of Orthodox Christianity. In 1462 Ivan III became grand duke, and in 1472 he married Sofia (Zoe), the niece of the last Byzantine emperor. Ivan III, called Ivan the Great, conquered Novgorod in 1478, extended his authority over the other Russian principalities, and checked the eastward expansion of Lithuania. In 1480, taking advantage of strife among Russia's Tatar-Mongol overlords, which had divided the Golden Horde into several separate khanates, Ivan refused to pay the annual tribute. The Tatar-Mongol forces attempted to reassert their authority but were defeated, and the date is traditionally regarded as the end of Tatar domination in Russia.

Ivan's grandson, later called Ivan the Terrible, was the first to bear the title tsar in 1547. In the same year he married Anastasia Romanovna, a member of the powerful Romanov family. Under Ivan's rule Moscow's military forces conquered the khanates of the Tatars and fought wars against the Poles* and Swedes. The pacification of the frontiers opened vast new territories to Russian colonization. During his reign the long struggle between the tsars and the powerful, landed nobility, known as boyars, became a serious threat to the state. Late in his reign Cossacks conquered Siberia, greatly extending the land area of his empire. The late sixteenth century also marked a growing discontent among the peasants, which followed a 1597 law that legalized serfdom and bound the serfs to the estates of the nobility.

The Rurik dynasty died out in 1598, initiating a period of anarchy and disintegration, the Smutnoye Vremya or Time of Troubles. The situation was at last resolved in 1613, when the national assembly, representing the chief towns and the church, elected Michael Romanov as tsar. Although social discontent had been one of the primary characteristics of the Time of Troubles, no real reforms were undertaken. The greatest effects of the period of chaos were the ruin of the old boyar nobility and the rise to power of a new class of small, landed gentry. In compensation, the boyars were granted vast estates and increasing rights over the masses of common people. Serfdom, near virtual slavery, provoked serious peasant revolts. Russia in the seventeenth and eighteenth centuries remained isolated from the rest of Europe, a semi-Oriental state distrustful of foreigners and innovations.

Two outstanding Romanov rulers greatly strengthened the Russian Empire. Peter the Great, who ruled from 1689 to 1725, forced the nobility to accept a series of reforms and "Westernized" Russia following his conquest of the lands up to the Baltic Sea. As a symbol of Russia's new position as a European power, Peter founded a new capital city, St. Petersburg, in the area in 1703. The city was to become his window on Europe, and the government moved there from Moscow in 1714. The second able ruler, a Romanov by marriage, Catherine the Great, who ruled Russia from 1762 to 1796, pursued a policy of enlightened despotism while continuing the aggressive foreign policy initiated by Peter. First, she turned her armies against the Ottoman Empire in order to acquire warm-water Black Sea ports necessary for trade. Vast territories were added in the south, while the partitions of Poland added new lands in the west. Catherine's domestic policies echoed the Westernization of Peter's reign. She chose French culture as her guide, and the liberal policies of the French Revolution were, for a time, espoused.

In the early nineteenth century under Tsar Alexander I, the first steps were taken to dismantle the system of serfdom, particularly the selling of serfs without land. The reform process was disrupted by Napoleon's invasion of Russia in 1812. Having burned Moscow, Napoleon was forced to retreat through the Russian winter, losing thousands of troops. The peace settlement formulated at the Congress of Vienna made Russia a leading European power.

Under the rule of Nicholas I Russia became the most reactionary state in Europe, acting as the policeman of the continent in combating all liberal tendencies. A clash between Russia and the Western powers in the Ottoman Empire led to the Crimean War, which revealed the inner weakness of the near-feudal Russian state. The liberal Alexander II, who became tsar in 1855, one year before the Crimean War ended, was determined to modernize his defeated country. Among his reforms was the liberation of the serfs in 1861. Alexander III succeeded the assassinated Alexander II in 1881. He quickly reversed most of the earlier reforms and instituted a reactionary domestic policy that suppressed all manifestations of free thought and progress. While great social, economic, and political change swept the rest of Europe, the Russians remained dominated by feudal agrarian traditions and the wasteful privilege of the aristocracy. Accomplishments such as the Trans-Siberian Railroad, finished in 1892, opened vast frontiers to development but failed to resolve the fundamental problems of the mass of the Russian people. He was succeeded in 1894 by Nicholas II, the last tsar of the Russian Empire.

The nineteenth century, a period of rapid change, saw a flowering of Russian literature, music, ballet, and drama, which included some of the greatest artists and works produced in Europe. The great names of Russian culture are among the greatest produced by Europe during the century. The cultural flowering continued until the early years of the twentieth century.

At the beginning of the twentieth century, Russia was the largest and most populous European state. Counting on numbers to overcome a lack of modern armament, Russia's generals blundered into the disastrous war with Japan in 1904–5, which made possible the success of the 1905 Russian Revolution. Tsar Nicholas was forced to grant a constitution and allow the formation of a parliament, the Duma, but reactionary forces soon gained control. Popular anger was channeled into anti-Semitic pogroms and other actions against non-Russian national groups.

The Triple Entente between Russia, France, and Great Britain was signed in 1907 as a balance against the Triple Alliance of Germany, Austro-Hungary, and Italy. Russia's aid to the Slavic nations against the weakened Ottoman Empire in the Balkans in 1911–13 established the Russian Empire as the protector of Europe's Slavic peoples. A new wave of worker unrest in Russia ended with the crisis that overtook Europe in 1914.

The Russians supported their fellow Serbs* against the Austrians* following the assassination of the Austrian heir by a Serbian nationalist. Serbia's defiance of demands by the Austrians set off a continental conflict that soon drew in all the major European powers. Poorly prepared and cut off from its allies in the West, Russia suffered serious military reverses and thousands of deaths. Inflation, corruption, food shortages, an exhausted population, and poor morale among the troops eventually provoked the February Revolution of 1917 and the abdication of the tsar.

A moderate, democratic regime oversaw a chaotic transfer of power, but its insistence on continuing to fight the Germans* and Austrians soon undermined its support. Finally, in October 1917 (November by the Western calendar) Lenin and his small Bolshevik faction seized control of the government and negotiated a humiliating peace. Provinces inhabited by non-Russians proclaimed their independence as anti-Bolshevik White forces mobilized against the Bolsheviks.

The disastrous civil war between Reds and Whites and the intervention of foreign forces finally ended in 1920 with the victory of the Red Army. In 1917 Russia was officially proclaimed the Russian Soviet Federated Socialist Republic, which formed the Union of Soviet Socialist Republics with newly reconquered Ukraine, Belarus, and the Transcaucasian Federation of Armenia, Azerbaijan, and Georgia in 1922. The devastated Soviet state, controlling considerably less territory than the former empire, was isolated and feared by the West.

Vladimir Ilyich Lenin, the Soviet leader, was faced with a ruined economy and peasant unrest. He finally instituted the New Economic Policy, which gave peasants the right to sell their grain surpluses. His policy on nationalities, cultural independence without political independence, was applied to the numerous non-Russian national groups, giving them some control over local affairs. The fundamental policy of the Russian Communist Party was, from its beginnings, complete state control of the economy and the redistribution of wealth.

Lenin's death in 1924 was followed by a collective leadership that was soon dominated by Iosif Vissarionovich Stalin, known as Joseph Stalin. After eliminating all rivals, Stalin began the forced collectivization and industrialization of Russia. Millions died in political purges and the vast penal and labor system or in state-created famines. The Soviet Union proclaimed that the historic process of the drawing together of nations and nationalities gave rise to a new historical community, the Soviet people. The term "Soviet people" came into official use in the 1930s, but the Russians dominated the state. In 1937, suspecting a plot, many of the Soviet army's officers were executed on Stalin's orders. Two years later the Soviet Union signed a nonaggression pact with Germany that effectively divided Central and Eastern Europe into Nazi and Soviet spheres. In 1941 his Nazi ally turned on Stalin and invaded the USSR. The Nazi invasion forced Stalin into an alliance with the Western powers, the United States and the United Kingdom and their allies.

The defeat of Germany and the Axis powers in 1945 left the Soviet Union as a leading world power despite its losses of some 20 million people during the war. Soviet authority was extended west to the Central European states liberated from Nazi rule, effectively dividing Europe into two hostile camps. In 1949 the USSR became the second state to test an atomic bomb, bringing the Soviet state superpower status. Under the influence of the Soviet government, Russian cultural works, unlike the flowering of the nineteenth century, were heavily censored, and many writers and artists fled to the West.

Stalin's death in 1953 began a partial thaw in Soviet society under the Khrushchev regime. The Russians, determined to retain their authority in the communist bloc, intervened against liberalization movements in Hungary in 1956 and Czechoslovakia in 1968 during the so-called Cold War. Attempts to install nuclear weapons in newly communist Cuba brought the world dangerously close to nuclear war in October 1962. While their government maintained a military stance that required the focus of the national economy, Russians lived in poverty.

A series of reactionary leaders between 1964 and 1985 did little to relieve the suffering of the Russian and Soviet peoples. Khrushchev was ousted in 1964, and Leonid Ilyich Brezhnev took power, but Brezhnev's rule was marked by growing economic problems and unrest in the non-Russian republics. Achievements such as launching the world's first space satellite or advances in military hardware did little to offset the growing poverty of the Soviet system. Most Russians lived in conditions little better than those of the poorer countries of Africa.

In 1985 Mikhail Gorbachev became president of the USSR. He embarked on a program that restructured the USSR's relations with the West, easing the tensions of the decades-long Cold War. His internal reforms, glasnost (openness) and perestroika (restructuring and reform), led to profound changes within the Soviet Union as Moscow's iron grip weakened. By 1989 ethnically based national movements had emerged in most of the union, and autonomous republics demanded greater autonomy and an end to government efforts to Russify their distinct languages and cultures. Ethnic Russians also rediscovered their roots and a nationalist sentiment buried under seven decades of Soviet rule. Dismayed by what they saw as the ungrateful stance of the peoples they had helped lead out of poverty and ignorance, a Russian backlash spurred the growth of a particular Russian national movement.

In 1989 the communist regimes of Eastern Europe, deprived of unconditional Soviet support, collapsed amid great rejoicing. The convulsions extended to the Westernized republics of the USSR in 1990, with demands for a looser union or, in some cases, complete independence. The Russians, who claimed that they had suffered the most under the Soviet regime, also pressed for greater freedom. On 12 June 1990 the Congress of People's Deputies of the Russian Federation passed a declaration of state sovereignty. One year later, on 12 June 1991, Boris Yeltsin became the first democratically elected Russian president.

The spasms affecting communism reached a politically decisive climax with an attempted coup against Mikhail Gorbachev in August 1991. One day after the coup leaders announced their takeover, on 20 August, Boris Yeltsin spoke to a large crowd from on top of a military tank; then he barricaded himself in the parliament building. On 24 August Gorbachev resigned as the head of the Communist Party, which was disbanded in the Russian Federation. On the same day Yeltsin, on behalf of the independent Russian Federation, recognized the independence of Estonia, setting the stage for the Russian recognition of Latvia and Lithuania and rapid disintegration of the Soviet Empire. Although legally the Soviet Union lasted for another four months, the Russian government from 24 August no longer recognized the authority of the Soviet government. The failed coup brought an unexpected end to the largest extant empire, the most influential political movement, and the most powerful state political party of the twentieth century. It also marked the resurgence of the formerly quiescent Russian nation, which had both created and been victimized by all three of these forces. The simultaneous collapse of communism and the Soviet Union intensified the Russian search for a new national identity.

Many Russian citizens had grown into the habit of feeling at home anywhere within the Soviet Union's frontiers. It had been a single country with a powerful center controlling an intricately linked command economy. Between 1930 and 1970 millions of Russians had settled in other parts of the Soviet Union in search of better pay, decent housing, and a higher social and professional status. These millions of ethnic Russians suddenly found themselves a diaspora of some 25 million people, often unwanted and unwelcome in the newly independent states.

The Russian Federation, the largest of the successor states of the Soviet Union, inherited its permanent seat on the United Nations Security Council, as well as the bulk of its foreign assets and debts. In 1992 the Russian government persuaded eleven of the fifteen former Soviet republics to form the Commonwealth of Independent States (CIS). A twelfth state, Georgia, joined the group in 1993. Russian nationalist groups often look on the CIS as a tool for safeguarding the large ethnic Russian populations left behind as the empire shrank back to the historic Russian lands.

The southern republic of Chechnya, which proclaimed its independence in 1991, was the scene of a humiliating attempt to reimpose Russian rule in 1994. On 1 December 1996 the Russian troops were withdrawn, having been fought to a standoff by the ill-equipped and much smaller Chechen forces. The Chechen rebellion, while the most far-reaching, is mirrored, to some extent, in many of the other republics where the process of de-Russification and autonomy movements have galvanized national movements across the vast Russian state.

The average Russian has a poor understanding of the benefits of democracy, often associating democratic institutions with social disorder, crime, corruption, and economic hardships. In spite of numerous setbacks in its democratic development, Russia has made some progress in governmental and human and group rights since independence in 1991. The turbulent events of Russian history often have led Russians to scapegoat "foreigners" and "others" for its internal problems. The humiliation of losing the Soviet Empire is no exception. The hardline Russian nationalist press targets Jews as the alleged agents both of the advent of communism and of its demise. Not only Jews but darker peoples, Armenians,* Azeris,* Chechens,* Georgians,* and Gypsies, bear the brunt of ethnic Russian suspicion and blame. A xenophobic view of non-Russian peoples has often vilified other national groups as foreigners in their native lands.

Once again Russia is entering a *smula*, a time of troubles. The reemergence of a nationalist Right, the first in Russia since 1920, has moved the whole spectrum of Russian politics. The reappearance of a Russian national movement, one firmly believing that Russia's rightful role as a great power can be achieved only by a strong authoritarian government, has alarmed Russia's other national groups and raised doubts about Russia's future prospects and intentions.

The deadlock over economic and political control within the Russian government, particularly conflicts between the Yeltsin presidency and the parliament, has allowed local governors and presidents to go their own way. The result is a Russia much more decentralized than it ever was in the past. Many regional governments have signed treaties with Moscow that give them a greater share and greater control over their resources. Crucial decisions on reform are increasingly made at the provincial and republican level.

The humbling defeat of the Russian army at the hands of the Chechen separatists in 1996 highlighted the decline of Russian military power. In 1996 some 500 soldiers committed suicide due to the harsh conditions and the lack of food and resources. In July 1997 President Yeltsin signed decrees that will shrink the military from 1.8 million to 1.2 million in three years. Giant ships molder in harbors around the country, and dissatisfaction with current conditions has demoralized all branches of the military service.

Six times over the past three centuries the Russians have turned toward the West, seeking to emulate the economic and social reforms there. The first five attempts, starting with Peter the Great and ending with Lenin, failed, and the autocratic Russian tradition reasserted itself. The sixth attempt, inaugurated by Boris Yeltsin in 1991, is still evolving, and the future for the Russian nation hangs in the balance.

In mid-1999, responding to an Islamic incursion into the southern republic of Dagestan and a spate of bombings in Moscow and other cities, the Russian government, in September, launched a military incursion against the Chechens.

The incursion, meeting strong Chechen resistance, again threatened a military disaster as in 1994, when the Chechen war cost some 80,000 casualties and caused widespread discontent and anti-government sentiment.

In the late 1990s President Yeltsin's failing health raised new concerns for the future of the Russian nation. The economy, already contracting, worsened in 1999, with the government seemingly unable to stop the collapse. Russia after the Yeltsin years could be a very different place, and the Russians themselves could again become a threat to European peace or fervent supporters of closer ties among the many European nations.

SELECTED BIBLIOGRAPHY

Hosking, Geoffrey. *Russia: People and Empire*. 1998.

Hosking, Geoffrey A. *Russian Nationalism, Past and Present*. 1998.

Jacobsen, Karen. *The Russian Federation*. 1994.

Milner-Gulland Robin. *The Russians*. 1997.

Shlapentokh, Vladimir, ed. *The New Russian Diaspora: Russian Minorities in the Former Soviet Republics*. 1994.

RUTULS

Rutal; Rutuly; Rutul'tsy; Chals;
Mukhads; Mjukhadars

POPULATION: Approximately (2000 e) 25,700 Rutuls in Europe, concentrated in the Rutul Rayon of the Dagestan Republic, a member state of the Russian Federation. A smaller Rutul community lives across the international border in Azerbaijan.

THE RUTUL HOMELAND: The Rutul homeland lies in the upper Samur River region of southern Dagestan in southeastern European Russia and northern Azerbaijan. The region, extremely mountainous, lies in the eastern Caucasus, with the population concentrated in twenty towns and villages in the high valley of the Samur River and its tributaries, the Ahty-Chai and Kara-Samur, with two Rutul communities, Shin and Kainar, situated in Azerbaijan. The most important of the Rutul towns are located on the banks of the region's rivers. The highland Samur valley has a severe climate, long, cold winters and cool, foggy, and windy summers, which the Rutuls claim has shaped their national character.

The Rutul region, called Rutulstan, has no official status other than that of a district or rayon of the Dagestan Republic. The Rutul capital and major cultural center is the town of Rutul, called Mjukhad by the Rutuls, which gave its name to the entire national group.

FLAG: The flag used by the Rutuls is the Dagestani national flag, a horizontal tricolor of green, pale blue, and red.

PEOPLE: The Rutuls are a Caucasian people who call themselves Mjukhadar, meaning inhabitant of Mjukhad, which is the chief town of the region. The name Rutul was early extended to the entire ethnic group in the region but only recently has come into general use. The small nation is still divided into clans, subclans, and village communities. The Rutuls are closely related to the Lezgins* and until the Russian Revolution were classified as ethnic Lezgins. Traditionally, the Rutuls had no general name for themselves but identified themselves with their home village. Within Rutul communities, patriarchal relations, with an important role played by the *tuhum* or clan, persisted until the early twentieth century. The introduction of a money economy brought a rapid separation of family from the clan. The process was completed in the 1950s and 1960s, relegating the clan to a cultural and historical entity. Frequent marriages between cousins, particularly in the eastern Rutul communities, persist as a remnant of the Rutuls' earlier endogamous marriage traditions.

The language of the Rutuls belongs to the Samurian branch of the Lezgin-Samur group of North Caucasian languages. Spoken in three closely related dialects, Shina, Ixreko-Muxrek, and Borch, although the dialects are not sharply defined and are spoken is numerous subdialects. The Rutul language is not a literary language, and the Rutuls used the related Lezgin language as their literary language until the 1950s, when Russian was imposed as the official language.

The Rutuls are Sunni Muslims, but although extremely devout, they have retained many pagan traditions. The worship of fire, a Zoroastrian custom, remains an important religious element, and one of the highest points in Rutulstan is called Tsailakhan, meaning "a place for fire." In spite of decades of official state antireligious policies, the Muslim religion retains a strong hold on the Rutuls, and fundamentalism in the 1990s has become a strong influence.

NATION: The Rutuls are thought to have lived in the Caucasus Mountains from at least the fifth century A.D. Ethnically and linguistically, the Rutuls were part of the larger cluster of indigenous Caucasian peoples called the Lezgins. In the seventh century the region came under Arab domination, and some clans were converted to Islam, but the Rutuls remained mostly animists with their own folk religion, although their homeland nominally formed part of the Arab administration of the region.

In the tenth century the Seljuk Turks overran the area and were succeeded by the Mongol-Tatar Golden Horde in the thirteenth century. In the fifteenth century, despite their own language and culture, they were treated as ethnic Lezgins in the historical records of the time. The names of Rutul towns first appeared in historical records between the thirteenth and sixteenth centuries. Their own local leaders were extremely powerful, which partially explains the ferocious resistance that the mountainous clans put up against foreigners attempting to impose effective political dominance in Rutulstan.

Persian traders moving north into the Caucasus Mountains in the fifteenth century introduced Islam to many of the isolated Rutul communities, even though Christianity, Zoroastrianism, and Judaism were making inroads in the region. The arrival of the Golden Horde brought Islam to even the most isolated communities. From the sixteenth through the eighteenth centuries, the Rutuls formed a powerful political confederation known as the Rutul Mahal. Each of the Rutul towns and villages had a civil and military leader who maintained contact with his counterparts in other towns and villages to develop common policies. The confederation grew as feudal relations developed in the region, often ruling non-Rutul regions.

Russian expansion in the early nineteenth century was fiercely resisted. In 1838 the Rutul leader, Aga-Bek, led a widespread uprising against Russian encroachment, but within a few years the Russians* had crushed the revolt. The Rutul Mahal was formally annexed to the Russian Empire in 1844. Russian rule led to a rapid decline in the patriarchal feudal relations of the Rutuls and the corresponding development of a capitalist economy. The Rutul Mahal in 1857 counted eighteen villages and towns, each with its mosque and religious leaders. The Rutuls, along with the other Caucasian tribes, fought an effective guerrilla war under the regional religious leader Iman Shamil. Thousands of Rutul warriors died in the final Russian victory over the Muslims in 1859, and many of the Rutul villages and towns were destroyed.

The establishment of firm Russian authority in the region forced the warlike Rutuls to concentrate on their livestock herds. As they had no winter pastures, the Rutul clans had to rent lowland grazing lands from the Azeris* for their herds. Between 1856 and 1913 the number of sheep in the Rutul herds tripled, and the number of cattle increased sixfold. During the winters, when the herds were being tended on the lowland pastures, many Rutul men left the region to work in the fishing and oil industries of Derbent and Baku.

In the early twentieth century the only consolidating force among the Rutul clans was their language and religion. The Rutuls had no form of national self-identification, and there was no accepted word in the Rutul language for "nation." The first secular educational establishment was created in Rutulstan in 1914, the year that war broke out in Europe. During the war the Rutuls generally supported the Muslim Turks against the hated Russians, but the war was far away and of little concern until the Russian Revolution in 1917. The collapse of civil government in the region left the Rutuls virtually independent. They participated in the new Muslim government created in the region but later supported the Bolsheviks, who promised autonomy in exchange for aid in fighting the anti-Bolshevik White forces in the region.

The final Red victory in 1920 was followed by the establishment of the Mountain Autonomous Republic in the Caucasus region, with Arabic as its official language. The Dagestan Autonomous Soviet Socialist Republic was created in 1921. In 1925 a government campaign against religion led to the closure of all Islamic schools, the elimination of Arabic, and the execution of many local religious leaders. In spite of harsh Soviet rule, the Rutuls made rapid strides in education, and a sense of national identity began to appear. The collectivization of the lowland Rutul herds was rapid. By 1926 there were already twenty-six collective farms in Rutulstan. By 1935 collectivization of lowland Rutulstan was complete, and the Soviet government began to forcibly resettle many Rutul clans from their villages in the high mountains to the lowlands, where they could be more effectively controlled.

Soviet manipulation of the Rutul identity began in 1925, when they were forced to adopt Azeri as the official language. In 1928 the Soviet government decreed that Azeris, Lezgins, Dargins,* and Avars* would all have official status in Dagestan but also decided that the Rutuls should merge into the larger Azeri ethnic group. Experts began to create a Latin alphabet for Rutul, but ten years later, in 1938, official policy supported the use of the Russians' Cyrillic alphabet. The constant cultural manipulation only increased Rutul resistance to Russification. The forced assimilation of the Rutuls had the effect of reducing the Rutul population from approximately 10,500 people in 1926 to a low of 6,700 in 1959. At the end of World War II, the Soviet government began to develop the region, one of the poorest in the Soviet Union. By 1948 the area under crops had doubled, and the foundations had been laid for horticulture, formerly unknown in the Rutulstan region.

The reculturation of the Rutuls began to take hold in the 1970s, when many Rutuls, registered as ethnic Azeris or Lezgins, began to rediscover their ethnic roots. The Rutuls' traditional community had preserved its integrity, although some migration to the area's cities led to the decline of traditional values. Until the 1970s the Rutuls were ruled by a rigid, endogamous, patriarchal clan system in which young people were encouraged to marry within extended families, particularly first or second cousins. The sense of clan cohesion was strengthened by the fact that land was owned by the extended family. During the 1960s and 1970s the Soviet state succeeded in establishing government cooperatives and in collectivizing many Rutul herds, therefore breaking the hold of tradition on daily Rutul life.

Ironically, the introduction of Russian as the official language in the 1950s has served as a kind of defense for the Rutuls during the uncertain years since the collapse of the Soviet Union in 1991. They continue to use Russian as a means of communicating with neighboring groups while maintaining Rutul as the language of daily life. The Russian language, at the moment, does not represent as strong a danger to the survival of the Rutul language and culture as that of the closer neighbors, the Lezgins and Azeris. The influence of Russian is indirect, as few Rutuls have direct contact with the Russians in the region.

The competition for jobs, government positions, and wealth in multiethnic Dagestan and Azerbaijan has led to calls for more autonomy for the small, divided Rutul nation. Many ethnic Rutuls are returning to the region from Derbent and other lowland areas where they were counted as members of other ethnic groups during Soviet censuses from the 1920s. The rapid growth of the Rutul national group is paralleled by demands for autonomy and protection of their small culture.

SELECTED BIBLIOGRAPHY

Akiner, Shirin. *Islamic Peoples of the Soviet Union*. 1986.
Benningsen, Alexandre, and S. Enders Wimbush. *Muslims of the Soviet Empire*. 1985.

Benningsen-Broxup, Marie, ed. *The North Caucasus Barrier: The Russian Advance towards the Muslim World.* 1992.

Gammer, Moshe. *Muslim Resistance to the Tsar: Shamil and the Conquest of Chechnya and Dagestan.* 1993.

Krag, Helen, and Lars Funch. *The North Caucasus: Minorities at a Crossroads.* 1994.

SAMIS

Sámis; Sammes; Saamis; Lapps;
Laps; Laplanders

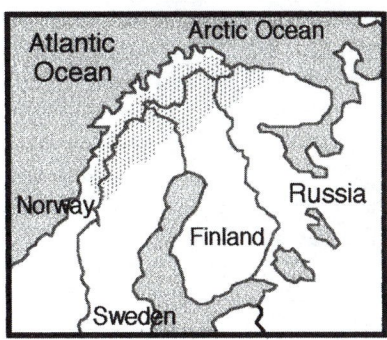

POPULATION: Approximately (2000 e) 105,000 Samis in Europe, concentrated in Scandinavia, with 70,000 in Norway, 22,000 in Sweden, 8,000 in Finland, and another 3,000 in the Kola Peninsula region of northwestern Russia.

THE SAMI HOMELAND: The Sami homeland occupies a vast region of Northern Europe, largely within the Arctic Circle. The western portion of the homeland is an area of fjords, deep valleys, glaciers, and mountains, the highest being Mt. Kebnekaise in Swedish Lapland, 6,926 feet (2,111 m.). Farther east, the region is mostly a low plateau, containing many marshes and lakes, the most important of which is Lake Inari in Finnish Lapland. The extreme eastern region of Lapland lies within the tundra region in Finland and Russia. The climate is Arctic, and vegetation is generally sparse, except in the forested southern zone.

Lapland, called Sápmi by the Samis, has no official political status. The region includes Finnmark and parts of Tromso and Nordland provinces of Norway, the eastern districts of Norrbotten and Vasterbotten provinces of Sweden, the northern districts of Finland's Lappi Province, and most of the Kola Peninsula of the Russian Federation. *Lapland (Sápmi)* has an area of about 150,000 sq.mi.–388,500 sq.km. and a population of about 210,000. The unofficial capital of the European Sami is Kautokeino, (2000 e) 3,000, located in Norwegian territory close to the Finnish and Swedish borders. Other important Sami cultural centers are Hammerfest, Kirkenes, and Vadso in Norway, Kiruna, Kvikkjokk, and Tärnby in Sweden, Sodankyla and Ivalo in Finland, and Pechenga in Russia.

FLAG: The Sami national flag is a blue field with a broad red stripe at the hoist divided from the blue by narrow vertical stripes of green and yellow, and bears a circle divided vertically blue near the hoist and red on the fly.

PEOPLE: The Samis are a distinct nation living in far Northern Europe in the Scandinavian and Kola Peninsulas. Popularly called Laps or Lapps, the Samis consider the name to be derogatory. About one-third of the Samis are nomadic, living during the winter in the interior and during the summer along the coast. This Sami minority, numbering about 30,000, has not settled in permanent homes, is the last nomads in Europe, and is often counted as the only ethnic Samis, with the settled populations counted as part of the majority nation. The majority of the Samis now live permanently in scattered settlements on the coast and fjords, and many are established in villages at the heads of valleys or on well-stocked lakes. The largest Sami population is in Norway, where they are commonly called Finns.

The total Sami population is a matter of conflict, as census figures often leave settled Sami populations out of the calculations. The definition of a Sami is still a matter of dispute, with unofficial census figures gathered by Sami experts much higher than those of the official government figures. Extensive intermingling has nearly erased the Samis' Asian origins, and although they are generally short and muscular, they are now nearly indistinguishable from their Scandinavian neighbors.

Sami society, divided by labor, includes the Mountain or Reindeer Samis, the Forest and River Samis, hunters and fishermen, and the Sea Samis, fishermen and whalers. The distinctive clothing and headgear, combining the bright colors of blue, red, yellow, and green, are still worn in many areas and proclaim the Samis' home regions. Only 10% of the Sami population still engage in reindeer herding, but that minority represents a continuation of traditional Sami culture. The majority of the Samis, as in the other Scandinavian nations, are Lutheran, with a small Orthodox minority mostly made up of Sami refugees from the former Soviet Union.

The language of the Samis is a Finnic language of the Finno-Ugric language group that is related to Finnish and other Finnic languages of Northern Europe. Spoken in three major dialects, North, South, and East, and over fifty subdialects, the Sami has great regional variety, and the dialects are not mutually intelligible.

NATION: Very little is known of the early history of the Samis, a people of early Mongol origins thought to have migrated west from Central Asia in prehistoric times. Mentioned as a separate tribal people living in the far north of Europe by the Roman historian Tacitus in A.D. 98, the Samis, nearly 2,000 years ago, were driven north into the barren Arctic by successive waves of Slavic, Finnic, and Gothic peoples. The Samis believe that they adopted their Finnic language in the last millennium B.C.

The nomadic Sami tribes pursued fishing, hunting, whaling, and, in the lands warmed by the Gulf Stream, some farming. The main activity of the Sami tribes revolved around the vast herds of reindeer. Traditionally, the Samis followed their reindeer herds, wintering in the lowlands and summering in the western mountains. On skis, a Sami invention, herders traveled great distances with their herds, which provided the resources for survival in the north and became the measure of wealth. The Samis lived in small communities known as *siidas*, each of which had its own territory. The *siidas* were also a central element of traditional Sami society.

Norwegians* and Swedes* conquered the western Sami tribes in the Middle Ages, beginning in the ninth century, but left the Samis to their traditional way of life as nomadic herdsmen and fishermen. The Scandinavians began constructing churches in the Sami regions in the twelfth century in an effort to begin the conversion of the pagan Sami populations. Between the thirteenth and eighteenth centuries, Norwegians, Swedes, and Russians* vied for authority in the Sami regions, with the Sami tribes often paying tribute to more than one of their more powerful neighbors. The majority of the Sami population was ruled by the Swedes from the thirteenth to the seventeenth centuries. In the east the Sami tribes of the Kola Peninsula came under the rule of the expanding Russian state in 1721. Long resistance to Christianity, finally overcome by Lutheran and Orthodox missionaries, led to the conversion of the last Sami tribes in the eighteenth century.

In the seventeenth and eighteenth centuries Scandinavian and Russian colonization of the Sami homelands began in earnest. The settlers concentrated on the most productive lands and mainly farmed, a source of livelihood that contrasted strongly with the traditional Sami occupations. The settlers erected permanent houses, but many adapted to the Sami way of life and copied the Samis' customs, attire, diet, and household practices.

The boundaries of the Sami homelands were not delimited until the mid-eighteenth century. The frontier between Sweden and Norway was agreed to in 1751, and the boundary between Norwegian and Russian territory was finally delimited in 1826. The official agreements on international boundaries effectively separated the various Sami tribes between several national states.

A change of official attitude began around the year 1850. Administrative reforms were introduced, particularly in Norway, starting with the area's schools. At the end of the nineteenth century, teachers were instructed to restrict the use of the Sami language. In Norway from 1902 it was forbidden to sell land to anyone unable to speak Norwegian.

In the twentieth century Norway, which split from Sweden in 1905, counted the largest number of Samis within their national territory. The second largest population, in the Kola Peninsula of northwestern Russia, came under Soviet rule in 1920. The Kola Samis, their herds collectivized and cross-border contacts with their kin forbidden, suffered discrimination and hardships under Soviet rule. Assimilation and the suppression of the Sami culture were pressed by all the area governments between the world wars. During the Russo-Finnish War in 1940, thousands of Samis fled Soviet territory for refuge in the West. By 1941 only about 2,000 of the 1939 Soviet Sami population of 15,000 remained in the Soviet Union.

The contemporary world intruded into the Scandinavian Sami homelands in

Northern Europe during World War II. The conflict brought bombs, tanks, and destruction to a people whose language has no word for war. Germany's scorched early policy in northern Norway in 1944 left virtually every building in Finnmark Province burned and the Sami herds slaughtered. The experience of war profoundly affected the peaceful Samis, raising the first demands for greater control of events that concerned their small and threatened nation.

The postwar increase of the Arctic region's non-Sami population began to curtail the traditional Sami way of life in the 1950s and 1960s, even though more liberal laws were applied in Norway, Sweden, and Finland. New mining towns were created, and roads, power stations, dams, and national parks crowded in on the Sami grazing lands. Confused by the differing national policies of Norway, Sweden, Finland, and the Soviet Union, Sami activists formed the Nordic Sami Institute in 1973. The organization's aim was to press for Sami political and land rights.

Pressed by environmental issues, Sami nationalism grew rapidly during the 1970s, and in 1983 Sami leaders from across the region declared the sovereignty of the divided Sami nation. In 1986 the Chernobyl nuclear disaster spread radiation across the Sami homeland. In September 1986 the Sami reindeer herds were found to be contaminated by the released radiation, making necessary the slaughter of most of the Sami reindeer herds. Two years later, in 1988, when the herds had begun to recover, national leaders demanded the creation of a Sami parliament that would have influence over planning and development of the region. In 1992 the Sami language was given equal status with Norwegian in Norway.

Sweden and Finland's entry into the European Union on 1 January 1995 provoked a serious debate on the future of the Sami nation. Sami leaders began a campaign to join the European Union as a separate European people, not Norwegian, Swedish, Russian, or Finnish, but Sami. Without full participation in the union as a separate nation, the Samis are skeptical of having to meet regulations, not of their making, that take no account of the unique conditions of life in the European Arctic.

SELECTED BIBLIOGRAPHY
Gaski, Harald. *Sami Culture in a New Era: The Norwegian Sami Experience*. 1998.
James, Alan. *Lapps: Reindeer Herders of Lapland*. 1989.
Stalder, Valerie. *Lapland*. 1971.
Valkeapaa, Nils-Aslak. *Greetings from Lappland: The Sami-Europe's Forgotten People*. 1983.
Vitebsky, Piers. *The Saami of Lapland*. 1994.

SANJAKIS

Sanjaki Muslims; Sandzhakis

POPULATION: Approximately (2000 e) 525,000 Sanjakis in Europe, concentrated in the Sanjak region of Yugoslavia.

THE SANJAKI HOMELAND: The Sanjaki homeland lies in southwestern Yugoslavia, occupying the mountainous region and the Sandzhak Plateau, which straddles the border between Serbia and Montenegro. Much of the region is mountainous, lying in the North Albanian Alps and the Zlatibor Mountains, which are southern spurs of the Dinaric Alps. The population is concentrated in the valleys of the Lim and Raska Rivers and their tributaries.

Sanjak has no official status. The historic Sanjak region formed the Turkish Sanjak of Novibazar and now forms the Sandzhak regions of the Yugoslav republics of Montenegro and Serbia. *Sandzhak (Sanjak)*: 2,943 sq.km.–7,625 sq.km. (2000 e) 803,000—Sanjakis 65%, Serbs* and Montenegrins* 30%, Albanians* 3%. The Sanjaki capital and major cultural center is Novi Pazar, called Novibazar by the Sanjakis, (2000 e) 91,000, the former capital of the region under Turkish rule. Other important Sanjaki cultural centers are Pljevla, called Tasildza by the Sanjakis, (2000 e) 22,000, and Ivangrad (Andrijevica), (2000 e) 20,000, in Montenegro, and Priboj (Pribol), (2000 e) 18,000, in Serbia.

FLAG: The Sanjaki national flag, the flag of the national movement, is a white field charged with a centered shield divided diagonally green over blue, separated by a white stripe, the green bearing three white crescent moons and the blue bearing three gold stars.

PEOPLE: The Sanjakis, also called Sanjak Muslims, are a South Slav nation related to the Bosnians.* Although ethnically related to the neighboring Serbs and Montenegrins, their conversion to Islam during the centuries of Turkish rule sets them apart both religiously and culturally. The Sanjaki culture is a Slavic culture that contains many Turkish traditions and customs and is closely tied to their Muslim religion. The descendants of early Slavs and a later Turkish military aristocracy, the Sanjakis are often called Turks, a derogatory term in the Balkans. The Serbs claim that the Sanjakis are not Slavs but are the descendants of Muslims settled in the region by the Turkish authorities in the seventeenth and eighteenth centuries.

The Sanjakis speak a dialect of Serbian that is written, like Serbian, in the Cyrillic alphabet. The dialect, called Sanjaki, is a western dialect of Serbian that has incorporated many borrowings from Turkish and Albanian, which is spoken in neighboring Kosovo.

NATION: South Slav tribes, probably from their original homeland in eastern Poland and Ukraine, settled the Lim River valley and the surrounding mountains in the seventh century A.D. The Slavs accepted the authority of the Byzantine Empire, which controlled the region, and by the ninth century the majority of the tribes had adopted the Christian religion of the Byzantines.

In the tenth century, the tribes living in the southern Dinaric Alps embraced a new faith brought to the region by travelers. The faith, a dualistic creed attributed to Bogomil, a Bulgarian priest, taught that every action has two sides, good and evil, life and death, light and dark, and so on. The creed, intensely nationalistic and political as well as religious, opposed Slavic serfdom, the authority and wealth of the church, and Byzantine cultural domination. The Slav believers in the region, called Bogomils, were branded heretics by church authorities and were subject to severe persecution; however, the Bogomil sect flourished from the tenth to the fifteenth centuries.

In the twelfth century a powerful Serb state emerged in the region. The Orthodox faith of the Serb majority became an integral part of the Serb culture of the state. The kingdom, with its capital at Raska, later called Novi Pazar by the Turks, gradually extended its authority into the isolated Bogomil valleys. Thousands of Bogomils died in massacres and planned heretic hunts from the twelfth to the fourteenth centuries.

The persecuted Bogomils looked to the Turks of the expanding Ottoman Empire for protection from Christian violence. Just to the south of the Bogomil homeland, at Kosovo Polje, the Field of Blackbirds, a coalition of Christian forces met defeat in one of medieval Europe's largest battles in 1389. The defeat opened the way for the expansion of the Turkish Ottoman Empire in the Balkan Peninsula. In 1456 the advancing Turks occupied the Bogomil heartland in the Lim valley. The Bogomils, hated and persecuted by both Orthodox and Roman Catholics, were offered salvation and largely converted to the Islamic religion of the Turks. As Muslims they became a favored minority and, with the Turkish military aristocracy settled on the lands of the annihilated Serb nobility, formed a ruling class that controlled large estates worked by Christian and Muslim serfs.

Under Ottoman Turkish rule the region grew prosperous, and the city of Novibazar gained importance as a regional trading center. The area around the

Lim valley, administered as a separate Turkish province or *sanjak*, called the Sanjak of Novibazar, separated Orthodox Serbia on the east from Orthodox Montenegro to the west. Surrounded by Orthodox majority territories, the region suffered sporadic Christian uprisings during the seventeenth and eighteenth centuries. In 1718 the Austrians occupied the province but made no changes to the existing social structure before withdrawing their administration in 1739.

A widespread uprising in Turkish territory in 1875 finally drew in Austrian military intervention and ultimately the Austrian occupation of Bosnia, Herzegovina, and Sanjak in 1878. In 1908, in partial compensation to the Ottomans for the Austrian annexation of Bosnia and Herzegovina, the Austrian authorities returned the Muslim majority Sanjak of Novibazar to Ottoman Turkish rule.

Serbian troops overran the region during the First Balkan War in 1912, and in 1913 the Sanjak region was partitioned between the Serb and Montenegrin states. The Balkan Wars left unresolved territorial conflicts that were partly to blame for the outbreak of World War I in 1914. The Serbs and Montenegrins, at war with the Austrians in 1914, were unable to impose changes, and the medieval social organization of the Sanjak is remained intact.

In 1917, in spite of Sanjaki opposition, the region became part of the newly constituted South Slav kingdom. At the end of the war in 1918, the Muslim landlords were ousted, and serfdom was outlawed. The Sanjakis, formerly the landed gentry of the region, became a despised, landless, Muslim minority in the intensely nationalistic and Christian state. Between the two world wars, they suffered official discrimination and periodic, often violent persecutions.

In 1941 Yugoslavia fell to the invading fascist forces of Germany and Italy. The Sanjak region became the focus of ethnic fighting, reprisals, and widespread atrocities perpetuated by all sides. Following the withdrawal of German troops from the region in 1944, thousands of Sanjakis fled as Tito's communist partisans took control of the region and systematically eliminated all opposition.

Tito's postwar division of Yugoslavia into six ethnic republics brought Sanjaki demands for the unification of the Muslim majority territories in Serbia and Montenegro and the creation of a separate Sanjak republic within the Yugoslav federation. Although the neighboring Montenegrins, with approximately the same national population, were given their own republic, Tito refused to consider the demands of the Muslim Sanjakis.

The Sanjakis, up to World War II, having identified themselves only by their religion or as Muslim Serbs or Montenegrins, in the decades after the war evolved a separate national identity. In the 1948 census, the Sanjakis were listed as Muslims, and in 1953 they were counted as undetermined Yugoslavs. Finally recognized, along with the neighboring Bosnians, as a separate Muslim nationality in 1969, they were again counted as simply Muslims in 1981.

Tito's death in 1980 began a slow unraveling of the federation he had held together. The collapse of communism in 1989 stirred the long-dormant Sanjaki nationalism. In late 1989 and early 1990 large demonstrations demanded national rights and protested growing Serb oppression. The disintegration of the

Yugoslav federation in 1990–91 stimulated a Sanjaki campaign to follow the other Yugoslav national groups to independence; however, their lack of arms and the threat of the powerful Yugoslav National Army (JNA) dampened pro-independence fervor, but not demands for cultural and political autonomy.

The Sanjakis in late October 1991 voted for autonomy in defiance of the Serb authorities. Just hours after the polls opened, Serb police moved in to forcibly close them, but the voting continued in secret. The Sanjakis boycotted the 1992 referendum that renewed the truncated Yugoslav federation of Serbia and Montenegro. In late 1993 violent incidents broke out between Sanjaki demonstrators and radical Serb nationalists but were quickly brought under control as the Serbs feared a violent confrontation within their own borders while their armed forces were fighting in Croatia and Bosnia and Herzegovina. In 1994 twenty-four Sanjaki nationalist leaders were arrested and put on trial, charged with plotting the secession of the Sanjak from Yugoslavia. The trial fueled Sanjaki nationalism but raised new fears that the repression suffered by the neighboring Albanians of Kosovo could easily be implemented in the Sanjak by the Serbian authorities.

In spite of Serbian charges, the spokesmen of the leading national organization, the Muslim National Council of Sanjak, in 1994 described allegations that the Sanjakis wished to unite with the Bosnians as pure imagination. Integration of the Sanjak, which is politically split between Serbia and Montenegro, with Bosnia-Herzegovina is a wish but is not politically possible.

On 3 November 1996 local municipal and federal elections were held in Yugoslavia. At the request of the Muslim National Council of Sanjak international monitors were dispatched to monitor the election process in Sanjak. Many of the monitors were told of election irregularities, particularly the absence of many voters' names from the voting lists and the absence of opposition or nationalist candidates' names on the voting forms. The nationalists, nevertheless, won the largest number of votes on a platform for cultural, religious, and economic autonomy.

The increasing violence in neighboring Kosovo and the growing rift between the Serbs and Montenegrins at the federal level in Yugoslavia have alarmed the Sanjakis in 1998–99. Should Yugoslavia again splinter, the Sanjakis want their homeland, which straddles the Serbian-Montenegrin border, to remain intact as a distinct European region and the homeland of the Sanjaki nation.

SELECTED BIBLIOGRAPHY
Kaplan, Robert D. *Balkan Ghosts.* 1993.
Margas, Branka. *The Destruction of Yugoslavia.* 1993.
Murvar, Vatro. *Nationalism and Religion in Central Europe and The Western Balkans.* Vol. 1: *The Muslims in Bosnia, Hercegovina and Sandzak: A Sociological Analysis.* 1990.
Silber, Laura, and Allan Little. *Yugoslavia: Death of a Nation.* 1997.
Thompson, Mark. *A Paper House: The Ending of Yugoslavia.* 1993.

SAN MARINESE

Sanmarinese; Sammarinese;
Sammarinesi

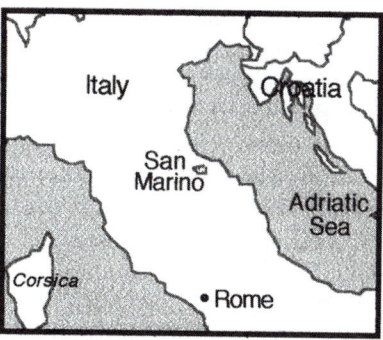

POPULATION: Approximately (2000 e) 31,000 San Marinese in Europe, with 19,000 concentrated in the Republic of San Marino and most of the others in Italy and France. Outside Europe the largest San Marinese population is in the United States.

THE SAN MARINESE HOMELAND: The San Marinese homeland lies in the Umbrian Apenines on the slopes of three-peaked Mt. Titano (2,424 feet/730 m.) near the Adriatic Sea in north-central Italy east of Florence. The world's smallest republic, the tiny enclave occupies a highland area southwest of the Italian city of Rimini and is completely surrounded by Italian territory. The tiny republic is watered by several streams, including the Ausa, Marano, and San Marino. Although agriculture remains important, manufacturing and tourism are now the main occupations. The other important source of income is the sale of postage stamps.

The republic, traditionally Europe's oldest existing state, was founded in the fourth century A.D. The independence of the republic was recognized by the papacy in 1631. *Most Serene Republic of San Marino (Serenissima Repubblica di San Marino)*: twenty-four sq.mi.–sixty-two sq.km. (2000 e) 26,300—San Marinese 75%, Italians* 23%. The capital and major cultural center is San Marino, (2000 e) 4,000, located on the slopes of Mt. Titano. The other important urban area is Serravalle/Dogano, (2000 e) 8,000, the most populous in the country.

FLAG: The San Marinese national flag, the official flag of the republic, is a horizontal bicolor of white over blue. The flag is often flown bearing the arms of the state within a wreath of oak and laurel.

PEOPLE: The San Marinese are an Italian people with a long and distinct history that traditionally dates from the fourth century A.D. The San Marinese culture is basically a Apennines mountain culture that incorporates distinct traditions and customs. The inhabitants of the tiny republic are extremely proud of their state and have a strong sense of their distinct identity. Like their Italian neighbors, the San Marinese are mostly Roman Catholic.

The official language of the republic is Italian; however, the language of daily life is the Sammarinese subdialect of Emiliano-Romagnolo, the dialect spoken in the neighboring Italian region of Emilia-Romagna. Sammarinese is spoken by an estimated 83% of the population of San Marino, while all but a few are bilingual, also speaking standard Italian, which is based on a Tuscan dialect.

NATION: According to San Marinese tradition, a Christian stonecutter, Marino (Marinus) of Dalmatia, took refuge on Mt. Titano during the barbarian invasions of Italy in the fourth century A.D. By the mid-fifth century, a community had formed on the slopes of the mountain, which was chosen for its defensible location. Refugees from the upheavals in the lowlands added to the gradually growing community.

Because of the community's inaccessible location and poverty, it was mostly ignored by the invaders that swept into Italy in the fifth and sixth centuries. Fortified towers, built on the three peaks of Mt. Titano, and stout city walls around their capital protected the tiny state from invaders. In 885 the San Marinese formally proclaimed the independence of their tiny state, which became a republic in the fourteenth century. The independence of San Marino was recognized by Pope Nicholas IV in 1291.

During the Middle Ages the San Marinese were threatened by the expanding city-states of the plains below. They found powerful protectors in the Montefeltro family of Urbino, who sent armed soldiers to repel incursions by the troops of the Malatesta family, the ruling family in Rimini and other nearby communes from the thirteenth to the sixteenth centuries.

The extension of papal control over the communes and small states of central Italy was extended to Urbino in 1631, when the remaining lands of the Montefeltro family were annexed. San Marino, formerly under the protection of the Montefeltros, was recognized by the papacy as an independent state. In spite of the wars and revolutions that periodically swept across the region, the San Marinese stubbornly clung to their cherished independence.

The tiny republic in 1849 gave refuge to Giuseppe Garibaldi, the Italian patriot and soldier during the revolutionary upheavals that swept Europe. Although a convinced republican, Garibaldi fought for the Sardinian kingdom against the Austrians,* and during his spectacular retreat across central Italy, he found refuge in the tiny mountain state of San Marino, where he was received as a hero who had fought against the Hapsburg's designs on central Italy, including San Marino.

In the 1860s, as the many independent Italian states began to unite, the San Marinese looked for support for their independence beyond Italy's borders. In

1861 President Abraham Lincoln of the United States accepted the honorary citizenship offered by the San Marinese during the American Civil War. Surrounded by Italian territory, the San Marinese in 1862 moved to formalize their relations with the Italian kingdom. That year the leaders of the republic signed a treaty of friendship with Italy, followed by formal agreements on economic issues between the two states. The treaty has been renewed and expanded several times.

During World War I and II, although San Marino had no army or conscription, many San Marinese volunteers fought with the Italian armies. In 1944 during World War II, Allied aircraft bombed factories producing war goods in the republic.

From 1945 to 1957 the republic was ruled by a communist-socialist coalition, with a communist majority in the Grand Council. The San Marinese communists, moderate and nationalist, were the forerunners of the Euro-Communists that emerged in Western Europe following the end of the Stalinist period in 1953. Under a Christian Democrat and Social Democrat coalition that governed the country from 1957 to 1969, women were given the vote. In 1973 women were granted the right to hold office in the republic.

A left-wing coalition again ruled the republic from 1978 to 1986, at which time dissident communists joined with the Christian Democrats to form a new government, which was reelected in 1988. Following the overthrow of communism, in 1991 the Communist Party of San Marino changed its name to the Democratic Progressive Party. In March 1992 the Christian Democrats formed a coalition government with the socialists, a status that continued after the May 1993 general election.

San Marino is governed by the Great and General Council, a legislative body of sixty members elected by universal suffrage for a term of five years. Two members of the council, called captains-regent, are elected for six months to preside over the country's executive body, the Congress of State. San Marino became a member of the United Nations in 1992.

SELECTED BIBLIOGRAPHY

Carrick, Noel. *San Marino*. 1988.

Catling, Christopher. *Regions of Italy: Umbria, the Marches and San Marino*. 1994.

Edwards, Adrian, and Chris Michaelides. *San Marino*. 1996.

Hearder, Harry. *Italy in the Age of the Risorgimento, 1790–1870*. 1983.

Prati, Alessandro. *San Marino: Recent Economic Developments*. 1996.

SARDS

Sardinians; Sardus

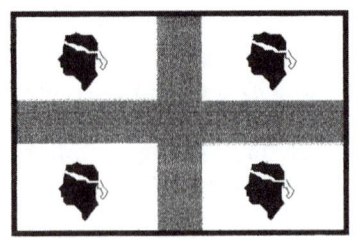

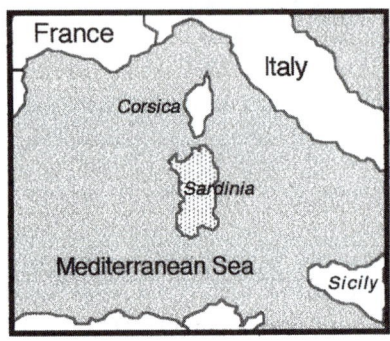

POPULATION: Approximately (2000 e) 2,225,000 Sards in Europe, 1,315,000 in Sardinia, with large Sard populations in other regions of Italy and in France, Switzerland, and Germany.

THE SARD HOMELAND: The Sard homeland is an island, the second largest in the Mediterranean. Sardinia lies in the western Mediterranean Sea some 100 miles west of the Italian mainland and just south of the French island of Corsica, which is separated from Sardinia by the Strait of Bonifacio, just seven miles wide at its narrowest point. The region of Sardinia also includes several smaller islands, Asinara, Caprera, San Pietro, and the La Maddalena Islands. The island is mostly mountainous, reaching its highest point at Mt. Gennargentu, 6,016 feet (1,834 m.). Natural pastures cover about half the island, while the major agricultural area is the large Campidano Plain, located in the southwest and watered by the Manno and Tirso Rivers.

Sardinia, called Sardigna in the Sard language and Sardegna in Italian, has formed a semiautonomous region of the Italian republic since 1948. *Region of Sardinia (Sardigna)*: 9,302 sq.mi.–24,098 sq.km. (2000 e) 1,644,000—Sards 80%, other Italians* 15%, Corsicans* 2%. The Sardinian capital and major cultural center is Cagliari, called Calaris in the Sard language, (2000 e) 207,000, an important port city on the Gulf of Cagliari on the island's southern coast.

FLAG: The Sardinian national flag, the official flag of the region, is a white field divided by a centered red cross, each white rectangle charged with a black Moor's head in profile.

PEOPLE: The Sards are a Romance people, the descendants of early Latins and later admixtures of the island's many conquerors. Traditionally, the Sards are more soft-spoken and reserved than the other Italian peoples, but traditionally, they are very proud and have often engaged in violent vendettas over points of honor. A small minority around the city of Algero has preserved much of the culture and language brought to the island by the Catalans.* The majority of the Sards are devoutly Roman Catholic, although church influence has decreased since World War II.

The Sards speak a distinct Romance language called Sardu. The language is the most similar to Vulgar Latin of all the Romance languages and is spoken in four major dialects, Campidanese in the south; Gallurese, influenced by the Tuscan and Corsican dialects in the northeast; Logurdese in the center; and Sassarese, influenced by the dialect of the Ligurians,* in the northeast. Each of the four dialects is further divided into regional subdialects, and none of the Sard dialects have been selected as the standard language. The Sard dialects are as close to ancient Latin as to modern Italian, with some of the dialects forming transition dialects to Spanish or Catalan. An estimated 8% of the Sards speak only Sardu, while around 80% are bilingual in Sardu and standard Italian.

NATION: The island of Sardinia was a very early center of Mediterranean culture. The Bronze Age Nuraghic civilization flourished from about 1800 B.C., leaving behind some 30,000 stone fortresses. Sardinia was mentioned in Egyptian chronicles of the thirteenth century B.C. as a distinct Mediterranean culture. About 800 B.C. Phoenicians established trading colonies on the island; however, according to Greek legends, the island was first settled by Carthaginians led by a sailor named Sardo about 500 B.C. The Greek name for the island, derived from Sardo, was adopted by other Mediterranean cultures. The Carthaginians established colonies that became the present Sardinian cities between 500 and 400 B.C.

The Romans conquered the island in 238 B.C. and gradually imposed their Latin culture on the Semitic Carthaginians and the Greek colonies. Thoroughly Latinized during six centuries of Roman rule, Sardinia has retained an indelible Latin imprint on the island's culture and language.

Roman power collapsed in the fifth century, leaving the island without defenses. Goths and Vandals from the mainland overran Sardinia but were expelled in 533 by the Byzantines of the Eastern Roman Empire. The Byzantines held the island until the eleventh century, but little material or cultural progress was made. Muslim Arabs from North Africa, called Saracens, conquered the island from the Byzantines but held it only briefly before being expelled by forces from the Italian mainland. The Saracens continued to raid and harass the Sardinian coastal regions from the eighth through the eleventh centuries.

In the eleventh and twelfth centuries the maritime republics of Pisa and Genoa fought for control of the island, which was finally divided between the two states in 1294. The Genoese took control of the northern districts, and the Pisans took the south, but three years later Pope Boniface VIII bestowed the island on the Catalan kingdom of Aragon. The Catalans ruled the island as part of their extensive Mediterranean Empire until the unification of Spain in 1479. Spanish administrators took control of the island from the Catalans, bringing yet another Romance language and culture to the island. The Pisans, Genoans, Catalans, and Spaniards* all influenced the evolution of the Sards' culture and language.

By the Peace of Utrecht in 1713 Spain ceded the island to the Austrians,* but in 1717 a Spanish force again occupied the island. The settlement of 1720 gave Sardinia to Victor Amadeus II of Savoy, who took the title king of Sardinia. In exchange he gave Sicily to the Holy Roman Emperor Charles VI. The kings of Sardinia, resident in Turin, maintained their royal residence at Cagliari on Sardinia. The House of Savoy ruled an area that included not only Sardinia but Piedmont, Savoy, Aosta, Liguria, Nice, and Menton on the Italian mainland. The island formed a neglected appendage where feudal privileges prevailed, while most of Sardinia remained poverty-stricken, bandit-ridden, and backward.

In the early nineteenth century the kingdom's administrators tried to establish some order on the island and finally abolished the nobility's feudal rights in 1835. In 1847 the island's administrative autonomy was abolished, which strengthened the hold of a handful of local nobles. The House of Savoy held the title king of Sardinia until 1861, when the House of Savoy became the Italian royal House and the Savoy kings became kings of united Italy. The adoption of a Tuscan dialect as the official language of united Italy was accompanied by the banning of regional dialects in education, publishing, or official use. The new language laws, in effect from 1870, relegated the Sard dialects to peasant dialects spoken in the countryside, while the larger towns and cities increasingly became Italian in language and culture.

In the late 1800s the Sards remained a basically peasant nation ruled by a small nobility of Italian culture and language. The Sard language, the language of daily life for the majority, was banned for use in education, administration, and publishing. The island's feudal conditions spawned a culture of violence and blood feuds, while banditry became a way of life for the disadvantaged Sards.

Feudal conditions continued well into the twentieth century, with vendettas and lawlessness widespread. The island remained virtually unchanged by the wars that swept across Europe in the early twentieth century. Only in the post-World War II period did some change begin to come to the island, mostly in the form of the growing tourist industry.

The importation of mainland Italian culture in the 1950s and 1960s galvanized a generation of Sards. Young Sards began to take a new interest in their language and culture in the 1960s, the Sard language becoming a rallying point of the growing national movement and its use a matter of pride for the young nationalists. In 1968 Sard nationalists attempted to stir up a separatist uprising on the island, but the movement collapsed following arrests and pressure by the Italian military. More moderate nationalist organizations used threats of separatism to pressure the Italian government for more autonomy and development for the economically backward and bandit-infested island.

Sard nationalism was revived and has increased dramatically since the late

1970s, the majority of the islanders supporting moderate nationalist demands for direct and autonomous management of the available resources to meet Sardinian needs. Long neglected by the Italian government, the island's agrarian sector is still characterized by large estates, and throughout the island work is scarce, utilities are primitive, and the schools are inferior. The island's neglect has created fertile ground for support of nationalist calls for independence from the inefficient and increasingly polarized Italian state. The language issue assumed great importance in the 1980s as Europe increasingly integrated with Sard leaders calling for separate Sard membership in the European Economic Community (EEC), later the European Union (EU). In 1985 Pope John Paul visited Sardinia and urged the Sards to overcome the traditional culture of violence rooted in ancient tradition, vendetta, ransom, destruction of property, degradation, and kidnapping.

Young Sards, unable to find work on the island but refusing the island's traditional outlet, emigration, turned to violence to publicize the island's plight in the 1980s. The campaign of violence escalated in the late 1980s and early 1990s. In 1991–92 over 200 bombings rocked the island. Militant Sard nationalists particularly targeted state-owned industries and Italian government offices.

European unification in the 1990s focused nationalist demands for recognition of the Sards as a separate European people. Growing numbers of Sards look to the European Union as the island's economic salvation, hoping the union will deliver the needed aid the Italian government has long promised but has not delivered. Bills providing economic aid for the island habitually fail to pass the Italian parliament.

Pressed by the growth of nationalism in several regions, the Italian government officially recognized minority languages for use in education, administration, and commerce in November 1991. The legalization of the Sard language ends a ban on the language that has been in effect since Italian unification. To the Sard nationalists seeking recognition as a separate European people the legalization of the language is only a first step to the realization of the Sards' national rights.

SELECTED BIBLIOGRAPHY
Altman, Jack, ed. *Sardinia*. 1996.
Gravette, Andrew. *Sardinia*. 1992.
Tykot, Robert H., and Tamsey K. Andrews. *Sardinia in the Mediterranean: A Footprint in the Sea*. 1992.
Waite, Virginia. *Sard*. 1977.
Webster, Gary S. *A Prehistory of Sardinia, 2300–500* B.C. 1995.

SAVOYARDS

Harpeitains; Mountain Occitans;
Valdotains; Valdostans;
Valdostanos

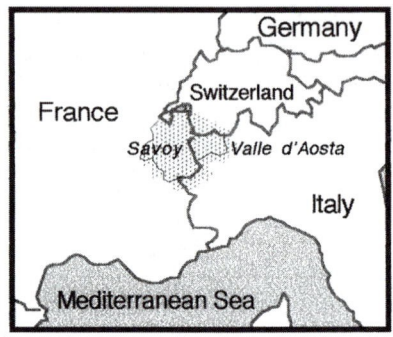

POPULATION: Approximately (2000 e) 1,115,000 Savoyards in Europe, 910,000 concentrated in the Savoy region of France, and 75,000 in the Valle d'Aosta region of Italy.

THE SAVOYARD HOMELAND: The Savoyard homeland lies in a mountainous region in eastern France, northwestern Italy, and southwestern Switzerland. Lying in the Savoy, Graian, and Penine Alps, the region commands many important Alpine passes that connect France, Italy, and Switzerland, including the historic Little Saint Bernard and the Mont Censis Passes and the highest of the Alpine peaks, Mont Blanc. Much of the region comprises the valley of the Rhône River and its tributaries south of Lake Geneva. The region contains several lakes, among them Bourget and Annecy, and a number of important mineral springs and spas.

Savoy has no official status and is divided between three European states, France, Italy, and Switzerland. French* Savoy is divided into the departments of Haute-Savoie and Savoie, Italian Savoy comprises the region of Valle d'Aosta, and Swiss Savoy comprises the southwestern districts of the canton of Valais. The region of Savoy has an estimated population of (2000 e) 1,175,000. The Savoyard cultural centers include Chambéry, (2000 e) 55,000, the historic capital of Savoy, and Annecy, (2000 e) 51,000, in French Savoy, Aosta, called Aoste in the Savoyard language, (2000 e) 37,000, the capital of Aosta region in Italy, and Martigny, (2000 e) 10,000, the largest town of Swiss Savoy.

FLAGs: The Savoyard national flag, the flag of the national movement, is a red field charged with a centered white cross. The flag of the Valdaostans is a vertical bicolor of black and red. The flag of the canton of Valais in Switzerland is a square vertical bicolor of red and white.

PEOPLE: The Savoyards, also called Harpeitians or Mountain Occitans,* are a distinct Gallo-Romanic nation that evolved from the Romanized Alpine tribes of the first century A.D. In Italian Savoy the inhabitants are popularly called Valdaostans. The unique Savoyard culture is an Alpine culture that incorporates borrowings from the French, Occitans, and Piedmontese.* The majority of the Savoyards are Roman Catholic, with a small, important Protestant minority, mostly in the high Alpine valleys of French Savoy. The Savoyards have shown an intractable resilience and have survived in their Alpine homeland since before the Roman conquest of the region.

Along with French or Italian, the Savoyards also speak their own Romance language called Harpeitanya or Franco-Provençal, a hybrid language that evolved from the mixing of forms and words from both Occitan (Langue-d'Oc) and French (Langue d'Oil). The language is spoken in a number of dialects, the most important being Savoyard and Dauphinois in France, Patoé Valdoten or Valdaostan in Italy, and Valaisien in Switzerland. Structurally, the language is separate from the neighboring language groups, Provençal, French, Piedmontese, and Lombard.

NATION: Home to Alpine Celtic peoples, the Allobroges and the Salassi, the western Alps region fell to the Romans in 121 B.C. and became part of the Roman province of Gaul. Between 25 and 15 B.C., the emperor Augustus directed several military campaigns against the tribes that held territory, effectively dividing the Roman Italy from Gaul and the Roman territories to the north. Some tribes were decimated during the campaigns, while others were sold as slaves and deported to far-flung corners of the empire.

The ensuing period of peace and the newly established unity of the empire allowed the construction of Roman roads leading to the passes through the high Alps. At the highest point, on the summit of La Turbie, the "Trophy of the Alps" was constructed in honor of Augustus, bearing the names of the forty-four tribes defeated by the Roman legions.

The Alpine valleys, appreciated for their cool weather and numerous thermal spas, became a favorite retreat for Roman officials and patricians of the large lowland cities. Roman influence became predominant in the culture and language of the region, and the native Celts adopted Latin norms. Many of the region's present cities and towns began as Roman trading posts or forts.

The empire began to disintegrate after three centuries of relative stability, and the Alpine tribes found themselves resisting successive invasions of Germanic tribes. The Burgundians* overran the region's last Roman defenses about A.D. 460. The Burgundians conquered the lowlands to the west in 480, and the combined territories were joined in the Christianized Burgundian kingdom. The Franks conquered the Burgundian kingdom in 534, and the Burgundian lands, including the highland region in the east, were incorporated into the Frankish kingdom. In the tenth century the region was included in the kingdom of Arles, which was ceded to the Holy Roman Empire in the eleventh century.

The population of the region from the tenth to the twelfth centuries expanded rapidly, assisted by a period of glacial retreat that raised the vegetation limits by as much as 6,561 feet (2,000 m.), allowing more extensive colonization of the valleys and an easier passage over the high passes.

A powerful feudal lord of Arles, Count Humbert the White-Handed, consolidated his small holdings in Savoy and gained control of various fiefs in Piedmont by marriage. In 1232 Humbert acquired Chambéry, which he made the capital of his expanding domain. From that point on, the history of the region was closely linked to the House of Savoy. His successors secured additional territories now in France, Italy, and Switzerland. The expanding bilingual Savoyard state emerged as the most powerful in the region. In the early fifteenth century, under Amadeus VIII, Savoy was an extensive, increasingly powerful state, which was raised to the status of a duchy in 1416.

By the beginning of the sixteenth century the rule of the Savoyard dukes had grown weak, and Savoy came under French and Swiss dominance. Savoy lost its Swiss territories, Vaud, Valais, and Geneva, between 1475 and 1536. The loss of territory shifted the center of power to the Savoyard territories in Piedmont in Italy. In 1559 Emmanuel Philibert moved the state's capital from highland Chambéry to Turin in his Italian territories, although the language and tone of the court remained French until the eighteenth century. The French language became the second language of the state, with the Savoyard language remaining the language of daily life in the western districts, while Piedmontese was the most widely spoken language in the eastern districts.

In the War of the Spanish Succession, Victor Amadeus II at first sided with the French but later switched sides and joined the forces of the Holy Roman Emperor led by his cousin, Eugene of Savoy. At the Peace of Utrecht in 1714, Savoy gained control of Sicily and in 1720 exchanged the island for the Austrian-ruled island of Sardinia. Duke Victor Amadeus of Savoy assumed the title king of Sardinia, applying the name of the island to his territories in Savoy, Nice, Menton, Piedmont and, after 1815, Liguria and Genoa. In 1792 the region was occupied by the French, but in 1815 the House of Savoy was restored, with additional territory added to the kingdom of Sardinia.

Italian Savoy was a center of the Risorgimento, and the House of Savoy led the movement for Italian unification. The Risorgimento, finally achieved with French aid in 1860, left only Rome and the Papal States outside the domains of the House of Savoy. Emperor Louis Napoleon of France, for his aid in the Italian unification, demanded the French-speaking parts of the kingdom, Savoy, Nice, and Menton. Only the French-speaking Aosta valley of the former Savoyard duchy remained part of Italy.

In the late nineteenth century, the centralized French and Italian kingdoms banned the official use of the Savoyard language and pressed assimilation, but the culture and dialect survived in the high mountain valleys. By the turn of the twentieth century the cities and towns of Savoy had become French-speaking, and in Aosta a sizable Italian-speaking minority settled in the towns; however, in the rural areas and the high Alpine valleys the Franco-Provençal dialect remained the language of daily life. The fascist Italian regime, in power in Italy from 1922, posed the first major threat to Savoyard culture in Italy. In the 1930s the fascist authorities banned both French and Harpeitanya and ordered all names, even family names, changed to Italian. Cultural repression increased during World War II but merely strengthened Savoyard resolve. In the latter years of the war, both French Savoy and the Valle d'Aosta were centers of dissent against fascism and the Nazi occupation.

The House of Savoy, held partially responsible for Italy's World War II defeat, was deposed following a 1946 referendum. As the new republican government of Italy began drafting a postwar constitution, the Savoyard nationalists in the Aosta Valley demanded secession from Italy and reunification with Savoy and part of the Swiss canton of Valais in an independent *Etat Montagne*. The movement gained considerable support in Savoy, but separatist sentiment died down after the Italian government separated the Aosta Valley from Piedmont and granted some political autonomy to the region in 1948.

The opening of several tunnels in the 1960s eliminated the seasonal accessibility of the region and brought an influx of outsiders. The tunnels turned the region into a major commercial route between France, Italy, and Switzerland, raising levels of traffic congestion, noise, and pollution. The scale of the growth of tourism has necessitated a vast expansion of local services and an imported workforce to man them, the majority of which originate in areas of different cultures and languages. The rapid expansion of tourist facilities and holiday homes sparked the first calls for linguistic and cultural autonomy across the region in the 1970s. In 1978 nationalists formed the National Savoyard Front (FNS) to work for the reunification and autonomy of Savoy within an integrated Europe.

The rapid changes brought to the region between the 1960s and 1970s have raised standards of living dramatically but also posed a serious threat to the Savoyard culture since, as the percentage of the indigenous population decreases and intermarriage increases, the language and traditions of the region are being lost.

The Savoyards, after centuries of resistance, are no longer threatened by armed invasion but are threatened by rural depopulation and the cultural and environmental impact of mass tourism. The Savoyard sense of identity remains strong, and in the 1990s there is a growing awareness that the limited autonomous powers allowed by the French and Italian governments have done little to prevent the increasing loss of their unique culture or the destruction of their fragile Alpine environment.

Valdaostan nationalists on 3 September 1991 set in motion the procedures for a referendum on secession from Italy, seen as a first step toward a reconstituted Savoyard state within a united European federation. In May 1993 the Valdaostan nationalists took 37.3% of the vote in local elections, the highest in their history. Radical separatists, vowing to secede and reunite with neighboring Savoy, took a surprising 5% of the vote. The militancy of the nationalists in Italian Savoy has fueled a strong regionalist and environmental movement in the Alpine regions of Italy, France, and Switzerland.

Regional autonomy in Italy and Switzerland and limited local powers in France have done little to prevent the growing threat to the unique Savoyard culture and language. However, in spite of the declining use of the local dialects, the sense of identity is still very strong in all three areas, which the Savoyards consider the heart of Europe.

SELECTED BIBLIOGRAPHY

Boers, Michael. *Europe under Napoleon 1799–1815*. 1996.

Brustein, William. *The Social Origins of Political Regionalism: France, 1849–1981.* 1982.

Cox, Eugene L. *The Eagles of Savoy: The House of Savoy in Thirteenth Century Europe.* 1983.

Grizell, Rex. *The Rhone Valley and Savoy*. 1991.

Pollard, John F. *The Fascist Experience in Italy*. 1998.

SAXONS

Sachsens; Saxonians; Old Saxons

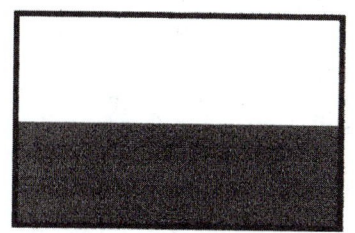

POPULATION: Approximately (2000 e) 7,771,000 Saxons in Europe, mostly living in east-central Germany.

THE SAXON HOMELAND: The Saxon homeland lies in southeastern Germany, a region of flat, fertile lowlands in the North German Plain, mostly in the valleys of the river Elbe and its tributaries, the Saale and the Spree, and the Neisse River, which forms the boundary between Saxony and Poland. In the south the land rises to a mountainous highland, the so-called Saxon Switzerland in the Erzgebirge (the Ore Mountains) and the Thüringer Wald (the Thuringian Forest). Formerly forming part of the German Democratic Republic (GDR), the region is heavily industrialized but also heavily polluted, mostly due to the mining of brown coal and uranium.

The historic region of Saxony as a geographic area has changed greatly in the course of its history. The present region inhabited by Saxons includes the German states of Saxony, Thuringia, and the southern districts of the state of Saxony-Anhalt. *State of Saxony (Sachsen)*: 7,078 sq.km.–18,337 sq.km. (2000 e) 4,877,000—Saxons 88%, Sorbs,* other Germans.* The Saxon capital and major cultural center is Dresden, (2000 e) 489,000 (metropolitan area 749,000), on the river Elbe. The other important cultural center is Leipzig, (2000 e) 502,000 (metropolitan area 684,000), the state of Saxony's largest city. Outside Saxony major Saxon cultural centers include Halle, (2000 e) 231,000 (metropolitan area 489,000), in the Saxon region of southern Saxony-Anhalt, and Erfurt, (2000 e) 205,000, the capital of the state of Thuringia.

FLAGS: The Saxon national flag, the traditional flag of the Saxon regions, is a horizontal bicolor of white over green. The flag of the Thuringian Saxons is a horizontal bicolor of white over red.

PEOPLE: The Saxons are a German people, the descendants of early Germanic tribes and Germanized Slavs. The traditions and culture of the Saxons reflect their long association with the neighboring Slavs. Formerly, the Saxons were often referred to as the Old Saxons, to distinguish them from the Saxon tribes that participated in the occupation of Britain between the fifth and seventh centuries A.D. In spite of centuries of disunity, the Saxons have retained an inbred sense of identity that even decades of communist rule failed to destroy. The majority of the Saxons are Lutherans, with a small Roman Catholic minority and a substantial number professing no religious beliefs.

The Saxon dialect of High German, Saxonian or Upper Saxon, is actually a group of nine dialects, four of them spoken only in Thuringia, and is the language of daily life in the region. The dialects, considerably different from standard German, incorporate extensive Slavic borrowings and, since German unification in 1990, have been giving way to standard German. Cultural groups in the region have begun efforts to save the unique Saxon dialects from extinction. Pronunciation, even of standard German, differs considerably from the pronunciation of the German heartland, and the Saxons can be distinguished readily by their characteristic types of pronunciation.

NATION: The Saxon tribes were first mentioned in the second century A.D. as inhabiting the area around the mouth of the river Elbe and the nearby islands in northwestern Germany. From their original territory, the Saxons extended their territory southward across the Weser River. In the fourth and fifth centuries the Saxon tribes split, some tribal groups joining the Angles and Jutes in the invasion and conquest of Angoland (England). Other Saxon tribes followed the river Elbe south to conquer Thuringia in 531. Partially subdued by the Franks in 566 and compelled to pay tribute, the Saxon lands were ultimately absorbed by the Frankish Empire, and the Saxons were forcibly Christianized in the seventh century.

In the eighth century the Saxons were brought under the control of Charlemagne's Empire. As part of the Carolingian Empire, the Saxons established a duchy in the ninth century. The Saxon duchy formed one of the five stem duchies of the Holy Roman Empire. Duke Henry I, called Henry the Fowler, was elected German king in 919. His son, Otto I, bestowed Saxony on a Saxon nobleman, Hermann Billung, whose descendants held the duchy until the extinction of the male line in 1106. During this period the Saxons expanded eastward, conquering and absorbing the new territory's Slav populations.

The Wettin dynasty, established as the ruling house of the increasingly powerful Margravite of Meissen in 1100, extended its authority to eventually control a large part of the Holy Roman Empire. In 1423 Margrave Frederick the Warlike gained control of Electoral Saxony, and in 1425 he became Elector Frederick I. In 1485 the Wettin lands were partitioned between the two sons of Elector Frederick. The division became permanent, with the Ernestine line taking control of the territories in the west and the Albertine branch retaining the ducal title in eastern Saxony. From the fifteenth century the Ernestine line divided Thuringia into a number of small states, the so-called Saxon duchies.

Martin Luther in 1571 pinned up a case for free choice in religion on the church door in Wittenberg. Luther's action began the momentous Protestant Reformation. The great popularity of Luther's works, written in the Saxon dialect, helped to standardize the Saxon dialects as a literary language. A Protestant stronghold during the wars of religion in the seventeenth century, Saxony emerged as one of the two most powerful of the Protestant German states, beginning a long and bitter rivalry with Brandenburg-Prussia.

The rivalry between Saxony and Brandenburg, later renamed Prussia, was a decisive factor in the history of the Saxon nation. The election of Augustus II, who was Frederick Augustus I as elector of Saxony, to the throne of Poland pulled the Saxons eastward but diminished their prestige. The death of Augustus III in 1763 ended the union with Poland, a period marked by economic and social decay but also a great flowering of Saxon culture and art, which was shared by the Saxon duchies to the west. Weimar, the capital of the duchy of Saxe-Weimar-Eisenach, became an intellectual center of Europe. Augustus II and Augustus II were patrons of art and learning and greatly beautified their capital, Dresden. Leipzig, with its famous university, led the rise of German literature and music.

The French Revolution and the rise of Napoleon pushed Saxony into an anti-French alliance with its antagonistic Prussian neighbor. In 1806 during the Napoleonic Wars, Saxony switched sides. Napoleon raised the Saxon elector to the status of king of Saxony, but the new king's failure to abandon his French ally before Napoleon's fall cost him the northern half of his kingdom. In 1815 a triumphant Prussia annexed northern districts of Saxony.

Passionately anti-Prussian and determined to recover the lost provinces, the Saxons mostly sided with the Austrians* during the Austro-Prussian War of 1866. Defeated by superior Prussian forces, the kingdom and the defeated Saxon duchies were forced to pay large indemnities and to join the Prussian-dominated North German Confederation. In 1871 Saxony and the Saxon duchies, under Prussian pressure, joined the German Empire. Saxony's abundant mineral wealth stimulated rapid industrialization in the late nineteenth century. The heavy industries established in the region, manned by a large urban proletariat, became centers of socialist ideals.

Important to the war effort after 1914, the industrial zones became centers of radical political movements, many supporting a 1917 movement for Saxon secession from Germany and separate peace with the Allies. In early November 1918 King Frederick Augustus III, along with the Wettin rulers of the small Saxon duchies and principalities in Thuringia, abdicated as revolution swept defeated Germany. On 19 November, inspired by the Russian Revolution, workers and soldiers councils took control of Saxony and declared the independence of the Soviet Republic of Saxony. The new government announced sweeping nationalization and expropriations. During the months that followed, violent clashes and running battles between communists, Saxon nationalists, and Pan-German groups left thousands dead and injured.

Saxony and the former Saxon duchies consolidated into the new state of Thuringia joined the German Weimar Republic, but in April 1919 the Saxon state severed all remaining ties to Germany. The action provoked an invasion of federal troops and the overthrow of Saxony's communist government. Called Red Saxony, in March 1920 there were an estimated 250,000 registered communists and many more who supported them. In March 1921 a new, armed revolt broke out, supported by the communist Hungarian government of Bela Kun, and in 1922 the communists again supported the separation of Saxony from Germany. The German government again dispatched troops to put down the separatists, and in 1923 the Saxon government was dissolved, and the Saxon Militia was disbanded.

The region remained a center of communist and socialist activities until the dissidents were driven underground by Hitler's Nazi troops in 1933. The communists and socialists of the region formed worker defense units, called hundreds, to secure the Saxon lands from fascist Nazi domination. In 1933, after Hitler became chancellor of Germany, the German government dispatched SS and SA troops to Saxony on the pretext that the Saxon authorities were unable to maintain order. The Saxon states lost all their former autonomy.

The mayor of Leipzig from 1930 to 1937, Carl Frederick Goerder, was the leader of the Saxon resistance to Nazism during World War II. He was arrested and executed in 1944. Dresden was severely damaged by British and American bombing in February 1945. Many of the city's famed art and architectural treasures disappeared in the firestorm that followed the bombing. Those art treasures that were saved were later stolen by the Soviets.

In 1945 the Saxon states fell to advancing American troops. The Americans later traded control of the region to the Soviets in exchange for Allied control of six boroughs of Berlin. The states of Saxony, Thuringia, and Saxony-Anhalt were reconstituted under Soviet military rule in 1947. Included in the communist German state created in 1949, many Saxons fled to West Germany, which was closely integrated into the Western Alliance. As part of the official opposition to regionalist sentiment, the Saxon states were abolished in 1952 and replaced with administrative units.

Resistance to Soviet domination remained strong, even though communism and socialism had a long history in the region. Economic hardships and suppression of all opposition stiffened resistance in the early 1950s, and serious anti-Soviet rioting broke out in the major Saxon cities in 1953 but was brutally suppressed. By the 1970s resistance had coalesced around the peace movement led by Lutheran clergy, but arrests and detentions drove the dissidents underground, even though the church remained a refuge for antinuclear groups during the years of the Cold War. In 1978 the Lutheran Church received concessions allowing limited freedoms.

In the 1980s the local communist authorities, faced with severe shortages, West German television, and the desire of many Saxons to leave for the West, appealed to German nationalism and the past glories of the Saxons. In 1984 the East German government finally had to arrange for the transmission of West German television into the Dresden area to alleviate absenteeism among workers leaving "Blind Dresden" to watch television in areas where reception was possible. In September 1988 demonstrations in Leipzig and other large cities were staged by Saxons demanding the right to leave for West Germany. The demonstrations underscored growing Saxon dissatisfaction with the ruling Communist Party.

Saxon nationalism, having survived over fifty years of communist rule, resurfaced in 1989 with demands for the partition of East Germany into Saxon and Prussian states. The rediscovered Saxon identity was put aside in the euphoria that accompanied the collapse of East Germany and the rush to German unification in October 1990. Disillusionment with reunification, which was followed by mass unemployment and economic hardship, spurred a nationalist resurgence. A poll in October 1993 demonstrated the growing despair: 25% saw themselves as the losers in unification, 15% were so disillusioned that they wanted a return to communist rule, and 20% expressed the opinion that independence for the Saxons would be a better alternative.

In the late 1990s, in spite of massive government investment and economic reforms, the Saxons remain relatively poor in comparison to the Bavarians* and Swabians* to the west. The continuing economic disparities between the former east and west Germans fuel the growth of regionalist feelings in the Saxon regions.

Nostalgia for the full employment and assured social services of the Communist past has given the reformed Communist Party, now called the Party of Democratic Socialism (PDS), a renewed popularity. From only about 10% of the vote in 1990, the PDS now has around 29% of the vote in the region. In state elections in Saxony and Thuringia, in 1999, the PDS became the second political party in both of the states of the Saxon heartland.

SELECTED BIBLIOGRAPHY

Fisher, Marc. *After the Wall: Germany, the Germans and the Burdens of History.* 1995.

Gedmin, Jeffrey. *The Germans: Portrait of a New Nation.* 1995.

Lapp, Benjamin. *Revolution from the Right: Politics, Class and the Rise of Nazism in Saxony, 1919–1933.* 1997.

Leyser, K. J. *Rule and Conflict in Early Medieval Saxony.* 1989.

Shlaes, Amity. *Germany: The Empire Within.* 1993.

SCANIANS

Skånes; Skanska

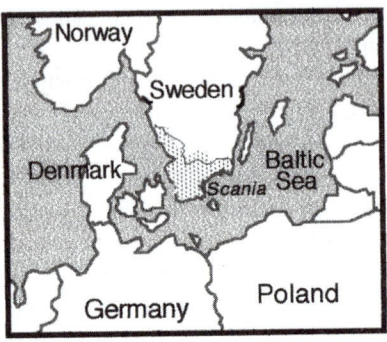

POPULATION: Approximately (2000 e) 1,648,000 Scanians in Europe, mostly in the Scania region of southern Sweden, the Danish island of Bornholm and the smaller islands surrounding it, and in neighboring regions of Denmark on the other side of the narrow body of water called the Oresund.

THE SCANIAN HOMELAND: The Scanian homeland, locally called Skåne or Skaneland, lies just south of the Smaland Plateau in southern Sweden but also includes the Danish island of Bornholm, forty miles southeast of the Scanian mainland. The region is surrounded by the Baltic Sea, the Oresund, and the Kattegatt and mostly consists of open plains in the south with wooded hills along the northern border with Smaland. Bornholm is a generally hilly, rocky plain about 270 feet (eighty-two m.) above sea level. The region's fertile plains are Sweden's major agricultural area, producing abundant crops of cash cereals and dairy products, while Malmo and the western coastal districts make up one of Scandinavia's major industrial zones.

Scania has no official status but constitutes four provinces of Sweden, Malmöhaus, Halland, Kristianstad, and Blekinge, and Bornholm County of Denmark. *Region of Scania (Skåneland)*: 7,660 sq.mi.–19,839 sq.km. (2000 e) 1,512,000—Scanians 91%, other Swedes,* other Danes.* Bornholm, or Danish Scania, has a population of (2000 e) 45,000. The Scanian capital and major cultural center is Malmo, (2000 e) 236,000 (metropolitan area 502,000), opposite Copenhagen on the Oresund. Other important Scanian cultural centers include Lund, (2000 e) 94,000, Scania's historic capital and an important university city. The most important town on the island of Bornholm is Ronne, (2000 e) 16,000, the capital of the Danish county of Bornholm.

FLAG: The Scanian national flag, the flag of the Scania region, is a red field charged with a yellow Scandinavian cross.

PEOPLE: The Scanians are a Scandinavian people of mixed Danish and Swedish descent, their culture and language incorporating customs and influences from both along with many unique traits. In spite of centuries of Swedish cultural and linguistic pressure, the Scanians have retained a strong sense of identity and consider themselves a separate Scandinavian nation. The Scanians mostly belong to the Lutheran faith, which forms an integral part of their culture.

The Scanian dialect, widely spoken in the region and claimed by nationalists as a separate Scandinavian language, is in some ways closer to Danish than to Swedish. The existence of a separate Scanian language is denied by the Swedish government, but the distinct Scanian dialect remains the language of daily life in the region. A closely related Danish dialect, called Eastern Danish, is spoken on Bornholm and the smaller islands of the group.

NATION: Germanic tribes occupied the region in ancient times but remained disunited and often warred among themselves. Remains of the ancient inhabitants include numerous dolmens and tumuli in the region. During the Bronze Age, close ties were established between the inhabitants of present-day Scania and the inhabitants of present-day Denmark. In A.D. 380 a tribal chieftain, Alaric, was the first to claim the title Rex Scaniae, king of Scania. Between 380 and 770 fifteen known kings ruled the region.

In 770 the Scanian king Ivar Vidfamne began to extend Scanian power to become the first empire builder in the Scandinavian region. The Scanians of the overpopulated coastal regions, unable to sustain the size of the growing population, participated in the great Viking expansion during the eighth and ninth centuries, which included the colonization of the island of Bornholm. Scanian Vikings, searching for land and plunder, raided Britain, Ireland, and Northern Europe.

The great king of the Danes,* Canute, in 811 united Denmark and Scania under the Danish crown. Canute eventually controlled Denmark, Scania, England, and Norway under his rule, which lasted until 1035. Growing rivalry between the Danes and Swedes led to the division of the island of Bornholm between Denmark and Sweden in 1149. Canute's line ruled the region until 1047, when Sven Estridsin, a Scanian, became king of Denmark. Sven Estridsin and his sons held the Danish throne until 1330. From 1330 to 1360 Scania was under the rule of Count Johan of Holstein, and although Canute's empire disappeared, Scania remained the heartland of the Danish kingdom. Danish rule of the rich Scanian provinces in the thirteenth century was increasingly challenged by the Swedes to the north.

Christianity gradually became the dominant religion in spite of fierce resistance. The archbishopric established at Lund in 1104 developed as the ecclesiastical center of all Scandinavia. The Scania region, the crossroads of Northern Europe, became a prosperous center of religious life and commerce. From 1327 to 1522 the archbishop ruled the island of Bornholm.

The Union of Kalmar united Scandinavia with the crowns of Denmark, Norway, and Sweden combined in 1397. Because the kingship was elective in all three countries, the union could not be maintained by inheritance and was dissolved in 1523. At the dissolution of the union the Danes retained control of Scania and Norway. The religious divide in Europe greatly affected the region, which was the ecclesiastical center of Scandinavia. The Protestant Reformation, accepted by the Danes in 1534, was accepted by the Scanians two years later, ending a serious religious rift between the Scanians and the Danes.

Danish control of both sides of the Oresund, the narrow strait between Denmark and the Scandinavian Peninsula, allowed the kingdom to halt trade and military traffic between the Baltic and North Seas during the frequent European wars. The Danes' control of Scania and the narrow Oresund allowed them to control shipping and compete with the powerful Hanseatic League, which controlled Bornholm, for Baltic trade. The Hansa city of Lubeck took control of Bornholm in 1525 and held it until 1576. Sweden's hostile relations with the Danish kingdom centered on a desire to annex Scania to attain a natural coastal frontier and to end Danish control of the Kattegat, the entrance to the Baltic Sea.

Sporadic wars between the Danes and Swedes in the seventeenth century resulted in the loss of Halland to Sweden in 1645. Renewed hostilities led to the Swedish conquest of the remaining Scanian provinces in 1658. War again broke out in 1660, and the invading Danes were aided by an ultimately futile Scanian uprising against Swedish rule. The Danes, however, took control of Bornholm. The Scanians again rebelled when the war resumed in 1675, welcoming the Danes as liberators from the hated Swedes. Swedish reprisals marked the return of the Swedish authorities to Scania when the Danes withdrew, and peace was agreed to in 1679.

In the years immediately following the Swedish annexation, the Scanians suffered for their active resistance to Swedish rule and from the repressive policies of the Swedish government. Through economic, political, and cultural pressure, the Swedish authorities gradually diminished Danish influence in the region, but the policy, instead of making the Scanians into Swedes, led to the evolution of a unique Scanian culture and language, which incorporated both Danish and Swedish influences. The evolution of a distinctive Scanian culture led to a decline of pro-Danish sentiment. When the Danes again invaded the region in 1709, the majority of the Scanians remained loyal to the Swedish kingdom or adopted a neutral stance.

Devastated by the long series of Danish–Swedish wars, Scania began to recover only in the mid-eighteenth century. To forestall Scanian unrest, the Swedish government relaxed cultural and linguistic restrictions in the nineteenth century. A Scanian cultural revival took hold in the 1880s, reversing over two centuries of gradual assimilation. Unlike many European minorities, the Scanian revival failed to evolve a strong nationalist sentiment. The revival, more cultural than most parallel European movements, focused on the modernization of the

Scanian language and a renewal of interest in Scania's folklore, crafts, and traditions. The Scanians benefited from neutral Sweden's avoidance of Europe's conflicts and its concentration on social development.

The Scanians cooperated with the Danes to save nearly all of Denmark's Jewish population during World War II. Sympathy for the Danish plight and cooperation with the Danish resistance to the Nazi occupation to closer ties to the Danes during and after the war. The Swedish government's murky relationship with Nazi Germany is still a controversial issue in Scania.

In the decades after the World War II, Sweden attained one of Europe's highest standards of living under liberal, democratic governments. The Scanians, their culture and language protected, had little motivation to espouse nationalism. However, a small movement in the 1970s began a campaign for a separate Scanian state in a Nordic confederation, arguing that if Scania were to become the sixth Scandinavian state, it would give the Scandinavians another voice in international forums such as the United Nations (UN) and the Council of Europe.

The assassination of Sweden's prime minister Olof Palme in 1986, followed by a series of government scandals and a sharp economic decline, politicized the formerly complacent Scanians. A resurgent national movement began to question the benefits and the social cost of Sweden's welfare state. In 1988 the first openly separatist political party, the Skånepartier, formed in Scania as the debate over membership in the European Community galvanized the population. A regionalist cultural organization, Skansk Framtid, was founded in 1989, with the final goal of a fully autonomous Scania.

Sweden's entry into the European Union, strongly supported in Scania, has raised the question of sovereignty within a united Europe. The Scanian national movement in February 1994 accused the Swedish government of betrayal when the government dropped Scania from an aid blueprint during negotiations on EU membership. The fervently pro-European Scanian nationalists have gained support for a sovereign Scania with close ties to both Denmark and Sweden in a united European federation.

In 1995 Scanian officials protested Swedish government attempts to divide the area among several regions under the policies of the European Union (EU). A new nationalist organization, Skansk Framtid, was formed by Scanians seeking a regional government for a reunited, historic Scania. The organization, with branches in the main Scanian provinces, is allied to a separate organization on the Danish island of Bornholm.

The ten-mile (sixteen km.) bridge joining Copenhagen and Malmo, scheduled to open in 2000, will create a city region, Copenhagen-Malmo, with a mixed Danish-Scanian population of over 2.3 million. The bridge, linking the Danish capital and Scania's largest city, is seen as strengthening the already strong ties between the Danes and the Scanians.

SELECTED BIBLIOGRAPHY
Gibbons, Eric. *Scania.* 1994.
Gordon, Raoul. *Sweden: Its Peoples and Industry.* 1976.

Kjrgaard, Thorkild, ed. *The Danish Revolution, 1500–1800: An Ecohistorical Interpretation.* 1994.

Lauring, Palle. *Denmark.* 1987.

Loiit, Aleksander. *National Movements in the Baltic Countries during the Nineteenth Century.* 1985.

SCOTS

Albans; Scotians

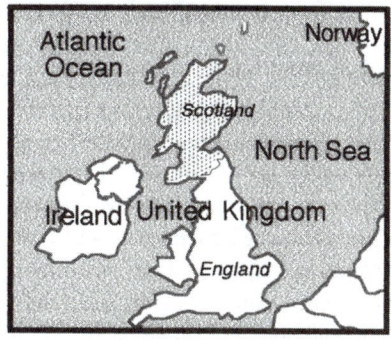

POPULATION: Approximately (2000 e) 5,765,000 Scots in Europe, mostly in Scotland but also in other parts of the United Kingdom. Other large Scottish communities live in Canada, the United States, Australia, and New Zealand.

THE SCOTTISH HOMELAND: The Scottish homeland occupies the northern third of the island of Great Britain, which it shares with England and Wales. Scotland is separated from England by the Tweed River, the Cheviot hills, the Liddell River, and Solway Firth. The terrain of Scotland is predominantly mountainous but is roughly divided into three distinct regions, the Highlands in the north, the Central Lowlands, and the Southern Uplands. Over half of Scotland's total area lies in the Highlands, the most rugged region on the island of Great Britain. Consisting of parallel mountain chains, the Highlands contain precipitous cliffs, moorland plateaus, mountain lakes, sea lochs, and thick forests. The Highlands are the most sparsely inhabited region of Scotland and are traversed by the Grampian Mountains, which include the highest summit in Great Britain, Ben Nevis, which rises to 4,406 feet (1,343 m.). To the south of the Highlands lie the Central Lowlands, a narrow belt constituting about one-tenth of Scottish territory but containing the majority of the population. The Southern Uplands, less elevated and rugged than the Highlands, consist largely of moorland plateau traversed by rolling valleys divided by low mountains, including the Cheviot hills on the border with England. The coastline is highly indented by fjord-like indentations called lochs.

Scotland forms a political division of the United Kingdom of Great Britain and Northern Ireland. *Scotland (Alba)*: 30,414 sq.mi.–78,772 sq.km.—(2000 e) 5,096,000—Scots 96%, English* 2%, Irish,* Indians, Pakistanis. The Scottish capital and major cultural center is Edinburgh, (2000 e) 434,000 (metropolitan area 688,00), on the south shore of the Firth of Forth. The other major cultural center is Glasgow, (2000 e) 651,00 (metropolitan area 1,927,000), Scotland's largest city. The population density is highest in the Central Lowlands, where nearly 75% of the Scots live, and lowest in the Highlands. About two-thirds of the Scots are urban dwellers.

FLAGS: The Scottish national flag, the official flag of Scotland, is a blue field charged with a white saltire. The traditional Scottish flag, the flag of the former kingdom, is a yellow field charged with a centered red rampant lion and bearing two thin red stripes near the perimeter decorated with spaced red pike heads.

PEOPLE: The Scots are a people of mixed ancestry, descended from the earliest inhabitants, the Picts, later Celtic migrants from Ireland, called Scots, and Norsemen, who controlled parts of Scotland for centuries. Scotland has a heterogeneous population, but despite different religions, languages, or locations, all consider themselves Scots. The Scottish culture, Celtic in origin, has been influenced by centuries of contact with the English but retains such symbols as the tartan, the bagpipe, and the cross of St. Andrew, the patron saint of Scotland. Celtic Scottish culture, although influencing the wider Scottish culture, remains most traditional in the Scottish Highlands, which are separated from the Lowlands by the Grampian Mountains. The Highland Scots have remained largely Roman Catholic, while the majority of the Scots are Protestant, mostly belonging to the national church, the Church of Scotland.

Clans, the traditional keystone of Scottish society, are no longer powerful, except in the Highlands. Originally, the clan, a grouping of an entire family with one head, or laird, was also important as a fighting unit. The solidarity associated with clan membership has been expanded into a strong national pride. The Puritan zeal of Scottish Presbyterianism, which is traceable to John Knox, the sixteenth-century religious reformer and statesman, also retains a strong hold on the Scottish culture.

The Scots speak standard English but also retain a distinctive Scots dialect, Lallans or Lowlands Scottish, which developed between the fifteenth and seventeenth centuries from medieval Northumbrian, a northern English language without the Norman French influence of standard English that is still spoken by the neighboring Northumbrians.* The first Lallans dictionary was being compiled in the late 1990s. Lallans, first known through the songs of the eighteenth-century Scottish poet Robert Burns, varies from standard English in pronunciation and in the number of words of Scandinavian origin. In the Highlands the inhabitants still use the Scots' original Celtic language, Eise, which is spoken by over 80,000 peoples. In bilingual areas, Eise is usually the first language of education. A form of Gaelic was brought to Scotland by Irish invaders in the fifth century, where it replaced an older Brythonic language. By the fifteenth century, with the accretion of Norse and English loanwords, the Scottish branch differed significantly enough from the Irish to warrant definition as a separate language. Scottish Gaelic exists in two main dialects, Northern and Southern, roughly geographically determined by a line up the Firth of Lorne to the town of Ballachulish and then across to the Grampian Mountains. The Southern dialect is more akin to Irish than is the Northern.

NATION: The Picts, of obscure origin, inhabited the northern part of the island of Britannia in prehistoric times. A fierce warrior people, the Picts defeated repeated Roman attempts to penetrate their homeland. The Romans finally constructed a series of fortifications across the island to divide Roman Britain from the wild tribal lands, which they called Caledonia, to the north, but even the Roman fortifications proved inadequate against the Pict and Celtic tribes. Although Roman influence remained slight, missionaries, particularly St. Ninian and his disciples, introduced the Roman religion, Christianity, to the region in the fifth century, a century and a half after the Roman evacuation. St. Columba, who came from Ireland in 563, spread the new creed through much of the region.

Scotland was divided into four small, warring kingdoms: that of the Picts in the north; that of the Scots who came from Ireland and founded Dalriada in the southwest; that of the Northumbrians, founded by the Angles and largely settled by Germanic migrants from the European mainland; and that of the Britons in Strathclyde. After the decline of Northumbrian power in the region, the kingdoms were the object of raids by Norse Vikings between the eighth and eleventh centuries. The Norsemen established colonies and ruled parts of the region.

The union of the Picts and Scots under Kenneth MacAlpine in 843 is considered the original formation of the Scottish kingdom, the Kingdom of Alba. MacApline, known as Kenneth I, established his rule over nearly all the territory north of the Firth of Forth. His descendants extended their rule into Northumbria. In 1018 the Scottish king extended his authority to the formerly independent Strathclyde kingdom and ruled all of Scotland except northern Pictland and the islands. The Norsemen were gradually pushed out of Scotland and were finally defeated in 1263, leaving only Orkney and Shetland, the homeland of the Zetlanders,* under Norse rule.

The English king in 1189 recognized the Scotland's independence, but the ambiguous terms of his recognition opened a long and bitter struggle between the two neighboring kingdoms. Edward I of England laid claim to Scotland in 1294, provoking a war that continued until his death in 1307. His son, Edward II, gathered the largest force ever raised on the island, and in 1314, 100,000 English troops moved north into Scotland, intent on conquest. Some 30,000 Scots, led by Robert Bruce, finally defeated the English at the Battle of Bannockburn, which secured the independence of the Scottish kingdom but not a cessation of English interference or the gradual Anglicization of the Lowland Scots. The Highland Scots, isolated from English influence, remained Gaelic and clannish.

For more than 200 years after Robert Bruce's death in 1329 and the accession of his infant son as Scotland's king, the region was the scene of almost continuous strife among the Scottish nobility. The feudal anarchy was especially pronounced because of the prevalence of the clan system in the Highlands and various other areas. In these regions, where close personal relations existed among the clan members and their leaders, the latter were powerful and contemptuous of royal authority. The period was also marked by almost uninterrupted warfare with the English.

In the sixteenth century the Protestant Reformation, led by the religious reformer John Knox, swept Scotland except for the Highlands, which remained resolutely Roman Catholic. The growth of Protestantism in Scotland led to opposition to the Scots' traditional alliance with the Roman Catholic French.* The general hostility to the pro-French monarchy was deepened by the marriage in April 1558 of Mary of Scotland to the dauphin of France. In 1560 the Scottish parliament abolished the jurisdiction of the Roman Catholic Church, and the Church of Scotland became the official church of the kingdom.

The long conflict with England, which was complicated by religious questions, ended when the Scottish king James VI succeeded to the English throne in 1603 and combined the two kingdoms in an uneasy dynastic union. A disastrous and expensive colonial adventure forced the Scots to choose independence and poverty or prosperity in union with England. In 1707 the Scots gave up their separate parliament and crown and joined the United Kingdom. Only the political and economic systems were united, and the Scots retained their separate legal system, educational structure, national church, culinary traditions, national sports, and popular culture. The union with England was opposed by many of the Highland Scots, who rose in support of the Stuarts in the Jacobite rebellions of 1708, 1715, and 1745–46. Following the defeat of the 1745–46 rebellion, the British government forced the breakup of the clan system in the Highlands.

At the same time that the Highlanders were in rebellion, Edinburgh, the home of the "Scottish Enlightement," was becoming one of Europe's most important cultural centers. Scottish thinkers in economics and philosophy won fame across Europe, and literary figures writing in English, such as Robert Burns and, somewhat later, Sir Walter Scott, became known throughout Europe and North America.

The union, unpopular with many Scots, was assailed by four unsuccessful rebellions to restore Scottish independence until the English forces decisively defeated the Scots at the Battle of Culloden in 1746. After the Scottish defeat the British government pressed assimilation of the Scots into English culture and banned the Scots' Gaelic language. The Roman Catholic minority, mostly in the Scottish Highlands, often suffered discrimination.

Scottish participation in the expansion of the British Empire included Scots' migration to many parts of the world. The empire brought industrialization and prosperity and the evolution of a large middle class, which necessitated reforms of the country's outmoded social institutions. In the eighteenth century a particularly Scottish renaissance developed, with such names as Hume, Adam Smith, Burns, and Scott known throughout the world. In the nineteenth century the Clyde region became one of the great shipbuilding regions of the world.

The Gaelic language, mostly replaced by Lallans or Broad Scots, related to the English of the Northumbrians, became the language of most Scots. With the loss of official status, this language, too, although still widely understood in the nineteenth century, began to give way to English, which was compulsory in education and administration.

The influence of the English culture and language became an issue in the early nineteenth century, as the industrialized Lowlands became an urbanized, largely English-speaking region. In the 1840s Scots' resistance to English influence grew into a nascent national movement. Nationalists formed the Society for the Vindication of Scottish Rights, the forerunner of the modern national movement. In 1872 the compulsory teaching of standard English threatened the Gaelic and the Lallans dialect spoken by the majority of the Scots.

Thousands of young Scots fought for Great Britain while munitions manufacture brought the Scots unprecedented wealth during World War I. In the postwar era, a declining economy after 1919 encouraged support for a nascent national movement. In 1928 Scottish nationalists formed the Scottish National Party to work for greater independence for the Scots.

Scottish participation in World War II again included thousands of Scottish soldiers fighting in many areas of the world. Scottish industries supplied Britain with much of its war material, but the Scottish cities, unlike those in England, were not heavily bombed. The nationalist controversy was briefly put aside during World War II; the debate resumed in 1945. Many prominent Scots signed the Scottish Covenant in 1949, binding its signatories to work for Scottish home rule. Young nationalists in 1953 stole the Scot's Coronation Stone from Westminster Abby, where it had been since 1707. They gave the growing submergence of the Scots within a British identity as their reason.

The Scottish National Party (SNP) remained a fringe party until the discovery of oil off Scotland's coast in 1971. Claiming the oil wealth for Scotland, the nationalists led a campaign for control of natural resources and the restoration of the Scottish parliament, the first step toward recovering Scotland's independence. Under the slogan "Rich Scots or poor Britains," the nationalists campaigned for a referendum on autonomy. A 1979 referendum on home rule was narrowly defeated by the Scottish voters, partly due to nationalist opposition to its continuing restrictions.

Growing economic problems and progress toward a united Europe spurred a nationalist resurgence in the 1980s. In the late 1980s the old-style Scottish nationalism of the 1960s and 1970s, with its heady mixture of Gaelic culture and left-wing rhetoric, quickly gave way to a more businesslike approach. The most pro-European of the British peoples, Scottish support for independence within a united Europe continued to win minority support, while devolution, home rule, and a separate Scottish parliament maintained widespread support. Strong English opposition prompted many Scots to look to the nationalists. Polling of public opinion in 1990 showed 36% favored independence. A similar poll in January 1992 revealed that separatist sentiment had risen to 50%, with only 15% favoring the status quo.

Nationalist groups, determined that Scotland take its place as a separate and ancient European nation, launched a campaign in March 1992 for a referendum on Scotland's future. The nationalist plebiscite proposal would offer the Scots three choices: independence, devolution and increased autonomy within the United Kingdom, or the maintenance of the Scotland's present semiautonomous status.

The Stone of Scone, also called the Stone of Destiny, taken from Scotland by the English king Edward I in 1296, was finally returned to Scotland in 1996, seven centuries after it was carried off by the English invaders. The stone, symbolic of the Scots nation, was incorporated into the English throne, and many English kings and queens were crowned on it. The stone was actually returned to Scotland during the Christmas season in 1950, stolen from Westminster Abbey by a number of Scottish students but was later recovered and returned to England.

In July 1997 the government minister for Scotland unveiled a proposal to devolve power from the British Parliament to a 129-member legislature in Edinburgh. On 11 September 1997 the Scots voted to approve the initiative. The first elections took place in 1999, and the legislature is scheduled to meet in 2000. Scottish representatives will make up part of all British delegations to the European Union (EU) and other international organizations.

SELECTED BIBLIOGRAPHY

Bruce, Duncan. *The Mark of the Scots.* 1997.

MacLeod, John. *Highlanders: A History of the Gaels.* 1997.

Mason, Roger, ed. *Scotland and England, 1286–1815.* 1987.

Scott, Paul, ed. *Scotland: A Concise Cultural History.* 1993.

Traquair, Peter. *Freedom's Sword: The Scottish Wars of Independence.* 1998.

SERBS

Serbians; Srbs

POPULATION: Approximately (2000 e) 8,727,000 Serbs in Europe, with 6,669,000 Serbs in the Serbian Republic, a constituent republic of the Federal Republic of Yugoslavia, and other large populations in Bosnia and Herzegovina, with a Serb population estimated at 875,000, Croatia, Germany, Sweden, and Switzerland.

THE SERBIAN HOMELAND: The Serbian homeland lies in Southeastern Europe in the northern Balkan Peninsula. Serbia is a largely mountainous country with short mountain ranges and spurs running in various directions in the south and west. The most productive region is the Danubian Plain in the northeast, which is drained by the Danube, Sava, Tisza, and Morava Rivers. In the east lie limestone ranges and basins, and in the southeast are ancient mountains and hills. In the south is the valley of the Sava River, and to the east and west of the Danube River basin lie the Serbian Highlands and the East Serbian Mountains. In the southwest, in Kosovo, are the basins of the Kosovo Polje and Metonija Rivers.

Serbia, with its semiautonomous provinces of Kosovo and Vojvodina, forms a constituent republic of the Federal Republic of Yugoslavia. The Serbians and Montenegrins* have asserted the formation of a joint independent state, but the federation of the two states has not been formally recognized by the United States. *Republic of Serbia (Republika Srbija)*: 34,117 sq.mi.–88,361 sq.km. (2000 e) 10,091,000—Serbians 66%, Albanians* 17%, Hungarians* (Magyars) 3.5%, Muslims 3.2%, Roms* (Gypsies) 2.4%, Romanians* 1.5%, Croats* 1.4%, Slovaks* 1%. The Serbian capital and major cultural center is Belgrade, (2000 e) 1,561,000 (metropolitan area 2,022,000), on the Danube River. The principal city of the Bosnian Serbs is Banja Luka, (2000 e) 195,000, in northeastern Bosnia and Herzegovina.

FLAGs: The Serbian national flag, the flag of the Serbian republic, is a horizontal tricolor of red, blue, and white. The flag of the Serbian dominated Federal Republic of Yugoslavia is a horizontal tricolor of blue, white, and red.

PEOPLE: The Serbs are a South Slav people, the most numerous of the South Slav peoples, which also include the Croats, Slovenes,* Macedonians,* Montenegrins, Bosnians,* and Bulgarians.* The Serbian culture and language have been greatly influenced by centuries of domination by the Muslim Turks.* The Serbs' national church, the Serbian Orthodox, through the centuries became an integral part of the Serbian culture and national heritage. The Serbs distinguish themselves culturally from the closely related Croats, Slovenes, and Bosnians through their adherence to the Orthodox faith and the use of the Cyrillic alphabet.

The language of the Serbs, called Serbian or Serbo-Croatian, is a western language of the South Slav group of languages. Serbian is very closely related to Croatian but uses the Cyrillic alphabet and has incorporated extensive Turkish borrowings. The language is spoken in four major dialects, Chakavian, Kajkavian, Stokavian, and Torlakian. The Serbian literary language is based on the Stokavian dialect.

NATION: Slavic tribes, the ancestors of the South Slav peoples, settled the Balkan Peninsula in the sixth and seventh centuries. In the seventh century some of the tribes were pushed across the Danube into Byzantine Moesia by the Avars.* In the east the tribes settled the fertile lowlands around the rivers Zeta, Tara, Piva, Drina, Ibar, and Morava. The eastern tribes, called Serbs, soon came under the hegemony of the Byzantine Empire and were converted to Orthodox Christianity.

The petty Serbian principalities were theoretically under a grand *zhupan*, who usually acknowledged nominal Byzantine rule. Civil strife and constant warfare with the neighboring Greeks,* Bulgarians, and Magyars characterized the early history of the Serbian nation. The first organized Serbian state was founded in the ninth century in the Bosnian mountains. It steadily expanded from the tenth century, but its authority was challenged by the Bulgars. Stephen Nemanja, recognized by the Byzantine emperor in 1159, founded the Nemanjic dynasty that ruled for two centuries. In 1217 his son assumed the title king of Serbia.

The Serb state, overshadowed by the Bulgarian kingdom, was a minor kingdom until the rule of Stephen Dushan, who became king in 1331 and had himself crowned tsar in 1346. Under his rule Serbia became the most powerful Balkan state. The multiethnic kingdom included Serbs, Greeks, Bulgars, and Albanians. The fourteenth century also marked the zenith of the Serbian Orthodox Church, which was central to the formation of the Serb culture and identity. Soon after Stephen Dushan's death in 1355, the Serbian Empire collapsed, and the Serbs came under pressure from the expanding Ottoman Empire of the Turks.

The Serbs were defeated by the Turks in 1371, but the decisive battle, the

Battle of Kosovo, which ended in defeat for the Serbs and their allies, sealed the fate of the Serbian nation in 1389. The Serbs rallied the Christian peoples of the region against the advancing Turks. On 20 June 1389 a large force of mostly Serbs, but also including Bosnians, Montenegrins, and Albanians, met the Ottoman army on the elevated plain called Kosovo Polje, the Field of Blackbirds, and was defeated. Serb legend tells of blackbirds feasting on the thousands of dead for weeks after the battle.

The Turks allowed the Serbs to remain semi-independent in a diminished and divided Serbia while paying tribute to the Ottoman sultans. In 1459 the Turks, taking advantage of quarrels over the Serb succession, finally annexed Serbia. In 1521 Belgrade and the other northern districts held by Hungary also came under Ottoman rule. During the centuries of Turkish domination, national traditions and the memory of Stephan Dushan's empire were preserved by the Serbian Orthodox Church, the repository of the Serb culture.

Turkish rule in Serbia was among the most oppressive in the vast Ottoman Empire. The Serbian nobility was mostly annihilated, and their lands were distributed to the Turkish military aristocracy. The Christian peasants, the *rayas*, were treated little better than slaves. Although the Serbs were forbidden to possess weapons, uprisings were frequent. Many Serbs fled to Austrian territory, where they joined the forces fighting the Turks. In 1683, while Vienna was surrounded by a huge Turkish army, the Serbs rose in rebellion, drawing off much-needed Turkish troops and supplies. Although Christian armies relieved Vienna and advanced into Turkish territory, the Serbs were again defeated.

Led by a religious leader, Patriarch Arsenija, some 200,000 Serbs, protected by the Austrian army, moved north out of Turkish-held territory. Known in Serbian history as the Great Serbian Exodus, the refugees were settled in the Austrian frontier regions in Slavonia and Vojvodina in 1690. Organized along military lines, the Serbian settlements were charged with guarding the frontier between the Austrian and Ottoman Empires.

In 1804 a Serbian patriot called Karageorge led a successful uprising against the Turks. In 1806 his forces captured Belgrade, where the entire Turkish population was massacred, and in 1808 he was proclaimed the hereditary chief of the Serbs. Karageorge joined the Russians in war on the Turks but was abandoned when the Russians made peace in 1812. By 1813 the Turks had recovered all the Serbian territories. In 1817 Milosh Obrenovich had Karageorge assassinated and was named prince of Serbia by the Serbian leaders. Obrenovich was recognized as hereditary prince in 1817, and the Serbs were granted limited self-government. Following the Russo-Turkish War of 1828–29, the Serbs gained greater autonomy, and the number of Ottoman garrisons in the region was reduced. Under the peace agreement, the Turks maintained nominal control over Serbia, which was convulsed by bloody feuds between the supporters of the Karageorgevich and Obrenovich families.

The major European powers at the 1856 Congress of Paris recognized Ottoman rule in Serbia but placed the territory under the collective guarantee of the leading powers. In 1867 the last Turkish troops were finally withdrawn. Serbia then signed a series of secret alliances with Montenegro, Romania, and Greece aimed at dividing up the remaining European territories of the Ottoman Empire. Serbian independence was settled by the Treaty of Berlin, which ended the Russo-Turkish War in 1878 but disappointed the Serbs' territorial ambitions by placing the former Turkish territories of Bosnia and Herzegovina under Austrian rule.

The Austrian presence in the Balkan Peninsula prevented a return of the Turks, but in the early twentieth century relations between the Austro-Hungarian Empire and Serbia soured. By 1905 Serbian policy had become openly nationalistic and anti-Austrian as the Hapsburgs were seen as frustrating Serbian aspirations to unite the South Slavs in an expanded Serbian-dominated state. Up to World War I, the region was in constant flux as shifting alliances between Serbia, Turkey, Bulgaria, and Greece led to two Balkan wars in 1912 and 1913. The wars allowed the Serbs to take control of the Turkish regions of Sanjak, Kosovo, and Macedonia and made Serbia the strongest state in the Balkans, which alarmed the Austrians.*

The ongoing conflict between Serbia and Austria was suddenly heightened by the assassination of the Hapsburg heir Archduke Francis Ferdinand by a Serb nationalist, Gavrilo Princip, on 28 June 1914. On 23 July the Vienna government sent a harsh ultimatum to the Serbian government. Supported by the Russians, the Serbs accepted parts of the Austrian demands but refused or hedged on others. On July 28 Austria-Hungary and its ally, Germany, declared war on the Serbs. Russian mobilization quickly extended the war to the east, and by early August most of Europe was at war.

The Serbian army held out for nearly two years until the autumn of 1915, when the army and the Serbian government were forced to withdraw to the Greek island of Corfu. On Corfu the representatives of the various South Slav nations proclaimed in July 1917 their eventual unification under the rule of the Serbian king. At the end of the war in November 1918, with the inclusion of former Austrian and Hungarian territories, the Kingdom of the Serbs, Croats, and Slovenes was formally proclaimed.

The South Slav state, beset by bitter ethnic feuds and the oppressive domination of the more numerous Serbs, lurched from crisis to crisis during the 1920s. In 1929 King Alexander proclaimed a dictatorship and changed the name of the country to Yugoslavia. He dissolved the parliament, and the internal borders were redrawn to erase the historic ethnic borders. The dictatorship ended in 1931, but the domination of the Serbs continued. In 1934 the government's conflict with Croatian and Macedonian nationalists culminated in King Alexander's assassination. Unresolved social issues, combined with the effects of the global depression of the 1930s, aided the growth of extremist groups on both the Right and Left.

In 1941 German, Italian, Bulgarian, and Hungarian forces invaded Yugoslavia, which was divided into several distinct regions. Hundreds of thousands of

Serbs died, many in massacres carried out by the forces of the fascist Croatian state allied to Germany. Although several partisan groups fought the fascists, the communist group led by Josip Broz, known as Tito, gradually gained control of Serbia as Axis defeat neared. In 1946 a Soviet-style constitution was adopted, which gave each of the member states of the federation cultural and some political autonomy, although power remained centered on Tito and the Communist Party. Internal ethnic divisions were suppressed during the Tito era, although not extinguished.

Tito's death in 1980 ended communist Yugoslavia's strong centralized leadership. In May 1981 the Albanian minority in Kosovo revolted against Serbian oppression, setting off a Serbian nationalist backlash. While the other republics distanced themselves from the central government, Serbs were allowed to dominate the Yugoslav Army (JNA) as well as key positions in the federal government. Serbian nationalism, which called for the solution of the national question in Yugoslavia by the creation of a Greater Serbia, uniting all ethnic Serbs in a single state, was endorsed by the Serbian Academy of Arts and Sciences in 1986.

In 1987 a hard-line communist, Slobodan Milosevic, was elected president of Serbia, and in 1988 he began moves to restrict the autonomy of Kosovo, setting off a serious crisis between Serbia and the western republics, Croatia and Slovenia, which supported the Albanians of Kosovo. Milosevic's embrace of extreme Serb nationalism deepened the crisis. The Serbian public mostly supported Milosevic and increasingly embraced radical Serbian nationalism. Serbian opposition groups and leaders were arrested or silenced.

The collapse of communism in most of Eastern Europe in 1989 loosened the ties between the constituent Yugoslav republics even further, and Serbian attempts to impose their control met strong resistance. In 1990 all of the republics elected nationalist governments, except Serbia and Montenegro, where the renamed communists, led by Milosevic, retained power. As friction between the republics increased, and the Serbian government became increasingly belligerent, Croatia, Slovenia, and then Macedonia pushed for independence, the Montenegrins mostly backed the Serbs, and in Bosnia and Herzegovina a three-way ethnic split between the Bosnians, Croats, and Serbs threatened violence.

Milosevic's Serbian government, dreaming of a Greater Serbia, demanded that existing borders be changed and encouraged the ethnic Serb minorities in Croatia and Bosnia to rebel. In October 1990 the Serb minority in the Croatian region of Krajina declared autonomy, while the Serb-led federal army intervened on the side of the Serbs. In June 1991 Croatia and Slovenia declared independence, ending hopes of holding the Yugoslav state together. Bosnia and Herzegovina and Macedonia soon followed. The federal army, the JNA, dominated by the Serbs, after suffering the humiliation of defeat in Slovenia, took control of one-quarter of Croatian territory before a cease-fire could be arranged and moved into Bosnia to support ethnic Serbs there. The deliberate targeting of civilian populations by Serb irregulars and the JNA outraged the international community, but feeble international attempts to intervene failed to halt Serbian aggression.

The Serb military, following victories in Croatia, firmly rejected any compromise with the other republics, while President Milosevic claimed to speak for all the ethnic Serbs in the former Yugoslavia. The international community branded the Serbs as the aggressors in the vicious Balkan wars and imposed economic sanctions that crippled the economy but did little to end the fighting in Bosnia. As the Bosnian war dragged on, stories of Serb atrocities and the policy of expelling civilian populations from Serb-claimed territory, called ethnic cleansing, further hardened the attitude of the world community toward the Serbs.

Within Serbia, Milosevic catered to the nationalist sentiment by further tightening restrictions on the non-Serb national groups, including a reign of terror directed against the large Albanian population in Kosovo. Extremist Serb national groups called for the cleansing of all non-Serbs from Serbian lands. The Kosovar Albanians responded with a nonviolent resistance. The European Community (EC) foreign ministers imposed economic sanctions on Serbia in November 1991.

On 11 April 1992 the largest and smallest of the former Yugoslav republics, Serbia and Montenegro, controlled by renamed communist parties, formally established the Federal Republic of Yugoslavia. On 27 April the federal assembly adopted a constitution of the new Yugoslav state, which claimed to be the direct heir of the former communist Yugoslav federation. The United States and the EC countries refused recognition. In December 1993, despite growing opposition to the Milosevic regime, the majority of the Serbian population voted to return his neocommunist administration in December 1993.

The United States, frustrated at ineffectual EC efforts to end the fighting in Bosnia, applied diplomacy and threats to force the Serbian government to agree to the 1995 Dayton Accords. President Milosevic represented the Bosnian Serbs, and although many of their leaders were dissatisfied with the accords, the situation on the battlefield, where they were losing much of their conquered territory, left them little choice. The accords split the Bosnian state into a Bosnian Serb statelet and a Muslim-Croat federation but specifically forbade the unification of the Bosnian Serb region with Serbia. Although the United States has refused to recognize Yugoslavia as the successor to the former socialist Yugoslavia, the European Union countries have mostly recognized the new federal republic following the imposition of the Dayton Accords in spite of continuing Serbian repression of the Albanian minority in Kosovo and the lack of freedom within the country.

Many Serbs, weary of war and their status as international pariahs and frustrated by economic chaos, in November 1996, after Milosevic annulled the results of Serbian municipal elections after early returns showed his party losing to the opposition, began a series of mass protests against the Serbian government. Hundreds of thousands marched through Belgrade and other urban centers.

The protests, led by Serbia's opposition leaders, failed to unseat Milosevic but forced the Serbian government to abandon some of its hard-line rhetoric. Bowing to domestic and international pressure, Serbia's parliament voted in February 1997 to reinstate the opposition victories.

A major stumbling block to better relations between Yugoslavia and the other former Yugoslav states is the lack of an agreement on the division of the properties and assets of the former Socialist Federal Republic of Yugoslavia (SFYR). The Serbian government wants to keep the bulk of the wealth and argues that the other states should get less because they voluntarily left Yugoslavia. The other governments want the assets divided on the basis of the republics' pre-1991 payments to the federal budget, to which Slovenia and Croatia were the principal contributors.

President Milosevic in July 1997 was elected president of the federal Yugoslav state, as the constitution of Serbia had prevented his seeking a third term as president of the constituent republic of Serbia. Until his election the presidency of Yugoslavia had been largely a ceremonial post, but he immediately set about gathering power to his new title. The dream of a "Greater Serbia" seems set to haunt the Balkan Peninsula well into the next century.

The Serbian defiance of international demands for an end to the ethnic cleansing and the spreading violence against the Albanians in Kosovo brought widespread condemnation in 1999. In late March North Atlantic Treaty Organization (NATO) forces launched attacks against Serbian military bases in an attempt to force the Serbs to grant the Albanians autonomy and to stop the military advance, which had already created an estimated 250,000 refugees in the province. The war was brought to an end in June, but only after widespread destruction in Serbia from NATO bombings and an estimated 1.5 million Albanians driven from their homes in Kosovo.

Many Serbs, already suffering economic hardships as a result of government policies and the months of bombings by North Atlantic Treaty Organization planes, gave their support to groups and political parties opposed to the continued rule of Slobodan Milosevic. In late 1999 thousands joined in marches and demonstrations demanding that Milosevic resign in order to remove the major obstacle to the reestablishment of the Serbians' ties to Europe and the rest of the world.

SELECTED BIBLIOGRAPHY

Anzulovic, Branimir. *Heavenly Serbia: From Myth to Genocide.* 1998.

Judah, Tim. *The Serbs: History, Myth and the Destruction of Yugoslavia.* 1997.

Levinsohn, Florence Hamlish. *Belgrade: Among the Serbs.* 1995.

Petrovich, Michael B. *A History of Modern Serbia, 1904–1918.* 1976.

Thomas, Robert. *The Politics of Serbia in the 1990s.* 1998.

SICILIANS

Sicilianos

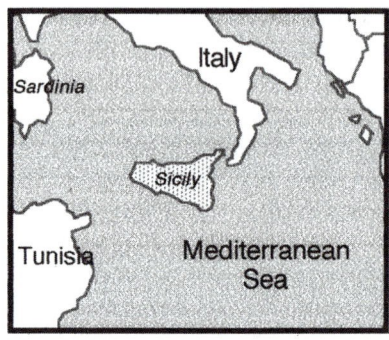

POPULATION: Approximately (2000 e) 7,814,000 Sicilians in Europe, 7,550,000 in Italy, concentrated in Sicily, but with sizable populations in other parts of the country. Other large Sicilian communities live in Germany, Switzerland, and France. Outside Europe there are Sicilians living in South America, especially Argentina and Brazil, the United States, Canada, and Australia.

THE SICILIAN HOMELAND: The Sicily homeland is an island off the southern Italian Peninsula, separated from the mainland by the narrow Strait of Messina. The region of Sicily comprises not only Sicily but also a number of smaller surrounding islands. The island, the largest island in the Mediterranean Sea, is roughly triangular in shape and is almost totally hilly or mountainous. Lying ninety miles north of the African coast, Sicily is mostly a broad, hilly plateau rising in the northwest to volcanic Mt. Etna, the island's highest point at 10,700 feet (3,261 m.). The only wide valley is the fertile plain of Catania in the east, mostly located along the lower Simeto River. There are narrow coastal strips in the south and west and a narrow fertile plain, the Conca d'Oro near Palermo, in the northwest. Sicily has long been known for its fertility, its pleasant climate, and its scenic beauty.

Sicily and the smaller islands, the Egadi Islands, the Lipari Islands, the Pelagie Islands, Pantelleria Island, and Ustica Island, form a semiautonomous region of the Italian republic. *Region of Sicily (Sicilia)*: 9,925 sq.km.–25,706 sq.km. (2000 e) 5,241,000—Sicilians 94%, other Italians,* Albanians.* The Sicilian capital and major cultural center is Palermo, (2000 e) 828,000 (995,000), the largest city on the island.

FLAG: The Sicilian national flag, the flag of the nationalist movement, has nine horizontal stripes of yellow and red and bears a blue canton on the upper hoist charged with three white legs. The unofficial flag of the region is a diagonal bicolor of red over yellow.

PEOPLE: The Sicilians are of mixed ancestry, being the descendants of the island's original Celtic and Latin inhabitants with admixtures of the island's many conquerors, Carthaginians, Greeks,* Romans, Vandals, Ostrogoths, Byzantines, Normans,* French,* Catalans,* Spaniards,* Savoyards,* Austrians,* and Piedmontese.* The insularity of Sicily's position in the Mediterranean aided the evolution of the distinct Sicilian culture, with its originality of customs, art, and traditions. The Sicilian culture, developed during 2,000 years of foreign rule, incorporates many customs and traditions not found on the mainland and has spawned the Mafia, Sicily's infamous export to the world. The Sicilians are devoutly Roman Catholic and among the most conservative of the Italian peoples.

The Sicilian dialect, claimed as a separate language, is a Romance language using borrowings from Greek, Spanish, and Arabic, as distinct from standard Italian as Romanian. The language is spoken in seven major dialects, Western Sicilian, Central Metafonetica, Southeastern Metafonetica, Eastern Nonmetafonetica, Messinese, Isole Eolie, and Pantesco, and is distinct enough from standard Italian to be considered a separate language. Sicilian remains the dialect of daily life for most of the islanders, although the majority are bilingual in standard Italian.

NATION: Originally inhabited by Sicani, Elymi, and Siculi tribes, probably of Celtic origin, the island early divided into numerous small territories. Between the eighth and sixth centuries B.C. Greeks founded colonies that grew into great and powerful cities. Syracuse, the island's leading Greek city, a center of Greek culture and Mediterranean trade, in the fifth century B.C. gained hegemony over the other Greek cities. The Syracusans successfully resisted a Carthaginian invasion at Himera in 480 B.C., but by the fourth century B.C. the western part of the island was under Carthaginian control. Carthaginian control of western Sicily involved the island in the conflicts between Rome and Carthage, the Punic Wars. In 246 B.C. Roman legions invaded the island and took control of Carthaginian Sicily, and by 210 all of Sicily had come under Roman rule. Rome's first overseas possession, the island was divided into large estates, a debilitating economic legacy that persists to the present. The chief events of Roman history in Sicily were two insurrections of slaves, in 135–132 B.C. and 102–99 B.C.

The collapse of Roman power left the island without defenses, and Germanic tribes from Northern Europe overran the island. The Vandals, led by Gaiseric, took control of the island in A.D. 440. In 493 the Vandals ceded the island to the invading Ostrogoths. The Byzantines of the Eastern Roman Empire, led by General Belisarius, took control of the island in 535, and Greek Byzantine culture was imposed.

Muslim Arabs, called Saracens, conquered the island from nearby North Africa in 827. The Saracens created a remarkable civilization on the island, incorporating the earlier Roman and Byzantine traditions into a enlightened, advanced culture. Sicily's Muslim rulers practiced a tolerance of the religious and ethnic minorities unknown in the rest of Europe. The enlightened Muslim government fostered education, agriculture, art, and the sciences and administered a civilized state far ahead of the European culture of the time.

The Norman conquest of Sicily mirrored the 1066 Norman conquest of England. A large force, led by Roger de Hauteville, left Normandy in 1061, his forces ultimately victorious in Sicily thirty years later. Under the Hauteville dynasty the Normans adopted much of the more advanced Saracen culture, particularly the tolerance that allowed a mixed population of Normans, Muslims, Latins, Greeks, and Jews to live in peace and to prosper. The most enlightened state in Europe from 1072 to 1266, Sicily's "golden age" was a forerunner of the later European Renaissance of the fourteenth to sixteenth centuries. The brilliant Hauteville court did much to introduce Arabic learning to Western Europe.

The pope, on the death of the last Hauteville heir, bestowed the kingdom on Charles of Anjou as king of Naples and Sicily. Harsh and intolerant French rule ended the brilliant Sicilian civilization of the Saracens and Normans. A 1282 Sicilian rebellion culminated in the massacre of all the French on the island, the so-called Sicilian Vespers. Freed of French rule, the Sicilians chose the Catalan king Peter III of Aragon as their new ruler in 1295. Ruled as a separate kingdom until 1409, Sicily then became part of Aragon. The merger of Aragon and Castile in 1479 in the united Spanish kingdom brought an end to all Sicilian autonomy.

With the accession of the House of Hapsburg to the Spanish throne in the early sixteenth century the government was further centralized, and Spanish governors were sent to Sicily to ensure imperial rule. Corruption increased, and the island came under the influence of a handful of powerful nobles and churchmen.

Sicily remained Spanish until 1713 and was held briefly by Savoy and Austria before coming under the Bourbon kings of the Kingdom of the Two Sicilies. Although the feudal privileges that had held the Sicilians in virtual serfdom were renounced in 1812, the island remained under the domination of the Neapolitans of the kingdom's capital. The Sicilians unsuccessfully rebelled against the Neapolitans in 1820 and 1848–49; however, during another rebellion in 1860 Giuseppe Garibaldi and 1,000 volunteers stormed ashore. Garibaldi relinquished his Sicilian conquests to a newly united Italian kingdom under the Piedmontese House of Savoy in 1861.

Even after unification, Sicily was neglected by the central government, and the island's basic economic and social problems remained. Dominated by the Piedmontese, the national government possessed little understanding of the southern regions of Italy. Sicily's traditional landholding system, control of the land by a few large aristocratic estates, remained unchanged, and the Sicilians remained poor and backward. Burdensome taxes and military conscription intensified Sicilian resentment and led to an abortive rebellion in Palermo in

1866. The Mafia emerged to serve a vital purpose, offering Sicilian peasants a means of justice outside the always unequal Italian law. Carried to the Americas by Sicilian immigrants, the Mafia remained a strong force among immigrant communities. Challenged by leagues of rebellious workers and peasants, in 1894 the Italian government proclaimed martial law in Sicily. Mutual suspicion characterized north–south relations in Italy until 1915, when the Italians entered World War I.

Promised glory and reforms, the Sicilians supported Mussolini's fascist takeover of Italy in 1922. However, Sicilian support of the fascists waned following government efforts to curtail the Mafia in 1927–28. Fervently antifascist by the time Italy joined World War II, a nascent nationalist movement provided fertile ground for British and, later, American agents. Encouraged by the Allies, the nationalists carried out a guerrilla war against the Italian fascists and their Nazi allies. Welcomed as liberators, Allied troops invaded Sicily in 1943.

Supported by the Allies, the nationalist leader, Turiddu Giuliano, declared Sicily independent on 10 July 1943 and began to organize the first independent Sicilian state in history. The Allies, to persuade the Italian government to withdraw from the war, abruptly ended their support of Sicilian separatism. In late 1943 Italian troops invaded the island, finally defeating the nationalists in a vicious, eight-week war. With widespread popular support, the rebels continued to fight a guerrilla war in the west of the island. In 1945 the Sicilian nationalists pled their case before the newly formed United Nations, but the Sicilian rebellion collapsed following the death of Giuliano in 1950.

Decades of neglect forced thousands to emigrate in the 1950s and 1960s to booming northern Italy or to the Americas. The forced emigration provoked strong resentment and a resurgence of nationalist sentiment in the 1970s. The polarization of Italy, marked by a rise of antisouthern sentiment in the rich northern regions, gave the nationalist movement new impetus in the 1980s.

Sicilians claim that collusion between the Italian government and the Mafia has maintained an iron grip on the island since the separatist war in the 1940s. The unholy alliance kept social protest to an absolute minimum until cooperation collapsed in the late 1980s. The reemergence of the nationalists showed in the voter support for nationalist issues in the March 1994 local elections. The nationalists claim that the unholy alliance between the government and the Mafia since World War II left Sicily as a neglected dependency with incomes little more than half the Italian average. The industrialization of the island has not absorbed the surplus labor force, and many Sicilians have migrated to northern Italy, Germany, Switzerland, North and South America, and Australia.

In local elections in 1996, small lists of candidates campaigned on a platform to split Sicily from Italy and to turn the island into the "Hong Kong of the Mediterranean." The openly separatist organizations gained one seat in the regional parliament. Also in the late 1990s Sicily has experienced a resurgence of the Mafia, which has become a serious problem to the development of the island.

SELECTED BIBLIOGRAPHY

Abulafid, David. *Italy, Sicily and the Mediterranean, 1100–1400.* 1987.

Duggan, Christopher. *Fascism and the Mafia.* 1989.

Finley, M. I. *A History of Sicily.* 1987.

Matthew, Donald. *The Norman Kingdom of Sicily.* 1992.

Riall, Lucy. *Sicily and the Unification of Italy: Liberal Policy and Local Power 1859–1866.* 1998.

SLOVAKS

Slovakians; Slovenska

POPULATION: Approximately (2000 e) 5,621,000 Slovaks in Europe, 4,556,000 in Slovakia, and 378,000 in the neighboring Czech Republic, 114,000 in Hungary, 106,000 in Yugoslavia, 45,000 in Poland, 40,000 in Romania, 26,000 in Ukraine, and smaller communities in other countries. Large Slovak populations outside Europe include over 500,000 in the United States and Canada and smaller communities in Australia, Argentina, and Brazil.

THE SLOVAK HOMELAND: The Slovak homeland is a landlocked territory located in the heart of Europe. Most of Slovakia is traversed by the Carpathian Mountains, including the Tatra and the Beskids. The northern High Tatra, which has rocky peaks, snowcaps, and traces of ancient glaciation, reaches the highest point at Mt. Gerlachovka, 8,711 feet (2,655 m.). In the south the mountains are lower and form the Low Tatra and the Slovak Ore Mountains. Mountains account for over one-third of the total territory and are generally heavily forested, with forests covering about 40% of the country. The Danube Lowlands in the southwest, the region's major agricultural area, are part of the Hungarian Plain and have the country's principal rivers, the Vah, Nitra, and Hron, which are tributaries of the Danube.

Slovakia separated from the Czech Republic and became an independent state on 1 January 1993. *Republic of Slovakia (Slovenska Republika)*: 18,923 sq.mi.– 49,023 sq.km. (2000 e) 5,385,000—Slovaks 85%, Hungarians* (Magyars) 11%, Roms* (Gypsies) 1.5%, Carpatho-Rusyns* 1.5%, Czechs,* Moravians,* Ukrainians,* Poles,* Germans.* The Slovak capital and major cultural center is Bratislava, (2000 e) 451,000 (metropolitan area 522,000), on the Danube River thirty miles (forty-eight kilometers) east of Vienna.

FLAG: The Slovak national flag, the official flag of the republic, is a horizontal tricolor of white, blue, and red bearing, near the hoist, a red shield, outlined in white and charged with the national symbols, three blue peaks surmounted by a white cross known as the Pribina Cross.

PEOPLE: The Slovaks are a West Slav people closely related to the Czechs to the west, the major differences between the two West Slav peoples being 1,000 years of separate history and the Slovak majority's Roman Catholic religion. The Slovaks tend to be more rural and less sophisticated than their Czech cousins, a result of their particular history. Domination by the Hungarians until World War I has greatly influenced the Slovak culture and language. The Slovaks are about 60% Roman Catholic, with Protestant, Orthodox, Uniate, and atheist minorities. About 58% of the Slovaks live in urban areas. The development of Slovak culture reflects the rich folk tradition, which has combined with the influences of broader European trends. The impact of centuries of culture repression and control by foreign authorities is also evident in much of Slovakia's art, literature, and music.

The language of the Slovaks is a Czech-Slovak language of the West Slav group of languages. Slovak or Slovakian is related to the languages of the Czechs, Poles, Sorbs,* and Kashubians.* The Slovak language is spoken in three major dialects, west, central, and east. All dialects of Slovak and Czech are inherently intelligible to all speakers of the two closely related languages. The Slovak literary language is based on the Bratislava dialect spoken in the Slovak capital and in the western upland region around Bratislava. Except for the expansion of vocabulary, the Slovak language has not changed significantly since the sixteenth century.

NATION: Slavic tribes, migrating from east of the Vistula River region, settled the Danube Basin in the sixth century A.D. United under the Slovak national hero, Prince Pribina, in the early ninth century, the various tribes remained under local chiefs in a loose confederation. Later in the same century the Slavic tribes of two different principalities, Morava and Nitra, were united in a West Slav state known as Great Moravia. The Christian religion spread to Slovakia through the missionary work of Czech priests moving into the pagan east.

The Magyars or Hungarians, originally nomadic horsemen from the region east of the Ural Mountains, terrorized the region for half a century before destroying the Great Moravian state in 906. Their victories over the West Slav peoples brought them into conflict with the Holy Roman Empire, which controlled the territories threatened by the Magyars just to the west. The Magyars, finally defeated near Augsburg in 955, retained their conquests, including the Slovak lands, but were compelled to settle in the river lowlands along the Danube and Theiss Rivers. All power in the Hungarian kingdom was concentrated in the hands of a clerical and secular nobility headed by the king. The Slovak lands were colonized by Hungarian nobles, and the Slovaks were gradually relegated to virtual serfdom on large Hungarian estates.

The Hungarian kings in the thirteenth century made concessions to the powerful nobles in order to gain their support for the expansion of the kingdom. The concessions gradually reduced the kingdom to a number of distinct regions ruled by feudal lords. The most powerful of the barons in the Slovak lands was Matus Cak of Trencin, who ruled over most of Slovakia. The Arpad dynasty of Hungary died out in 1301, further weakening the kingdom, and the expanding Ottoman Empire took control of part of the Hungarian kingdom, including eastern Slovakia, in 1526. The Magyar capital, Buda, fell to the Ottoman Turks in 1541, forcing the Hungarians to transfer their administrative center to Bratislava, called Pozsony in the Hungarian language. The Slovaks were pressured to give up their language and cultural identity and become Hungarian. Mainly rural, landless peasants, the Slovaks had little economic status and virtually no role in the political life of the kingdom.

The Austrian Hapsburg Empire took control of the remaining Hungarian lands in 1687. The Hapsburgs added the kingdom to their vast empire. In the eighteenth century, under Empress Maria Theresa and Emperor Joseph II, who abolished serfdom, the Slovaks were subjected to intense Germanization. Bratislava remained the center of the Hungarian kingdom until 1789, when the capital was returned to Budapest. However, the Hapsburg Hungarian kings were crowned in Bratislava's cathedral until 1835. The city remained an important Hungarian cultural center but at the same time became the focus of growing Slovak nationalism.

The nationalist ideal, led by the Slovak Catholic clergy, gained support during the mid-1800s, particularly during the upheavals that shook the Austrian Empire in 1848. The revival of the Slovak language and culture was paralleled by a new determination to win the right to determine their own future free of Hungarian domination. The use of the Slovak language, codified by Anton Bernolák in the 1700s and reformed a century later by L'udovít Stúr, became a potent nationalist issue.

The Hungarians forced the Austrians* to share power in the empire in 1867, forming the Austro-Hungarian Empire. The compromise between the Hapsburg Empire's two most powerful nations reinforced official policy aimed at assimilating the smaller nations into Austrian or Hungarian culture. The Slovaks, in the Hungarian half of the empire, reacted to renewed assimilation pressures by espousing Slovak nationalism. Backward, neglected, and oppressed, the only opportunity for education and advancement was the Catholic priesthood, which resulted in ever closer ties between the Roman Catholic Church and the growing Slovak national movement. To escape grinding poverty, Slovaks began to emigrate in large numbers in the 1880s, mostly to North America.

Stirred by the large emigrant population in the United States and Canada, Slovak demands for political and cultural autonomy gained momentum up to World War I. The Slovak National Council, formed by immigrant groups in the United States, initiated close cooperation with parallel Czech national groups. At the outbreak of World War II in 1914, Slovak nationalist leader Milan Stefanik joined with Czech leader Thomas Masaryk to promote Slovak-Czech independence from the United States. Thousands of unhappy Slovak conscripts in the Hungarian armies deserted to the Allies.

The collapse of the defeated Austro-Hungarian Empire gave the nationalists the opportunity they had waited for. The Czechs declared their independence from Austria on 28 October 1918, and the Slovaks followed by declaring their independence of Hungary on 30 October. In an attempt to prevent the Slovak secession, Hungarian troops invaded the new state on 3 November but were forced by the Allied powers to withdraw. On 14 November 1918 the Czech lands and Slovakia united in the new Czecho-Slovak republic.

Roman Catholicism, the dominant religion in Slovakia, was unpopular at the time, being seen as a remaining tie to the former Austro-Hungarian Empire. Only when the tensions between the Czechs and Slovaks had relaxed in the early 1920s did the Roman Catholic Church regain its popularity among the Slovaks.

The new Czech and Slovak government adopted agreements drawn up by nationalists in the United States that provided for major Slovak cultural and religious autonomy within the new republic of Czechoslovakia. According to the preindependence agreements, Slovakia was to be a partner, with only defense, foreign affairs, and internal security overseen by the federal government in Prague.

On 28 March 1919 a resurgent Hungary declared war and proceeded to reconquer all of Slovakia. A Hungarian minority of about 1 million inhabited southern Slovakia, one of the new state's most urgent problems. When Romanian troops invaded Hungary, the Hungarian forces were forced to withdraw from Slovakia, and leftist Slovaks proclaimed a Slovak Socialist Republic, which lasted for four weeks until overthrown by Czechs and moderate Slovaks.

Slovaks differed in many important ways from their more numerous Czech neighbors. The Slovak economy was more agrarian and less developed than that of the Czech lands to the west. The question of religion also divided the two people. The majority of Slovaks were practicing Catholics, while the Czech leadership believed in limiting the power of the church, and the Slovak people had generally less education and experience in self-government than the Czechs. These disparities, compounded by centralized Czech control of the government, produced discontent among the Slovaks with the structure of the new Czech and Slovak state.

The 1920 Czecho–Slovak constitution set up a democratic, although highly centralized, government, which seriously damaged relations between the two nations. The Slovaks, neglected under Hungarian rule, had not developed trained bureaucrats or military officers to lead Slovak regiments in the new Czecho–Slovak army, so Czechs from more advanced Bohemia were dispatched to administer Slovakia. The anticlerical stance of the Prague government caused much tension with the devoutly Roman Catholic Slovaks. The Catholic Church supported Slovak agitation for the autonomy promised in the preindependence agreements.

Slovakia's status remained that of an ordinary province, even though the separate Slovak language was allowed. In the 1930s, as fascist governments took power in Germany and Hungary, more radical groups emerged in Slovakia, many espousing the fascist ideals. Slovak nationalism, led by Father Andrej Hlinka and his successor, Father Jozef Tiso, supported by Nazi Germany, veered rapidly toward fascism in 1938 following the Munich Agreement, which effectively dismembered Czechoslovakia. Germany allowed its ally, Hungary, to annex the Hungarian-populated districts of southern Slovakia, while promoting the fascist Slovak nationalist movement in Slovakia. Tiso declared Slovakia independent under German protection on 14 March 1939.

Many Czechs were expelled from the new Slovak state, and all the trappings of a fascist dictatorship were created, including anti-Semitic laws. Tiso erected a one-party, authoritarian regime and allowed German troops to garrison the republic. With the outbreak of World War II, the Slovak state entered the war as a German ally, while a large, antifascist underground grew steadily in opposition to the fascist regime. During the course of the war, Slovakia's 67,000 Jews were massacred with the active participation of many of the traditionally anti-Semitic Slovaks.

In 1944 the Slovak underground launched a popular rebellion, paving the way for the Soviet occupation of the region. In 1945 Tiso was hanged, and his fascist state was dismantled, and Slovakia was again integrated into a reconstituted Czecho–Slovak republic. Slovakia was finally granted autonomy in 1945. Many ethnic Hungarians were expelled from southern Slovakia, but a move to deport the remaining half million Hungarians from Slovakia was blocked by the Allies. In the 1946 elections, 66% of Slovak voters gave their support to conservative political parties supported by the Catholic Church.

The 1948 communist takeover of Czechoslovakia again raised the old antagonism between the Czechs and Slovaks, aggravated by the new communist regime's attacks on the Slovaks' cherished Catholic religion and the abolition of Slovakia as a separate region. Harsh repression in the 1950s targeted Slovak nationalism and the Slovak Catholic hierarchy. Thousands of priests, bishops, and nuns were herded into concentration camps amid a wave of show trials of Slovak Catholic leaders.

A Slovak national revival beginning in 1963 gained wide expression in the late 1960s. Alexander Dubcek, an ethnic Slovak, became the Communist Party leader in Czechoslovakia. His liberalization and reforms led to the so-called Prague Spring, the flowering of the Czech and Slovak cultures. The brief liberalization of the Czech and Slovak cultures, which threatened the communist hold on Eastern Europe, was crushed by invading Warsaw Pact tanks in 1968. Many Slovak leaders fled or were imprisoned.

The reimposition of authoritarian communism was accompanied by the adoption of a new, federal constitution in Czechoslovakia. On 1 January 1969 Slovakia became a separate republic in a federal state with equal rights to the partner Czech Republic; however, the Communist Party remained the only center of power. Following the Warsaw Pact invasion and the creation of the federal republic, tensions between the Czechs and Slovaks worsened. Many Czechs accused the Slovak communists of cooperating with the Soviets in the "normalization" of the republic.

In the 1970s and early 1980s the Slovaks urbanized and industrialized but carefully avoided the painful subject of politics. By 1986 heavy industries had been established in many Slovak towns and cities, and only 15% of the Slovak population tilled the land. The national revival, interrupted by the 1968 invasion, gradually regained support as controls relaxed in the late 1980s. Minority factions of the national movement took on a vehement anti-Hungarian, anti-Czech, and anti-Semitic rhetoric that outraged moderates seeking closer ties to Western Europe. Joseph Tiso, executed as a war criminal in 1947, became a national hero to the more reactionary factions.

Tens of thousands of Slovak Catholics marched through Bratislava in March 1988 to protest the lack of religious and political freedom. Police used riot sticks, dogs, and tear gas to break up the demonstration, the first important defiance of the communist government in Slovakia. Loyalty to the Catholic Church became stronger than in past decades as young Slovaks saw the church as the spearhead for increasing freedom.

In April 1988 the Czecho–Slovak government, following the Soviet lead, began a series of limited economic reforms but continued to suppress demands for political reforms. The most conservative government in the communist bloc, the Czechoslovak government refused to institute reforms like those in neighboring Poland and Hungary and even in the Soviet Union. In October 1988 the communist leadership of Slovakia resigned amid the first tentative cultural and economic liberalization. The federal government reacted to the burst of political activity with a wave of police repression, using force to crush unauthorized demonstrations and raiding the homes of dozens of Slovak dissidents.

The overthrow of communism in Czechoslovakia in 1989, the so-called Velvet Revolution, allowed nationalist sentiment to reemerge, stimulated by conflicts with the Czechs over the name of the federal state, demands for greater autonomy, and the growing economic differences. Mass demonstrations in Bratislava and other Slovak cities by nationalists demanded autonomy, more economic support, and a new name for the country. In March 1990 nationalist passions were further aroused by the ongoing issue of a new name for the federal republic. The Slovaks demanded that the name clearly identify their nation as an equal partner.

A new movement called Public against Violence (PAV) was formed in Slovakia, bringing together political dissidents, intellectuals, and Catholics to lead the transition to an open democratic society. The federation's first free elections since 1946 were held in June 1990 and were won by PAV in Slovakia and Vaclav Havel's Civic Forum in the Czech lands. Havel was chosen as president of Czechoslovakia, and Marian Calfa, a Slovak, became vice president.

The economic reforms set in place following the dismantling of the communist command economy began to be felt in mid-1990. While the Slovaks demanded greater economic aid for their unprofitable and aging heavy industries, many Czechs complained that Slovakia already received too big a share of federal revenues and jobs. Czech demands for cuts in spending further alienated many Slovak nationalists.

Czecho–Slovak president Vaclav Havel was authorized by the federal parliament in July 1991 to call a national referendum on separation. On 17 July 1991 the Slovak parliament declared the sovereignty of the republic with the federation. Continuing disagreements over a new federal constitution deepened until Czech and Slovak leaders finally agreed to the peaceful division of the federation into two sovereign states in August 1992. The Republic of Slovakia was declared an independent republic on 1 January 1993. The so-called Velvet Divorce between the Czech Republic and Slovakia split the former Czecho-Slovak state peacefully, although disputes over the distribution of state funds, industries, and infrastructure continued.

Slovakia by 1997 had fallen behind the Czech Republic in several important areas. The Slovaks' democracy and civic rights are primitive compared with those enjoyed by the Czechs. The Slovak state increasingly interferes with the Slovak economy, which has been hit harder than the Czechs' by postcommunist economic reforms. The Slovak government has signed an array of agreements with Russia ranging from arms transfers and the sharing of intelligence to supplies of oil and gas. The government, in spite of its lack of reforms, continues to measure Slovakia's progress in comparison to that of the Czech Republic.

The authoritarian regime of Vladimir Meciar was ousted by a pro-Western coalition in October 1998. When the new coalition took control of the government, over 2,000 officials, many former communists of the former government, were dismissed. The new coalition, however, is not a united front but includes four political blocs made up of ten political parties. The coalition partners have little in common except their opposition to the corrupt Meciar regime and their desire to join the North Atlantic Treaty Organization (NATO) and the European Union (EU).

SELECTED BIBLIOGRAPHY

Delfiner, Henry. *Slovakia 1938–1939: A Case Study of Subversion.* 1974.
Drobna, Olga, ed. *Slovakia: The Heart of Europe.* 1996.
Kirschbaum, Stanislav J. *Historical Dictionary of Slovakia.* 1998.
Kirschbaum, Stanislav J. *A History of Slovakia: The Struggle for Survival.* 1995.
Leff, Carol Skalnik. *The Czech and Slovak Republics: Nation Versus State.* 1996.

SLOVENES

Slovenians

POPULATION: Approximately (2000 e) 1,992,000 Slovenes in Europe, 1,795,000 in Slovenia and other large communities of 78,000 in Austria, and 120,000 in Italy, 25,000 in the Prekmurje region in eastern Croatia near the Hungarian border, and smaller groups in Hungary and Ukraine. Outside Europe Slovene communities are found in the United States, Canada, and Australia.

THE SLOVENE HOMELAND: The Slovene homeland lies in South-Central Europe at the head of the Adriatic Sea. Most of Slovenia occupies the Karst Plateau, an area of Alpine highlands in the Carnic, Karawanken, and Julian Alps that rise to their highest point at Mt. Triglav, 9,395 feet (2,864 m.). In the south a northern spur of the Dinaric Alps and the limestone Karst Plateau slopes down to a short coastline of about thirty miles (forty-eight km.) on the Gulf of Trieste just south of the city of Trieste. The Slovenian lowlands lie in the east and along the Adriatic coast. The region has several important *bled*, or glacial lakes, and other lakes in the Karst Plateau.

The Slovenes declared their independence from Yugoslavia in 1991 and were recognized as an independent nation in 1992. *Republic of Slovenia (Republika Slovenije)*: 7,819 sq.mi.–20,251 sq.km. (2000 e) 1,998,000—Slovenes 90%, Croats* 3%, Serbs* 2%, Muslims 1.5%, Italians,* Germans,* Friulis.* The Slovene capital and major cultural center is Ljubljana, (2000 e) 324,000, on the Sava River about seventy-five miles west-northwest of Zagreb, Croatia.

FLAG: The Slovene national flag, the official flag of the republic, is a horizontal tricolor of white, blue, and red charged with the Slovenian shield, an image of Mt. Triglav on the upper hoist, bearing three white peaks crossed by two wavy lines and surmounted by three, six-pointed, yellow stars.

PEOPLE: The Slovenes are a South Slav nation, the most northerly of the South Slav peoples of the Balkan Peninsula. Historically, the Slovenes have been dominated by the German-speaking Austrians to the north, their basically Alpine culture showing many Austrian influences. The Slovene culture is centered on the cities of Trieste, Italy, called Trst in Slovenian, and Klagenfurt, Austria, called Celovec, which with Ljubljana historically made up the three historic centers of the Slovene culture and nation. The most Westernized and advanced of the South Slav peoples, the Slovenes have achieved the highest standard of living of the newly independent states. The inhabitants of the new country have maintained close contacts with the prosperous Slovene minorities in Italy and Austria. Overwhelmingly Roman Catholic, the Slovenes are closely allied to the neighboring Catholic Croats, and most Slovenes are bilingual in Croatian, a closely related South Slav language.

The Slovene language is a western South Slav language showing a marked German admixture and written in the Latin alphabet, with the exception of the letters q, w, and y. The language, spoken in two major dialects, Lower Carniola and Upper Carniola, is further divided into forty-six subdialects. The Slovene literary language is based on the subdialect of Dolenjsko, which is between the two main dialects. The oldest identifiably Slovenian text dates from about 1000.

NATION: Slavic tribes moved into the area east of the Adriatic Sea in the sixth century A.D. The migrating Slavs reached the Karst Plateau, traditionally in A.D. 568, and settled the valleys of the Sava, Drava, and Mura Rivers. Under pressure from the Avars,* the Slavic tribes spread out across the Friuli Plains, north to the Danube and along the Adriatic Sea. Historically, the ancestors of the Slovenes settled in four distinct areas, Styria, Carniola, Carinthia, and Gorizia. A period of rule by the Bavarians* ensued, during which most of the Slovenes converted to Roman Catholicism.

The Slovene tribes formed a separate state called Karantanja, later known as Carinthia. In 745 the Slovene duchy was included in the Frankish Empire of the Carolingians, the forerunner of the Holy Roman Empire. In the ninth century the German peoples directly took control of the Klagenfurt region, while most of Slovenia was ruled by a succession of German princes until its piecemeal incorporation into the Hapsburg Austrian Empire between 1278 and 1335. In 1364 the Slovene territories became hereditary possessions of the House of Hapsburg. The central districts were erected as the titular Duchy of Carniola, while the eastern districts came under the authority of the Hungarian kingdom. Under Hapsburg rule the region became Westernized, and the German language was predominant.

The Austrian imperial government refused to recognize the Slovenes as a minority, and intense pressure was applied to assimilate the Slovenes into German Austrian culture. The cities and towns became Germanized, while the Slovene language and culture survived as peasant dialects in the rural areas. In 1551 a Protestant minister published the first book written in the Slovene language, and in 1584 the first Slovene grammar was written. Not until 1750 were

Slovenian schoolbooks produced by Marko Pohlin, an opponent of Germanization.

Over the next centuries the Slovene culture was preserved only as rural traditions, and the Slovene language survived as a group of peasant dialects. Only in the nineteenth century did a sense of nationhood begin to appear among the various Slovene groups. In 1848, during the nationalist upheavals in the empire, a group of Slovene intellectuals issued the first political program for a united Slovenia within the Hapsburg Empire. The first Slovene political and nationalist organizations appeared in 1860, the forerunner of the later political parties.

Increased access to education and the spread of nationalist ideas stimulated a Slovene national revival in the 1880s and 1890s. The most advanced of the South Slav peoples of the Austro-Hungarian Empire, the Slovenes led the campaign for Slovene autonomy within the empire, only later espousing the creation of an autonomous South Slav state equal to the Austrian and Hungarian partners in the empire.

Slovene nationalism won widespread support as the Austro-Hungarian Empire slowly collapsed during World War I. At Allied urging, the Slovenes sent a delegation to a meeting of the leaders of all the South Slav peoples in 1917, where they reluctantly agreed to join a sovereign state made up of the South Slav nations of the Hapsburg Empire, along with the less advanced, but more numerous, Orthodox South Slavs of Serbia and Montenegro. At the collapse of Austria-Hungary, Slovene leaders in Ljubljana proclaimed the country's independence, and although the Slovenes feared domination by the Orthodox Serbs in the new South Slav kingdom, they feared even more the neighboring states to the east, west, and north.

By the terms of the 1919 Treaty of St. Germain between Austria and the Allies over Slovene protests, the western portions of historic Slovenia, including the city of Trieste, with an Italian majority, were transferred to Italy, and northern Slovenia, with the city of Klagenfurt, was included in the new Austrian republic. The territorial dispute soured relations between the South Slav state and the neighboring states between the wars. Irredentist claims to Slovene-populated regions of Italy and Austria kept the region in turmoil in the 1920s and 1930s.

Still the least enthusiastic for South Slav union, the Westernized, Roman Catholic Slovenes greatly resented the domination of the new kingdom by the less-developed Orthodox Serbs. Serb control of power in the kingdom provoked widespread discontent and demands for Slovene autonomy. The wealthier Slovenes resented the revenue from their lumber and mining taken by the central government for projects in Serbia and the poor southern regions of the kingdom. The government of the state, renamed Yugoslavia in 1929, to blunt local nationalisms, divided the national regions into counties, effectively partitioning the various ethnic and religious groups. During the 1930s and early 1940s the Yugoslav kingdom lurched from crisis to crisis, further alienating the various national groups.

In April 1941 the armies of the Axis powers invaded Yugoslavia. A pro-fascist Slovene, General Rupnik, became the head of an Italian-occupied puppet state, called the Province of Ljubljana. Other portions of Slovenia were placed under direct German and Hungarian rule. Soon after the occupation the Slovenes under Italian authority rebelled and were joined by the Julian Slovenes under German rule. The Slovene rebels formed the Freedom Front (OF), which became the center of Slovene resistance. The Slovene uprising was the first rebellion by a national group against the Italian and German fascists.

The Italian government changed sides in 1943, and German troops occupied the territories formerly held by the Italian forces. Until then the Slovene nationalist resistance had maintained its independence of the communist partisans led by Josip Broz Tito, himself partly of Slovene origin. The communist resistance pressed for control, and the "Dolomite Proclamation" was approved by the assembly of activists. The proclamation gave the Slovene Communist Party a leading role in the resistance, and many noncommunist partisan groups, called White Guards, were massacred, reportedly on Tito's direct orders. Another 40,000 noncommunist Slovenes were massacred by the communists at the end of World War II, including many who had fled to Allied-occupied territory. It reportedly took eight days to kill the Slovenes and dispose of their bodies in mass graves. The British military had agreed to the forced repatriation of the Slovenes in return for a Yugoslav withdrawal from Austrian Carinthia.

Tito, the communist resistance leader, gained control of all of postwar Yugoslavia and organized the state as a federation under firm communist control in 1946. Slovenia was joined to the new communist federation as a constituent republic under the control of the League of Communists of Slovenia (LCS).

Yugoslav claims to the traditionally Slovene city of Trieste (Trst), also claimed by Italy, resulted in the creation of a separate Free territory of Trieste under United Nations (UN) auspices in 1947. The Free territory, after seven years of independence, was in 1954 divided between Yugoslavia, which received the rural southern region mostly populated by Slovenes, and Italy, which gained the city of Trieste and its immediate area with its large Slovene minority. The border region remained a source of tension between Yugoslavia and Italy from World War II to the signing of a final agreement on Trieste in 1975.

The Yugoslav republic of Slovenia developed as Yugoslavia's wealthiest and most advanced region, while the Slovenes resented Yugoslav government policies that heavily taxed them for development projects in Serbia and the poorer southern republics of the federation. In 1962 the Slovene republican government threatened secession over the "economic nationalism" of the Serb-dominated federal government. Growing demands for economic and political autonomy ended with purges and arrests of Slovene leaders in 1971 and 1976. With less than 8% of the Yugoslav population, Slovenia earned between 25 and 30% of the country's foreign exchange between the 1960s and the 1980s.

Tito's death in 1980 dramatically loosened decades of centralized, firm communist control. The Slovenes' dissatisfaction with the Yugoslav federation grew during the 1980s, with increased nationalist sentiment expressed by all segments of the population. Fueled by a severe economic crisis, the Slovenes moved to separate their more prosperous republic both economically and politically from the Serb-dominated Yugoslav federal government.

In the summer of 1988 the military trial of three young Slovene journalists and an army officer led to the first calls for Slovene independence. Along with political unrest, economic problems mounted, and Yugoslav inflation hit 1,200%. Amid the growing economic and political crisis in 1989 communism began to collapse, and a radical Serb nationalist group took control of the federal government.

A nationalist crisis in Kosovo, an autonomous province of Serbia, where the Serbian government had ousted the provincial government and imposed military rule, further alienated the Westernized Slovenes from the Yugoslav heartland in Serbia. In February 1989 the Slovene communist leadership publicly protested the state of emergency imposed on Kosovo, fearing that the liberalizing Slovenia would be the next target of the Serb-dominated Yugoslav army (JNA). In late 1989 the federal government imposed an economic embargo on Slovenia because of its stand on Kosovo.

The Yugoslav republic of Slovenia and neighboring Croatia demanded reforms and the formation of a confederation of sovereign states in Yugoslavia but were blocked by the Serbs. A coalition of nationalist groups, Demos, won Slovenia's first free elections in April 1990, stimulating more demands for a looser Yugoslav federation. Milan Kucan, a communist turned nationalist, was elected president of the republic. The largest of the republics, Serbia, under a neocommunist government, strongly resisted the decline of its traditional domination of the federation. On 23 December 1990 a Slovene referendum on independence resulted in overwhelming support, giving the Slovene government a mandate to negotiate a less restrictive political relationship with Belgrade within six months or to complete the process that would lead to independence. Amid a continuing political crisis, the Slovene leadership declared the independence of the Republic of Slovenia on 25 June 1991.

The Serb-dominated Yugoslav army, the JNA, on 27 June 1991 picked the Slovenes as an easier target than neighboring Croats. The army moved in to secure the borders and take over important government buildings in Ljubljana. The Slovenes resisted, set up blockades, and attacked advancing JNA armored columns. After a ten-day war, on 7 July 1991 the army called off further intervention, but the Slovene government, acting on a European Community proposal, accepted a three-month moratorium on the country's independence while attempts were made to bring about a peaceful resolution to the crisis.

After the three-month wait, on 7 October 1991 the Slovenes took control of their borders, and on 25 October 1991 the last Yugoslav soldier left the country. Germany promised that diplomatic relations would be established on 15 January 1992. On that date the presidency of the European Community announced that its member states had decided to recognize Croatia and Slovenia, but not the other former Yugoslav states.

The first Slovene national elections on 6 December 1992 were a high point for newly independent Slovenia. The Slovenes bucked the trend in the former communist states by rejecting militant nationalism and electing a liberal, democratic government. In June 1993 they celebrated two years of independence and their status as the richest, most stable state to emerge from the collapse of communism. The new republic looked to the West for security as former Yugoslavia dissolved into war. Along with Macedonia in the south, Slovenia escaped the general Balkan war that convulsed the former Yugoslav republics of Croatia and Bosnia-Herzegovina.

Relations with the other former Yugoslav republics, particularly Yugoslavia, the federation of Serbia and Montenegro, which claims to be the sole successor to Tito's state, became increasingly tense in 1994–95. The distribution of the assets of the former Socialist Federal Republic of Yugoslavia (SFRY), which Yugoslavia claims, has become an issue for Slovenia and continues to cloud relations between the two successor states.

In March 1995 the European Union granted a mandate for negotiations to begin between the European Union (EU) and Slovenia on an association agreement. Slovenia's market economy and democratic politics made the country one of few in the former communist bloc to meet EU requirements for association. The Slovene government signed an association agreement with the EU in June 1996, and in July 1997 Slovenia was among the countries named to take part in talks leading to the European Union's first expansion into Central and Eastern Europe. On 14 July the Slovene parliament voted to amend the constitution to permit foreigners to own property, an EU requirement. The property issue is politically sensitive because many Slovenes fear that lifting the ban might lead to a massive influx of foreign buyers, particularly Italians whose families left the region in the wake of World War II.

SELECTED BIBLIOGRAPHY

Baker, Thomas Mack. *The Slovene Minority of Carinthia.* 1984.

Benderly, Jill, and Evan Kraft, eds. *Independent Slovenia: Origins, Movements, Prospects.* 1996.

Hafner, Danica Fink, ed. *Making a New Nation: The Formation of Slovenia.* 1997.

Plut-Pregelj, Leopoldina. *Historical Dictionary of Slovenia.* 1996.

Prunk, Janko. *A Brief History of Slovenia: Historical Background of the Republic of Slovenia.* 1993.

SORBS

Srbi; Sorbischs; Sorabes; Lusatians;
Wends

POPULATION: Approximately (2000 e) 643,000 Sorbs in Europe, most in the eastern German states of Brandenburg and Saxony, and with some 40,000 in adjacent areas of Poland.

THE SORBIAN HOMELAND: The Sorb homeland lies in east-central Germany and southwestern Poland, a region of rolling hills and forests, particularly the large Spree Forest around Cottbus. The region extends north from the Lusatian Mountains, lies mostly between the Elbe and Oder Rivers, and is traversed by the basin of the Spree River. The hilly and fertile southern section is known as Upper Lusatia, and the sandy and forested northern part is Lower Lusatia.

Lusatia, the Sorb homeland, has no official status; the historic region forms the districts of Bautzen, Görlitz, Kamenz, Niesky, and Zittau of the German state of Saxony, and Callau Cottbus, Forst, Guben, Hoyerswerda, and Weisswasser districts of Brandenburg state, along with the Zgorzelec district, the western part of the Polish province of Jelenia Gora. The historic district, called Luzicka Serbja by the Sorbs, is called Lausitz in German and Luzyce in Polish. *Lusatia/Luzyce (Luzicka Serbja)*: 4,933 sq.mi.–12,776 sq.km. (2000 e) 1,271,000—Germans* 54%, Sorbs 43%, Poles* 2%. The Sorbian capital and major culture center is Bautzen, called Budysin in the Sorbian language, (2000 e) 52,000, the historic capital of Upper Lusatia. Other important Sorbian culture centers are Cottbus, called Khociebuz in Sorbian, (2000 e) 124,000, on the Spree River, and Görlitz, including the Polish half of the city, called Zgorzelec, with a combined population (2000 e) 127,000.

FLAG: The Sorb national flag, the unofficial flag of the Lausitz region, is a horizontal tricolor of blue, red, and white.

PEOPLE: The Sorbs are a West Slav nation, also called Lusatians or Wends. They call themselves Srbi. The smallest of the West Slav nations, they are related to the neighboring Poles and Czechs* but have retained their distinct culture and language. In the Middle Ages the term "Wends" was applied by the Germans to all the Slavs inhabiting the area between the Oder, Elbe, and Saale Rivers. Culturally, the majority of the Sorbs have assimilated into German culture while retaining their own traditions and customs. Part of the Sorbian population, in the Spree Forest, has preserved its traditional dress. The Sorbs have retained their traditional ties to the neighboring Poles and Czechs, and since 1989 there has been a general revival of the Sorbian culture and language. The German-speaking Sorbs, speaking a German dialect with marked Slavic admixtures, retain many Slavic characteristics and are increasingly aware of their unique culture and heritage. The majority of the Sorbs are Lutheran, the only Slav nation with a Protestant majority. The Roman Catholic minority is concentrated in the border districts on both sides of the Polish border.

The Sorbian language, of the West Slavic language group, is spoken in two major dialects, Upper Sorbian, resembling Czech, and Lower Sorbian, in its spoken form closer to Polish. A third dialect, called Eastern Sorbian, considered a subdialect of Upper Sorbian, is spoken in Polish Lusatia. In Germany a majority of the Sorbs now speak German, with only some 200,000 able to understand Sorbian and only 60,000 using the language as the language of daily life. Since German unification, Sorbian has been accepted as a minority language and is authorized in local government and education.

NATION: The Slavic Milceni and Luzici tribes settled the region east of the river Elbe in the seventh and eighth centuries. The tribes controlled most of present Saxony and founded towns that later developed into the great Saxon cities, Dresden, Leipzig, and Chemnitz. They continued to migrate west until their expansion was checked by Charlemagne's Franks in the ninth century. Called Wends, the German term for all Slavs, they soon came into conflict with the Germanic peoples moving into their territory in the tenth century.

Saxons* and Brandenburgers launched a crusade to Christianize the Wends in 1147. The Wends had already begun to adopt Christianity, so the crusade served German expansion rather than the propagation of the faith. The German onslaught drove many of the Slavs east across the Oder and Neisse Rivers. German nobles and merchants colonized the conquered lands and reduced the Wends to serfdom. The Germans relegated urban Slavs to restricted sections or to districts outside the city walls of their conquered towns and cities.

Seven Sorb cities in the southeast, free cities of the Holy Roman Empire, formed a defensive alliance in 1346, the Lusatian League. The cities preserved considerable independence from the surrounding German states and maintained the Sorb language and culture. The Czechs of Bohemia took control of Lusatia in 1368, temporarily easing the pressure to assimilate into German culture. Divided into two margravates, Upper and Lower Lusatia, in the fifteenth century, the Sorb lands were partitioned and often changed hands. The Saxon annexation of the margravates reunited the area under Saxon rule in 1635, while the majority of the Sorbs gradually absorbed German culture and language.

The majority of the Sorbs accepted the Lutheran Reformation in 1530, their conversion to Protestantism inciting a cultural and national revival. A written form of the Sorbian language was devised in order to publish the New Testament in the language in 1548; a Lutheran catechism followed in 1574. In the Spree Forest and the highlands the Sorbian language remained the first language of the Slav population, the isolated regions becoming bastions of the beleaguered language and culture. In the Germanized lowlands and in the towns and cities, German slowly gained prominence as the language of daily life.

The Saxons, allied to Napoleonic France, lost the northern districts of the Saxon kingdom, including Lower Lusatia, to victorious Prussia in 1815. The Prussians instituted an intense Germanization policy in the region, forcing the Sorbs of Lower Lusatia to adopt German names and to relinquish their language and Slavic traditions. The Sorbs of Upper Lusatia, under more lenient Saxon rule, published the first grammar in the Upper Sorbian dialect in 1830 and the first dictionary in 1840. Reunited in the German Empire in 1871, the Sorbs experienced a national revival with the first grammar in Lower Sorbian published in 1891. Resistance to forced assimilation sparked the growth of Sorb nationalism. To escape harsh Prussian rule, many Sorbs emigrated, mostly to Texas and Australia.

The nationalism that swept Poland and the Czech lands in the mid-nineteenth century acquired many parallels in Lusatia. The first openly nationalist organization, Macica Serbska, formed in the late nineteenth century. The German parliament in 1908 declared that German must be the spoken language of the empire and placed official restraints on the Sorb cultural and national revival. Domowina (Nation), formed in 1912, pressed for Sorb secession from the German Empire.

Conscripted to fight fellow Slavs in 1914, the Sorbs' opposition to German domination expanded rapidly. In November 1918, as defeated Germany collapsed in revolution, Sorbian leaders declared the autonomy of Lusatia and dispatched a delegation to Berlin to negotiate the peaceful secession of Lusatia from Germany. Rebuffed by the German government, the Sorbs declared Lusatia independent of Germany on 1 January 1919. A Sorbian delegation traveled to the Paris Peace Conference in 1919 to seek recognition under U.S. president Wilson's call for the self-determination of Europe's minority peoples. Their appeals ignored, the Sorbs were forced to surrender to invading German troops. In the postwar German reorganization the states of Saxony and Prussia again divided the Sorbian homeland.

In 1920, due to intense pressure to assimilate, only 170,000 used Sorbian as their first language, with over 600,000 able to speak both Sorb and German. The number of Sorbian speakers fell rapidly under the policies of the postwar German government. In 1929 the Sorbs won the right to use their language in education and religion, but the concessions fell far short of the cultural autonomy demanded by Domowina and other national organizations.

National Socialists, called Nazis, in control of Germany from 1933, persecuted the Sorbs as subhuman Slavs and banned the use of their language. All remnants of the Sorbian culture were suppressed. In 1938 Domowina was banned, and its leaders were condemned to Nazi concentration camps. Finally liberated by the German defeat in 1945, the Sorbs again attempted to win Allied support for independence. In an exchange of territories the Americans withdrew from the region and allowed the Soviets to occupy Saxony and Lusatia. The portion of Lusatia east of the Neisse River was ceded to Poland. The Soviet authorities, unsympathetic to national movements in Eastern Europe, quickly suppressed the Sorbian national movement and imprisoned the nationalist leaders.

In 1952, over Sorbian protests, their homeland remained divided among two of the new districts that were created out of East Germany's historic regions. Emulating the Soviet policy on nationalities, the East German authorities encouraged Sorbian culture but quickly suppressed all signs of nascent nationalism. The government encouraged Sorbian education and made Sorbian an official language in Lusatia. Ethnic awareness revived in the 1960s and 1970s as the Sorbs created cultural centers, newspapers, radio stations, theaters, schools, folk ensembles, and publishing houses.

Sorb nationalism reemerged as communism in East Germany collapsed in 1989. The nationalists dared to show their forbidden flag at a national rally in Bautzen for the first time since 1945. Sorbian nationalist leaders, citing the medieval Lusatian League as justification for their claims to sovereignty, put forward plans for an autonomous Sorbian homeland. Nationalist demands for a separate Sorb state within united Germany were ignored in the rush to German reunification in October 1990.

Mass unemployment and economic hardships followed unification, giving rise to a wave of German intolerance of "foreigners," including the Sorbs, who do not fit the vision of a pure "Fatherland" propagated by the more radical German national organizations. The Sorbs have resisted assimilation for over 1,000 years and now focus on formalizing their position as the first Slav nation in the European Union (EU).

SELECTED BIBLIOGRAPHY

Engerrand, George Charles. *The So-Called Wends of Germany and Their Colonies in Texas and Australia.* 1991.

Lundman, B. J. *Races and Peoples of Europe.* 1984.

Neilsen, George R. *In Search of a Home: Nineteenth Century Wendish Immigration.* 1989.

Shlaes, Amity. *Germany: The Empire Within.* 1991.

Stone, Gerald. *The Smallest Slavonic Nation: The Sorbs of Lusatia.* 1972.

SPANIARDS

Spanish; Españoles; Castilians;
Castellanos

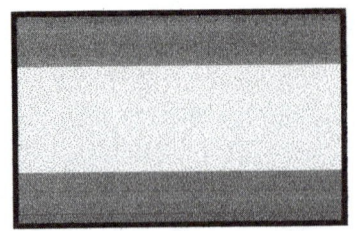

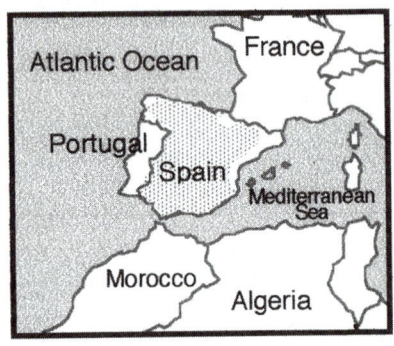

POPULATION: Approximately (2000 e) 36,243,000 Spaniards in Europe, with 28,744,000 in Spain and large communities in France, Germany, Switzerland, the Netherlands, and Belgium. Large concentrations outside Europe live in the Americas and North Africa.

THE SPANISH HOMELAND: The Spanish homeland lies in Southwestern Europe, occupying the major part, about 85%, of the Iberian Peninsula. The region extends from the Pyrenees, which separate it from French* territory, to the Strait of Gibraltar, which separates Spain from North Africa. The center of Spain, the Castilian heartland, is a vast plateau, the Meseta Central, which extends from the Cantabrian Mountains in the north to the Sierra Morena in the south. The long, unbroken mountain chain, the Pyrenees, extending from the Bay of Biscay to the Mediterranean Sea, forms the northern border of the Spanish homeland. Only a small part of Spain is forested, and woodlands are located mainly on mountain slopes.

The Spanish state is a kingdom comprising seventeen autonomous region, including those of the Basques,* Catalans,* and Galicians.* *Kingdom of Spain (Reino de España)*: 194,881 sq.mi.–504,742 sq.km. (2000 e) 39,601,000—Castilian Spanish (including Andalusians*) 72%, Catalans 16%, Galicians 8%, Basques 2%, Roms* (Gypsies), Arabs, Latin Americans, Chinese. The Spanish capital and major cultural center is Madrid, (2000 e) 3,104,000 (metropolitan area 5,264,000), which forms a separate autonomous region within the kingdom.

FLAG: The Spanish national flag, the official flag of the kingdom, has three horizontal stripes of red, yellow, and red, the yellow twice the width of the red stripes. The national emblem is often shown in the center.

PEOPLE: The Spaniards are an Iberian nation, the descendants of early Iberians, Celts, and Romans, with later admixtures of many different national groups. The Spanish culture is also a mixture of many distinct influences from both Europe and North Africa, and like the Spaniards themselves the culture is a mixture of Mediterranean, Teutonic, and Semitic elements. The large Rom population, called Gitanos, which is not counted separately, has had an important historic influence on the music, food, and culture of Spain, particularly in the southern regions. Long ties to Latin America have also influenced Spanish culture and music, which includes many borrowings from Cuban and Latin American cultures. The Spaniards are increasingly urban, with more than 80% of the population living in towns and cities. Roman Catholicism is professed by about 97% of the population, and although modern Spanish society is highly secular, any consideration of Spanish culture must stress the tremendous importance of religion in the history of the nation and in the life of the individual.

The language of the Spaniards is one of the most widely spoken of world languages. It is the official language not only of Spain but also of nineteen Latin American states. Spanish is descended from the Vulgar Latin brought to the peninsula by the soldiers and colonists of ancient Rome, with later admixtures of Arabic and other languages. Although Castilian became the dominant dialect by the thirteenth century, seven major dialects are still spoken in Spain, Andalusian, Murcian, Aragonese, Navarrese, Castilian, Leonese, and Canarian, along with a number of regional languages and mixed dialects.

NATION: The Iberian Peninsula has been inhabited since the Stone Age. The strategic position of the peninsula, which guards the Strait of Gibraltar, was known to the ancient peoples of the Mediterranean. The region became the first invasion point for the Iberians, originally a North African people, who, about 1000 B.C., became the most prominent and gave the peninsula their name. The other important people in the peninsula were the Celts, who entered it in a mass migration from the north. The Celts almost completely absorbed the indigenous inhabitants. A subsequent intermingling of Celts and Iberians formed the so-called Celtiberians, living chiefly in the center and the west and along the northern coast.

The Phoenicians established colonies, and later the Carthaginians settled on the east coast and the Balearic Islands, where Greek colonies were also founded. The Roman defeat of the Carthaginians in the second of the Punic Wars, 218–201 B.C., resulted in the expulsion of the Carthaginians. The fall of Numantia in 133 B.C. marked the end of organized resistance to Roman rule. Except for the Basques in the far north, the inhabitants of the region became thoroughly Romanized and Latin in culture. Roman rule brought political unity, economic prosperity, and the rule of law. The Roman religion, Christianity, was introduced, and traditionally, St. Paul visited Spain, and St. James the Greater is the apostolic patron of the later Spanish nation.

The decline of Roman rule allowed Germanic tribes to overrun the remaining Roman defenses. In A.D. 409 Spain was conquered by the Teutonic Suevi and the Vandals. They were followed by the Visigoths, who forced the Vandals to cross into North Africa. The Visigoths established their kingdom in northern Spain and southern France in 419, with Toulouse as its capital. At its fullest extent the Visigothic kingdom included territory from the Strait of Gibraltar north to the Loire River. Following the Frankish conquest of the Visigoths' Gaulish territories, the capital was transferred south to Toledo in Castile.

In the sixth century the Roman and Visigothic elements of the peninsula were merged into a single people, although the fusion was very slow, and a common law for all inhabitants was not imposed until 654. Byzantine cultural influences became important, but less so than those of the Jews, who settled in Spain in large numbers and suffered persecutions from the seventh century. The Visigothic kings remained weak, with the Roman Catholic Church acquiring broad secular powers. The kingdom, weakened by the clash of Germanic, Hispano-Roman, and Jewish influences, collapsed in 711, following defeat by an invading army from North Africa.

The Berber Muslims, called Moors, led by Tariq ibn-Ziyad, soon conquered almost the entire peninsula. The Moors' northward progress was arrested by a battle fought in France in 732 by the Frankish ruler Charles Martel. Cordoba in Andalusia, called Al-Andalus by the Moors, was made the Moorish capital and became the center of a brilliant, tolerant civilization, which combined Muslim, Christian, and Jewish cultures. The Moorish civilization under the Umayyad dynasty was far in advance of that of the rest of Europe. Numerous schools were established, many of them free and for the education of the poor. At the great Muslim universities medicine, mathematics, philosophy, and literature were cultivated. The works of the Greek philosopher Aristotle were studied long before they were well known in Christian Europe. The Umayyad rulers also encouraged trade and commerce and constructed an extensive irrigation system in the dry southern districts.

The Umayyad dynasty died out in 1036, and the caliphate split into a number of independent, mutually hostile kingdoms. To the petty nobles and Christian kings of poor northern Spain, the flourishing, prosperous cities and the irrigated lands of the Moorish territories were a constant temptation. At the decisive Battle of Navas de Tolosa in 1212, Alfonso VIII of Castile defeated the Moors, and his descendants conquered most of Andalusia.

Christian Spain in the Middle Ages consisted of two great kingdoms, Castile and Leon in the west, center, and south, and Aragon in the northeast and along the Mediterranean. The unified northwestern kingdom of Aragon and Catalonia, economically more prosperous than the other kingdoms, took little part in the Moorish wars, leaving the Castilians to complete the conquest of Moorish Spain, and Castilian nobles formed the nucleus of an aristocratic class that formed the ruling class in Spain for centuries. Castile and Aragon were united by the marriage of Ferdinand and Isabella in 1479. The last of the great Moorish kingdoms, Granada, fell to their combined military forces in 1492.

To achieve religious unity and fill a depleted treasury, the Catholic rulers of

Spain expelled the Jews from the kingdom and confiscated their extensive properties. Until 1492 the Jews and Muslims had been allowed to live in the reconquered territories; however, from the time of the Spanish Inquisition, set up in 1478, attempts were made at forcible conversion, including confiscation of property, torture, and murder, usually in ritualized mass burnings. The Inquisition was not restricted to Jews and Moors but was also applied to those who did convert but remained suspect. The expulsion of the Jews and, in 1609, of the remaining Muslims deprived the Spanish kingdom of its most useful and active populations. Later, the Spanish government, by fostering the exploitation of central Spain for sheep grazing, unwittingly prepared the ruin of many districts that had been fruitful under Moorish rule.

The economic and political revolution that began under Ferdinand and Isabella, the opening of the New World to Spanish exploitation, eventually grew into a vast empire. Gold and silver, the primary objectives of Spanish colonial expansion, flowed into Spain in fabulous quantities. In the sixteenth century, called the Golden Century, Spain was the premier world power, with fleets on every sea and a brilliant cultural, artistic, and intellectual life. In the Italian Wars from 1494 to 1559, the Spaniards triumphed over their chief rivals, the French, and added Naples and other Italian and European territories to their empire.

Charles I, the first of the Hapsburg kings in 1516, began the centralization of Spain. On his accession, the Spanish homeland remained divided into separate kingdoms and principalities and the semi-independent cities, which enjoyed great privileges and independence. Under his successors the centralization of the kingdom continued against the resistance of the historically independent Basques, Catalans, Valencians, Aragonese, and Navarrese.

During the sixteenth century the Roman Catholic Church enlarged its already dominant position. The Spanish Inquisition reached its greatest power, and at the same time the Catholic Counter-Reformation was advanced. The Dutch* of the Netherlands shook off Spanish rule, although the southern, Catholic provinces, later called Belgium, were again subjugated. The Dutch rebellion and other reverses in France began a long decline in Spanish military power. The rivalry on the seas between Spain and England culminated in the attempted conquest of England by the ill-fated Spanish Armada in 1588. The Spaniards lost control of Portugal, and prolonged wars with France continued until 1659. In the same year a serious revolt broke out in Catalonia, which ended only when the region's autonomous rights were restored.

Spain's declining prestige and power were exacerbated in the late seventeenth century by the complicated succession at the death of Charles II. The War of the Spanish Succession broke out in 1701 and continued until 1714 and the Peace of Utrecht, which confirmed the succession of the Bourbons in the person of Philip, the grandson of France's King Louis XIV.

Spanish power continued to decline during the eighteenth century, with widespread poverty among the Spanish lower classes, while the declining revenues from the overseas colonies became a drain on the treasury. The population of

Spain had greatly increased, and the vast majority, the peasants, lived in misery, many on inefficiently run estates owned by absentee landlords. The Spanish government and court decayed in an atmosphere of bigotry, incompetence, and corruption. The church had largely abandoned its constructive role and was using its influence for the perpetuation of the existing order.

Drawn into the French Revolutionary Wars of Napoleon, the Spaniards suffered their greatest humiliation in 1808 with the successive abdications of the king and his son and the installation of Joseph Bonaparte, Napoleon's brother, on the Spanish throne. The Spaniards refused to recognize Joseph as king and organized resistance. By 1814 the Spanish resistance forces, aided by the British, had expelled the French forces, and the Spanish Bourbons were restored under a new constitution that restricted the powers of the monarchy, did away with the special privileges of the nobility and the church, and formally ended the Inquisition. By 1825 nearly all of Latin America had gained independence. In Spain itself the king's refusal to honor the liberal 1812 constitution led to revolution in 1820, which was put down by French troops. The question of succession led to the Carlist Wars, which raged until 1839 and further weakened the decayed kingdom. In 1868 a constitutional monarchy was created, but the abdication of the chosen candidate, Amadeus, duke of Aosta, in 1873 was followed by the short-lived first Spanish republic and yet another civil war, which ended in 1876.

The Bourbon Alfonso XII was placed on the throne by a coalition of moderate political parties. By the end of the nineteenth century, the socialists and anarchists had gained broad support, particularly in the industrial cities in the north and the rural, backward regions of the south. Strikes and uprisings, usually suppressed with great brutality, became characteristic of the twentieth century. The Catholic Church, identified with the nobility and the exploitative landlords, was hated by many, and anticlerical feeling was strong.

The ill-prepared Spanish forces lost the remaining colonial territories in war with the United States in 1898. The Spanish defeat prompted a period of cultural examination and produced a modest rebirth of the arts, music, and culture. Under Alfonso XIII the Spaniards remained neutral in World War I. Colonial uprisings in Morocco and renewed rebellion in Catalonia in 1923 resulted in the establishment of a military dictatorship under Primo de Rivera. Widespread opposition finally forced Rivera's resignation in 1931.

A republican victory in municipal elections in 1931 resulted in the overthrow of Alfonso XIII and the establishment of the second republic. A large-scale program of irrigation and other public works was undertaken. Education was secularized, and all church–state ties were ended. The government's reform program was difficult to carry out against the entrenched conservative interests, particularly in the backward southern regions, and the process alienated many groups. The reforms, including the distribution of the vast church properties, met widespread opposition among conservative groups.

The Popular Front, made up of communists, republicans, socialists, and syndicalists, were victorious in elections in 1936, but before the new government could begin to function, a military rebellion precipitated the Spanish civil war. The insurgents, called the Nationalists, led by General Francisco Franco, embraced the most conservative groups in Spain, the monarchists, the army officers, the Catholic Church, the landowners, and the small industrial middle class. United in the fascist Falange, the Nationalists received massive military aid from Nazi Germany and Mussolini's Italy. Because of the nonintervention policy of France and Britain, the Loyalists of the Popular Front, supported by the Catalan and Basque nationalists, received virtually no outside help other than foreign volunteers and limited Soviet military aid. In spite of internal division and military inferiority, the Loyalists made a remarkably strong stand against the Franco forces, but by 1938 the territory they held had shrunk drastically. By early 1939 the war was virtually over. Thousands of Loyalists and their supporters fled to France, and a politically centralized dictatorship under Francisco Franco was established. The Falange was made the only legal political party, and the savage civil war was followed by an unusually vindictive peace. Franco made no attempt at national reconciliation, and the defeated Loyalists were seen as "Reds" who had supported a treasonous "anti-Spain" campaign. Hundreds of thousands were imprisoned, and an estimated 37,000 were executed during the first four years after the war.

Franco gave aid to the Axis powers but carefully remained neutral during World War II. In 1946 the newly created United Nations (UN) urged its members to break diplomatic relations with the Spanish state. In 1947 Spain was declared a monarchy, although no king could assume the throne unless Franco died, was incapacitated, or decided to step down. In 1950 the UN declaration was rescinded, and the Spaniards were finally admitted in 1955.

The citizens of the country remained among the poorest in Europe until mass tourism, promoted by the government, began to bring in much-needed revenues in the 1960s and 1970s. The long coastlines experienced an unprecedented building boom, with lines of high-rise hotels fronting the most beautiful of the Mediterranean beaches. Jobs in the tourist industry provided employment and contact with peoples from less restrictive societies, but unemployment remained the highest in Europe, and unbridled development destroyed much of the coastline. While the Spanish standard of living remained among Western Europe's lowest, the economy surged because of industrial growth, the extraordinary rise in tourism, and money sent home by the numerous Spanish workers in Northern Europe.

Political unrest, particularly over the succession to the Franco dictatorship, became serious in the early 1960s. New laws separated the posts of head of government and chief of state, made religious freedom a legal right, and ended Falange control of labor unions. Press censorship was ended in 1966, but strong guidelines remained. The death of Franco in 1975 was a turning point for the Spanish nation. The restoration of the Bourbon dynasty in the person of King Juan Carlos was carried out peacefully, and the king greatly helped the transition from a Latin American-style dictatorship to a modern democratic state. In 1981 an attempted coup by right-wing military officers was thwarted by the king, and Spanish democracy was more firmly established.

To reinforce the nascent Spanish democracy, the European Economic Community (EEC) granted full membership in 1986. Membership, which included generous development funds, aided the dramatic expansion of the Spanish economy in the 1980s and 1990s. The economic expansion, paralleled by the growth of a middle class, drastically changed Spanish society, and although unemployment remains the highest in Europe, the hidden economy, the so-called black, or underground, economy, is thought to absorb much of the region's excess labor.

The socialists, led by Felipe Gonzalez, held power through four consecutive elections from 1982 to 1993, then peacefully yielded power. The peaceful transfer of power demonstrated the maturity of the Spaniards' democratic traditions; however, revelations about a dirty war against Basque separatists during the 1980s clouded the socialists' record. In early elections in March 1996, the socialists lost their majority to the conservative Popular Party (PP), the centrist descendant of the Falange, led by Jose Maria Aznar. The PP failed to gain an outright majority, however, and was forced to form a coalition government with the moderate Catalan nationalists, who control the regional government of Catalonia.

Once known for rural poverty, black-clad widows, and Latin American-style government, the Spaniards have become part of Europe's mainstream. Although incomes remain below the European average, a growing middle class has embraced modernity, including contraception. The Spaniards now have Europe's second lowest fertility rate, superseded only by that of the Italians.* The Spanish economy, which continued to perform well, was one of the stars of the European Union (EU).

SELECTED BIBLIOGRAPHY
Douglass, Carrie B. *Bulls, Bullfighting, and Spanish Identities*. 1997.
Kern, Robert W. *The Regions of Spain: A Reference Guide to History and Culture*. 1995.
Pluckrose, Henry. *Spain*. 1998.
Ross, Christopher J. *Contemporary Spain: A Handbook*. 1997.
Truscott, Sandra, and Maria Garcia. *A Dictionary of Contemporary Spain*. 1998.

SWABIANS

Schwäbisch; Suabians

POPULATION: Approximately (2000 e) 8,853,000 Swabians in Europe, mostly in southwestern Germany, but with communities in Berlin and other areas of the German Federal Republic. Large communities outside Europe are concentrated in the United States and Canada.

THE SWABIAN HOMELAND: The Swabian homeland lies in Southwestern Europe, a fertile region drained by the Rhine, which forms the international border between Germany and France, and the upper Danube and the Neckar Rivers. The southern districts are mostly rolling hills and include the Black Forest, the Lake of Constance (the Swabian Sea), and the Swabian Jura Mountains. Much of the region is forested, although the river valleys, particularly along the Rhine, are among the most fertile regions in Europe. The region has numerous warm springs that have been frequented since Roman times.

The territory known as Swabia is divided, with most of the region included in the German state of Baden-Württemberg, with the smaller eastern region part of the state of Bavaria. *State of Baden-Wurttemberg (Land Baden-Württemberg)*: 13,803 sq.mi.–35,750 sq.km. (2000 e) 9,912,000—Swabians 88%, Bavarians* 8%, French* 2%, other Germans,* Turks,* Spaniards,* Italians,* Portuguese.* The Swabian capital and major cultural center is Stuttgart, (2000 e) 591,000 (metropolitan area 2,245,000), the capital of Baden-Wurttemberg. Other important Swabian cultural centers are Karlsruhe, (2000 e) 277,000 (metropolitan area 571,000), the historic capital of Baden, and Augsburg, (2000 e) 254,000 (metropolitan area 415,000), the leading city of Bavarian Swabia.

FLAG: The Swabian national flag, the basis of the official state flag, is a horizontal bicolor of black over yellow.

PEOPLE: The Swabians are a southern German people related to the Bavarians, the Alsatians,* and the Swiss-Germans.* The Swabian nation includes four historically distinct divisions, the Swabians in the center, the Badanese in the west, the Franconians in the north, and the Eastern Swabians in Bavaria. The Swabians tend to be more blond and Nordic than other southern Germans, although culturally, they have much in common with the neighboring Germanic peoples. The Swabian culture has many borrowings from the French due to the close geographical proximity. Religiously, the Swabians are divided, with the Protestants concentrated in the northern districts and the Roman Catholics in the southern districts and Bavaria.

The Swabian language, which is only about 40% intelligible with standard German, is spoken throughout the region, although all are bilingual in standard German. Swabian is spoken in two major dialects, Black Forest and Alpine, while a closely related dialect, Alemannic or Alemannisch, is spoken by the Badenese in the west. Swabian and Alemannic differ from other German dialects in not having undergone the second *lautverschiebung*, or vowel change. The Swabians can be readily distinguished by their characteristic type of pronunciation of both the Swabian dialects and standard German.

NATION: The decline of Roman power and the eventual evacuation of Roman troops allowed the Germanic Alemanni and Suevi or Suebi tribes to occupy the region in the first and second centuries A.D. The mingling of the peoples of the region evolved a unique and Germanic-Celtic-Roman culture, which flourished under nominal Roman rule.

The region remained stable until the fourth century, when pressure from Goths and Burgundians* forced the Suevi to expand westward. Shortly after the fall of Roman power in A.D. 476, the Alemanni tribes set up an independent state embracing present Alsace, most of Switzerland, and southwestern Germany. Farther east, the Suevi were conquered by the Franks under Clovis in 496 and remained part of the Mergovingian and Carolingian Frankish Empires until the ninth century. The Alemanni came under Frankish rule in the sixth century.

The Frankish Empire at Charlemagne's death in 843 was divided between his three sons. By the Treaty of Verdun, the Carolingian lands were formally distributed, with Swabia becoming part of the kingdom of Louis the German. As part of the German Empire, the southern districts were included in the duchy of Swabia, and the north was added to the Franconian duchy. The region, known as Alamannia or Alemannia, became one of the five stem duchies of medieval Germany. The name Aleman or Alemanni is still used by the French and Spanish to mean German. In 1079 the duchy was bestowed on the House of Hohenstaufen, which became the imperial dynasty in 1138. On the extinction of the dynasty in 1268, Swabia broke up into a number of small secular and ecclesiastic lordships and lost its political identity.

The most powerful of the regional states were Baden in the west and Wurttemberg in the east, while the Hapsburgs gained control of Briesgau and other districts in southern Swabia in the fourteenth century. Most of the Swabian towns had obtained the status of free imperial cities, virtually independent city-states, by 1300. Their wealth, built on commerce and industry, made them the most powerful element in the region. They consolidated their power in a series of leagues starting in 1331. The Swabian League of 1376–89 successfully opposed the German emperor but was eventually defeated by the count of Wurttemberg. The most important Swabian League was that of 1488–1534, which was formed for the purpose of maintaining internal stability in the Swabian homeland. When the Holy Roman Empire was organized in circles in the sixteenth century, the Swabian Circle was created with its capital at Augsburg.

The commercial revolution in Europe in the fifteenth and sixteenth centuries decreased the power of the imperial cities as international trade became more important than local agriculture or crafts. The activities of the Fugger and Welser banking families, based in Augsburg, made Swabia a center of trade between Northern and Southern Europe.

The majority of the petty northern Swabian states, including the Hapsburg fiefs, accepted the Protestant Reformation in the sixteenth century, but the countryside remained divided between Catholics and Protestants, as it has to the present. When the Holy Roman Empire was organized, the Swabian territories were included in the Swabian Circle, which included most of the present Swabian region.

During the French Revolution in the late eighteenth century, the Swabians were forced to choose as Europe descended into war. Baden and Wurttemberg initially joined the Allies fighting Napoleon and French expansion but were later forced by French pressure to switch sides at the Peace of Luneburg in 1801. Napoleon in 1806 raised the duke of Baden to the title grand duke and the duke of Wurttemberg to the status of king. Most of the small Swabian ecclesiastic and feudal holdings were annexed by Baden, Wurttemberg, and Bavaria. Baden and Wurttemberg again switched sides before Napoleon's final defeat and participated in the Congress of Vienna as victorious states. Massive Swabian migration to eastern Europe, particularly Galicia and Bukovina, reinforced earlier German migrations to the region.

French influence in Swabia, always strong, resulted in the adoption of liberal constitutions. The social and cultural life of the Swabian states reflected their ties to the West, while conservative Prussia held sway in most of the German states. Anti-Prussian sentiment, which remains today, resulted from heavy-handed Prussian pressure to join the Zollverein, the German Customs Union in 1835, and the suppression of popular revolutions during the upheavals of 1848–49. Between 1849 and 1851 tens of thousands of Swabians emigrated to escape grinding poverty or domination by the hated Prussians. In 1866 Baden and Wurttemberg sided with the Austrians* in the Austro-Prussian War and shared Austria's defeat. The south German states were forced to pay large indemnities and to sign military alliances with Prussia.

Prussian influence increased, and in 1870 Baden and Wurttemberg joined the North German Confederation and, a year later, the Prussian-dominated German

Empire. The Swabians fought as Prussian allies in the Franco-Prussian War of 1870–71, although many Swabians felt that they had more in common with the neighboring French than with the Protestant Prussians of eastern Germany. Prussia, with 65% of the German Empire's area and 62% of its population, was able to exert enormous pressure on the smaller German states. In 1890 the German Empire became more militaristic under the rule of Emperor William II, who was very unsympathetic to the Catholic-dominated southern German states.

In 1914 the armies of Baden and Wurttemberg joined those of the other German states in war against the Allies. The Swabians, whose territory lay on the border with France, felt they would lose no matter who won the war, but with initial German victories, war fever blunted Swabian misgivings. Following a French air raid on the Badenese capital, Karslruhe, in 1916, the Badanese government attempted to secede from the empire and to negotiate a separate peace with the Allies but was prevented by Prussian troops.

As defeat for the Central Powers loomed in October 1918, strikes and anti-Prussian rioting erupted across the region. Strong movements for secession from Germany gained support, but in November the German government surrendered. Revolution swept Swabia, and the rulers of Baden and Wurttemberg were deposed. Provisional republican governments were formed in Karlsruhe and Stuttgart. An attempted communist coup in Berlin had local repercussions as separatism again gained support. The French, who saw the breakup of the German Empire as a solution to their security problem, supported separatism in Baden and Wurttemberg, but in 1919 the two states joined the new Weimar Republic, a new federation dominated by Prussia. In 1921 membership in monarchist organizations was made a criminal offense.

Throughout the turbulent 1920s and 1930s the Swabians continued to oppose Prussian domination of the German Federal Republic, and anti-Prussian sentiment remained a strong ingredient in the Swabian nationalist movement, which continued until the early 1930s. The rise of the Nazis in Germany was also resisted. The Swabians, with their long tradition of stable democracy, included one of only five districts in Germany to elect stable, democratic parties to state governments in the postwar period. In 1933, when Adolf Hitler came to power, on the pretext that the Baden and Wurttemberg state governments were unable to maintain order, he sent in SS and SA troops to quell the remaining Swabian opposition. Many of the Swabian opposition leaders were sent to concentration camps, while others fled across the frontier into France.

In the late 1930s the Swabians, along with the other German peoples, supported Hitler's nationalist, anticommunist crusade. Air raids and heavy fighting in the northern districts devastated Swabia, especially the cities of Mannheim, Karslruhe, and Heidelberg. In early 1945 Baden and Wurttemberg were occupied by French and American troops.

Following the German surrender, the region was divided into new states, Baden, Wurttemberg-Baden, and Wurttemberg-Hohenzollern. In 1952 the states were united to form the new state of Baden-Wurttemberg. Stuttgart, the Swabian capital since 1482, was chosen as the capital of the new, united Swabian state.

Swabia formed an important element in the postwar German economic recovery. The culture of the region in the postwar years became less Swabian and took on more of the Pan-German culture. Standard German became the language of the cities. The industrialized cities of the region were rebuilt and were among the most prosperous in Germany in the 1960s and 1970s.

In the 1970s the Swabians began to take a new interest in their unique culture and dialects. Centuries of close contact with the French and other nations on their borders made the Swabians among the most enthusiastic for closer European integration in the 1970s and 1980s. The Swabian cultural revival and the growth of regionalist sentiment grew from the rivalry between the northern and southern German states in the late 1980s. The Swabians, unlike the northern Germans with their aging heavy industries and high unemployment, consistently had the lowest unemployment in Germany and very high economic growth, with only the Bavarians surpassing them.

The Swabians continue to press for more autonomy and a greater say in the European Union (EU). Nationalists and regionalists cite the medieval Swabian Leagues as the model for a sovereign Swabia within united Europe. Swabians generally oppose moving the federal capital from Bonn to Berlin, fearing a return of Germany's former centralized government.

SELECTED BIBLIOGRAPHY

Craig, Gordon A. *The Germans*. 1991.

Elias, Norbert, ed. *The Germans: Power Struggles and the Development of Habitus in the Nineteenth and Twentieth Centuries*. 1996.

Gress, D. R. *A History of West Germany, 1945–1988*. 1989.

Shlaes, Amity. *Germany: The Empire Within*. 1991.

Todd, Malcolm, ed. *The Early Germans*. 1995.

SWEDES

Suedes

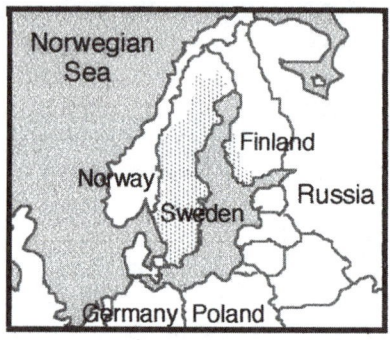

POPULATION: Approximately (2000 e) 8,496,000 Swedes in Europe, 8,090,000 in Sweden, 338,000 in Finland, and other sizable groups in Norway, Denmark, and Germany. Outside Europe large Swedish communities, totaling over 1 million, live in the United States, Canada, and Australia.

THE SWEDISH HOMELAND: The Swedish homeland occupies the eastern part of the Scandinavian Peninsula in Northern Europe and includes the large islands of Gotland and Öland in the Baltic Sea. Sweden is roughly divided into two geographical areas, the north, called Norrland, comprising about two-thirds of the country, which is mountainous except for a narrow coastal strip on the Gulf of Bothnia, and the south, Svealand and Götaland, mostly low-lying plains. About 55% of the total land area is forested, and only 8% is arable. The region is drained by a number of rivers and contains several large lakes. The plains of Scania occupy the southeastern tip of the Scandinavian Peninsula. Sweden is the largest of the Scandinavian countries in both area and population.

Sweden is one of the oldest of the European states and once controlled a vast empire in Northeastern Europe. *Kingdom of Sweden (Konungariket Sverige)*: 173,665 sq.mi.–449,792 sq.km. (2000 e) 8,831,000—Swedes (including Scanians*) 91%, Finns* 3%, Croats,* Greeks,* Danes,* Norwegians,* Samis.* The Swedish capital and major cultural center is Stockholm, (2000 e) 624,000 (metropolitan area 1,546,000), which is built on fourteen islands and is often called the "Venice of the North."

FLAG: The Swedish national flag, the official flag of the kingdom, is a blue field bearing a yellow Scandinavian cross.

PEOPLE: The Swedes are a Scandinavian people, related to the Danes, Norwegians, and other Scandinavian peoples of Northern Europe. Tall and often very fair and with light eyes, the Swedes are descended from the early Vikings, the Norsemen of European history. Most of the Swedes live in the more temperate southern provinces where the largest cities, Stockholm, Göteborg, and Malmö are located. Virtually all Swedes, about 94%, belong to the Evangelical Lutheran Church, whose metropolitan see is in the ancient university city of Uppsala. About 85% of the population is classified as urban.

The Swedish language is an East Scandinavian language of the North Germanic group of languages. The language is spoken in five major dialects, Northern, Central, Southern, Eastern, and Dalecarlian, and a number of subdialects, all divided into two groups, the northern Göta group and the southern Svea dialect group. The literary language is based on the dialect spoken in Svealand. The language is written in the Roman alphabet, with the addition of three symbols, å, ä, and ö.

NATION: The Swedes are believed to have lived in southern Sweden, their present homeland, for at least 5,000 years, longer than any other European nation. In early historic times, Svealand was inhabited by the Svear, mentioned in the first century A.D. by the Roman historian Tacitus as the Suiones. The Svear, also called Sviones, engaged in long wars with their southern neighbors in Götaland, the Gothones, traditionally, the ancestors of the Goths. The two tribes, although united by religious beliefs, were generally at war with each other. By the sixth century A.D. the Svear had conquered the Götar or Goths, with whom they merged.

The early Swedish tribes were often combined with other Scandinavian tribes in groups of piratical raiders called Vikings or Norsemen. From the ninth to the eleventh centuries, the Vikings plundered areas of Europe to the south and east of the Scandinavian Peninsula. The Swedes alone, known as Varangians, extended their influence over northern Russia and as far away as the Black Sea. Before the tenth century, details of Swedish history are obscure.

The Swedes often warred with their Danish and Norwegian neighbors but were usually divided into tribes and clans that precluded the unification of the region. St. Ansgar introduced the Swedes to Christianity, traditionally in A.D. 829, but traditional religious beliefs remained in force until the twelfth century. The introduction of Christianity allowed the Swedish tribes to unite in a loose confederation under an elected king in the eleventh and twelfth centuries. In the twelfth century the Christian Swedes began to expand their conquests to the pagan east, particularly in Finland. The authority of the Swedish king was weakened in the thirteenth century by the rise of an independent feudal class. The Swedish cities also began to acquire wide rights at that time and were strongly influenced by the Hanseatic League.

Originally, all the inhabitants of the Scandinavian region spoke a common language, known as Dansk tunga, or Danish tongue, even before the early Middle Ages. The Swedish branch of this common tongue developed into a separate language during the period from the tenth to the sixteenth centuries and is called

Old Swedish. Until after 1200 the only records of the language are runic inscriptions, cut primarily on tombstones and memorial stones. The Latin alphabet was introduced in the thirteenth century; periods of further differentiation followed, and some approximation to Danish occurred. The written language, based on two of the most widely spoken dialects, was made uniform throughout all of Swedish territory in the fourteenth century.

Feudalism became the controlling influence in the Swedish lands in the thirteenth and fourteenth centuries. As the power of the monarch waned, that of the wealthy aristocracy grew. In 1319 much of Scandinavia was united under Magnus VII, but in 1389 the Swedish nobles forced Albert of Mechlenburg to renounce the throne, which was given to Margaret I, queen of Denmark and Norway. In 1397 Queen Margaret united the crowns of Sweden, Norway, and Denmark through the Union of Kalmar. Margaret's successors were unable to control the Swedes, and real power in Sweden was held for long periods by regents, particularly of the noble Sture family, chosen by the Swedish diet. King Christian II of Denmark in 1520 ordered a massacre of Swedish nobles at Stockholm, which stirred strong Swedish resistance to Danish rule. In 1523 the Swedes chose Gustavus Vasa, the founder of the modern Swedish state, as their king. Lutheranism was established as the state religion in the 1520s.

King Gustavus eliminated the influence of the Hanseatic League and strengthened the authority of the monarchy. In 1544 he made the kingship hereditary in the Vasa dynasty and made Lutheranism the official state religion. Under his rule the Swedes began a campaign of territorial expansion. In 1558 the Swedes took territory from the Danes in the south and moved east to conquer the Estonians* in 1561, the Karelians* and Ingrians* in 1617, and the Livonians* and Latvians* in 1629. Participation in the Thirty Years' War won the Swedes additional territory in the Baltic Sea and on the German mainland and made Sweden the leading Protestant power in Europe. Swedish colonial expansion, New Sweden in North America, proved short-lived, but the kingdom expanded its territories in Germany and Poland in the seventeenth century.

Swedish expansion in the north was contested by Russia, and in 1700 war between the two states broke out. In 1709 the Swedes were completely routed by the Russians at the Battle of Poltava, which marked the collapse of the Swedish kingdom and its replacement by Russia as the dominant power in the Baltic region. The Northern War, which lasted for twenty-one years, finally ended in Swedish defeat and the loss of much territory to Russia, the German states, and Poland. Relations with Russia dominated Swedish politics during most of the eighteenth century, with distinct factions favoring aggressive or conciliatory policies in relations with their powerful neighbor to the east.

King Gustavus IV, who ruled from 1792 to 1809, was a despotic leader who restored the absolute power of the monarchy and involved Sweden in the Napoleonic Wars and renewed war with Russia. He was overthrown in 1809, when Sweden lost Finland to Russia, and a constitutional monarchy was established.

From 1810 Swedish affairs were handled by one of Napoleon's generals, the adopted heir of King Charles XIII, who led the Swedes against Napoleon in 1813 and participated in the Congress of Vienna at the head of a victorious state. The congress compensated Sweden for the loss of Finland by uniting Sweden and Norway in personal union under the Swedish crown. When the fighting ended in 1814, the Swedish kingdom proclaimed its perpetual neutrality.

The nineteenth century was one of progressive liberalization in government and social legislation. Notable legislation established freedom of the press in 1844 and enfranchised the growing middle class in 1865. The rapid industrial growth of the latter nineteenth century was accompanied by the rise of the Social Democratic Party, which later dominated Swedish politics in the twentieth century. Extreme rural poverty was met by mass emigration. Between 1870 and 1914 about 1.5 million Swedes emigrated, mostly to the United States and Canada.

The early twentieth century brought great changes to the Swedish nation. Relations with the Norwegians were strained throughout the nineteenth century, and in 1905 the union of Norway and Sweden was peacefully dissolved. The country, among the most progressive in Europe, passed a series of welfare legislation, including taxpayer suffrage and workmen's compensation. On the basis of its neutrality, the kingdom averted participation in World War I and World War II, although the Swedish government's relations with the German government during World War II are still a matter of suspicion and speculation.

At the end of World War II, Sweden's traditional neutrality precluded inclusion in the newly formed North Atlantic Treaty Association (NATO) in 1949 or the economic and political association that later became the European Union (EU) in the 1950s. The conviction of many Swedish military leaders that the state would be unable to preserve its neutrality in the event of another general war in Europe prompted many Swedes to question the traditional policy of neutrality. In March 1957 a report issued by twelve Swedish defense experts recommended that the armed forces be equipped with atomic arms.

Expensive social welfare schemes in the 1960s and 1970s slowed economic expansion and led to unemployment and social unrest. The Swedes remained carefully neutral during the long decades of the Cold War, but the country continued to decline economically. Swedish opposition to the war in Vietnam damaged relations with the United States beginning in the late 1960s; many young U.S. opponents of the war received political asylum in Sweden. Criticism of American military actions by Prime Minister Palme in 1972 brought U.S.-Swedish diplomatic relations to the verge of severance until 1974. The Social Democrats, usually in coalition, continued to govern the country, and the prime minister, Olaf Palme, was assassinated in 1986, which marked a turning point in Swedish history.

Sweden continues to have a wide-ranging welfare state, but many Swedes in the 1980s and 1990s were concerned about the high cost of the state services and the high taxes they must pay to support the schemes. However, the Swedes have the highest fertility rate in the European Union (EU) and the highest rate of births outside wedlock, with over 50% of all children born to unwed mothers.

In 1991 the Social Democrats, who had created the Swedish welfare state, were defeated by a coalition of center and right-wing parties, which favored cutting government spending. The Social Democrats returned to power in the 1994 elections and vowed to reform the welfare state and bring Sweden closer to the other European states. The end of the Cold War following the collapse of the Soviet Union in 1991 forced the Swedes to rethink their treasured neutrality. Swedish voters approved membership in the European Union on 13 November 1994, and Sweden became a full member of the EU on 1 January 1995.

In elections during the 1990s, particularly in 1998, the traditional political parties, the Social Democrats and the moderates, were increasingly challenged by the Left, which became the third largest political group in Sweden. The Swedes' adhesion to the EU has allowed more latitude in political expression after decades of neutrality during the Cold War.

SELECTED BIBLIOGRAPHY

Barton, H. Arnold. *A Fold Divided: Homeland Swedes and Swedish Americans, 1840–1940.* 1994.

Dohlman, Ebba. *National Welfare and Economic Interdependence: The Case of Sweden's Foreign Trade Policy.* 1989.

Fleisher, Wilfrid. *Sweden, the Welfare State.* 1973.

Misgeld, Klaus. *Creating Social Democracy: A Century of the Social Democratic Labor Party in Sweden.* 1993.

Sather, L. B., and Alan Swanson. *Sweden.* 1987.

SWISS-GERMANS

Schwyzerdütsch; Schwytzertuetsch

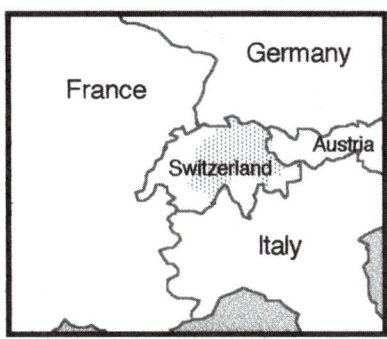

POPULATION: Approximately (2000 e) 4,807,000 Swiss-Germans in Europe, 4,651,500 in German Switzerland and small communities in other parts of Switzerland, Austria, and Germany. Large Swiss-German communities outside Europe are located in the United States, Canada, Argentina, and Brazil.

THE SWISS HOMELAND: The Swiss-German homeland lies in West-Central Europe, mostly a region of highlands known as the Swiss Plateau, which contains four-fifths of the Swiss population. The Rhine River and the Lake of Constance (Bodensee) separate the region from Germany in the north, and on the south and east are the high peaks of the Swiss Alps. The Swiss Alps are part of the largest mountain system in Europe and are famous for their jagged peaks and steep gorges. The region has many lakes, the largest being Zürichsee, Lake Zurich, the Lake of Lucerne, and the Thunersee. Much of the region is upland pasture, with dairy herds and truck farming, and fruit growing.

The region, German Switzerland or Schwyzerdütschland, forms the parts of Switzerland that are made up of German-speaking cantons of Aargau, Appenzell Ausser Rhoden, Appenzell Inner Rhoden, Baselland, Baselstadt, Bern, Glarus, Luzern (Lucerne), Nidwalden, Obwalden, Santk Gallen (St. Gall), Schaffhausen, Schwyz, Solothurn, Thurgau, Uri, Zug, Zurich, the eastern districts of Valais and Fribourg, and the northern and central districts of Graübunden (the Grisons). *German Switzerland (Schwyzerdütschland/Schweiz)*: 10,228 sq.mi.–26,490 sq.km. (2000 e) 4,954,000—Swiss-Germans 92%, Romands* 3%, Yugoslavs 2%, Spaniards* 2%, Italians,* Portugese,* Turks.* The Swiss German capital and major cultural center is Zurich, (2000 e) 342,000 (metropolitan area 827,000), a center of finance and manufacturing. Other important Swiss-German cultural centers include Bern (2000 e) 128,000 (metropolitan area 307,000), the capital of the Swiss Federation.

FLAG: The Swiss-German flag, the official flag of the Swiss Federation, is a square red field bearing a centered white cross.

PEOPLE: The Swiss-Germans are an Alemannic German people, a distinct national group ethnically and culturally closely related to the neighboring Swabians* and Vorarlbergers.* Mainly a mixture of Alpine and Nordic heritage, the Swiss-Germans are separated from Europe's other Germanic nations by their unique culture and dialects and by centuries of a distinct history. The culture of the Swiss-Germans and Vorarlbergers is a distinctive Alpine culture that developed in the mountain valleys and the highlands of the Swiss Plateau. The culture was strong enough for the Vorarlbergers to resist the baroque style so popular in the Austrian Empire. The Swiss-Germans and their Vorarlberger kin clung to the unique Alpine style in rebellion against what they saw as the extravagances of the Hapsburgs. The Swiss-Germans, except the Vorarlbergers, who are mostly Roman Catholic, are divided almost evenly between Protestants and Roman Catholics. About 68% of the Swiss-Germans are classified as urban.

The Swiss-German language, called Schwyzerdütsch, is actually a group of twenty to seventy related dialects that belong to the Alemannic group of German languages. The major Swiss-German dialects are the Bernese, Zurich, Luzern, Basil, and Obwald dialects. The dialects, which differ from canton to canton, have a strong social function, as they maintain the cantonal borders and strongly differentiate the Swiss-Germans from the neighboring Germanic nations. The majority of the Swiss-Germans also speak standard High German, although about 94% speak the Swiss-German dialects as the language of daily life, and 66% speak dialects only. Standard German is the official language, but Schwyzerdütsch is increasingly used in education and religion.

NATION: Celtic tribes, the Helvetii and other Alpine tribes, occupied the region during the Celtic expansion across most of Europe. In 58 B.C., during the Gallic Wars of Roman emperor Augustus, the Celtic tribes were conquered, and the region was incorporated into the Roman Empire as part of the province of Rhaetia. The region prospered under Roman rule, and many of the cities of the present region began as Roman towns or forts.

The collapse of Roman power was followed by invasions of Germanic tribes from the north in the fifth century, particularly the Alemanni, whose language and culture became predominant. In the sixth century the region passed to the control of the Franks. In 843, at the dissolution of Charlemagne's Frankish Empire among his sons, the region was included in the Swabian territory of Louis the German and in 1033 became part of the Holy Roman Empire under the rule of noble feudal families.

The rise of the powerful Hapsburg family supplanted the feudal rulers from the thirteenth century. The Hapsburgs acquired most of the region piece by piece between the thirteenth and sixteenth centuries. Hapsburg encroachments on the traditional privileges of the three small, mountainous territories of Uri, Schwyz, and Underwalden resulted in the conclusion of a defensive league, the Everlasting League of Forest Cantons, among the three. The legend of William Tell springs from the defiance of the so-called Forest Cantons against their Austrian rulers. In 1308 the league revolted against Hapsburg rule and in 1315 defeated the Austrians* at Morgarten. Luzern, called Lucerne in English, joined the league in 1332. Enlarged by the inclusion of the territories of Zurich, Zug, Glarus, and Bern, the League decisively defeated the Hapsburg forces in 1386 and 1388.

By the fifteenth century the Swiss Confederation had become a major European military power. Hapsburg territories, including Aargau and Thurgau, were conquered and ruled as subject territories. Solothurn and Fribourg joined the confederation in 1481. The Swiss were victorious against the Burgundians* and later against the forces of Emperor Maximilian I, who granted the confederation virtual independence in 1499. Basel joined in 1501 and Appenzell in 1513, bringing the number of cantons to thirteen, which stayed constant until 1798.

The Protestant Reformation in German Switzerland started in 1518, when a country pastor named Huldreich Zwingli began to denounce the sale of indulgences by the Roman Catholic Church. Subsequently, under Zwingli's leadership, the inhabitants of the city of Zurich revolted against church dogma by burning relics, banning the adoration of saints, and releasing clerics from their vows of celibacy. Vigorously backed by the merchant class, such innovations further asserted the city's independence from both the Roman Catholic Church and the Holy Roman Empire. Other Swiss towns, such as Basel and Bern, quickly adopted similar reforms.

Because of their skill and bravery in war, Swiss mercenaries became famous throughout Europe. In the course of the wars between Italy and France in the early sixteenth century, Swiss troops, fighting with the French as mercenaries, were able to annex the Italian districts and towns that later formed the canton of Ticino. The Swiss troops then fought against the French and were defeated in 1515. This led to the introduction of Switzerland's neutrality policy. In 1536 the Bernese Swiss took Lausanne and various territories from the Savoyards.*

The conquest of Vaud by the Bernese and close alliances with other free cities and regions, including St. Gall, the Grisons, and Geneva, increased Swiss political power, but the confederation's military power was broken by a French* victory in 1515. A "perpetual alliance" with France, signed in 1516, and neutrality became the basis of confederation policy. Swiss mercenaries, however, continued to serve in many European armies, including those of the papacy.

The Swiss cantons, although united by history, culture, and their German dialects and bound by a federal diet and by individual treaties, were often torn by internal feuds and dissension, and the confederation was seriously split by the Protestant Reformation. The Catholics, led by the leaders of the Four Forest Cantons of Uri, Schwyz, Unterwalden, and Lucerne, defeated the Protestant Swiss forces in battle. The Treaty of Kappel in 1531 preserved Roman Catholicism in the Forest Cantons, Zug, Fribourg, and Solothurn. National unity nearly disappeared over the next 200 years, but the Swiss cantons remained carefully neutral throughout the Thirty Years' War, which devastated Europe. At the end of the war in 1648, the Swiss Confederation's independence was formally recognized by the Peace of Westphalia.

In the late seventeenth and eighteenth centuries, powerful oligarchies formed the governments of many of the cantons and remained prosperous, while the farmers and peasants became poorer. The confederation lost its remaining political power in eighteenth century but remained an island of prosperity in Europe while developing as an intellectual and cultural center.

The cantonal oligarchies opposed the liberalization of the French Revolution but were unable to stop the invading French in 1798. The French deposed the cantonal rulers and joined the individual cantons in the Helvetic Republic. Napoleon's Act of Mediation in 1803 partially restored the old confederation, and in 1815 the Congress of Vienna confirmed the reestablishment of the confederation, with the addition of nine new cantons, many with non-Germanic populations. By the terms of the Treaty of Paris in 1815, the neutrality of the new, multiethnic confederation was guaranteed for all time.

A severe economic depression in the nineteenth century caused large-scale emigration to North and South America, and generally reactionary rule in many of the Swiss German cantons gave rise to the Radical Party, which favored greater governmental centralization. Opposition to centralization centered in the Catholic rural cantons, which in 1845 formed the Sonderbund defensive alliance. After a brief and almost bloodless civil war in 1847, the victorious Radicals transformed the confederation into one federal state under a new constitution.

The national unity of the multinational Swiss Confederation was reconfirmed by a revised constitution in 1874. Much social legislation was passed, and the Swiss cantons prospered as manufacturing and banking centers. Armed neutrality, the Swiss policy since 1815, kept the small confederation out of the continuing European wars, including World War I. However, after World War I, Switzerland joined the League of Nations.

The Swiss were again neutral during World War II, although revelations about Swiss ties to Nazi Germany continue to surface. After the war the Swiss were excluded from the new United Nations because its charter makes Swiss membership impossible without some modification of the strict Swiss interpretation of neutrality. In 1959 the Swiss Confederation became a member of the European Free Trade Association (EFTA) and in 1972 signed an industrial free-trade agreement with the expanding European Economic Community (EEC), later the European Union (EU). In February 1971 women, for the first time, were allowed to vote in federal elections and to hold federal office.

From the 1950s the French-speaking inhabitants of the western district of Bern Canton agitated, with some violence, for separation from the German-speaking majority. The desire of the inhabitants of the Jura region to separate opened the first serious divisions between the two largest of the Swiss nationalities, the

Swiss-Germans and the French-speaking Romands. In 1978 the majority French-speaking districts of northwestern Bern voted to form a new canton called Jura, but the separatists failed to win enough votes in the mixed districts around Lake Bienne (Biel). The controversy opened a bitter rift between the French and German cantons of Switzerland.

The economic realities of post–Cold War Europe propelled the Swiss into closer cooperation with their European neighbors. In May 1992 the Swiss government formally applied for membership in the European Economic Community (EEC) and in December held a referendum on a joint EEC-EFTA trading area. To the chagrin of the pro-European Romands, the referendum was defeated due to the majority opposition of the Swiss-Germans.

The growing popularity of the People's Party among the Swiss-Germans has reinforced their growing sense of national identity. The political party, which is anti-European Union and against immigration to Switzerland, has had success challenging the traditional hold of the Christian Democratic Party on the Swiss German cantons.

The growing split between the two largest national groups in Switzerland has exacerbated the perception that the German Swiss are increasingly usurping Swiss identity and shunting the non-Germans to the margins of Swiss political life. The so-called fried potato ditch, the *Rösti-Graben*, has become more than just the imaginary line dividing the two largest of the Swiss national groups. For centuries Swiss identity has been defined in negative terms, not German, not French, not part of any international organization, but in the late twentieth century the Swiss-Germans are being forced to reevaluate their traditions and national identity as a distinct European nation.

SELECTED BIBLIOGRAPHY

Bonjour, Edgar, ed. *Short History of Switzerland.* 1985.
Hilowitz, J. B. *Switzerland in Perspective.* 1991.
Mayer, K. B. *The Population of Switzerland.* 1982.
Steinberg, Jonathan. *Why Switzerland?* 1996.
Murray, J. L. *History of Switzerland.* 1985.

SZEKLARS

Szekely; Szekelers

POPULATION: Approximately (2000 e) 1,825,000 Szeklars in Europe, 1,774,000 in the Transylvania region of Romania, with other communities in Hungary.

THE SZEKLAR HOMELAND: The Szeklar homeland lies in East-Central Europe in a highland region plateau called the Transylvanian Basin, an eastern extension of the Great Hungarian Plain, which rises to the Transylvanian Alps and the Eastern Carpathian Mountains in the east and south. In the west are the Western Carpathians, including the Bihor, Apusem, Trascau, and Metaliferi Mountains. The Transylvanian Plateau, 1,000 to 1,600 feet (305 to 488 m.) high, is drained by the Muresul River and other tributaries of the Danube.

The Szeklar region of Transylvania has no official status and forms a number of administrative counties of the Romanian republic. Historically, the Szeklars constituted one of the three privileged nations of Transylvania. *Transylvania (Erdély)*: 21,292 sq.mi.–55,146 sq.km. (2000 e) 6,824,000—Romanians* 48%, Szeklars 26%, Roms* (Gypsies) 14%, Magyars (Hungarians*) 7%, Germans* 3%, Serbs,* Tatars,* Ukrainians*. The Szeklar capital and major cultural center is Cluj-Napoca, called Kolozsvár in Hungarian, (2000 e) 322,000, the historic capital of Transylvania.

FLAG: The Szeklar national flag, based on the colors of the flag of the Hungarians, is a horizontal tricolor of red, green, and white.

PEOPLE: The Szeklars, who call themselves Székely, came into Transylvania either with or before the Magyars, the Hungarians. Their traditional organization and hierarchy were of the Turkic type, and the Szeklars were probably of Turkic origin, possibly related to the Avars.* The Szeklar culture is basically Hungarian, with Szeklar traditions and customs surviving mostly in isolated communities; however, the Szeklars remain a separate nation and are recognized by the Romanian government as a distinct national group.

The language of the Szeklars is a dialect of Hungarian, which they adopted by the eleventh century. Their dialect, called Szekely, is the easternmost of the Hungarian dialects and comprises many borrowings from Romanian, German, and Turkish. It is not inherently intelligible to speakers of standard Hungarian, which is also spoken by the Szeklars.

NATION: The Transylvanian highlands formed part of the Roman province of Dacia, with Latin culture and speech predominant in the region. From the third century A.D. the region was overrun by tribes moving into the weakened Roman Empire. The Visigoths, Huns, Gepidae, Avars, and Slavs moved across the region, destroying Roman culture, but not the Romans' language, which became the basis of the later Romanian language. Magyar tribes are thought to have entered the region in the fifth century.

In the ninth century, the Szeklars, Turkic-speaking tribes, were known to have settled the valleys of the east and southeast. It is not known whether they came into Transylvania with or before the Magyars. In 1003 the region, with its mixed population, was brought under the control of the Hungarian crown. By the eleventh century the Szeklars had adopted the Magyars' Hungarian speech and much of their culture. Wars with Bulgars* and Petchengs forced the majority of the Magyars to move farther west into present Hungary, leaving the Hungarianized Szeklars in the Transylvanian Basin to form the eastern districts of the Hungarian kingdom.

In the Middle Ages, Hungarian kings promoted the development of the region by inviting Germans to settle in the area. In the twelfth and thirteenth centuries, German colonists, called Saxons,* settled in the south and northeast. German influence among the Szeklars became more pronounced in the early thirteenth century, when King Andrew II of Hungary called on the German Teutonic Knights to protect Transylvania from the Cumans and, later, the Mongols. Large numbers of Romanians, called Vlachs, were living in the region by 1222, although the exact date of Romanian settlement is disputed. Originally seminomadic herders, they later settled as farmers.

The administration of Transylvania was headed by a royal governor, a vaivode, and society was divided into three privileged nations, the Szeklars, the Magyars, and the Saxons, and the nonprivileged class of serfs, mostly Vlachs. Following a Vlach peasant revolt in 1437, the three privileged nations renewed their historic alliance, and suppression of the Vlach peasants increased. The majority of the Szeklars formed part of the landed gentry, owning large estates worked by Vlach serfs, although a minority were urban dwellers.

The Szeklars, with their own military and civil organization, enjoyed broad autonomy under the Hungarian crown and were, without exception, regarded as of noble birth and were exempt from taxation. In the sixteenth century the majority of the Szeklars accepted the Protestant Reformation, most adopting

Calvinism as their religion, while others became Unitarians or remained Roman Catholic. The Turks defeated the Hungarians in 1526, and Transylvania was separated as an autonomous principality under Turkish protection and nominal Turkish rule.

The Báthory family, which came to power in Transylvania in 1571, ruled the region as princes under Ottoman, and briefly under Austrian Hapsburg, suzerainty until 1602. In 1604 Stephen Bocskay led a rebellion against Austrian rule, and in 1606 he was recognized by the Austrian emperor as prince of Transylvania. Under Bocskay's successors Transylvania experienced a golden age as the bulwark of Protestantism in Eastern Europe and the only European country where Roman Catholics, Calvinists, Lutherans, and Unitarians lived in relative peace and mutual tolerance. Only the Orthodox Vlachs were denied equal rights.

The Turkish defeat near Vienna in 1683 increased Austrian influence in the region, and in 1699 the Ottoman Empire ceded Transylvania to the Austrians.* The Szeklars vainly fought the growing Austrian authority, and a widespread Szeklar revolt delayed the creation of an Austrian civil government in the region. In 1711 the Szeklars were defeated, and Austrian control was firmly established.

The Austrians maintained the status of the three privileged nations, but during the eighteenth century their privileges declined. Austrian attempts to press the Szeklars into service as border militia met with widespread resistance. In 1763 a large number of Szeklars who sought to escape recruitment were massacred at Madefalva. Many Szeklars fled Austrian territory to settle in Bukovina and Moldavia under Turkish rule. In 1791 the Vlachs petitioned Emperor Leopold II for recognition as the fourth "nation" of Transylvania and for equality for their Orthodox religion, but the Transylvanian Diet rejected their petition.

The revolutionary upheavals of 1848 were greeted in Transylvania by a proclamation of the union of the region with Hungary. The proclamation, supported by the Magyars and Szeklars, was opposed by the Saxons, the Vlach Romanians, and the Austrians. The Szeklars and Magyars promised the Romanians abolition of serfdom in exchange for their support, but the Romanians rejected the offer, and a revolt spread among the Romanian peasants. In the fighting that followed in 1849, the Szeklars and Magyars were defeated and lost their remaining autonomy and privileges. Austrian military rule from 1849 to 1860 was disastrous for the Szeklars but greatly benefited the Romanian peasants, who were given lands confiscated from the defeated Szeklars and Magyars.

In the 1867 compromise, the *Ausgleich*, which established the equality of the Hungarian and Austrian nations within the Austro-Hungarian Empire, Transylvania became an integral part of Hungary. The Romanian population, forming about half the Transylvanian population, having enjoyed brief equality, was again reduced to the domination of the Szeklars and Magyars.

At the end of World War I, many parts of the defeated Austro-Hungarian Empire broke away to form separate independent states. The privileged nations of Transylvania attempted to erect an independent republic to perpetuate their own favored positions. The minority-dominated diet of Transylvania declared the independence of the province on 28 October 1918 but was opposed by the Allies and Romanian claims to the region on ethnic grounds and earlier Allied promises. The Transylvanian Romanians on 1 December 1918 declared the union of Transylvania and Romania, and Romanian troops invaded the region and suppressed the independence movement. By the terms of the Treaty of Trianon, Hungary formally ceded the entire region, including the Szeklar homeland, to Romania.

The Romanian government quickly moved to suppress the former privileged nations. The large estates were broken up, and holdings were limited to 300 acres, while holdings in the "old kingdom" Romania were allowed up to 1,250 acres. In 1921 the Szeklars, along with the Magyars and Saxons, complained of Romanian suppression of the 1,000-year-old Transylvanian institutions by Orthodox officials sent to the region from the east. In 1929 the government placed restrictions on language and religious rights in an attempt to assimilate the non-Romanian population.

When World War II broke out, both Hungary and Romania were allied to the Axis powers. In 1940, over strong Romanian protests, the Vienna Award gave Hungary about two-thirds of Transylvania, including the majority of the Szeklar districts. In 1944 war broke out between the two states, opening the way for the Soviet occupation of both countries.

A communist government installed in Bucharest at the end of the war moved to integrate the non-Romanian minorities; however, a small, autonomous region was created for the primarily Szeklar region in eastern Transylvania. During the 1956 Hungarian Revolution there was rioting in Szeklar and Magyar areas in support of the aims of the revolutionaries. The demonstrations led to executions and imprisonment in 1957 for the leaders accused of separatist plotting.

In 1967 relations between the Romanian and Soviet governments worsened, and the Soviets encouraged the Hungarian government to continue to pressure Romania over Transylvania and the Magyar and Szeklar minorities in the region. In 1971 the government prohibited the use of the ancient place-names and allowed only the Romanian names to be used. New decrees, passed in 1974, undermined the foundations of Transylvania's Szeklar and Magyar past. Hungarian-language schools and publications were forcibly closed.

In the 1980s, under Romania's communist dictator Nikolai Ceauşescu, new restrictions were placed on the non-Romanian minorities, and the government pressed assimilation. Those wishing to emigrate, particularly to Hungary, were forced to pay a heavy departure tax to compensate the Romanian state for education and public services. The tax was revoked only when the U.S. government threatened to end Romania's favored trading status. In October 1985 the government further curtailed Szeklar-Magyar cultural activities. The sorry state of the Romanian economy aggravated tensions in the region, as the Szeklars and Magyars tended to be more prosperous than the majority Romanians.

The Romanian government in mid-1988 announced plans to raze 8,000 Transylvanian villages and to rehouse their inhabitants in new, high-rise housing in nearby towns. The excuse, to free up much-needed agricultural lands, was disputed by the Szeklar-Magyar population, which charged the government with attempting to eradicate their ancient culture in the region. In August 1988 the communist presidents of Hungary and Romania met in an effort to solve the long-standing dispute over Transylvania, but relations between the two Warsaw Pact allies remained tense. By the end of 1988 the Hungarian government had taken in some 35,000 refugees from Romania, many of them ethnic Szeklars, who easily adjusted to life in Hungary.

In the late 1980s the Szeklars and Magyars of the region looked to liberalizing Hungary, as Romania remained under the Stalinist-style Ceauşescu regime. Decades of oppression and communist mismanagement had impoverished the potentially prosperous region, but Transylvania remained the most advanced of the Romanian regions. In December 1989 government attempts to silence a Magyar Protestant minister in the city of Timisoara, in the southwestern region of Banat, sparked a revolution that spread rapidly across Transylvania and the rest of Romania. Fighting and violence accompanied the overthrow of the Ceauşescu dictatorship.

The end of the communist suppression opened the old disputes in Transylvania with renewed demands for language, cultural, and religious rights. In March 1990 radical Romanian nationalists, formerly supported by the communist government, provoked attacks on Magyars and Szeklars in the city of Tirgu-Mures. The attacks were the most serious ethnic violence in Europe since World War II, superseded only by the later ethnic conflicts in the Balkans involving the Croats,* Serbs, and Bosnians.*

SELECTED BIBLIOGRAPHY

Joo, Rudolf, and Andrew Ludanyi. *The Hungarian Minority's Situation in Ceausescu's Romania.* 1994.

Lehrer, M. G. *Transylvania: History and Reality.* 1987.

Livezeanu, Irina. *Cultural Politics in Greater Romania: Regionalism, Nation Building, and Ethnic Struggle, 1918–1930.* 1995.

Treptow, Kurt W., and Marcel D. Popa. *Historical Dictionary of Romania.* 1996.

Verdery, Katherine. *Transylvanian Villagers: Three Centuries of Political, Economic, and Ethnic Change.* 1983.

TABASARANS

Tabassarans; Tabasaran Zhvi;
Tabasarantsy; Ghumghums

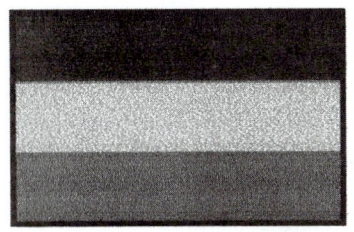

POPULATION: Approximately (2000 e) 119,000 Tabasarans in Europe, concentrated in the Dagestan Republic of southern European Russia.

THE TABASARAN HOMELAND: The Tabasaran homeland lies in the foothills of the high Caucasus Mountains of Dagestan near the Russian-Azeri border. The Tabasarans inhabit the valleys of the rivers that cut through the high mountains of the region, the Darvag, Rubas, Tshirakh-Tshay, and Karchag-Su Rivers. Some Tabasaran villages are in regions that are virtually inaccessible during the winter months. The region is traditionally divided into Upper and Lower Tabasaran, and the more favorable climatic conditions of Lower Tabasaran support the cultivation of industrial and garden crops, while the highlands are mostly used as pasture for herds of cattle, goats, and sheep. The Tabasaran homeland is watered by the Tshirakh-Tshay and Kurakh-Tshay Rivers.

The region, called Tabasaran, lies in the Tabasaran and Khiv Rayons of the Dagestan Republic. Due to migration to the lowlands, there is now a sizable Tabasaran population in Derbent Rayon on the Caspian Sea. Many of the Tabasaran settlements in the highlands remained isolated until the construction of a highway from Kashumkent to Khiv. The Tabasaran capital and major cultural center is the most important of the Tabasaran towns, Khiv, on the Tpig-Kashumkent Highway. The other major Tabasaran center is Khuchni, the capital of Tabasaran rayon.

FLAG: The flag used by the Tabasarans is the Dagestani national flag, a horizontal tricolor of green, pale blue, and red.

PEOPLE: The Tabasarans are a Caucasian people, and although there is little information about their origins, they are believed to be an indigenous nation of the Caucasus. Formerly, they were grouped together with the Lezgins,* Aguls,* and Rutuls,* but in recent decades they have asserted their separate ethnic identity. The small Tabasaran nation is divided into two groups, northern and southern, divided by habitat and dialect. The number of Tabasarans has grown rapidly since the Soviet census of 1979, when many ethnic Tabasarans registered as Lezgins or Azeris* for political reasons. After the Legzins, the Tabasarans are the second largest of the Lezgian-Samur peoples of the region. Like the other Lezgian nations, the Tabasarans are characterized by dark pigmentation, thin faces, and sharp features. In recent decades Tabasarans have been settling the lowlands around the city of Derbent.

The language of the Tabasarans belongs to the southeast group, the Samurian or Lezgi-Samur group, of the Caucasian languages. The language is spoken in two major dialects, North Tabasaran or Khanag and Tabasaran or South Tabasaran. The dialects correspond to the two major divisions of the Tabasaran nation. The literary language is based on the South Tabasaran dialect.

The Tabasarans are Sunni Muslims of the Shafi theological school. They are extremely devout, and like other nations of the region, they have been influenced by the religious fundamentalism of the 1990s. In spite of over seventy years of official atheism, the Tabasarans' fundamental religious institutes and traditions remain intact. Many pre-Islamic traditions have persisted, including celebrations of sowing and plowing, the worship of old trees, and superstitions about spirits and omens.

NATION: Little is known of the early history of the Tabasarans, although they were the first nation, along with the Lezgins, mentioned in the historical archives of the Armenians.* References to the Tabasarans go back to the Armenian historian Eghisgi in the fifth century, as one of the eleven nations inhabiting the vicinity of Derbent, and to the Armenian geography of the seventh century, where they appeared among a list of Caucasian peoples.

In the seventh century a small Tabasaran state emerged in the foothills of the Caucasus Mountains, which expanded in the twelfth century to form a *maisum* state, so named for the *maisum*, the ruler or governor. The state, known as the Maisumat of Tabasaran, became one of the three great political entities of medieval Dagestan. Between the thirteenth and fifteenth centuries, the Tabasarans came under the nominal rule of the Khanate of Derbent.

Throughout the centuries the Tabasarans have repelled numerous invaders of their homeland. Traditionally, they would withdraw to mountain strongholds, which proved too costly for invaders to attack. In the seventh century Arab invaders from the south introduced Islam, and Derbent became a major cultural and political center of the powerful Arab Empire. The Arabs were succeeded by the Seljuk Turks* in the tenth century, and in the thirteenth century the Mongols and Tatars* of the Golden Horde overran the region. By the sixteenth century, the Ottoman Turks dominated the region, and Islam became the majority religion. In the early eighteenth century, the Persians extended their influence in the region.

In the eighteenth and nineteenth centuries the Tabasarans were divided into two political entities, Upper Tabasaran and Lower Tabasaran. Upper Tabasaran was ruled by a *maisum*, and Lower Tabasaran was ruled by a *gadi*. In the eighteenth century, an estimated 7,000 people inhabited Upper Tabasaran, and 10,000 lived in Lower Tabasaran. The petty nobles and gentry, the *beks*, were granted powers and lands by the rulers and enjoyed unlimited powers. Some small communities in the high mountains existed as free communities ruled by a village elder and a village assembly. Traces of the kin-village system still remain in the highland Tabasaran communities.

In 1806 the Russians* took control of the Tabasaran homeland. Under Russian rule, the *beks* retained their feudal privileges and powers. Tabasaran resistance to Russian rule, led by Muslim teachers and leaders, grew and became part of the widespread Muslim rebellion that broke out in the region in 1816. Under the charismatic religious leader Iman Shamil, the Caucasian peoples of the region resisted the Russian advance in a bloody and often heroic war that continued for forty years. Many Tabasarans were either killed or forced to emigrate to Ottoman Turkish territory.

In 1860 the territories of both Tabasaran feudal units were united in a new political unit called Kaitag-Tabasaran. The new region was under the rule of a *naib* and a tsarist bureaucracy. Under the Russians, local village administrations were formed, and the traditional powers of the landlords, the *beks*, were ended. New crops were introduced, including fruit and wine grapes. Tabasaran carpets became internationally renowned. In the late nineteenth century, with the introduction of a cash economy, great changes took place in the Tabasaran social order. The patriarchal clan, the *tukhum*, began to disintegrate, and family units began to predominate. Social and family relations were regulated by *adat*, or customary law, and Sharia, Islamic law. This process accelerated in the twentieth century.

The isolated nation was little touched by World War I until the Russian Revolution. A conference of local Muslim leaders, attended by delegates of the Tabasarans and the other Muslim tribes, elected Mullah Gotinsky as their political and religious leader in May 1917, but the Bolshevik takeover of the Russian government in October 1917 created chaos in the region as local Bolsheviks attempted to take power. The Muslim peoples formed a separate republic in March 1918 and attempted a cooperative defense as the Russian civil war spread south. The anti-Bolshevik forces, the Whites, took control of the region in January 1919, but forced conscription of Muslims incited strong resistance. Promised local autonomy, the Dagestani peoples mostly went over to the Reds. The last of the defeated Whites withdrew from Tabasaran in January 1920.

The Dagestani leaders, representing a number of tribes, disappointed at their treatment by the Soviet authorities, demanded the promised autonomy. Rebuffed by the Soviets, the Dagestani nations rebelled and held out until finally subdued in May 1921, at a cost of over 5,000 Soviet casualties. A hypothetically autonomous Dagestani republic, created in early 1921, joined the new Soviet Russian

Federation. In 1925 the Soviets launched an antireligious campaign that included closing religious schools, eliminating the use of Arabic, and executing many local religious leaders.

In 1928 Tabasaran was made an official language in Dagestan. That year the Soviet authorities began to create a Latin alphabet for the Tabasaran language, but that program was abandoned in 1938, and the Russian Cyrillic alphabet was introduced. Gradually, over the next decades, the Russian language was imposed on education and local governments in Dagestan.

Under Soviet rule, the Tabasarans made rapid cultural and economic advancements during the period of Soviet consolidation. The area of cultivated land was rapidly expanded, new crops were introduced, and farming was mechanized. Collectivization of agriculture, completed in Dagestan in 1940, was a regression, and economic activity passed from private hands to the state. Ambitious programs, with little regard for local conditions or customs, were initiated and often failed.

In the 1950s and 1960s the Soviet authorities launched a program to increase wine production in the region. Whole Tabasaran villages were forcibly moved from the mountains to the plains to provide the needed manpower. The industrialization of the Tabasaran towns brought with it the problem of unemployment. Whole villages were abandoned. In 1926 only 1% of the Tabasarans lived in towns, but by 1959 the percentage had grown to 8.8%, and in 1970, 16.2% of the Tabasarans lived in urban areas. The urbanization of the Tabasarans challenged the traditional way of life as more consumer goods were purchased, and contact increased with people of other nations.

In the 1990s, following the collapse of Soviet power, the Tabasarans have begun to recover the lost parts of their culture. Suppressed by decades of Soviet rule, they have developed a fervent anti-Russian feeling. The use of the Russian language, except as a lingua franca, is declining, and an estimated 98% of the Tabasarans now use their own language as the language of daily life. A steadily increasing birthrate and the cultural and national revival of the 1990s seem to ensure the future of the small Tabasaran nation.

SELECTED BIBLIOGRAPHY

Benningsen, Alexandre, and S. Enders Wimbush. *Muslims of the Soviet Empire.* 1985.

Goldenberg, Suzanne. *Pride of Small Nations.* 1995.

Hewitt, B. G. *The Times Guide to the Peoples of Europe.* 1994.

Olson, James S., ed. *An Ethnohistorical Dictionary of the Russian and Soviet Empires.* 1994.

Wixman, Ronald. *Language Aspects of Ethnic Patterns and Processes in the North Caucasus.* 1980.

TALYSH

Talish; Tolish; Talush; Talyshi;
Talesh

POPULATION: Approximately (2000 e) 141,000 Talysh in Europe, mostly in the southern districts of Azerbaijan. An estimated 120,000 to 200,000 Talysh live in the adjoining regions of Iran.

THE TALYSH HOMELAND: The Talysh homeland, called Talyshtan, lies in Southeastern Europe on the geographical dividing line between Europe and Asia. Most of the region in the southern districts of Azerbaijan is flat plains between the Viliazh-Chai River, the Caspian Sea, and the Iranian border and includes the Talish Mountains along the Azeri-Iranian border. The region, called Talyshstan, lies along the Caspian Sea just east and south of the Narimanabad Peninsula and includes the subtropical region of the Lenkoran Lowlands in southeastern Azerbaijan and northern Iran.

Since the independence of Azerbaijan in 1991, many younger Talysh have rejected the assimilation projected by the Azeri government. New interest in their language and culture has spurred the formation of an autonomy movement with a small, but growing, separatist movement in the Talysh homeland in the south. Government figures estimate the Talysh population of Azerbaijan at less than 2% of the population, but nationalists claim a much higher number, some 11% of the total population of Azerbaijan. The different figures would seem to be based on language rather than ethnic origins. Nationalists claim that the combined Talysh population of Azerbaijan and Iran numbers over 2 million.

The region comprises four districts of the Republic of Azerbaijan, Astara, Lenkora, Lerik, and Masally. *Talyshstan*: 1,299 sq.mi.–3,364 sq.km. (2000 e) 218,000—Talysh 64%, Azeris* 33%, Iranians,* Russians.* The Talysh capital and major cultural center is Astara, (2000 e) 31,000, with its twin city, also called Astara, on the other side of the Iranian border. The other important Talysh cultural center is Lenkoran, (2000 e) 48,000, where Talysh have been settling in large numbers since the early 1980s.

FLAG: The Talysh national flag, the flag of the nationalist movement, is a horizontal bicolor of red over green bearing two white stars on darker squares near the hoist.

PEOPLE: The Talysh are an Iranian people of mixed Iranian and Caucasian ancestry known throughout Azerbaijan for their intellectual abilities and literacy. They tend to be more highly educated and more literate than the surrounding peoples. The Talysh culture, close to that of the Azeris, combines elements of Caucasian, Turkish, and Iranian origin but has retained customs and traditions not found among other groups in the region. Traditionally a rural people whose economy and culture revolved around cattle raising, the Talysh since the late 1970s have been urbanizing at a rapid rate. In 1979 only about 1% of the Talysh lived in towns, but by 1994 an estimated 22% lived in urban areas. The Talysh, like the majority of the Azeris and Iranians, are mostly Shi'a Muslims.

Talysh nationalists claim that the ethnic Talysh account for 11% of Azerbaijan's population, numbering about 835,000. The Azeri government claims that the Talysh make up under 2% of the total population. The difference is in language, as many ethnic Talysh during the Soviet era were forced to adopt Azeri as their first language. Increasingly, the Azeri-speaking Talysh are being drawn back into the revived Talysh culture and language. The language of the Talysh is a northwestern Iranian language with a strong admixture of Caucasian and Azeri borrowings. The language is spoken in four major dialects in Azerbaijan that roughly correspond to the four regions with Talysh majorities, Astarin, Lenkoran, Lerik, and Massalin. Under Soviet policies, the Talysh literary language disappeared, and Azeri is now used as the literary language. The majority are bilingual, speaking both Talysh and Azeri, and some are even trilingual, also speaking Russian or Iranian.

NATION: The Talysh are believed to be an ancient people, whose roots are in the Talish Mountains thousands of years ago. Nomadic Caucasian tribes as early as 1500 B.C. migrated south to settle the fertile plains and marshlands along the Caspian Sea. Traditionally, the Talysh economy revolved around cattle raising in the highlands. The Talysh culture evolved around the seasonal activities associated with their herds. In their early history, both Persian and Caucasian peoples settled in the mountains, and the Talysh evolved from the mixture of the two peoples.

By the sixth century B.C. most of the Talysh lands were included in a satrapy (province) of the ancient Persian Empire. Conquered by the Greeks of Alexander the Great in 334–331 B.C., the region later formed part of the Greek province of Media Atrophene. In the second century B.C. the Persians reconquered the Caspian region.

Muslim Arabs conquered the region in A.D. 641 and introduced Islam. From the coastal settlements, the new religion was carried into the Talish Mountains, and the Talysh tribes, over many decades, were finally converted. From the tenth century, Talyshstan formed part of the newly established linguistic and culture frontier between the Turkic peoples, who had conquered the territory to the north, and the Iranian peoples. Devastated by the Mongols in the thirteenth century and by the forces of Tamerlane a century later, Talyshstan had declined to a poor, backward region when the Persians regained control of the Caspian provinces in 1592.

English traders, moving south from Russia, reached Talyshstan in the late sixteenth century and opened trade routes to the west. Russian explorers and Cossacks, spearheading the Russian expansion into the Turkish and Persian lands, soon followed. Cossacks overran the Talysh lowlands in 1636 and caused considerable damage before withdrawing. In 1722 the Russians took Talyshstan from Persia and held the region for ten years, finally returning the region to Persia in exchange for territorial concessions in the Caucasus.

In the mid-eighteenth century Seid Abbas established the Talysh Khanate. His son inherited the throne in 1747 and expanded Talysh control to the lowlands. At his death in 1786, both Russia and Persia were competing for influence in the region. The Talysh resented Persian encroachments, and the khanate developed a pro-Russian policy. The Talysh khan, Mir-Mustafa, began appealing to the Russians for protection against the Persians in 1795, and in 1802 the Russian government proclaimed a protectorate over Talyshstan.

The Persians contested Russian influence in the region until they signed the Treaty of Turkmanchai, which recognized Russian authority in the region. The heartland of the Talysh khanate officially became Russian territory, and the political sovereignty of the Talysh was dissolved. Under British pressure, the Persian government delineated the northern border in the late nineteenth century, effectively dividing the Talysh nation between the Russian and Persian Empires.

In Persian Talyshstan, opposition to the excesses and neglect of the Persian monarchy erupted in open rebellion in 1905. A British–Russian agreement signed in 1907 divided the weak Persian state into spheres of influence. In 1909 Russian troops crushed the rebellions in northwestern Persia, which reformed as an anti-Russian movement in 1912. In 1917, with their country collapsing in revolution, the Russian troops withdrew from Gilan.

In 1920 the Soviets victorious in the Russian civil war, established control over the northern Talysh region. In May 1920 Soviet forces invaded Iran in support of the rebels fighting the Persian government. The rebels, aided by Soviet troops, declared the region independent of Persia as the Persian Soviet Socialist Republic, and a new government began to redistribute lands traditionally held by absentee Persian landlords, religious bodies, the Persian state, and the crown. The Talysh enthusiastically supported the Soviets in the hope that their divided nation would be reunited, but in 1921, in exchange for generous oil concessions, the Soviet forces were withdrawn, and the rebel republic collapsed. The border was reestablished, and Talyshstan remained divided.

Soviet policy encouraged the assimilation of the Talysh into the more numerous Azeri community. To further this aim, the authorities in 1939 abolished the Talysh Latin alphabet and replaced it with the Russian Cyrillic script, forcing those Talysh who were literate to turn to Azeri publications. Azeri, along with Russian, was the official language of the region, and education, local administration, and entertainment were all in Azeri. By 1959 relatively few people in the region identified themselves as Talysh. Soviet ethnographers assumed that the Talysh, as planned, were disappearing as a separate nation and were being absorbed by the more numerous Azeris, with whom they shared many cultural traits and their Shi'a Muslim religion.

The Soviet authorities, convinced that the Talysh had disappeared, did not try to count them in the censuses of 1970 or 1979; however, in the early 1980s agitation and demands for limited cultural freedom forced the authorities to reconsider. In the late 1980s it became increasingly clear that there was a core of Talysh who clung to their mother tongue and culture and refused to assimilate into either Azeri or the Russian-dominated Soviet culture. The reforms to Soviet society, introduced by Mikhail Gorbachev in 1987, allowed the Talysh to organize and loose a torrent of grievances. The Soviet authorities, forced to count the Talysh as a separate ethnic group in the 1989 Soviet census, were surprised to find that 21,914 people in the region registered themselves as Talysh.

Since the independence of Azerbaijan in 1991, many younger Talysh have rejected the assimilation projected by the Azeri government. New interest in their language and culture has spurred the formation of an autonomy movement with a small, but growing, separatist movement in the Talysh homeland. Government figures estimate the Talysh population of Azerbaijan at less than 2% of the population, but nationalists claim a much higher number, estimating that 11% of the total population of Azerbaijan is ethnic Talysh. The different figures would seem to be based on language rather than ethnic origins. Nationalists claim that the combined Talysh population of Azerbaijan and Iran numbers over 2 million.

SELECTED BIBLIOGRAPHY

Lenczowski, George. *Russia and the West in Iran 1918–1948: A Study in Big Power Rivalry*. 1968.
Olson, James S., ed. *An Ethnological Dictionary of the Russian and Soviet Empires*. 1994.
Swietochowski, Thadeusz. *Russia and Azerbaijan*. 1995.
Tapper, Richard, ed. *The Conflict of Tribe and State in Iran and Afghanistan*. 1983.
Wixman, Ronald. *The Peoples of the USSR: An Ethnographic Handbook*. 1984.

TATARS

Tatarians

POPULATION: Approximately (2000 e) 7,121,000 Tatars in Europe, 6,620,000 in Russia, and with smaller numbers in Belarus and Ukraine. Outside Europe, sizable Tatar communities live in Siberia, the Central Asian States, and the Russian Far East.

THE TATAR HOMELAND: The Tatar homeland lies in eastern European Russia, occupying the steppe lands, the low, rolling hills of the Volga and Kama River valleys. The Volga, Kama, Belaya, and Vyatka Rivers are important for both transportation and irrigation. In the east the region rises to wooded uplands. Rich in natural resources, Tatarstan is a leading producer of oil and natural gas and is the starting point for the Friendship pipeline to Eastern Europe. The republic has important deposits of brown coal, gypsum, dolomite, limestone, and marl.

Tatarstan, the heartland of the Tatar homeland, is a member state of the Russian Federation, although the Tatars refused to sign the treaty that established the federation on 31 March 1992. *Tatar Republic (Tatarstan)*; 26,255 sq.mi.–68,000 sq.km. (2000 e) 3,768,000—Tatars 51%, Russians* 40%, Udmurts* 4%, Chavash* 3%, Maris* 2%. The Tatar capital and major cultural center is Kazan, (2000 e) 1,109,000 (metropolitan area 1,238,000), on the Volga River.

FLAG: The Tatar national flag, the official flag of the republic, is a horizontal bicolor of red over green, the colors separated by a narrow white stripe.

PEOPLE: The Tatars are a Turkic nation of mixed ancestry. The name is derived from Tata or Dada, a Mongol tribe that originated in northeastern Mongolia in the fifth century. Extensive mixing with the Finnic and Slav peoples of the Volga River basin over the centuries has changed the physical aspect of the

Tatars, who are now European in culture and appearance. Since 1991 there has been an influx of Tatars from the other states of the former Soviet Union. Russia's largest non-Slav minority, the Tatars are the most northerly of the Muslim peoples, and the majority of the Tatars are Sunni Muslims; however, there is an important Orthodox Christian minority, called the Kreshen, who number about 320,000 and have helped to maintain historic Tatar ties to the neighboring Christian Finnic and Slav peoples. About 71% of the Tatars live in urban areas.

The language of the Tatars is a Uralian language of the Western Turkic language group of the Altaic languages. Spoken in three major dialects, Middle Tatar or Kazan, Western Tatar or Mishar, and Eastern Tatar or Siberian Tatar, the language is further divided into a number of subdialects and several mixed dialects, including Astrakhan, Kasim, Tepter, and Uralic. Assimilation, or Russification, government policy during the Soviet era had a special impact on language. Between 1959 and 1989 more than 8% of the Tatar population adopted Russian as their preferred language; however, since 1991 that trend has reversed.

NATION: Nomadic tribes, called the Tata, are thought to have originated in northeastern Mongolia in the fifth century A.D. Migrating west, the Tata mixed with the Kypchak and other Turkic peoples and first appeared in the lower Volga River basin in the eighth century. From the ninth to the twelfth centuries the Tatars formed a national state in the region with its capital at Bolgary Velikiye. Mixing with the Finnic, Slavic, and Bulgar peoples of the Volga region, the Tatars' physical aspect became more European with each generation. Traditionally, an embassy from the Muslim Caliphate in Baghdad came to the region in the year 922. A congress of the tribes met and adopted the new religion, Islam, as the state religion, replacing their ancient Turkic script with the Arabic of the Muslim emissaries.

The adoption of Islam and contacts with the Muslim peoples to the south stimulated a great explosion of art and learning. In 1212 the first extant work of Tatar literature, the epic poem *Tale about Yusuf* by Kul-Gali, was written.

In 1236 the Tatars were conquered and absorbed into the Golden Horde, and the Mongol armies that invaded Europe in the thirteenth century were largely composed of Turkic peoples. The Mongol and Turkic peoples of the Golden Horde merged and became known in Europe as Tatars. The invasion, led by Batu Khan, into Central Europe in 1241 is known as the Tatar invasion.

Following the disintegration of the enormous Mongol Empire, the Tatars established several successor states, such as the khanates of Astrakhan and Kazan. Kazan, founded as the capital of the Volga Tatars in 1401 in the Volga-Kama region, became the capital of the new Khanate of Kazan in 1445. In 1502 the Tatars defeated the remnant of the Golden Horde and expanded west to the Ural Mountains. The powerful khanate extracted tribute from the Slav states west of the Urals, including the Muscovite state, as the price for their continued independence. Rich on tribute and trade, the khanate fostered a great flowering of

Tatar culture, arts, and literature. In 1486 the khanate and the growing duchy of Moscow signed a treaty of eternal peace.

The Tatars' former vassals, the Russians, led by Ivan IV, called the Terrible, the grand duke of Moscow, ignoring the treaties between his state and the khanate, invaded and conquered the Tatar Kazan state in 1552–53. The Tatar capital, Kazan, finally fell following a two-month siege by Russian troops. The victorious Russians, as part of the official policy of suppressing Islam, tore down the city's main mosque and built an Orthodox cathedral on the same site. The Tatar Khanate of Astrakhan was conquered in 1556. Even though Ivan ruthlessly suppressed the Tatars' Islamic religion, the family of the last khan and the Tatar aristocracy were absorbed into the tsarist aristocracy, greatly facilitating the annexation of the vast region. The most advanced of the Turkic peoples, the Tatars became the middlemen between the imperial government and newly conquered Turkic peoples over the next three centuries. Tatar administrators and officials dispersed to many parts of the vast Russian Empire.

Stubborn Tatar resistance to Russification and forced conversion to Orthodox Christianity generated sporadic revolts and violence in the region in the seventeenth and eighteenth centuries. The Tatar revolts prompted a new imperial policy, the colonization of the vast Volga Basin by more reliable Christian Slavs. In 1708 Kazan became the center of the Slavic colonization of the Volga Basin. Persecution of the Muslims reached its peak in 1742, when new and more repressive laws were adopted. Thousands of Slav colonists settled in the area over the next century. The resilient Tatars, despite steady pressure to assimilate, tenaciously clung to their language and culture. Their Islamic religion, banned for two centuries, was again allowed during the reign of Catherine the Great in 1788.

The Volga Tatars by the 1880s had evolved a large middle class, the first Turkic people to do so. The high literacy rate and well-developed national culture stimulated a national revival in the late nineteenth century. The first openly nationalist group formed in 1906, advocating independence, socialism, and the expulsion of the Slavs from traditional Tatar lands.

Officially exempted from military conscription until 1916, the Muslim Tatars felt little of the effects of World War I until revolution swept the empire in February 1917. As civil government collapsed, Tatar nationalists and moderate Slav Mencheviks took control of the Volga region. Vehemently opposed to the atheism of the Bolsheviks following the October 1917 coup and threatened by advancing Bolshevik forces, the Tatar leaders declared independence on 24 January 1918. In April 1918 the Bolsheviks overran the breakaway state and suppressed the Tatar national movement.

Militarily allied to the anti-Bolshevik Czech Legion, freed prisoners of war, the nationalists routed the Bolsheviks in the region. With the other non-Russian peoples of the Volga, the Tatars formed a federation, the Idel-Ural Federation, which was declared independent on 30 September 1918. The expanding Russian civil war brought violence and destruction to the Tatar homeland as the Whites and Reds fought for control. In 1920 the victorious Soviets took control of the Tatar lands, which were absorbed into the new Soviet Russian Federation as an autonomous republic.

Although the Tatars were one of the largest nations of the new Soviet Union, they were not granted union republican status as were the Armenians,* Azeris,* Georgians,* Belarussians,* and Ukrainians* but were given only autonomous status within the autonomous Soviet Russian Federation. Soviet leader Joseph Stalin later reportedly spoke scornfully that the Tatars had as much chance of achieving union republic status as of seeing their ears. The boundaries of the new autonomous republic were drawn to include only about one-third of the total Tatar population and to ensure an ethnic Russian majority. The Tatars, feared and hated since the Mongol-Tatar conquest of Russia, were still not trusted by the new Soviet regime.

The discovery of extensive petroleum reserves in Tatarstan during World War II hastened industrialization but drew in a large influx of Slav workers. By 1975 the Tatar population of the republic had fallen to just 37% of the total. Minority status quickened a national revival that converged with the liberalization of Soviet life in the late 1980s. In 1989 the Tatars celebrated the 1,100th anniversary of the adoption of Islam in the Volga region.

The disintegration of the Soviet Union in August 1991 set in motion a strong Tatar nationalist movement and sparked huge pro-independence rallies in Kazan. A number of nationalist groups formed, including the Tatar Public Center and *Ittifak*, the National Independence Party. In August 1990 the Tatar Supreme Soviet adopted a declaration of state sovereignty of the Republic of Tatarstan. A referendum on sovereignty in March 1992 resulted in a vote of 61% favoring greater independence. The Tatar national movement led a campaign for complete separation from Russia, but more moderate groups advocated some form of continued ties to Russia. As a result of the referendum later in March, the Tatar government refused to sign a new federation treaty, and in November the Tatar parliament approved an amendment declaring Tatarstan a sovereign state freely associated with the Russian Federation.

Tatar national leaders, in spite of growing pressure from the Russian government, stubbornly insisted that Tatarstan's relations with Russia and other states must be governed by treaty. In July 1993 the Tatars negotiated twelve bilateral treaties with Russia. In February 1994 the Tatar leaders of the republic approved the treaty that normalized relations with the Russian Federation and finally signed the 1992 federation treaty. The treaty, revised through two years of often acrimonious negotiations, covers a number of the points that the Tatars insisted on, including the recognition of Tatarstan as a sovereign state freely associated with the federation and the right to legal secession from the federation. Russian leaders, including President Boris Yeltsin, denounced Tatar separatism and warned that the loss of Tatarstan would be a strategic and economic disaster for the Russian Federation.

The Tatars outside Tatarstan, including the related nations such as the Bashkorts,* have established closer economic and cultural ties since the demise of the Soviet Union. In August 1997 the second World Congress of Tatars was held in Kazan, with representatives of the many Turkic nations in Russia and the former Soviet Union and delegates from the large Tatar diaspora.

SELECTED BIBLIOGRAPHY

Frank, Allen J. *Islamic Historiography and "Bulghar" Identity among the Tatars and Bashkirs of Russia.* 1998.

Izhbolden, B. S. *Essays on Tatar History.* 1963.

Khazanov, Anatoly M. *After the USSR: Ethnicity, Nationalism, and Politics in the Commonwealth of Independent States.* 1995.

Parker, Edward Harper. *A Thousand Years of the Tatars.* 1989.

Rorlich, Azade-Ayse. *The Volga Tatars: A Profile in National Resilience.* 1986.

TEREK COSSACKS

Kazaki Terek; Kazaky Terek

POPULATION: Approximately (2000 e) 1,050,000 Terek Cossacks in Europe, mostly in the Stavropol Krai and North Ossetian Republic of southern European Russia.

THE TEREK COSSACK HOMELAND: The Terek Cossack homeland lies in the North Caucasus, occupying the Stavropol Plateau and the Terek River basin between the Kuma and Kuban Rivers in southern European Russia. The northern foothills of the main Caucasian range lie in the southern part of the region, while the north, including the Stavropol Plateau, is mostly dry steppe lands. In the north is the Manych Depression, with oil and natural gas deposits. The region, once drought-ridden, has been irrigated since 1945.

Terek has no official status; the region, one of the three Cossack provinces of the North Caucasus, forms Stavropol Krai (territory) of the Russian Federation. *Stavropol Krai (Terek)*: 25,676 sq.mi.–66,501 sq.km. (2000 e) 2,292,000—Russians* 51%, Terek Cossacks 24%, Ukrainians* 18%, Chechens* 3%, Karachais,* Nogais,* Turkmens. The Terek Cossack capital and major cultural center is Stavropol, (2000 e) 332,000, founded as a Cossack fort in 1777. The other major cultural center is the city of Vladikavkaz, (2000 e) 337,000, the historic capital of the Terek host and the present capital of the Ossetians.*

FLAG: The Terek national flag, the flag of the former republic, is a horizontal tricolor of black, green, and red.

PEOPLE: The Terek Cossacks, the third largest of the Cossack peoples of Russia, are concentrated in the east and southeast of the Stavropol Territory. They evolved from Don Cossacks* moving south in the eighteenth century. A major subgroup, the Greben Cossacks, also called the Skoi, still inhabit the northern districts close to the territory of the Don Cossacks. The Terek Cossack culture is laced with North Caucasian elements, which reflect long association with the Ossetians, Circassians,* and Nogais. In the north among the Greben Cossacks, cultural borrowings from the Chechens are more important. Not recognized by the Russian government as a separate cultural and national group, the Terek Cossack claim to national status is based on their history, dialect, and geographic location.

The language of the Terek Cossacks is a Cossack language that incorporates Russian, Ukrainian, Caucasian, and Turkic elements. The language, not inherently intelligible to speakers of Russian, is spoken in two major dialects, Terek in the south and east and Greben in the northern districts.

NATION: The Russians began to expand into the North Caucasus, the Muslim lands between the Black and Caspian Seas, in the sixteenth century. The Slavs captured the region traversed by the lower Volga River in 1554–56 and pushed into the North Caucasus region in 1557. Although claimed by Russia in 1598, the Ottoman Turkish resistance to the Russians delayed colonization for over two centuries. In 1777 Cossacks established a fort at present Stavropol, which became the center of the Slavic colonization of the North Caucasus. In 1784 the key fortress of Vladikavkaz was founded by the Cossacks in traditional Ossetian territory.

The Don Cossacks spearheading the Russian expansion governed themselves under elected leaders called *atamans* in return for military service and an oath of personal loyalty to the Russian tsar. The Cossacks moving south from Stavropol took the name of the river that marked their southern boundary, the Terek. In 1861 the Terek Cossack lands were combined with the newly conquered highlands of the Caucasus Mountains to form Terek Province. The lands of the Muslim Chechens and Ingush* north of the river were confiscated, and the Muslims were driven into the mountains.

In return for military service the Cossacks settled on the frontier were allowed to govern themselves under elected leaders called *atamans* or *hetmans*. Although their traditional rights were curtailed in the eighteenth and nineteenth centuries, their military skills allowed the Cossacks to continue as a group distinct from the general public. The Terek Cossacks' pride in being completely free was replaced by pride in soldierly service. Total loyalty to the tsar, but not the Russian state, became a tradition among the Cossacks.

The Terek Cossack communities, holding their land in common, became large-scale landlords in the late nineteenth century. The abolition of serfdom in Russia sent a wave of landless peasants to the region, most settling on the Cossacks' communal lands as tenant farmers. The better educated and more prosperous Cossacks dominated a large area of the North Caucasus up to World War I. The Orthodox Christian Terek Cossacks, personally loyal to the tsar, were charged with keeping the Muslim tribes included in Terek Province under close military control. In the latter part of the nineteenth and the early part of the twentieth centuries, the tsarist government used Cossack troops to perpetrate pogroms against the Jews. Cossack troops were used on a large scale in the suppression of the Russian Revolution of 1905 and during the strikes and demonstrations that erupted during World War I.

Formed into elite military units when war began in 1914, the Terek Cossack units sent to the front were decimated. In February 1917 the discontented Terek Cossacks, freed from their oath to the tsar by revolution, began to desert and return to their homeland. In March 1917 the Terek Cossacks elected a new *ataman* and formed a military government to fill the void as the tsarist civil government collapsed.

The Muslim peoples and the Terek Cossacks put aside decades of tensions as a new force threatened them both. The Bolshevik coup in October 1917 forced the peoples of the region to participate in a cooperative government. On 20 October 1917 the Terek-Dagestan government declared its sovereignty as a temporary expedient until a legitimate Russian government could be reestablished. The cooperative state, called Terek-Dagestan, collapsed in December 1917 as fighting broke out between the Terek Cossacks and the Chechen-Ingush, the Muslim tribes attempting to recover lands lost to the Cossacks in the eighteenth and nineteenth centuries.

Two Bolshevik statutes officially reduced the Cossacks to the status of other Russian peoples. The statutes, greatly resented among the Terek Cossacks, fueled support for the nascent national movement in the region. The Terek Cossack military government on 4 March 1918 declared Terek independent of Bolshevik Russia. The Terek leaders tried to ensure the security of their new republic by proposing a union of the states seceding from Russia or, failing that, a federation with the other Cossack peoples of the North Caucasus, the Don Cossacks to the north and the Kuban Cossacks* to the west.

In November 1918 invading Bolsheviks overran the Terek Cossack republic, beginning a reign of terror against the anti-Bolshevik groups in the region. The Soviet authorities confiscated Cossack properties and lands, redistributing them to the pro-Bolshevik Russians and their Chechen and Ingush allies. The Soviets allowed the looting of Cossack towns and villages while thousands of Terek Cossacks faced eviction and persecution. In January 1919 the anti-Bolshevik forces drove the Soviets from the Terek, but by 1920 the victorious Red Army had regained military control of most of the region.

The new Soviet authorities ended all the Cossacks' traditional privileges and dismantled the Terek Cossack military structure. The Terek Cossack leaders who failed to escape were deported or executed, and thousands of Cossacks died in purges between 1920 and 1938. Despite resistance, in the early 1930s the Cossacks were engaged in collective farming, Cossack cavalry units were forbidden, and many Terek Cossacks were resettled in Kazakstan and in a number of areas in Siberia. The Soviets banned the use of the Cossack language and reclassified the Cossacks as ethnic Russians, carefully suppressing their separate history and culture. Not until 1936 were the Cossacks again allowed military training and to serve in the Red Army.

Fervently anti-Soviet, thousands of Terek Cossacks joined the Nazi German government's anticommunist crusade during World War II, often facing Cossacks serving in the Red Army. The German advance on the Caucasus reached the Terek homeland in 1942, and the invaders were often welcomed as liberators from hated Soviet rule. The Soviet authorities meted out punishment for the collaboration with deportations and mass executions in 1944–46, and the severe oppression continuing until Joseph Stalin's death in 1953.

A Cossack cultural and national revival, begun among exile groups in Europe and the United States after World War II, started to slowly penetrate the closed territory in the 1960s and 1970s. The exile publication of the first Cossack dictionary, along with works on Cossack culture and history, stimulated a renewed interest in the suppressed Terek nation. The revival accelerated in the late 1980s with the introduction of reforms to the Soviet system by Mikhail Gorbachev in 1987. The cultural national sentiment revived the traditional hostility between the Terek Cossacks and the Chechen Muslims of Chechenia to the south. In April 1990 serious ethnic clashes erupted as the conflict, frozen but not resolved by communist rule, again became a factor in the politics of the region.

During the last years of the USSR, Terek Cossack organizations experienced a sudden revival in the region. In 1990 Cossack associations were formed in traditional areas of Terek lowlands. At first the goals of the Terek Cossack associations were cultural and historical in nature—to preserve Cossack traditions and promote historical accuracy of Cossack lifestyles. But the associations soon became involved in politics and armed conflicts, spurred, in part, by the slaying of five Terek Cossacks in the North Caucasus in mid-1991. The Terek Cossacks began to demand local self-administration and the return of traditional lands.

The disintegration of the Soviet Union in August 1991 split the growing national movement. One faction, centered on Stavropol, demanded official recognition as a separate people and republican status within the reconstituted Russian Federation. The other faction, based in the old Terek Cossack capital, Vladikavkaz, now in North Ossetia, resumed the ancient Cossack tradition of defending Russia's southern frontier with the Muslim lands. Terek Cossacks fought for the Russian-dominated Trans-Dniester Republic against the Moldovans* and joined the Serbians* in the wars that raged through the Balkans.

In mid-1992 a decree signed by Russian president Boris Yeltsin rehabilitated the Cossacks. The decree granted them the status of a distinct ethnic group and gave them the right to receive land free of charge. The decree also called for the use of Cossack forces to protect Russia's borders, although some Terek Cossacks have refused military duty outside their traditional homeland.

In July 1993 the Stavropol regional parliament began a debate on whether to declare the territory a republic and to restore the name Terek, banned by the Soviets in 1920, but as the differences between the republics, regions, and territories making up the Russian Federation began to blur, sentiment for republican status waned. In the late 1990s the Terek Cossacks pressed for the replacement of local governments, in areas with Terek Cossack majorities, with the traditional *hetman* boards of government.

The Terek Cossacks in the later 1990s became more politically assertive. In 1995 tensions in the region erupted in violent clashes between Terek Cossacks and neighboring Caucasians, leaving several dead and many wounded. Since that time, the Terek Cossacks, with their long military history, have again organized along their historic, militaristic lines.

In the summer of 1997 a Terek Cossack supported group called Russian Warrior organized camps for 700 young adults in Stavropol Oblast, seeking to instill the historical values of the Cossack horde in the region's younger generation. Many of the graduates of the camps were enlisted in elite military units that participated in the capture of traditional Terek Cossack territory in Chechenia north of the Terek River in the autumn of 1999.

SELECTED BIBLIOGRAPHY

Groushko, Mike. *Cossack: Warrior Riders of the Steppes.* 1993.

Hindus, Maurice. *The Cossacks: The Study of a Warrior People.* 1970.

Longworth, Philip. *The Cossacks.* 1970.

McNeal, Robert H. *Tsar and Cossack: 1855–1914.* 1987.

Seaton, Albert. *The Horsemen of the Steppes: The Story of the Cossacks.* 1985.

TSAKHURS

Tsakhighali; Tsakhury; Tsaxurs;
Caxurs

POPULATION: Approximately (2000 e) 26,000 Tsakhurs in Europe, concentrated in the border region between the Russian Federation and Azerbaijan.

THE TSAKHUR HOMELAND: The Tsakhur homeland lies in the high mountain valleys of the eastern spur of the Greater Caucasus Mountains. Their mountain valleys, among the most geographically isolated in the region, lie in the region between the Samur and Alazani Rivers. Traditionally, the Tsakhurs have herded cattle and sheep, moving with the seasons between the lowland and highland pastures. In the last decades a growing number have turned to agriculture, particularly fruits and garden vegetables. Until recent decades contact was possible only when the high mountain passes were open during the summer, but the construction of a highway through the region in the 1960s ended its geographic isolation.

The region, called Tsakhurshan, the Land of the Tsakhurs, comprises thirteen towns and villages in the upper reaches of the Samur Valley in Rutul Rayon of the Russian Republic of Dagestan and the Zakataly, Kakh, and Belokany Rayons of the Azerbaijan Republic. The Tsakhur capital and major cultural center is Tshaikhi in Dagestan.

FLAG: The Tsakhurs use a variation of the flag of the Confederation of Caucasian Highland Peoples that has seven green and white stripes with a large blue canton at the upper hoist bearing bearing seventeen small white stars.

PEOPLE: The Tsakhurs are a Dagestani people, one of the small Caucasian nations of the Caucasus Mountains region. Ethnically, they form part of the Samurian peoples of southern Dagestan. Until the disintegration of the Soviet Union in 1991, the Tsakhurs in Azerbaijan had been assimilated by the Turkic

Azeris,* but with the imposition of an international border through their traditional territory the Tsakhurs have mobilized to reunite and to save their small nation. The most widely scattered of the small national groups of the eastern Caucasus, about one-third of the Tsakhurs live in Russia, and two-thirds live in adjoining areas of Azerbaijan. Throughout their history, the Tsakhurs have maintained close contact with their neighbors, the Azeris and Rutuls.* The Tsakhurs are Sunni Muslims, although they retain many pagan rites and traditions.

The Tsakhur language belongs to the southeastern group of the Lezgi-Samur branch of Dagestani languages. The language, called Tshajhna-Miz by the Tsakhurs, is spoken in three distinct dialects, Kirmico-Lek, Mikik, and Misles. The literary language is based on the Kirmico-Lek dialect. About 95% of the Tsakhurs continue to use their language as the language of daily life, although most also speak Azeri or Russian.

NATION: There is little known about the early history of the Tsakhurs. The earliest written records of the Tsakhur nation date back to ancient records of the Georgians* and Armenians,* where the Tsakhurs were called Tsakhaiks. Historically, the Tsakhurs lived in the most geographically remote valleys of the Caucasus Mountains, where they constructed mighty buildings and fortresses.

The isolation of their valleys somewhat protected them from the many invaders that crossed the Caucasus between Europe and Asia, but the Tsakhurs had to fight a succession of fierce and bloody battles to maintain their freedom. The Arabs in the seventh century took control of the lowlands, but their authority was only nominal in the upland valleys. Islam, introduced to the Tsakhurs by the Arabs in the eighth century, became the predominant religion, but their pagan traditions and beliefs continued alongside the new Islamic rituals.

The Mongols in the thirteenth century drove the Tsakhurs into their mountain fortresses, and a century later, in 1396, their homeland was overrun by the forces of Tamerlane. Threatened by outsiders, the Tsakhur clans underwent a process of political consolidation by the fourteenth century. The clans established a confederation, at first led by a khan and later, with further consolidation, by a Tsakhur sultan.

From the twelfth to the fourteenth centuries, the shahs of Shirvan attempted to exert control, and in the seventeenth and eighteenth centuries the Transcaucasian peoples, the Georgians, Armenians, and Azeris, claimed nominal control of the Tsakhur sultanate, but foreign rule was rarely enforced, and the sultanate remained an independent political entity.

Initially, the Tsakhur sultans governed only areas in present Dagestan, but they gradually extended their authority to territories in present Azerbaijan, which were conquered and settled by Tsakhurs. Until the seventeenth century, the sultan's residence was the town of Tsakhur, which gave its name to the national group, but it was later transferred to Elisu, and many Turkish and Persian sources refer to the state as the Elisu Sultanate.

The Russians, expanding their authority into the Caucasus, reached Tsakhurstan in 1803, and the Tsakhurs became subjects of the Russian Empire. The sultanate was allowed to continue with limited autonomy under the ultimate control of Russian administrators. In the early nineteenth century Tsakhur society was rural and patriarchal, with each village headed by an elder. All decisions were made at village community meetings. Despite the supremacy of the sultans, the Tsakhur communities retained their autonomy. To preserve their position, the Tsakhur clans maintained a confederal union, with its highest body an open forum to which every community was entitled to elect an envoy, a *kevh*. In time an aristocracy developed that usurped the seats of the *kevhs* and made them hereditary. In the 1830s Sultan Daniel-Bek, with the aid of tsarist troops, succeeded in subordinating most of the Tsakhur communities in Dagestan and Azerbaijan.

In 1836 Iman Shamil, a Muslim religious leader, declared the independence of Dagestan and imposed Sharia law. At first the Tsakhurs fought the rebels as allies of the Russians, but in 1844, outraged by Russian policies, Sultan Daniel-Bek switched sides, and the Tsakhurs joined the Muslim forces fighting the Russians. In 1852, in retaliation, the victorious Russians forcibly deported the entire Tsakhur population from Dagestan to Azerbaijan, and the sultanate was dissolved. In 1860, at the end of the Muslim rebellion, the Tsakhurs were permitted to return to their ancient homeland in Dagestan.

In spite of the hardships, the Tsakhurs experienced an economic boom period from 1856. The development of limited industrialization and demand for livestock led to a twofold increase in the number of horses and a threefold increase in the sheep herds, and the number of cattle in the Tsakhur herds increased sixfold. During the period of rapid economic expansion, the Tsakhurs also moved into other economic areas and were valued as stonemasons, shoemakers, and tailors. Their metalwork, particularly jewelry, and leather goods found their way into markets far beyond the Tsakhur homeland.

In the late nineteenth century Russianization of the Tsakhurs became the official government policy. Illiteracy was widespread in the region. In 1887 only forty-eight Tsakhurs were considered literate, and most were religious leaders able to read Arabic. Pressure to assimilate into Orthodox Russian culture triggered a religious and national revival. By the turn of the twentieth century, religious fervor had become a part of the Tsakhur culture. The economic development, which had changed Tsakhur life, ended with the onset of hostilities between the Russians and the Turks in the region in 1914.

The Tsakhurs, although exempted from military conscription, covertly supported their fellow Muslims, the Turks,* as the war neared their homeland. When the Russian Revolution toppled the monarchy in 1917, there were riotous celebrations in the region, but the growing Russian civil war soon spilled over into the region, and the Tsakhurs, as they always had, retreated to their mountain strongholds.

In the spring of 1920 the victorious Soviets established their rule in the region and brought numerous changes to the Tsakhur communities. Their homeland was divided; part was included in the Mountain Autonomous Republic established by the Soviet authorities, and part was included in the Azeri republic within the Soviet Union. In the late 1920s the Soviet government conducted an intense anti-Islamic campaign that included the execution of local religious leaders, the closing of religious schools, and the suppression of Islamic rituals.

The Tsakhurs, in spite of the hardships of Soviet rule, made advances materially and culturally. The government tried to develop a Latin alphabet for the Tsakhurs in 1932, but the effort was abandoned, and the Russians' Cyrillic alphabet was imposed. Avar was then declared the literary language of the Tsakhurs, but in 1938 Russian became the only official language of the region.

During World War II, the Germans invaded the North Caucasus, but the Tsakhurs, preferring to leave the Christians to do battle, withdrew into their inaccessible mountains. At the end of the war, the Soviet government began to construct roads into the high Caucasian valleys, and communications were facilitated. The collectivization of the Tsakhur herds was completed in 1947, and in 1949 new winter pastures were allocated. The end of their long isolation brought the Tsakhurs into contact with new ideas and peoples.

The Soviet government in the 1960s began a campaign of assimilation of the Dagestani peoples. State policy prohibited the teaching of Tsakhur and other Dagestani languages in the region's public schools. As well as cultural suppression, the Soviet authorities Sovietized the Tsakhur economy.

The material improvement of the Tsakhur living standards eliminated the traditional practice of migrant Tsakhur workers. In decades past, nearly all Tsakhur men had undertaken migrant work, but by 1970 only about one-third continued to do so.

The rapid changes that led to the disintegration of the Soviet Union in 1991 brought new challenges and problems to the Tsakhurs. The division of the Soviet state into a number of new states again divided the Tsakhur nation among the new Russian Federation and the Republic of Azerbaijan. Although the Tsakhurs have maintained contact among the scattered Tsakhur clans, the new international boundaries have made national life much more difficult.

In the late 1990s the Tsakhurs are among the most nationalistic of the peoples of the Caucasus region. An estimated 99% of the Tsakhurs use their language as the language of daily life, and the sense of Tsakhur identity has only intensified since 1991. A concerted campaign to unite their nation has become the primary nationalist issue.

SELECTED BIBLIOGRAPHY

Abtorkhanov, Abdurahman, and Marie Bennigsen Broxup. *The North Caucasus Barrier: The Russian Advance towards the Muslim World.* 1992.

Bennigsen, Alexandre, and S. Enders Wimbush. *Muslims of the Soviet Empire: A Guide.* 1986.

Krag, Helen, and Lars Funch. *The North Caucasus: Minorities at a Crossroads.* 1994.

Olson, James S. *An Ethnohistorical Dictionary of the Russian and Soviet Empires.* 1994.

Wixman, Ronald. *The Peoples of the USSR: An Ethnographic Handbook.* 1984.

TURKS

Türkçe; Türkisch; Anatolians

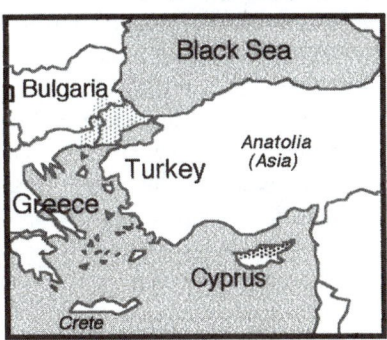

POPULATION: Approximately (2000 e) 9,587,000 Turks in Europe, 6,135,000 concentrated in the European provinces of Turkey, and with large Turkish populations in other parts of Europe, 1,780,000 in Germany, 835,000 in Bulgaria, 188,000 in the Netherlands, 145,000 in Cyprus, 138,000 in France, 131,000 in Greece, and smaller communities in Belgium, the United Kingdom, Switzerland, Macedonia, Yugoslavia, Azerbaijan, Georgia, and Russia.

THE TURKISH HOMELAND: The Turkish European homeland, commonly called Thrace or Eastern Thrace, lies in Southeastern Europe occupying the southeastern tip of the Balkan Peninsula. The region, corresponding to the Balkan territory east of the Maritsa River, is separated from Anatolian Turkey by the Sea of Marmara, the Bosporus, and the Dardanelles, which together form a sea link between the Black Sea and the Mediterranean. Most of European Turkey is a central plain of rolling agricultural lands drained by the Maritsa and Ergene Rivers. The region is a fertile, well-watered area of which slightly more than one-quarter is farmed. The region includes the European half of the city of Istanbul, which is divided into European and Asian parts by the waters of the Bosporus.

The region, the only European territory left to Turkey following the Balkan Wars and World War I, comprises the provinces of Edirne, Tikerdag, Kirklareli, and the western districts of the provinces of Istanbul and Cankkale. *European Turkey (Eastern Thrace)*: 9,041 sq.mi.–23,416 sq.km. (2000 e) 6,135,000— Turks 97%, Bulgarians* 1%, Armenians,* Greeks.* The Turkish capital is Ankara in Asia Minor, but the cultural capital is Istanbul (2000 e) 7,212,000 (metropolitan area 11,073,000), formerly known as Constantinople.

FLAG: The Turkish national flag, the official flag of the Turkish republic, is a red field bearing a white crescent moon and five-pointed star. The flag of the Turkish Bulgarians is a white field with narrow, red stripes at the top and bottom.

PEOPLE: The Turks are an Altaic people, the most numerous of the Turkic peoples of the Middle East and Central Asia and the largest of the Turkish nations in Europe, which include the Azeris,* Balkars,* Crimean Tatars,* Karachais,* Kumyks,* Nogais,* and Tatars.* Turkish culture and ethnic heritage demonstrate their geographic position between Asia and Europe and the extensive mixing with the many nations of the vast Ottoman Empire from the fifteenth to the twentieth centuries. The Turks are mostly Sunni Muslims, and the European Turks tend to be secular and pro-European in their outlook.

The language of the Turks, called Turkish or Anatolian Turkish, belongs to the Oghuz branch of the Altaic language group. Turkish is spoken in nine distinct dialects, four of which are spoken in European Turkey, Danubian, Karamanli, Rumelian, and Edirne. The language was written in the Arabic script until 1928, when the Roman alphabet was adopted. The language is the official language of Turkey and is one of the official languages of Cyprus and is spoken by the Turkish populations in the Balkans. The literary language is based on standard Turkish, the dialect originally spoken by educated people in the city of Istanbul.

NATION: The name Turk was first used by the Chinese in the sixth century A.D. to designate nomadic tribes that controlled a vast empire from Mongolia to the Black Sea. The Turkic Empire, which was divided into two independent parts, was forced to accept nominal Chinese rule in the seventh century, although the northern part of the empire regained its independence in 682. The oldest known inscriptions in the Turkish language relate to the events leading up to the independence of the northern Turks in 682.

In the next centuries the Oghuz Turks lost control of the vast territory to other Turkic peoples, the Uighurs and Kyrgyz. The Oghuz tribes formed a powerful federation that migrated to the west. In the seventh century the Muslim Arabs overran most of the Middle East, bringing the Oghuz Turks into contact with the new religion. The tribes embraced the Sunni branch of Islam, which became the predominant religion and part of the Turkish culture.

One Turkic group, the Seljuks, a member of the Oghuz confederation, moved west into the territory of the Greek Byzantine Empire and had a great impact on the history of Southeastern Europe. In the eleventh century the Seljuk Turks, led by Togrul, conquered most of Central Asia and Iran. Under his successor, Alp Arslan, the Turks overran Georgia, Armenia, and Anatolia. In 1071 the Turks defeated the Byzantines at Manzikert, leaving the Byzantine Empire, except for a small area around Constantinople, open to Turkish occupation. The arrival of the Turks placed a distinctive stamp of Turkish language and culture on the population they found there, and it was the instrument by which Islam replaced Christianity in this territory.

At the beginning of the twelfth century the Seljuk Turk Empire began to fragment, and various states emerged. The weakened empire fell to the Mongols in the thirteenth century, and many Turks were absorbed into the Mongol hordes.

A minor tribe of the Oghuz confederation, the Osmanlis, in the thirteenth century had been assigned by their Seljuk masters to the border area of the Byzantine Empire. Their position on the volatile frontier allowed the Osmanlis to develop a highly disciplined military organization. Osmanli expansion into Europe began in the fourteenth century. The Osmanlis or Ottomans emerged in history as the leaders who fought the Byzantines in northwestern Anatolia.

The Turks began to camp in the Gallipoli (Gelibolu) Peninsula and to mount raids on the remaining Byzantine possessions in Europe. The Ottomans expended their conquests in Europe at the expense of the Byzantine Empire, Bulgaria, and Serbia. Adrianople, the present Edirne, fell to the Ottoman Turks in 1361 and was made the capital of the expanding Ottoman state. Great military victories over the Christian Europeans at Kosovo Poloje in 1389 and at Nikopol in 1396 brought large parts of the Balkan Peninsula under Ottoman rule and awakened Europe to the approaching danger. Called the Osmanli or Ottoman Empire, the state absorbed surrounding Turkish states, and in the late fifteenth century the Osmanli rulers ended all other local Turkish dynasties in Asia.

The appearance of Tamerlane forced the Ottomans to lift their siege of the Byzantine capital, Constantinople, in 1402. The Ottomans soon rallied and in 1453 captured Christian Constantinople. Within a century the Ottomans had changed from a nomadic people to the heirs of the Byzantine Empire, the most ancient surviving empire of Europe. The Turks' success was due partly to the weakness and disunity of their Christian foes and partly to their superior military organization. Their armies employed numerous Christians, both conscripts and volunteers. Turkish expansion reached its peak in the sixteenth century, accompanied by a golden age of literature, art, and architecture. Turkish migrant communities were begun in the European territories and on the island of Cyprus, which had a mostly Greek population.

Turkish power began to wane in the later sixteenth century, following the death of Sultan Süleyman I in 1566. The first serious blow by Europeans, mostly Venetians* and Spaniards,* was the Ottoman defeat at the naval battle of Lepanto in 1571, which opened the Mediterranean to more extensive European trade. In the seventeenth century Turkish power was temporarily restored, and in 1683 a huge Turkish army surrounded Vienna. The relief of Vienna by the Poles* began a new decline. In 1699 the Turks negotiated a peace with the victorious Europeans, which cost the Turks control of Hungary and other European territories.

The Turkish Empire remained a feudal state, mostly unaffected by the social developments in the rest of Europe. The sultanate had become infamous for indolence, depravity, and the murder of rivals. The actual rule of the empire fell to the grand viziers, many of whom were able administrators, although corruption and bribery had been raised to a system of civic administration. Public officials, the governors of provinces, and the rulers of vassal states purchased their posts at exorbitant prices. They recovered their fortunes by extorting still more taxes from their subjects, which further reduced the peasantry to abject misery. The despotic Ottoman administration was mitigated only by the observance of Muslim law.

The downfall of the Ottoman Empire gained impetus with the Russo-Turkish Wars of the eighteenth century. The Russians* expanded their boundaries at Ottoman expense, who were then forced to grant autonomy to the Slavic peoples of the empire, particularly the Serbs.* The Russian Empire took on the role of protector of the Slav nations under Ottoman rule. Drastic reforms were introduced in the late eighteenth and early nineteenth centuries, but they came too late to save the empire. By the nineteenth century the Ottoman Turkish Empire was known as the sick man of Europe.

The Turks' weakening hold on their European territories was further eroded by a rebellion of Slavs in Bosnia and Herzegovina in 1875, which precipitated the Russo-Turkish War of 1877–78. The Turks were defeated in spite of a vigorous stand. The territories of the Romanians,* Serbs, and Montenegrins* were recognized as independent states, while the Bosnians* passed under Austrian rule, and further territory was lost to the Bulgarians. In 1878 the British took control of the island of Cyprus, with its mixed Greek and Turkish population. Military defeat began a period of reform. A liberal constitution was framed, and the first Turkish parliament opened in 1877 but was soon dismissed, and the sultan began despotic rule. The deteriorating situation in the empire was partly to blame for the massacres of Armenian Christians in the late nineteenth century, in which an estimated 1.5 million Armenians perished. The massacres turned world public opinion against Turkey.

Reformers, particularly the Young Turk movement, became strongly nationalist and grew steadily as chaos overtook the empire. In 1908 the Young Turks forced the restoration of the constitution of 1876, and in 1909 the parliament, dominated by the reformers, deposed the sultan and put Muhammad V on the throne. However, the Ottoman Empire continued to weaken, and in the Balkan Wars of 1912 and 1913 the Turks lost nearly all their European territories. A coup d'état, led by Enver Pasha, established a virtual dictatorship. The Turks joined the Central Powers at the outbreak of war in 1914, and despite initial gains, particularly in the Balkans, the war further undermined the fragmenting empire. In 1918 Turkish resistance to the Allies in Europe collapsed. An armistice was concluded, and the ancient empire of the Turks came to an end.

The Treaty of Sèvres confirmed the dissolution of the empire and virtually abolished Turkish sovereignty. The Turks lost their last Asian territories except Anatolia, Armenia became a separate republic, and the Greeks gained control of parts of western Anatolia, including the city of Smyrna, later renamed Izmir. In Europe the Turks were forced to cede the Aegean Islands to Greece and the Dodecanese and Rhodes to the Italians,* retaining only Constantinople and its environs, including the Zone of the Straits, which was neutralized and internationalized. The treaty was accepted by the government of the sultan but was rejected by a rival nationalist government led by Kemel Ataturk. The nationalists defied the authority of the sultan, took the offensive against the Allies in Anatolia, and concluded a separate treaty with the USSR in 1921. The Greeks, encouraged by the Allies, launched an offensive against Ataturk's forces from their base at Izmir, but in the war that followed the Greeks were routed, and the Turks captured the territories held by the Allies in western Anatolia. On 1 November 1922 the Ataturk government deposed the sultan, and the nationalists took control.

Pressed by the new nationalist Turkish republican government, a conference was convened at Lausanne, Switzerland, to revise the Treaty of Sèvres. The subsequent Treaty of Lausanne, signed in 1923, established the present boundaries of Turkey, including European territories returned to Turkey by Bulgaria and Greece. Under a separate agreement, 1.5 million Greeks living in Turkish territory were repatriated to Greece, and approximately 800,000 Turks from Greece and Bulgaria were resettled in Turkey.

In October 1923 Turkey was formally proclaimed a republic, with Ataturk as the first president. He was reelected in 1927, 1931, and 1935. Under his leadership the Turks were encouraged to adopt Western dress, and the Roman alphabet was adopted. Ataturk's reforms changed the religious, social, and cultural bases of Turkish society. In 1925 the government intensified its antireligious policy, abolished religious orders, forbade polygamy, and prohibited the wearing of the traditional headgear, the fez. In 1928 Islam ceased to be the state religion, and in 1930 the city of Constantinople, replaced by Ankara as the Turkish capital in 1923, was renamed Istanbul. Women, who had few rights under Ottoman rule, were given suffrage and were fully emancipated in 1934. In the next year every adult Turk had to adopt a family name. Kemel Ataturk died in 1938, leaving a nation well on its way to becoming a state on the European model.

The Turks remained neutral during World War II; however, the onset of the Cold War worsened relations between the Turks and the neighboring Soviet Union. From 1947 military aid from the major Western states pulled the Turks into the Western camp. In 1952 the Turkish state became a full member in the North Atlantic Treaty Organization (NATO).

Relations with other European states were generally good, with the exception of those controlling areas with large Turkish populations. Tensions with Greece over the island of Cyprus, with its volatile Turkish minority, began in the mid-1950s and continued after Cyprus was granted independence in 1960 with Greece, Turkey, and the United Kingdom as the guarantors of the Cypriot sovereignty. Relations with the neighboring Bulgarians, exacerbated by the Cold War, also involved the large Turkish minority in that country.

Demands for greater freedom from the 1960s led to a series of unstable civilian governments and military coups. Suppression of student and reform movements caused widespread unrest. Increasing tensions with Greece over Cyprus became serious in the early 1970s. In 1974, following a Greek Cypriot attempt to unite the island to Greece, the Turkish government sent troops to invade the island. The Turkish troops took control of the northern third of the island, while Turks from the south fled to the north, and Greeks fled south to escape the Turkish occupation. Only the intervention of the governments of the United States, the United Kingdom, and the United Nations (UN), prevented war between Turkey and Greece.

Political instability led to the declaration of martial law in 1980, and in the civil violence over 2,000 people were killed. The military seized control of the government and forcibly restored order before allowing the civilian government to again take charge. A new constitution was approved in 1982, and in 1987 martial law was lifted in all but four provinces. The separatist war of the Kurds in southeastern Anatolia continued to generate bloody and violent confrontations and denunciations of the Turkish government's lack of respect for basic human rights.

The Turks, considering themselves Europeans, applied for membership in the expanding European Economic Community (EEC) in 1987 but were not accepted for immediate membership. Better relations with Greece, a prerequisite for membership, were pressed from 1988. The next year a new crisis erupted when 300,000 ethnic Turks from Bulgaria fled across the Turkish border to escape Bulgarian government attempts to forcibly assimilate them.

The millions of ethnic Turks in Western Europe, particularly in Germany, have lived as second-class citizens or as semilegal noncitizens. Under rules proposed by the new German government in October 1998, the Turks in Germany could now become German citizens. Other Turkish populations in Western Europe are smaller but have begun to demand their rights.

The long-standing dispute over Cyprus was still under discussion in 1999, with little progress to report. The two sides, the Greeks and the Turks, remain far from a political settlement. According to Rauf Denktash, the leader of the Cypriot Turks, "There is no Turkish-Cypriot nation; there is no Greek-Cypriot nation; there is no Cypriot nation." There are only Turks and Greeks, who happen to live in different parts of one island.

SELECTED BIBLIOGRAPHY

Barkley, Karen. *Bandits and Bureaucrats: The Ottoman Route to State Centralization*. 1997.

Graber, G. S. *Caravans to Oblivion: The Armenian Genocide, 1915*. 1996.

Heper, Metin, and Ahmet Evin, eds. *State, Democracy, and the Military: Turkey in the 1980s*. 1988.

Lewis, Bernard. *The Emergence of Modern Turkey*. 1986.

MacFie, A. L. *The End of the Ottoman Empire 1908–1923*. 1998.

TYROLEANS

Tiroleans; Tirolese; Tirolos

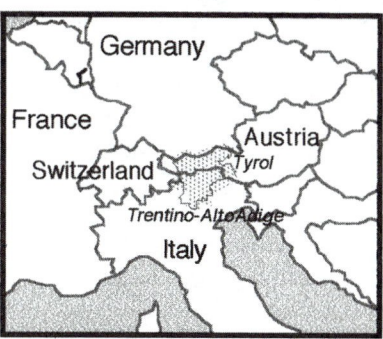

POPULATION: Approximately (2000 e) 1,388,000 Tyroleans in Europe, mostly in the Tyrolean regions of Austria and Italy.

THE TYROLEAN HOMELAND: The Tyrolean homeland occupies a mountainous region of high Alpine valleys between the Bavarian Alps in the north and Ötzal Alps in the south. The region is traversed by the Inn, Lech, and Adige Rivers. Tyrol is famed for its idyllic beauty but has only limited natural resources, so tourism is the major industry. Pasture farming, cattle raising, forestry, and dairy farming are the main occupations in the rural areas.

Tyrol, divided in 1919 between Austria and Italy, forms the Austrian state of Tyrol and the Italian region of Trentino-Alto Adige. *Region of Tyrol (Tirol/ Tirolo)*: 10,139 sq.mi.–26,259 sq.km. (2000 e) 1,521,000—Tyroleans 91% (Tyroleans 633,000, Trentines 492,000, South Tyroleans 263,000), other Austrians,* other Italians.* The Tyrolean capital and major cultural center is Innsbruck, (2000 e) 120,000, the historic capital of the region. Other important Tyrolean cultural centers are Bolzano, called Bozen in German, (2000 e) 99,000, the capital of South Tyrol in Italy, and Trento, called Trient in German and Trent in English, (2000 e) 102,000, the capital of the Trentine Tyroleans.

FLAGs: The Tyrolean national flag is a horizontal bicolor of white over red bearing, on a centered white disc, the national symbol, the red Tryolean eagle. The Tyrolean eagle centered on a white field is the flag of the South Tyrol. A horizontal bicolor of red over white is the flag of the Trentino.

PEOPLE: The Tyroleans are an Alpine people comprising the Tyroleans, including the South Tyroleans in the north, and the Trentines (Trentinos, Trentini) in the center and south. The two Tyrolean peoples share a collective history as Tyroleans that spans over 1,000 years of coexistence in their mountain home-land. The Tyroleans also share their Roman Catholic religion and a common Alpine culture that supersedes the linguistic diversity of the region.

The language of the Tyroleans is German, with the majority of the Tyroleans and South Tyroleans being fluent in both standard German and the Tyrolean dialect, which is closely related to the language spoken by the Bavarians* to the north. The Trentines are mostly Italian-speaking, using both standard Italian and a distinct Gallo-Italic dialect that remains the language of daily life in Italy's Trento Province. Many of the Tyrolean peoples speak both German and Italian.

NATION: The mountainous region north of Roman Italy was the home to a number of Celtic tribes that prevented communications between Italy and the Roman possessions in Gaul and Germania. Between 25 and 15 B.C. the emperor Augustus directed several military campaigns that ultimately defeated the Celtic tribes. Some of the tribes were decimated, while others were sold as slaves and deported to far-flung corners of the empire. The surviving tribes readily adopted the Romans' Latin speech and culture and became influential citizens of the vast empire.

Periodic overpopulation and land hunger, combined with pressure from re-mote peoples and the attraction of the wealth of the peaceful Roman provinces, drove tribes of Germanic peoples to attack the provincial frontiers at various times starting in A.D. 166. The frontiers completely broke down during the fourth century, and the Germanic tribes moved south. By the mid-sixth century the Bavarians had occupied Tyrol. Avars* moving into the region from the east contended with the Bavarians for control of the Danube River valley. The Avars left only superficial traces in the country, but the Bavarian clans that settled in the Tyrol developed a distinctive Alpine culture and eventually split from the Bavarians as a separate people. In the eighth century, the Franks absorbed the region into their expanding empire.

The southern Tyrolean districts came under the rule of the powerful bishops of Trent and Brixen in the eleventh century. In the north the counts of Tyrol and Montfort gained control of the Tyrolean districts. In 1342 the Tyrolean peoples adopted a constitution, the first of its kind in Europe. The Hapsburgs gained control of the northern part of Tyrol in 1363, gradually extending their influence throughout the region. The castle of Tyrol, which gave the region its name, is now in Italian territory.

The capital of the County of Tyrol was at Meran (Merano) until 1420, when it was transferred to Innsbruck in the northern districts. The Protestant Refor-mation, which brought much violence to the region, was the cause of a serious peasant uprising in the region in 1525. At the end of the religious wars in the sixteenth century, the majority of the Tyroleans retained their Roman Catholic religion.

Over the next centuries the Tyroleans and Trentines developed a common Alpine culture unique to the region. The common culture and religion transcended the linguistic issues, while the majority of the population used the Tyrolean German dialect for communication between the region's isolated Alpine groups.

The secularized bishoprics of Trent and Brixen were awarded to Austria in 1802 during the upheavals of the Napoleonic Wars. Three years later defeated Austria ceded all of Tyrol to Napoleon's ally, Bavaria. Andreas Hoffer, now a Tyrolean national hero, united the diverse Tyrolean peoples to drive the Bavarians and French* from the region. Hoffer was captured and executed in 1809, but his followers held out in mountain strongholds until Tyrol returned to Hapsburg control in 1815. The rebellion strengthened the ties among the Tyrolean peoples.

The Tyroleans formed a distinct national group in the multiethnic Hapsburg Empire, with ties of loyalty to the Hapsburg monarchs but not to the Austrians, seen by the Tyroleans as a distinct, lowland nation. In the latter part of the nineteenth century, as revolutionary ideas fed nationalist movements across Europe, the Tyroleans developed a distinct nationalism, seeking greater cultural and political freedom within the empire.

Italian irredentism, the movement to incorporate Italian-speaking parts of the Austro-Hungarian Empire into newly united Italy, gained some support in Trentino after 1878, but the majority of the Italian-speaking Trentines, separated from Italian influence since the fourteenth century, remained markedly unaffected by calls to Italian unity. Progressive and prosperous, in the 1880s and 1890s the Tyrol was one of the few regions of the vast Hapsburg Empire where ethnic strife remained virtually unknown.

The Italian government, promised the Italian-speaking areas of Austro-Hungary, joined the Allies in 1915. Italy's entry into World War I turned Tyrol's pristine Alpine valleys into battlefields and opened a serious rift between the German-speaking Tyroleans and Italian-speaking Trentines.

A growing national movement, opposed to the ongoing war and rejecting Italian territorial claims, gained support among the Tyroleans in the north. In October 1918, as defeat for the Austro-Hungarian Empire became apparent, the Tyroleans took control of the local civil administration. The Tyrolean authorities, hoping to save their nation from division, organized a referendum in the Tyrolean diet, which voted overwhelmingly for secession and independence.

Tyrolean nationalist leaders, citing point number ten of President Wilson's Fourteen Points, independence for the non-Austrian peoples of the empire, rejected both Austrian and Italian claims to the Tyrol. When it became clear that the Italian government was determined to annex the southern districts, including the German-speaking South Tyrol, the nationalists declared the Tyrol independent on 24 April 1919. The Tyrolean nationalists began to erect a confederation of Swiss-style autonomous cantons, with German, Italian, and Ladin as official languages, but again the Allies intervened to prevent secession. At the Paris Peace Conference the Allies assigned northern Tyrol to the new Austrian republic. The mainly Italian-speaking Trentino and the South Tyrol, with its 250,000 German-speaking Tyroleans, came under the authority of the Italian kingdom.

The fascist government of Italy, installed in 1922, and the leftist Austrian government pressed assimilation in their respective Tyrolean territories. In the south, despite promises of autonomy for the South Tyroleans, the fascist authorities closed all Tyrolean schools, newspapers, and publications and in 1926 ordered the South Tyroleans to change all place and family names to Italian. The fascist government sponsored immigration from the backward and culturally and dialectically distinct southern Italian regions that raised tensions in the region, not only with the German-speaking Tyroleans in South Tyrol but also between the immigrants and the culturally distinct Trentines. By 1939, 95% of all public offices in Italian Tyrol were held by Italians.

The tensions in Italian Tyrol reverberated in Austrian Tyrol. A militia sent from "Red Vienna" to suppress the Tyrolean national movement brought the region close to civil war in the early 1930s. The German annexation of Austria in 1938, welcomed in the anti-Austrian, but pro-German, Tyrol, proved a disaster for the region. The German annexation of South Tyrol, following Italy's World War II surrender in 1943, briefly reunited the region, and over 60,000 Tyroleans had moved to the North Tyrol before Germany's defeat in 1944.

A democratic postwar Austrian government began to champion the cause of the German-speaking South Tyroleans. Agreements between Austria and Italy provided for limited autonomy in 1964, the accord designed to head off a growing campaign of violence and sabotage by South Tyrolean nationalists in Italy. The Südtiroler Volkspartei became the major political party in German-speaking South Tyrol. The party, seeing that the revision of borders and the unification of the Tyrol were impossible, worked for increased autonomy for the South Tyrolean minority in Italy.

In the 1960s the concept of a collective historical past emphasizing the shared Alpine culture gained support among both German- and Italian-speaking Tyroleans. As tensions increased between the Tyrolean peoples and the influx of newcomers from southern Italy, new demands were put forward for increased autonomy for the entire Trentino-Alto Adige region. In 1970 the region was granted limited political autonomy.

Only after the escalation of terrorist acts by radical South Tyrolean groups in the late 1960s did the Italian government acknowledge the ethnic problem in the region. In 1972 the Italian government instituted a new autonomy statute for the region. The idea of a common Tyrolean fatherland grew during the 1960s and 1970s. In Austrian Tyrol the idea was paralleled by the growth of a strong regional movement. On the Italian-Austrian border nationalists erected signs showing the artificially and unjustly fragmented Tyrol with "Never forget Tyrol" printed on large signs. Radical Tyrolean nationalists put forward a plan for an autonomous federation of Tyrol, South Tyrol, Trentino, and Vorarlberg.

The increasing Italianization of the region was demonstrated by the language issue. In 1987 only 67% of the population of the province of Bolzano, called South Tyrol, spoke German as their first language, down from over 90% in 1919. The language issue fueled the growth of more radical groups in the 1980s, particularly Ein Tirol (One Tyrol). A series of bombings kept the separatist issue in the news in the late 1980s and early 1990s.

The increasing integration of Europe and the reunification of Germany stimulated a resurgence of Tyrolean nationalism in the 1990s. Resentment of the mass migration from southern Italy, beginning in the 1950s, has reversed decades of assimilation and reinforced the Trentine participation in the common Alpine nationalism. Political groups formed across the region, including the Trentino-Tyrol Autonomist Party of Trento, the Heimat Bund (Homeland Alliance), the South Tyrolean German Group, and Schutzen.

On 15 September 1991 nationalists from all the Tyrolean areas demonstrated on the frontier at the Brenner Pass, demanding a referendum on reunification of Tyrol within a united Europe. Faced with rising nationalism, the Italian government agreed to greater autonomy in 1992.

The Tyroleans are unusually pro-European, hoping that a united Europe will hasten the reunification of their homeland. When Austria became a member state of the European Union (EU) on 1 January 1995, the two halves of the Tyrolean nation were in theory, but not in reality, reunited within the union. For the Tyrolean nationalists seeking a politically united and autonomous Tyrol within a European federation, the fact that both Italy and Austria belong to the European Union does not alter their goal.

SELECTED BIBLIOGRAPHY

Alcock, Anthony Evelyn. *The History of the South Tyrol Question.* 1989.

Levy, Miriam. *Governance and Grievance: Hapsburg Policy and Italian Tyrol in the Eighteenth Century.* 1988.

Proctor, Alan. *The Tyrol.* 1986.

Toscano, Mario. *Alto Adige, South Tyrol: Italy's Frontier with the German World.* 1994.

Ward, Martha C. *The Hidden Life of Tirol.* 1993.

UDMURTS

Votiaks; Votyaks; Ary; Arianes;
Otiakis

POPULATION: Approximately (2000 e) 1,123,000 Udmurts in Europe, concentrated in the Udmurt Republic, a member state of the Russian Federation, but with sizable communities in neighboring republics of Bashkortostan and Tatarstan and the Russian regions of Kirov, Perm', and Sverdlovsk. The only large community outside Russia is the 16,000 Udmurts living in Kazakhstan in Central Asia.

THE UDMURT HOMELAND: The Udmurt homeland lies in eastern European Russia, mostly a highland region between the Vyatka and Kama Rivers and the forested foothills of the Ural Mountains. The region, lying 620 miles (1,000 km.) northeast of Moscow, is largely low and hilly, with wide river valleys. Railroads are the main form of transportation, with important trunk lines crossing Udmurtia, which forms part of the Ural industrial region. Although soil fertility is low, cereal crops are cultivated.

The Udmurt Republic, raised to the status of an autonomous republic within Soviet Russia in 1934, since 1992 has formed a member state of the Russian Federation. *Udmurt Republic (Respublika Udmurt)*: 16,255 sq.mi.–42,101 sq.km. (2000 e) 1,655,000—Russians* 48%, Udmurts 41%, Tatars* 8%, Maris* 1%, Bashkorts* 1%. The Udmurt capital and major cultural center is Izhevsk, called Ischewsk in the Udmurt language, (2000 e) 684,000, an important industrial center. The other important Udmurt cultural center is Glazov, (2000 e) 109,000, the historic capital of the Udmurt nation.

FLAG: The Udmurt national flag, the official flag of the republic, is a vertical tricolor of black, white, and red bearing a red, eight-pointed star, representing the sun, centered on the white.

PEOPLE: The Udmurts are a Finnic people, one of the nations that make up the eastern branch of the Finno-Ugric peoples concentrated in the Volga River basin of eastern European Russia. The Udmurt nation is made up of two major divisions, the Udmurts in the south and the Besmerians or Besermyans of Tatar or Chavash* origin but assimilated into the Udmurt culture and language. Known for their folk crafts, embroidery, weaving, and wood carving, the Udmurts have retained their traditional culture in spite of centuries of assimilation pressures. Along with the Irish,* the Udmurts have the highest proportion of red-haired people in Europe. The Udmurts are mostly Russian Orthodox, but with a minority that has retained traditional beliefs, which include ancestor worship.

The language of the Udmurts is a Permian language of the Finno-Permian branch of the Finno-Ugric languages. The language, related to the language of the Komis,* is spoken in two major dialects, North Udmurt or Vesermyan (Besermyan), spoken by the Besmerians, and South Udmurt, also known as Southwestern Udmurt, spoken by the Udmurts. The two Udmurt dialects are distinct but are mutually intelligible. The literary language is based on a transitional dialect between the North and South dialects. The Cyrillic alphabet used by the language was developed in the eighteenth century.

NATION: Archaeological findings place the ancestors of the Udmurts in the region between the Kama and Vyatka Rivers in Neolithic times, and they emerged as an identifiable ethnic group in the sixth century A.D. Divided into tribes, the Udmurts practiced a shamanistic religion revolving around the veneration of their ancestors. The tribes survived by slash-and-burn agriculture, hunting, fishing, and trade with neighboring peoples. Until the conquest of their homeland by the Chavash in the eighth century, the Udmurts controlled a large territory north of the Volga River. Influenced by the Bulgar Chavash, the Udmurt tribes settled in agricultural villages in the fertile river valleys. The Udmurts remained under nominal Chavash rule until the thirteenth century.

Slavic explorers from the Novgorod republic explored the northern Udmurt districts in the early twelfth century, and in 1174 Novgorodian colonists founded fortified settlements north of the Vyatka River. The Udmurts fiercely resisted the Slav colonization but gradually lost ground to the Slavs and abandoned their traditional lands in the north. Originally called Arans by the Russians, they were later referred to as Perm, a term also applied to a number of different Finnic peoples, and even later they were called Votyaks.

The Mongols, advancing from the southeast, conquered and devastated the Udmurt lands in 1236–37, forcing many Udmurts to take refuge in the unconquered Slavic region to the north. At the breakup of the Mongol Golden Horde in the fourteenth century, the southern Udmurts came under the rule of the Tatars and were included in the Khanate of Kazan. The Udmurts in the north came under the control of the Slavic Vyatka Republic. By the late fourteenth century most of the Udmurts had accepted the Christian religion brought to the region by Orthodox monks, although their traditional beliefs were also retained.

The northern Udmurts came under Russian rule in 1489 following the conquest of the Vyatka Republic by the expanding duchy of Moscow. The conquest of Kazan in 1552 reunited the Udmurt peoples under Russian rule, although Udmurt rebels continued to fight the Russians until 1558. Then began the period of Christianizing the Udmurts. They were sometimes offered tax incentives or exemption from serving in the imperial army, but more often soldiers would arrive in Udmurt villages and force all the inhabitants to stand in the snow while an Orthodox priest read the liturgy and the *zakon bozhii*, God's Law, to them, and they were then considered Orthodox Christians and were given Christian, that is, Russian, family names.

The best and most fertile lands were confiscated and controlled by absentee Russian landlords, and poverty became widespread in the region. The local Udmurt population, including the large Orthodox community, suffered a harsh Russian colonial rule. By the seventeenth century most Udmurts were tied to the large Russian estates in the region as serfs, unpaid agricultural workers. Kept in ignorance and poverty, the Udmurts' only escape was the lower ranks of the Orthodox priesthood. The small Udmurt population in the Kama River area produced the first educated minority, the spark that began an Udmurt cultural revival in the late nineteenth century.

The majority of the rural Udmurt population lived in isolation until World War I. In 1910 the first literary works appeared in the Udmurt language, the development of a separate literary language accelerating the cultural and national revival. Thousands of illiterate Udmurt soldiers sent to the front in 1914 began to desert and return home following the overthrow of the tsar in February 1917. The returning soldiers formed a self-defense force as civil government collapsed in the region. In the summer of 1917 the Udmurts convened a national congress, which voted for autonomy in a federal, democratic Russia as promised by government agents. The Bolshevik coup in October ended the debate and thrust the non-Russian peoples of the Volga Basin into closer cooperation. The Udmurts began to erect a state as part of a federation of non-Russian states in the region.

Invading Bolshevik forces occupied Udmurtia in March 1918. The new Soviet authorities quickly suppressed the Udmurt national movement and transferred the capital of the region from the Udmurt city of Glazov to the mostly Russian industrial city of Izhevsk. To win Udmurt support, the Soviets distributed the lands of the great Russian estates to the former Udmurt tenant farmers.

Following the Soviet victory in the Russian civil war, the regional authorities, as part of the Bolsheviks' nationalities policy, established an autonomous Udmurt province on 5 January 1921. The provincial government then moved to confiscate the agricultural lands distributed to the Udmurt farmers in 1918, which provoked a widespread revolt in the region. Between 1920 and 1922 thousands of Udmurts perished in the fighting or from famine and disease. In the 1930s the remaining Udmurt lands were confiscated and collectivized, and their dispossessed owners were forced to settle on government communes.

In spite of the harshness of Soviet rule, the Udmurts advanced in education and culture, particularly after gaining republic status in 1934. In 1922 only 22% of the region's population was literate, and only 10% of that small number were ethnic Udmurts. By the time World War II began in June 1941, Udmurt literacy had become widespread.

The Udmurt region, part of the Ural industrial zone, during World War II received large industries and populations displaced by the war farther west. The Slavic influx reduced the Udmurts to a minority in their homeland, their minority status stimulating the first stirrings of modern Udmurt nationalism in the late 1940s and early 1950s. During the Stalin years, until Stalin's death in 1953, the Udmurts, like the other non-Slav peoples of the region, were under intense pressure to assimilate into the wider Soviet culture, and all signs of dissent or Udmurt nationalism were harshly suppressed.

In the 1970s the Udmurts urbanized, with the populations of many regional towns and cities doubling between 1969 and 1979. Urbanization produced a modern generation of Udmurts, little aware of their unique history and educated in Russian. Udmurt assimilation, well advanced by 1980, began to reverse as young Udmurts took a new interest in their culture and language in the 1980s. The Soviet liberalization of the late 1980s, the reforms introduced by Mikhail Gorbachev, accelerated the reculturation of the Udmurts. As strict Soviet controls disappeared, cultural and nationalist groups formed, demanding official status for their language, the opening of a specifically Udmurt university, and a change from the Russian Cyrillic alphabet to the Latin alphabet used in the West.

The Udmurt republican government, pressed by the growing Udmurt national movement, declared Udmurtia a sovereign state in October 1990. The Udmurt parliament then declared that federal laws were valid in the republic only when confirmed by the parliament. Following the disintegration of the Soviet Union in August 1991, militants advocated independence within a Volga federation, but the majority of the Udmurts fear the uncertainties of independence while asserting their rights within the Russian Federation. The moderate nationalist groups believe that real autonomy will ensure that the Udmurts have not replaced Soviet domination for an equally oppressive Russian domination.

In the years since Russian independence from the collapsing Soviet Union, the number of ethnic Udmurts has risen dramatically. To escape persecution or for economic advantages during the Soviet era, many Udmurts had registered as ethnic Russians, but since 1991 many have again assumed their traditional designation as ethnic Udmurts. The government of their homeland, the largest part of which forms an autonomous republic within the Russian Federation, has fostered the use of the Udmurt language and sponsors cultural activities, including traditional religious rituals. Political organizations, such as the Udmurt National Center, an umbrella coalition of nationalists, ecologists, and cultural groups, work for greater autonomy for the Udmurts.

In spite of centuries of assmiliationist pressure, the Udmurts in the 1990s demonstrate a cohesive sense of identity. In the late 1990s more than 80% of the Udmurts still spoke Udmurt as their first language, and an estimated one-third of the total Udmurt population did not understand Russian. They also retained many elements of their traditional animistic religion.

SELECTED BIBLIOGRAPHY

Colton, Timothy, and Robert Levgold, eds. *After the Soviet Union.* 1992.

Kirkow, Peter. *Russia's Provinces: Authoritarian Transformation versus Local Autonomy.* 1998.

Kozlov, Viktor. *The Peoples of the Soviet Union.* 1988.

Milner-Gulland, R. R., ed. *Cultural Atlas of Russia and the Former Soviet Union.* 1998.

Smal-Stocki, Roman. *The Captive Nations: Nationalism of the Non-Russian Nations and Peoples.* 1960.

UKRAINIANS

Ukraintsi; Ukraintsy; Okrainans

POPULATION: Approximately (2000 e): 51,668,000 Ukrainians in Europe, 38,291,000 in Ukraine, and another 4,685,000 in Russia, 1,524,000 in Poland, 316,000 in Belarus, and smaller numbers in other former Soviet republics, Slovakia, Hungary, and Romania. Outside Europe large Ukrainian populations live in Siberia, Kazakhstan and the other Central Asian republics, Canada, the United States, Brazil, Argentina, and Paraguay.

THE UKRAINIAN HOMELAND: The Ukrainian homeland lies in East-Central Europe, mostly a vast fertile plain, the Ukrainian Steppe, which extends from the Carpathian Mountains and the Volhynian-Pololian uplands in the west to the Donets Ridge in the southeast. The Ukraine Steppe is drained by the Dnieper, Dnestr, Southern Bug, and Donets rivers. The Dnieper divides Ukraine into two historic areas, left-bank and right-bank Ukraine. In the north and northwestern districts is the wooded area of the Pripat Marshes, and in the south is the black earth region with its fertile, treeless, grassy steppe. The richness of the Ukrainian soil has historically rendered the region the "breadbasket of Europe." The region, which lacks natural defenses, straddles the historic trade and invasion routes between Europe and Asia.

Ukraine in 1922 was a constituent republic of the new USSR. Significantly enlarged by the addition of the Western Ukraine in 1939 and the Crimea in 1954, Ukraine became an independent state at the dissolution of the Soviet Union in 1991. *Ukraine (Ukrayina)*: 233,089 sq.mi.–603,701 sq.km. (2000 e) 51,584,000—Ukrainians 74%, Russians* 18%, Poles* 3%, Moldovans* 2%, Jews, Belarussians,* Roms* (Gypsies), Crimean Tatars,* Greeks,* Bulgarians,* Hungarians.* The Ukrainian capital and major cultural center is Kiev, called

Kyyiv in Ukrainian, (2000 e) 2,691,000 (metropolitan area 2,913,000), one of the oldest cities in Europe, often called the "Mother of Cities."

FLAG: The Ukrainian national flag, the official flag of the republic, is a horizontal bicolor of pale blue over yellow.

PEOPLE: The Ukrainians are a Slavic people, the second largest, after the Russians, of the East Slav nations. Their geographic position at the crossroads of the Eurasian Plain has shaped the Ukrainians' complex racial and cultural mixture, and some scholars believe that Ukraine was the original home of the Slavic peoples. Historically and geographically, the Ukrainians are divided into three major ethnographic groups that correspond roughly to the major dialectic zones. The Central-Eastern or Southeastern group is centered in the mid-Dnieper region, where the modern Ukrainian nation formed; the Northern, closer to the other East Slav nations; and the Western, culturally, religiously, and historically distinct, more influenced by contacts with the nations of the non-Slav West. The majority of the Ukrainians are urban, about 68%, while nearly one-third, large by European standards, remains rural. The majority of the Ukrainians belong to the Orthodox churches, particularly the Ukrainian Orthodox churches banned from 1930 to 1990. In western Ukraine a large number are Uniate Eastern rite Catholics, or Roman Catholics.

The most notable demographic trend among the Ukrainians has been a decline in population, with an estimated loss of nearly 1 million between 1991 and 1999. The population decline is due to death rates exceeding birthrates. Leading factors in the low fertility and high mortality rates are environmental pollution, poor diet, alcoholism and heavy smoking, and a severely deteriorating medical care system.

Their language, an East Slav language related to Russian and Belarussian, is spoken in three major dialects, Northwest, Southwest, and East, and numerous subdialects. Dialectical differences are slight, but in the border regions the language has been influenced by neighboring languages, and most Ukrainians are bilingual in Russian. The dialect spoken in the Kiev-Poltava region became the literary language in the nineteenth century. Since independence in 1991, there has been a movement to purge the language of excessive Russian influence.

NATION: Archaeological evidence shows that the region was inhabited in ancient times. The known history of the region began with the establishment of Greek cities on the Black Sea coast. Called Sarmathia, the region later formed the frontier of Roman power, and the first Slavic elements, the Sclaveni, are mentioned in Roman chronicles of the first century A.D. The formation of the Ukrainian nation began with the great Slav migrations of the sixth and seventh centuries A.D. Tribal peoples, the Slavs slowly formed alliances and unions, the most important becoming tribal states.

The formation of the medieval state called Kievan Rus' or Rus'-Ukraine goes back to at least the sixth century A.D., but Kievan prominence dates from the arrival of the Varangian (Viking) Rurikid dynasty in the ninth century. Around 875 A.D. Kiev emerged as the center of the first East Slav state, a loose empire extending south to the Black Sea. The city evolved as the earliest center of East Slav culture and learning. The Kievan Rus' state extended its authority to the Gulf of Finland and Karelia in the north, to the upper course of the Volga River in the east, to the Syan and Western Sub Rivers in the west, and to the Crimean Peninsula in the south. From the ninth to the twelfth centuries the Slav Empire was the leading power in Europe.

The age of Varangian barbarism ended with Prince Vladimir the Great, called St. Volodymyr in the Ukrainian language. In order to marry the sister of the Byzantine emperor, Vladimir accepted Christianity in 988. On his orders his subjects were baptized in mass ceremonies in the Dnieper River. Kiev became the first center of Slavic Orthodox Christianity. By the eleventh century the East Slavs began to separate into national groups, with the Ukrainians, Russians, and Belarussians emerging as the largest of the East Slav groups.

In the 1130s the state began to break up into smaller feudal states. While Kiev remained the center of the most powerful of the states, other centers of power developed, the most important the Galician and Volynian principalities in the northwest. In 1169 the Russian prince of Suzdal seized and sacked Kiev, which shifted the center of power away from the Ukrainians. Thirty years later, the Volynian prince Roman Mstyslavovych united the lands of Galicia and Volynia in a powerful medieval state.

The Mongol invasions sealed the fate of the Kievan state. The city fell to the invaders in 1240 and was completely destroyed. Most of the remaining Ukrainian principalities fell one by one to the Mongol-Tatar Golden Horde. Separated from the Slav heartland by the Mongol-Tatar invasion, the Galician-Volynian principality survived as the new power center of Ukraine. The principality declined after 1349 and in 1386 was conquered by the Lithuanians.* Other Ukrainian territories later came under the rule of Poles and Turks.* The Roman Catholic Poles and the Lithuanians united in 1569, bringing the northern Ukrainian districts together under Polish rule. The southern regions continued under the rule of the Tatar successor state to the Golden Horde, the Khanate of Crimea, which controlled the Crimean Peninsula and a large territory of the southern Ukrainian Steppe.

The advance of serfdom and the persecution of the Ukrainian Orthodox Church sparked widespread opposition to Catholic Polish rule in the seventeenth century. Resistance centered on a warrior group called the Zaporozhye Sich, the Zaporozhye Cossacks, which formed in southern Ukraine in the early sixteenth century. Bohan Khmelnitski (Khmelnytsky), the *hetman* (chief) of the Cossacks, led a national rebellion against Polish domination in 1648.

The Cossacks were successful and established an independent Cossack state, but, too weak to resist the powerful Polish-Lithuanian army, Khmelnitski turned to the Russians. In 1654 Khmelnitski signed a treaty with Moscow recognizing that state's authority over the Zaporozhye Cossack territories. The Treaty of Pereyaslav, which formed a political and military alliance, was to give protection to the mostly independent Ukrainian Cossack state; however, Russian encroachment on Ukraine's independence alienated many Ukrainians, who signed a separate treaty with Poland in 1658, setting off war between Russia and the Polish-Lithuanian state, which ended with the partition of Ukraine in 1667.

Under foreign rule, the Ukrainian upper classes adopted Polish, Lithuanian, or Russian culture and language and often the Roman Catholic religion. Hetman Mazeppa of the Zaporozhye Cossacks tried, from 1687, to break free of foreign rule. He formed an alliance with Sweden and joined the Northern War between Sweden and Russia. In 1709 the allies were defeated by the Russians at Poltava by Peter the Great. The defeat sealed the fate of the Ukrainian territories as Ukrainian autonomy was further curtailed. Between 1764 and 1775 the Zaporozhye Sich was suppressed by the tsarist government, and all political autonomy was eventually ended.

Western Ukraine, called Galicia, with a mixed population of Ukrainians and Poles, became part of Austria as a result of the first Polish partition in 1772. The southeastern region around Chernivtsi, called Bukovina, was added to Austrian Galicia three years later. The revolutionary events in the Austrian Empire in 1848 gave rise to a number of reforms in Galicia. Serfdom was abolished, a regional parliament was created, and Galicia became a full province of the empire. Austrian rule, less oppressive than Russian, allowed the growth of Ukrainian nationalism as part of the European nationalist revival in the mid-nineteenth century.

The national movement in Austrian territory stimulated a Ukrainian cultural and political revival in Russian Ukraine. Under the influence of the romantic and liberal ideas, young Ukrainians began to take a renewed interest in their particular history and traditions. Among the leading intellectuals to embrace Ukrainian nationalism was Taras Shevchenko, a poet and artist who exercised an immense influence on the development of a Ukrainian national consciousness in the nineteenth century.

Under Russian imperial rule, the eastern Ukrainians were subjected to a policy of intense Russification. A cultural revival in the 1870s and 1880s stimulated the spread of Ukrainian national sentiment, leading to renewed oppression and a government ban on the use of the Ukrainian language in 1876. The revolution of 1905 and the reforms adopted in its wake resulted in some relaxation of the harsh tsarist restrictions. The ban on the Ukrainian language was abolished and Ukrainians were allowed to form political organizations.

In the early twentieth century two major revolutionary movements gained support, one seeking to overthrow the tsarist autocracy, and the other a particular Ukrainian nationalism. The first, heavily socialist in nature, promoted a universal culture and remained divided among the various factions as in Russia; the second, based on the Ukrainians' separate history, language, and outlook, advocated autonomy within Russia, while more militant factions demanded support for separation from the Russian Empire and the unification of all Ukrainian lands.

Millions of Ukrainians served in the tsarist armies during World War I, with many of the soldiers later forming the nucleus of a Ukrainian national army when revolution swept the empire in February 1917. Nationalists formed a *rada* (parliament) in Kiev and demanded a status within democratic Russia equal to that of Finland and Poland, the two Russian possessions promised autonomy by the new provisional government of Russia. The demand for autonomy was denied as it felt that Russia could not survive without Ukraine's grain, coal, and other natural resources. The overthrow of the provisional government by a small band of Bolshevik plotters in October 1917 ended efforts to win autonomy within a federal, democratic Russia.

In the west, as the defeated Austro-Hungarian Empire disintegrated, Ukrainian nationalists took control of Galicia and on 14 November 1918 proclaimed the independent Republic of Western Ukrainia. In the east on 22 January 1918, with support from Germany and Austria, the Ukrainian nationalist leaders declared the independence of Russian Ukraine as the Ukrainian National Republic. In January 1919, threatened on all sides, the two Ukrainian states were merged but faced renewed threats from the opposing Red and White Russian forces as well as from Polish and German troops in the region.

In February 1918 Bolshevik troops invaded, and turmoil in the state increased as defeated Germany and Austria withdrew their troops in November. Driven from Kiev by Bolshevik soldiers, the Ukrainian government fought a multisided war as armies and guerrilla bands of every political stripe plundered the state. In late 1919 the Bolshevik Red Army won control, and on 17 February 1920 a Soviet republic was proclaimed. Newly independent Poland, at war with the Soviets, conquered the Catholic majority provinces in western Ukraine, while newly independent Czechoslovakia was awarded Ruthenia (Transcarpathia) by the Allies, and the Romanians* took control of the southwestern territories of Bessarabia and Bukovina.

Joseph Stalin, the Soviet dictator after 1924, was determined to crush the rebellious Ukrainians for all time. Over 3 million died during the collectivization of the rich Ukrainian agricultural districts in 1929–32, and another 6–7 million perished in a systematically planned famine in 1932–33. Uncounted millions died in labor camps and the mass executions that accompanied the periodic Stalinist purges between 1932 and 1937. In 1930 the Ukrainian Autocephalous Orthodox Church, labeled "counterrevolutionary," was officially banned, and its properties were confiscated by the officially sanctioned Russian Orthodox Church.

In the western districts, Western Ukraine and Carpatho-Ukraine (Transcarpathia), although conditions were less severe than in the Soviet Union, Ukrainians in Polish Galicia and Czechoslovak Ruthenia were denied the autonomy the governments had agreed to in the post–World War I settlements. Ruthenes and Ukrainains were mostly excluded from all administrative positions and were under intense pressure to assimilate.

The rise of Nazism in Germany first impacted the Ukrainian lands in Czechoslovakia. In 1938 Ruthenia, called Carpatho-Ukraine, was made an autonomous province with its own government. Amid the continuing Czech crisis, the government of the province declared Carpatho-Ukraine independent on 2 March 1939, but in accordance with a secret pact between Hungary and Germany, the Hungarian troops occupied the small state on 14–15 March.

Soviet troops, as part of a Nazi-Soviet nonaggression pact signed in September 1939, occupied Polish Western Ukraine in November and in 1940 took control of Bukovina from the Romanians. Western Ukrainian ties to the Vatican and the West provoked severe Soviet repression. Up to 1 million people in the region were killed or deported, including anyone having the smooth hands of an intellectual. The Nazis turned on their ally and invaded the Soviet Union in June 1941. Shortly before the German troops reached Lviv, the capital of Western Ukraine, nationalists proclaimed the restoration of the Western Ukrainian republic on 30 June 1941. The Nazis ignored the proclamation and arrested the nationalist leaders. The Western Ukraine was turned into a German colony, and thousands volunteered or were conscripted into the German army or deported as laborers to Germany.

In September 1941 the Germans entered Kiev and were welcomed by many Ukrainians as liberators from the hated Soviets. A nationalist government was formed under Stephen Bandera. The war divided the Ukrainian nation, with Ukrainians often facing each other on the battlefield. During the war the large Jewish population of over 1 million was destroyed, often in massacres with Ukrainian participation. The Ukrainian nation lost about 6 million people through death or deportation during the war.

Retaken by the Red Army in 1944, thousands of Ukrainians were arrested and deported. In 1945 the Soviet Union annexed and added to Soviet Ukraine the Galician region of Poland, Ruthenia from Czechoslovakia, and northern Bukovina and eastern Bessarabia from Romania. Overlooking the contribution made by millions of Ukrainians to the Soviet war effort, Stalin accused the entire Ukrainian nation of collaboration in 1945. Only sheer numbers saved the majority of the Ukrainians from the mass deportations that Stalin inflicted on many smaller nations, although tens of thousands disappeared into Stalin's slave labor camps or were executed. At Stalin's insistence at the end of the war, the Ukrainian Soviet Socialist Republic was numbered among the founding members of the United Nations in 1945. In the western provinces, the Uniate Catholic Church of Western Ukraine was banned and absorbed by the Russian Orthodox Church in 1946. While the Russian Orthodox hierarchy received state subsidies, Uniate Catholic priests, nuns, and laymen filled Stalin's slave labor camps.

The state terror of the Stalin era somewhat relaxed following his death in 1953, but the Stalinist policy of encouraging ethnic Russians to settle in the Ukrainian territories continued. In a conciliatory gesture, the Crimean Peninsula was transferred from the Russian Federation to Soviet Ukraine in 1954 to mark the 300th anniversary of the union of Ukraine and Russia.

Until the mid-twentieth century, Ukrainian society remained traditionally agrarian and village-based, but with Soviet industrialization came the urbanization of the local workforce. The urbanization of the Ukrainians aided the growth of a local nationalist sentiment. A modest national revival begun in the 1960s was ended in 1972 with many arrests. Driven underground, most nationalist activity was centered in the large Ukrainian populations in Canada and the United States and among exile groups in Western Europe. In the western provinces, the least assimilated portion of the population remained the least willing to assimilate into the wider Soviet culture dominated by the ethnic Russians.

Underground Ukrainian nationalism, stifled for over four decades, began to resurface with the Soviet liberalization in the late 1980s, slowly gaining support from its strongholds in the western Ukraine and Kiev. Nationalists formed the Ukrainian Popular Front (RUKH), which worked for Ukrainian autonomy and later led the calls for separation and independence. Growing opposition to the republic's conservative communist government forced a change in the leadership of the republic in 1989. The new communist government of the republic, led by Leonid Kravchuk, rapidly took on the nationalist coloring necessary to survive in the atmosphere of renewed Ukrainian nationalism. Members of RUKH denounced Moscow's control of 95% of Ukrainian industry and the 90% of profits that was taken from the republic. The economic colonization, they claimed, had no historical precedent, not even in colonial Africa.

Ukrainian activists in January 1990 organized a human chain stretching 311 miles from Kiev to the western Ukrainian capital at Lviv to symbolize the unity of the historically divided Ukrainian nation. After fifty years of silence, communist officials admitted to the man-made Ukrainian famine of 1932–33. The Ukrainian Orthodox Church and the Ukrainian Autocephalous Orthodox churches were legalized, and some properties were returned. In the western provinces the Uniate Church, loyal to the Vatican, was also legalized, leading to bitter confrontations over the disposition of confiscated properties.

Ukrainians elected their first real parliament since 1918 in March 1990. Despite the fact that over two-thirds of the deputies in the parliament were Communist Party members, on 16 July 1990 the parliament voted, with only six against, to declare Ukraine a sovereign state. In December the parliament declared Ukrainian the national language of the state.

In the aftermath of the abortive coup against Mikhail Gorbachev in Moscow on 24 August 1991, the Ukrainian parliament proclaimed independence. The Ukrainians' refusal to join a revamped union was the final blow to the disintegrating Soviet Union. On 1 December 1991 the citizens of the new state voted overwhelmingly in support of the independence declaration and on the same day elected Leonid Kravchuk as the country's first president.

The new Ukrainian state, determined to establish an effective independence, was increasingly at odds with the neighboring Russian Federation over the disposition of the former Soviet military assets on its territory, particularly the huge naval base at Sevastopol in the Crimea. The economy, already in crisis, contracted rapidly under the forces of a free market and the loss of many of its former sources of raw materials in Russia. The euphoria over independence soon faded in the face of mounting problems.

In July 1994 in free elections, Leonid Kuchma, a former communist turned nationalist, was elected to the office of president. The democratic transfer of power was the first in Ukraine's history. Giving high priority to the division of power within the government and the revival of the economy, President Kuchma sought a wide range of political and economic ties beyond the Commonwealth of Independent States (CIS), the grouping of former Soviet republics. In 1996 Ukraine became the third largest recipient of U.S. aid, after Egypt and Israel. At the same time the Ukrainian government attempted to settle remaining differences with the Russian Federation. On 31 May 1997 Ukraine and the Russian Federation signed a treaty of friendship and settled the prickly question of Sevastopol and the Black Sea Fleet.

In August 1997 President Kuchma announced two major changes of Ukraine's security policy. He stated that the Ukrainians did not intend to join the North Atlantic Treaty Organization (NATO), although future cooperation was possible, and that the republic would no longer be bound by the provisions of the CIS, which effectively moved Ukraine further from Moscow's influence, although Russia remains Ukraine's largest trading partner and probably the largest direct investor.

The Ukrainian republic, the largest state wholly within Europe, faces a continuing economic crisis, the threat of Russian separatism in the eastern provinces and the Crimea, and vast regional differences due to the separate histories and cultural development of its various regions. The Ukrainians, who began to see modest benefits from the free market only in 1997, are, despite economic and political unrest, determined to survive as the first successful, independent Ukrainian state in modern history.

SELECTED BIBLIOGRAPHY

Clay, Rebecca. *Ukraine: A New Independence.* 1997.

Kuzio, Taras. *Ukraine: State and Nation Building.* 1998.

Magocsi, Paul Robert. *A History of Ukraine.* 1996.

Pawliczko, Ann Lencyk, ed. *Ukraine and Ukrainians throughout the World: A Demographic and Sociological Guide to the Homeland and Its Diaspora.* 1994.

Wanner, Catherine. *Burden of Dreams: History and Identity in Post-Soviet Ukraine.* 1998.

VENETIANS

Venezianos

POPULATION: Approximately (2000 e) 3,671,000 Venetians in Europe, mostly in the northeastern Veneto region of Italy. Other Venetian communities live in other parts of Italy, particularly Rome, and an estimated 100,000 inhabit the parts of the republics of Croatia and Slovenia. Outside Europe there are important Venetian communities in the United States and Argentina.

THE VENETIAN HOMELAND: The Venetian homeland is made up of two distinct topographical areas: the mountain ranges of the Carnic and Dolomite Alps in the north and the Venetian Plain in the south. The lowland region, the Venetian Plain, lies on the Gulf of Venice, an arm of the Adriatic Sea, and includes the valleys of the lower Adige, Po, and Piave Rivers. Along the coast much of the land is low and marshy. The northern part of Veneto is mountainous, with the foothills and high peaks of part of the Dolomites and the Carnic Alps. In the east scenic Lake Garda makes up part of the border with Lombardy.

The region, coextensive with the ancient region of Venetia, forms a semiautonomous region of the Italian Republic. *Region of Veneto (Venezia)*: 7,095 sq.mi.–18,376 sq.km. (2000 e) 4,389,000—Venetians 78%, Lombards* 3%, Ladins,* Tyroleans,* Fruilis,* other Italians.* The capital and major cultural center of the Venetians is Venice, Venezia to the Italians, (2000 e) 318,000, built partly on 118 islands in the Lagoon of Venice. Other important Venetian cultural centers are Verona, (2000 e) 253,000, on the Adige River, and Padua (Padova), (2000 e) 218,000, twenty-two miles (35 km.) west of Venice.

FLAG: The Venetian national flag, the flag of the region of Veneto, is a yellow field charged with a red square on the hoist bearing the Lion of Venice in yellow, and outlined in a yellow and red design, the same design reflected in six horizontal stripes on the fly.

PEOPLE: The Venetians are a northern Italian nation, the descendants of the medieval Venetians, who created a vast Mediterranean Empire. The Venetian culture, which incorporates both Mediterranean and Alpine influences, has borrowed many traits and customs from the peoples once ruled by the Venetian Empire. The Greeks* of the former Byzantine Empire had great influence on the culture, particularly Venetian architecture. More oriented to Vienna and the north than to Rome and the south, the Venetians have maintained their distinct identity, which has strengthened in recent years. The majority of the Venetians are Roman Catholic, with a Protestant minority, mostly in the mountainous districts in the north.

The language of the Venetians is a distinctive dialect that has incorporated many influences from the neighboring Slavic and Germanic peoples. The dialect is very different from standard Italian, and the Venetians are bilingual. Venetian is spoken by 60% of the inhabitants of the region and is used as their first language by 35% of the population. The language, claimed by Venetian nationalists as a separate Romance language, is spoken in three major dialects, Istrian, Trentine, and Venetian.

NATION: The Veneti, an Illyrian people, are thought to have settled the Venetian Plain by 1000 B.C. In the north the high mountain valleys were home to various Celtic tribes. In the second century B.C. the region came under Roman rule, and the regions of Venetia and Istria were joined by Emperor Augustus to form a separate province with its capital at Aquileia. Aquileia and the second city of the Roman province, Padua, dominated the region and evolved as centers of Roman culture. Padua eventually became an important city of Roman Italy, second only to Rome in wealth and culture.

Roman power began to collapse in the third century, and eventually the remaining Roman defenses were overrun. Barbarian tribes invaded the Venetia province in the fifth century A.D. In 452 the Huns, led by Attila, moved across the Venetian Plain, destroying everything in their path. Germanic Lombards later invaded the region from the west. The inhabitants of the once-flourishing city of Aquileia, to escape the destruction, fled to the defensible islands of the Venice Lagoon. Byzantium, the eastern part of the Roman Empire, gained control of the region in the sixth century.

The small island communities united in 697 to elect the first doge (duke) to rule over the unified island state. Well situated to control the flourishing maritime trade, the island communities grew and prospered. In the ninth century the central islands joined to form the city of Venice. On the mainland the towns of the region began to reacquire importance, first under the rule of local bishops and later as free communes.

Not until the tenth century did important towns and, later, free communes develop in the region. Cities such as Verona and Padua grew powerful under the rule of noble families, but the republic of Venice gradually became dominant. Over the next century Venice gained power and eventually broke free of Byzantine rule and began to expand its authority over nearby mainland territories. The Venetians won control of the plains east of the Adige River and expanded to conquer the islands and coastal regions of Dalmatia across the narrow Adriatic. Venetian control of both sides of the Adriatic Sea allowed the republic to control trade between Europe and the East.

In 1204 the Fourth Christian Crusade, led by the Venetian doge Enrico Danolo, instead of moving on to free the Holy Land from Muslim rule, turned on the Byzantine capital, Constantinople. The treasures looted from Christendom's largest and wealthiest city financed Venice's rise to power. Venice emerged from the venture as the ruler of a colonial empire made up of several Mediterranean islands, including Crete, and parts of the Greek mainland.

All Venetian citizens shared in the bounty of the golden age of the republic, but the patrician merchants increasingly obtained political power and eventually formed a ruling oligarchy. In reaction to an unsuccessful conspiracy in 1310, the Council of Ten was instituted to punish crimes against the state. The Ten, supported by a formidable secret police, acquired increasing power, and the doge became a figurehead.

In 1380–81 Venice, known as the "queen of the seas," defeated the rival Republic of Genoa to become the premier Mediterranean maritime power. In the fifteenth century, at the height of its power, Venice extended its rule to the former free cities of the eastern Po Valley to become an extensive Italian state, one of the wealthiest and most powerful in Europe. The Venetians' ambassadors, the creators of the modern diplomatic service, represented Venetian interests in every court in the known world. The Most Serene Republic of Venice was the most powerful state of the Western world.

The emergence of the Turkish Ottoman Empire in the East challenged Venetian dominance of the Mediterranean, and the decline of Venice is usually dated from the fall of Byzantine Constantinople to the Turks* in 1453. Sporadic wars between the fifteenth and eighteenth centuries gradually shrank the republic's overseas empire as colony after colony fell to Turkish rule. Even though the republic declined in power, its cities experienced a great flowering of culture and arts between the fourteenth and sixteenth centuries, the Renaissance. The naval Battle of Lepanto in 1571 gave the Venetians renewed standing in Europe by undoing predominant Turkish seapower, but the respite was not to last. The decline of Venetian power was accompanied by a growing intolerance, particularly of Jews, and the growing power of the Inquisition between 1550 and 1670. The empire continued to decay, losing Cyprus to the Turks in 1571, Crete in 1669, and the Peloponnisos in 1715. The territorial losses ended Venetian dominance of trade in the eastern Mediterranean.

Politics in the Venetian state in the eighteenth century were aristocratic and stagnant. The republic, in spite of frantic efforts to maintain its neutrality, fell, without a shot, to Napoleon's forces in 1797. Napoleon traded most of the Venetian territories to Austria in exchange for lands in the Low Countries.

Briefly joined to Napoleon's Kingdom of Italy from 1805 to 1814, Venice returned to Austrian rule following Napoleon's final defeat.

During the Risorgimento, the unification of Italy, the Venetians, led by Daniele Manin, rebelled against Austrian rule in 1848 and heroically resisted a siege until 1849. The rebels proclaimed Venetian independence as the Republic of St. Mark. Opposed to Venetian moves to unite with the Kingdom of Sardinia, Manin resigned but returned in 1849 to lead Venetian opposition to the reimposition of Austrian rule. The Kingdom of Italy, united in 1860–61 under the Sardinian king, sided with Prussia in the European war called the Austro-Prussian War of 1866. As a reward Prussia backed the Italian annexation of the Venetian territories from defeated Austria.

The new Italian kingdom adopted a Tuscan dialect spoken around Florence as its national language. The dialect, very unlike the Venetian dialect, was generally rejected in the region. Linguistic nationalism increased as the Veneto industrialized in the late nineteenth century, bringing the first migrants from southern Italy, part of the same migration that sent millions of southern Italians to the Americas. The first recorded incidence of violence between the migrants and anti-immigrant Venetians took place in Verona in 1889.

Italy remained virtually a collection of regions until the early twentieth century. The Italian fascist government launched a campaign to eradicate Italy's many regional languages in 1922, although the campaign was largely unsuccessful in Veneto. The beginning of radio broadcasts in the 1930s helped to spread standard Italian to the region, but the predominance of the Venetian language continued through World War II.

After World War II, 60% of the Venetian population still used the Venetian dialect in daily life. The percentage began to decline only with the arrival of mass media in the 1950s and 1960s. The postwar economic boom in northern Italy further eroded the use of the Venetian dialect. Standard Italian became the lingua franca used by Venetian supervisors and the thousands of southern Italians moving north to work in the booming industries in the postwar period.

Resentment of the dialectically and culturally different southern Italians became an issue in the region in the 1960s. Serious anti-immigrant sentiment and violence began to grow in the 1970s, along with an increasing frustration with the notoriously inefficient and overstaffed government in Rome. Moves toward European integration raised fears that Veneto and the other industrialized northern regions would be unable to compete in Europe while hampered by Rome's bloated bureaucracy and the need to channel northern taxes and massive development aid to the corrupt and backward southern regions. In the late 1980s nationalists formed the Liga Veneta, the Venetian League, which formed part of the autonomist Northern League, which grouped several autonomist organizations from regions across northern Italy.

Venetian nationalism, exemplified by the dramatic spread of national sentiment in the late 1980s and early 1990s, is still mainly autonomist, the majority of the nationalists favoring political and economic autonomy within a federal

Italy. In late 1994 nationalists in the city of Venice accused members of the Italian government of having more interest in looting the public purse than in the neglected heritage of Venice and other decaying historic cities in the region.

In September 1996 Umberto Bossi, leader of the coalition Northern League, declared the "federal republic of Padania" independent from the rest of Italy. The so-called republic consists of a region stretching from the Po River to Italy's northern border and includes the cities of Turin, Milan, Bologna, and Venice. The declaration was not to take effect for up to twelve months to enable a Northern League provisional government, formed earlier in the year, to negotiate a treaty of separation with the Italian government. While the Northern League and the regional autonomist organizations were founded on a federalist platform, Bossi had redefined the coalition's goals and had begun calling for the region's secession. Although opinion polls showed little support for secession in Veneto, analysts said that the movement tapped into a growing discontent among northerners, who have accused the national government of economic mismanagement and squandering northern tax revenues to finance projects in poorer regions. In response to such concerns, the Italian parliament had been working to pass constitutional reforms aimed at giving local leaders a stronger voice in national government and changing the country's tax structure.

The massive corruption and crime scandals that have reached the highest circles of the Italian government and the economic elite have spurred the growth of Venetian nationalism and the increasing calls for a separate Veneto state, tied to a federal Italy or an independent Padania, within a united, federal Europe. The Venetians, with their long and separate history, often see the Italian government as a semiforeign presence in their homeland.

SELECTED BIBLIOGRAPHY
Carello, Adrian N. *The Northern Question: Italy's Participation in the European Economic Community and the Mezzogiorno's Underdevelopment.* 1989.
McNeill, W. H. *Venice: The Hinge of Europe, 1081–1797.* 1974.
Morris, James. *The World of Venice.* 1985.
Nichol, Donald M. *Byzantium and Venice.* 1992.
Norwich, John Julius, and Peter Dimock, eds. *A History of Venice.* 1989.

VEPS

Vepse; Vepslaines; Bepslaanes;
Lyyudiniks; Lyudinikad; Lüdilaines;
Chukhars; Kayvans; Tyagalazhet;
Vepsians

POPULATION: Approximately (2000 e) 38,000 Veps in Europe, some 20,000 in Finland, and 18,000 in Russia, concentrated in the Republic of Karelia and the region of St. Petersburg. Outside Europe there is a Vep community in Kemerovo Oblast in Russian Siberia. Vep activists claim a national population in excess of 70,000 in Russia.

THE VEP HOMELAND: The Vep homeland, part of the East European Plain, lies in northwestern European Russia between Lake Ladoga and Lake Onega and around the Oyat, Kapscha, Pascha, and Ivoda Rivers east of Lake Ladoga. The Vep homeland was much larger in the past. The region, mostly lowlands between the lakes or in the river valleys, is fertile and mostly rural. In the area east of Lake Ladoga there are lowland marshes and swamps. A region of cold winters and short, hot summers, the growing season is correspondingly short, but farming remains the major economic activity of the region.

The homeland of the Veps has no official status in Russia, although since the foundation of the independent Russian Federation in 1991, the Veps have worked to unify the three Vep territories into a single autonomous unit. The northern Veps, called the Äänis, live in the Republic of Karelia around the town of Äänisjärv on the southwestern shore of Lake Onega south of the Karelian capital, Petrozavodsk. The central Veps, the most numerous group, live in the St. Petersburg region on the Oyat River and its tributaries. The southern group lives on the border between St. Petersburg and Vologda Oblasts, on the Lid River. Some Veps live in St. Petersburg or other nearby towns.

FLAG: The Vep national flag, the flag of the regional movement, is a pale green field bearing a light blue Scandinavian cross outlined in yellow.

PEOPLE: The Veps are a Finnic people culturally and linguistically related to the neighboring Karels.* Called Chud until the Russian Revolution, the name "Vep" was retained only by the southern Veps, but the name has been revived as part of the Vep national movement. Vep nationalists claim a much larger ethnic population in the region, as many registered as ethnic Russians for political or economic reasons in successive Soviet censuses. There are a growing sense of Vep identity and a desire to revive their unique culture and language. The Vep population in Finland, mostly refugees who fled the Vep homeland during the Winter War and World War II, has provided financial and educational aid to the Vep national revival. The majority of the Veps belong to the Orthodox Church.

The language of the Veps, called Vepsian, is a Balto-Finnic language closely related to Karelian and Finnish. The language, written in the Latin alphabet, is spoken in three major dialects, Southern Veps, Central Veps, and Prionezh or Northern Veps. The dialects correspond to the three major divisions of the Vep nation. The language is now taught in some primary schools but is not compulsory. Most Veps are bilingual in Russian and often speak Karelian or Finnish. The Vep language is now recognized as one of the official languages of the Republic of Karelia, a member state of the Russian Federation.

NATION: The Finnic peoples from the Volga River basin migrated to the west and settled the territories around the Baltic Sea and Lakes Ladoga and Onega in the eighth century. By the ninth century, as mentioned in Slavic chronicles, the Veps were known as a separate people that populated the region between the large lakes in clan-organized groupings, with few ties beyond the clan level. In the tenth century they were mentioned as a people called the Visu in Arab travel journals.

Most of the Vep clans came under the political control of the Slavic Republic of Novgorod, which was founded by Vikings, called Varangians, as a merchant state. The Vep homeland was invaded by crusading Germans* and Swedes* expanding their territories to the east, but the majority of the clans remained under Novgorodian rule until 1478, when Great Novgorod fell to the expanding Russian state called Muscovy or Moscow, and in 1485 the Vep territories were annexed to the growing Russian Empire.

The constant northward expansion of Russian settlement soon made the Veps a minority in their traditional homeland. Russian colonists formed a wedge in the Süväri Basin, which divided the Northern and Central Veps. The intrusion of Russian colonists on the tributaries of the Süväri and Jüvenjoe Rivers also divided the Northern Veps from the related Ingrians* and Karels. The forcible conversion to the Orthodox religion, schooling only in the Russian language, and the close proximity of Russian settlements began the long process of the assimilation of the Veps into Russian culture.

The Finnic nations of the region were often in the middle of the quarrels between the expanding Swedish and Russian states. The western Vep clans formed part of the medieval Karel state, which came under Swedish rule in

1617. At the end of the Northern War between Sweden and Russia in 1721, all the Vep territories came under the rule of the Russians.* Under tsarist rule, the region became backward and poverty-stricken and was known chiefly as a place of exile for political prisoners and criminals.

In the mid-nineteenth century, under the influence of the Westernized Finns,* the Veps, then numbering over 70,000, experienced a cultural revival, with renewed interest in their language, literature, and culture. The Finns, incorporated into the Russian Empire in 1809, became the champions of the smaller Finnic nations of Russia.

An official government policy of Russification was introduced in 1899, and the Veps came under intense pressure to assimilate. Their language was prohibited in publications and in education, but materials smuggled into the region from Finland kept the Veps in touch with the nationalist movement that was growing among the related Finns. In the past, in Russian sources, the Veps and also the other Finnic peoples of the region were disparagingly called Chukhars or Chukhnas.

During the Russian Revolution of 1905 the first stirrings of Vep nationalism were felt, and many activists took to the streets to call attention to a long list of grievances. Among the concessions granted by the Russian government were an end to the policy of Russification of the Finnic minorities and more linguistic and cultural freedom. The opening of Vep schools and availability of Finnish publications began to reverse decades of forced assimilation.

The outbreak of war in 1914 accelerated the growth of nationalism in nearby Finland, with a parallel increase in activity in the Vep territory. The overthrow of the tsarist government in 1917 threw the region into chaos, with escaped prisoners and political exiles suddenly freed from the many prison camps. As the tsarist administration collapsed, the Veps, following the lead of the Finns, created a nationalist administration to administer their region and the official national population of over 35,000. The Vep government, opposed by many of the local Russians, remained, for the most part, a government in name only.

In March 1918 the arrival of British troops gave the Veps some protection. The British and Allied troops, landed at Murmansk and Archangel in support of an anti-Bolshevik government, took control of much of the territory, driving local Bolsheviks underground. During the Russian civil war, the Finns invaded the region and were welcomed by the Veps as liberators from hated Russian rule. The Western Interventionist forces were withdrawn in 1919 as the Red and White Russian forces fought for control of Russia.

In early 1920 the Red Army defeated the remaining White forces in the region, and the last of the foreign troops were withdrawn. The imposition of Soviet rule, particularly the Soviets' nationality policy, was quite promising for the Veps and even had the appearance of aiding the national awakening that began in the nineteenth century. The Soviet authorities created twenty-four administrative units in the Vep homeland, part of which were grouped into two national districts, Vidla in the Leningrad region and Shoutjärve in the Karelian

Autonomous Republic. Before a third autonomous district, Shimjärve, in the Leningrad region could be formed, those national districts already in existence were liquidated.

The collectivization of Vep agriculture in the late 1920s caused severe disruptions. In 1928, to escape the forced collectivization, some Southern Veps left the region and migrated as homesteaders to the new lands in Siberia, particularly the Kemerovo Oblast. In spite of the hardships of collectivization, Vep culture advanced under Soviet rule. Schools in the Vep language were opened, and a written language in the Latin alphabet was created on the basis of the Central Vep dialect. A department of minorities was established at the Leningrad District Council, which engaged in compiling the Vep written language. A system of spelling was worked out similar to the Latin alphabet system created for the Karels of Tver. The first book published in the Latin alphabet was a primer, in 1932, and altogether more than thirty books were printed in the Vep language. By 1934 all the Vep schools had been supplied with textbooks in their native language. Finnish academics, visiting the Vep region in 1934, reported a national population of over 50,000, with large families and the widespread use of the Vep language in domestic life.

The period of Soviet support was short-lived. The Stalinist policy of the violent oppression of minorities, begun in 1937, hit the Veps particularly hard. All national cultural activities were stopped, and the assimilation of the Veps by "accelerated methods" was ordered. Vep schools were closed, textbooks were burned, teachers were imprisoned, and many intellectuals disappeared or were executed. Politically, the Vep autonomous district in Leningrad Oblast was abolished in 1939, and other national districts were parceled out between the Karelian Associated Soviet Socialist Republic (ASSR) and Leningrad and Vologda Oblasts. The Veps of Shimjärve, fleeing the oppression in their district, abandoned their homes and settled in the villages and towns of the Northern Veps.

The Winter War between Finland and the Soviet Union in 1939–40 divided the Veps between those wishing to aid the related Finns and those so terrified of the Soviet administration that they wished to ignore the painful subject of politics. During World War II, called the War of Continuation by the Finnic peoples, Finnish troops occupied part of the Vep region. The occupation authorities established a Finnish educational system, and many Vep volunteers joined the Finnish military, where they formed the Kindred Battalion.

In 1944 the Finns and their German allies in the region were defeated and were driven back into Finland by the Red Army. Thousands of Finnic refugees fled their homelands as the Russians advanced, including an estimated half of the total Vep population, some 25,000 people. Those who stayed or were unable to escape faced severe punishment for collaborating with the Finns.

In the postwar period younger Veps began a mass migration to the towns, moving into a Russian linguistic and cultural environment. Although Soviet census figures were always suspect, the data from the 1959, 1970, and 1979 censuses were not objective but reflected the arbitrary power of local officials in recording nationalities. In identification documents and house registers of the village Soviets, the nationality of the Veps was often misrepresented out of fear or false shame at admitting to Vep nationality. By the late 1970s the population claiming Vep nationality was mostly over age forty, reflecting the assimilation of the younger Veps into the urban Russian population. The feeling of national identity was very low, and hopes for the future were bleak.

The reforms introduced into Soviet society by Mikhail Gorbachev in the late 1980s began the reculturation of the Veps. Under Gorbachev's administration, Soviet officials admitted the Stalinist terror that had decimated the Veps in the late 1930s. A national district was reestablished for the Northern Veps, but aspirations of forming a united administrative unit for all the present Vep regions were met with powerful Russian resistance. A Veps Cultural Society was formed in 1989, the first openly Vep association since 1937.

The Vep language was adopted as an official language by the government of the Republic of Karelia following its declaration of sovereignty in 1990. Following the collapse of the Soviet Union and the creation of the new Russian Federation in 1991, various Vep nationalist associations were formed to promote the revival of the Vep culture and language. In 1998 Vep activists in Finland estimated the national population, both declared and registered as other nationalities, at over 70,000 in Russia.

SELECTED BIBLIOGRAPHY

Allison, Roy. *Finland's Relation with the Soviet Union 1944–84*. 1985.
Kirkow, Peter. *Russia's Provinces: Authoritarian Transformation versus Local Autonomy*. 1997.
Maude, George. *The Finnish Dilemma: Neutrality in the Shadow of Power*. 1976.
Paasi, Anssi. *Territories, Boundaries and Consciousness: The Changing Geographies of the Finnish-Russian Boundary*. 1997.
Watson, Jane Werner. *The Soviet Union: Land of Many Peoples*. 1973.

VOLGA GERMANS

Russian Germans

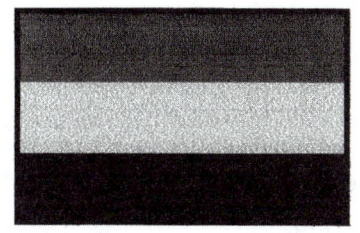

POPULATION: Approximately (2000 e) 788,000 Volga Germans in Europe, most in the southern provinces of European Russia, but with an estimated 100,000 in Germany. Outside Europe the largest of the Volga German populations are in Central Asia, particularly Kazakhstan. The total German population of the Russian Federation and the other former Soviet republics is thought to exceed 2 million.

THE VOLGA GERMAN HOMELAND: The Volga German homeland, formerly called the German Volga Republic, occupies the rolling steppe lands in the valley of the middle Volga River on the arbitrary divide between Europe and Asia. Situated on the east bank of the Volga, the region borders on Kazakhstan on the east. Most of the land is fertile steppe, part of the great Volga River basin, formerly called the breadbasket of Russia. The Volga Germans, deported during World War II, now live scattered across the Russian Federation, from the Kaliningrad Oblast on the Baltic Sea, to Siberia and the Russian Far East. There are also Volga German colonies in most of the former Soviet republics.

The Volga German homeland has no official status; the region forms the eastern districts of Saratov Oblast. The Russian and German governments have agreed to the re-creation of an autonomous Volga German state in the region they occupied before 1941, but as yet nothing more has been accomplished. Other proposals include an autonomous homeland in Kaliningrad Oblast, formerly part of German East Prussia with its capital at Königsberg, now Kaliningrad, and the establishment of national districts in German areas of Siberia and around the city of Orenburg, the only major Russian city whose German name was not altered by the Soviet authorities. *Proposed Volga German Region*: 10,888 sq.mi.–28,200 sq.km. (2000 e) 1,346,000—Russians* 85%, Ukrainians* 10%, Volga Germans 3%, Kazakhs, Tatars.* In 1941 the region had a population of 656,000, Volga Germans 67%, Russians 20%, Ukrainians 12%. The major German cultural centers in Russia include Engels, (2000 e) 213,000, the former capital of the Volga German Autonomous Soviet Socialist Republic, and Kaliningrad (Königsberg), (2000 e) 418,000, the former capital of German East Prussia.

FLAG: The Volga German flag, the flag of the republican movement, is a horizontal tricolor of red, pale blue, and black.

PEOPLE: The Volga Germans originated with eighteenth-century colonists, mostly from the southern German states. The Volga or Russian German culture is a mixture of both German and Slavic influences, incorporating traits and customs that have long since disappeared in Germany and borrowing from the Slavs they have lived among for over two centuries. Deported from their Volga and Black Sea homelands in 1941, the Germans have lived dispersed among the majority Russian population across a wide region of the Russian Federation, Kazakhstan, and other parts of Central Asia and other areas of exile.

The languages of the Germans remain the Bavarian, Danubian, and Swabian they brought with them from southern Germany in the late eighteenth century. In 1989 only 60% of the Russian Germans listed German as their first language; however, since the collapse of the Soviet Union and the reunification of Germany a rapid reculturation has taken hold in the German-populated areas with a revival of the German dialects. Few of the Russian Germans speak the standard modern German language, and those emigrating to Germany have difficulty with the language and culture.

NATION: German settlement in territory that eventually came under Russian rule began in the thirteenth century with the German knights who conquered the region now included in the Baltic States, the homelands of the Estonians,* Latvians,* and Lithuanians.* In 1720, at the conclusion of the Northern Wars between Sweden and Russia, the Germans in the Baltic region were the first to come under Russian authority.

Tsarina Catherine II of Russia, known as Catherine the Great, was born in the southern German state of Anhalt-Zerbst in 1762. To strengthen her empire and to exploit the rich southern agricultural lands newly won from the Turks* and Tatars, the tsarina issued an invitation to the inhabitants of the German states to settle in the region. The inhabitants of the southern German states, suffering from overpopulation, crop failures, and religious conflicts, responded in large numbers. Catherine's manifesto, issued in 1763, guaranteed the colonists and their descendants free lands, exemption from military service, freedom of religion, local autonomy, use of their own languages, local control of schools, and many other incentives designed to appeal to the industrious German peasants.

Catherine's invitation, particularly appealing to the Bavarians,* Swabians,* and Rhinelanders* of the southern German states that had suffered extensive devastation during the just-ended Seven Years' War, provided a less costly alternative to emigration to America. Between 1764 and 1768 thousands of German colonists settled the newly conquered frontier districts north and east of the Black Sea. Some 27,000 Germans moved farther east to establish over 100 farming communities along the middle course of the Volga River. Catherine's manifesto provided the settlers with a thirty-year exemption from taxes as well as a ten-year, interest-free loan for homes and farm machinery. The colonists, isolated and self-sufficient, prospered as farmers and merchants in close-knit communities having little to do with the neighboring Slav villages. Dialects, cultures, and traditions that gradually changed or disappeared in Germany continued in the region, eventually forming part of a distinctive Slav-influenced German culture.

The German settlers suffered great hardships as they spread out across the steppe lands of southern Russia and Ukraine. The lack of trees evolved a distinct type of dwelling, the sod house, similar to those constructed on the plains of North America. The Russian government's determination that the region produce grains was embodied in a 1767 decree prohibiting the German settlers from engaging in any occupation other than farming. The decree violated Catherine's 1763 manifesto and reduced the German immigrants to serfs in all but name.

Frequent crop failures were worsened by the inability of the Russian government to deliver grain seeds on time each spring. Often planting took place as late as May or June. The mixture of privations, government interference, and raids by Tatars and bandits took their toll on the settlers. Some returned to Germany, and others fled to Russia's Baltic provinces, while many emigrated to North America, where they founded settlements in the Great Plains region of the United States and Canada that remained distinct from nearby German settlements. The emigrants retained their distinct Slavic-German culture wherever they eventually settled. The German settlers who persevered had their first good harvest in 1775, and production improved markedly with the introduction of improved farm machinery imported from Germany.

Catherine's successors on the Russian throne progressively abolished the Germans' privileges. By 1870 all of Catherine's guarantees had disappeared. Over the next decade an official policy of assimilation and Russification closed German schools, publications, and institutions. The authorities introduced military conscription. Resistance to assimilation and conscription led to the growth of a German national sentiment in the 1880s and 1890s. The German national movement evolved as a cultural campaign to preserve their language and culture but also became antigovernment.

Suspected of pro-German sentiment when war began in 1914, the tsarist government imposed harsh new restrictions on the Germans. In 1916 the government issued a decree ordering the deportation of all Germans, the order to be implemented in April 1917. The decree, suspended when revolution swept Russia in February 1917, was finally rescinded, along with all other tsarist decrees, by the Bolsheviks who overthrew the Russian provisional government in October 1917.

The Bolshevik takeover of Russia further divided the Russian Germans. In the western provinces, the Germans generally supported the anti-Bolshevik Whites, but in the Volga region and Ukraine, the German minority often supported the Reds, partly due to Bolshevik promises of land. Local German leaders took control of the region, with some preparing to declare independence and to seek assistance from the German military units occupying Russian territory to the west. However, in late 1917 Bolshevik forces overran the region and pro-Bolshevik Germans organized an autonomous administration, the first ethnic group to be organized under the Bolsheviks' nationalities program. In 1919 the region was raised to the status of an autonomous republic within the new Soviet Russian Federation. Outside the Volga republic the Soviet authorities created seventeen autonomous districts for the scattered German populations.

The Germans of the German Volga Republic, created as a model showcase to encourage the spread of communism in Germany, suffered harsh repression when the post–World War I communist uprisings failed in Germany. As relations between the Soviet Union and Germany worsened during the late 1920s and early 1930s, the repression of the German population of Russia increased. Soviet repression eased only when the Soviet Union signed a friendship treaty with Nazi Germany in 1939. By 1940 more than 25% of the total German population of the Soviet Union lived in the German Volga Republic.

The Nazi invasion of the Soviet Union in June 1941 ended the short period of leniency. Soviet leader Joseph Stalin accused all Soviet Germans of collaboration. In August 1941 the 440,000 Volga Germans and between 250,000 and 350,000 mostly Black Sea Germans were shipped east in closed cattle cars. The deportees, often without food or shelter, were dumped at rail sidings across Siberia and Central Asia under close KGB control. Another 350,000 Germans, living in areas overrun by the German armies, were evacuated by the German army to Germany. Over 200,000 of the evacuees, rounded up by Soviet troops in defeated Germany in 1945, were forcibly repatriated and sent directly to slave labor camps, where they remained until granted amnesty after Stalin's death in 1953.

In the west, in violation of agreements among the Allies, the Soviets occupied the German region of East Prussia. Most of the region's population was forcibly expelled, but thousands who failed to escape were arrested and shipped east to exile or slave labor camps. The region, turned into a military base and an important port on the Baltic Sea, remained off limits to non-Russians even after the rehabilitation of the exiled Soviet Germans.

The postwar Soviet government began a radical denationalization program, whereby Germans were denied the opportunity to maintain their language and culture. The policy of forced assimilation, carried out with considerable force and brutality, was considered a success. According to the 1959 Soviet census, only 43% of the ethnic Germans in the Soviet Union stated that they spoke German in their daily lives.

Not rehabilitated with the other deported peoples in 1956–57, the Germans were finally exonerated in 1964 but were not allowed to return to their homes in the Volga River basin, the Black Sea region, or Kaliningrad Oblast on the Baltic Sea. Their petitions and appeals constantly rebuffed, the German exiles developed a sense of grievance that stimulated the growth of nationalism. In 1975 a Volga German national movement formed to work for the reestablishment of an autonomous German homeland on the Volga. Improved relations between the Soviet Union and Germany allowed a small number to emigrate, but the numbers were limited by Germany's inability to absorb all who wished to leave Russia.

The reestablishment of an autonomous German republic within Russia was first raised by Leonid Brezhnev in 1972. But each time the government issued a statement implying or clearly stating an intention to reestablish a German republic in the Volga region, it has been met with demonstrations and strong opposition from the Russian population settled in the region following the German deportation in 1941.

Support for the creation of an autonomous German homeland in Kaliningrad Oblast became widespread in the 1980s, following the liberalization of Soviet life in 1987–88. Among the arguments for the creation of a German republic in Kaliningrad were the Germans' historical ties to the region. The need for a German homeland in Russia was discussed in March 1991 during a meeting between President Mikhail Gorbachev and the German foreign minister, Hans-Dietrich Genser, but the subsequent events, including the collapse of the Soviet Union in August 1991, left the question of an autonomous homeland unsettled.

Although cool to the idea of yet another minority nationalism, the Russian authorities, badly in need of Germany's political and financial assistance, in a series of meetings with German officials finally agreed. The long delay in implementing the accord has stimulated more militant groups and demands and has provoked the emigration of over 100,000 a year to Germany in the 1990s. An estimated half of the ethnic Germans living in the Soviet Union in 1991 have left for Germany, taking advantage of the German government's offer to return to their historic homeland. The majority of the returning Germans are descendants of the Volga Germans deported from their Volga homeland in 1941. However, in the later 1990s, Germany's economic problems and high unemployment have blunted the Russian Germans' welcome in Germany and again raised the question of a German-financed homeland on the Volga.

A 1996 meeting of the initiative group uniting major cultural and nationalist organizations of Russia's ethnic Germans adopted a resolution on starting the formation of the Russian or Volga Germans' national-cultural autonomy, the first of its kind on the territory of the Russian Federation. The participants in the meeting approved the membership of the organizing committee, which carried the Germans' case for autonomy to the various ministries, departments, and local administrations of the Russian Federation.

SELECTED BIBLIOGRAPHY

Curran, Alfred A. *Soviet-German Nationalism.* 1986.

Ingsborg, Fleischhauer, and Benjamin Pinkus. *The Soviet Germans: Past and Present.* 1986.

Kloderdanz, Timothy J. *Thunder on the Steppe: Volga German Folklife in a Changing Russia.* 1994.

Koch, Frederick C. *The Volga Germans: In Russia and the Americas 1763 to the Present.* 1987.

Sinner, Peter. *Germans in the Land of the Volga.* 1989.

VORARLBERGERS

Alemannis

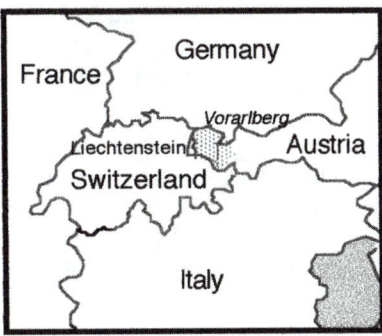

POPULATION: Approximately (2000 e) 326,000 Vorarlbergers in Europe, mostly concentrated in the Vorarlberg state of Austria, but with substantial populations in Vienna and other parts of Austria and in Switzerland and Germany.

THE VORARLBERGER HOMELAND: The Vorarlberger homeland lies in the extreme western portion of Austria. Called Vorarlberg for the Arlberg Mountain, which lies on the border between Vorarlberg and Tyrol, the name means "Land before or beyond the Arlberg." The region is noted for its Alpine scenery and for its cattle and dairy herds. Although the most industrialized of the Austrian states, Vorarlberg remained isolated from the rest of Austria until modern times.

Vorarlberg forms a state of the Federal Republic of Austria. *Vorarlberg*: 1,004 sq.mi.–2,601 sq.km. (2000 e) 335,000—Vorarlbergers 88%, Tyroleans* 8%, other Austrians.* The Vorarlberger capital and major cultural center is Bregenz, (2000 e) 28,000. The other important Vorarlberger cultural center is Dornbirn, (2000 e) 40,000, the state's largest city.

FLAG: The Vorarlberger national flag, the official flag of the state, is a horizontal bicolor of red over white.

PEOPLE: The Vorarlbergers are an Alemannic people closely related to the neighboring Swiss-Germans,* but not closely related to the neighboring Tyroleans or the Austrians. In the isolation of their mountain homeland, the Vorarlbergers developed a distinctive Alpine culture. The baroque style so popular in Austria was not accepted in Vorarlberg, whose people developed a uniquely Alpine style in rebellion against what they saw as the extravagances of the Hapsburgs. Like the other Austrian nations, the Vorarlbergers are mostly Roman Catholic.

The language of the Vorarlbergers, spoken along with standard German, is a distinctive Alemannic dialect related to Swiss-German. The Vorarlbergers are the only group in Austria to speak an Alemannic dialect.

NATION: Originally inhabited by Ilyrians and Celts prior to the Roman conquest of the region, the area around the Lake of Constance was long a crossroads. The region west of the Arlberg formed part of the Roman province of Rhaetia, present Switzerland, from the first century A.D. At the collapse of the Roman Empire in the fifth century, barbarian tribes from outside the empire invaded the region. By the sixth century the region had been occupied by Germanic Alemannic tribes. The Alemannic tribes later came under the rule of the Franks, and their homeland formed part of the Frankish kingdom of Charlemagne.

In 843, following Charlemagne's death, Vorarlberg formed part of the eastern Frankish kingdom, one of the successor states to his empire. The eastern kingdom, ruled by Louis the German, later expanded to become the German Empire. In the thirteenth and fourteenth centuries, there was a strong immigration from the present Swiss region of Valais, the migration forming the basis of the present Vorarlberg nation.

The Alemannic territories split into a number of small holdings, with Vorarlberg coming under the rule of the counts of Montfort. Between the fourteenth and sixteenth centuries, the region was acquired piecemeal by the Hapsburgs. In 1523 Vorarlberg became a Hapsburg crownland administered from neighboring Tyrol. For hundreds of years the Vorarlbergers formed a separate German-speaking nation in the multinational Austrian Empire.

In the early nineteenth century, during the Napoleonic Wars, the French leader Napoleon gave Vorarlberg and Tyrol to his Bavarian ally in 1805. In 1809 the Vorarlbergers joined the Tyroleans in a revolt against the Bavarians* In 1814, following Napoleon's defeat, Vorarlberg returned to Austrian rule. In 1861 a bishopric was established in Bregenz, the beginning of separation from neighboring Tyrol.

Although the Vorarlbergers remained isolated from the rest of Austria until the construction of a tunnel under the Arlberg in 1884, their province was one of the most progressive in the empire. The Vorarlbergers had the first telephone, the first electric light, and the first hydroelectric turbine in the empire. A Vorarlberger was the first in the empire to drive an automobile. In some aspects, the region's schools were a century ahead of those in other parts of the empire. Industrialized, due to the abundant hydroelectric power, in the late nineteenth century, the region was one of the most advanced in the Austro-Hungarian Empire by the turn of the twentieth century. Proud of their achievements and of their unique culture, the Vorarlbergers in the late nineteenth century developed a zealous local patriotism.

Insulated from the war by their mountains, the Vorarlbergers were unprepared for the defeat and collapse of the empire in November 1918. The strong separatist movement in the Tyrol caused the Vorarlbergers to separate administratively and to proclaim themselves a separate non-Austrian, Germanic people. Vorarlberger leaders set up a separate administration as the civil government of the empire collapsed. The Vorarlbergers, in spite of historic ties to Austria, held a plebiscite and voted for independence and an alliance with neighboring neutral Switzerland, with which they have economic, geographic, and linguistic ties. When the neighboring Liechtensteiners* declared their independence of the empire, the Vorarlbergers followed, declaring the independence of the Republic of Vorarlberg on 3 November 1918. The new Vorarlberger government began to establish close ties to the Swiss Confederation.

The secession of Vorarlberg from Austria was blocked by the Allies and the new Austrian republican government. Under strong economic and political pressure, the Vorarlbergers finally joined the new Austrian republic, becoming an autonomous land or state with a separate provincial assembly.

The unstable Austrian government, dominated by socialist, anticlerical Vienna, was constantly at odds with the nationalistic Vorarlbergers. In April 1919 over 80% of the Vorarlbergers voted to secede from Austria and to ally to Switzerland, but they were again blocked by Allied opposition. The powerful provincial diet retained considerable autonomy, and another movement for secession in 1921 was defeated only following Allied intervention.

In the 1920s Vorarlberg's autonomy was curtailed by the socialist government in Vienna, but political turbulence kept the nationalist movement active during the late 1920s and early 1930s. In 1938 Austria was annexed by Nazi Germany, and the Vorarlbergers lost all their remaining autonomy. Initial enthusiasm for union with Germany waned following the bombing of the industrial cities in Vorarlberg in 1944. In 1945 French troops occupied the region. The Allied occupation of Austria ended in 1955.

Standard German mostly replaced the Vorarlbergers' Alemannic dialect by the 1960s, but the region's unique Alpine culture flourished with renewed vigor. Austria's state neutrality and prosperous postwar economy benefited industrial Vorarlberg during the Cold War of the 1970s and 1980s.

Vorarlberg had the fastest growing population in the Alpine region of Europe, growing 94% between 1923 and 1971. By the 1980s guest workers from Southern Europe constituted about 20% of the workforce in the region, raising social tensions with the close-knit Vorarlberger community. In September 1979 an autonomist group, Pro-Vorarlberg, published an appeal in which it demanded a special statute for Vorarlberg within the Austrian republic. The appeal led to an initiative by the provincial diet to conduct negotiations with the government in Vienna on financial and fiscal autonomy and increased control of local education, commerce, forestry, agriculture, and communications. The Vorarlbergers also demanded the right to conclude contracts with neighboring states, such as Germany, to which it sells substantial amounts of hydroelectric power. The autonomy initiative was approved by a provincial referendum on 23 June 1980 and was passed by almost 70% of the electorate but was opposed by the Austrian government and was never implemented.

In the 1990s the Vorarlbergers continue to claim that theirs is an independent nation, freely associated with the post–World War II Austrian republic. Strongly oriented to the Swiss, the Vorarlbergers have retained a strong provincial patriotism. Although the Vorarlbergers have close economic and historic ties to neighboring Switzerland and Liechtenstein, due to the rugged nature of their homeland and the struggle of its citizens to glean a livelihood from the meager resources, the Vorarlbergers have retained a very strong sense of their separate culture. Their national flag is flown more often than the Austrian national flag, and local heroes take precedence over Austrian heroes.

The integration of Europe, both economically and politically, has stimulated demands for greater economic and political autonomy. The Vorarlbergers' position on the Swiss and German borders has led to a decided preference for greater local control of their trade and economy.

SELECTED BIBLIOGRAPHY

Greene, Carol. *Austria*. 1986.
Jelavich, Barbara. *Modern Austria: Empire and Republic 1815–1986*. 1987.
Luther, Kurt Richard, and Peter G. J. Pulzer, eds. *Austria 1945–95: Fifty Years of the Second Republic*. 1998.
Sked, Alan. *The Decline and Fall of the Hapsburg Empire, 1815–1918*. 1989.
Steiner, Kurt, ed. *Modern Austria*. 1981.

WALDENSIANS

Waldenses; Valdese

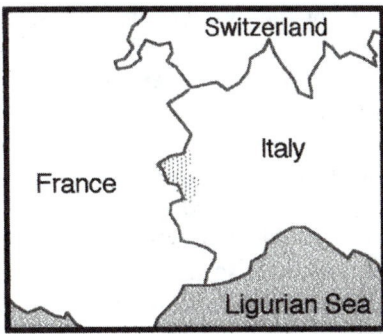

POPULATION: Approximately (2000 e) 33,000 Waldensians in Europe, mostly in the Waldensian valleys in northwestern Italy, but with some across the border in France. Outside Europe the largest Waldensian population, some 15,000, lives in the Rio Plate region of Argentina and Uruguay, with smaller numbers in the United States and Canada.

THE WALDENSIAN HOMELAND: The Waldensian homeland, often called Waldensia, lies in the Cottian Alps, occupying seven valleys traversed by the Pellice and Germanesca Rivers, on the French border southwest of Turin in northwestern Italy. The region, mostly high Alpine valleys in the rugged Alps, remained one of Europe's most isolated until the 1950s, when new roads linked the region to the towns of Piedmont, particularly Turin.

Waldensia has no official status; the region forms a historic area in the Italian region of Piedmont. *Waldensian Valleys (Valli Valdesi)*: 1,136 sq.mi.–2,943 sq.km. (2000 e) 62,000—Waldensians 50%, Occitans* 32%, Italians,* French.* The Waldensian capital and major cultural center is Torre Pellice, (2000 e) 6,000, historically the nucleus of the Waldensian valleys, the center of the Waldensian Church, and the seat of the Waldensian Synod.

FLAG: The Waldensian flag is a blue field with a narrow red horizontal stripe at the bottom divided from the blue by a narrow white stripe. In the center is a white candle with an oval of yellow light around the flame surrounded by seven white stars.

PEOPLE: The Waldensians are a division of the Occitan people who inhabit northwestern Italy and the Occitania region of southern France but are historically and religiously distinct as the oldest surviving Protestant nation in the world. The descendants of the followers of the first Protestant religious dissidents in the twelfth and thirteenth centuries, the Waldensians became a nation through centuries of persecution, massacres, and isolation. The Waldensian culture, protected by their self-imposed isolation, combines the original Occitan Latin culture with influences from the Piedmontese* and the Romands* in Switzerland.

The Waldensians speak an Alpine dialect of Occitan that has been heavily influenced by Piedmontese, the predominant language of the region. The majority of the Waldensians also speak standard Italian, and many also speak French.

NATION: In the latter half of the twelfth century, in 1170, a wealthy merchant in Lyon, Pietro Waldo, also called Valdo or Valdesius, ceded his fortune to his family and took a vow of poverty. He began a life of religious devotion and poverty, vowing vengeance on the money he believed had reduced him to a form of slavery and made him more obedient to it than to God. He entreated people to place their hope in God and not in riches. Dedicating his life to meditation, he soon gained a following, known as the "Poor of Lyon."

Waldo and his followers questioned the existing religious doctrine and attempted to return Christianity to the simplicity and purity of the early Christian Era. They demanded of the church hierarchy the freedom to worship in their regional Occitan vernacular and to that end published the Bible in the dialect. Waldo advocated a return to the era when the church and the Bible dealt only with religious matters and rejected the papacy, purgatory, indulgences, and the opulence of the mass. Contrary to prevalent church teachings, Waldo laid great stress on gospel simplicity.

Their outspoken condemnation of the corruption and opulence of the Roman Catholic Church gained Waldo and his followers powerful enemies. In 1179 Pope Alexander III forbade Waldo and his followers to preach. The dissidents' refusal to comply prompted the church leaders to excommunicate them as heretics, but as they believed that they acted according to pure religious doctrine, they were not swayed by threats or the church's official condemnation. In the late twelfth century the Waldensians were driven from Lyon and at the Council of Verona in 1184 were condemned as heretics and excommunicated.

Increased persecution included the burning of more than eighty as heretics at Strasbourg in 1211. In spite of persecution, the Waldensians gradually gained support, and groups formed in France and Italy. In 1215 the pope formally declared Waldo and his believers heretics, and the congregations were forcibly dispersed. The dissidents were separated, and Waldo himself fled to Bohemia, where he died in 1217.

In spite of church edicts that forbade Waldensian contacts with Catholic believers, the movement continued to win followers. Many of the Waldensians suffered torture, burnings, and crusades of extermination called up by the church authorities. Many Waldensian communities in France and Italy were virtually wiped out. In 1487 at the instigation of Pope Innocent, most of the people in

Waldensian colonies in Dauphine, west of the Alps, were massacred. The Waldensian survivors fled to a seven-valley redoubt in the high Cottian Alps in Piedmont. Their simple pre-Reformation doctrines are set forth in the Waldensian Catechism, which was published around 1489.

In the late fifteenth century the Waldensian valleys came under the authority of the Savoyards.* Pressed by the Inquisition, the duke of Savoy led the first systematic attempt to annihilate the Waldensians in 1494. The duke's troops overran many Waldensian towns, murdering and pillaging. Waldensian women threw themselves off high cliffs to escape the shame of rape by the rampaging soldiers. The Waldensians, although numerically fewer and more poorly armed, eventually repulsed the ducal troops and forced the duke to grant a peace treaty lasting forty years.

The religious strife spreading through Europe, the Reformation in the sixteenth century again threatened the Waldensians. In 1532 the Waldensians joined the Protestant movement and thus reignited official church enmity. They paid for the publication, in Switzerland, of the first French Protestant version of the Bible in 1535 as the Waldensians became openly Calvinist. In 1550 anti-Waldensian attacks reached a peak of ferocity and cruelty.

The persecution continued through the Thirty Years' War in the early seventeenth century. In 1685 the French king insisted that his cousin, the duke of Savoy, deal with the Waldensians as he had dealt with the Protestant Huguenots. The duke's Catholic soldiers swept through the Waldensian valleys killing thousands in horrible massacres. Most of the captives were imprisoned in cruel, crowded conditions. Only 3,000 Waldensians survived the duke's bloody crusade. The survivors, after their release from the duke's prisons, migrated to Switzerland with the Waldensian leader, Henri Arnaud, or to other parts of Protestant Europe. In 1689 a small band of Waldensians, under the leadership of Henri Arnaud, left their homes near Geneva and, in what is called the "Glorious Return," fought their way back to their ancestral valleys against strong French and Savoyard resistance. The Waldensians finally defeated the forces sent against them and liberated their valleys, one after another. The Waldensian victory ended the wars and massacres, but not the persecution they suffered as church-labeled heretics. The recuperation of their beloved valleys began a long process of revival and renewal of the Waldensian nation.

Genuine freedom for the Waldensians came only in 1848, when King Charles Albert of Sardinia granted them full civil and religious rights within his kingdom. In spite of the official rehabilitation, the continuing hardships and hatred they faced drove many to emigrate. In the latter half of the nineteenth century many left for South America to begin anew. One group of Waldensians settled in the United States at Valdese, North Carolina, and others settled on Staten Island, New York, and in Missouri. In 1855 the Waldensians founded a school of theology in Torre Pellice, their modern headquarters.

The Waldensians, before and during World War II, actively opposed Italy's fascist government with its enforced religious and national conformity so alien to their ideas of freedom. Many joined partisan units during the war, and the communities suffered official reprisals, particularly after the German occupation of northern Italy in 1943. Whole villages were destroyed in retaliation for the Waldensians' unbending opposition to fascism.

The small Waldensian nation knew peace only after World War II. In 1979 the 130 congregations in Italy federated with the Methodist Church of Italy and moved to end their centuries of self-imposed isolation. The Waldensians began to participate in national and international religious affairs and began to organize their national life as a separate people.

In the 1990s, although not threatened by neighboring peoples, the Waldensians are threatened by unconstrained development, particularly Alpine tourism. An active movement to win greater say over development projects in the 1980s evolved a more militant activism to save their unique culture and traditions from extinction. The Waldensians have become one of the latest of Europe's ethnic and religious mosaic to emerge as a separate nation.

The small Waldensian nation, which survives as a religious and historical minority within a very strong Catholic tradition in Italy, in the 1990s has experienced a cultural and religious revival that blends a strong Calvinist tradition and an Alpine Occitan culture to sustain a unique national group. Increasingly, ties are being reestablished between the European Waldensians and the diaspora Waldensians in the Americas.

At the end of the twentieth century the Waldensians, faced with a decline of the traditional industries, such as mining, have increasingly integrated into the industrial society of the towns of the Piedmont Plain. Mixed marriages between Waldensians and Catholics, modern problems such as drugs, and the end of the Waldensian isolation threaten the integrity of the small Waldensian nation.

SELECTED BIBLIOGRAPHY

Léonard, E. G. *A History of Protestantism.* 1967.

Symcox, Geoggrey. *Victor Amadeus II: Absolutism in the Savoyard State 1675–1730.* 1983.

Tourn, Giorgio. *You Are My Witnesses: The Waldensians across Eight Hundred Years.* 1989.

Tourn, Giorgio. *Waldensians: The First Eight Hundred Years, 1174–1974.* 1975.

Wye, J. A. *History of the Waldenses.* 1980.

WALLOONS

Walons; Wallons

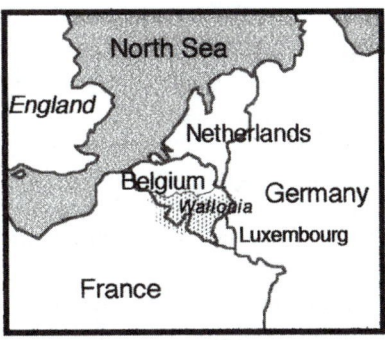

POPULATION: Approximately (2000 e) 4,102,000 Walloons in Europe, most in southern Belgium, but with over 200,000 in adjacent areas of France.

THE WALLOON HOMELAND: The Walloon homeland, Wallonia, lies in southeastern Belgium, part of the North European Plain. The region occupies an area of low plains rising to wooded hills, the Ardennes, in the south. The Meuse and Sambre Rivers, which traverse the region, are the major rivers, and the region around the rivers, the Sambre-Meuse valley, is one of the most fertile in Northwestern Europe. The only heavily wooded area is in the Ardennes, which contain native beech, birch, elm, and oak, while the majority of the region is farmlands and pasture.

Most of Wallonia forms an autonomous region of the Kingdom of Belgium. The small southern region, lying within France, forms Givet, Fourmies, and Maubeuge districts. *Wallonia (Walonia)*: 6,504 sq.mi.–16,845 sq.km. The Walloon capital is Namur, (2000 e) 104,000, but the traditional capital and major cultural center is Liège, (2000 e) 189,000 (metropolitan area 889,000), Wallonia's largest urban area.

FLAG: The Walloon national flag, the official flag of the region, is a yellow field bearing a red rooster centered.

PEOPLE: The Walloons are a Latin people, the most northerly of the Latin peoples in Europe. The descendants of Latinized Celts and Gauls who pushed into the region when the Germanic peoples overran northern France, the Walloons tend to be shorter and darker than the Flemish* of northern Belgium. A large Walloon population of about 200,000 inhabits the eastern part of France's Nord Department and has retained its separate culture and dialect. The culture of the region retains more Latin influences than that of the neighboring French. The Walloons are overwhelmingly Roman Catholic. Many Walloons also claim the city of Brussels, which is 80% French-speaking, but not necessarily Walloon.

The Walloons speak French, the official language of the region, and 450,000 also still speak Walloon, a dialect closer to Old French than standard modern French. The language is described as a Romance language with a Celtic substratum and Germanic influences. Walloon is spoken in two major dialects, Walloon and Picard. The language has a substantial literature but no official status in Wallonia and is not officially taught in the region's schools. In the disputed city and suburbs of Brussels, both French and Dutch are officially recognized, although French speakers, but not necessarily Walloons, are the larger group.

NATION: A Celtic tribe in the region north of the Ardennes, the Belgae, after fighting for seven years, fell to the Romans under Julius Caesar in 57 B.C. The Celtic inhabitants of the Roman province of Belgica, under Roman rule for over 400 years, became thoroughly Latinized and adopted the Latin culture and language.

In the fourth century, traditionally in A.D. 358, Salic Franks moved down from the northeast, and the Latin-speaking population took refuge in the Ardennes. The pressure of the Germanic settlers gradually pushed the Latins to a line approximating the present linguistic frontier between the Walloons in southern Belgium and the Flemish of the northern provinces.

The region split into a number of small, independent states soon after Charlemagne's Frankish Empire was divided by his heirs in 843. While Flanders became a dependency of France, Wallonia became part of the middle kingdom, Lotharingia, later called Lorraine. Reunited in the fifteenth century under the Burgundians,* the Low Countries passed by marriage to the Hapsburgs in 1477. In the sixteenth century the Low Countries, called the Netherlands, which included present Belgium, became a center of world commerce. Rule of the Walloon provinces passed from the Austrian Hapsburgs to the Spanish Hapsburgs in 1555. The southern districts of the Hapsburg province of Hainault, with a large Walloon population, came under French rule in 1678.

The French took the provinces from the Spanish in 1792, and Napoleon annexed Wallonia to the French state in 1801. The Congress of Vienna, convened in 1815 to reorganize Europe at the end of the Napoleonic Wars, added the Roman Catholic, former Hapsburg provinces to the predominantly Protestant Dutch* kingdom. A shared antipathy to Protestant rule united the Walloons and the Flemish in a revolt against Dutch rule in 1830. Supported by the United Kingdom and France, the Catholic provinces in Flanders and Wallonia united in a separate kingdom called Belgium in 1831.

The distinct Walloon dialect, often called Old French, remained the language of administration for the first three decades of Belgian independence, but standard French gradually took precedence in the 1860s. Industrialized Wallonia dominated the kingdom in the nineteenth century. The French language became the predominant dialect in Wallonia and Brussels and was the only official language of the kingdom. Prosperous and assured, the Walloons thrived in the 1870s and 1880s, easily dominating the rural, agricultural Flemish provinces. The Walloon culture experienced a great flowering of art and literature, the cultural revival centered on the Walloon metropolis, Liège.

The decline of religion in Belgian politics made language the center of Belgian disagreements. A new Flemish assertiveness after World War I challenged Walloon domination of the Belgian kingdom. United only by a common religion, the language issue emerged as the kingdom's primary preoccupation in the 1920s and 1930s. Amid growing cultural and linguistic tensions the Belgian government finally recognized Flemish as an official language for some uses in the late 1930s, ending over 400 years of Walloon domination.

The tension between the two peoples escalated after World War II, fanned by economic changes. Wallonia's outdated heavy industries declined rapidly, while new industries shifted to Flanders nearer the Flemish port cities. The shift of economic and political power to Flanders fed a growing Flemish nationalist movement, stimulating Walloon nationalism in response. In 1961 Walloon socialists demanded a new state structure, with local autonomy for the two Belgian nations. Demonstrations broke out in the Walloon cities in 1961–62, and serious nationalist clashes occurred in Brussels and the linguistic border regions. In 1963 a law was passed establishing three official languages within Belgium: Flemish was recognized as the official language in the north, French in the south, and German along the eastern border. Language rights spurred the growth of nationalism, and vacationing Walloons clashed violently with Flemish nationalists in Oostend in 1965.

Nationalist attitudes hardened in the 1970s as both the Walloons and the Flemish demanded greater political and economic autonomy. Teaching the Walloon language in regional schools was granted government permission in 1983. In August 1990 Wallonia and Flanders won major autonomy, opening a bitter debate over control of the Belgian capital, Brussels. The mainly French-speaking, but not Walloon, inhabitants of the capital evidenced little interest in the dispute, while the predominantly Flemish suburbs agitated for the metropolitan area's inclusion in Flanders.

The bitter communal dispute made Belgium all but ungovernable as administrations formed and fell on the linguistic and autonomy issues. In 1988 a bitter dispute prevented agreement on the component parties of a coalition, leaving Belgium without a constitutional government for over four months. In 1989 the Brussels metropolitan area became a third Belgian autonomous region, a compromise reluctantly accepted by the Walloon and Flemish authorities. A serious constitutional crisis in late 1991 again left Belgium without an effective administration, bringing the dissolution of the kingdom ever closer. Nationalists on both sides proposed that Brussels, the center of European integration, become a separate European capital district with Wallonia and Flanders independent states within a federal Europe. Nationalists claim that the European option would formalize the division that has virtually turned Belgium into a geographic area occupied by two distinct nations.

The official devolution of additional powers to the regions in February 1993 effectively partitioned Belgium. Walloon authority, including control of the southern part of Brabant, called Barents, was augmented by the implementation of a federal state in mid-1993. The few powers left to the Belgian government, powers that will eventually become European responsibilities, are the only official ties left between Wallonia and Flanders. When the Belgian government surrenders the responsibilities to the European government, Belgium will effectively cease to exist, and Wallonia and Flanders could become separate states in a federal Europe. In parliamentary elections held in May 1995, the pro-devolution coalition was returned to power; the election signaled the completion of the conversion to a more decentralized form of government.

In the late 1990s the Walloons have increasingly resented Flemish domination of the Belgian state. Walloon leaders claim that the Flemish have usurped political and economic power in Belgium, which they contend now serves only one nation, Flanders, and marginalizes the Walloons. Nationalist organizations, such as the Francophone Front, are increasingly winning support for their demands for a separate Walloon state within the European Union (EU).

SELECTED BIBLIOGRAPHY

Enloe, Cynthia H. *Ethnic Conflict and Political Development.* 1986.

Esman, Milton J. *Ethnic Conflict in the Western World.* 1977.

Fitzmaurice, John. *The Politics of Belgium: Crisis and Compromise in a Plural Society.* 1983.

Lijphart, Arend, ed. *Conflict and Coexistence in Belgium: The Dynamics of a Culturally Divided Society.* 1981.

Pateman, Robert. *Belgium.* 1996.

WELSH

Cymry; Cymraeg

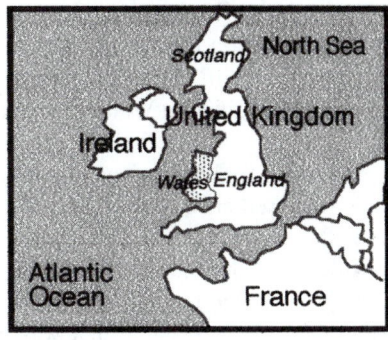

POPULATION: Approximately (2000 e) 3,075,000 Welsh in Europe, most in Wales and other parts of the United Kingdom. Outside Europe, Welsh populations live in Australia, New Zealand, Canada, the United States, and Argentina.

THE WELSH HOMELAND: The Welsh homeland lies in the extreme west of the island of Great Britain, a large, rectangular peninsula between the Irish Sea and the Atlantic Ocean west of the land border with England. Most of the region is uplands, known generally as the Cambrian Mountains, which includes the Snowdon Massif, the highest point in Wales. The major rivers are the Dee in the north, the Severn in the east, and the Conwy in the north. There are numerous lakes and smaller rivers.

Wales forms a separate principality of the United Kingdom. *Principality of Wales (Cymru)*: 8,016 sq.mi.–20,761 sq.km. (2000 e) 2,902,000—Welsh 88%, English* 11%, other British. The Welsh capital and major cultural center is Cardiff, called Caerdydd in Welsh, (2000 e) 253,000 (metropolitan area 658,000), the official capital of Wales since 1955.

FLAG: The Welsh national flag is a horizontal bicolor of white over green, bearing the Welsh national symbol, a red dragon, centered.

PEOPLE: The Welsh, calling themselves Cymry and their country Cymru, are a Celtic people with a vigorous and unique culture. Generally darker and shorter than people in the other British nations, the Welsh have retained much of their historic appearance. The Welsh culture, highly developed before the eleventh-century Norman conquest, is closely related to the cultures of the Cornish* and Bretons,* who inhabit the peninsulas to the south. About three-quarters of the Welsh population in Wales is concentrated in the large urban areas in the south. The majority of the Welsh belong to the Protestant Methodist Church, the religion closely tied to the Welsh culture.

English is now the first language of Wales. Only 60,000 Welsh speak just the Welsh language, and only one-quarter of the population is bilingual, although the numbers are increasing. The language, Cymraeg, belongs to the Brythonic branch of the Celtic languages and has a long literary history. Essentially, the Welsh language was the language spoken throughout Celtic Britain and much of Europe in pre-Roman times. The language has been revived since World War II as part of the Welsh cultural resurgence. Welsh has borrowed words throughout history from Latin, Anglo-Saxon, and Norman French and extensively from English, but it still has a large native vocabulary of Celtic origin. Forty dialects have been identified in Wales. Standard Welsh has both a Northern and Southern variety.

NATION: The original inhabitants of the region are thought to be Iberians, the earliest settlers of most of the island of Great Britain. Celtic tribes, originally from the European mainland, populated the western mountains by the early Bronze Age. The Iberian and Celts often mixed and bore the general name of Cymry. Under nominal Roman rule from 55 B.C., the Cymry were subjugated only after a long struggle that was completed during the reign of the Roman emperor Vespasian, A.D. 69–79. The highland tribes retained their culture and language, while the Celtic lowlands to the east and south became Latinized in culture and speech. The declining Roman Empire gradually abandoned Britannia in the early fifth century. In 410 the Romans withdrew their military garrisons, leaving the island open to invasion.

Overrun by Germanic tribes from Northern Europe, the Celtic defenders fell back on the less accessible areas to the west, the peninsulas of Wales and Cornwall, and eventually crossed the channel to Brittany. The Celtic inhabitants of Britain, fleeing the wave of Anglo-Saxon invaders, took refuge in the Welsh mountains, where, in time, they merged with the Cymry and maintained their independence. The Anglo-Saxon invaders called the native Celts *waelisc*, meaning foreign, eventually corrupted to "Welsh." The Germanic invaders were unable to conquer the highland Celts, but their advance separated the Celtic populations north and south of the Bristol Channel. The Welsh defeated all attempts to invade their peninsular strongholds and continued to raid the lowland communities. During the reign of Offa, king of Mercia, a defensive earthwork extending the length of the Welsh border was erected, which helped to further isolate the Welsh from the Anglo-Saxons. In the sixth century the scattered bands united to form a viable nation. A Welsh king, Hywel Dda, in the tenth century collected Welsh law and custom in a unified code for the kingdom.

The Norman invaders from continental Europe conquered England in 1066, but fierce Welsh resistance halted their invasion at the Welsh border. The Norman leader William the Conqueror declared himself lord of Wales in 1071, even though the Normans gained only a foothold in south Wales in 1093. Dissension in Norman England eased the military pressure on Wales in the twelfth century, the respite stimulating a great flowering of medieval Welsh culture. For over 200 years the Welsh repulsed sporadic attempts to conquer their homeland but ultimately failed to stop the English onslaught. Wales fell to English rule in 1282. Edward I of England in 1301 named his eldest son and heir as Prince of Wales.

Harshly treated by the English as a conquered nation and resentful of unjust laws and administration, the Welsh rebelled under the leadership of Owen Glyndwr (Glendower) in 1400. Initially successful, the Welsh rebels formed a government and created a representative parliament, one of the first in Europe. Defeated nine years later, the victorious English gradually curtailed the principality's rights.

In 1536 Wales was joined to England in a political union. The language of the conquerors, English, was made the official language of the principality, provoking fierce resistance. The Welsh were given seats in the English parliament, but all Welsh laws were replaced by English laws. In spite of forced assimilation, the Welsh retained their culture and language.

The Protestant Reformation, particularly the English version, also fueled Welsh opposition. In the late eighteenth century most of the Welsh finally accepted Protestantism, but not the Anglican sect of England. The Welsh adopted the teachings of John Wesley, derisively called the Methodist for his methodical attention to study and religious duty. The Methodist creed became closely tied to the reviving Welsh culture over the next century.

The industrialization of south Wales in the late nineteenth century brought an influx of English industrial workers. Industrial evils and rural poverty forced many Welsh to emigrate, while between 1870 and 1911 over 120,000 English settled the southern counties. The Welsh industrial expansion continued through World War I, but a serious decline began in 1918. The grave economic problems of the 1920s aroused Welsh nationalist sentiment. In 1925 nationalists formed Plaid Cymru, the Welsh national party.

The spread of education in English after World War II decreased the number of Welsh able to speak their own language. The percentage of Welsh speakers declined by half during the 1950s. The decline of the language and culture stimulated the emergence of a modern nationalist movement based on the effort to save the language and culture from extinction. The Welsh nationalist movement surged during the 1950s with emphasis on the revival of the language.

An organized campaign to win some say in local administration spurred the growth of nationalism in the 1950s and 1960s. In 1964 the British government created a specific Welsh affairs office in London, with a separate government secretary for Wales. The nationalists denounced the offices as continued colonialism. In 1966 Plaid Cymru, advocating national status within a federal United Kingdom, elected its first member to the British parliament.

European integration in the European Economic Community pushed the continent's Celtic nations to reestablish ancient ties. Annual congresses, folk festivals, and cultural exchanges increased and revitalized the Celtic cultures in the

1970s and 1980s. The renewed Pan-Celtic ties gave the Welsh a reinforced determination to win self-rule and equal status for the Welsh language in education and administration.

Radical nationalist organizations formed in the 1960s and 1970s developed close ties to other European groups and received support from Libya and other states. A Libyan group, the Arab Social Union, at the invitation of Plaid Cymru, visited Wales to discuss educational exchanges with the Welsh nationalists. Other nationalist groups, such as the Welsh Socialist Republican Movement and Free Wales, turned to terrorism with attacks on English targets.

A referendum on the devolution of administrative power to a Welsh parliament went down in defeat in 1979. The groups opposed to the devolution stressed British as opposed to Welsh nationalism. Discontented with the result of the referendum, militant nationalists launched a campaign of arson, burning holiday homes and real estate offices dealing with the people buying them, the "foreigners" from across the English border.

Economic success in the 1980s and 1990s has enhanced the Welsh confidence that their country no longer needs the monetary subsidies that have tied Wales to England for centuries. In January 1992 nearly three-quarters of the Welsh demonstrated support for devolution and a separate Welsh assembly. For the nationalists the vote represented a first step toward the goal of a separate Welsh state in an integrated Europe. The rising tide of Welsh nationalism won a concession on the language. In May 1992 the British government finally granted Welsh equal status with English in the principality.

On 18 September 1997 the Welsh voted on a devolution plan. Approval of the initiative set up a sixty-seat legislature, which will not have major financial responsibilities or even the power to make laws on the Welsh language; however, the Welsh nation will have a form of self-government for the first time in over six centuries of English domination. Welsh nationalists approved the devolution of power but continue to work for greater autonomous powers for the new Welsh legislature.

SELECTED BIBLIOGRAPHY
Davies, John. *A History of Wales.* 1993.
Ellis, Peter B. *The Celtic Revolution.* 1988.
Morgan, K. O. *Rebirth of a Nation: Wales 1880–1980.* 1981.
Smith, Dai. *Wales! Wales?* 1984.
Williams, David. *A Short History of Modern Wales.* 1962.

ZETLANDERS

Islanders; Shetlanders; Orcadians

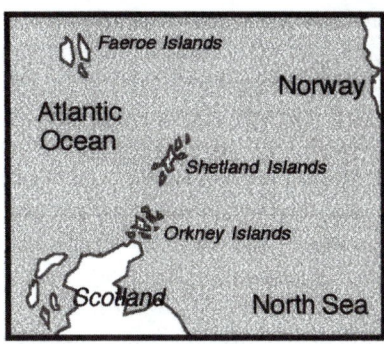

POPULATION: Approximately (2000 e) 55,000 Zetlanders in Europe, mostly in the Shetland and Orkney Islands of the northern British Isles.

THE ZETLANDER HOMELAND: The Zetlander homeland comprises two groups of islands lying just north of Scotland in the North Sea. The islands, the most northerly territory of the United Kingdom, form a long archipelago north of the mainland of Scotland. The Orkney Islands, comprising about 100 islands and islets, make up the southern group, of which less than 30 are inhabited. The closest of the Orkney Islands is only ten miles north of the mainland, from which it is separated by Pentland Firth. The Shetland Islands, 70 islands and islets, 19 inhabited, lie fifty miles north of the Scottish mainland. The islands are generally low-lying and treeless.

Zetland has no official status, but separately the Shetland and Orkney Islands form administrative regions of Scotland in the United Kingdom. *Zetland (Shetland and Orkney Islands)*: 927 sq.mi.–2,401 sq.km. (2000 e) 41,000—Shetlander 52%, Orcadians 45%, other Scots.* The Zetlander capital and major cultural centers are the capitals of the island groups, Lerwick, capital of the Shetlands, (2000 e) 8,000, and Kirkwall, capital of the Orkneys, (2000 e) 7,000.

FLAG: The Zetlander national flag, the flag of the national movement, is a dark blue field charged with a white Scandinavian cross.

PEOPLE: The Islanders number approximately 30,000 Shetlanders and 25,000 Orcadians in the United Kingdom. The Shetlanders and Orcadians, who call themselves Islanders, are the descendants of early Viking settlers with a later Scottish admixture. Ethnically, the Islanders are more closely related to the Icelanders* and Faeroese* than to the other peoples of the British Isles.

The island dialects, Shetlandic and Orcadian, claimed as dialects of a separate Zetland language, are virtually unintelligible to mainlanders and combine Old Norse, Celtic, and English influences. Culturally, the Islanders remain more Scandinavian than Scottish, many of the earlier Norse traditions and customs having survived to the present. Radio transmissions since the 1970s have been made in the local dialects. Island children, until the 1970s, were rebuked for speaking the dialects in school, but they have now taken on a new authenticity.

NATION: The islands, originally settled by Bronze Age Picts from the mainland, came under Norse Viking rule in the eighth century as part of the Viking expansion in the North Atlantic. By the ninth century Scandinavian colonists had settled many of the islands, the earlier inhabitants absorbed into Viking culture. Annexed by Harold Fairhair, the first king of Norway, the islands were organized as a separate earldom in 875. Details of the Norse conquest and settlement are recounted by the *Orkneyinga Saga*, a Norse epic.

The islands, called Zetland, meaning high land, remained a Norwegian dependency until the Norwegian kingdom, along with its possessions and dependencies, passed to Denmark in 1397. The Danish king Christian I in 1468 pledged the islands to James III of Scotland as security for the dowry of Margaret of Norway on her marriage to the Scottish king. King James, not in receipt of the dowry, annexed the islands to his kingdom in 1472.

Scotland's union with England in 1707 began a long campaign in the islands for separation from Scotland and for a distinct legal status within the United Kingdom. The Islanders demanded the political and economic autonomy that would recognize their distinct culture and history, a status similar to the autonomy granted Manx* or the Guernseyites* and Jerseyites.* Relative isolation and a small population facilitated the efforts to preserve the unique island culture and dialects, even though the English language spread to the isolated islands in the eighteenth and nineteenth centuries. A lack of industry and high unemployment caused the islands' population to decline from 1871.

The Shetland and Orkney Islands developed as the United Kingdom's major fishing region, while excess population left for the mainland, keeping the population nearly constant during the early decades of the twentieth century. The relative prosperity of the region renewed the island campaign to win separate legal status within the United Kingdom.

The islands, particularly the important anchorage at Scapa Flow in the Orkneys, became important to the British fleet during both world wars. In November 1939 the islands were the target of the first German air raids on the United Kingdom following the outbreak of war in Europe.

The population of the islands began to drop after World War II and the postwar decline of the fishing industry. The Islanders, forced to leave in search of work, denounced the lack of opportunities as the result of their colonial political status. The discovery of oil in the North Sea off the islands in 1970 reversed the population decline. The islands became a center of the North Sea oil industry with oil workers from many parts of the world brought in by the British and international oil companies.

The idea of home rule for the islands north of the Scottish mainland emerged in 1962 after a local delegation visited the Faeroese homeland. The vigor of the autonomous government of the Faeroe Islands stimulated the growth of local nationalism in Zetland. Their culture and way of life threatened by the massive influx of oil workers and companies, the Islanders began to mobilize during the 1970s. Nationalist organizations demanded autonomy and separate legal status to protect their unique culture and to give them local control over the ecological damage done by the oil companies. In 1979 the Islanders threatened secession as their pristine islands were practically overrun by the oil companies going after the rich oil deposits in the North Sea. Local groups, the Shetland Movement and the Orkney Movement, led the campaign for greater autonomy.

The region's oil wealth, which stimulated Scottish nationalists to demand that the British government leave the control of the booming industry to the Scots, also roused island demands that the Scots keep their hands off Zetland's oil. The nationalist upsurge, with growing support for island control of development and the offshore oil fields, and demands for a fairer share of the oil revenue, added another element to the dispute between Scotland and the government of the United Kingdom over control of natural resources.

Scottish nationalism, advocating independence within a united Europe, stimulated Zetlander sentiment for separation from Scotland in the 1980s and 1990s. The Islanders, culturally and historically distinct, in numerous polls expressed their preference for separate legal status within the United Kingdom; a large minority favored eventual independence within a European federation, with pro-Scottish opinion a distant third. In the 1990s pro-European sentiment is gaining support with the realization that future European regulations and funding will be more important to the islands than decisions made in either Edinburgh or London.

The Shetlanders and Orcadians, part of Scotland through a quirk of history, mostly oppose Scottish nationalism and, if loose ties to the United Kingdom are not possible, look with some confidence to independence. An independent Zetland within a European framework, including the part of the North Sea oil production within their territorial waters, valued at around $18 million a day, would be a viable, even wealthy sovereign state.

SELECTED BIBLIOGRAPHY

Crumley, Jim. *Shetland: Land of the Ocean.* 1996.
Ritchie, Anna. *Shetland.* 1998.
Ritchie, Anna, ed. *Orkney.* 1997.
Simpson, Grant. *Scotland and Scandinavia 800–1800.* 1990.
Tudor, John R. *The Orkneys and Shetland: Their Past and Present State.* 1963.

European National Groups with 2000 Population Estimates and Major Geographic Location(s)

Nation	Population	Major Geographic Location(s)
Abaza	38,000	Azazashta region of the Karacheyo-Cherkess Autonomous Region, Russian Federation.
Abkhaz	122,000	Republic of Abkhazia (proclaimed independent in 1992), Georgia.
Adyge	128,000	Republic of Adygea, Russian Federation.
Aguls	24,000	Dagestan Republic, Russian Federation.
Ajars	260,000	Ajar Republic (Ajaristan), Georgia.
Alanders	65,000	Autonomous Region of the Aland Islands, Finland.
Albanians	6,200,000	Republic of Albania; Kosovo (Kosova), Republic of Serbia, Yugoslavia; northwestern Macedonia.
Alsatians	2,123,000	Alsace and Lorraine regions and the Territory of Belfort, Franche-Comté region, France.
Andalusians	9,458,000	Autonomous Region of Andalusia, Spain.
Andorrans	25,000	Principality of Andorra.
Armenians	4,650,000	Republic of Armenia; Russian Federation.
Austrians	6,920,000	Republic of Austria.
Avars	622,000	Dagestan Republic, Russian Federation.
Azeris	7,332,000	Republic of Azerbaijan.
Azoreans	300,000	Autonomous Region of the Azores, Portugal.

Nation	Population	Major Geographic Location(s)
Balkars	95,000	Balkaria region, Kabardino-Balkaria Republic, Russian Federation.
Bashkorts	2,310,000	Republic of Bashkortostan, Russian Federation.
Basques	2,338,000	Euzkadi-Pais Vasco and Navarra autonomous regions, Spain; three districts of Pyrénées-Atlantiques Department, France.
Bavarians	10,512,000	State of Bavaria, Germany.
Belarussians	11,650,000	Republic of Belarus; Russian Federation; Ukraine.
Bosnians	1,900,000	Republic of Bosnia and Herzegovina.
Bretons	2,825,000	Historic region of Brittany (Bretagne), the Region of Brittany and the Loire-Atlantique Department of Pays de la Loire Region, France.
Bulgarians	8,520,000	Republic of Bulgaria.
Burgundians	2,582,000	Region of Burgundy (Bourgogne), France.
Canarians	1,750,000	Autonomous Region of the Canary Islands, Spain.
Carpatho-Rusyns	1,500,000	Zakarpats'ka Oblast (Transcarpathia Province), Ukraine; Presov region, Slovakia; Lemko region, Poland.
Catalans	9,855,000	Northwestern Spain; southern France.
(Catalans)	(6,238,000)	—Catalonia (Catalunya) Region, Spain.
(Valencians)	(2,854,000)	—Valencia Region, Spain.
(Balearic Islanders)	(521,000)	—Balearic Islands, Spain.
(Northern Catalans)	(242,000)	—Roussillon Region, France.
Chavash	2,255,000	Chavash Republic, Russian Federation.
Chechens	1,020,000	Chechen Republc, Russian Federation.
Cherkess	76,000	Karachai-Cherkess Autonomous Region, Russian Federation.
Cornish	590,000	County (and Duchy) of Cornwall, England, United Kingdom.
Corsicans	390,000	Region of Corsica, France.
Crimean Tatars	332,000	Autonomous Republic of Crimea, Ukraine.
Croats	5,450,000	Republic of Croatia.
Czechs	10,550,000	Czech Republic.
Danes	5,129,000	Kingdom of Denmark.
Dargins	337,000	Dagestan Republic, Russian Federation.

Nation	Population	Major Geographic Location(s)
Don Cossacks	2,250,000	Rostov-na-Donau Oblast, Russian Federation.
Dutch	14,076,000	Kingdom of the Netherlands.
English	47,640,000	Kingdom of England, United Kingdom.
Estonians	1,025,000	Republic of Estonia.
Faeroese	54,000	Autonomous Faeroe Islands, Kingdom of Denmark.
Finns	5,128,000	Republic of Finland.
Flemish	6,092,000	Flanders and Brussels regions, Kingdom of Belgium.
French	52,117,000	French Republic.
Frisians	865,000	Autonomous Province of Friesland, Kingdom of the Netherlands.
Friulis	762,000	Fruili region, Fruili-Venezia Giulia Region, Italy.
Gagauz	225,000	Republic of Gagauzia, Moldova; Bessarabia region, Ukraine.
Galicians	3,585,000	Autonmous Region of Galicia, Spain.
Georgians	4,211,000	Republic of Georgia.
Germans	83,885,000	Federal Republic of Germany.
Gibraltarians	35,000	British Crown Colony of Gibraltar.
Greeks	11,616,000	Hellenic Republic (Greece).
Guernseyites	84,000	Bailiwack of Guernsey, United Kingdom.
Hungarians	12,948,000	Republic of Hungary.
Icelanders	257,000	Republic of Iceland.
Ingrians	360,000	Saint-Petersburg Oblast, Republic of Karelia, Russian Federation; Estonia; Finland.
Ingush	289,000	Republic of Ingushetia, Russian Federation.
Irish	5,895,000	Republic of Ireland.
Istrians	412,000	Historic region of Istria, Croatia, and Slovenia.
Italians	57,125,000	Republic of Italy.
Jerseyites	102,000	Bailiwack of Jersey, United Kingdom.
Kabards	412,000	Kabarda region, Kabardino-Balkaria Republic, Russian Federation.
Kalmyks	212,000	Kalmyk Republic, Russian Federation.
Karachais	159,000	Karachai-Cherkess Autonomous Region, Russian Federation.

Nation	Population	Major Geographic Location(s)
Karels	504,000	Republic of Karelia, Russian Federation; Finland.
Kashubians	250,000	Kashubia region (Kaszuby), Poland.
Komis	567,000	Komi Republic and Komi-Permyak Autonomous Region, Russian Federation.
Kuban Cossacks	1,730,000	Krasnodar Oblast (Kuban), Russian Federation.
Kumyks	287,000	Dagestan Republic, Russian Federation.
Ladins	36,000	Historic Ladinia region, Trentino-Alto Adige Region, Italy.
Laks	133,000	Dagestan Republic, Russian Federation.
Latvians	1,632,000	Republic of Latvia.
Lezgins	458,000	Dagestan Republic, Russian Federation.
Liechtensteiners	34,000	Principality of Liechtenstein.
Ligurians	1,859,000	Region of Liguria, Italy.
Lithuanians	3,275,000	Republic of Lithuania.
Livonians	100,000	Historic region of Livonia, Latvia and Estonia.
Lombards	8,721,000	Region of Lombardy, Italy; Ticino Canton, Switzerland.
Luxembourgers	310,000	Grand Duchy of Luxembourg.
Macedonians	2,250,000	Republic of Macedonia; Greece; Bulgaria.
Madeirans	354,000	Autonomous Region of Madeira, Portugal.
Maltese	405,000	Republic of Malta.
Manx	89,000	Isle of Man, United Kingdom.
Maris	768,000	Republic of Mari-El, Russian Federation.
Meskhtekians	100,000	Georgia; Azerbaijan; Russian Federation.
Moldovans	3,804,000	Republic of Moldova.
Monégasques	5,800	Principality of Monaco.
Montenegrins	643,000	Republic of Montenegro, Yugoslavia.
Moravians	1,528,000	Region of Moravia, Czech Republic.
Mordvinians	1,848,000	Republic of Mordvinia, Russian Federation.
Nogais	128,000	Dagestan Republic and Karachai-Cherkess Autonomous Region, Stavropol Oblast, Russian Federation.
Normans	4,031,000	Haute-Normandy and Basse-Normandy regions, France.

Nation	Population	Major Geographic Location(s)
Northumbrians	3,496,000	Metropolitan county of Tyne and Wear, and the nonmetropolitan counties of Cleveland, Cumbria, Durham, and Northumberland, England, United Kingdom.
Norwegians	4,452,000	Kingdom of Norway.
Occitans	12,200,000	Historic Occitania region, southern France; Region of Piedmont, Italy; Monaco.
Ossetians	722,000	Republic of North Ossetia (Alania), Russian Federation; South Ossetia, Republic of Georgia.
Piedmontese	3,750,000	Autonomous Region of Piedmont, Italy.
Poles	44,880,000	Republic of Poland; western Ukraine; Belarus; Lithuania; Russian Federation.
Portuguese	11,872,000	Republic of Portugal; France; Luxembourg.
Rhinelanders	13,765,000	North Rhine-Westphalia and Rhineland-Palatinate states, Germany.
Romands	1,428,000	Swiss Romande, western Switzerland.
Romanians	23,723,000	Republic of Romania; Ukraine; Russian Federation; Yugoslavia; Hungary.
Romansh	71,000	Grisons (Graubünden) Canton, Switzerland.
Roms	8,000,000 to 10,000,000	Hungary; Romania; Russian Federation; Ukraine; Belarus; Yugoslavia; Germany; France; Italy; Spain; United Kingdom.
Russians	112,847,000	Russian Federation; Ukraine; Belarus; Latvia; Estonia; Georgia; Moldova; Germany.
Rutuls	25,700	Dagestan Republic, Russian Federation.
Samis	105,000	Historic Lapland region, Norway, Sweden, Finland, Russian Federation.
Sanjakis	525,000	Historic Sanjak region, Serbia and Montenegro, Yugoslavia.
San Marinese	31,000	Most Serene Republic of San Marino.
Sards	2,225,000	Autonomous Region of Sardinia, Italy.
Savoyards	1,115,000	Savoie and Haute-Savoie departments, Rhône-Alpes Region, France; Valle d'Aosta Region, Italy.
Saxons	7,771,000	Saxony, Saxony-Anhalt, and Thuringia states (lander), Federal Republic of Germany.
Scanians	1,648,000	Historic region of Scania, Sweden.

Nation	Population	Major Geographic Location(s)
Scots	5,765,000	Kingdom of Scotland, United Kingdom.
Serbs	8,727,000	Republic of Serbia, Yugoslavia.
Sicilians	7,814,000	Autonomous Region of Sicily, Italy.
Slovaks	5,621,000	Republic of Slovakia.
Slovenes	1,992,000	Republic of Slovenia.
Sorbs	643,000	Historic region of Lusatia, Saxony and Brandenburg states, Germany.
Spaniards	36,243,000	Kingdom of Spain; France; Germany; Switzerland.
Swabians	8,853,000	Historic region of Swabia, Baden-Wurttemberg and Bavaria states, Germany.
Swedes	8,496,000	Kingdom of Sweden; Finland.
Swiss-Germans	4,807,000	German (eastern) Switzerland.
Szeklars	1,825,000	Historic Transylvania region, Romania.
Tabasarans	119,000	Dagestan Republic, Russian Federation.
Talysh	141,000	Republic of Azerbaijan.
Tatars	7,121,000	Tatarstan Republic, Russian Federation.
Terek Cossacks	1,050,000	Stavropol Olbast, Russian Federation.
Tsakhurs	26,000	Dagestan Republic, Russian Federation; Azerbaijan.
Turks	9,587,000	European provinces of Turkey; Bulgaria; Cyprus; Greece.
Tyroleans	1,388,000	State of Tyrol, Austria; Autonomous Region of Trentino-Alto Adige, Italy.
Udmurts	1,123,000	Udmurt Republic, Russian Federation.
Ukrainians	51,668,000	Republic of Ukraine; Russian Federation; Moldova; Belarus.
Venetians	3,671,000	Autonomous Region of Veneto, Italy.
Veps	38,000	Republic of Karelia and St. Petersburg Oblast, Russian Federation; Finland.
Volga Germans	788,000	Russian Federation; Germany.
Vorarlbergers	326,000	State of Vorarlberg, Austria.
Waldensians	33,000	Piedmont region, Italy.
Walloons	4,102,000	Autonomous Region of Wallonia, Belgium.
Welsh	3,075,000	Principality of Wales, United Kingdom.
Zetlanders	55,000	North Sea north of the Scottish mainland.
(Shetlanders)	(28,000)	—Shetland Islands, Scotland, United Kingdom.
(Orcadians)	(27,000)	—Orkney Islands, Scotland, United Kingdom.

Appendix B

European Language Groups

Altaic

West Altaic
   Bulgaric (Bolgar)
      Chavash
      Turkic
   South (Oghuz)
      Azeri; Crimean Tatar; Gagauz; Turkish
   West (Kipchak)
      Aralo-Caspian
      Nogai
      Ponto-Caspian
      Balkar; Karachai; Kumyk
      Uralian
      Bashkort; Tatar (Volga Tatar)
East Altaic
   Mongolian
      Kalmyk

Arabic

Western
   Maltese

Caucasian

Northern Caucasian
  Northwest Caucasian
    Abkhazo-Adygheian
      Abkhaz-Abazin
        Abkhaz; Abaza
    Circassian
      Kiakh (Lower Circassian)
        Adyge; Cherkess
      Upper Circassian
      Kabard
  North-Central Caucasian
    Chechen-Ingush
      Chechen; Ingush
Northeast Caucasian
  Dagestani
    Avaro-Andi-Dido
      Avar
    Lak-Dargwa
      Dargin; Lak
    Samurian (Lezgian)
      Agul; Lezgin; Rutul; Tabasaran; Tsakhur
Southern Caucasian (Kartvelian)
  Georgian; Guruli (Ajar); Meskhtekian

Basque

Basque

Indo-European

Baltic
  Latvian; Latgalian; Lithuanian
Celtic
  Brythonic
    Breton; Cornish; Welsh
  Goidelic
    Irish; Manx; Scots Gaelic
Germanic
  North Germanic (Scandinavian)

Germanic (*continued*)

    East Scandinavian

        Danish; Norwegian (Riksmal)

        Swedish

          Alander; Scanian

    West Scandinavian

        Faeroese; Icelandic; Norwegian (Landsmal)

West Germanic

  High German

    Alsatian; Austrian; Bavarian; German; Letzburgish (Luxembourger); Liechtensteiner German; Rhinelander; Saxon; Swabian; Swiss German; Tyrolean; Volga German; Vorarlberger

  Low German

    Dutch; Flemish

    Anglo-Frisian

      English

        Channel Islands English (Guernseyite, Jerseyite); Gibraltarian English; Lallans (Lowland Scots); Northumbrian; Zetlander (Shetlander, Orcadian)

      Frisian

Greek

  Greek

Indo-Iranian

  Indo-Aryan

      (Rom) Romani

  Iranian

      Ossetian; Talysh

Italic

  Romance

    Eastern

      Romanian

      Moldovan

    Gallo-Romance

      North

        Franco-Provençal (Savoyard); Romand

        French

          Burgundian (Bourgignon/Franc Comtois); Walloon

          Norman

            Guernesíais (Guernsey Norman); Jèrriais (Jersey Norman)

Italic (*continued*)

    Western

      Ligurian

      Lombard

        Ticinese (Swiss Italian)

      Piedmontese

        Waldensian (Highland Piedmontese)

   Ibero-Romance

   Central

     Spanish (Castilian)

       Andalusian; Canarian; Yanito (Gibraltarian Spanish)

    Eastern

     Occitan

      Monégasque

    Western

     Catalan-Valencian-Mallorquin

       Andorran Catalan; Catalan; Valencian; Mallorquin

     Galician

     Portuguese

      Azorean; Madeiran

   Italo-Romance

    Sicilian; Venetian

    Italian

     San Marinese

   Rhaeto-Romanic

    Friulian; Ladin; Romansh

   Southern

    Corsican; Sardinian

Slavic

 East Slavic

  Belarussian; Carpatho-Rusyn; Ukrainian

  Russian

    Cossack (Don, Kuban, Terek)

 South Slavic

  Eastern

   Bulgarian; Macedonian

Slavic (*continued*)

    Western

        Bosnian; Croatian; Slovenian

        Serbian

            Montenegrin

            Sanjaki Serbian

    West Slavic

        Kashubian; Polish; Slovak; Sorbian

        Czech

            Moravian

Thraco-Illyrian

    Albanian

Thraco-Phrygian

    Armenian

Uralic

Finno-Ugric

    Finnic

        Balto-Finnish

            Finnish; Estonian; Ingrian; Karelian; Livonian; Olonetsian (South Karelian); Vepsian

        Cheremisic

            Mari (Cheremiss)

                Low Mari; High Mari

        Lappic

            Saami (Sami)

        Mordvinic

            Erzya; Moksha

        Permian

            Komi; Komi-Permyak; Udmurt

    Ugric

        Hungarian (Magyar)

        Szeklar (Transylvanian)

Index

The page numbers set in **boldface** indicate the location of the main entry.

About the Author

JAMES B. MINAHAN is an independent researcher living in Barcelona, Spain. He is the author of *Nations Without States: A Historical Dictionary of Contemporary National Movements* (Greenwood, 1996), which was named in ALA/ RASD 1996 Outstanding Reference Source, and *Miniature Empires: A Historical Dictionary of the Newly Independent States* (Greenwood, 1998).